Carl A. SPAATZ
and the Air War in Europe

General Carl A. Spaatz, 1945.

Carl A. SPAATZ
and the Air War in Europe

Richard G. Davis

**Center for
Air Force
History**

Washington, D.C.

1993

Library of Congress Cataloging-in-Publication Data

Davis, Richard G.
    Carl A. Spaatz and the air war in Europe / Richard G. Davis.
       p. cm--(General Histories)
    An expansion of the author's thesis.
    Includes bibliographical references (p.) and index.
    ISBN 0-912799-75-7 (casebound).--ISBN 0-912799-77-3 (perfectbound)
      1. Spaatz, Carl, 1891–1974. 2. Generals--United States--Biograpby. 3.
United States. Air Force--Biography. 4. Aeronautics, Military--United States-
-History. 5. World War, 1939–1945--Aerial operations, American 6. World
War, 1939–1945--Campaigns--Western
I. Title. II. Series.
UG626.2.S66D38 1992
358.4'0092--dc20
[B]   92-14889 CIP

For Sale by the Superintendent of Documents, U.S. Government Printing Office,
Washington, D.C. 20402

Foreword

Carl A. Spaatz and the Air War in Europe offers the first detailed review of Spaatz as a commander. It examines how the highest ranking U.S. airman in the European Theater of Operations of World War II viewed the war, worked with the British, and wielded the formidable air power at his disposal. It identifies specifically those aspects of his leadership that proved indispensable to the Allied victory over Nazi Germany.

As Chief of the Air Corps Plans Section and, beginning in 1941, as first Chief of the Air Staff, Spaatz helped prepare the United States for war by overseeing an unprecedented buildup of military air capability. As Commander of the Eighth Air Force, he expanded and maintained a network of bases from which his bombers could strike at Germany from England. As General Eisenhower's adviser and Commander of the Northwest African Air Forces, he reorganized and vastly improved dispersed and difficult-to-supply Allied air activities. After assuming command of all U.S. Strategic Air Forces in Europe, he controlled the American contribution to the Combined Bomber Offensive.

Spaatz's forces destroyed the Luftwaffe, first by employing new long-range fighters in vigorous counter-air actions and then, when the Luftwaffe assiduously avoided further engagements, by forcing it to fight to defend the petroleum industry that fueled it. Only after a protracted debate concerning which targets—oil or transportation—were to receive top priority did he win the right from skeptical Allied principals to mount strategic bombing missions against German oil production facilities. With the Luftwaffe effectively paralyzed, Spaatz moved against bridges, ports, railyards, and roads and, finally, crushed the Nazi war economy.

The Anglo-American partnership, although triumphant in the end, was not easy. Its lines of authority were frequently and hotly debated. Through portraits of major Allied civilian and military personalities, this study describes several contentious interactions around which Spaatz maneuvered adroitly to achieve his broad military objectives.

Author Richard Davis contrasts American and British grand strategy, battle tactics, and operations, laying bare the political considerations that necessarily influenced Allied planning. He demonstrates how clashes among only a few individuals can profoundly affect command decisions and the successful prosecution of coalition warfare. Lessons contained in his study have implications even now in the post-Desert Storm era. That the Air Force today is able to project global strength is due in large measure to the foresight and tenacity of Carl Spaatz, who freed air power to become the dominant force of modern warfare.

RICHARD P. HALLION
Air Force Historian

United States Air Force
Historical Advisory Committee
(As of July 1, 1992)

Professor Roger E. Bilstein
University of Houston
Clear Lake

Col. Donald S. Lopez
USAF, Retired
National Air and Space
Museum

Dr. Christopher J. Bowie
The RAND Corporation

Mr. Felix C. Lowe
Smithsonian Institution Press

Lt. Gen. Charles G. Boyd
Commander, Air University

Dr. Peter Paret
Institute for Advanced Study

Professor Wayne S. Cole
University of Maryland
College Park

Ms. Ann Petersen
The General Counsel, USAF

Lt. Gen. Bradley C. Hosmer
Superintendent
USAF Academy

Gen. Bryce Poe, II
USAF, Retired
Air Force Historical
Foundation

Introduction

This study is an expansion of a doctoral dissertation I began in 1982. Initially I sought to tell the story of the air war in Europe from a new perspective—that of the senior U.S. Army Air Forces (AAF) officer in the theater, General Carl A. Spaatz. Little did I realize the magnitude of the task. I discovered a man who had stood close to the central events of the conflict in Europe. Without Spaatz and his insistence on bombing the German oil industry, the war in Europe might have lasted several more months. Spaatz commanded more men than Patton or Rommel ever led. By the end of May 1945 his forces could deliver more destructive power than any force before the advent of nuclear weapons. Thus, an understanding of the part Spaatz played in the victory of the Allied coalition is necessary to any serious study of World War II.

In the course of investigating Spaatz's activities during the war, I soon realized that many of the conventional interpretations of the role of the U.S. Army Air Forces in Europe sprang from the imrediate post-World War II era when the AAF was in the last rounds of its fight to gain independence from the U.S. Army. As a consequence, early U.S. air historians tended to downplay the shortcomings of air power and to emphasize the advantages of centralized command of air power by airmen operating autonomously. In this work I have attempted to present a more balanced view of the effectiveness of air power.

By its very nature this study of the military life of Carl A. Spaatz is virtually a history of U.S. military aviation from its beginnings to the end of World War II in Europe. To place Spaatz in the context of his times, I found it necessary to examine the development of U.S. military aviation thought and technology. From his tour as Commandant of the Issoudun Pursuit Training Center in France in 1917, where he first displayed his skills as an administrator and trainer of men, through his service as special observer during the Battle of Britain in the summer of 1940, Spaatz's career reflected the continual changes in air power.

Immediately after World War I, Spaatz commanded the sole pursuit group stationed in the continental United States and led the flight of its air elements from Texas to Michigan without the loss of a man or machine (no mean feat in 1922). Once in Michigan, he established his group at Selfridge Field, which had been abandoned two years earlier. Leaving Selfridge in 1924, he attended the Air Corps Tactical School at Langley Field near Norfolk, Virginia.

At that time and place the school was far removed from the future period of intellectual and doctrinal ferment in which it produced the American theory of daylight precision bombing. Next, Spaatz served in Washington, D.C., in the Air Service's Training and Operations Section. There he testified as a defense witness in the controversial court-martial of Brig. Gen. William "Billy" Mitchell.

During the late 1920s and 1930s Spaatz switched from commanding fighters to commanding bombers—a career move that mirrored the Air Corps' change in emphasis from pursuit to bombardment aviation. At the same time, he absorbed the new theories that preached the ability of the heavily armed bomber, flying a tight defensive formation, to penetrate successfully deep into enemy territory to destroy vital economic targets and to return, all the while unescorted by friendly fighter aircraft. Even subsequent firsthand experience of the British and German failure to bomb effectively in daylight failed to persuade him to modify his belief in unescorted bombing.

Before U.S. entry into World War II, Spaatz, as Chief of the Air Corps Plans Section and, upon the formation of the AAF in June 1941, as first Chief of the Air Staff, helped to plan and supervise the vast expansion of U.S. military air power. On July 1, 1939, the Air Corps had a force of 1,239 combat aircraft, 570 training planes, 20,191 enlisted men, 633 aviation cadets, and 2,502 officers. Many of the aircraft were obsolescent; there were no advanced training aircraft; and all but 45 of the officers were rated pilots. Thirty-two months later, on March 1, 1942, the AAF had 2,393 combat aircraft (2,182 rated as modern), 10,087 trainers (2,541 advanced), 312,405 enlisted men, 32,896 cadets, and 27,446 officers (13,631 nonpilots).[1] These figures represented an increase of more than 1,000 percent in every category except combat aircraft, which increased only 200 percent.

With the onset of war, Spaatz took command of the Eighth Air Force and helped prepare a base capable of sustaining the thousands of planes scheduled to operate against Germany from Britain. After Spaatz had launched only a handful of heavy-bomber missions against nearby French targets, however, Lt. Gen. Dwight D. Eisenhower summoned Spaatz to the North African Theater to advise him and, eventually, to command all Allied air power there.

In North Africa the organizational chaos of his geographically scattered command tested his logistical and organizational abilities to the utmost, but by the finish of the Allies' campaign against the Axis forces in Tunisia, Spaatz had produced a well-run, efficient force. Also in North Africa, he played a significant role in solving the dispute between the Army ground and air elements about the effectiveness of the AAF's handling of close air support.

The fall of Tunisia led to the Allied invasion of Sicily and Italy and a period of frustration for Spaatz. After overseeing the reduction of the Island of Pantelleria by air power, Spaatz saw his influence on operations decline as Eisenhower increasingly relied on British Air Chief Marshal Arthur Tedder. In the summer and autumn of 1943, Spaatz concentrated on perfecting the organization of the AAF in the Mediterranean and on obtaining and establishing a new strategic American air force to operate against Germany from its unprotected southern flank.

At the end of 1943, Spaatz left Italy for London where he assumed command of the two American strategic air forces operating against the Germans.

As the strategic air commander, he made his two most decisive contributions to Allied victory. With the help of an influx of long-range fighter-escort aircraft, he launched, in the first five months of 1944, an intensive counter-air campaign that emasculated the Luftwaffe fighter force. By the time of the invasion of Normandy, the German air force no longer had the strength to interfere with the invasion or to defend German industry from each large American bomber mission.

Shortly before the invasion, Spaatz, after a long policy struggle within the Allied coalition, began a strategic bombing campaign against the German oil industry. This campaign damaged vital cogs of the Nazi war machine by grounding a large portion of the Luftwaffe starving it of aviation fuel, and by impairing the mobility of the *Wehrmacht*, leaving it almost helpless to counter the maneuvers of its enemies.

Under Spaatz's leadership, in the autumn and winter of 1944–1945, the U.S. Strategic Air Forces in Europe (USSTAF) helped to bring the German war economy to a halt by adding the transportation network to its target priorities. Spaatz's forces also participated in the most controversial bombing raid of the European war when they joined with British Bomber Command to level the center of Dresden on February 14, 1945. An exemplar of AAF bombing policy and operations, this raid carried a high proportion of incendiary bombs, was directed at a railroad marshaling yard, and was executed in nonvisual bombing conditions. It was not carried out to induce terror but was intended to give direct assistance to the Soviets' winter offensive by destroying a transportation center in eastern Germany. In contrast, the February 3, 1945, mission against Berlin was specifically ordered by Spaatz to shake the morale of the German High Command and government.

In the middle of April 1945, Spaatz ended the strategic bombing campaign. Thereafter, the bombers devoted their efforts to aiding the ground forces and flying supplies to alleviate famine in Holland. Spaatz attended the German surrenders to the Allies at Reims and Berlin on May 7 and May 9, 1945.

This work is neither a full-scale biography of Carl A. Spaatz nor a comprehensive history of the USAAF in action against the European Axis powers from 1942 to 1945. Instead it studies Spaatz as a military leader by examining his thoughts and actions within the context of his times. By hewing to Spaatz's perspective I could not follow the entire course of the American strategic bomber offensive in Europe. Those readers looking for a description of the Eighth Air Force under Ira Eaker's leadership or of Spaatz's valuable contributions in the postwar era must look elsewhere. But a year-long trip to North Africa and the Mediterranean enabled me to take a close look at the birth pangs of modern American tactical air power, to explore the creation of the under-appreciated Fifteenth Air Force, and to thoroughly study the last eighteen months of the American air effort in Europe once Spaatz had returned to the strategic cockpit in London.

Acknowledgments

Many archivists, colleagues, and professors contributed to this work. Mary Wolfskill at the Library of Congress; Will Mahoney at the Modern Military Division of the National Archives; and my friends at the Suitland, Maryland, National Records Center—Richard L. Boylan, Henry Mayer, and Bill Getchell—all contributed particular expertise. Col. John F. Shiner, former Deputy Chief, Office of Air Force History; Herman S. Wolk, Senior Historian, Center for Air Force History; Brig. Gen. Harris Hull, USAF (Ret.); Dr. Richard Kohn, former Chief, Office of Air Force History; and Professor Wesley Newton of Auburn University read several versions of the manuscript and served as final review panelists. Their advice proved crucial in the last revision. David Mets, historian at the Armament Division, Eglin Air Force Base, Florida, and author of a biography of General Spaatz, reviewed the manuscript and supplied advice from his own extensive knowledge. William Heimdahl, Chief, Historical Support Division, Center for Air Force History, and MSgt. Roger Jernigan spent considerable time locating obscure documents in the microfilm collection. Dr. Daniel R. Mortensen, a tactical air power historian at the Center for Air Force History, shared his research on North Africa and helped to refine the treatment of several topics. Patrick E. Murray, Chief Historian, Third Air Force, England, made a special trip to the Imperial War Museum in London to locate photographs.

Other colleagues with the Center for Air Force History deserve special credit, having learned more about Spaatz than they probably ever wished to. Jacob Neufeld, Director of the Center for Air Force History, gave me generous amounts of time to work on the manuscript. Dr. Richard I. Wolf proofread large sections of the manuscript and helped me with printers and word processors. Two very hard working and professional editors, Mary Lee Jefferson of the Center for Air Force History and Priscilla Taylor of Editorial Experts, Inc., spent many hours smoothing my prose and forcing me to clarify, in as few words as possible, points and concepts I had glossed over or abbreviated. Ms. Jefferson then patiently shepherded the book through the publishing process, coordinating the efforts of many others. Dr. Alfred M. Beck, Chief, Histories Division, corrected my haphazard German spelling. Editor David R. Chenoweth designed and typeset the statistical appendices. Anne E. Johnson, Chief, Editorial Services, lent moral and technical support in the last phases of publication. Members of the Graphics Office for the Air Force District of Washington made outstanding contributions. Susan Linders, Chief, Conventional Graphics, oversaw production of the book's artwork. Bruce John and Protean Gibril prepared the maps; Tracy Miller prepared the charts. Kathy Jones finalized all illustrations, and Lori Crane, designed the cover.

ACKNOWLEDGMENTS

   Professor Charles J. Herber of George Washington University, who
directed this work as a dissertation, was a helpful advocate and editor.
Professors Robert W. Kenny and Peter P. Hill read and commented on
earlier drafts. Professor J. Kenneth McDonald ably directed my first years
of study; and one of the finest scholars and gentlemen associated with
George Washington University, Professor Roderic H. Davidson, made my
studies in European diplomatic history a joy. Martin Blumenson, historian,
and Col. John Schlight, USAF (Ret.), former Chief, Southeast Asia Branch,
Office of the Chief of Military History, U.S. Army, attended my dissertation
defense and gave useful criticism.

The Author

Richard G. Davis received his B.A. from the University of Virginia; his M.A. from the University of North Carolina, Chapel Hill; and his Ph.D. from George Washington University. Before joining the U.S. Air Force Historical Program in 1980 he worked for the National Archives and Records Administration as an archivist specializing in the declassification of classified documents. His earlier works include *The 31 Initiatives*, a study on Army/Air Force efforts at cooperation and reform, and *Tempering the Blade: The Development of American Tactical Air Power in the North African Campaign*. Dr. Davis has also published several articles in professional journals. He is currently researching the U.S. offensive air campaign in the Persian Gulf War of 1991.

Contents

Part One. Carrying the Flame
From West Point to London
1891–1942

Part Two. Tempering the Blade
The North African Campaign
November 8, 1942–May 14, 1943

Part Three. Mediterranean Interlude
From Pantelleria to London
May–December 1943

Part Four. The Point of the Blade
Strategic Bombing and
the Cross-Channel Invasion
January–June 1944

Part Five. The Mortal Blow
From Normandy to Berlin
June 6, 1944–May 9, 1945

Maps

Tables

Charts

Photographs

Statistical Appendices

Part One

Carrying the Flame
From West Point to London
1891–1942

Flight Trainee 2d Lt. Carl A. Spatz, 25th Infantry, spring 1916.

Chapter 1

Spaatz's Early Career (1891–1938)

The candidate should be naturally athletic and have a reputation for reliability, punctuality and honesty. He should have a cool head in emergencies, good eye for distance, keen ear for familiar sounds, steady hand and sound body with plenty of reserve; he should be quick-witted, highly intelligent and tractable. Immature, high strung, overconfident, impatient candidates are not desired.[1]

—*Army Specifications for Flyers, 1917*

Carl Andrew Spatz* was born on June 28, 1891, in Boyertown, Pennsylvania, and lived there throughout his youth. He was the second child, and first son, in a family of two boys and three girls. Both his Prussian immigrant grandfather and his American-born father published the local newspaper, at first in German, later in English. As a boy, he learned to set type by hand and to run the paper's printing press. He graduated from high school at the age of fourteen, a fact that says less about his academic abilities than it does about the simplicity of the local curriculum. To remedy his academic deficiencies, his parents sent him to Perkiomen Preparatory School for two more years. Years later Spaatz classified himself as a poor student who read what he wanted and never studied,[2] traits he continued throughout his life. When his father was badly burned attempting to rescue persons trapped in a local opera house fire in January 1908, Carl returned home to run the newspaper. Afterwards he attended the Army-Navy Preparatory School in Washington, D.C. On March 1, 1910, at the age of eighteen, he entered the United States Military Academy at West Point.

---

* In 1937 Spatz, at the urging of his wife and three daughters, legally changed his name to Spaatz. He hoped that the additional "a" would encourage the correct pronunciation of his name, which sounded like the word "spots."

Spaatz himself never revealed why he chose to attend the Academy. His attendance at the Army-Navy Preparatory School could have indicated a leaning toward the military profession or merely a desire to secure sound credentials before attending any college. His wife has said that his family could not afford to continue his education. The offer of an excellent free education, coupled with an honorable career that stressed the outdoor life he enjoyed all his life probably persuaded him to apply for and accept appointment to a service academy.[3]

He had an undistinguished sojourn in the Corps of Cadets. Less than three weeks after his entrance, he attempted to resign but was dissuaded from doing so.[4] Why he attempted to resign remains obscure. Given his easy-going temperament, it seems probable that the hazing and other traditional indignities inflicted on entering cadets almost proved too much for him. Later, although guilty, he dodged expulsion for having liquor in his room by escaping court-martial conviction on a technicality.[5] In academics he stood 57th out of 107. In conduct, he ranked 95th. His behavioral shortcomings reflected a distaste for "bull" or spit and polish. He received demerits for neglecting to sweep the floor, to dust his shoes, to fold his bedclothes, and to keep his rifle clean. In fact, Spaatz maintained a rumpled look throughout his career. Rumor has it that on his graduation day he was still walking punishment tours.

He never gained cadet rank, remaining a "cleansleeve" for his four years at the Point. What interested him—bridge, poker, and the guitar—he pursued vigorously. His classmates especially relished his repertoire of risqué songs. The *Howitzer,* the West Point yearbook, caricatured him with guitar in hand. The editors commented on his silent demeanor, noted his ability to recite with confidence on a subject he had not read, and spoke of his indifference to demerits and "independent attitude generally."[6] By his graduation on June 12, 1914, his independence, taciturnity, and impatience with stultifying routine had become fixed. He had also acquired a permanent nickname, "Tooey," because of a chance resemblance to upperclassman, Francis J. Toohey.

Spaatz left the Academy determined to become a flyer. In his third month at West Point, on May 29, 1910, he had seen Glenn Curtiss fly by on a 150-mile trip from Albany to New York City. (Curtiss stopped only once to refuel, thereby setting a new world record of 87 miles nonstop flight.)[7] The sight so impressed Spaatz that he then and there decided to fly.[8] In 1914 the U.S. Army's few aircraft belonged to the Aviation Section of the Signal Corps. Before Spaatz could join the Signal Corps he was required to serve one year in a line or combat unit.

On joining the 25th Infantry Regiment at Schofield Barracks, Hawaii, he served in an all-black infantry company. Thirty years later, he testified to the Gillem Board, which was investigating the place of the black soldier in the post-World War II armed forces, "I must say that I enjoyed that year of service with that outfit as much as any year of service I have ever had—as a white officer in a Negro outfit, I would just as soon serve with them any time." He thought his men made "fine soldiers easily disciplined by white officers and easily kept under control." He also told the Gillem Board that blacks should not serve in integrated units and that they would be more effective in support and service units than in combat units.[9] Throughout his career Spaatz evinced the paternalistic attitude of his rank and station toward blacks. He never appeared to question their low status within the military; he was simply a man of his time.

Spaatz made no lasting mark on the 25th Infantry, but he did succeed in making an indelible impression on the teen-aged daughter of a cavalry colonel also stationed in Hawaii. She became his bride two years later.

When his year in the infantry ended, Spaatz reported to North Field in San Diego, California, on November 25, 1915, to begin flight training. This preparation consisted of two to five hours' dual instruction, learning how to inspect the plane for safety, and how to disassemble its motor. On his first solo flight, the engine quit,[10] but he glided the plane to a safe landing and continued to fly. In his initial air assignment, May 1916, Spaatz flew to the U.S.-Mexican border for a tour of duty in the 1st Aero Squadron with Brig. Gen. John J. Pershing's punitive expedition in Mexico. The commanding officer of the 1st Aero Squadron, Capt. Benjamin D. Foulois, later became Chief of the Army Air Corps. A month after U.S. entry into World War I, Spaatz, one of only sixty-five flying officers in the Army, was promoted to major and given command of the 5th Aero Squadron at Fort Sam Houston in Texas. On July 26, two weeks before his departure for Europe, he married twenty-year-old Ruth Harrison, whose father had also been transferred to Fort Sam Houston. The couple gave the bride's parents less than twelve hours' notice.

By September 19, 1917, Spaatz found himself in France, where his unit was broken up for replacements. He spent the next three weeks in Paris in charge of the mechanical training of enlisted men, followed by a month at Chaumont assigned to the Supply Section of the aeronautical area of Pershing's headquarters. While at Chaumont, Spaatz participated in his first combat mission, flying as an observer on a French bombardment sortie on the night of October 29. He also flew with French observation and reconnaissance squadrons.[11] On November 15, 1917, he became the Commander of the 3d Aviation Instruction Center at Issoudun, France.[12] He received this posting because as both a Regular Army officer and a trained flyer, he was one of the very few men qualified to fill the job.

There were no planes suitable for advanced training or pilots qualified as instructors in the United States at the outbreak of the war. The Aviation Section of General Pershing's American Expeditionary Force (AEF) thus had no choice but to establish large training centers in Europe, where pilots could practice flying on up-to-date aircraft supplied by the French and the English. Although the Aeronautical Training Section of the AEF, Aviation Section, selected Issoudun in June, construction on flight training facilities did not begin until August 18. By autumn conditions there, thanks to delays in the arrival of construction materials, were, as an official report noted, "to say the least, disheartening."[13] The center did not receive its first French aircraft until October, and the provisional flight school did not start operation until October 24. Barracks and shops were of the crudest construction, and the rainy season had started before roads were in place, making the center a sea of mud. On the flying field, mud churned up by aircraft wheels broke propeller blades as fast as they could be replaced. The center had no machine shops or material to erect them.[14]

The morale of all personnel under these conditions plummeted. Primary training cadets, who had joined the Army Air Service for the romance of flying, particularly resented their lot at Issoudun, which had no facilities for primary or introductory flight training. The center had to accept the primary cadets because the French and British initial training schools could not find space for them. When pressed into laboring on the center's essential construction projects, they reacted with little enthusiasm.[15] This was the initial situation that confronted Spaatz, who had no training in aviation instruction and had never flown a modern service plane.

He spent most of the next nine and one-half months either as commanding officer of the school or as the officer in charge of training. Spaatz did his job well. By the time he left in September 1918, Issoudun had become the largest training field in the world and the Army Air Service's chief facility for training pursuit or fighter pilots. It had 14 airfields, 84 hangars, and numerous warehouses, shops, and barracks.[16] The machine shops could completely overhaul more than 100 engines a week (each requiring at least 100 man-hours) and rebuild from salvaged parts 20 aircraft a week (each plane required 32 mandays). The school averaged 500 to 600 flying hours a day. In all, it graduated 766 pursuit pilots.[17] This accomplishment was not without cost; Issoudun suffered 56 training fatalities during Spaatz's tenure. In August 1918, for example, 17 students died.[18] In all, the Army Air Service suffered 128 combat fatalities and 244 training fatalities in France and 262 training fatalities in the United States.[19] Spaatz also reestablished discipline. One of his trainees recalled fifty years later, "The students all thought he was a stiff necked little German," adding, "but he was fair, and that's all you can expect out of a good officer."[20]

The assignment gave Spaatz invaluable experience as a trainer and administrator of a fledgling air force. He had successfully accomplished his assignment—so successfully, in fact, that Brig. Gen. William "Billy" Mitchell, one of Pershing's chief aviation officers, wanted to return him to the United States to upgrade Air Service training there. Instead, Spaatz, not known for his loquaciousness, spoke up. He wangled permission for two weeks at the front with the 1st Pursuit Group, which included the 94th Aero (Hat-in-the-Ring) Squadron, one of whose members was Maj. Edward "Eddie" V. Rickenbacker. Rickenbacker, who ended the war as the highest-ranking American ace, with twenty-six kills, had served at Issoudun under Spaatz for several months.

When Spaatz arrived, he found the 1st Pursuit out of the line and not flying combat missions, so he went on to the 13th Aero Squadron, 2nd Pursuit Group.[21] Upon his arrival, Spaatz won over the outfit's pilots, mostly second and first lieutenants who had first entered combat five weeks before his arrival, by removing his major's insignia of rank and becoming one of them.[22] When his first two weeks were up, he ignored his orders and stayed two more weeks.[23]

On September 16, 1918, despite the repeated jamming of his machine guns, Spaatz shot down his first German aircraft.[24] Ten days later, he earned a Distinguished Service Cross in a stunt that made the *New York Times*: "Flying officer shoots down three planes—two German and his own."[25] Spaatz had focused so intently on his dogfighting that he had neglected to check his fuel gauge, causing the loss of his own Spad. Fortunately, when he crash-landed his plane near the trenches, he fell into French hands. The friendly *poilu* started an alcoholic celebration, which Spaatz's compatriots continued upon his return to base. When Spaatz left for the United States, Mitchell told him, "I will be glad to have you command a group at any time under my command."[26]

Spaatz landed in New York City on October 13. He traveled to Washington, D.C., where he was assigned to the Aviation Service's Training Department as Inspector of Pursuit Training and met Col. Henry H. "Hap" Arnold for the first time. The two eventually became fast friends—to the lasting benefit of both their careers. Spaatz had already heard much about Arnold, who was very close to Spaatz's wife's family, the Harrisons. Next, Spaatz began an inspection tour of pursuit facilities. He boarded a train for Dayton, Ohio, where he tested various types of planes, presumably trainers. Just outside El Paso, on November 11, 1918, he learned that the war had ended. The next day he finished his tour in San Diego, California. He emerged from the war as a recognized expert on air training and pursuit aviation.[27]

He also emerged convinced that Army air power deserved more autonomy. By the end of World War I, many air officers, such as Mitchell and Foulois, had become dissatisfied with the place of aviation in the Army. They had encountered too many officers who had gained command of air units without the least knowledge of aviation or who, worse still, had no appreciation of aviation's potential.[28] Other officers, such as Arnold, had found little sympathy or support from War Department bureaucrats in Washington.[29] Nor did Secretary of War Newton D. Baker demonstrate remarkable insight in his Annual Report of 1919, which condemned the principle of bombing civilian areas,[30] and by extension, all strategic bombing. At the time of the postwar congressional hearings on the place of air power within the military establishment, Spaatz said, "My own feeling was all in favor of getting it out of the Signal Corps. . . . I wanted air force on the same level as infantry."[31] Within a few years, Spaatz and many other Army air officers wanted not just autonomy within the Army but independence from it.

In 1919 Spaatz began the typical treadmill existence of an American officer between the world wars—repeated changes of post, lack of public regard, low pay, and agonizingly slow promotion. Although from 1918 to 1920 he changed posts twenty times,[32] he had two advantages over some of his fellow officers— flight pay, a cause of much jealousy among non-flying officers, and seniority as a major. For all but three months of the next seventeen years, when he temporarily became a captain, Spaatz remained a major, unlike many of his compatriots who lost their wartime ranks and toiled for years as captains or even lieutenants.

The U.S. Army filled its officer ranks by means of an unmodified seniority system. A thorough knowledge of the workings of the Army promotion system provides a key to understanding the position of the Air Service and of Spaatz within the Army.* The promotion list, a conservative personnel system long in use throughout the world's civil and military services, worked strictly by seniority or time in grade. Unlike many foreign services, which limited the unmodified seniority list to captain and below, the U.S. Army's system extended up through colonel.[33] Each commissioned officer entered the U.S. Army officer corps as the most junior 2d lieutenant and, if he lived long enough, advanced to colonel as the men on the list ahead of him left the service. Considerations of merit or ability did not modify one's relative position on the list, and there was no selection scheme to advance deserving and active officers over the heads of the superannuated. The system provided for voluntary retirement at thirty years of service and mandatory retirement at age sixty-four. The list did not apply to general officers' promotions, which were by selection.

Strict adherence to the promotion list had the advantage of allowing every officer to know his promotion prospects precisely and gave assurance that there could be no favoritism or nepotism. In practice, of course, the choice assignments still went to the favorites who had the rank to qualify for them. The disadvantages of the system included lack of reward for initiative and ability, slow promotion, and bureaucratic routine.

Before World War I, each branch within the U.S. Army (such as cavalry, infantry, artillery, and quartermaster) had maintained its own separate promotion list, so some officers were promoted faster than others of equal ability and time of service. To remedy this perceived flaw, Congress, in the National Defense Act of 1920, combined all Regular Army promotion lists into a single list, providing that no officer would hold a relative position on the combined list lower than the one he held on his branch list at the time of the bill's passage. In the same act Congress established the Air Service as a separate branch within the Army; specified that at all times 90 percent of its officers must be rated flyers, balloonists, or observers; and required that all command positions be filled by rated officers.

---

* The air branch of the U.S. Army underwent three name changes from 1919 to 1941: from 1919 through the first half of 1926 it was officially the Army Air Service; from July 1926 through June 1941 it was the Army Air Corps; and from June 1941 to September 1947 it was the Army Air Forces.

8

These provisions created a closed shop. Officers elsewhere in the Army could not transfer into the Air Service unless they passed flight training. Such a switch proved difficult for field-grade officers (major and above). Their age (mid-thirties, at best) and the extremely high physical standards for pilots almost guaranteed failure to gain a rating. Hence accretions to the Air Service's and Air Corps' Regular Army officer ranks came, for the most part, at the 2d lieutenant grade, from West Point graduates and from Reserve Officers, Flying Cadets, and enlisted pilots earning regular commissions.

So stringent were the air branch's physical standards that only the finest specimens entered its training programs. Men who flew in open, unheated cockpits at altitudes well over 10,000 feet at all times of the year, without oxygen, in aircraft lacking most types of power-assisted controls required extraordinary stamina. The air branch's basic and advanced flight training eliminated a large percentage of would-be pilots. On the average, about 40 percent of each entering class completed both stages of training, although in some classes as few as 25 percent graduated. Charles A. Lindbergh, who underwent flight training in 1924, recalled that only 17 of 103 members of his class completed training, and the Air Corps passed only 128 of 592 students in fiscal 1928.[34] Moreover, from 1921 to 1938, 95 flying cadets died in air accidents.[35]

Because the Air Service (and its predecessors) had existed only since 1907, it had had no time to develop its own higher-ranking officers. Even Hap Arnold,

Maj. Gen. Mason Patrick, Chief of the Air Service, and Brig. Gen. William "Billy" Mitchell, early 1920s.

one of the very first Army pilots, was only a major and barely in the upper 40 percent of the major's ranks of the promotion list. In July 1923, Arnold was the fifteenth-ranking major in the Air Service but only 909th of 2,250 majors in the entire Army. At the same time Spaatz was the 88th ranking major (of 89) in the Air Service and stood 2,207 on the majors list. It took Arnold almost nine years to reach lieutenant colonel (February 1932) and Spaatz more than twelve years (September 1935) to advance through the entire major's portion of the list to lieutenant colonel.

The Army's air branch had a much lower percentage of field-grade officers than the remainder of the Army. (See Table 1, Distribution of Regular Army Rank in the Air Service and Air Corps Compared with the Army as a Whole 1922–1941.) From 1923 to 1935, the Air Corps had an average of less than 11 percent of its Regular Army officers in field grades. The remainder of the Army averaged a little less than 33 percent field-grade officers for the same period. This imbalance resulted in underrepresentation of the Air Corps' views and lack of understanding of the Air Corps' difficulties at the senior levels of the Army. But if the lack of field-grade officers hurt the Air Corps as an institution within the Army, in the long run it may have advanced the careers of officers within the Air Corps itself.[36]

The lack of rank within the Air Corps—even within the field grades the great majority of officers were majors—meant that officers assumed responsibility and gained experience at levels far above their actual rank. The 1930 Annual Report of the Chief of the Air Corps noted that Air Corps Tables of Organization called for a major to command each squadron. Yet, of 53 squadrons, majors led only 5, and 4 of those majors doubled as base commanders. One squadron was led by a second lieutenant of less than four years' service.[37] From 1921 to 1938, if not beyond, the same 75 to 90 field-grade officers, many of whom became AAF generals in World War II, controlled the inner workings of the air arm. Spaatz, who served as a major for most of the period between 1921 and 1938, was always one of the 100 most senior officers in his branch. In an institution in which considerations of rank and seniority dominated personnel assignments, Spaatz's seniority kept him constantly in important command and staff positions.

If the Air Corps had a paucity of field grade officers, it had an overabundance of junior officers (captain and below), partly by design. In the early 1920s, Air Service thinking estimated a pilot's active flying career at eight years under wartime conditions and, at most, fourteen years under peacetime conditions.[38] Because the air branch insisted on officer pilots, it required only first and second lieutenants to operate individual aircraft, with captains to command flights. Once a man's flying career ceased, about the time he might expect to become a major, he could be transferred, sent to the reserves, or discharged. The operation of aircraft by officer pilots necessitated a force heavy in junior officers. In 1924 the Air Service used a figure of 85 percent captains and lieutenants as the optimum,[39] not

Table 1

Distribution of Regular Army Rank in the Air Service and Air Corps Compared with the Army as a Whole, 1922–1941

Year	Col	Lt Col	Maj	Capt	1st Lt	2d Lt	Total
1922	3/627	10/797	115/2,760	605/3,204	605/3,204	19/202	919/12,711
1923[a]	3/509	11/682	86/2,182	124/4,073	544/2,783	127/1,184	895/11,413
1924	3/507	13/685	90/2,177	129/4,079	516/2,764	116/1,051	867/11,264
1925	3/504	13/689	97/2,163	127/4,142	510/2,695	163/1,519	913/11,712
1926	2/500	13/688	98/2,157	127/4,148	502/2,688	142/1,431	884/11,612
1927	2/530	16/675	97/2,139	126/4,140	507/2,717	172/1,547	919/11,748
1928	2/549	16/658	97/2,127	132/4,139	507/2,726	207/1,605	961/11,804
1929	3/556	16/663	99/2,188	153/4,112	494/2,753	294/1,691	1,059/11,963
1930	6/571	18/665	92/2,447	158/3,815	492/2,787	441/1,754	1,207/12,039
1931	6/567	21/674	90/2,482	228/3,751	431/2,820	460/1,816	1,236/12,110
1932	7/559	26/697	90/2,528	298/3,706	375/2,786	458/1,857	1,254/12,133
1933	10/557	30/717	84/2,509	341/3,741	373/2,757	444/1,754	1,282/12,035
1934	8/553	33/737	80/2,468	391/3,767	384/2,746	403/1,940	1,299/12,208
1935[b]	9/557	30/725	85/2,419	430/3,778	519/2,812	230/1,680	1,303/11,971
1936	18/727	54/1,087	96/3,259	579/4,009	530/2,113	82/856	1,359/12,051
1937	24/745	58/1,230	97/3,136	599/4,009	504/2,156	126/973	1,408/12,249
1938	27/764	57/1,553	114/2,821	649/4,066	488/2,222	97/1,022	1,432/12,448
1939	25/793	56/1,605	130/2,858	729/4,094	416/2,146	314/1,471	1,670/12,967
1940	26/854	61/1,637	297/3,051	675/3,899	378/2,238	773/2,085	2,210/13,764
1941	29/852	161/3,834	398/2,482	493/2,386	418/2,344	845/2,338	2,344/14,236

a. The Dickman Board demoted 236 majors, 750 captains, and 800 first lieutenants by January 1, 1923.

b. The Promotion Act of 1935 shifted the World War I "hump" one rank higher from first and second lieutenant to first lieutenant and captain.

Compiled from the Official Reports of the Secretary of War.

far from the 90 percent average of 1923 to 1935. Throughout the interwar period the air branch supplemented its number of officer pilots by using reserve officers; for most years the air branch had by far the largest number of reservists on duty for periods exceeding fifteen days of any branch.[40] In practice the single promotion list thwarted the expectations of the Air Service and the Air Corps.

Instead of an even distribution of officers with like times of service throughout, the list had instances of many individuals crammed into a small time-of-service bracket. Officers who joined the Army in World War I formed one such logjam. At the rear of that jam was what the air officers called the promotion "hump." When men joined the Army at the beginning of the war, those wishing to fly went to flight training, in some cases for twelve to eighteen months. The flyers received their commissions only after they had completed flight training. They were thus well behind the men who joined other branches and earned their commissions months earlier. In the interwar period this placed a large percentage of Air Corps junior-grade officers at the bottom of the promotion list, with little prospect of ever reaching field grade. In 1930, 400 of the 494 Regular Army first lieutenants in the Air Corps had wartime experience.[41] The most senior of them would have to advance 3,800 places through the captains' ranks and one-third of the way through the entire list to reach major—a daunting prospect. The effect on the entering second lieutenants, who could not even make captain until the hump cleared, also must have been dramatic. The limited promotion potential coupled with the lack of personnel turnover contributed to the aging of the small officer corps. (Table 2 for the year 1931, the mid-point between the wars, illustrates the interwar relation between age and rank.) It was no wonder that the bulk of resignations from the whole officer corps, not just the air branch, consisted of junior-grade officers. From 1924 through 1933, 3 colonels, 8 lieutenant colonels, 81 majors, 239 captains, 231 first lieutenants, and 391 second lieutenants resigned from the Regular Army, an average of 95 a year from a force of approximately 12,000.[42] As always, those with the least invested in the service and the worst prospects of advancement were most likely to resign. Well over 90 percent of the officer corps chose to stay with the colors.

The officer corps as a whole formed a conservative, all-white society removed from the mainstream of American life. Postings to isolated forts and bases, lives spent in the military ghetto of officers' on-base housing, a promotion policy of glacial slowness, and a professional ethos that led to concentration on the technical aspects of their work and to the avoidance of participation in the partisan civilian world accounted for much of the Regular Army officers' segregation. The officers of the Air Service and Corps formed a small band of brothers set apart even from the officer corps at large.* They numbered no larger than the student body of a medium-size urban high school and they spent much of their careers in small groups of a few dozen or less on primitive airfields. Their agita-

---

* Regular officers left the air branch by three routes: death, resignation, or retirement. Only a statistically insignificant number of them were dismissed or discharged. From 1925 through 1935, 131 regular officers died in air crashes, 35 died of other causes, 126 resigned, and 72 retired. At the same time, the air branch grew from 913 regular officers to 1,303. As one would expect, retirements were concentrated in the years after 1928 (70 of 72), as senior officers who joined the service at the time of the Spanish-American War and later reached retirement age departed. Resignations peaked in 1930, with 27, as the junior officers resigned to join the newly established commercial airlines, and trailed off drastically during the Depression; only 16 regular officers resigned from 1931 to 1935. Figures were compiled from the Annual Reports of the Chief of the Air Corps, 1921–1935.

Table 2
Age and Rank of the U.S. Army Officer Corps, 1931

Age	Maj Gen	Brig Gen	Col	Lt Col	Maj	Capt	1st Lt	2d Lt	Total
64	2	1	8						11
63	2	3	19						24
62	1	5	25	1	1	1			34
61	1	5	18	2	4	1	1		32
60	1	7	36	2	9	5			60
59	4	6	41	4	5	9	1		70
58	1	4	42	7	13	7			74
57	5	7	60	12	11	16	5		116
56	2	2	65	21	10	15	2		117
55		1	64	23	26	22	2		138
54		4	43	44	19	20	2		132
53			28	57	18	35	9		147
52		1	12	70	15	40	11		149
51	1		6	33	24	53	6		123
50			2	75	22	50	7		156
49			1	77	54	70	7		209
48				49	50	84	9		192
47				31	77	56	14		178
46				12	113	73	13		211
45				7	136	124	18		285
44					139	134	25		298
43					144	128	31		303
42					132	172	30		354
41					169	230	52		451
40					159	317	59		535
39					146	376	101		623
38					116	381	115		612
37					61	382	143		586
36					29	400	213		642
35					2	188	248		438
34					1	14	295	6	316
33						3	261	14	278
32							249	19	268
31							270	40	310
30							258	71	329
29							178	136	314
28							66	182	248
27							10	265	275
26								286	286
25								259	259
24								260	260
23								155	155
22								69	69
21								18	18
Total	20	46	470	527	1,725	3,406	2,711	1,780	10,685

Extracted from the July 1, 1931 Army List and Directory.

tion for a separate promotion list,[43] the flight or danger pay they earned while on flying status (which many in the rest of the Army resented), and the fight between the air arm and the rest of the service over the air portion of the budget set the air arm apart from the Army as a whole. Although the leading cause of accidental death* for the entire Army from 1927 to 1936 was automobile accidents (660), the second leading cause of death was airplane accidents (459)[44]— a category confined to only one branch of the service. (See Table 3, Flight Accident Statistics, 1921–1938.) This danger exclusively to themselves, their low positions on the promotion list, and their mutual participation in an exhilarating, yet highly technical, occupation bound the air officers together.

Understandably the division of the budget and other service resources created some of the fiercest tension in the Army. From 1920 to 1934, the total cost of Army aviation ranged between 13.1 and 22.7 percent of the Army budget, averaging 18.2 percent a year. This included not only direct appropriations to the air arm but also indirect expenses such as pay, quartermaster and medical services, ordnance, subsistence, construction, and issue of supplies from the war reserve from other Army accounts.[45] Such expenses in an era of unremitting fiscal belt-tightening created bitterness within the rest of the Army as the financially conservative Coolidge administration, the Depression-ridden Hoover administration, and the first Roosevelt administration sought to reduce War Department expenditures without regard to military capability.[46]

Spaatz's life in the interwar years was not uneventful. In 1919 he led the Far West Flying Circus in mock dogfighting and stunting exhibitions as part of the Air Service's contribution to the Liberty Loan drive. In December of that year, he received a letter of commendation for his achievements in the Transcontinental Reliability Endurance Flight. Spaatz won elapsed time west to east, finished third west to east all types, and won second place west to east DH-4 class.[47] Colonel (ex-Brig. Gen.) Mitchell, now head of the Air Service's Training and Operations Group, had organized the flight of about eighty service aircraft as a promotional effort to generate public enthusiasm for aviation.[48] By October 1919, Spaatz had already, in the course of his career, amassed 600 hours of flight time; checked out in eighteen types of French, British, and American aircraft (including the treacherous Morane monoplane); and crashed five times.[49]

In April 1919, Spaatz became one of only six men to ever receive the rating of Military Aviator on the grounds of distinguished service.[50] Before World War I, Congress had authorized the Aviation Section of the Army Signal Corps to award Junior Military Aviator and Military Aviator ratings for piloting skill; the ratings carried temporary increases in rank and pay. Spaatz himself had qualified as a Junior Military Aviator. Congress discontinued the ratings in 1916 but allowed their retention by those who had earned them. During the war, Congress

---

* Fatalities resulting from illness were the leading cause of all deaths for the officer corps.

Table 3
Flight Accident Statistics, 1921–1938

	1921	1922	1923	1924	1925	1926	1927	1928	1929	1930	1931	1932	1933	1934	1935	1936	1937	1938	Total
Aircraft Accidents																			
Aircraft hours (1,000s)	75	65	66	98	150	158	141	183	263	325	396	371	433	374	449	501	513	591	3,252
Number of accidents	361	330	283	275	311	334	227	249	390	471	456	423	442	412	453	430	358	375	6,158
Number of fatal accidents	45	24	33	23	29	27	28	25	42	37	21	33	28	35	33	42	27	38	606
Number of fatalities	73	44	58	34	38	42	43	27	61	52	26	50	46	54	47	59	48	62	864
Number of injured	98	97	89	55	119	79	60	52	72	82	76	89	82	83	75	69	53	63	1,393
Details of Fatalities																			
Regular Army, officers	35	21	28	15	17	14	18	12	9	19	8	13	9	15	12	21	15	15	296
Regular Army, enlisted men	17	15	18	8	11	10	5	5	26	9	3	9	13	14	12	17	16	13	221
Regular Army, flying cadets	13	7	1	3	1	0	9	4	10	9	3	6	3	8	3	3	3	9	95
Reserve Corps, officers	0	1	7	5	8	14	9	4	13	11	9	20	18	16	7	9	12	20	183
Miscellaneous	8	0	4	3	1	4	2	2	3	4	3	2	3	1	13	9	2	5	69
Accident Rates (per 1,000 flying hours)																			
Fatalities	0.94	0.86	0.88	0.35	0.25	0.27	0.31	0.15	0.23	0.16	0.07	0.13	0.11	0.14	0.10	0.12	0.09	0.11	0.27
Accidents	4.67	5.06	4.30	2.81	2.07	1.96	1.61	1.36	1.48	1.45	1.15	1.14	1.02	1.10	1.01	0.86	0.70	0.63	1.89

Compiled from the Official Reports of the Chief of the Army Air Service Corps.

reinstated the award of ratings but for distinguished service instead of skill in aviation. Aside from the honor, the rating entitled Spaatz to a flight pay of 75 percent of base pay, an emolument he continued to draw even after the National Defense Act of 1920 limited all flight pay, except for distinguished Military Aviators, to 50 percent. This benefit loomed even larger when Congress passed the Pay Classification Act of 1922, compressing the differences between pay for rank and emphasizing longevity of service. Under the new act Spaatz's base pay, for a major with less than 23 years' service, was $2,400 per annum.

Throughout the period between the two world wars, Spaatz probably earned more per year than any other nongeneral officer in the Army. The family apparently lived comfortably with little left over from day-to-day expenses. In 1925, in planning for his expected retirement with thirty years' service in 1940, Spaatz bemoaned his financial status, saying, "I have $300 in the bank and owe about $2,000."[51] His finances continued to do no better until very late in his career. Nonetheless, the extra money certainly gave him the advantage of relative peace of mind and the comfort of a lifestyle unavailable to many of his peers. It may well have allowed him to concentrate on his profession without the distraction of worry.

In 1921 Spaatz and Arnold, who had sealed their friendship during a mutual tour of duty in California, served up a wacky public relations ploy. They persuaded the chef of a San Francisco hotel to prepare the first egg to be laid and fried in flight. On the day of the great Egg Festival at Petaluma, the chicken capital of California, Tooey and the chef added a prize hen to the crew and headed back for the bay area. They arrived *sans poulet*—the hen jumped ship at several hundred feet and dived into San Francisco Bay. But the flight did not exactly lay an egg; the chef threw a bash to celebrate his own safe arrival while the newspapers carried the story.[52]

From 1922 to 1924, Spaatz commanded the 1st Pursuit Group—the only pursuit group in the Air Service—at Selfridge Field in Michigan, just outside Detroit. By June 1922, the nation's military aviation had shrunk to a force of fewer than 10,000 officers and enlisted men.[53] At Selfridge, he earned a reprimand for neglect of duty. One of Spaatz's great qualities as a leader was his ability to delegate authority and to allow his subordinates to do their jobs with minimum interference from above. This time the trait backfired: his finance officer, 1st Lt. Howard Farmer, embezzled $15,000. A court-martial sent Farmer to prison, and a review of its findings led to an official reprimand for Spaatz, who, aware of Farmer's weakness for drinking and gambling, should have removed him from temptation. Instead, he had accepted the officer's pledge not to gamble while entrusted with government funds.[54] Although Spaatz was very upset at the deserved reprimand, it was a measure of his force of character that he did not overcompensate by too closely circumscribing the actions of future subordinates.[55]

During his stay at Selfridge Field, Spaatz cemented his relationship with the

16

Assistant Chief of the Army Air Service, Brig. Gen. Billy Mitchell, who regarded the 1st Pursuit Group as his favorite organization.[56] After an inspection trip in August 1922, Mitchell remarked, "I have had the First Pursuit Group in the air every day that I have been here. Their work is extremely satisfactory." He added, "I don't think we could have a better Commanding Officer of the Group."[57] During the course of these seignorial visits, Mitchell invariably expected Spaatz to procure a powerful motor car, usually from Rickenbacker Motor Corporation, for his personal use. On one occasion Mitchell shipped six of his own horses to Detroit, asking Spaatz to find a government veterinarian, forage, and men to fix up some stables.[58] Within three days Spaatz had fulfilled the general's request.[59]

In the course of his many trips to Selfridge, Mitchell, one of the most ardent air power enthusiasts, took pains to imprint his views on Spaatz. Although Mitchell predicted that bombardment aviation would someday have its principal value in "hitting an enemy's great nerve centers," he gave primacy of place to pursuit aviation.[60] Mitchell believed that gaining air superiority over the enemy air force was the first and the most necessary task of the air arm. Without freedom to operate, air could not perform any of its other missions or deny enemy air the ability to conduct its own missions. Mitchell emphasized that friendly pursuit aircraft must locate the enemy, concentrate against him, and drive him from the sky. Only then could friendly air proceed with the bombardment of enemy forces and installations.[61]

In accordance with these theories and others developed from World War I experience, the Air Service organized three types of combat units: pursuit, bombardment, and attack. Pursuit had counterair and ground-strafing roles. Bombardment would attack naval vessels and enemy industrial centers and other key areas behind enemy lines and assist in attacks against field targets. Official manuals, which were approved by the ground officers who dominated the War Department General Staff, paid little attention to the planning or conduct of strategic bombing. Instead, they concentrated on bombardment's role in ground operations. Attack aviation would conduct low-level attacks with heavy machine guns, cannon, and bombs against battlefield targets. Airmen who believed such low-level attacks would expend both men and machines to little purpose were overruled by ground officers who valued front-line morale-boosting missions against immediate tactical targets.[62]

Spaatz took Mitchell's theories to heart. In February 1922, he wrote to the Chief of the Air Service that he conceived of four distinct types of pursuit missions—offensive, defensive, night, and attack—each requiring a plane of different design.[63] As commander of the only pursuit group, he participated in the writing of several pursuit training and tactical manuals, including overall pursuit aviation training regulations, as well as regulations for the pursuit pilot, squadron, group, and wing.[64] In only one case did Spaatz envisage the employment of pursuit in an exclusively defensive role. "The first bomb dropped by an enemy on

A snow-covered ramp at Selfridge Field filled with Boeing and Curtiss pursuits. Frozen Lake Michigan appears in the background, early 1930s.

one of our cities," he stated, "will cause such a clamor that no executive would be strong enough to withstand it." Spaatz noted, however, that defensive pursuit would be anything but defensive once airborne.[65] When asked to comment on the attack aviation manuals, Spaatz indicated that "pursuit forces should not accompany the attack forces in the manner of an escort but should be concentrated over the objective of the attack at the time the attack forces arrive to deliver the attack." Spaatz added, "The attack forces must be prepared to disperse a small force of the enemy pursuit which may molest them on their way to and from the objective."[66] It is important not to make too much of the influence of this early thinking on his subsequent actions, but it seems that Spaatz was at least predisposed to accept a doctrine that called for loose escort of bombers by fighters and aggressive employment of fighter aircraft at all times.

While serving in Michigan, Spaatz had his first encounter with "drop tanks," jettisonable aviation fuel tanks carried externally by fighter aircraft. He observed, "This arrangement, of course, permits pursuit to penetrate to much greater depth without destroying its characteristics."[67] Here was part of the solution to the long-range fighter-escort problem that would plague Spaatz and other bomber commanders twenty years later. Spaatz had recognized one piece of the long-range escort puzzle, but, like most other Air Corps officers, he was unable to fit that piece into place, to fully realize that drop tanks would give an aircraft of fighter performance a bomber's range.

Spaatz left the 1st Pursuit Group in 1924 to attend his branch of service's professional school, the Air Service Tactical School at Langley Field, near Norfolk, Virginia, where he had time for reflection—especially when he was hospitalized for a neck abscess that almost led to blood poisoning. While at Langley, he kept a diary, a practice he would not resume until he went to England in May 1940. Spaatz, in an introspective mood, attributed the death of one of his classmates in an air accident in part to reflexes slowed by age. Thirty-three years old at the time, he himself had just had a close call and wondered whether his own skills were slipping.[68] In one of the few personally revealing notes in his papers, he analyzed himself as follows:

CHARACTER ANALYSIS CAUSES AND REMEDIES

1. Tendency to false illusion that nothing is worth-while except that done by myself.

2. Tendency to be opinionated without sufficient knowledge.

3. Mental laziness . . . resulting in ability to group quickly certain things but with no retentiveness, also resulting in inability to form definite conclusions and pursue consistent line of thought.

4. Tendency to assume everyone acts with right motives hence no effort to differentiate between men to separate those whose mental makeup prevent[s] their acting with right motives as in case of Farmer [the erring finance officer].

5. Egotism which impels me to make authoritative statements on subjects or about things with which I am unfamiliar or only vaguely informed.

6. Tendency to trust instinct rather than make effort to employ reason.

7. Shyness induced by egotism (hating to admit lack of knowledge), mental laziness.[69]

This gloomy self-evaluation accurately highlighted several aspects of Spaatz's personality. He had a quick mind but he was not an air power intellectual or philosopher. He relied on instinct and intuition rather than on systematic thought. Nor did he have any illusions regarding his depth of knowledge on most subjects; throughout most of his career he displayed no great interest, knowledge, or sympathy with affairs other than those directly affecting aviation. Finally, he admitted his "shyness," which manifested itself in a painfully wooden manner in staff conferences or formal briefings requiring a rapid interchange of ideas.

Before graduating from the Tactical School in June 1925, Spaatz traveled to Washington, D.C., to attend the hearings of the House Military Affairs Committee on the Curry Bill for a "separate Air Service." A month later he gave testimony to the Lampert Committee of the House of Representatives which was investigating U.S. aviation. After stating that he personally knew 60 to 70 percent of the Army's flyers, Spaatz gave his views on the place of aviation in the U.S. military: "The general feeling is that under present conditions we are not getting anywhere." He went on to express his feeling that, as a new medium of combat, the Air Service required its own unique regulations, training doctrines, and methods of conducting warfare. He objected to the then current arrangements under which "we follow the doctrines laid down by the Army for their operations so far as the Army is concerned." He added that "any work we may do is based on the effect it has on the Army's operations. . . . No well-defined policy of independent operations by an air force acting independently of the Army is being developed under present conditions." Finally, he noted the prevalent opinion within the Air Service that the next war would start in the air and that if it were to do so soon, "this country is absolutely defenseless."[70]

After Langley, Spaatz was posted to Washington, D.C., as Assistant G-3 for Training and Operations in the Office of the Chief of the Air Service. Arnold occupied the office next door. Spaatz's four-year stay in Washington opened with the controversial court-martial of his old commanding officer, Billy Mitchell, during October and November 1925, in which Spaatz and Arnold loyally supported Mitchell. Spaatz participated in the ensuing *cause célèbre* as one of the first defense witnesses, testifying about the current strength of the Air Service. In his judgment, 1,300 of the 1,800 planes available were obsolete and only 400 were "standard." Of those 400, more than half were of World War I vintage; furthermore, only 26 of them were bombers and only 39 were observation planes. Spaatz noted that the U.S. Air Service had only 59 modern planes fit for duty. "By dragging all administrative officers from their desks," Spaatz said that he could put 15 pursuit planes into the air, adding, "It is very disheartening to attempt to train or do work under such circumstances."[71] In a key exchange, the defense counsel asked Spaatz if he thought the War Department was slowing the development of air power. The prosecutor objected that the question called for a conclusion on the part of the witness, but in the accompanying hubbub, Spaatz replied, "I do."

The defense counsel pressed, "Would the recommendation made by Colonel Mitchell have improved the Air Service in the technical and other divisions?" The prosecutor objected, and Spaatz was forbidden to say whether flyers were sufficiently trained in gunnery to fight a war. Members of the court also questioned Spaatz. One particularly sharp exchange took place between Spaatz and the president of the court, sixty-one-year-old Maj. Gen. Robert L. Howze. Howze, an old Indian fighter who had earned a Congressional Medal of Honor fighting the Sioux after Wounded Knee (the award of the medal was announced the day the court-martial opened) and had commanded a division in France, asked who was to blame for any shortcomings. Spaatz replied that, where gunnery was involved, the squadron commanders were at fault. Howze continued, "Is there anybody higher up than the commander of this unit who is responsible for the gunnery work?" Spaatz responded, "Well, in the case of the First Pursuit Group [his old command], the commander of the VI Corps Area has charge of it." Spaatz's pointed rejoinder drew the blood of the VI Corps Area Commander, who happened to be a member of the court.

Maj. Gen. William S. Graves, leader of the U.S. Expeditionary Force in

Brig. Gen. William Mitchell addressing his court-martial, Washington, D.C., October 28, 1925.

Siberia, 1918–1919, asked whether his office had ever denied help to the air squadron. Spaatz responded that when the people of Oscoda, Michigan, had offered to rent a gunnery practice field to the Air Service for a dollar a year, he had had trouble persuading the War Department to pay. The crowd laughed, but Graves won the point when Spaatz was unable to recall specifically which office had delayed the matter.

Neither Spaatz's nor Arnold's testimony swayed the court, which was even less impressed with Mitchell's decision to conduct an all-out defense designed to take advantage of the circus atmosphere engendered by the trial's heavy press coverage. The court-martial suspended Mitchell from active duty for five years, and he resigned.[72]

The statements Spaatz made at the court-martial illustrate the intensity of his convictions about preparedness and the status of the Air Service. Despite warnings that his appearance might jeopardize his career, Spaatz, who believed in loyalty up and loyalty down, supported Mitchell. He displayed equal amounts of courage and tactlessness in bluntly describing Air Service conditions and in fixing responsibility for them. Spaatz later commented, "They can't do anything to you when you're under oath and tell them answers to their questions."[73]

During his first tour in Washington, D.C., Spaatz demonstrated another unusual facet of his character, his respect for the independence and intelligence of women. Although anything but a ladykiller or a Don Juan, Spaatz liked and appreciated women. As the father of three daughters and no sons he became used to living in a feminine household and he endured much good-natured teasing about his "harem." He developed many deep friendships with remarkable ·women in the course of his career. While in Washington, he encouraged his wife to accept what was then a remarkable opportunity. For three years Ruth Spaatz became the member of a professional standing acting troupe at the National Theater. She eventually played leading roles. Given society's attitudes toward working mothers and actresses, Spaatz's support of his wife seems all the more unusual.[74] Later, he would be one of the first and most enthusiastic supporters of the Women's Army Corps (WAC), in World War II. In fact, his executive officer for most of World War II was a WAC, which made him probably the only officer of his rank in the U.S. armed services to have a woman serving in such a role.

Spaatz continued on staff duties until the end of 1928, when he received orders to command the 7th Bombardment Group at Rockwell Field in southern California. One of his first actions there involved a publicity stunt conceived by a close friend, Capt. Ira C. Eaker. Eaker proposed to set a new world record in flight endurance. In the moderate, predictable weather of southern California the flight would be safer, less stressful, and free of weather-imposed interference. There was also easy access to the media in nearby Hollywood. The idea appealed to Spaatz's adventurous instincts and he quickly endorsed Eaker's proposal.

Between January 1 and 7, 1929, the flight of the *Question Mark*, a Fokker trimotor transport aircraft, commanded by Major Spaatz and crewed by Captain Eaker, Lt. Elwood R. Quesada, and Lt. Harry A. Halverson, set a world flight endurance record of 150 hours, 40 minutes, and 14 seconds, shuttling between Los Angeles and San Diego and gaining national and international attention. The *Question Mark*, so named because no one knew when it would come down, had its fuel tanks filled in the air 37 times, received 5,600 gallons of hand-pumped fuel, and traveled 11,000 miles. Perceptive observers noted that if Spaatz and his crew could man a craft that long, so could bomber crews.[75] Less technologically oriented observers had different opinions. When Ruth Spaatz pointed out the aircraft flying overhead to the Spaatz's oldest daughter, seven-year-old Tattie, and remarked, "That's your daddy, and he's been up there longer than any human being has ever been in the air before. Isn't it marvelous?" Tattie crushingly replied, "I think it's sort of dumb."[76]

Early in the flight—on January 1, as the plane flew over the Rose Bowl football game—the converted fire hose lowered for in-flight refueling came loose from the tank opening above the *Question Mark* and drenched Spaatz with 72-octane gasoline. Quesada headed for calmer weather over the ocean while the other crew members removed Spaatz's clothes and rubbed him down to prevent burns. Spaatz told them, "If I'm burned and have to bail out you keep this plane in the air, and that's an order."[77] When refueling recommenced, the unharmed major, clad only in a parachute and a grin, stood halfway out an open hatch to make sure nothing separated again.

On January 4, heavy fog prevented supply ships from locating the *Question Mark*, which had flown inland toward the Imperial Valley and clearer skies. When the *Question Mark* finally contacted a refueler, both aircraft almost hit the ground after entering an air pocket. Throughout the flight, supply ships delivered box lunches prepared by Air Corps wives or purchased from local diners, and when the standing endurance record was broken, ground crews sent up five jars of caviar, cheese, figs, and ripe olives.[78] Engine trouble finally forced the plane down.

The feat earned the *Question Mark*'s crew Distinguished Flying Crosses. Spaatz's citation read in part, "By his endurance, resourcefulness and leadership, he demonstrated future possibilities in aviation which were heretofore not apparent and thus reflected great credit upon himself and the Army of the United States."[79] Of course, fleeting international fame and medals carried no weight with penny-pinching clerks at the War Department. They forwarded the flight's meal vouchers, approximately $75 per man, to the Comptroller General of the United States, who refused payment, noting:

> The fact that in the performance of the duty here in question the officers could not procure subsistence in the usual manner or at the accustomed places and that it was necessary to procure subsistence by means otherwise than ordinarily procured, creates no status giving a right to have the subsistence furnished them at the expense of the United States.[80]

The flight inspired several imitators and by the end of the year civilian aviators had set an endurance record of 420 hours.[81]

The *Question Mark* flight again demonstrated Spaatz's skill as an administrator and logistician. He set up more than adequate refueling and resupply arrangements and showed his intense desire to fulfill his duty—even at risk to himself. The drive to complete a task, in spite of obstacles, was his hallmark.

After three years at Rockwell Field, Spaatz assumed command of the 1st Bombardment Wing at March Field in Riverside, California. From California, Spaatz traveled back to the Potomac in 1933 where he served for two years as Chief of the Training and Operations Division in the Office of the Chief of the Air Corps (OCAC). In 1935 he received his first promotion in seventeen years— to lieutenant colonel.

With the promotion came orders to attend the Army Command and General Staff School at Fort Leavenworth in Kansas. Most officers looked forward to this posting because it was a mandatory stepping-stone to the rank of general officer. Spaatz objected that he was too old (forty-four and only six years from retirement) and that he had no interest in the operation of an infantry division. He wrote Arnold, "I am going to Leavenworth not because I expect it will do me any good, but primarily because I am ordered there and secondarily to get away from here [Washington]."[82] He felt some relief, though, that the course had been reduced from two years to one.

True to character, Spaatz, as he had done twenty-one years earlier at West Point, did barely enough course work to pass, finishing 94th out of 121. He made little attempt to conceal his contempt for the failure of the courses to contain a meaningful appreciation of air power. This attitude earned him an unfavorable recommendation for any further training in general staff or high command duty.[83] The school had little influence on him and he apparently learned almost nothing of value there.

Organization and Doctrine of the Prewar Air Corps

Upon leaving Leavenworth in July 1936, Spaatz became Executive Officer, 2d Wing, of the recently created General Headquarters (GHQ) Air Force, Langley Field in Virginia. The three wings of GHQ Air Force were far larger than the units that had previously held that designation in the Air Corps. As a consequence, in going from a wing commander at March Field in 1933 to the new post in one of the three major combat units in the service, Spaatz assumed a position entirely in keeping with his seniority. The only operational squadron of B-17s in the Air Corps made up part of the 2d Wing's order of battle. The assignment to the big four-engine bombers showed how far Spaatz and Army air power had come since the Mitchell court-martial.

Although the Air Corps Act of July 2, 1926, had changed the designation of the Army Air Service to the Army Air Corps and had authorized an expansion to 1,800 aircraft and 20,000 officers and men, extra funds had never come and the change of name had left the Air Corps' status unchanged; it remained one of the Army's combat branches. Over the next nine years, numerous bills on air reform were introduced in Congress, but not one received a favorable committee report. The failure to obtain independence had led many Air Corps officers, including Maj. Gen. Benjamin Foulois, to settle for something more obtainable. They proposed to divide Army aviation into two components: (1) observation planes normally assigned the armies, corps, mobile units, and fixed harbor defenses; and (2) remaining tactical support and striking force units grouped under the GHQ Air Force. The GHQ Air Force would operate under the wartime Army Supreme Commander (Army planning did not envisage a two-front war) to locate and attack the enemy; to assist the Army ground forces by attacking enemy rear areas; and to give direct support and cooperation, when required, to the ground forces. Spaatz served under Col. Frank M. Andrews on an Air Corps board that was authorized by the War Department to plan the creation of the GHQ Air Force, a concept Spaatz supported.

On March 1, 1935, with the strong support of the Army Chief of Staff, General Douglas MacArthur, GHQ Air Force became a reality, gathering under

Maj. Gen. James E. Fechet, Chief, U.S. Army Air Corps, discussing the *Question Mark*'s flight with its crew. *Left to right*: **1st Lt. Elwood R. Quesada, Capt. Ira C. Eaker, Fechet, Maj. Carl A. Spaatz, and Sgt. Roy G. Hooe.**

its aegis all the tactical units based in the United States. It formed three combat wings, one at its headquarters at Langley Field and the other two at Barksdale Field in Louisiana and March Field in California. This measure at least brought much of the Air Corps' combat strength into a single cohesive command structure.

Unfortunately, this reorganization grafted GHQ Air Force onto the already existing Air Corps. Both the Chief of the Air Corps, who retained responsibility for matériel procurement, personnel recruitment, and individual training and indoctrination of air crews, and the Commanding General, GHQ Air Force, reported directly to the Army Chief of Staff. This duality led to friction and competition between the two separate parts of the Air Corps—a situation of divide and rule not unforeseen by the War Department. In March 1939, under the pressure of rearmament and possible war in Europe, both GHQ Air Force and the Office of the Chief of Air Corps became directly responsible to the Chief of the Air Corps.

Technology and doctrine both underwent considerable changes in the post-Mitchell Air Corps. Spaatz, who had started the 1920s as one of the Air Service's pursuit (fighter) experts, ended the 1920s and spent most of the 1930s as a bombardment commander, first as Commanding Officer (CO), 7th Bombardment Group, from May 1929 to October 1931; then as CO, 1st Bomb Wing,

The *Question Mark* Flight, January 1929. Scenes from the aerial experiment. *Clockwise from above*: The interior of the *Question Mark* reveals the positions of an auxiliary gas tank on the floor, refueling apparatus on the roof, and berths. A chase aircraft with its chalked message *(opposite, above)* shows one means of communication before the introduction of reliable airborne radios. The gravity-fed transfer of gasoline proceeds between aircraft *(opposite, below)*. Spaatz *(below)* wrestles with the refueling hose as it reaches the *Question Mark*.

from November 1931 to June 1933; and finally as Executive Officer of the 2d Wing, GHQ Air Force, from July 1936 to January 1939. This change in the technical focus of Spaatz's career reflected the changes in aircraft and philosophy that influenced the Air Corps in the 1930s.

Between 1930 and 1932, two fast, all-metal, monoplane twin-engine bombers entered the Air Corps inventory, the Boeing B-9 and the Martin B-10. The B-10, with a speed of 207 mph and a ceiling of 21,000 feet, outclassed any other bomber then in use in the world and most of the fighters as well. No sooner had the B-10 entered production than the Air Corps accepted bids on a newer generation of bombers, which resulted in the B-17. The B-17 weighed 35,000 pounds (compared with the B-10's 9,000), and had four engines and a service ceiling of 30,000 feet. At 14,000 feet, at a top speed of 250 mph it could carry 2,500 pounds of bombs 2,260 miles. The prototype model first flew in August 1935, yet the B-17, suitably modified and upgraded, remained a first line bomber in the AAF fleet until the end of World War II.[84]

As bombardment aviation prospered, pursuit aviation languished. The Air Corps, squeezed with limited funding, concentrated its appropriations on bomber development. The B-10 and the B-17 appeared not to need escort against enemy fighters. Also, the B-17 could attack an enemy before he came within range of sensitive American targets. With the enemy held at arm's length, the value of a large force of defensive fighters depreciated. As a result, the 1931–1935 period was the nadir of U.S. pursuit aviation and pursuit airframe development. The Air Corps' top fighter, the P-26, had an open cockpit, nonretractable landing gear, a range of 360 miles, and a top speed of 235 mph. This lag in development left the United States almost a full generation of fighter aircraft behind the world's other major aviation powers.[85]

The most outspoken advocate of pursuit aviation in the service, Capt. Claire Chennault, head of pursuit instruction at the Air Corps Tactical School (which had moved in July 1931 from Langley Field to Maxwell Field in Alabama, just outside Montgomery), fought for a more balanced doctrine. He emphasized both the offensive and the defensive nature of fighter aircraft. Contending that pursuit aircraft could successfully intercept and destroy bombers as well as enemy fighters, he enunciated four major principles:

1. Attainment of air supremacy depends upon the success of the pursuit force.
2. The primary function of pursuit is to gain air supremacy.
3. The first objective of pursuit is to destroy enemy pursuit.
4. Success of pursuit depends upon equipment, selection and training of pilots, numbers, tactics, and organization in units large enough to provide effective concentration of force.[86]

His pleading did not convince the leaders of the Air Corps, who distrusted him. Chennault retired on the grounds of ill health in 1937 and subsequently led a volunteer American pursuit unit, the American Volunteer Group, known as the

Flying Tigers, for the Nationalist Chinese forces fighting the Japanese. There he showed that his concepts were workable even under adverse conditions.

Chennault left behind a few converts, such as Capt. Earle Partridge, who, with other officers, slightly revived pursuit aviation in the late 1930s. Through their efforts the Air Corps designed and accepted the P-40 fighter, which outclassed the P-26, although it proved inferior to the first-line fighters of other major aviation powers. The German Messerschmitt (Bf 109), the British Spitfire, and the Japanese Zero—all designed and brought into production at the same time as the P-40—surpassed it.

Air Corps doctrine in the post-Mitchell era shifted materially. Fueled by the changes in technology, by Mitchell's new writings (free of the need to conciliate the powers that be), and by the theories of Giulio Douhet (the Italian air power enthusiast and theoretician), most of the Air Corps accepted bombardment aviation rather than pursuit aviation as the most important arm of the service. Mitchell and Douhet advocated a form of aerial warfare that went far beyond the mere support of ground armies. Air power, they argued, could strike directly at a nation's means of production, its lines of transportation, the morale of its population, and the will of its leadership.[87]

This aggressive and unofficial doctrine (official War Department doctrine focused on defending the continental United States) found a home in the Air Corps Tactical School (ACTS), where the instructors, mostly junior officers, adopted it and taught it to their classes.[88] The major tenets of the ACTS included the following:

1. The national objective in war is to break the enemy's will to resist and to force the enemy to submit to our will.

2. The accomplishment of the first goal requires an offensive type of warfare.

3. Military missions are best carried through by cooperation between air, ground, and naval forces, although only air can contribute to all missions.

4. The special mission of the air arm is the attack of the whole of the enemy national structure to dislocate its military, political, economic, and social activities.

5. Modern warfare has placed such a premium on material factors that a nation's war effort may be defeated by the interruption of its industrial network, which is vulnerable only to the air arm. The disruption of the enemy's industrial network is the real target, because such a disruption might produce a collapse in morale sufficient to induce surrender.

6. Future wars will begin by air action. Thus we must have an adequate standing air force to ensure our defense and to begin immediate offensive operations. We must place ourselves in a position to begin bombardment of the enemy as soon as possible.

7. The current limited range of our aircraft requires the acquisition of allies to provide forward bases in order to begin action against the enemy.

8. Assuming the existence of allies and forward bases, the air force would

have the power to choose between attacking the armed forces or the national structure of the enemy. The latter should be the primary objective.[89]

The foregoing doctrine, given the inevitability of the small prewar force, dictated a specific composition for strength available. The force would require a preponderance of long-range bombers to operate offensively. Bombers would maximize their effectiveness by extreme accuracy—10 tons of bombs on target would do as much damage as 100 tons of bombs dropped with 10 percent accuracy. Precision bombing meant daylight bombing; current and foreseeable technology could not provide for precise night bombing. Daylight bombing deep into enemy territory, given current technology, meant that bombers would operate without fighter escort and would need the ability to outrun or outgun enemy defensive fighters. The B-17, with its highly accurate and super-secret Norden bombsight, fit this specification perfectly, as would its successors.

ACTS doctrine contained many assumptions that eventually proved invalid. It underestimated the capacity of a modern industrial nation and its populace to survive repeated and heavy bombing. It overestimated the ability of air technology to develop bombs big enough to damage heavy equipment or reinforced concrete and the ease with which those new bombs could be manufactured. It discounted the possibility of improvements in air defense and fighter technology that would reverse the advantage held by the bomber. In their most extreme position, heavy-bomber enthusiasts assumed that fighter defenses would be unable to locate bombers until they had dropped their bombs. Because bombers could strike with seeming impunity, the best defense was a good offense. Enemy forces would resort to their own attacks. Then the sky would fill with aerial armadas passing each other virtually undisturbed until the side with the most effective strength subdued the other.

In only one other nation did the advocates of strategic bombing gain a decisive voice in shaping doctrine and affecting airframe design and acquisition—Britain. There the followers of Marshal of the Royal Air Force (RAF) Hugh Trenchard, the first Chief of Staff of the RAF, a service independent of the British army and navy, also adopted a bombing philosophy similar to that of Douhet and Mitchell. They, too, committed themselves to daylight bombardment, believing, in the words of Prime Minister Stanley Baldwin, in 1931, that "the bomber will always get through. The only defence is offence, which means you have to kill more women and children more quickly than the enemy if you want to save yourselves."[90] In Germany, France, Japan, and Italy, however, the air services, even if nominally independent, found themselves subservient to theories or general staffs that bound them to tactical support of their country's land or naval forces.

The advent of radar and highly organized ground-spotter organizations, both unforeseen by Air Corps bomber advocates, solved the defensive problem of tracking the bomber force. One ACTS instructor, Maj. Haywood S. Hansell, a leading Air Corps bomber theoretician, who led the 3d Bomb Wing in Europe in 1943 and the XXI Bomber Command in Guam in 1944, later admitted, "If our air theorists had had knowledge of radar in 1935, the American doctrine of strategic bombing in deep daylight penetrations would surely not have evolved."[91]

Similarly, improvements in fighter design led to faster, more heavily armed types that could best the B-17 and could be overcome only if they were prevented from reaching the bombers. The Air Corps, however, had rejected the idea that fighters should escort the bombers deep into enemy territory. Current technology seemed incapable of producing an aircraft that could (1) carry the combined weight of fuel necessary for long missions and armament superior to its opponents' and (2) retain the speed and agility to survive a dogfight unburdened by the necessary weight penalties of long-range flight. In addition, the Air Corps would never have the funds to build both a prewar bomber fleet and an escort fighter fleet under a particularly parsimonious Congress. The Air Corps maintained its stance against long-range escort through 1940. Only the fortuitous development of the long-range P-51 and drop tanks for the P-47, as well as their deployment in late 1943 and early 1944, saved American air power from a costly mistake.

During the 1930s, Spaatz articulated few views on air doctrine. What can be gleaned from his actions and writings as air observer during the Battle of Britain, as Chief of the Air Staff, and as combat commander in World War II suggests a clear affinity with the Air Corps Tactical School branch of air doctrine. He had a close relationship with Arnold, a leading bomber man; Spaatz had served on the development boards for the B-17, the B-24, and the B-29,[92] and he believed in their ability to defend themselves. But there were indications that, with regard to the tactical sphere of operations, Spaatz still adhered to Mitchell's early dictum regarding the absolute necessity of establishing air superiority before proceeding to other air operations.

Spaatz's Association with Arnold and Eaker

During the interwar years, Spaatz remained roughly one step behind Henry H. Arnold and one step ahead of Ira C. Eaker, two of his closest friends in the service. In many ways the careers of the triumvirate reflect the experience of the entire Air Corps for the period.

Arnold to Spaatz to Eaker was not the double-play combination of a professional baseball team but the eventual chain of command for American heavy-bomber forces in the British Isles. Henry H. Arnold (born June 25, 1886), Carl A. Spaatz (born June 28, 1891), and Ira C. Eaker (born April 13, 1896) had a long association with one another. The three had first served together at Rockwell Field in San Diego, California, in December 1918. Their task of demobilizing units of the Air Service had been diametrically opposed to their future effort of building up a strategic bombing force. Their friendships, both personal and professional, had deepened through the years. Spaatz and Arnold were the closest of confidants from 1918 until the latter's death in 1950. Eaker was almost as close to both. Yet the three had different backgrounds, personalities, and approaches to life.

Arnold graduated from West Point in 1907. Like Spaatz, he graduated in the lower half of his class academically and did not achieve cadet rank. Four years (and ten days of flight training) later he became one of the Army's first four licensed pilots and one of the first twenty-nine licensed pilots in the country. Wilbur Wright even served as one of his instructors. Until slowed by a series of heart attacks at the height of his career in 1941, Arnold was an extremely energetic advocate of U.S. military aviation. He believed it should become an independent armed service, and he dedicated his life to seeing that it did. Although Arnold was highly intelligent, he was intellectually undisciplined; thus he tended to endorse a variety of contradictory ideas in rushing to accomplish his goals. He was, on the one hand, astute enough to support the very long-range bomber, the B-29; he was, on the other, naive enough to see merit in what was derisively dubbed the "bats in the belfry" project to drop fire-bomb-carrying bats on Japanese cities. He had little patience with people who opposed his ideas but had an ability to get things done, especially when dealing with production and personnel.

To his friends, Arnold demonstrated a charm, openness, and exuberance that helped earn him the sobriquet "Happy" or just plain "Hap." To his opponents he was "a real S.O.B." One of his great regrets was missing the chance to serve in a combat command during World War I. Instead he had become the Army's youngest full colonel at age thirty-one and had spent the war in Washington, D.C., serving on the War Department Staff, where he saw first-hand the difficulties of organizing an air force from the ground up.

After the war, he stayed in the Air Service, rising to Assistant Chief of the Air Corps in 1935; upon the flying death of Maj. Gen. Oscar Westover in 1938, he became Chief of the Air Corps. Highlights along the way include testimony at Mitchell's court-martial, attendance at the Command and General Staff School in 1929, and the winning of the Mackay Trophy in 1934 for commanding a flight of B-10 bombers from Bolling Field in Washington, D.C., to Fairbanks, Alaska, and back. Late in life, Spaatz said of Arnold, "I know he had confidence in me, because of the relationship we had before. With me, he might sound impatient, but when I responded and gave him the reason for what I was doing, that would end it."[93]

Ira C. "Iree" Eaker took a reserve commission in the Infantry after graduating from Southeastern State Teachers College in Oklahoma in 1917. In November 1917, he transferred to the Signal Corps, Aviation Section; ten months later he received his pilot's rating. From 1919 to 1922 he served in the Philippines, and from 1922 to 1924, at Mitchel Field in New York. From 1924 to 1926, he was a pilot for the Chief of the Air Service, Maj. Gen. Mason

Patrick; the Assistant Chief, Brig. Gen. James Fechet; and the Assistant Secretary of War for Air, Trubee Davison. Unlike the fiery, hard-driving Arnold or the taciturn Spaatz, Eaker was the diplomat of the trio. Although not asked to testify at the Mitchell court-martial, because he served as assistant defense counsel at Maj. Gen. Patrick's orders, he stayed up nights helping Spaatz and Arnold prepare their statements.

In the late 1920s and 1930s, Eaker pursued his career. He participated in the Pan-American Flight goodwill tour of 1926 and 1927 and the flight of the *Question Mark*, and he graduated from the Air Corps Tactical School in 1936 and the Command and General Staff School in 1937. In 1936 he completed the first transcontinental flight purely on instruments, flying the entire trip with a canvas hood over his cockpit.

In 1932 the Army sent Eaker to the Journalism School at the University of Southern California; he earned a B.A. in journalism in September 1933. This education helped him to write three books with Arnold. The most significant was *The Flying Game*, published in 1936. By 1941, he had gained his full colonelcy and the command of the 20th Pursuit Group at Mitchel Field. Both Spaatz and Arnold trusted him completely. That trust, Eaker's skill in gaining the respect of others, and his undeniable skills as an air leader and pioneer made him Arnold's logical choice to arrange for the arrival of AAF combat forces in England in 1942. When Arnold chose Spaatz to lead the U.S. Eighth Air Force to Britain, both men mentally penciled in Eaker as second in command.[94]

By the end of 1938, Carl Spaatz had spent twenty-eight years in the United States Army, twenty-three of them as a flyer. From his days at West Point through his course at the Command and General Staff School he showed little appreciation of, if not disdain for, the academic side of the military profession. He had independently conceived no profound or original thoughts concerning his specialty—military aviation. His mind did not turn to systematic thinking but worked intuitively. He was not an intellectual leader, but he became, nonetheless, an early convert to many of the advanced aviation ideas of his era. He formed close associations with men such as Mitchell, Andrews, and Arnold, and he absorbed their ideas as his own. Spaatz believed that U.S. military aviation ought to be independent, and he placed great faith in the doctrine of strategic daylight precision bombing. Similarly, he did not display great enthusiasm for the technical aspects of airframe and engine research and development. He served on numerous aircraft development boards and participated in the *Question Mark* flight, but he was never assigned to his service's technological areas.

If Spaatz's intellectual and scientific prowess did not raise him above his peers or catch the eye of Arnold, his breadth of experience in training, operations, administration, and staff work as well as his self-confidence, honesty, loyalty, and courage did. Spaatz was a man of action who invariably accomplished the tasks set for him—an invaluable trait for any officer. At Issoudun he had demonstrated the ability to train and organize from the ground up. At the front

Maj. Carl A. "Tooey" Spatz, ca. 1930.

A jaunty Lt. Col. Henry H. Arnold and actress Bebe Daniels pose in front of a Boeing P-12 "Peashooter," Long Beach, California, October 30, 1932.

he had shot down three planes in as many weeks. He had gained insight into the problems associated with both pursuit and bombardment as group leader and wing commander. In his tours in the operations, training, and plans sections of the Office of the Chief of the Air Service/Corps, he had learned the bureaucratic intricacies of the War Department and had developed a great dislike for repetitive staff work. As a commander he would use his staff to insulate himself from routine in order to free himself for decisions.

It was Spaatz's ability to make quick, correct decisions based on his wide experience, common sense, and intuition, coupled with the moral courage to face such decisions, that would make him an outstanding combat Air Force leader.

Chapter 2

Prewar Planning
(January 1939–November 1941)

It takes close coordination with the Army to obtain maximum misuse of air power.[1]

—*Spaatz's Battle of Britain Diary, August 28, 1940.*

On January 12, 1939, Spaatz officially left the GHQ Air Force to assume command of the Plans Section of the Office of the Chief of the Air Corps (OCAC). He rejoined his friend Arnold, who had become head of the Air Corps on September 29, 1938. Toward the end of November 1938, a few weeks after the Munich crisis in Europe had ended, Arnold temporarily reassigned Spaatz from Langley Field to Washington, D.C., and ordered him to draw up in secret an expansion plan that would bring the Air Corps up to a strength of 10,000 planes within two years. This marked the first step of the Air Corps' planning and preparation for World War II. For the next three years in roles as Chief of the Plans Section, as a special Military Air Observer to Britain, and as Chief of the Air Staff of the AAF, Carl Spaatz contributed to the Air Corps' preparations for war.

Rearmament of the Air Corps

On November 14, 1938, the day the United States recalled its Ambassador from Berlin and a week after the mid-term elections had returned reduced but still overwhelming Democratic majorities in both houses of Congress, Arnold attended a special meeting with President Roosevelt at the White House. Also present were Harry Hopkins, head of the Works Progress Administration and one of Roosevelt's chief advisers and troubleshooters; Robert H. Jackson, Solicitor General of the United States; Louis Johnson, Assistant Secretary of War; Herman Oliphant, General Counsel of the Treasury Department; General

Malin Craig, Army Chief of Staff; and his deputy, Brig. Gen. George C. Marshall. The President apparently called the meeting in response to a series of disturbing European events. In late September the Munich Conference, which resulted in the German occupation of the Czech Sudetenland on October 3, further revealed the unrelenting nature of Hitler's territorial demands. A meeting with the U.S. Ambassador to France, William C. Bullitt, on October 13, confirmed for Roosevelt the dangerous state of European politics. And the increasingly barbaric behavior of the Nazis toward the German Jews, displayed in such incidents as "Crystal Night" on November 8, 1938, amply illuminated the viciousness of the German state's internal policies. These events, the culmination of years of Hitler's foreign and domestic policies, conclusively demonstrated to Roosevelt the rogue nature of the Nazi regime. They convinced him that the United Stated needed to enlarge its airplane production capacity greatly in order to counter the mounting security threat to the United Stated posed by the Germans. Roosevelt intended these planes not only for the Air Corps but for the French and British as well. Apparently FDR hoped that making an increased U.S. manufacturing capacity available to the French and British would enable them to procure enough aircraft either to forestall an attack by Hitler or to help them defeat him if war came.[2]

At the meeting on November 14, the President did most of the talking. He noted the weakness of U.S. defenses and pointed out that Germany had a reported air strength almost double the combined Anglo-French total. The President sought an Army Air Corps of 20,000 planes, with an annual productive capacity of 2,000 planes per month. He knew, however, that such a program would not pass Congress. Therefore he asked the War Department to develop a plan for building 10,000 aircraft and for constructing new plant capacity for an additional 10,000 aircraft per year. Although his meeting concentrated on airplanes, it supplied the spark for all subsequent Army and Army Air Corps prewar matériel and manpower expansion as the War Department sought not only new planes but funds to provide a balanced, combat-ready Army.[3]

On November 17, Arnold detailed Spaatz along with Col. Joseph T. McNarney and Col. Claude Duncan to draw up within the next month the Air Corps' plan to meet the President's requests. This plan served as the blueprint for further expansion of an Air Corps that in the autumn of 1938 had only 1,600 aircraft on hand. Plants working on aircraft contracts for the Air Corps had a productive capacity of only 88.2 planes per month.[4] Even six months later (June 1939), the Air Corps still had only thirteen operational B-17s and 22,287 personnel, only twice the strength of the Cavalry.[5]

In January 1939, Spaatz became Chief of the Plans Section of the OCAC. Aside from fourteen weeks as a special observer in Britain during the summer of 1940 and one month as head of the Matériel Division, he remained in that post until July 1941 when he became the first Chief of the Air Staff, Army Air Forces. The major tasks of the Plans Section were the preparation of the Air

38

Maj. Gen. Henry H.
Arnold, Chief, U.S.
Army Air Corps, 1938.

Corps annexes to the Army war plans; the integration of the lessons of the war in Europe into current Air Corps planning and training; the establishment of aircraft production priorities; the coordination of all research and development projects associated with combat aircraft; and, most important, the creation and management of the various air expansion and rearmament programs introduced in the prewar period.[6]

The first significant problem to face the Plans Section was Roosevelt's rejection of the expansion plan presented to him by the Army and the Air Corps. He had asked for $500 million in Air Corps planes, but the Army and the Air Corps had requested an additional $200 million for Army matériel, $100 million for Navy aircraft, plus unstated amounts for air bases and air training. The President, who was not at all sure Congress would approve the additional $500 million in the first place, redistributed the funds giving $200 million of the $500 million to the Army matériel branches, earmarking $120 million for air bases and other non-plane air items, and leaving $180 million for procurement of 3,000 combat aircraft. He promised to find the Navy's money elsewhere. Congress passed the expansion bill in April 1939, authorizing an Air Corps ceiling of 5,500 aircraft.[7]

Spaatz spent much of his time dealing with the nuts and bolts of training and procurement. The problem of aircraft for the French and British proved vexing from the beginning. On January 23, 1939, an advanced model U.S. Army dive-bomber crashed during a flight test, killing the American co-pilot and injuring the French pilot and ten others. This accident gave ammunition to members of Congress and others who wished to build up U.S. forces before aiding Britain and France or who sought to avoid sending aid to any belligerent in the hope of avoiding entanglement in the coming war.

Yet the accident also established a precedent permitting a policy of more liberal release of advanced aircraft. Within weeks the British purchased 650 aircraft worth $25 million, while the French added another 615 planes worth $60 million. In the course of the year Canada, Australia, Belgium, Norway, Sweden, and Iraq placed further orders. Although the American aircraft industry accepted the orders, it feared that U.S. neutrality laws might prevent delivery in the event of war and was reluctant to expand production facilities. In the face of this reluctance, the French agreed to underwrite the cost of expansion for engines from Pratt and Whitney and airplanes from Wright Aeronautical. By November 1939, the British and French had invested more than $84 million in engine plants alone.[8]

These large orders ran head-on into the Air Corps' own 5,500-plane program. In July and August 1939, the Air Corps let contracts of $105 million, more than the entire business of the industry in any peacetime year prior to 1938. Congress spent an additional $57 million to buy new manufacturing equipment for the aircraft industry. By the end of 1939 there was a backlog of orders worth $630 million, with $400 million attributable to foreign purchases.[9]

The outbreak of war on September 1, 1939, the same day that George C. Marshall officially became Chief of the War Department General Staff, increased the pressure from the Western Allies for aid. On March 25, 1940, the Allies received permission to purchase all but the most advanced models of U.S. combat and trainer types. Aircraft available to the Allies included the B-17, B-24, B-25, B-26, A-20, and P-40, all front-line aircraft in the Air Corps inventory. After the fall of France, the British took over all French contracts and added more of their own. Their orders soon reached 14,000 planes, and after Dunkirk the administration continued its policy of filling Britain's immediate combat needs over the requirements of Air Corps expansion.[10] As a result, the Air Corps was short of aircraft for training and for equipping its new and existing units.

The entire process left Spaatz shaking his head in disagreement; years later he remarked, "In 1939, when the British Mission was here, my own feeling was that we should build up our own air force rather than build up someone else's."[11] In a memo to Arnold he remarked, "It might be difficult to explain in the case of the collapse of England and the development of a threat against the Western Hemisphere or our possessions how we can agree that any airplanes can be diverted at a time when we have only sufficient modern airplanes to equip a paltry few squadrons."[12]

Spaatz Observes the Battle of Britain Firsthand

In May 1940, Spaatz took on a new assignment as Assistant Military Attaché (Air) to Britain, or as he put it, "a high-class spy."[13] Arnold sent him to Europe to get a firsthand view of the current state of the air war. Officially, he went to study Royal Air Force (RAF) training and tactics. Unofficially, he went to discuss British aircraft requirements in light of U.S. production and training programs. As Chief of Air Corps Plans, a position he resumed soon after returning from Britain, Spaatz had unique knowledge of the status of the Air Corps' capabilities, including its readiness, training, procurement, and war plans. He would find this knowledge invaluable as he assessed the British experience. He could immediately apply whatever he learned from the RAF to the Air Corps' programs.

The position Spaatz occupied came about as a direct result of the intervention of President Roosevelt. In early 1940, the President and General Marshall visited an Air Corps display; afterward the President asked for the number of air attachés accredited to London. On learning that the embassy had two air attachés, he suggested doubling the figure.[14] The Air Corps promptly asked the British for permission to send two specialist officers as assistant air attachés and requested the British to share the tactical and technical lessons in the war to date. These officers would have diplomatic status as attachés, but they were actually technical observers. Their official orders referred to them as "Military Air Observers." Although not explicitly stated, the Air Corps apparently intended to fill the two attaché positions with a series of technical and administrative experts, on relatively short assignments, to obtain access to the most recent combat developments.

Although the RAF Director of Plans, Air Commodore John Slessor, gave the suggestions qualified support, other sections of the Air Ministry greeted the propositions with suspicion. The Chief of the Air Staff, Air Chief Marshal Cyril Newall asked, "What guarantee have we that this information will not find its way back to our enemies?" He added, "I am not prepared to be rushed by the Americans, who, as always, wish to have the best of both worlds. They would like to be our allies, but without any obligations, and they are not blind naturally to the pecuniary advantages of such a state of affairs."[15]

The Air Ministry's delay elicited a protest from the British embassy in Washington. The British ambassador, the Marquis of Lothian, noted the unfavorable impression created by the delay, especially in light of the President's interest. He emphasized the advantages to be gained by having American manufacturers build more combat-ready aircraft, and concluded, "I regard an early and favorable decision as highly desirable."[16] On March 11, influenced by the interest of Lothian and the President, the Chief of the Air Staff recommended approval of the proposal on the conditions "that information made available to these Air Attachés should be treated with complete secrecy, and that we should

expect to obtain a reasonable amount of information in return for what we give."
The Chief of the Air Staff retained the full right to refuse the American attachés
any information.[17] The British subsequently decided to deny the American
attachés access to all operations rooms and details of their workings,* to tell
them nothing about any aspect of radar, to give no information about stabilized
automatic bombsights, and to share no detailed drawings of power-operated turrets.[18]

The first pair of observers arrived in Britain in April 1940. Instructions from
the Office of the Chief of the Air Corps required them to report on the ability of
bombardment aircraft to penetrate active antiaircraft defenses, on the use of
escort fighters, on the effectiveness of aerial bombing, on methods proposed to
increase bomber aircraft effectiveness, and on methods proposed to increase pursuit aircraft effectiveness.[19] Significantly, the Air Corps sent one of its leading
ordnance, armaments, and bombing technical experts, Lt. Col. Grandison
Gardner,[†] and an expert in aircraft engines, Maj. Franklin O. Carroll. Gardner
stayed in Britain until the beginning of the German offensive in the west in May
1940. He became convinced of the need to incorporate either existing British
power-operated machine gun turrets, or if British designs could not be obtained,
the development of American turrets, into the construction of all future
American heavy bombers.[20] Both American officers reflected conventional Air
Corps opinions. Neither expected America to take an active part in the war.
However, Gardner did suggest that in the event the Americans supplied the RAF
with a number of B-17s, experienced reserve Air Corps officers proceed to
Canada to serve as civilian instructors to British crews.[21]

Spaatz and Capt. Benjamin S. Kelsy were the second set of Military Air
Observers sent to Britain. They received the same instructions as Gardner and
Carroll.[22] Two weeks before their arrival, the acting American military attaché
in England, Col. Martin F. Scanlon, wrote the RAF Director of Intelligence,
whose branch had responsibility for supervising and escorting foreign military
visitors, to arrange inspections of RAF installations. Scanlon asked permission
for Spaatz and Kelsey to observe the headquarters of RAF Fighter, Bomber, and
Coastal Commands, to visit one station belonging to each command, and to
inspect one of each type of training school.[23] This itinerary matched Spaatz's
expertise, as one of the chief Air Corps planning officers assigned to create and
sustain an up-to-date and expanding Air Corps training program. The RAF's
methods of coping with the rapid expansion of its force had a direct bearing on
his own responsibilities.

---

* Within the operations rooms, RAF air defense fighter squadrons plotted all incoming information (including radar bearings) on aircraft over Britain.

† Lt. Col. Gardner's previous assignment had been in the Air Matériel Division as Chief,
Armaments Laboratory, Experimental Engineering Section. For two years before that he had served
as the operations officer and then the executive officer of the 19th Bombardment Group.

Air Chief Marshal Cyril Newall, Chief of the Air Staff, RAF, 1937–1940.

Imperial War Museum

On May 28 Spaatz sailed into Genoa, Italy, on the U.S. liner *Manhattan.* U.S. neutrality laws forced him to sail on neutral shipping that avoided the blockade announced by the warring powers. Three days later, after a journey through still-neutral Italy and belligerent France, he arrived in London. The Dunkirk evacuation was in full operation, and the Allied coalition prepared for the hopeless second phase of the Battle of France. The next morning, June 1, he was presented to the American ambassador, Joseph P. Kennedy. More important for the purpose of his mission, Spaatz also renewed his personal contacts with the principal embassy attachés for air, Col. Martin F. Scanlon and his assistant, Maj. George C. McDonald. They provided his entree to the RAF.

On June 1, Spaatz's first full day in Britain, he lunched with Air Chief Marshal Newall.* He also met the RAF Chief of Intelligence, Air Commodore Archibald Boyle. Two days later he lunched with his British opposite number, Air Commodore Slessor.[24] During these early meetings, Spaatz noted that after

---

* RAF-AAF equivalent ranks:

Marshal of the RAF	General of the Army
Air Chief Marshal (ACM)	General
Air Marshal (AM)	Lieutenant General (Lt. Gen.)
Air Vice-Marshal (AVM)	Major General (Maj. Gen.)
Air Commodore (A/Cmdr)	Brigadier General (Brig. Gen.)
Group Captain (GC)	Colonel (Col.)

43

only nine months of war both the Germans and the British had begun to run short of trained crews. He learned that the British had captured German pilots with less than 100 hours' flying time and that, for the British themselves, a shortage of trained crews, not lack of aircraft, was the biggest bottleneck in fielding a large force. He also learned that the RAF "apparently thinks as we do, but [has] been hindered by higher-ups" with regard to the feasibility and desirability of strategic bombing of the German economy.[25]

For the next ten days, Spaatz visited the RAF's Training Command, Technical Training Command, and training bases. The initial training system of the British impressed Spaatz, but he considered their bombing accuracy low and doubted the effectiveness of night bombing. Spaatz and the two other American attachés who accompanied him agreed that, in the event of active U.S. participation in the war, the most useful immediate contribution the United States could make would be high-altitude long-distance bombers.[26] This conclusion was probably based more on the predilection of Army Air Corps officers toward the use of large bombers than to any lessons directly related to their visit. In almost every other phase of air activity, their observations must have shown them that the RAF had outpaced 1940 Air Corps practice.

Meanwhile, the French, whose army had been shattered by the *Wehrmacht*, on June 17 asked for an armistice. During this dark period of the war, Spaatz initiated informal staff talks to discuss the details of America's "almost inevitable" entry into the war.[27] Spaatz's authority to begin such extraordinary discussions was unclear. No secret instructions or hints of any have surfaced in Roosevelt's, Arnold's, and Spaatz's personal papers. Given Spaatz's presence as an observer in an ongoing program (the Air Corps continued to send short-term Military Air Observers to England until the U.S. entry into the war) and his assignment to the post before the outbreak of the German offensive on May 10, 1940, it seems unlikely that any higher authorities would have anticipated the need for immediate emergency aid to England or would have authorized him to initiate such negotiations.* Spaatz probably initiated these discussions on his own.

---

* Absence of proof, however does not mean that such instructions could not have been passed to Spaatz after he went to Britain. Spaatz arrived in London during the repercussions of the Tyler Kent affair. Kent was a code clerk in the American embassy. On May 20, 1940, the British informed the Americans, using incontrovertible evidence, that Kent had totally compromised U.S. diplomatic codes. As a result, all communications of the U.S. diplomatic service were blacked out for two to six weeks between Dunkirk and the fall of France, while scores of special couriers delivered new codes to all U.S. embassies. It may well have been that higher-ups in Washington could not have told Spaatz to begin negotiations even if they had wanted to, unless, of course, a courier hand-carried instructions from Washington to him. See David Kahn, *The Codebreakers: The Story of Secret Writing* (New York: Macmillan, 1967), pp. 494–495, for more on Tyler Kent. On the other hand, instructions could have reached Spaatz through the U.S. naval or military attachés' office. Because of known slackness in State Department signal security, important message traffic to and from London, such as that between Roosevelt and Churchill, came via the Navy message center.

Such a step was probably less radical than it might at first appear. As Spaatz probably knew from his tour as Air Corps Chief of Plans, the U.S. and British navies had come to a preliminary meeting of minds on war-fighting strategy as early as December 1937.[28] In late May 1940, as Spaatz may well have known, the U.S. Naval Attaché in London, Capt. Alan G. Kirk, with the approval of the British Admiralty, had recommended to his superiors the assignment of U.S. naval officers as observers with British fleet units, which was agreed to.[29] On June 10, President Roosevelt gave strong public support to the British and French in the famous "stab in the back" speech delivered at Charlottesville, Virginia. The next day, at the President's insistence, the War Department transferred to the British "surplus" war matériel, including 500,000 Enfield rifles, 129,140,708 rounds of ammunition, 80,583 machine guns, 316 three-inch mortars, 20,000 revolvers, 25,000 Browning automatic rifles, and 895 seventy-five mm guns with a million rounds of ammunition, through an intermediary company of the U.S. Steel Corporation.[30] On June 15, the British Admiralty set up a committee, under the direction of Admiral Sidney Bailey, to consider questions arising from possible naval cooperation with the United States.[31] As a result, Spaatz ran little risk in opening exploratory talks of his own with the RAF; their public disclosure would have added little fuel to the measures already approved or undertaken. Nor did he commit his country to more than information finding. In any case, this *démarche* was one of the first efforts in combined U.S.-British operational military planning.

On June 13, the day before the fall of Paris, Major McDonald, after discussing the subject of direct U.S. aid to the British with Spaatz, visited the RAF Director of Intelligence. He informed Air Commodore Archibald Boyle that military officers at the U.S. embassy were considering the possibility that the United States would contribute directly to the war in the air over Europe. Acting on the assumption that entry of the United States into the war was "almost inevitable," McDonald suggested that plans be prepared for the dispatch of fifty B-17s to Britain. If the proposal received a favorable hearing in the United States, then pilots could be trained and special targets studied. Bearing out Spaatz's responsibility in initiating this matter, McDonald indicated that if the RAF "thought there was anything in it, he could arrange for the *necessary papers* [emphasis in original] to be sent to General Miles [the senior U.S. Military Attaché in London] and General Arnold in the U.S.A. at once."[32]

The Director of Intelligence passed the McDonald-Spaatz suggestion on to Slessor, who was "all for the plan" in principle. On June 16, Spaatz, McDonald, and Slessor fully discussed the proposal and agreed on the details of a small air expeditionary force.[33] After this session Slessor circulated the plan to the appropriate branches of the Air Ministry so that each could contribute its share to the final plan. The targets suggested by the RAF included oil plants at Vienna, Regensburg, Leuna, Stettin, and Magdeburg; aircraft factories at Munich, Berlin, Magdeburg, Dessau, and Kassel; and targets in northern Italy. They were

Air Commodore John Slessor, Director of Plans, Air Staff, RAF, 1940–1942.

Imperial War Museum

beyond the range of current RAF bombers or were small, requiring precision attacks.[34]

Before these talks could progress further, on June 17, the British ambassador in Washington, D.C., Lord Lothian, proposed to the President that talks between the combined armies, navies, and, if necessary, air forces of the United States and Britain might be useful. Roosevelt consented.[35] This agreement in principle was immediately passed to the British armed services. On June 20, Slessor informed the Air Staff, "The President of the U.S.A. has authorized immediate secret staff conversations on naval and air matters. . . . Major MacDonald and Colonel Spaatz (the U.S.D. of Plans) have already asked me to give them an outline plan for the reception and operation of one heavy-bomber group and one fighter group."[36] Both the RAF and Spaatz seem to have regarded these talks as nothing more than courtesies, preliminary to the opening of formal staff conversations.

Prime Minister Churchill, however, dithered over accepting the President's offer. He feared that the Americans would use the occasion to insist on discussing the transfer of the British fleet to transatlantic bases in the event of Britain's defeat. Foreign Minister Lord Halifax pressed the Prime Minister for an early decision, explaining that Roosevelt might cool to the idea, that the situation in the Far East needed coordination, and that the service ministers were all in favor of talks.[37] On June 30, Churchill agreed to the talks provided they occurred in London where the British could ensure security. The President, who wished to minimize publicity before the November 1940 national elections, was happy to agree.[38]

After further delay, on July 20, Lord Lothian learned that Rear Adm. Robert L. Ghormley, Assistant Chief of Naval Operations, and Brig. Gen. George V. Strong, Assistant Chief of Staff (head of the War Plans Division), had been appointed members of a U.S. military delegation destined for London for talks with British military leaders. Lothian thereupon pressed for the inclusion of an air expert, which resulted in the addition of Maj. Gen. Delos C. Emmons, Commanding General, GHQ Air Force. The true purpose of their visit was covered by an announcement that they had come for a meeting of the Anglo-American Standardization of the Arms Committee. The combined military talks began in London on August 20.[39] These higher level contacts superseded the initial Spaatz-McDonald-Slessor talks, and Spaatz returned to observing the war.

On July 10, the first phase of the Battle of Britain began with Luftwaffe attacks on channel ports and shipping. Spaatz, who had requested and received permission to stay beyond his sixty-day tour of duty,[40] watched these events closely. A new British disclosure policy made his observations even more valuable. A request by Spaatz and the other American air attachés to spend three or four days at a British fighter or bomber station in order to get a thorough look into the operational use of the aircraft there had forced the Air Ministry's hand. The workings of the operations room and of radar could not be concealed without great embarrassment to all concerned. Therefore, the Air Intelligence section in charge of escorting foreign officers requested instructions.[41]

The situation had changed drastically since April 1940. The British no longer had allies outside the Commonwealth and, as Slessor pointed out, the Germans had probably gained more information on radar from the French than was likely to result from leakage from America. Furthermore, the Prime Minister had agreed to exchange almost any sort of secret information with the Americans, subject to his personal review.[42] On July 3, the Air Ministry ruled that there was "no reason whatever why these officers should not be told of the existence of R.D.F. [radio direction finding equipment, or radar—radio detection and ranging], its purposes and its achievements."* The ministry added that "in fact there is every reason why they should be told, so that they may report to their own country that we have valuable items which would make an exchange of technical information worthwhile from the American standpoint."[43] At the same time, the Air Ministry opened operations rooms and all variations of radar to the Americans, but did withhold all technical details and design information.

Spaatz spent the last two weeks of July with Bomber Command observing tactics and methods. Nine of those days he spent with a Wellington twin-engine night-bomber group. There Spaatz saw the small scale and ineffectiveness of

---

* The British used the term RDF to refer to all types of radar devices.

current British night bombing. He therefore, not unnaturally, saw little reason to question U.S. daylight precision doctrine.[44] Concerning the Wellington he remarked, "Although night bombing has resulted in few losses, believe answer to bombardment is altitude, speed and daylight attack, preceded by weather reconnaissance plane in uncertain weather." A few of the more frank British flyers, he added, "have doubts as to the effectiveness of their night attacks."[45]

At this time neither Bomber Command nor the German night fighter defenses had reached the high degree of effectiveness they achieved later in the war. Nor had the British begun their policy of city area bombing to destroy civilian housing and demoralize the German work force. Instead, confronted with a situation even worse than the prewar "worst case" estimates, Bomber Command, since June 20, 1940, had targeted the German aircraft industry, but proved ineffective. Less than a month later the head of Bomber Command, Air Chief Marshal Charles A. Portal, ruefully confirmed Spaatz's observations: of the ten primary aircraft industry targets "only three can be found with any certainty in moonlight by average crews. Expert crews may be expected to find the remainder on clear nights with a full moon, and average crews will sometimes find them after a good deal of time has been spent in searching." In addition, Portal pointed out that the air industry targets were in sparsely inhabited sites so that bombs missing the plants fell on empty ground. Because the vast majority of the bombs dropped missed, the raids had no disruptive effect on the German economy. Portal suggested bombing rail centers instead.[46] Rail yards occupied the center of many German cities. Portal, who became Chief of the Air Staff in October 1940, would have the authority and opportunity to see that his suggestions were carried out until the end of the war. The RAF's ineffectiveness in hitting specific targets at night would eventually lead to the institution of the mass fire-raising attacks in which hundreds of four-engine heavy bombers would drench the center of a city, such as Hamburg or Dresden, with thousands of incendiary bombs.

The performance of the RAF against the Luftwaffe persuaded Spaatz that the British could beat any German invasion attempt. On July 31, he informed Arnold that if the Germans did not launch their invasion in August, they would have to postpone it indefinitely: "Unless the Germans have more up their sleeve than they have shown so far," Spaatz commented, "their chance of success in destroying the RAF is not particularly good. In air combat, German losses in daylight raids will be huge. In night attacks, the accuracy of their bombing is of very low order." An all-out attempt might win for the Germans, but Spaatz noted, "if not, it would be the beginning of the end for German air supremacy."[47]

On August 2, Spaatz repeated these views at a breakfast meeting in Claridge's, where the embassy's military attachés met with William J. Donovan, a "special observer" from President Roosevelt. Donovan, a World War I hero and an old friend of the President, had come to assess Britain's chances of staying in the war.[48] After speaking out at the luncheon, Spaatz noted in his diary that Donovan had agreed with his—Spaatz's—estimates of the threat of a direct

Imperial War Museum

Bomb damage to London, autumn 1940.

German invasion of Britain. Both Donovan and Spaatz felt that the Germans would try an alternative strategy of closing the Mediterranean and harassing British ports and shipping with air raids and U-boats.[49] Donovan reported to the President that the British would successfully resist invasion and were resolved to continue fighting.[50] The extent to which Spaatz's advice aided Donovan in reaching his eventual decision cannot be determined. As an authoritative American military observer, however, Spaatz must have helped counter what Donovan termed "a great deal of hopelessness [that] had been coming over those in our high command here." At the end of August 1940, Donovan informed Air Chief Marshal Newall, "I still have confidence that my judgment as to your power of resistance to invasion and of your resolution is still right."[51] It is not unreasonable to assume Spaatz's similar views must have influenced the President's special observer.

During August, when Reich Marshal Hermann Goering, Commander in Chief of the Luftwaffe, ordered his men to begin the decisive phase of the Battle of Britain, Spaatz spent much of his time with Fighter Command, particularly with No. 12 Group under Air Vice-Marshal Trafford Leigh-Mallory. (See Map 1 for RAF Fighter Group defensive sectors.) At that point he finally got a good look at radar, including its early warning, ground-controlled intercept (GCI), and Identification Friend or Foe (IFF) variants. This equipment enabled the RAF accurately to track and to intercept German raids, as well as to distinguish its aircraft from enemy aircraft. Spaatz and Lt. Col. Frank O'D. Hunter, an Army Air Corps pursuit expert who had originally been sent to observe the French air

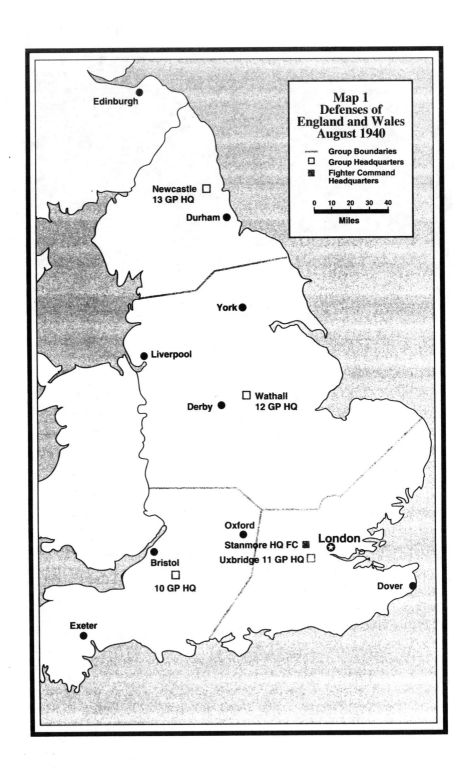

Map 1
Defenses of
England and Wales
August 1940

Group Boundaries
Group Headquarters
Fighter Command
Headquarters

0   10   20   30   40
Miles

Edinburgh

Newcastle
13 GP HQ

Durham

York

Liverpool

Derby   Wathall
               12 GP HQ

Oxford
Stanmore HQ FC   London
Uxbridge 11 GP HQ

Bristol   Dover
10 GP HQ

Exeter

force, spent all of August 9 in the operations room at No. 12 Group getting a full explanation of night and day procedures.[52] Spaatz recommended the construction of similar underground bomb-proof control facilities in the Panama Canal Zone and Hawaii. He noted favorably the efficiency of female RAF personnel, which may have encouraged his own subsequent wartime support of U.S. Army female personnel. Spaatz may also have formed an unfavorable opinion of Air Vice-Marshal Leigh-Mallory's abilities. Spaatz criticized what he termed "too much rigidity of control by the higher command, which as stated above, extends even to the point of Group control of individual sections of a squadron."[53]

In mid-August, Spaatz spent three days at Dover, where he witnessed German air attacks and watched British heavy antiaircraft artillery fire inaccurately on friend and foe alike. During his stay at Dover, Spaatz, dressed in his rumpled civilian tweeds, wandered away from his escort and was promptly detained by a British naval commander as a spy when he blundered into a restricted area. It took some hours to establish his identity. Spaatz took the incident with his usual good humor and a few days later signed himself in at an RAF field as "Col. Carl A. Spaatz, German spy."[54] At the British Technical Establishment, he examined downed German aircraft. Detailed reports on each plane soon found their way to Arnold. As for the performance of the Luftwaffe, Spaatz noted that its bombing had been "particularly lousy," and he suspected that it had been "too hastily constructed" to stand up for long to the apparently better trained RAF Fighter Command.[55]

In the last week of August, Spaatz maintained his close contacts with the RAF. On August 24, he attended bomber crew debriefings. From this and other experiences in Britain he deduced, "General opinion is that German fighters will not attack a well-closed-in day-bombing formation."[56] Three days later, he discussed tactics and operations with Slessor's deputy, Group Captain Baker, and with McDonald and Hunter. They agreed that a modern, well-dispersed air force could not be destroyed on the ground.[57] They further noted the unsuitability of dive-bombers against well-defended targets and the relative effectiveness of rapid-firing, light antiaircraft weapons. In discussing the jealousy between the British army and the RAF, which Spaatz had previously noted,[58] they stated, "It takes close coordination with the Army to obtain maximum misuse of air power."[59] In other words, the more an air force conformed to the wishes of its army, the less effective it would be.

On August 30, Spaatz informed the acting senior U.S. military attaché in London, Col. Raymond E. Lee, that there would be no blitzkrieg of England in 1940 and that, therefore, he would just as soon "go home and get to work."[60] The next day he received his orders to return home. Before he left on September 9, a week before the British broke the German air offensive, he talked several times with Slessor and experienced the first of the major Luftwaffe night raids on London. Of Hitler's terror raids Spaatz noted, "Apparently indiscriminate bombing of London has started."[61] During one of the night raids he dined with

American press correspondent Drew Middleton. When Spaatz heard the bombs drop, he recognized that the Germans had switched from their counterair campaign to terror bombing, conceding air superiority to the British. He remarked to Middleton, "By God, that's good, that's fine. The British are winning." Spaatz continued, "The Germans can't bomb at night—hell, I don't think they're very good in daylight—but they haven't been trained for night bombing. Nope, the British have got them now. They've forced them to bomb at night. The Krauts must be losing more than we know."[62] Spaatz recommended that B-17s be shipped at once to the British to add strength to the long-range British striking force.

After leaving England, Spaatz spent ten days in Lisbon. There he saw first-hand the pitiful state of refugees fleeing Nazi-occupied Europe, which further hardened his attitude toward the Germans. At lunch at the U.S. legation he told those present, including the ex-governor of New Hampshire, John G. Winant, who was on his way to London to replace Joseph P. Kennedy as ambassador to England, "The English have developed real air power, whereas the Germans so far appear to have developed a mass of air geared to the Army and [are] lost when confronted with properly applied air effort."[63] By this Spaatz meant that, despite the ineffectiveness of its current night-bombing campaign, the RAF had laid a solid foundation for development into an effective force; whereas the Luftwaffe was flawed at its creation and rickety in its structure and, thus, would

John G. Winant, U.S. Ambassador to Britain, 1940–1945.

be unable to sustain its early successes. Spaatz noted that Winant seemed impressed with his views. A week later, with Generals Strong and Emmons, Spaatz left Lisbon for Washington.

Spaatz's stay in England had shown him the current state of air warfare, but it had not shaken his belief in some key Air Corps doctrine. He had seen, for instance, no reason to modify views concerning long-range escort fighters. The Air Corps held that a formation of self-defending bombers did not need escort, especially because such escort, in order to carry enough fuel internally, would have to be larger, and therefore would be less maneuverable and combat capable, than lighter, shorter-range defending fighter aircraft. The performance of the German heavy twin-engine fighter, the Bf 110, against the nimble, shorter-range, lighter British single-engine Hurricanes and Spitfires, confirmed this conviction. Spaatz also observed from German operations that close fighter escort, in any case, did "not insure immunity from attack by hostile fighters on the bombers. A comparatively fewer number of hostile fighters can, by determined effort, break up the large [bomber] formation."[64]

After talking to RAF bomber pilots Spaatz also reaffirmed his belief in the necessity of daylight precision bombing for accurate results and in the defensive strength of large, heavy-bomber formations. Explaining away the apparent contradiction between the assumption that determined fighter attack would break up bomber formations and the assumption that a well-flown bomber formation could defend itself, he observed that so far the Germans had not demonstrated the ability to mount a determined attack on British bombers. Spaatz apparently had not fully realized that the British had switched to night operations because of excessive casualties suffered in daylight operations. These beliefs, typical of those of many Air Corps leaders, would be modified only by costly direct actions with "determined" German fighter planes in 1943.

But, as already noted, Spaatz had seen the ineffectiveness of the close escort tactics the Germans employed to protect their bombers. In close escort German fighters stayed with the bombers until British fighters attacked, at which time the escorts tried to break up the intercepting fighters' assault. This tactic had proved ineffective. It robbed the German fighters of their aggressiveness by forcing them to react to British attacks instead of launching their own. In contrast, distant escort freed the fighters to leave the slow-moving bomber formations and to attack enemy fighters when they made their appearance. This observation may have helped Spaatz reach his brilliant wartime decision, in January 1944, to free the Eighth Air Force's fighters from the bombers by authorizing them to search out and destroy enemy fighters. At the same time, Spaatz discarded one of the tenets of prewar air thinking—that air bombardment could shatter a civilian population's willingness to resist. Spaatz left Britain convinced that the morale of the British and probably that of the German civil populations would not collapse in the face of bombardment.

Spaatz's stay in Britain also exposed him to technical innovations, such as

The Battle of Britain. Contending aircraft reflected the advanced aviation technology of the era. *Clockwise from above*: The twin-engine Vickers-Armstrong Wellington was one of RAF Bomber Command's principal models. With a 4,500-pound bomb load and a maximum speed of 235 mph, it was among the best of its type. Hawker Hurricanes *(opposite, above)* were the most numerous British fighters in the battle and bore the brunt of early engagements with the Luftwaffe. Each was armed with eight Browning .303 caliber machine guns and attained a speed of 350 mph. Marks 1 and 1A Supermarine Spitfires *(opposite, middle)* confronted the Luftwaffe in the later days of the battle. As heavily armed as Hurricanes but faster, the Spitfires outfought and outlasted most German adversaries. The Bf 109E fighter *(opposite, below)* was the Luftwaffe's mainstay in Germany's five-month effort to dominate British skies. It was a formidable opponent at 350 mph and combined machine gun and cannon armament. Its fuel-injected engine enabled pushovers into sudden dives, giving its pilot the advantage in initiating and breaking off combat, but a short range limited its ability to protect German bombers over Britain or to engage the RAF at will. The Bf 110 *(below, right)*, designed as a long-range "destroyer" (*Zerstörer*), fared poorly as a fighter and escort in the battle. The Heinkel 111 medium bomber *(below, left)*, carrying 4,410 pounds of ordnance and a crew of four, had only light defensive armament. In the absence of German fighter escorts with sufficient staying power, the graceful but slower Heinkels took heavy losses in the German aerial assault on the British Isles.

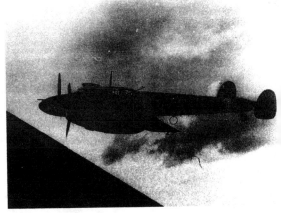

THE AEROPLANE

radar and IFF equipment that electronically identified friendly or enemy planes on radar scopes; new combat tactics, especially night bombing and defensive fighter deployment; and organizational and manufacturing problems and solutions which would help his own planning in the United States. Unfortunately, Spaatz appears not to have recorded any opinions he may have formed during this trip of RAF leaders. He had only a brief meeting with Portal, Air Officer Commanding (AOC) Bomber Command. A colonel, even one from a favorably disposed neutral country, simply did not hobnob with officers at the highest levels of command, especially when they were in the midst of their nation's single most important battle since Trafalgar or, perhaps, Hastings.

Among the more junior RAF officers, however, Spaatz made several friends, including Slessor, who became Chief of the Air Staff after World War II. In his memoirs Slessor recorded a lively picture of the American air observer, whom he described as "a man of few words but with a dry sense of humor that can reduce me to a state of schoolboy giggles quicker than anything I know." Spaatz was, Slessor continued, "a man of action rather than of speech, rather inarticulate but with an uncommon flair for the really important issue and a passionate faith in the mission of air power."[65] Spaatz's acquaintance with RAF leadership and methods, acceptability to the RAF, his optimistic reports that contradicted gloomy predictions from other sources, and offers of help in Britain's darkest hour had much to do with his selection a little over a year later to command U.S. air power in Britain.

Spaatz's time in Britain did not turn him into an ardent Anglophile; even after his return to the States he continued to oppose sending aircraft to Britain at the expense of U.S. Air Corps requirements. Yet he had been exposed to the latest aviation technology and tactics available, and he had gained a better understanding of the RAF, the force most likely to be allied with the U.S. Air Corps after America's certain entry into the war. Spaatz's initiation of negotiations for Air Corps entry into the war, even though superseded, and his often-stated belief in the ultimate victory of the RAF earned him the respect of his British associates. More important, Spaatz's transmittal of his faith in the RAF to Arnold and to Donovan may have helped persuade the President to increase U.S. assistance to Britain and, as a result, made Spaatz a key contributor to the growing Anglo-American relationship.

Spaatz's failure to draw correct conclusions from the German and British experiences about the survivability of daylight bomber aircraft also had important consequences. He did not realize that procurement of an effective daylight long-range fighter escort aircraft was a top priority or that Air Corps bomber formations were no more likely to survive in daylight than RAF or Luftwaffe bomber formations. If he had decided that the Air Corps, too, could survive only at night, or that it needed to begin development of appropriate escort fighters immediately, then the American strategic bombing effort in World War II, which he was eventually to direct, might have taken an entirely different path, with incalculable results.

Spaatz and Prewar Strategic Planning

On May 16, 1940, two days before Spaatz left for England, the Air Corps, at the President's behest, increased its expansion plans. Spaatz's plan of December 1938 had called for an increase in annual military pilot training from 300 to 4,500 pilots. In the spring of 1939 the Air Corps had adopted a planning goal of 24 combat-ready groups—that is, fully equipped, completely trained, and capable of fulfilling their assigned missions by June 30, 1941. But the May 16 expansion raised these goals to 7,000 pilots per year and 41 groups. Barely 2 months later, on August 8, newer plans called for 12,000 pilots and 54 combat-ready groups. The August 8 plans also called for 21,470 planes and a total of 119,000 personnel, almost 6 times the personnel envisaged in the summer of 1939. These were the changes Spaatz found when he resumed his post as Chief of the Plans Division (upgraded from a section in May 1940), Headquarters, Air Corps, in November 1940. In another month, on December 17, 1940, a new program called for 30,000 pilots a year.[66]

Between his return from England in September and his resumption of duty in the Plans Division, Spaatz spent a month as Chief of the Air Corps Matériel Division. Although the Matériel Division did the bulk of its work at Wright Field in Dayton, Ohio, a recent Air Corps reorganization had moved the Office of the Chief of the Matériel Division to Washington, D.C. This was probably done in the hope of integrating the technical, aeronautical, and procurement knowledge of the Matériel Division into the Headquarters of the Air Corps, where it was desperately needed for planning purposes. It also made the Matériel Chief readily available to Congress, where he had to justify his decisions. Soon after Spaatz's brief occupancy of it, the Office of the Chief of the Matériel Division returned to Dayton, where it has remained. Spaatz merely occupied the post for a month while waiting for his appointment as an Assistant Chief of the Air Corps, with its accompanying rank of brigadier general,* to become effective so that he could return to the Plans Division.

As the authorized strength of the Air Corps ballooned, its structure underwent reorganization. In October 1940, General Marshall began a new study of Air Corps needs, which resulted in the unsuccessful[67] reorganization of November 19, 1940, under which General Arnold became Acting Deputy Chief of Staff for Air, but the GHQ Air Force was removed from his authority and placed under the authority of the Army Chief of Staff in peacetime and under the control of the Headquarters of the Commanding General of the Army in wartime. This scheme, which once again separated the Air Corps' combat function from

---

* The posts of Chief of the Air Corps and the three Assistant Chiefs of the Air Corps endowed their occupants with the ranks of major general and brigadier general respectively. The rank stayed with the job; former occupants reverted to their Regular Army ranks, usually colonel or lieutenant colonel.

Robert A. Lovett,
Assistant Secretary of
War for Air, 1941–1945.

its supply and training function, could not long survive. By the end of March 1941, Marshall initiated new studies that resulted in the final prewar air organization.[68]

On June 20, 1941, the War Department issued a revised edition of Army Regulation 95-5, which governed the status, function, and organization of the air arm. It created the Army Air Forces (AAF) headed by a chief, who also became the Deputy Chief of Staff for Air and had the authority to supervise and coordinate the work of the Office of the Chief of the Air Corps, the GHQ Air Force (redesignated Air Force Combat Command), and all other air elements. The regulation further created an Air Staff to assist the new deputy chief, which freed the air arm from much of the dominance formerly exercised over it by the ground officers who controlled the War Department General Staff. At Arnold's behest, Spaatz became the first Chief of the Air Staff at the end of June 1941. This organization sufficed until March 9, 1942, when a final rearrangement of positions gave the Army Air Forces equality with the Army Ground Forces and greatly reduced the power of the General Staff.[69] In another War Department organizational move, in December 1940, Robert A. Lovett became Special Assistant to the Secretary of War on all air matters. The following spring Lovett advanced to the post of Assistant Secretary of War for Air, a position left vacant by the Roosevelt administration since 1933. Lovett would prove a powerful, friendly, and effective civilian advocate for the AAF.

Negotiations with the British and strategic planning kept pace with air expansion and reorganization. On January 29, 1941, committees from the U.S. and British armed forces began secret meetings "to determine the best means whereby the United States and the British Commonwealth might defeat Germany and her allies should the United States be compelled to resort to war."[70] President Roosevelt had personally read, edited, and approved the U.S. delegation's initial statement of views, presented to the British at the conference's first session.[71] The final report, American-British Staff Conversations No. 1 (ABC-1), submitted on March 27, 1941, stated, "The Atlantic and European area is considered to be the decisive theatre."[72] Both parties agreed to the principle of defeating Germany first and, if necessary, Japan second. ABC-1 also provided for a joint planning staff, a joint transport service, prompt exchange of military intelligence, unity of command within each theater, integrity of national forces, and for "U.S. Army air bombardment units [to] operate offensively in collaboration with the Royal Air Force, primarily against German Military Power at its source."[73]

A second report on these staff conversations (ABC-2) dealt with air matters. In it, the Americans agreed that until the United States entered the war, all aircraft production from newly constructed manufacturing capacity would go to the British. This decision, of course, delayed the Air Corps' 54-group program. It was also agreed that, if the United States entered the war, new manufacturing capacity would be split 50-50.[74] Spaatz, in his capacity as Chief, Plans Division, had vigorously objected to the agreement because of its open-ended commitment to supply aircraft to the British, which would reduce the reinforcement of U.S. overseas possessions and the number of aircraft available for hemispheric defense.[75] Arnold, who agreed with Spaatz and protested that a shortage of aircraft reduced "to the vanishing point the present low combat strength of this force," nonetheless reluctantly agreed to defer full implementation of the 54-group program.[76]

In April 1941, the two powers agreed to exchange military delegations to facilitate exchange of information and planning. A British Military Mission, with joint army-navy-air representatives, came to Washington, and two separate "Special Observer Groups," one U.S. Army and one U.S. Navy, crossed the Atlantic to London. Because the largest initial combat force contemplated for deployment to Britain was drawn from the Air Corps, an air officer, Maj. Gen. James E. Chaney, headed the "Special Army Observer Group."[77]

Under the impetus of ABC-1, U.S. military planners updated and further developed Joint Army and Navy Basic War Plan RAINBOW No. 5. This plan accepted most of the strategic assumptions of ABC-1 and gained the approval of the Secretary of War and the Secretary of the Navy in May 1941. RAINBOW No. 5 provided detailed breakdowns and deployment schedules for Army (including air) and Navy units allocated to areas of anticipated conflict.

On July 9, President Roosevelt requested the Joint Board of the Army and Navy—the predecessor of the current U.S. Joint Chiefs of Staff—to prepare an estimate of the "over-all production requirements required to defeat our potential enemies."[78] When the President's request descended on the War Department General Staff, the War Plans Division (WPD), the staff's most prestigious section and its major military planning component, was already swamped. WPD's chief, Brig. Gen. Leonard T. Gerow, appointed Maj. Albert C. Wedemeyer to head the group preparing the estimate. Wedemeyer, in turn, expected Lt. Col. Clayton Bissell and other air personnel in the WPD to prepare an air annex. Bissell went to Col. Harold George of the newly formed Air War Plans Division (AWPD), part of Spaatz's new Air Staff. Bissell asked George to bring over a team to help out. George objected and went to Spaatz, his immediate superior. Both he and Spaatz realized that if the WPD prepared the air plan, Army ground officers would base their estimates on tactical close air support needs while shortchanging strategic air war needs. The two went to Arnold, who supported their position. Arnold suggested to Gerow that because WPD already had an overload of work, the Air Staff would help draw up the air requirements. Gerow acquiesced. He and Spaatz "discussed the over-all problem prior to the work being conducted."[79]

George and three other air officers, Lt. Col. Kenneth H. Walker, Maj. Laurence S. Kuter, and Maj. Haywood S. Hansell, prepared the air annex in one week, August 4–11, 1941. Because of its clear definition of the AAF's strategic aims and its call for a gigantic air arm to accomplish those aims, the Army Air Forces Annex, "Munitions Requirements of the AAF for the Defeat of Our Potential Enemies" (AWPD/1), proved to be a key document in the AAF's preparation for the war. It defined three AAF tasks in order of importance: (1) to wage a sustained air offensive against Germany; (2) to conduct strategically defensive operations in the Orient; and (3) to provide air actions essential to the defense of the continental United States and Western Hemisphere. The air offensive against Germany had four goals: (1) reducing Axis naval operations; (2) restricting Axis air operations; (3) undermining "German combat effectiveness by deprivation of essential supplies, production, and communications facilities" (a strategic bombing campaign); and (4) supporting a final land invasion of Germany.[80] To accomplish its mission, AWPD/1 called for 2,164,916 men and 63,467 aircraft, of which a total of 4,300 combat aircraft (3,000 bombers, 1,300 fighters) were slated for Britain.

In mid-August, Gerow reviewed and accepted AWPD/1. Marshall followed suit on August 30, as did Secretary of War Henry L. Stimson on September 11. AWPD/1 reached the President's desk a few days later. Along with the Army and Navy requirements, it formed the beginning of the Victory Program on which the government based its initial industrial mobilization. Stimson's and Marshall's agreement with the plan meant that the AAF had the approval of the War Department's top civilian and military officials for its ambitious wartime expansion.

During 1941, Spaatz may have made what in retrospect seems one of the biggest mistakes in his professional life. He has been accused of having had in his hands, but not having appreciated, the solution to the long-range escort-fighter problem. Spaatz apparently failed to realize that available technology in the form of expendable, externally carried fuel tanks, called drop tanks, could satisfactorily solve the problem of range extension. One scholar has stated,

> Literally hundreds of crewmen lost their lives because escort fighters of suitable range were not ready when needed. The lack of escort fighters jeopardized the whole effort to prove the feasibility of strategic air power. What an irony that he who was to command the Eighth Air Force and suffer the brutal losses incurred in ramming home the Combined Bomber Offensive in 1943 and 1944 had it in his power in 1941 to provide the solution but did not.[81]

Although it is true that the Army Air Corps did not fully realize the possibilities of drop tanks, singling out Spaatz as the man responsible for this situation on the basis of one questionable document seems unfair. As the basis of his charge, the scholar cited a broadly written memorandum composed by Maj. Hoyt S. Vandenberg and signed by Spaatz. The scholar concentrated on the doctrinal aspects of the memorandum, noting its opposition to the "carrying of bombs" and "provision of excessive range" (drop tanks), both of which "require additional and *unnecessary* [sic] weight and operational complexities that are incompatible with the mission of pursuit." Furthermore, bombs and additional range would "provide opportunities for improper tactical use of pursuit types."[82]

Despite its language, however, this memorandum addressed aircraft production more than doctrine. It disapproved production change no. 3[83] (the addition of both a 75-gallon auxiliary fuel tank and provisions for carrying either 300-pound or 600-pound bombs) for 623 P-39D aircraft. In a background memorandum to Spaatz, Vandenberg justified the refusal on the ground that all the proposed changes "would tend to slow up production and reduce the combat effectiveness of the airplane." Vandenberg also suggested that only essential changes be approved.[84] Spaatz's Plans Division, faced with desperate aircraft shortages throughout its training and readiness programs, concentrated on pushing aircraft through the production system. As a consequence, Vandenberg argued that "a determined effort should be made to keep the pursuit airplane as simple as possible."[85] As a technical detail it should be noted that the P-39D aircraft's design limited it to operations under 12,000 feet, and at no time did the Air Corps seriously consider using the plane as an escort for heavy bombers. Production, not doctrinal considerations, motivated Spaatz's action.

Although the Air Corps began a limited-range extension program in 1940 and expanded it in 1942,[86] Spaatz's and Vandenberg's attitudes toward long-range fighter escort typified prevailing prewar Air Corps views. The authors of AWPD/1, in August 1941, showed equal shortsightedness. "It has not yet been demonstrated," the plan stated, "that the technical improvements to the bombardment airplane are or can be sufficient to overcome the pursuit airplane."

Consequently, the plan observed, "It is unwise to neglect development of escort fighters designed to enable bombardment formations to fight through to the objective." The aircraft envisioned by the plan was not an aircraft of pursuit performance with extended range, such as the P-51, but, instead, was a convoy defender like the YB-40 (a B-17 modified by the addition of extensive armor plate and several additional .50 caliber machine guns). AWPD/1 called for the funding of an experimental squadron of thirteen such planes.[87] In combat with the American Eighth Air Force over Germany, in 1943, the YB-40 proved a costly failure. Similar opinions appeared in the AAF's last prewar review of its pursuit aircraft requirements. In October 1941, Spaatz, as Chief of the Air Staff, and at Arnold's behest,[88] appointed a board of pursuit and air matériel officers to recommend "the future development of pursuit aircraft." The opinions of the board's members, which included Col. Ira C. Eaker and Col. Frank O'D. Hunter, illustrated the thinking of the AAF on the eve of the war.

Eaker, in particular, would have played a key role in this board's decisions. He had just returned from England, where he had served as Special Air Observer until October 1, 1941. His primary mission had been to determine the feasibility of integrating the radio systems of American ground echelons, pursuit formations, and aircraft into British operations.[89] However, Arnold had also instructed Eaker to conduct "a broad study of all phases of fighter operations." This included obtaining "the best thought now prevalent on the subject of escort fighter protection."[90] Eaker did a thorough job. He not only talked to many senior RAF officers, he came back with dozens of copies of British reports concerning British and German fighter tactics and performance. He undoubtedly shared the information he collected with the pursuit panel.

The views of the RAF on bomber escort aircraft, as Eaker accurately reported, paralleled those of the AAF. Eaker's visit to England came just at the conclusion of a limited upsurge in RAF daylight bombing missions. The RAF directed those missions, nicknamed "circus" raids, at targets on the French coast within range of British fighter planes. The purpose of these raids was to produce attritional combat between escorting RAF fighters and attacking German fighters. They failed because the Germans soon adopted a policy of engaging only when they held the advantage. The Germans could adopt such a policy because the limited range of the RAF escorts did not allow bombing of targets vital to the German war effort.[91] Circus operations reinforced the prevailing RAF opinion that short-range fighter aircraft could not provide strategic escort.

In May 1941, shortly before launching the operation, the Chief of the Air Staff and a former head of Bomber Command, Air Chief Marshal Portal, had replied to a query from Churchill on fighter escorts by noting, "Increased range can only be provided at the expense of performance and maneuverability." He added, "The long-range fighter, whether built specifically as such, or whether given increased range by fitting extra tanks, will be at a disadvantage compared with the short-range high-performance fighter."[92] On September 28, Portal expressed similar views to Eaker, drawing the logical conclusion "that the proper escort fighter will be a ship exactly like the bomber it is going to escort." This heavily armored and armed aircraft would take station at weak points in the bomber formation and by "expel[ling] heavy caliber fire in all directions," make it "very difficult for the light single seater fighters."[93] The commander of the RAF Test, Research, and Experimental Unit spoke to Eaker of the impossibility of the large fighter getting through a screen of small fighters, saying, "They will sting it to death."[94]

The organization and design of the RAF contributed to its inability to conceive of aircraft combining bomber range and fighter performance. The *raison d'etre* of Fighter Command was the air defense of Britain. Its planes, especially the superb Spitfire series, had been designed and built for that purpose alone. Therefore, they emphasized performance over endurance, which was not needed for defense of English air space. Fighter Command had little operational need to develop long-range fighters. Likewise, Bomber Command had committed itself, despite limited circus operations, to the strategic bombing of Germany at night. Night operations depended on avoiding and deceiving the enemy's defenses, not fighting through them, which would have required escort aircraft. Bomber Command, too, had little operational need for escort aircraft. Given the perceived lack of need and the limited resources available, the RAF's refusal to invest in escort aircraft and its failure to pursue technical solutions to fighter range extension were understandable. In fact, the RAF never developed or employed substantial numbers of long-range fighter escort aircraft during the war.

These strongly held opinions of a future major ally, with over two years of hard-won direct combat experience, which had been confirmed by AAF observers, undoubtedly influenced the AAF pursuit board. Eaker, himself, continued to advocate the development of a convoy defender until its experimental employment, under his own command, demonstrated the fallacy of the idea in actual operations. In any case, the board's officers had probably held views similar to those of the RAF even before their exposure to Eaker's reports and documents.

The AAF pursuit board, like the RAF, could not overcome the seeming tautological improbability of the successful long-range fighter escort and made no recommendation whatever for one. Instead, the board suggested consideration of a "convoy defender." "Only with the assistance of such an airplane," warned the board, "may bombardment aviation hope to successfully deliver daylight attacks deep inside enemy territory and beyond range of interceptor support." Yet the board feared that the size and expense of such a convoy defender would interfere with other production and development projects. It thus gave low priority to development of a convoy defender prototype, concluding:

> The Board is unable to say whether or not the project is worthwhile, and can only point out the need for furnishing day bombardment with the very maxi-

mum attainable defensive firepower if that form of attack is to be chosen to gain a decision in war against any other modern power.[95]

The board also considered a long-range pursuit aircraft with a range of 2,000 miles and an operating altitude above 25,000 feet, which would have sacrificed climb and maneuverability for range and endurance. But the board did not recommend the development of a prototype, nor did it envisage the use of drop tanks by this plane.[96]

Operational employment and accessory equipment also received attention by the board, which recommended the high-priority development of nineteen items of new equipment, including new gunsights, pressurized cockpits, new means of aircraft propulsion, and "expendable external auxiliary-fuel tanks." The board defined pursuit's mission in these words: "The general mission of our pursuit aviation is to seek out and destroy, by air combat, hostile aircraft which attack or threaten to attack our vital installations on the ground or our friendly aviation in the air. *The principal target is the hostile bomber*" [emphasis added].[97] Here the board enunciated a principle embraced by none other than Hermann Goering, the Luftwaffe's commanding officer. Interestingly enough, almost all students of great strategic bombing campaigns of World War II cite Goering's directives to attack Allied bombers in preference to Allied fighters as a key tactical error.

The board saw a need for adding drop tanks and for increasing the safety of bombers on deep penetration raids. Yet it never connected the single-engine pursuit aircraft and drop tanks with the bomber protection problem. Neither did the rest of the AAF until almost too late. Ironically, a future commander of the Eighth Air Force did have the solution to the fighter escort problem in his reach, but failed to grasp it. However, that failure, if failure it be, applies more to Eaker, who sat on the development board, than to Spaatz.

The refusal by Spaatz, Eaker, and the board to place a high priority on fighter escort stemmed more from technical considerations than from a denial of the necessity for it. The recent observations of both men in Britain had shown the disadvantages of the Bf 110 against the Spitfire and Hurricane. RAF technical personnel were convinced that a plane capable of both long-range combat and successful dogfighting could not be built—a view shared by Spaatz and Eaker and reflected in the board's findings. Eight years earlier Spaatz had written Arnold concerning a long-range fighter prototype: "If this plane used as a single seater operates to its full range of 1,000 miles, it would undoubtedly be used for the purpose of accompanying bombardment." In that case, Spaatz thought that the fighter "would be forced to meet interceptor pursuit of the enemy which, with a much lower cruise range, will have greatly superior performance."[98]

Spaatz and Eaker, of course, had seen the British and the Germans both resort to night bombing because their bombardment aircraft could not survive in hostile daylight skies. They discounted that experience by calculating that the B-17 flew higher, was more rugged, and carried more and heavier guns than any European bomber. They also assumed that the Americans would maintain tighter defensive formation than the British or Germans.

Events proved the Americans and British correct in their assumption that no heavy fighter could successfully perform long-range escort in Europe. The P-38, an American twin-engine fighter, had its greatest impact in the Pacific against a very different foe. The P-38, because of its higher operating altitude and faster diving speed, a factor of its greater weight, was not helpless against German aircraft; it just operated at a disadvantage in a melee because of its relative lack of maneuverability, especially when opposing pilots were of equal ability. The P-38 performed better than the Bf 110 in the strategic escort role, but as soon as sufficient numbers of long-range single-engine fighters became available, the AAF hastened to replace it.

Ironically, the aircraft that proved the ultimate solution to the long-range escort problem, the P-51 (Mustang), had its maiden flight in October 1940, a year before the pursuit board met. The Mustang was the direct result of a contract between the British government and the North American Aviation Corporation. The contract, signed in January 1940, specified completion within 120 days of a prototype single-engine fighter aircraft. Within 117 days, North American rolled out the plane, complete except for its engine. The design incorporated lessons learned from the early days of the war and included simple lines, for ease of production; an in-line water-cooled engine, frowned upon by the AAF because of its vulnerability to damage compared with a radial air-cooled engine; and an advanced laminar-flow wing section design for improved performance. As recompense for giving permission to the British to produce the aircraft in the United States, the AAF took delivery of two of the initial ten aircraft for testing.

The original U.S.-produced and -designed Allison engine of the P-51, the same used in the P-40, did not provide enough power and limited the P-51's best performance to altitudes below 15,000 feet, an operational ceiling unsuitable for escort of heavy bombers. The British, who appreciated the possibilities of the Mustang's sleek airframe, replaced the original engine with their own powerful Rolls-Royce Merlin engine. The mating of one of the outstanding piston-driven aircraft engines ever made and a superb airframe resulted in a hybrid of distinguished performance, perhaps the best propeller-driven fighter of World War II.

The Americans, too, made a key contribution to the Mustang's development. In their search for a suitable long-range escort they added increased internal tankage, which extended the P-51's escort range to 475 miles (the maximum range of a P-47 with drop tanks) and 108-gallon drop tanks, which extended its escort range to more than 650 miles (to Berlin and beyond). These improvements made the P-51 the preferred escort for the American heavy bombers and the dominant fighter over Europe for the last year of the war. Unfortunately, it did not come into mass production in the United States until 1942 and did not reach American fighter groups in England until December 1943. It reached the Eighth Air Force just in time to help turn the tide of the air war, in conjunction with the yeoman-like service of P-47s equipped with new longer-range drop tanks, and to prevent the U.S. strategic bomber effort from foundering because of excessive losses sustained in unescorted deep-penetration missions into Germany.[99]

Moreover, the aircraft was a bargain; in 1943, each P-51 cost $58,824, compared with $105,567 for a P-38 and $104,258 for a P-47.[100] An aircraft privately designed and built in less than four months, with no government research and development input, cost less, was easier to produce, and outperformed the two aircraft the AAF had spent years bringing to fruition. Perhaps the P-51 was a technological freak aided by wartime combat experience and superior British engine technology, or perhaps the Air Corps aircraft development program had limited itself to overly conservative engineering.[101]

As 1941 drew to a close, the most important and dramatic portion of Spaatz's career lay before him. In the three years prior to U.S. entry into World War II, Spaatz had worked at the center of U.S. air expansion. Few officers could equal his many years of command experience or his breadth of knowledge of the current state of AAF readiness and plans for future production. He understood his force's lack of training and the long delays to be expected in securing replacement aircraft, and this knowledge may account for much of his subsequent reluctance to commit his command in Britain to combat until it was fully ready. Finally, his trip to Britain, which gave him knowledge of modern combat and acquainted him with senior RAF officers, made him an obvious choice for leadership when the United States entered the war in Europe. His seniority entitled him to a large role, but he could keep such a role only by successful performance.

Chapter 3

Spaatz Commands the
Eighth Air Force
(December 1941–November 1942)

> If we fold up here, where will it stop? It could be an
> irreparable blow to our side, at the very time our Allies are
> hanging on by a hair absorbing terrible punishment, and
> counting on us to live up to our big promises. We're the
> only force in U.S. uniforms capable of hitting the number-
> one enemy for a long time.[1]
>
> —*Maj. Gen. Pritchard to Brig. Gen. Savage,*
> *Archbury Field, England, late 1942*

Early in the afternoon of December 7, 1941, Spaatz at home in Alexandria, Virginia, answered his phone. He exclaimed "Christ, no!," slammed down the receiver, and headed for the front door.[2] The Japanese had attacked Pearl Harbor. Almost ten years earlier, after participating in maneuvers based in Oahu, Hawaii, Spaatz had written that the exercises had, "conclusively demonstrated the ineffectiveness of carrier based airplanes against land based airplanes." To be fair to him, one should note that he had also suggested the dispersal of Army aircraft in Oahu to forty or fifty airfields—a move that would have rendered the Japanese attack against the AAF much less effective.[3]

Like many officers in Washington, D.C., in late 1941, Spaatz had braced for an imminent outbreak of hostilities with Japan, but the date and location of the attack, Pearl Harbor, instead of the Philippines, had surprised him. The next day, Congress, after President Roosevelt's dramatic "day of infamy" speech, declared war on Japan. On December 11, Hitler declared war on the United States. Hitler's action allowed the Allies to implement the decision that formed the bedrock of all U.S. and combined Anglo-American prewar planning—Germany first. Hitler had not even obtained a Japanese declaration of war on the Soviet Union in return.

In the next year, Spaatz would devote all his energies to defeating the Nazi regime. He would organize, lead to Britain, and send into combat the first increments of an armada destined to rule the daylight skies over Europe. He would defend the AAF's doctrine, its public image, and the integrity of his forces against all comers. And he would oversee the allocation and organization of much of his force for participation in the Allied invasion of North Africa in November 1942.

When Spaatz reached his office on December 7, he and several others who had also just arrived discussed what to do. Spaatz placed the Air Staff and AAF Headquarters on a round-the-clock manning basis. Next, he ordered the 31st Pursuit Group to the Seattle area and the 1st Pursuit Group to the Los Angeles area, and he activated the Western Aircraft Warning Service.[4] The destruction of the fleet left the West Coast wide open to attack.

Among those present at Spaatz's office in the Munitions Building on the mall in Washington, D.C., were Robert A. Lovett, Assistant Secretary of War for Air, and Maj. Lauris Norstad, Chief of Intelligence for the Air Force Combat Command. They all sat on the floor with their backs toward the wall and listened to a hasty and inadequate intelligence briefing on Japanese strengths and intentions. They discussed the applicable war plans and settled on RAINBOW No. 5 which provided for a two-front war, with the main thrust in Europe and holding action against Japan. Because Arnold was on a trip to the West Coast, Spaatz was, to use Norstad's phrase, "sitting in the seat," the man responsible for making decisions. He promptly decided to implement the plan. In less than an hour after the news of the attack broke, Spaatz was calling AAF units and ordering them to fulfill their roles in RAINBOW No. 5.[5]

Rapidly unfolding events in the Pacific soon destroyed the strategic basis of the plan. The attack on Pearl Harbor eliminated whatever chance the U.S. Navy might have had of preventing an all-out Japanese attack on the Philippines and the tiny U.S.-held islands of Guam and Wake. Moreover, the loss of the British capital ships HMS *Prince of Wales* and HMS *Repulse* on December 10 plus the impotence of the U.S. Navy and the incompetence or unpreparedness of the defenders produced further disasters in Malaya, Burma, the East Indies, the Philippines, and the Pacific islands. These events forced the Americans to divert considerable air resources to the war against Japan, but not to abandon their commitment to defeat Germany first.

At the first of the great series of Allied strategic planning conferences, the ARCADIA Conference held in Washington, D.C., from December 24, 1941, to January 14, 1942, the Americans and the British agreed that Germany remained the chief enemy. Among the decisions made, two affected the AAF's hope of launching a bomber offensive from Britain: the Allies reluctantly decided (1) to send additional troops to the Pacific and (2) to mount an invasion of French

North Africa. The Americans would garrison the stops on the air ferry route from Hawaii to Australia; supply more garrisons for islands such as Christmas, Borabora, and Samoa; and station a large number of troops in New Caledonia to help the French. Because the British could not meet their strategic commitments to Australia and New Zealand, the Americans sent 61,000 troops and over 500,000 tons of cargo to help defend both countries.

Troops sent to the Pacific required more shipping than troops sent to Britain because those units sailing to the Far East expected to enter combat soon after arrival. This meant that they had to carry all equipment required for combat with them which had to be combat loaded, i.e., completely assembled and packed on the ship in a manner that enabled the off loading of essential weapons, ammunition, and supplies first. Loading for combat emphasized combat necessity, not efficient use of a ship's storage space. Hence, combat loading consumed more shipping tonnage.[6] In contrast, troops going to Britain still had months of training and preparation before them and did not have to travel combat loaded. The diversion of shipping to the Pacific war slowed AAF deployment to Britain.

Roosevelt and Churchill further complicated matters by directing an invasion to be mounted against French North Africa known as SUPER-GYMNAST. The British, whose 8th Army had just relieved Tobruk and seemed to have defeated the Germans and Italians, had great interest in a North African invasion. The Americans, except for Roosevelt, had less enthusiasm. They had to find shipping to send a force across the Atlantic and were not about to allow the siren song of their ally to bring them to grief in the Mediterranean. This alternative kept more shipping tied up and unavailable for carrying men and matériel to the British Isles.[7]

An Axis resurgence in Libya undercut the planning to invade North Africa by bringing into question the attitude of the Vichy government, which gave every indication that it would support the Germans as long as they continued to win. On March 3, 1942, the Combined British and American Chiefs of Staff (CCS) dropped SUPER-GYMNAST as an operational possibility.[8] The Americans advanced a new alternative. One American in particular, the new head of the War Plans Division, Brig. Gen. Dwight D. Eisenhower, had already sent two important memoranda to General Marshall proposing that the Allies launch an early invasion of Europe. Eisenhower had good reasons for the suggestion. It placed a minimum strain on shipping. It did not disperse the escorts vital to the North Atlantic line of communications to Britain. A buildup in England would force the Germans to put a larger garrison in western Europe, leaving fewer troops to fight the Soviets. Once ashore in France, the invaders would find better land communications than anywhere else in Europe. Numerous airfields already existing in England allowed for the establishment of the large air force necessary to gain air superiority over the beachhead. An invasion of western Europe would allow the British to employ offensively a maximum portion of their combat power because they would not have to leave behind a large force to defend the home islands. And the attack would cause the Germans to fight on yet another front.[9] One can find no better statement of the U.S. Army's rationale for an invasion of northwestern Europe. Eisenhower made passing reference to a U.S.-British air attack designed to clear the way for the landing but no mention of a strategic bombing campaign against the Reich.

By the end of March 1942, the Operations Division (OPD), the successor to the War Plans Division under the Army reorganization of March 9, delivered yet another plan to Marshall emphasizing the need for a massive assault from England to France. Marshall, of course, needed no convincing. He and Secretary of War Stimson urged the President to approve the project. Instead, Roosevelt approved the idea of developing a plan and clearing it with London. Within two days of the President's decision, OPD produced a draft invasion plan, including an analysis of troop readiness and availability, supply requirements and shipping resources, and an AAF outline for attacks on either September 15, 1942, or April 1, 1943. Marshall and Stimson presented this latest design to Roosevelt, who approved it, authorizing Marshall and Harry Hopkins, FDR's chief aide, to travel to London to secure British agreement to a common strategy. The President made clear to the British his support of the plan by sending Marshall not only as Chief of Staff but as an envoy or negotiator "in the name of the President."[10]

The U.S. delegation arrived in London on April 8. It included an air planner, Col. Howard A. Craig. The Americans repeated the arguments of Eisenhower's memoranda and stated that if all preparations went forward, a combined force of 5,800 aircraft and 48 divisions could begin the attack against northwestern Europe. The plan had three phases. The preparatory phase (code-named BOLERO) was to include development of a logistics base, movement of troops and equipment, establishment of a preliminary front using England to stage commando raids and to mount strategic air attacks against occupied Europe and Germany on an increasing scale, and contingency planning for a possible emergency offensive in 1942. The second phase (SLEDGEHAMMER) was the cross-channel invasion to seize beachheads in the Le Havre-Boulogne area. The third phase (ROUNDUP) was the expansion of the beachhead and breakout. The Americans promised to have 1 million men, 30 divisions, and 2,550 combat aircraft ready by April 1, 1943, but only 3½ divisions and 700 combat aircraft by September 15, 1942.[11]

For the next six days the British and American planners and the British Chiefs of Staff discussed the "Marshall Memorandum," as the British dubbed the plan. On April 14, the British accepted the plan with one proviso—that all necessary measures be taken to prevent a joining of Japanese and German forces.[12] The Americans had no objections.[13] The Marshall Memorandum, especially the BOLERO phase, was the strategic foundation for Spaatz's own plans for the buildup of the U.S. Eighth Air Force in England. By the end of July 1942, the ground under this foundation had shifted, threatening to bring down the planning basis of the AAF in Europe.

The decisions at the ARCADIA Conference and the acceptance of the Marshall Memorandum substantially modified AWPD/1. The diversion of shipping to the Pacific overturned deployment predictions, and the preparation for a land invasion meant less time for the strategic bomber offensive and an increased emphasis on the creation of tactical air power to support the invasion. On February 12, 1942, General Arnold announced that the AAF would send to the British Isles 16 heavy-bombardment groups, 3 pursuit groups, and 8 photo-reconnaissance squadrons, 512 heavy bombers, 225 fighters, and 96 reconnaissance planes. In a personal telegram to Churchill, which examined the disposition of U.S. armed forces throughout the world, Roosevelt supplied a tentative schedule for the arrival of the AAF in Britain:

> July 1942—3 heavy-bomber groups (105 planes), 1 medium-bomber group (57 planes), 3 light-bomber groups (171 planes), and 5 fighter groups (400 planes);
> October 1942—11 heavy-bomber groups (385 planes), 3 medium-bomber groups (171 planes), 5 light-bomber groups (285 planes), and 7 fighter groups (560 planes);
> January 1943—15 heavy-bomber groups (525 planes), 7 medium-bomber groups (399 planes), 7 light-bomber groups (399 planes), and 13 fighter groups (1,040 planes).

The President explicitly noted that the fighters were "to be used as fighter escort for daylight bombing and for offensive sweeps."[14] The man intended to prepare the way for this armada, Brig. Gen. Ira C. Eaker, arrived in England on February 20 and established the VIII Bomber Command on February 23.

On February 2, 1942, Arnold made Spaatz Commander-designate of the AAF in Britain. Spaatz also became Commanding General of the Air Force Combat Command (the successor to GHQ Air Force). The position carried with it the rank of temporary major general. For the next three months, Spaatz applied his organizational skills to preparing the AAF for overseas movement. He suggested on March 31 that the Eighth Air Force be made the intermediate command head-quarters between the U.S. Army European Theater of Operations and its subordinate AAF commands. Thus, the Commanding General of the Eighth Air Force would be not only the chief of all AAF units in the theater but also the airman responsible for overseeing both a large strategic and a large tactical air force. Official orders established the Eighth as such exactly one week later, on April 7.

When Spaatz assumed command of the Eighth Air Force on May 10, the initial movement of personnel and matériel had already begun. Some potential organizational and command problems had also been solved. ABC-1 established the principle that the theater air forces of each nation would be treated as separate entities under the strategic direction and command of one of the Allies. Moreover, Arnold gained Marshall's agreement that the U.S. Army in Britain would be organized along functional lines. Instead of dividing Britain into geographically denominated corps or army areas, each composed of a force of all arms, the senior officers of the Army Ground Forces, the Army Air Forces, and the Army Services of Supply in the theater would command only their own branch and be directly subordinate to the theater commander. Arnold had hewn to one of the cardinal rules of air power: Air power must be concentrated to be most effective. Spaatz would command an air force composed of all air and aviation support units in the theater. Air components would not be split up and parceled out to army ground generals in charge of subregions. This arrangement relieved the theater commander of the administrative and tactical details of operating an air force and provided flexibility enough to accommodate the vast air armada then contemplated for deployment to Britain. The Headquarters of the Eighth Air Force, as the highest level AAF headquarters in England, was therefore responsible for the theater's air power.

The Eighth consisted of an air force headquarters and four subordinate commands, each carrying the number of the overall headquarters: VIII Bomber Command, VIII Fighter Command, VIII Air Support Command, and VIII Service Command. The composition of these commands corresponded to expected functions. The VIII Bomber Command, consisting of heavy-bombardment groups, each containing 32 aircraft, would carry out the operational aspects of the strategic bomber offensive. Later in the war, the Eighth's heavy-bombardment groups gained authorization for a front-line strength of 48 planes. The VIII Air Support Command, made up of the medium-bombardment groups, the light-bomber groups, and the dive-bomber groups (all of 52 planes each), would provide tactical support and interdiction for the ground troops invading France from England. The VIII Fighter Command, made up of the fighter groups (75–80 planes each), would escort, according to the situation and its range capabilities, the planes of either the Bomber Command or the Air Support Command. If required, Fighter Command could also join the Air Support Command in direct assistance to the ground troops. The functions of VIII Service Command included supply and maintenance of all items peculiar to the Air Force. As the size of the Air Force increased, additional echelons appeared between the commands and the groups. First came wings, formed of several groups. Next, for the heavy bombers only, came bombardment divisions containing three to five wings.

Combat aircraft equipping the three fighting commands varied in quality from poor to excellent. The B-17E, although somewhat undergunned by later standards, outclassed any other daylight heavy bomber in the world. In addition to speed and high-altitude capability, the B-17E had a rugged construction that allowed it to absorb unbelievable amounts of battle damage and still return to base. Variants of the B-17 served as the backbone of the Eighth's bombers throughout the war. The B-17E had a combat radius of approximately 750 miles.*

---

* The combat radius is the straight distance a plane can fly from its base and return. It takes into account taxiing, taking off, forming up, and landing, and is calculated at 3/8 to 2/5 of the aircraft's rated range.

Brig. Gen. Ira C. Eaker,
Commanding General,
VIII Bomber Command,
1942.

Brig. Gen. Frank O'D.
"Monk" Hunter,
Commanding General,
VIII Fighter Command,
1942–1943.

The B-25 Mitchell medium bomber had a combat radius of about 500 miles and a bomb load of 3,000 pounds. It was usually operated at altitudes below 20,000 feet and thus was unable to attack targets defended by heavy antiaircraft guns, which usually guarded strategic targets. It was sturdy and fairly heavily armed.

American fighters did not measure up to world standards. The P-39 (Aircobra), although fast, lacked the maneuverability and altitude to contend with German fighters. It had a combat radius, allowing 10 minutes of combat, of 150 miles. The P-40 (Warhawk) had a similar combat radius. But given proper tactics and disciplined pilots, it could hold its own against the German fighters at lower altitudes. By 1942, the AAF official history acknowledged its obsolescence.[15] The twin-engine P-38 (Lightning) was a good high-altitude heavy fighter with a combat radius more than double that of other American fighters. It could hold its own at high altitudes against German aircraft but its engines reacted badly to the unique combination of high humidity and extreme cold found over northwestern Europe during winter; it operated more satisfactorily in the warmer Mediterranean and the Pacific.

Upon taking over command, Spaatz immediately began the final preparations for sending the Eighth to England. Contrary to what one might suspect, the headquarters personnel of the Eighth Air Force did not consist of a group of elite officers hand-picked by Spaatz and Arnold for their dedication to the ideals of daylight strategic bombardment. In fact, Spaatz had inherited the Eighth Air Force Headquarters because its previous assignment, preparing for a possible invasion of French North Africa, had lapsed, leaving it available for reassignment. The Eighth's former Commander, Col. Asa N. Duncan, became Spaatz's Chief of Staff, and Duncan's staff continued its work for Spaatz. The new staff faced an abrupt change in focus from planning a tactical mission in support of a possible small-scale invasion to planning both the major ground support and the major strategic air campaigns of the American armed forces in Europe. Spaatz's staff faced a daunting challenge; in spite of the grandiose numbers and missions described in AWPD/1, the AAF appears to have done little operational planning for combat over Europe. In early April 1942, Maj. Henry Berliner, a personal friend of Spaatz and the Eighth Air Force Assistant Chief of Staff for Plans, approached Col. Richard D'O. Hughes of the target planning section of the AAF Air Staff. Major Berliner admitted that Spaatz had sent him to find out if any serious planning existed concerning the Eighth's mission. Hughes shared target intelligence he had gathered and an impressed Berliner asked him to meet Spaatz the next day. At the meeting, Spaatz, as usual, said little, but he absorbed everything that Hughes related. A few days later General Marshall ordered the Eighth Air Force to prepare and to present to him in ten days a complete operational plan. Berliner and his staff promptly appeared, hat in hand, at Hughes's door. Hughes noted, "they had none of them ever made an operational war plan before in their lives, none of them had had the opportunity to study the problems involved, and a more scared and nervous bunch of officers I have seldom seen." Hughes agreed to help and within five days he prepared a slick and plausible plan. Shortly thereafter he found himself transferred permanently to Spaatz's headquarters.[16]

On May 10, Spaatz and Arnold met at Bolling Field to discuss the movement of the Eighth to Britain and Hughes's plan. Spaatz "expressed the hope that the force would not be stampeded into premature action by political pressures and other influences."[17] He warned against exaggerating AAF strength and cautioned that he intended to operate on the basis of 100 percent reserves at all times, until the pipeline of replacement combat crews and machines had been put in place and filled. Spaatz wanted it understood that he would not begin combat operations until his force was ready.[18]

Four days later Spaatz and Marshall met, and Spaatz again presented his (and Hughes's) basic concept of operations. The Americans meant to draw the Luftwaffe into combat and destroy it in a battle of attrition. A great air force, as Spaatz had observed in England, could not be destroyed in one or two battles. He had seen how constant action had broken the German air offensive while bringing the British themselves to the brink of defeat. It would take months of constant bleeding of experienced pilots and loss of first-line machines to draw the sting of the Luftwaffe and make a cross-channel invasion possible.[19]

To force the Luftwaffe to come up and fight, the Americans intended to bomb targets of such economic or military importance that the Germans would have to defend them or lose the war. General Spaatz contended that "the full or partial destruction of Ploesti would force the enemy to defend many of those targets now considered unimportant." Once Hitler's chief source of natural petroleum in Ploesti, Romania, dried up, the synthetic oil plants of the Reich would have to be defended or Germany would be helpless to fight a modern war.[20]

Given the Marshall Memorandum, tactical air plans for the European invasion ranked high on the agenda at this meeting. Marshall discussed the strength of Nazi defenses and the necessity of reducing them. He next turned to the need for air superiority over Allied preinvasion troop concentration points and asked what the AAF could do to counter night movement of enemy armored formations. Marshall also expressed concern about the AAF's capability to protect the invasion areas. Spaatz, in turn, suggested that timely reconnaissance and properly stationed planes would solve those problems. He defined for Marshall the difference between air superiority and air supremacy. Air superiority meant that the stronger force could operate with freedom but could not guarantee that the opposing air force would be unable to execute damaging air raids. Air supremacy meant that the opposing air force would be completely unable to operate effectively. Spaatz emphasized that the cross-channel invasion required air supremacy before October, when bad weather would tie up the air arm and the plan. Marshall accepted a weather deadline of "early October" and asked Spaatz to brief Secretary Stimson.[21]

**Henry L. Stimson,
Secretary of War,
1940–1945.**

The next day Spaatz explained his basic concepts a third time to the Secretary of War. Stimson noted that the strategic targets differed from those of AWPD/1. Spaatz replied that the original conceptions of AWPD/1 "involved the usage of Air Power—supported by ground forces," but that the present planning "involved Air Power—*supporting ground forces* [emphasis in original]." Spaatz then spoke of having two U.S. expeditionary air forces, one of which "would attack vital enemy industries and interior installations" while the second would "establish air supremacy over a limited area—permitting ground forces a necessary latitude to carry out the mission." Clearly, Spaatz conceived of two separate American expeditionary air forces—one strategic, one tactical. Both would operate under the same overall commander. Stimson promised his full support to Spaatz.[22]

On May 16, 1942, Spaatz and company terminated their series of conferences with nearly two hours of discussion with Maj. Gen. Robert C. Richardson, Jr., Marshall's personal representative, who was to leave shortly for a tour of Pacific combat zones. Richardson's task was to determine for the Chief of Staff the minimum amount of Army resources required to hold the line against Japan. This rationale would enable Marshall to devote the remainder of his forces against the more powerful foe in Europe.

After the obligatory explanation of the basic concepts and exhortations against premature commitment, discussion turned to more technical matters of

General George C. Marshall, Chief of Staff, U.S. Army, 1939–1945.

compatibility of AAF and British equipment and of target selection. Spaatz mentioned railroads, waterways, and troop concentrations. Richardson pointed out the importance of submarine production as a key target. Both generals discussed the effect of combined Anglo-American command on target selection and agreed that the Americans should retain the right to select their own targets. During the targeting discussions, Spaatz included German aircraft production, noting that the necessary rate of destruction would be twenty planes a day. With regard to fighter escorts for the bombers, Spaatz expressed the then standard AAF opinion on the defensive prowess of the B-17 as a gun platform.[23]

Finally, discussion turned to methods of sending the Eighth to England. Spaatz presented a plan to fly the Eighth's aircraft over a Maine–Labrador–Iceland–England ferry route. Richardson was impressed, and as he departed, indicated that Marshall, too, had expressed great optimism about the plan's success. The key element of the plan was its provision of aircraft and crews in England as early as possible. Aircraft that arrived crated and disassembled via sea transport would need to be assembled and checked out. Their entry into combat would be thus delayed. Each B-17 heavy bomber would lead four P-38 fighters. The flying of hundreds of planes across the relatively undeveloped North Atlantic route required detailed and accurate scheduling to assure the presence of vital supplies and navigation aids along the way. The plan also sacrificed future combat strength for immediate effect, because the inexperienced crews ferrying the planes would suffer attrition at a fairly high rate, while all seaborne airplanes and crews would arrive intact, provided German submarines did not sink them. Once the route had been established, as it was later in the war, regular ferry crews, rather than combat crews, delivered the planes.[24]

In these conferences Spaatz left no doubt in the minds of his superiors, military and civilian, about what he intended to do and how he meant to do it. The Eighth Air Force, when fully prepared and only then, would be hurled en masse against vital German targets that absolutely had to be defended by the Luftwaffe. The Luftwaffe would destroy itself on the guns of the Eighth's bombers and, if possible, those of its short-range fighters. And as the battle of attrition continued in the air, the Eighth would also throttle the Luftwaffe on the ground by destroying the aircraft production industry. This action would ensure air supremacy for the invasion of Europe and severely damage Germany's capacity to wage war.

Spaatz's knowledge of the Luftwaffe's size, strength, and deployment came almost entirely from British intelligence. The AAF official history admitted, "When the war began, the AAF probably was more deficient in its provisions for intelligence than in any other phase of its activities." The same source also stated that the AAF remained dependent on British intelligence for the combat status of the Luftwaffe and for target information for the balance of the war.[25] The British possessed reasonably accurate reports on those matters in part because of their European intelligence network[26] and in part because of their breaking of top-secret German codes (known as the ULTRA secret), especially those of the Luftwaffe. The breaking of the codes enabled the British to obtain accurate readiness, location, and order of battle information on Luftwaffe combat formations.* This information gave Spaatz confidence in his assumptions that the Germans would continue to deploy the bulk of their air power on the Eastern Front or Mediterranean. Furthermore, code breaking could give him quick warning of any change in enemy air plans.

Spaatz's strategy, given the disposition of the Luftwaffe and the on-time delivery of the aircraft promised him, did not seem unreasonable. The Luftwaffe had between 4,000 and 4,400 front-line combat aircraft for most of 1942, 60 percent of them deployed against Russia, a little less than 10 percent assigned to the night fighter defenses of Germany,[27] and a large contingent in the Mediterranean. Spaatz may have faced no more than 400 to 500 machines of all types, which gave a large statistical edge to his own initial strength of 512 heavy bombers and 225 fighters, plus the several thousand British bombers and fighters stationed in Britain. Any major German redeployment or upset of Spaatz's timetable would invalidate his calculations.[28] Postwar examination of captured Luftwaffe records revealed that Spaatz faced a larger force than he had antici-

---

* It is doubtful that in May 1942 the British were directly sharing the ULTRA secret with the AAF. However, information derived from ULTRA, but not attributed to it and suitably disguised, would have figured in the British appreciation of German air strength made available to Spaatz.

pated. German day fighters on the Western Front began the year numbering 292 aircraft and ended the year numbering 453. In September, German day fighter strength reached a high of 574 and then dropped to 500 for the following two months.[29]

The most salient point of Spaatz's plans was the emphasis on destroying the Luftwaffe rather than on conducting a strategic bombing campaign against the German war economy. Spaatz would strike at important economic targets primarily to force the Luftwaffe to defend them and only secondarily to damage German production. He apparently muted his own beliefs in the effectiveness of strategic bombing in order to present to Marshall and Stimson views more in keeping with the role of the Eighth Air Force as only one part of the U.S. forces to be employed against Germany. To concentrate on strategic bombing at the expense of tactical air operations in support of U.S. ground units would hardly have persuaded his listeners of the AAF's willingness to join the combined-arms team envisaged for Europe. Lack of cooperation may have cost Stimson's and Marshall's support for AAF logistics priorities. Or, practical as always, Spaatz may well have realized that the destruction of the Luftwaffe was a necessary preamble to the freeing of American air power to conduct both strategic and tactical operations at will.

On May 21, Spaatz learned of the first of the diversions of strength that eventually hamstrung the Eighth's ability to engage in an effective strategic bombing campaign in 1942. Admiral Ernest J. King, Commander in Chief of the U.S. Fleet and Chief of Naval Operations (CNO), insisted that the Eighth divert four B-17Es to the defense of Alaska. Spaatz, unaware that King had foreknowledge (thanks to the breaking of Japanese naval codes) of the upcoming Midway Island campaign, viewed the action with a jaundiced eye. Such withdrawals, in his opinion, were merely the entering wedge of a whole series of possible diversions that could only hinder the creation of a stable air force.[30] Spaatz complained about the diversion of the B-17s to Alaska; he strongly protested the dissipation of his force and the disruption of his movement to England. In the interest of safety, Spaatz said he could not allow the B-17s to shepherd more than four fighters each across the Atlantic. Arnold regretted the diversion of the B-17s but insisted that "certain pressure" (King) made it necessary.[31]

Later that morning Spaatz met with Arnold and Maj. Gen. Millard F. Harmon, Spaatz's successor as Chief of the Air Staff. The three analyzed a letter Spaatz had just received from Eaker expressing "the opinion that the R.A.F. would attempt the dispersal of our units and absorb them within the British Command."[32] Because both parties accepted the assumption that the U.S. bombing force would operate semiautonomously, this dispute centered on the control and basing of U.S. fighters. During the ABC talks in January and February 1941 and in a final report of March 27, 1941, the Americans had agreed to undertake the air defense of the bases of U.S. naval units in British waters and of certain other areas as well.[33] In the summer of 1941, the Air Ministry and the U.S.

Observer Group made concrete plans to station U.S. pursuit groups in Northern Ireland, with the clear intention of having the Americans assume full responsibility for the air defense of that sector. The Observer Group further agreed to allow individual pursuit squadrons to gain operational experience by working with British units in different sectors of the British air defense network.[34]

The rapid buildup of tactical air forces required by the Marshall Memorandum and the AAF's intention of building up a large strategic bombing force led the Americans to change their opinion on the proper basing for the pursuits. Arnold expounded the new strategy to Portal in mid-April 1942. In order to gain air supremacy over Europe and to divert the Luftwaffe from the Russian front, Arnold said, the United States and Britain would have to concentrate the greatest mass of aircraft as soon as possible in England. Because night bombing alone could not wear the Germans down in time for the cross-channel invasion, daylight bombing must resume. In its first stages, daylight bombing would necessitate a large force of fighter escorts to hold down losses from enemy fighters. Once the day bombers had gained greater defensive firepower and perfected formation flying, they would extend their attacks beyond the range of their fighter escorts.[35] American pursuit units would have to have fields close to the French beaches and within escort range of their bombers.

This new policy encountered British opposition. When Maj. Gen. James E. Chaney, head of the U.S. Observer Group in Britain, presented Arnold's new plan to the British on May 8, the head of Fighter Command, Air Chief Marshal Sholto Douglas, insisted that U.S. fighters become part of the British integrated air defense establishment, the Air Defense of Great Britain (ADGB).[36] Chaney replied that his instructions were to limit the use of U.S. fighters to bomber escort and invasion support. The British appealed to the RAF Delegation in Washington to explain the British position to Arnold. It was not possible "to accept for operational training in the front line between 200 and 300 American fighters without V.H.F. [radios] or I.F.F. or any knowledge of routing and recognition or flying control or, in fact, of any procedure at all." In the event of an enemy raid, "the Americans could not cross their fingers and say they were not playing. They must take their share in the defence of what was in fact an Anglo-American air base."

In a reply that the Air Ministry found most unsatisfactory, the RAF Delegation said, "You are up against a very strong determination on the part of Arnold, Spaatz, and others to concentrate the training and employment of their forces in the U.K. entirely upon proving the daylight bombing offensive can be made a success." Attempts to explain the technical difficulties to Spaatz in particular had failed, but the RAF Delegation thought that he might come to accept universal fighter control once he reached Britain and experienced those difficulties. The delegation warned that the Americans would not easily be turned from their determination to use their pursuits primarily as escorts.[37]

On May 12, Chaney delivered a new proposal asking to put two fighter groups on fields near U.S. bombers (in the Huntingdon area) and to delay the arrival of an additional five groups. Portal rejected it. The delay jeopardized the Marshall Memorandum objectives. The plan to occupy Northern Ireland had already gained the approval of the Combined Chiefs of Staff; moreover, the RAF had no objection to the proposal that the primary task of the U.S. fighters be offensive and had already offered cooperation in the early stages of the bomber offensive. Portal insisted, however, that U.S. pursuit units in RAF sectors have not only offensive tasks but convoy escort and air defense duties as well. The Chief of the Air Staff proposed that the United States eventually take over British No. 12 Group's sector, the second most important sector for the defense of eastern Britain and the sector defending the U.S. bomber bases.[38] The issue remained at an impasse until Arnold's visit to Britain at the end of May 1942, to discuss the reallocation of U.S. aircraft production with the British.

While in Britain, Arnold apparently agreed to station the first two and the last U.S. fighter groups in the Huntingdon area and the second two in Northern Ireland. British sources state that he further agreed to the fitting of one fighter squadron into each active RAF Fighter Sector (to gain operational experience) and to the eventual takeover of the Northern Ireland and other group sectors.[39] Given Arnold's subsequent instructions to Spaatz, which forbade the integration of U.S. fighters into British air defense schemes, either Arnold changed his mind or the British assumed agreement where there was none.

While Arnold preceded him to London, Spaatz, with what must have been a sense of relief, left the round of conferences in Washington to supervise the overseas movement of his forces. On May 23, he flew to Fort Dix in New Jersey and inspected all units. From there he motored to Mitchel Field in New York City, and, on May 25, he flew into Grenier Field in New Hampshire. His command's aircraft had already started to arrive—57 P-39s and 3 B-17s. By May 28, the total had risen to 76 P-39s and 17 B-17s, with an additional 78 P-38s at Dow Field in Bangor, Maine, and 31 transports at Westover Field in Massachusetts.[40]

The next three days were taken up by meetings with Maj. Gen. Harold L. George, the head of Ferry Command, who controlled the ferry route itself, not the planes traveling through it; Maj. Gen. Sherman Miles, the Army Corps Area Commander for New England; and Col. Howard A. Craig of the Air Staff. George agreed that Ferry Command had the responsibility for the proper functioning of the movement route and would establish communications and provide housing, supplies, and weather reports. General Miles agreed to provide ground security. Spaatz said that the Eighth could provide its own air defense.[41]

On June 1, Spaatz began his flight for Prestwick, Scotland, the first leg of which ended at Presque Isle.[42] Thanks to the Battle of Midway in the Pacific, the trip to Scotland took seventeen days. On the evening of June 1, as Spaatz, George, and Craig worked to perfect plans, they received a priority call from Brig. Gen. Laurence S. Kuter relaying orders from Marshall to halt all movement. Midway had claimed its first casualty—the Eighth's departure for England. At

8:30 P.M. Kuter issued orders placing all units on six-hour alert for movement to the West Coast, where they would pass to the control of the Fourth Air Force.[43] Spaatz relayed the changes to his subordinates and ordered the transports to Presque Isle to unload 80,000 pounds of supplies and then to comply with War Department orders. By June 3, Spaatz had returned to the District of Columbia.

Victory at Midway unscrambled the Eighth's plans. On June 6 and 11, the 1st Fighter Group and 97th Heavy Bombardment Group returned to Spaatz's control. He escaped Washington on June 10 and arrived at Grenier Field that evening. Winging into Presque Isle by 11:30 the next morning, Spaatz inspected each item covered in his previous visit.[44] On June 12, Spaatz tried twice to fly the 569 miles to Goose Bay, but thunderstorms and icy conditions forced him to turn back. Communications remained unsatisfactory. Weather and communications failed to cooperate on June 13 as well. Frustrated, Spaatz wired Arnold to send "the best communications expert in the country" to Presque Isle at once. On June 14, Spaatz landed in Goose Bay—two hours ahead of his staff. Despite more unfavorable weather reports, Spaatz wished to get a first-hand idea of the difficulties involved in the 776-mile flight to Bluie West I (B.W.I.) Field, Greenland, so he pushed on to Greenland on June 15. Once there, he received a wire from Arnold asking when the first contingent would start for Britain. Spaatz replied that the B-17s not needed for escorting fighters or for weather patrols would start at once; the 1st Pursuit Group could start in a week. On June 17, Spaatz's party flew the 779 miles to Reykjavik, Iceland. They completed the last leg (884 miles) to Prestwick on June 18.[45]

Spaatz alighted at Prestwick to the greetings of Brig. Gen. Ira Eaker, who had done a thorough job in preparing Britain for the initial presence of the AAF. Soon after his arrival on February 20, 1942, Eaker had set up the first AAF headquarters in Europe. He then proceeded to RAF Bomber Command Headquarters, where he began studies of its staff procedures. Next, he drafted recommendations for training, equipment, and employment of U.S. units. He found time to examine British airfields intended for American use, to present a plan for reception and assignment of bombers, to prepare a scheme for supply and administration of such units, and to take appropriate steps toward close coordination of effort with the RAF. On February 22, two days after Eaker arrived at Bomber Command, Air Chief Marshal Arthur T. Harris replaced Air Marshal Richard Peirse.

On June 19, Spaatz and Eaker motored to London to pay a call on the U.S. theater commander, Maj. Gen. Chaney. (The next day Maj. Gen. Eisenhower relieved Chaney and assumed command of the European Theater of Operations [ETO].) The two airmen then called on the American ambassador, John G. Winant, a great air enthusiast who had been a Navy pilot in World War I. He wished to visit all of the Eighth's installations. Spaatz invited Winant to accompany him on his first inspection trip. Before completing his last call of the day, on Portal, Chief of the RAF Air Staff, Spaatz held a press conference. Unlike current press conferences, those of World War II tended to be mannerly, with newspaper men throwing slow pitches and off-the-record comments staying off the record. Spaatz did well. Quentin Reynolds, Drew Middleton, Ed Beattie, and the rest of the press corps liked Spaatz's straightforward answers as well as his honest desire to stay out of the limelight. The correspondents honored Spaatz's request that his presence in the British Isles not be mentioned. In that, they had no choice. Strict U.S. military censors subjected all news stories to their flinty-eyed gaze before release, pruning them of information valuable to the enemy. If Spaatz could keep his presence secret a while longer, perhaps the Germans might be less prepared for the AAF's first raids. Perhaps more important, the American public might be less inclined to demand immediate action if it remained unaware of the Eighth's arrival in Britain.[46]

On June 20, Spaatz held a full-scale staff conference at High Wycombe. After a complete briefing, he set the tone for his command. First, he complimented Eaker for "his splendid work and accepted any commitments made by him *in toto*." He stressed the necessity for a "pleasant" relationship between his staff and the British. "The 8th must do well," he noted, "otherwise our prestige would suffer at home as well as with the British who depend on the U.S. effort." Spaatz ended on a cautionary note. The Eighth should take advantage of British experience, not British tactics. The B-17s and daytime operations must start under fighter escort and not count on their own firepower until they had to make penetrations beyond escort range.[47] Spaatz's remarks about the defensive power of the B-17s demonstrated, at this point, more concern about lack of numbers, skill at formation flying, and gunnery training than any lack of faith in the ability of the B-17s to conduct unescorted deep penetration missions. He would need his fighters for the early shallow penetrations and for supporting the upcoming invasion.

For the next two weeks Spaatz threw himself into the task of preparing a logistics and base structure for his command capable of sustaining the Eighth for a prolonged campaign. (See Map 2, Eighth Air Force Installations, 1942.) He flew all over England and Ireland, laying the groundwork for large-scale air force repair and supply depots. These large facilities would serve as the backbone of the Eighth's logistics efforts. They would be the first recipients of new planes and supplies from the United States and would condition them for dispatch to the combat units. In addition, they would handle complex repairs and overhauls beyond the capacity of the forward depots assigned to the combat groups. Spaatz reported to Arnold that by January 1, 1943, he would have 3 million square feet of storage for air supplies, which would enable the depots to operate at full capacity. These main depots would require at least 25,000 additional personnel. Spaatz also planned for 20 forward supply depots to serve the combat groups.[48] Kay Summersby, Spaatz's British driver during the summer of 1942 and later General Eisenhower's driver and confidante, remembered Spaatz at this time as a "serious man, serious to the point of grimness, and certainly the hardest working man in the whole U.S. Army Air Force [*sic*]."[49]

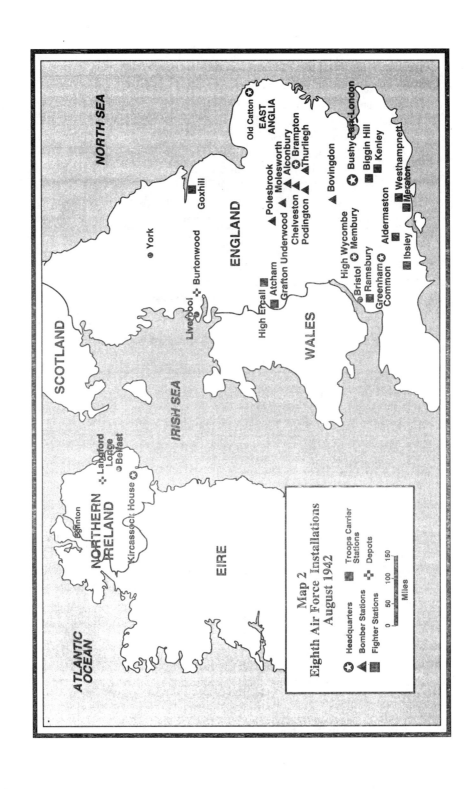

Map 2
Eighth Air Force Installations
August 1942

Headquarters
Bomber Stations
Fighter Stations
Troops Carrier Stations
Depots

0 50 100 150
Miles

ATLANTIC
OCEAN

NORTHERN
IRELAND

EIRE

SCOTLAND

IRISH SEA

NORTH SEA

ENGLAND

WALES

Eglinton
Langford Lodge
Belfast
Kircassock House

Liverpool
Burtonwood
York
Goxhill

Old Catton
EAST ANGLIA

High Ercall
Atcham
Grafton Underwood
Polesbrook
Molesworth
Alconbury
Chelveston
Podington
Brampton
Thurliegh
Bovingdon

High Wycombe
Bristol
Ramsbury
Greenham Common
Membury
Aldermaston

Bushy Park-London
Biggin Hill
Kenley
Westhampnett
Merston
Ibsley

The first bottleneck Spaatz encountered was the shortage of labor and construction supplies in the British Isles. The British, although willing to help, found difficulty in squeezing either commodity out of their overstrained war economy. At one point, when Air Marshal Christopher Courtney, the RAF's chief supply officer, humorously promised that the bases for the first six groups would be ready on time even if they lacked "plush chairs," Spaatz replied that his units would sleep in tents if necessary.[50]

Next, Spaatz traveled to Northern Ireland to inspect newly created Eighth Air Force training facilities. He planned to set up a training command to give a final polish to newly arrived combat crews from the United States.[51] The British agreed to hand over seven airfields and a headquarters facility. On July 4, 1942, the AAF activated the Eighth Air Force Composite Command at Bolling Field in Washington, D.C.,[52] which was soon transferred to Ireland. Spaatz knew full well that Arnold would send him crews as soon as they could make the trip—well before they had finished their training.

Two factors prevented this training command from completing its mission: (1) the scarcity of active U.S. combat formations (new groups were sent into combat very soon after arrival, before their training could be enhanced) and, by midsummer 1943, (2) the higher training level of arriving groups. In fact, because of diversions to North Africa and elsewhere, combat crews did not arrive in Northern Ireland for training until September 1943. The few replacements reaching the Eighth were easily handled at one of the two AAF training fields in England.[53] The Eighth disbanded the training command by the end of 1943.

The aircraft needed for operations arrived after a painfully slow journey over the ferry route. The first two, a B-17 bomber and a C-47 transport, arrived on July 2. Six days later a grand total of eight B-17s, seven P-38s, and five C-47s had arrived. Spaatz's reception plans for his forces were not helped by constant changes in the number of aircraft scheduled for the theater. By June 19, Arnold's original promise of February had grown by one heavy-bomber group (32 bombers), nine fighter groups (675 fighters), six medium- and six light-bomber groups (624 planes), eight transport groups (480 transports), and four observation groups (144 planes). Many of these additional 2,000 aircraft were intended to provide support for the cross-channel invasion.[54] Subsequent strategic decisions sending groups to the Pacific or to North Africa caused numerous delays in the planned shipments for England. Not until July 27, 1943, did the Eighth report a strength of sixteen heavy bomber groups—the original figure promised by Arnold in February 1942.[55]

Establishing the Autonomy of the Eighth Air Force

Aside from the primary task of readying his force and deploying it in battle, Spaatz had to establish the autonomy of the AAF in England, not from the U.S.

85

Army—whose overall leader in Britain, Eisenhower, faithfully adhered to the agreements allowing the Eighth to operate as a whole—but from the Royal Air Force. The RAF, at this stage in the war, was far larger than the AAF in Britain and incomparably more experienced. The RAF had committed itself to night bombing because its own operations had shown that daylight bombing raids against Luftwaffe-defended targets produced unacceptable losses of men and machines. Therefore, the RAF wanted the Americans to abandon their attempt to bomb in daylight and to join with them in night raids. Initially, at least, the British also wanted to employ U.S. fighters to augment their own air defenses.

On June 22, Spaatz paid an informal call on Rear Adm. St. G. Lyster, British Chief of the Naval Air Staff. Lyster suggested U.S. fighter protection for British shipping, a suggestion that Spaatz resisted. His fighters' primary function was U.S. bomber protection, and the instructions given to him from Arnold through Eisenhower were clear: U.S. fighters would not "be integrated with British fighter units employed in the defense of the United Kingdom, or into the British Fighter Command."[56]

The following day Spaatz and Eaker drove to RAF Fighter Command to confer with Air Chief Marshal Sholto Douglas.[57] Spaatz again emphasized that the primary function of U.S. fighters was to support U.S. bombers. He did concede, however, that his fighters would be trained in air defense procedures to assist the RAF in the unlikely event that it could not cope with a renewed German air offensive against Britain. Douglas suggested that the most expeditious way to acquaint American pilots with operations was to blend U.S. squadrons with British wings until they learned procedures. Spaatz agreed to consider this suggestion. Next, Douglas "expressed the hope that eventually the U.S. Air Forces would take over an entire sector."[58] Spaatz pointed out that the Americans would then have to assume responsibility for the air defense of that sector. Douglas admitted "that if U.S. forces did take over a sector, U.S. Air Forces might be called upon to furnish Fleet Arm protection."[59] Spaatz deferred his decision.

He continued his delaying tactics on other occasions during the summer when the RAF again made tentative attempts to gain closer operational control of the AAF in Britain. On July 7, Douglas repeated his attempt to pin down Spaatz on sector air defense. Finally, on July 15, Eisenhower and Spaatz met with Douglas and Slessor and obtained British agreement to the principle "that the integrity of the 8th Air Force must be maintained in any organizational set-up—but there was no objection to all Air Powers being under one Command."[60] If not in this meeting, then at some time during the summer, Spaatz made substantial concessions to the British. He allowed the attachment of his fighter squadrons to British groups for final training and acclimatization and agreed to the eventual assumption of control of British sector and group areas.[61] Spaatz might well have taken the calculated risk that the integration of his fighters both

Air Chief Marshal Sholto Douglas, Air Officer Commanding, Fighter Command, RAF, 1942.

Imperial War Museum

offensively and defensively into the British air control network would be a liability only if the Germans launched attacks on Britain—a possibility that he discounted. Spaatz probably did not object to the responsibility for the air defense of his own fields, if needed. In return, he gained a well–functioning control network with which to coordinate his own operations. In any case, Spaatz's accommodation became unnecessary with the unanticipated transfer of all his active fighter groups* to the North African operation, and it came too late to head off unfavorable press reports. One, which appeared on the front page of the August 8 issue of the *New York Times*, began, "The widely advocated British-American air offensive against Germany is not being carried on because of British-American inability to agree on methods or objectives."[62] The article added that British air officers doubted the ability of U.S. heavy bombers "to do the job." Instead, according to the *Times*, the British wanted the Americans to build night bombers. Although the American and British publics may have failed to grasp the import of the RAF's suggestion, professional air officers knew that the AAF's switch to night bombing would bring the entire American air effort under total British control. Three days later the *New York Times* printed Spaatz's rebuttal on page two.[63] He asserted that the dispersal of men and planes dictated

---

* The Eighth did retain the British-trained ex-RAF Eagle squadrons just transferred to its control.

by strategy, bad weather, and the necessity of putting American crews through advanced operational training—not disagreement over tactics—had delayed the start of the joint air offensive.

The opening of Park House, where Spaatz and most of his staff lived and took their meals, allowed him to entertain high-ranking RAF officers in comfort and privacy. Spaatz also visited them often at their offices or over a working lunch. On occasion, his diary recorded the subject of discussion. On August 8, for example, he and Air Chief Marshal Wilfred Freeman, Vice-Chief of the Air Staff, "conferred" on the transfer of the Eagle Squadrons—fighter squadrons composed of American citizens who had joined the RAF to fight the Nazis before Pearl Harbor—from the RAF to the AAF. (In September the three squadrons of combat-experienced pilots became part of the Eighth Air Force, forming the 4th Fighter Group.)[64] Between August 11 and 21, Spaatz saw Air Vice-Marshal Norman H. Bottomley, Assistant Chief of the Air Staff (Operations), five times.[65] Although some of their conversations must have centered on coordination for the first U.S. heavy-bomber raid on August 17, Bottomley was the officer, subject to Portal's and possibly Churchill's approval, who defined operations. If he accepted operational independence for the AAF, the goal was three-quarters gained.

Bottomley and Spaatz had lunch on August 11 and dinner at Park House on August 13 for a preliminary round of negotiations. Five days later, probably after both sides had reviewed the original scheme, the two met again. The next day Spaatz sent Bottomley a letter, perhaps a draft proposal, and the two dined that evening at Park House.[66] Although speculative, this scenario fits with subsequent events.

On August 20, Spaatz forwarded to Eisenhower a draft proposal on Anglo-American operations. The same day, in light of the commencement of active U.S. operations on August 17, the Eighth Air Force and the Air Ministry together held the first of a series of weekly meetings to discuss operational questions. At the first two meetings, both attended by Spaatz and chaired by Slessor, the chief order of business was consideration of a joint U.S.-British directive on daylight bomber operations involving fighters.[67] Modifications to suit both staffs and the approval of Eisenhower and the British resulted in the promulgation, on September 8, of the "Joint American/British Directif [sic] on Day Bomber Operations Involving Fighter Co–operation."

The joint directive divided the development of the day bomber offensive into three successive phases and provided command procedures for implementing each. In phase 1, U.S. bombers would fly with combined U.S.-British fighter cover. In phase 2, U.S. fighters would escort the bombers while the British supplied diversions and withdrawal cover. In phase 3, the AAF would operate independently in cooperation with the RAF, a phrase ambiguous enough to allow the AAF complete control over its own operations. The directive did, however, imply U.S. coordination and adjustment of operational intentions with British air control plans. The joint directive effectively laid to rest the question of integration of U.S. forces into the RAF.[68] Spaatz had convinced the RAF that the AAF should retain its operational integrity.

Although Spaatz had fended off too close an embrace from the RAF, the "Joint Directif," at least in the minds of the RAF's top leaders, merely allowed the AAF to continue its experiment in daylight bombing.[69] The British, as the *New York Times* had implied, did not believe it would succeed. Portal flatly predicted failure. On September 26, 1942, he stated to Archibald Sinclair, the Secretary of State for Air, with remarkable accuracy the conditions the U.S. strategic bombers would face in October 1943:

> The Americans will eventually be able to get as far as the Ruhr, suffering very much heavier casualties than we now suffer by night, and going much more rarely. They will in effect do area bombing with the advantage of the absence of decoys. If it can be kept up in face of the losses (and I don't think it will be), this will of course be a valuable contribution to the war, but it will certainly not result in the elimination of the enemy fighter force and so open the way to the free bombing of the rest of Germany. I do not think that they will ever be able to regularly penetrate further than the Ruhr or perhaps Hamburg without absolutely prohibitive losses resulting from being run out of ammunition or from gunners being killed or wounded.[70]

Called Peter by his close associates, Portal was the youngest of the Combined British and American Chiefs of Staff. He had begun his military career in 1914 as a motorcycle dispatch rider. A year later he joined the Royal Flying Corps, earning a Distinguished Flying Cross and shooting down several German aircraft before the end of the war. Between the wars he served as Commander, British Forces, Aden; as instructor at the Imperial Defense College; and as Director of Organization on the Air Staff. Personally somewhat remote and cool, he nonetheless established excellent working relationships with Spaatz, Eaker, Arnold, and Eisenhower. The British Chiefs of Staff and Churchill respected him for his strategic ability and brilliant intellect. Because he was virtually unflappable, he could weather the storms of Churchill's fanciful military ideas, often hurled with insulting vehemence by the Prime Minister at the Chiefs of Staff, and temper those ideas with wisdom. Portal worked exceedingly long and hard hours during the war, leaving behind him a voluminous official, but scant personal, correspondence.

Despite his sincere doubts about U.S. daylight bombing policy, which he believed would delay the Americans' eventual and necessary conversion to night bombing until 1944 or later, he loyally supported the AAF's determination to build up the largest possible force in Britain. Always a realist, he probably accepted the political fact that the Americans were so wedded to daylight bombing that only repeated setbacks and not advice could divorce them from it. He may also have recognized that vocal opposition to daylight operations could only work against British interests in the long run. Any undermining of the AAF buildup would result in the dispersal of units slated for Britain to other theaters.

Early Operations

Even as Spaatz fended off the British with one hand, he had to use the other to restrain Arnold. Arnold wanted AAF aircraft operating from Britain against the Germans as soon as possible. He had promised Churchill action by July 4, nine days before Spaatz arrived in Britain.[71] As Commanding General of the AAF, Arnold naturally had priorities very different from those of the leader of a combat air force like the Eighth. Arnold had to justify AAF appropriations to the President, the Congress, and the public. In addition, he had to maintain AAF production and strategic priorities in the face of challenges from the British and the U.S. Navy. All this required a perception of the AAF as a successful and aggressive weapon actively being used against the enemy.

In the summer of 1942, the AAF's image needed bolstering. Navy air had won at Midway while the public still wondered about Army air's performance at Pearl Harbor and in the Philippines. Furthermore, Arnold knew that Roosevelt wanted to see results from the AAF which would justify the massive aircraft production program and shipping priorities slanted toward the projection of air power. On June 28, Spaatz received orders from Arnold to schedule a raid for Independence Day. Because his B-17s had not yet arrived and his 31st Fighter Group had just received its unfamiliar Spitfires, he chose a squadron of light bombers assigned to the VIII Air Support Command. The unit had landed in Britain months earlier as part of a token U.S. force. Spaatz and Eaker viewed the raid as a premature commitment.

The results, from Spaatz's viewpoint, justified his counsel against forcing action too early. The morning of July 4 six American crews and six British crews, all in RAF Boston Bombers and all flying in a joint formation, with the Americans in relatively protected positions, attacked German airfields in Holland. Two of the planes with American crews were downed and two more failed to reach their target. The attacks inflicted little damage. From Arnold's point of view, however, the raid was successful. Not only had Americans been bloodied, but one of their pilots had heroically managed to bring home his severely damaged plane. Capt. Charles C. Kegelman was promptly promoted to major and awarded the first Distinguished Service Cross (DSC) earned by a member of the Eighth Air Force. British and American papers gave the story of the raid headline treatment. To complete the episode Spaatz personally pinned the DSC on Kegelman on July 11. His command diary sourly noted, "The cameramen and newspapermen finally got what they wanted—and everybody seemed contented."[72] But not Arnold, who continued to press Spaatz for more AAF action and publicity.

Spaatz not only had to meet Arnold's demands, he had to satisfy Dwight D. Eisenhower, the new head of the European Theater of Operations (ETO). Spaatz and Eisenhower had not known each other well before their current assignments. They had crossed paths only three times—once at West Point, where Eisenhower

**Air Chief Marshal
Charles A. Portal, Chief
of the Air Staff, RAF,
1940–1945.**

Imperial War Museum

graduated a year after Spaatz, in 1915; again in Washington, D.C., from 1933 to 1935, when Spaatz served in the Office of the Chief of the Air Corps and Eisenhower was in the Office of the Chief of Staff; and, finally, during the first six months of the war, when both men had served in high Army and AAF staff positions. Although the new theater commander was not an air enthusiast, he was much less closed-minded about the AAF than many staff and ground officers; he even had a private pilot's license. Marshall had selected him for his current position and had promoted him to lieutenant general. Eisenhower had spent the previous seven months working hand in hand with the Chief of Staff as head of the Operations Division of the War Department's General Staff and had prepared the Marshall Memorandum, which set out the invasion plans for northwestern Europe agreed to by the Anglo-American Allies. Having written the plan, he would now execute it.

On June 26, Spaatz had his first appointment with his new commanding officer. It was the start of an effective, close, working relationship that did much to advance the cause of the Allies and, to a lesser extent, the AAF. This first meeting proved typical. Spaatz agreed to notify Eisenhower one week before his units were scheduled for combat or to telephone him at any time day or night that AAF units entered combat. Eisenhower, as the officer responsible for conducting the amphibious assault on the Continent, was naturally concerned that VIII Air Support Command (VIII ASC) had not yet set up its headquarters in

Maj. Gen. Carl A. Spaatz congratulating newly-promoted Maj. Charles C. Kegelman to whom he has just awarded the first Distinguished Service Cross earned by a member of the Eighth Air Force.

Britain. Spaatz sent a cable "asking for Colonel [Robert C.] Candee to get here immediately with Air Support Headquarters." Then Spaatz and Eisenhower agreed to locate VIII ASC Headquarters at Maj. Gen. Mark W. Clark's II Corps Headquarters. In this they adhered to the essential principle of co-location of a tactical air headquarters with the headquarters of the ground unit it supported. Clark's II Corps Headquarters commanded all Army Ground Forces in Eisenhower's theater and was scheduled to have direct tactical control at the invasion beachhead.[73]

Spaatz did not walk away empty-handed from his first meeting with Eisenhower. He obtained support for his position against the British on the role of U.S. fighter aircraft in England. In a letter to Arnold dated the day of the meeting, Eisenhower confided:

> We intend to insist that the American squadrons should be looked upon as an offensive force with the result that our fighter squadrons will be fully engaged fighting over hostile territory. If we are going to provoke a fight, we have got to have the close support units to fight with, and they must not be worn out by keeping them on regular alerts.[74]

Apparently Spaatz had drawn Eisenhower's attention to the fact that any

Eighth Air Force fighter assigned to air defense over England and naval support over the English Channel might be a fighter unavailable for tactical air missions over a beachhead.

The Spaatz-Eisenhower relationship eventually grew into what Spaatz later termed "a rather close personal relationship, and I think on both sides that mutual confidence made it unnecessary to have long detailed explanations for courses of action."[75] From July 1 to October 31, 1942, the two generals "conferred," to use the term employed in Spaatz's Command Diary, fifty-five times.

On June 26, after dinner at High Wycombe, Spaatz, Eaker, Winant, and Air Chief Marshal Harris retired to Eaker's apartment for drinks and discussion. Harris had met Spaatz and come to a first-name basis with him during a trip to the United States as a member of a British purchasing commission in 1938, and again when he headed the permanent RAF Delegation to the United States in late 1941. That evening Spaatz and Harris agreed that, given 5,000 bombers, they could end the war in three months. When Winant pointed out that current production schedules should soon supply that force, Spaatz noted that attrition, operational damage, and commitments to other theaters had significantly altered the situation. As Spaatz's Command Diary narrated, Spaatz and Harris disagreed at only one point. Spaatz "contended that the war could not end until the Allies gained a foothold on some point now occupied by Germany, and operated from that territory against the enemy." Harris insisted that "a prolonged bombing of the enemy's vital industry alone could finish the job." Placing troops on occupied soil meant supporting them, thereby jeopardizing other operations. Harris also raised the possibility of another Dunkirk disaster. Spaatz replied that "no such effort should be attempted until the Allies were certain of the results and that the propitious moment was *only* when and if the Allies gain complete SUPREMACY [*sic*] in the air."[76]

This discussion neatly summarized the differences between these two great practitioners of strategic bombing: Spaatz, the flexible, pragmatic disciple of Billy Mitchell, who, despite his belief that strategic bombing alone could defeat Germany, also anticipated and accepted having a large percentage of his force assigned to tactical air missions supporting an invasion of France; and Harris, the inflexible student of the great British air power advocate, Trenchard, who insisted in the face of all opposition that his bombers could win if he was given a chance to prove it. Almost two years later, when the two men actually had 5,000 bombers between them, they would find themselves unable to end the war within their self-imposed deadline, perhaps because diversions prevented them from applying the full effort of their bombers.

In June 1942, Spaatz and Harris had much in common. Both had received their commands in February, and neither led a large force. Spaatz hoped to have at least 500 modern heavy bombers by January 1, 1943. Harris, despite taking great risks to get 1,000 bombers in the air for a raid over Cologne, hoped to have a similar number. Harris had mounted this large raid only by including 370 aircraft and their half-trained crews from his operational training units and by having his regular units put up every bomber airframe they had, including second-line aircraft.[77] When he took charge, he found a total operational force of only 374 medium and heavy bombers, of which only 44 were four-engine Lancaster heavy bombers—the mainstay of the British night-bomber campaign.[78]

Harris also found a new directive for operations, dated February 14, 1942, which authorized him to employ his effort "without further restriction" in a campaign whose primary objective "focused on the morale of the enemy civil population and in particular, of the industrial workers." This directive continued a policy first enunciated in a directive of July 9, 1941, which called for attacks against civilian morale and the inland transportation system in Germany. The Air Ministry issued the February directive to take advantage of a newly developed radio navigational aid, Gee, which promised greater accuracy in night bombing of targets within its range, 350 miles from Mildenhall. The accuracy of the system varied from 0.5 mile to 5 miles.[79] Targets within range included Germany's chief industrial area (the Ruhr) and the coastal ports of Bremen, Wilhelmshaven, and Emden.[80]

The bombing of Germany to reduce the morale of its civilian population, especially the work force, which emphasized the targeting of city centers rather than precision targets and the use of large numbers of incendiary bombs, became an *idée fixe* with Harris. He had observed how the RAF had scattered its effort in vain attempts to bomb the Germans' transportation system, synthetic oil industry, and capital ships at Brest. From these failures he drew firm conclusions that Bomber Command lacked the accuracy to destroy precision targets and that any attempt to divert his forces to such targets should be resisted at all costs. He dubbed plans that promised to end the war by knocking out a single system of key targets "panaceas" and those who advocated them "panacea mongers."

A study issued on August 18, 1941, six months before Harris's assumption of command, had already drawn attention to Bomber Command's inaccurate night bombing. The Butt Report, named for its author, D. M. Butt, a member of the War Cabinet Secretariat, had concluded, after examination of 633 photos taken by attacking aircraft, that only one aircraft in five dropped its bombs within five miles of its target. Only 7 percent of the British bombers attempting to demolish the Ruhr dropped their bombs within five miles (or within seventy-five square miles) of the target.[81] The Butt Report, with its damning indictment of RAF night navigation, spurred the development of electronic navigation aids, such as Gee. The report may also have tipped the scales toward adoption of the area-bombing policy embraced by the February 14 directive by eliminating any option featuring precision night bombing. The Butt Report could only have strengthened Harris's mistrust of precision targeting.

Like the majority of high-ranking British and American airmen, Harris had spent his adult life in the service. In 1914, he had joined the Rhodesia Regiment and had fought as a mounted infantryman during the conquest of German South-

Air Chief Marshal Arthur T. "Bomber" Harris, Air Officer Commanding, Bomber Command, RAF, 1942–1945.

Imperial War Museum

West Africa. Forswearing the infantry, he had trekked to England where he joined the Royal Flying Corps and finished the war as a major. For the next fifteen years he had commanded various bomber formations throughout the British Empire. He had served on the Air Staff for five years before going to the United States in 1938 to head a British purchasing commission. At the start of the war, he commanded the crack No. 5 Group, where he displayed his talent as a hard-driving director of bombing operations.

Harris had a forceful personality and was prone to wild overstatement of his views. In support of his opinion that the Army would never understand air power, he was said to have remarked, "In order to get on in the Army, you have to look like a horse, think like a horse and smell like a horse."[82] In an even more pungent utterance Harris was supposed to have said, "The Army will never appreciate planes until they can drink water, eat hay, and shit!" When stopped for speeding on a road between High Wycombe and London, he replied to the constable's admonition that he might kill someone, "Young man, I kill thousands of people every night!"[83] Harris also enjoyed a special relationship with Churchill, which, if not personally close, was at least founded on a mutual interest in advancing Bomber Command. Churchill needed a means to strike at Germany proper before the cross-channel invasion, and Harris wanted as large a force as possible to bomb Germany into surrender by air alone. Harris had "direct contact" with the Prime minister.[84] The proximity of High Wycombe

95

(Headquarters, Bomber Command) and Chequers (Churchill's country residence) facilitated frequent and frank exchanges of views between the two men. This easy availability for face-to-face discussions often gained Harris the advantage of Churchill's support and a strengthened position with the Air Ministry.

Spaatz, whose position in dealing with the AAF staff was also strong, although it rested on his relationship with Arnold rather than with the head of government, nonetheless came under increasing pressure to commit his forces to combat. Throughout July, the combat aircraft of the Eighth trickled in. On July 1, the 97th Heavy Bombardment Group's first B-17 landed at Prestwick, but it was not until July 27 that the entire group and its ground echelon were completely assembled.[85] The 1st Fighter Group's initial P-38 touched down in England on July 9, but the group was not operational until mid-August. The 31st Fighter Group completed its conversion to Spitfire MK Vs, becoming operational on August 12. All of the groups had been rushed overseas after receiving only minimal unit training in the United States. The 97th lacked experience in formation flying, high-altitude operations, gunnery, and navigation. When Spaatz and Eisenhower inspected a bomber group in late July, they flew a gunnery training mission with a crew that had never fired on the range before, had just arrived from the United States, and had not even initiated crew training. After the flight Eaker chewed out his subordinate in a furious letter, asking:

> What would you think of an infantry regimental commander who, when told the commanding general was coming to inspect his regiment, assigned the latest recruit to put on the effort as representative of the organization? That is exactly what General Eisenhower, General Spaatz, and I think of you and your judgment and that of your organization commanders. It was a disgraceful performance. It wasted their time and gave them an erroneous idea of the state of your crews.[86]

Practice missions alleviated many of these problems and, on August 9, the 97th received orders for its first mission, which weather postponed until August 17.

For Arnold back in the States, mission no. 1 could not come too soon. He had asked, then requested, then cajoled, and eventually prodded Spaatz for action. On July 16, Arnold had noted, "The movement of the First Pursuit Group with its accompanying heavy bombardment has not progressed by a long shot as I had hoped." On August 9, he had written, "I am personally gravely concerned over the apparent extension of the time period which you had anticipated necessary to complete the training of our units prior to their actual entry into combat." He continued, "The strategic necessity for the immediate or early initiation of effective, aggressive American Air Force offensive operations becomes more and more apparent here daily." The harried AAF leader closed by admonishing, "Where doubt exists as to the ability of our units to acquit themselves adequately, I urge that you do not be over conservative."[87]

Arnold needed results to justify the retention of top priority for allocation of air resources to the strategic bomber offensive in Britain. Perhaps even more than Marshall he had opposed the newly agreed upon invasion of North Africa (TORCH).* The diversion of heavy-bomber groups to North Africa delayed the bomber offensive from England called for in AWPD/1. The longer the delay, the greater the gathered momentum of the demands generated by other theaters. On July 24, as part of the final settlement concerning the invasion decision, Marshall had allotted to Admiral King fifteen heavy- and medium-bomber groups for use in the Pacific. In addition, the U.S. Chiefs of Staff shifted heavy- and medium-bomber groups from the scheduled buildup in England to the North African operation. In November 1942, the Eighth would have to transfer four heavy-bomber and four fighter groups already in England to TORCH. North Africa, where the battle was against German and Italian ground units, would be a ground forces theater. The Pacific would be either a Navy show (in the central Pacific) or the ground Army's (in MacArthur's area of operations). In 1943, at least, the European Theater of Operations with its scheduled air offensive against the enemy's homeland, would be the theater that got the AAF its share of newsprint, but only if Arnold could get results.

The press stories of disagreement between American and British airmen added to Arnold's desire for action. On August 15, Arnold felt compelled to call a press conference to defend the AAF. The conference, which the *New York Times* described as "perhaps the most active military press conference held in Washington since the war began," had extensive off-the-record portions. In reply to a question on the bombing of Germany he could only say it was "merely a question of getting the planes over there."[88]

The next day, in the *Sunday Times* of London, Peter Masefield, a well-regarded British aviation expert, roundly condemned the American heavy-bomber effort. Masefield echoed the view of the RAF Air Staff, which had concluded that the B-17 and the B-24 were unsuitable for day operations in Europe. In January, on the basis of its experience with twenty early model aircraft, the Air Staff had concluded that "unless the Fortress or the Liberator can be adapted for employment at night they are unlikely to achieve more than intermittent harassing operations in daylight in a European theatre and in the face of modern air defenses."[89] Masefield suggested that the Americans produce and operate British-designed heavy bombers at night alongside the RAF.[90] The American papers also carried the story.

The day after Masefield's article appeared, Spaatz held a joint AAF-RAF press conference to emphasize cooperation between the two forces and to finally launch mission no. 1.

Spaatz had intended to lead the mission himself.[91] Eisenhower approved these arrangements,[92] with the proviso that both Eaker and Spaatz not fly on the

* The decision to invade North Africa is discussed later in this chapter.

same mission, but apparently, the British objected. What would happen, they asked, if a ranking officer were downed over occupied France and ended up in the hands of German military intelligence? Spaatz and Eaker reluctantly accepted the British view but decided that the psychological value of a general flying was worth the risk. Spaatz, however, had already learned one of the most important secrets of the war; the British had already fully briefed him on the ability of the British Government Code and Cypher School (GC and CS) at Bletchley Park to decrypt the messages of the German top-secret Enigma enciphering machine (used by all the German armed services and many civil and police organizations as well).* Spaatz obviously knew too much. Therefore, Eaker, Spaatz's deputy and Commander of VIII Bomber Command, who did not yet know the ULTRA secret,[93] led Eighth Air Force heavy-bomber mission no.1, directed at the Rouen-Sotteville railroad marshaling yards.[94] The targeting officer of the Eighth Air Force, Col. Richard D'O. Hughes, selected the marshaling yards because they were far enough from the town to minimize killing French civilians and because they fell well within the range of escorting Spitfires.[95]

The attacking planes bombed with reasonable accuracy; approximately half of the 18.5 tons of bombs released fell in the general target area. They damaged ten of twenty-four lines of track, destroyed some rolling stock, and scored direct hits on two large transshipment sheds in the center of the yard. The attack may have temporarily disrupted service, but it caused no lasting injury to the Germans. Serious damage to such a target required the attack of a far larger number of bombers.[96] An overjoyed Spaatz greeted Eaker as soon as the latter alighted from his aircraft.

After the first raid Spaatz enthusiastically told Arnold, "It is my opinion and conviction that the B-17 is suitable as to speed, armament, armor, and bomb load. I would not exchange it for any British bomber in production." Arnold sent Spaatz's message directly to the President, adding, "The above more than vindicates our faith in the Flying Fortresses and precision bombing."[97]

As Arnold's letter to Spaatz on August 19, 1942, indicated, the news of the Rouen raid was the perfect tonic which Arnold couldn't wait to share with the "highest authorities." He told Spaatz:

> You can't blame me for being a little impatient, because I have been impatient all my life. . . . I was very glad to get the information covering the operation of the bombers over Rouen. That mission came just at the right time to act as a counter-irritant to the British report that our airplanes were no good, etc. etc. As a matter of fact, the President had me up to Hyde Park day before yester-day, asked me about that article, and told me he was much concerned. I assured him that there was no reason for being concerned. I hope we are right.

---

* The high-grade signal intelligence material produced by the British Government Code and Cypher School was tightly controlled and distributed under the code name ULTRA. Hence references to GC and CS as the ULTRA organization and to the material as ULTRA or the ULTRA secret.

Lt. Gen. Dwight D. Eisenhower, Commanding General, European Theater of Operations, and Eighth Air Force commanding generals, summer 1942. *Left to right*: Lt. Gen. Robert Candee (Commander, VIII Air Support Command), Brig. Gen. Frank Hunter (Commander, VIII Fighter Command), Col. Asa Duncan (Chief of Staff, VIII Bomber Command), Maj. Gen. Walter Frank (Commander, VIII Service Command), Eisenhower, Maj. Gen. Carl Spaatz (Commander, Eighth AF), and Brig. Gen. Ira Eaker (Commander, VIII Bomber Command).

Arnold was still greatly worried about "the tendency of the Strategic Planners to take aircraft away from the European Theater and throw it in the Southwest Pacific Theater." He lamented, "We are so dispersing our effort that we will have an overwhelming superiority in no theater. This in itself violates the approved conception of employment of aircraft." Arnold asked Spaatz whether he could "get Eisenhower and Portal together and for you to get everybody over there to stand up on their hind legs for the Air Force that is needed?"[98]

In quick succession, on August 19, 20, and 21, the Eighth sent out three raids. None consisted of more than twenty-four B-17s, and the last one sent against the Rotterdam shipyards was recalled at the French coast after being sixteen minutes late for its escort. Attacking German fighters damaged one of its planes, but the bombers seemed to have defended themselves well. Spaatz sent reports of these pinpricks to an impatient Arnold. In a hurried letter, hand-carried to Arnold, Spaatz wrote that the latest operations indicated "we can bomb accurately from high altitude." Spaatz further commented favorably on his bombers' ability to maintain formation, fly formation through flak, and defend themselves against the Germans' best fighter, the Focke-Wulf 190 (FW 190).[99]

The King and Queen of England inspecting an Eighth Air Force field with Maj. Gen. Carl A. Spaatz, summer 1942.

Earlier the same day Spaatz, who said he had delayed judgment until operational experience allowed him to gauge with accuracy the value of U.S. training and equipment, had justified his actions to Arnold. "First let me say that I can imagine what a strain this inaction has been on you and what a lot of gripes you have had to put up with and answer. But I really believed we were justified in withholding action with our B-17s until we could get off to a good start and am following a similar policy with the P-38s." Then Spaatz told Arnold that critics had begun to recant:

> In spite of the *London Times,* Seversky or anyone else the B-17s are far superior to anything in this theater and are fully adequate for their job. The British themselves admit this and say that with similar equipment and training they too would day-bomb. They are unanimous in their praise of our Bombing accuracy about which they had their fingers crossed until now.[100]

Arnold, recognized that Eisenhower because he had Marshall's complete confidence and would soon be a power in his own right, should have the best air advice available, especially if he were in charge of American air power's most important theater. Arnold tried to supply Eisenhower's staff with high-quality officers. On July 30, Arnold informed Spaatz that to help him meet TORCH planning obligations he was sending him Colonels Vandenberg and Norstad. Arnold wanted Eisenhower to accept Spaatz's headquarters as his own air planning unit.

100

"Get him to use you in that way as he is the head of all U.S. Army Forces in Europe." Arnold added, *"I want him to recognize you as the top air man in all Europe* [emphasis added]." A few days later Arnold rather querulously observed, "I am not satisfied that Ike is using you and your staff to the extent that we hoped he would. Perhaps geographical separation, or other factors not in evidence here lead him toward decisions without the advice and counsel of the air-thought represented in your command." Arnold had wanted to offer Eisenhower "any officer in the Army Air Forces whom he might wish to have as his Chief of Staff" but was unable to derail Brig. Gen. Walter Bedell Smith's assignment as Eisenhower's Chief of Staff.[101]

Spaatz replied on August 11, "Hansell will be the top planner for air and as such under the present instructions will be the Theater Commander's Air Planner." Spaatz went on to point out that Hansell would live in the same house with him and other key officers of the Eighth. Norstad and Vandenberg were assigned to Headquarters, ETO, as air planners for the cross-channel invasion and Operation TORCH respectively.[102]

The complexity of these arrangements apparently caused Spaatz some concern. On August 14, he told Arnold, "I am certain that it would be a mistake for two large Air Staffs to be built up here."[103] Spaatz suggested a solution to Arnold and Eisenhower, and so, on August 21, Arnold, at Ike's request, gave Spaatz additional duties as Air Officer for ETO and appointed him head of the Air Section of the ETO staff, thus assuring the Eighth of active participation in theater planning.

Earlier, on July 7, Arnold had given Spaatz a second hat by appointing him Commanding General, AAF, ETO, which did not add a plane or private to Spaatz's command, but did elevate him a step on the ETO organization charts. Before that, as Eighth Air Force Commander, Spaatz was a tactical commander and therefore was organizationally outranked by the Commanding Generals of the Service of Supply, ETO, John C. H. Lee, and Army Ground Forces, ETO, Mark Clark, who had theaterwide administrative training and doctrinal responsibilities.

Spaatz now wore three hats (CG, Eighth Air Force; CG AAF, ETO; Chief, Air Section, ETO Staff) with one goal—keeping air power and its advocates at the forefront of the theater scheduled to receive the preponderance of U.S. wartime air strength. When Eisenhower was officially transferred to the Mediterranean in January 1943, an airman succeeded him. General Marshall's selection of Lt. Gen. Frank M. Andrews as CG, ETO placed the theater in the hands of a man committed to daylight strategic bombing.

In September 1942, Arnold, eager for more materials with which to wage his air power publicity campaign on the home front, applauded Spaatz for suggesting photographs of bombing results. "People believe more readily what they see than what they hear," he noted, "Every daily paper in the United States will feature the pictures if you can get them to us."[104] Arnold extolled the value of posi-

Maj. Gen. Carl A. Spaatz, according to his driver, "the hardest working man in the whole U.S. Army Air Forces," summer 1942.

tive publicity, saying: "Within the borders of [the] continental United States, two most important fronts exist, namely, aircraft production and public opinion. Nine months have passed since Pearl Harbor, and the American public now wants to see pictures, stories and experiences of our Air Forces in combat zones. The public is entitled to expect us to furnish . . . them." Arnold directed Spaatz to give the subject of publicity and news coverage "his full and immediate cooperation."[105]

Spaatz had probably borrowed the idea of bomb damage photos from Harris, who habitually trotted them out to impress the Prime Minister and others with his efforts. Eventually Arnold, too, kept albums stuffed with strike photos, dutifully supplied by Spaatz, in his office to spring on unsuspecting visitors. He circulated the photos and even a glossy monthly magazine entitled *Impact** throughout Washington. Air power publicity was rapidly growing. On September 7, 1942, for instance, the lead story in *Time* magazine covered the Eighth and its commander.

Spaatz also cultivated the press, though less ebulliently than Arnold. Several times he invited correspondents such as Ed Beattie and Joe Morrison of United

---

* *Impact* was a security classified publication, but it appears to have circulated freely throughout the AAF and official government circles. In fact, its security classification may have lent it a certain cachet, making readers think they were "in the know."

Press, as well as Walter Lippmann and Wes Gallagher of Associated Press for dinner and late-night poker at his residence in London. He held press conferences in July and August. On August 23, Spaatz even allowed Arthur Sulzberger, publisher of the *New York Times*, to accompany him on a flight to High Wycombe where Eaker would be decorated with the Silver Star. The flight almost ended in tragedy when the pilot of their plane ground-looped on landing, wiping out the props and landing gear. Happily, everyone in the plane walked away from the crash.[106]

After a while, General Marshall, who did not want one part of the Army praised at the expense of another, cabled Eisenhower on August 19, questioning the advisability of all the attention given U.S. air raids and airmen. The next day Eisenhower passed the word to Spaatz, who temporarily muted his public relations activities. Spaatz persuaded *Time* to take him off the cover of the September 7 issue (but not out of the lead story) and had his chief of staff substitute for him on a March of Time radio broadcast scheduled for that very evening.[107]

In the meantime, Spaatz and the Eighth continued to struggle toward full operational readiness. In August, the Eighth Air Force sent out eight heavybomber missions, including one completely aborted. The largest August raid had only 30 B-17s. In September, the Eighth launched only four heavy-bomber missions, including another aborted mission. It lost its first 2 B-17s to enemy action on September 6 and had two new heavy-bomber groups (the 301st and 92d) enter combat on September 5 and 6. On its busiest day it sent out 76 heavy bombers.

The next month the Eighth mounted only three raids, the largest of which numbered 108 heavy bombers. Two more groups (the 93d and 306th) entered combat, while the Eighth Air Force lost its first B-24 in combat. Yet for every few steps forward there would be one backward. On October 21, the 97th Bomb Group, the Eighth's most experienced heavy-bomber formation, transferred to the Twelfth Air Force, which the Americans had formed to support the Allied invasion of French North Africa, scheduled for early November 1942. Its second most experienced group, the 301st Bomb Group, went to the Twelfth Air Force on November 8. In November, the Eighth finally matched the number of missions flown in August—eight. It put 91 bombers in the air for the month's largest mission and had three additional groups enter combat (the 44th, the 303d, and the 305th.)[108]

These first short steps failed to please Arnold. His records showed 178 heavy bombers in England by September 30,[109] but as yet no single mission had come close to matching that figure. He sent Spaatz the first of a series of messages that would continue for the next sixteen months and were directed at the U.S. bomber commanders in England. Arnold sarcastically noted, "It is believed that some powerful reason must obtain which limits your heavy-bomber operations to an apparent average of less than one per week. Weather conditions alone are not believed the cause, nor the preparation of some of the two hundred heavy bombers under your control in England for use in other theaters. Request full information on the subject."[110]

Arnold, who had never led a unit in combat, never seemed to appreciate fully the difficulties involved. Spaatz, Andrews, and Eaker repeatedly had to defend their seemingly dismal operational readiness rates which, in the autumn of 1942, could be attributed in large part to bad weather and training requirements. Before Spaatz could field all the bombers on hand, he had to finish training their crews, all of which arrived unready for combat. Weather played a far larger role than Arnold would acknowledge. An authoritative postwar study of weather as it affected heavy-bomber missions stated that weather reduced "the potential effort planned on a monthly basis by 45 percent."[111] This figure included the summer months, which, of course, contained the best flying weather.

Spaatz and Eaker, however, were encouraged by their progress. In a series of memos written for internal AAF use, Eaker gave his and Spaatz's views. After the first four missions, he confidently stated his conviction that "in the future, successful bombing missions can be conducted beyond the range of fighter protection."[112] Six weeks later, after suffering his initial losses from German fighters, Eaker reiterated his beliefs:

> Our bombing experience to date indicates that the B-17 with its twelve .50 caliber guns, can cope with the German day fighter. There will be losses, of course, but there is no evidence that the losses will be of such a high order as to make day bombing uneconomical. I think it is safe, now, to say that a large force of day bombers can operate without fighter cover against material objectives anywhere in Germany, without excessive losses.

Such losses as did occur could be much reduced, Eaker thought, with the provision of a B-17 type convoy defender aircraft, already existing in prototype, "with extra ammunition supply and extra armor, flying on the flanks of the bomber formations." He requested the shipment of a group or squadron of such planes as soon as possible.[113]

Eaker seems not to have yet accepted the technical feasibility of a long-range escort fighter. He did not ask for more P-38s or for the development of an even longer-range fighter. In reply to Arnold's criticism, Eaker wrote, "Three hundred heavy bombers could attack any target in Germany with less than four percent losses." A smaller number of bombers, which would lack the self-defensive strength of the larger force, would suffer greater losses. "The daylight bombing of Germany with planes of the B-17 and B-24 types is feasible, practicable and economical."[114] In the next year, the Luftwaffe day-fighter force would amply demonstrate the inaccuracy of Eaker's and Spaatz's initial assessments.

Spaatz's Command Style

In early August, Spaatz settled Eighth Air Force Headquarters (code-named WIDEWINGS) in Bushy Park, on the outskirts of the Hampton Court palace grounds, southwest of London. Spaatz himself occupied a comfortable house nearby in Wimbledon. He continued seeking out comfortable if not palatial residences throughout the war—a habit that gave rise to ill-concealed jealousy among critics. They complained that such self-indulgence and Sybaritism were only to be expected of a fly-boy general. Spaatz did like his comforts, but there was a method in his practice: Spaatz made his quarters his command post, a command post where he housed many of his staff officers and held daily staff meetings.

Shortly after the war one officer told an interviewer, "General Spaatz apparently does not like an office. He likes to be alone, to relax in the atmosphere of his home, and so we used to take major things out to him." Spaatz's deputy or chief of intelligence would take documents to him at lunch time. "At the end of the day," the officer continued, "you found yourself with a collection of papers, cables, etc. to go out to Park House because most of the key people lived there."[115] The same officer further observed:

> We lived and messed there and there was nearly always some key personnel around there day and night—it operated on a 24-hour basis. I can remember being there at two o'clock in the morning, rushing over to General Spaatz's house; General Anderson came out in his bathrobe, and General Spaatz served us tea. During a big night we were up all night in some cases.[116]

Living and working together fit in with Spaatz's philosophy of leadership. Spaatz once said of himself, "I may be peculiar in that I refuse to be seated at a desk with a bunch of papers in front of me to pore over."[117] In the same context Spaatz philosophized, "I doubt you can run any big outfit . . . immersed in all the details . . . so you must delegate responsibility." He went on, "It has always been a fetish of mine that you can't delegate responsibility without delegating authority with it."[118]

A long-time friend also spoke of Spaatz's attitude toward routine:

> Tooey, like some literary characters, was inclined to get up very late and work very late. He was a night worker more than a day worker. So actually [he did] much of [his] work in pajamas in a messed up bedroom at 10 or 11 o'clock in the morning. That's just the way he worked; I'm not disparaging him. He was firmly in command. . . . The last thing in the world he wanted was an 8 o'clock officers' call someplace with everybody sitting down at desks pushing papers around. He just didn't want to be bothered with administration or minor matters. He refused to be.[119]

Spaatz ran a military household that had much more in common with the staffs of Lee and Napoleon than the German General Staff. By keeping his senior officers close at hand, messing, drinking, and even gaming with them, he established a firm and deep rapport with his subordinates. He did not make a habit of issuing long, detailed orders. Former Air Force Chief of Staff, General Curtis LeMay, who served under Spaatz in both the Pacific and European theaters of World War II, recalled many years later that he "never got any direct orders from General Spaatz on anything," but after a few hours of sitting at the same poker table in the evening, he understood what Spaatz wanted him to do.[120]

Not everyone appreciated Spaatz's methods. The informality of his head-quarters led some to believe that he was lazy, lax, or merely a good old boy prone to cronyism. As late as June 1943, after a year's close association with Spaatz, Eisenhower wrote of "the only weakness" he had found in Spaatz:

> I have an impression he is not tough and hard enough personally to meet the full requirements of his high position. He is constantly urging more promotions for subordinates and seeking special favors for his forces. My belief in this regard is further strengthened by the type of staff he has accumulated around him. He has apparently picked officers more for their personal qualifications of comradeship and friendliness than for their abilities as businesslike, tough operators.

Repeated urgings from Eisenhower to correct this perceived defect produced no change. Spaatz's request for a liquor ration for his units also raised Eisenhower's ire.[121]

By freeing himself from the mundane chores of excess paperwork, Spaatz freed himself not only for decisions but for personal leadership. Throughout the war his relative freedom from his desk enabled him to visit and inspect the combat, training, and supply units under his control. Of course these units "prettied" themselves up for his visits, but he had far too much experience doing the same thing himself not to know how and where to look for any shortcomings. Because of his desire to avoid personal aggrandizement and his less than charismatic personality, these visits had none of the flamboyant trappings that similar visits from Patton or Montgomery might have had. Spaatz went to see, not to be seen.

The Eighth Air Force and the North African Invasion

Even as Spaatz labored to create an effective force in England, events in the Middle East drastically changed the Allies' strategic plans. German Field Marshal Irwin Rommel launched an offensive in the Libyan desert that, after overcoming fierce British resistance, captured the fortress of Tobruk, shattered his enemies, and sent them reeling back to El Alamein, Egypt, the last defensible position in front of the Suez Canal. The debacle in the Middle East, the locale of Britain's major effort against the European Axis powers, threatened one of the basic strategic underpinnings of the Eighth—that Britain would be the base for an Anglo-American ground offensive against Germany in either 1942 or 1943.

Churchill, already jolted by the disasters to British arms suffered at the hands of the Japanese in Malaya, Burma, and the East Indies, now needed to shore up a rapidly crumbling situation in the Mediterranean. Added strength for that theater could come only from forces designated for the cross-channel invasion; Churchill set out to divert them to North Africa. As he remarked in his memoirs, "During this month of July, when I was politically at my weakest and without a gleam of military success, I had to procure from the United States the decision which, for good or ill, dominated the next two years of the war." He had to ask the United States to abandon plans for a cross-channel invasion in 1942 to undertake the occupation of French North Africa in the autumn or winter by a large Anglo-American expedition. "I had made a careful study of the President's mind and its reaction for some time past," remarked Churchill, "and I was sure that he was powerfully attracted by the North African Plan." The time had come, Churchill believed, to shelve the cross-channel invasion, "which had been dead for some time."[122]

Roosevelt himself needed American troops in action against the Germans in 1942,[123] if possible before the congressional election of November 1942. Although leaning toward the proposed North African operation, the President gave General George C. Marshall, the outstandingly talented U.S. Army Chief of Staff and one of the strongest supporters of the cross-channel invasion, one last chance to persuade the British Chiefs of Staff to carry it out in 1942.[124]

Marshall, Admiral Ernest J. King, Chief of Naval Operations, and Harry Hopkins, arrived in London on Saturday, July 18. They immediately closeted themselves with Eisenhower, Spaatz, and Admiral Harold R. Stark, chief American naval officer in the British Isles. Over the weekend, the Americans discussed a revision hurriedly thrown together by Eisenhower's staff, of the previous cross-channel invasion plans. This revision called for the establishment of a secure foothold on the Cotentin Peninsula of Normandy.[125] Eisenhower, who had been recommended for command of the American forces in Britain by his mentor, Marshall, supported it, as did Spaatz.

During the weekend Spaatz contended that a cross-channel invasion in 1942 had a better chance than one in 1943. He based his reasoning on the condition and disposition of the Luftwaffe. In July 1942, the German summer offensive had taken Sevastapol and broken through Soviet defenses toward Stalingrad. This offensive had absorbed the bulk of the Luftwaffe's resources and would obviously do so for several more months. During the winter months the Luftwaffe could rehabilitate itself and would therefore be a much more formidable opponent in 1943 than in 1942.[126]

Spaatz repeated this position,[127] but he and the rest of the Americans failed to move the British in ensuing meetings. On the day Marshall arrived in England, Churchill and the British Chiefs of Staff met and unanimously decided that the proposed autumn 1942 cross-channel invasion "was not a feasible or sensible operation."[128] Because the British would be supplying most of the resources required in any action, their refusal to go along ended all prospects of an early invasion. When the U.S. delegation reported this impasse to the President, he replied with a list of alternative U.S. actions against Germany, but indicated a preference for U.S. actions against French North Africa. Marshall bowed to the inevitable and agreed to a U.S.-British invasion of French North Africa code-named Torch. By July 30, Roosevelt and Churchill made their tentative agreement on a North African campaign.

The Allies' decision to invade French North Africa by November 1942 had important long-term and short-term effects. It undermined large-scale U.S. heavy-bombardment operations launched from the British Isles and postponed the cross-channel invasion until 1944. More immediately, Torch or its ramifications required that Spaatz substantially modify his plans and expectations from midsummer to the end of 1942 and beyond. On August 6, he received a letter from Arnold detailing, with what turned out to be undue optimism, the final results of the Marshall-King-Hopkins mission to London:

1. The cross-channel invasion would be abandoned for the year.
2. The air buildup in Britain would continue.
3. Torch would be executed.
4. More aircraft might be diverted to the Pacific.
5. A Torch planning unit would be created in London.

The letter contained a postscript: "I have just agreed with General Marshall that Doolittle will go to England at once as Commander of Air Forces for Torch."[129] By selecting Brig. Gen. James H. Doolittle, America's reigning air hero, Arnold at least assured the AAF that it would receive extensive press coverage of its role in Torch, whatever that role might be. Subject to Spaatz's and Eisenhower's approval of Doolittle, the Eighth had made its first contribution to the North African venture—its air commander. Doolittle had been slated to command the 4th Bombardment Wing (Medium) for the VIII ASC. He checked into Widewings the same day, August 6.

Torch not only delayed the cross-channel invasion, it slowed the buildup of the Eighth. In mounting the North African invasion, the Allies had accepted the necessity of assuming a defensive posture in operations against the Germans from Britain. As a consequence, Britain for the time being no longer required a rapid buildup in air power to support a ground offensive. The North African invasion would consume resources and shipping originally destined for Britain. All this meant that the U.S. bomber offensive mounted from England would start considerably later and with far less force than that envisaged prior to July 1942.

The shift to Torch disconcerted Spaatz. He believed that the Eighth was making great progress. He had even somewhat optimistically convinced himself that "the presence here now of 200 B-17's would be a major factor in crippling German air power and insuring air supremacy next spring."[130] In a letter to Arnold, he wrote that he was "much concerned about possible diversion of units from the Eighth Air Force. . . . Regardless of operations in any other theater, in my opinion this remains the only area from which to gain air supremacy over Germany, without which there can be no successful outcome of the war."[131]

Four days before the Eighth's first B-17 raid over Europe on August 13, Eisenhower cabled Marshall that the current air plan, with which Generals Spaatz, George S. Patton (one of the ground force commanders), and Doolittle agreed, called for forming "the nucleus of TORCH Air Force from the Eighth Air Force—to be supplemented as necessary direct from the United States."[132]

Eisenhower required the Eighth to contribute two heavy-bomber groups, three medium-bomber groups, two P-38 groups, two Spitfire groups, one transport group, and one light-bomber group. To compensate for these losses, he asked for five additional heavy-bomber groups in Britain.

By August 18, Spaatz had been charged with the planning, organization, and training of a new air force, the Twelfth, code-named JUNIOR, which would command the AAF units assigned to the North African operation. Spaatz directed each of his various command headquarters to sponsor the creation of a corresponding unit of JUNIOR. On September 23, Doolittle assumed command, with Vandenberg as his chief of staff.[133] By October 24, the day Headquarters Twelfth Air Force embarked for North Africa, the Eighth had supplied 3,198 officers, 24,124 enlisted men,[134] and 1,244 planes for JUNIOR. Until well into January 1943, 50 percent of the Eighth's on-hand supplies and much of its maintenance work were devoted to the Twelfth. Well might Spaatz ask, "What is left of the Eighth Air Force after the impact of TORCH? We find we haven't much left."[135]

The creation of the Twelfth Air Force prompted a disagreement between Spaatz and Eisenhower. On September 8, the two discussed the problems caused to the AAF, ETO, by having to raise the Twelfth while the Eighth simultaneously flew operational missions. Eisenhower solved the problem very simply. He ordered Spaatz to cease all combat air operations by the Eighth at once.[136] The next day Eisenhower cabled Marshall his proposals on how to conceal the halt.[137]

From Spaatz's point of view, Eisenhower's decision was the worst possible. It delayed the entire AAF bomber offensive for an indeterminate period. If it provided an opportunity to justify the diversion of yet more AAF strength to subsidiary theaters, it might prove fatal to AAF hopes and deleterious to the morale of the Eighth's service and combat personnel. Spaatz apparently wasted no time in appealing to Arnold. On September 10, Arnold cabled Eisenhower, "You and Spaatz are urged to continue intensive air operations until the last possible moment as the Eighth Air Force is now accomplishing the mission for which it was intended: (a) draw the GAF [German Air Force] from other fronts, (b) attract the attention of German fighters, (c) reduce German war effort by bombing important targets."[138]

On the same day, Spaatz gave Eisenhower a draft cable he wished to send to

Arnold in which he forcefully expressed his disagreement with Eisenhower's order to halt operations. Spaatz was certain that missions from North Africa would not be as effective against the Luftwaffe and German war strength as those from Britain. He argued that "new operations jeopardize acquisition of air supremacy over Germany and may have serious effect on successful outcome of war"[139] and warned that air operations would be delayed for at least two months.

Eisenhower persuaded Spaatz not to send the cable. Instead, he modified his position, cabling Marshall: "Ground elements of U.S. Air Squadrons in U.K. that are set up for service in the expeditionary force are compelled to begin packing of equipment immediately. Nevertheless, provision is being made to carry on at least two bombing missions a week."[140] Apparently, Spaatz was able to convince Eisenhower that the Eighth could devote maximum attention to organizing the Twelfth while continuing to bomb Europe. As long as Spaatz realized that TORCH had overriding priority, Eisenhower was willing to allow him to salvage the bomber offensive. In the end, harsh northern European weather limited the Eighth's bombers to four raids in September, three in October, and eight in November. Although the rate of operations was only half of that authorized by Eisenhower and far less than that hoped for by Spaatz and Arnold, it at least gave the crews and commanders experience and probably kept some German attention focused on northwestern Europe.

While the Eighth continued to aid JUNIOR, Spaatz pursued two courses of action with equal vigor. He provided unstinting cooperation in all phases of the Twelfth's growth while doing everything possible to maintain the Eighth as a viable fighting force capable of sustaining a strategic offensive against Germany. He failed in the latter but not through lack of effort. In a series of letters to Arnold, whose views were identical to his own, Spaatz attempted to further his fight for the AAF bomber offensive. Noting unanimous British praise of the Eighth's bombing accuracy, he began, "I am more confident than ever before that the war can be won in this theater if we are permitted to carry out the policies which were built up under your command." Daylight precision bombing would be decisive, provided the Eighth received an adequate force in time. "For God's sake," Spaatz exclaimed, "keep our Air Force concentrated here so we can polish off the Germans and get on with the war."[141] Three days later, he wrote:

> In so far as my advice is requested, and often when it is not requested, I have reiterated the folly of attempting to fight the war all over the world. In my opinion unless the powers that be come to a full realization of the necessity for concentration of the Air Forces in this theater, we stand an excellent chance of losing the war.[142]

The three raids the Eighth had flown so far had convinced him that accurate, high-altitude bombing could be performed by unescorted bombers penetrating into the heart of Germany. Because TORCH was turning the ETO into "a 100%

air theater of operation" until the mounting of a cross-channel invasion, Spaatz wrote that, in conjunction with the RAF, he needed only 20 heavy-bomber groups (960 planes), 10 medium-bomber groups (570 planes), 10 fighter groups (800 planes), 10 photo reconnaissance/weather squadrons, and 2 transport groups (supply carriers) to attain "complete aerial supremacy" over Germany within a year.

Spaatz's and Arnold's advocacy of a continued air buildup in England did not stem from a desire to prove their air power beliefs at the expense of the remaining U.S. war effort. As their correspondence shows, they both genuinely feared a complete German victory over the Soviet Union or a stalemate on the Eastern Front that would allow the Luftwaffe to recuperate and redeploy to the west in the winter of 1942–1943.[143] Although convinced that unescorted deep-penetration bombing was feasible, they did not believe that it could then succeed against the entire Luftwaffe or even against serious German counterbombing over Britain. They also had justifiable concerns about the German summer offensive in the Soviet Union which had, by late August, progressed through Sevastapol, Voronezh, and Rostov; penetrated far into the Caucasus; and reached the Volga River a few miles above Stalingrad.

Roosevelt's August 24 request for production requirements necessary "for complete air ascendancy over the enemy"[144] gave Arnold a chance to open a second front of his own in the war to mount the European bomber offensive. Arnold assembled a team of air planning experts to produce a new document for the allocation of the nation's economic assets toward aircraft production, called Air War Plans Division plan for 1942 (AWPD/42). When he received the President's request, Arnold sent a priority cable to Spaatz ordering him to detail Brig. Gen. Haywood S. Hansell, one of the authors of the AAF's prewar planning blueprint, AWPD/1, to Washington for an important conference. Hansell woke Spaatz at midnight, August 26, to inform him of the message's contents, and Spaatz and his staff worked until six in the morning to gather background material.[145]

Spaatz and Eaker enthusiastically supported Arnold's attempt to refocus U.S. strategic thinking. Spaatz, deciding to send Eaker along with Hansell because he recognized the "vital importance of the forthcoming decision," wrote to Arnold:

> Hansell is thoroughly familiar with my ideas, and Eaker's ideas as of operations, etc., exactly parallel mine. I hope the idea can be put across that the war must be won against Germany or it is lost. The defeat of Japan, as soul-satisfying as it may be, leaves us no better off than we were on Dec. 7. The war can be lost very easily if there is a continuation of our dispersion. It can be won and very expeditiously if our effort is massed here and combines its strength with the RAF.[146]

Although Arnold could not get Eaker in to see the President, he did order him to make presentations to the Chief of Staff and the Secretary of War. Arnold remarked to Spaatz, "Our major program is more or less bogged down due to the diversity of interest. It has been dispersion, dispersion, and more dispersion in our unity of thought for the main effort."[147] Arnold told Harry Hopkins that the frittering away of air units and resources had sapped AWPD/1. Arnold pleaded for a revival of AWPD/1 because "it represents the only way in which we can vitally affect the No. 1 enemy at once. Given twenty heavy groups of bombers—700 bombers—operating from U.K. bases this fall and winter, I believe that we can prevent the rehabilitation of the German Air Force this winter."

Arnold further promised to dislocate or depreciate the German submarine effort by destroying the five U-boat bases in southwestern France.[148] Failure to deliver on those promises would cost him in a coinage he could ill afford—credibility. Arnold's pressure on subordinates to perform—as well as his penchant for counting raw numbers of aircraft in a theater instead of only those operationally ready—stemmed directly from the practice of painting himself into corners with promises.

AWPD/42, issued September 9, was the AAF's official response to TORCH and to the Navy's demands in the Pacific. In its strategic intent AWPD/42 closely resembled AWPD/1, arguing that conducting simultaneous effective air offensives against both Germany and Japan was impossible with the resources available. Because the vital industrial areas of Japan were currently out of range of U.S. aircraft, Europe had to be the target for the one offensive that could be launched.

The projected offensive would destroy the German war economy by combining a U.S. force of 2,225 operational bombers, based in Britain and deployed by January 1944, with RAF Bomber Command. The AAF would concentrate on the "systematic destruction of vital elements of the German military and industrial machine through precision bombing in daylight," whereas the RAF would specialize in "mass air attacks of industrial areas at night to break down morale."[149] In addition, AWPD/42 called for priority production of large numbers of aircraft, which clashed head on with the Navy's projected shipbuilding programs and the Army's anticipated heavy-equipment requirements.[150]

When the U.S. Joint Chiefs of Staff met to discuss the availability of the fifteen groups (two of them heavy-bomber groups) promised by Marshall to King in mid-July 1942 and destined for the Pacific, Arnold used AWPD/42 as the basis for his argument in favor of delay. The Navy objected and the battle was joined, finally to be decided by the President. Roosevelt, in typical fashion, gave each side half a loaf; the Navy got the groups for the Solomons campaign, but AWPD/42's basic assumptions and all but 8,000 of its production requirement of 139,000 planes in 1943 were approved. By the end of the year, production realities reduced the aircraft goal in 1943 to 107,000.[151]

In conjunction with AWPD/42, Arnold asked Spaatz to enlist the aid of key commanders in the ETO for the AAF position.[152] Spaatz complied, producing messages from Patton, Clark, and Eisenhower. Eisenhower's message to

Marshall on September 5 shows Spaatz's handiwork: "We are becoming convinced that high altitude daylight precision bombing is not only feasible but highly successful and that by increasing the scale of attack, effective results can be obtained."[153] Eisenhower's request for the 20 heavy-bombers, 10 medium-bombers, and ten fighter groups that Spaatz had already determined would be needed so pleased Arnold that he told Marshall, "I believe that this cable is of such great and immediate importance as to warrant the presentation of its contents to the President and to the Joint Chiefs of Staff." Arnold asked Marshall to make the presentations to enhance its effect.[154] Apparently he did.

TORCH siphoned off the Eighth's operational groups and changed its bombing priorities. Transatlantic shipping, which formed the centerpiece for the operation's logistical planning, had become the objective of both the German and Allied navies in the Battle of the Atlantic, the outcome of which was still in doubt between September and November 1942 as German submarines continued to sink Allied shipping as fast as it could be produced. Thus, the Eighth embarked on a campaign against German submarine bases in France, particularly those at Brest, St. Nazaire, L'Orient, Bordeaux, and La Pallice. Their suppression would ease the pressure on the Allied navies and increase the chances of safe passage for the TORCH convoys as they sailed for North Africa.

After preliminary discussions beginning at least as early as September 25, Eisenhower, on October 13, ordered Spaatz to make the submarine pens and bases his top-priority targets and to estimate the size of the campaign to be mounted and the extent of British cooperation.[155]

The next afternoon, Spaatz met with Air Marshals Harris and Portal to discuss Eisenhower's order. They agreed that RAF Bomber Command lacked the equipment to precision-bomb the submarine bases during the day and that night bombing would be ineffective. Therefore, the RAF would bomb submarine-manufacturing installations in Germany while the Eighth hit the submarine pens.[156] At the time, this latter task seemed perfectly suited to the limited reach and punch of U.S. bomber forces. Spaatz, Eaker, and Arnold apparently expressed no objection to the new priority. The Luftwaffe would certainly defend its submarine bases, start the battle of attrition in earnest, and realize the AAF's desire to draw it into combat and destroy it. Only later did the AAF's lack of proper ordnance (it had no bombs heavy enough to penetrate the massive concrete roofs of the submarine pens) and its concentrating on a limited and predictable set of targets, become painfully obvious.

In a letter to Spaatz dated September 3, Arnold first voiced a theme that he would sound well into 1943. As with so much else, TORCH was its inspiration. "Please understand," he wrote, "that the decision for undertaking the special operation is now completely out of my hands and it is upon that basis that I have insisted that it and the United Kingdom operations are complementary." Because TORCH could not be averted, perhaps it could be deflected or at least be made to serve other AAF goals. TORCH should go forward with all possible support;

therefore any units that helped to ensure its success, such as the Eighth, should be as strong as possible, too.[157]

Arnold soon concluded that coordinating the efforts of the Eighth and Twelfth would best be accomplished by a single USAAF commander supervising operations in both Britain and Africa. That officer would be directly subordinate to the overall U.S. commander, Eisenhower. Arnold also concluded, *pari passu*, that only one man had the proper qualifications for the post—Spaatz. As Maj. Gen. George E. Stratemeyer, Chief of the AAF Staff, noted, Arnold had expressed a desire for Spaatz to remain at Eisenhower's side and provide him with AAF advice. Stratemeyer told Spaatz, "You really should be designated as the Commanding General, American Air Forces in Europe," not just of the ETO. Such "a request to place you in that position should come from Eisenhower, and I am sure that it would be approved here."[158] Spaatz discussed the suggestion with Eisenhower, but then rejected it on the ground that the already thin ranks of experienced staff officers would be diluted if yet another headquarters were created.[159] This was not an idle objection; throughout the war, the Achilles heel of the AAF was its shortage of adequately trained staff officers.[160]

Although Eisenhower had initially agreed with Spaatz that an overall USAAF commander was not needed, he gradually came to side with Arnold, but for his own reasons. He accepted the AAF's contention that a bombing offensive should be waged from Britain but thought it should come after the conclusion of Torch. He wanted to strengthen the Eighth immediately to use it as a reinforcement pool for North Africa,[161] believing that once bases were set up along the African Mediterranean littoral, Africa and Britain would form a "single air theater" in which air power could be concentrated at any point to take advantage of weather conditions or strategic opportunity.[162]

On October 29, Eisenhower requested Spaatz's support for his own plan of a unified AAF command "from Iceland to Iraq." He had apparently obtained clarification on the War Department's view of a unified command. A single theater would help keep resources from the Pacific, an appeal that two separate theaters—Europe (Britain) and North Africa—competing against each other would lack. If Torch succeeded so that a unified command was possible, Eisenhower intended to place Spaatz in the position of "Supreme Commander of all U.S. Army Air Forces which came under his command, and to advocate the inclusion of U.S. Army Air Forces in the Middle East also in that same command."[163] He instructed Spaatz to prepare a plan for implementation of his proposal within thirty days.[164]

By the eve of the invasion, which started on November 8, 1942, Spaatz seems to have resigned himself to being Eisenhower's chief air officer in North Africa, although he would far rather have stayed in Britain to direct the Eighth Air Force. In a series of mid-November letters, Arnold and Stratemeyer urged Spaatz's appointment. On November 13, Stratemeyer wrote Spaatz, "You should get yourself appointed as overall commander of his Air Force."[165] Two days later, Arnold wrote in a letter to Spaatz,

> With all due respect to everybody concerned, you are sidetracked. In my opinion, this whole problem of air operations in Europe must be controlled by one man. Are you in a position in England to give the best advice to Eisenhower in Gibraltar on such matters? It appears to me that if something is not done we will find the air being used more as a support for the ground arms than it should be, particularly so, when *if there ever was a time to use it strategically that time is now* [emphasis added]. It may be that you should take a trip down to see Eisenhower and talk this matter out.[166]

The same day Arnold wrote to Eisenhower, "Sticking my neck out considerably, I suggest that you have Tooey join you at your present headquarters."[167] Finally, Stratemeyer put it most succinctly, "You should be in Ike's pocket."[168] All these communications illustrate Arnold's perception of Eisenhower as the most important and influential American officer in Europe. (Eisenhower's European Theater of Operations command already included all U.S. Army and AAF units assigned to Iceland, Britain, and North Africa.)[169] Arnold's and the AAF's best interests lay in providing him with the best possible advice on air matters. Naturally, in Arnold's opinion, only Spaatz could give that advice.

Stratemeyer's last exhortation proved unnecessary. By the time Spaatz received it, he had already flown to North Africa to inspect the Twelfth and from there on to Gibraltar, where he met with Eisenhower and accepted the job as Theater Air Commander. Eaker moved up to command the Eighth Air Force.

At a meeting at Headquarters, Eighth Air Force, on November 23, Spaatz explained to his staff the general function of the new theater air command. He saw its chief duty as strategic control, not operational or administrative control. It would be organized as follows:

Eighth Air Force (in command of all U.S. air forces in Britain)
Twelfth Air Force (in command of all U.S. air forces in North Africa)
Iceland air forces.

The theater air forces commander would exercise technical supervision and control of units attached to ground forces. General directives would be issued on strategic bombing, on allocation of units between the Eighth and Twelfth Air Forces, and on the readiness of heavy- and medium-bombers in each air force to support operations throughout the theater.[170]

The questions of the final operational objectives and strength of the Eighth and Twelfth Air Forces and the organization of a combined Allied air command would be settled only after successful initial landings in North Africa. But at the end of November 1942, it probably appeared to Spaatz that he had guaranteed the attainment of the strategic goals of AWPD/1. He had gained a position from which, subject to Eisenhower, he could direct the strategic bombardment of

German-occupied Europe from any point between London and Baghdad. He could also concentrate his forces to operate in those areas most favored by the weather, wherever they may be in his vast command.

Disillusionment would soon come in muddy Tunisia.

Part Two

Tempering the Blade
The North African Campaign
November 8, 1942–May 14, 1943

Part Two

Tempering the Blade

temper\'tem per*vb*\: to make stronger and more resilient through hardship: to put in tune with something.[1]

Current and long-standing USAF tactical air power doctrine defines five combat functions for tactical air power: counterair or air superiority, close air support, air interdiction, tactical air reconnaissance, and tactical airlift operations. USAF doctrine adds that the governing principle for determining the priority given to each function is the neutralization of "the enemy threat having the most profound and continuing influence on the total mission of the area [theater] command." Air Force Manual 2-1 further notes that "all five combat functions are performed concurrently because they are mutually supporting."[2] Although the next three chapters touch on all the combat functions of tactical air power, they concentrate on three: counterair-air superiority, close air support, and air interdiction. They also give not only an in-depth analysis of the tactical air power experience of another major air service, the Royal Air Force (RAF), but trace the influence of thought within the RAF on the emergence of AAF doctrine.

During the campaign in North Africa (see Map 3, Operation TORCH Area), the U.S. Army Air Forces in Europe and their commanding general, Carl A. Spaatz, met and overcame fundamental problems in the employment of air power. At the campaign's opening, Spaatz left his task—that of introducing the strategic U.S. Eighth Air Force to limited combat operations from a secure and logistically sophisticated base area in Britain—to assume entirely different duties in North Africa. There he directed combined Anglo-American strategic, tactical, and coastal air forces in the midst of sustained combat at the end of an attenuated supply line. As the leader of tactical forces, Spaatz met and mastered three primary tasks of air in the support of ground operations:

    1. The achievement of air superiority throughout the theater of operations and above the battlefield;

    2. The provision of close air support to the ground forces; and

    3. The interdiction of enemy supplies and reinforcements to prevent their utilization at the front.

If superiority had rested simply in numbers of machines, the Allies would have had it throughout the campaign. Mere numbers, however, were decisive only if all other factors—training, logistics, organization, doctrine, weapons and geographic position, as well as the morale, combat experience, and condition of available manpower—were equal. These variables had to be factored into any

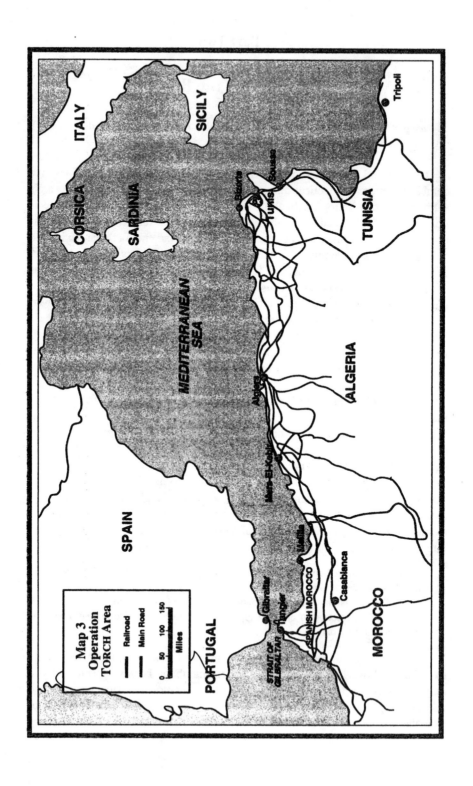

Map 3
Operation
TORCH Area

Railroad
Main Road

Miles
0   50   100   150

PORTUGAL

SPAIN

ITALY

SICILY

CORSICA

SARDINIA

MEDITERRANEAN
SEA

Gibraltar
Tangier
STRAIT OF
GIBRALTAR
SPANISH MOROCCO

Melilla

Casablanca

MOROCCO

Mers-El-Kebir

Algiers

ALGERIA

Bizerte

Tunis
Sousse

TUNISIA

Tripoli

meaningful calculation of Allied versus Axis air strength throughout the campaign. When initial Axis advantages are considered, the inability of the more numerous Allied air forces to achieve their goals becomes clear.

The delivery of close air support proved one of the most nettlesome problems because it depended on the resolution of other shortcomings and on the personal relationships between the air and ground commanders. Close air support was the application of aerial firepower in coordination with the movement and fire of friendly ground formations against hostile targets near ground combat operations. Successful close air support required attainment of air superiority over the field of ground combat operations. It also required the maintenance of a mutual spirit of cooperation between the ground elements and the air forces providing support. During the early phases of the North African campaign, the Allied air and ground forces could achieve neither air superiority nor satisfactory teamwork. Consequently, from November 1942 through mid-February 1943, Allied close air support was ineffective.

Interdiction proved far easier to solve. The complete dependence of the Axis powers on supplies transported to Africa from Italy, the few ports available to receive those supplies, the shortage of suitable shipping, the limited number and constricted nature of shipping lanes, and the paucity of protected air transport fields made the Axis extremely vulnerable to any logistical disruption. Allied breaking of Axis codes, which enabled precise tracking of supply convoys and routes, added immeasurably to the ease with which Allied air power could locate and attack the many weaknesses in the Axis logistical network. Any problem stemmed chiefly from the difficulty of obtaining sufficient striking power.

By using his managerial, organizational, and, above all, operational skills, Spaatz played a vital role in Allied tactical air power's reversing the variables that prevented Allied attainment of air superiority. In the later stages of the campaign, Spaatz improved the team work between Allied air and ground elements, which had been noticeably lacking in both the American and British components of Operation TORCH's invasion force. As for interdiction, Spaatz was instrumental in keeping the heavy bombers on interdiction tasks and in disrupting the Axis air transport system. Spaatz's treatment of air superiority, close air support, and air interdiction is explored within the next three chapters.

Chapter 4

The Race for Tunisia
(November 1942–January 1943)

Perhaps the most glaring error in the higher planning was the decision not to have a unified Air Command. The separation of the Air Forces into two separate commands with two distinct areas of responsibility was a stab in the back from which they never recovered until they were re-organized under Air Chief Marshal Sir Arthur Tedder.[1]

—AHB Narrative, ca. 1950

Initial Invasion Operations

On November 8, 1942, three Anglo-American task forces landed in French North Africa. After overcoming half-hearted French resistance, they occupied their initial objectives—Casablanca, Oran, and Algiers. Fortunately, Admiral Jean Francois Darlan, Commander in Chief of the Vichy French armed forces and second in command to Marshal Petain himself in the Vichy regime, happened to be in Algiers in the midst of an inspection trip of France's colonial possessions in Africa. Darlan ordered all French forces to cease fighting on November 10. The Nazi invasion of unoccupied France, part of the German response to the North African invasion, led Darlan to agree to place French military forces under Eisenhower's command and to order the French civil administration to cooperate with the Allies. This agreement, signed on November 13, secured Morocco and Algeria for the Allies and allowed them to turn their energies toward the liberation of Tunisia, much of which the Axis had taken over from the Vichy French at the start of the invasion. The Axis powers, aided by the confusion and inaction of the Vichy French government in Tunisia, rushed to forestall the Allies by hurrying troops and equipment across the narrow stretch of the Mediterranean separating Sicily and Cape Bon, Tunisia.

The stresses engendered by the race to acquire Tunisia revealed weaknesses in Allied logistics, organization, and doctrine, particularly in the area of airpower. AAF personnel had played a minor role in preinvasion planning. Chief U.S. Army and Navy planners had limited the role of AAF personnel to providing air details concerning tactical support to the invasion task forces rather than to employing air power in the Mediterranean at large. Ten days before the operation started, Spaatz confessed to Doolittle that he had never understood the "what, when, and where" of the Twelfth Air Force's assigned mission and function.[2] AAF planners did, however, convince Eisenhower on one point—that the British and American air forces should be commanded directly by Eisenhower rather than by a subordinate air commander in chief.[3]

The original invasion plan had called for an overall air commander, but Eisenhower said, "I accepted representations made to me, principally by American airmen in whom I had the greatest confidence, that the projected use of the American and British air forces involved such a wide geographical dispersion that unified command would be impracticable."[4] This advice, consistent with his thinking, probably came directly from Spaatz. The abortive air plan for the autumn invasion of France that Spaatz prepared and presented to the Combined American and British Chiefs of Staff (CCS) during the King-Marshall-Hopkins mission of July 1942 provided for an organization exactly like the one Eisenhower adopted for TORCH. The July plan explicitly admonished that "there must be no subordination of U.S. Air Units, and no attachment to R.A.F. units." Instead, the plan specified, "there will be unity of command through the Task Force Commander. He will use his two air forces, British and American, as a Corps Commander would use two division commanders, without subordinating one to the other."[5] Even when the two air forces operated in the same area, let alone widely separated ones, the AAF would not subordinate itself to the RAF. This failure to set up a combined air command before the invasion hamstrung the efficient application of Allied air power during the first crucial month of the campaign.

Spaatz erred in his resistance to possible RAF domination. Although understandable, his loyalty to the AAF weakened his military judgment. Of course, the example of General John J. Pershing, Commander of the American Expeditionary Forces to Europe for World War I, influenced the U.S. Army leaders of World War II who had served their apprenticeships in the ranks of his forces. (Except for a few cases of extreme emergency, Pershing had adamantly refused to place his forces under the command of his French or British allies.) In other preinvasion planning for TORCH, only the U.S. Navy consented to a combined command with its British counterpart. The U.S. Army and the AAF, for whatever reasons, did not.[6]

For the landing phase of the invasion, the inexperienced Twelfth Air Force, designated the Western Air Command, assumed responsibility for supporting the Casablanca and Oran task forces, both composed entirely of U.S. forces. Plans called for the Twelfth to attain an eventual strength of 1,244 aircraft, including 282 in reserve. The combat-experienced RAF supplied the Eastern Air Command (EAC) to assist the chiefly British Algiers task force. The EAC had a planned force only one-third the size of the Twelfth's—454 planes of all types, many of them short-ranged Hurricane and Spitfire fighters. The EAC also had responsibility for air operations to the east of Oran, including Tunisia. Once French North Africa capitulated and Fascist Spain appeared quiescent—a situation that released the Allied forces assigned to watch those areas—the Twelfth had no strategic role other than to support the drive on Bizerte.[7]

Inexperience hampered the AAF's effectiveness. Twenty-nine years later Doolittle admitted, "I was a brand new Air Force commander, and I had never commanded anything bigger than about a flight prior to that time, so there were a great many things I had to learn, and I endeavored to learn them very rapidly. For one, I had to learn my job, and I worked hard at learning it."[8]

Doolittle, the short, stocky, forty-five-year-old son of a carpenter, had a devil-may-care image that masked a man of surprising substance. In the 1920s and 1930s, he won several international airplane speed races, including the Schneider Trophy for seaplanes in 1925 and the first Bendix Trophy for transcontinental speed in 1931; in taking the Thompson Trophy in 1932, he also set a new speed record. As one of the most famous pilots of his day, he had the same aura of mystery and death-defying courage that clings to modern-day astronauts. Doolittle had, on occasion, shown bad judgment. On a trip through South America in 1926, when he was under the influence of alcohol during a stopover in Santiago, Chile, he fell from a second-story window ledge and broke both ankles. Yet he finished the journey, including air shows and stunts, by flying in leg casts. On other occasions Doolittle engaged in wingwalking or sat on a biplane's wheel spreader or axle while it landed.

Unlike many AAF leaders, Doolittle was not a career officer or a West Pointer. He had joined the Army in April 1917, transferred to the Aviation Section, and served there for thirteen years, until early 1930, before resigning to join Shell Oil. While in the Air Corps he earned a doctorate in aeronautical engineering from the Massachusetts Institute of Technology. At Shell, Doolittle worked to develop 100-octane aviation fuel, a prerequisite for the advanced and more powerful piston-driven engines that would equip U.S. aircraft in World War II. Recalled to duty as a major on July 1, 1940, he acted as a troubleshooter at various aircraft plants. In late January 1942, Arnold assigned Doolittle, by then a lieutenant colonel, to command Special Project No. 1, a combined Army-Navy effort to strike Tokyo with Army bombers flying from a Navy aircraft carrier.

"Doolittle's Tokyo Raid," sixteen B-25s launched from the USS *Hornet* on April 18, 1943, once more catapulted Doolittle into national prominence. He again demonstrated his great physical courage by leading the flight and taking off with the shortest run. When a Japanese picket boat spotted the Navy task

Brig. Gen. James H.
Doolittle, Commanding
General, Twelfth Air
Force, 1942.

force before the planned launch time, he displayed the ability to take a calculated risk and demonstrated the moral courage needed for high command by
ordering the flight to leave early, lengthening the journey by 250 miles.
Rewards followed. The AAF and the nation, saddened by the surrender of U.S.
and Filipino forces in Bataan in early April, rejoiced over a genuine hero. By
May 5, the day before the surrender of Corregidor in Manila Bay, Doolittle
was jumped to brigadier general. On May 19, President Roosevelt pinned a
Congressional Medal of Honor to his chest. Arnold assigned him the command
of the Eighth Air Force's 4th Bombardment Wing, a medium-bomber wing
being formed. When the British and the Americans agreed on the North
African invasion, Arnold reassigned him to command the Twelfth Air Force,
which in the initial planning had not been large but which grew substantially
with the invasion. Doolittle was definitely a man of parts, most of them excellent.[9]

For all his abilities, however, Doolittle was slow to gain Eisenhower's confidence. Eisenhower wrote in his postwar memoirs, "It took him [Doolittle] some
time to reconcile himself to shouldering his responsibilities as the senior United
States air commander to the exclusion of . . . going out to fly a fighter plane
against the enemy."[10] The first meeting between Doolittle and Eisenhower
sometime shortly after Doolittle's arrival in Britain on August 6 proved disastrous, for Doolittle had managed to convince Eisenhower only of his brashness
and his ignorance of the job.[11]

Although the AAF official history implies Eisenhower's acceptance of

Doolittle as the American air commander for TORCH prior to August 6, any such agreement must have been tenuous.[12] On September 13, Eisenhower wired Marshall that he personally preferred and strongly recommended Eaker for the command of the Twelfth. He suggested Doolittle for the XII Bomber Command or command of the air supporting the Casablanca invasion force. The next day Eisenhower suggested to Marshall that Maj. Gen. Walter H. Frank, Commanding General, VIII Air Service Command, was equally acceptable. Both Frank and Eaker had already gained invaluable experience establishing and preparing an air force for a major operation.[13]

Eisenhower's second message crossed with Marshall's reply to the first. Marshall gave Doolittle an exceptional recommendation: "Arnold and I both feel very strongly that Doolittle is a much more effective organizer and leader for the U.S. air force and Casablanca. He is a leader par excellence and both highly intelligent and strongly persistent in work of preparation." Marshall had just finished taking Doolittle on a trip to the West Coast and noted as a result that with "his combination of industry, intensity, technical knowledge and level headed bearing he greatly impressed me as probably the outstanding combat leader type in our Air Corps."[14] Marshall added that, despite what he had just said, the decision was of course Eisenhower's to make. A few days later Marshall, in a hand-delivered note to Eisenhower, expressed his full confidence and approval of all but two actions—the appointment of Frank instead of Doolittle, which he termed a "tragic error" and the selection of Maj. Gen. Russell P. Hartle to command the Center (Oran) Task Force for TORCH. Marshall offered to send any of eight other generals.[15] Eisenhower selected Maj. Gen. Lloyd R. Fredendall and retained Doolittle. On September 23, Doolittle officially assumed command of the Twelfth.

It took Doolittle months of hard work to change Eisenhower's opinion. The Twelfth's top remaining leaders had little or no more combat and administrative experience than their commander.

North Africa, in the winter of 1942–1943, proved an unforgiving locale for the conduct of air operations. The division of the Twelfth into two parts, each directly subordinated to its invasion task force commander (Maj. Gen. George S. Patton in Casablanca and Maj. Gen. Lloyd R. Fredendall in Oran), put the two sections of the air force 365 miles apart by air. The route traveled by the ground echelons from Casablanca and Oran to the front would, naturally, be more arduous and less direct. Furthermore, the task force commanders' reluctance to give up command of their air assets prevented the Twelfth from gathering its full force. Part of the Twelfth remained tied to the U.S. Fifth Army in Morocco to watch the Spanish. Although portions of the AAF would eventually travel the entire 1,065 miles from Casablanca to Tunis, the Luftwaffe and the *Reggia Aeronautica* (Italian Royal Air Force) were more favored by geography. They had major depots in Sicily, which was 160 miles from Tunis, and Naples, 375 miles from Tunis. The Axis powers also seized the only four all-weather, hard-surface airfields in the

Tunisian plain,* which gave them a considerable advantage over the Allies, who operated from unimproved dirt fields in the eastern Algerian highlands. When the rainy season began in December 1942, these fields immediately turned into mud puddles. The Allies had only one hard-surface field east of Algiers, at Bône, 115 miles from the front. (See Map 4, Allied and Axis Airfields on the Northern Tunisian Front.) To add to the confusion in the initial phases of the campaign, RAF and AAF units operated from the same airfields. All supplies for the forward units of the Twelfth would have to move along the feeble colonial road network and one overworked, single-track rail line from Algiers.

In addition, the Twelfth lacked mobility. Aircraft might travel far and swiftly, but they remained tethered to their ground echelons. The ground echelons required considerable motor or rail transport to keep pace with the rapidly changing front lines characteristic of modern warfare. Already hampered by frangible French railways, the AAF in North Africa had to prevail over a chronic shortage of motor transport. The Twelfth started the Tunisian campaign understrength in trucks because invasion planners, facing the usual premium on shipping space confronting any large-scale amphibious invasion and envisaging a static role for the AAF, had pared the Twelfth's motorized components to a minimum. The Oran task force carried no two-and-one-half ton trucks, and only 50 percent of all types of organizational vehicles. The Casablanca task force sailed with 100 percent of its men but only 50 percent of its matériel.[16] U.S. ground units moving to support the advance of Lt. Gen. Kenneth A. N. Anderson's 1st British Army into Tunisia aggravated the transportation shortage by stripping away much of the Twelfth's shrunken allocation of motor transport.

The Eastern Air Command suffered the same hardships. It had requested shipping for enough motor transport to make its ground echelons 100 percent mobile, but was allocated only half of its request.[17] Many vehicles immediately fell into different hands. One air observer reported that new units' "Senior Officers and others were in the habit of commandeering vehicles as soon as they were unloaded in ALGIERS, without regard to whether they were consigned to their unit or not. When no longer needed, these vehicles were abandoned by the wayside."[18]

The original strategic plans placing the Twelfth Air Force in a static role, far to the west of the combat area, added to the organizational chaos. Doolittle had difficulty regaining command of his widely separated forces from the task force commanders. Each of the task force commanders (ground force generals who were the equivalent of corps commanders) for the Casablanca and Oran invasions had received control of approximately one-half of the Twelfth Air Force to

---

* One, El Aouina, was only 20 miles from the front lines, and another, Sidi Ahmed, was 25 miles away.

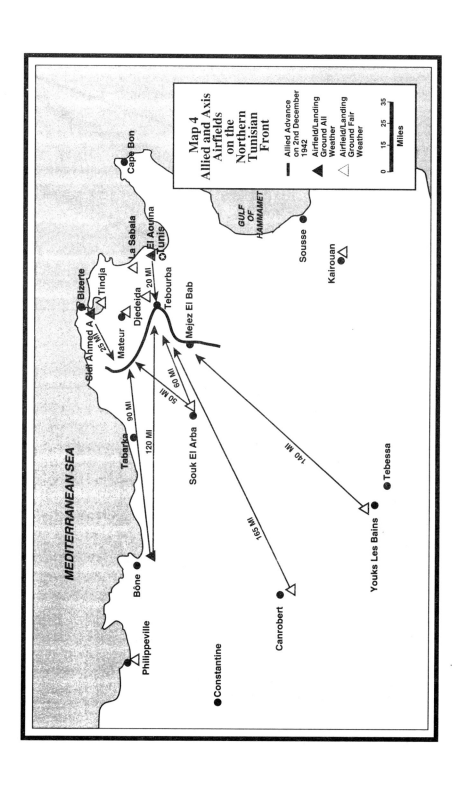

Map 4
Allied and Axis
Airfields
on the
Northern
Tunisian
Front

Allied Advance
on 2nd December
1942

▲ Airfield/Landing
Ground All
Weather

△ Airfield/Landing
Ground Fair
Weather

Miles
0   15   25   35

MEDITERRANEAN SEA

Cape Bon

GULF
OF
HAMMAMET

Sousse

Kairouan

La Sabala
El Aouina
Tunis
Bizerte
Tindja
Mateur
Djedeïda
Sidi Ahmed A
Tebourba
Mejez El Bab
20 MI
25 MI
Tabarka
90 MI
Souk El Arba
50 MI
60 MI
60 MI
120 MI
140 MI
Tebessa
165 MI
Bône
Youks Les Bains
Philippeville
Canrobert
Constantine

provide support for their invasion assault. After the assault, the task force commanders only reluctantly released their attached air forces. The confusion compounded when new air and ground elements landed in Algiers, in order to enter
the fighting in Tunisia immediately, while their rear echelons landed half a continent away in Casablanca. The Twelfth had other units still in Britain or the United
States, or on convoys in the middle of the Atlantic.

Communications and intelligence problems also plagued the Twelfth at the
start of the campaign. The French telephone system, at best primitive and inefficient, soon failed under the demands placed on it. Atmospheric conditions
unique to North Africa hindered radio transmission, as did lack of modern
equipment and half-trained signals personnel.[19] In many instances motorcycle
couriers had to carry the load.[20] Moreover, the Twelfth had no military intelligence. All its operational information came from the British; there were thus
delays in planning and consequent delays in missions.

U.S. Air Support Doctrine Before Operation TORCH

U.S. ground and air forces started the North African campaign with an
untested air support doctrine. Because of the AAF's position as a combat arm
subordinate to the Army rather than as a service independent from the Army like
the RAF, the ground forces, rather than air, had the decisive voice in determining official doctrine. In 1926 this dominance was reflected in War Department
Training Regulation 440-15 (TR 440-15), which stated categorically, "The mission of the Air Service is to assist the ground forces to gain strategical and tactical successes by destroying enemy aviation, attacking enemy ground forces and
other enemy objectives on land or sea, and in conjunction with other agencies to
protect ground forces from hostile aerial observation and attack." TR 440-15
also stated that the "Air Service is an essential arm in all major operations. The
organization and training of all air units is based on the fundamental doctrine
that their mission is to aid the ground forces to gain decisive success."[21] TR
440-15 authorized strategic bombardment operations under favorable conditions
and after the defeat or neutralization of a hostile air force if it was "based on the
broad plan of operations of the military forces."[22]

The advent of General Headquarters Air Force (GHQ AF) in 1935 led to the
revision of TR 440-15. This revision placed GHQ AF under the commander in
chief in the field in wartime, and under the Chief of Staff of the Army in peacetime. The revision gave the GHQ AF three functions:

1. Operations beyond the sphere of influence of the ground forces;
2. Operations in support of the ground forces; and
3. Coastal frontier defense.

Operations beyond the ground forces' sphere of influence were still required

130

to conform to the Army strategic plan, prepared by a section of the War Department General Staff dominated by ground officers. In addition, the GHQ Air Force Commander could be directed by the commander-in-chief in the field to "support designated operations of an army with all or with a specified part of GHQ Air Force in accordance with the instructions of such army commanders."[23] Yet the 1935 version of TR 440-15 represented a significant step forward in the eyes of air officers, in that it recognized a role for strategic bombardment equal to that of ground support.

It is important to remember that strategic bombing offered the airmen an institutional advantage not offered by tactical operations. Strategic operations were independent of the Army and could be used to justify an independent air arm. Tactical operations, in contrast, would always be in cooperation with ground forces and difficult to separate from them—hence the airmen's constant attempts to advance strategic air and their lack of interest in tactical air.

Adolf Hitler's aggressive, *revanchist* foreign policy of 1936–1939 and the outbreak of war in Europe led to the reexamination of U.S. Army air doctrine. On April 15, 1940, War Department Field Manual 1-5 (FM 1-5) superseded TR 440-15 of October 15, 1935. The authors of FM 1-5 intended it to be the comprehensive rubric for the employment of all types of U.S. military aviation. As such, it defined the basic doctrines for strategic bombardment, antiaircraft defense, support of ground and naval forces, and air operations in lieu of naval forces. This manual was based on the recommendations of a War Department Air Board, appointed by Secretary of War Harry H. Woodring on March 23, 1939. Woodring designated Arnold president of the board, and its membership included Maj. Gen. Frank M. Andrews (recently appointed by Marshall to head G-3, Operations of the General Staff) and Brig. Gen. George V. Strong (head of the War Plans Division). After polling the components of the Army and the Air Corps, including GHQ Air Force, and the Air Corps Tactical School the board submitted its findings to the Chief of Staff on September 1, 1939. With only minor changes these findings became FM 1-5.[24]

Although the manual emphasized the role of air power in the defense of the United States and its possessions, it provided for a strategic air offensive to "decisively defeat important elements of the enemy armed forces" or to "deprive the enemy of essential war material."[25] In its discussion of air operations in support of ground forces it laid down the following instructions:

> The hostile rear area is the normal zone of action of support aviation, since operations in this area permit the full utilization of striking power against concentrated targets with the minimum of losses and the maximum of results. Support aviation is not employed against objectives which can be effectively engaged by available ground weapons within the time required.

FM 1-5 also observed that "aviation is poorly suited for direct attacks against small detachments or troops which are well entrenched or disposed."

The manual addressed the control of tactical air as well, stating that, in general, centralized control at the theater level maximized effectiveness, but noted:

> When decentralization becomes necessary in situations requiring immediate tactical support of specified units, the superior commander may attach to or place in support of specified large units a part or all of his support aviation. Support aviation may thus act with greater promptness and better understanding in meeting the requirements of the supported unit. When combat aviation is employed for immediate tactical support of surface forces, the requirements of the supported force will be of paramount importance in the selection of objectives for air operations.[26]

In theory, the manual should have supplied a reasonable compromise solution to the ground forces' desire for control of support aviation in a battle situation and the desire of elements of the Air Corps to centralize the control of all tactical air under an airman. In practice, all would depend on the attitude of the theater commander, who would almost certainly be a ground officer. In that case, Air Corps officers feared that he would routinely attach air support units directly to his field armies or corps and ignore the strictures on centralization of air command. Army and corps commanders, whose attention would be focused solely on the attainment of their own immediate objectives, would be slow to release the attached air units and would invariably be unable to cooperate effectively with each other in a timely enough manner to take advantage of air's ability to concentrate all of its forces over a single objective. FM 1-5, however, reflected the increased influence of the Army Air Corps within the structure of the Army and the development of an aircraft capable of strategic bombardment, the B-17. No longer, as in 1926, could the ground forces impose doctrine by fiat.

A series of important prewar Army maneuvers in Louisiana and North Carolina in 1941 showed the extent of the rift between the ground forces and the air forces. As the Army ground forces sought to adapt to the German method of blitzkrieg warfare, they clashed with the Army Air Forces, which had a different set of priorities. The ground forces, looking at the war in Europe and seeing the successes of the German army acting in close concert with the Luftwaffe, a force designed for ground support, formed armored divisions and an armored corps to fight the new war. To work effectively, these new corps required large-scale close air support to form a combined-arms team capable of fighting the Germans on equal terms. Thus they needed modern planes for training and an air support communications network and support team to function at full capacity. The AAF had difficulty supplying those items.

The AAF, studying the war in Europe, realized it would need an air defense network and a strategic bombing campaign to weaken the Germans before attempting an invasion of the Continent, if that proved necessary. The needs of the ground forces took lower priority. The Western Allies were buying hundreds of modern warplanes and the AAF's own training programs were consuming

132

most remaining aircraft production, leaving few aircraft for air support training. Given these conflicts, prewar maneuvers had proved unsatisfactory.

Ten days before the attack on Pearl Harbor, Arnold noted the poor coordination between ground and air during the North Carolina and Louisiana maneuvers that he and Marshall blamed on the "lack of knowledge of fundamentals on the part of both the Air and Ground elements."[27] Air and ground officers did not know air communications techniques and procedures, proper employment of their own forces for air operations, and the characteristics and limitations of air itself. Arnold informed Spaatz that Marshall wished to hold a series of command post exercises at Fort Benning in Georgia for all major combat commanders of the Army. "The first one should be started off," recommended Arnold, "with a general discussion by all present as to exactly what Air Support means and how it is to be carried out, so that the fundamentals may be discussed frankly and all present get some ideas of what can and should be expected."[28]

U.S. entry into the war increased the intensity of the dispute between air and ground. The Army reorganization of March 9, 1942, institutionalized the dispute by giving air and ground the same degree of power and prestige. In that reorganization the AAF and the Army Ground Forces (AGF) became separate and equal organizations under the Army General Staff and the War Department. If, as in 1926, one arm or the other could have imposed its will, at least one of them would have been content. Or if a virtually unlimited number of planes had been available, both sides could have had adequate air resources for strategic bombing and ground support, as was the case in 1944–1945.

On April 9, 1942, the War Department promulgated a manual on air support based on the lessons of the prewar exercises, War Department Field Manual 31-35 (FM 31-35), "Aviation in Support of Ground Forces." Air historians have charged that it created many of the AAF's ground support woes early in the war. The AAF official history said of FM 31-35, "The outstanding characteristic of the manual lay in its subordination of the air force to ground force needs and to the purely local situation."[29] Yet the AAF itself had issued the manual. The Army Air Support Staff Section had drafted the manual. Its successor in the March 1942 reorganization, the Directorate of Ground Support, had produced the finished copy.

In fact, the manual attempted to reconcile irreconcilable air and ground positions. It was not intended to speak to any aspect of air power other than air support. The manual devoted more than half of its text to a detailed exposition of the air-ground communications network rather than to doctrines of employment. It placed an air support command—along with fighter, bomber, and base commands—within a theater air force, all under the control of an airman. The manual offset this arrangement by noting that the air support command would be habitually attached to or designated to support a particular field army. Within the air support command, all control was centralized in the hands of its commander, an airman, who would assign missions as the needs of the ground units developed.

133

If required, however, an aviation unit could be "specifically allocated" to the support of subordinate ground units.[30] In such a case, the aviation unit would receive its orders from an air support control unit commanded by an airman and co-located at the command post of the supported unit. The overall air support commander retained the right to assign other air support missions to the "specifically allocated" unit. The manual went on to state:

> Designation of an aviation unit for support of a subordinate ground unit does not imply subordination of that aviation unit to the supported ground unit, nor does it remove the combat aviation unit from the control of the air support commander. It does permit, however, direct cooperation and association between the supporting aviation unit and the supported ground unit and enables combat aviation to act with greater promptness in meeting the requirements of a rapidly changing situation. Aviation units may be *attached* [emphasis in original] to subordinate ground units. This is exceptional and should be resorted to only when circumstances are such that the air support commander cannot effectively control the combat aviation assigned to the air support command.[31]

The manual assumed that in most instances air control would be centralized at the theater level.

FM 31-35 began its consideration of the method of employing air support aviation with the following obvious, but often ignored, homily: "The basis of effective air support of ground forces is teamwork. The air and ground units in such operations form a team. Each member of the team must have the technical skill and training to enable it to perform its part in the operation and a willingness to cooperate thoroughly."[32] The first factor affecting employment was the establishment of local air superiority to ensure air support without excessive losses. Next came economy of force, defined as hitting the right target at the right time rather than using a few aircraft to hit widely scattered targets. Other factors included attention to time and space factors (distance from air bases, speed of communications, readiness status of aircraft, etc.), the inherent flexibility of air power to concentrate on short notice, and the necessity of the air support command to cooperate with other air elements in the same area.

The manual's procedures for selecting targets raised the ire of pro air power critics, who focused on one paragraph: "The most important target at a particular time will usually be that target which constitutes the most serious threat to the operations of the supported ground force. The final decision as to priority of targets rests with the commander of the supported unit."[33] This lifting of one paragraph from its context distorted the balanced intent of the entire manual, which was not an encomium for the doctrinal positions held by the ground forces. Ground force officers objected to the centralized control of air support aviation inherent in the air support command; they favored the direct attachment of air units to the units they supported.[34] FM 31-35 satisfied neither the ground forces nor the air forces, which was perhaps the true measure of its attempt at objectivity. If it proved wanting on the battlefield, it was because most of the American air and ground commanders in North Africa were inexperienced in combat and half-trained in the air support procedures laid down by FM 31-35 or ignorant of its provisions.

The issuance of FM 31-35 did little to solve the U.S. Army's and AAF's ground support training deficiencies. In front of War Department, Navy, and British army observers the AAF botched its share of a corps-level demonstration at Fort Benning on June 13, 1942.[35] This demonstration, conducted under the command of Maj. Gen. Lloyd R. Fredendall, included units of the 1st Infantry Division. Both the division and Fredendall would play large roles in North Africa. In July 1942, Maj. Gen. Jacob L. Devers, the Commander of the U.S. Armored Force, the chief armored training unit of the Army, complained to Marshall that the armored forces did not have a single combat plane working with them. When informed of the complaint, Arnold tartly replied that the armored forces had the best the AAF could supply and that he hoped to have sufficient quantities of light bombers and observation planes to meet ground force requests in full by the end of the year.[36]

In September Devers complained directly to Arnold of "lots of talk but no real action because there is a great shortage of equipment." He pointed out specific shortcomings in bombardment, observation, and communications units attached for training. "I stick to my opinion," said Devers bluntly, "that there is no air-ground support training. We are simply puttering. Cannot something be done about it?" Arnold replied that he had no modern heavy-bombardment, medium-bombardment, or fighter units available because all such units and their replacements were committed to active battle fronts. He had already allocated his only uncommitted light-bombardment group to one of the Armored Forces' major training establishments, the Desert Training Center. He attempted to reassure Devers by observing: "When our ground forces are committed to an active combat theater, I believe that they may look upon practically the entire Air Force in that theater as support aviation, as it is in North Africa today."* Arnold concluded by saying that he would continue to push for modern aircraft for training as soon as they became available.[37]

If the state of air-ground training of the armored forces, which had the highest priority, needed bolstering as late as September 1942, one can only imagine the status of the Army's remaining divisions and of the forces assigned to the North African invasion. Lt. Gen. Leslie J. McNair, Commander of the Army Ground Forces, admitted on December 30, 1942, "So far as I know, there is no U.S. ground unit overseas which had air-ground training before leaving the U.S., other than the superficial occasions incident to large maneuvers."[38] Clearly

---

* Arnold's mention of North Africa referred to Egypt where the British Western Desert Air Force (assisted by a handful of AAF units) was supporting Lt. Gen. Bernard L. Montgomery's British 8th Army against German Field Marshal Irwin Rommel's German-Italian *Panzer* Army.

the invasion ground and air forces were woefully untrained for the task ahead of them.

Despite the benefit of Britain's more than three years at war, the British 1st Army, Eisenhower's chief British ground formation, entered battle with air support doctrine and practice hardly superior to those of Eisenhower's American troops. The British air planners for the invasion, perhaps constrained by security considerations, which prevented direct contact, took no notice of the combat proven air support advances made by their own forces in the Middle East.[39] The British 8th Army and the Western Desert Air Force (WDAF), thanks to the hard lessons learned at the hands of the German *Afrika Korps*, had developed both an effective air support team and a modified air support doctrine based on close air-ground planning and communications. The British North African contingent for TORCH ignored that example and instead produced a plan similar to that of the advanced air striking force that had accompanied the British Expeditionary Force to France in 1939.[40] That plan had proved deficient because it did not provide close enough cooperation between the RAF and the British army. The TORCH invasion plan in general suffered from the same defect.

Nor were the British troops appreciably better trained in air-ground operations than the Americans. The British 1st Army, under Lt. Gen. Kenneth A. N. Anderson, was a hastily assembled force that had never operated together as a whole. Nor were its troops of the highest quality; the British had skimmed their home country units (units stationed in metropolitan Britain) of their best manpower and starved them of modern equipment in order to maintain the British 8th Army in the desert war against Rommel. In particular, the home forces had been forced to divest themselves of almost all their organic light antiaircraft artillery to augment that of the desert forces. This deficiency was not corrected before British units embarked for the invasion.[41] The shortage of antiaircraft weapons left the British 1st Army vulnerable to even light air attacks unless it received adequate protection from friendly fighter forces.

The Eastern Air Command, the RAF force responsible for the 1st Army's air support, had also been created for the TORCH invasion. It had not worked or trained with the 1st Army. Its staff had come together at the last moment, with no opportunity to form a team. Its squadrons had worked together, but its administrative and service troops were a hastily amalgamated hodge-podge of men with no training for field service or field conditions. They suffered severely in the North African countryside, where virtually no supplies could be obtained locally. The EAC had responsibilities beyond its means. It not only had to give air support to the 1st Army, it also had to provide for the air defense of all ports east of and including Algiers, escort and protect reinforcement convoys and shipping, and support the operations of the Allied fleet. Until it gained experience, the EAC's own manpower and organizational deficiencies, not to mention the unfavorable airfield situation and totally inadequate supply lines, would hinder its performance.[42]

Lt. Gen. Kenneth A. N.
Anderson, General Officer
Commanding, British 1st
Army, 1942–1943.

Imperial War Museum

In the long run, these shortcomings merely slowed the eventual victory of the Allies. The Axis powers could only delay the inevitable, given the decisive Anglo-American advantages in men and matériel—advantages, in turn, augmented by the priceless information supplied by the British signal intelligence organization, which decoded German Air Force, Navy, and Army as well as Italian air force and navy ciphers at both the strategic and the tactical levels. The British breaking of Axis codes, known as ULTRA, may have contributed more decisively to the North African campaign than to any other in the European Theater.

Operations in November–December 1942

The Allies had originally planned to capture airfields at Bône, Bizerte, and Tunis with airborne and commando troops, but uncertainty about the reaction of the French forces in Tunisia led to the cancellation of those ambitious plans. (See Map 5, Eastern Algeria and Northern Tunisia.) On November 10, a fast convoy left Algiers to occupy the port of Bougie, a little less than 100 miles away but still beyond the practical escort range of the EAC's Spitfires flying from Algiers. This convoy and a slow reinforcement convoy initially had air cover from the British carrier *Argus*. In the meantime, high surf foiled an attempt to land aviation fuel at the airfield at Djidjelli, on the coast a few miles

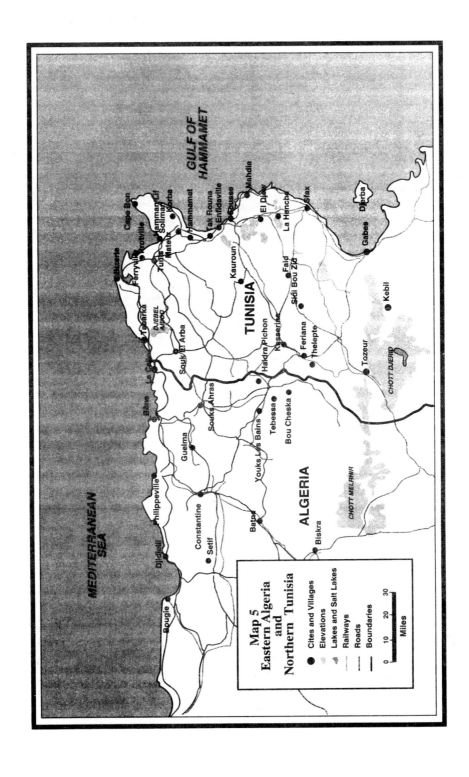

MEDITERRANEAN SEA

GULF OF HAMMAMET

Bougie
Djidjeli
Phillippeville
Bône
La Calle
Setif
Constantine
Batna
Biskra
Guelma
Youks Les Bains
Tebessa
Bou Cheska
Souk Ahras
Souk El Arba
Tabarka
DJEBEL ABIOD
Bizerte
Ferryville
Tunis
Mateur
Sollman
Sidi Nsir
Cape Bon
Hammamet
Oak Rouna
Enfidaville
Hammam Lif
Djerba
Sousse
Mahdia
El Djem
La Hencha
Sfax
Gabes
Djerba
Kebil
Kairouan
Sidi Bou Zid
Faid
Hadra
Pichon
Kasserine
Feriana
Thelepte
Tozeur
CHOTT DJERID
CHOTT MELRHIR

ALGERIA

TUNISIA

Map 5
Eastern Algeria
and
Northern Tunisia

- ● Cities and Villages
- ▲ Elevations
- ▨ Lakes and Salt Lakes
- ----- Railways
- ——— Roads
- ━━━ Boundaries

0   10   20   30
Miles

east of Bougie, grounding a squadron of just-arrived Spitfires. An attempt to supply fuel by truck from Bougie, a distance of 60 miles by road, misfired when the British 36th Infantry Brigade commandeered the designated trucks for reconnaissance purposes.[43] As a result, when the *Argus* withdrew in the afternoon, according to schedule, the unloading ships at Bougie had no air protection. The Luftwaffe promptly took advantage of this situation to sink three transports.

On November 12, a small British landing force seized the port of Bône, 125 miles east of Bougie and 185 miles by road from Bizerte. Bône had the easternmost hard-surface all-weather airfield available to the Allies for the bulk of the campaign. It served as the forward air base for the RAF Eastern Air Command. It also had unloading facilities for twenty-two ships—an important consideration when the relative ease of sea transport was compared with the difficulties encountered on the only two roads eastward from Algiers and the single-track railroad. It took trains four to six days to reach the advanced railhead at Souk el Arba (taken on November 16 by British paratroopers) from Algiers, and the line could sustain only six military trains a day with a daily capacity of only 2,000 tons.[44] The rail line underwent a change in gauge just east of Constantine, which added the delay of transshipment and the threat of another bottleneck in the line of supply.[45]

General Anderson, despite the grandiose title of his command, had only the understrength British 78th Division to send overland from Algiers. Its main body started its advance from Algiers on November 14. Its spearheads reached Djebel Abiod, about 25 miles from Bizerte, on November 17. At that point the British ran into tough German paratroops advancing from Bizerte and halted to organize for a general attack.

U.S. Twelfth Air Force units began to arrive at British forward fields by the third week of November. They placed themselves at the disposal of Air Marshal William L. Welsh, but not under his command. He could not order U.S. squadrons to specific objectives, and "the targets were decided on a day in advance after exhaustive discussion."[46] A week later, reinforced by units from the U.S. 1st Armored Division, the British resumed their advance. Overcoming counterattacks supported by tanks and dive-bombers, the Allies advanced to the outskirts of Djedeida, twelve miles from Tunis, on November 28. Concentrated German dive-bombing attacks and newly arrived antitank guns halted them there. The next day the heaviest air attacks to date hit exposed Allied tanks and infantry, while the Germans organized their defense.

By November 27, the 1st Army had one squadron of Twelfth Air Force P-38s (25 planes) at Youks-les-Bains, two squadrons of RAF Spitfires (36 planes) at Souk el Arba, and two squadrons of RAF Spitfires and one of Hurricane fighter-bombers (54 planes) at Bône available for both air superiority and close air support operations. These planes had a serviceability rate of only 50 percent and Spitfires had no bombing capability. The aircraft at Bône provided air defense for the port and arriving convoys and were not always available. In fact the

British did not use fighter bombing to support their front-line troops in the campaign until December 15.[47]

The Luftwaffe countered those planes with a force of approximately 81 fighters and 28 dive-bombers based in Tunisia. In the entire Mediterranean the Germans possessed 1,220 aircraft, of which more than 512 were operating against TORCH by November 12 and some 850 by December 12. At the same time they raised the number of their transport aircraft from 205 to 673.[48]

Anderson naturally found the air situation unsatisfactory. He called off his attack on November 29 partly because "the strain of persistent dive-bombing was beginning to tell." He complained further that air attacks on Bône had seriously disrupted his supply lines and said, "This week was notable for the heavy scale of enemy air attack, particularly by dive-bombers, to which the leading troops were subjected, and which our own air forces were at this stage unable to prevent."[49] Here, the inexperience of Anderson's troops, their light scale of anti-aircraft armament, and their lack of ammunition proved nearly disastrous. The slow-flying dive-bomber was a terrifying weapon, especially against untried troops who lacked the firepower to keep it at a respectful altitude.

In the first phase of the campaign, the Allies did not provide adequate close air support because they could not obtain air superiority and because no air-ground team existed. The EAC's Commander, Air Marshal Welsh, had appointed Air Commodore G. M. Lawson to operate the forward squadrons. Upon arrival at 1st Army Headquarters and later at 78th Division Headquarters, Lawson found communications chaotic. "Quite candidly," he acknowledged, "I am astonished at every point I have visited [by] the lack of knowledge of the operational setup and of the urgency of the drive in getting proper communications established."[50] Without communications, air-ground coordination ceased. Anderson complicated matters further by insisting on repeated attacks on Tunis, Bizerte, and Axis airfields elsewhere, as well as defensive patrols, known as "air umbrellas," over his own troops. These demands stretched the EAC far beyond its limited ability. Welsh did not help the situation by establishing his headquarters six miles outside Algiers, isolated not only from Anderson and Doolittle but also from Eisenhower and his headquarters, known as Allied Force Headquarters (AFHQ).[51]

On November 13, the day before Anderson began his advance toward Tunisia, Eisenhower telegraphed Spaatz: "I continue to look to you not only for control of the United States air in the United Kingdom but as *my most trusted air advisor*. . . . It may be best for us to confer immediately in light of what has so far transpired."[52] Eisenhower referred to the Axis powers' prompt and vigorous decision to establish a bridgehead in Tunisia, surprising the Allies, since invasion planners had discounted any possibility of such action. The Allied command had expected a cakewalk into Tunis once they had overcome the Vichy French.[53] Four days later, on November 17, Spaatz's B-17 touched down at Gibraltar, the site of Eisenhower's headquarters for the initial phase of the campaign. Doolittle met Spaatz, who had come to the Rock at Eisenhower's request.

Air Commodore G. M.
Lawson, Air Officer
Commanding, No. 242
Group, RAF, 1942–1943.

Imperial War Museum

By the time of their meeting, Eisenhower had already received from Bletchley
Park, the location of the British Government Code and Cypher School, signal
intelligence revealing an unexpectedly heavy Axis response. British cryptolo-
gists had cracked the particular Enigma machine key setting (Locust) employed
by the German Supreme Commander in the Mediterranean, Luftwaffe Field
Marshal Albert Kesselring, and could read the intercepted traffic without
delay."[54] As the daily intercepts arrived, confirming increased totals of Axis
men, aircraft, and tanks, Eisenhower redoubled the pressure on his subordinates
to secure Tunisia.

Thus Spaatz, who had arrived expecting to discuss the plan for a single theater air force (see previous chapter), instead found himself enmeshed in
Eisenhower's anxious attempts to hurry the Twelfth to the east and to interdict
the flow of Axis reinforcements. The confused state of Doolittle's command
took priority over all other air concerns. At the meeting, Spaatz and his commanding officer "decided to postpone the discussion of the organization of the
Air Force until I [Spaatz] could complete a brief visit to the principal establishments in the North African Theater."[55]

As Spaatz emerged from the Gibraltar meeting, he learned that his chief of
staff, Brig. Gen. Asa N. Duncan, had ditched his B-17 into the Atlantic. Subsequent air search unearthed no trace of his plane, its crew, or passengers. The
AAF had lost a valuable, experienced officer, and Spaatz had lost a friend.

The tour itself was hardly a case of *veni, vidi, vici* for Spaatz. On his tour of the theater he found much to correct while obtaining few concrete results. He and Doolittle left Gibraltar for Africa on the morning of November 18. At Oran, Spaatz noted its excellent repair facilities and "great numbers of [AAF] men who knew what they were doing and who were going about it in a fast and orderly fashion." He gathered a somewhat different impression at Algiers, particularly of its major air facility, Maison Blanche, which he found overcrowded as well as unsuitable for deployment of B-17s. Its location put the heavy-bombers too close to the front, leaving them too exposed to enemy counter-strikes. Typically, Spaatz observed that "the place lacked organization." After a quick stop at Gibraltar to inform his superior of his findings, he flew to Casablanca on November 20. There he conferred with Brig. Gen. John K. Cannon, Commander of the Twelfth Air Support Command (XII ASC). "Uncle Joe" Cannon, although not one of the top AAF decision makers, was only a step below the Arnold, Spaatz, Eaker, and Andrews echelon. Cannon had taken flight training in 1921, had graduated from the Air Corps Tactical School and the Command and General Staff School in the 1930s, and had led the First Air Force's Interceptor Command in 1941. His specialties, pursuit aviation and training, neatly complemented the responsibilities he faced in North Africa. Spaatz reported to Arnold that "my impressions at Casablanca were very favorable"; he noted excellent shop facilities, but added that Casablanca's turf-covered main aerodrome was muddy.[56]

That evening Spaatz returned to Gibraltar once again and spent the next day conferring with Eisenhower and his staff. These conversations resulted in an agreement on the single theater air force that Spaatz and Arnold had championed for months. Eisenhower informed both airmen that he "was going to put in a firm recommendation to that effect but would await, for the moment, the "out-come of the Tunisian fight."[57] This caveat proved the undoing of the unified air plan. The fight in North Africa dragged on so long and absorbed so many resources that it required the creation of a new theater of operations, which made permanent the split in AAF European resources. The most concrete result of the November 21 meetings was Spaatz's transfer from England to North Africa as Eisenhower's chief air adviser.

Spaatz returned to England on November 23. He designated Eaker to command the Eighth Air Force, and shortly thereafter he informed Arnold that "plans are underway for a Theater Air Force Headquarters and integration of the Eighth and Twelfth under its command. . . . With a very small staff I rejoin Eisenhower."[58] Arnold approved these moves and Spaatz flew back to Gibraltar on December 1. The same day the Germans, strongly supported by tanks and air, attacked—driving back the advance elements of the 1st Army. By December 3, the Germans had defeated the 78th Division and substantial portions of the U.S. 1st Armored Division operating under British control. The air superiority the Germans had established over the battlefield proved a decisive factor in their victory.

Also on December 3, Eisenhower appointed Spaatz Acting Deputy Commander in Chief for Air of the Allied forces in North Africa. Spaatz's appointment marked Eisenhower's first attempt to improve the effectiveness of the Allied air forces in his command. Spaatz would coordinate air operations rather than command them, because his new position had only advisory functions. Eisenhower noted, "This arrangement is to meet an emergency."[59] Spaatz wrote to Stratemeyer, the Chief of the AAF Staff, "This is a temporary solution to a situation which will eventually require further clarification."[60]

Temporary or not, Spaatz immediately made his presence felt. On December 2, he had met Doolittle, Brig. Gen. Howard A. Craig, and Vandenberg, who enumerated the difficulties facing them. The Twelfth's leaders especially objected to Eisenhower's directive to both the Twelfth and the EAC to give General Anderson and his 1st Army "everything he asked for."[61] In effect Eisenhower gave complete control of air operations to Anderson, which, as the assembled airmen all agreed, "resulted in misuse of air power."[62] Anderson's daily demands for maximum effort in the defense of his front-line troops meant the dedication of all missions to air defense and ground support operations—an ineffective practice resulting in terrific wear and tear on crews, aircraft, and maintenance personnel. Anderson, in the airmen's opinion, also failed to allot them necessary road and rail transport for their forward fields. Eisenhower's directive chafed the U.S. airmen because its restrictions placed them under the command of a ground force general whose ideas of air power seemed, at best, hazy. Spaatz agreed to broach these problems to Eisenhower as soon as possible.[63]

On December 3, Spaatz established his headquarters. Craig had responsibility for liaison between the Twelfth and Eisenhower's headquarters, AFHQ, while Air Vice-Marshal James M. Robb would handle liaison duties between the EAC and AFHQ. Spaatz also decided to assign deep bombing missions (in current USAF terminology, "deep interdiction" missions) against enemy supply lines to the Twelfth and support of ground operations to the EAC. The light- and medium-bomber units of the Twelfth would be attached to the EAC when the congested supply situation in the forward fields eased.[64]

Spaatz's decision to divide his forces, with one force devoted exclusively to bombing missions behind the enemy's lines and the other devoted solely to the support of ground operations, departed from the then current AAF doctrine of a composite air force, a self-sustaining unit capable of all types of combat and support missions. Of course, the composition of the forces at hand made his decision almost mandatory. The EAC was equipped largely with fighter and other light aircraft, whereas the Twelfth had the only heavy bombers dedicated entirely to the theater. This functional division of December 1942 cleared the way for the AAF to concentrate on daylight precision bombing while giving to the RAF the responsibility of ground support for the 1st Army. It also helped to relieve the increasing congestion of aircraft in the forward airfields. Doolittle and the Twelfth Air Force had literally marched to the sound of the guns, flying groups into the fields before their ground echelons arrived and crowding the EAC. To remedy the situation, the Allied airmen decided to withdraw four squadrons of fighters (out of twelve) from the front to Constantine and to recommit them when the land offensive started.[65]

At Spaatz's insistence, the flow of ULTRA intelligence to the AAF in North Africa greatly increased. Spaatz arranged to have ULTRA and other intelligence reports delivered to him each day by eleven o'clock. Then he and his staff would discuss and analyze the information before he made his daily call to Eisenhower. Spaatz brought the Eighth Air Force Chief of Intelligence, Col. George C. McDonald, from Britain to organize the U.S. intelligence setup. Spaatz had worked closely with McDonald, then Assistant U.S. Military Attaché for Air, during the Battle of Britain and during their stint with the Eighth. McDonald had twenty years' experience in intelligence with a specialty in photographic reconnaissance, to which he had added several months' experience in operations, and a familiarity with ULTRA.[66]

On December 3, Eisenhower, Anderson, Spaatz, and Doolittle met to discuss current operations and future plans. The shortcomings of Allied air power, highlighted during the successful German counterattack of December 1, ranked high on the agenda. Eisenhower reported to the Combined Chiefs of Staff that "the scale of possible air support is not sufficient to keep down the hostile strafing and dive bombing that is largely responsible for breaking up all attempted advances by ground forces."[67] Anderson expressed his attitude in 1st Army's situation report for December 3:

> Unusually heavy dive bombing in the morning. The attempt will definitely be made tomorrow to operate fighters from Medjez el Bab aerodrome in the hope of alleviating the burden this continued dive bombing places on very tired troops whom I cannot relieve for at least three days. Until this air threat can be properly dealt with, there seems no possibility of lessening the effort which I must demand from the R.A.F. and U.S. Squadrons now supporting me.[68]

Spaatz and the other air commanders argued for a partial pause in the air effort in order to arrange for the completion of advanced airfields, the arrival of additional air maintenance troops in the forward area, the positioning of spare parts and supplies in the advanced airfields, and the provision of radar warning and antiaircraft defenses for the forward area.[69]

The current scale of operations could not continue, the airmen contended, if the ground forces wished to have any planes left to support them for the next attack. The EAC, for instance, reported on December 2 almost 100 percent wastage of its Spitfire squadrons. Eisenhower agreed to wait while his air forces improved their logistics and to accept reduced air operations. The bombers, as Spaatz had promised his AAF colleagues, switched to the ports. The fighters would mount a counterair campaign against German airfields. This pause would last until December 9, when the offensive would renew.

Unfortunately, this delay proved the first of many. The rainy season arrived with a vengeance, turning the North African terrain—roads and airfields in particular—into viscous mud that quickly sapped the Allies' desire to advance. As early as November 29, one of the Twelfth's main airfields, Tafaraoui, located a short distance from Oran, had a hard-surface runway but no hard-surface dispersal areas. It reported 285 planes mired in the mud,[70] giving rise to a ditty about "Tafaraoui where the mud is deep and gooey."

In the three weeks from the December 3 meeting to Christmas Eve, Spaatz drove himself and his staff to prepare for a renewal of the Allied offensive. He called the theater's four aviation engineer battalions from Oran and set them to work east of Algiers. Despite the loss of two battalions' worth of equipment in ships that did not reach North Africa and despite confused unloading at the overcrowded North African ports, the engineers performed well. By December 12, the 809th Aviation Engineer Battalion had finished a single well-drained airstrip at Telergma, the start of a medium-bomber airfield complex. Spaatz sent the heavy bombers to Biskra at the end of a spur of the French rail system, on the fringes of the Sahara desert. There an engineer company completed a field in four days.[71] Spaatz ordered every available air transport to ferry bombs, ammunition, fuel, and supplies of all sorts to the front in order to keep his forward fields supplied. As usual, he traveled, visiting Maison Blanche on December 15 (where he noted little improvement since his November 18 inspection), to Anderson's headquarters on December 20 (where Anderson expressed concern that Welsh would not properly support Lawson), and to Biskra on December 21 to check bomb supplies. To increase the effectiveness of planning he prodded his chief of intelligence to get photo reconnaissance in order, especially in front of the 1st Army, so that both the army and air forces could determine bombing targets. Next, he ordered daily early-morning flights over the front line to give air planners some idea of the weather. He did his best not only to improve communications between his headquarters and forward airfields but also to establish links that would enable a unified air command for the theater. All this attention to detail had little immediate effect. Spaatz did not command "general weather."[72] On December 24, after three days of rain had rendered all forward airfields unserviceable,[73] Eisenhower postponed any major offensive for six weeks.

By the end of December, Allied air had not gained air superiority or established effective air support arrangements. Air attempts to cut down the flow of supplies across the Mediterranean to the Axis bridgehead also had encountered difficulties. From November to December, Axis seaborne supply tonnage received in Tunisia increased by 60 percent from 12,627 tons to 21,437; airborne supply tonnage grew sixfold, from 581 tons to 3,503. But because a portion of this increase represented a partial diversion of shipping from Libyan ports overrun by the British, whose supply tonnage dropped by 19,000 tons in December, the total amount of supplies received by the Axis forces in Africa actually decreased by 8,000 tons or almost 25 percent.[74]

Despite the increase in Axis tonnage to Tunisia, Allied interdiction of Axis shipping to Tunisia improved, too—from no Axis supplies shipped to Tunisia lost in November to 23 percent lost in December.[75] Throughout the Mediterranean the Allies sank 17 ships of over 500 tons deadweight in November (12 by air) and increased that total to 32 (14 by air) in December.[76] Apparently most of the shipping losses to air occurred on runs to the Libyan ports. American heavy and medium bombers concentrated their attacks on Tunisian ports, causing disruption, delays, and some damage. Because Tunisian dock workers refused to unload under the constant bombing,[77] debarking troops had to spend a day at the docks unloading supplies before marching to the front—an irritating but not damaging loss of time. Allied air power had a measurable, but not an immediately decisive, effect on Axis supplies.

As the forward movement, but not the fighting, stopped in the Tunisian hills, Eisenhower struggled to set up an effective air organization.[78] In doing so he turned not only to Spaatz, but also to Air Chief Marshal Arthur Tedder, the Air Officer Commanding, Middle East, and one of the premier airmen of the RAF.

In May 1941, at the age of fifty-one, Tedder became Air Officer Commanding in Chief, Middle East. He found himself in the midst of crises on several of the fronts he oversaw. Rommel swept all before him in the Western Desert; the Italians still held out in Abyssinia; dissident Arabs attacked RAF airfields in Iraq; daily air raids struck Malta; and the final stage of the Commonwealth evacuation from Greece had begun. The disastrous battle of Crete and stern fighting in the Western Desert lay ahead. By December 1942, Tedder had already served more than two years fighting the Axis in the Mediterranean. He had learned the bitter lessons of Crete and Tobruk and supplied lessons of his own at El Alamein and during the Axis retreat to Tripoli. No American air commander at that stage of the war matched Tedder's combat experience and practical knowledge of conducting air operations in the face of the German and Italian air forces. Under his and his subordinates', particularly Air Vice-Marshal Arthur Coningham's, leadership, the RAF in the Middle East had become the Allies' most effective ground support air force. Tedder placed himself at Eisenhower's disposal—a display of inter-Allied cooperation much appreciated by the American commander.[79]

Before joining the British army in 1914, Tedder had taken a degree in history from Cambridge and won the Prince Consort Prize for an essay on the Royal Navy during the 1660s. In 1916, he transferred to the Royal Flying Corps. After the war, he served as an instructor at the RAF Staff College; in 1934, he served on the Air Staff as Director of Training in charge of the Armaments Branch; and in 1936, he commanded the Far Eastern Air Force in Singapore where he observed firsthand the interservice disputes that presaged the mismanaged defense of Malaya in 1941–1942.

In 1938, he became Director General of Research and Development and virtually deputy to Air Marshal Wilfred Freeman, in charge of all RAF aircraft production until 1940. Upon leaving the Ministry of Aircraft Production, Tedder joined Air Marshal Arthur Longmore as Deputy Air Officer Commanding in Chief, Middle East. For the next five months he assisted in the operations and administration throughout the vast theater under Longmore's purview. From December 1940 through January 1941, Tedder had direct command of the air forces assisting Lt. Gen. Richard O'Conner's Western Desert Force in its destruction of the Italian *Tenth Army* and the conquest of Libya. When Churchill and Portal lost patience with Longmore's inability to do the impossible, they relieved him and appointed Tedder.[80]

Unlike Harris or Spaatz, Tedder was not identified with a particular type of aviation. Instead, during his wartime service in the Mediterranean, he had spent more than two years in the pit of joint army-navy-air action. He had learned how to balance the conflicting demands of the services while maintaining his own and his service's integrity. He became, out of self-defense, an expert in unified command, acquiring a deep-seated belief in the necessity of joint service operational planning and unity of command for air power under air leaders. After the war he said simply,

> Each of us—Land, Sea, and Air Commanders—had our [*sic*] own special war
> to fight, each of us had his own separate problems; but those separate problems
> were closely interlocked, and each of us had responsibilities one to the other.
> Given mutual understanding of that, you get mutual faith; and only with mutual
> faith will you get the three arms working together as one great war machine.[81]

Tedder had definite opinions on the North African command situation. A visit to Algiers in late November left him deeply disturbed. Eisenhower and his American staff had taken up quarters in a large hotel. The British had taken residence in the naval commander's flagship because of its excellent communications facilities. The two air forces had occupied headquarters miles from each other and from Eisenhower's AFHQ. On November 27, Tedder, after having observed that Doolittle refused to cooperate on a mission requested by the EAC, objected to the "almost crazy" existing air organization. The two separate air forces needed a single commander, preferably an American with a "first class" British deputy. Tedder obviously realized that the Americans, who furnished the majority of the aircraft, would not consent to an overall British air commander. He hoped to bolster the American head with a proven British backup.[82]

In late 1942, Tedder rendered more than advice to the Americans. When he returned to Cairo from North Africa on December 17, he took Brig. Gen. Howard A. Craig with him "for the purpose of furthering his education."[83] In Cairo, Craig visited the Combined War Room and the Joint Operations Staff, where Royal Navy, Army, and Air Force, staffs worked hand-in-hand on operations, intelligence, and planning. When engine trouble delayed Craig's return flight, Tedder urged him to visit Air Vice-Marshal Arthur Coningham, Air Officer Commanding, Western Desert Air Force (WDAF), at Marble Arch, Tripolitania. The WDAF provided close air support to General Bernard Montgomery's British 8th Army.[84]

**Air Chief Marshal
Arthur W. Tedder, Air
Officer Commanding,
Mediterranean Air
Command, RAF,
1941–1943.**

Imperial War Museum

Coningham, a New Zealander who had fought in the Australian-New Zealand Army Corps in World War I, had earned the nickname "Maori," which was soon corrupted by pronunciation to "Mary." A large man with a surprisingly high voice, he impressed most observers with his physical presence and his fervent championship of newly developed British air support doctrine, which he claimed as his own. Before his posting at Tedder's request to the Western Desert, in July 1941, he had commanded No. 4 Group in Great Britain and had been exposed to the machinery of air support being studied and developed by officers of the RAF Army Co-operation Command.[85]

Although many airmen consider Coningham the father of air support doctrine—and he did serve as a conduit of that doctrine to the AAF—the method and technique of air-ground cooperation he used in the desert did not originate with him. As two modern British military historians have pointed out, the growth of cooperation necessary to form and successfully operate a combined-arms team of any sort—be it artillery-infantry, tanks-infantry, or air forces-army—was slow and delicate, requiring time, copious amounts of goodwill, constant human contact, and careful training. Combined-arms cooperation did not become fully functional instantly or merely by decree.[86]

In their excellent history of British military theory, Shelford Bidwell and Dominick Graham present a thorough history of the development of British air support. They begin by noting that the RAF had begun the war with the inten-

148

tion of intervening on the battlefield only in ground emergency. The dividing line between ground and air operations would be the range limit of army artillery.[87] When this plan proved unworkable during the campaign in France, it was discarded in favor of closer air force-army cooperation, which the RAF fostered by forming the Army Co-operation Command. Its commander, Air Marshal Arthur Barrett, and his two chief subordinates, Army Lt. Col. J. Woodall and Group Captain A. Wann, produced an outstanding solution to the problem based on an army-air control system created entirely by Woodall as a result of logical analysis.[88]

Woodall's system had four chief components:

1. The requirement for a properly equipped air formation reserved for the direct support of the field army but under RAF control. This formation would have two tasks: to shield the army from air attack by offensive action against enemy air and to apply airborne firepower on the battlefield itself, coordinating closely with ground operations.

2. A specially trained army staff (Air Liaison Officers—ALOs) able to explain air methods and limitations to soldiers and army methods of operation, planning and situation to pilots assigned to the missions.

3. A joint command post or control center, the Army Air Control Center (AACC), staffed by army and air force officers.

4. A communications network of two links, one from the joint air-army headquarters directly to brigade or lower-level subordinate fighting formations in the

Air Vice-Marshal Arthur Coningham, Air Officer Commanding, Western Desert Air Forces, RAF, 1941–1943.

Imperial War Museum

field, which bypassed intermediate headquarters, and another link direct from the joint command post to the airfields, where the ALOs had access to it. This linking of ground units to the air formations supporting them through only one intervening element greatly speeded up the delivery of air support to the forces needing it. In addition, each headquarters in an army had a signals section, called a "tentacle" (because of its appearance on an organization chart of the communications network), with a signals officer and a staff officer trained in air support.[89]

When Coningham arrived in the desert, he found the WDAF and the British 8th Army smarting from the rough handling they had received in a costly, failed attempt to relieve the Axis siege of Tobruk (Operation BATTLEAXE). Both services saw the need to integrate their efforts. Into the breach stepped "Mary," who added the newly created air-ground method to ongoing joint exercises. In September the British army and the RAF published "Middle East Training Pamphlet No. 3: Direct Air Support." The communications network envisaged by this pamphlet mirrored the network proposed by Woodall and even called the jointly staffed Air Support Control Headquarters (ASCs) established at each corps and armored division headquarters "tentacles." Coningham had apparently gone Woodall one better by providing joint RAF-army staffing for the forward links in the system. The ASCs accompanied the 8th Army for Operation CRUSADER, which relieved Tobruk in late November 1941.[90]

In May 1942, the RAF joined the rest of the British forces in the retreat to El Alamein. Once there, the new system proved its worth during early September, in the defense of Alam Halfa, Montgomery's first battle as commander of the 8th Army. Before the battle, Montgomery, a firm believer in army-air cooperation, and Air Vice-Marshal Coningham had moved their headquarters to a common site, which allowed the AACC to remain in close touch with both army and air staffs. By October 1942, the British 8th Army had virtually perfected the system and used it with decisive effect in the Battle of El Alamein and the pursuit of Rommel's defeated forces.[91]

By the end of the campaign in the desert, Coningham had modified Woodall's system, which had been originally designed to insulate the RAF from army command while providing the army with air support. In the desert the most difficult problem was not preventing the army's command of RAF units but, rather, coordinating the operations of the RAF units themselves. The control of the air and of aircraft in the air revolved around the fighter. As Coningham said, "The fighter governs the front."[92] The fighter gained air superiority over the enemy's fighters, defended against the enemy's strikes, and escorted friendly bombers. As a result, Coningham created a fighter group with a headquarters and an air control center and placed it at a command level directly below the adjacent 8th Army/Western Desert Air Force Headquarters. The fighter group relieved Coningham's headquarters of the burden of detailed operational control, leaving WDAF Headquarters free to concentrate on planning and overall direction of operations.

The fighter group control center contained an army gun operations room,*
an air controller, a duty signals intelligence officer ("Y"), an operations officer,
and two forward bomber control officers. They plotted aircraft tracks on their
operations table and had the radio equipment for controlling aircraft. All bomber,
fighter-bomber, and tactical reconnaissance missions were coordinated through
the control center. The fighter group headquarters and control center were
located as close as possible to the majority of the airfields, which enabled rapid
communications by secure ground lines.[93] This modification curtailed the role
of the AACC and the tentacles, reducing them to the status of a specialized communications network divorced from command.

Coningham's cardinal principle was that the enemy air force had to be driven
from the sky before any other air operations could succeed; hence maximum
force must be focused on an initial counterair campaign. He deplored the employment of air assets in scattered groups and small numbers, called "penny
packets," tied closely to ground troops and conducting purely defensive functions. Penny packets prevented the concentration of force necessary to win the
crucial counterair battle. The achievement of air superiority by aggressive offensive action against enemy aircraft and airfields freed friendly air forces to exercise their flexibility and capacity for rapid concentration at the decisive point.
When conditions did not require concentration, an air force which possessed air
superiority could roam over and behind the battlefield at leisure, harassing or
destroying enemy ground formations and supply lines. As a corollary, Coningham
believed in the centralized control of air operations by an airman working
closely with, but not directly under supervision of, the ground commander.

Although Coningham put his air headquarters in a tent adjacent to Montgomery's own, he maintained that air officers had trained for their task and ought
to be allowed to do it without kibitzing from soldiers with little idea of, or sympathy with, air problems. The RAF's independence from the army greatly assisted
Coningham in the realization of his ideas.[94] Coningham lost no time inculcating his
strictures to Craig, who proved a willing convert. Criag's initial report gave Spaatz,
and through him the AAF hierarchy, additional insight into British methods.

Unfortunately, Coningham's and Montgomery's newfound skills made little
difference in the early stages of the North African campaign. The Americans had
yet to put their doctrine into practice, and the British had not yet fully assimi-
lated the lessons of the Western Desert. Not until February 1943, did the hard-
learned experience of the Western Desert Air Force begin to influence all the
Allied forces in Africa.

---

* The army gun operations room coordinated RAF activities with army artillery to prevent guns
and aircraft from interfering with each other's missions and from attempting fire missions better
suited to either air or ground capabilities. For instance, aircraft could not safely fly into an area
already under artillery fire, but could fly sorties beyond artillery range. There was no need to send
aircraft to attack a target undergoing the more accurate fire of artillery.

Within a few days after Christmas 1942, Eisenhower concluded that the lull in intensive air activity provided the opportunity to jettison the temporary command arrangements of early December. This decision resulted in a short lived, but significant, reorganization, which increased Spaatz's authority and revealed the complexities of inter-Allied politics as they concerned high-level personnel assignments. Eisenhower informed Marshall after careful study and discussions with Tedder, Spaatz, and Coningham, "I have come to the conclusion that a single air commander is necessary."[95] Eisenhower at first wanted Tedder for the position, but upon further consideration chose Spaatz. Eisenhower noted of Spaatz: "He is a sound organizer and has gained, through operating as my deputy commander for air, a very fine picture of our problem here, as well as its relationship with the Mideast and with Great Britain. He is a fine officer and will do a good job."[96]

If Marshall approved of the proposal, Eisenhower intended to present it to the U.S.-British Combined Chiefs of Staff (CCS). Eisenhower did not expect the British to object to the naming of an American to the position because they knew Spaatz and because the Americans would supply the bulk of the bombers and a considerable portion of the fighters to the new command.[97] Two days later, writing to Marshall, Eisenhower explained that he considered it essential for his air commander to retain control of the U.S. heavy bombers in Britain.[98] As long as Spaatz remained the Commanding General, AAF, in the European Theater of Operations, he could call down reinforcements from Britain, whereas a British commander, because of the need to ensure the protection of his homeland, would have a more difficult time doing this. Eisenhower wanted to guarantee his ability to obtain timely air reinforcements.

Churchill and Portal did not care for the appointment of a man with little field experience in the command and administration of a mixed air force to the command of all Allied air forces in North Africa.[99] After some grousing, however, they consented on condition that Spaatz appoint a British officer as his deputy and that his staff contain a British officer experienced in maintenance and supply.[100] Their acquiescence also hinged on their perception that the proper air command arrangements in North Africa would soon be reconsidered at the meeting of President Roosevelt, Prime Minister Churchill, and their Combined Chiefs of Staff at Casablanca in mid-January.[101]

Eisenhower found the British stipulations acceptable. On January 5, 1943, he appointed Spaatz Commander of the Allied Air Force and Air Vice-Marshal James M. Robb as deputy. Eisenhower attempted to follow British suggestions on the internal structure of the Allied Air Force. The British recommended that all their own and U.S. aircraft, irrespective of nationality, be grouped according to their functions, logistic possibilities, and tactical requirements. Because both British and U.S. statutes tied military promotions, discipline, and other functions to the existing Twelfth Air Force and EAC, Eisenhower did not wish to dispense with those organizations. Consequently, he gave the EAC control of general reconnaissance, a striking force to hit enemy shipping, and an air support force to cooperate with the British 1st Army. The Twelfth was assigned the tasks of conducting strategic heavy-bombing missions and providing close air support to the U.S. II Corps in Tunisia. The two existing organizations had by now solved many of the tough administrative and logistical problems facing them in North Africa and their dissolution might reopen Pandora's box.

These new arrangements, which lasted until mid-February 1943, did not ease the Twelfth's basic logistics problem. Spaatz reported to Eisenhower on January 1 that lack of transport prevented any air buildup to support a ground offensive. Two days later, Spaatz repeated to Eisenhower that stockpiles of supplies and preparations were needed at the front. He also asked for a higher priority in allocation of supplies sent forward. The day before his departure for Casablanca on January 19, Spaatz instructed his forces to take advantage of the lull in fighting to strengthen the buildup of repair and maintenance capability and to get replacement aircraft to the front as rapidly as possible. On January 20, he inspected Marrakech, the African terminus of the AAF South Atlantic air ferry route, to clarify the responsibilities of the rear area services of supply and training. All these actions helped to ensure maximum effort in the task of untangling the knotted logistics situation.[102]

The Germans halted the Allied drive or Tunis twenty-five miles short of its goal, a margin of Allied defeat so narrow that a slight change in any of several factors might have brought a different outcome. The men on the spot could not hold back the rainy season, or overcome an overloaded transport system, or build hard-surface airfields in an instant, or correct badly loaded ships. For both air and ground forces, the first phase of the Tunisian campaign was a logistical nightmare. By the end of November, the forward airfields were so overloaded that Eisenhower's Assistant Chief of Staff for Air, Air Vice-Marshal A.P.M. Sanders, reported that it was "imperative that no more U.S. air squadrons should be brought to the East from the Oran and Casablanca areas until the situation regarding airfields and supplies to them can be improved." Sanders added sternly, *"It is useless to send operational air units to them* [forward airfields] *until transportation and communications to keep them effectively supplied and controlled can be established"* [emphasis in original].[103]

In December 1942, Spaatz made solid, if unspectacular, progress toward solving logistical problems, but because of those problems he made less headway in the gaining of air superiority, the provision of close air support, and the interdiction of enemy supply. Successful tactical air operations required superiority in aircraft at the front—and superiority could be achieved only by having an overwhelming number of aircraft at all points or by concentrating the planes available at key points. Both necessitated better logistics. More planes needed more fields and supplies. Concentration at key points needed better command and control of available aircraft.

The Allied Air Force was created to clarify lines of command and thereby ease the ability to concentrate both air forces on one objective. Control of aircraft in the air, which would greatly increase the offensive and defensive power of Allied fighters, awaited the delivery and installation of adequate radio and radar equipment, another function of the logistics system.

In the next phase of the campaign Spaatz directly addressed the problem of tactical air.

Chapter 5

Failure and Reorganization (January–March 1943)

> I have mentioned the need for mutual understanding and mutual faith. This, in the ultimate, comes down to personalities. One thing I have learnt in this late war is that the personality of the few men at the top—commanders and staff—matters far more than conceived.[1]
>
> —*Sir Arthur Tedder, January 9, 1946*

The Casablanca Conference

From January 14 to 24, Winston Churchill, Franklin Roosevelt, and their Combined Chiefs of Staff met at Casablanca, in French Morocco, to settle the Western Alliance's war strategy for 1943. They decided, after putting aside American alternative suggestions, to continue the main effort against the Axis powers in the Mediterranean and to postpone the major invasion across the English Channel into France until 1944. This decision affected both the forces then fighting the Axis in North Africa and the buildup of forces in Britain.

The conference divided Allied forces fighting the European Axis powers into two separate theaters, North Africa and England. Thereupon, the Americans, for their own administrative purposes, formed a separate North African Theater of Operations (NATO) to support the campaign in Tunisia and subsequent operations in the Mediterranean, while maintaining the previously established European Theater of Operations (ETO) to support the strategic bomber offensive against Germany and to prepare for the cross-channel invasion. An AAF officer, Lt. Gen. Frank M. Andrews, replaced Eisenhower as Commanding General, U.S. Army, ETO, and Eisenhower became Commanding General, U.S. Army, NATO. Eisenhower also retained his position as overall Allied Commander in North Africa. Andrews's responsibilities included the prosecution of the U.S. portion of the U.S.-British Combined Bomber Offensive. This offensive,

Lt. Gen. Frank M. Andrews, Commanding General, European Theater of Operations, 1943.

directed against Germany and occupied Europe, received the endorsement of the conferees, who called for "the heaviest possible bomber offensive against the German war effort,"[2] with the ultimate goal of "the progressive destruction and dislocation of the German military, industrial and economic system, and the undermining of the morale of the German people to a point where their capacity for armed resistance is fatally weakened."[3]

The selection of Andrews to fill this post disappointed Spaatz. He wanted to direct the Combined Bomber Offensive himself and had even asked Arnold at Casablanca whether he could return to the Eighth to do so. Arnold told him no, because the new assignments had already been planned at the "very highest levels."[4] Spaatz did not allow this setback to weaken his efforts in North Africa.

The Casablanca Conference spawned yet another reorganization of Allied air power in North Africa, this one along the lines suggested by the British in their earlier proposals. Air Chief Marshal Arthur Tedder became Air Commander in Chief, Mediterranean, in charge of Allied air forces in both the North African and the British Middle East theaters of war. He had two principal subordinates—an air commander for the Middle East (Air Commander in Chief, Middle East, Air Chief Marshal Sholto Douglas) and an air commander for Northwest Africa (Spaatz). Spaatz's combat elements, the U.S. Twelfth Air Force and the British Eastern Air Command (EAC) plus the Western Desert Air Force (WDAF) (including the U.S. Ninth Air Force), which had not yet arrived from Tripolitania, would split to form three functional commands. Doolittle, recently promoted to major general, would oversee the Northwest African Strategic Air Force (NASAF), composed of heavy and medium bombers and their escorting fighters. This force would bomb Axis ports in Italy and Tunisia, attack Axis shipping in transit, and assist the other two air forces if necessary. Air Marshal Arthur Coningham would head up the Northwest African Tactical Air Force (NATAF), composed of Allied fighter-bombers, light and ground-attack bombers, and a force of fighters. This force would provide ground support for the newly formed 18 Army Group, which would take command of all Allied ground forces in Tunisia. Air Marshal Hugh P. Lloyd would command the Northwest African Coastal Air Force (NACAF), composed of fighters, long-range reconnaissance aircraft, and antisubmarine planes. This force would protect Allied shipping and ports.[5]

At the Casablanca Conference Arnold had an opportunity to propound the AAF's strategic views before Roosevelt, Churchill, and their combined military staffs. The AAF also had to stave off a last British attempt to shunt the U.S. bomber force from daylight bombing to night operations. This proposal had the support of the Prime Minister, who became Arnold's major target in a campaign to preserve daylight precision bombing.

The AAF's inability to mount a single bombing raid on the German home-land in the thirteen months since the United States had entered the war had stimulated the Prime Minister's doubts. As late as mid-September 1942, Churchill expressed unreserved support of Spaatz and U.S. daylight heavy bombing. In a personal message to Roosevelt he asked for more B-17s, observing,

> A few hundred fortresses this autumn and winter, while substantial German Air Forces are still held in Russia, may well be worth many more in a year's time when the enemy may be able greatly to reinforce his Western Air Defences. I am sure we should be missing great opportunities if we did not concentrate every available fortress and long range escort fighter as quickly as possible for the attack on our primary enemy.[6]

Within a month, however, the Prime Minister began to take the opposite tack. Opinion within the Air Ministry split. Portal expressed skepticism at the claims of fighters downed by the B-17s and the chances of successful bombing of Germany. "It is rash to prophesy," he told Churchill, "but my own view is that only very large numbers (say 400 to 500) going out at one time will enable the Americans to bomb the Ruhr by daylight with less than 10% casualties and I doubt even then the bombing will be very accurate."[7] Portal indicated a willingness to delay tackling the problem with the Americans until the end of the year, after the U.S. elections and after the AAF had had a chance to ride out a press uproar over the inferior quality of its fighter aircraft.[8]

The Assistant Chief of the Air Staff (Policy), Air Vice-Marshal John Slessor, the RAF senior officer with perhaps the clearest understanding of U.S. determination to carry through with daylight precision bombing, and the civilian head of the RAF, Secretary of State for Air Archibald S. M. Sinclair, warned of the dangers of appearing to thwart U.S. designs. While admitting that Spaatz and his other American friends were "a bit unwarrantably cockahoop" over the success of their early raids, Slessor spoke of their professionalism and resolve to succeed, concluding, "I have a feeling they will do it."9

On October 16, Churchill sent a message to Harry Hopkins that the achievement to date by the B-17s' shallow penetrations, under mainly RAF escort, "does not give our experts the same confidence as yours in the power of the day bomber to operate far into Germany." Churchill asked Hopkins to look into the matter "while time remains and before large mass production is finally fixed."10 The Prime Minister expressed himself more bluntly within his own government. In a note on air policy he predicted a disaster for the Americans as soon as they ventured out from under British escort. Churchill suggested diverting the Americans to antisubmarine patrols and night bombing. As for U.S. aircraft production, Churchill urged that the Americans take up night-bomber production on a large scale.11

Sinclair immediately took up the challenge. The Americans had come to a critical point in their allocation of air priorities, he said, and if the Prime Minister pressed for conversion to night bombing, setting himself "against their cherished policy of daylight penetration," he would confound the very groups in the U.S. military that wished to build up big bomber forces in England during 1943 and 1944:

> It would be a tragedy if we were to frustrate them on the eve of this great experiment. To ally ourselves with the American Navy against General Spaatz and General Eaker and the United States Air Force in this country, and to force them into diverting their highly trained crews to scaring U-Boats instead of bombing Germany would be disastrous. It would weaken and alienate the very forces in the United States on which we depend for support in a European as opposed to a Pacific strategy and for the production of heavy bombers as distinct from the types which it is so much more easy to produce in quantity.12

The Prime Minister replied that Sinclair's impassioned plea had not convinced him of the "merits" of daylight bombing or of the tactics to pursue toward the Americans.13

A few days later, Sinclair, speaking for himself and Portal, reiterated his arguments:

> We feel bound to warn you most seriously against decrying the American plan for daylight attack of GERMANY. We are convinced that it would be fatal to suggest to them at this of all times that the great bomber force they are planning to build up is no good except for coastal work and perhaps ultimately night bombing.

Sinclair pointed out the difficulties Spaatz had encountered in training and keep-

**Archibald Sinclair,
British Secretary of State
for Air, 1940–1945.**

Imperial War Museum

ing an adequate force and spoke of his determination not to fly over Germany
with inadequate numbers and half-trained gunners.[14]

In November Portal advised the Prime Minister against premature scuttling
of the U.S. effort: "I do not think we can decide what to do until we have balanced the probability of success, which may not be very high but is not negligible, against the results of success, if achieved." Success would have tremendous
consequences in wastage for the Luftwaffe fighter forces and destruction of
German industry: "It is solely because of the great prizes that would be gained
by success that I am so keen to give the Americans every possible chance to
achieve it."

Portal suggested that the Americans also be encouraged to press on with
night adaptations and alternative day methods in case daylight precision bombing failed. He, too, repeated the fear that premature opposition to daylight
bombing would lead to the commitment of U.S. resources to other theaters.[15] On
November 21, Portal took the additional step of asking the RAF Delegation in
Washington to press Arnold for an attack on Germany "at the earliest possible
moment without waiting for the build-up of a very large force." The inability of
the AAF to bomb the Reich weakened Portal's defense of not only the shipping
priorities for the aviation fuel, personnel, and supply requirements of the Eighth
Air Force but U.S. bombing policy as well.[16]

Churchill remained unconvinced. In mid-December he noted that the effect of the U.S. bombing effort judged by the numbers of sorties, bombs dropped, and results obtained against the enormous quantities of men and material involved "has been very small indeed." During the previous two months he had "become increasingly doubtful of the daylight bombing of Germany by the American method." If his ally's plan failed, "the consequences will be grievous." The collapse of daylight bombing would stun U.S. public opinion, disrupt an industrial effort increasingly committed to production of bombers unsuitable for night work, and render useless the tens of thousands of American air personnel and their airfields in Britain.[17] Perhaps for domestic political reasons (a certain percentage of the British population objected to the ubiquitous presence of their Allies*), the large, seemingly useless mass of AAF personnel in Britain (which would eventually be dwarfed by the million Americans in Britain before the Normandy invasion) particularly raised the Prime Minister's ire. He returned to it time and again in the course of the debate. Nonetheless, Churchill had fixed his policy:

> We should, of course, continue to give the Americans every encouragement and help in the experiment which they ardently and obstinately wish to make, but we ought to try to persuade them to give as much aid as possible (a) to sea work and (b) to night bombing, and to revise their production, including instruments and training for the sake of these objects.[18]

Churchill's persistence in recommending antisubmarine work reflected the uncertain status of the Battle of the Atlantic in late 1942. The British were losing merchant shipping faster than they could replace it. British import tonnage, the life's blood of an economy not blessed with overwhelming native supplies of raw materials and agricultural resources, had fallen from a prewar annual average of 50 million tons to 23 million tons in 1942. Even the most stringent shipping measures could not close the gap between imports and domestic requirements, which forced the British to consume internal stocks, reducing them to the minimum needed to support the British war effort. In early November, the British came hat in hand to Washington to plead for an additional 7 million tons of U.S.-built shipping, a request Roosevelt granted without even consulting military leaders.[19] But it would take months for American yards to deliver the ships. In the meantime, Churchill felt that a diversion of the U.S. bombing effort to sea work would pay greater dividends in saved shipping, while a reduction in U.S. forces stationed in Britain would conserve tonnage.

---

* The British reduced this resentment to a single phrase: The Yanks were "overpaid, oversexed and over here!" At the end of August 1942, Eighth Air Force personnel in Britain numbered approximately 30,000. By the end of November 1942, transfers to the Twelfth Air Force left only 23,000 AAF personnel in England. The January 1943 rolls carried 36,000 personnel. See Craven and Cate, *Torch to Pointblank*, pp. 599–600. American forces as a whole dropped from 228,000 in October to 135,000 at the end of the year, and to 105,000 by the end of February 1943. See Leighton and Coakley, *Global Logistics*, p. 487.

Sinclair continued to resist what he considered a doubtful policy. He admitted that the RAF might be wrong in its perception that the Americans would pick up their toys and go to the Pacific if threatened, but his officers were convinced that "any attempt to divert the American Air Forces from the function for which they have been trained to a subsidiary role over the sea or in secondary theaters would be fiercely resented and vigorously resisted." If daylight bombing proved unsuccessful, the Americans themselves would abandon it and turn to night action. "They will not turn aside from day bombing," estimated Sinclair, "till they are convinced it has failed; they will not be convinced except by their own experience."[20] Writing just a few days before the Casablanca Conference, Sinclair counseled patience, advising that at the present stage it would be wrong to discourage the Americans from what might still be a successful experiment.[21]

All this drew an exasperated retort from Churchill. The Americans had not even begun their experiment and when they did, it could take four or five months to convince them one way or the other:

> Meanwhile I have never suggested that they should be "discouraged" by us, that is to say we should argue against their policy, but only that they should not be encouraged to persist obstinately and also that they should be actively urged to become capable of night bombing. What I am going to discourage actively, is the sending over of large quantities of these daylight bombers and their enormous ground staffs until the matter is settled one way or the other.[22]

Churchill had not decided against daylight precision bombing, but the time was obviously fast approaching when daylight precision bombing must begin to justify itself by deed rather than potential. Without results the Prime Minister could no longer accept the expenditure of resources devoted to the project. But his threat to halt the buildup of U.S. heavy-bomber groups could, in the end, jeopardize the entire experiment. The precision bombing concept, whatever its emphasis on bombing accuracy, included a large measure of attrition, for both friend and foe, in its formula for success. Without sufficient logistical backup, including large numbers of air crews and bombers, the U.S. effort could not succeed.

The Americans probably first learned officially of Churchill's attitude in an exchange of memorandums between the American and British Chiefs of Staff in late December and early January. Within these memos, which served as the basis of initial discussion at Casablanca, each staff expressed its view on the most advantageous strategy for the Allies to follow in 1943. The Americans wished to hold the North African and Pacific theaters to minimum commitments while mounting a large-scale invasion from England into France. The British favored a continued offensive in the Mediterranean and a more gradual buildup of ground forces in Britain.[23] The clash between the Allies' positions constituted the major story of the conference. The British, who had the majority of troops under arms, aircraft, and shipping, won the dispute, much to the chagrin of Marshall and the Americans. Overall, U.S. air power in 1943 played a minor role in the struggle between U.S. advocacy of the direct strategy versus British support of the indirect approach.

In their initial policy memos, both countries called for air offensives against Germany and Italy. The Americans urged "an integrated air offensive on the largest practicable scale against German production and resources, designed to achieve a progressive deterioration of her war effort."[24] The British Chiefs echoed that call and recommended a combined U.S.-British heavy- and medium-bomber force of 3,000 planes in Britain by the end of 1943. Although the British fully endorsed night bombing, they questioned the efficacy of day bombing:

> In spite of the progress made during recent months by the United States Bomber Command in the bombing of targets in occupied territory, it is still an open question whether regular penetration of the defenses of Germany by daylight will be practicable without prohibitive losses. While every effort should continue to be made to achieve success by day, it is important to arrange that, if the daylight bombing of Germany proves impracticable, it will be possible to convert the United States Bomber Command from a primarily day to a primarily night force with the least possible delay and loss of efficiency.[25]

If he had not earlier received warnings from friends on the RAF staff, Arnold must have quickly learned from them after receiving the memo that it reflected the Prime Minister's opinions.

The abandonment of day bombing, the rock on which all AAF hopes stood, was unthinkable. No matter how reasonable the British suggestion at least to consider and prepare for the possible failure of the experiment may have appeared, it could not be accepted lest it in any way undermine the concept. Once Arnold learned of Churchill's determination to question U.S. bombing, he marshaled some of his biggest guns—Spaatz, Andrews, and Eaker—to help persuade "Big Boy" (Churchill's code name in the preconference planning) to change his mind. The night before the conference opened, January 13, Eaker was ordered to Casablanca. There he worked frantically to prepare a brief to present to the Prime Minister, who had consented to see him.[26] On January 20, Spaatz, Andrews, and Eaker all met Churchill.

Eaker proved by far the most convincing. Writing his memoirs eight years after the event, Churchill admitted his frustration with U.S. bombing: "It was certainly a terrible thing that in the whole of the last six months of 1942 nothing had come of this immense deployment and effort, absolutely nothing, not a single bomb had been dropped on Germany." The intensity of Eaker's defense, which included a promise to attack Germany proper with 100 bombers a minimum of two or three times before February 1 and frequently thereafter,[27] and the telling point he made concerning the advantages of round-the-clock bombing of Germany, changed the Prime Minister's mind. "Considering how much had been staked on this venture by the United States and all they felt about it," stated

Churchill, "I decided to back Eaker and his theme, and I turned around completely and withdrew all my opposition to the daylight bombing by the Fortresses."[28] Eaker recalled that Churchill merely agreed to allow the AAF more time to prove its case.[29]

Eaker's recollection seems more probable. As Churchill had said ten days before the conference, he was not opposed to daylight bombing; he simply wished to encourage nighttime bombing as a reasonable alternative. What Spaatz, Andrews, and Eaker accomplished was to confirm the advice the Prime Minister had already obtained from the RAF Staff and the Secretary of State for Air. The Americans would not abandon daylight bombing until they were convinced it had failed—and they were willing to devote vast amounts of human and material resources to ensure success. And an attack on daylight bombing could not help alienating the AAF, jeopardizing British aircraft allocations, and slowing the bomber buildup in Britain. The Americans had bet enormous stakes on daylight bombing and the Prime Minister, who always felt that night bombing would offer a quicker payoff, realized that they could not be asked to hedge their bet at this particular time. Having won the main point of the conference by keeping the Mediterranean front open (discomforting the U.S. Army and its Chief of Staff in the process), the British knew it would be folly to risk the good will of the AAF and create hard feelings over a matter that would prove itself one way or the other in a few months.

On January 27, Eaker partially fulfilled his promise to the Prime Minister. He dispatched ninety-one heavy bombers against the Emden U-boat yards. Four more raids into Germany, none of which was carried out by more than ninety-three planes, followed in February.[30]

During his twenty-four-hour stay at Casablanca, Spaatz talked to both heads of government. He apparently left his meeting with Churchill and went directly to Roosevelt, with whom he met from 10:00 A.M. to 11:30 A.M. No official record of the meeting exists, and Spaatz did not refer to it in his records. Only Elliott Roosevelt, one of the President's sons, left an account. According to the younger Roosevelt, Spaatz explained the operational difficulties encountered in Tunisia, such as the lack of replacement planes and hard-surface runways, and spoke of the problems of combined command and the difficulty of serving under Tedder.[31] The reference to Tedder does not ring true. In fact, as of January 20, 1943, Spaatz had yet to come under that officer's command. What Spaatz may have explained was the difficulty of coordinating the operations of the EAC and the Twelfth Air Force around inadequate signal organizations and different staff procedures. It seems likely that Spaatz also spoke of daylight bombing, given (1) the British threat to it, (2) his familiarity with the AAF's troubled efforts in Europe, and (3) Roosevelt's, Churchill's, and Portal's questioning of Arnold during the conference on the Eighth Air Force's failure to bomb Germany.[32] If Churchill continued to press for conversion to night bombing, Roosevelt would have to be persuaded to resist. Churchill's reversal, however, eliminated the need for special and immediate support from the President.

While at Casabianca, Spaatz also discussed operations and organization with Marshall, Portal, and Arnold.[33] Arnold, no less frustrated than Churchill over the Eighth Air Force's inability to bomb Germany, had hard questions. Spaatz did his best to lance his chief's frustration before it came to a head. Years later Spaatz recalled, "I remember having a heart to heart talk with Hap, walking along the beach. We talked very, very frankly about daylight bombing and whether it should be carried out or not."[34] Spaatz went on to predict that, in time, British night losses would exceed American daylight casualties. Arnold did not find Spaatz's or Eaker's arguments completely convincing. A month later he complained to Stratemeyer that both "gave the usual and expected reasons for not operating against Germany. Their reasons for not operating more frequently, however, seemed very weak."[35]

On January 21, the Combined Chiefs of Staff issued their first directive on the bomber offensive from Britain. They ordered British and U.S. bomber commanders to "take every opportunity to attack Germany by day, to destroy objectives that are unsuitable for night attack, to sustain continuous pressure on German morale, to impose heavy losses on the German day-fighter force, and to contain German fighter strength away from the Russian and Mediterranean the-

Lt. Gen. Henry H. Arnold, Commanding General, U.S. Army Air Forces, and Air Chief Marshal Charles A. Portal, Chief of the Air Staff, RAF, at the Casablanca Conference, January 1943.

aters of war." The directive specified five targets in priority order: the Germans' submarine construction yards, aircraft industry, transportation, oil plants, and other targets in the German war economy. The directive also authorized attacks on Berlin, "which should be attacked when conditions are suitable for the attainment of especially valuable results unfavorable to the morale of the enemy or favorable to that of Russia." Finally, the directive ordered the Allied bomber commanders to support the Allied armies when it came time for the cross-channel invasion.[36]

Eaker had gained his chance to conduct the daylight bombing experiment. Unfortunately for him, the calls of other theaters for shipping and planes effectively reduced the Eighth Air Force to the lowest priority, starving him of resources and hamstringing him throughout his tenure in England.

Operations, Personalities, and Teamwork

The postponement of the Allied offensive in late December because of bad weather, exhaustion of front-line troops and aircraft, and the need to bring up reinforcements, most of them American, led to the formation of an overall U.S. ground command in Tunisia, the U.S. II Corps, which would occupy central Tunisia, taking a position to the right of the Allied line. The British 1st Army occupied the Allied left, while the under-equipped French XIX Corps occupied defensive positions in the relatively impassable center of the Allied lines. If all went well, Eisenhower hoped to have II Corps drive to the coast, separating the Germans in Tunisia from Rommel's forces retreating from Libya. Eisenhower exercised direct operational control over the U.S., British, and French national contingents. At the front no unified ground command existed. (For a view of the terrain in Tunisia, see Map 6.)

The air organization paralleled the ground forces' division into national contingents. Spaatz ordered the EAC to support the British 1st Army and the Twelfth Air Force to support U.S. II Corps and all U.S. land forces in North Africa.[37] The French had a small air force but depended on their Allies for air support. Neither the EAC's No. 242 Group nor the Twelfth's XII Air Support Command, the subordinate organizations charged with cooperating with the land forces, was assigned directly to the land forces they assisted.[38] In fact, at no time during the campaign were AAF combat units, as opposed to observation and reconnaissance units, ever directly assigned or attached to U.S. Army units.

When the Allies began to contemplate moving a large U.S. ground formation into the front line, they may have considered creating an American army rather than an American corps to control the U.S. ground forces in Tunisia.[39] On December 30, Spaatz and Lt. Gen. Mark Clark, the Commanding General of the American Fifth Army, then forming and training in the western TORCH area, toured the battle area. Political considerations probably scotched the move. An American army would have competed for prestige with Anderson's 1st Army

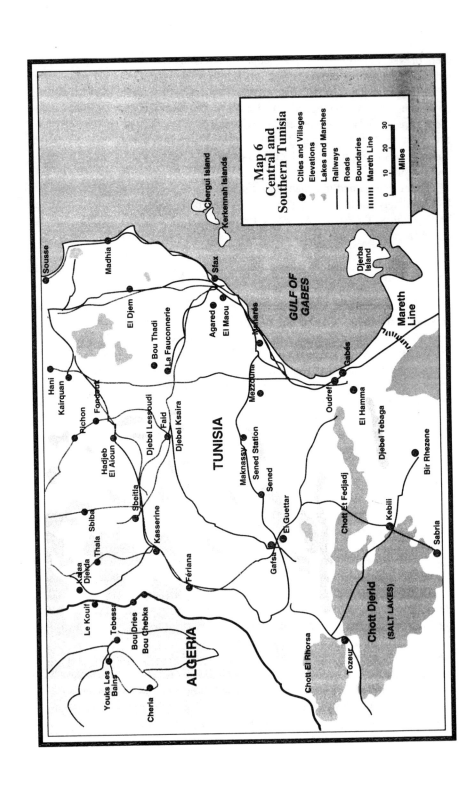

Map 6
Central and
Southern Tunisia

Cities and Villages
Elevations
Lakes and Marshes
Railways
Roads
Boundaries
Mareth Line

Miles
0 10 20 30

GULF OF
GABES

Chergui Island
Kerkennah Islands

Djerba
Island

Mareth
Line

Sousse
Madhia
Sfax
El Djem
Bou Thadi
La Fauconnerie
Agared
El Maou
Mahares
Gabés
Oudref
El Hamma
Djebel Tebaga
Bir Rhezene

Hani
Kairouan
Pichon
Fondouk
Djebel Lessoudi
Faïd
Djebel Ksaïra
Hadjeb
El Aioun
Maknassy
Sened Station
Sened
Mezzouna
Sbeitla
Kasserine
El Guettar
Gafsa
Fériana
Sbiba
Thala
Kalaa
Djerda
Le Kouif
Tebessa
Bou Dries
Bou Chebka
Youks Les
Bains
Cheria

TUNISIA

ALGERIA

Chott El Fedjadj
Kebili
Sabria

Chott El Rhorsa
Tozeur

Chott Djerid
(SALT LAKES)

Maj. Gen. Lloyd R. Fredendall, Commanding General, U.S. II Corps, North Africa, January–March 1943.

and if defeated would have lost a commensurate amount for the inexperienced Americans. Furthermore, the size of the contemplated U.S. force, little more than a reinforced division to start with, hardly justified an army headquarters. Therefore, Eisenhower decided to assign a corps to the area. He then faced the problem of selecting an officer to head the largest American unit to fight the European Axis to date.

Eisenhower quickly narrowed the choice to two men close at hand, the commanders of the U.S. invasion task forces—Maj. Gen. George S. Patton in Casablanca and Maj. Gen. Lloyd R. Fredendall in Oran. Both had some experience in corps commands and in actual combat against the Germans. Patton, fifty-six years of age, had served in the cavalry after graduating from West Point. After his service in World War I, he had transferred to the armored forces. He played a large part in the great prewar (1941) Carolina and Louisiana maneuvers and, at the time of his selection for TORCH, commanded the I Armored Corps at the Desert Training Center. It was during Patton's tenure there that Devers and others had become dissatisfied with the AAF support given to training.

Patton, scion of one of the wealthiest families in California and a thoughtful, extremely well-read student of his profession, was a man of extraordinary strengths and failings. Perhaps the finest American combat ground commander of

167

World War II, he was also an egomaniac and a mystic. Subject to violent emotions, he was a great actor who was not above throwing tantrums or kisses to get his way. At this stage of the war his eccentricities, such as rabid Anglophobia, seemed to outweigh his potential, so Eisenhower picked Fredendall instead.[40]

Maj. Gen. Lloyd R. Fredendall, at age fifty-eight, had done well in the Army, despite his failure to complete West Point. His specialty was training, and he had previously commanded the II Corps before it went overseas. It was during his command of II Corps in May 1942 that the AAF had botched a large-scale air-ground exercise at Fort Benning. Marshall had recommended him for TORCH and Eisenhower had asked for him. He, like Patton, was senior to Eisenhower in service, but seniority never seemed to have been a serious problem. The short, stocky Fredendall projected a gruff image every bit as rough as Patton's. He was outspoken and did not hesitate to criticize either his superiors or his subordinates. He formed judgments rapidly, often with insufficient or inaccurate information, but was impatient with the recommendations of his subordinates. He had a habit of issuing bombastic, colorful, but imprecise messages. At a key point in the Kasserine engagements, for example, he told a subordinate, "I want you to go to Kasserine right away and pull a Stonewall Jackson. Take over up there." Although he did not lack personal courage, Fredendall, for reasons that are still obscure, ensconced himself in an elaborate dug-in headquarters established far behind the front, which he seldom left. The complex amazed and disgusted almost all outside observers.[41] Soon after taking over on January 1, he developed extremely bad relations with Maj. Gen. Orlando P. Ward, the commander of his principal combat unit, the 1st Armored Division. He soon began to ignore Ward to deal directly with one of Ward's subordinates, Brig. Gen. Paul M. Robinett. Nor did Fredendall have any affection for the French or the British; he particularly disliked General Anderson.[42] (See Chart 1, Allied Chain of Command, January 6, 1943.)

Fredendall certainly appears to have been misjudged by Eisenhower given his failure in battle seven weeks later and his replacement by Patton. On December 10, Eisenhower rated Fredendall behind Patton, remarking, "Patton I think comes closest to meeting every requirement made on a commander. Just after him I would rate Fredendall, although I do not believe the latter has the imagination in foreseeing and preparing for possible jobs of the future that Patton possesses."[43] On February 4, Eisenhower recommended promotions to lieutenant general for both Patton and Fredendall, after assuring Marshall that he had "now eliminated from my mind all doubts I had as to Fredendall."[44] Yet, also in a February 4 message, Eisenhower critized Fredendall's complaints about the British, his command's lack of road discipline which caused extensive traffic jams and offered tempting targets to Axis aircraft, and the "habit of some of our generals in staying too close to their command posts."[45] The letter indicated that Eisenhower may not have rid himself of doubts after all.

Fredendall, surprisingly, had no problems getting along with the successive

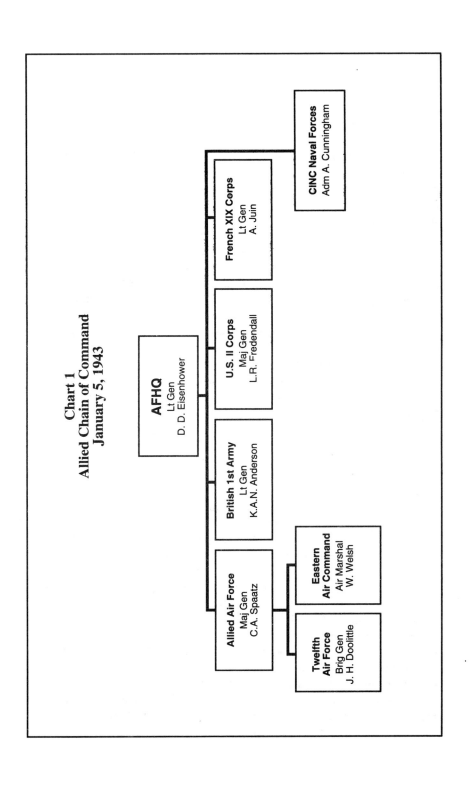

Chart 1
Allied Chain of Command
January 5, 1943

commanding officers of the XII Air Support Command (XII ASC), the Twelfth Air Force unit charged with II Corps air support. Because he did not move his headquarters, the commanders of the XII ASC, who had co-located their headquarters with Fredendall's, had no problem maintaining contact with him or setting up semipermanent communications facilities with their subordinate air units. And despite his refusal to help the French, Fredendall did not interfere unduly with the operations of the XII ASC. Col. Paul L. Williams, who led the XII ASC from late January to the end of the campaign, noted in an official report, "General FREDENDALL and General PATTON both stated in substance, 'Don't wait for us to order air missions, you know what the situation is, just keep pounding them.'"[46]

The lack of air-ground teamwork between II Corps and XII ASC was more the fault of XII ASC than of II Corps. Frequent changes of command, assignments, and stations robbed the XII ASC of the continuity of training and cooperation with familiar ground units necessary for ground support work. Doolittle had hastily formed the XII Air Support Command, under the command of Brig. Gen. John K. Cannon, even later than the rest of the Twelfth Air Force when the Casablanca invasion was added to TORCH. Once ashore in Casablanca, more than 1,000 miles from Tunis, the XII Air Support Command trained with Clark's Fifth Army. When II Corps entered Tunisia, XII ASC split in two, part going with II Corps and a small part, XII ASC Detachment, staying with Clark. Cannon took over XII Bomber Command, and Brig. Gen. Howard A. Craig left Spaatz's headquarters to take over XII ASC. This would seem to have been an inspired choice, because Craig had just received the tablets containing the commandments governing the application of close air support from the hands of Coningham, but Craig failed to gain Doolittle's confidence. In the midst of the German counterattack of January 18–25 (described later), Doolittle wrote to Spaatz that although Craig was a brilliant staff officer and one of the AAF's exceptional planners and organizers, his current job did not suit his capabilities. Doolittle suggested that Craig move to the XII ASC Detachment with Clark and that Col. Paul L. Williams replace him. Of Williams, Doolittle said, "Williams is better suited as a result of experience and temperament to command and lead combat units in support of ground troops in an extremely active forward area."[47] The next day, January 21, Spaatz sent Williams to the XII ASC, noting that Craig would become Tedder's chief of staff in the coming Casablanca-dictated air reorganization.[48] The XII ASC now had its third commander in three weeks, two of whom had had no chance to become acquainted with its personnel, its condition, and the troops and ground commander it supported. This switch occurred precisely when a German counterattack against the French XIX Corps contributed to the Allies' disjointed air response.

Beyond its unfamiliar leaders the XII ASC suffered under many operational handicaps. The rainy season limited operations and turned the airfields to mud. The airfields themselves were too distant from the front lines and meagerly equipped. Insufficient logistics and lack of experience, already cited, contributed to a very low operational ready rate, subtracting even more planes from the command's order of battle. The XII ASC had two further problems. (1) It lacked radar coverage of its front. This cut down its warning and reaction times to German air operations and forced it to rely on chance sweeps to catch German aircraft aloft or on their fields. The Germans, who had complete radar coverage, avoided these sweeps. Their dive-bombers would merely land for five minutes or so until the Allied aircraft passed and then resume their deadly work. (2) By mid-January the command had already fought several of its units to exhaustion. Doolittle reported to Spaatz that the Twelfth's entire striking force consisted of nine groups with a total of 270 planes—only 48 percent of their full strength.[49] Doolittle's figures included the Twelfth's heavy bombers. The XII ASC operations report showed only twenty-six P-40s, nineteen P-39s, and thirty-eight A-20s operational on January 13—numbers that rose to fifty-two P-40s, twenty-three P-39s, twenty-seven A-20s, and eight DB-7s by January 26.[50] Under these circumstances the chances that II Corps and XII ASC could form an effective air-ground team in a few weeks were nil.

The British half of Spaatz's Allied Air Force suffered from many of the same problems, but personalities played an even greater role in disrupting its operations. Lt. Gen. Kenneth A. N. Anderson, because of his wartime experiences, had simply never acquired an understanding of air operations. During the fall of France, he had served as a brigade commander in the British Expeditionary Force. Shortly before Dunkirk, he took over a decimated division and, for the next two and one-half years, he trained troops in England. His only memories of air were searing ones of the overwhelming ground-support effort of the Luftwaffe and the inadequate response of the RAF. His first experiences in North Africa confirmed these memories as his supply ships went down at Bougie, his forward lines were dive-bombed incessantly, and the Luftwaffe maintained air superiority over his front. Understandably, he tended to be defensive-minded as far as air was concerned.

Nor did Anderson's personality facilitate cooperation. He was an unusually reserved and reticent Scot, stubborn in his opinions and congenitally pessimistic in his assessments of military operations.[51] During the preparations for TORCH, these qualities occasionally manifested themselves. He clashed with the British navy over use of landing craft. His American subordinate for the Algiers invasion, Maj. Gen. Charles W. Ryder, was warned, upon receiving his assignment, to get along with Anderson "no matter how difficult it may be."[52] Anderson's chief of staff, Brigadier C.V.O'N. McNabb, had all of Anderson's poor qualities, in spades. He was reticent to the point of secretiveness, and few Americans could approach him, let alone come to know him.[53]

Anderson's relations with the RAF commanders proved particularly acrimonious. RAF semiofficial histories admit that Air Marshal William Welsh's and Anderson's mutual antipathy took precedence over the conduct of their duties.[54]

Almost immediately after the EAC and 1st Army landed in North Africa, arrangements between the two men broke down. Anderson and Welsh were to arrange air support together, but they soon went their separate ways. Welsh stayed in Algiers to supervise air defense and convoy protection while Anderson moved forward to a spartan headquarters, deficient in signal organization but close to the front. Welsh's failure to follow disappointed Anderson. Instead, Air Commodore G. M. Lawson, with a small RAF command post, moved forward with Anderson and attempted to meet his air-support demands. Further forward, EAC had a wing commander with the 78th Division and with British 5th Corps, which took over the British front at the end of November. Both men had insufficient rank for their task of cooperating with Army counterparts who outranked them by at least two grades. The formation of No. 242 Group, a headquarters unit commanding all British aircraft assigned to the support of the 1st Army, its placement under Lawson's command, and its co-location with 5 Corps improved the system slightly. However, EAC Headquarters failed to maintain close liaison with No. 242 Group. In addition Welsh, consumed by his other duties, made few planes available to No. 242 Group and when Lawson ordered his fighter squadrons out on ground strafing missions, Welsh stopped him. By January 4, 1943, Lawson had only a handful of fighter-bombers available to him.[55]

Neither the Americans nor the British had a fully functioning air-ground support team. By the middle of February this lack of air-ground cohesiveness would hamper the Allied response to the German counterattack at the Kasserine Pass.

As II Corps came into the line during the first two weeks of January, the Allies planned to use it for a drive to the coast to separate the Axis forces in Tunisia from Rommel's retreating forces. Fredendall made preparations for that attack until mid-January, when logistical difficulties and an unexpectedly rapid approach by Rommel led Eisenhower to order him to assume a defensive stance. From January 18 to 25, a counterattack by the Axis forces in Tunisia on the center of the Allied line gained important mountain passes and alarmed the Allies before it was contained. Allied tactical air flew several useful missions in the course of this assault.[56] A few days later, from January 30 to February 3, the sparring between Allied and Axis forces shifted to the south. Once again, the Axis gained key passes from the French, especially the Faid Pass, which could serve as a jumping-off point for attacks on II Corps' main supply depot at Tebessa and the airfields at Thelepte. Sandy soil conditions, which promoted excellent drainage, allowed Thelepte to operate in any weather, a crucial factor in Tunisian air operations. Axis dive-bombing attacks harassed the Americans, particularly during an unsuccessful U.S. attack on the village of Maknassey. One German air attack on January 31, 1943, struck a U.S. infantry battalion aboard a truck convoy in daylight, causing substantial casualties.[57]

The Allies remained on the defensive at the beginning of February as Rommel's forces joined their comrades in Tunisia and prepared to take the offensive before Montgomery's British 8th Army could come to the assistance of Eisenhower's forces. The Germans began the so-called "Battle of the Kasserine Pass" by breaking out of the Faid Pass and seizing the important crossroad at Sidi Bou Zid. They continued forward, capturing several positions, including Thelepte, by February 17. On February 20, under the eyes of Rommel himself, Axis forces stormed the Kasserine Pass, badly damaging several units of the U.S. 1st Armored Division. At that point Allied defenses stiffened. The Axis, concerned about the approach of Montgomery and their own lack of supplies, began to withdraw from the Kasserine Pass on February 22. They were pursued only hesitantly by Allied ground forces, who reoccupied the entire pass by February 24. This withdrawal ended the largest Axis attack of the campaign and gave them a tactical victory but produced no strategic effect. The Allies soon replaced their heavy losses in men and matériel.

This summary of ground operations outlines the campaign's events in the winter of 1942–1943. The activities of Spaatz and of Allied air-ground operations during the period are the subjects of the following pages.

Before the decisions affecting air organization made at Casablanca could take effect, the German counterattack of January 18 to 25 struck the boundary between the British and French forces in Tunisia, forcing them to give ground and, in the process, revealing serious deficiencies in overall coordination among the different Allied forces. In one instance, the XIIth Air Support Command, acting under Fredendall's orders, refused to send planes over an area for which RAF No. 242 Group had responsibility.[58]

Spaatz, after inspecting facilities in Marrakech, returned to Eisenhower's headquarters (AFHQ) in Algiers on January 21. There he participated in an emergency conference on the German attack against the French, during which he informed Eisenhower of the new air arrangements mandated at Casablanca.[59] The conference minutes noted, "It was evident also that collaboration by air forces was faulty to date, due particularly to the absence of an air headquarters with executive authority as far forward as Advanced Headquarters [General Anderson's headquarters in Constantine]."[60] Eisenhower remedied this problem by directing Spaatz "to place at Advanced Headquarters immediately an officer who will be in executive control [in command of] the air forces supporting General Fredendall and General Anderson."[61] Eisenhower authorized that air officer to secure the assistance of the Northwest African Strategic Air Force if specifically requested, but required him to "receive his instructions for battle from General Anderson so far as they affect all air forces allotted to the support of the ground armies."

Eisenhower had taken a large step toward improving air support, but in making the air commander subordinate to the ground commander he overlooked an essential piece of the more successful British method developed under Coningham—the equality of land and air. In his own mind, at least, Eisenhower remained faithful to the strictures of FM 31-35. As late as January 15, 1943, he could write, "We have a published doctrine that has not been proved faulty."[62] On January 22, Spaatz assigned Brig. Gen. Laurence S. Kuter as Acting Chief of the Allied Air Support Command (AASC). When Coningham arrived, he relieved Kuter. (See Chart 2, Allied Chain of Command, January 30, 1943.)

In another action resulting from the emergency conference, Eisenhower charged Anderson with the task of "co-ordinating" the entire front. Three days later, on January 24, Eisenhower made Anderson responsible for the employment of U.S. forces, and that evening the French commander, General Alphonse Juin, agreed to place his forces under Anderson. The western Tunisian front now had one overall ground and air commander. It did not yet have an air-ground team.

At this point, Spaatz replaced Brig. Gen. Howard A. Craig with Col. Paul L. Williams as Commander of the XII Air Support Command. Williams, who had specialized in attack and observation aviation before the war and had commanded air support formations in the prewar maneuvers, stayed with XII ASC until the campaign's end. Spaatz had brought him to Britain and then to North Africa precisely because of his experience in army cooperation. The XII ASC and No. 242 Group made up the bulk of Kuter's new command.[63]

In Algiers, Spaatz began a round of meetings that would take him to Cairo and back. On January 24, he met Arnold, who had come directly from Casablanca. They decided to equip all AAF fighter units in Britain only with P-47s—a decision that would free all P-38s then based in Britain for deployment to Africa. This key decision, based in part on operational necessity and in part on logistical considerations, deprived the Eighth Air Force of the long-range escort fighters it would need to protect its deep-penetration operations over Germany. It demonstrated the AAF's refusal to accept the need for long-range escort for strategic bombers as the highest priority. Late on January 26, Spaatz left Algiers for Cairo and, upon arriving the next morning, joined in three days of discussions with Tedder, Arnold, Andrews, and Maj. Gen. Louis H. Brereton, the Commanding General of the Ninth Air Force, to settle the details of the new Allied organization in the Mediterranean.[64] He returned to Algiers on January 31.

On February 4, in the wake of another Axis thrust, Spaatz flew to Constantine. That evening he and Brig. Gen. John K. Cannon called on Maj. Gen. Lucian K. Truscott, Eisenhower's representative at the front, to inform him of their intention to visit Fredendall's II Corps Headquarters the next day. During their visit, Spaatz elaborated on his own views toward the use of aviation in conjunction with ground operations: "It was a mistake to use up all of one's force in an indecisive operation; the air force should be used to hit the soft parts of the enemy and in return to protect the soft parts of one's own force; and only in the event of an all-out decisive engagement was the loss of a whole force to be risked."[65]

The next day, Spaatz and his party traveled to Tebessa to meet Anderson, who had apparently come south to discuss future operations with Fredendall.[66] Once again, the conversation turned to air support. Brigadier McNabb,

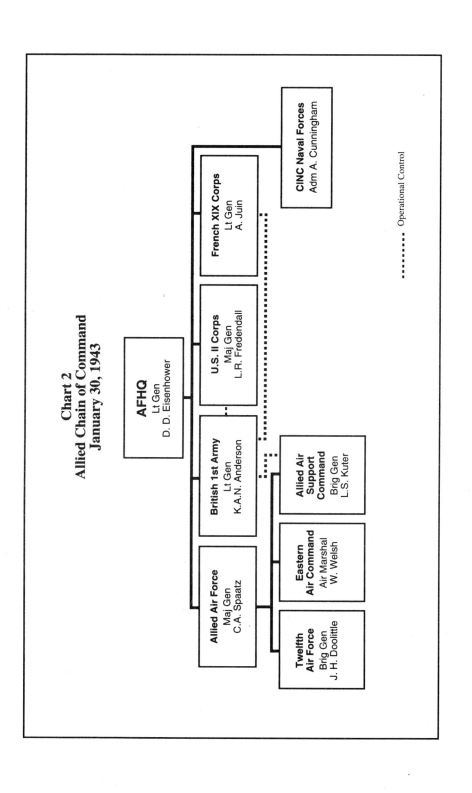

Chart 2
Allied Chain of Command
January 30, 1943

AFHQ
Lt Gen
D. D. Eisenhower

British 1st Army
Lt Gen
K.A.N. Anderson

U.S. II Corps
Maj Gen
L.R. Fredendall

French XIX Corps
Lt Gen
A. Juin

CINC Naval Forces
Adm A. Cunningham

Allied Air Force
Maj Gen
C.A. Spaatz

Eastern
Air Command
Air Marshal
W. Welsh

Allied Air
Support
Command
Brig Gen
L.S. Kuter

Twelfth
Air Force
Brig Gen
J. H. Doolittle

••••••••• Operational Control

Anderson's chief of staff, referring to a local Allied counterattack planned for the next day,[67] gave the 1st Army's views:

> . . . General Anderson wanted the whole air effort put on the ground positions immediately in front of our troops in the coming offensive, in as much as the ground striking force was weak in artillery. General Anderson had stated the day before that this should be the main effort of all air strength available, that this was the primary job to be done and that he was not interested in the bombing of enemy airdromes such as that at Gabes.[68]

Here was an airman's bête noire. Anderson wanted to ignore counterair operations to use support aircraft as artillery pieces.

After lunch, the party proceeded to General Fredendall's dug-in command post, where they encountered more evidence of the Allied ground commander's parochial view of air support. Generals Spaatz, Fredendall, Truscott, and Kuter and Colonel Williams all participated in an informal discussion. Fredendall, no doubt recalling the Axis dive-bombing against his troops in the recent attack on Maknassey, wanted full air cover for the first two days of his attack in order to protect his troops and artillery. Spaatz observed: "He wanted his men to see some bombs dropped on the position immediately in front of them, and if possible, some dive bombers brought down in sight of his troops." Spaatz had practically used up his medium-bomber and P-40 fighter groups in air support, and the replacement rate of both pilots and machines would not allow for continued wastage on such an extravagant scale. He preferred that the air force hit enemy airfields, tank parks, troop convoys, and motor transport concentrations while protecting Allied vulnerabilities such as supply lines. If he "maintained a constant 'umbrella' over one small section of the front, with only shallow penetration by [his own] bombers and fighters, then [his] available force would be dissipated without any lasting effect." Spaatz insisted that the "hard core" of any army ought to have the ability to defend itself against dive-bombing. Fredendall granted the last point, but admonished that if he did not get forty-eight hours' air cover from the start, the offensive would fail.[69] In any case, Eisenhower canceled the contemplated offensive, and the exact nature of air cover for the land forces was unresolved.

This was not the first run-in between Spaatz and Fredendall. On January 17, Spaatz had flown to Tebessa, at Doolittle's urging, to straighten out air support matters. Doolittle had passed word that Craig, the Commander of the XII ASC, could not "adequately" handle the situation. Spaatz discovered that Craig would have brought the situation under control if it had not been for the interference of Fredendall who, among other things, willfully compromised the security of the highly secret radar on the night-fighting British Beaufighters. He had ordered them to patrol over Axis air space—an action contrary to Anglo-American agreements. Spaatz went on to II Corps Headquarters to try to hammer out some *modus vivendi*. He laconically noted in his diary:

Informed him that the arbitrary decisions made by him with reference to the use of air forces by Craig at Tebessa resulted in confusion, and recited the instances. Told him that the only logical place for the Ground Support Commander was alongside of him to prevent him from making damn fool decisions.

Fredendall agreed temporarily to abide by Craig's decisions.[70]

When Spaatz returned to Algiers the following day, he flew on the same aircraft as Brig. Gen. Ray E. Porter, an infantry officer returning from Fredendall's staff for reassignment as the Assistant Chief of Staff, Organization and Training Division, G-3, in Washington, D.C. This was a key post for the approval of official War Department doctrine, and Porter would later have a hand in incorporating the North African experiences into new air doctrine. Porter expressed views on air support that Spaatz must have found refreshing. He noted that the vast majority of all U.S. casualties attributable to dive-bombing resulted from the single Axis raid near Maknassey in which an incompetent battalion commander had brought his men forward, in daylight, in a truck convoy jammed nose to tail. Porter "further stated that after one or two dive bomber attacks, the men could take care of themselves and were no longer seriously affected in their morale." Finally, Porter echoed an opinion becoming increasingly common at the front: "He believed a defensive fear complex was being built up at 2nd Corps as evidenced by their elaborate bomb proofs for their Headquarters, which in its initial location was so well concealed as to present very little chance for a bombing attack."[71]

After three months of combat operations, the top Allied ground commanders and the top Allied air commander were still unable to agree on a satisfactory ground-support method. Fredendall, backed by his interpretation of War Department doctrine, and Anderson, untutored in the air-ground experiences of the British 8th Army, wanted to use aircraft either as artillery or as an aerial defensive garrison over key points. The airmen rejected these ideas as impracticable. They wished to employ their forces to attack the enemy air force and other vulnerable areas behind the front lines. At the point of combat, the airmen reasoned, the ground troops had the equipment and training to fend for themselves; in their view, infantry, armor, and artillery did not constitute the "soft points" of the army. The ground commanders found this stand unacceptable. The logjam would continue until mid-February when the major German attack at the Kasserine Pass and Coningham's arrival to command the Northwest African Tactical Air Force would offer the beginnings of a solution.

Reorganization and the Kasserine Pass

Spaatz remained hard at work on the air reorganization until its implementation. He wrote to Arnold on February 8 that he hoped to have the first stage in place in a few days. His staff had already prepared the orders and they were only awaiting Tedder's return from London to issue them.[72] To the Chief of the Air Staff, Maj. Gen. George Stratemeyer, Spaatz confided:

> The most serious difficulty which I see confronting us is the different conception which obtains in the RAF and in our own War Department as to the place of aviation. It is difficult to have aviation treated as a co-equal with the Army and Navy in our set up, whereas the RAF will not submit to being considered in any other way. A number of instances have developed indicating that the ground general considers his air support as a fundamental part of his forces, even to the point of dictating as to how to do the job. Such employment, I am afraid, will not be accepted by the RAF. With Coningham, a full-fledged veteran of the Battle of the Mediterranean with all of his prestige behind it, at the head of our Air Support command, it can readily be seen that something is bound to break out in a very short period.[73]

Tedder and Coningham returned from London on February 14, the same day the Germans launched their greatest attack of the campaign. In the midst of this series of engagements, which included the sanguinary American defeat at the Kasserine Pass, the Allies instituted the command changes agreed on at Casablanca: Fleet Adm. Andrew Cunningham became Naval Commander in Chief, Mediterranean; General Harold L. Alexander became Deputy Commander in Chief of the Allied Force and head of the 18 Army Group, comprising the British 1st and 8th Armies, the French XIX Corps, and the U.S. II Corps; Tedder became head of the Mediterranean Air Command (MAC). (See Chart 3, Organization of Allied Air Power, February 18, 1943.)

MAC Headquarters consisted of a small policy and planning staff, "a brain trust without executive authority or domestic responsibilities."[74] In the North African Theater, MAC's operations came under AFHQ's control. There MAC operated through its own subordinate command, the Northwest African Air Forces (NAAF), under the command of Spaatz. NAAF began operations on February 18, when the Allied Air Force disbanded. The U.S. Twelfth Air Force and British Eastern Air Command, joined on February 21 by the Anglo-American Western Desert Air Force, made up NAAF's major subelements: the Northwest African Tactical Air Force (NATAF), the Northwest African Coastal Air Force (NACAF), and the Northwest African Strategic Air Force (NASAF). Spaatz's own headquarters was transferred virtually intact from the Allied Air Force. Spaatz set up an operational headquarters in Constantine, near Doolittle's and Coningham's headquarters, and left an administrative section in Algiers. Throughout the NAAF and its subordinate air forces, AAF and RAF personnel occupied alternating command and staff positions down to, but not including,

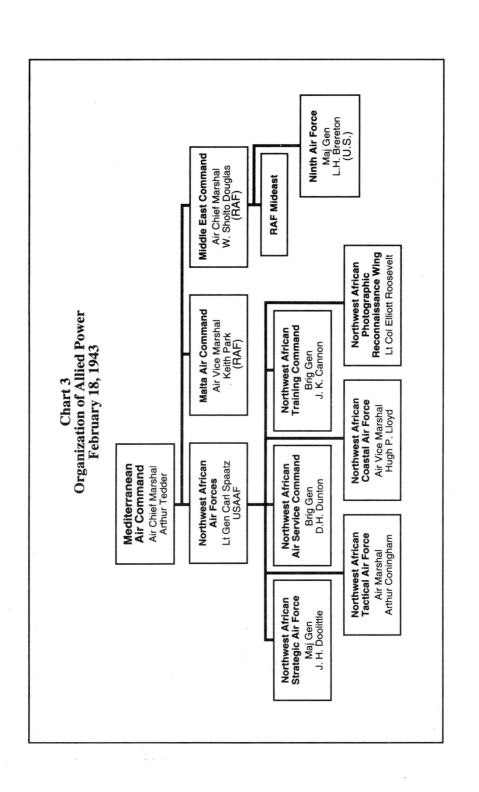

Chart 3
Organization of Allied Power
February 18, 1943

Mediterranean Air Command
Air Chief Marshal
Arthur Tedder

Northwest African Air Forces
Lt Gen Carl Spaatz
USAAF

Malta Air Command
Air Vice Marshal
Keith Park
(RAF)

Middle East Command
Air Chief Marshal
W. Sholto Douglas
(RAF)

RAF Mideast

Ninth Air Force
Maj Gen
L.H. Brereton
(U.S.)

Northwest African Strategic Air Force
Maj Gen
J. H. Doolittle

Northwest African Tactical Air Force
Air Marshal
Arthur Coningham

Northwest African Air Service Command
Brig Gen
D.H. Dunton

Northwest African Coastal Air Force
Air Vice Marshal
Hugh P. Lloyd

Northwest African Training Command
Brig Gen
J. K. Cannon

Northwest African Photographic Reconnaissance Wing
Lt Col Elliott Roosevelt

Imperial War Museum

The new Allied leadership, February 18, 1943. *Bottom row, left to right*: **General Dwight D. Eisenhower, Air Chief Marshal Arthur W. Tedder, General Harold R. L. G. Alexander, and Admiral Andrew B. Cunningham;** *top row, left to right*: **Harold Macmillan (British Minister, AFHQ), Maj. Gen. Walter Bedell Smith, Commodore Royer M. Dick, and Air Vice-Marshal H. E. P. Wigglesworth.**

the individual combat unit level. This interleaving greatly expanded the practice of combined British and U.S. headquarters that the Allies had begun with the establishment of AFHQ before the North African invasion.[75]

The concept of dedicating entire air forces to separate, yet cooperating, tactical or strategic roles became AAF standard operating procedure throughout the European and Mediterranean Theaters of Operations. In the case of NAAF, however, it should be noted that the designation *Strategic* was something of a misnomer, in that the Northwest African Strategic Air Force did not attack strategic industrial targets but confined itself to what could be called grand tactical targets, enemy lines of supply, and logistical support.

NAAF also absorbed the British air cooperation doctrines conceived by Woodall and employed by Coningham. Allied ground leaders would henceforth grudgingly concede the principle that a single airman must command all the air forces committed to the ground battle, because aircraft, unlike other combat arms, had free rein over the combat zone and should deploy in overwhelming force at the decisive points and not fritter away their strength in penny-packet formations at the ground commander's whim.

The organization of a combined Allied staff to the lowest feasible level served as a template for the organization of the Allied Expeditionary Force, which later conducted the cross-channel invasion into France. This close association with the RAF had an important side benefit for the AAF, which managed to cloak itself in the RAF's independent status and thus free itself from some of the more irksome restrictions inherent in its role as a subordinate part of the U.S. Army. Spaatz, for example, participated in Allied command conferences as an equal to his ground and naval opposite numbers rather than as an air adviser to the American ground force commander.

The reorganization also embraced the logistical support of Allied air power in North Africa. Brig. Gen. John Cannon became the head of the Northwest African Training Command, and Brig. Gen. Delmar Dunton formed the Northwest African Air Service Command from the XII Air Service Command and the maintenance organization of the Eastern Air Command.[76]

In one of their first actions after establishing the NAAF, Spaatz and Tedder met Eisenhower on February 17 and gained his agreement

> that air support should function very much along the principles previously in operation with 8th Army and Alexander. It was understood that this means in general that the decision and needs of the ground army are of paramount importance, and that the element of decision as to type of operation must rest with the Army commander.

Eisenhower, however, allowed the air commander to determine all matters of technique and forces employed.[77] This concession by Eisenhower gave XII ASC more operational flexibility.

Coningham's arrival at 18 Army Group Headquarters on the same day, February 17, allowed Allied air power to widen this initial and significant concession by Eisenhower. Upon assuming command on February 23, the New Zealander promptly put the Northwest African Tactical Air Force into operation according to his own principles. The flying of defensive umbrellas over ground formations was to cease at once. All future missions would be offensive and would be conducted as aggressively as possible. Furthermore, the prime target would be unarmored motor transport and troops; there would be no more concentration on "tank-busting."[78] These directions, however, did not come into force until March 2, after the Kasserine fighting had ended.[79] The location of Coningham's headquarters with Alexander's ended Anderson's de facto control of tactical air.

General Alexander's assumption of the command of the 18 Army Group also proved beneficial. Alexander, the British Army Commander in Chief, Mediterranean, and Eisenhower's deputy in charge of land forces, had served as Montgomery's and Coningham's commanding officer in the El Alamein campaign. He, too, had absorbed the new methods of air support, and his acceptance of them greatly eased the heretofore strained relations between the ground and

Imperial War Museum

Air Marshal William L. Welsh, Air Officer Commanding, Eastern Air Command, 1942–1943, inspecting an honor guard before his departure to the United States as head of the RAF's delegation in Washington, D.C.

air forces. On February 23, Spaatz's diary noted with satisfaction: "General Alexander supports the Air Force fully in their objection to the air umbrella rather than air offensive operations. This is a complete reversal of the previous attitude of the Army under Anderson and Fredendall."[80]

The assumption of command by Coningham, the centralization of control of tactical air under him, and his location with Alexander solved the personality problems of the old EAC. Anderson, with his defensive attitude, was removed from his position in charge of allocation of tactical air. Welsh and Lawson were replaced and sent elsewhere. Welsh spent the rest of the war exiled to the United States as head of the RAF Delegation. When Spaatz took over the Allied Air Force in the beginning of January he had recognized the pair's inability to cope with Anderson. Because Spaatz controlled them and not Anderson, he had recommended their replacement then and there. Portal, who apparently assumed that Spaatz wished to dispose of Welsh because Welsh outranked him, objected to U.S. interference in internal RAF matters,[81] reprieving Welsh and Lawson for six weeks. By that time Tedder presumably had informed Portal about the true state of affairs.

182

No matter how effective the experienced Alexander-Coningham air-ground team would prove in the long run, it could not change the situation in a day. Allied tactical air did not make its presence felt during the Kasserine engagements until after the Germans had begun their voluntary withdrawal. On the first day of the offensive, February 14, the XII ASC mounted 391 sorties as opposed to 360 to 375 German sorties.[82] The Germans were more effective, but the large number of U.S. sorties gave a hint that the balance might soon tip in the Allies' favor. By February 16, the XII ASC reported a total operational strength of seventy-six Spitfires, twenty-seven P-39s, and twenty-four A-20s. The 33d Fighter Group and its P-40s had withdrawn to refit on February 9. The Spitfires of the 31st Fighter Group and two-thirds of the 52d Fighter Group replaced it.[83] Both air forces maintained their effort through February 16, but bad weather for the next five days hampered Allied air operations. On February 18, the enemy advance forced the XII ASC to evacuate its forward fields at Thelepte, requiring it to destroy thirty-four unserviceable planes and 50,000 gallons of aviation fuel. In two days the Americans had lost forty-two planes. The clouds and rain finally cleared on February 22, when the XII ASC, disorganized by its retreat from Thelepte and operating from one overcrowded field (Youks-les-Bains) with only a single steel-plank runway, flew 304 sorties and lost only eleven planes.

On the evening of February 22 the Germans began their retreat, and for the next few days British and U.S. aircraft punished their retiring columns with increasing effect. Rommel later recorded, "The bad weather now ended and from midday [February 23] onward we were subjected to hammer-blow air attacks by the U.S. air force in the Feriana-Kasserine area, of weight and concentration hardly surpassed by those we had suffered at Alamein."[84] During the critical period of February 20 to 24, Coningham had also had the strategic bombers placed at his disposal. Instead of complaining about delays imposed by enemy air, ground leaders began to note improvement. On February 25, Eisenhower observed, "The Air Force is now better organized, is well sorted out and operating efficiently."[85]

In January and February 1943, Allied ground and air leaders sought to answer the question of who should have ultimate control of the theater's limited air assets. Later in the war such a question would not have arisen because the overwhelming number of aircraft then available to the Allies made it possible to supply simultaneously the need of the ground commanders for battle-line support and the need of the air commanders for counterair and supply-line strikes. The Casablanca Conference imposed an air command structure on the theater that supplied an air chain of command separate from the ground forces. This formal structure, however, would have meant little if Eisenhower had continued to allow his ground commanders to set air priorities. He who sets priorities controls the allocation of resources. Spaatz, alone in January, and, with Tedder's help in February, persuaded Eisenhower to allow air commanders a greater voice in the control of their own forces. Eisenhower probably assented in part because he had lost confidence in his American ground force commander, Fredendall, whom he relieved on March 6.

Once the air commanders could determine their own priorities, the Casablanca reorganization became decisive because it provided an efficient means to control available air power. Coningham's ability to call in all the Allied power needed (an ability denied his predecessors) allowed him to contest the air over the Kasserine Pass and to heavily attack the retreating German columns. In the next eleven weeks, the air commanders' ability to coordinate all of their resources on key points would prove important to Allied success.

Chapter 6

The Collapse of the Axis Bridgehead (February–May 1943)

So far as I know, Spaatz and I see eye to eye on every single thing that comes up; and we believe that we have learned lots of things that were, before the war either not understood, or not fully appreciated, either by our Ground Forces or our Air Forces.[1]

—Eisenhower to Arnold, May 2, 1943

The reorganization that produced the Northwest African Air Force (NAAF) and introduced the air support team and new procedures enhanced the efficiency of Allied air power. It was the catalyst that enabled the disparate air elements present in North Africa to redirect their efforts to the task at hand—defeating the enemy. The improved logistical situation, which occurred at approximately the same time as the reorganization, proved an equal factor in advancing Allied air fortunes. The end of the rainy season in mid-April allowed the Allies to greatly accelerate operations from their forward fields. At the same time, increasingly effective Allied interdiction of Axis supplies forced the Luftwaffe in North Africa to cut back its operations. All of the factors that had previously favored the Axis air effort no longer weighed heavily in the scales, while Allied air power had overcome the obstacles in its path.

Spaatz spent his energies late in the winter and spring of 1943 reinforcing and employing the new strength derived from the final restructuring, the exploitation of fresh doctrine, and the improvement of overall logistics. He nurtured the new organizational arrangements; won over recalcitrant air and ground commanders to the new theories; and attempted to perfect the procurement, maintenance, and transportation of his men, matériel, and facilities.

In the aftermath of Kasserine, the Allies refitted and prepared for the offensive that would drive the Axis into the sea. On March 1, in addition to his post as Commander, NAAF, Spaatz became Commanding General of the Twelfth Air

Force. This new title did not add to his duties, because the Twelfth had virtually ceased to exist except on paper, but it did regularize his position in the formal War Department hierarchy. Spaatz also worked to increase the proficiency of the NAAF.

Signal intelligence revealed that more than 80 percent of the Axis supplies (49,600 tons) dispatched to North Africa in February had arrived safely.[2] The NAAF was thus compelled to improve its antishipping effort, which depended on the Northwest African Strategic Air Force (NASAF). On March 1, Spaatz, Tedder, and Doolittle inspected the Telergma area airfields assigned to the NASAF. Spaatz wanted the flow of "all intelligence data" and results of all photo reconnaissance, including Malta flights, promptly sent to Doolittle's command. Evidently, he wanted to ensure that Doolittle received a full and timely share of ULTRA intercepts, some of which revealed the movement of Axis shipping between Italy and North Africa. To track this movement, the Allies routinely used aerial reconnaissance. Aerial reconnaissance was the perfect cover. It verified the intercepts and kept their source a secret. Spaatz also wanted the lateral communication links with the Northwest African Tactical Air Force (NATAF) and the Northwest African Coastal Air Force (NACAF) strengthened, as well as a radio intercept station at NASAF HQ to intercept spotting reports from Malta and Coastal Air Force reconnaissance aircraft.[3]

From the NASAF fields around Telergma, Spaatz moved forward to the NATAF airfields around Bône in the north and Youks-les-Bains in the south. These visits played up the importance of one of the technological components of the new air-support doctrine—the need for radar coverage of the battlefield and beyond. Radar coverage allowed the air-support commander to form a quick and accurate picture of the position of his own and of the enemy's frontal aviation. Complete coverage enabled the air commander to divert or abort tactical bomber and reconnaissance flights from enemy fighters and, at the same time, made it possible for him to use friendly fighters either defensively to break up incoming enemy air attacks or offensively to strike enemy aircraft on or over their airfields. This made the centralization of control of air-support forces not only necessary but easier and more effective.

During the initial rush from Algiers to Tunisia, the Allies sent forward as many aircraft as they could. They neglected, however, to send forward their ground-based early warning radar. Spaatz, who had seen its effectiveness in the Battle of Britain, moved at once to get ground control intercept (GCI) and early warning radar sets deployed as rapidly and as far forward as possible. In his diary he emphasized the importance and urgency of radar coverage at the front in obtaining effective use of fighters on both the defensive and the offensive:

> The nearer the RDF [radio direction finding or radar] coverage can read the enemy airdrome areas and check them up on take off, the more effective our operations will be. This makes the location of sites for RDF stations of almost

as great importance as the terrain for airdromes as an objective for the ground forces. This necessity has been lost on our buildup of units, and must be emphasized in order that our Air Forces can be properly balanced.[4]

Spaatz reiterated the point in a letter to Arnold, dated March 7:

> The ability of the enemy to attack our troops with dive bombers indicates that the enemy has control of the air or our forces are improperly controlled or that essential equipment is lacking. The solution lies in an acceptance of the principle that the first prerequisite to the support of the ground army or armies is the establishment of a fighter defense and offense, including RDF, GCI and other types of Radar equipment essential for the detection of enemy aircraft.[5]

The arrival of the radar-equipped U.S. 3d Air Defense Wing and additional British radar for XII ASC and No. 242 Group allowed the NAAF to establish a radar net covering the front by April.[6]

Continuing his inspection of tactical fields, Spaatz lunched with Colonel Williams and General Fredendall at Le Kouif, a field northeast of Youks-les-Bains, on March 3. He found the attitude of the soon-to-be-relieved Fredendall concerning air altered: "General Fredendall, in contradiction to the last visit . . . has considerably broadened in his viewpoint of air importance. He realizes the necessity of seizing and holding airdrome areas and high or dominating ground necessary for proper RDF coverage."[7] Fredendall had learned, too late, the role of tactical air. In his after-action report he wrote:

> Ground forces should have it explained to them that it is not necessarily true that the air should furnish them with a visible "umbrella," but that air is being furnished in the average operation even when our planes are not visible from the ground. Also that this air support includes not only cover and reconnaissance over' them, but also bombardment of enemy troops and airdromes.[8]

From Williams, Spaatz received a testimonial on the efficacy of air support parties—AAF liaison teams with the forward elements of the ground troops, each equipped with a VHF radio mounted on a 1½-ton truck. These units had supplied the higher commanders some of the quickest and most accurate information on combat situations. AAF formations had made it a habit to pass within range (fifteen miles) of the air support parties in order to get exact information on conditions in the target areas. At least once, an air support party (ASP) called down a strike on enemy forces in close contact with its own forces.[9]

Spaatz's front-line inspections revealed a morale problem in NASAF as compared to NATAF. Acute shortages of replacement planes and crews accounted for much of the problem in NASAF's medium-bomber and fighter groups.[10] This issue had become particularly severe in February, but thanks to increased ferrying of new aircraft from the United States and the unsnarling of the replacement pipeline through France's African possessions, the AAF corrected half of the problem by the end of March, when Spaatz could report to

Maj. Gen. Carl A. Spaatz, Marshal of the RAF Hugh M. Trenchard, Brig. Gen. James H. Doolittle, and actress Vivien Leigh *(far right)* **enjoying a light moment in North Africa. Brig. Gen. Hoyt S. Vandenberg is seated directly behind Spaatz.**

Stratemeyer, "Tell the Boss that there is a very, very noticeable improvement in the airplane situation."[11] The lack of replacement crews, unlike the airplane shortage, did not lend itself quite so readily to a production-line solution. In fact, the problems of war-weariness and the rotation of experienced crews continued to haunt Spaatz and the AAF's other numbered air force commanders until the war's end. Initial rotation policies seemed to imply that crews could go home after fulfilling a minimum of 30 combat missions or 200 hours of combat flying. Many crews who felt they had fulfilled their duty were dismayed when circumstances required additional missions. Their morale plummeted.[12]

Spaatz did what he could to improve their spirits. On several occasions he ordered "more attention to awards and decorations." He attempted to ensure that daily AFHQ press communiques gave the NAAF its full share of credit and did not subordinate its activities to ongoing naval and ground actions. Spaatz even ordered the photos of bombing results released to the crews.[13] This action relieved the fear "that the missions were a waste of time, material, and life"[14] common among men who flew over the same target mission after mission, yet never saw the damage they did because of the smoke of their own bombs or because of their own evasive action to avoid enemy antiaircraft fire.

Like Union General Joseph "Fightin' Joe" Hooker, who faced a similar morale problem in the Army of the Potomac after its defeat in the Battle of

188

Fredericksburg, Spaatz took simple, but apparently well-calculated, measures to improve the camp life of his soldiers and to supply them with the creature comforts dear to American fighting men. He replaced unfamiliar and unpopular British tents and rations in the combat units with American versions.[15] He ensured that flying personnel had cots and he established messes and recreation rooms. He set up separate rest camps for officers and enlisted men, improved facilities in all camps, and requested greater Red Cross support. He also tried to place motion picture projectors in each station,[16] made sure each unit had religious services available to it, and ordered his surgeon's section to survey the entire area for malaria. Morale, according to his staff, took a decided upturn.[17]

After completing his tour of the front, Spaatz inspected the rear echelons. He flew to Marrakech on March 6. There he decided to keep the airfield complex under the control of the NAAF rather than to transfer it to the Air Transport Service. Thus, control of the terminus of the transatlantic ferry route would stay in his hands. He also issued a standardized set of specifications for airfield construction. As a result of this action, plus aviation engineer reinforcements, the arrival of heavy construction equipment above the normal table of organization, and a decision to retain all aviation engineers under the control of the NAAF, the size and number of forward airfields greatly increased[18] and multiplied the force available to Coningham and Spaatz.

By March 12, Spaatz returned to Algiers, where he learned of his promotion to lieutenant general. He appreciated the honor and the increased status it gave him. Coningham, as an air marshal, had, until then, technically outranked him, but as Spaatz noted in a letter on the total AAF personnel situation in North Africa, "I have been much less concerned about promotion for myself than adequate promotion for a number of officers who are doing a General's job without the rank."[19] This remained a problem until June 1943, when Eisenhower, after repeated requests from Spaatz, promoted four AAF officers.[20]

The Air War Against Axis Supply Lines

In the middle of March 1943, NAAF Headquarters moved from Algiers to Constantine. The move placed it closer to the front and enabled it, in Spaatz's words, "to control the Strategic and Tactical Air Forces during the Tunisian Battle."[21] In Constantine, on March 17, Spaatz, Doolittle, and Allied air officers of the Coastal Air Force met to analyze the effectiveness of the antishipping campaign. From ULTRA sources they knew the daily unloading returns from Tunis and Bizerte.[22] These confirmed that "the shipping strikes have not been sufficient to bring down the amount of supplies into Tunisia below the danger point to the Germans."[23] Spaatz recommended singling out tanker shipping and concentrating all forces on it. Photo reconnaissance and "other intelligence" would show the tankers' locations.

189

By January, ULTRA could already determine the full details of 60 percent of all cargoes.[24] Of course, it could not supply the Allies every detail necessary to their plans of attack. The conference hammered out responsibilities for photo reconnaissance (NACAF), minimum forces exclusively devoted to antishipping (two squadrons of the NASAF), and chain of command (the NACAF would notify NASAF Headquarters of targets and the NASAF would decide composition of the force). The conferees also agreed to strengthen communication links between the two air forces.

The settling of jurisdictions, better flying weather in March and April, and the end of the crisis on the ground which had diverted the NASAF's strength to ground-support strikes, combined to greatly increase the ship-killing opportunities for Doolittle's command. Adding to the strength and effectiveness of Doolittle's antishipping blows were improvement in aircraft replacement rates; reinforcement by one medium-bomber group and two heavy-bomber groups; and the transfer, in March, from Cairo to Algiers, of an intelligence group that specialized in the study of the enemy supply situation and the selection of shipping targets.[25]

British aircraft flying out of Malta and night patrols by Royal Navy ships and submarines put further pressure on the Axis which, in March, unloaded 43,125 tons of supplies, as compared with 49,600 tons in February. In the following month unloadings plunged to 29,233 tons.[26] Postwar figures show that in March and April, 41.5 percent of seaborne cargoes dispatched to Tunisia failed to reach North Africa; loss of Axis shipping in March, not made good in April, accounted for that month's lower tonnage. Only four ships exceeding 3,000-tons dead weight reached Africa in April. Furthermore, daily unloadings steadily declined throughout the period from 1,300 to 700 tons.[27] By the end of April, the Allied tactical air forces had joined the fray and they, too, began to fly antishipping strikes.

Naturally, the Axis increased their resupply effort in the face of the Allies' onslaught. They diverted as much high-priority seaborne supply as possible to small ferries, landing craft, and naval vessels. The Axis also turned to air transport. As a British official history states, "Enigma [ULTRA] made it plain that his higher rate of fuel consumption [the principal air transport cargo] and the increasing destruction of his shipping had made the enemy critically dependent on air supply."[28]

Throughout the Tunisian campaign, German air transport ferried large numbers of personnel and amounts of supply to the Axis bridgehead in North Africa. This transport proved an invaluable aid in November and December 1942, when the surprise Allied landings called for a rapid response. In those two months the Luftwaffe brought in 37,000 men and 9,000 tons of matériel. After the initial surge, traffic declined to between 50 and 20 landings a day at the end of the year. German transport landings then began to climb until they reached 150 a day by late March 1943. In February 1943, air transport brought in 11,000 personnel and 4,000 tons of supplies. In all, excluding March, this airlift conveyed 71,000 troops and 23,000 tons of supplies to North Africa.[29]

No one appreciated this herculean effort of the Luftwaffe more than Spaatz. On January 16, he instructed his staff to draw up plans "to get after" the daily parade of Junkers Model 52 (Ju 52) traffic across the straits.* Two days later, January 18, he "told Cannon to send out a strong fighter force occasionally to swat the Ju 52 daily procession coming across the Straits."[30]

The British, too, developed plans to disrupt Axis air transport. Eastern Air Command drew up plans for such an operation on February 5 and expanded the plans to include the XII Bomber Command. This operation, code-named FLAX, ran afoul of the exigencies of the Kasserine crisis, which siphoned off all available air, causing the cancellation of the strike.[31] In March, Spaatz returned to the scent. At an NAAF staff meeting on March 4, he directed the NASAF to include in its priorities attacks against Axis air transportation.[32] When the NAAF drafted a plan to ruin any attempted Axis evacuation from Tunisia, the destruction of German air transport received first priority.[33]

At the beginning of April, Tedder, Spaatz, Doolittle, and Coningham met for a "Dunkirk" conference to complete plans for action against the expected attempt by the Axis to withdraw completely from Tunisia. Spaatz, supported by Coningham, disagreed with Tedder about whether the chief target priority should be air or sea transport. Spaatz said, "At the present time we are in doubt as to whether we are justified in getting away from sea transport and hitting air transport; but on the evacuation, unless we can believe air is the most important, we will be continuously in doubt as to what to do."[34] As the discussion continued, it turned to implementing FLAX. Tedder agreed "emphatically" with FLAX as a separate operation, but not as a general or continuing plan. He remarked that Eisenhower would probably agree to FLAX as a specific operation to take priority over everything.

Tedder objected to waging an air campaign exclusively against air transport and rejected Spaatz's suggestion that air transport be assigned first priority; instead, Tedder "insisted" that shipping remain the prime target. ULTRA intercepts tended to confirm Tedder's judgment. They showed that shipping carried eight to ten times more tonnage than aircraft to the bridgehead in February and March.[35] Once Tedder had driven that point home, he gave his subordinate authority to attack "air transport when specific targets arise." That satisfied Spaatz, who observed that in any case of sea versus air transport, the value of the individual target would always determine its selection.[36]

Eisenhower apparently accepted the plan. On April 5, the NASAF conducted the first FLAX strike. A morning fighter sweep splashed eleven Ju 52s and five escorts into the sea. Next, B-17s struck Tunisian landing fields, where the transport shuttle terminated, with fragmentation bombs. Around noon more B-17s and

---

* The Germans used the trimotor Ju 52 as their chief transport aircraft.

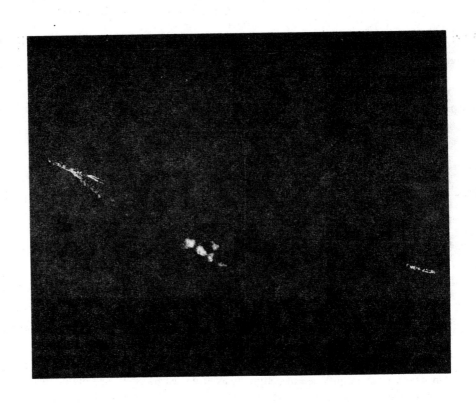

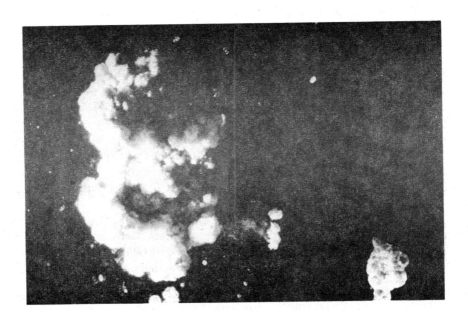

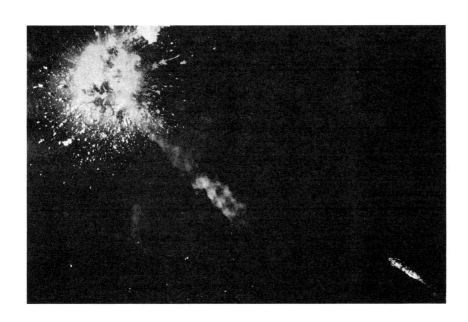

The end of two Axis supply ships off Bizerte, Tunisia, March 1943.

A six-engine Messerschmitt Me 323 Gigant transport *(above)* and low-flying Junkers (Ju 52) tri-motor transport *(below)*. The ubiquitous *"Tante Ju"* was the workhorse of Luftwaffe airlift.

B-25s finished off the affair by dropping fragmentation bombs on the Sicilian airfields at Boccadifalco, Trapani, and Borizzo, where the second daily flight for Tunisia usually formed up. These actions totally disrupted service, because an afternoon P-38 sweep found the straits empty. The bomber raids caught Axis aircraft bunched together on their fields and inflicted heavy damage. The Luftwaffe acknowledged losses of 14 Ju 52s shot down, 11 transports destroyed on the ground, and 67 transports damaged. The AAF claimed 201 enemy aircraft destroyed, and admitted its loss of 3 aircraft with 6 unaccounted for. Additional attacks on April 10 and 11 resulted in claims of 67 transports and 13 escorts destroyed.[37]

Spaatz wrote to Eaker in England describing the carefully set trap. Before executing FLAX, the Allies had observed enemy air transport activity via photo reconnaissance and radar coverage, but had not interfered with daily flights. As a result, the methodical Germans were lulled into establishing a regular schedule and became more vulnerable to the initial Allied attacks.[38] Because of extremely sensitive ULTRA information, Spaatz avoided mentioning its contribution to the success of the operation. The breaking of the code used by the Luftwaffe's Enigma cipher machine gave details of cargoes, variation of convoy routes, flight cancellations, and German defensive measures. RAF "Y," the RAF's tactical intercept service added more information with its readings of local Luftwaffe and Italian Air Force (IAF) air transport radio traffic. "From the study of this traffic the intelligence staffs derived their familiarity with points of arrival and departure, the time taken to unload and turn around, the normal routes, and the strength of the escorts."[39] The signal security of the German air force was notoriously poor.

After April 17, the Western Desert Air Force (WDAF) took over the execution of FLAX from the NASAF. The following day, the WDAF, operating from newly captured airfields around Sousse, a coastal city on the Gulf of Hammamet only 90 miles from Cape Bon (one-third of the distance from NASAF fields), staged the "Palm Sunday Massacre." WDAF P-40s and Spitfires attacked a homeward-bound air convoy and sent between 50 and 70 of the 100 transports and 16 escorts spinning into the Mediterranean. The next day they added 12 out of 20. The Axis, in desperate condition on land and sea, persevered in the face of this pounding. They brought in air transport reinforcements and kept flying. Even instructor crews participated in the one-sided fight.[40] On April 22, the Germans lost an entire flight of 21 Messerschmitt Model 323s (Me 323s). These six-engine converted gliders had four times the cargo capacity of Ju 52s but little maneuverability; they generated barely enough speed to keep themselves airborne, lacked armor and self-sealing gas tanks, and had no chance against the Allied fighters which pounced on them. Three days later, ULTRA revealed the order of the Commander in Chief of the Luftwaffe, Reich Marshal Hermann Goering, to switch all transport flights to night. This step greatly reduced air resupply into Tunisia and ended FLAX.[41]

Throughout the FLAX operation the NASAF had continued its raids on Axis staging airfields. These raids completed the destruction of the German air transport fleet and resulted in the loss of numerous Axis escort and antishipping aircraft as well. Of the 263 German transports available at the beginning of April, the Luftwaffe had lost 157 by April 27,[42] not including Italian transports and Axis bomber aircraft pressed into transport service. One estimate placed total losses at 432 aircraft. These losses, combined with casualties suffered by the German Air Transport Service in its attempts to supply the German *Sixth Army* in the Stalingrad pocket of southern Russia, crippled German air transport for the remainder of the war.[43]

Operation FLAX and the equally successful strangulation of seaborne traffic doomed the Axis land forces in Africa. Only forty tons of diesel and motor fuel remained in the bridgehead at the time of their surrender.[44] Allied intelligence had selected its shipping targets so carefully that the only surplus remaining was food, which the Allies had purposely not sunk in anticipation of feeding Axis prisoners of war.[45]

The interdiction campaign, like the adoption of British air-support techniques, provided an example of the victory of wartime improvisation over prewar doctrine. Neither subject had captured the imagination of the interwar Army Air Corps theorists, yet both these aspects of the Tunisian campaign have served as models for future AAF and USAF doctrine. Never again has U.S. air power participated in such an effective supply interdiction effort or had so many advantages over the enemy. The Allies broke almost every major cipher used by the enemy; they had overwhelming air and naval superiority, which they could freely apply to the restricted area of the Cape Bon–Sicily narrows; and they fought an overextended and, to some extent, disheartened enemy.

Spaatz contributed to the success of the operation in two ways. He insisted that airborne as well as water transport be interdicted, thereby closing a vital supply line that specialized in the delivery of petroleum products—a necessity for the Axis forces in the bridgehead. Second, like other senior air officers, he seized the opportunity to demonstrate air power's effectiveness against the Axis forces' vulnerability to an aggressive air interdiction campaign.

Heavy-Bombardment Aviation in Tunisia

The pride of the AAF, heavy-bombardment aviation, performed well and sometimes spectacularly well during the Tunisian campaign. From November 1942 through May 1943, the B-24s of the Ninth Air Force and the B-17s of the Twelfth Air Force flew 7,041 combat sorties, only 900 fewer than the medium and light bombers of the two air forces,[46] and lost only 81 aircraft (1.1 percent) to combat or accident.[47] The B-17s suffered only 24 combat casualties; enemy fighters accounted for 8 of them, flak and other causes taking the other 16.[48] In a letter summarizing the campaign, Spaatz wrote to Arnold, "The impact of the

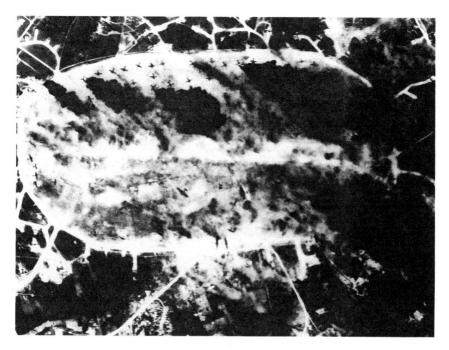

After an air raid on Castelvetrona, Sicily, April 1943. Direct hits on forty-two air-craft, including twenty transports, were observed.

A German Siebel ferry, typical of the watercraft used to supply the Axis bridgehead, spring 1943.

well flown B-17 formation into the European air picture has been tremendous and, in my opinion, will be the decisive factor, unless the Germans find some means of opposing it better than they have now."[49]

After a slow start, the heavy bombers made their first raid beyond North Africa on February 7, 1943, when they hit a major airfield in Elmas, Sardinia. This raid, according to its planners, damaged a large percentage of the Axis anti-shipping capability stationed at Elmas, thereby enabling an Allied convoy to escape further losses.[50] Two more raids in February struck port facilities in Cagliari, Sardinia, and Palermo, Sicily. These missions established the pattern for subsequent months; NASAF medium bombers (B-25s and B-26s) concentrated on shipping, while heavy bombers (B-17s and B-24s) attacked the loading and unloading facilities at both ends of the Axis supply lines. Occasionally, the B-17s went after convoys or ships in harbor.

Two raids produced dramatic results that helped enhance the AAF's faith in the destructiveness of its preferred weapon system. On April 10, B-17s sank the Italian heavy cruiser *Trieste* with 1,000-pound bombs dropped from 19,000 feet. The same raid damaged the *Goriza*, one of Italy's two remaining heavy cruisers. Dramatic before and after pictures received full circulation during the war, and even the postwar U.S. Army and Air Force official histories selected them for publication.[51] Four days earlier, B-17s had blown up an ammunition ship in convoy to Tunisia; that pyrotechnic display also earned wide coverage.

As usual, Arnold pressed Spaatz and his other combat commanders to provide the public and the President with evidence of destruction by bombing. Spaatz's and Doolittle's unprecedented permission given to the glamorous *Life* magazine photojournalist Margaret Bourke-White to fly a B-17 combat mission over Tunisia and the resultant story failed to assuage Arnold,[52] nor did *Time* magazine's cover story of March 22 on Spaatz.[53] The AAF commander was concerned that an unsophisticated public would not understand why "our early units were not as well trained as units committed to combat should be," why "we did not suddenly have a great striking force prepared to operate against Germany," and why the AAF required "a necessary 'feeling out' period."[54] Arnold needed proof of accurate and devastating bombing. On April 10, he cautioned Spaatz that "many people in high places" were asking hard questions about the exact details of damage inflicted by Spaatz's forces. "It will help us a great deal in defending your operations," noted Arnold, "and in building up a correct picture of the results being accomplished if you will make a special effort to have a summary on the subject gotten back here about every two weeks."[55]

Eleven days later, in response to an earlier request by Arnold for information on Kasserine Pass and antishipping operations, Spaatz wrote that he hoped Arnold had received his daily operations reports, the weekly intelligence summaries, and "the special folders of significant heavy bomber operations."[56] Spaatz cited four special folders already sent: (1) the March 22 Palermo raid, which Spaatz earlier called one of the most destructive of the war;[57] (2) the April 6 ammunition ship strike; (3) the sinking of the *Trieste*; and (4) an April 13 mission against the Castelvetrano airfield in Sicily. These four special folders should have helped Arnold greatly in his defense of precision bombing.

Spaatz did not mention a devastating raid by the 97th Bombardment Group on airfields in the Souk el Arba area on February 22, the high point of the German Kasserine attack. In an interview more than thirty years later, General Kuter still remembered the incident well—the B-17s used "anti-personnel bombs, hundreds of them all over, and killed a lot of people."[58] Unfortunately, the base belonged to the RAF; the bombers had missed their intended target by a hundred miles. Prompt apologies and a thorough investigation by the NASAF mollified the British, who chalked up the incident to the fortunes of war.[59] It was no wonder Spaatz did not send a special folder on this mission.

Appropriately, when Spaatz quietly chose to join a limited number of combat missions, he flew on the heavies—on at least three occasions that can be verified in his diary and probably two or three more times. On March 31, he rode in the nose of one of the 97th Bombardment Group's B-17s on a mission over Decimonannu airfield in Sardinia. Next, he flew with the 301st Bombardment Group on the April 13 Castelvetrano airfield raid. Two weeks later, on April 27, he observed the bombing of Villacidro airfield from one of the 97th Bombardment Group's fortresses.[60] The Castelvetrano raid lost one airplane to antiaircraft fire. According to Eisenhower's personal naval aide, Capt. Harry Butcher, who knew Spaatz well and often participated in his late-night poker games, Spaatz told him, but not Eisenhower, that he had flown on a raid over Palermo on April 14 in which three planes were lost, two to fighters and one to flak. That trip "wasn't the first by any means."[61] Given the information in Spaatz's papers and Butcher's diary, Spaatz apparently flew no fewer than four or five missions. It appears reasonable to conclude that he flew a strike with each of the heavy-bombardment groups in his command: the 2d, 97th, 99th, and 301st.

Spaatz's flights demonstrated bravery, but did they demonstrate another quality essential to command—wisdom? If the casualty figures can be accepted, he personally witnessed one-sixth of all B-17 combat losses for the campaign. He did not choose milk runs. In fact, he appears to have exposed himself to great danger and to have run real risks. If his plane had gone down and he had been captured, the enemy might have forced the ULTRA secret from him, to the significant detriment of the Allied effort. His loss in battle might also have damaged AAF prestige and shaken faith in the possibility of daylight bombing.

But Spaatz's flights do demonstrate a cardinal principle of good command—leadership. He had a morale problem in the NASAF. What better way to help ease it than to let his men know "the old man" shared their risks? How better could he understand the physical, mental, and organizational problems of flying a wartime raid? Military history abounds with examples of leaders who failed because of plans based on absolute physical impossibilities. One need only remember the apocryphal tale of the World War I British staff officer who burst into tears on his first visit to the front when he realized the hopelessness of the attacks he had helped to plan.

Nor did Spaatz, in this instance, take absurd chances. B-17 strikes had far lower loss rates than antishipping or ground-support attacks. He apparently participated as an observer only and did not interrupt normal crew procedure or put himself in the cockpit. By confining himself to raids on coastal targets he lessened the danger of capture should he and his crew be forced to abandon their plane. They could parachute from it or ease it into the water with the hope of encountering Allied rescue parties. Moreover, recent evidence shows that the ULTRA secret had become known at levels far lower than his. Because he was usually not the only one who knew about it on the missions that he flew,[62] he probably did not jeopardize it unduly. On balance, Spaatz's combat missions seem to have been justified. He achieved a positive effect on his own and his men's morale and gained invaluable insight into the day-to-day workings of his command. As a commander he had a duty to lead by example in combat. He fulfilled that duty without indulging in it to the extent that he compromised his capacity to carry out higher responsibilities. Of course, if he actually had been lost, his flights could be condemned as ill-considered and foolish—such is fate. Spaatz, in this instance, had at least stacked the deck in his favor.

Such experiences did not dampen his belief in precision bombing. In late May he summed up the performance of the heavy bombers this way: "In our day to day operations at the present time, we feel any area can be completely neutralized, even blown into oblivion, by high altitude attacks, without incurring any serious losses on our part." He went on to bemoan the loss of a year in mounting a massive strategic campaign against Germany—an attack that would have been decisive, in his view, had it been properly followed up.[63]

Ground Operations and Air Support

As the NASAF tightened its grip on Axis supply lines, Allied ground forces, assisted by the newly formed NATAF, shattered enemy land forces in a nine-week-long assault on the Italian-German bridgehead. Under the able leadership of Coningham, the U.S. XII Air Support Command, the Western Desert Air Force, and No. 242 Group soon gained air superiority. Fighter-bombers and light bombers of the NATAF roamed the battlefield unhampered by the Luftwaffe.

Coningham's appointment to head the NATAF improved the performance of the tactical forces but did not provide a universal nostrum to the ills of air-ground cooperation in North Africa. Not all ground or air commanders succumbed to the New Zealander's messianic expressions of the new support arrangements. Nor did "Mary's" combative temperament ease his path. In his view, the Americans, with less than six months' wartime experience, had nothing to teach him. In the subsequent campaign in Sicily, he made his view abundantly clear to Spaatz in a scene that one observer described as "the first time I saw personal Anglo-American relations go wrong at that level."[64]

Coningham had begun to develop an obsessive and splenetic hatred of Montgomery, believing that he had filched from him and the air arm the laurels of victory at El Alamein.[65] As a result, Montgomery began to place increasing reliance in the abilities of Air Vice-Marshal Harry Broadhurst, Coningham's replacement in command of the WDAF. The Montgomery-Broadhurst collaboration proved extremely effective in supplying tactical air support to the ground troops under Montgomery's command through North Africa, Sicily, Italy, and Normandy—and served as proof of the importance of personal compatibility in the air-ground equation.[66] Spaatz, while scrupulously declining to interfere with Coningham's overall direction of the tactical battle, spent a great deal of time calming the waters in Coningham's wake and convincing American officers of the value of the new doctrine, if not of the value of its bearer.*

Although Coningham's appointment to head the NATAF improved the performance of the tactical forces, neither Spaatz nor the AAF in North Africa accepted his system *in toto*. The Americans disagreed with his orders of March 17, which forbade NATAF planes from communicating with air-support parties (as mentioned, AAF-manned liaison teams equipped with a VHF radio on a $1\frac{1}{2}$-ton truck that traveled with the forward ground elements and provided immediate contact with planes overhead). To Coningham, the practice by which U.S. aircraft checked in with the air-support parties smacked of excessive control of air by the ground commander and thus violated the principle of unity of air command. It also threatened to short-circuit the whole British system by providing a direct link between pilots and individual ground units. Such a link abbreviated the functions of the Fighter Wing Control Room, reducing control by the overall air commander.[67]

Colonel Williams, the commanding officer of the XII ASC, after discussion with his group leaders and pilots, advised his superior that the air-support parties did not command or control his planes, but merely provided a quick and valuable communications link with the ground forces at the point of combat.[68] Spaatz intervened in support of Williams's position, and the air-support parties continued to provide their useful services.[69]

American use of air-support parties illustrated certain differences in Allied air coordination practices. Although the Americans absorbed many lessons from the British, the two organizations did not form mirror images. The Americans regarded the air-support parties as the equivalent of British "tentacles," but they did not follow the example of assigning an air liaison officer at each forward airfield. Instead, the ground unit receiving support sent one of its own officers to the airfield to brief the air commander. In the WDAF/8th Army scheme, the 8th

---

* See discussion of the RAF's and Coningham's air support doctrine in Chapter 4.

Army processed air requests from subordinate units, decided on priorities, and at that point presented requirements to the WDAF, which had control over all operational aspects of the mission.

The Americans also used different communication channels. Instead of II Corps Headquarters developing air requests from its subordinate units, XII ASC Headquarters developed requests received directly from the air-support parties. The air-support party's commander not only served as air-ground liaison but doubled as a member of the ground unit's staff. After allocating its aircraft to specific strikes, XII ASC then confirmed its decisions with II Corps G-3 (Operations). If G-3 approved, XII ASC carried out the missions according to its own plans and force available. The Americans believed in the superiority of their procedure since it introduced qualified air opinion at the beginning of a request process, thereby preventing air commitment to unsuitable or impossible tasks. Coningham had learned from the Americans through Williams that aircraft command and control was technically reserved to XII ASC Headquarters and not to the air-support parties, but he was, apparently, either uninformed or uncomprehending of the essential role played by those parties in the American scheme of ground support.[70]

Coningham's original order, had it remained in effect, would have totally disrupted American air-ground cooperation. The Americans resisted this attempt to impose British methods from the top. In practice, however, both the British and the American schemes worked equally well. In 1944 Spaatz took the American procedures with him to Britain where they were applied by the U.S. Ninth Air Force. With Spaatz's departure in 1944, the Mediterranean Theater adopted British procedures.

Even before Coningham's arrival to command the NATAF, Spaatz had observed to Stratemeyer that with Coningham "at the head of our Air Support Command, it can readily be seen that something is bound to break out in a very short time."[71] Air-ground relations remained tranquil until April 1. After the Kasserine crisis, Allied ground and air units prepared to renew attacks on the Axis. The logistical situation improved dramatically after early December and January. Spaatz could report that the forward fields had sufficient bombs and gasoline for operations.[72] The NAAF needed only one item to remove the principal bottleneck remaining in its logistics—motor transport. On March 30, Spaatz complained that II Corps still had 450 AAF trucks. Seven days later, he asked Eisenhower for more transport to move the air force forward, even if it had to come from II Corps.[73]

After a pause to reorganize following the defeats of mid-February, II Corps resumed the offensive. Although Coningham now held operational control of XII ASC, he followed the earlier and logical practice of ordering each of his air contingents to support its own land forces. In keeping with his ideas, however, XII ASC gave first priority to counterair operations rather than to ground support for II Corps.

On March 17, following intensive artillery and air preparation, Patton's II Corps took Gafsa and began to attack toward the sea coast, seventy-five miles away. By then, XII ASC's operational strength had risen to 116 Spitfires, 49 P-39s, and 4 photographic reconnaissance planes.[74] The Support Command's medium bombers had transferred to the Tactical Bomber Force, a centralized tactical bomber command directly under Coningham's control. Spitfires had short endurance and could not drop bombs. The P-39s served only as fast ground-attack planes because of their inability to compete in dogfights with superior Axis fighters in the theater. The XII ASC had two responsibilities for this phase of the battle: (1) to protect the forward move of II Corps and (2) to obtain and hold air superiority over opposing air forces to free the entire WDAF for the 8th Army attack on Rommel at the Mareth Line. The Tactical Bomber Force, composed of both British and American medium bombers, would supply striking power to XII ASC for hitting Axis airfields. Coningham also had the power to require Strategic Air Force missions on enemy fields during critical days of the offensive.[75]

Rain grounded portions of the NATAF and mired II Corps in mud, postponing the offensive until March 29. For the next twelve days II Corps made little progress against heavy German resistance. A number of fruitless and costly attacks, which gained negligible results, made the period between March 28 and April 2 particularly frustrating for Patton. On the morning of April 1, a German air attack killed one of his personal aides, Capt. Richard N. Jenson, and landed a bomb within a few feet of Maj. Gen. Omar N. Bradley, deputy corps commander.[76] Jenson's death upset Patton greatly;[77] he manifested his grief, in part, against Allied air support, which he felt had abandoned him.

This attitude represented a *volte-face* for Patton. Just before the attacks, Spaatz, on a trip to the front, had elicited from him on March 24 and from Maj. Gen. Terry Allen, Commander of the 1st Infantry Division (the "Big Red One") on March 25 expressions of approval concerning their air support;[78] on March 23 and 24, XII ASC had successfully bombed and strafed enemy tanks, motor transport, and troops in the El Guettar (1st Division) sector.[79] Neither general may have been fully aware that XII ASC's priority mission was conducting counterair operations, not ground support.[80]

By April 2, however, Patton, as on other occasions during the war, could no longer contain his anger. He proceeded to issue a situation report ("sitrep") highly critical of the air effort. "Forward troops," the sitrep stated, "have been continuously bombed all morning. Total lack of air cover for our units has allowed German Air Force to operate almost at will."[81] Patton gave the report wide circulation. Predictably, Coningham reacted by giving even wider circulation to a choleric message of his own. After first noting that XII ASC had provided 260 sorties on the day in question and that, furthermore, enemy air action had resulted in only four killed and a small number wounded, he stated: "On receipt of sitrep it was first assumed to be seasonal first April joke." then he continued:

It is assumed that intention was not to stampede local American air command into purely defensive action. It is also assumed that there was no intention to adopt discredited practice of using air force as an alibi for lack of success on the ground. . . . It can only be assumed that Two Corps personnel concerned are not battleworthy in terms of present operation. . . . [Finally NATAF's commander requested] that such inaccurate and exaggerated reports should cease. XII ASC have been instructed to not allow their brilliant and conscientious support of Two Corps to be affected by this false cry of wolf.[82]

Coningham angrily complained at Tedder's headquarters that Patton's provocations were "particularly intense," consisting of "a solid 48 hours of sitreps, signals and telephone calls, three of them being to General Alexander." In the meantime, "there were no communications to General Williams commanding American air, nor to my headquarters, but all the other addresses of my signal were included. They were all based on false information because General Patton is living 40 miles away from his airmen and does not know the air position."[83]

Because the Patton-Coningham fracas was potentially damaging to both air-ground and inter-Allied relations, Spaatz, Tedder, and Eisenhower reacted sharply. Tedder, in his memoirs, claimed that he corrected the situation himself. After receiving a copy of Coningham's message, Tedder phoned Eisenhower and explained that as Air Officer Commanding, Mediterranean Air Command, he had instructed Coningham to cancel his message and to accompany him to Gafsa to apologize to Patton in person. This meeting, Tedder claims, resolved the situation and converted Patton to a friend. Tedder added that his prompt handling of the problem prevented Eisenhower's resignation.[84]

Spaatz's command diary entries, recorded at the time of the event, contradict Tedder's account. Spaatz and, presumably, Tedder had received copies of Patton's original message as they were leaving a joint MAC-NAAF staff meeting that put the final touches on the "Dunkirk" plans. The "inaccuracy" and "unjustness" of the sitrep and its wide distribution had provoked "great concern."[85] The next morning Spaatz and Tedder, in the midst of preparing to fly to the front, received Coningham's intemperate reply. They flew to Thelepte, met Kuter and Williams, and investigated the lack of air support reported by Patton. The WDAF, they found, had scheduled 160 fighter sorties for April 1, but weather had interfered. The XII ASC had not attacked a tank concentration because the ground forces had canceled their planned attack when artillery moved into range of the tanks. Finally, they discovered a lack of radar coverage to the east of Gafsa, which prevented effective employment of the fighters stationed there.[86]

The four then motored from Thelepte to visit Patton at his headquarters in Gafsa. They must have been dumbfounded when he informed them of his satisfaction with current air support. Nonetheless, they expressed their misgivings over his having moved too far forward of Williams to communicate with him.[87] The separation of Patton and Williams violated the spirit of the new doctrine,

Lt. Gen. Carl A. Spaatz, Lt. Gen. George S. Patton, and Spaatz's Chief of Intelligence, Col. George C. McDonald, Constantine, Algeria, March 1943.

which required the co-location of air and ground headquarters for the proper supervision of forces.

By a quirk of fate, two to four German aircraft suddenly interrupted conversation, strafing and bombing Patton's headquarters area and prompting one of his guests to remark, "I always knew you were a good stage manager, but this takes the cake." Patton replied, "If I could find those sonsabitches who flew those planes I'd mail them each a medal."[88] In a far less celebrated incident, the airmen had a measure of revenge on the Luftwaffe the same day, when XII ASC fighters intercepted a Stuka (dive-bomber) formation and shot down thirteen of sixteen planes.[89]

That afternoon Tedder and Spaatz flew on to visit the WDAF at Medinine, behind the 8th Army's front. Spaatz saw, firsthand, that the 8th Army had much more effective air support than the other Allied land forces in Tunisia. With Williams and Patton's chief of staff in tow, Spaatz provided some on-the-job training by inspecting joint WDAF/8th Army Headquarters. He noted that Montgomery, unlike Patton, left his main headquarters adjacent to air headquarters, even if he personally moved an advanced command post closer to the fighting.[90] The German masters of the blitzkrieg, Generals Irwin Rommel and Heinz Guderian, employed similar methods in directing their own armored attacks.

During their visit to the front, Spaatz and Tedder talked at great length about Coningham's reply to Patton. When they returned to Williams's headquarters on

April 4, Tedder wrote a reprimand to Coningham, which he sent to Spaatz, who forwarded it to NAAF Headquarters for transmission to its recipient. Tedder then called Eisenhower with an explanation and directed Coningham to see Patton post haste.[91] Coningham met Patton at noon the same day, and the two immediately engaged in a shouting match, both protesting their faith in their own men. Once it stopped, the atmosphere cleared and the two officers got down to business. Coningham, as ordered, apologized. Patton graciously accepted as if he himself had done no wrong, and they both agreed to cancel and withdraw their respective messages. Patton recorded in his diary, "We parted friends, and I think we will now get better air support than ever before." As Patton well knew, the squeaky wheel gets the grease.[92]

In a contrite letter to Tedder's deputy, Air Vice-Marshal H.E.P. Wigglesworth, Coningham said of Patton, "I like him very much, he is a gentleman and a gallant warrior. But on the slightest provocation he breathes fire and battle, and as I also like fighting I could not resist the challenge when he turned the barrage on to me."[93] Coningham sent out a new message, in which he expressed regret that his original signal might have been interpreted as a slight to U.S. forces and laid the cause to an egregious error in transmission: "Two Corps" had been wrongly substituted for "Few corps." The new signal concluded with the withdrawal of his offending message and an indication that he considered the matter closed.[94]

Eisenhower, however, had the last word. As Spaatz's chief of staff, Col. Edward (Ted) Curtis, recalled, the Coningham-Patton dispute angered Eisenhower considerably.[95] His steam was still up on April 5 when he wrote Marshall, "The past week has been a very trying one and was notable for one incident that disturbed me very much. This involved a very unwise and unjust criticism of II Corps by a senior member of the British Air Force." Eisenhower concluded, "There was really no excuse for the thing happening."[96] Later that morning, Spaatz and Eisenhower met in conference, where the incident became the chief topic of conversation. Spaatz defended Coningham, arguing that Patton had initiated the affair with a sitrep so accusative that notice had to be taken of it; Patton should restrict his "grousing" to proper channels. Moreover, Patton's movement of his headquarters to a spot inaccessible to Williams's headquarters could only have decreased the possibility of effective support. Spaatz pointed out that, in any case, Patton had obtained 160 sorties from the WDAF. Eisenhower responded by suggesting a large-scale air operation in support of II Corps, a suggestion Spaatz forwarded to Coningham.[97] The squeaky wheel had gotten the grease.

This meeting apparently changed Eisenhower's view of the affair. That afternoon he wrote to Patton suggesting that the matter be dropped in the interest of *"the great purpose of complete Allied teamwork"* [emphasis in the original]. He chided Patton for demanding an additional "pound of flesh" and observed, "In connection with this matter I am since informed that there was a certain amount of unwise distribution of your sitrep." He warned Patton that in future any criticism of another service or collaborating agency should be made by means of a "confidential" report through the proper chain of command or, better yet, with "a friendly and personal conference with the man responsible." He concluded:

> You and Spaatz, with your respective subordinates, are at the moment carrying the burden of battle command for the American side of the house. In both of you I have the most tremendous confidence and I therefore feel that you have every right to have my opinions on these matters as accurately as I am able to express them.[98]

Patton noted, "Ike told me later that he could not punish Coningham because he was a New Zealander and political reasons forbade."[99] This ended the incident, but the problem of perfecting air-ground cooperation remained.

On several occasions in April and May, Spaatz went to the front to try to correct close air support arrangements. He was incensed by what he found on his visit to the U.S. 34th Infantry Division on April 8. This untried division, recently detached from II Corps and assigned to the British 9 Corps, had failed to reach its objective, partly because of confusion over a planned air attack. The 9 Corps canceled the air attack around midnight April 7–8 and so notified 34th Division. At 8:00 A.M. Maj. Gen. Ryder, 34th Division Commander, realizing that his infantry had not advanced so far or so quickly as planned, tried to reinstate the air attack for 8:30 A.M., but no planes appeared and at 9:30 A.M. the division called off the air attack once more.[100] In following up the lack of support for the 34th, Spaatz discovered that air-ground communications had failed. The 34th had not realized that it could call for air support directly to XII ASC through its own air support party. The XII ASC, assigned to support II Corps, had just moved seventy-five miles to the northeast (from Thelepte to LeSers), too far from both American II and British 9 Corps Headquarters. Nor had XII ASC been aware of its continuing responsibility for the 34th Division. To make matters worse for the pride of the 34th Division, the British assault went well and at its end the British 9 Corps commander recommended the withdrawal of the 34th from combat and the retraining of its junior officers at the rear under British guidance.[101]

Spaatz attributed the air-ground problem to the ground forces' own confusion about lines of authority: XII ASC could not effectively cooperate with two widely separated masters. Upon his return to Constantine, Spaatz suggested the formation of a new army headquarters to supervise both corps. This headquarters, sited alongside Williams's headquarters, would allow XII ASC to do its job effectively. "Any organization which had air forces available but could not get their machinery in motion to apply them was faulty," Spaatz wrote in his diary. Williams had had the forces to aid the 34th, but because of poor control could not apply them.[102] Eisenhower rejected Spaatz's suggestion. Because a new army headquarters would have had to be American, and he may not have felt that the time was right to discuss its formation.

Meanwhile, Montgomery continued his pursuit of the retreating Italian-German army group. His march along the Mediterranean coast, from the Mareth Line to Enfidaville, moved the southern boundary of the bridgehead one hundred miles north. This left the U.S. II Corps with no front to occupy. Anticipating this "pinching out," Allied commanders had already ordered II Corps to prepare to transfer to the far northern edge of the bridgehead, where it could advance on Bizerte. This move, begun on April 12, placed II Corps under Anderson's 1st Army. The shrunken size of the Axis-occupied area left room for only two air control sectors, and because XII ASC supported II Corps, now under the operational control of the 1st Army, XII ASC joined No. 242 Group, the 1st Army's air support formation, as a subordinate unit. WDAF had the other air control sector.[103]

As II Corps completed its move across the 1st Army's entire line of communication and the 8th Army's drive stalled at Enfidaville, a lull in the fighting ensued. Spaatz, mindful of previous deficiencies in cooperation between II Corps and XII ASC, used this breather to try to strengthen the bond between the two organizations. He observed the air liaison officer at II Corps, found him unimpressive, and replaced him.[104]

This personnel move did not halt the flow of complaints from General Bradley, who had replaced Patton as the Commander of II Corps, or from Anderson. The 1st Army initiated its new offensive on April 22, the same day the Luftwaffe began a general withdrawal from its African bases. From that point on, the Luftwaffe ceased to play a significant role in North Africa, and the Tactical Air Force discontinued airfield attacks as a matter of policy, turning instead to ground support.[105] Because this offensive was the major effort of the theater, 1st Army had a great say in the allocation of air on its front and had the responsibility of joint planning with air for its attacks. Anderson proved he had learned nothing new about air operations. For the final breakthrough Coningham placed the entire NATAF and all the medium bombers the Strategic Air Force could spare under the operational control of No. 242 Group, the air headquarters co-located at 1st Army headquarters.[106]

In preparing the final plan for the defeat of the Axis forces in Tunisia, the 1st Army never consulted No. 242 Group—not even about zero hour. It chose dawn but Allied tactical aircraft could not take off from their primitive airfields before first light and, thus, could not bomb their first objective targets in time to assist the ground assault. The bombing of second and third objectives played a great part in the army's breakthrough. This, however, was a case of good fortune because the target, the Medjez Valley, normally had a seasonal morning mist from 9:00 to 10:00. For each of the four days before the attack the mist had come and had obscured the second and third objectives.[107]

According to No. 242 Group, Allied air made every effort to satisfy the ground forces and even employed several nonstandard procedures. Provided the Army limited its requests to one or two attacks a day, No. 242 Group would attack any target, regardless of suitability. The group also placed at 1st Army's disposal a considerable force for its use as artillery, with little result; No. 242 Group claimed that 1st Army dissipated the force made available in seventy different attacks against forty-four separate targets.[108]

On April 29, Eisenhower visited Spaatz at his villa in Constantine to discuss Bradley's and Anderson's dissatisfaction with their air support. Spaatz concluded that the generals' complaints resulted from their inability to get exactly what they wanted when they wanted it. He told Eisenhower that he would go forward to straighten out the matter the next day, April 30.[109] During his visits to both headquarters, Spaatz found the conditions he expected: lack of communication, not aircraft, proved to be the problem.

Anderson needed reassurance. The appearance of newly identified German units on his front had convinced him that the air force had not done enough to stop enemy movement. He did not realize that these German groups were actually remnants of units already broken by Montgomery in the south. Spaatz pointed out that the chief priority of the NASAF and, more recently, of the WDAF was the interruption of enemy reinforcements and supply. No doubt the latest ULTRA intercepts, which reflected the steep decline in unloadings, strengthened Spaatz's defense of the effectiveness of the air effort.[110]

At II Corps, the NAAF's commander found dissatisfaction with photo reconnaissance and the level of air support received. He traced both problems to 1st Army Headquarters, rather than to a lack of desire by XII ASC to provide assistance to II Corps. Bradley's command did not get all the air missions it requested because 1st Army, which set air priorities for all the forces it controlled, did not approve all of II Corps requests. Spaatz had no authority to change that arrangement, although he did attach XII ASC's tactical reconnaissance squadron directly to II Corps and tied II Corps G-2 (Intelligence Staff) into reconnaissance pilot briefings.[111] In attaching one of his air units directly to the ground unit it supported, Spaatz, of course, violated the doctrine of concentration of air assets. Once again, he demonstrated his refusal to allow doctrine to overcome common sense. He thought it better to bend a rule than to adhere to theory and leave the army blind.

Spaatz could do nothing, however, about 1st Army's allocation of air missions. The 1st Army denied II Corps' requests because all available air strength was being employed in front of the 1st Army's British troops to help them blast through stiff German opposition. A return visit by Spaatz on May 4 revealed improvements in the situation and greater satisfaction with air support.[112] Spaatz checked the time elapsed from a II Corps request for air and its clearance through army headquarters and discovered no great delay. He did find, however, that 1st Army Headquarters had refused requests when its judgment of particular needs and conditions differed from that of II Corps.[113]

Later, Spaatz reminded Eisenhower of his previous warnings that the arrangements for the new battle would prove unsatisfactory. Because matters would not improve until his forces had their own independent army or corps commanders with their staffs located alongside XII ASC's headquarters, he recommended no change. Bradley's corps would have to continue under the current structure. Spaatz also informed Eisenhower that the heavy sortie rate of tactical aircraft demonstrated that 1st Army had used its available air resources to the maximum.[114] The collapse of the bridgehead and its final surrender on May 13, 1943, ended the Tunisian campaign. This speedy finish obviated the need for further tinkering with the air-ground relationship.

At the conclusion of the North African campaign, Tedder and Spaatz thought it necessary to formalize NAAF and MAC command arrangements. But the British and American staffs separately drew up complicated organizational charts, began bickering over respective rank and seniority, and insisted on instituting procedures unique to their own service. Tedder's "back hairs began to bristle." At his morning meeting on May 12, disagreements came to a head. Spaatz complained that Mediterranean Air Command would usurp NAAF headquarters' functions by going direct to NAAF's subordinate commands. This, Spaatz said, indicated improper organization. Tedder shot back, "If you want a divorce, you can have one here and now, repeat now!" Only a few moments later, reason returned, and the parties agreed to shelve their draft documents and to get on with fighting the war.[115]

This exchange undoubtedly influenced Spaatz's final judgment on headquarters' arrangements. On May 24, 1943, he wrote to Arnold that the organization had been made to work and had proved adequate for the job at hand, "but it is too dependent on personalities to be sound." Nonetheless, Spaatz believed that the Americans had learned much from the British, particularly the handling of administration, operations, and intelligence.[116]

Spaatz and Changes in AAF Air Support Doctrine

The AAF emerged from the campaign in North Africa with a new and clearly defined doctrine of air support, much of which stemmed from RAF developments. Spaatz absorbed this doctrine, expounded it to Arnold and the AAF hierarchy, and oversaw its development in his command. In addition to the constant stream of information he sent back in his numerous letters and reports to Arnold, Spaatz found time, while on an inspection trip to Marrakech on March 7, to write a long and thoughtful letter in which he described the shortcomings of current official AAF doctrine on air support and suggested seminal changes:

> I cannot believe that the situation here is of such a special nature that it requires
> a peculiar form of organization, but rather that it approximates the conditions

under which our land forces will be confronted at least during the European phase of the war. It has become evident that what we considered the Air Support Command and the air support forces are not adequate for the purpose either in composition or organization, and by their very term give an erroneous impression to the ground army.

Spaatz argued that the air support command needed access to heavy- and medium-bombardment units when the situation required them, that the ASC could not operate effectively, and that the army could not advance until the air force had achieved air superiority. Because air formations could move freely in flight, ignoring terrain, the control of air should be centralized and not divided into small packets among armies or corps. Spaatz listed five requirements for support of the ground army:

> 1. The establishment of a fighter offense and defense, including a complete radar network;
> 2. The use of the fighter force to protect the army and to gain air superiority;
> 3. The creation of a tactical reconnaissance force to meet the needs of the army;
> 4. The creation of a fighter-bomber force to attack targets in the battle area; and
> 5. The employment of a bomber aircraft capable of operation at altitudes up to 10,000 feet.

Once those five elements were achieved, they could be combined to form a tactical air force. In fact, Spaatz suggested eliminating the term *air support command* altogether. In a postscript, Spaatz also mentioned the invaluable role played by the air support parties and commented on the importance of personalities in the coordination of air and ground efforts: "It must be based on the principle that the airman knows his job and the ground man knows his job, with a mutual respect for each others' capabilities and limitations. . . . The ground or the air commander should be eliminated who cannot get along with his opposite number."[117]

Arnold gave wide circulation to this and other letters from Spaatz describing operations and lessons learned.[118] Some of the new air doctrine even reached the American public when *Time* magazine in its March 22, 1943, issue quoted Tedder:

> Air war is a separate war, though linked to those on land & sea. . . . [*sic*]
> Command of the air determines what happens on land & sea. . . . [*sic*] The
> essential lesson learned in the Middle East is that an air force is a separate
> offensive entity, striking at the enemy in cooperation with the army.[119]

Spaatz's March 7 letter to Arnold echoed many of the principles found in War Department Field Manual (FM) 100-20, Field Service Regulations, "Command and Employment of Air Power," issued July 21, 1943. FM 100-20 institutionalized many of the lessons of the North African campaign drawn by Spaatz and disseminated by him to the War Department. The proximate cause of FM 100-20, however, was a note from Assistant Secretary of War for Air Robert A. Lovett to Marshall. Lovett sent Marshall a copy of a pamphlet published by General Montgomery. Montgomery, because of his ballyhooed victories over Rommel in the desert, had a prestige that no other Allied ground commander could match at this stage in the war, thus his statements on the art of command took on a particularly authoritative air.

On February 16, 1943, he and Coningham addressed an assemblage of Allied admirals and generals in Tripoli. Montgomery distributed a pamphlet entitled "Some Notes on High Command in War," in which he spelled out several tenets concerning the use of air power. Air power's greatest asset was flexibility, which enabled it to be concentrated for use as a striking force of prime importance. To gain concentration, air control must be centralized, and command should flow through air force officers. Montgomery specifically forbade the dissipation of air resources into "small packets." He suggested that each army commander have an air headquarters with him to command all aircraft allotted to army support. These air forces would not, however, be under the "direct command" of the army commander.[120]

Coningham added some RAF clarification to Montgomery's remarks. He put the WDAF/8th Army experience into its simplest form saying, "The soldier commands the land forces, the airman commands the air forces; both commanders work together and operate their respective forces in accordance with a combined Army-Air plan, the *whole operation being directed by the Army Commander*" [emphasis added]. The difference between "direct command" and "direction" had been solved for a time in the Western Desert. The difference between the two remained to be resolved between the AAF and the Army Ground Forces (AGF). Coningham also pointed out that the air force had two tasks: first, to gain air superiority, and afterward, to apply 80 to 90 percent of its hitting power to the enemy ground forces.[121] Within days Spaatz sent Arnold a copy of the pamphlet.[122]

On April 18, Lovett sent a copy of the pamphlet to Marshall, claiming that on page 2 it confirmed the principles of the War Department reorganization of June 1941, which established the Army Air Forces as a semiautonomous entity within the Army. Lovett then observed, "General Montgomery's statement with respect to the use of air power contains much material which, although accepted by the Army in principle, has not been formally embodied in our written doctrine, as far as I know."[123] Marshall apparently referred the matter to the War Department General Staff's Organization and Training Division, G-3, asking were the doctrines acceptable to the Army, should they be embodied formally in Army literature, what action had been taken so far by G-3, and what did G-3 recommend?

G-3 replied that the AAF and the AGF held opposing views on Montgomery's doctrine, none of which had been incorporated into official U.S. Army procedures. It also pointed to previous attempts by an AAF-AGF air support board appointed on December 2, 1942, to reconcile those views and to create an entirely new air doctrine. The board failed to agree and postponed any reconsideration of FM 31-35 pending further proof gained by combat. If anything, the board revealed a hardening of positions. The AAF insisted on change in the direction of RAF air support doctrines as tested in the Western Desert, whereas the AGF wished to decentralize air control to levels below division and to emphasize close-in, on-call missions which would expand the zone of friendly artillery fire. In view of the AAF-AGF failure to compromise, G-3 recommended the revision of FM 31-35 and other appropriate War Department publications.[124]

The Operations Plans Division (OPD), the Army's Washington command post, approved but, noting G-3's concentration on the air-ground view, addressed the larger question of overall command and employment of air units at the combat theater level. The OPD told Marshall that in its opinion the theater supreme commander should exercise his command through the senior officer of each service and, in all cases, the "*direct*" [emphasis in original] command of AAF forces must be exercised by the AAF commander. Nor should the supreme commander attach AAF units to units of the ground forces except when ground units were operating independently or were isolated by distance or lack of communication.[125] OPD recommended a position far closer to the AAF's than the AGF's.

The Training Division began informal work on doctrinal revision in early May. Despite the objections of AAF officers in the General Staff,[126] elements of the AGF were polled, and they denounced any change. Not only was FM 31-35 basically sound, but British air support methods, "particularly those of the Eighth Army" had been fully considered and their best features adopted in FM 31-35. Likewise, the U.S. air mission request system came from a study of the tentacle system. The AGF, reading between the revision's lines, raised the following objections:

   1. Ground and air forces would be more widely separated.
   2. There would be little or no air support without air superiority.
   3. Air support, when available, would be furnished on a basis dictated by
the air commander.
   4. Air units would not be attached to ground units, and
   5. Air support would not be decentralized.

The AGF rejected the placement of air superiority at the highest priority, calling the deferment of air support until its attainment an unsound practice which "would impose a serious and at times insurmountable handicap on the ground force commander concerned."[127]

The AGF's protest had no effect on the General Staff. On May 31, a career air officer, Lt. Gen. Joseph T. McNarney, the Deputy to the Chief of Staff, acting for Marshall, instructed the Training Division to change the necessary training publications. McNarney specified that the U.S. Army's new doctrine concerning command and employment of air power would include the following four points:

1. Land and air forces were co-equal and independent,

2. Gaining of air superiority was the first requirement for the success of any major land operation, therefore air would concentrate against the enemy's air forces until the obtainment of air superiority,

3. Flexibility was air's greatest asset allowing concentration of the whole weight of air power on a specific target, and

4. Control of air power must be centralized and exercised through air channels of command; the theater commander would exercise command of the air force through the air force commander; and the theater commander would not attach AAF units to the ground forces unless the ground forces were operating independently or were isolated.[128]

The first section of FM 100-20, when published, consisted entirely of these four points and repeated almost exactly the wording in McNarney's instructions to the Training Division.[129] By the end of June, McNarney and Arnold had personally approved a draft of the new manual.[130] Eight officers (including five generals) representing the infantry (2), the field artillery (1), the coast and antiaircraft artillery (1), and air (4) had also carefully reviewed and approved the draft.[131] Three of those general officers (Stratemeyer, Kuter, and Porter) either had acquired combat experience in North Africa or had recently visited the theater. All three had had extensive discussions with Spaatz on the changes needed in air doctrine.[132]

FM 100-20 reflected several of the thoughts Spaatz had expressed in his March 7, 1943, letter to Arnold: "In order for the Army to advance, the air battle must be won." FM 100-20 stated, "The gaining of air superiority is the first requirement for the success of any major land operation."[133] Spaatz had observed, "The control of the air units must be centralized and command must be exercised through the Air Force commander. . . ." FM 100-20 specified, "CONTROL OF AVAILABLE AIR POWER MUST BE EXERCISED THROUGH THE AIR FORCE COMMANDER."[134] Spaatz had suggested a tactical air force composed of fighters, fighter-bombers, medium bombers, reconnaissance aircraft, and radar warning and control equipment; so did FM 100-20.[135] FM 100-20 also accepted almost word for word Spaatz's admonition concerning the necessity of establishing a fighter-radar network: "The first prerequisite for the attainment of air supremacy is the establishment of a fighter defense and offense, including RDF [radio direction finder], GCI [ground control interception], and other types of radar equipment essential for the detection of enemy aircraft and control of our own."[136]

FM 100-20 reversed the strictures of earlier manuals. For example, FM 31-35 (April 9, 1942), "Aviation in Support of Ground Forces," allowed the army commander specifically to allocate aviation units to the support of subordinate ground units whenever operations required it.[137] FM 100-20 severely circum-scribed that prerogative: "The Superior Commander will not attach Army Air Forces to units of the Ground Forces under his command except when such Ground Force units are operating independently or are isolated by distance or lack of communication."[138] The new manual also followed Spaatz's injunction that, in times of vital and decisive action, the strategic air force may join the tac-tical air force and be assigned tactical objectives.[139] In practice FM 100-20 did not significantly change the methods of air-ground cooperation established by the U.S. Army in Tunisia because, thanks to Spaatz, Tedder, Coningham, and Eisenhower, they were already being used.

So well had Spaatz educated Arnold and the War Department that, when Kuter arrived back in the States shortly after the end of the campaign, he wrote to Spaatz, "My fiery conviction that air support to be effective must come from an air force co-equal and cooperating with the top ground force meets with prac-tically no excitement." According to Kuter, the War Department's Bureau of Public Relations had released the subject to the press "without batting an eye."[140]

A month later Arnold informed Spaatz, "With particular respect to the Tactical Air Force, the ideas you have worked up and forwarded to me are being implemented by Kuter and happen, at present, ⁺o be going full ball [sic] through-out the Air Forces and the War Department." He also noted that the War Department would issue FM 100-20 in the Field Service Regulation format which would be theoretically binding on the theater commander, rather than in the field-manual format, which had served as a guideline only.[141]

The perfection of their own version of air-ground support doctrine was not the only item on Arnold's and the Air Staff's agenda. They also wished to enhance the position of the AAF in the postwar fight for air force independence. After the war Kuter, for instance, admitted that "my own writing during the period was slanted toward the formation of a separate air force."[142] He added that because his primary focus was on independence, he had slighted the tactical air power position. The AAF authors of the manual could not resist the opportu-nity to integrate this agenda with the lessons of North Africa. Thus FM 100-20 became a vehicle proclaiming the independence of air power. Its entire first sec-tion, cast completely in capital letters, was a unilateral declaration of indepen-dence. It began by stating, "LAND POWER AND AIR POWER ARE CO-EQUAL AND INTERDEPENDENT FORCES; NEITHER IS AN AUXIL-IARY OF THE OTHER."[143]

The manual's assignment of missions to the Tactical Air Force named close air support as the third and last priority after attainment of air superiority and the prevention of the movement of troops and supplies into or within the theater of operations. In its discussion of this third priority the manual noted, "In the zone of contact [between the opposing land forces], missions against hostile units are most difficult to control, are most expensive, and are, in general, least effective," and "only at critical times are contact zone missions profitable." Finally, the manual prescribed adjacent or common headquarters for the air and ground forces only when third and last priority targets were attacked.[144]

The Army Ground Forces, as noted, did not concur in the publication of FM 100-20.[145] They feared that centralization of all air power under an air commander might fatally damage the AGF's concept of a combined-arms force in which all Army strength, including air and ground, could be massed at a decisive point.[146] The AGF found it significant and almost insulting that FM 100-20 would supersede the recently published revision of the AAF's principal manual, Army Air Forces Field Manual (FM) 1-5, "Employment of Aviation of the Army," dated January 18, 1943. This manual, which was not widely circulated, was certainly known to the AGF and AAF Headquarters and just as certainly unknown to most, if not all, of the U.S. forces in North Africa. Based in large part on information gathered by prewar observers in England, this manual authorized two practices banned by FM 100-20. It stated that when early warning facilities and communications were lacking, air defense aviation must conduct patrols. The manual added,

> In some situations, and particularly along the line of contact between opposing ground forces, such patrols may also be employed to afford some measure of general protection for friendly aircraft in flight. The primary purpose of such patrols is, however, the protection of surface objectives rather than protection of friendly aircraft in flight.[147]

The manual further noted that such patrols demanded an excessive number of planes and that issuance of antiaircraft artillery to such units was a better alternative. Nonetheless, the manual authorized the penny-packet employment favored by the ground forces, albeit as a last resort. FM 1-5 allowed for the practice of "control or target designation by certain units directly from an air support control, or air support officer *to aircraft in flight*" [emphasis added].[148]

FM 1-5 of January 1943 was the wartime culmination of the entire series of prewar manuals. It took an evolutionary rather than a revolutionary approach. More than the earlier manuals, it addressed the conduct of strategic air operations in a manner close to that advocated by air power enthusiasts. It spoke of a strategic air offensive, emphasized the necessity of staying with a single strategic target system and avoiding diversions, and discouraged using heavy and medium bombardment in direct ground support.[149] FM 1-5's treatment of ground support, as mentioned, reflected the views of the AGF. Yet, it emphasized the interdiction mission of tactical air power rather than that of close air support: "The hostile rear area is the most profitable zone of action for air support aviation. . . . Support aviation is not generally employed against objectives which can effectively be engaged by available ground weapons within the time required."[150] The manual recognized that the aircraft was a theater-level weapon best employed under centralized control; it allowed the direct attachment of air to ground units only under abnormal circumstances. But at the crucial point of the land battle, and only then, "would the requirements of the supported force be paramount."[151] These provisions attempted to satisfy the ground commander's need to employ every available asset when necessary, against the airman's desire to conduct independent counterair and interdiction missions. The AGF was loath to abandon FM 1-5 for FM 100-20.

Observations from North Africa must have confirmed this reluctance. The report of AGF personnel in North Africa revealed anything but the satisfaction Kuter and Spaatz reported back to Washington. Maj. Gen. Walton H. Walker, Commanding General, IV Armored Corps, arrived in Algiers on April 21 and left about May 8, a period when the Allies had almost complete control of the air. Just when Spaatz went forward to make last-minute inspections and adjustments Walker reported, "Air-ground cooperation as envisaged in training and maneuvers of ground force units in the United States appeared to be non-existent in the North African Theater."[152] Both Patton and Bradley informed him that air support had been unsatisfactory, but Bradley did note recent improvement. Particularly criticized were the quantity and frequency of air photographic reconnaissance and the AAF's reliance on planned as opposed to on-call air strikes—two areas of perennial ground force dissatisfaction that still defy agreement between air and ground.[153]

When Spaatz observed that the ground commanders seemed dissatisfied because they could not get all the air support they wanted when they wanted it, he had hit the nail on the head. Both Coningham's and FM 31-35's cumbersome communication links, which required ground requests for air to go from the ground to an air headquarters and from there to an airfield, lent themselves to concentration and centralization of air command and control by airmen. By the same token, this communication system did not lend itself to speedy response to immediate ground requests for air support. Throughout the campaign, ground combat officers complained of the lack of on-call, or immediate-response, air strikes. Brig. Gen. Paul M. Robinett, Commander of the 1st Armored Division's Combat Command B, which suffered heavy casualties under British command, wrote to Marshall: "The coordination of tank attacks with infantry and air attacks has been perfect on the German side. On our own side it has yet to be achieved." Robinett strongly implied that placing all air and ground forces attacking an objective under the ground commander could solve the problem.[154] At the campaign's end, Col. William B. Kern, a battalion commander of the 1st Armored Division, remarked, "I believe that we will have to come to some simple system of requesting air support. The present system of going back through so many channels is wrong. We haven't time for it." Maj. Gen. Charles W. Ryder, Commander of the 34th Infantry Division, added, "The system of calling through two or three different headquarters for air support simply will not give the support desired at the time desired. Adequate air support can only be obtained by direct call from the division to the air. Any other system," observed the general, "is too slow and will result in loss of opportunities."[155]

Given good two-way radio communication between pilots in the air and ground observers (a practice that Coningham forbade and that technology, at that point, could not then guarantee) and a great many airplanes available for ground support missions (not available until later in the war), the close air support problem could be overcome in wartime. During the campaign in northwestern Europe, for instance, overwhelming numbers of fighter-bombers and innovations such as two-way radios installed in the leading tank elements of attacking Allied armored units allowed Allied tactical air forces to supply massive amounts of airborne firepower to the battlefield. FM 100-20 replaced FM 1-5, not FM 31-35. It left in place the clumsy, slow methods of air-ground communications found in FM 31-35, which stayed in effect until postwar revisions. In practice, however, the troops in the field appear to have ignored FM 31-35 in favor of local air-ground arrangements.

The high-level centralization of "photo recon" tended to delay the timely dissemination of its products for use in fluid combat situations. Spaatz attempted, but only at the end of the North African campaign, to solve this problem by attaching XII ASC's photo reconnaissance squadron directly to II Corps.* The AGF's nonconcurrence gave the promulgation of FM 100-20 the aura of an AAF putsch. As Kuter remarked to Coningham, "More people were defeated in Tunisia than Germans and Italians."[156] Why Marshall agreed to sign the manual remains a mystery. Perhaps he felt that this concession to the AAF would mute its increasingly public agitation for independence.

Although he fully understood the new doctrine, Spaatz did not regard it as the last word in the Army versus the AAF. In summing up their relationship he said, "The situation is normal. If it was not for the disturbance which would ensue, I would probably announce the urgent necessity of a separate Air Force." Even the most understanding contacts and intentions at the high command level could not offset the ground-air difference, "which permeates the entire structure." In Spaatz's opinion, the minor day-to-day problems, not the strategic or tactical application of forces, proved the stumbling block of interservice relations. "I will emphasize," he told Arnold, "that air operating under the command control of a ground officer will most probably be improperly used."[157] In an interview in 1965, Spaatz restated this point in answer to a question about the major lessons of World War II: "I think the first lesson was the one about air being indivisible and in order to develop effectively, it must be controlled by air people that developed it, and not under the Army or any other form of organization other than the Air Force."[158]

At the beginning of the campaign in North Africa in November 1942, the AAF and its commander encountered three problems that hampered their efforts

---

* In addition to its employment difficulties, air reconnaissance presented a "political" problem to the AAF in North Africa because the commander of the chief photo reconnaissance unit was one of President Roosevelt's sons, Elliott Roosevelt.

to defeat the Axis: faulty organization, poor logistics, and the lack of an effective air-ground team. By the time of the fall of Tunis and Bizerte in May 1943 the Allies had built an organization, the NAAF, capable of employing air power in a flexible and coherent manner against the enemy. The functional separation of the Northwest African Air Force into a ground support force and a long-range bomber force necessitated by British experience in air-ground cooperation on the one hand, and the AAF's virtual theaterwide monopoly on long-range bombers on the other hand, proved so sensible that the practice continues in the USAF to this day. The relatively smooth functioning of its combined staff served as a model for later Allied organizations.

Spaatz played no small role in the success of the NAAF. Perhaps his supreme ability as a commander was his willingness to delegate authority and responsibility. He resolutely refused to interfere with the day-to-day operations of either Doolittle or Coningham. He trusted them to do the jobs they had trained for, while he served as a theater-level air spokesman. With Tedder, Spaatz kept Eisenhower aware of the needs and limitations of air power. On several occasions he served as Eisenhower's air troubleshooter. When the campaign was two weeks old, Eisenhower ordered him to North Africa to bring order to the chaotic air situation. When the campaign had only two weeks to go, Eisenhower sent him forward to solve Anderson's and Bradley's air support problems.

The Americans, despite claims to the contrary, did not develop an air-ground team. Spaatz himself had to spend days at the front during the campaign's finale, tinkering with arrangements and dealing with Army complaints. Complaints continued into the Sicilian campaign. Brig. Gen. Paul L. Williams, XII ASC's Commander and therefore the senior officer most closely connected to the ground forces, apparently identified with his mission of close air support rather than with air independence. In one of his reports he made the mistake of saying: "I am thoroughly convinced that the organization of an Air Support Command based on the principles of FM 31-35, is sound, workable, and I strongly recommend that all such commands be organized in this manner with certain modifications as indicated herein." He added, "I and my principal staff officers lived and operated with the Corps Commanders during most of the period. This is absolutely essential."[159]

Not surprisingly at the end of the campaign Williams found himself transferred from the XII ASC to a troop carrier wing where he could cooperate to his heart's content with Army airborne troops while not being allowed to overidentify with close air support. After the war an Air Staff officer who had reviewed FM 100-20 before publication and had gained experience in North Africa described the publication of Williams's report as "premature" and ascribed it to a misguided chauvinistic adherence to American concepts. The officer noted that Spaatz neither supported nor endorsed the report.[160] But in fact, Spaatz suggested to Arnold that the report be "given the highest consideration"[161] and demonstrated that, as a combat officer, he did not take so hard a line on air-ground doctrine as the AAF staff in Washington.

Perhaps the most telling statistic on the AAF's attitude toward close air support concerned the training status of the U.S. Army's ground divisions in the United States on January 1, 1944, six months before the invasion of France. Thirty-three still needed aviation for joint training and initial air-ground tests, twenty-one had not witnessed a recognition demonstration of the various types of aircraft, and forty-eight had had no opportunity to participate in the comparative air-ground firepower demonstrations required by regulations.[162]

Although close air support still did not quite meet the mark, it had improved from the beginning of the campaign. The interdiction and counterair phases of tactical air power proved spectacularly successful once the command and control arrangements of air improved enough to allow flexibility. This flexibility allowed (1) the concentration of all forces at the crucial time and place, as with FLAX or the close air support effort for Anderson's April offensive; (2) the encouragement of specialized functions, such as daily antishipping strikes by the Strategic Air Force; and (3) the day-to-day supply of close air support by the Tactical Air Force.

For the relatively modest butcher's bill of 1,433 casualties (277 killed in action, 406 wounded, and 750 missing, interned, or captured),[163] and 666 aircraft of all types lost on combat missions,[164] the AAF acquired a revision of air-ground support doctrine and gained recognition of the principle of equality between air and ground on the battlefield. More important, the AAF had gained valuable combat experience and demonstrated its ability both to overwhelm the Luftwaffe and to interfere with the operations of German ground forces. Carl Spaatz was instrumental in that watershed development of U.S. air power.

Part Three

Mediterranean Interlude
From Pantelleria to London
May–December 1943

Part Three

Mediterranean Interlude

During the second half of 1943, Spaatz and his command fought to maintain a significant role in determining air strategy in the Mediterranean, to assert AAF independence from the U.S. Army and RAF, and to participate in the Combined Bomber Offensive aimed at the German heartland. During late May and early June, the NAAF conducted operations against Pantelleria, a small Italian-occupied island in the straits between Tunisia and Sicily. The surrender of this island on June 11, 1943, demonstrated that, in certain instances, air power alone could force the surrender of a fortified position. Pantelleria also provided a case study in combined operations, air-ground cooperation, and AAF-RAF relations.

The AAF and Spaatz contributed to the success of the Anglo-American invasion of Sicily on July 10, 1943, and of Italy at Salerno on September 9, 1943, by providing air-ground support and air cover for the invasion fleets. During the Allied drive up the Italian peninsula to the Cassino Line, American air power in the Mediterranean continued to provide air-ground support and began to prepare to participate in the Combined Bomber Offensive against Germany by forming a new U.S. air force with a strategic bombardment mission—the Fifteenth.

In early December 1943, Stalin, Churchill, and Roosevelt met in Tehran, Iran, where they agreed on future strategy for the conduct of the war against the Nazis. The planned cross-channel invasion of France was scheduled for spring 1944, and Eisenhower received the top command of the invasion, code-named Operation OVERLORD. Tedder became Eisenhower's deputy.

The British and American Chiefs of Staff also approved both the appointment of an American strategic bomber commander to command and coordinate the Eighth and Fifteenth Air Forces and the transfer of Spaatz to fill the post. The move coincided with Arnold's replacement of Eaker with Doolittle as Eighth Air Force Commander. Arnold had become increasingly disenchanted with the Eighth's combat performance and had assigned Eaker to replace Tedder in the Mediterranean. By January 1, 1944, Spaatz had arrived in London to assume his new command. From there he would direct U.S. participation in the Combined Bomber Offensive and assume de facto direction of U.S. air-ground support of OVERLORD and the subsequent campaigns through to the final defeat of Germany.

Chapter 7

Pantelleria and Sicily
(May–August 1943)

If the fates decree what I would love most is to have the old
gang reassemble at Rehoboth. Whatever is happening now
is a nightmare, with some few pleasant interludes.[1]

—*Spaatz to a friend, June 18, 1943*

General Spaatz came to see me. As usual he was dirty and
unshaved.[2]

—*Lt. Gen. George S. Patton's diary, August 5, 1943*

Pantelleria

After the Axis surrender in Tunisia on May 13, 1943, and before the Allied
invasion of Sicily, on July 10, 1943, the Northwest African Air Force (NAAF)
concentrated its force first against Pantelleria (code-named Operation
CORKSCREW) and then against the German and Italian air forces in Sicily,
Sardinia, and the lower half of the Italian Peninsula. (See Map 7, Pantelleria.)
Pantelleria occupied a key position between Tunisia and Sicily, fifty-three miles
from the former and sixty-three miles from the latter. German radar on the
island, which had a range of eighty miles, could detect any large movement of
shipping or aircraft from Tunisia to southern Sicily. Pantelleria also had an airfield capable of holding eighty fighter aircraft, as well as the capacity to serve as
a base for Axis reconnaissance aircraft and as a fuel and munitions depot for
submarines and motor torpedo boats. Allied capture of the island would not only
deny it to the enemy, but would gain a forward base for one group of short-range
P-40 or Spitfire fighters to cover the Sicilian invasion fleets and landing
beaches. Fighters based at North African fields had insufficient range to reach
Sicily, and the Malta fields could hold no more aircraft. In addition, crippled

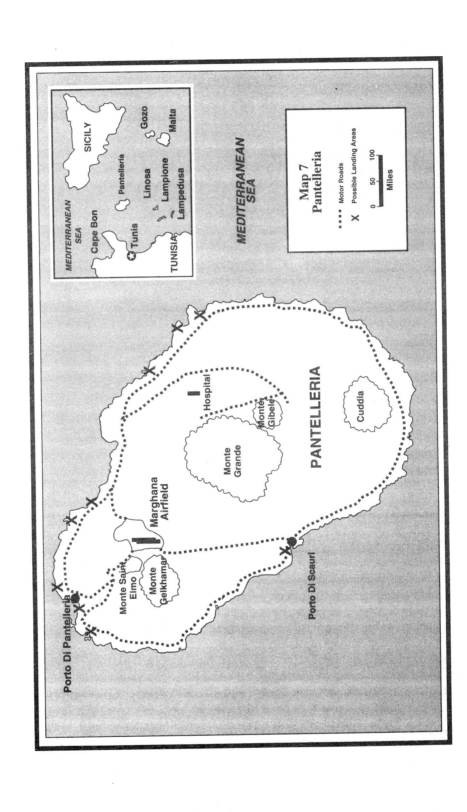

Map 7
Pantelleria

· · · · Motor Roads

X   Possible Landing Areas

0   50   100
Miles

SICILY

MEDITERRANEAN SEA

Cape Bon

Tunis

TUNISIA

Pantelleria

Linosa

Gozo

Malta

Lampione

Lampedusa

MEDITERRANEAN SEA

Hospital

Monte Grande

Monte Gibelè

Cuddia

PANTELLERIA

Marghana Airfield

Monte San Elmo

Monte Gelkhamar

Porto Di Pantelleria

Porto Di Scauri

Allied aircraft would be able to use Pantelleria's airfield if they could not return to their own base. The neutralization of the island became even more important when the final plans for the Sicilian invasion required an assault on the southern beaches near Licata and Gela. The U.S. invasion forces headed for those beaches would have to sail within easy range of Pantelleria.[3]

Pantelleria, a military zone forbidden to unauthorized persons by the Italian government since 1926, presented a potentially tough nut. Its one small beach suitable for amphibious assault had tricky offshore currents and high surf. The island's surface of volcanic lava and ash could not support vehicular traffic and was cut by numerous ravines. The Italians had reinforced these natural defenses with more than a hundred concrete gun emplacements supplemented by fortified positions and pillboxes imbedded in the cliffs. Sturdy peasant farmhouses and hundreds of high, thick stone walls, which delineated each farmer's fields, presented further military difficulties. But Pantelleria had a weak spot—its defending garrison. Before the invasion, Allied intelligence judged the morale of the garrison doubtful—a surmise strengthened by the poor performance of Pantelleria's antiaircraft batteries during the end of the Tunisian campaign.[4] The island's approximately 12,000 defenders were mostly overage and inexperienced; many had homes and families on the island.[5] In addition, the island was effectively deprived of help from the mainland because Allied air superiority over the entire area prevented resupply and reinforcement.

After the fall of Tunisia Operation CORKSCREW became the Allies' chief priority. Allied planners in charge of the invasion of Sicily had begun to consider an assault on Pantelleria as early as February 1943.[6] On May 9, Eisenhower started preliminary preparations. He ordered Tedder to make the full strength of Spaatz's NAAF available for action to remove Pantelleria as a bottleneck to Allied ambitions in the Mediterranean. He further directed Admiral Andrew Cunningham of the Royal Navy to provide naval striking force and protection for the movement of a division to the island.[7] Finally, he set up a combined command consisting of Spaatz, Maj. Gen. Walter E. Clutterbuck, Commander of the British 1st Division, which would land on the island, and Rear Adm. R. R. McGrigor of the Royal Navy, commander of the naval forces in the assault, to oversee the operation. Eisenhower authorized his commanders to postpone the landing, but he reserved the right to abandon the project if losses or opposition grew too heavy.[8] By virtue of his recent promotion, Spaatz outranked the British officers heading up the other sections of the combined operation. This fact, at least, made the air component *primus inter pares*.

Two days later Eisenhower informed the U.S.-British Combined Chiefs of Staff (CCS) that he desired to take Pantelleria in order to use its airfield to support the western portion of the invasion. In the same message he noted that he thought the Allies could "crack this place" because its garrison consisted entirely of Italians.[9]

Operations against Pantelleria presented an excellent opportunity to display

Maj. Gen. W. E. Clutterbuck (*right*)**, General Officer Commanding, 1st British Infantry Division, 1943.**

Rear Adm. R. R. McGrigor, Royal Navy, 1943.

the prowess of air power. The island required a heavy and sustained bombardment to reduce its defenses. Air had to supply this firepower because army artillery could not reach the island and Allied naval commanders would not risk their heavy units in the submarine- and mine-infested narrows, which remained subject to attack by the still-respected Axis air forces. In contrast, the island lay well within striking distance of Northwest African Strategic Air Force (NASAF) fields in Cape Bon. On May 13, Eisenhower told Marshall,

> I want to make the capture of Pantelleria a sort of laboratory to determine the effect of concentrated heavy bombing on a defended coastline. When the time comes we are going to concentrate everything we have to see whether damage to material, personnel and morale cannot be made so serious as to make a landing a rather simple affair.[10]

Spaatz meant to pass his superior's test of air power. He committed to the assault the entire Strategic Air Force and part of the Tactical Air Force, an armada of four heavy-bomber groups, seven medium-bomber groups, two light-bomber groups, and eight fighter groups, a total of slightly more than 1,000 operational aircraft.[11] Against this concentration the Axis had 900 operational combat planes within range of the island, most of them committed to tasks other than defending Pantelleria.[12]

Spaatz met with his British Navy and Army colleagues on May 16 and presented the air plan of operations. It called for three days and nights of increasingly violent attacks, at the end of which the Navy would approach the island to test the remaining strength of enemy defenses. On the fourth day, the Allies would summon the garrison to surrender. Refusal by the garrison would be followed by a "high order" of air attack on the afternoon and night of the fourth day and the landing of troops on the morning of the fifth day. Apparently the Army and Navy accepted the plan, although General Clutterbuck expressed great concern about the amount of residual resistance his troops might have to overcome.[13] Spaatz discounted Clutterbuck's complaints and, in the privacy of his personal headquarters mess, began to refer facetiously to Clutterbuck as "Clusterbottom."[14]

The next day, May 17, Spaatz expressed to Eisenhower his belief that the air component ought to control the operation, while the Army and Navy should conform to the air commander's decisions. He also emphasized that the current bombing of Pantelleria constituted only part of a larger Allied air effort to suppress the German and Italian air forces in anticipation of the battle for Sicily.[15]

The preparatory bombing of Pantelleria began on May 19. Fifty medium-bomber and fifty fighter-bomber sorties a day struck Pantelleria's airfield and port in an effort to prevent any resupply of the island. These attacks, supplemented by a naval blockade, increased in tempo on May 23 and by the end of the month had almost completely cut the island's supply lines. Additional raids against Axis airfields in Sicily, Sardinia, and the toe of Italy helped to prevent

Axis air interference with the Pantelleria operation and the all-important invasion of Sicily.[16]

Just before the initial bombing of the island got under way, Spaatz started an inspection trip of the NAAF's rear echelons. He flew from Eisenhower's headquarters in Algeria to Casablanca on the evening of May 17. There he met Brig. Gens. John K. Cannon and Delmar Dunton, who commanded the Northwest African Training Command (NATC) and the Northwest African Service Command (NASC) respectively. The next day, Spaatz inspected the air depot at Casablanca and found it well stocked and efficient, a far cry from its state during his initial inspection in November 1942. Later that day, the three generals flew to Marrakech where they decided to release the facilities there from the purview of the NAAF and place them under the Air Transport Command. On the following day, the party flew from Marrakech east to Oujda, where they inspected the 99th Fighter Squadron (Separate).[17]

The 99th was the first all-black AAF combat unit to reach an overseas combat theater. Its thirty-year-old commanding officer, Lt. Col. Benjamin O. Davis, Jr., a West Point graduate and son of Brig. Gen. Benjamin Davis, the first black general in U.S. history, caught Spaatz's eye. Spaatz's diary recorded that "Lieutenant Colonel Davis impressed me most favorably, both in appearance and intelligence." Spaatz also noted that the squadron would be attached to the 33d Fighter Group for use in ground support and would receive the same treatment as any similar white squadron.[18]

On May 20, Spaatz returned to Oujda and reviewed troops of the 82d (Airborne) Division. He hosted a lunch followed by a meeting with Lt. Gen. Mark W. Clark, Commander of the U.S. Fifth Army, Clark's chief of staff, Maj. Gen. Alfred M. Gruenther, and Maj. Gen. Matthew B. Ridgway, Commander of the 82d Division. They agreed on the advisability of employing a battalion of the 82d in the upcoming Sicilian invasion. When talk began to drift to further operations, Spaatz expressed some wildly unorthodox viewpoints on future courses of action. To avoid slogging through Sicily, Sardinia, and Italy the Allies could, he suggested, buy Spain off very cheaply and secure the necessary control of the air to cross the Pyrenees. Once they crossed the Pyrenees and reached the Bay of Biscay, they could eliminate the submarine threat, "the only chance Germany had of still winning the War." An invasion "through Spain was the best way of putting an Army on the continent of Europe."[19] Spaatz did not stop there. He suggested that the Americans exclude the British from the Iberian operation and thus more easily persuade the Spanish to cooperate.

Clark not only agreed with Spaatz but added that on an earlier occasion he had discussed a similar idea with Marshall, who had proved sympathetic. Marshall had told Clark that Churchill opposed the idea. The generals concluded their session after deciding that, because the Americans were supplying the majority of combat forces, their plan for invading Spain ought to have priority over operations in the Mediterranean, which supported purely British national interests. Clark said he would present the results of this brainstorming to Eisenhower that very afternoon.[20]

If he did, they went no further. Whatever his limitations, if any, as a field commander, Eisenhower had far too much political and diplomatic talent and knowledge to seriously consider any such plan. It revealed an abysmal ignorance of Spanish politics and demonstrated a cavalier disregard of the numerous logistical and geographical difficulties involved. Nonetheless, it reflected the impatience of some Americans in the higher military echelons toward the strategic direction of the war forced on them by the necessities of coalition warfare.

On May 22, Spaatz flew to meet Eisenhower, Cunningham, Alexander, and Tedder. Among other matters they discussed preparations for the Pantelleria operation. Admiral Cunningham, with certain reservations, backed Eisenhower in approving them.[21] Alexander, the top ground commander in the theater, had his doubts.[22] The consequences of failure, such as raised Italian morale, worried him greatly. Spaatz replied that if the Allies could not accomplish the reduction of the island, "we might as well pack up and go home."[23]

Later the same day Spaatz met with Clutterbuck and McGrigor to discuss operational specifics. At the end of the meeting, the three agreed to draw up a final plan and present it to Eisenhower. Spaatz went over its outlines with Eisenhower the next day and received his approval to go ahead with it.[24] It followed the original recommendation that an increasing level of air bombardment culminate with a final intensive bombing attack on the five days prior to landing, scheduled for June 11. Apparently, Clutterbuck still had objections because Eisenhower noted in a letter to Marshall on May 25 that some of those responsible for carrying out the invasion "are shaking their heads."[25] In fact, Clutterbuck visited Eisenhower to tell him of his doubts about the attack and said that he "feared that he would have a great number of his men slaughtered."[26]

On May 24, at his forward headquarters in La Kroub, Spaatz again met with McGrigor and Clutterbuck to conclude their plans for convoys and lines of communication. They also scheduled rehearsals for three days (D-3) and one day (D-1) before the actual invasion. Two days later, Spaatz flew to Malta and met its air commander, Air Vice-Marshal Keith Park, who agreed to allow NAAF planes to use Malta as a refueling point and to cooperate fully in mounting the operation.

On his return from Malta, Spaatz found that Professor Solly Zuckerman, a medical doctor and research anatomist who had temporarily vacated an appointment at Oxford to conduct studies on the effects of bomb damage, had arrived at NAAF Headquarters in Constantine. The British Chief of Combined Operations, Lord Louis Mountbatten, had brought Zuckerman into his organization. There the professor became friends with the Deputy Chief of Combined Operations for the air element, Air Vice-Marshal James Robb, who later became Deputy Commander of the NAAF under Spaatz. Robb had introduced Zuckerman to Spaatz in March 1943, and the two apparently hit it off. Zuckerman wrote about his first dinner with Spaatz's staff that "they were men who were learning, as I was learning, and unlike some professional military people whom I had met, there was no assumption of superior knowledge, and no assurance that they knew how Germany was going to be defeated."[27]

Two months later, Zuckerman, then in London, received a request by telegram from Robb to go to North Africa. Upon his arrival on May 22, Zuckerman met Tedder, another old friend, who sent him to Spaatz's headquarters with instructions to comment on the feasibility of the forthcoming Pantelleria operation. After a two-day study in which he applied the statistical and quantitative methods he had employed in his scientific and anatomical studies, Zuckerman replied that the forces available could silence Pantelleria's shore defenses.[28] From then until he issued his final report on the island's damage in July 1943, Zuckerman became a part of Spaatz's staff. He roomed with Brig. Gen. Lauris Norstad,[29] Assistant Chief of Staff for Operations, NAAF, and attended all planning sessions.[30]

Zuckerman's first task after demonstrating the feasibility of the operation was to help prepare a detailed bombing plan. He had constant exchanges with Spaatz, Robb, Norstad, and McDonald, who, according to Zuckerman, made it plain that they had every confidence in his ability to produce an effective and precise bombing plan of a kind that had not been designed before.[31] The professor repaid the airmen's confidence by producing one that (1) provided precise aiming points; (2) called for detailed reports and analysis of each sortie; (3) required extensive photo reconnaissance; and (4) demanded the plotting of every bomb burst on a grid, with attention paid to the relationship of bombs identified to total dropped, the position of burst in relation to gun positions, and any damage caused. As a last proposal, Zuckerman called for an extensive ground survey of the island after it was captured.[32]

Even before the professor presented his plan's final draft, Spaatz's forces began to execute it. Photos and reports poured into the schoolroom where Zuckerman, with a small staff and photo interpretation experts, assessed damage and assigned new targets. The plan called for enough bombs to be dropped on each battery to destroy only one-third to one-half of its guns; peripheral bomb damage would inactivate the rest of the battery by damaging gun sights and communications and storage facilities and would bury everything in rubble. Once the analysts had determined that a battery had received sufficient explosives, they redirected their effort. On each of the twelve days prior to the invasion, Zuckerman submitted a report to Norstad, who forwarded it, with appropriate changes of orders, to each command.[33]

While the professor orchestrated the bombing, Spaatz coordinated other aspects of the invasion within the NAAF and with the Allied ground and naval forces. On May 28, he met with Brig. Gen. Elwood R. Quesada, Deputy Commander of the Coastal Air Force, and with a representative of Air Marshal Arthur Coningham, Commander of the Tactical Air Force. Spaatz made it clear to both that the Pantelleria invasion would have priority over any other task facing their commands and that he would accept no excuses for failure.[34] When difficulties arose on June 3–4, during a preinvasion test exercise involving the Royal Navy command ship, HMS *Largs*, a five-year-old, 4,500-ton vessel designated a Landing Ship Headquarters and packed with communications gear, Spaatz flew to Sousse on the coast of northeastern Tunisia, the location of invasion task force headquarters.

Clutterbuck and McGrigor reported an almost complete failure in air cooperation with both army and navy elements of the invasion force. Although final test results indicated three satisfactory communication links—between the ship and individual planes, between the ship and NAAF headquarters, and between the ship and task force headquarters at Sousse—the communication links between the ship and the Tactical Air Force and the XII Air Support Command (XII ASC) failed. Spaatz ordered the air inspector to investigate. The XII ASC, at Spaatz's orders, would begin flying a daily mission against Pantelleria under the sole direction of the naval command ship and was to maintain constant communication with it at all times. In addition, Coastal and Tactical Air Forces would henceforth maintain full-time liaison officers at task force headquarters. Spaatz returned to Constantine convinced that much of the doubt in the minds of the British Army and Navy commanders stemmed from their own interservice rivalry with the RAF.[35] Upon returning to his headquarters Spaatz instructed Robb to "inform Coningham that my impression was that he was a trifle too indifferent in his arrangements for CORKSCREW, particularly in connection with exercises."[36]

Meanwhile, the bombardment of Pantelleria steadily increased in fury. On June 1, the first B-17s attacked the island. Together with P-40 fighter bombers they dropped 141 tons of high explosives; on June 4, heavy, medium, and fighter bombers unloaded an additional 200 tons of bombs. Between May 18, when the bombing began, and June 4, the NAAF flew 1,700 sorties flinging 900 tons of ordnance, many of them 250- or 500-pound high-explosive bombs, on the harbor and airfield and 400 tons on Pantelleria's gun positions.[37] Starting with June 7, D-day minus four (D-4), the level of attack increased daily, especially when General Doolittle, Commander of the Strategic Air Force, lowered the bombing altitude after disappointing results.[38]

On June 7, Spaatz flew back to Sousse. At 5:30 the next morning, (D-3), he boarded Admiral McGrigor's flagship, a small Hunt Class destroyer-escort, HMS *Whaddon*, for a personal look at the effects of bombing and naval gunfire on Pantelleria. Clutterbuck and Zuckerman were also on board. In addition to the eight destroyers of McGrigor's task force, five cruisers from the British Mediterranean Fleet joined in the shelling. One of them, HMS *Aurora*, had Eisenhower and Admiral Andrew Cunningham on board. They, too, wished to view the proceedings.[39]

As the *Whaddon* approached the island around 10:00 A.M., Clutterbuck became visibly upset, complaining about the spasmodic nature of naval fire and what he considered excessive intervals between air strikes.[40] When the *Whaddon* joined in the bombardment, firing 36-pound shells from its twin 4-inch guns, Spaatz muttered to Zuckerman, "What the hell kind of damage do they think these small shells will do?"[41] This sentiment was echoed by the professor, who noted in his memoirs that photo interpretation throughout the campaign never revealed any significant damage by naval fire.[42] A little before 11:00 A.M. the medium bombers attacked two gun batteries. Then came the *pièce de résistance.* Doolittle's B-17s rumbled over Pantelleria at 12,000 feet; their bomb salvos, aimed at two of the island's batteries, completely obscured the coastline with smoke and dust. This sight even encouraged Clutterbuck.[43]

Throughout the bombardment of June 8, only three Italian batteries attempted to engage the ships offshore, and the garrison did not put up a heavy barrage against the attacking aircraft. After the B-17s completed their mission, fighter-bombers dropped surrender leaflets and the Allies declared a unilateral six-hour cease-fire. These overtures elicited no response from the Italians, and so the attack resumed in the afternoon. The ships returned to harbor. Eisenhower, who had spent the day on a 6,000-ton cruiser, reported to Marshall that he and Cunningham "were highly pleased both with the obvious efficiency of the air and naval bombardments, and with their coordination achieved as to timing."[44]

Those who had spent their day baking in the Mediterranean sun on an unstable 1,000-ton destroyer-escort returned to port in a much more irascible frame of mind. Spaatz grumbled in his diary,

> This particular show has been 95% air, and would have been difficult under any circumstances, but has been doubly so by the reluctance of AFHQ [Eisenhower] to place an Air Officer in complete charge of the show. It has been only by virtue of my outranking the other officers that air has been able to take control, but it could have been easier . . . had this authority been vested in me, or an Air Officer.[45]

Spaatz also directed that the next time Eisenhower observed an air attack he should have an air officer at his side to prevent his getting too big a dose of navy attitude. Apparently upon disembarking, Clutterbuck immediately fired off messages to Tedder and Eisenhower, complaining that communication failures in the test exercise and the XII ASC's "lack of interest in" the operation had jeopardized the success of the invasion.[46]

Eisenhower and Tedder responded promptly to Clutterbuck's signals. Eisenhower sent his chief of staff, Maj. Gen. Walter Bedell Smith, and Tedder sent two men, his chief deputy and his chief of staff, Air Vice-Marshal H.E.P. Wigglesworth and Brig. Gen. Patrick W. Timberlake, to invasion force headquarters at Sousse, apparently with instructions to investigate the operation's air-ground cooperation arrangements. When the extra stars arrived on June 9 (D-2), Spaatz noted tartly in his diary that "having so many fingers in the pie at the last minute does not lend much help to the operation at this stage of the game."[47]

Tedder's men tested the signal arrangements, found them satisfactory, and returned to Tedder's headquarters in Algiers with what Spaatz hoped was a "clearer picture of the trouble which can be caused by one nervous ground force man."[48] Bedell Smith stayed to the end of the operation, partly because Eisenhower had begun to be apprehensive regarding its ultimate conclusion—a case of nerves caused in some measure by "a number of long faces" at his own headquarters.[49]

Over and above his meetings with Bedell Smith, Timberlake, and Wigglesworth, Spaatz double-checked arrangements for the invasion. He talked with AAF Brig. Gen. Aubry C. Strickland, one of the supporting aircraft pilots in the *Question Mark* flight who now commanded the NAAF Air Service Command troops scheduled to prepare the island's airfield for its new Allied occupants. Strickland's 2690th Base Command would also tend to the occupation chores involving Pantelleria's civil population.[50] Strickland reported that he had collected his troops and, at the moment, had that no further problems. Spaatz also instructed his supply officers to make sure that no stoppages occurred in the air supply line. He wanted definite assurances that NAAF planes had sufficient bombs, ammunition, and fuel to maintain maximum effort on both D-day and the days immediately preceding and following it.[51]

By 11:00 the next morning, June 10, Spaatz and his staff boarded the HMS *Largs,* from which they observed the last day of air activity and the dispatch of the invasion fleet. By 8:30 the next morning on D-day, June 11, the *Largs* had sighted Pantelleria and within an hour had sailed to within ten miles of it. By 10:30 A.M. the assault boats had formed up and awaited only the signal to start their final run to the beach, timed to coincide with the end of the naval bombardment and a last B-17 strike. The Tactical Air Force completed its bombing by 10:00 A.M., and the Strategic Air Force's heavy bombers pounded the island one last time at 11:30 A.M., an instant before the first troops hit the beaches. On board the *Largs,* Clutterbuck continued to exhibit unease, even though the ship's display boards showed that all bombing had followed schedule and that 300 additional sorties had punished the island since 10:00 A.M. Spaatz's command diary noted scornfully, "Timidity on his part has been prevalent throughout the entire operation."[52]

The landing itself proved anticlimactic. As troops hit the beach, offshore observers noted a white flag flying over the island. During the night of June 10–11, Vice Adm. Gino Pavesi, the Italian military governor of Pantelleria, had informed Rome that the Allied bombing was unendurable.[53] On the morning of June 11, Pavesi held a staff meeting. All present agreed that the situation had become untenable. There was no water (bombing had destroyed the water plant), no communications, and nearly no ammunition. In addition, almost all 24,000 people on the island were exhausted. Before he sighted the invasion fleet, Pavesi had already made the decision to surrender by 11:00 A.M. on June 11.

The already low morale of the defenders had crumbled under incessant bombardment and the shortages of basic supplies. Many of the local militia, who manned the antiaircraft batteries, had deserted in order to assist their families.[54] From May 8 to June 11, the NAAF had dropped 6,200 tons of bombs and had flown 5,285 sorties, with the loss of fourteen aircraft destroyed or missing. AAF planes accounted for 5,000 tons of bombs and 4,387 sorties.[55] Naturally, Spaatz was pleased, as was Robert A. Lovett, Assistant Secretary of War for Air, who had come to North Africa in late May and had stayed to witness the conclusion of the operation. The two sent a telegram to Arnold briefly describing the battle and concluded by saying, "The boys have really done a grand job."[56]

The Allies transferred their attention and air strikes to the Pelagies (a group of three small islands: Lampedusa, Linosa, and Lampione also located between Africa and Sicily), which surrendered the next day.

A day after the surrenders, Spaatz sent Zuckerman to Pantelleria to prepare a thorough report on the exact nature and effectiveness of the bombing. This prompt action reflected Spaatz's concern that studies by the ground forces or navy hostile to air might downgrade the effectiveness of the air effort.[57] While waiting for the professor's final report, which he did not receive until July 20, Spaatz drew some immediate conclusions from the experience which led him to recommend three improvements: (1) longer-range radar for command ships; (2) manning of opposite ends of communications links by members of the same service and country; and (3) coordination of all bombing, whether tactical or strategic, with and through the control ship.[58]

In Spaatz's mind, at least, Pantelleria had confirmed the most extreme theories of air power enthusiasts: air power *alone* could defeat a major power. While still in the afterglow of the Pantelleria success, Spaatz wrote to a friend:

> The application of air power available to us can reduce to the point of surrender any first class nation now in existence within six months from the time that pressure is applied. In applying the pressure, any or all of the air must be directed against anything which can prevent or interrupt our air effort. Any conception of modern Warfare which does not fully recognize the foregoing is marking time in place.[59]

Two days later, Spaatz forwarded to Tedder the preliminary analysis of damage by Zuckerman and in his cover letter expressed his conclusions a little less boldly: "Precision bombing deserves a precise plan, and air forces properly employed can destroy or reduce the operational effectiveness of defenses to a point where the will to fight ceases to exist." In a bow to Zuckerman, Spaatz acknowledged, "Air force operations must be planned to employ scientifically forces adequate to secure the degree of material destruction necessary to reduce the objective. A by-product of such operations will almost certainly be complete demoralization." Again referring to Zuckerman's application of the scientific method, Spaatz wrote, "The force necessary to destroy communications and to isolate a given area is a matter of mathematical calculation. In this instance, the

236

Pantelleria, June 1943. Wrecked Italian Fiat and Macchi aircraft litter a field *(above)* on the island of Pantelleria after an Allied raid. The entrance to an underground hangar *(below)* indicates the protection such aircraft were afforded.

force employed succeeded in paralyzing what can be regarded as a front of fifteen miles, with a reasonable factor of safety."

Spaatz had two more points: (1) an ascending and continuous scale of bombardment coupled with deliberate and successive elimination of strong points will markedly affect the defenders' morale and paralyze their repair facilities and services; and (2) "unless topographical features exist, which allow the precise definition of targets and bombing lines, the air cannot be expected to provide a precise barrage immediately in front of ground or naval forces."[60]

These were the views of an air power zealot. Fortunately for himself and the AAF, Spaatz reserved most of them for his Command Diary. The Pantelleria operation merely confirmed his long-held opinion that air, in order to exert its dominant role in warfare, required equality with the army and the navy and that equality could come only with independence for the air forces. As Spaatz explained to Zuckerman, "There was one 'A' too many in the designation U.S.A.A.F."—the 'A' that stood for Army—and Pantelleria would help get rid of it.[61]

The operation also provided an opportunity for one of the pioneering efforts in the application of scientific analysis and quantification to combat, particularly in operations research for the AAF and the closely related field of operations analysis. Zuckerman's methods and results predisposed airmen, such as Spaatz, to seek more opportunities to apply them. Zuckerman's work received mention in Eisenhower's dispatch on the fall of Pantelleria:

> A less intense bombardment might, in the light of later knowledge, have subjugated the island, but there would have been lacking essential data for the study of the tactical possibilities of scientifically directed air bombardment of strongpoint[s], and the most economical disposal of available air strength. Professor Zuckerman's exhaustive report on the subject may prove of as much value in the fight against the Axis as the capture of the island.[62]

Zuckerman's final report showed that although the batteries received bombing on a scale of 1,000 tons of bombs per square mile, the amount of firepower lost to each battery ranged from 10 percent to 75 percent, with an average of more than 40 percent lost for all batteries.[63] Only two batteries received direct hits and the attacks neutralized forty-three of the eighty guns, ten of them permanently.[64]

Not all analysts of Operation CORKSCREW have agreed with Spaatz's most extreme conclusions. Clutterbuck pointed out the failure of the XII ASC and the *Largs* command ship to establish satisfactory communications links during practices. He argued that communications between the two would have failed disastrously had they been needed.[65]

Montgomery's recent biographer, Nigel Hamilton, condemned the effort expended in the conquest of Pantelleria as an "unfortunate distraction" and bemoaned the casualties "sacrificed to this airman's fantasy of how the Axis enemy could be defeated by air power alone."[66] Hamilton implied that the effort could have been better spent by softening up Sicily, as if the initial German counterattack on the Sicilian beachheads could have been totally prevented by air power. To blame many of Montgomery's problems in Sicily on inadequate preinvasion air bombardment does air power and Montgomery no service. Without the presence of the 33d Group's P-40s and Spitfires flying from Pantelleria's field, Montgomery would have had even less support.

As the AAF official history admitted, "In the final analysis the morale of the defenders was the determining factor in the failure of Pantelleria to put up a strong and prolonged resistance. The air assault not only hurt the enemy's ability to resist; it broke his will."[67] The AAF's conclusions were literally true, but the extremely low morale of the garrison was not so much the product of air bombardment as of other factors. The air bombardment probably provided a face-saving excuse for an action the garrison would have taken in any case. A more resolute defending force, despite the damage inflicted by Allied air power, would certainly have made the landing a far bloodier affair.

Preinvasion Planning and Air Preparations for Sicily

At the Casablanca Conference in January 1943, the Anglo-American allies decided to continue their campaign in the Mediterranean by invading the island of Sicily after the fall of Tunisia. Planning for HUSKY, the code name for the operation, began in February 1943. The Allies did not complete the main elements of the plan until May 13. Before that date they had intended to land on two widely separated points on the island. The Americans would land on the northwest near the key port of Palermo, and the British would land in the southeast near the port of Syracuse. However, thanks in part to the strenuous objections of General Montgomery,[68] Commander of the British 8th Army which would conduct the British portion of the landing, the final arrangements called for the Americans to land on the left flank of the British at Licata, Gela, and Scoglitti, with the immediate seizure of the large airfield complexes of Ponte Olivo, Biscari, and Comiso as their first objective. The British would land near the port of Syracuse and move inland. Spaatz's Northwest African Air Force would carry the brunt of the air responsibility for the invasion.

The NAAF first had to destroy or neutralize Axis air power prior to the assault. Next, it had to provide close air support to the naval, ground, and airborne assault forces. It also had to shield the invasion area, ongoing naval operations, and the assault convoys from enemy air attack while taking the offensive against enemy shipping and naval forces. Additional air units based in Malta and the Middle East would aid the NAAF in its endeavors.[69]

The NAAF's plans placed all units in Malta under the command of the Air

Officer Commanding, Malta, who in turn came under the general direction of the Commander of the Northwest African Tactical Air Force, Arthur Coningham. Air plans further ensured the maximum amount of flexibility by arranging for a high degree of coordination between the Northwest African Tactical and Strategic Air Forces; depending on the situation, either air force might come under the operational control of the other.[70]

The air plan had three main phases. The first phase, from the defeat of the Axis in Tunisia to July 3, called for the NAAF to bomb systematically Axis air forces and Italian industry over a widely dispersed area so as not to give away the invasion target. The heavy bombers would bomb airfields in Sardinia, Sicily, and southern Italy, along with the ports of Naples, Messina, and Palermo and industrial targets in southern Italy. Harris's Bomber Command would strike targets in northern Italy, in the hope of keeping some Axis air forces out of the invasion area. The second phase of the bombing, the week before the invasion, would switch attacks to enemy communications with Sicily and concentrate on enemy airfields with round-the-clock bombing. This phase ignored landing beaches in the hope of maintaining tactical surprise. The third phase, after the invasion, would keep the Allied air forces continuing their counterair attacks while maintaining air superiority over the island.[71]

The AAF official history notes that "the air plan dealt for the most part with broad policies and it had not been integrated in detail with ground and naval plans. This was deliberate and the result of sound strategic and tactical considerations."[72] Unlike the North African campaign, the Sicilian operation would ensure the air forces the maximum flexibility in their employment and prevent the immobilization of air resources caused by parceling air out to specific units or sectors. As the operation began, 4,900 operational Allied planes faced 990 German and 700 Italian air force operational aircraft.[73]

As the invasion approached, the photographic and signal intelligence section at Spaatz's headquarters in La Marsa put together the products of both sources of information on an hourly basis.[74] Spaatz, as usual, paid special attention to ensuring rapid dissemination and use of the fruits of the intelligence effort. On June 18, he ordered a direct communications link set up between the NAAF War Room in La Marsa and the forward command posts of the Tactical, Strategic, and Coastal Air Forces. He also directed that each air force's forward command post have present for duty at all times an officer with the authority to make binding decisions for that air force.[75] These measures increased his control over subordinates and helped to enable all elements of the NAAF to respond quickly to the latest German moves.

Throughout the Sicilian campaign, the NAAF performed its many tasks successfully. Before the invasion, its heavy- and medium-bomber groups, aided by the bombers attached to the U.S. Ninth Air Force and by its own fighter-bombers, kept up their attacks on the Axis air forces. These attacks, which started with strikes assisting the NAAF's April 1943 assault on German air transport into the Tunisian bridgehead and continued through and after the anti-air strikes supporting the Pantelleria operation, rose to a crescendo in the week preceding July 10 (D-day). Spaatz firmly believed in the necessity of conducting a vigorous counterair offensive before other land, sea, or air operations began. On June 24 he observed to Arnold, "The German Air Force becomes very cocky when it has a few successes. It then becomes necessary to give them a thorough beating on their airdromes as well as in the air."[76]

By the beginning of June, the Luftwaffe had started to transfer bombers from Sicily and southern Italy to southern France and northern Italy. This move diminished its ability to attack the ports where the Allied invasion forces assembled. ULTRA, however, revealed an increase in Luftwaffe fighter and fighter-bomber activity on Sicily, which continued until July 3. At that point the NAAF began a final week of intensive bombardment, which reduced the number of fighters by one-third and caused the fighter-bombers to withdraw. Diversionary and counterair raids on Sardinia in the week before the invasion reduced the 130 Luftwaffe fighter-bombers there to 35 percent serviceability and denied them the aviation fuel necessary for sustained operations. Added to the invaluable information gained from signal intelligence was detailed aerial photographic reconnaissance. NAAF aircraft took special photos of industrial areas and communication lines and daily pictures of the Corsican, Sardinian, Sicilian, and Italian airfields and the ports berthing the major surface combat units of the Italian fleet.[77]

By July 10, only two airfields on Sicily remained entirely serviceable. Also, NAAF strikes against communications lines had totally disrupted the Sicilian rail network by destroying rolling stock and repair facilities. As a final fillip, on July 9, NAAF Spitfires shattered the Hotel San Domenico at Taormina, the Luftwaffe's headquarters on Sicily. This raid, prompted by the pinpoint accuracy of signal and other intelligence, dislocated the Luftwaffe's response on the day of the invasion.[78] The NAAF's effective preinvasion attacks of Sicily helped to limit to 12 ships the losses among the invasion fleet of 3,000 craft as a result of Axis air action, as opposed to the original estimate of possibly 300.[79]

When the Allied troops reached the shore, Coningham's Northwest African Tactical Air Force once again shouldered its responsibilities for air-ground cooperation. Allied air had an equal voice in air-ground arrangements. It had not in the invasion of North Africa in 1942. Montgomery's 8th Army continued its excellent relationship with Air Vice-Marshal Harry Broadhurst and the Western Desert Air Force. On the U.S. side Spaatz had spent considerable energy providing support for Lt. Gen. George S. Patton's U.S. Seventh Army.

On May 13, Spaatz, Tedder, and Coningham met and agreed on new command arrangements for air support and cooperation. Col. Paul Williams, Commander of the XII Air Support Command (XII ASC), the principal U.S. component of the Tactical Air Force, was to move over to Troop Carrier Command (TCC), a unit charged with the delivery and supply of airborne troops in the combat zone. Col. Lawrence P. Hickey would take command of XII ASC

241

Headquarters, which would become a glorified air support party attached directly to Patton's headquarters. The fighter units of XII ASC would join the Third Air Defense Wing directly under Coningham's command, while Brig. Gen. John K. Cannon replaced Kuter as Coningham's second in command and principal American deputy. Finally, Tedder was to meet with all army commanders and senior air officers before the invasion in order to completely clarify arrangements. The conferees also agreed that when U.S. forces had firmly established themselves on Sicily, the XII ASC would reconstitute itself as a major combat unit.[80] According to Spaatz, these moves resulted from his feeling that the Tactical Air Force had not given the U.S. II Corps enough help in the just-completed campaign.[81]

The new arrangements left Patton unsatisfied. He noted in his diary on May 22, "Tedder controls the air with Spaatz, a straw man, under him. . . . Conyngham [*sic*] commands the tactical air force and the close support air force by another British Vice Air Marshall [*sic*]. Our close support force is commanded by a Colonel. . . . The U.S. is getting gypped."[82] Patton took his complaints to Alexander, who passed them on to Spaatz. For his part, Spaatz assured Alexander that he had placed Cannon in Coningham's headquarters precisely because Patton had more faith in Cannon than in any other air force officer. Spaatz promised to send Cannon to Patton as soon as the former had a chance to become familiar with his new job.[83]

Lt. Gen. Carl A. Spaatz receiving a report from members of the 90th Photographic Intelligence Wing, North Africa, July 1, 1943.

Two days later on May 24, Spaatz met with Cannon, told him of the earlier promise to Alexander, and instructed him to see Patton within the week. Spaatz also noted that Patton had expressed apprehension to Eisenhower as well and instructed Cannon to inform Patton that the air reconnaissance squadron attached to his headquarters would receive its orders directly from XII ASC and not Coningham.[84]

Before the landing Spaatz made one major change in the implementation of the air support command arrangement. He replaced Colonel Hickey, who had apparently never gained the confidence of Coningham,[85] with Maj. Gen. Edward J. House. This change mollified both Coningham and Patton while making the rank of the Commander of XII ASC equal to that of Air Vice-Marshal Broadhurst's, Air Officer Commanding the Western Desert Air Force.[86]

Air Power and the Invasion of Sicily

With few exceptions, air power performed successfully throughout the Sicilian campaign. Although the NAAF's efforts minimized friendly ground and naval losses to enemy air power, air-ground cooperation again proved unsatisfactory to the U.S. ground forces. For most of the campaign on-call air support remained non-existent. Maj. Gen. John P. Lucas, Commander of VI Corps, voiced an apparently widespread opinion: "Air missions took too long to accomplish even after the planes had been moved to Sicily. Authority to fly this mission could be obtained in about three hours whereas the mission itself took only 20 or 30 minutes."[87]

Near the end of the fighting, however, the Allies introduced the "Rover Joe" (in British usage, the "Rover" tentacle), a communications unit located with front-line divisions or brigades or sometimes smaller units, consisting of an armored scout car equipped with radio sets and a joint staff of army officers and one RAF officer. It communicated with the Army Air Support Control, the joint Army-RAF communications group at the WDAF/8th Army Headquarters; with the Air Liaison Officer at the wing or group airfield; and, by means of a VHF radio, directly with aircraft over the target area. The staff of the tentacle kept in close touch with the local army unit commander. If he approved an air strike, the liaison officer at the wing was briefed. When the planes arrived, the tentacle's RAF officer directed them to the target. The U.S. Seventh Army and XII ASC used a similar system based on the jeep.[88]

The partial failure of airborne operations as well as the failure to prevent the Axis evacuation of Sicily by completely interdicting the Straits of Messina marred the air effort. The initial paratroop and glider forces landed on D-day (July 9), seized many of their objectives, and caused great confusion to the island's defenders. Nonetheless, the landings proved costly in terms of manpower; and, because the troops were so widely scattered, their effect on operations was disappointing.

Subsequent missions did not remedy initial problems, and one reinforcement mission flown on the night of July 11 resulted in heavy losses for little discernible gain. This mission was scheduled to drop the 504th Parachute Regiment's 2,300 soldiers into the friendly American beachhead at Gela at about 11:00 P.M. Its approach route took it over friendly ships offshore and then over American-occupied positions in Sicily. Generals Patton, Bradley, and Matthew B. Ridgway (the parachutists' commander) all took extreme care to inform the Army, especially the antiaircraft crews, of the drop and instructed them to hold their fire. They also received assurances from the Navy that guaranteed antiaircraft-free passage over ships offshore.

Unfortunately, the mission arrived on the heels of the last Axis air attack of several that had hit the area during the day. An earlier attack had blown an ammunition ship sky-high. A gunner in the fleet, confused and nervous from a day of Axis bombing and perhaps uninformed of the drop, opened fire on the slow, low-flying, troop-carrying aircraft. Within seconds every antiaircraft gun on ship and shore joined him. They slaughtered the unprepared and ungainly transports, shooting down 23 and damaging 60 of the 144. The 504th Regiment reported 81 dead, 132 wounded, and 16 missing.[89] Pilots lost formation and geographical bearings and proceeded to scatter the paratroops from Gela to the east coast.[90]

Eisenhower demanded an immediate investigation by both Patton and Spaatz, exclaiming, "If the cited report is true, the incident could have been occasioned only by inexcusable carelessness and negligence. . . . You will institute within your command an immediate and exhaustive investigation into the allegation with a view of fixing responsibility." Eisenhower also asked for a complete statement of disciplinary action taken, if any proved necessary.[91]

Spaatz visited both the 51st and 52d Troop Carrier Wings on July 13 and met with all group commanders who had led missions on the nights of July 9 and 11. As he informed Arnold in a letter the next day, he found morale high despite the losses. Spaatz had several pertinent observations for Arnold, who enthusiastically supported airborne operations: (1) airborne operations can avoid excessive casualties only by achieving surprise; (2) excessive losses will occur if troops are dropped on organized battle positions; (3) ground and naval units need extensive training to prevent them from firing on friendly aircraft; and (4) surface forces should get ample warning before an airborne overflight of their positions and should be forbidden to fire on any planes during the designated time of the overflight.[92] Tedder endorsed the report, adding, "A.A. firing at night is infectious and control almost impossible."[93] The lessons Spaatz, Eisenhower, and the advocates of airborne operations gleaned from the Sicilian operation paid dividends in the planning for the airborne phase of the cross-channel invasion.

In addition to the supervision of combat operations, which, of course, required much of Spaatz's time and effort, two other related matters received

244

significant attention: the question of a separate postwar U.S. Air Force and the establishment of an all-American, all-AAF, Mediterranean-wide command. In summing up the Tunisian campaign, Spaatz had written to Arnold, "If it were not for the disturbance which would ensue, I would probably announce the urgent necessity of a separate Air Force."[94] This comment reflected not only his opinion of the just-completed campaign but also the experiences and conclusions over his entire career. In 1925, at Brig. Gen. William "Billy" Mitchell's court-martial, Spaatz had stated that the air arm could not function properly under the aegis of the War Department, and the eighteen years after the trial had only served to reinforce that opinion. On June 1, Spaatz, in a conference with Doolittle and Maj. Gen. Follett Bradley, who commanded one of the U.S. continental air forces charged with training and had just arrived from Eaker's Eighth Air Forces Headquarters in Britain on a trip at Arnold's behest, agreed that, although the current air organization was adequate for the defeat of Germany, the final campaign against Japan would require the separation of the U.S. Army Air Forces from the U.S. Army. Spaatz added that the AAF ought to disentangle itself from the British Army and the RAF as well. This action would enable the AAF to set up all-U.S. strategic and tactical air forces whose commanders would have equal rank with the Army Ground Forces commander. The overall air commander would outrank the ground force commander.[95] These musings did not leave AAF circles.

Spaatz also believed that air power should have a preeminent place not only in the Sicilian invasion but in any amphibious operation. Before the Sicilian landings he observed, "The next operation will be successful, but the same mistake is being made which was made in the Pantelleria assault—that of placing air as a secondary power to the ground forces and not giving them the top command when air success is first in importance in making the operation a success."[96] A few days later, on July 5, he codified his ideas on the proper role of air power in future operations as follows: (1) air power isolates the area where the ground forces will attack; (2) air power will attain air supremacy over that area; (3) enemy forces and fortifications will be reduced by a rising scale of attack à la Pantelleria; and (4) only after the completion of the foregoing actions will ground forces, fully supported by tactical and strategic air, begin their assault. Spaatz added that, in operations having a further lead time for planning than HUSKY/Sicily, the air commander should have the supreme command and army and navy forces should start their combat operation only after the air commander had given the go-ahead.[97]

It should also be noted that Spaatz did not view the Strategic and Tactical Air Forces as units that operated entirely independently of one another. Many times he made it clear that strategic forces should be employed in roles that provided direct support to the ground forces when required—during, for example, preinvasion and breakthrough operations. On at least one occasion he complained to Eisenhower that Tedder tended to overcompartmentalize strategic and tactical air activities.[98]

In August, Spaatz had another opportunity to advance the AAF's drive for independence and equality. U.S. Senators of the Select Committee to Visit the War Theaters, after spending time in England with Eaker's Eighth Air Force, flew into Marrakech to tour the North African Theater. On August 13, Spaatz and Tedder met with Sen. Henry Cabot Lodge, Jr., of Massachusetts, the committee's Republican member. Two days later, Spaatz met with three Democratic members, Sens. Richard B. Russell of Georgia, Albert B. Chandler of Kentucky, and James M. Mead of New York, and with Sen. Bennett C. "Champ" Clark who, although not appointed to the select committee, had apparently attached himself to it. At both meetings Spaatz emphasized the necessity of separating the air force from the ground army.[99] He even asked General Wilson, the group's escort, to keep that thought "foremost" in any conversations he had with the Senators.[100]

Spaatz's papers contain a rather florid draft of a statement that he apparently used in his conversations with the committee members. Entitled "Separation and Efficiency," dated August 3, 1943, the ten-page draft, which may or may not have been personally written by Spaatz, presents an AAF insider's argument for the division of the U.S. armed forces into three equal branches for the purposes of combat and economic efficiency. "Why," asks the paper, "does the one major service that has demonstrated its powers remain a divided weapon, existing in many forms under several services but consolidated and coordinated nowhere?" After a lengthy examination of the differences in the handling of air power between the Army Air Forces and the Navy, in which the latter is found wanting, the paper suggests a reform of the U.S. Joint Chiefs of Staff which would grant to the air force an equal vote with the two other services and to the head of the Joint Chiefs the power and responsibility to make final decisions. The paper also recommends the establishment of theater commands on the same joint bases. The complete separation of the AAF Air Staff from the War Department General Staff would accompany reform.[101] The select committee proved infertile soil for such proposals. As Spaatz probably realized, serious congressional consideration of the proper position of the AAF in the U.S. military hierarchy would have to wait until after the war. Upon its return to Washington in October 1943, the committee merely noted, "Close integration of our land, sea and air forces has been accomplished in most theaters and works extremely well. It points the way to a sound post-war military policy."[102]

Along with his desire for the eventual independence of a U.S. air force within the U.S. military structure, in the summer of 1943 Spaatz had a more immediate goal—independence from the Royal Air Force. The February 1943 reorganization of Allied air power in North Africa had set up the Northwest African Air Forces and had provided the NAAF with a combined U.S.-British staff from Spaatz's headquarters down to, but not including, the combat group level. From the Kasserine Pass crisis to the Axis surrender in Tunisia, the NAAF's arrangements had worked well, although Spaatz believed that the goodwill of the individuals involved had been more responsible than any intrinsic merit or stability in the structure itself.[103]

Spaatz also found the air arrangements between the NAAF and Air Chief Marshal Arthur Tedder's Mediterranean Air Command (MAC) less than perfect. he "expressed the fear that MAC was becoming too operational, and that there was an increasing tendency for that command to go direct to elements of the NAAF."[104] The practice of bypassing Spaatz's headquarters, especially in communications between Tedder and Coningham, rankled the Americans. On May 24, Spaatz had a conference with Coningham's American deputy, Brig. Gen. John K. Cannon; Spaatz stated that "the Tactical Air Force has the tendency to consider itself an independent air force" and that he expected Cannon to keep him "informed of any tendencies or concrete action in this direction." Spaatz added that he ultimately aimed to group all American tactical units under American command. In the meantime, Spaatz cautioned Cannon, the reconnaissance squadron attached to the U.S. II Corps should not come under the command of Western Desert Air Force, a British command, or Tactical Air Force, nor would he permit the reorganization or breaking up of any American groups.[105]

On June 1, Spaatz told Doolittle that he preferred to have all American Tactical and Strategic Air Force units under a U.S. commander and that he thought it best to "extricate" the AAF from the RAF. Three days later Spaatz noted in his diary a disagreement between himself and Coningham about which particular American officer should command the XII ASC, an all-U.S. unit. On June 6, Spaatz became extremely irked when Coningham treated the Pantelleria operation in a particularly offhand manner. Later, through his deputy, Air Vice Marshal Robb, he advised Coningham that a change of attitude would be desirable. On June 12, at the conclusion of the Pantelleria operation, Cannon and Spaatz met again at Sousse. Cannon reported that MAC had sent a signal moving the U.S. 33d Fighter Group from the Tactical to the Coastal Air Force three days prior to the final assault. This action had clearly intruded into Spaatz's realm of authority as Commanding General, Twelfth Air Force, and Commanding General, NAAF. Spaatz instructed Cannon to tell Coningham that "if he carried out any future orders received direct from MAC he would be relieved of his command—that all orders should come direct from NAAF." Spaatz further spelled out his view in person to Tedder on June 21: "MAC does not have the right to exercise control over units under the command of NAAF," Spaatz claimed, "unless [that] order is coordinated through HQ, NAAF."[106]

The establishment in mid-June of a joint MAC-NAAF advanced command post at La Marsa blurred further the lines of authority. This command post, which served as the control center for the Sicily operation for both Tedder and Spaatz, had direct radio links to all of the NAAF's and MAC's subordinate commands. It also served as a collection and analysis point for photographic and electronic intelligence. Access to this communications network and intelligence made it easier for MAC to assume a larger operational role at Spaatz's expense. By June 27, Spaatz's American chief of staff, Brig. Gen. Edward P. Curtis, had begun to suggest that the joint command post wasted too much staff. Spaatz replied that he expected an early break, with NAAF Headquarters moving forward while MAC stayed behind.[107]

By July 12, Spaatz apparently had decided to ensure his control of U.S. air units even if it meant completely bypassing the British. On that date he ordered the creation of a new communications network manned entirely by Americans. The system, which would operate only between senior U.S. officers, would have no central filing system; copies of messages would be kept only by sender and recipient. Spaatz wanted the system, which soon became known as REDLINE, in effect by August 1. The first link was to be established between Cannon and XII ASC, presumably to give XII ASC a way to circumvent Coningham. Spaatz also wanted the network so flexible that even missions already airborne could still be recalled. When established, the system would give Spaatz complete control, without British interference, over all AAF units and personnel in the Mediterranean.

Spaatz planned to go even further in separating his forces from the RAF. On July 12, he instructed Generals Cannon and Quesada "to have officers in training so that you will have them ready to take over. I want the 12th Fighter Command built up so that key personnel will be trained when the Americans are in complete control." Spaatz also wanted American officers in each function of the Tactical and Coastal Air Forces who could take over at a moment's notice.[108] The next day Spaatz told Doolittle that future plans for the NAAF were unstable.[109]

Eventually, REDLINE grew into a swift and effective all-American communications system. REDLINE traffic reveals that the most voluminous message files deal with Cannon at the Tactical Air Force. Spaatz used this link as a means of asserting his control over the U.S. units in Coningham's command, where responses to his regular orders were consistently delayed. He simply had copies repeated to Cannon over REDLINE. An early exchange of messages typifies the traffic. On August 7, Spaatz testily wired Cannon, "It is stated in the Tactical Air Force Operations Report for August 5 that Desert Air Force sent three A-36 missions to toe of Italy et cetera. On my visit yesterday I was assured that A-36 groups are operating under command control of 12 Air Support Command. Answer immediately as to what circumstances Desert Air Force gives orders to A-36 groups?"[110] Three hours later Cannon replied, "Tactical Air Force Operations Report for August 5 is in error. Desert Air Force never repeat never under any circumstances gives orders to A-36 groups or to any other organizations assigned to 12 ASC."[111] In contrast, Spaatz and Doolittle seldom resorted to REDLINE since their regular channels had no British middlemen and, of course, Doolittle responded to Spaatz, his American commanding officer, with a great deal more alacrity than he did to Coningham. Cannon, for his part, could not use regular channels because they ran straight through Coningham.

On the morning of July 18, Spaatz and Eisenhower met to discuss the reorganization of the AAF in the Mediterranean Theater. Butcher, Eisenhower's naval aide, described in his diary how Allied Force Headquarters viewed Spaatz's status: "This situation has resulted in Spaatz being virtually squeezed out of his job, yet the vast majority of all aircraft in operation are American. Ike is keenly aware that there may be American reactions against the current arrangement."[112]

Later in the day Spaatz visited Eisenhower with a long message for Marshall which, after some discussion, Eisenhower sent. "After careful examination and test of the U.S. air organization in the Mediterranean, Spaatz and I," wrote Eisenhower, "have concluded that the Ninth Air Force should be abolished as a separate entity and incorporated into the Twelfth." Eisenhower gave six considerations that influenced his decision. The first three concerned the advantages in having only one AAF headquarters with a single logistical and administrative organization. The last three addressed Spaatz's and the AAF's problems with the RAF. Eisenhower explained:

> Under the existing setup the entire air force is under the strategic control of the Air Chief Marshal [Tedder], yet his principal American assistant [Spaatz] has direct control over only part of the American force. In other words the American Air Force and principal American commander do not have that prestige that should be theirs.

In his next point Eisenhower explained that recent operations had shown the need for the consolidation of Tedder's and Spaatz's headquarters, in order "to permit the constant and instant coordination of all air forces in the Mediterranean." Furthermore, in the heat of intensive fighting, tactical and strategic air force operations merged into one problem that was virtually impossible to coordinate through more than one headquarters. Thus, if Spaatz had a secure position as commanding general of all AAF forces in the Mediterranean, the NAAF could disappear and Spaatz could serve as Tedder's deputy. This post would give Spaatz "a position of great strength, prestige, and influence," while allowing the British to maintain the overall strategic responsibility for the theater allotted to them by the directives of the Combined Chiefs of Staff. The scheme would also "provide absolute continuity of American command of all American units from top to bottom."[113]

In his reply to Eisenhower's message, Marshall accepted the outline of the plan. Eisenhower asked Spaatz to prepare a response, which he sent out under Eisenhower's signature on July 26.[114] On August 22, Eisenhower joined the units of the U.S. Ninth Air Force to those of the U.S. Twelfth Air Force.* This action placed every AAF unit in the theater under Spaatz and administratively moved the units belonging to the defunct Ninth Air Force from the control of the British Desert Air Force to the U.S. Twelfth Air Force. In practice the Ninth's units continued to perform their old roles in the Strategic and Tactical Air Forces. The move did not solve the problem of overlapping functions between MAC and NAAF which continued to plague the two organizations until they joined to form Headquarters, Mediterranean Allied Air Forces (MAAF), on December 10, 1943.

Eisenhower and Spaatz met in Algiers on August 4 where Spaatz informed his superior that he and Tedder disagreed on air reorganization "primarily because of the extent to which I insist that American units be commanded by American commanders all the way up to the highest command." Eisenhower agreed to return Tedder's headquarters from La Marsa to Algiers, to separate Tedder from day-to-day operations while keeping him where he could supply advice on air matters close at hand. Back at his headquarters, Spaatz told his staff that the NAAF had just reverted to its status prior to the establishment of the NAAF-MAC Combined Command Post—in other words, the NAAF had direct control of operations. He added that Tedder would accept this arrangement before they returned to Algiers.[115]

This state of affairs lasted five days and then Eisenhower reversed himself. In Tunis, on August 9, in a meeting with Eisenhower, Tedder, Coningham, and Alexander on planning for the invasion of Italy, Spaatz had an opportunity to present organizational problems. He noted that the current situation left Coningham in doubt as to the chain of command. The situation could be corrected if orders to Coningham and Doolittle came from the NAAF, not from a combined NAAF-MAC headquarters or from MAC alone. In addition, MAC Advance Headquarters should be disbanded, and morning meetings between MAC and NAAF no longer held.

After the meeting, Eisenhower told Spaatz that he had changed his mind, perhaps succumbing to urgings from Tedder. As a result, Spaatz and Eisenhower were back to the position they had taken in their July 18 message to Marshall. Eisenhower "stated that he did not want anything to develop which would indicate that the RAF and the USAAF could not operate together." He wanted MAC as the "top over-all" headquarters, with the Twelfth Air Force as an administrative head for all U.S. units. Spaatz complied and directed his staff to send to MAC all nonadministrative functions of the NAAF. Spaatz noted in his diary, "This is a compromise organization and will be successful only if senior staff officers are very careful to consider the proper prerogative of staff officers of other headquarters."[116]

---

* Headquarters, Ninth Air Force, was transferred to England to lead the U.S. tactical air force intended to support the cross-channel invasion. The Ninth Air Force had been part of the Northwest African Air Forces.

In fact although not in name, Spaatz became Tedder's deputy. He maintained a voice in overall strategic direction and zealously championed the administrative separation of the British and U.S. air forces in all but the top command levels. Yet despite his stand, day-to-day operational control of Allied air power in the Mediterranean increasingly tended to become Tedder's preserve. Spaatz would have found much to agree with in the postwar statement of his successor as deputy, John Slessor:

> The position of deputy commander is not an easy one: he is rather liable to be neither fish, flesh, fowl nor good red herring and his responsibility is not easy to define. As in all these things, it depends largely on personalities, and on friendly arrangements between the commander and his deputy about who does what—an arrangement easier to agree upon than to make known to all subordinate commanders.[117]

Spaatz had succeeded in gathering the disparate AAF elements in the theater under a single U.S. commander, and he remained Eisenhower's principal American air adviser. But he had failed to separate the AAF from the RAF completely, and the two would remain harnessed together, thanks to Tedder's preeminent position as overall Air Commander in Chief.

This squeezing out of Spaatz left Coningham with what amounted to independent control of the theater's tactical air forces. Spaatz could not and Tedder did not control him. Several errors in judgment by Coningham, which went uncorrected by higher air authority, may have contributed to the unsuccessful air interdiction of the Axis evacuation from Sicily across the Straits of Messina to Italy. From August 11 to 17, the Germans and Italians, working independently, evacuated more than 100,000 men, 9,800 vehicles, 47 tanks, 150 guns, and 17,000 tons of munitions and stores.[118] Three German divisions escaped to fight again. The Allies had made no plans as they had in the Tunisian campaign to halt this retrograde movement, which earned the Allied command structure and each of the three services equal shares of the reproaches from postwar analysts.

Land forces, particularly the British, did not press the Axis forcefully enough to prevent them from disengaging the vast majority of their troops. The naval forces would not risk the loss or damage of their heavy units by bringing them into the confined waters of the straits in order to sink the evacuation ships. The Allied high command structure, influenced perhaps by Hitler's previous refusal to evacuate Tunisia, not only did not anticipate the evacuation but failed to realize it had begun until very late in its progress. Neither Eisenhower nor his three chief subordinates, Alexander, Cunningham, and Tedder, pushed hard enough or coordinated readily enough with their colleagues to mount the combined ground, naval, and air effort necessary to close the Straits of Messina.[119]

Finally, the air forces, under Coningham, made several mistakes. Coningham assumed that the evacuation would take place largely at night, and he anticipated heavy air opposition over the straits. Both these reasonable assumptions proved wrong, but he did not abandon them. Although he had the authority to request the assistance of Strategic Air Force's heavy bombers, medium bombers, and fighters, with twelve hours' advance notice, subject to Doolittle's approval, Coningham apparently never requested the American daylight bombers after August 9. From July 29 to August 17, NAAF heavy bombers flew only 142 sorties over Sicily.[120] Most of the NASAF therefore devoted itself to attacks on the Italian mainland distant from the straits, in preparation for the upcoming invasion of Italy. On the day the main German withdrawal began, Coningham notified Tedder that, should a big withdrawal develop, "we can handle it with our own resources and naval assistance."[121] In fact, Coningham overestimated the ability of the NATAF to halt the evacuation. The Axis powers had brought up numerous heavy and light antiaircraft guns to defend the crossing. These put up such intense fire that NATAF's light bombers and fighter-bombers could not operate effectively against Axis shipping, which also carried heavy antiaircraft armament.[122] Nor did Coningham press home his attacks, perhaps because he and his superiors sensed no emergency. On August 16, the last full day of the evacuation, with an available force of 970 aircraft, he sent only 317 sorties against the straits.[123] After the war, Coningham himself concluded, "The escape of a large number of the enemy at Messina proved that a density of flak can be provided so lethal that air attack can be held off sufficiently to maintain communications."[124]

Coningham apparently believed that his orders should come from Tedder rather than Spaatz. This was the view that Spaatz, who at the time of the evacuation had lost much of whatever control he ever had over Coningham, expressed to Eisenhowever on August 9.[125] Tedder had taken over strategic direction and allocation for theater air power, thereby forcing Spaatz to concentrate primarily on purely American administrative matters.

Spaatz's papers contain no references at all to the Axis evacuation. Given his intense interest in the details of the operation against supply lines in Tunisia and in the bombing of Pantelleria, it seems reasonable to conclude that he had become detached from day-to-day operations, especially the tactical sphere of responsibility. Instead, during the time period of the evacuation he found time to campaign for air force independence with visiting senators and to inspect bomb groups in North Africa. In addition, he oversaw the AAF in the Mediterranean's first Combined Bomber Offensive mission—against fighter assembly plants in Wiener-Neustadt, Austria, on August 13—and discussed plans for AAF reorganization and the coming invasion of Italy with Eisenhower and Tedder.[126]

In short, Spaatz had no hand in stopping the evacuation. There were indications that if he had he would have, at the very least, used the U.S. heavy bombers more frequently on evacuation targets. On August 4, shortly before the evacuation, he said, in Eisenhower's presence, at a general officers' meeting, "It is my belief that it [air] should have been used exclusively in Sicily to expedite the battle there." In his diary Spaatz added, "Too much insistence exists in the mind of Tedder that there be a differentiation between Tactical and Strategic Air Forces. Under certain battle conditions they should be considered as one Air Force and should be applied [together] as was done in the case of Pantelleria."[127]

Spaatz's remark on Tedder's mindset found an echo in the criticism of the air effort in official Royal Navy and U.S. Army histories.[128] Both point out shortcomings in Tedder's and Coningham's performances. The U.S. Army history, in particular, takes Tedder to task for continuing to employ the heavy B-17 and B-24 bombers of the NASAF too far from crucial evacuation ports. Coningham contributed by releasing the heavy bombers from interdiction responsibility on August 11 and by overestimating the effectiveness of his own tactical forces. If Spaatz had had more responsibility for this phase of the operation, he might have been more flexible in his use of heavy bombardment, which in any case would not have been the panacea that U.S. Army historians implied it might have been, because the Germans evacuated over open beaches, targets much less suitable to heavy bombers than the local ports at each end of the straits.

During July and certainly by the beginning of August, Tedder supplanted Spaatz as Eisenhower's chief air adviser, although propinquity rather than ulterior purpose accounted for much of the change in Spaatz's status. By the nature of his job, Tedder stayed physically closer to Eisenhower and occupied a link in the chain of command between Spaatz and Eisenhower. As a result, Eisenhower, who based his entire command philosophy on Allied unity and teamwork, not only listened more often to Tedder, but went out of his way not to appear to seek Spaatz's views because they were American. Nor did Spaatz make Eisenhower's task easier. As Spaatz began to lose influence on Allied operations, he naturally began to concentrate more and more on a sphere over which he had greater control—the administration and strategic policy of the AAF in the Mediterranean. Fortunately, Eisenhower, Tedder, and Spaatz liked and respected one another personally and professionally. This triangle, which could have produced emotional and institutional fireworks, eventually became a sound working relationship, with occasional tiffs and disagreements, instead of a Mycenaen epic with heroes sulking in their tents while the battle raged outside.

Chapter 8

Salerno and London
(July–December 1943)

It was very dark indeed on September 13, but thanks to a
full effort by Air, enemy counterattacks were slowed up
and finally on the 14th pretty much knocked in the head.[1]

—*Spaatz to Eaker, September 18, 1943*

The Invasion of Italy

On July 26, the day after Mussolini fell from power, the Combined Chiefs of
Staff (CCS) directed Eisenhower to proceed with the plans his command had
drawn up for an invasion of Italy at Salerno, a city just south of Naples. The
Allies chose Salerno chiefly because their relatively short-range fighter aircraft
in Sicily could not operate effectively farther north. The Germans made the
same calculations and marked the area as a likely invasion spot. They based a
panzer division there, and a good road network enabled them to reinforce the
area rapidly if the Allies did indeed arrive.

After taking power, Mussolini's successors began secret peace negotiations
with the Allies. Marshal Pietro Badoglio's government agreed to a secret
armistice timed to coincide with the invasion. The Allies hoped that chaos
within the Italian armed forces and in their relationship with their German part-
ners resulting from the surprise cessation of hostilities would ease the way for the
invading forces. Allied air power also sought to smooth the path. The Strategic
Air Force, in particular, spent much of the five weeks prior to the invasion in
counterair and supply and in the communications line interdiction strikes that had
become standard. By the time of the invasion on September 9, the Luftwaffe and
the Italian rail network had suffered severely.

Once again the Northwest African Air Forces (NAAF) protected the invasion fleet effectively, despite a temporary resurgence of Luftwaffe activity. Only

five major Allied ships were sunk and nine were heavily damaged.[2] When the German counterattack against the beachhead reached its peak on September 13 and 14, the Northwest African Strategic Air Force (NASAF) joined the Northwest African Tactical Air Force (NATAF) in a maximum effort against German units, strong points, and communications on the front line or immediately behind it. Because all of the NAAF's striking forces were directly supporting the beachhead, Eisenhower requested the CCS to transfer three heavy-bomber groups from the Eighth Air Force to the NAAF. In addition, he asked the CCS to order the Eighth to bomb Northern Italian communications from England. The CCS promptly complied.[3] In all, from September 12 to 15, the NAAF dropped 3,500 tons of bombs and flew 6,000 sorties over the Italian battlefront.[4]

Allied naval support forces also played an important part in repelling the counterattack. During the entire Salerno operation they pumped 11,000 tons of shells, the equivalent of 72,000 field artillery shells (105mm), into German positions.[5] Given the advantage in accuracy of naval gunfire over bombing, Allied navies contributed somewhat more than Allied air in breaking up the German assault. Nonetheless, Eisenhower, Alexander, and Clark, Commander of the U.S. Fifth Army, which had operational control of the invasion, had nothing but praise for the air support given by the NAAF. Alexander wrote to Spaatz on September 17 that the air attacks had greatly aided the morale of the ground units and inflicted heavy losses on the enemy. In addition, said Alexander, the air strikes "have seriously interfered with his movements, interrupted his communications and prevented his concentration of the necessary forces to launch large scale attacks. You have contributed immeasurably to the success of our operations."[6] Alexander also passed on Clark's "acclaim of the close and continuous air support given his army." And Eisenhower told Lt. Gen. Joseph T. McNarney, U.S. Army Deputy Chief of Staff, on September 16, "I cannot say too much for our Air. . . . Our airmen hit what they are aiming at, and their effect in this campaign has been remarkable."[7]

Following this activity the U.S. air effort in the Mediterranean began to fall off, mainly because of weather and manpower problems. The wet fall and winter of 1943–1944 caused the cancellation of many missions, which, of course, reduced the effect of air power on land operations and on the interdiction of enemy supplies and communications. Fine flying weather in the summer contributed to the shortage of manpower by allowing aircraft to undertake almost daily missions; as a result, air crews completed their fifty-mission combat rotation more quickly than anticipated.* The ability to fly almost incessantly also

---

* The number of required combat missions for air crews varied throughout the war depending on theater, type of aircraft, and intensity of combat. In the summer of 1943, heavy-bomber crews in the Mediterranean, where enemy opposition was light, had to fly fifty missions before returning home. At the same time, heavy-bomber crews in Britain, who faced much heavier opposition (and hence had a shorter life expectancy), had a combat tour of twenty-five missions.

256

led to increased fatigue among air and ground crews, causing more depletion of the human resources needed to conduct the air battle.[8] The replacement situation had become severe even before the invasion of Italy. Spaatz reported to Arnold:

> As the extent to which air has assisted the ground action becomes more widely known increasing demands are made for its employment. We are faced with a rather difficult problem in this respect in that weather almost never interrupts flying and between 70% and 80% of our airplanes are kept in commission. Combat crew fatigue has become the main problem.[9]

The following day Eisenhower sent, at Spaatz's behest, an "Eyes Only" cable to Marshall in which he pleaded for an immediate increase of the replacement rate from 15 percent per month to 25 percent per month. Eisenhower noted, "It now appears that we must either fail to meet demands or gradually reduce our groups' effectiveness as a result of attrition." Alluding to the surrender negotiations with Italy and the worsening Axis position on Sicily, Eisenhower added, "We have reached a critical position in this area which requires that any favorable development, military or political, be fully and immediately exploited. Air forces, of course, provide our most effective means of rapidly applying pressure where necessary."[10]

The Salerno operation only exacerbated the shortfall. At the height of the German counterattack, Spaatz wrote to Arnold:

> In addition to communications, the biggest worry at present is the old one of replacement crews. Our frequency of operation in spite of all efforts to hold it down to a minimum, is continuously greater than the replacement rate warrants, and crews are becoming war weary faster than replacements will arrive to relieve them.[11]

Eisenhower, too, pleaded with Marshall for more men: "Our actual use of air has greatly exceeded that which was planned. I consider that reducing the scale of our present air effort might prove disastrous." Eisenhower urged Marshall to take remedial action at once; otherwise "our strength will drop below that essential for conduct of operations."[12]

Arnold and Marshall, however, could do little to meet these appeals. They temporarily sent down eighty B-24s (two groups) from the Eighth, but the vagaries of U.S. military manpower recruitment and procurement, especially in the AAF, had produced a manpower crisis that particularly affected air crews. The low point in the supply of trained manpower for the AAF occurred in the summer of 1943, leaving Arnold and the AAF unable to meet more than the minimal planned replacement flows.[13]

During this replacement crisis Spaatz confronted another delicate personnel problem—evaluating the performance of the pilots of the 99th Fighter Squadron, the only black AAF unit then in combat. In an "Eyes Only" cable on August 17, Spaatz alerted Arnold to a possible problem. General Cannon, Deputy Commander of the NATAF, reported that the 99th was "beginning to show evidence of tiring." Cannon compared the unit's performance unfavorably to that of the 33d Fighter Group, which was operating from the same airfield under the command of Col. William W. Momyer, and noted, "It is indicated that the colored pilot cannot stand up under [the] same pressure as [the] white pilot." Cannon, however, noted the mitigating fact that although Lt. Col. Benjamin O. Davis, Jr., the 99th's commanding officer, reported that he had been promised four replacement pilots per month when he went into action in May 1943, he had received a total of only four replacements by mid-August. As Spaatz and Cannon well knew, a shortage of replacement pilots meant that a unit had to work overtime to maintain its sortie rate. The 99th, operating under added strain for a continued period, was worn out compared with white units with more replacements. Spaatz personally requested "that no conclusion be drawn until further study and experience."[14]

Even as Spaatz warned Arnold, *Time* magazine began to prepare a story on the 99th. Both apparently had gotten advance warning of the story, which appeared in the September 20, 1943, issue. The story accurately stated that "unofficial reports" from the Mediterranean suggested that "the top air command was not altogether satisfied with the 99th's performance" and was thinking about transferring the unit to the Northwest African Coastal Air Force (NACAF).[15]

On September 10, either in response to Spaatz's warning or to the impending story in *Time*, Arnold requested the preparation of "as detailed a confidential report as the facts now in your possession warrant" on black pilots without delay. Arnold further noted, "We have received from many unofficial sources second hand tales of the fact that the Negro pilot tires very easily, and that he loses his will to fight after five or six missions." Arnold knew that Spaatz would realize "the urgency required for this information in view of the fact that we contemplate building additional Negro units at once."[16]

As ordered, Spaatz directed Cannon, despite his involvement in the fighting associated with the Salerno invasion, to expedite the completion of a comprehensive report on the 99th.[17] On September 18, Cannon replied by forwarding a report prepared by the Commanding General, XII ASC, Maj. Gen. Edwin J. House. Citing an unnamed officer[18] "who has been in the best position to observe carefully the work of the 99th squadron over its entire combat period," House severely censured the 99th's performance. Although the unnamed officer noted that the 99th's "ground discipline and ability to accomplish and execute orders promptly are excellent," he concluded:

> Based on the performance of the 99th Fighter Squadron to date, it is my opinion that they are not of the fighting caliber of any squadron in this group. They have failed to display the aggressiveness and desire for combat that are necessary to a first class fighting organization. It may be expected that we will get less work and less operational time out of the 99th Fighter Squadron than any squadron of this group.

House added his own observations. He recommended that the squadron be reequipped with obsolescent P-39s and reassigned from the XII ASC to the less active NACAF. He also remarked:

> On many discussions held with officers of all professions, including medical, the consensus of opinion seems to be that the Negro type has not the proper reflexes to make a first-class fighter pilot. Also, on rapid moves which must be part of this Command, housing and messing difficulties arise because the time has not yet arrived when the white and colored soldiers will mess at the same table and sleep in the same barracks.

Finally, House suggested, "If and when a colored group is formed in the United States, it be retained for either the eastern or western defense zone and a white fighter group be released for overseas movement."[19]

In his endorsement of the report to Spaatz, Cannon wrote, "The pilots of the 99th Fighter Squadron fall well below the standard of pilots of other fighter squadrons of this Command," in categories such as eagerness for combat, aggressiveness, will to win or reach the objective, stamina, and ability to fight as a team. Black pilots had "no outstanding characteristics in which they excel in war over the pilots of other squadrons of this Command."[20]

The report contradicted what Spaatz had recorded in early June 1943, that Colonel Davis had told him the "men have lost a little of the eagerness they had before any combat missions, but are proving themselves."[21] In any case, Spaatz forwarded the report to Arnold, expressing his "full confidence in the fairness of the analysis" made by Cannon and House, observing: "I feel that no squadron has been introduced into this theater with a better background of training than had by the 99th Fighter Squadron."[22]

The report came to the attention of the McCloy Committee, a special committee established by the War Department to oversee black troop policies. On October 16, Colonel Davis testified before the committee and effectively refuted House's and Momyer's criticisms.[23] The 99th remained in combat in Italy and was eventually joined by the all-black 332d Fighter Group.

At the very least, the foregoing report demonstrated the inability of the Army hierarchy to conduct an objective evaluation of black soldiers in the U.S. Army of World War II. The incident may have affected Spaatz's evaluation of them. After the war he told the Gillem Board, which was investigating the possible future roles of black soldiers in the AAF, that they should not serve in integrated units and that they would be more effective in support and service units than in combat units.[24]

Throughout World War II, the War Department specified a policy of strict segregation requiring separate but equal accommodations, training, and treatment. Spaatz, accordingly, did not brook egregious discrimination. In the autumn of 1943, he became aware that AAF rest facilities on the Island of Capri, in the harbor of Naples, were not admitting black officers. He had the situation rectified.[25] The AAF built a separate rest facility on Capri for black AAF combat officers (the approximately thirty black pilots assigned to the 99th). Not until May 1944 did the AAF in the Mediterranean begin construction of a rest camp for the enlisted personnel of the 99th or for black officers and enlisted men assigned to AAF service organizations.[26]

The Mediterranean Theater and Strategic Bombing

Once it had defeated the Nazi counterattack on the Salerno beachhead, the U.S. Fifth Army captured Naples on October 1. On the same day, the British 8th Army, advancing from the toe of Italy, occupied the great airfield complex of Foggia, eighty miles to the northeast of Naples. The capture of Foggia gave the AAF the capability to open up a second front in the Combined Bomber Offensive against Germany by putting it well within range of Austrian and south German industrial targets.

This new aspect of the air war had been part of the AAF's plans since the promulgation of AWPD/1 in September 1941. AWPD/1 had provided for a bomber force of very long-range B-29s (still on the drawing boards in 1941) operating against Germany from bases in the Suez region. Similarly, at the inception of the North African invasion, Arnold and Spaatz had persuaded Eisenhower as the European Theater Commander to agree tentatively to a single air force for Britain and North Africa, which would allow the strategic bombing of Germany from both areas.

At the end of the Tunisian campaign, Eisenhower forwarded to Marshall a suggestion from Spaatz that "this theater would offer a very fine region from which to use some of the new B29s."[27] Eisenhower also sent the Combined Chiefs of Staff his recommendations on the course of action to follow after the fall of Sicily. To this document (CCS No. 223) Tedder added a statement in which he pointed out the advantages of launching strategic bomber missions from Italy. These feelers went unnoticed by Marshall and the rest of the Combined Chiefs, who met in Washington, D.C., from May 12 to 25, 1943. There they accepted Eaker's plan for the Combined Bomber Offensive (CCS No. 217), which called for a rapid buildup of an Eighth Air Force powerful enough to defeat Luftwaffe fighter forces and bomb key German industries.[28]

At Arnold's insistence, however, the Combined Chiefs authorized a one-time-only, low-level B-24 raid against the Romanian oil fields and refinery complex at Ploesti, provided Eisenhower approved, which he did in early June. In addition to two B-24 groups (the 376th and 98th) from the Ninth Air Force, the CCS diverted one group (the 389th) scheduled to reinforce the Eighth and two of the Eighth's own groups (the 93d and 44th) to the Ploesti raid (code-named TIDALWAVE). These 177 bombers launched the first Mediterranean raid to participate in the Combined Bomber Offensive by attacking the Ploesti oil targets on August 1. They lost 54 aircraft and 532 crewmen and inflicted heavy, but not decisive, damage to their targets.[29]

Before flying the Ploesti raid, these groups joined the NAAF and flew several hundred sorties in the Sicilian campaign. They also participated in two other strategic missions before leaving the theater, one before and one after the Ploesti raid. On July 19, with the medium bombers and B-17s of the Twelfth Air Force (more than 500 planes in all), they also bombed airfields near and two railroad marshaling yards in Rome. They damaged the fields and the rail yards severely, but one bomb landed a thousand feet from one of the yards in the nave of the Basilica of San Lorenzo where it caved in the roof and front facade, destroying thirteenth- and fourteenth-century frescos and mosaics.[30] Reported casualties were 700 killed and 1,600 wounded.[31]

This raid in the classical terms of Douhet, the Italian air theorist, was aimed against the will of a nation. Few other single strokes could have produced the blow to national pride and spirit or so forcefully demonstrated the failings of Mussolini's ramshackle Fascist state to the Italian people than this raid. On August 13, 259 heavy and medium bombers returned to Rome's marshaling yards and inflicted heavy damage, closing the line to Naples for five or six days and killing 221 persons and wounding 565 more. The next day, the Italian government declared Rome an open city.[32]

Spaatz and the NAAF had planned the initial raid many weeks before its execution. On June 1, Spaatz discussed the prospects of bombing Rome with Churchill, Marshall, and Alan Brooke, British Chief of the Imperial General Staff, who had come to the Mediterranean to obtain Eisenhower's views on post-Sicilian operations. In his description of the Prime Minister's visit, Eisenhower related that "long discussions were carried on regarding the desirability of bombing the marshalling yards near Rome." The CCS authorized the raid on June 15.[33] In addition, Spaatz emphasized the necessity of capturing northern Italy for use in air operations against Germany.[34]

Two weeks later Spaatz and Tedder, while planning support operations for the upcoming Sicilian assault, decided to interdict rail yards in both Naples and Rome as part of the overall campaign to disrupt supply and communications in Italy. Spaatz suggested that Naples should receive not only bombs but surrender leaflets as well.[35] He did not make clear whether he thought the latter might render the port susceptible to a *coup de main* or prove effective as a psychological ploy in the war against Italian morale. Spaatz may have felt that a hard double blow at those two key cities might undermine Italian morale and weaken opposition to the invasion. He noted that if air power could not be concentrated against those two targets, the entire effort should fall on Sicily itself. In private, Spaatz had earlier expressed great faith in the psychological impact of bombing. On May 8, he wrote to a friend in Washington, D.C., that, in the B-17, the United States had discovered the principal weapon for concluding the war successfully. "We have ample evidence," remarked Spaatz, "to clearly indicate they can blast their way through any defenses and destroy the will to fight in any nation which may oppose us."[36]

Nine days after the Sicilian landings the AAF struck Rome in a raid that showed precision bombing at its best and helped to topple Mussolini's regime six days later.[37] Naturally, Spaatz sent a special report to Arnold:

It [the raid] should prove of particular interest to our air force supporters, but definitely has very little interest from an air force standpoint. It was too easy. Seven other raids are now under study and of these the one on NAPLES is certain to hit them in the eyes, especially the "Sunday-morning quarterbacks."[38]

Arnold and Spaatz usually tried to stay a step ahead of any critics of air power.

Shortly before their return to England, the Eighth's three groups, joined by the Ninth's two groups, executed a strategic mission against German fighter plants at Wiener Neustadt, Austria. On August 13, the groups left their bases around Benghazi, Tripoli, and flew more than 1,200 miles to their target. They achieved complete tactical surprise and inflicted severe damage on hangars and grounded aircraft and on the fighter construction and assembly plants of Wiener-Neustaedter Flugzeugwerke A.G.; for much of the remainder of the year, production at the plants slowed noticeably.[39] This was the first time that Allied bombers based in the Mediterranean had attacked a target in Greater Germany.

The attacks on Rome, Ploesti, and Wiener Neustadt strengthened Spaatz's conviction that bombers based in his command should participate in raids on Germany. A week after the Wiener Neustadt raid Spaatz wrote to Lovett, "I am increasingly convinced that Germany can be forced to her knees by aerial bombardment alone. The process can be accelerated by us if suitable bases are available in the Mediterranean area as well as those now available in England."[40] This statement reflected views that Spaatz had expressed for months. On June 24, he had written to Arnold that the fate of the air forces after the next two operations (Sicily and Salerno) concerned him greatly. He also believed that the heavy-bomber effort against Germany ought to come from more than just one base area: "If we can establish ourselves in Italy, much of Germany can be reached from there with better weather conditions at our airdromes than prevail normally in England. This would immediately, when applied, force a dispersion of the German fighter and anti-aircraft defenses."[41] Spaatz suggested that the necessary heavy-bomber force could be obtained by converting his existing B-25 and B-26 groups to B-17 groups. The excess medium bombers could then go to the French.

After talks with Doolittle, Spaatz reiterated most of his foregoing suggestions in a July 14 letter to Arnold. Spaatz did modify the proposal slightly by observing that not all of his medium-bomber groups could convert because ground support missions required aircraft with the medium bombers' operating characteristics. Again he pointed out the advantages of strategic bombing from Italy:

I am confident we will progress up the Italian Peninsula, and before too many weeks have passed, will be in a position to bomb the fighter production plants

262

in the vicinity of Vienna and other places now beyond the effort out of U.K. I believe points we can reach amount to 97% of their production.[42]

Arnold held different views. In late July, he told a member of the RAF Delegation in Washington that the fall of Sicily and potential fall of Italy did little for the Allies against Germany. Because the bombing offensive against Germany must come from Britain, the three B-24 groups on loan to Spaatz should be returned immediately. The best way to finish the war was to attack by the shortest way—across the channel. Arnold regarded Eisenhower's call for reinforcements in the Mediterranean as an extravagance that could compromise the cross-channel invasion.[43] When the RAF Delegation reported these opinions to Portal, he instructed his mission in Washington to present the RAF's case for strategic bombing from Italy, especially from the central (Rome) and north (Po Valley) Italian areas. Portal, like Spaatz, pointed to the advantages of spreading German fighter defenses and placing more vital targets within easy range. He believed that without question the Allies should create in Italy the largest bomber force that a logistical base could support. He accepted the fact that the limiting element of logistics would mean a smaller total force in Italy than the one stationed in Britain.[44]

Air Marshal William Welsh, the head of the RAF Delegation, discussed Portal's ideas with Arnold on August 1 and reported considerable modification of Arnold's views. Arnold agreed completely on the need for a bomber force flying from northern Italy. A decisive factor in changing Arnold's mind may have been British intelligence indicating significant dispersal of German fighter assembly and manufacturing capacity to Austria and other southern European targets beyond the range of the Eighth Air Force's heavy bombers.[45] But Arnold added a new wrinkle. He suggested that the Allied bomber offensive required a single overall commander to coordinate the strategic bombing forces in both Italy and Britain in order to avoid competition, overlarge liaison staffs, and constant appeals to the Combined Chiefs of Staff for decisions. Welsh warned Portal that Arnold would bring up the matter of command when they next met.[46]

In the meantime, AAF Headquarters rejected Spaatz's proposals to reequip his medium-bomber groups because it wished neither to delay the B-17 buildup in Britain nor to deprive Eisenhower of support.[47] Similarly, the CCS rejected Eisenhower's request for a loan of four of the Eighth's B-17 groups for the Salerno operation. Lt. Gen. Jacob L. Devers, U.S. European Theater Commander, and Eaker, the Eighth Air Force Commander, strongly supported the turndown because they feared that such a transfer would wreck the current Combined Bomber Offensive.[48] Marshall also refused to transfer four medium-bomber groups from Britain, and Arnold rejected the request by Eisenhower, Spaatz, and Tedder to keep the Eighth's three B-24 groups that had bombed Ploesti in the Mediterranean theater.[49] On September 2, Arnold informed Spaatz that he would receive no more P-38 replacement aircraft for six weeks.[50] These actions enraged Eisenhower,[51] but Marshall and Arnold pointed out that the

NAAF already outnumbered the entire Luftwaffe and that the needs of POINTBLANK*—the U.S. daylight precision bombing portion of the Combined Bomber Offensive against Germany that was a prerequisite to the cross-channel invasion—overrode all other considerations.[52]

If Eisenhower and Spaatz had lost their campaign to acquire some of Eaker's assets, at least they had helped to gain recognition of the point that Italy would serve as an admirable base for future attacks on Germany. At the Quebec Conference, August 14 to 25, 1943, Roosevelt, Churchill, and the Combined Chiefs agreed on "strategic bombing operations from Italian and Central European bases, complementing POINTBLANK."[53] The British Chief of the Air Staff, Portal, remarked, "If we could have a strong force of Heavy and Medium Bombers there [northern Italy] in the near future, Germany would be faced with a problem insoluble."[54] Arnold, in the midst of the conference, wrote to Spaatz that "a planned and sustained strategic bombing attack on German key industrial targets from Mediterranean bases" warranted the top priority.[55]

Two days after the conference, Arnold requested Spaatz to return to Washington for ten days to two weeks. With Eisenhower's approval, Spaatz scheduled a trip to Washington for the beginning of October. He told Eisenhower that he would emphasize the replacement crew problem and the "utilization of the Mediterranean base area for heavy bombers including B-29s."[56]

Once the CCS had accepted Italy as a base for strategic bombing, details of command, control, strength, and coordination with the Eighth Air Force needed attention. Eisenhower signaled Marshall on September 19, "Forward movement into Italy necessitates immediate planning on my part for extension of bomber effort into Germany." He went on to inquire about the exact number of aircraft to be sent and, after stating his own and Spaatz's belief in the effectiveness of that aspect of the Combined Bomber Offensive conducted from Italy, informed Marshall that Spaatz would arrive in Washington prepared to discuss numbers and "the overall organization and control of strategic air forces as Tedder, Spaatz, and I see it."[57]

By October Arnold and his staff had drawn up plans for a new strategic air force—the Fifteenth Air Force. On October 9, the day Spaatz landed in Washington, Arnold submitted to the U.S. Joint Chiefs of Staff (JCS) his design for turning the Twelfth Air Force into a tactical air force and establishing the Fifteenth as a strategic air force. Both forces would operate under the theater commander, but the Fifteenth would occasionally receive directives from the CCS for employment in the Combined Bomber Offensive. The Fifteenth would receive the Twelfth's six heavy groups and fifteen more from the continental United States.

---

* POINTBLANK's first objective was to destroy the German daylight fighter forces, after which it would attack the German aircraft industry, the ball-bearing industry, and other high-value economic targets.

Eaker and Devers objected vigorously, arguing that the plan diverted forces from Britain and sacrificed the principle of concentration of force, thereby jeopardizing POINTBLANK and OVERLORD. The JCS, after discussions with Bedell Smith and Spaatz, approved Arnold's plan. The JCS then submitted the matter to the Combined Chiefs of Staff, who had overall control of the Combined Bomber Offensive. The CCS agreed with a proviso inserted by the British that if logistical problems prevented the stationing of heavy-bomber groups in the Mediterranean, then the excess bombers would go to Britain.[58] The CCS directed Eisenhower to employ the Fifteenth Air Force against strategic targets. They allowed him to use units of the Fifteenth that had been reassigned from the Twelfth Air Force (six heavy-bomber groups, and two long-range fighter groups) primarily against political targets in the Balkans and in support of the land forces in Italy rather than against POINTBLANK objectives, until the land forces secured air bases north and east of Rome.[59]

Spaatz, who had returned to La Marsa on October 22, the same day the CCS approved the formation of the Fifteenth, quickly assured Arnold on the logistical capabilities of southern Italy. Spaatz immediately obtained an authoritative statement on logistics from a West Point classmate, Lt. Gen. Brehon B. Somervell, the crusty Commanding General, Army Services of Supply. Somervell, the Army's chief logistics and supply officer with a status virtually equal to Arnold's, had visited the Italian theater and Spaatz at the end of October. Armed with Somervell's estimate and the results of a recent inspection of Foggia and its supply line back to Taranto, Spaatz sent out a telegram, over Eisenhower's signature, minimizing supply difficulties. Eisenhower appended a staff report from Bedell Smith which indicated somewhat more soberly that Italy could support the planned influx of bombers and escorts. Smith's report gave Arnold the ammunition he needed to refuse to discuss the issue when the British again questioned the capability of Italy to support additional strategic groups.[60]

For their part the British had come to question not the eventual need for the Fifteenth, whose existence they had already approved, but the timing of its increase. Portal had always favored strategic attacks from Italy because he assumed that the central and northern portions of the peninsula would be available for bases. Hitler's decision to defend Italy south of Rome and Field Marshal Kesselring's successful execution of that policy upset his calculations, however, and he began to question the effectiveness of basing bombers at the Foggia fields in the south.[61] In London, Eaker took issue with the rate of the Fifteenth's bomber and fighter group buildup specified in Eisenhower's instructions. He privately protested to the British that the nine heavy-bomber groups scheduled to go to Italy in November, December, and January should come to Britain, even if Italy could support them logistically.[62]

On October 26, the British Chiefs of Staff, reflecting Portal's and Eaker's positions, suggested to the CCS in Washington that the fifteen heavy-bombardment groups scheduled for Italy be redirected to their original destination—

Britain. They further asked that the six heavy-bombardment groups already in Italy be assigned primarily to POINTBLANK even before the fall of Rome.[63] Churchill seconded these suggestions. He instructed Portal not to allow the strategic buildup to interfere with the battle for Rome but to give the armies and their tactical air support first priority. Churchill emphasized that the goal from the British must be "saturation" or overwhelming strength for the American daylight attacks.[64]

When the British Joint Staff Mission in Washington presented that position to the CCS, the Americans brushed it aside. At the October 29 meeting, Arnold, referring repeatedly to assurances given him by Spaatz, said that the buildup of the Fifteenth did not interfere with the strengthening of Eisenhower's tactical air or ground forces. Arnold maintained that bombers in Italy would be more effective than those in Britain and renewed his promise to send to Britain all the groups that the Fifteenth could not supply or operate effectively. Marshall reminded the British that Eisenhower himself had called for a strategic air force in Italy, in part to have those forces at his disposal in case of a ground emergency, during which he could decide relative priorities. With the losses during the Schweinfurt mission of October 14 in mind, Marshall observed that strategic forces in Italy would help reduce "very heavy casualties" incurred in daylight bombing over northwest Europe.[65] Having already accepted the creation of an additional U.S. strategic air force, the British could hardly continue to object to the way the Americans divided their own assets, especially in light of assurances that POINTBLANK remained the prime objective and that the Americans could supply their own forces.

The creation of the Fifteenth Air Force, whose headquarters would serve as the hub of the strategic bombing campaign based in Italy, naturally consumed much of Spaatz's ten-day sojourn in Washington. In addition to the always vexatious problem of replacements, Spaatz and Arnold probably discussed arrangements for the overall control of strategic air forces in Europe—a complex problem of great concern not only to the AAF and the RAF but to the theater commanders and the Combined Chiefs as well.

The theater commanders, Eisenhower in Italy and Devers in Britain, wanted total authority over all air forces in their commands. Had this authority been allowed, the coordination of strategic bombing against Germany would have been hamstrung, especially if both the Mediterranean and the European Theaters of Operation possessed competing strategic forces. The CCS, charged with the overall strategic direction of the war, also had a stake in the problem. They had decided at the conferences in Washington in May 1943 and in Quebec in August 1943 that the successful invasion of the Continent required a successful strategic bombing campaign. The first objective of such a campaign would be to so damage the Luftwaffe that it could not contest Allied air supremacy over the invasion area. Competing with the requirements for strategic bombing in the eyes of the CCS were the equally valid claims of the invasion commanders and ground troops for tactical support of preinvasion preparations, the landings, and post invasion operations.

The AAF and the RAF had separate agendas on the issue of command and control. Arnold and the AAF wanted a single Allied Strategic Air Force Commander in charge of the Eighth and Fifteenth Air Forces and Bomber Command, with headquarters in London and a status equal—presumably with four-star rank—to that of the European and Mediterranean theater commanders. This idea, if approved, would in a stroke make the AAF's and the RAF's strategic air forces independent of the ground forces' leaders and allow untrammeled pursuit of the strategic bomber campaign against Germany—the *raison d'être* of both air forces. In addition, the airman who held the post would emerge with a prestige that at least matched that of the war's other theater commanders, such as Generals Eisenhower and MacArthur and Admiral Chester Nimitz. Arnold probably assumed that the commander would be a member of the AAF, principal supplier of aircraft. Even if an RAF officer got the job, Arnold would still have taken a large step toward eventual postwar autonomy for the AAF.

Next, Arnold wanted a U.S. Strategic Air Force Commander in Europe (also based in London) who would take operational control of both U.S. strategic air forces (the Eighth and Fifteenth) and administrative control of the U.S. air forces in Britain (the Eighth and Ninth). The AAF would thus acquire control over all of its heavy bombers directed toward Germany. Without such a headquarters, the two strategic air forces, each under a separate theater commander, might well fail to coordinate their efforts adequately. Such a command would also be at least equal to Bomber Command in prestige and stature and would certainly exceed it in numbers of heavy bombers. Because this headquarters would be in London, it could still take advantage of British intelligence and cooperate with Bomber Command—a unit already headed by an officer with the equivalent of four-star rank. His U.S. opposite number would probably have the same rank, which would reflect well on the AAF. By giving the U.S. Strategic Commander administrative control of the Ninth (Tactical) Air Force, which was slated to provide tactical air support for the cross-channel invasion, Arnold may have hoped to influence what promised to be the major U.S. land campaign of the war and to augment the power and prestige of the head of the U.S. Strategic Bomber Command.[66]

Although Arnold's plan stemmed from both his proposal for a combined bomber command in the summer of 1942 and his and Spaatz's advocacy of a single theater air force in the fall of 1942, his campaign for the acceptance of a new strategic command began no later than August 1, 1943, when he informed the head of the RAF Delegation in Washington, Air Marshal Welsh, of his idea for an overall commander.[67] Arnold continued to explore the idea during a trip to visit Britain and Eaker in September 1943. After spending three days inspecting the Eighth, Arnold visited Air Chief Marshal Harris at Bomber Command on September 5. That evening he and Harris discussed the subject of a combined command "in generalities." Arnold favored the plan because it allowed more efficient use of aircraft. Harris objected chiefly, as Arnold noted in his trip journal, because the British would then lose control of the bomber offensive. Harris, who operated with virtual autonomy from the RAF staff, could hardly be expected to accept an American superior when he had already freed himself from a British one.[68] Arnold also discussed his plan with Portal,[69] who probably indicated that he found it impractical.

By early October, Arnold had carried his ideas to Harry Hopkins, Franklin Roosevelt's alter ego, who endorsed them and presented them to the President.[70] A month later, Marshall, who by and large supported Arnold's position, advised him not to press the question until after the settlement of the more important questions of a unified Mediterranean command proposed by the British and the appointment of a single supreme commander for all U.S.-British forces fighting against the Germans.[71]

Nevertheless, Arnold persevered in his advocacy of new command arrangements. When the President made the first leg of his trip to the initial Big Three meeting with Churchill and Stalin at Tehran, Iran, in November 1943, he sailed on the brand-new U.S. battleship *Iowa*. The U.S. Chiefs traveled with him and added the finishing touches to their presentations and plans for the Cairo Conference with Churchill and Chinese leader Generalissimo Chiang Kai-shek, November 22–26, and the Tehran Conference, November 28 to December 1. During the voyage Arnold succeeded in gaining the backing of his fellow chiefs and the President for his command scheme. In a JCS memo for the President dated November 17, 1943, the JCS stated that from the military point of view the operation of the British and American strategic bombers required unity of command. The memo, which offered different proposals depending on how the British reacted to the American push for a supreme Allied commander in Europe, specified a single bomber command whether the British agreed to an overall supreme commander or not.[72]

The next day Arnold obtained the American Chiefs' agreement for the formation of a new U.S. headquarters to command and control all U.S. strategic bomber forces in Europe. The U.S. Strategic Air Forces in Europe (USSTAF) would command both the Eighth and Fifteenth Air Forces from London, where it could coordinate action with British Bomber Command. The theater commanders retained the right, upon notification of the Commanding General, USSTAF, to deploy bombers in the event of a tactical or strategic emergency. The JCS also agreed to Arnold's suggestion for a commanding general, Carl A. Spaatz. His name went forward to the President with the rest of the package.[73] Arnold chose Spaatz to head USSTAF for both professional and personal reasons. Spaatz had the seniority required for the post; he had the confidence of Portal, Tedder, and other high-ranking RAF officers; he possessed experience in conducting strategic bombing operations under wartime conditions; he had demonstrated his ability to function smoothly and effectively in theater-level Anglo-American operations; and he was personally loyal to Arnold, supporting his beliefs as to the wartime and future roles of the AAF.

The RAF diametrically opposed Arnold's proposals. It wished, for the most part, to maintain the status quo, which best served its interests. The RAF Chief of Staff, Portal, had received from the Combined Chiefs of Staff the task of coordinating the Eighth Air Force and British Bomber Command effort from Britain. On paper and subject to concurrence by the AAF, therefore, the British were in charge of the Combined Bomber Offensive, and Bomber Command remained an independent part of the offensive. This maintenance of Bomber Command's role was important, because the balance of heavy-bomber strength, heretofore in favor of the British, would swing dramatically in favor of the Americans during 1944. The British objected, too, that a new command would disrupt the excellent relations between the Eighth Air Force and the RAF, create a new unnecessary headquarters staff, and move the responsibility for coordination to Washington from London, which already had intelligence and communications personnel trained and ready to work. As for the Fifteenth Air Force, the British asserted that tight, direct coordination between that force and the forces in Britain would be impossible to attain and that shuttle bombing when, for example, British-based bombers striking a target in southern Germany continued on to land in Italy rather than on their home base, was not practical because bombers rapidly lost effectiveness when away from their own dedicated ground maintenance and supply echelons.[74]

On November 20, the *Iowa* docked in Oran, where Eisenhower met Roosevelt at the quay and flew with him to Tunis. The following day Roosevelt and Hopkins went sightseeing; the President went to selected Tunisian battlefields with Eisenhower; Hopkins went to Spaatz's headquarters. Roosevelt and Hopkins used their visits to evaluate the two generals with an eye to future reassignment. Hopkins questioned Spaatz closely about his views concerning the entire war strategy in Europe and about the feasibility of assisting the Soviets in their advance westward. Spaatz cited the Ploesti oil refineries and Balkan targets of a "psychological" nature, such as rail centers and depots, but noted that continued destruction of fighter and munitions factories in Germany would advance the Soviet cause as much as any other targets.[75]

Next, Hopkins asked Spaatz for his views on the Combined Bomber Offensive and its relationship to the cross-channel invasion and to operations in the Mediterranean. Spaatz replied boldly that once the weather cleared over Germany in April and May, thus allowing continuous operations from Britain and Italy, Germany would give up in three months. OVERLORD, Spaatz thought, was neither necessary nor desirable. From the point of view of air power, further gains in Italy would bring the bombers closer to Germany and represented a better investment in men and matériel than the cross-channel invasion.

Hopkins was impressed but unconvinced.[76] He belonged to the Marshall/War Department Operations Planning Division school of strategy, which upheld the primacy of the OVERLORD cross-channel invasion over all other operations. But apparently Spaatz's personality, sincere advocacy of air power, and determination to get the job done at any cost must have persuaded Hopkins that Arnold had been wise in championing him for the command of the strategic air forces in Europe.

Once the chiefs of state and their military leaders assembled in Cairo on November 23, Arnold's proposals encountered stiff opposition from the British. Although Marshall and Roosevelt, on separate occasions, brought up the issue of an overall Allied strategic air force with Churchill, they could not overcome British resistance. To Roosevelt's observation that "our strategic air forces from London to Ankara should be under one command," Churchill replied that a decision on the matter could be deferred until after OVERLORD—and that the current system worked well enough.[77] The dispute was not resolved until after the Tehran Conference, which dealt mainly with inter-Allied relations and assurances to the Soviets of American and British intentions to open a second front against Germany in the spring of 1944.

At the Second Cairo Conference, December 3–7, the Americans and the British settled their chief outstanding differences concerning strategy, strategic priorities, and operations. On December 6, Roosevelt announced his decision to appoint Dwight D. Eisenhower as Supreme Commander, Allied Expeditionary Force (SCAEF), from which position he would direct the invasion of France. Marshall, who had wanted the command and had many reasons to think he would get it, was disappointed. He was to continue as Army Chief of Staff. The President told him, "I could not sleep at night with you out of the country."[78] It was the most important personnel decision of the war; Eisenhower achieved greatness in his new role as commander of the cross-channel invasion, while Marshall continued to perform admirably his taxing and equally important chores in Washington.

At the Second Cairo Conference, the Americans abandoned their quest for an Allied Strategic Air Force and a supreme commander. The Allies did agree to institute the U.S. Strategic Air Forces in Europe (USSTAF). The British declined to interfere in what they regarded as an unwise, but purely American, decision.[79]

USSTAF would establish its headquarters in London and employ its strength primarily against POINTBLANK targets in accordance with directives issued by the CCS. In so doing it would continue to coordinate activities with RAF Bomber Command and ensure that in assignment of supplies and services between tactical and strategic operations POINTBLANK had first priority. Arnold as Commanding General, U.S. Army Air Forces, would continue to have direct channels to the Commander, U.S. Strategic Air Forces "on matters of technical control, operational and training techniques, and uniformity of tactical doctrine." The implementing directive to the American theater commanders and Commanding General, Strategic Air Forces, stated that the Strategic Air Forces would continue under the direction of the Chief of the Air Staff, RAF, as agent for the Combined Chiefs of Staff, until coming directly under the control of the Supreme Allied

Commander (for OVERLORD only) "at a date to be announced later" by the CCS. Should a tactical emergency arise, the theater commanders could employ the strategic forces upon notification of the CCS and Commanding General, Strategic Air Forces.[80] Before accepting this directive the British Chiefs stipulated that Arnold should consult Eisenhower, Tedder, and General James Maitland Wilson, British Commander in Chief, Middle East, and Eisenhower's replacement as Supreme Allied Commander in the Mediterranean.[81]

Also at the Second Cairo Conference, during a meeting of the Combined Chiefs of Staff on December 4, Arnold left no doubt in Portal's or his other listeners' minds about his unfavorable view of Eaker's efforts as commander of the Eighth Air Force. He complained of a "lack of flexibility in operations" despite numerous inspections and reports; a 50 percent aircraft availability rate* (in an industrialized country) as opposed to 60 to 70 percent in other (more primitive) theaters; and the dispatch of only one 600-aircraft operation in the whole month of November. He said, "The failure to destroy targets was due directly to the failure to employ planes in sufficient numbers. A sufficient weight of bombs was not being dropped on the targets to destroy them, nor was the proper priority of targets being followed."[82]

Arnold found that failure intolerable. The hostile tone in his memoirs describing his September inspection of the Eighth revealed a growing disenchantment with Eaker's progress. He was very angry, for example, as he listened to radio reports during his flight to England of B-17s running out of fuel on the ferry route through Gander, Newfoundland, and Prestwick. Arnold had worked himself into a heart attack to get planes for the AAF and in Eaker's command they, with their needed crews, were lost before ever reaching combat. "I was not satisfied," he remarked.[83] Also, while Arnold stayed in England, the Eighth suffered the misfortune of a large raid's misfiring over Stuttgart. Not a single one of 338 B-17s sent out reached its primary target. Arnold noted darkly, "Certain features of the operation never did find their way into reports sent up through channels."[84] On December 2, 1943, Arnold had a talk with his staff—Kuter, Vandenberg, and Hansell. He expressed to them the same dissatisfaction he would show two days later to the Combined Chiefs.[85]

On December 7, Arnold met Wilson for the first time and lunched with Tedder. He discussed the new air arrangements with both and found that neither objected to them.[86] On December 8, he flew to Sicily where he met the President, Eisenhower, Bedell Smith, and Spaatz, all of whom had traveled on the same C-54 aircraft from North Africa to Sicily.[87] Arnold consulted first with Eisenhower and Bedell Smith, who approved of his choice of Spaatz to command the Strategic Air Force.[88] Even though they were still puzzled as to the

* The availability rate is the number of aircraft and crews officially listed in the theater or unit divided by the number of aircraft and crews actually available for combat. A 50 percent rate meant that Eaker had only half of the number of his planes ready to fight.

exact task and position within the command hierarchy of the strategic air commander, both Bedell Smith and Eisenhower preferred to have a known and friendly quantity, such as Spaatz, in the job rather than a stranger who might not appreciate the needs of the ground commanders. In his trip notebook Arnold noted, "Both agree Spaatz was the man for the job. Wouldn't take anyone else, not even Tedder."[89] After Eisenhower and Bedell Smith endorsed the selection of Spaatz, Arnold presumably obtained a final ratification from the President. Roosevelt, who had used his flight and the previous days' meetings and dinner with Eisenhower and Spaatz in Tunis to add to impressions collected earlier, raised no objection.

Then Arnold and Bedell Smith informed Spaatz of his appointment to the post of Commanding General, U.S. Strategic Air Forces in Europe. Spaatz himself would have preferred not to set up an overall strategic headquarters,[90] but he told Arnold that once the new headquarters went into operation "it must come under Eisenhower's control not later than March 1 to be properly tied in with OVERLORD."[91] He added that it might be possible to increase the rate of operations in Britain but that congested conditions there might prevent the full use of aircraft. Finally, he explained the complicated air command arrangements in the Mediterranean to Arnold and warned that the contemplated shift of personnel (such as Tedder and himself) might well upset the delicate balance between the RAF and the AAF there.[92]

This last point may have been the final consideration in Arnold's decision to remove Ira Eaker from command of the Eighth Air Force and transfer him to the Mediterranean. As Arnold and Spaatz had confirmed that day, Tedder would soon vacate his post as Air Officer Commanding, Mediterranean Allied Air Forces (MAAF) to go to England as Eisenhower's deputy commander (not as deputy for air). Eaker's transfer south would allow the AAF to fill the chief air command in the Mediterranean—a position promised to the Americans during the general reorganization of the commands in the theater—with a widely experienced combat officer.

After their meeting Arnold and Spaatz talked briefly with Eisenhower; they recommended Eaker's transfer and Eisenhower agreed.[93] In addition, Spaatz reiterated to Eisenhower what he had told Bedell Smith—when the cross-channel battle began, Spaatz should serve directly under Eisenhower so that all of the power of the strategic air forces could assist the invasion.[94] The three generals left the conference unsure about exactly what form the subordination of USSTAF to the Supreme Allied Commander would take and when it would occur.[95] Two and one-half weeks later, on Christmas Day, Eisenhower confessed to Marshall, "To be perfectly frank, this assignment for Spaatz leaves me somewhat puzzled as to purpose and . . . position of such a command in an American organization, since we always, in each Theater, insist upon a single commander."[96]

After these brief meetings, all of which took place in little more than an hour, Spaatz returned to Foggia and his palatial headquarters with Arnold, where they spent the night. The next evening, December 9, Arnold, Spaatz, Doolittle, and Cannon met over dinner to discuss the new organization and the future of the Twelfth and Fifteenth Air Forces. As for personnel, Spaatz reaffirmed his recommendation that Eaker be transferred to the Mediterranean and suggested that Doolittle replace him as commander of the Eighth, that Brereton retain command of the Ninth (the tactical air force designated to provide American direct support for OVERLORD), and that Cannon keep the Twelfth while becoming head of MAAF's Tactical Air Force.* Arnold was also finally convinced that the Fifteenth could handle the fifteen additional heavy-bombardment groups scheduled for the Mediterranean Theater.[97]

On December 12, Arnold completed his talks with Spaatz, finished his inspection of the AAF in Italy, and departed for Tunis to complete arrangements with Eisenhower. They agreed to the personnel changes recommended by Spaatz with the addition of Maj. Gen. Nathan F. Twining, who at that time commanded the Thirteenth Air Force in the South Pacific, to command the Fifteenth. By December 15, Arnold had returned to Washington greatly pleased. In his memoirs he wrote, "As far as the Army Air Forces were concerned the thing we wanted most of all had been gained at the [Cairo] Conference. We had received confirmation of our present plans for bombing the interior of Germany to a pulp."[98]

Upon his return to the Pentagon, Arnold set in motion the personnel changes to which he, Spaatz, and Eisenhower had agreed. Eaker's transfer to the Mediterranean immediately became a cause célèbre. Eaker must have known he stood on slippery turf. Both before and after Arnold's inspection tour in September he had received from Arnold's headquarters an increasingly querulous string of inquiries demanding higher rates of operations, greater employment en masse of available aircraft, and more spectacular bombing results.[99] Only a month before, however, he, Spaatz, and Tedder had met at Gibraltar to discuss the coordination of the Combined Bomber Offensive between the Eighth, the Fifteenth, and RAF Bomber Command. They agreed to put Eaker on Spaatz's REDLINE and to exchange messages at least twice a day. They further divided Germany into bombing zones and allocated targets for each American air force; and they provided for exchanging target material, posting liaison officers in each headquarters, and sharing blind-bombing (bombing through clouds with the use of radar) techniques. They also allowed the Fifteenth to station a permanent intelligence liaison officer in London as its representative on all British Air Ministry intelligence matters.[100] At the end of the conference the three Allied air-

---

* The current MAAF Tactical Air Force Commander, Air Marshal Coningham, had already been selected to command the British 2d Tactical Air Force which would support the British ground forces in OVERLORD. The Northwest African Air Forces (NAAF) had been redesignated Mediterranean Allied Air Forces (MAAF) in the fall of 1943.

Maj. Gen. John K. Cannon, Commanding General, Northwest African Tactical Air Force; Lt. Gen. Carl A. Spaatz, Commanding General, Northwest African Air Forces; Lt. Gen. Mark W. Clark, Commanding General, Fifth Army; and General Henry H. Arnold, Commanding General, U.S. Army Air Forces, awaiting departure in front of an idling Piper L-4 Grasshopper, after a visit to the Fifth Army front in the Pesenzano area, Italy, December 11, 1943.

men sent word to Arnold, "We are in complete agreement on all matters."[101]

Apparently, Eaker had his first intimation that Arnold remained dissatisfied with his operation during a visit on December 14 from Portal, who asked him to answer the criticisms that Arnold had expressed during the three conferences at Cairo and Tehran. Eaker's defense satisfied Portal, who forwarded it to Arnold and concluded, "I found Eaker thoroughly alive to need for earliest possible attacks on POINTBLANK targets and to importance of using maximum force available. I am confident you will see great achievements as soon as weather gives him a chance."[102] Four days later Eaker received the official message transferring him to the position of Commanding General of the Mediterranean Allied Air Forces.

Arnold put the best possible face on the move; "As a result of your long period of successful operations and the exceptional results of your endeavors as Commander of the Air Force in England you have been recommended for this position."[103] But Eaker objected to being "kicked upstairs." He felt as if he had been kicked in an even more sensitive area. More than twenty years later, he remarked, "The darkest hour for me was when I was ordered to the Mediterranean

Maj. Gen. James H. Doolittle in front of a Martin B-26 Marauder at Maison Blanche, Algeria, October 15, 1943.

and relieved of my command of the 8th Air Force."[104] To Maj. Gen. James E. Fechet, a former head of the Air Corps and an old friend, Eaker said, "I feel like a pitcher who has been sent to the showers during a world series game."[105]

Shocked and angry, Eaker fought to retain control of the command that he had nurtured over the previous thirteen hard months. With an abundant supply of heavy bombers and new P-51 long-range escort fighters filling the supply pipeline from the United States and beginning to reach the units in England, Eaker knew that he had success within his grasp. He immediately wrote to Arnold:

> Believe war interest best served by my retention command Eighth Air Force; otherwise experience this theater for nearly two years wasted. If I am to be allowed any personal preference, having started with the Eighth and seen it organized for a major task in this theater, it would be heart-breaking to leave it just before climax."[106]

Then Eaker went to Devers, his theater commander, who was also ticketed for a Mediterranean berth (although he was ignorant of it at the time) and then to the U.S. ambassador to Britain, John Winant. Eaker even approached Portal. Finally, unaware that they had already approved of his transfer, he telegraphed Eisenhower and Spaatz for a reprieve.[107] Portal attempted to help Eaker, writing frankly to Arnold that he disagreed with some of the impending personnel moves. "To move him now that we approach the climax of the air war over

Western Germany would be a grave mistake. I therefore greatly hope that when the final decision is made you will feel able to leave Eaker here."[108] Portal also thought Doolittle ought to stay with the Fifteenth and, in a backhanded slap at Brereton, who already commanded the Ninth Air Force, he said, "I do not know Twining, but if you should decide to send him to 9th Air Force to take Brereton's place I can assure him a warm welcome and a receptive ear for his Pacific experience."[109] All this was to no avail.

Arnold's replies to Portal and Devers (written by Kuter) emphasized the need for a man of Eaker's qualities in the Mediterranean (to fill the vacuum left by Spaatz). To Devers, Arnold added, "This move is necessary from the viewpoint of world wide air operations."[110] To Portal, Arnold replied that General Wilson would find Eaker topnotch in the Mediterranean and "the Spaatz-Doolittle-Anderson team a vigorous and effective one in the U.K."[111] Arnold did his best to quash any hope Eaker retained of staying with the Eighth: "I extend to you my heartfelt thanks for the splendid cooperation and loyalty that you have given me thus far and for the wonderful success of your organization, but I cannot, repeat, not see my way clear to make any change in the decisions already reached."[112] Spaatz, after receiving Arnold's approval, replied in a variation on the same theme: "Command of an Air Force in either place is relatively of less importance as compared to overall requirements, particularly since Eighth Air Force under new setup will function as an operating headquarters more nearly approximating Eighth bomber command."[113]

Eaker's appeals did not go completely unheeded. On December 23, Bedell Smith informed Spaatz, that "strong objections are being raised to the transfer of Eaker from the U.K." Spaatz, who replied that he would not go to England unless Ira Eaker came to the Mediterranean, [114] still believed that the AAF in the Mediterranean required Eaker's leadership to replace his own.[115] In a postwar interview he said:

> I know this—that I would have been satisfied to have stayed down in the Mediterranean and command the Mediterranean Air Force, if I hadn't had to go up on that cross-channel operation. . . . I didn't look forward at all to England at that time. I felt my job down in the Mediterranean was just the job I wanted to have.[116]

From Bedell Smith, Spaatz learned that his position would be clarified by Eisenhower in a cable to Marshall, [117] and he recorded in his Command Diary his irritation at what he regarded as Arnold's backsliding on the subject. Arnold had not strongly enough sold Marshall on the changes, and now Eisenhower would have to bail them both out. "My original estimation of Eisenhower's fairness has been strengthened," noted Spaatz, "by the way . . . he is taking this and the way he is standing by me in my decision."[118]

But before Eisenhower could send his explanation, he found a stinging telegram on his desk from Marshall, who had received Eaker's *cri de coeur* on

December 22, when he returned to Washington from a Pacific tour following the Second Cairo Conference.[119] Marshall, tired after a long tour and still deeply disappointed from his own failure to gain the OVERLORD command, reacted with an uncharacteristically emotional display, especially for a man who exemplified the Virginia Military Institute tradition, derived from George Washington and Robert E. Lee, of complete imperturbability in the face of stress. After questioning the tendency to "gut" the Mediterranean theater of leadership, Marshall said, "I believe I was more disturbed over the pressure of TEDDER and SPAATZ to move EAKER to the Mediterranean because to me he did not appear particularly suited for that theater and I am forced to the conclusion that their attitude is selfish and not purely objective."[120] Arnold seemed to have created the impression that not he, but Spaatz and Tedder, wanted Eaker ousted.

On Christmas day in Tunis Eisenhower told Spaatz that he would send a message to Marshall in which he would give Spaatz's views as his own. Spaatz again remarked in his diary, "General Eisenhower has [been] and is firm in [his] decisions and I consider him one of the finest men I know."[121] In his "Eyes Only" cable to Marshall, Eisenhower gave assurances that he had studied the proposed personnel changes for some time and had a "completely objective" attitude in recommending them. Then Eisenhower justified the transfer by pointing out Eaker's ability and noting the waste of talent involved in having him and Spaatz in the same theater. The only other air officer he would consider for the Mediterranean, Maj. Gen. Lewis H. Brereton, had just set up his Ninth Air Force in England to serve as the U.S. tactical air force in support of OVERLORD. Brereton's selection might disrupt that vital phase of the invasion.

Noting Spaatz's intention to stay in the Mediterranean if Eaker stayed in London, Eisenhower implied that he needed Spaatz in London and that he accepted conditions concerning Eaker. Eisenhower emphasized to Marshall that in Spaatz he had one of the few senior officers experienced in air-ground support, a practice "that is not repeat not widely understood and takes men of some vision and broad understanding to do . . . right. Otherwise a commander is forever fighting with those air officers who, regardless of the ground situation, want to send big bombers on missions that have nothing to do with the critical effort."[122]

Later in the day Eisenhower wrote to Eaker, stating of the new move that Arnold (with no mention of Spaatz) had proposed it during his stopover in Sicily and that he had agreed to it "because of the absolute necessity of finding an outstanding man for the post of Air CINC of the Mediterranean." He then added his own opinion that if Spaatz left for Britain, Eaker must come south, for "we do not repeat not have enough top men to concentrate them in any one place."[123]

The day after Christmas Spaatz flew from Tunis to Algiers for further discussion about the new posts with Eisenhower, who showed him the message from Marshall questioning Eaker's transfer. At first Spaatz bristled and told him that he would write to Marshall to explain; but upon reflection he decided against such a move.[124] It would accomplish nothing except to prod Marshall on a sore point and make Spaatz appear self-serving. Besides, the transfer had been confirmed and Spaatz would leave for England in two days. At the same meeting Spaatz told Eisenhower that in order to prevent disputes, presumably about logistical, matériel, and replacement priorities between the Eighth and Ninth Air Forces, Eisenhower needed to appoint a Commanding General, Army Air Forces, European Theater of Operations. As in the Mediterranean, a single AAF general officer could then arbitrate between the competing demands of the strategic and tactical air forces. Spaatz also told Eisenhower that, instead of dealing directly with the Fifteenth Air Force, he intended always to go through the Commander of the Mediterranean Allied Air Forces, in this case, Eaker.[125]

In the Eaker incident, Eisenhower had taken a straightforward position. He welcomed Arnold's and Spaatz's recommendation because he wanted Spaatz in England with him. When objections arose, he backed Spaatz. When Spaatz made it clear he would not go to Britain unless Eaker was transferred, Eisenhower persuaded Marshall to bow to the new arrangements.

Spaatz, too, had taken a straightforward position during the Eaker transfer. At no point in his wartime papers or postwar interviews did he criticize Eaker's performance in command of the Eighth. Unlike Arnold, Spaatz had extensive personal experience with difficulties involved in the mounting of large-scale heavy-bomber missions and with the frustrating and peculiar weather conditions in England and Western Europe. Spaatz believed in Ira Eaker's great ability, especially as a military diplomat, and wanted him in the Mediterranean to advance the war effort and the AAF's cause as the new Commander of the Mediterranean Allied Air Forces. Knowing that Eisenhower wanted him in London, Spaatz told Arnold: "If I go to England, then Ira must have command of the air forces in the Mediterranean."[126] He did not consider Eaker's move a demotion;[127] in fact, Spaatz later credited himself with the original recommendation that Eaker move.[128] He wanted Eaker in the Mediterranean because he knew that, given the complex and intermingled operational and administrative controls over the American air forces in Europe in which he and Eaker would operate, he needed a man he knew and trusted.[129]

There was no hint that Spaatz advocated Eaker's transfer in order to remove a rival or a possible center of opposition from England.

Unlike Eisenhower and Spaatz, Arnold had mixed motives in removing Eaker. AAF official historians said in 1949, "If Arnold's dissatisfaction over the rate of Eighth Air Force operations entered into the decision, the record apparently has left no evidence of it."[130] The diplomatic record of the Cairo Conference, published in 1961, and Arnold's own memoirs, published in 1949, contradicted them. Arnold probably did feel that Eaker's talents could be more effectively applied in the Mediterranean, but he did not lose sight of his main goal—removing Eaker from the Eighth Air Force for not fully employing the resources supplied him to pursue the ultimate purpose of the Combined Bomber Offensive.

He seized on the command shuffle stemming from the Cairo and Tehran conferences to cloak a decision he had probably already reached. In his own mind, at least, he had saved face for himself, Eaker, and, most important, for his beloved AAF. Eaker might be broken-hearted and a friendship of twenty-five years' standing shattered, but Eaker and Spaatz had been moved to where the Commander of the AAF wanted them.

In February 1944, Arnold explained to Spaatz his reason for assigning him to London in a highly emotional and confidential letter. Arnold had advanced the Strategic Air Force for a purely military consideration—unity of command for the British and Italian portions of the bomber offensive. But he went on:

> Another and perhaps equally important motive behind the formation of the United States Strategic Air Forces in Europe was my desire to build an American Air Commander to a high position prior to the defeat of Germany. It is that aspect particularly which has impelled me in my so far successful fight to keep your command parallel to Harris' command and, therefore, parallel to Ike's. If you do not remain in a position parallel with Harris, the air war will certainly be won by the RAF, if anybody. Already the spectacular effectiveness of their devastation of cities has placed their contribution in the popular mind at so high a plane that I am having the greatest difficulty in keeping your achievement (far less spectacular to the public) in its proper role not only in publications, but unfortunately in military and naval circles and, in fact, with the President himself. Therefore, considering only the aspect of a proper American share in credit for success in the air war, I feel we must have a high air commander some place in Europe. Today you can be that commander.[131]

After an exchange of messages on personnel matters between Eisenhower and Marshall, the latter accepted Eisenhower's recommendations almost *in toto*. Marshall acquiesced in Spaatz's transfer with the proviso that no large new staff organization be created as a consequence of it.[132]

On December 28, 1943, Spaatz boarded his B-17 on the first leg of the flight to England. For thirteen months he had advanced the effectiveness and importance of the AAF in the war against the Axis in the Mediterranean Theater of Operations. His personal involvement in the day-to-day operations of the NAAF had waned as Air Chief Marshal Arthur Tedder actively assumed his own role as Eisenhower's Commander in Chief for Air. Spaatz had directed the bombing of Pantelleria, controlling the combined operation's planning, execution, and air, naval, and land coordination. From that high point of broad responsibility his influence had steadily diminished until, by the end of the Sicilian campaign, he apparently exercised little control over his RAF subordinate commander for the Tactical Air Force, Air Marshal Arthur Coningham.

As a result of the peculiarities of the Allied command structure in the Mediterranean, Spaatz found himself reduced to the de facto position of head of the Northwest African Strategic Air Force. After the merger of Spaatz's and Tedder's operational headquarters by Eisenhower in late summer 1943, Tedder felt free to go directly to the RAF Commander of the Tactical and Coastal Air Forces, but constrained to go through Spaatz to give orders to Doolittle, an American officer. That this situation did not cause a great deal more anger and mistrust than it did is a tribute to the personalities of Tedder and Spaatz, especially Spaatz, who subordinated himself for the mutual good.

Spaatz concentrated his energies on consolidating the AAF's position within the theater and expanding its part in the Combined Bomber Offensive. He succeeded in both endeavors. By the end of his tenure in the Mediterranean he had a fully functional all-American communications network, REDLINE, in place, which enabled him, as AAF chief in the Mediterranean, to retain close administrative ties with his units, independent of the RAF or any combined Allied organization. REDLINE also allowed him to retain what minimal control of operations he had.

Spaatz held the strongest belief that an air force based in the Mediterranean Theater could, by attacking from the south, increase Germany's defense burden and advance the goal of the Combined Bomber Offensive. His convincing Arnold and Eisenhower and, then, the three's convincing the Combined Chiefs of Staff of the soundness of that belief resulted in the establishment of the Fifteenth Air Force. He may also have felt, at least until his appointment as head of U.S. Strategic Air Forces in Europe, that commanding the Fifteenth rather than serving as Tedder's deputy would give him a chance to contribute more to the war effort.

When Spaatz departed for London he left behind two large, well-organized, and well-supplied American air forces. Of course, a year's worth of combat experience and the fruits of America's vast industrial effort did much to improve their status. Spaatz also deserves credit as a military administrator. The responsibility for military administration rested in his headquarters, not in Tedder's Mediterranean Air Command or the Strategic, Tactical, and Coastal Air Forces. They dealt only with operations.[133] Without Spaatz's efforts there might have been not only one air force, but one air force dominated by the RAF and devoted to the close support of the army. Spaatz's establishment of a strategic air force, over the objections of those favoring a stronger heavy-bomber buildup in England, would also prove important in the long run. Bombers based in Britain did not have the range to hit the vital Axis oil targets of southeastern Europe. Without the Fifteenth Air Force, the Allied bombing campaign would have achieved substantially fewer results. Arnold might well have refused to consider splitting his forces in the face of the enemy and handing part of them over to an officer he did not know as well or trust as completely as Spaatz.

Part Four

The Point of the Blade
Strategic Bombing and the
Cross-Channel Invasion
January–June 1944

Part Four

The Point of the Blade

Strategic Bombing bears the same relationship to tactical
bombing as does the cow to a pail of milk. To deny immediate aid and comfort to the enemy, tactical considerations
dictate upsetting the bucket. To insure eventual starvation,
the strategic move is to kill the cow.[1]

—*U.S. Strategic Bombing Survey, November 1945*

On January 1, 1944, Lt. Gen. Carl A. Spaatz officially assumed command of
the United States Strategic Air Forces in Europe (USSTAF). This new headquarters had operational control of two U.S. strategic air forces, the Eighth in Britain
and the Fifteenth in Italy. Under the direction of the Chief of the Air Staff, RAF,
who acted as an agent for the U.S.-British Combined Chiefs of Staff, Spaatz was
responsible for directing the U.S. portion of the Combined Bomber Offensive—
the U.S.-British strategic bombing campaign against the German war economy
and military machine. At some unspecified future date, before the invasion of
France from Britain (OVERLORD), Spaatz would come under the command of the
Supreme Allied Commander of the invasion force. Once under Eisenhower's
control, USSTAF would apply its forces to the preinvasion air campaign, to the
assault, and to subsequent phases of the campaign.

Spaatz would play a far stronger and more prominent role in the deliberations
of the Allied high command and enjoy greater prestige and autonomy than his predecessor, Ira Eaker, because he was much friendlier with Eisenhower and Tedder,
because he would oversee a much larger, more generously supplied, more effective,
and more organizationally independent force, and because, in the last analysis, he
would exercise a more forceful personality.[2] In the beginning of 1944, the focus of
Anglo-American operations shifted from the Mediterranean to northwest Europe,
where the decisive ground operation to overthrow Germany would be launched.
This fact magnified the importance of the commanders and their decisions.

Spaatz faced two problems: he had to (1) get the maximum number of bombers
over the target (which meant using escort fighters because not enough unescorted
bombers would survive to reach their destinations) and (2) get the greatest possible accuracy from bombs delivered. Spaatz was compelled to substitute sheer
tonnage for precision when his bombers failed to destroy their targets—this
practice required bombing in less-than-perfect weather conditions and using
radar for navigation and sighting.

By January 1944, the Americans' operational plan for their part of the Combined Bomber Offensive, known as POINTBLANK, had three high-priority targets: (1) single-engine fighter plane production, (2) twin-engine fighter plane production, and (3) German antifriction bearing manufacturing.[3] As a single overriding prerequisite to the neutralization of these targets, POINTBLANK called for the destruction of the Luftwaffe's fighter forces in being—the chief obstacle to the success of the Combined Bomber Offensive. POINTBLANK had its origins at the Casablanca Conference in January 1943, where Roosevelt, Churchill, and their military staffs had agreed to a bomber offensive against Germany. In May 1943, at the Washington Conference, the Combined Chiefs of Staff approved a plan for the Combined Bomber Offensive drawn up by Eaker and the Eighth Air Force. This plan was based on priorities originated by an AAF-supported study group (the Committee of Operations Analysts) and agreed on, with some modifications, by experts of the British Ministry of Economic Warfare and the RAF Air Staff.[4]

The plan gave the highest priority to German fighter plane production. Early elimination of fighter manufacture was essential to the accomplishment of the rest of the Combined Bomber Offensive and would heighten the chances of success for the cross-channel invasion by reducing expected air opposition. Allied planners had identified antifriction, or ball, bearings as crucial in the production of German war matériel. The effects of their unavailability, although not imme-

Air Chief Marshal
Trafford Leigh-Mallory,
Commander, Allied
Expeditionary Air Force,
1943–1944.

Imperial War Museum

diately felt in enemy front-line strength, would eventually touch all types of high-speed military equipment. The Allies believed from their own experience that ball bearings could not be stockpiled and that only large plants could manufacture a complete range of them. In addition, more than half of all German production was concentrated in one locality within range of bombers based in Britain—Schweinfurt.[5] But the Allies soon learned that the Germans were not so dependent on ball bearings as predicted. Moreover, the Eighth Air Force, because of heavy losses, had been unable to follow up attacks on Schweinfurt in August and October, which had alerted the Germans and led them to disperse the industry and redesign their equipment to use less of its vital product.

While attempting to carry out their mission under POINTBLANK, Spaatz and his headquarters became increasingly involved in the planning and the conduct of the preinvasion air campaign. A protracted dispute eventually developed between Spaatz and the Commander of the Allied Expeditionary Air Force (AEAF), Air Chief Marshal Trafford Leigh-Mallory. Spaatz became, almost by default, the chief spokesman for a faction of the Allied high command that objected to the massive antirailroad and transportation interdiction plan supported by Tedder and advocated by Leigh-Mallory, who had operational control of all tactical combat air forces directly assigned to Eisenhower's invasion force.

These two interwoven threads of POINTBLANK and OVERLORD dominated Spaatz's thoughts and actions for the crucial period between New Year's Day 1944 and the invasion of France on D-day, June 6, 1944.

Chapter 9

The Luftwaffe Engaged
(January–February 1944)

We look upon our attacks against Germany now as major
battles that are phases of a campaign. Each of these battles
has all the elements of a major land or sea engagement,
involving movement over tremendous distances, involving
holding forces, involving penetrations and involving envel-
opments.[1]

—Spaatz to Arnold, January 10, 1944

Reports of the actual dispatch of over 800 heavy bombers
against German fighter targets on 2 successive days and
your ability and intention to repeat on the 3rd day are the
brightest items that have crossed this desk for a long time.[2]

—Arnold to Spaatz, January 31, 1944

Upon his arrival in London on December 29, 1943, Spaatz found the Eighth
Air Force facing a crisis. For two and a half months it had flown no deep-penetration bombing missions into Germany during clear weather.[3] As the Army Air
Forces offical history admitted, "The Eighth Air Force had for the time being
lost [the battle for] air superiority over Germany."[4] The AAF had learned during
the October 14 Schweinfurt mission, in which it lost 60 of 320 bombers dispatched, wrote off 7 bombers as not repairable, and counted 138 more as damaged,[5] —"that such operations without fighter protection were impossibly
costly."[6] Portal, in his capacity as the coordinator for POINTBLANK, informed the
Combined Chiefs of Staff on December 4, 1943, that "the program was, in fact,
some three months behind [schedule]."[7] As of early January 1944, Eighth Air
Force statistics, only slightly skewed by the disastrous Schweinfurt mission,

showed that only 26 percent of those crews beginning operational tours in the theater could expect to complete twenty-five missions (the minimum needed to return to the States); 57 percent would be dead or missing; and the remaining 17 percent would fail to complete their tours because of combat fatigue, accidental death, transfer, or administrative reasons.[8] Arnold reported only slightly less discouraging statistics to Marshall, noting that the Eighth's 3.8 percent loss rate per mission from July through November translated into a loss of 64 crew members* out of every 100.[9]

Spaatz, however, would soon take advantage of opportunities and resources unavailable to his unlucky predecessor, Ira Eaker. In a campaign that bore some resemblance to that of Ulysses S. Grant versus Robert E. Lee in the spring of 1864, Spaatz would use every opportunity to close with the Luftwaffe and force it to bleed and die. Similarly, just as the relative contributions of Grant and George G. Meade, the actual commander of the Union Army of the Potomac, blurred and merged, so, too, did those of Spaatz and his chief subordinate Maj. Gen. James H. Doolittle. Grant's drive from Fredericksburg to Petersburg destroyed the offensive potential of Lee's army and tied it to a trench system that it could not successfully defend. Spaatz, in the upcoming campaign, would pull the Luftwaffe's teeth, forcing it to defend only the most preeminently important target systems, such as oil, while allowing the AAF daylight air supremacy over Germany. Also like Grant, Spaatz benefited through the prodigal output of men and material from an industrial economy whose production was overwhelming.

The pipeline that had supplied Eaker with only a slowly increasing force overflowed in late 1943 and early 1944 for Spaatz. The Allied victory in the Battle of the Atlantic and massive U.S. merchant shipping production turned the constricted flow of supplies that had slowed the U.S. buildup in Britain for the first one and a half years of the war into a fast-flowing river. As a consequence of delays caused, in part, by a January 1943 decision by Arnold and Spaatz to divert P-38s to the North African Theater, Eaker's first operational P-38 "Lightning" long-range fighter group (the 55th) of approximately seventy-five aircraft became operational the day after the Schweinfurt mission. The P-38s of the 20th Fighter Group went into action in December 1943, as did the first long-range P-51B Mustang fighters (the Ninth Air Force's 354th Fighter Group). In March the P-51 began to use new external fuel tanks (drop tanks), which enabled it to go as far as any bombers in the theater.[10]

As of December 30, 1943, the Army Air Forces in England comprised 4,618

---

* A loss rate of 3.8 percent per mission meant that 3.8 percent of the original force was lost on each mission. By the end of 25 missions the cumulative loss suffered by the original 100 air crews was therefore 64 air crews, even though only 3.8 percent, on average, were lost in a single mission. Reinforcement of the original 100 crews would have no effect on their chances for statistical survival because new arrivals would be lost at the same rate.

Lt. Gen. Carl A. Spaatz, Commanding General, U.S. Strategic Air Forces in Europe; Maj. Gen. Nathan F. Twining, Commanding General, Fifteenth Air Force; and Lt. Gen. Ira C. Eaker, Commanding General, Mediterranean Allied Air Force.

Maj. Gen. Lewis H. Brereton, Commanding General, Ninth Air Force; Lt. Gen. Carl A. Spaatz, Commanding General, U.S. Strategic Air Forces in Europe; and General Dwight D. Eisenhower, Supreme Commander, Allied Expeditionary Force, studying a photograph of a Ninth Air Force medium bomber field, April 22, 1944.

aircraft, 4,242 of them combat aircraft, divided into 45¾ groups (26¾ of heavy bombers, 12 of fighters, 4 of medium bombers, 2 of troop carriers, and 1 of reconnaissance).[11] Despite constant attrition from September 1943 to May 1944, the number of fully operational heavy bombers in Eighth Air Force tactical units rose from 461 to 1,655. During the same period the Eighth's fighter aircraft also jumped from 274 to 882[12] and the number of personnel assigned to the Eighth went from 150,000 to 400,000. By February 19, 1944, another part of Spaatz's command, the Fifteenth Air Force, would contribute an additional 12 heavy bomber and 4 fighter groups.[13]

Before taking on the Luftwaffe, Spaatz instituted a system in which operations and administration received equal attention. This arrangement stemmed from Spaatz's dual responsibilities as the Commander of USSTAF, in operational control of the Eighth and Fifteenth Air Forces, and as the head of the AAF in Britain in charge of administration for the Eighth and Ninth Air Forces. The Ninth, a tactical air force, made up the U.S. contingent of Air Chief Marshal Leigh-Mallory's AEAF. Spaatz appointed Brig. Gen. Hugh J. Knerr as his Deputy for Administration, assigning directorates subordinate to him for personnel, supply, maintenance, and administration.[14] Maj. Gen. Frederick L. Anderson became Spaatz's deputy for operations over directorates for operations and intelligence. (See Chart 4, U.S. Strategic Air Forces in Europe, May 1944.) The official AAF history comments that this arrangement "integrated operations and logistics in one headquarters to a degree never before attained and represented a triumph for the concept that logistics was of equal importance with operations."[15]

By elevating logistics to the same command level as operations Spaatz increased the status and morale of his logistics organizations. He placed his administrative control of the Ninth Air Force at the same level as his operational control over the Fifteenth Air Force. By tying the Eighth and Ninth together administratively, Spaatz made it harder for the Ninth to separate itself completely from his headquarters. He also emphasized the separateness of the AAF from both the RAF and the U.S. ground forces. A few months later Spaatz wrote to Arnold, "The Maintenance and Supply functions of our Air Forces cannot be integrated into the British Maintenance and Supply system for obvious reasons. Therein we have a firm foundation upon which to build our effort to regain and retain complete control of all U.S. air units in all theaters." Not only did the new organization help to maintain independence from the British; it helped also to maintain institutional independence from the U.S. Army Service Forces (ASF). In the same letter he added, "We must always be alert that the A.S.F. does not extend its control of ground services to the Air Forces through lack of an organization of our own capable of rendering all manner of base services to air units in the combat zone."[16] In keeping with Spaatz's desire to avoid as much administrative detail as possible, the reorganization reduced the number of people reporting directly to him to three—the two deputies and his chief of staff.

290

Chart 4
U. S. Strategic Air Forces in Europe
May 1944

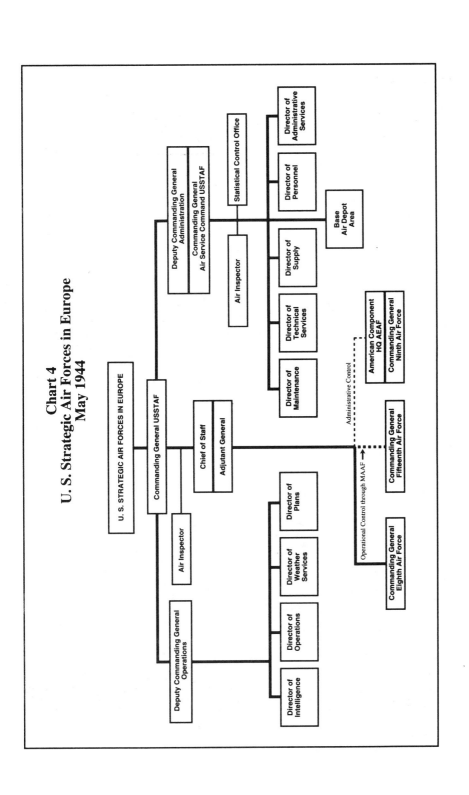

Lt. Gen. Carl A. Spaatz on an inspection tour, arriving at an Eighth Air Force base.

Lt. Gen. Carl A. Spaatz meeting his oldest daughter, "Tattie" (Katharine) *(left)*, a Red Cross worker, England, January 1944.

Lt. Gen. Carl A. Spaatz and his command plane, a B-17 named for his youngest daughter, "Boops" (Carla), Italy, 1944.

Spaatz overcame the worries of Portal and Marshall that his headquarters would graft a new and large layer of bureaucratic staff onto already awkward air command arrangements in England. His new headquarters simply moved in on Eighth Air Force Headquarters, abolished it, absorbed most of it, and sent the rump on to the headquarters of VIII Bomber Command, which, in turn, became Doolittle's new headquarters, redesignated Headquarters, Eighth Air Force.

Maj. Gen. Walter Bedell Smith, Eisenhower's chief of staff, participated in the discussions for the new organization. On January 1, he assured Eisenhower, who had returned to the United States for a short visit, that "the . . . planned Organization represents NO repeat NO increase in personnel and NO repeat NO increase in the number of Headquarters."[17] The same day, Spaatz and Bedell Smith agreed to locate Eisenhower's Supreme Headquarters with USSTAF at Bushy Park, code-named WIDEWINGS.[18] Spaatz believed that this arrangement overcame one of the basic flaws of the Mediterranean organization, which had allowed the different service commanders to locate their headquarters in areas widely separated from the theater commanders and each other.

The decision to co-locate USSTAF and SHAEF (Supreme Headquarters Allied Expeditionary Force) together gave Spaatz an advantage over the other air leaders. Their very distance from Eisenhower would assure Spaatz greater access to the ear of the Supreme Commander. Bedell Smith's and Spaatz's agreement ruined the plans of the Commander in Chief of the Allied Expeditionary Air Force, Air Chief Marshal Leigh-Mallory in his complex at Stanmore. He had intended to move Eisenhower into Bushey Heath, a group of adjacent buildings. Stanmore, the Headquarters of No. 11 Group, had perhaps the finest communications network in Britain. Much of the Battle of Britain had been directed from Stanmore, and its facilities had since expanded. Before Leigh-Mallory and Lt. Gen. Frederick Morgan, the principal planner for OVERLORD designated Chief of Staff Supreme Allied Command (COSSAC), could explain the situation to Smith, however, several battalions of U.S. engineers had descended on Bushy Park and erected Eisenhower's headquarters. When Bedell Smith learned that Morgan and Leigh-Mallory had meant to place SHAEF at Stanmore, he remarked, "My God, I've married the wrong woman."[19] From the beginning of the campaign, Spaatz gained a leg up in the fight over the air command arrangements that would plague the Allies until April 1944.

Spaatz further strengthened his command by supporting and pursuing far-sighted personnel management practices. He continued the enlightened racial policies of his predecessor, Ira Eaker. As the number of black AAF personnel in England began to increase above 3,000, Eaker instructed his staff to "stop arguing as to reasons why they [blacks] were sent here and do our best to cooperate with the War Department in making their employment here satisfactory to all concerned." Eaker believed that "90 percent of the trouble with Negro troops was the fault of the whites" and told his staff "to give serious thought to handling this important problem."[20] As a result, in August 1943, the Eighth Air Force reorganized all black AAF units into the Combat Support Wing, a name carefully chosen to give black soldiers a feeling of contributing to the war effort. This move gave black AAF units a single strong commander with a good organization and an efficient supervisory headquarters. The commanding officers of the Combat Support Wing were sensitive to racial problems and they recognized the circumstances unique to their black units. Spaatz and Eaker also made it clear that they would allow no discrimination and expected their troops to avoid derogatory remarks and altercations.[21]

Spaatz also enthusiastically supported the assignment of Women's Army Corps (WAC) personnel to USSTAF. So determinedly did he press for WACs that in February 1944 General Arnold succeeded in obtaining a USSTAF allocation of them separate from that of the European Theater of Operations. The AAF in Europe had a quota of 4,448 WACs as opposed to a quota of only 1,727 for the ETO. By June 6, 1944, the AAF had female personnel assigned throughout its Bomber, Fighter, and Troop Carrier Commands and its bombardment divisions, even down to individual combat wings.[22] Spaatz's own executive officer, Capt. Sally Bagby, ran his unique personal/military headquarters. Spaatz was the highest-ranking officer in the theater to have assigned a woman to such a position.

Maj. Gen. Frederick L. Anderson, Commanding General, VIII Bomber Command, December 1943.

Maj. Gen. Earle E. Partridge, Deputy Commanding General, Eighth Air Force, spring 1944.

Brig. Gen. Curtis E. LeMay, Commanding General, 3rd Bombardment Division, Eighth Air Force, 1943.

Initial Operations

On January 3, Spaatz was briefed on the V-1, a German jet-propelled pilot-less bomb, and the threat that it posed. The new weapon badly frightened British leaders, who immediately decided to concentrate a special effort on knocking out its launch sites and rendering it inoperable. This effort to eliminate the sites, code-named CROSSBOW, would divert, over Spaatz's continued objections, much of the AAF's strength from both strategic and preinvasion bombing. After this first experience with CROSSBOW Spaatz noted, somewhat acerbically, that it was "very apparent from all conversations so far" that "everyone" accepted the CROSSBOW diversion from the main air effort. Spaatz went on to observe that if the Germans considered CROSSBOW so important, why had fighter opposition to raids on the sites decreased from November to December?[23]

From the beginning of January to February 15, the weather and CROSSBOW proved almost as adversarial to the U.S. daylight bombing offensive as the Luftwaffe. In that period the Eighth's heavy bombers flew combat missions on twenty-one days. Only six of those bombing missions went forward under completely visual conditions, and only two of those six attacked strategic targets in Germany. Nine other missions struck V-1 launch sites in France.[24] In eleven of the thirteen missions over Germany the AAF resorted to bombing directed by an early, inaccurate system of radar which enabled the Eighth to conduct only area bombing. Area bombing tormented the Germans but did not provide results anywhere close to those obtained by visual means. The Eighth had only twelve B-17s

296

equipped with H2X radar equipment. They arrived in October 1943 with hand-built equipment and served as pathfinders (PFF), or lead planes, for bomber groups.[25] Spaatz and Doolittle worked them hard. Their crews became exhausted.

The American H2X derived from the British-developed H2S radar bombing system. H2X was critically important in increasing American bomb tonnage dropped on Europe because it enabled operations in overcast conditions. Its contribution to the weight of the U.S. bombing effort in 1944–1945 was second only to the success of the U.S. long-range fighter escorts in preserving the bombers themselves. That H2X stemmed from British, not American, efforts constituted another indictment of prewar U.S. military air thinking. America's failure to anticipate the need for long-range fighter escort and to develop as early as possible the ability to locate and bomb targets through clouds left U.S. strategic bombers operable at only a fraction of their strength and almost ruined the efforts of the AAF. The Americans owed a great debt to the RAF not only for the P-51 but for H2X as well.

Ever mindful of public perception, Arnold instructed Spaatz to abjure the term "blind bombing" for the H2X technique, because it gave "both the military and the public an erroneous impression."[26] Spaatz agreed to use such terms as "overcast bombing technique," "bombing through overcast," "bombing with navigational devices over clouds extending up to 20,000 feet."[27] He also pressed

Lt. Gen. Carl A. Spaatz and his executive officer, Capt. Sally Bagby, Women's Army Corps, spring 1944.

Arnold for more radar-equipped planes, explaining that the "results of the past two months' extensive use of Pathfinder (H2X) aircraft in the Eighth Air Force have shown the equipment offers enormous possibilities for further intensification of the bombing offensive against Germany." He drove the point home by adding, *"The most critical need of the Strategic Air Forces is for more Pathfinder aircraft. A few H2X airplanes now will profit our cause more than several hundred in six months"* [emphasis in original].[28]

The bombing of Germany by nonvisual means continued a policy begun under Eaker in the last quarter of 1943. Although nowhere nearly as accurate as precision bombing, radar bombing allowed more frequent operations, maintained the pressure on German cities, and forced the Luftwaffe to intercept under adverse weather conditions. Its adoption of this policy marked the AAF's acceptance of the reality that daylight precision bombing alone could not win the air war. The implications of this belated acknowledgment were little remarked on at the time. Yet, at this point the AAF, without ever publicly or privately admitting it, abandoned its unquestioning faith in prewar bombing doctrines.

Once he assumed command, Spaatz wanted to go after the Luftwaffe immediately. The POINTBLANK directive under which he operated left the means for doing so up to him. Spaatz's approach differed significantly from that of his predecessor. Because of his lack of long-range escort fighters, Eaker had had no choice but to rely on a bomber-based strategy. The Eighth under Eaker's command had attempted to ruin the Luftwaffe fighter force by bombing the German air industry. The Americans had hoped that attrition inflicted on all battle fronts and by short-range U.S. and RAF fighters out of Britain would destroy the damaged German air industry's ability to replace losses. Eaker may have focused too heavily on his bombers and their task. His fighters appear to have concentrated on their escort duties to the detriment of their possible employment in counterair and ground sweeps. This philosophy was made clear during an Eighth Air Force Commanders' meeting in September 1943, where the prevailing sentiment was that "fighters must escort the bombers whether they bring down any German fighters or not."[29] In any case, Eaker had few fighters to waste.

Official doctrine supported Eaker's tactics. AAF Field Manual 1-15, "Tactics and Techniques of Air Fighting," of April 10, 1942, and AAF Field Manual 1-5, of January 18, 1943, emphasized pursuit's air defense and escort roles, with a bow to ground support. The replacement for the latter manual, War Department Field Manual 100-20, sent a mixed message. In addressing the role of fighters belonging to a strategic air force, such as the Eighth, it stated, "Accompanying fighter aviation, where its radius of action permits, is also used to increase [the bomber's] security. Fighter aviation also furnishes air base defense for bombardment bases."[30] That passage offered little encouragement for aggressive action.

The direction given a tactical air force such as the Twelfth, differed radically from the advice given the strategic air forces. Whereas the mission of the strate-

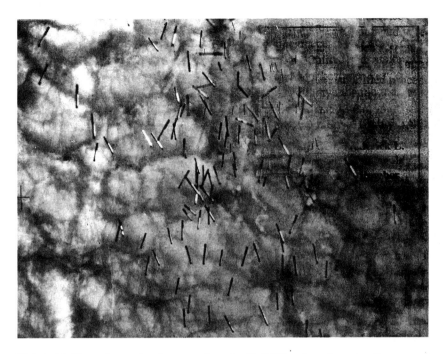

Eighth Air Force heavy bombers, equipped with H2X radar, dropping four-pound incendiary bombs "blind" in overcast skies over Kiel, Germany, December 13, 1943.

gic air force was "the defeat of the enemy nation,"[31] the first priority of a tactical air force was the gaining of air superiority "by attacks against aircraft in the air and on the ground, and against those enemy installations which he requires for the application of air power."[32] Fighters formed the air-to-air component of the counterair team, and light and medium bombardment formed the air-to-ground segment. The manual's tactical section reflected Spaatz's experience with the AAF in North Africa, as the strategic section reflected Eaker's experience with the Eighth Air Force in Europe.

Unlike Eaker, Spaatz and Doolittle decided on or before their arrival in Britain to intensify the campaign against the Luftwaffe by using their fighters in an offensive air-to-air role, instead of purely as escorts. Spaatz also intended to use the Ninth (Tactical) Air Force to assist in the counterair effort, despite the fact that Leigh-Mallory intended to use it for preinvasion operations. Shortly after Spaatz's visit to Washington two months earlier, Arnold had expressed to Marshall similarly aggressive sentiments which were probably reflective of his own combative temperament but could have come, in part, from Spaatz. Spaatz might have discussed his experiences in the Mediterranean campaign with Arnold. In any case, Arnold recommended in a memo to Marshall that the Allied air forces "seek out and destroy the German Air Force in the air and on the

299

ground without delay. The defensive concept of our fighter commands and air defense units must be changed to the offensive." He called for more imaginative use of fighters as ground strafers, as fighter bombers, and as air-to-ground rocket launchers to assist the OVERLORD assault.[33] Spaatz could be sure of Arnold's support for a more active fighter force. Both men must have realized and counted on the fact that a changeover to offensive fighter tactics would impose a far higher rate of attrition on both the Luftwaffe and the AAF. Arnold would have to support Spaatz with many replacement fighter pilots and aircraft.

On several occasions, especially in his first meetings with Eighth Air Force staff personnel, Spaatz reiterated his desire to close with the Luftwaffe. On January 9, he visited the Eighth's War Room. There he met an old acquaintance, Col. Richard D'O. Hughes, Assistant Chief of Intelligence, and the principal link between the Eighth Air Force and the Enemy Objectives Unit (EOU) of the Economic Warfare Division of the U.S. Embassy, London. The EOU served as the de facto target planning staff of the Eighth. Hughes, an expatriate British subject with numerous British decorations and long-time service in the British Indian Army, served his new country ably not only by applying his considerable intellect to the complicated issues of targeting but also by using the British "old boy" network to gain entrée to British intelligence and targeting agencies.[34]

Spaatz told Hughes of his main objective to knock out the Luftwaffe by hitting it in the air, on its airfields, and at its fighter factories:

> It is my belief that we do not get sufficient attrition by hitting fighter factories, therefore we must place emphasis on airdromes and knocking them down in the air. Our mission is destroying the German Air Force, and that we will hit primary objectives when weather permits, but at other times will choose targets as stated above, which will bring fighters into the air.[35]

Spaatz had voiced this concept of targeting vital economic objectives to force Luftwaffe attrition almost two years earlier,[36] and it remained one of his guiding principles throughout the war.

On subsequent days Spaatz repeated to Hughes and to his operational commanders, Anderson and Doolittle, that he considered his chief mission the destruction of the Luftwaffe and that he would not even wait for "proper weather [in which] to bomb the priority targets."[37] Spaatz's official "Operational Directive" instructed Doolittle to hit the airframe factories and the German fighters "in the air and on the ground."[38] On January 21, in the first of a weekly series of "Eyes Only" reports to Arnold, Spaatz optimistically wrote that he needed only a few days of visual bombing to wreck the remaining fighter and ball-bearing factories. Then, "all other attacks will be made on the basis of destroying enemy air force in air and on ground. Such attacks will be made so far as possible under conditions most favorable to ourselves and normally will be against objectives which force German fighters into combat action within range of our fighters."[39]

By late January, Spaatz had come to the realization that "we must continue to attrit the German Air Force on the ground whenever we can operate." In a letter to Arnold, Spaatz stated his policy:

> I feel you would become very impatient with me if this very large striking force spent most of its time on the ground or in training flights, waiting for the few days when visual bombing permits hitting our primary targets—the aircraft factories. I also feel sure that to confine our operations to that alone would not deplete the German Air Force at the necessary rate.[40]

Neither Arnold nor Eaker, who had held similar views while leading the Eighth, disagreed with these sentiments. What made Spaatz's formulation unique was his insistence on attacking the Luftwaffe on the ground as well as in the air. Thanks to Spaatz's experience in Tunisia and particularly in Sicily, he had first-hand knowledge of the devastating effect of a prolonged counterair campaign on the Axis air force bases in the Mediterranean. Hundreds of German planes, many repairable, had littered Sicilian airfields and fallen into Allied hands. Spaatz reiterated this point to Arnold: "I feel personally that this matter of hitting airdromes from U.K. requires a shot in the arm, both as to methods of attack and frequency of attack. I believe that in our penetration into Germany that advantage must be taken of the use of intruder aircraft."[41] Spaatz expressed similar views to the Assistant Secretary of War for Air, Robert A. Lovett:

> I believe that some of the methods applied in the Mediterranean are applicable here. . . . My tendency will be to place a little bit more emphasis upon swatting the enemy on his airdromes whenever possible and [on forcing] him to fight under conditions most advantageous to us.[42]

Spaatz also communicated this insistence on attacking the Luftwaffe before it could become airborne to Eisenhower and Tedder. On January 22, Spaatz discussed his plans for USSTAF with Eisenhower. They were, first, to attack fighter and ball-bearing plants whenever conditions permitted visual bombings and, second, to attack "targets in Germany under conditions most favorable to obtain maximum destruction of German fighters in the air and on the ground."[43] Later in the day Spaatz discussed his plans with Tedder. They "agreed that attacks so far on airdromes had been unfruitful here, possibly due to wrong method of attack."[44]

By choosing to attack the Luftwaffe rather than to defend against it, Spaatz had found the way to break the German fighter force. After December 1943, the number of U.S. fighter aircraft on hand in fully operational tactical units dramatically increased. The AAF had the means as well as the method of taking the battle to the Luftwaffe.[45] By April 1944, American fighter sweeps and intruder missions, which Spaatz and Doolittle had launched once they had sufficient long-range fighter aircraft, were disrupting all types of German air activity—trainee pilots could not even be assured of practicing in the air unmolested. The sweeps also caught many German night fighters and bombers on their fields.

Fortune and the impatience of Arnold also favored Spaatz and Doolittle with the right man to command their fighters. In August 1943, Arnold replaced the Commanding General of the VIII Fighter Command, Maj. Gen. Frank O'D. Hunter, with Maj. Gen. William E. Kepner. Hunter, in Arnold's opinion, had failed to fully support and understand the need for a long-range fighter program.[46] Kepner, however, not only firmly believed in the feasibility of long-range fighter escort but had helped to push through the AAF's range extension program in the spring and summer of 1943.[47] Kepner subsequently told an interviewer that until Spaatz and Doolittle arrived he had never had enough fighters to do other than "stick close to the bombers." Furthermore, even though he had wished to get the fighters out to scour the skies for German fighters, his superiors thought "that the time hadn't come to do that." As soon as Spaatz and Doolittle arrived, they had "directed that I take such steps as I felt necessary to lick the German Air Force. If it meant getting out and scouring the skies, even by thinning down the escort, that would be okay with them. . . . It certainly wouldn't have been possible without their help."[48]

As it had so often before, British signal intelligence greatly helped Spaatz accomplish his goals. By the time he arrived in London, ULTRA intelligence intercepts indicated that fuel shortages and deficiencies in pilot training had already begun to impair the Luftwaffe's readiness. The Germans had reduced their number of reconnaissance flights and had called in test pilots and ferry

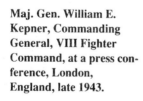

Maj. Gen. William E. Kepner, Commanding General, VIII Fighter Command, at a press conference, London, England, late 1943.

pilots to operate fighters against U.S. daylight raids. In January ULTRA revealed Hitler's orders to cut back Luftwaffe meteorological operations and shorten the recuperation period for wounded pilots. By February 6, ULTRA supplied further evidence of a Luftwaffe comb-out of its noncombatants to provide pilots and to meet the needs of the land forces.[49] The knowledge that the enemy's resources were becoming ever tauter must have added to Spaatz's determination to maintain and increase the pressure on the foe.

Spaatz knew that if enough Luftwaffe fighter planes went down, Germany could neither defend its industry nor contest the air over the beachhead. The requirements of both POINTBLANK and OVERLORD for air superiority necessitated knocking out the Luftwaffe by no later than May 1. Spaatz had 120 days in which to ruin the offensive power of a large, modern air force.

An examination of the Eighth's first mission of the year, on January 11, proved typical of many of the missions of the next few weeks. Weather forecasters predicted clear weather over key aircraft plants at Oschersleben and Halberstadt and in the Brunswick area. The nature and location of these targets, some less than a hundred miles from Berlin, assured a heavy and active defense effort by the Luftwaffe. The Eighth's eleven groups of P-47s, joined by two groups of P-38s, provided cover from the Dutch coast to within fifty to seventy miles of the targets. A lone P-51 group would escort the first of the bomber formations all the way to and from the target.[50]

As the heavy bombers left their bases in Britain, the weather deteriorated, making takeoff and assembly difficult. Nevertheless, 663 B-24s and B-17s left their fields. Weather continued to worsen, causing the 2d (B-24s) and 3d (B-17s and B-24s) Bombardment Divisions to abort their flights short of their primary targets. Instead, they bombed targets of opportunity in western Germany. The remaining 291 bombers hit their targets but suffered severely from fierce Luftwaffe reaction. Using improved tactics and fuel tanks developed in the summer and fall of 1943, the German fighters waited until most of the escorts had left and then attacked the bombers. Forty-two American heavy bombers failed to return—13 percent of the force engaged. All 44 American P-51s fought well, but weakened their effort by spreading themselves over too large an area in an attempt to defend the widely dispersed U.S. bomber formations. Even so, the P-51s were credited with more German aircraft kills than 177 P-47s which had escorted the bombers part of the way to the target area. Obviously, the Germans had been able to avoid the P-47s but not the P-51s,[51] but the P-51s also reached the initial rendezvous point too soon, and thus had insufficient fuel to cover the bombers on their return from the targets to the P-47s and P-38s providing withdrawal escort. Meanwhile, the weather over England degraded further, and the returning 1st Bombardment Division planes had to land on unfamiliar runways belonging to the 2d and 3d Divisions. Subsequent air reconnaissance revealed that the plant at Oschersleben had suffered severe damage, and one of the Brunswick targets, Waggam, site of an aircraft production complex, had received

Early model P-47s over England, summer 1943.

direct hits on almost every one of its assembly plants.[52]

Spaatz and Maj. Gen. Barney Giles, Chief of Staff of the AAF, who had come to England to witness the birth of USSTAF, spent January 11 in the VIII Fighter Command operations room observing the mission. They shortly discovered for themselves another of the problems that had hampered Eaker—the need of AAF Headquarters in Washington, D.C., for favorable reports on the bombing effort. The Eighth Air Force's report on the mission of January 11 was not released in Washington until the morning of January 13. In the meantime, U.S. newspapers, working on copy from London that was based on intercepts of German propaganda broadcasts, headlined stories in the evening editions of January 11 of "123 United States aircraft lost over Germany." The next day the press picked up German claims of 135 U.S. planes lost. The Eighth's statement, scheduled for 9 A.M. that day, did not appear, making it seem that the AAF had decided to conceal a disaster.

When the Eighth's statement finally came out on January 13, the public, according to AAF headquarters, showed greater interest in the dispute over total losses than in the damage claims of the AAF. Brig. Gen. Laurence Kuter, acting as Arnold's representative, told Spaatz in a telephone conference, "We adjure that future initial releases will come as early as possible to avoid undisputed prominence in the U.S. press to items released by German radio." Kuter also "adjured" that future releases should contain graphic references to damage done rather than tales highlighting German fighter defenses. If Spaatz objected to

Filling the pipeline: Replacement B-17s for the Eighth Air Force, England, March 1944.

"needling" from Washington and wanted to avoid future "embarrassment," his reports had better get to Washington as quickly as possible.[53]

The January 11 mission evoked an outburst from Arnold, who, angered by its negative coverage in the press, complained about the small number of bombers actually attacking significant targets. He felt that the mission had jeopardized the entire principle of daylight bombing: "I cannot understand why with the great number of airplanes available in the Eighth Air Force, we continually have to send a boy to do a man's job. In my opinion, this is an uneconomical waste of lives and equipment." Although he realized that because of the recall, only forty-seven planes had bombed Brunswick, what deeply worried him was "the concept of small forces split up all over Europe instead of some good smashing blows." Instead of pecking away at the German aircraft industry, he asked, couldn't the AAF send out a really large number of aircraft and simply level a target? Arnold asked Spaatz for "some new thoughts and new lines of approach."[54]

For eighteen days after the January 11 mission, although high clouds or bad conditions over the bases prevented the bombing of Germany itself, USSTAF launched three missions against CROSSBOW installations. On January 21, Spaatz observed to Arnold, "Basically the principal enemy we face is weather."[55] Two days later Spaatz wrote to Lovett:

> The weather here is the most discouraging of all factors and I am sure that it
> will result in the loss of remaining hairs on my head, or at least will turn what is

left of the red into white. Nothing is more exasperating than trying to run an Air Force continuously hampered or grounded by weather."[56]

On January 29 and 30, conditions over England improved enough to allow the dispatch of large missions against Frankfurt-am-Main (over 800 heavy bombers) and Brunswick. Unfortunately, both missions had to bomb through heavy overcast with the assistance of H2X.

By the end of January 1944, little time remained before POINTBLANK's subordination to OVERLORD. Spaatz had at most two months to devote the full force of USSTAF to strategic objectives because by April 1, sixty days prior to the scheduled launching of the cross-channel operation, the needs of the invasion would take primacy. On January 26, Spaatz wrote Eaker, "I have reviewed the problem of strategic bombing of our enemies, and the thing that has struck me most is the critical time factor. We have very little time in which to finish our job."

On February 3, the Eighth sent more than 700 bombers in a pathfinder-led attack on Wilhelmshaven. Bad weather caused 100 of those bombers to abort and another 61 to bomb targets of opportunity in Emden. The next day, another pathfinder/bombing-through-clouds raid directed at Frankfurt-am-Main suffered from weather and navigational problems, and only 233 of 433 bombers sent out bombed their primary target. The remainder again bombed various targets of opportunity. This pattern, but on a lighter scale, continued until February 19.[57]

On February 17, Portal issued a new bombing directive to both Spaatz and Harris confirming target priorities agreed on in mid-January. The primary objective remained the destruction of the Luftwaffe. Single- and twin-engine fighter airframe and airframe component production and Axis ball-bearing industry targets were again accorded first priority; second priority went to installations supporting German fighter air forces and other objectives such as CROSSBOW, "Berlin and other industrial areas," and targets in southeastern Europe, such as cities and transportation targets. The plan further instructed Spaatz and Harris that preparation and readiness for the direct support of OVERLORD "should be maintained without detriment to the combined bomber offensive."[58]

Two features of this directive are noteworthy: (1) as of mid-February, POINTBLANK still had priority over OVERLORD in strategic operations, and (2) Berlin was singled out for special attention. This mention of Berlin, in part, was an *ex post facto* authorization of Harris' Battle of Berlin begun in November 1943. But the directive also specifically authorized area attacks by U.S. forces on the German capital and any other German city within range:

> Attacks should be delivered upon Berlin or other important industrial areas by both Bomber Command R.A.F. and U.S.S.A.F.E. (latter using blind bombing technique as necessary) whenever weather or tactical conditions are suitable for such operations and unsuitable for operations against the primary objective.

Leigh-Mallory and the AEAF

During January, Spaatz had to deal with the frustrations created by the confused Allied command structure as well as those caused by nature. Eisenhower, as the Supreme Commander, Allied Expeditionary Force (SCAEF), commanded all military forces directly assigned to the cross-channel invasion. Tedder was Deputy Supreme Commander. Under them came Admiral Berthram H. Ramsey, Naval Commander, Allied Expeditionary Force; Air Chief Marshal Trafford Leigh-Mallory, Commander in Chief, Allied Expeditionary Air Force; and General Bernard L. Montgomery, Commander, 21 Army Group. Montgomery's army group, composed of the British 2d Army under Lt. Gen. Miles Dempsey and the U.S. First Army under Lt. Gen. Omar N. Bradley, would conduct the ground assault. After Montgomery had established and enlarged the beachhead, the Allies would create additional Commonwealth and American armies, whereupon Bradley would form an all-American army group (the 12th). Bradley's first additional army would be the U.S. Third Army under the redoubtable Lt. Gen. George S. Patton.

Each of the service components of the Allied Expeditionary Force had a clearly defined mission. The naval forces would convoy amphibious assault troops to Normandy, prevent German naval interference (minimal at best), keep the seaborne supply lines to France open, and provide naval gunfire support to the troops. The 21 Army Group would force its way ashore, form and expand a beachhead, and, after a few weeks, break out of the beachhead and begin an offensive across France and as far as necessary into Germany to defeat the Third Reich. The AEAF would maintain air supremacy over the invasion convoys, the beachhead, and subsequent operations of the ground forces. It would further interfere with and delay as far as possible the movement of German reinforcements toward the beachhead, would transport and supply the airborne assault forces, and would provide necessary air support for the ground forces. (See Chart 5, Chain of Command, Allied Expeditionary Force, February 13, 1944.)

To accomplish his mission Leigh-Mallory had two Allied air forces assigned to his operational control, the British 2d Tactical Air Force under Air Marshal Arthur Coningham and the U.S. Ninth Air Force commanded by Maj. Gen. Lewis Brereton. Coningham's force consisted of three groups: the newly formed No. 83 and No. 84 Groups made up of fighters and fighter-bombers taken from Fighter Command, reconnaissance aircraft acquired from the dissolution of Army Co-operation Command, and No. 2 Group of light bombers and Mosquito Intruder aircraft transferred from Bomber Command. These transfers consumed two-thirds of Fighter Command, which received the new designation, Air Defence of Great Britain (ADGB). Leigh-Mallory also retained his responsibilities for the home defenses, and the new chief of ADGB, Air Marshal Roderic M. Hill, reported directly to him.[59]

Brereton's air force consisted of three components: IX Fighter Command

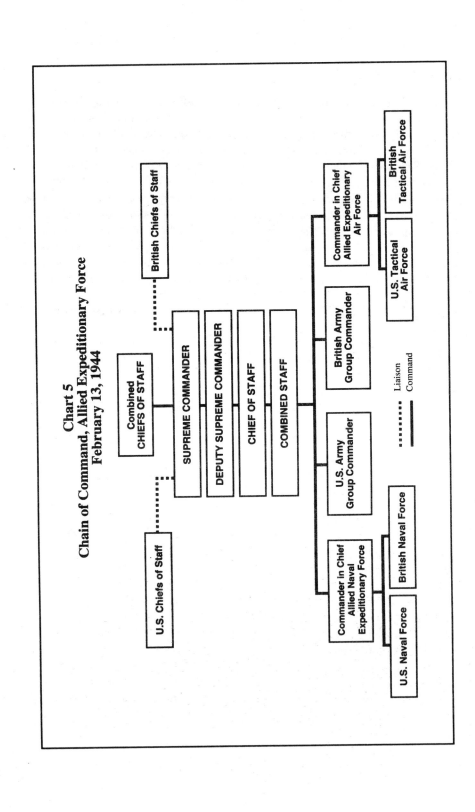

Chart 5
Chain of Command, Allied Expeditionary Force
February 13, 1944

(Maj. Gen. Elwood P. Quesada commanding), IX Bomber Command (Maj. Gen. Samuel E. Anderson commanding), and IX Troop Carrier Command (Maj. Gen. Paul L. Williams commanding), plus assorted service and antiaircraft troops. The IX Fighter Command had two subordinate units: IX Air Support Command would work with U.S. First Army, while XIX Air Support Command would assist U.S. Third Army. The medium and light bombers of IX Bomber Command could aid either support group or perform other tasks required by the theater. The IX Transport Command would supply theater air transport requirements and provide all airlift needed for U.S. airborne operations. (Under Allied agreements, IX Transport Command would provide a substantial portion of British combat airlift as well.) The chief function of the Ninth Air Force was to give air support to U.S. ground forces participating in the OVERLORD invasion. Thus Brereton was the American airman responsible to, not under the direct command of, Bradley, the overall U.S. ground force commander. Although the Ninth would have eight medium-bomber, three light-bomber, fourteen transport, and eighteen fighter groups by invasion day, in mid-January 1944 the Ninth had only five groups—four of medium bombers transferred from the Eighth Air Force and one of P-51 fighters.

What confused Allied command arrangements was not the organization of the expeditionary force, but the role Spaatz's USSTAF and the large RAF metropolitan commands (Fighter, Coastal, and Bomber) would play in supporting the invasion. It would take three months to arrive at a solution that was barely satisfactory. At the beginning of 1944, Leigh-Mallory assumed that these forces would to a great extent come under his control. This assumption met stiff resistance from the independent air leaders, in particular Spaatz and Air Officer Commanding, Bomber Command, Arthur Harris. In addition, the Ninth Air Force, more than twice the strength of the British 2d Tactical Air Force, served two masters: Leigh-Mallory had operational control, but Spaatz had administrative control. Because the two men had very different missions and irreconcilable conceptions about the correct employment of the Ninth, this dual control soon led to discord.

At first glance Leigh-Mallory seemed a sound choice as Commander in Chief, Allied Expeditionary Air Force. He had specialized in army cooperation (that part of the RAF assigned to supporting the ground forces) and in the offensive use of fighter aircraft. In World War I he had served as an army cooperation pilot and, by 1927, he had become Commandant, RAF School of Army Cooperation.[60] Shortly before World War II he transferred to Fighter Command and led No. 12 Group, which defended the Midlands in the Battle of Britain. At the very end of the battle he replaced Air Vice-Marshal Keith Park, a defensive fighter expert, as Commander, No. 11 Group, which defended London and southeastern Britain. At that point the RAF switched to the offensive, carrying the air campaign to the Germans with fighter sweeps over France.[61]

Eventually Leigh-Mallory became Air Officer Commanding, Fighter Command and, in November 1943, he officially gained his post as head of the

AEAF. His name had been mentioned in connection with such posts as early as the summer of 1942, when the British had begun to plan the rearrangement of their air commands for future large-scale ground operations in France. On March 11, 1943, Leigh-Mallory learned privately, from Portal, of his selection as Commander in Chief, Allied Air Force (Designate), by the British Chiefs of Staff and its approval in principle by the Combined Chiefs of Staff at Casablanca. By the end of June 1943, the CCS had authorized him to begin discussing air matters with OVERLORD's planners. On August 20, he was recognized as interim head of the AEAF, but he still had no directive on operations from the CCS.[62]

A closer look at Leigh-Mallory reveals weaknesses that hampered his ability to participate in coalition warfare. He has been described "as a man of driving egoism," with a habitually haughty manner[63] and "an assertive temperament."[64] Even his apologists admit that he "was so typically English, [and] sometimes tactless, almost pompous in appearance and naive in character without any finesse, that it certainly was difficult for the Americans to assess his ability, and they did little to try to understand him."[65] Once Leigh-Mallory absorbed an idea it became almost immutable.[66] This characteristic proved a grave defect, not because he adopted impractical ideas but because he defended his own beliefs with an uncompromising ferocity and thus exasperated his opponents.

During the Battle of Britain he engaged in a heated controversy with Air Vice-Marshal Keith Park, Commander, No. 11 Group, and Air Chief Marshal Hugh Dowding, Air Officer Commanding, Fighter Command, over the proper employment of fighters. Leigh-Mallory favored launching a large force, assembling it in the air, and using it all at once against the enemy. The problem was that by the time this "big wing" had assembled, the German raiders, as often as not, had delivered their bombs. Nonetheless, Leigh-Mallory stubbornly refused to change his tactics. In fact, Dowding had resolved to remove Leigh-Mallory, but before he could act, was removed by Churchill.[67] Dowding's abrupt replacement by Sholto Douglas and Park's replacement by Leigh-Mallory offended many of Fighter Command's senior officers. Likewise, Leigh-Mallory's obdurate adherence to his own strong ideas about air preparations for OVERLORD would intensify his conflict with other air leaders.

Leigh-Mallory had little gift for interpersonal relationships. Not only did his dispute with Dowding and Park worsen, but, after his elevation to the AEAF, he did not get along with his American deputies, Vandenberg and Brig. Gen. Frederic H. Smith,[68] or with his subordinate air force commanders Air Marshal "Mary" Coningham and Maj. Gen. Lewis H. Brereton.[69] The fates had dealt unkindly with Leigh-Mallory in supplying his associates. He and Tedder differed in personality, experience, and outlook. Without his knowledge, Leigh-Mallory's appointee as the head of the 2d Tactical Air Force, Air Marshal J. H. D'Albiac, was replaced by Tedder with Coningham. At the time, Leigh-Mallory assumed that Montgomery had consented to this change, but, in fact, Montgomery would have picked any air leader over Coningham. Then, the Commander of No. 83

Group, the fighter and fighter-bomber group assigned to cooperate with the British 2d Army, was replaced with Air Vice-Marshal Harry Broadhurst at Montgomery's insistence. Leigh-Mallory assumed that Coningham approved of this move, but in fact Coningham would have picked any air leader over Broadhurst. Neither Broadhurst nor Coningham had much use for Leigh-Mallory.[70]

Nor did Spaatz and other American airmen view him without suspicion.[71] They mistook his natural reserve for hostility and were put off by his somewhat ponderous and inarticulate speech.[72] In general, they returned his abruptness in kind. Leigh-Mallory's first American deputy, Brig. Gen. Haywood S. Hansell, was a highly regarded officer and a personal friend of Spaatz, but was promoted by Arnold and sent to the Pacific to begin B-29 operations. It might have been better for all concerned if he had stayed in London. Leigh-Mallory's second American deputy, Maj. Gen. William O. Butler, lacking the dynamic personality necessary to attract and keep high-quality American staff officers, did not help his chief. The American contingent at AEAF Headquarters needed high-quality officers to counterbalance domination by Leigh-Mallory's appointments from Fighter Command. The staffing of AEAF Headquarters called for 150 RAF officers and 80 AAF officers. Butler had purposely kept the American contingent small and did not even intend to use all of his authorized billets.[73] At one point Eisenhower even suggested that Butler be replaced with the more forceful Maj. Gen. Frederick L. Anderson.[74]

Air Vice-Marshal Harry Broadhurst, Air Officer Commanding, No. 38 Group, RAF, 1944.

Imperial War Museum

311

AEAF Headquarters remained an essentially British organization throughout its existence, which gave the AAF additional reason to view it with suspicion.[75] The Americans either did not understand or refused to acknowledge that Leigh-Mallory had such a large British staff because he also served as Air Officer Commanding the home defenses. If his British staff had merely been equal in number to the American staff assigned to Headquarters, AEAF, it would have been vastly overburdened.[76]

Spaatz's and Leigh-Mallory's disparate personalities added a note of personal acrimony to their differences, but their widely divergent views on the employment of air power and of the place of air power in the command structure of the Allied invasion force would have brought the two men into conflict in almost any case. The gulf between the two became apparent at their meeting of January 3 on plans for OVERLORD. Spaatz noted in his diary, "Am not sure whether L-M [Leigh-Mallory] has proper conception of air role. Apparently accepts possibility of not establishing Air supremacy until landing starts."[77] Spaatz believed that delaying the battle for air supremacy until the invasion would be too late not only for the invasion but for the bomber offensive as well. Spaatz believed that the Luftwaffe had to be crushed as soon as possible. If Allied air forces had to fight for supremacy over the beaches, they could provide no support for the ground forces and might not be able to provide air cover for the invasion fleet; paratroop drops could not be guaranteed without air supremacy.

In contrast, Leigh-Mallory's perspective came from his four years' experience in successfully defending against Luftwaffe attacks. Since 1941, the Germans had refused to engage in daylight combat with Fighter Command, and Fighter Command, with its short-range defensive fighters, could not force the Germans to fight if they chose not to. Leigh-Mallory welcomed the thought that the Germans would once more have to fly into territory he defended.

A few days later, Spaatz and OVERLORD's planners, including Leigh-Mallory and Lt. Gen. F. E. Morgan, the head of the Allied planning group that had drawn up the original plans for the invasion, clashed over command prerogatives. Morgan and Leigh-Mallory, who at this stage regarded himself as the commander in chief of all Allied air power necessary for the invasion, which included USSTAF,[78] insisted that three American P-38 long-range fighter groups move from the Mediterranean to Britain to help provide air cover. Spaatz objected on the dual grounds that only he, and not the Allied planning staff, had the authority to order such a move, and that he would not strip the Fifteenth Air Force of its escorts and, in the process, weaken it and POINTBLANK for an unnecessary fight over the beachhead. Spaatz pointed out to Butler that the matter concerned neither Morgan nor Leigh-Mallory and that the decision rested entirely with him.[79] Morgan appealed to Eisenhower in Washington.

Eisenhower had not yet arrived in London to take up his new command and, at Marshall's insistence, he had returned to the States for rest and consultation with the Army Staff. Eisenhower, who had his own ideas about the air situation, apparently backed Spaatz, for the three groups stayed permanently in the Mediterranean. Marshall, too, clarified the matter in a January 15 message to Spaatz and Morgan in which he confirmed that Spaatz alone had the authority to transfer USSTAF units.[80]

By the time Eisenhower arrived in London on January 16, air command arrangements in the British Isles had become a veritable Gordian knot, and the Supreme Commander seemed as confused as anyone. When he had originally learned of his selection in early December 1943, Eisenhower had requested that Tedder, whom he intended to install as his commander in chief for air, be transferred at the same time. On December 17, Eisenhower had written to Marshall,

> We would go into the operation with an operational organization set up largely according to the one we now have here [The Mediterranean]. Tedder would be my chief air man and with him I would have Spaatz who would have control of the Strategic Air Forces. Under Tedder will be one officer in charge of coordinating the tactical air forces.[81]

Two weeks later, after receiving a message from Bedell Smith, who had already become alarmed at the fuzziness of command arrangements, Eisenhower sent a message to Marshall: "I have received information from General Smith in London that is disturbing in its implication. He states that the British Chiefs of Staff have forwarded to the American Chiefs of Staff a paper which proposes that the Combined Chiefs of Staff shall dictate in detail the organization of tactical air forces for OVERLORD."[82]

Eisenhower objected strongly, asking Marshall to employ his full authority to oppose the scheme. He also pointed out that he and other veterans of the Mediterranean had learned several hard lessons in air power, which he did not want thrown away by "rigid directives." Eisenhower particularly objected to a proposal for two separate tactical air forces: "I simply cannot conceive of such an idea." He had come a long way from the general who had condoned the parceling out of air power in Tunisia. Eisenhower continued, "I hear that Tedder, who I have assumed to be my chief air man, is really intended to be an officer without portfolio, and that a man named Mallory is to be my chief air man."[83] Eisenhower did not object to Leigh-Mallory, whose qualifications as a fighter expert, he thought, would be most useful at critical stages of the campaign. What he resented was his being unable to use Tedder as he wanted because of high-level British interference.[84]

After meetings with Marshall and Arnold in Washington, Eisenhower warned Bedell Smith on January 5 that he anticipated trouble in securing the necessary approval for the integration of all forces essential to the success of the cross-channel invasion. Eisenhower noted, "I suspect that the use of these air forces for the necessary preparatory phase will be particularly resisted. To support our position it is essential that a complete plan for use of all available aircraft during this phase be ready as quickly as possible." Eisenhower therefore requested that Tedder proceed to London at once and consult with Spaatz and others on the plan.[85]

Eisenhower assumed that the British would object to having their metropolitan air forces, particularly Bomber and Coastal Commands, placed under the operational control of the Supreme Commander of the Allied Expeditionary Air Force. Nevertheless, he intended to ensure the employment of every resource, including all air power in Britain, to achieve the ultimate success of his mission. After their Stateside meeting, Eisenhower knew he had Arnold's backing. Arnold confirmed that both USSTAF and Bomber Command should be placed directly under the Supreme Commander for the "impending operation." Arnold made clear his support, saying, "It is my desire to do all that is possible here to further the simultaneous transfer of these two strategic bombing organizations from their present status to your command when you feel this transfer should take place."[86]

Spaatz and Eisenhower agreed that USSTAF must come under the operational control of the Supreme Commander. In December, when they both had learned of their new appointments, Spaatz fully expected to be under Eisenhower's command at least sixty days before the invasion. All subsequent disputes over preinvasion preparations concerned the place and use of strategic bombers under Eisenhower, not the basic principle that the invasion required the support of heavy bombers to succeed. In fact, during the initial phases of organizing USSTAF, Spaatz told the Chief of Staff of the AAF in Washington, Maj. Gen. Barney Giles, that Eisenhower had learned through Marshall that USSTAF would not be under him operationally. Spaatz, believed that it should be under Eisenhower both administratively and operationally. Giles agreed that Spaatz and Eisenhower would be left to settle command arrangements between themselves.[87]

In the afternoon of Eisenhower's first day of work as Supreme Commander, January 17, he and Spaatz met. Eisenhower admitted that he had received no clarification of the "present confused air situation" while in Washington.[88] Both agreed to soft-pedal any dramatic action and to proceed with the current cumbersome arrangements. Eisenhower directed his chief of staff immediately to publish an order giving Spaatz administrative responsibility for all U.S. air units in the theater. He also approved the plan to place his own headquarters at WIDEWINGS, Bushy Park, putting himself and Tedder near USSTAF Headquarters.[89]

On January 22, Spaatz and Tedder discussed air command assignments. They both believed that their old Mediterranean methods would serve admirably for Operation OVERLORD; Tedder should preside over a joint command post, and RAF Bomber Command, the Eighth Air Force, and the tactical air forces should all have representatives present at daily meetings held in USSTAF'S War Room. These flexible proposals so pleased Spaatz that he told Tedder that all he needed to know was what to hit and when.[90] On January 24, both confirmed this preliminary discussion and agreed that the "operation must be conducted the same as in the Mediterranean area, no matter what type of organization was directed by topside."[91]

While Spaatz and Eisenhower sought to pin down USSTAF'S place in the command structure, Arnold, Portal, Spaatz, and others simultaneously tried to define its immediate objectives. The Eighth Air Force had not received a new bombing directive from Portal since the implementation of POINTBLANK in June 1943. The advent of USSTAF, the imminence of the invasion, and the effectiveness of the Luftwaffe fighter defenses all indicated the necessity of a new directive. After initial proposals had passed back and forth across the Atlantic, Spaatz, Portal, Harris, Air Vice-Marshal Norman H. Bottomley (Deputy Chief of the Air Staff), Air Marshal Douglas Evill (Vice-Chief of the Air Staff), and Leigh-Mallory met on January 19 to hammer out a modified bombing directive. Targets and priorities remained unaltered. Coordination of effort between the Eighth and Fifteenth Air Forces, between the Eighth Air Force and Bomber Command, and between the strategic and tactical air forces in the Mediterranean could continue as presently constituted. They also chose to continue to have Portal coordinate between the tactical and strategic air forces in England. This later decision was made over Spaatz's objections. He advocated, instead, an overall air command under the Supreme Allied Commander as a necessary condition "for efficient operations in preparation for conduct of OVERLORD."[92] This suggestion met the united opposition of the British, who had rejected similar actions of the AAF at the Cairo Conference. The RAF would not countenance any arrangement that might subordinate it to the AAF. Eisenhower, with his usual political acumen, realized this fact and struck the suggestion from Spaatz's report to Arnold.[93] He counseled Spaatz to drop the idea, observing that "the political situation would not permit an over-all air commander at this time." Eisenhower told Spaatz that he did not require a designated overall commander; all that he required was that operational control of all air power, at the proper time for OVERLORD, "be assured by a single air commander." Spaatz admitted that USSTAF could fulfill its functions without an overall air commander, but he believed that its lack might jeopardize the ultimate success of the invasion.[94]

Thus, by the end of January, Spaatz had reaffirmed his personal and USSTAF's organizational commitment to placing control of the AAF's heavy bombers in the hands of the commander of the forces assaulting the Continent. This commitment did not mean that he had abdicated his position as the chief proponent in England of strategic daylight precision bombing; rather, it meant that, in practice, he would employ those techniques in the way that he thought could most effectively contribute to the invasion as a first priority. Spaatz did not abandon the theory that air power alone could bring about the defeat of Germany, but, as a good soldier, he meant to do all in his power to guarantee the fulfillment of OVERLORD's objectives. He noted with resignation in his diary:

Launching of OVERLORD will result in the calling off of bomber effort on Germany proper from one to two months prior to invasion. If time is as now contemplated, there will be no opportunity to carry out any Air operations of sufficient intensity to justify the theory that Germany can be knocked out by Air power. . . . Operations in connection with OVERLORD will be child's play compared to present operations and should result in very minor losses.[95]

The still unsettled air command arrangements prevailing in late January and in February complicated operations in no small measure. The Ninth Air Force was having difficulty dividing its resources to assist the Eighth's strategic mission, as it was obligated to, while it carried out its own tactical responsibilities. This difficulty would not be easily overcome. Also, the assignment of early- and late-model P-51s between the two air forces' fighter groups, originally decided by General Eaker in 1943, was a matter of growing concern. Eaker had sent most of them to the Ninth Air Force because of their abilities as fighter-bombers. Early model P-51s were limited by their relatively short range. (The P-51 had fought in Africa as the A-36 and had formed fighter-bomber groups assigned to the Northwest African Tactical Air Force.) When drop tanks, improved internal fuel tanks, and other modifications vastly increased the later model's tactical radius of operations and combat ceiling, it became the strategic escort fighter par excellence of World War II.

Spaatz thus believed that the late-model P-51s' newfound capabilities as escorts far outweighed their capabilities as ground-support fighters, and he felt justified in questioning the way the aircraft had been allocated between the Eighth and Ninth Air Forces. He had the authority, through enabling directives, to order the transfer of aircraft and personnel as he wished, but because the transfer of the P-51s to the Eighth Air Force would affect the operations of the Ninth, he was required to consult with Leigh-Mallory.

On January 20, Spaatz discussed his decision to move the P-51s first with General Brereton, the Ninth's commander, who objected to it, and then at a meeting with Brereton, Tedder, Leigh-Mallory, Doolittle, and Kepner, Commander, VIII Fighter Command. Spaatz overrode Brereton's protests, declaring that the P-51s were "absolutely essential throughout all operations to cover the bombers in deep penetration."[96] On January 24, the generals finally accepted Spaatz's compromise proposal; of the nine P-51 groups scheduled for the European Theater of Operations, the Eighth would get seven and the Ninth would retain two. Spaatz commented in his diary, "Leigh-Mallory's attitude in this was surprising to me, since after hearing arguments on both sides, he agreed to P-51's going to Eighth Air Force, based on over-all situations."[97]

Leigh-Mallory proved less amenable in matters involving the Ninth Air Force's participation in strategic bombing missions. Strategic missions consisted of much more than simply flying the heavy bombers and escorts to their objectives and returning them. Punishing the Luftwaffe as well as destroying targets required large-scale assistance from the Ninth. The Ninth's fighter-bombers and medium bombers would fly diversionary raids or strike Luftwaffe fighter fields in missions timed to coincide with the takeoff, assembly, and landing of Luftwaffe defensive fighter forces. In addition, the Ninth's formations would help to confuse German fighter controllers by cluttering up the early warning system with hundreds of additional planes.

Spaatz called these coordinated strikes "absolutely essential" to the maximum protection of heavy-bomber formations and the destruction of the Luftwaffe. Spaatz took note of the fact that in two major operations at the end of January no medium bombers had supported strategic strikes. They bombed CROSSBOW (V-1 launch sites in France) targets for which Leigh-Mallory, in his purely British capacity as head of Air Defense of Great Britain, had prime responsibility. This situation appeared to Spaatz to be symptomatic of the problems the AAF would confront "if and when" USSTAF came under Leigh-Mallory's control. "Leigh-Mallory's concern with what is in front of him," said Spaatz "may hamper POINTBLANK Operations."[98]

Spaatz, supported by his Deputy for Operations, Maj. Gen. Frederick L. Anderson, continued to press for clarification of control over the Ninth Air Force during strategic missions. On February 4, Anderson, Brig. Gen. Earle E. Partridge (Deputy Commander, Eighth Air Force), and Maj. Gen. William E. Kepner (Commander, VIII Fighter Command) representing the Strategic Air Forces, met with Leigh-Mallory, his British deputy (Air Vice-Marshal Arthur Saunders), Maj. Gen. W. Butler (his American deputy from the AEAF), Maj. Gen. L. H. Brereton (Commander, Ninth Air Force), Brig. Gen. Elwood R. Quesada (Commander, IX Fighter Command), and Brig. Gen. Samuel E. Anderson (Commander, IX Bomber Command-Medium). Leigh-Mallory opened the meeting by observing that the AEAF had done all that USSTAF required. Anderson expressed USSTAF's view that "the Mediums were not paying their way; that they should extend their operating range to the maximum which is, at present, 350 miles; that this should be done at least a couple of times beyond fighter escort, if necessary to ascertain the Hun reaction."

This statement reflected both Anderson's and Spaatz's determination to bloody the Luftwaffe, whatever their own losses. Leigh-Mallory responded that sending a portion of the medium bombers against the Eighth's targets while reserving the remainder for CROSSBOW attacks might satisfy strategic requirements. Anderson insisted that the Eighth's missions required maximum medium-bomber support and that experience had shown that CROSSBOW bombing produced unsatisfactory diversionary raids. Although Leigh-Mallory indicated that he would ask Portal for a final determination, he compromised by issuing the medium bombers additional targets to support the Eighth's efforts. Anderson, in turn, reaffirmed the Eighth Air Force's commitment to CROSSBOW when weather over Germany made strikes there impossible.[99]

Leigh-Mallory's appeal to Portal proved futile. Portal, after receiving Leigh-Mallory's brief and one from Spaatz, supported by Arnold, voted in the latter's

Maj. Gen. Frederick L. Anderson, Deputy for Operations, U.S. Strategic Air Forces in Europe, conferring with meteorologists on weather conditions over various targets.

favor. On February 15, he wrote to Spaatz, "I have had the various directives looked up and it seems quite clear that A.C.M. Leigh-Mallory is bound by his directive (COSSAC [43] 81 dated 16 November 1943) to lend maximum support to the strategic air offensive."[100] Portal added that Leigh-Mallory owed support to the Eighth not only in visual but in overcast conditions; furthermore, Leigh-Mallory's own directives to the Ninth Air Force and the British 2d Tactical Air Force gave priority to support of the Eighth's operations over all others. Finally, Portal required Leigh-Mallory to add to his target lists of airfields all of those designated by USSTAF.[101]

On February 19, the day before the great week-long USSTAF attack on Germany subsequently known as "Big Week", Spaatz, having already bested Leigh-Mallory, clipped Brereton's wings as well. Brereton, who had visions of a Ninth Air Force independent of both USSTAF and the AEAF,[102] and his chief of staff, Brig. Gen. V. H. Strahm, met with Spaatz, Anderson, and Doolittle to discuss the "use of 9th Air Force Fighters with the 8th Air Force." Brereton "agreed" that (1) IX Fighter Command would inform VIII Fighter Command daily of planes available; (2) VIII Fighter Command would issue *"Primary"* [emphasis in original] field orders giving specific jobs by time and group assigned to IX Fighter Command; and (3) whenever the effort might be delayed by transmitting orders through Ninth Air Force channels, VIII Fighter Command

318

could deal directly with Ninth Air Force wing commanders after or immediately before takeoff.[103]

In case Brereton retained any illusions of independence, Spaatz followed up this meeting with an official letter stating, "The Commanding General, USSTAF, will exercise control of all administrative and training matters pertaining to the Ninth Air Force and will assume direct responsibility to higher headquarters for the proper performance of those functions."[104] Because Spaatz's administrative control of the Ninth and Eighth Air Forces in England included the power of promotion, he held the whip hand over any U.S. officer who desired to advance his career.

Of course, Leigh-Mallory and Brereton saw Spaatz as a "noncooperator" with preinvasion tactical air plans. Both men had been charged with fielding air forces trained in close air support. They could not do so as long as Spaatz insisted that they devote maximum effort to supporting POINTBLANK. As usual, when training demands and operational necessity clashed, the immediate needs of the active forces at the front took precedence. Spaatz was destroying airplanes, killing German pilots, and bombing factories while the tactical airmen wanted to conduct training exercises.

"Big Week"

The final settlement of the Ninth's role came at a most opportune moment. On February 19, 1944, USSTAF's weather forecasters predicted an event eagerly awaited by the American heavy-bomber leaders in Europe: the breaking up of the cloud cover over central Europe for an extended period. Headquarters, USSTAF, ordered Operation ARGUMENT to begin the next day. This operation, planned since early November 1943, called for a series of combined attacks by the Eighth and Fifteenth Air Forces against the Combined Bomber Offensive's highest-priority objectives. During these attacks, RAF Bomber Command agreed to make night area bombing attacks on the same targets. (See Map 8, Greater German Air Industry Targets.)

Because the attacks called for a joint effort by both of its component air forces, Headquarters, USSTAF, departed from its normal supervisory and policy-making activities to take direct responsibility for mounting operations. Accordingly, as a courtesy to his old friend, Spaatz alerted Eaker* first rather than Twining, Fifteenth Air Force Commander, of the impending implementation of ARGUMENT, requesting that forces bomb the Regensburg and Augsburg aircraft assembly plants or the ball-bearing works at Stuttgart. Spaatz also

---

* Although he was Commander of the Mediterranean Allied Air Forces (Twelfth U.S. Air Force and British 1st Tactical Air Force), Eaker had only administrative, not operational, control over the Fifteenth. Spaatz, however, always treated Eaker as if the latter had operational control of the Fifteenth, in effect making a new line of command.

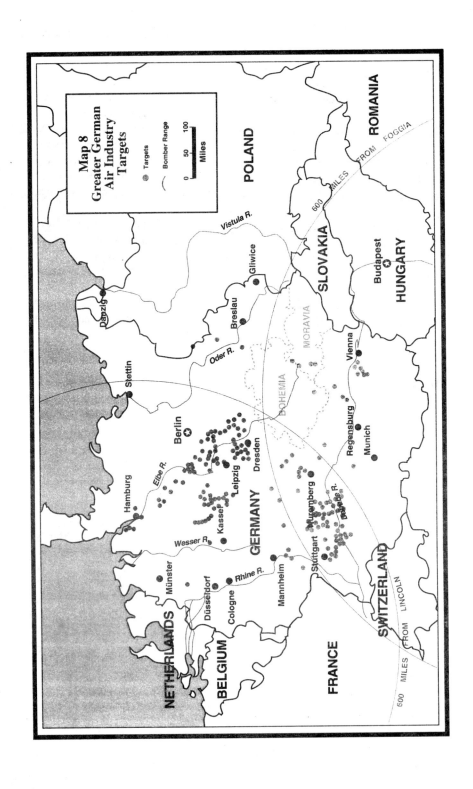

Map 8
Greater German
Air Industry
Targets

⊕ Targets

⌒ Bomber Range

0   50   100
Miles

POLAND

ROMANIA

SLOVAKIA

HUNGARY

Budapest ✪

600 MILES FROM FOGGIA

Vistula R.

Gliwice

Breslau

Oder R.

MORAVIA

Vienna

Danzig

Stettin

BOHEMIA

Regensburg

Munich

Berlin ✪

Elbe R.

Leipzig

Dresden

Nuremberg

Danube R.

Hamburg

Kassel

Wesser R.

Stuttgart

GERMANY

Münster

Düsseldorf

Cologne

Rhine R.

Mannheim

SWITZERLAND

NETHERLANDS

BELGIUM

FRANCE

600 MILES FROM LINCOLN

600

directed that "All forces of the 15th Air Force should use an area attack on Breslau as their secondary mission."[105] He thus demonstrated his willingness to countenance area bombing if it furthered a legitimate military objective. The simultaneous attack by the Fifteenth's twelve heavy-bomber groups and four fighter groups, or even a diversionary attack on Breslau, the alternative target, would prevent some of the German defenders from concentrating on the Eighth as it came from England and give it a better chance of successful bombing.

Eaker informed Spaatz that the Fifteenth could not fly its scheduled strategic mission because he had committed it to the tactical support of the Anzio beach-head, where a German counterattack had come dangerously close to driving the Allies into the sea. Eaker believed that if the Fifteenth did not support Anzio, the Allied theater commander, British General James Maitland Wilson, might declare the situation a ground emergency and exercise his right to take direct control of the Fifteenth from USSTAF for the duration of the critical situation. Eaker wished to avoid that declaration because it would rob him of all flexibility and establish a troublesome precedent. Eaker also objected because his weather fore-casters had predicted overcast skies covering the Fifteenth's targets. The Fif-teenth, which lacked H2X equipment, could not bomb them effectively.[106]

Spaatz disagreed. POINTBLANK, too, had reached a climactic stage. He and Anderson had previously agreed to accept extraordinary risks to ensure the com-pletion of ARGUMENT prior to March 1, even if it meant the loss of 200 bombers in a single mission.[107] Spaatz went to Portal with a draft telegram for Eaker that read, in part, "Because of critical status of POINTBLANK, it is absolutely neces-sary that we make our maximum effort under visual conditions. Eighth Air Force will attack targets as indicated. Therefore, I believe it essential that the maximum heavy effort possible be used in southern Germany for diversionary purposes."[108] Spaatz went on to request that at least some of the Fifteenth's planes fly against their proposed targets or Breslau as a secondary target. Portal, after consulting Churchill, who ruled that all available forces should support the Anzio battle, told Spaatz that he could not agree to the transmission of such a cable to Eaker. Spaatz agreed to cancel the message.[109]

The failure to obtain the use of the Fifteenth added to the tension at Spaatz's headquarters on the night of February 19–20. Even as the Lancaster heavy bombers of RAF Bomber Command mounted a heavy strike over Leipzig, one of the Eighth's principal targets for the next day, Spaatz's subordinates debated the wisdom of following up the RAF's effort with a Sunday punch. The meteorolo-gists of the Eighth and Ninth Air Forces had conducted their own auguries and arrived at a forecast less sanguine than USSTAF's. Doolittle and Brereton there-fore doubted the feasibility of a large-scale raid for the next day.[110] Kepner believed that expected conditions would produce icing on the wings of his fight-ers, cutting the efficiency of the P-38s in half and lowering the efficiency of his P-47s and P-51s.[111]

The P-38, on which great hopes rested, was beginning to prove itself unsuited for operations over Europe. Its engines reacted badly to the combination of extreme cold and high humidity encountered in winter operations. On February 17, VIII Fighter Command reported that 40 percent of its P-38 force was affected by engine trouble.[112] In all, more than half of all P-38 losses in the theater were attributable to engine malfunction.[113]

Anderson vehemently opposed the naysayers. As each call came in from the Eighth or Ninth, he encouraged Spaatz to continue the operation.[114] Anderson tenaciously scrambled to maintain the viability of the mission throughout the long night. Anderson's deputy, also present that night at Park House, described the scene:

> Anderson prepared to stay the night because he knew that he must be there, by the telephone, knowing that in all military operations there was the chance of something uncontrolled going on and the whole thing fizzling out and being a catastrophe, and he was determined to keep the mission on. He knew also that the public reaction to the possible loss of 200 bombers would be very strong, even though the mission was a success.[115]

To Anderson's deputy Spaatz seemed "on the fence" and less strongly committed to the launch.

That view misinterprets Spaatz's position or, at least, his style of command. Spaatz allowed his subordinates wide latitude and encouraged them to state their opinions. Until the decision had to be made in the early morning, he would naturally have listened carefully to both sides. Nor should silence on his part be construed as waffling. Never a garrulous man, in times of stress Spaatz kept a poker face and retreated into quiet. The decision rested squarely on his shoulders. Brig. Gen. C. P. Cabell, formerly Commander of the 45th Bomb Wing but at that time serving on Spaatz's staff and present at Park House, told Brig. Gen. Haywood S. Hansell,

> Finally, when the last moment for action had arrived, the decision was left in the lap of General Spaatz. The risks were so great and the conditions so unfavorable that none of the subordinate commanders was willing to take the responsibility for the launch. General Spaatz quietly and firmly issued the order to go.[116]

Sixteen combat wings of heavy bombers (over 1,000 bombers), all seventeen AAF fighter groups (835 fighters), and sixteen RAF fighter squadrons (to assist in short-range penetration and withdrawal escort) began their takeoff runs, assembled, turned to the east, and headed for twelve major assembly and component plants that constituted the heart of Hitler's fighter production. As part of the largest force dispatched to date by the Eighth, six unescorted bomber wings flew a northern route to bomb targets near Posen and Tutow. The rest of the bomber force, escorted by the entire fighter force, flew toward Leipzig and Brunswick in central Germany. They would show up on German radar screens in time to attract the bulk of the fighter reaction to themselves and away from the northern force.

322

In addition, 135 medium bombers from the Ninth Air Force, two-thirds of which aborted because of weather, assisted by attacking airfields in western Europe. In contrast to the loss of 41 bombers against the same targets on January 11, only 21 heavy bombers failed to return to base. The raid seriously damaged four plants manufacturing Ju 88 (night-fighter/bomber) aircraft in the Leipzig area and two plants manufacturing Bf 109 (day-fighter) aircraft. The AAF official history, basing its assertions on examination of postwar records, cited a delay of one month's production of Ju 88s and severe damage to about 32 percent of Bf 109 manufacturing capacity. But other official histories admitted that the raids, like most AAF raids, damaged the machine tools less severely than the buildings that surrounded them. Those tools, when cleared of rubble and dispersed to other parts of Germany, would continue to produce more aircraft.[117]

When the results reached Park House on the evening of February 20, Spaatz, according to one witness, was euphoric, "on the crest of the highest wave he had ever ridden."[118] That evening Spaatz gave all the credit to Anderson for having persevered in his fight to save the mission.[119]

For the next five days, until the weather once again closed in, the Eighth and the Fifteenth Air Forces fought their way to and from targets deep inside the Nazi homeland. The Luftwaffe reacted savagely, provoking heavy and prolonged combat with great attrition on both sides. The Fifteenth Air Force, which lacked P-51s, lost 89 bombers, compared with 158 lost by the Eighth, but actually suffered a higher percentage loss.[120] In all, USSTAF lost at least 266 heavy bombers, 2,600 air crew (killed, wounded, or in German hands), and 28 fighters.[121] Almost half of those losses occurred on the last two missions, when the Germans took advantage of mistakes that left the bombers unescorted or underescorted.[122] In February, the Eighth wrote off 299 bombers, one-fifth of its force,[123] whereas the Luftwaffe wrote off more than 33 percent of its single-engine fighters and lost almost 18 percent of its fighter pilots.[124]

According to the AAF official history, the damage inflicted by the week's missions caused a two-month delay in German fighter aircraft production.[125] At the end of February, Luftwaffe Field Marshal Erhard Milch, in charge of aircraft production, informed Albert Speer, German Minister for Armaments Production, that he expected the March production figures to equal only 30 to 40 percent of the February total.[126] As a result of this meeting, the two set up a "Fighter Staff" to push through a large increase in fighter production. The Fighter Staff estimated that, at the time of its establishment at the end of February, 70 percent of the original buildings of the German aircraft industry had been destroyed. Damage to machine tools was less severe.[127]

The delay in German fighter production was even more significant than the actual number of fighters never produced. By the time the aircraft industry recovered in late spring and early summer, the Luftwaffe's situation had totally changed. The Eighth Air Force's attacks on German synthetic oil targets, begun in May 1944, produced severe aviation gasoline shortages, which resulted in

Defenders of the Reich. In increasingly desperate efforts to stem Allied attacks on German industries and cities, the Luftwaffe relied on a collection of new and aging aircraft, the older of which were pressed into new roles. *Clockwise from above*: The veteran Ju 88 medium bomber, shown with the search antenna of Liechtenstein airborne radar, served as a night fighter to counter RAF incursions. A second antenna in the starboard wing homed on warning radar in the tails of British bombers. Radar also appeared in the night-fighting version of the Bf 110 *(opposite, top)*, some of which could fire on enemy aircraft overhead with a unique upward-aiming cannon. The Bf 109 *(opposite, middle)*, in production since 1937, had evolved by 1944 into a nearly 400-mph fighter armed with machine guns and a 30mm cannon. The lightweight, nimble, and heavily armed FW 190 *(opposite, below)*, introduced in 1941, outclassed the early Spitfire but was handily mastered by later Allied fighters such as the P-47 and P-51. The world's first mass-produced jet fighter, the Me 262 Swallow (*Schwalbe*) *(below)*, entered combat in June 1944. As an interceptor the Me 262 carried four 30mm cannon and flew at 540 mph. Adolf Hitler unwittingly reduced its effectiveness by decreeing that the new aircraft be used solely as a bomber.

the catastrophic curtailment of training programs and operations. By July 1944, hundreds of the newly assembled fighters were grounded from lack of fuel. Had they been delivered in April or May when fuel was available, they might have made POINTBLANK a more risky undertaking.

Big Week also affected replacement production by persuading the German leadership and aircraft industry to undertake a large-scale and immediate dispersal program. This program eventually rendered the aircraft industry relatively invulnerable to bombing, but it caused more production delays and increased indirect labor costs by 20 percent[128] while heightening demands on the German railway system. This situation further strained the economy and left production even more dependent on uninterrupted transportation.[129]

Although postwar research has shown that the missions between February 20 and 25 accomplished less than was originally estimated by the Allies, what made Big Week "big" was not the physical damage inflicted on the German fighter industry and front-line fighter strength, which was significant, but rather the psychological effect it had on the AAF. In one week, Doolittle dropped almost as much bomb tonnage as the Eighth had dropped in its entire first year. At same time, Bomber Command conducted five heavy raids over Combined Bomber Offensive targets losing 157 heavy bombers for a loss rate of 6.6 bombers per 100 sorties, which slightly exceeded the American rate of 6 bombers per 100 sorties.[130] In trial by combat, the AAF had shown that daylight precision bombing not only operated as claimed, but at no greater cost than the supposedly safer and less accurate night area bombing. What is more, USSTAF, thanks to its fighter escorts, claimed the destruction of over 600 enemy aircraft, while Bomber Command could claim only 13.[131]

In their own minds, Spaatz and other high-ranking American air officers had validated their belief in their chosen mode of combat. Spaatz fairly glowed in a letter he sent to Arnold summarizing the month: "The resultant destruction and damage caused to industrial plants of vital importance to the German war effort and to the very existence of the German Air Force can be considered a conspicuous success in the course of the European war."[132] Spaatz went on to compare the relative contributions of the month by both the AAF and the RAF. The Eighth flew 5,400 more sorties than Bomber Command and dropped some 5,000 more tons of bombs, all with a lower loss rate.[133] The AAF had come of age; the long buildup in Britain had produced results at last:

> During the past two years as our forces slowly built up and the RAF carried the great part and weight of attack some circles of both the Government and the general public have been inclined to think that our part in the battle was but a small one. I trust that this brief comparison of effort will enable you to erase any doubts that may exist in some minds as to the great importance of the part now being played by the United States Army Air Forces in Europe in the task which has been set us—the destruction of Germany's ability to wage war.[134]

Although the Luftwaffe fighter force actually increased its bomber kills in March and April, Big Week, *in the minds* of Spaatz and other U.S. airmen, was the beginning of the end for the German daylight fighter. Most of the American airmen in Europe probably agreed with USSTAF's Assistant Director of Intelligence, Col. Richard D'O. Hughes, who said three weeks later, "I consider the result of the week's attack to be the funeral of the German Fighter Force."[135] According to Hughes, USSTAF now realized that it could bomb any target in Germany at will—a realization that led USSTAF and Spaatz to begin the hunt for the one crucial target system to bomb, now that the first objective, the suppression of the Luftwaffe, seemed to have been accomplished.[136] In short order they agreed on the German synthetic oil industry as that critical target system.

The Transportation Plan and Air Command Arrangements

No spent .50-caliber brass shell casings littered the hallways of WIDEWINGS, Park House, Norfolk House, Stanmore, or the Air Ministry at Whitehall, nor did hospital wards receive a single casualty. Yet from late January to late March, 1944, Spaatz and Harris, supported at times by Winston Churchill, engaged in a heated dispute with Leigh-Mallory, his AEAF staff, and OVERLORD's planners over the contribution expected of the strategic air forces in supporting preparations for the invasion of France. Eisenhower and Tedder, as hardly disinterested parties, refereed this dispute with varying degrees of impartiality. Each of the contestants took up distinct positions, which, depending on the fortunes of his own command, his commitment to the invasion, and the imminence of the invasion date, he defended at length.

Unlike Harris, Spaatz never questioned the basic premise that at some point prior to the invasion his force should come under the direct control of the Supreme Commander, Allied Expeditionary Force. Naturally, given his personal and professional biases, he differed, at times sharply, with Leigh-Mallory and others over the timing, the direction, and the degree of effort demanded of his forces.

Spaatz insisted that any plan adopted must lead, at least, to air parity over the invasion area by the time the troops left their ports to hit the beaches.[137] He believed that his forces should begin close assistance to the invasion sixty days before launching. Support begun earlier would duplicate effort and perhaps neutralize the effects of his strategic bombing campaign against Germany by preventing any follow-up of the blows he intended to deliver. Spaatz also believed that USSTAF possessed sufficient forces to devote a large simultaneous effort to the invasion and to the strategic campaign. He would resist any invasion plan that he believed would require his forces to participate beyond the point of diminishing returns. Overconcentration of effort on preinvasion operations would threaten the painfully gained momentum of his strategic campaign and thereby deny him the chance to try to defeat Germany by air power alone.

Spaatz's determination to support the invasion and to do all in his power to achieve its success did not keep him, as an air strategist, from questioning its basic utility. In November 1943, according to Capt. Harry Butcher, Eisenhower's naval aide, Spaatz told President Roosevelt's adviser, Harry Hopkins, that, given three months of clear weather, he could defeat Germany and render the invasion unnecessary. Therefore, he favored, as a better investment, the strengthening of Allied forces in Italy to gain the Po River Valley and position the bombers even closer to Germany.[138]

After the war, Spaatz implied that Butcher had not gotten his argument "quite straight" and claimed that, instead of mounting the vast, expensive cross-channel operation, he favored "sweeping around" to and through the Balkan states.[139] This somewhat Churchillian strategy of attacking upward from southern Europe reflected Spaatz's doubts about the possibility of gaining and maintaining another successful lodgment in Europe in the face of determined opposition. The Salerno campaign had come close to failure against an enemy not nearly so well prepared or fortified as would probably be encountered in France.

In mid-February, Spaatz, in a private conversation with the U.S. Ambassador to England, John G. Winant, detailed his fear that the Germans would voluntarily shorten their extended defense line on the Eastern Front, freeing fifty to seventy-five divisions, "which would have a good chance of destroying any force we put on the continent."[140] At the same time, he expressed his mistrust of what he viewed as Leigh-Mallory's overconcentration on the invasion's tactical air power. Spaatz did not see the possibility of a successful assault if the ground troops had only the benefit of air power applied tactically for their immediate support. "Strategic bombing of sufficient intensity is necessary first," Spaatz believed: "The landing of ground troops should be the pushing over of a toppling wall."[141] He would, naturally, resent attempts to cut back the Combined Bomber Offensive before it had undermined the German war economy.

As late as April 10, Spaatz, in a conference with Vandenberg, who had arrived in London to assume the post of the senior American officer and Deputy Commander of Leigh-Mallory's Allied Expeditionary Air Force, questioned the whole basis for OVERLORD and suggested alternatives. He characterized the operation as "highly dangerous." Its outcome was "extremely uncertain," and its failure would "have repercussions which may well undo all of the efforts of the strategic bombing efforts to date." H2X enabled USSTAF to bomb through overcast, overcoming its greatest obstacle, weather, and, hence, provided one more reason not to launch OVERLORD. Spaatz continued:

> If I were directing overall strategic operations, I would go into Norway where we have a much greater chance of ground force success and where I believe Sweden would come in with us. Then, with air bases in Sweden, we would attack Germany from four sides (U.K., Italy, Russia and Sweden) simultaneously. Why undertake a highly dubious operation in a hurry when there is a surer way to do it as just outlined? It is better to win the War surely than to undertake an operation which has . . . great risks.[142]

This curious proposal of Spaatz's may have had, if successful, the geopolitical advantages of denying Swedish iron ore and ball bearings to the Germans and of closing the Baltic, while imposing upon the Germans the requirement to defend another large air sector. The proposal revealed not only a complete rejection, if not a basic misunderstanding, of the whole ground strategy behind OVERLORD, but also an abysmal ignorance of international relations. The Swedes probably would not have declared war on Germany because of the Allied liberation of Norway, nor would the Soviets have regarded such an operation as the long-promised Second Front. This implausible scheme, apparently never seriously advocated by Spaatz, illustrates that he hoped to conquer Germany from the air and to avoid a large and costly land campaign in northwestern Europe. Spaatz also feared that the supremacy the AAF had gained in daylight might fade abruptly if the Germans introduced jet-propelled fighters. Spaatz even doubted the fighting capacity of U.S. ground forces. His North African experience had "indicated the inability of American troops to cross areas heavily defended by land mines, and . . . the beaches of OVERLORD are certain to be more heavily mined than any area in Africa."[143]

Spaatz did not allow his doubts about the utility and feasibility of the cross-channel invasion to handicap him in the performance of his duties. His fears, though broad, were not often deep. It is a measure of his self-confidence and sense of duty that he did not allow his doubts either to unman him or to cause him to slacken his labors on behalf of the ultimate success of the invasion of France.

Harris held views even less acceptable to Leigh-Mallory: (1) Bomber Command's operational limitations made it tactically incapable of hitting any night targets save those in the broad-based area bombing it already pursued, and (2) any switch from the current operational program would undo everything achieved to date, allowing Germany the time to harden and disperse its industries and to use its production lines in an uninterrupted period just before the invasion. Thus, any subordination of Bomber Command to a detailed tactical plan might actually have a detrimental effect on OVERLORD.[144]

Two events, however, combined to undercut Harris's contentions. His winter bombing campaign over Germany encountered increasingly resourceful, accurate, and costly interception from the German night-fighter force, which, by the end of March 1944, had become tactically dominant. Bomber Command's losses mounted steeply and could no longer be sustained by its machines and air crews.[145] In the first three months of 1944 its losses from all causes were 796 aircraft, compared with 348 in the same period in 1943.[146] Then, in early March 1944, Portal ordered a series of experimental night precision bombing attacks on French targets, including railway marshaling yards. These attacks produced outstanding results, unequivocally demonstrating the abilities of Harris's units to pulverize the OVERLORD targets scheduled for them.[147] By the end of March Harris had lost much of his credibility and with it a decisive voice in the preinvasion air debate.

The target of Spaatz's and Harris's fulminations, Leigh-Mallory, indomitably and in his own phlegmatic fashion, pressed for the adoption of the preinvasion plans drawn up by the AEAF. He had originally assumed that, as commander of the air forces in direct support of the invasion, he would also assume the command of the strategic bomber forces when they passed to the control of the Supreme Commander. This assumption, which soon proved illusory, did not endear him to either Spaatz or Harris, nor did their opposition to Leigh-Mallory's claims endear them to him. The chief architect of the AEAF's plan, Professor Solly Zuckerman, a personal friend of both Tedder and Spaatz, had returned to London in January 1944 from the Mediterranean, where he had completed his studies of the bombing campaigns in Pantelleria and Sicily. There he reached his own judgments about the effectiveness of the campaigns and the ways to improve upon them. In London, Zuckerman read the preliminary plan, which he judged inadequate, and he agreed to work with Leigh-Mallory's staff to prepare a new one. By the end of January, he had produced a plan fully accepted by Leigh-Mallory.[148]

Zuckerman, like Spaatz, Leigh-Mallory, Tedder, Portal, and most other preinvasion planners, started from the assumption that air superiority over the beachhead was a sine qua non. Therefore, he recognized the necessity for the continuation of POINTBLANK to promote the attrition of the Luftwaffe's fighter force. Similarly, he accepted as a given the diversion of resources to CROSSBOW. The professor then divided the remainder of the preinvasion bombing plan into three target systems: airfields, coastal defenses, and German lines of communication. The bombing of the airfields 130 miles or less distant from the beachhead would begin approximately twenty-four days prior to the invasion; the bombing of coastal defenses would begin immediately before the assault. The campaign against communication lines would begin on March 1, ninety days before the invasion. The bombing of the German transportation system was the most controversial element of Zuckerman's plan. His studies had convinced him of the necessity of an intensive attack on the Belgian and northern French railway system, directed in particular at rail marshaling yards and associated maintenance facilities. This attritional attack on the railways would so lower their carrying capacity that the German response in units and material to the invasion would be fatally slowed. Zuckerman's transportation bombing required the participation of all Allied air forces because of the large number of targets to be destroyed and kept suppressed. It also provided for 45,000 tons of bombs, out of an entire preinvasion program of 108,000 tons, to be dropped on the communications system. In his estimates of the bomblift required to neutralize the system, Zuckerman called for the Eighth Air Force to supply 45 percent of the preinvasion effort. Bomber Command, with a bomblift capacity 60 percent greater than the Eighth's, would supply 35 percent of the preinvasion effort, and the Ninth Air Force would supply the remaining 20 percent. Zuckerman allotted only 20 percent of the Eighth's effort to POINTBLANK.[149]

A captured German photo of damage to the Fieseler aircraft plant, Kassel, Germany, after RAF and Eighth Air Force raids.

The AEAF plan's use of all available air power strongly appealed to both Eisenhower and Tedder, who found themselves in the position of having to yoke the AEAF, USSTAF, and Bomber Command into the invasion program. Eisenhower needed direct control over all available planes in Britain to guarantee their support for the invasion. He therefore sought a preinvasion air plan that could employ all available air forces. Tedder agreed. Unlike Leigh-Mallory, Harris, and Spaatz, each of whom was identified with a particular type of air warfare, Tedder had not risen to prominence through a fighter or bomber background. Rather, he had come to the fore as a leader of large air forces consisting of all types of aircraft that cooperated closely, both strategically and tactically, with the overall theater command. It was Tedder who had first called Zuckerman to the Mediterranean and then dispatched him to London to assist planning there. Tedder firmly believed in the professor's analysis of the lessons learned from the Mediterranean campaign and favored his plan.[150]

On January 24, Zuckerman and Leigh-Mallory presented a draft of the scheme at a preinvasion air planning conference. Everyone agreed on the necessity of bombing the airfields and coastal defenses. This lines-of-communication bombing proposal, or, as all concerned soon called it, the transportation plan, immediately raised USSTAF's dander. USSTAF Assistant Director of Intelligence, Col. Richard D'O. Hughes, told Leigh-Mallory that Spaatz had already said "that a large percentage of his available bomber effort was available to assist OVER-LORD." He went on to note that "if it were considered the right course of action,"

331

Spaatz was prepared to initiate attacks against rail targets in Germany immediately with a priority second only to POINTBLANK. Leigh-Mallory then said he would have the Air Ministry issue a directive instructing the strategic forces to bomb such targets in Germany and would add some French rail targets to USSTAF's list, at which point Hughes began to object: the Eighth did not have the resources to bomb more than the thirty-nine German rail targets assigned to it; CROSSBOW had priority over northwest France when weather permitted; and the French rail targets did not have political clearance. Leigh-Mallory discounted Hughes's assertions. His proposed directive would not place responsibility for bombing the targets on USSTAF. He would consider anything destroyed in the next month as a bonus before the plan went into effect (March 1). As for relief from CROSSBOW obligations and obtaining the political clearances to bomb France, he would arrange them.[151]

As Hughes realized, Spaatz did not object to attacking rail yards in Germany. Such targets might lure the Luftwaffe into coming up to fight and could serve as secondary targets of opportunity when weather conditions over the primary targets made bombing impossible after the start of a major raid. Such a program did not represent a major diversion of strategic forces from POINTBLANK. In contrast, marshaling yards in northwest France yielded none of the advantages of German targets. They interfered with USSTAF's secondary priority of CROSSBOW and, because of their position inland, did not constitute acceptable targets of opportunity for CROSSBOW diversions. Nor would the Luftwaffe be inclined to contest the air over French targets in strength. Finally, bombing French targets would have detrimental political effects for the Allies. When some bombs missed the yards and fell into populated areas, as they surely would, the Germans would gain free grist for their propaganda mills, while the Allies might earn the opprobrium of an occupied people whose goodwill could greatly benefit the invasion.

Meanwhile, Leigh-Mallory's use of the Ninth Air Force in aid of the strategic campaign and his oft-stated belief that the decisive battle for air supremacy would occur at the time of the invasion troubled Spaatz, who increasingly resisted placing his forces under the AEAF and a commander whose competence he doubted and whose advocacy of the transportation plan he could not support. In a message he wrote, but did not send to Arnold, Spaatz remarked, "Proposal now under consideration for recommendation to CCS to place Strategic Air Forces (AAF) under Eisenhower nominally, actively under Leigh-Mallory, in immediate future. This places CG, USSTAF in impossible position."[152] A week later he informed Eisenhower, "I have no confidence in Leigh-Mallory's ability to handle the job and . . . I view with alarm any setup which places the Strategic Air Forces under his control."[153] Spaatz and USSTAF would take every opportunity to speak out against the transportation plan, sincerely believing that it misapplied their forces. They could not advocate command and control over strategic bombers by Leigh-Mallory. The two issues of tactical target selection and overall air command and control had become intertwined.

On February 15, after telling Eisenhower how he felt about Leigh-Mallory, Spaatz attended an air planning meeting at Stanmore, Middlesex, a London suburb and site of Leigh-Mallory's headquarters. Leigh-Mallory, Tedder, Harris, F. L. Anderson, Butler, Hughes, and Zuckerman also participated in what became, at times, a heated discussion. Leigh-Mallory began the meeting by presenting a definitive version of Zuckerman's bombing plan, which assigned 41 percent of the total preinvasion bomb tonnage to the transportation plan and only 11 percent to POINTBLANK. The Eighth Air Force would provide 45 percent of the total preinvasion bomb tonnage on all target systems, with Bomber Command contributing a total of 35 percent.* Spaatz, whose staff had received copies of the plan three days before the meeting and had prepared rejoinders, immediately said that the AEAF's plan "did not show a full understanding of the POINTBLANK operation."[154] Spaatz disagreed with the plan's premise that "air supremacy cannot be assured until the joining of the decisive air battle which will mark the opening of the OVERLORD assault."[155] Air supremacy must be achieved before the assault, Spaatz said, adding that the AEAF had not consulted USSTAF in the preparation of a plan that called for a massive commitment of strategic forces, and that such a plan would not be approved until USSTAF had the opportunity to participate in its development.

Leigh-Mallory argued that the Luftwaffe would rise to prevent the destruction of the rail system. Spaatz did not agree. The German fighter force might not take the bait, he said, and if it did not, he had to retain the authority to attack any target necessary to make the Germans fight—otherwise he could not accomplish his primary task of destroying the German fighter force. In other words, Spaatz would not agree to a scheme that allowed Leigh-Mallory to set his targets. Leigh-Mallory then suggested that the Combined Chiefs of Staff and the Supreme Commander settle the issue.[156]

Spaatz reemphasized the different phases of the Combined Bomber Offensive: (1) the destruction of the German fighter force, (2) the exploitation of that destruction to reduce the German will and means to continue the war, and (3) the direct support of the invasion.[157] Then Spaatz asked when the strategic air forces would come under Leigh-Mallory's operational control. Leigh-Mallory shot back, "March 1." At that point, according to Zuckerman, Spaatz commented, "That's all I want to know; I've nothing further to say."[158] According to Colonel Hughes's minutes of the meeting, Spaatz told Leigh-Mallory that "he could not concur in a paper at cross purposes to his present directive."[159]

Spaatz and Leigh-Mallory also wrangled over when the Luftwaffe would be destroyed. Leigh-Mallory again suggested that higher authorities settle the mat-

---

* Forty-eight percent of the preinvasion tonnage apparently was assigned to airfields and coastal defenses. Likewise, the AEAF would apparently provide 20 percent of the total effort.

ter. Spaatz said that "until a new directive was issued to him, he felt compelled to make recommendations as to the proper employment of the forces under his command to higher authority."[160]

Leigh-Mallory and Harris engaged in an equally unproductive dialogue concerning Bomber Command's role. Harris reiterated his prediction that the transportation plan would not succeed and that the air forces would be blamed for its failure. Finally, Spaatz entered the fray once again to reject the tonnage and effort figures in the plan. At this point, Tedder proposed a joint planning committee, as Spaatz had suggested earlier, with representation from USSTAF, Bomber Command, and the AEAF "to draw up a plan to suit the capabilities of all concerned."[161] All present accepted Tedder's recommendation.

After the meeting, Spaatz and Tedder had more talks in which they agreed not to request a change in the current Combined Bomber Offensive directive until the planning committee produced a scheme acceptable to all parties; meanwhile the current command system would apply. Spaatz also informed Tedder "that Americans would not stand for their Strategic Air Forces operating under Leigh-Mallory."[162] For the Americans the suggestion that they come under Leigh-Mallory's control was not just a function of their mistrust of the Commander of the AEAF. The shifting of their priorities to OVERLORD by March 1 would undercut the strategic bombing campaign. Spaatz had originally assumed that March 1, which he had accepted as the date of USSTAF's beginning operations under OVERLORD, would mark a period sixty days before an early May invasion, but the possible postponement of the invasion until June confronted him with a ninety-day delay in the strategic campaign if he remained committed to a March 1 date. As of February 15 USSTAF had not yet accomplished even its minimum strategic goals. To have the transportation plan proposed to USSTAF before the Luftwaffe's fighter force had been defeated or the destructive effects of bombing on the German economy proved was unacceptable. Already frustrated by the weather, which prevented his forces from going after the Germans, and pressured by Washington to push the Combined Bomber Offensive home, Spaatz naturally reacted sharply to another threat to the success of his strategic mission.

Two days after the February 15 meeting, Eisenhower met with Spaatz. Eisenhower had already explained to Marshall that he intended to have his "Air Preparation" plan accepted as "doctrine" by everyone under his control, including Spaatz,[163] whose previous complaints concerning Leigh-Mallory he found worrying. Eisenhower, quietly attempting to change Spaatz's mind, suggested that "proper credit had not been given to Leigh-Mallory's intelligence." Spaatz stood firm, indicating to Eisenhower that his views "had not and would not change."[164]

A draft press release from the Ninth Air Force that afternoon added fuel to the fire. The release described Leigh-Mallory as the "Air Commander in Chief." Spaatz promptly complained to Tedder, who replied, reasonably enough, that the term had already been released previously. This response failed to satisfy

An Avro Lancaster, backbone of RAF Bomber Command, 1943–1945. "Lancs" had impressive payloads, but weak defensive armament and protection.

Spaatz. He then called Harris, who supported his position. Through their combined pressure the offending phrase was squelched.

Later that day, Spaatz, Anderson, Hughes, and Col. C. P. Cabell (one of USSTAF's representatives on the Joint Planning Committee) had dinner at Park House with Zuckerman. Unlike many of his staff and other ranking American air officers, Spaatz never let his intense opposition to the transportation plan turn into antagonism against the plan's creator. Zuckerman recorded that Spaatz during the dinner asked him why didn't he stop working "with that man Leigh-Mallory and join us?"[165] In a discussion after dinner, the Americans attempted to explain their position to the professor. They emphasized the importance of continual missions over Germany and expressed their hope to have at least a small force over Germany every day and a larger one when weather permitted visual bombing. In any case, the small forces, in seeking visual targets through the clouds, would hit small German towns and their marshaling yards, destroying both with, they hoped, important effects.[166] Their unsystematic method failed to convince Zuckerman, whose plans, as the Americans well knew, required extensive bombing of French targets by the strategic forces.

On February 19, Eisenhower and Spaatz met again to review air command arrangements. Eisenhower asked Spaatz how the current system could be made to work with Leigh-Mallory in his present position. Spaatz replied that no system that left Leigh-Mallory in command of the strategic air forces would

335

work.[167] He recommended as "the only practical solution" the formalization of the Joint Planning Committee, which was already working on the POINTBLANK program and on a plan to merge it into OVERLORD. After he and Harris had ensured that this plan conformed to the limitations and capabilities of their forces,[168] the CCS could issue a new bombing directive redefining target priorities and transferring the strategic air forces to Eisenhower's direction. Spaatz implied he would not approve any plan that allowed Leigh-Mallory control of all air operations for an extended period prior to the invasion. He conceded, of course, that "plans for the employment of Air in the actual assault of OVERLORD, including the softening immediately prior thereto, must of necessity be drawn up by Leigh-Mallory, with representatives from RAF Bomber Command and USSTAF familiar with the capabilities of these forces."[169] While Spaatz did not object to Leigh-Mallory's operating within his own area of expertise, he was determined to have a voice in the use of U.S. forces.

Eisenhower accepted this plan with two modifications. He asked that Portal have representation on the committee, and second, that from time to time the plan be checked against actual bombing results and modified if necessary. These changes brought the RAF Chief of Staff formally into the process, increasing the probability that the RAF and the CCS would approve any plan drawn up by the committee. Portal would also balance Harris, who tended to operate semi-independently. Eisenhower's second change allowed him the flexibility to change air plans as events dictated.[170]

Spaatz apparently assumed that this agreement with Eisenhower would enable him to carry POINTBLANK a step or two closer to completion. Later that day, after lamenting, "Operations this week insignificant because of weather," he summarized for Arnold the February 15 meeting and the new agreement with Eisenhower. Spaatz emphasized his fear of a "premature shifting from POINTBLANK to direct preparation for OVERLORD and its consequent indication of willingness to delay attainment of air supremacy until air battle over beachhead." He also noted that Eisenhower would insist on putting RAF and AAF strategic forces under his own control.[171] In his reply, Arnold wholeheartedly agreed with Spaatz that "premature diversion of POINTBLANK and failure to achieve air supremacy prior to the assault would have tragic results." Arnold further approved of Eisenhower's gaining some measure of control of the strategic air forces.[172] Fortified with Arnold's support, Spaatz prepared to fight for a continuation of the Combined Bomber Offensive.

As Spaatz and Eisenhower reached their agreement, Harris introduced a new complication. He appealed directly to Churchill to prevent the subjugation of Bomber Command to the Supreme Commander of the Allied Expeditionary Force, especially if that meant control by Leigh-Mallory.[173]

Spaatz's and Harris's fractious attitude had so discouraged Eisenhower's second in command, Tedder, that he wrote to Portal on February 22:

I am more and more being forced to the unfortunate conclusion that the two strategic air forces are determined not to play. Spaatz has made it abundantly clear that he will not accept orders, or even coordination from Leigh-Mallory, and the only sign of activity from Harris' representatives has been a series of adjustments to the records of their past bombing statistics, with the evident intention of demonstrating that they are quite unequipped and untrained to do anything except mass fire-raising on very large targets.[174]

Tedder went on to warn Portal that if the British Chiefs of Staff and Churchill continued to withhold Bomber Command from Eisenhower's control "very serious issues will arise affecting Anglo-American co-operation in OVERLORD," issues that would result in "quite irremediable cleavage" between the Allies.[175]

On February 28, Eisenhower had dinner at No. 10 Downing Street with Churchill, whom he found impatient for progress on air planning and much disturbed at the thought of Leigh-Mallory's commanding the strategic air forces.[176] Eisenhower explained that he was waiting for a coordinated plan on which all could agree and requested that the Prime Minister refrain from acting on the matter. The next morning Eisenhower wrote a memo to Tedder urging him to work more quickly to complete a solid plan before the Prime Minister came "in this thing with both feet."[177] This memo sounded the death knell for Leigh-Mallory's claim to command all air power cooperating with the invasion. Eisenhower wrote:

I'm quite prepared, if necessary, to issue an order saying I will exert direct supervision of all air forces—through you—and authorizing you to use headquarters facilities now existing to make your control effective. L.M.'s position would not be changed so far as *assigned forces* are concerned but those *attached* for definite periods or definite jobs would not come under his *command* [emphasis in original].[178]

Even as Eisenhower signified his willingness to limit Leigh-Mallory to command of only the U.S. Ninth Air Force and the British 2d Tactical Air Force Churchill waded into the air tangle. On February 29, the Prime Minister voiced his own ideas on OVERLORD's air organization. Tedder should serve as "the 'Aviation lobe' of Eisenhower's brain," with the power to use all air forces temporarily or permanently assigned to the invasion in accordance with the plan approved by Eisenhower.[179] Furthermore, Churchill charged Tedder to draw up, with the assistance of Leigh-Mallory's AEAF staff, a plan satisfactory to the Supreme Commander. Leigh-Mallory would prepare plans and execute orders received from Tedder in Eisenhower's name. As Deputy Commander, Tedder would be empowered to issue orders to Spaatz, Harris, and Air Chief Marshal Sholto Douglas, head of Coastal Command, for any employment of their forces in OVERLORD sanctioned by the CCS.[180] This outline would eventually become the command structure accepted by the Allies.

Churchill's minutes of February 29 may have suggested the solution for the chain of command for air, but Eisenhower found other sections of it objectionable.

Although the minutes admonished that "the 'OVERLORD' battle must be the chief care of all concerned, and great risks must be run in every other sphere and theater in order that nothing should be withheld which could contribute to the success," Churchill, in the same document, proceeded to violate his own dictum. "There can be no question," he ruled, "of handing over the British Bomber, Fighter, or Coastal Commands as a whole to the Supreme Commander and his Deputy." The three commands had other functions as well as those assigned by OVERLORD. In addition, Churchill felt that the CCS should retain the right to vary assignments to the invasion "should overriding circumstances render it necessary."[181]

Upon reviewing these minutes, Eisenhower accepted Tedder's command role and responsibility for drafting an air plan, but balked at having anything less than total operational control of both strategic air forces. Further conversations with Churchill proved unfruitful. In the beginning of March, Eisenhower told Churchill that if Bomber Command did not come under his control, he "would simply have to go home."[182]

Eisenhower conceded that Coastal Command, which occupied a lesser place in the invasion plan, could remain under separate control, but he insisted that Bomber Command receive its direction through the headquarters of the Supreme Commander, as agreed by the Combined Chiefs of Staff at Cairo in December 1943. Portal, for his part, denied that the CCS had ever intended to place more than a portion of Bomber Command under Eisenhower. At this juncture, Churchill told Portal to negotiate an agreement with Eisenhower and indicated that he would accept whatever arrangement the two men agreed to.[183] In the end, during April, the strategic air forces came under Eisenhower's control.

By the end of February 1944, Spaatz had only partially solved the basic problems confronting his command. Two months of bad weather had reduced the opportunity for visual daylight bombing of Germany to a handful of days. To their credit, Spaatz, Fred Anderson, Doolittle, and their men had taken maximum advantage of those days to damage key German aircraft assembly and production targets. Those strikes, in conjunction with bombing-through-overcast missions, had pushed the loss rate of the German fighter force to an unsustainable level. The Luftwaffe lost to all causes 12.1 percent of its fighter pilots in January and another 17.9 percent in February.[184] Thus, in two months almost one out of every three of Germany's fighter pilots had been killed or disabled, including some of its most skilled aviators. Wastage of machines was high, too. Luftwaffe fighter units wrote off 33.8 percent of their total strength in January and another 56.4 percent in February, a 90 percent turnover in two months.[185] The Eighth, too, had suffered severely, losing 211 heavy bombers (19.5 percent of its force) in January and 299 (20.2 percent of its force) in February.[186] The Eighth also lost 172 fighter aircraft in combat and 190 fighter pilots to combat or accidents for the first two months of the year.[187]

Spaatz, however, thanks to resources of men and matériel reaching him, not only sustained such losses but actually increased his strength on hand. His command had not brought the Luftwaffe to earth, but had substantially weakened it. In those two months a measure of confidence returned to the Eighth, which, thanks to increasing numbers of long-range escort-fighters, was no longer afraid to fly deep into Germany. This restoration of spirit, the attrition of the Luftwaffe, and the damage to Germany's air industry, although not decisive in themselves, were three large steps toward the accomplishment of POINTBLANK.

In comparison with the steady strides forward on the operational side of the war, Spaatz and USSTAF remained enmeshed in disputes concerning the transportation plan and air command arrangements. The latter, at least, gave some hope of speedy resolution, while the former would drag on, not completely resolved, almost until the invasion.

Chapter 10

The Luftwaffe Defeated
(March–April 1944)

A concentrated effort against oil, which would represent the most far-reaching use of strategic air power that has been attempted in this war, promises, I believe, more than any other system; a fighting chance of ending German resistance in a shorter period than we have hitherto thought possible.[1]

—*Spaatz to Arnold, March 6, 1944.*

In the three months before the invasion of Normandy on June 6, 1944, the AAF gained daylight air superiority in the skies above occupied Europe and Germany and began a campaign against the Axis oil industry, the success of which contributed greatly to preinvasion air preparations. Neither of these tasks proved easy. The Germans opposed each step with their usual dogged resistance, and disputes among the British and Americans threatened to misdirect the employment of Allied air power, dissipating its force and jeopardizing the accomplishment of the goals before it. Spaatz, as the senior AAF officer in the European Theater of Operations, played a key role in these events by his supervision of the U.S. air effort and by his participation as the chief AAF representative in Europe in the contentious negotiations that worked out Allied air command arrangements (See Chart 6, Chain of Command, Allied Expeditionary Force, April 7, 1944.) and U.S. strategic air forces contributions to preinvasion bombing.

Air Command Arrangements for OVERLORD Are Settled

In the beginning of March, the Allies settled the air command arrangements for OVERLORD. Tedder served as go-between as the British Chief of the Air Staff, Portal, and the American Supreme Commander, Eisenhower, wrestled to

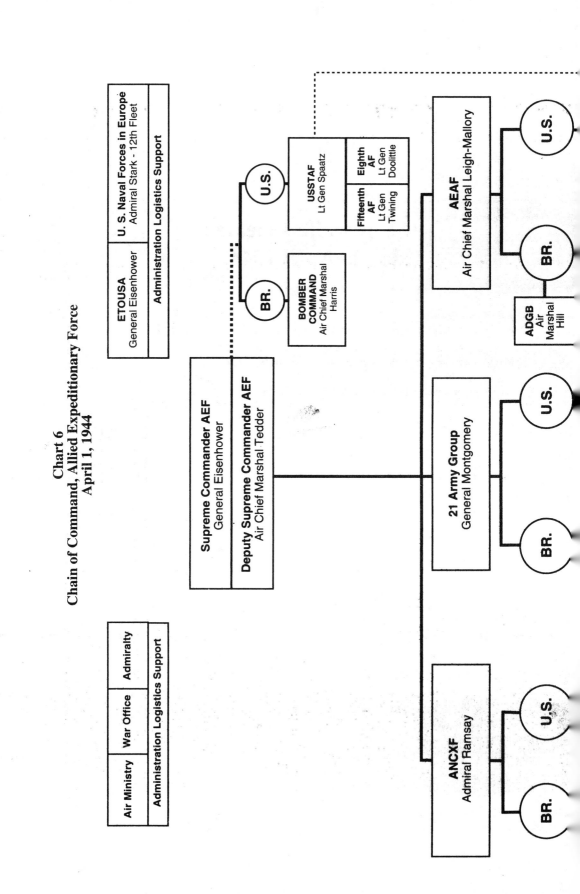

Chart 6
Chain of Command, Allied Expeditionary Force
April 1, 1944

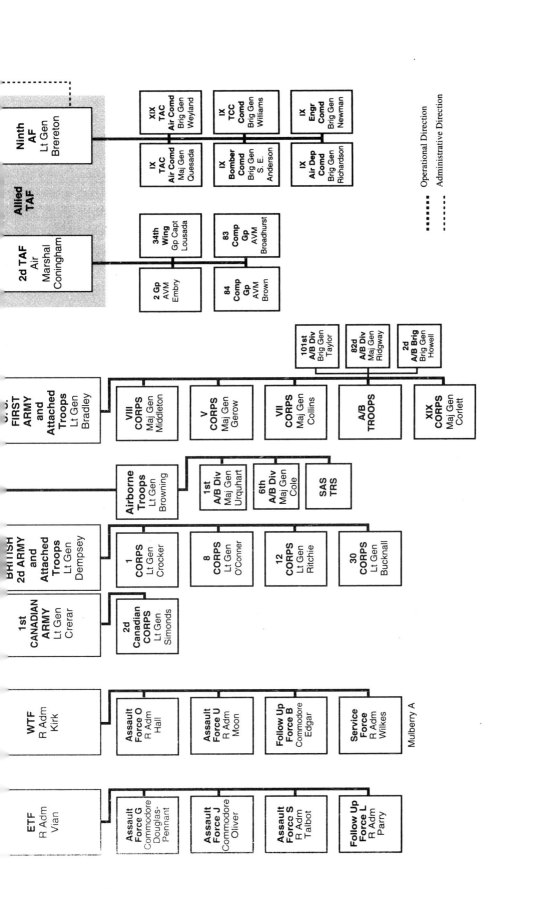

ETF R Adm Vian

- **Assault Force G** Commodore Douglas-Pennant
- **Assault Force J** Commodore Oliver
- **Assault Force S** R Adm Talbot
- **Follow Up Force L** R Adm Parry

WTF R Adm Kirk

- **Assault Force O** R Adm Hall
- **Assault Force U** R Adm Moon
- **Follow Up Force B** Commodore Edgar
- **Service Force** R Adm Wilkes

Mulberry A

1st CANADIAN ARMY Lt Gen Crerar

- **2d Canadian CORPS** Lt Gen Simonds

BRITISH 2d ARMY and Attached Troops Lt Gen Dempsey

- **1 CORPS** Lt Gen Crocker
- **8 CORPS** Lt Gen O'Conner
- **12 CORPS** Lt Gen Ritchie
- **30 CORPS** Lt Gen Bucknall

Airborne Troops Lt Gen Browning

- **1st A/B Div** Maj Gen Urquhart
- **6th A/B Div** Maj Gen Cole
- **SAS TRS**

U.S. FIRST ARMY and Attached Troops Lt Gen Bradley

- **VIII CORPS** Maj Gen Middleton
- **V CORPS** Maj Gen Gerow
- **VII CORPS** Maj Gen Collins
- **A/B TROOPS**
  - **101st A/B Div** Brig Gen Taylor
  - **82d A/B Div** Maj Gen Ridgway
  - **2d A/B Brig** Brig Gen Howell
- **XIX CORPS** Maj Gen Corlett

2d TAF Air Marshal Coningham

- **34th Wing** Gp Capt Lousada
- **2 Gp** AVM Embry
- **83 Comp Gp** AVM Broadhurst
- **84 Comp Gp** AVM Brown

Allied TAF

Ninth AF Lt Gen Brereton

- **XIX TAC Air Comd** Brig Gen Weyland
- **IX TAC Air Comd** Maj Gen Quesada
- **IX TCC Comd** Brig Gen Williams
- **IX Bomber Comd** Brig Gen S. E. Anderson
- **IX Engr Comd** Brig Gen Newman
- **IX Air Dep Comd** Brig Gen Richardson

.... Operational Direction
--------- Administrative Direction

reconcile their differences. Portal, following Churchill's dictates, sought to preserve some autonomy for RAF Coastal, Fighter, and Bomber Commands, whereas Eisenhower wished for complete control, particularly of Bomber Command. By March 9, Portal produced a draft agreement incorporating elements of both positions. Eisenhower described it as "exactly what we want,"[2] and a day later informed Marshall, "All air forces here will be under Tedder's supervision as my agent and this prospect is particularly pleasing to Spaatz."[3]

Spaatz wrote to Arnold in a similar vein, "I feel that this is a logical, workable plan and, under the conditions which exist, cannot be improved upon."[4] Tedder would coordinate the operation of the strategic forces in support of the invasion, and Leigh-Mallory, under Tedder's supervision, would coordinate the tactical air plan. Eisenhower accepted the right of the Combined Chiefs or the British Chiefs to impose additional tasks on the strategic forces if necessary. Finally, once assault forces had established themselves on the Continent, both parties agreed to undertake a revision of the directive for the employment of the strategic bomber force.[5]

The British then passed the draft agreement to the Combined Chiefs. In their covering memos, the British stated that when the air plan for support of OVERLORD met the approval of both Eisenhower and Portal, acting in his capacity as the agent of the Chiefs for the Combined Bomber Offensive, "the responsibility for supervision of air operations out of England of all forces engaged in the program, including the United States Strategic Air Force and British Bomber Command, together with any other air forces that might be made available, should pass to the Supreme Commander."[6] Eisenhower and Portal would jointly supervise those strategic forces not used by the invasion in accordance with agreements they had previously reached. The British Chiefs added that, at present, they had no plans to use the reservations inserted into the agreement, and, if they did, they would immediately inform the U.S. Joint Chiefs of Staff.[7]

The U.S. Joint Chiefs balked at once. This proposal did not give Eisenhower unquestioned control of the strategic air forces. The British protested that the Supreme Commander himself found the plan acceptable—to no avail. Even Eisenhower had second thoughts and insisted on untrammeled control of the strategic bombers for the invasion period. Once again, he thought of resigning if the matter continued to drag on *ad infinitum*.[8] On April 7, barely two months before the invasion, the Combined Chiefs agreed that the strategic air forces would operate under the Supreme Commander's "direction." This was apparently less ambiguous than allotting him "the responsibility for supervision." At the same time, the Combined Chiefs approved, with a few exceptions on targets, the air plan developed for the invasion. Formal direction of the strategic air forces passed to Eisenhower on April 14,[9] confirming the informal command structure already in place.

The Dispute over Strategic Targeting

Simultaneously, the strategic air forces, through their representatives on the Joint Planning Committee for the OVERLORD air plan, spent much of March arguing the merits of Zuckerman's transportation plan versus USSTAF's oil plan. The strategic air forces would come into the Supreme Commander's hands only after approval of the air preparation plan. Until the airmen could agree on a plan, the formalization of the air command structure would hang fire.

For practical purposes, however, the strategic air commanders had no intention of actually employing their veto. Spaatz and, by now, even Harris accepted the necessity of some strategic support for the invasion. Moreover, Eisenhower would surely override any veto by appealing to the CCS, who would defer to him in any matter directly touching on the success of the invasion. Their veto power gave the strategic air commanders leverage in obtaining a command system and a plan for air employment more in keeping with their own ideas than might otherwise have been possible. Although their positions were not invulnerable, Eisenhower would find it difficult and very disruptive to replace them with more malleable commanders, who would probably lack their expertise and prestige.

By late February, Spaatz and others had recognized that the Combined Bomber Offensive had progressed to a point, thanks to the attrition of the Luftwaffe's fighter forces inflicted in January and February, at which time the destruction of targets other than the German aircraft industry was not only feasible but desirable. Spaatz thus ordered the formation of a USSTAF planning committee to consider future actions. He did so partially in response to the transportation plan, which the AEAF had presented to him in February—a plan that USSTAF regarded as unsound. He laid down three guiding principles for the committee: (1) the plan must provide for air supremacy at the time of the invasion; (2) the plan should take into account a possible early collapse of Germany prior to the invasion; and (3) if Germany did not collapse, the plan should nevertheless make a maximum contribution to the success of OVERLORD.[10]

With pressure for adoption of the transportation plan gaining momentum every day, Spaatz urgently required a viable alternative on which to base his opposition. He pushed the planning committee to complete its work; they prepared a final draft in thirty-six-hours,[11] presenting to Spaatz on March 5, a "plan for the Completion of the Combined Bomber Offensive."

Quickly dubbed the oil plan it called for a "re-clarification" of POINTBLANK directives and, after examining ten discrete target systems, selected three German production programs—rubber, bomber aircraft, and oil. To those three, it added the already accepted targets of German fighter production and ball bearings. Oil received top priority followed by fighters and ball bearings, rubber, and bomber aircraft. The plan emphatically rejected railroad transport as a strategic target. Such a system had too many targets, had built in too much noncritical civilian traffic and long-term industrial traffic that could be suppressed or diverted before military traffic would be significantly reduced, and its destruction would take too long to have a significant military effect. In contrast, the oil plan required fifteen days' visual bombing for the Eighth Air Force and ten for the Fifteenth Air Force.[12]

The plan assumed that the destruction of only fourteen synthetic oil plants and thirteen refineries would account for more than 80 percent of production and 60 percent of readily usable refining capacity. These losses would reduce the total German supply of fuel by 50 percent, thereby cutting materially "German military capabilities through reducing tactical and strategical mobility and frontline delivery of supplies and industrial ability to produce weapons and supplies." Furthermore, the plan contended that the Germans, under fire, would immediately reduce consumption of oil products in order to conserve their stocks.[13] This postulate, although logical, could not be verified by intelligence before the attacks. USSTAF insisted that the immediate cut would have great effects in the battle for the beachhead, but the oil plan's critics countered by claiming that it did not guarantee a significant impact on German fighting ability before the invasion assault. Almost everyone agreed that the plan had long-range potential devastating to the Nazis. Nonetheless, factors that improved the chances of the imminent invasion appealed more to Eisenhower than schemes that promised important but delayed benefits.

The oil industry's configuration added to its suitability as a target system. Ploesti, the enemy's major source of natural petroleum, was vulnerable to the increasing power of the Fifteenth Air Force. Once operations there ceased, the synthetic oil plants of Germany would become the enemy's chief source of supply. These plants, most of which were well within bomber range of Britain, constituted a compact target system. Their destruction would produce dramatic results before the cross-channel attack and leave an adequate reserve of unused American force available for containing the aircraft industry or striking at other targets of opportunity.[14]

The synthetic oil plants also presented a practical bombing problem, which was not as important in early 1944, when strategic airmen had only minimum disposable force, as it would become in the winter of 1944–1945, when they had enormous bomber fleets. For technical and logistical reasons the Germans had chosen to build their synthetic oil plants away from urban areas. These plants could only be bombed if they could be located by visual means. The American H2X radar's resolution or return was so inaccurate that it could only locate a city area. Although synthetic plants were huge, they were considerably smaller than a city. Hence, bombing oil plants meant using the very few days of visual bombing weather to hit targets outside German cities. In the winter of 1944–1945 synthetic oil targets absorbed all visual bombing days. The Americans were left with little choice but to resort to H2X-assisted raids on targets within German cities for the majority of their bombing effort, with calamitous results for the German civilian population.

Upon receiving the plan on the evening of March 5, Spaatz and his staff, as usual, began their discussion before dinner and continued it into the wee hours. Walt W. Rostow, then a first lieutenant in the Enemy Objectives Unit (EOU) of the Office of Strategic Services, which served as USSTAF's unofficial target intelligence section, recorded in 1981, "Despite the effort to emphasize, within the plan, the will to complete the attacks on the POINTBLANK systems, General Spaatz quickly appreciated that it was to all intents and purposes an Oil Plan." Spaatz then "explored at length the issues at stake, especially the capabilities of the Eighth and Fifteenth Air Forces with respect to the number of targets involved. He then ordered the plan completed for prompt presentation to Portal and Eisenhower."[15]

In sending the plan to Eisenhower, Spaatz stated his own views: "I consider that the plan provides for the optimum use of Strategic Air Forces between now and the time for close support in the immediate tactical area. Our calculations of the possible results are considered to be conservative." He added that the plan's results were "pitched in terms of so lowering the German fighting efficiency on existing fronts that the German ability safely to move strategic reserves will be impaired; and in the months following D-Day, the capacity of the German ground armies effectively to continue resistance must inevitably be exhausted."[16]

The oil plan offered a strategically based rebuttal of the transportation plan. Another plan, drawn up by the EOU, challenged the transportation plan on tactical grounds. EOU's plan called for the bombing of french supply dumps and bridges rather than rail marshaling yards. Both plans provided rallying points for the critics of Zuckerman's plan. The counterattack mounted by these critics brought Tedder fully into the field in support of the transportation plan because he might lose face if the Allies rejected it. He believed that the plan offered a partial solution to the air command difficulties by providing a set of targets requiring the coordination and cooperation of the strategic and tactical air forces. Tedder wrote Portal that in order to derive full use of Allied air power, he needed a target system based "on one common object toward which all available air forces can be directed. . . . Concentration against one common system, by both day and night, is essential."[17] Tedder's reasoning was, of course, apparent to the adherents of both plans. The oil plan allowed a non-centralized air command system under which the strategic air forces would operate without close cooperation with the tactical air forces. The transportation plan required a unified air command in order to yoke both the strategic and tactical air forces into a coordinated attack on a complex, wide-spread, resilient target system.

The dispute between the adherents of the transportation plan and its opponents, who criticized it on strategic and tactical grounds, continued until mid-May 1944. During a series of meetings held throughout March the transportation plan's detractors mobilized increasing opposition. Field Marshal Alan Brooke, Chief of the Imperial General Staff, the equivalent of the American Chairman of the Joint Chiefs of Staff, and others questioned the plan's effectiveness,[18] as did segments of the British Air Staff and Ministry of Economic Warfare. Spaatz, on the day of the AAF's first major raid over Berlin, wrote Arnold enthusiastically:

> We do, however, feel sure that a new range of tactical possibilities in operation are open to us, and that it would be a misuse of our force and of the opportunities we have created not to push strategic bombing to its ultimate conclusion, in that period available to us. A concentrated effort against oil, which would represent the most far-reaching use of strategic air-power that has been attempted in this war, promises more than any other system, a fighting chance of ending German resistance in a shorter period than we have hitherto thought possible.[19]

Arnold began cudgelling his own superior, Marshall, to support the oil plan. In a memo dated March 13, he explained, "In view of the recent progress made against the GAF, the ball-bearing industry and Berlin, and the imminence of OVERLORD, it is evident such a plan is required." After denigrating plans based "upon only cold, mathematical-like tables of performance data [the transportation plan]," Arnold concluded, "The tremendous force available to us must not be permitted to waste its substance on any but potentially decisive operations."[20]

These pleas did not change Marshall's determination or that of the War Department to leave the major decisions concerning the military policy of the invasion to the invasion commander, Eisenhower. On March 16, the AAF Chief of Staff, Maj. Gen. Barney Giles, told Spaatz that because Portal, Harris, and, above all, Eisenhower had not committed themselves to the oil plan, the Joint Chiefs of Staff were unlikely to take action on it. He pointed out that the most recent CCS directive on strategic bombing already gave Spaatz the authority to start attacks against the systems he had selected. Then Giles asked for new initiatives from Spaatz:

> What concerns us most here is whether or not you are going to be able to sell Eisenhower on the necessity for letting you go ahead with your Plan without insistence that you be diverted prematurely. I feel that if Eisenhower makes an issue of a system or of a date he will be backed up by the U.S. Joint Chiefs of Staff—so that places it right in your lap.[21]

In order to "sell" Eisenhower, Spaatz would have to "sell" Tedder, who had already told Portal, "I am frankly skeptical of the Oil Plan, partly because we have been led up the garden path before, partly because the targets are in difficult areas . . . and partly because I am not sure of the real vulnerability of the new synthetic oil plants."[22] On March 16 the Joint Bombing Committee met again. Tedder began the meeting completely in favor of the transportation plan, but the united opposition of the RAF Assistant Chiefs of Staff for Plans, Bomber Operations, and Intelligence caused him to waver and he, with Portal and Eisenhower, referred the transportation plan to the British Joint Intelligence Committee for review. Spaatz noted optimistically, "Hoped by all concerned here that Tedder will repudiate AEAF Plan of his own accord," an action that would avoid hard feelings all around.[23] Tedder, however, did not abandon the transportation plan, even in the face of the Joint Intelligence Committee Report, which supported the oil plan. The latter report, according to Tedder, was based on unsubstantiated and invalid assumptions.[24]

Meanwhile, Eisenhower had reached the end of his tether. If a meeting scheduled for March 25 did not decide between the competing plans, he stated, "I am going to take drastic action and inform the Combined Chiefs of Staff that unless the matter is settled at once I will request relief from this command."[25]

At the March 25 bombing policy conference which would decide between the competing plans, Spaatz, Tedder, and Eisenhower were joined by Portal, Harris, Leigh-Mallory, and various intelligence officers and experts on Axis oil. During the preceding week Spaatz and Tedder had prepared and circulated briefs detailing their positions and had marshaled last-minute agreements to attract further support for their proposals. Apparently, Tedder persuaded Portal to back the transportation plan. Harris, too, gave the plan lukewarm support. He opposed the oil plan because he disagreed with the concept of designing a strategic bombing strategy around a single-target system. Choosing such a "panacea" diverted his forces from area bombing, which he thought was the most effective method of conducting the bomber offensive. In addition, British bomber operations in March demonstrated the night bomber's surprisingly high capability for the precision bombing of marshaling yards while simultaneously revealing an alarming rise in the effectiveness of the German night-fighter force, which reached its apogee in the winter of 1943–1944 and inflicted "prohibitive" casualties.[26] These two factors undercut Harris's original objections that he could not bomb precision targets and that city-busting raids offered a more decisive alternative.

Spaatz, not to be outdone, took advantage of Eaker's visit to London—they visited each other's headquarters monthly and coordinated bombing operations and policy—to use his friend's close ties with the British and his expertise to try to win converts to the oil plan. On the morning of March 25, Spaatz and Eaker, who had just stepped off his plane, went to lobby both Eisenhower and Tedder. After discussing air command arrangements in Britain and the proposed directive for air support of OVERLORD, Eisenhower asked for Eaker's views on the oil versus transportation debate. Although he declined to comment on the oil plan because he had not studied it, Eaker told Eisenhower that the Luftwaffe must receive top priority and recommended that no attacks on communications lines south of the Rhine should occur before D-day. His experience in Italy, said Eaker, had shown him that communication attacks, unsupported by sustained friendly ground action to pressure the enemy and force him to consume supplies, had little effect. The two AAF generals then spent an hour with Tedder going over the same subjects,[27] but they did not change his mind.

That afternoon Portal, chair of the bombing policy conference called on Tedder to present the transportation plan. During the presentation and the ensuing discussion three salient points emerged. First, all present agreed that the bombing of Luftwaffe targets, including ball bearings producers, had top priority, and, therefore, the meeting would consider the allocation to a specific target system of only the effort *remaining after* bombing the highest priority system. Second, Tedder believed that only an all-out attack on the transport-action system would sufficiently disrupt enemy movement before and after D-day to give the invasion the greatest chance of success. Third, Eisenhower asserted that "the greatest contribution that he could imagine the air forces making" was the hindering of enemy movement and "that everything he had read had convinced him that, apart from the attack on the G.A.F., the Transportation Plan was the only one which offered a reasonable chance of the air forces making an important contribution to the land battle during the first vital weeks of OVERLORD." In fact he did not believe that there was any other "real alternative."[28]

Then the group examined the oil plan. Spaatz and F. L. Anderson, the only Americans present besides Eisenhower, presented their case. Several factors affected the manner of their exposition. Spaatz, congenial, even convivial, in his mess or at ease, usually performed woodenly at set-piece conferences,[29] as he did at this one. He had already circulated his views in his brief and so he confined himself to reiterating three of its conclusions: (1) strategic attacks on the railways would not affect the course of initial battle or prevent movement of German reserves from other fronts, whereas the oil plan might do both; (2) attacks on the rail system would not, in an acceptable length of time, weaken enemy resistance on all fronts simultaneously, which the oil plan would do while it also hastened the postinvasion success of OVERLORD; and, most important, (3) attacks on rail targets would not provoke a strong reaction from the Luftwaffe, whereas attacks on oil targets would.[30] This spare, straightforward presentation aided the advocates of the transportation plan. A presentation of EOU's tactical plan would have strengthened his case.

As Rostow has pointed out, other organizational, bureaucratic, and personal factors also affected the presentation. Spaatz, because he commanded a strategic force, chose not to present the tactical plan, which would require the participation of forces not under his control. Although he harbored genuine, continuing doubts as to the invasion's chances of success in achieving a foothold on the Continent, he would accept almost any plan Eisenhower backed because he did not want it said that he had not done his utmost to support the attack. A member of his staff, Carl Kaysen, recalled that a week or so before the meeting Spaatz told his staff, "I won't take the responsibility. This ——— [*expletive deleted in original*] invasion can't succeed, and I don't want any part of the blame. After it fails, we can show them how we can win by bombing."[31]

Anderson followed Spaatz's short discourse with the observation that although the oil plan could not guarantee a decisive influence on the initial stages of OVERLORD, it could, within six months, have a devastating effect on the enemy. Conversely, USSTAF doubted that the transportation plan would ever have a decisive effect on the enemy. A British oil expert from the Ministry of Economic Warfare, Oliver Lawrence, commented that if USSTAF attacked its twenty-seven targeted oil installations within a three-month period, the Germans would have to cut their current military consumption by 25 percent. Lawrence added that the Germans had large reserve stocks in the west, so they might not immediately cut back operations in France, but they would certainly feel the pinch in the west four or five months after the plan's start.

Portal immediately seized on Lawrence's comments to administer the coup de grâce to the immediate adoption of the oil plan stating that they "showed conclusively that the oil plan would not help OVERLORD in the first few critical weeks." He softened the blow by strongly suggesting that, once the initial invasion crisis had passed, the oil plan had "great attractions." Eisenhower agreed. This ended the meeting's consideration of Spaatz's alternative to the transportation plan.[32]

Talk then turned to the use of strategic bombers. Harris doubted that he could carry out precision attacks against all twenty-six targets allotted to him in the time period before D-day. Despite a rising rate of casualties, he wanted to continue his attacks over eastern Germany for as long as he had enough hours of darkness. Eisenhower, conceding that the transportation plan would cause Bomber Command very little change in its programs, said, "The more important question was whether the 8th and 15th Air Forces could achieve their part in [the transportation plan]." Spaatz replied that one-half of his visual bombing attacks would have to strike Luftwaffe targets and the other half would have to hit a target system capable of producing "at least some enemy fighter reaction, and so attrition." He had chosen the oil plan over the transportation plan precisely because the former would guarantee constant air battles and consistent attrition of the Luftwaffe's fighter force.

Portal disagreed. He believed that the Luftwaffe would defend the railways once it realized the Allies had begun an all-out campaign against them. Spaatz emphasized the importance of the location of the targets chosen; his forces must fly well into Germany in order to generate the maximum amount of air fighting, and for tactical reasons some of the transportation targets ought to be in the same area as Luftwaffe targets. Tedder agreed, anticipating that he would have no problem coming up with targets to fit Spaatz's requirements. Portal then raised another problem—the large numbers of civilian casualties almost certain to result from bombing the marshaling yards in or adjacent to French towns. He reserved to the British government the opportunity to consider the possible consequences.[33] This caveat, which few at the time remarked on, would eventually delay complete execution of the transportation plan for several weeks until Churchill could satisfy himself that the bombing would not redound to Britain's discredit.

The bombing policy conference ended with Portal and Eisenhower giving Tedder, not Leigh-Mallory, instructions on coordinating the execution of the plan with the air commanders involved.[34] At this time Portal and Eisenhower also stated their intention to put in place the air command arrangements on which they had previously agreed, subject to final approval by the Combined Chiefs of Staff.[35] From that point on, Eisenhower, using Tedder as his executive for air, began to exercise de facto control of the strategic bomber forces.[36] The decision that Tedder coordinate the execution of the transportation plan had the character of a compromise. Eisenhower accepted Leigh-Mallory's preinvasion plan but did not require that Spaatz, who questioned Leigh-Mallory's capabilities, place himself under the man.

Thus concluded what a British official history termed "the historic occasion."[37] Eisenhower chose the transportation plan over the oil plan, and the air command arrangements agreed on between Eisenhower and the British went into effect. Critics have disputed the wisdom of the Supreme Commander's choice ever since. Much ink and emotion have flowed over the benefits derived from the transportation plan. On tactical grounds its critics maintain that a campaign of bridge busting and bombing of supply dumps would have consumed less force with equal results.[38] On strategic grounds critics bemoan the "national disaster"[39] of the delay in the oil campaign, which, when executed, severely restricted Germany's ability to wage war.

How did Spaatz react to this conference—an event Eisenhower biographer Stephen E. Ambrose described as "a crucial moment in his [Spaatz's] life"?[40] Did he complain bitterly to everyone of the obtuseness of his plan's opponents? No, neither his character nor his thirty years' service as a Regular Army officer fitted him for the role of chronic malcontent. As in the Mitchell court-martial nineteen years earlier, he presented and defended a position in which he believed passionately. Once Eisenhower had reached a decision, however, Spaatz supported it with grace and, in fact, left the meeting not displeased, but cheered that the command arrangements acceptable to him had prevailed. In a letter to Arnold, Eaker, who had dinner with Spaatz that evening, said of Spaatz's reaction:

> I have never seen him quite so jubilant and overjoyed. He had won out completely on the command set up. The strategic British and American Air Forces were not to be put under Leigh-Mallory. The communication plan had won out over the oil plan, but Tooey was not too displeased about this, since all had firmly agreed that the German Air Force was to be an all-consuming first priority.[41]

The day after the meeting, in his weekly "Eyes Only" summary for Arnold, Spaatz commented:

> I believe decision reached was justified based on all factors involved, which are predominantly the absolute necessity to insure the initial success of OVERLORD. I feel satisfied with the command set-up as now being established. . . . I feel the

time has arrived now when the most essential thing is the full out coordination of the air effort in support of OVERLORD.[42]

Spaatz's actions and words after the meeting betray little sense of defeat or angst at the thought of forfeiting what he considered an excellent chance to hit Germany in its most vital organs. Postwar information gathered by the Allies reveals that the anti-oil campaign was decisive once it began in earnest in the summer of 1944. Spaatz, in March 1944, might have had a hunch that the oil campaign would yield immediate crucial results, but he had no proof. He accepted the transportation plan because he would only have to divert, at most, half of his effort, much of it on days the Eighth could not bomb Germany using visual means in any case. He could employ the remainder of his force with a free hand to continue increasing the Luftwaffe's already ruinous attrition rate. The latest version of the transportation plan also assigned RAF Bomber Command twenty-six rail targets in France, thus ensuring Harris's participation and removing a specter that had troubled Spaatz since the plan's inception. In early February he had remarked to Zuckerman, "What worries me is that Harris is being allowed to get off scot-free. He'll go on bombing Germany and will be given a chance of defeating her before the invasion while I am put under Leigh-Mallory's command."[43] It is also possible that Spaatz had not given up on the oil plan. If he could demonstrate that bombing oil targets could produce a violent air reaction by the Germans, then selecting oil targets would clearly fall into the purview of his directive to destroy the Luftwaffe.

Spaatz may have lost a round on points but he had not lost the fight. On March 31 he stepped back into the ring with memos to Portal and Eisenhower titled "The Use of Strategic Bombers in Support of OVERLORD," in which he accepted the proposition that French railways required heavy attacks. But, after noting that neither the oil plan nor the transportation plan had, as yet, a qualitative measure of effectiveness, he rejected an attack on German railways and suggested that oil targets would be just as easy to bomb and more effective in the long run:

> The effect from the Oil attack, while offering a less definite input in time, is certain to be more far-reaching. It will lead directly to sure disaster for Germany. The Rail attack can lead to harassment only. In weighing these two, it appears that too great a price may be paid merely for a certainty of very little.[44]

Spaatz then offered the possibility of simultaneously executing both the oil and transportation plans. Eighth Air Force fighter-bombers could bomb both French railway targets and synthetic fuel plants in the Ruhr. RAF Bomber Command could also make daylight attacks against French rail targets or bomb synthetic fuel plants in Stettin or, if they wished, the Ruhr at night. In Romania, the Fifteenth Air Force might bomb transportation targets, and the

Russians might advance far enough to send their limited-range planes against Ploesti. To Spaatz, bombing the transport lines around Ploesti was the key to hampering German military operations in the Balkans and the southern USSR, restricting the flow of refined and crude petroleum from Ploesti, and contributing to the general dislocation of the German rail system. If the Soviets could take or neutralize Ploesti, the Germans would be extremely vulnerable to air attacks on the synthetic fuel plants, Hitler's only remaining significant source of oil. "These possibilities," in Spaatz's opinion, "therefore, lend weight to the advantage of early attack upon the synthetics in order to obtain the earliest possible threat. That impact might well be far earlier than currently estimated."[45]

Finally, Spaatz recommended the following target priorities in order of importance for his two air forces:

> For the Eighth:
>   1. The Luftwaffe and ball bearings,
>   2. The nineteen rail targets already selected in occupied countries, and
>   3. The thirteen major synthetic oil plants.
>
> For the Fifteenth:
>   1. The Luftwaffe and ball bearings,
>   2. Rail transport in Romania and selected targets in southern France,
>   3. Synthetic oil plants in southern Germany, and
>   4. Political targets in the Balkans.[46]

At the end of March, the transportation plan was in; Spaatz was persevering in his push for oil; and Leigh-Mallory was out, reduced to the same status as Spaatz and Harris, with Eisenhower, acting through Tedder, in command. Spaatz had achieved a position satisfactory to himself on several issues. The strategic bombers would remain under strategic commanders. He also expected U.S. representation within the AEAF to become more vigorous with the replacement of the lackluster Butler by the ambitious Brig. Gen. Hoyt S. Vandenberg, Spaatz's personal friend. Vandenberg, a former member of the prewar Air Corps Plans Division and former Chief of Staff of the Twelfth Air Force and of the Northwest African Strategic Air Forces, received his second star in order to have the requisite rank for the new assignment.

Spaatz and Eisenhower had earlier agreed on Butler's transfer. On March 1, Eisenhower cabled Marshall that he found Butler "*not* [emphasis in original] suitable for his present assignment."[47] On March 6, Eisenhower, presumably in response to Marshall's and Arnold's request for further information, added, "The difficulty with General Butler is that he is completely negative,"[48] with nothing constructive to offer either ally. The Supreme Commander then suggested Vandenberg. "The importance of the American contingent of this staff is obvious, and it must be headed by a strong, able type whose word and opinions will carry some weight."[49] Marshall, who rubber-stamped almost all of Eisenhower's personnel requests, promptly complied. Vandenberg, leaving his post as AAF Deputy Chief of the Air Staff, arrived in London on March 24, where he immediately saw Spaatz. With him came another AAF general, Brig. Gen. Frederic H. Smith, Jr., the son-in-law of Admiral Ernest J. King, Chief of Naval Operations. Smith's marital connections gave him greater influence and importance than his rank might suggest. He would serve as Vandenberg's deputy and Chief of AEAF Operations.

At their initial meeting and at another three days later concerning the role and responsibilities of the Deputy Commander, Allied Expeditionary Air Force, Spaatz clarified his reasons for asking Eisenhower to appoint Vandenberg. Vandenberg pointed to the dual nature of his roles: (1) serving as a loyal subordinate to his commander, Leigh-Mallory, and (2) "guarding the operational use and fulfilling the administrative requirement of the American component." Spaatz responded that Vandenberg's top priority ought to be "safeguarding the interests of the American component" and gaining Eisenhower's concurrence in this matter. Spaatz added that with Eisenhower's agreement, he meant to route all matters of major policy concerning the Ninth Air Force through Vandenberg. Vandenberg would "inform" General Brereton to direct through him all matters requiring decisions by higher authority. The two generals then consulted with Eisenhower, who concurred in their decision, and with Tedder concerning the position of AEAF and the other air commands in England. Vandenberg finished his rounds by going off alone for dinner with Leigh-Mallory at AEAF Headquarters.[50]

By placing his own man in the deputy commander slot and making him the de facto commander of the entire U.S. contingent in the AEAF, Spaatz tightened his control over the nonstrategic AAF elements in Britain. He eliminated Butler, who, in addition to his other failings, had supported the transportation plan.[51] He also subordinated Brereton, a congenital maverick who had visions of playing an independent role in the tactical sphere of operations, to a member of the Arnold-Spaatz AAF ruling faction. Brereton, too, had committed the sin of supporting the transportation plan.[52] Vandenberg's selection had the further advantage of making available to Leigh-Mallory an efficient, energetic officer familiar with strategic operations. In the long run, Vandenberg's appointment would improve the effectiveness of the AEAF as an Allied and a combat headquarters.

A week before the new man's arrival, Spaatz and Leigh-Mallory had clashed again over the role of the Ninth Air Force's fighters. On March 10, Leigh-Mallory, eager to implement the transportation plan and to initiate greater training in ground-air tactics and cooperation for his forces, had ordered that, except for two groups of P-51 aircraft, the Ninth Air Force would "operate exclusively under the Allied Expeditionary Air Force . . . released from its commitment to assist U.S. VIIIth Air Force POINTBLANK operations under arrangements made by that Force."[53] Leigh-Mallory added that the Ninth's medium-bomber attacks would be planned to coincide with the Eighth's deep-penetration flights. Spaatz

Maj. Gen. Hoyt S.
Vandenberg, Deputy
Commanding General,
Allied Expeditionary Air
Force, spring 1944.

Brig. Gen. Frederic H.
Smith, Jr., Chief of
Operations, Allied
Expeditionary Air Force,
spring 1944.

strenuously objected that the loss of the fighters would deprive him of the much-needed services of five recently activated P-47 groups, some 300 to 375 aircraft which, thanks to a newly developed 150-gallon drop tank, had achieved an escort range of 475 miles in February. They were able for the first time to escort to objectives just beyond an arc drawn from Hamburg to Frankfurt. The relative shortage of P-51s plus new drop tanks made the P-47s the backbone of the Eighth's escort fighters for the winter of 1943–1944.

In his reply to Leigh-Mallory, Spaatz pointed out that the former's instructions violated previous agreements:

> It is my understanding that all three types of U.S. fighters are at the disposal of the Eighth Air Force to assist . . . in POINTBLANK operations. Further, inasmuch as I have been made responsible for the training of the Ninth Air Force, it will be my responsibility to determine how much diversion from POINTBLANK will be allowed for training.

Spaatz did reaffirm, however, his commitment to release Ninth Air Force fighters to the AEAF "whenever possible."[54]

Three days later, Spaatz protested again to Leigh-Mallory and appealed to Eisenhower. Spaatz agreed that the Ninth's medium bombers could fulfill their POINTBLANK obligation by timing their tactical strikes in conjunction with the Eighth's strategic missions. He then drew Leigh-Mallory's attention to the current operations directive of the Combined Chiefs of Staff, which unequivocally gave support of the strategic air forces as the present primary mission of the Ninth Air Force. To Eisenhower, Spaatz wrote one blunt paragraph:

> I think this is a matter of utmost importance in our operations. Unless the Eighth Air Force operating out of U.K. can be assured of the availability of all long-range fighters, including P-47's, their deep penetrations will result in greatly increased heavy bomber losses, and we will be losing many opportunities to deal punishing blows to the German Air Force.[55]

The matter obviously required a decision from higher authority. On March 20, after a regular commanders' conference, Spaatz insisted to Eisenhower[56] that they meet with Tedder and Leigh-Mallory to resolve the issue. Eisenhower ruled in favor of Spaatz;[57] the Ninth Air Force remained undivided. The incident, like earlier ones, did little to help the relationship between the two men and their organizations. The AAF official history, not known for criticism of its own, noted of the situation:

> The failure to achieve cooperation between USSTAF and AEAF, coupled with other differences over the training of Ninth Air Force units and over the control of the strategic air forces themselves, created an atmosphere of distrust and suspicion between the two headquarters, which was an exception rather than the rule in Anglo-American relations in the European theater.[58]

Operations

This bureaucratic and policy trench-fighting in March 1944 had no effect on operations. Both Allied air forces and the Luftwaffe suffered brutal and unprecedentedly high losses as the skies of occupied Europe served as a battlefield by day and by night in the continued struggle for mastery of the air. As mentioned, the German night-fighter forces during March reached such a level of effectiveness that RAF heavy-bomber losses became prohibitive. As a result, RAF Bomber Command temporarily discontinued night attacks over Germany. The month culminated in the disastrous Nuremberg raid on the night of March 30–31, in which it lost 96 out of 795 bombers—the greatest number of Allied heavy bombers ever lost on a single mission.[59] The mission went so awry that the citizens of Nuremberg never even knew that an RAF force had been directed toward their city. The Eighth Air Force also suffered its worst single day's loss on March 6, when the Reich's air defenses downed 69 out of 730 bombers during the Eighth's first major attack on Berlin.[60] For the month, Bomber Command lost 278 heavy bombers, while the Eighth lost 232 fighters and 299 heavy bombers (plus 41 heavy bombers written off as not repairable). In addition, the Eighth had 3,111 bombers with repairable damage.[61] The Fifteenth Air Force reported 99 bomber losses, most incurred on non-POINTBLANK missions.[62] The German fighter force, too, suffered astronomical casualties, losing 511 pilots (21.7 percent of its force) and writing off 56.4 percent of its aircraft, its worst percentage loss of the war.[63] Aircraft the Luftwaffe could replace, but experienced pilots it could not. Luftwaffe fighter casualties, the vast majority incurred in daytime combat, reflected not only the intensity of the fighting but changes in American tactics and a surge in the number of American long-range escort fighters. By the end of March, USSTAF had taken a large step toward its goal of daylight air supremacy over Germany and Europe.

The operational confidence gained during Big Week, fueled by over-optimistic intelligence reports of damage inflicted, led Spaatz and his subordinates to change both bomber and fighter tactics. Between March 3 and March 9, the Eighth launched five major attacks, none with fewer than 500 heavy bombers, on Berlin. Spaatz reported to Arnold, "The operations during the past week had the major purpose of forcing the German fighter force into battle. Three attacks were made without any attempt at deception, the route followed on each attack being exactly the same."[64] More important than the direct routing of heavy bombers was the more aggressive employment of U.S. fighter forces.

Four developments contributed to this change:

1. The freeing of the U.S. fighters from the restrictions of close escort,
2. The arrival of large numbers of U.S. long-range fighter aircraft,
3. The development of the relay fighter escort system, and
4. The increased strafing of German ground targets by U.S. fighter aircraft.

Upon their arrival and throughout the first three months of 1944, Spaatz and Doolittle had insisted that the Eighth go after the Luftwaffe at every opportunity. Maj. Gen. William Kepner, head of VIII Fighter Command, said in July 1944, "The minute Spaatz and Doolittle came here they directed that I take such steps as I felt necessary to lick this German Air Force. If it meant getting out and scouring the skies, even . . . thinning down the escort, that would be okay with them."[65]

On January 21, in one of his first meetings with the Eighth's subordinate leaders, Doolittle announced the new theme,[66] which he based on his experience in the Mediterranean.[67] He emphasized that although "the role of protecting the bombardment formation should not be minimized," fighters "should be encouraged to meet the enemy and destroy him rather than be content to keep him away."[68] Spaatz agreed with this view. A year earlier in North Africa, when he had also confronted a situation of air parity or slight inferiority, Spaatz had highlighted certain principles on air employment. His third principle addressed close escort of bombers: "*Do not give close support to Heavy Bombers* [emphasis added]. This was not followed in early operations, causing heavy losses in fighter units, particularly of P-38's."[69] Upon his return to Washington, in February 1944, AAF Chief of Staff Maj. Gen. Barney Giles reported the tactical changes to the Air Staff, noting that Doolittle had instructed his fighters "to attack enemy fighter formations even though such formations are not pressing attacks on bomber formations."[70] Doolittle's order freed the long-range escort fighters from the restrictions of close escort heretofore applied. Before that time, standard procedure had tied U.S. fighters to bomber formations, which they were forbidden to desert to pursue German fighters.[71]

Prewar and early wartime field manuals had reinforced the use of close escort. FM 1-5, "Employment of Aviation of the Army," in both its April 1940 and January 1943 incarnations, stated,

> A pursuit force may be employed to furnish close or immediate protection for a particular formation engaged in an important air operation. The only method by which pursuit forces are able to provide close protection for aircraft in flight is by accompanying those aircraft and by engaging any and all enemy aircraft which threaten the security of the formation.[72]

Here the use of the word "engaging" rather than "attacking" seems to imply surrender of the initiative to the enemy's fighters. The manuals went on to state that the need for close support depended on the effectiveness of the enemy fighter forces and was required when the defensive fire power of the escorted aircraft was inadequate. Somewhat ambiguously the manuals noted, "All aircraft in flight possess a measure of inherent security, and most aircraft possess considerable defensive power."[73] That clause limited provision of close escort to essential missions against developed air defenses. Even so, if a plane had sufficient defensive firepower, as the B-17 and B-24 in theory did, it might not ever need escort (which, until January 1944, it could not get on deep-penetration raids in any case).

AAF Field Manual 1-15, "Tactics and Technique of Air Fighting," April 10, 1942, made the task of close escorts clear: "Their mission precludes their seeking to impose combat on other forces except as necessary to carry out their defensive role."[74] When it addressed recommended tactics for escorts, the manual stressed their defensive nature: "Forces in special support counterattack immediately when hostile fighters make direct attacks on the defended formation. When possible, withdrawal from combat will be made when a threat against the defended formation has been removed."[75] At no time did either FM 1-5 or FM 1-15 refer to any type of escort other than close escort. Medium and loose escort, both employed by the Twelfth Air Force in the Mediterranean, apparently became useful to the AAF through combat experience. It would seem that Eaker and his fighter commander, Maj. Gen. Frank O'D. Hunter, hampered by insufficient numbers of escorts, poorly trained groups, and inadequate range for the fighters they did possess, had erred chiefly in following "the book" too closely. As FM 1-15 acknowledged, "Distance from the supported force will be influenced by relative speeds, escort strength, and visibility conditions."[76] Spaatz, Doolittle, and Kepner had the "escort strength" their predecessors lacked, and could thus place their fighters in loose escort. The doctrine of ultimate pursuit introduced by Spaatz and Doolittle, however, stood official doctrine on its head. It turned the escorts into aggressors, which attacked rather than counterattacked and did not withdraw from combat but pursued from the tops of the clouds to the tops of the trees.

By the end of January, the Eighth abandoned pure close escort, substituting a system based on the doctrine of "ultimate pursuit," which allowed U.S. fighters to follow the enemy, wherever he might be, until they destroyed him in the air or on the ground.[77] By the end of February, the escorting fighter groups spread out in formations twenty-five to thirty miles wide and frequently sent a squadron or more directly ahead to sweep the routes in front of bomber formations.[78] If no enemy aircraft attacked the bombers or hovered nearby, two-thirds of the fighters were permitted to search both flanks and above and below the bombers for enemy fighters. As a result, combat took place at all altitudes, and small formations of U.S. fighters returned from Germany at a low level, which encouraged them to shoot up targets of opportunity en route.[79] Luftwaffe Maj. Gen. Adolph Galland, commander of the German day-fighter force, recorded the effect of the new U.S. tactics in his postwar memoirs: American fighters

> were no longer glued to the slow-moving bomber formation, but took action into their own hands. Wherever our fighters appeared, the Americans hurled themselves at them. They went over to low-level attacks on our airfields. Nowhere were we safe from them, and we had to skulk on our own bases. During take-off, assembling, climb and approach to the bombers, when we were in contact with them, on our way back, during landing, and even after that the American fighters attacked with overwhelming superiority.[80]

Coincident with the arrival of Spaatz and Doolittle, large numbers of long-range P-38 and P-51 fighter aircraft appeared in the theater, while the P-47, already present in large numbers, increased its escort range by one hundred miles. (See Maps 9 and 10 and Table 4, which illustrate increases in range and number of escort fighters.)

These increases in numbers and range helped the Americans refine their escort technique. The escort ranges represented only a fraction of the fighters' rated capabilities. But several factors—the necessity to provide for an emergency combat reserve for each plane; the fuel consumed by delays in takeoffs, landings, and forming up; and less than optimum weather conditions—combined to limit their range to, at best, three-eighths of their rated maximum. Escort imposed further range restrictions because of the speed difference between the bombers and their "little friends."

On penetration, the bombers, usually carrying their full wartime emergency weight overload, averaged 150 mph (indicated air speed). The fighters, throttled back for optimum gas consumption, averaged at least 100 mph (indicated air speed) faster. For example, P-47s that were not flying escort duty conducted sweeps well beyond Berlin—far beyond their escort range. To maintain stations with the bombers, the fighters had to weave back and forth, so that side-to-side mileage had to be subtracted from their straight-line range.

To maximize the amount of escort available to medium- and long-range missions, the Eighth Air Force developed a relay escort system. In this system, a single fighter group, instead of providing escort to a single bomber formation all the way to and from a target—an impossibility given its range—would fly straight to a prearranged rendezvous point, meet the formation, escort it 150 to 200 miles to another rendezvous point, hand it over to a second fighter group, and then fly home.[81]

This system minimized the fuel consumed in weaving back and forth, extended the fighters' range, and provided escort all the way to and from the target. As the deep-penetration raids flown in 1943 had shown, if bombers did not have escort all the way, the Luftwaffe would simply wait until they had flown beyond their escort and then attack. At first glance, this system had the apparent disadvantage of using several times more fighters than necessary for a given mission, but this was not the case. The relay system maximized escort throughout the entire mission. During the first half of 1944, before it had converted all but one (the 56th Fighter Group) of its fighter groups to P-51s, the Eighth employed three types of fighter aircraft, each with a different range. The relay system allowed the P-47s to escort the shallow-penetration leg of the mission, the P-38s to escort the medium-penetration section of the mission, and the P-51s to provide deep-penetration and target support.[82] This system proved of special value in February and March when the shorter range P-47s formed the bulk of available escort aircraft. Overlapping the P-47, P-38, and P-51 relays allowed the long-range fighter groups to double the bombers' protection for a few min-

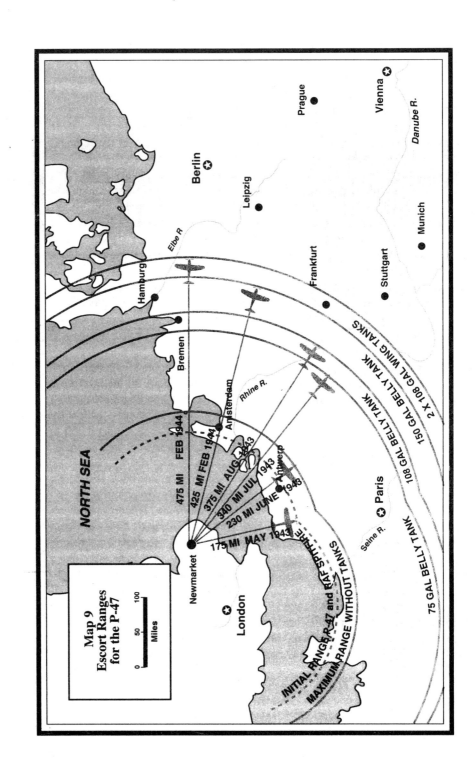

Map 9
Escort Ranges for the P-47

Miles
0   50   100

NORTH SEA

London

Newmarket

175 MI MAY 1943
230 MI JUNE 1943
340 MI JUL 1943
375 MI AUG 1943
425 MI FEB 1944
475 MI FEB 1944

INITIAL RANGE P-47 and RAF SPITFIRE
MAXIMUM RANGE WITHOUT TANKS

Paris

Seine R.

Antwerp

Amsterdam

Rhine R.

Bremen

Hamburg

Elbe R.

Frankfurt

Stuttgart

Munich

Leipzig

Berlin

Prague

Vienna

Danube R.

75 GAL BELLY TANK
108 GAL BELLY TANK
150 GAL BELLY TANK
2 X 108 GAL WING TANKS

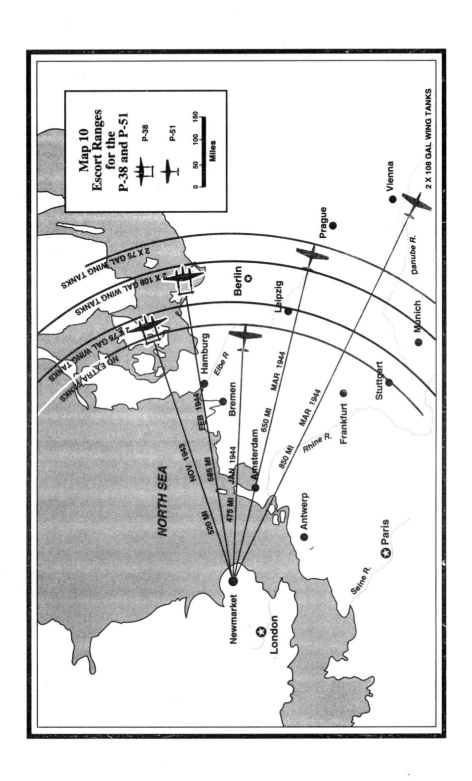

Map 10
Escort Ranges
for the
P-38 and P-51

P-38
P-51

Miles
0   50   100   150

2 X 108 GAL WING TANKS

2 X 75 GAL WING TANKS
2 X 108 GAL WING TANKS
2 X 75 GAL WING TANKS
NO EXTRA TANKS

NORTH SEA

Newmarket

London

Antwerp

Paris

Seine R.

NOV 1943   520 MI
585 MI
FEB 1944
JAN 1944   475 MI
Amsterdam
650 MI   MAR 1944
850 MI   MAR 1944
Rhine R.

Frankfurt

Stuttgart

Munich

Bremen
Elbe R.
Hamburg

Berlin

Leipzig

Prague

Vienna

Danube R.

utes or enabled one group to leave the bombers five minutes early, drop down to low altitude, and sweep all parts of western, central, and southern Germany.[83]

Until the end of March 1944, the RAF Spitfire squadrons of Leigh-Mallory's AEAF supplemented the fighters of the U.S. Eighth and Ninth Air Forces by providing the escort for initial penetration and final withdrawal legs of the heavy-bomber missions. The RAF's contribution allowed the Americans to extend the range of their own escort fighters during the early months of 1944 and to provide fighter cover all the way to the target. By the end of March, however, the increase in the number of available American long-range escorts, the decline in the efficiency of the Luftwaffe fighter force, and the Germans' tactic of concentrating their fighter defenses over Germany itself permitted the Americans to dispense with the RAF's assistance.[84] Leigh-Mallory, who had had to delay his ground support training programs for both his U.S. Ninth Air Force and British 2d Tactical Air Force while their fighters supported the Eighth's deep-penetration missions, was probably overjoyed to regain full use of some of his force.

In any case, German ground controllers almost never managed to get all of the fighters available to them massed for a single blow, thus the escort seldom had to deal with overwhelming numbers of attackers. The Germans depended on carefully timed assaults by intact formations to knock down the heavy bombers.

Table 4
**Eighth and Ninth Air Force Fighter Escort Missions
January–April 1944**

Month	P-38	P-47	P-51
January	597	4,011	295
February	1,038	7,032	1,030
March	1,468	8,717	2,397
April*	1,962	6,483	3,281

*April's figures, unlike those for January, February, and March, do not include hundreds of missions flown by Ninth Air Force P-47 fighter groups.

Compiled from Freeman, *Mighty Eighth War Diary.*

**Maj. Gen. Adolph Galland,
Commanding General,
Luftwaffe Day Fighter
Forces.**

Fighters attacking in formation could mass their firepower, downing several aircraft on each pass. A relatively few escorts, even if they shot down no enemy fighters, could disrupt German formations and timing, causing them to lose much of their effectiveness. Even in the worst case, the Germans would have time for only one or two passes against the B-17s and B-24s before some of the escorts arrived to disrupt them. It took a brave, determined, and skilled pilot to make a successful attack on a heavy-bomber formation alone.

The relay system led directly to the increased strafing of German ground targets by U.S. fighters. Sometime in February, individual fighter pilots on their own began to fly close to the ground on return relay flights and to strafe German aircraft, facilities, and other targets of opportunity.[85] To encourage this practice and to invite the pilots to focus on Luftwaffe fields and facilities, the Eighth began to record official "kills" for planes destroyed on the ground. Finally, by March all fighters were routinely ordered to descend to low altitude and conduct fighter sweeps on their return trips.[86]

Although given a unique twist by its application to the relay system, the practice of pursuit aircraft strafing ground targets while returning from other missions had a certain measure of doctrinal approval. In April 1940, FM 1-5 had ruled:

> The attack of surface objectives by pursuit may be combined with the performance of other missions of a higher priority. Opportunities may be presented

for the attack of appropriate targets by pursuit forces returning from missions without having expended all their ammunition. In such cases the attack of appropriate surface objectives as a part of a specific mission or as a general procedure is normal.[87]

This clause in the FM 1-5 of April 1940 probably reflected U.S. analysis of the aggressive and freewheeling tactics employed by the German Condor Legion in Spain and by the Luftwaffe in the Polish campaign of 1939, when aircraft apparently used every opportunity to strafe columns of retreating, disorganized enemy military personnel and civilian refugees, neither of whom presented a significant antiaircraft threat. FM 1-5 of January 1943 rescinded the entire clause following U.S. experience in Tunisia and British experience in the Western Desert. Unlike the Poles and the French, Germans both at and behind the front in North Africa had the ability to put up deadly amounts of light anti-aircraft fire. Such volumes of fire made it extremely costly for fighters to attack appropriate ground targets, such as personnel and light vehicles. The manual forbade the use of fighter aircraft for ground attack missions unless (1) no other aircraft were available, (2) fighters were not needed to gain or maintain air superiority, and (3) fighter aviation did not need to be conserved for future employment in its normal role.[88] The writers of the January 1943 FM 1-5 apparently envisaged fighter ground attack as a tactic of attrition used only in extraordinary circumstances.

Reich Marshal Hermann Goering, Luftwaffe Commander in Chief, with German pilots.

In effect, Doolittle, Spaatz, and Kepner created a system that simultaneously employed fighters primarily as escorts and secondarily as attackers of counterair targets on the ground. Because the Germans soon supplied their airfields with liberal amounts of light flak, ground strafing became a battle of attrition on both sides. By then, however, the Eighth Air Force had established air superiority over Germany and could afford some losses. Given Spaatz's and Doolittle's counterair experiences in North Africa, Sicily, and Italy, the doctrinal underpinnings of their tactics, although interesting, appear to have had no discernible effect on the development of their relay/ground attack system.

In the relay system, as elsewhere, ULTRA and other signal intelligence greatly aided the U.S. fighters' efforts. In March ULTRA intercepts revealed the damage done by the low-level fighter attacks. On March 8, a Luftwaffe intercept stated, "The enemy has recognized our own tactics of taking off and getting away from the airfield with all serviceable aircraft before attacks on our ground organization. In the event he has recently put aside a part of the escorting force to attack these aircraft and has achieved successes in this connection."[89] Sixteen days later, as Allied fighter pressure increased, the command organization of the Luftwaffe's home fighter forces reported repeated attacks on aircraft landing at bases in the home war zone. The report further noted American tactics: "They imitate the landing procedures of German fighters or effect surprise by approaching the airfield in fast and level flight. The difficulty of distinguishing friend from foe often makes it impossible for flak artillery to fire on them."[90] With such direct encouragement, the Eighth had decided by April to launch pure fighter sweeps in weather unsuitable for bombers to keep up the pressure over western and central Germany. In addition to ground attack sweeps, the Americans began to launch "free sweeps" toward German fighters in suspected concentration areas in order to disperse them before they could mount attacks on the U.S. bombers.[91]

Tactical signal intercepts gave further impetus to the new sweep tactics. RAF "Y" Service, a tactical intercept organization, cooperated fully with the Eighth. Upon detecting through in-the-clear transmissions of German ground controllers large concentrations of German fighters assembling to attack the bombers, "Y" Service vectored groups out on sweeps into the German formations.[92] By the end of March, although the Germans had ceased to use radio telephones, British intelligence had worked out new methods of timing P-51 sweeps. The British intelligence official history claims that these new methods "contributed a good deal to the Eighth Air Force's success in its policy of deliberately seeking out German fighters and forcing them to accept combat."[93]

Attacking German ground targets took a heavy toll of American fighter pilots, who suffered five times more casualties in strafing than in air-to-air combat.[94] By the end of March, Spaatz reported that USSTAF was 500 fighter pilots short of its goal of 2 pilots per plane[95] to prevent individual pilots from being pushed to the breaking point.

The increasing intensity of the U.S. daylight heavy-bomber offensive and the new tactics of the fighter escorts posed an insoluble problem to the Luftwaffe's day-fighter forces. These forces already labored under the self-imposed handicaps of faulty organization and incompetent higher leadership. From October 1943 through March 1944, Goering, Commander in Chief of the Luftwaffe, attempted to cope with the deteriorating air situation by strictly enforcing a policy of ignoring the fighter escort and attacking the heavy bombers.[96] Maj. Gen. Adolph Galland, who commanded the Luftwaffe day-fighter force, protested vociferously against this directive, claiming that it unnecessarily handcuffed his pilots. German pilots under orders to avoid American fighters were put on the defensive and robbed of the aggressiveness needed for successful fighter-to-fighter combat.[97]

Other German wartime critics advocated attacking the escorts at the earliest possible point to force them to jettison their drop tanks and reduce their range.[98] This apparently simple stratagem demonstrated the depth of the German defensive problem. The Luftwaffe did not base substantial numbers of fighters in France for three reasons: they would be vulnerable to harassing raids from medium bombers and fighter-bombers, their bases would require additional manpower for heavy antiaircraft defenses and for ground defense against partisans, and their supply dumps would stretch logistical links as well as offer targets to air raids. To catch incoming U.S. fighters, German fighters would have to scramble from western Germany or eastern France. Provided enough of them avoided and survived the RAF fighter sweeps vectored precisely by radar and "Y" Service, and provided they distinguished American from hunting British groups, the German fighters would then have to compel all the Americans to strip (jettison) their tanks. Otherwise an American group would leave behind one squadron to deal with the few penetrating Germans and continue onward. Of course, all Luftwaffe fighter aircraft committed to this operation would be unavailable to attack the heavy bombers over Germany.

If the Luftwaffe had waited until the RAF was out of range to begin its attack on the U.S. fighters, much of the advantage of forcing the stripping of tanks would have evaporated. In any case, the Eighth's fighter groups actively sought combat with the Luftwaffe, whether flying to or departing escort duty. It is difficult to see what the tactic of forcing the Eighth's fighters to jettison early would have accomplished other than to play directly into Spaatz's and Doolittle's hands by provoking air battles not only within range of all AAF fighters but within the reach of short-range RAF fighters as well. If the Luftwaffe wished to begin the battle over France instead of deep over the Reich, all the better. Given the growing technical inferiority of German aircraft, the relative lack of training and experience of German fighter pilots, and the superior numbers of Allied fighter aircraft, such a policy could have only one result: even greater disaster for the Luftwaffe.

To some extent the charges against Goering were typical of the postwar scapegoating indulged in by German generals. Goering and Hitler presented obvious, large, and defenseless targets. After March 1944, when the Luftwaffe's situation had worsened, Goering authorized one fighter group from each fighter division to attack and divert American escorts.[99] Granting permission for diversionary operations instead of all-out attacks on American fighters did not, of course, return the initiative to the German fighter pilots, but it showed more flexibility on Goering's part than his subordinates tended to attribute to him. Also at the end of March, Goering responded to the pleas of his subordinates by consolidating the three defensive air commands facing the American bombers. He gave operational control of three of the most important of the Reich's western air defenses to the Luftwaffe's *I Fighter Corps*.[100] Before then the *I Fighter Corps*, (responsible for northern air defense sectors, coastal areas devoted to naval operations, the Berlin area, and industrial districts of the Rhineland, Westphalia, and central Germany), the *7th Fighter Division* (responsible for the defense of southern Germany, especially the industrial areas of Frankfurt-am-Main, Mannheim, Stuttgart, Nuremberg, Munich, and Augsburg), and *Fighter Command Ostmark*, (charged with defending vital Austrian targets such as Vienna, Wiener-Neustadt, Steyr, and Linz) had operated semiautonomously. Each had forces inadequate to defend its sector, but there was no central operational control mechanism capable of forcing the commands to cooperate with each other. This was an important factor in the Luftwaffe's inability to concentrate all of its defensive strength on the attacking U.S. forces. The shortage of fighters to apply against its opponent was as much a function of the Luftwaffe's own inefficiency as it was of the heavy losses inflicted by the Americans.

Ever larger numbers of American long-range escorts succeeded in wrecking the combined interceptor tactics the Germans had developed to combat deep-bomber penetrations. Before February 1944, the Germans almost always waited to attack until the escort had left the bombers to return home, which happened on any deep-penetration raid in 1943. Waiting to attack until the escort left allowed for basing deep within Germany, and for defensive aircraft to be concentrated after the bombers had committed to a specific route and probable destination. Fighters could concentrate without being attacked. During the Schweinfurt missions and later, German twin-engine fighters had stayed beyond range of the bombers' defensive armament and shelled them with 210mm rockets, adapted from the German rocket mortar and known by the ground troops as the "screaming meemie." When the bombers loosened their positions to avoid rocket explosions, the single-engine fighters would attack the attenuated formation. In the face of vigorous escorts this tactic did not work. Not only were concentration areas liable to attack, so were home airfields. The performance of the American single-engine fighter escorts so outclassed that of the twin-engine German heavy fighters as to make the latter virtually helpless. If the Germans wished to employ their heavy fighters at all, their light fighters had to escort the twin-engine fighters, much to the detriment of German morale and firepower

Men of the 91st Bomb Group being briefed prior to a raid.

directed against the bombers. By the end of March, the twin-engine fighters seldom arose to defend against American daylight raids.[101]

The increasing numbers of American escorts forced the Luftwaffe to modify
its single-engine fighter tactics. As early as mid-December 1943, map exercises
at *I Fighter Corps* Headquarters had demonstrated that commitment of individual single-engine fighter groups alone had little chance of success. A single
group would become too involved in fighter-to-fighter combat with the escorts.
On December 29, 1943, *I Fighter Corps* ordered future attacks on Allied heavy-
bomber formations to employ a wing formation of at least three closely aligned
groups to ensure that at least one group of fighters penetrated to the bomber
stream.[102] These larger formations required longer time to marshal, offered targets that were easier for Allied air controllers to identify, and proved difficult for
increasingly inexperienced German fighter pilots.

Throughout March and for the rest of the air war against Germany, U.S.
fighter escorts so efficiently accompanied their bombers that large U.S. losses
resulted only when navigational or timing errors by either bombers or fighters
caused them to miss their rendezvous, or when a small contingent of the escorts
was overwhelmed by large numbers of enemy fighters, which then broke
through to attack the bombers.[103] The March 6, 1944, Eighth Air Force mission
to Berlin, which will be discussed in detail below, illustrates many of the tactical
and operational changes involved in the increased use of escort fighters.

The harsh weather of the winter of 1943–1944 continued unabated in March.

It allowed only two days of visual bombing over Germany—on March 8, when the Eighth lost 37 of 623 bombers dispatched against the Erkner Ball Bearing Works in Berlin and on March 18, when it lost 43 of 738 bombers that attacked airfields and aircraft assembly plants in central and southern Germany. The 80 bombers lost in those two days made them, aside from the 69 of 730 lost in the March 6 mission on Berlin, the worst two days of the month. A lack of visual bombing opportunities did not prevent the Eighth from launching full-scale efforts of 400 or more heavy bombers on fifteen of the month's days.

The Eighth had attempted to launch two large missions against Berlin on March 3 and 4. Bad weather had stopped both in their tracks, but not before fighters, which missed the recall, appeared over Berlin on March 3 and a lone wing of B-17s (the 13th Combat Wing from Curtis LeMay's 3d Bombardment Division), became the first of the Eighth's bombers to hit the German capital by pushing through heavy clouds on March 4. These efforts alerted the Germans to the Eighth's intentions.

On March 6, a total of 730 American bombers, taking three hours to assemble and climb to bombing altitude (24,000 to 27,000 feet), formed up over England and headed due east to Berlin. German radar spotted them and their RAF Spitfire escort as soon as they left their bases and tracked them for the entire mission. American escort consisted of 801 fighters (thirteen Eighth Air Force and four Ninth Air Force groups). Eleven groups of P-47s (615 aircraft) provided the second leg of the penetration escort. Three groups of P-38s (86 aircraft), one of which turned back because of an excessive number of engine failures, supplied medium-range escort, and four groups of P-51s (100 aircraft) flew deep escort. Three groups of the P-47s flew two missions, providing return escort on their second flight.[104] For the far reaches of the trip the bombers had none too many escorts.

Seventy miles east of the Dutch-German border, at the practical P-47 range limit, the B-17s of the 3d Bombardment Division grouped in a sixty-mile-long column of combat wing pairs and ran smack into the middle of a concentration of perhaps 150 German single-engine fighters. The small number of P-38s operationally available for that leg of the relay left the bombers underescorted. German ground controllers, having detected an escort gap in the center of the column, sent small forces to the head and tail of the U.S. force to distract and pin the escort, and then threw the remaining 100 fighters at the momentarily unprotected center. In less than thirty minutes the aggressive German attack downed perhaps twenty bombers of the 3d Bombardment Division.

The attack singled out the 100th Bombardment Group. In fierce air combat at 24,000 feet and at 43 degrees below zero the group took a fearful beating. As it had so often before and would again, the sky over Germany filled with the carnage of air battle. Bf 109s and FW 190s dived and twisted through the bombers' formation, whose gunners tried futilely to keep them at bay. At one point an attacking Bf 109 dived through the formation, apparently enveloped in flames.

Three gunners on three different bombers claimed and were awarded a sure kill.* After diving below the clouds, the German pilot landed his slightly injured aircraft at his home field.

As the fight continued, the American pilots, sweating profusely despite the cold, in leather clothes and restrictive oxygen masks, dared not try any but the slightest wobble of evasive action for fear of crashing into each other in formation. Once a bomber spouted smoke or flames and, laboring, fell back from the safety of the formation, the fighters finished it off like predators stalking a herd.

The crew of a fatally injured bomber had little time to escape before hundreds of gallons of fuel or six thousand pounds of bombs exploded. If the bomber began to spin, the centrifugal force it generated trapped the crew within it. Many airmen were crushed and broken by the tail surfaces of their own bombers when the slipstream grabbed them as they exited and brutally pushed them to the rear. Anyone who bailed out started a five-mile descent to ground by falling through other bomber formations, perhaps meeting grisly death on props and leading wing edges. Soon the sky filled with falling men, loose hatch covers, ejected shell casings, and spinning pieces of debris. Parachutes—white U.S. and brown German, either of which could be collapsed by the close passage of aircraft—dotted the sky.

The Germans did not have things all their own way. When the slow twin-engine Bf 110s and Me 210s, made even clumsier by the large racks and rockets carried under their wings, attempted to close within rocket range of U.S. bombers, American escorts sliced through their formations killing or scattering the *Zerstörers* (destroyers), leaving the survivors shaken. On March 6, *Zerstörergeschwader Horst Wessel* scrambled nine aircraft: two aborted because of mechanical problems, one was damaged, five were lost in air-to-air combat (with one pilot killed and four wounded), and the unit's commander landed his damaged plane at a different airfield.[105] When the single-engine FW 190s and Bf 109s formed up to assault the bombardment divisions, squadrons of P-51s

---

* The matter of actual kills versus claims by Eighth Air Force bomber gunners was a matter of controversy. The number claimed always exceeded the number actually lost by the Germans by a factor of at least eight or nine to one. In part, these inflated claims resulted from the inability of any one gunner to be sure that his bullets and not someone else's accounted for a particular plane. The natural confusion of the battle compounded the inability of the participants to assess enemy casualties correctly and accurately. Nor did the Eighth have a remotely foolproof method of debriefing the returning crews to eliminate multiple counting. For morale and propaganda purposes the AAF could not admit that men pointing sticks would have been hardly less effective than .50 caliber machine guns in killing German fighters. However, the heavily armed bombers certainly had enough deterrent firepower to force the Luftwaffe pilots to launch disciplined, coordinated attacks from a respectful distance, which cut down by an unknown, but large, factor the total number of attacks delivered and losses inflicted during any one raid. In this book, the author used as a rule-of-thumb U.S. fighter claims, not bomber claims, to approximate actual enemy losses. Any overcount in fighter claims, possibly one or two in ten, would be cancelled out by the actual losses inflicted by the bomber gunners. For an official discussion of this problem, see Craven and Cate, *Torch to Pointblank*, pp. 221–224.

struck them first, disrupting their attack formations and pursuing them as they sought, as ordered, to avoid the escort and close with the bombers.

As the fighters dueled, a P-51 stuck on the tail of an FW 190, shredding it with bullets from its six .50-caliber machine guns. The German pilot huddled behind the armor in his cockpit, finally abandoning his ruined aircraft. Back in England, review of P-51 gun cameras clearly showed the German leaving his plane, which blew up a few moments later. The American pilot gained a kill and another small brightly painted swastika on the side of his plane. Eighth Air Force public relations officers passed the film to the press, which recorded for the American home front the death of another of the Nazi's vaunted fighter planes.

The 2d Bombardment Division, just behind the 3d, saw only two German fighters in the same defensive area. Over Berlin the Germans concentrated seventy-five twin-engine day and night fighters, escorted by about twenty-five single-engine fighters. They attacked the leading elements of the 1st Bombardment Division, the first division over the city, and attempted to saturate the defending escort. They were the only heavy opposition and they ceased as the 1st left the target area.

One of the bombers lost over Berlin that day carried to earth with it the Commander of the 4th Combat Wing, Brig. Gen. Russ Wilson. In all, enemy fighters accounted for 41 bombers, 4 more landed in Sweden, and the remaining 24 fell victim to antiaircraft fire or accidents. Six more heavy bombers had sustained enough damage to be not repairable. The totals amounted to 75 heavy bombers lost or not repairable, 347 heavy bombers damaged, and 11 escort fighters lost. Nor had the bombing been accurate; most of the 1,648 tons of bombs and 2,448,000 propaganda leaflets fell on areas other than their primary targets, the industrial suburbs. USSTAF admitted, "Generally poor results were obtained in Berlin area."[106] Spaatz reported to Arnold that the Eighth had hit none of its primary targets.[107] Perhaps its crews were tired or rattled by their losses. An Allied intelligence report aptly summed up the day: "Thus, on this occasion, due no doubt to skillful handling, a good appreciation of our intentions, and good flying weather, the Luftwaffe gave few of the expected indications of rigor mortis."[108] On the return trip American fighters claimed 1 German aircraft destroyed and 12 damaged on the ground.[109] Ten hours after takeoff the bombers landed back in England.

A comparison of this raid with the Schweinfurt raids of August 17, 1943, and October 14, 1943, reveals how the air war had changed. One indication of the intensity of bomber versus fighter combat is the number of fighters claimed by bomber gunners. The numbers claimed had no relation whatever to actual German losses, but they did indicate the frequency of attack, the activity of the gunners, and the ferocity and duration of the attack perceived by the bomber crews. During the August 17, 1943, Regensburg-Schweinfurt mission (Eighth Air Force Mission no. 84) 346 bombers lost 60 of their own and claimed 288 German fighters destroyed, 37 probably destroyed, and 99 damaged.[110] In fact,

The Eighth Air Force Unleashed. American daylight strikes on Hitler's Europe were unrelenting in the months before the Normandy invasion. *Clockwise from above*: **B-17s of the 381st Bomb Group run up for a mission.** *Top to bottom*, **the P-38 Lightning, the P-51 Mustang, and the P-47 Thunderbolt were the three principal escort types on which U.S. bombers depended. German flak** *(below)* **acquires the altitude of a bomber formation over Kassel, Germany. Each burst scattered some 1,400 metal fragments, any of which could cripple a bomber. A pair of B-17s** *(opposite, below)* **maneuver with H2X radar domes fully deployed. The H2X radar dome replaced the standard B-17 belly turret and was used to identify and bomb objectives through cloud cover. A gun camera registers the beating given a German flak tower** *(opposite, left, above)* **by an Eighth Air Force fighter in the low-level sweeps that ceaselessly harassed German defenders. Spotters** *(opposite, right, above)* **man the plotting table at the control center of the 65th Fighter Wing at Saffron-Walden, Essex, in England.**

The Germans lost 34 fighters shot down, 12 damaged beyond repair, and 25 damaged.[111] On October 14, 1943 (Eighth Air Force Mission no. 115), the 291 attacking American bombers again lost 60 of their own number and claimed 186 German fighters shot down, 27 probably destroyed, and 89 damaged.[112] The Luftwaffe actually lost 31 destroyed, 12 written off, and 34 damaged.[113] On March 6, the 730 American bombers lost 69 but claimed only half of the number of Germans as in the earlier two contests: 97 German fighters destroyed, 28 probably destroyed, and 60 damaged. A far larger force had suffered a 9.5 percent loss rate (half of that of the two earlier missions) and suffered far less contact with enemy fighters. Antiaircraft fire accounted for one-third of the bombers lost in the Berlin raid, a much higher percentage than in the Schweinfurt raids, that reveals the decline in German fighter effectiveness.

As to escort statistics for the three raids, in August 1943, VIII Fighter Command dispatched 240 short-range P-47s; they claimed nineteen kills, three probables, and four damaged. In October, 196 P-47s newly outfitted with small drop tanks, escorting their bombers as far as Aachen, claimed thirteen kills, one probable, and four damaged. In the Berlin raid, however, the P-47s, whose range had just reached its maximum in February 1944 with the employment of new, larger tanks, claimed thirty-six kills, seven probables, and twelve damaged. The P-38s, which had an ineffective day, claimed three kills and one damaged. The P-51s, which defended the bombers over the target and during deep stretches when desperate Luftwaffe pilots could no longer wait for them to depart and had to attack before they themselves ran out of fuel, claimed fourty-three destroyed, one probable, and twenty damaged. One hundred P-51s bore the brunt of the battle and, in losing only five of their number, achieved an 8-to-1 kill ratio.[114] The claims of the American fighters were many times more accurate than those of the bombers. Each American fighter came equipped with gun cameras, which verified their scores by actually picturing bullet strikes on German aircraft.

The war diary of the Luftwaffe *I Fighter Corps*, however, only acknowledged that eighteen of its fighters had been destroyed and thirty-nine had been more than 60 percent damaged. The *I Fighter Corps* claimed that ninety-five bombers and fifteen American fighters had been definitely destroyed and ten bombers probably destroyed.[115] Obviously, aircraft combat claims were subjective. The Germans had lost heavily enough that they offered no concentrated opposition over the return route, even though they had sufficient time to land, refuel, and rearm. Some of them managed to pick off several stragglers.[116]

Two subsequent raids on March 8 and 9 met less opposition, even though the weather on March 8 allowed visual bombing and, therefore, excellent conditions for Luftwaffe takeoffs, landings, and air-to-air interceptions. The Americans lost 37 bombers and 18 fighters, while their fighters claimed 79 destroyed, 8 probables, and 25 damaged, plus 8 destroyed, 4 probably destroyed, and 7 damaged on the ground.[117] In this attack, few twin-engine fighters presented themselves, presumably because they had suffered severely two days earlier. The March 9

Eighth Air Force heavy bombers hitting the outlying factory area of Berlin.

mission, conducted in complete cloud cover all the way to, over, and from Berlin, encountered only 15 interceptors. The Germans did not wish to expend their force in questionable takeoff and landing conditions. For the week, the Eighth wrote off 153 heavy bombers lost attacking Berlin, only 25 fewer than during Big Week.[118]

By the end of March 1944, the Eighth had written off 349 heavy bombers—23.3 percent of its force.[119] Ominously for the Germans, so heavily had the Eighth been reinforced that this figure represented a sortie loss rate of only 3.3 percent—a drop from both January and February.[120] The AAF official history claimed that "by April 1, 1944 the GAF was a defeated force."[121]

The events of April 1944, a black month for the Eighth, tend to refute that claim. The weather in April, as in March, proved poor. Nevertheless, the Eighth launched strikes of more than 400 heavy bombers on fifteen of the month's days, thirteen of the attacks on targets inside Germany;[122] nine of those strikes employed, for at least some of the groups involved, visual methods of sighting. The first raid of the month, on April 1, set the tone for the entire month—it was a fiasco. Of 440 heavy bombers dispatched, only 165 bombed targets, and some of those bombed the town of Schaffhausen in neutral Switzerland, angering the Swiss and causing both the AAF and the U.S. government a great deal of expense and embarrassment. Half of the force ran into heavy weather and turned back. The remainder scattered widely throughout southwestern Germany and bombed targets of opportunity; some bombed 120 miles south of their assigned objectives. Luckily, the weather played no favorites and prevented the Germans from taking full advantage of the Eighth's scattered formations—only 12 bombers failed to return. The Germans may also have chosen to conserve their fighter forces depleted in March's air battles.

On April 22, the Germans initiated a new tactic by infiltrating the bomber stream as it approached its bases to land and shooting down fourteen late-returnees as they tried to touch down in the dark. This tactic, fortunately not repeated, sent a chill throughout the Eighth, which feared that the Germans had finally begun to take advantage of the heavy bombers at their weakest moments —when they milled about, out of formation, in the air over their congested airfields waiting to land in the evening or to form up in the morning. These periods, sometimes hours long, were clearly visible to the Germans on their radar equipment.

On April 29, the Eighth lost sixty-three heavy bombers over one of the Reich's most heavily defended targets, Berlin. In this raid, as in others, the heaviest losses were taken by groups that failed to meet their escorts.[123] Brig. Gen. Orvil A. Anderson, the Eighth's operations officer, had an immediate first impression that the April 29 mission was "the poorest operation . . . I've seen during the year . . . I've been here." Calling the mission "poorly executed all the way through," Anderson said, "It can go down on the records as one of the dumbest ones we've done. From the point of execution it just didn't click— nothing clicked."[124] The last major raid of the month had proved more costly and just as poorly managed as the first.

The Eighth embarked on a more successful tack when it initiated the practice of flying fighter sweeps in weather unsuitable for bombers. On April 5 and 16, hundreds of fighters attacked airfields in western and central Germany. Spaatz, reporting to Arnold on previous sweeps, said, "Eighth Air Force fighters inaugurated a series of sweeps against airdromes, transportation, and Flak towers, which will be increased in scope and should prove very demoralizing to the Hun."[125] A week later, Spaatz instructed the AAF Public Relations Office in Washington:

> In order to destroy the Luftwaffe it is essential that emphasis be given to the destruction of planes on the ground as well as in the air and that our pilots be encouraged in strafing operations by official and public credit for their accomplishments. . . . Recommend that Public Relations policy in US be adjusted to support present need for emphasis on strafing.[126]

In an account of April 5, Spaatz emphasized to General Giles that properly conducted fighter sweeps inflicted real attrition on the Luftwaffe by destroying its aircraft on the ground and demoralizing personnel. Spaatz added,

> Inasmuch as *the pilots are briefed to shoot up any moving target within Germany*, [emphasis added] 750 or 1000 fighter aircraft roaming deep into

Germany is evidence to the German people of the GAF's weakness and no amount of Goebbels' propaganda can counteract this impression. It is my plan to keep this type of attack going.[127]

The rise in the number of claims of enemy aircraft damaged or destroyed on the ground by Eighth Air Force fighters amply illustrates the increasing use of the counterair sweep; from 1 plane in the last two weeks of January to 40 in February, to 113 in March and 712 in the first twelve days of April.[128] This tactic was not employed without cost. Combined with fighter attacks in support of preinvasion operations, it sent fighter losses up from 232 in March to 338 in April to 475 in May.[129] Many of the best of the Eighth's fighter pilots lost their lives or spent the rest of the war in prisoner-of-war (POW) camps because of the intense light antiaircraft fire they encountered. Although they were hated by their pilots, these missions increased Luftwaffe attrition.[130]

In April 1944, the Eighth Air Force wrote off as lost or not repairable 422 heavy bombers,[131] more than in any other month of the air war over Europe. This represented a loss of about 25 percent of the heavy bombers on hand in tactical units, an increase of 1.3 percent over March's figures.[132] Despite the addition of 6 new heavy bombardment groups,[133] which raised the Eighth to a total of 39 heavy bombardment groups and 1,872 heavy bombers, the sortie loss rate climbed to 3.6 percent from March's 3.3 percent.[134] The heavy-bomber losses of the Fifteenth Air Force jumped from 99 to 214,[135] many of those the result of POINTBLANK missions. German losses remained high, too. Some 447 Luftwaffe fighter pilots, 20 percent of the total force, would never fly combat again, nor would 43 percent of their fighter aircraft.[136] The Luftwaffe's home fighter command lost 38 percent of its pilots.[137] These figures had declined from the previous month, but the loss of trained pilots could never be made good.

Morale Problems

All the work of the fighters flying escort and conducting ground attacks did not prevent the loss of hundreds of U.S. heavy bombers to enemy fighters. In March, the morale among American heavy-bomber crews began to buckle, as thirty-seven crews chose internship on the Continent. In April, fifty-two crews, or one of every eight planes lost, chose to land and present themselves for internment in either Sweden (twenty planes) or Switzerland (thirty-two planes).[138] In contrast, from December 30, 1943, to February 29, 1944, only five crews had landed in neutral countries.[139] Most of the crews interned during April in Sweden had participated in exceptionally deep missions into Poland. They might have despaired of achieving a safe landing in far-away England and selected the easier course. That excuse seems questionable, however, in light of the fact that the Eighth's crews had bombed some of the same targets before, yet had chosen to return to their bases. Of course, some planes, many heavily damaged, may have survived to land on neutral territory because the Luftwaffe fighter force had lost its ability to pick off those that had fallen out of formation on their return flight. Despite these extenuating factors, too many crews voluntarily, for whatever reason, did not return to their bases.

Another symptom of poor morale was displayed by Eighth Air Force crews sent back to the United States on thirty days' leave at the end of their combat tours. In early April Arnold wrote to Spaatz: "Reports reaching me from trustworthy sources, as well as my own personal observations, lead to the conclusion that the behavior of returned combat personnel does not always reflect credit upon the AAF." Arnold concluded with the admonition, "Whatever the method, however, it is imperative that immediate and adequate measures be taken to improve the attitude, conduct, and military bearing of AAF personnel being returned to this country."[140]

The air crews were sunk in pessimism; they had worked and fought to exhaustion to send out a full effort almost every other day for weeks. Their reward, given the high loss rates, was apparently a far better than even chance of ending up killed in action or being taken prisoners of war in Germany rather than returning to the States. As overwork, exhaustion, and high losses bred depression, so did changes in the crew rotation policy initiated by Arnold and introduced by Spaatz and Doolittle. The heightened pace of bomber operations meant that a bomber crew, after three and one-half to four months of training, could complete a tour in as little as two months. The AAF could not afford such waste.

On January 30, Doolittle introduced a policy of retaining selected crew members after they had completed their twenty-five-mission tour, anticipating by almost two weeks a similar change in rotation policy throughout the AAF.[141] In mid-February, Doolittle explained to his commanders his reasons for doing so: (1) the AAF had completed its expansion program, it no longer needed experienced crews to be returned to the United States to form new units; (2) the coming cross-channel invasion meant as many as two missions a day, making a tour of twenty-five missions impractical; (3) greatly increased fighter support had lowered the loss rate, making it possible for more crews to complete their tour; and (4) increased experience raised the effectiveness of the force. Doolittle added a final exhortation:

> This Air Force is now approaching the most critical phase of the war with Germany. During the next few months it is mandatory that we secure complete air superiority over the German Air Force in this Theater. In order to accomplish this end in the time allotted, we must adopt every expedient to improve the effectiveness of the Air Force and to keep it at a high level of operational efficiency.[142]

In March, Doolittle sought to convince his combat crews that when they finished a tour they were not "through with the war."[143] He notified them that "hereafter relief of combat crew personnel from regular participation in operations will not take place upon completion of any specified number of sorties." He added, "Combat crews have also been informed that they are relieved from duty only to provide time for suitable rest and recuperation. At the end of this period, they are considered to be again available for combat assignment." To give the crews a goal to strive toward, Doolittle further ruled that combat crews would be *eligible* for relief after thirty sorties.[144] In practice, unit commanders routinely relieved crews after thirty missions, but the threat of indefinite assignment lingered to the detriment of morale.

On March 13, Spaatz and Doolittle saw for themselves how brittle morale had become when they visited the 100th Heavy Bombardment Group at Thorpe Abbotts. The 100th had lost fifteen bombers on the March 6 Berlin raid. During dinner in the officers' mess a drunken young second lieutenant swayed up to Doolittle, poked him in the chest, and announced, "You think we don't know what you're here for? Well, let me tell you we do. You're here to improve our morale and if there's anythin' goin' to ruin our morale it's havin' a bunch of generals around here tryin' to fix it." Spaatz was not amused.[145] The Air Surgeon, Maj. Gen. David N. W. Grant, visited England at the end of March and found Spaatz "disturbed over the effect on morale of the discontinuance of returning air crew members to the U.S. upon the completion of 25 missions."[146]

A British announcement at a regular RAF press conference on April 12, 1944, threatened to snap the Eighth's already taut mood. RAF spokesman Air Vice-Marshal Richard Peck, Portal's principal public information deputy, stated that Luftwaffe fighter strength had increased by 200 to 300 machines since November 1943, with the whole of the increase directed to the western air defenses of the Reich. This, he added, brought Germany's fighter defenses to their numerically strongest state of the war; only the weather had been responsible for the light opposition that U.S.-British bombers had met on some occasions. "The onslaught against the German Air Force on the ground and in the air has certainly succeeded in reducing the reinforcement of the enemy's air defenses to a point far below what we had planned," said Peck, but "it has not prevented some continued strengthening."[147] Naturally, the British papers headlined the news, which may have confirmed suspicions harbored by top AAF officers, such as Doolittle and Fred Anderson, that members of the British press had embarked on "an anti-American bombing effort."[148] Both had complained earlier that the British press seemed out to "belittle" the American effort, and they suspected a "sinister movement" to discredit the AAF.[149]

Spaatz, whose own intelligence estimates showed a 300-fighter decrease in the Luftwaffe since January, objected mightily to Peck's statements and insensitive timing. On the previous day, April 11, the Eighth had suffered its second worst casualty total of the war, losing sixty-four planes, including nine interned in Sweden. The 3d Bombardment Division sustained particularly high casualties because it had conducted an unescorted raid aimed at Poznan, well inside Poland. The Germans, free to employ their twin-engine fighters, handled it roughly. This, or the worsening weather over the primary target, had led the 3d to bomb Stettin and Rostock, targets far short of Poznan, and to return early.[150] The bombers may have unloaded on German targets because Eighth Air Force policy forbade the use of H2X bombing methods over occupied countries— reflecting the attitude that any collateral civilian casualties inflicted by relatively inaccurate bombing-through-clouds techniques ought at least to be German and that any bomb dropped on Germany would do some harm, no matter how infinitesimal, to the enemy war effort.

Spaatz conducted both a front-door and a back-door campaign to ameliorate the effects of the RAF statement. He and his staff at Park House that evening decided not to try to conduct a countercampaign in the British press.[151] They probably recognized that any such effort might backfire. Instead, Spaatz wrote a stinging letter to Portal but did not sign it or send it through official channels, which, of course, kept it out of official records. Spaatz gave a copy of the letter to U.S. Ambassador John G. Winant, a trusted friend. He informed Winant of the possible consequences of Peck's statement.[152] Winant, whose son, a heavy-bomber pilot, had been shot down over Germany in October 1943 (this event had been reported in the British press only two hours after it occurred),[153] lost no time in taking the letter to Churchill, who, with equal celerity, sent it unoffi-

Air Vice-Marshal Richard Peck, Air Chief Marshal Portal's principal RAF public information deputy, 1944.

Imperial War Museum

cially to Portal.[154] The method of transmission through the American ambassador and the Prime Minister underlined the seriousness of Spaatz's protest:

> The effects of statements of the kind made by the RAF spokesman on our bomber crews and fighter pilots could reach the point of being very serious morale problem. Such ill advised statements, not substantiated by facts, discrediting American effort, certainly are disastrous to British-American relationships.[155]

The next day, April 14, Portal, without disavowing Peck's statement, apologized:

> I am extremely sorry that any statement should have been made which could result in discouraging the crews engaged in the combined bomber offensive against Germany. I am still more sorry that anything should be said which could be interpreted as discrediting the efforts of the Allied Air forces, and particularly of the American 8th and 15th Air Forces, to destroy the German fighter force.[156]

A few days later Archibald Sinclair, the British Secretary of State for Air, replied abjectly to Winant:

> The Prime Minister has drawn my attention to a statement made by an officer of the Royal Air Force. . . . I was very distressed to hear from [Churchill] and from Portal [who had heard it from Spaatz] that this statement had made a most unfavorable impression on officers of the USAAF and that you were much concerned about the effect which it produced.[157]

These expressions of concern, however, could not wipe out the doubts created in the minds of the Eighth's flyers. Portal and Spaatz agreed to put their staffs to work on a statement documenting the reduction in German aircraft manufacturing capacity since November. Portal proposed to follow up that document with a press handout on the same subject and suggested that in the future the two headquarters should coordinate their statements.[158]

Spaatz agreed to these palliatives while attempting to reinforce them on his own. On April 17, he invited three high-powered American correspondents, Ed Beattie, Wes Gallagher, and Helen Kirkpatrick to lunch. He asked them to help counteract Peck's statement, telling them that he had no desire to "sell" anything to the people back home or to "boast" of USSTAF's accomplishments. Instead, he desired "that all crews be made aware of the overall effect of the work they are doing. The crews must be made to know and believe that these losses have been worthwhile." Later that evening he had dinner with Robert Sherwood, head of the London Office of the American Office of War Information, the U.S. government's official public relations and propaganda agency. The two agreed to ensure the accuracy of any information on bomb destruction released to the crews.[159]

A week after Peck issued his statement, Spaatz inspected the 355th Fighter Group at Duxford. He talked to the group commander, who had lost five planes that day, and learned, not surprisingly, that the group was "most skeptical as to the truth of information we have been giving them that Germany's fighter force is being knocked down." Next, Spaatz discussed the problem with the Commander of the 1st Bombardment Division, Brig. Gen. Robert B. Williams, "who said other group commanders have expressed their doubts . . . that the true story is being given to them."[160] Spaatz concluded that "our most important job just now is keeping up the morale of these boys who are doing the fighting, and only by convincing them with facts can we prove to them that the results obtained are worth the effort they are putting into the job."[161]

The next day, April 20, Spaatz showed Doolittle and a group commander from the 1st Bombardment Division advance copies of the joint AAF-RAF press release. They approved, but the group commander said that "it will be hard to make the crews believe anything just now—they're dubious of anything they read."[162] On April 22, USSTAF handed out a combined RAF-USSTAF press release, with no quantifiable effect. Two days later, the Eighth lost forty bombers in raids over central Germany, fourteen of which landed in Switzerland. Spaatz continued his inspections and other gestures, such as sending autographed bottles of scotch to new fighter aces. One can only speculate if these or any of his actions helped. No substantive evidence has yet turned up to prove that they did. At least Spaatz recognized the problem and did what he could to solve it. In the end, the noticeable drop in casualties in May did as much as anything to keep morale from breaking.

The Oil Plan Is Salvaged

At the end of March, Spaatz had informed both Portal and Eisenhower of his continued support for the oil plan, and during April, he managed to gain the partial acceptance of oil as a high-priority target. He had recognized as early as May 1942[163] that the bombing of the Romanian oil fields and refinery complex at Ploesti was the logical first step in his campaign and a prerequisite for the bombing of the synthetic oil plants.[164] The elimination of the 25 percent of German petroleum production derived from the Romanian fields would wipe out all reserves in the Axis oil network and make oil hydrogenation plants even more valuable targets. Spaatz, however, had difficulties with the British when it came to freeing the Fifteenth Air Force from its other responsibilities to neutralize Ploesti. The latest Combined Bomber Offensive directive pertaining to the Fifteenth, issued by Portal on February 17, limited its targets to "cities, transportation targets and other suitable objectives in the Balkans and in the Satellite countries of southeastern Europe whenever weather or tactical conditions prevent operations against 'POINTBLANK' objectives or in support of land operations in Italy."[165]

Morale visit: Maj. Gen. Lewis H. Brereton, Lt. Col. Sherman R. Beaty, General Dwight D. Eisenhower, and Col. Herbert B. Tatcher inspecting a Ninth Air Force medium bomber group, April 22, 1944.

As early as March 5, USSTAF had requested clearance from the Air Ministry for the Fifteenth Air Force to hit Ploesti,[166] which apparently was not forthcoming. On March 17, after the Fifteenth had informed Spaatz that the weather for the next few days would be favorable, he twice asked for permission to proceed with the bombing. In both instances Portal replied that such an attack did not fall within current directives; he stated that the Fifteenth should direct its activities toward Sofia, Bucharest, and Budapest. Spaatz then appealed to Eisenhower, who agreed with him, whereupon Spaatz met Portal once more and explained that he intended to appeal to Arnold as well. At this point Portal agreed not to object if the Combined Chiefs of Staff approved. The Air Staff in Washington told Spaatz that Arnold would raise the subject of Ploesti at the next CCS meeting in two hours' time.[167] Apparently this *démarche* to the CCS produced no results. Portal, after consulting with Churchill, ruled Ploesti off-limits on March 18. In any case, the weather closed in, ending the opportunity. In the meantime, ground operations in Italy consumed the energies of the Mediterranean Allied Air Force and the Fifteenth. The third Battle of Cassino, which began on March 15 and produced many casualties but little change in the front lines, ground to a halt by March 23. By then the MAAF had commenced Operation STRANGLE, an air campaign directed against Axis rail transportation in Italy. Unlike Zuckerman's transportation plan for OVERLORD, STRANGLE concentrated on all aspects of the transportation, system, not just marshaling yards and

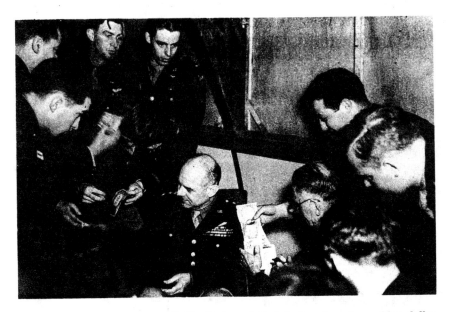

Morale visit: Lt. Gens. James H. Doolittle and Carl A. Spaatz autographing dollar bills at a dinner held to mark the completion of a bomber group's 100th mission, April 21, 1944.

repair facilities. It proved relatively successful but drew the Fifteenth away from Balkan and POINTBLANK targets.[168]

This diversion and a new bombing directive issued on March 22 by General Wilson, the Allied theater commander in the Mediterranean, provoked another outburst from Spaatz in London. Wilson, seeking to weaken Balkan support for the Nazis, whose south Russian front seemed hard hit by the Soviets' winter offensive, ordered the Fifteenth "to act immediately and in the fullest possible strength" against the marshaling yards in Bucharest, Ploesti, other suitable Romanian targets, and Sofia or other Bulgarian targets. Budapest, conversely, should not be bombed under any circumstances.[169] The Fifteenth replied that it would put a maximum effort over Bucharest as soon as conditions permitted, but Ploesti, as far as they knew, remained on the restricted list and would have to be cleared with USSTAF in London. Before Spaatz could send an answer, Portal instructed Wilson, " . . . have recently considered whether to add oil installations at Ploesti to list of bombing targets in Southeast Europe, but after discussing matters with Chiefs of Staff and His Majesty's Government, . . . have reached conclusion that this would not be advantageous at present time."[170]

After reading Wilson's orders to the Fifteenth and Portal's decision on targets, Spaatz wondered just who actually commanded the other half of his organization. To Arnold, Spaatz complained:

Too many agencies are giving orders to the 15th Air Force. . . . It has been my understanding that the 15th Air Force operates under my instructions, except when the tactical situation of the ground forces in Italy demands otherwise. I cannot accept responsibility for the direction of the 15th Air Force unless this situation is clarified.[171]

Spaatz objected to the bypassing of his authority by Wilson and Portal and to the bombing of political rather than economic targets in the Balkans. This stand placed Spaatz squarely in the U.S. military tradition, with its emphasis on the destruction of the enemy, as opposed to the British-European military tradition, which tended not to divorce war from politics and diplomacy.

Arnold assured Spaatz that he would take action with the CCS to unsnarl command arrangements.[172] He also reviewed his conception of USSTAF's place in the European war in a message to Portal and complained that the Fifteenth Air Force appeared to have been directed to help the battle in Italy rather than to support USSTAF's priorities. Arnold added,

Over and above clarifying operational channels we are concerned that undue diversion from the primary mission of the Fifteenth US Strategic Air Force may result. Although we recognize that there are many attractive targets in the Balkans we desire that the higher priority of POINTBLANK targets in possible weather conditions be observed.[173]

Arnold followed up that message with a protest to Field Marshal John Dill, head of the British Military Delegation in Washington. Arnold expressed his, Marshall's, and King's concern about the bypassing of Spaatz.[174] Portal replied on March 25, before he attended the transportation versus oil plan conference that day. He stated that he regretted any difficulties regarding command channels, citing his objections at the Cairo Conference to the formation of USSTAF. At no time had he meant to give strategic direction to the Fifteenth through Wilson rather than Spaatz. He would correct the circumstances that led Spaatz to think otherwise. As for using the Fifteenth in the Balkans, Portal responded, "In my opinion and in that of the other British Chiefs of Staff, the situation in Rumania and Bulgaria now ranks as a strategic emergency though it is the Germans and not we who are threatened."[175] He therefore asked Arnold to agree to authorize "a few heavy attacks on Balkan targets." Bucharest, according to Portal, could be attacked a few times without loss to OVERLORD.

Through a more confidential channel, Portal gave further reasons for his decisions. The ban on bombing Hungary was a political decision imposed by the British government, which was in communication with anti-German elements in the Hungarian government. The British did not want to compromise a possible anti-German uprising. The Germans, however, forestalled any further Hungarian wavering by deposing the government of Admiral Miklos Horthy and installing their own puppet regime; following this development, Portal hoped to have the bombing ban on Hungary removed. However, he still objected to bombing Ploesti on military grounds—it would require more visual bombing days than would likely be available, and it would detract from the Fifteenth's responsibilities to POINTBLANK and Italy. Portal believed that greater damage could be done to Romanian oil exports by bombing not the oil refineries in Ploesti but the marshaling yards in Bucharest.[176]

For his part, Spaatz continued on the warpath. He had just learned of a British proposal to the CCS that would allow theater commanders to direct strategic air force attacks against political-strategic objectives "when they considered such action desirable." Spaatz viewed this proposal as threatening to the entire POINTBLANK offensive because it gave the theater commanders power to replace his attacks on German "industrial and military systems," the effects of which were measurable, with area bombing, the effects of which were not, in order to break down German morale. Not only would such a proposal increase the theater commanders' power at Spaatz's expense, "it will probably nullify my control of Combined POINTBLANK operations at critical times with no balanced judgments [with] regard to issues involved." Spaatz urged Arnold to advocate that the CCS "adopt a policy of resisting all but genuinely necessary demands for diversion of effort." Spaatz added that he did not regard OVERLORD as a diversion and that he was of course prepared to come under Eisenhower's control to support it.[177]

On the other side of the Atlantic, Arnold sought to achieve a solution to the Fifteeth's command problems. The CCS, with Arnold's agreement, approved a cable to Portal authorizing him "to capitalize on favorable opportunities for

Morale visit: Lt. Gen. Carl A. Spaatz and Brig. Gen. Robert B. Williams *(far right)* **chatting with a member of the 381st Bomb Group, April 19, 1944.**

heavy attacks on important political and military targets in Southeast Europe."[178] This wording allowed the British to pursue political targets and the Fifteenth to go after military targets, specifically oil. Arnold cabled to Portal his agreement that the bombing of certain Balkan targets would not only aid OVERLORD but would do more damage to the German cause than other targets already on the priority lists. However, Arnold saw that the priority of Balkan targets might vary with the course of the war, and he maintained that any such bombing had to be tied to POINTBLANK. Fortunately, the weather would hardly ever be favorable over both Balkan and POINTBLANK targets at the same time. Balkan targets could, therefore, be bombed, provided careful supervision limited the diversions from OVERLORD and coordinated the bombing effort. Arnold concluded with a remonstrance:

> In order to get full effectiveness from the United States units and equipment Spaatz must be informed at all times of what is expected of his units. The USSTAF is building up an extremely powerful force of bombers and it must be used efficiently. I appreciate your assurances of maintaining the channel of command.[179]

Portal agreed with Arnold on all points. He promised to work closely with Spaatz and not to authorize diversions "unless really important results can be expected."[180]

Thereupon, Portal added Balkan and Hungarian political targets to the Fifteenth's strike list. His refusal to target Ploesti stemmed from the confrontation over the oil versus transportation plans going on in London at the same time the dispute over command channels erupted. Because Ploesti represented 25 percent of total Axis production, it was the single most lucrative target in any oil campaign. It made little sense for the Allies to damage Ploesti, forcing the Germans back on their synthetic production, and then ignore the remaining highly vulnerable plants in Germany proper. A successful raid on Ploesti would put a high trump in Spaatz's hand and might well allow him to gather enough support to carry the day for oil. Thus Spaatz adamantly pressed for a strike on Ploesti, and Portal just as adamantly resisted it.

On April 2, the Fifteenth struck ball-bearing targets in Steyr, Austria. For the next two days it hit marshaling yards in Budapest and elsewhere in the Balkans. On April 5, it went after Ploesti's marshaling yards, but actually hit oil targets—each refinery complex had its own commercial railway yard, and "sloppy" bombing of the yards inflicted damage on the oil centers. As the AAF official history states, "It was thought wise to begin the undertaking surreptitiously under the general directive which called for bombing transportation targets supporting German forces who were facing the Russians." With some satisfaction the history notes, "Most of the 588 tons of bombs, with more than coincidental inaccuracy, struck and badly damaged the Astra group of refineries near by."[181]

Twice more, on April 15 and 26, hundreds of U.S. heavy bombers returned to Ploesti, where they inflicted "incidental" damage to oil refineries. These raids alerted the Germans. By the time the Fifteenth obtained Portal's official permission to blast Ploesti, in May 1944, they had greatly intensified their artificial smoke screen, antiaircraft artillery, and fighter defenses. As a result, H2X bombing and a much greater expenditure of effort were required to achieve the accurate delivery of the required amount of high explosives on target.[182] But German imports of finished oil products, mostly from Romania, fell from 186,000 tons in March to 104,000 tons in April to 40,000 tons in June.[183] The April raids obviously had inflicted great damage.

Even as the Fifteenth Air Force began its clandestine oil offensive, setting the stage for attacks on synthetic plants, Spaatz continued to seek a way for the Eighth to begin one as well. Although approved by Eisenhower, the transportation plan had at least temporarily failed to gain Churchill's endorsement. When Churchill and the British War Cabinet reviewed it on April 3, they blanched at an attached Bomber Command estimate predicting 80,000 to 160,000 French civilian casualties from the bombing of marshaling yards.[184] Churchill, who well remembered the disastrous effect of the decision to bombard the French fleet in July 1940, regarded these figures with apprehension.[185] He wrote to Eisenhower,

> The Cabinet today took rather a grave and on the whole an adverse view of the proposal to bomb so many French railway centres, in view of the fact that scores of thousands of French civilians, men, women, and children, would lose their lives or be injured. Considering that they are all our friends, this might be held to be an act of very great severity, bringing much hatred on the Allied Air Forces.[186]

After consulting with Tedder, Eisenhower replied on April 5 that the loss projection of civilians was "grossly exaggerated"; that senior airmen agreed that the only viable air target, other than the Luftwaffe, was transport; and that the French people were "slaves" with the biggest stake of all in the success of the invasion.[187]

Churchill did not agree. That evening the Prime Minister began a month-long series of Defence Committee meetings during which he questioned the necessity for the transportation plan. In the meantime he wished to limit transport attacks to those with estimated civilian casualties of no more than 100 to 150 per raid.[188] With the full execution of the transportation plan on hold, Spaatz and USSTAF perceived an opening for the implementation of the oil plan.

Even as Spaatz prepared to reopen the oil plan with Eisenhower, another diversion threatened to occupy his force's efforts. In mid-April, British concern over V-1 launch sites intensified. On April 15, the day after Bomber Command and the Eighth Air Force came under Eisenhower's direction, the air leaders met to decide which transport targets to attack in relation to the Luftwaffe and CROSSBOW. Tedder opened with a statement that a directive for the use of the strategic effort had been agreed upon. Air Vice-Marshal Norman H. Bottomley, Deputy Chief of the RAF Air Staff, immediately disputed him, pointing out that Portal had not approved any such directive because the Prime Minister had not cleared the plan for political reasons. In his response, Tedder noted that all but two of USSTAF's targets had been cleared.

Discussion turned to CROSSBOW. Tedder suggested four priorities for USSTAF: (1) the Luftwaffe, (2) CROSSBOW, (3) transport targets in France, and (4) transport targets in Germany. Spaatz noted that such a ranking "greatly prejudiced" USSTAF's chances of destroying the nineteen transport targets assigned to it in France. Tedder said he would accept that price if it meant neutralizing CROSSBOW targets.[189]

On the afternoon of April 19, Tedder phoned Spaatz's Deputy for Operations, Fred Anderson, to give him a new bombing directive. CROSSBOW had priority even over the destruction of the Luftwaffe. The British War Cabinet and the British Chiefs of Staff, alarmed by recent intelligence showing a dramatic increase in V-1 launch sites, declared the security of the British Isles at risk and invoked the escape clause in the air agreement.[190] This may have been the final straw for Spaatz, whose forces Tedder proposed to divert from POINTBLANK for a target system chosen solely for British domestic political considerations.

That evening, Spaatz took his dissatisfaction to Eisenhower, who had retired to his house and the two had a stormy meeting. The Supreme Commander's "obvious agitation" before Spaatz's visit was described in a diary belonging to his naval aide who was on the scene. Eisenhower had just received word of a breach of security by one of Spaatz's general officers, Maj. Gen. Henry J. F. Miller, West Point 1915, and Commanding General of the Ninth Air Force's Air Service Command. On the night of April 18, Miller became drunk at a large London hotel and proceeded loudly to take bets that the invasion would come before June 15.[191] Eisenhower brought the incident up as soon as Spaatz entered. Spaatz showed his displeasure by walking to the phone and calling the Ninth's chief of staff, Brig. Gen. Victor H. Strahm. He ordered Strahm to arrest Miller and confine him to quarters.[192] Eisenhower subsequently removed Miller from his post, reduced him to the permanent rank of colonel, and returned him to the United States, where he soon retired.[193]

Spaatz, too, had emotional issues to discuss. He strongly protested Tedder's decision to give CROSSBOW overall priority. As he told Tedder later that evening, if the rocket sites so upset the British, they should send the RAF to get them.[194] Eisenhower supported Spaatz's basic position: POINTBLANK had priority over CROSSBOW.[195] Spaatz also reopened the oil plan debate.

Earlier that day Spaatz had decided to ask Eisenhower for permission to bomb oil targets during the next two days with suitable visual weather conditions.[196] Spaatz based the decision on several factors. Discussions that morning with his staff had developed a consensus that German fighter opposition had appreciably lessened.[197] On April 18 and 19, two strikes of more than 775 heavy bombers each, directed against Berlin and Kassel respectively, had lost a combined total of only 15 bombers.[198] Spaatz and USSTAF wanted to experiment with the oil targets to see whether striking them could continue to force attrition on the Luftwaffe.[199] Spaatz personally still believed that oil should have priority second only to the destruction of the Luftwaffe.[200] Finally, the morale of his command needed boosting.[201] If oil bombing proved as successful as he suspected it would be, his men would see that their efforts were effective. If Spaatz could not gain Eisenhower's approval, he feared that the entire AAF strategic effort in Europe might fail, or at least fail to keep the Luftwaffe out of the air over the invasion beaches.

Apparently, Eisenhower was hard to convince. At one point in the meeting Spaatz may have threatened to resign if he could not have a greater voice in the employment of his force.[202] Such an act would probably have completely soured Allied air relationships at a critical stage prior to OVERLORD. Spaatz had done his best to keep his disputes with the RAF out of the public eye. A more flamboyant airman would have had less respect from the British and might have been harder to deal with than Spaatz, who, in every case except this, had proved himself a loyal and self-effacing subordinate. Spaatz's departure and his reasons for it could not have been concealed any better than Patton's notorious slapping incident. The press would undoubtedly have given the story top play, bringing air strategy arguments out into the open and exposing them to public criticism. In any case, convinced either by the logic and vehemence of Spaatz's arguments or by his promise to give up his command, Eisenhower gave him verbal permission to take the two days he needed.[203] It must have seemed a small price to pay given the possibly disruptive consequences of strictly adhering to the transportation plan. During the meeting Eisenhower may also have taken Spaatz to task for his laggardly performance on behalf of the transportation plan. As of April 19 the Eighth had not bombed a single one of its assigned rail targets.

Furthermore, Eisenhower and Spaatz both knew that the weather seldom granted the bomber force visual access to targets deep in Germany and on the French coast during the same day. Eisenhower kept no record of the meeting, and Spaatz's diary merely lists the points under discussion, giving little hint of any conversation or emotions. He laconically noted,

> Received permission from Eisenhower to use two days of visual target weather
> to attack oil targets for purpose of determining German's willingness to send up
> defensive fighters against our bombers—must find some way to force them into
> the Air so that the strength of the German Air Force can continue to be
> decreased. . . . [204]

As the official AAF history states, "Somehow it seemed important to the two U.S. leaders not to go on record as taking the initiative in opening this new offensive."[205]

392

General Dwight D. Eisenhower, Supreme Commander Allied Expeditionary Force, in the cockpit of a B-26, April 11, 1944.

On the morning of the next day, April 20, Spaatz went to Tedder's office where the two reached a decision on CROSSBOW's priority. At first Tedder insisted that the bomber force make the V-1 launch sites their primary objective. At Spaatz's urgings he agreed to a compromise. On the first suitable day the Eighth would bomb CROSSBOW, and on the next two suitable days it would attack oil targets.[206] That very day Spaatz and Doolittle sent 892 B-17s and B-24s against CROSSBOW targets in France. The Luftwaffe offered no opposition, and the Eighth lost 9 bombers to antiaircraft fire.[207] On April 21, Spaatz and Doolittle, on board their own B-17, watched their bombers form up for the first oil attack. The weather turned foul; strong winds and clouds extended to 30,000 feet, causing the entire mission to abort. Even Spaatz, despite high hopes, admitted that he was glad the Eighth had canceled the mission rather than attempt it in impossible circumstances.[208] Not until May 12 would the right combination of weather over bases and targets allow the first blow against oil. Meanwhile, the Eighth conducted nine CROSSBOW missions, sending out 2,941 sorties and losing 33 bombers to flak or the junk heap of non-repairable aircraft.[209] Two days after his meeting with Eisenhower, Spaatz sent the Eighth over its first transportation target—Hamm, Germany, the largest rail marshaling yard in Europe. This action may have fulfilled his bargain with the Supreme Commander.

In March and April 1944, the battle of air attrition between USSTAF and the Luftwaffe fighter force continued over German-occupied Europe. In the first week of March a single raid on Berlin lost 69 heavy bombers; in the last week of April a mission to the same target lost 63. The number of the Eighth's bombers attributed lost to enemy fighters climbed from 178 in March to 314 in April.[210] The fierceness of these battles reflected the AAF's and Spaatz's policy of forcing combat at every opportunity. New techniques—employing long-range escorts on deep-penetration sweeps and encouraging aggressive tactics and attitudes against the enemy in the air and on the ground—paid dividends in March and April 1944, as the Luftwaffe fighter force had an almost 100 percent turnover of aircraft and a 40 percent turnover of pilots.[211] By the end of April, despite its own losses, USSTAF had defeated the Luftwaffe fighter force. In May, the Eighth lost 100 fewer bombers to enemy fighters than in April; in June it lost 200 fewer than in April. By the beginning of May Luftwaffe fighter forces could no longer mount continuous heavy opposition to the Allied strategic bombing campaign, nor did they retain the strength to interfere with the impending cross-channel invasion.

Spaatz contributed greatly to the defeat of the Luftwaffe. He put his whole authority behind the decision to employ aggressive, loose-escort tactics, which freed the fighters to seek out the enemy but left the bombers more vulnerable. The heavy losses his forces suffered did not cause him to flinch from his objectives. Years later, he recalled that after a mission with heavy losses Eisenhower asked him whether the air forces could continue to take such losses:

> I said, "What's that got to do with it?" [Eisenhower asked] "Are we getting control of the German Air Force?" I said, "If we have to take these losses to control them, then we have to. . . . You can't have a war and worry about that. What you have to worry about is whether you're winning or not."[212]

In addition, Spaatz drove his senior commanders to use their forces to the fullest. On March 2, Spaatz informed Doolittle and Twining:

> Our effort requiring the enemy to oppose us on our terms must be pushed relentlessly every day it is humanly possible to operate over Germany. Standard operational limitations which have been wisely used in the past will not be applicable to the present emergency situation. Greater risks are justified, and infinitely greater demands on personnel are mandatory. Further, for the immediate future it is even desirable to invite an opposition when we have fighter escort, rather than . . . to evade it.[213]

Doolittle later recalled that, once, after he had canceled a mission, Spaatz told him "If you haven't got the guts to run a big Air Force, we'll get someone else."[214]

Spaatz never doubted that he could overcome the Luftwaffe, undermine the German economy, and guarantee air supremacy over Europe and the invasion beaches provided he had suitable weather, replacement of his losses, and freedom to use his force. Meteorological conditions provided just enough usable weather. Arnold not only made good the losses but increased the force. And Spaatz, steering carefully through the labyrinthine disputes over command, control, and policy, maintained his close working relationships with Tedder and Eisenhower, pursued his chief objectives: the Luftwaffe and oil targets.

Chapter 11

Final Preparations
for the Invasion
(May–June 1944)

Your concern over the reaction of the G[erman] A[ir] F[orce] when OVERLORD is launched is shared by me. He [the enemy] is undoubtedly attempting to ration his forces to the greatest extent possible at this time in order to maintain an adequate force against a threat of invasion from the West. I have stressed in all my conferences with Eisenhower, Tedder, and others that a continuation of POINTBLANK operations is vital in order to maintain wastage of the GAF. The primary purpose of these POINTBLANK operations to date has been the depletion of the GAF. At this time it is the sole purpose. Targets selected are those which we anticipate will force the GAF into the air against us.[1]

—*Spaatz to Arnold, May 10, 1944*

The Oil Plan Is Implemented

In the five weeks before the Allied landings at Normandy, the AAF continued to execute its main tasks: the elimination of the Luftwaffe, the neutralization of V-1 launch sites, and the interdiction of the German transportation system in France. In the days just preceding and during the assault phase of OVERLORD, USSTAF put aside these tasks to provide maximum direct support of the invasion. Spaatz contributed substantially to the attainment of the Allies' and the AAF's goals.

The Eighth Air Force entered May with 39 operational heavy-bombardment groups, to which the Fifteenth added another 20, for an authorized front-line strength of 2,832 B-17s and B-24s. Spaatz used this force in a manner calculated to provoke combat with the Luftwaffe so as to inflict fatal attrition upon it. Despite the fact that German day fighters shot down 100 more American heavy bombers in April 1944 than in any other month of the war,[2] USSTAF Headquarters had perceived a weakening in the enemy's fighter reaction. The nonexistent Luftwaffe reaction to missions flown against CROSSBOW and transportation targets in late April and the first week of May confirmed speculation.

This decline produced not cheer but apprehension within USSTAF and suspicion that the Luftwaffe meant to conserve its forces for action against the expected invasion. On May 6, at an Allied air conference held at AEAF Headquarters, Stanmore, Spaatz admitted his fear that the Germans "were conserving their effort against the threat of invasion" and that they might leave the homeland undefended in order to bring all their fighters to bear on the beachheads.[3] Spaatz probably based his assessment on reports received from the RAF's Air Intelligence Branch (AI). On April 30, AI noted that the Luftwaffe had maintained its strength and predicted a German air strength of 1,950 aircraft spread from Norway and northern Germany to southern France, with 750 immediately available to oppose the invasion. Estimated strength increased throughout the month. On May 25, AI placed total German strength in the west at 2,350 planes; the 900 immediately available included 500 bombers and 220 single-engine fighters.[4] But AI, in information gleaned from ULTRA, attributed this situation to a conservation policy stemming from a shortage of pilots. In February, for example, decrypts indicated Luftwaffe intentions to use aircraft from flying schools and training units in case of emergency.[5]

Spaatz believed that attacking oil targets would nullify the Germans' intention to conserve their aircraft and pilots and force the Luftwaffe up to protect its sources of fuel. On May 12, weather conditions finally permitted a full-scale visual attack on several crucial synthetic oil-producing plants. Aside from two costly strikes on April 29 and May 8 over Berlin, which usually produced heavy German reaction, this attack attracted the heaviest opposition in three weeks. Fifteen combat wings—886 heavy bombers plus 735 escorting fighters left Britain to bomb their targets. The leading division, the 3d, which was underescorted because one of its assigned fighter groups had mistakenly rendezvoused with a trailing division, saw its remaining escort swamped by a large force of German fighters, which, in forty minutes, downed 32 bombers before they could reach their targets. This single massed blow accounted for most of the 46 bombers lost. The other two bombardment divisions lost only 2 bombers to enemy fighters and 12 to antiaircraft fire.[6] The Eighth wrote off an additional 9 bombers as unrepairable[7] (See Map 11, Greater German Synthetic Oil Plants.) The American escort lost 4 P-47s and 3 P-51s, claiming in return 61 German aircraft destroyed and 11 damaged in the air as well as 5 destroyed and 2 damaged on the ground. German records confirmed the accuracy of those claims, counting 28 pilots dead, 26 injured,[8] and 65 aircraft lost.[9] Surviving bombers dropped 1,718 tons of bombs, through ground haze and low clouds, on synthetic oil plants at Zwickau,

396

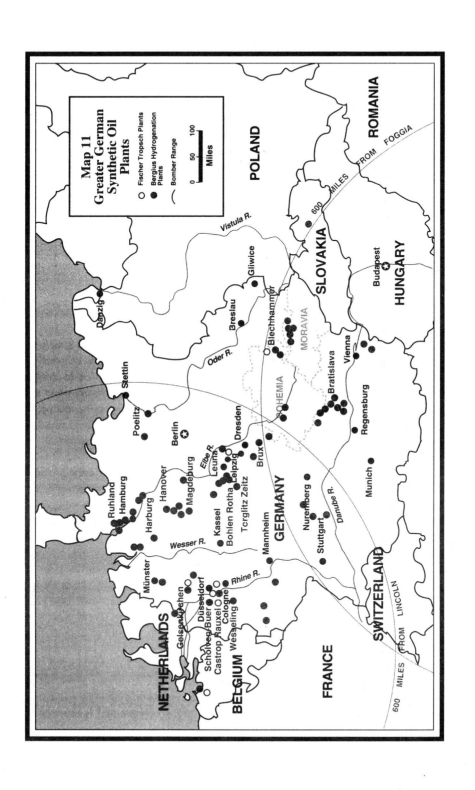

**Map 11
Greater German Synthetic Oil Plants**

○ Fischer Tropsch Plants
● Berglus Hydrogenation Plants
⌒ Bomber Range

0   50   100
Miles

Merseburg-Leuna, Brux, Lutzkendorf, Bohlen, and Zeitz, while, coincidentally and unknown to the Allies until after the war, destroying at Merseburg-Leuna, a building engaged in heavy-water experiments for Germany's atom bomb program.[10] Albert Speer, Nazi Minister of Armaments and War Production, spoke of USSTAF's work that day in his postwar memoirs:

> I shall never forget the day the technological war was decided. Until then we had managed to produce approximately as many weapons as the armed forces needed, in spite of their considerable losses. But, with the attack of nine hundred and thirty-five daylight bombers of the American Eighth Air Force upon several fuel plants in central and eastern Germany, a new era in the air war began. It meant the end of German armaments production.[11]

A week later Speer reported to Hitler, "The enemy has struck us at one of our weakest points. If [he] persist[s] at it this time, we will soon no longer have any fuel production worth mentioning. Our one hope is that the other side has an air force General Staff as scatterbrained as ours!"[12]

Commitments to Crossbow and Overlord and the weather delayed the next oil mission until May 28, when 400 heavy bombers attacked plants at Ruhland and Magdeburg and restruck Merseburg-Leuna, Zeitz, and Lutzkendorf. The next day the Eighth sent 224 B-24s to bomb the synthetic plant at Politz, while the rest of the force bombed aircraft industry targets deep in eastern Germany and Poland. A combined total of 66 bombers and 19 fighters were lost in the two raids. American escorts claimed 100 destroyed, 2 probably destroyed, and 11 damaged in the air and 21 destroyed and 22 damaged on the ground.[13] Only the month's three raids on Berlin and the previous oil raid met opposition of similar intensity.

These oil strikes proved two of Spaatz's contentions: First, the enemy would come up to resist them, but would not defend V-1 launch sites or marshaling yards. Second, the bombing of the German synthetic oil plants would have immediate and serious consequences for the German war economy. Ultra intercepted an order, dated May 13, showing that the previous day's mission had greatly alarmed the Germans. This order, from the Luftwaffe Operations Staff in Berlin, stripped heavy and light antiaircraft guns from the Eastern Front and from the fighter-manufacturing plants of Oschersleben, Leipzig-Erla, and Wiener Neustadt for the protection of hydrogenation plants at Zeitz and Politz.[14] A history of USSTAF and Ultra called this intercept "one of the most decisive and timely pieces of intelligence received in this war."[15] It gave proof that the Germans regarded oil as the target system of paramount importance—even above the production of fighter aircraft. A week later the Allies intercepted an order directing the German armed forces to convert an even higher percentage of their motor transport to power supplied by highly inefficient wood fuel generators.[16] When he learned of these messages, Tedder dropped his opposition to the oil plan and is reported to have remarked, "I guess we'll have to give the customer what he wants."[17]

The first oil raid: Bomb damage to a synthetic oil plant in Bohlen, Germany, May 12, 1944.

After the war, captured documents from Speer to Hitler revealed the dramatic and almost instantaneous effect of May's bombings. On June 30, Speer reported the state of production of aviation fuel to Hitler. In April, the Luftwaffe consumed 156,000 tons of the 175,000 tons of aviation gasoline manufactured by the synthetic plants; the average daily production in April was 5,850 tons. The attack of May 12 reduced that average to 4,821, but production had recovered to 5,526 tons per day by May 28, when the Allies completely knocked out the plant at Leuna. The May 29 attack stopped all production at Politz, and the two strikes combined dropped daily production to 2,775 tons. The total output for May of 156,000 tons fell 14,000 tons short of essential planned consumption. In June, thanks to more attacks, production rose above 3,000 tons on only two days.[18] On June 7, ULTRA deciphered the following message, dated June 5, from the Luftwaffe Operations Staff,

> As a result of renewed encroachment into the production of a/c [aircraft] fuel by enemy action, the most essential requirements for training and carrying out production plans can scarcely be covered with the quantities of a/c fuel available. In order to assure the defense of the Reich and to prevent the readiness for defense of the G.A.F. in the east from gradually collapsing, it has been necessary to break into the strategical reserve.[19]

Portal sent a copy of this decryption to the Prime Minister, saying, "I regard this as one of the most important pieces of information we have yet received."

Portal also recommended a concentrated bombing attack on synthetic oil targets by all Allied strategic bombers as soon as they could be spared by the invasion. Piecemeal attacks spread over a long period by small forces, warned Portal, would only allow the enemy time to increase his flak and smoke defenses. Churchill replied, "Good."[20]

Even as the Eighth Air Force staggered the Germans under punishing round-house blows, the Fifteenth Air Force continued pounding Ploesti. As a result of Spaatz's visit to the MAAF and the Fifteenth at the end of April, USSTAF finally obtained Portal's approval of oil as a legitimate target.[21] Spaatz persuaded Portal that the Fifteenth had grown so large that for tactical reasons it should hit other important targets, such as refineries, near the Ploesti marshaling yards.[22] No longer obliged to conduct on the sly its missions against oil, the Fifteenth sent almost 500 heavy bombers to Ploesti on May 5 and followed with 700 on May 18, 460 on May 31, and 300 on June 6. Results were, for the most part, excellent. It also bombed small crude oil targets in the Balkans while the RAF kept up a heavy mining campaign in the Danube River.[23] A postwar examination of captured German records reveals that, at the time of the Fifteenth's bombing of Ploesti and other Balkan petroleum targets, German imports of finished oil products had fallen from 186,000 tons in March 1944 to 104,000 in April and 81,000 in May. By August, when the Russians occupied the gutted ruins of Ploesti, German oil imports had dropped to a mere 11,000 tons.[24] On June 4, Eisenhower's headquarters publicly proclaimed the existence of the oil offensive.[25]

Churchill Delays the Transportation Plan

By May 1, five weeks after the transportation plan had been endorsed by Eisenhower, it had not been endorsed by Churchill, who remained worried about the potential political side effects of killing and maiming French civilians. Spaatz, too, worried. He believed that, although actual casualties might vary widely, the Germans would greatly exaggerate their number for propaganda purposes.[26] On April 22, after discussion with his personal staff and Bedell Smith, Spaatz met with Eisenhower on the subject,[27] bringing the draft of a letter with him in which he spelled out his objections and proposed an alternative:

> I would feel seriously remiss in my duty if I did not bring to your attention the serious implications involved with these attacks. Many thousands of French people will be killed and many towns will be laid waste in these operations. I feel a joint responsibility with you and I view with alarm a military operation which involves such widespread destruction and death in countries not our enemies, particularly since the results to be achieved from these bombing operations have not been conclusively shown to be . . . decisive. . . . [28]

Spaatz then pointed out the necessity for all air forces to give direct support to OVERLORD, but he observed:

> The use of these forces in a manner which involves so much destruction to our Allies on the continent may far outweigh the advantages gained by the attacks as planned. We must evolve a scheme of employment of our Air Forces which better achieves the basic aim of maximum direct assistance to OVERLORD.

He suggested considering the possibilities of cutting rail and road lines at points outside town centers and of attacking concentrations of German troops, their supply and ammunition depots, and their tank parks.[29]

Eisenhower replied that he had examined the problem and understood the political repercussions in a postwar Europe, but he argued that the primary consideration was the absolute necessity of winning the war quickly.[30] Although not completely convinced by Eisenhower's rejoinder, Spaatz acquiesced to Eisenhower's wishes.[31]

The next day Ambassador Winant lunched with Spaatz at Park House. The two discussed their concern over the bombing of populated areas in occupied territory but agreed that they had faith in Eisenhower and would abide by whatever he decided.[32] Spaatz accepted the continuation of the transportation plan but did what he could to mitigate its consequences for French civilians living in harm's way. He emphasized to his subordinates the importance of being careful in all operations against French targets: only the best lead bombardiers would be used, no indiscriminant bombing and no H2X bombing would be permitted. "The crews must be impressed with the need for air discipline in order to avoid needless killing. . . . "[33]

The Prime Minister, whose political senses were perhaps more acute than those of the U.S. generals, delayed his final decision. On the night of April 19, Churchill still doubted that any suffering caused by the transportation plan justified its results. He raised the possibility of attacking synthetic oil targets,[34] but Portal and Tedder repeated their opinion that such a tactic could not succeed by D-day. Even after the British Chiefs of Staff asked for a speedy decision, Churchill demurred, although he admitted that the longer the decision remained in question, the stronger the case for the transportation plan became.[35]

On April 26, the Prime Minister agreed to put the matter before the War Cabinet. Portal drew up a list of targets, the bombing of which would cause no more than 100 civilian casualties each. At a meeting the next day, the Cabinet agreed to revise the transportation plan to include only attacks that would inflict no more than 150 civilian casualties each. Churchill was to visit Eisenhower and then send a message to Roosevelt for a definitive American opinion.[36]

On April 29, Churchill suggested to Eisenhower that USSTAF, perhaps in conjunction with the Air Ministry, produce a plan for employing heavy bombers which would sacrifice no more than 100 French lives per attack. If it failed to inflict sufficient damage to the key portions of the French rail system, the full transportation plan, whatever its cost to civilians, would be strengthened.[37] Slowing or delaying the movement of German ground units toward the beachhead had to have priority over other considerations.

Eisenhower remained adamant. To abandon the transportation plan at this juncture was unthinkable. He wrote to Marshall, "There is no other way in which this tremendous air force can help us during the preparatory period, to get ashore and stay there. The Prime Minister talked to me about bombing 'bases, troop concentrations and dumps.' "[38] Churchill's reference to dumps and troop concentrations echoed Spaatz's letter on civilian casualties to Eisenhower; such similarity of phrasing points to close collaboration between Spaatz's headquarters and Churchill's staff. On April 22, Doolittle, for instance, attended a dinner at 10 Downing Street where he was prepared to discuss and support USSTAF's views on the oil plan.[39] In the space of a week, both Churchill and Spaatz, using virtually the same language, proposed to Eisenhower that the use of American heavy bombers in the transportation plan be restricted.

On May 2, Eisenhower sent Churchill a more detailed reply, written for the most part by Tedder,[40] which patiently reviewed the rationale behind the transportation plan—it was intended to weaken and confuse the rail network at a critical time, rather than to choke it off entirely. Next, Tedder and Eisenhower took note of the March 25 meeting and of USSTAF's alternative suggestions, which they had "fully and sympathetically considered" but rejected because "they do not, themselves, in any way constitute a plan by which our air power can, in the final stages, effectively delay and disrupt enemy concentrations." After noting that a limitation to 100 to 150 casualties per mission would "emasculate" the transportation plan, the reply concluded with Eisenhower's typical reaction against any challenge to his wishes: "The 'Overlord' concept was based on the assumption that our overwhelming Air Power would be able to prepare the way for the assault. If its hands are to be tied, the perils of an already hazardous undertaking will be greatly enhanced."[41]

That night the War Cabinet considered the reply. Churchill spoke of the hazards of interfering with Eisenhower's plans for political reasons, yet said he had not realized "that our use of air power before 'Overlord' would assume so cruel and remorseless a form."[42] Foreign Secretary Anthony Eden feared the adverse reaction of the western Europeans. Support for the transportation plan came from the British Chiefs of Staff. Alan Brooke, Chief of the Imperial General Staff, supported the plan more vigorously than he had before because of the effort already expended on it. Finally, the Cabinet agreed that the Prime Minister "should consider further the air plan for support of 'Overlord'."[43]

On May 3, the British Defence Committee met for the last time on the subject. Before the meeting Tedder had convinced the Prime Minister of South Africa, Field Marshal Jan Smuts, who happened to be in London for a meeting of the British Commonwealth, of the necessity of the transportation plan. Smuts, who had been instrumental in establishing the RAF as an independent service in

1917, held great influence over Churchill and pressed him on the plan before the meeting,[44] but any waivering he might have induced in Churchill did not start at the subsequent Defence Committee meeting. The transportation plan, said Churchill, "will smear the good name of the Royal Air Force across the world." Churchill asked whether the plan could be implemented at a cost of less than 10,000 dead. Tedder expressed his hopes of keeping the number of French dead below that number, although he could make no guarantees. The committee then considered a suggestion from Lord Cherwell, Churchill's chief scientific adviser, that bridges might be better alternative targets than rail centers. Tedder rejected the suggestion out of hand. In the end, the committee instructed Tedder to report its discussion and conclusion to Eisenhower, after reviewing the transportation plan to ensure no more than 10,000 French casualties.[45]

On May 7, Churchill informed Roosevelt of the British government's concern over the "slaughter" of French civilians, which might "leave a legacy of hate." He noted "the great differences of opinion in the two air forces—not between them but crisscross about the efficacy of the 'railway plan' as a short-term project." Then he asked for Roosevelt's opinion:

> It must be remembered, on the one hand, that this slaughter is among a friendly people who have committed no crimes against us, and not among the German foe, with all their record of cruelty and ruthlessness. On the other hand, we naturally feel the hazardous nature of 'OVERLORD' and are in deadly earnest about making it a success. Whatever is settled between us, we are quite willing to share responsibilities with you.[46]

Roosevelt replied on May 11,

> However regrettable the attendant loss of civilian lives is, I am not prepared to impose from this distance any restriction on military action by the responsible commanders that in their opinion might militate against the success of 'OVERLORD' or cause additional loss of life to our Allied forces of invasion.[47]

This ended the matter. Having received no support from the Combined Chiefs of Staff or the President and having been opposed by Eisenhower, Churchill allowed the transportation plan to proceed without interference. Happily, civilian casualties from rail center attacks before D-day proved to be less than half of those predicted; approximately 4,750 were killed.[48]

Whereas Churchill had opposed the transportation plan on political grounds, Spaatz attempted to overturn it on practical grounds. He had already gained Eisenhower's permission for two days' visual bombing of oil targets; these missions demonstrated the effectiveness of the oil plan as a strategic alternative. In addition, by late April and early May, he began to offer a tactical alternative to the transportation plan. He pushed for an interdiction campaign directed first against the Seine and Loire River bridges, important rail junctions, and open stretches of track, and then against ammunition and fuel dumps, ordnance depots, and other military establishments large enough to offer a suitable target.[49] He chose not to present those plans on March 25 because he did not want to appear to overstep his authority. Churchill's opposition to the transportation plan, however, kept alive the possibility of a replacement. Thus Spaatz sought to substitute his oil and interdiction campaign.

The details of USSTAF's interdiction campaign, which the Enemy Objectives Unit had prepared in mid- and late February,[50] circulated throughout the Allied air establishment and beyond. This was apparently done sub rosa or by word of mouth, perhaps with Spaatz's approval. Churchill, at one point, advocated the adoption of portions of the plan to Eisenhower. Lord Cherwell kept suggesting bridge attacks. By May, additional information supporting the interdiction advocates' position had become available with the completion of Operation STRANGLE, a campaign conducted by Allied air over a period of almost two months in Italy against all types of targets along whole sections of track rather than one type of target. By the end of the operation, May 12, it had switched primarily to attacks on bridges, because they had proved to be better targets.[51]

On trips to Italy at the end of April, Spaatz and Anderson had the chance to review STRANGLE's results first hand and brought back enthusiastic reports of its success in bridge breaking. Experts had predicted that the tactic would require the expending of huge numbers of bombs and had thus deemed it unrewarding. STRANGLE had demonstrated that it was entirely feasible with modest numbers of bombs and that it was, moreover, a highly effective block to enemy movement.[52] RAF Air Intelligence joined USSTAF in backing bridge attacks. AI reports of bridge attacks in Italy during February and March, based on photographic reconnaissance and high-grade signal intelligence, testified to the tactic's "not unimpressive" effect.[53]

Given this evidence and Churchill's ongoing political concern, a concern that certainly percolated to Spaatz's headquarters, the experimental bombing of the Vernon rail bridge over the Seine on May 7 assumed special significance. It occurred when Churchill, who had run out of time in fighting the transportation plan, needed some hard evidence to quiet its advocates. Spaatz also had to provide a demonstration of the effectiveness of his alternative tactical proposal. Their chance came when Montgomery's 21 Army Group Headquarters requested the destruction of several bridges by the air force to interfere with the enemy's ability to ship reinforcements to the Normandy area. This request dovetailed neatly with Spaatz's effort to introduce bridge-bombing operations. By mid-April, his chief of intelligence had already passed along to Brig. Gen. Frederic Smith, Vandenberg's deputy at AEAF, a "suggestion" to bomb bridges. Smith and four other brigadier generals prepared a plan to bomb those spanning the Seine River between Paris and Rouen.[54]

On May 3, at a target meeting, Leigh-Mallory rejected Smith's bridge plan, but suggested that, if it were technically possible, the Eighth's heavy bombers destroy several bridges and other likely communications sites.[55] This suggestion

Anthony Eden, British
Foreign Secretary,
1941–1945.

British Prime Minister Winston Churchill and his War Cabinet. *Standing from left to right*: **Archibald Sinclair, Albert Alexander, Lord Cranborne, Herbert Morrison, Lord Moyne, David Mergesson, and Brendan Bracken;** *seated from left to right*: **Ernest Bevin, Lord Beaverbrook, Anthony Eden, Clement Attlee, Churchill, John Anderson, Arthur Greenwood, and Kingsley Wood.**

merely confirmed Spaatz's low opinion of Leigh-Mallory. Spaatz wired Arnold, "Extremely heavy program of attack against communications and other precision targets submitted by AEAF for OVERLORD. Preparations may compromise POINTBLANK if approved and weaken OVERLORD if not completed."[56] Spaatz did not object to targeting the bridges; he objected to doing so with the least-efficient aircraft available for the job—heavy bombers. Their use not only would divert them from POINTBLANK and CROSSBOW but also would produce high figures of bomb tonnage versus bridge destruction, confirming Zuckerman's, Leigh-Mallory's, and Tedder's opinion that bridge breaking did not offer an effective alternative to transportation targets. Operations in Italy had shown the superior effectiveness of the fighter-bomber for the task.

After the meeting of May 3, USSTAF attempted to reverse Leigh-Mallory's decision to allocate the bridges to heavy bombers. Thirty-five years later, Smith recalled that on May 4 he received a call from Fred Anderson requesting that he stay late in his office where a captain of the Horse Guards, the unit that guarded the Prime Minister, would pick up a copy of the bridge-bombing plan Smith had proposed at the May 3 meeting. The Guards officer duly arrived and, Smith believed, whisked the plan off to Churchill, who pressed Leigh-Mallory to reverse his stand.[57] If Smith's memory and surmises were accurate, they give ample evidence that Spaatz's and Churchill's people, at least on this occasion, cooperated closely in trying to determine the details of preinvasion bombing operations. (See Map 12, Normandy Transport Network.)

On May 6, at another target conference, Spaatz, Leigh-Mallory, Tedder, and many of their deputies once more reviewed the target priorities of their respective organizations. After committing the Eighth Air Force to a limited program of airfield bombing, termed "preinvasion post-holing" because of the cratering of the runways caused by high-explosive bombs, Spaatz brought up the subject of bridges. He quoted a report from Italy on fighter-bomber effectiveness. Leigh-Mallory attempted to cut off discussion by announcing that "bridges were a difficult target and he did not want to see a waste of effort at this time." Then the 21 Army Group Planning Officer, Brig. Gen. Charles Richardson, spoke up, stating that the ground forces wanted the destruction of eight bridges. "This," he said, "would be of more decisive value than pin-pricking on rail communications." Coningham lent support to bridge bombing, which he wanted done on an experimental basis first, because it would hamper road movement as well as rail movement and, in the invasion area itself, would compel the enemy to rely more heavily on motor transport than rail. Leigh-Mallory, perhaps bowing to Spaatz's and Coningham's arguments or perhaps feeling the pressure from 10 Downing Street, agreed to experimental attacks on bridges over both the Seine and the Meuse. He added diversionary attacks on the Meuse to deceive the Germans. He also excused the Eighth from participating.[58]

Little did Leigh-Mallory realize the alacrity with which the AAF would pursue this initiative. General Smith immediately selected the Seine bridge at

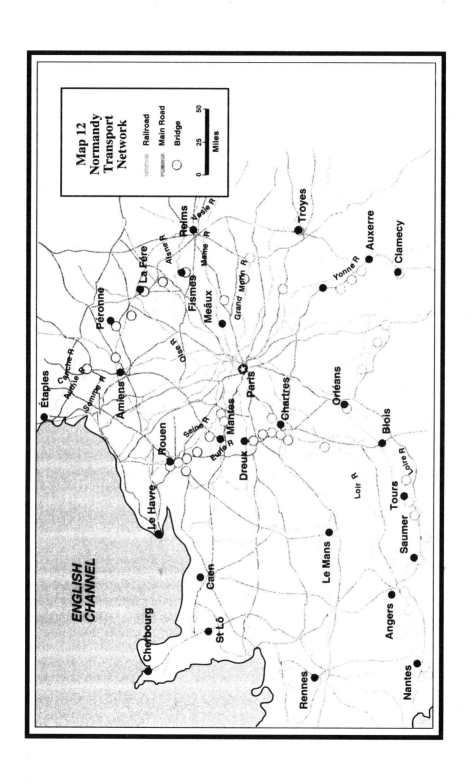

Map 12
Normandy Transport Network

Railroad
Main Road
○ Bridge

Miles
0   25   50

ENGLISH CHANNEL

Cherbourg

St Lô

Caen

Le Havre

Étaples

Côuche R
Authie R
Somme R

Amiens

Péronne

La Fère

Reims
Aisne R
Vesle R
Marne R

Fismes

Meaux

Grand Morin R

Troyes

Auxerre
Yonne R

Clamecy

Oise R

Rouen
Seine R
Eure R
Mantes

Paris

Chartres

Orléans

Blois

Dreux

Loir R

Tours
Loire R

Saumer

Le Mans

Angers

Rennes

Nantes

Vernon, called his roommate Brig. Gen. David Schlatter of the Ninth Air Force, and told him to go ahead.[59] Just before noon the next day, a flight of fighter-bombers from the 365th Fighter Group, specially trained in low-level bombing, left England for France. Twelve planes and escorts attacked the bridge at Vernon, and another twelve with escorts attacked additional bridges. Within a few minutes and under the gaze of German Field Marshal Irwin Rommel, who happened to be there,[60] the P-47s, with only six tons of bombs, destroyed the bridge and a nearby ammunition factory, at the cost of two planes lost and five damaged. The flight leader reported "the most intensive light flak they had yet encountered."[61] Another flight damaged three more bridges at Oissel, Orival, and Mantes-Gassicourt the same day.[62] This brilliant piece of beginner's luck was the most accurate bridge raid of the campaign in northwestern Europe; the typical bridge cut took 173 tons.[63]

The next morning, May 8, every major figure in the bombing plan controversy found a set of post-attack aerial photographs on his desk showing the bridge lying at the bottom of the Seine. Like the ULTRA intercept on German oil, they removed all doubt about the cost-effectiveness of attacking bridges with fighter-bombers rather than heavy bombers.[64] On May 10, Leigh-Mallory, after assessing the raid's effectiveness, ordered his tactical forces to begin cutting the bridges over the Albert Canal in Belgium and along the Meuse. Because of security considerations, the AEAF did not bomb the Loire bridges until D-day.[65] Tedder ceased his opposition.[66] As its advocates had claimed, pre-D-day bridge-breaking also proved easier on the French civilian population than bombing marshaling yards. Less than 1,000 French civilians died as a result of it.[67]

Almost as an afterthought the British and the Americans finally asked an official representative of General Charles de Gaulle's Free French government-in-exile its opinions on the matter of killing French civilians. Churchill, who had little love for the stubborn French general or his government, opposed the consultation, saying:

> It is therefore in my opinion not necessary that a psychological effect should be obtained by a French transport expert being consulted by the Target Committee. His presence would only constitute a complication, and a suggestion to de Gaulle of this kind would only give another opportunity of obtruding himself.[68]

Nonetheless, on May 16, Eisenhower sent his chief of staff, Bedell Smith, to call on the Commander of the French Forces in Britain, Maj. General Pierre Joseph Koenig. After Smith explained the situation, Koenig grimly replied, "C'est la guerre [This is war]." He added, "It must be expected that people will be killed. We would take twice the anticipated loss to be rid of the Germans."[69]

Preinvasion Operations

The King of England, his Prime Minister, the Supreme Allied Commander, and most of the senior officers responsible for the planning and execution of OVERLORD met for a formal presentation of the invasion plan on May 15 at the

Headquarters of 21 Army Group, at St. Paul's School in London. After Eisenhower spoke, each of the major commanders delineated the tasks assigned to his troops. Spaatz, as usual, performed woodenly in public, reading from a prepared text. It bored Alan Brooke and Leigh-Mallory, but Patton commented that, "Bradley and Spaatz made short and good speeches."[70] Spaatz left the description of the Combined Bomber Offensive and the invasion air plans to Harris and Leigh-Mallory respectively, instead concentrating on the battle against the Luftwaffe. He claimed that German fighter and bomber production had declined by about 50 percent since January 1. He also touched on the transportation plan, informing his listeners that the Eighth Air Force had struck eighteen of its twenty-two assigned targets. In concluding, he repeated his favorite theme—the attrition of the Luftwaffe: "In addition to the destruction of the transportation and airdrome targets assigned the 8th Air Force prior to D-day, the 8th will continue its operations into Germany with the primary objective of further depletion of the German Air Force in being."[71]

General Montgomery probably made the day's most impressive presentation. Always the master of the set piece, be it a battle or a briefing, Montgomery strutted through the ground invasion plan. In the course of his talk he produced maps showing phase-lines of the anticipated advance, which indicated the capture of Caen by D-day plus three or four days. Those present were all professional military men who understood that Montgomery's maps represented only planning estimates. Nonetheless, the phase-lines and the tenor of his presentation left the clear impression that he would obtain a large beachhead fairly rapidly.[72]

The size of the beachhead was a matter of particular concern to the British airmen of the 2d Tactical Air Force. Their short-range fighters and fighter-bombers would be launched from airfields in Britain averaging 130 miles from the Normandy beachhead. Thus their time directly over the beachhead itself would be severly restricted. Consequently, they deemed the establishment of landing strips and airfields in Normandy a matter of the first importance. The airfields had to be able to accommodate the storage and management of necessarily huge quantities of ordnance and fuel. A large initial beachhead would allow a greater proportion of the British tactical air force to move to advanced stations on the Continent. The 130-mile gap was much less important to the American airmen, all of whose fighter aircraft had drop tanks that extended their range.

On May 20, the intelligence staff of Eisenhower's headquarters (SHAEF, G-2) reported that the bombing of the railway marshaling yards had yet to produce as intended. Rail traffic in France had dropped by only one-third—or to the point where the more enthusiastic transportation plan proponents had predicted that German military transport would begin to suffer.[73] Leigh-Mallory, however, was able to supplement the plan because Tedder had just lifted the ban on strafing trains—a ban the Allies had heretofore observed because they had difficulty distinguishing civilian from military traffic.[74] He therefore ordered a series of fighter sweeps against moving trains. These so-called "Chattanooga Choo-Choo" missions on May 21, 25, and 29 and June 2, 3, and 4 damaged hundreds of locomotives, cut the rails in numerous places, and forced the Germans to bring in train crews of their own nationals to man the trains along dangerous lines after the French crews deserted in large numbers. Daylight traffic almost completely halted.

The bridge campaign also continued. From May 11 through May 26, Allied aircraft attacked bridges in Belgium and northern France. On May 24, the ban on the Seine bridges, imposed because of security considerations, was removed, and by D-day, June 6, all Seine River rail and road bridges below Paris were at the bottom of the river or otherwise unusable, all at the cost of about 220 tons of bombs per bridge.[75]

While the medium bombers and fighter-bombers of the AEAF downed bridges and shot up trains, the Eighth Air Force lent its efforts to pre-D-day preparations. On April 22, it's bombers inaugurated their part in the transportation plan by striking the largest railroad marshaling yard in Europe, at Hamm, Germany. Hamm was the rail gateway to the Ruhr, Germany's largest industrial area, and the Eighth's bombs left it crippled for the rest of the war.[76] On May 1 and 11, its fighters participated in the "Chattanoogas" while its heavy bombers conducted large-scale raids on French rail center targets. In the two weeks before the invasion, USSTAF delivered the bulk of its tonnage on transportation targets. In missions on May 23, 25, 27, and 30 and June 4, it delivered more than 13,000 tons of bombs. Of the twenty-three rail centers assigned to it, the Eighth damaged fifteen so severely that they needed no additional bombing. It also inflicted great damage on the remaining eight.[77]

RAF Bomber Command participated more heavily against rail centers than USSTAF, dropping 46,000 of 71,000 tons expended. Spaatz's initial fear that Bomber Command would get off scot-free while he had to tie himself to the transportation plan never materialized. German rail transport was reduced by another one-third from the beginning of January 1944.[78]

The authorities and participants, both Allied and German, have continued to dispute the relative effectiveness of the various methods employed against rail traffic. Tedder and Zuckerman naturally claimed that the transportation plan was the most important contributor to its decline.[79] The official AAF history, in contrast, quoted just as many sources with the opposite opinion and concluded with a statement by the AAF Evaluation Board: "The pre-D-day attacks against French rail centers were not necessary and the 70,000 tons involved could have been devoted to alternative targets."[80] The fact remains that the pre-D-day air campaign imposed severe and damaging injuries to the German military's mobility and logistics, which undoubtedly hurt the German effort on D-day and after.

In conjunction with its interdiction campaign, Allied air power also sought to neutralize all 100 usable enemy airfields within a 350-mile arc from the planned invasion beaches. The British wanted the airfields within 130 miles of the invasion area singled out in order to put the Luftwaffe at the same operational disadvantage as their own aircraft operating from British bases. The Eighth, which flew its first antiairfield mission of the campaign on May 9, executed the lion's share of this phase of pre-D-day preparations. Of the airfields within 130 miles of Caen, the left flank of the invasion, Bomber Command had responsibility for 8, AEAF for 12, and USSTAF for 20. The Eighth and the Fifteenth also had responsibility for neutralizing the 59 fields more than 130 miles but less than 350 miles from Caen. Large missions by the Eighth on May 23, 24, and 25 and missions by the Fifteenth damaged many but when it became evident, probably from ULTRA sources, that the Luftwaffe had not begun to occupy its advanced bases in France, the Allies discontinued their attacks.[81]

As air preliminaries for the invasion proceeded, Leigh-Mallory laid the groundwork for the final phase of preinvasion activities. In the week before the invasion he would have control of all assisting air forces. On May 23, less than two weeks before D-day, scheduled for June 5, he inaugurated a series of daily morning Allied Air Commanders' Conferences on projected operations and the allotment of tasks between the various forces involved.[82] Tedder, Spaatz, Doolittle, Harris, and senior AEAF officers attended this initial session in the Battle Room of Advanced AEAF Headquarters in Uxbridge.

Afterwards, in a gesture typical of his obtuseness, Leigh-Mallory complained that the American officers assigned to the Battle Room, from which he planned to conduct and monitor the daily combat activities of the Allied air forces over the beachhead, were not carrying out procedures "according to his ideas," and he asked Vandenberg that they be transferred elsewhere and replaced by British officers. Vandenberg acquiesced, but later called Spaatz and, characterizing Leigh-Mallory's actions as "outrageous," offered to "bring a very fine fight out in the open." After thinking it over, Spaatz instructed Vandenberg "to carry on at present, say nothing to upset relations." Once they got the troops ashore, said Spaatz, the whole question of command and use of the American air forces would have to be reexamined.[83] Not surprisingly, sour relations between Leigh-Mallory and senior American air officers continued until the invasion and beyond.

By the end of May, USSTAF had still not completed the details of its participation in the first day of the invasion. All agreed that its first bomber mission should drench the invasion beaches just before the assault forces landed. USSTAF and AEAF parted company, however, on the objectives for the second mission of the day. On June 1, Leigh-Mallory, Vandenberg, and his deputy, Brig. Gen. Frederic Smith, all rejected as operationally unsound USSTAF's proposal to strike enemy troop and road movement behind the front lines from an altitude of 15,000 feet. The bombers would be unable to locate German troops in the thickly wooded country of Normandy, and they would further congest the already crowded airspace. AEAF wanted USSTAF to stick to bombing desig-

U.S. Army Air Forces fighters bringing an engine to its last stop on a "Chattanooga Choo-Choo" strafing sortie, May 1944.

nated villages and towns in order to block the roads with rubble and impede German movement.[84]

That evening during dinner, Vandenberg with Spaatz and Maj. Gen. Laurence S. Kuter, Assistant Chief of the Air Staff for Plans, who had just arrived from Washington, agreed that USSTAF's plans for bombing troop movements could not work. Spaatz, who feared that the Luftwaffe's capabilities for D-day might have been greatly underestimated, instead, wanted to post-hole one more time all airfields within fighter range of the beachhead. Vandenberg demurred on the ground that the bombers would be spread too thin. He advocated bombing only key airfields, Spaatz agreed, Vandenberg would present the new plan to Leigh-Mallory the next day.[85]

This proposal fit in well with instructions Spaatz had received earlier in the day from Tedder. Tedder, still bound by Churchill's desire to minimize French civilian casualties, required that Spaatz obtain clearance for any targets in France near a town or city center.[86] This dinner session was typical of Spaatz's *modus operandi*. He purposely used the relaxing atmosphere of his comfortable house and table to facilitate compromise and discussion in a convivial setting far removed from an office or conference room where everyone would be on guard.

The next day, Leigh-Mallory disapproved the key airfields plan, whereupon

Vandenberg suggested that he consult Tedder. This Leigh-Mallory did and reported back to Vandenberg that not only Tedder but Eisenhower had approved his own plan to bomb the road choke points between German reinforcements and the beachheads. Reluctantly, Vandenberg then signed the order for an attack on eleven French cities.[87]

On June 3, Tedder, Spaatz, and others trekked to Stanmore for the daily Air Commanders' meeting. Spaatz suggested changes in the employment of the strategic forces. In his view, the plan for strategic air support after the initial D-day strike was too rigid and it lacked provisions for any counterair effort. He probably based his appraisal on the need for a counterair effort on the reports emanating from RAF Air Intelligence. On May 25, AI predicted that approximately 1,600 German aircraft would be engaged against the beachhead by D-day plus four days and that there would be 1,100 to 1,250 German sorties on the day of the invasion.

On May 30, ULTRA identified only ten groups (280 planes) of single-engine fighters in Germany, because of the transfer of other groups to the west.[88] Spaatz proposed withholding a reserve for airfield bombing and the flexible employment of his force according to the flow of the ground assault, rather than the execution of a set scheme of attacks on targets fixed before the battle. Leigh-Mallory ridiculed the suggestion, maintaining that fighters and fighter-bombers could provide the necessary counterair effort. But Spaatz persisted, believing that Leigh-Mallory had committed the Eighth Air Force to "using a doubtful means of delaying enemy ground movements and neglecting a punitive means of reducing his air efforts."[89] Leigh-Mallory would not reconsider his position, and, as Vandenberg noted in his diary, "a slightly acrimonious air prevailed as the meeting was adjourned."[90]

Later, Spaatz met separately with both Eisenhower and Tedder at WIDEWINGS, where he continued to press his views on the employment of heavy bombers. Spaatz complained to Eisenhower that the more bombers he had, the more missions the ground commanders planned to send them on.[91] Eisenhower sympathized but apparently would sanction no changes in the AEAF's plan.

Early Monday morning, June 5, Eisenhower, despite marginal weather conditions, made his fateful decision to commit his forces to the assault the following day, June 6. That evening Spaatz and Vandenberg had dinner at Eisenhower's house and spent the evening at Vandenberg's quarters. There they kept track of the Ninth Air Force's Troop Carrier Command, which had just left its bases to drop two American airborne divisions behind the invasion beaches. For the rest of the night the two continued to receive reports on airborne operations and the lack of German air opposition. They had both worried that the airborne troops, whose route took them directly over portions of the invasion fleet, might encounter the same murderous antiaircraft fire from their own forces as they had during the Sicilian invasion. Around 4:00 A.M., June 6, when the last of the main drops had ended, Spaatz left Vandenberg's residence and returned to his own headquarters to follow the invasion from there.[92]

Each segment of the AAF played its own distinctive part in the operations on D-day. The IX Troop Carrier Command began the American assault on Normandy with its airborne drop during the night of June 5–6. The VIII Fighter Command began patrolling the outer perimeter of the invasion area as the troop carriers and night bombers withdrew. The Eighth's fighters kept up their patrols until the troops landed, whereupon they moved to an area just outside the beachhead to patrol and to attack any legitimate targets. The IX Fighter Command and the RAF (with their shorter-endurance fighters) covered the beaches and provided fighter-bomber support. Five groups of P-38s, one from the Ninth Air Force and four from the Eighth, maintained an all-day umbrella over the invasion convoys delivering the ground assault troops to the beaches. Just before H-hour* the bombers of the Eighth and Ninth attacked the beach defenses. Low clouds forced the heavy bombers to employ H2X. The medium bombers of the Ninth had to come in under the clouds to drop their payloads, exposing themselves to heavy coastal antiaircraft fire. Weather interfered with the Eighth's second mission of the day, and only three groups, approximately 90 aircraft out of 528 bombers dispatched, released their bombs on road choke points outside the beachhead. Other Eighth Air Force missions bombed Caen and transportation targets in a wide arc from Coutances in the west to Lisieux in the east. For the day, the Eighth and Ninth launched 8,722 sorties and lost 71 aircraft, mostly fighters, to flak.[93]

As for the Luftwaffe it could mount barely 100 sorties (70 by fighters) on the first day of the invasion, and only 175 more completely ineffectual sorties on the night of June 6–7. In all of France it possessed 815 aircraft, including 325 bombers, 170 single-engine fighters, 45 twin-engine fighters, and only 75 ground attack aircraft.[94] As Spaatz stated in late June 1944, "The concentrated attacks on the Luftwaffe, production, and product, paid the dividends that we always envisioned, the dividend being beyond expectation. During the entire first day of the invasion enemy opposition in the air, either fighter or bomber, was next to nil."[95]

The battle for air supremacy over the beachhead never occurred, because the AAF had already defeated the Luftwaffe over Germany. D-day and the Luftwaffe's feeble reaction in the following weeks amply proved Spaatz's oft-repeated contention that the greatest contribution the strategic air forces could make to OVERLORD was the smashing of the German fighter force. This offensive achievement ranked with the defensive victory of the RAF in the Battle of Britain. The demise of the German fighter force was a turning point in the air war.

---

* H-hour, the time when the first assault craft would land and release its troops onto the beach, was 6:30 A.M. for the American invasion beaches (Omaha and Utah) and 7:00 A.M. and 7:30 A.M. for the British landings. Among the factors dictating selection of H-hour were at least an hour of daylight before it (for preliminary bombardment) and tide at half-flood (to expose German obstacles) and rising (to ensure two high tides in daylight for maximum unloading of supplies).

When Spaatz returned to London from the Mediterranean in late December 1943 to form the U.S. Strategic Air Forces in Europe, he had two primary tasks: to justify and execute the AAF's portion of the Combined Bomber Offensive against Germany and to ensure the success of the U.S.-British cross-channel invasion to the best of his ability. These tasks required him to serve two masters, Arnold and Eisenhower, both of whom had, at times, very different conceptions of the part they wished him to play.

Arnold had fought for the creation of USSTAF because he believed that the American strategic air forces in Italy and England should have a single, able airman to coordinate, control, and command them. Arnold had another objective as well. As he told Spaatz in late February 1944:

> The other, and perhaps equally important, motive behind the formation of the United States Strategic Air Forces in Europe was my desire to build an American Air Commander to a high position prior to the defeat of Germany. It is that aspect particularly which had impelled me in my so far successful fight to keep your command parallel in stature to Harris' command and, therefore, parallel to Ike's.

Arnold further felt the need to ensure the AAF a proper share of the victory. He told Spaatz:

> If you do not remain in a position parallel with Harris the air war will certainly be won by the RAF, if anybody. Already the spectacular effectiveness of their devastation of cities has placed their contribution in the popular mind at so high a plane that I am having the greatest difficulty in keeping your achievement (far less spectacular to the public) in its proper role not only in publications, but unfortunately in military and naval circles, and in fact, with the President himself. Therefore, considering only the aspect of a proper American share in credit for success in the air war, I feel we must have a high air commander some place in Europe. *Today you can be that commander* [emphasis added].[96]

Eisenhower, in contrast, wanted control of the strategic forces in order to guarantee the success of OVERLORD. He required that control as early as possible—far longer than desired by Arnold, who initially conceded only that the heavy bombers would come under the Supreme Commander during the assault phase of the invasion. In addition, Eisenhower intended to use his control of the strategic air forces to implement a plan whose aims, requirements, and methods of execution raised profound doubts in the minds of many senior airmen, including Spaatz.

Spaatz, of course, had his own ideas; he did not meekly follow the dictates of his powerful superiors. Against Arnold's hopes, he did not do his utmost to maintain a position independent from Eisenhower's. He did not object to coming under Eisenhower's control, provided he was not subordinated to the AEAF and provided Bomber Command came under equal and parallel control. Spaatz's willingness to come under Eisenhower, however, did not mean that he abdicated his responsibility as a professional airman to employ his units to inflict maximum damage on the enemy. An examination of Spaatz's actions from New Year's Day 1944 to D-day, June 6, 1944, shows that he not only served his masters well but did so while remaining his own man.

From the beginning of his tenure, Spaatz clearly saw that the attainment of the goals of both POINTBLANK and OVERLORD depended on a single factor—the destruction of the Luftwaffe. Once he had severed Hitler's air arm, he could pulverize Germany's war economy and ensure air supremacy for the land campaign. Spaatz remorselessly pursued that goal, pushing the men under his command almost to the breaking point. Doolittle, under the watchful eyes of Anderson and Spaatz, sent his men and machines into the air day after day. By March, the Eighth Air Force often abandoned deception tactics and flew straight to their targets in order to provoke attrition. The primary reason the Eighth made the long, hard, costly trip to Berlin was not just to bomb Hitler's capital but to force the Luftwaffe into the air. At last, when their losses in machines and pilots forced the Germans to adopt a policy of conservation, Spaatz insisted, over the objections of Tedder and Portal and the resistance of Eisenhower, on launching the strategic attack on the German oil industry. The absolutely necessary defense of that target system exposed the Luftwaffe to further punishing attrition.

Spaatz's championship of the oil plan exemplified his ability to fight for and gain his own goals while not irreparably damaging the teamwork and unity demanded by successful coalition warfare and interservice cooperation. Spaatz believed that if he could smash the oil industry, he could quickly and fatally weaken Germany. He would not allow anyone or anything to permanently divert him from that goal. First, he presented an alternative to the transportation plan. When that failed, he sought an opportunity to demonstrate the effectiveness of his policy. When the Germans showed signs of conserving their fighter force, Spaatz had the leverage he needed to obtain Eisenhower's approval of a limited trial of oil bombing. As Spaatz had opined, the actual bombing revealed the acute sensitivity of the Germans to threats to their oil.

Spaatz did not simply advocate the oil plan. He took risks with his career by authorizing the clandestine bombing of the Ploesti refineries. Such a move, if unsuccessful, might have been difficult to explain and could have earned him a reprimand or worse. But again, by keeping that bombing sub rosa, he allowed the British to ignore it when they heard of it, which presumably they did soon after the raids.

Spaatz used variations of this same subterfuge in his unsigned letters to Portal on morale and to Eisenhower on civilian casualties, and in obtaining permission to interdict bridges. In these instances, the results justified Spaatz's actions and judgments. That he did not show similar restraint in his dealings with Leigh-Mallory is understandable. He did not believe that Leigh-Mallory was competent to perform his duties or, because of his high-handedness and insensitivity, deal with Americans. Because Leigh-Mallory insisted on having a headquarters top-heavy with British personnel and tried to interfere with his relationship with the Ninth Air Force, Spaatz apparently decided that, in this instance, the rules of Allied unity need not apply. Spaatz continued to question Leigh-Mallory's plans until the eve of the invasion.

The efforts of the AAF in this period cost dearly in blood and matériel. From January 1 through May 31, the Eighth and Fifteenth Air Forces lost 2,351 heavy bombers on combat missions. They wrote off another 254 from accidents and unrepairable battle damage. The Eighth and Ninth Air Forces lost 983 fighters and suffered 18,403 casualties (5,427 killed in action, 11,033 missing in action or interned, and 1,943 wounded). Ninety percent of those men, most of whom were missing in action or prisoners of war, would not fight against Germany again. The Fifteenth and Twelfth Air Forces lost 595 fighters and sustained 7,285 casualties (2,780 killed in action, 3,452 missing in action, and 1,053 wounded). The Fifteenth probably suffered 80 percent of the AAF's personnel losses in the Mediterranean. This expenditure of resources gained the Allies air supremacy over Europe. With air supremacy came the freedom to bomb at will any target in Germany and the freedom invade France without Luftwaffe interference.

The achievement of air supremacy over France and the invasion area and of air superiority over Germany before D-day was the decisive contribution of Spaatz and USSTAF to OVERLORD. Battling for control of the skies on the day of the invasion might have ruined Allied objectives. By forcing the Luftwaffe to concentrate its chief defensive effort over Germany, USSTAF left the Luftwaffe unable or unwilling to oppose the Allied interdiction air campaign in northern France. The Eighth's contribution to the transportation plan, although not niggardly, amounted to less than one-third of Bomber Command's—13,000 tons to 46,000 tons.[97] For the first three months of 1944, 70 percent of the Eighth's bombs hit German soil.[98] In April, the Eighth Air Force dropped 62.5 percent of its bombs on Germany; in May, 57 percent of its bombs fell on Germany.[99] Given the increase in bombers available to Doolittle in April and May, actual tonnage on the Reich went up in both months. Thus, preinvasion bombing, although a diversion, did not greatly damage the Combined Bomber Offensive. For the first five months of 1944, CROSSBOW targets received more tonnage— 16,082 tons—than transportation targets.[100] This represented a dead loss to the Eighth's war effort, because CROSSBOW neither involved Luftwaffe fighter opposition nor substantially delayed German deployment of V-1 pilotless jet propelled bombers. Transportation bombing at least aided the invasion.

Spaatz's bridge campaign may have been at least as important as the transportation plan. The bridge campaign consumed only 4,400 tons of bombs and for the first phase of the invasion greatly reduced the Germans' ability to shift heavy units rapidly to the invasion beachhead. The units eventually arrived but battered, piecemeal, and late, which gave the Allied ground forces the time they needed to consolidate their positions.

417

In the first six days of June, the Eighth bombed only tactical targets in France in support of the Overlord assault. Out of 14,230 tons dropped, the Eighth dropped 7,018 on the Pas-de-Calais coastal defenses as part of Allied preinvasion deception efforts, and 4,852 on D-day.[101] Aside from in some measure keeping Hitler's attention fixed on Pas-de-Calais as the most probable invasion site, this effort probably contributed little to the success of the invasion. There was no testimony among the German defenders at the Normandy beaches of any discomfiture attributable to Allied heavy bombers.

USSTAF's preinvasion bombing certainly damaged the Germans, but those efforts seem small compared with the efforts of Bomber Command and the AEAF, which by themselves would have sufficed to fulfill the Allies' goals for preinvasion air operations. If USSTAF had spent that same effort demolishing the German oil industry, the Allies might have won the war earlier. Spaatz did everything in his power to keep his bombers over Germany where they could bomb oil targets and maintain air supremacy.

Part Five

The Mortal Blow
From Normandy to Berlin,
June 6, 1944–May 9, 1945

Part Five

The Mortal Blow

During the last eleven months of the war in Europe the Anglo-American Allies successfully established themselves on the Continent, broke out of their beachhead to drive across France to the German border, fought an arduous campaign to penetrate the German border defenses, repelled Hitler's last-gamble counteroffensive, crossed the Rhine River to meet the westward advancing forces of the Soviet Union, and finally forced the unconditional surrender of the German state. The Army Air Forces and its senior officer in Europe, Carl Spaatz, played a large role in achieving Allied victory. Operating under Dwight Eisenhower's direct control from June to September 1944 and thereafter independently, the United States Strategic Air Forces in Europe crushed the already defeated Luftwaffe while seeking a balance between its strategic mission of destroying the German war economy and its tactical responsibilities to aid the advance of the Allied ground armies by all means possible.

Because his dual positions as the commander of both USSTAF and the AAF in the European Theater of Operations gave Spaatz administrative control of all AAF units in the theater, he became the de facto leader of almost all U.S. Army Air Forces fighting the Nazis. Even Ira Eaker, AAF commander of the Mediterranean Allied Air Forces, often consulted with Spaatz and tended to defer to his judgment. The head of the AAF, Arnold, certainly viewed Spaatz as the principal U.S. airman in Europe. Arnold did his utmost to support Spaatz with men and matériel while charging him with the task of enhancing the image and status of the AAF at every opportunity.

Thanks in part to his close and easy relationships with the Supreme Commander Allied Expeditionary Force, Eisenhower, and the Deputy Supreme Commander, Tedder, Spaatz balanced the competing and sometimes contradictory demands on his command's capabilities with an *éclat* that brought promotion for himself and, more important, prestige and credit to the AAF.

Chapter 12

Summer 1944:
CROSSBOW, THUNDERCLAP,
and Strategic Bombing
(June–September 1944)

My own opinion of the present situation is that so far the
Germans have been very successful in that all the power of
the Americans and the British is being contained in a narrow beachhead by fourteen half-baked . . . divisions,
thereby relieving Germany of the pressure of the bombardment to which they have been subjected during the past six
months.[1]

—*Spaatz's Command Diary, June 17, 1944*

From June to mid-September 1944, the fighting on the ground between the
Western Allies and the Germans divided into two distinct phases: (1) the landing
and expansion of the beachhead (June 6 to July 24) and (2) the breakout from
the beachhead and pursuit of the defeated Germans to the French-German border
(July 25 to September 10). Whereas the operations of the Allied tactical air
forces had to adapt to the exigencies of the ground situation, the operations of
the strategic air forces developed differently. Spaatz, although subordinate to
Eisenhower until the middle of September, had his eyes on a perspective beyond
that of some ground and tactical air leaders who wished to put themselves into a
position from which they could attack and destroy Germany. Spaatz already had
the means available to attack deep within Germany. He fought to retain his
forces for the Combined Bomber Offensive, while the ground soldiers continually pressed him to divert his planes to tasks on the front line or relatively close
behind it. They believed that a well-timed, heavy air strike might provide the
final element needed to achieve the decisive breakthrough.

This argument could never convince a strategically minded airman like Spaatz. He pleaded that large formations of heavy bombers did not easily lend themselves to concentration on a single decisive point necessary for the support of a land attack. The Eighth often launched missions consisting of several hundred heavy bombers, but when they reached their target area, they separated into component bomb wings (100 to 150 bombers) or bomb groups (40 to 50 planes) to deliver their ordnance on individual targets. This practice increased bombing accuracy and avoided possible problems when too many bombers hit the same target at too close intervals. These problems included dust and smoke clouds obscuring the target, antiaircraft artillery, and air congestion disrupting formations and causing highly spread bomb patterns. In any case, the Army did not need, except in cases of emergency, the constant support of heavy bombers and their escorts when the tactical air forces had ample numbers of fighter-bombers and medium bombers at the beck and call of the ground forces. Spaatz's efforts to maintain the strategic bomber offensive in the face of diversions to retard the German V-1 attacks on England, to support the ground forces, and to engage in morale bombing as opposed to precision bombing over Germany constitute the theme of this chapter.

Initial Operations

Before the invasion Spaatz had agreed to aid the assault phase of the operation. For that critical phase the Eighth Air Force ceased its attacks directed against German industry and devoted its efforts to the bombing program called for in preinvasion and invasion deception plans. From May 30, when the Eighth struck aircraft production targets in Germany and then temporarily halted strategic attacks, until June 18, when it resumed missions against industrial targets in Germany, the Eighth flew exclusively in support of the invasion. In June the Eighth dropped 44,209 tons of bombs on France, almost 76 percent of its effort for the month.[2]

The Germans, too, meant to put their maximum air power into the skies over the beachhead. To that end, in the four days following D-day they sent more than 300 single-engine fighter aircraft in addition to the 170 already in France to fly ground support for the troops battling the Allies.[3] This action, however, proved disastrous. The Luftwaffe drew its planes from the fighter force defending the homeland against attacks by Allied heavy-bomber forces and assigned them to fledgling pilots, who had just replaced the veteran pilots killed or disabled in the spring, were minimally trained for antibomber operations, and had no ground support training. In their flights to the forward airfields they suffered an accumulation of losses not only from Allied aircraft, who knew their flight plans from signal intelligence decryptions,[4] but also from their own faulty navigation and from landings on unfamiliar fields.[5]

The Luftwaffe literally telegraphed its punches to the Allies. Throughout

Lt. Gen. Carl A. Spaatz and General Henry H. Arnold visiting the first Ninth Air Force air strip constructed in the Normandy beachhead, June 1944.

this phase of the campaign in the west, the Allied ULTRA signal intercept organization read and distributed the Luftwaffe's messages at least as quickly as the intended recipients.[6] The Luftwaffe Enigma machine was simpler than its army and navy equivalents in that it possessed one less code-setting wheel or rotor. Consequently, the ULTRA organization had fewer difficulties deciphering the Luftwaffe's messages than those of the other German armed forces. As early as 2:30 P.M. on June 6, ULTRA learned that eighteen fighter groups had left Germany for France.[7] By June 8, it learned that seven more groups had arrived, and it passed their exact locations on to Allied operational units. Within six days of the invasion, June 12, ULTRA knew that because of the fierce pressure exerted by the Allies, the Luftwaffe had given up on fighter-bombing, ordering the removal of bomb racks and the reconversion of their aircraft to their pure fighter configuration.[8] This action, which eliminated the fighters' capacity to deliver bombs, proved that the Luftwaffe had abandoned its ground support role and had been forced entirely into defense against Allied air attacks. By the end of the first week, the Luftwaffe's strength stood at 1,100 machines, its highest of the campaign.

The British Air Ministry greatly overestimated this force at 1,615 aircraft, but noted a very low serviceability rate, 33 percent for fighters and 16 percent for fighter-bombers. The average daily fighter effort ranged from 250 to 300 sorties. RAF Air Intelligence noted that bomber groups operated at only 65 percent of establishment.[9] Heavy attacks by the Eighth over airfields on June 14 and 15—based on information from ULTRA intercepts—applied the coup de grace. On June 16, the Luftwaffe withdrew five shattered groups for refitting in Germany. Their replacements at the front, also drawn from domestic air defense duties, fared little better. During the month of June 1944, the total fighter force available for German home defense fell from 700 to 370.[10]

The diversion of the Eighth Air Force from the strategic bombing campaign to the immediate support of the invasion could not have been avoided. It was unlikely that Eisenhower, who had ultimate control of the heavy bombers and most of the other high-level Allied commanders, would ever have allowed the Combined Bomber Offensive to continue unabated while the Luftwaffe and the German Army rushed units toward the beachhead. Spaatz had accepted this fact from the day he learned of his appointment to USSTAF. In any case, the Luftwaffe was unable to use the temporary halt in POINTBLANK to any advantage. Instead, Hitler and Goering stripped the homeland of half of its defending aircraft to send them into the maelstrom over Normandy, where overwhelming Allied air power quickly dashed them to bits. When the Combined Bomber Offensive resumed, it found much less opposition.

Operation CROSSBOW

The first major diversion of the strategic bombing forces, after operations flown in direct support of OVERLORD, began within a few days of the invasion. On the night of June 12–13, the first V-1 robot bomb, designated by the Germans as *Vergeltungswaffe eins* (Reprisal Weapon No. 1) and called, among other names, "flying bomb," "buzz-bomb," or "doodlebug" by the Allies, struck England. In the next few days, the rate of the attack, directed mainly toward London, increased. In retrospect, this weapon caused much more alarm among the English people and their political leaders than was warranted. Nonetheless, at the time, the V-1, with its near-total unpredictability and unnerving buzzing sound that shut off just before impact, provoked extraordinary anxiety and led to extreme pressure on the Allies to reduce the threat.

In all, between June 13 and September 1, 1944, 5,890 flying bombs landed in England. They killed 5,835 persons and seriously injured an additional 16,762. London suffered 90 percent of all casualties.[11] Each weapon killed, on the average, one person and seriously injured almost three more. In contrast, during the ten-day Battle of Hamburg in July 1943, the RAF and the AAF killed almost 50,000 German civilians, most as the result of a single fire storm on the night of July 27–28.[12] (See Map 13, Operation CROSSBOW Network.)

Because the Allied armies had bogged down in Normandy and could not break out to occupy any launch sites farther up the French coast and because they needed most of the tactical air forces' efforts for their own support, the burden of countering the V-1 fell to the strategic air forces. The British wanted the

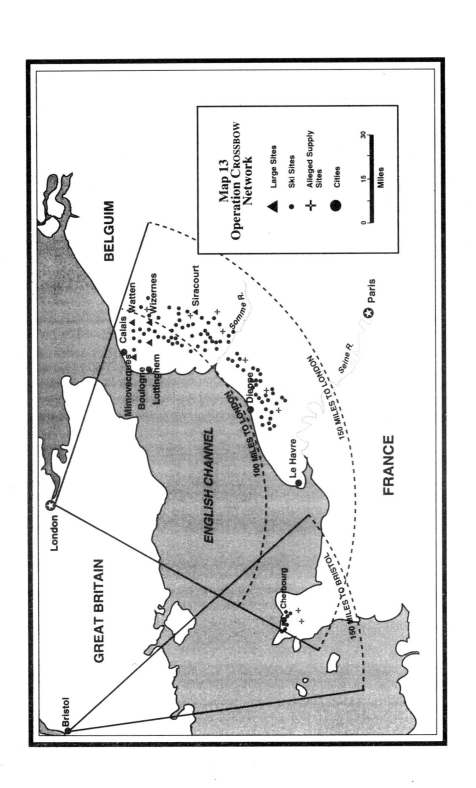

GREAT BRITAIN

BELGUIM

London

Bristol

ENGLISH CHANNEL

FRANCE

Calais
Watten
Mimoyecques
Wizernes
Boulogne
Lottinghem
Siracourt
Somme R.
Dieppe
Le Havre
Cherbourg
Seine R.
Paris

100 MILES TO LONDON
150 MILES TO LONDON
150 MILES TO BRISTOL

Map 13
Operation Crossbow
Network

▲ Large Sites
• Ski Sites
✚ Alleged Supply
   Sites
● Cities

0   15   30
          Miles

launch sites bombed into inoperability, and they wanted counterterror raids conducted on the German people. Spaatz objected to both solutions; previous bombings of launch sites had proved ineffective and terror bombing could produce no predictable result to justify the abandonment of precision bombing.

At first the Allies failed to react, but the firing of 300 buzz bombs on the night of June 15–16 necessitated some countermeasure. On June 18, Churchill visited Tedder and Eisenhower at the latter's headquarters at WIDEWINGS in the London suburb of Teddington. Churchill persuaded them to designate V-1 sites as the chief targets of the strategic air forces.[13] Eisenhower passed the decision along to the airmen at the Daily Air Commanders' Meeting and emphasized to all present the seriousness with which he viewed the situation. He approved the use of USSTAF and Bomber Command and every other "means practicable for stopping the pilotless aircraft."[14] At the end of the meeting, Eisenhower told Maj. Gen. Fred Anderson to carry the word to Spaatz that CROSSBOW would "receive first priority over all other targets, either in France or Germany."[15] Eisenhower followed up his message with a call to Spaatz that afternoon, and Spaatz promised to set aside a small force for exclusive use against V-1 sites.[16]

Spaatz and Doolittle responded promptly. They had already resumed CROSSBOW strikes on June 16 and 18, and on June 19 they stepped up their effort by sending 703 heavy bombers out to hit V-1 launch sites. During six of the remaining eleven days of the month, the Eighth sent out CROSSBOW missions of at least 125 planes each. In addition to hitting the launch sites, the Eighth broadened its attack to include electrical switching and power stations that supplied the weapons as well as storage areas. Bomber Command took even stronger measures, and the Ninth also contributed 1,500 medium-bomber sorties starting on June 23. For the latter half of June, Allied air power dispatched 8,310 bomber sorties and dropped 23,431 tons of bombs.[17] As AAF official historians acknowledged, "CROSSBOW Operations during the second half of June indicated that the Germans had again created for the Allies a diversionary problem of the first magnitude."[18]

From the beginning of this new phase of CROSSBOW, Spaatz voiced his objections to the amount of force he had to devote to it and to the targets selected for it. Like most of the AAF's commanders in Europe, Spaatz believed that mass bombing of the launch sites accomplished little. The Germans had hardened the large sites with vast amounts of concrete, making them impervious to the most powerful bombs. They had, for the most part, abandoned the large sites to concentrate on small, well-camouflaged positions almost impossible to spot from the air. Spaatz wished to bomb the electrical system in Pas-de-Calais, which would stymie the functioning of the large sites and supply areas. The British, who controlled the V-1 targeting selection from the Air Ministry, incorporated these proposals into their plans but did not emphasize them.[19] They continued to expend most of the heavy-bomber effort on large launch sites, with negligible results. Spaatz asked Arnold to direct the air proving grounds in

Winston Churchill wearing the uniform of a Marshal of the RAF at an antiaircraft gun line in Britain.

Florida to begin experiments using war-weary planes loaded with explosives. Spaatz hoped to fly the planes by remote control to crash into otherwise impregnable targets. At the same time he initiated within the theater a similar program variously called APHRODITE or WEARY-WILLIE.[20]

Finally, he offered two suggestions closer to his true purpose—that of maintaining the Combined Bomber Offensive. He offered to bomb the German factories making the V-1's gyroscopes and the large, recently discovered V-1 storage depots in France.[21] The bombing of factories in Germany would serve Spaatz's twofold purpose of halting the V-1 attacks and of luring the Luftwaffe into the sky.

On June 29, he hand-carried a letter to Eisenhower expressing his views on the main tasks facing USSTAF. In it he pointed out that the defeat of the Luftwaffe had taken place over Germany and not the occupied countries: "I consider the primary tasks of the Strategic Air Forces now to be the denial to the German ground . . . of the means with which to effectively continue resistance and the continuation of the neutralization of the German Air Force." To accomplish these tasks Spaatz asked Eisenhower to make the following policy decision: "On those days when weather conditions over Germany are favorable for visual bombing, such operations should have overriding priority over all others." Spaatz allowed for two exceptions—a major emergency involving the ground

429

forces and operations against the large installations being prepared to launch the German rocket-propelled V-2. The V-2 was a supersonic rocket whose advent the Allies feared perhaps even more than that of the V-1. No defense, save the destruction of its takeoff platform, could work against the swift, powerful V-2. Spaatz did not believe that operations against V-1 firing sites could be sufficiently decisive on any one day to justify diverting the strategic air forces from their primary tasks on the few days of favorable weather over Germany. As for the use of heavy bombers in support of the ground forces, Spaatz noted, "In the absence of a major ground force emergency, I do not believe that the results from the tactical use of heavy bombers will constitute as much support to OVERLORD as the use of the same force against critical German targets." Spaatz explained that the "normal weather cycle" ensured enough unsuitable weather over Germany to provide a large proportion of the available heavy-bomber effort for employment against tactical objectives in Normandy.[22]

Although Eisenhower privately regarded the V-1 as "very much of a nuisance,"[23] his ranking of air priorities naturally differed from Spaatz's. In a memo to his chief of staff, Maj. Gen. Walter Bedell Smith, he observed that by September 20 good flying weather over Europe would cease. Therefore, for the next sixty to ninety days he ranked "direct attacks against Germany" sixth in priority below normal close support of the ground army, disruption of communication lines, neutralization of CROSSBOW, airborne operations, and supply of troops by air. However, he allowed an escape clause: "In any event there will unquestionably be sufficient days, when other types of operations are impracticable, to continue the striking [air] assault upon Germany, and there will be days during the winter when this can likewise be carried out."[24]

When he received Spaatz's letter, June 29, Eisenhower appended it to a memo for Deputy Supreme Commander Tedder in which he issued a new bombing directive giving CROSSBOW top priority with the proviso, " . . . when we have favorable conditions over Germany and when the entire Strategic Air Force cannot be used against CROSSBOW, we should attack—a. Aircraft industry; b. Oil; c. Ball bearings; d. Vehicular production."[25]

Spaatz's resentment of and resistance to the CROSSBOW diversion continued into July. When he received an allocation of targets giving the Eighth Air Force sixty-eight CROSSBOW targets as compared to thirty for Bomber Command and only six for the AEAF, he strongly protested to Eisenhower, "If we are to consider all these targets as a high priority obligation, the implementation of our strategic bombing plans will be seriously hindered."[26] At the forefront of Spaatz's objections lay the realization that long summer days provided unparalleled opportunities for his own forces but denied opportunities to Bomber Command, which could not penetrate deeply into Germany during the short summer nights in northern Europe. A short winter's day later could not replace a long sunlit summer's day, which gave the U.S. bomber formations license to penetrate as deeply as possible into German-occupied Europe. Spaatz pointed out to Eisenhower:

Germans preparing to launch a V-1 flying bomb across the English Channel.

It must be borne in mind that the U.S. Strategic Air Force is the only force presently in a position to make deep penetrations in strength beyond the Ruhr and therefore must be responsible for the largest share of the strategic task of denying to the enemy the means with which to effectively continue resistance.[27]

Spaatz also noted that CROSSBOW would interfere with USSTAF's tactical target assignments (bridges, POL [petroleum, oil, and lubricants] dumps, and airfields). Because of the "present restricted operational capabilities" of Bomber Command and the limited range of the tactical air force, he recommended that they be directed to maintain a fixed percentage of their force for CROSSBOW. For his part, he promised to put in a strong effort against the V-2 launch sites when he could not fly over Germany. "Such an arrangement," he stated, "should insure adequate effort against the CROSSBOW installations and . . . will not force one command to carry a greater burden than another to the detriment of the other priority tasks and the war effort as a whole."[28]

On the same day Spaatz discussed the CROSSBOW situation with Tedder. They agreed that current crazy-quilt air command arrangements interfered with the coordination of the CROSSBOW campaign. Spaatz used this chance to emphasize the need to continue operations over Germany in order to shorten the war and to continue the destruction of the German fighter force. He hoped to strain the Luftwaffe's depleted daylight fighter force to such an extent that its crack night fighter force would have to join daylight battles. "If this is not done now," Spaatz told Tedder, "the British night bomber force will not be able to operate without excessive losses when the nights get longer."[29] Tedder, despite the pressure on him from the British government to bomb CROSSBOW sites, agreed to work with Spaatz in persuading Eisenhower to free USSTAF from excessive commitment to CROSSBOW.[30] Finally, Tedder, Portal, and Eisenhower, at Spaatz's urging,[31] set up a Joint CROSSBOW Committee to coordinate among the relevant air agencies but it proved ineffectual, in the opinion of USSTAF.[32] In any case, there was no need for it after the V-1 launch sites were eliminated by ground forces in late August.

From July and August until Allied ground troops overran the sites around September 1, Bomber Command, USSTAF, and the AEAF rained bombs on the entire identified V-weapon target system—from the German experimental rocket research station at Peenemunde on the Baltic, through the manufacturing plants at Russelsheim and Ober Raderach, through the power stations and electrical switching sites in France, to the storage areas and launch sites in Pas-de-Calais. The campaign lasted seventy-seven days. In just two months—July and August—the Allied air forces expended 16,566 sorties and one-fourth of their total tonnage on CROSSBOW targets,[33] all, however, to little avail. The AAF official history admits that the rate of V-1 firings continued "essentially unhindered,"[34] and concludes, "The CROSSBOW campaign of the summer of 1944 must be regarded generally as having failed to achieve its objectives. Indeed it seems to have been the least successful part of the over-all effort."[35]

Reprisal Bombing and THUNDERCLAP

The ineffectiveness of CROSSBOW raised the specter of another diversion of the strategic bombing effort. The failure of the rate of V-1 firings to drop by early July 1944, which was apparent to residents of London, led to demands for the diversion of the strategic air forces to retaliation or counterterror raids over Germany. These demands were behind Air Chief Marshal Harris's request to schedule Bomber Command with the Eighth on a daylight mission over Berlin on June 21, 1944. Portal informed Churchill that he, Spaatz, Tedder, and Eisenhower favored the operation. More than 2,000 bombers, including 700 from Bomber Command, would drop 6,500 tons of bombs. "At the lowest," said Portal, "it will be a pretty good answer to the results achieved in the last few days by the 'flying bomb'."[36] Operational considerations, such as the effectiveness of the German night fighter force and the lack of night-time flying hours (at the time of the summer solstice in European latitudes), also influenced Harris's decision to participate in a daylight raid.

However, at 1:00 A.M. on June 21, Harris, with Tedder's concurrence,[37] scrubbed the mission. Base weather did not look favorable. Harris did not approve of Doolittle's decision to send only half of his bomber force over the main target area, which increased the risk of flak to the low-flying RAF. He also had misgivings because mission plans revealed that the number of escorts supplied the British might drop from 300 to 150 or less.[38] This decision was greeted with relief by Spaatz and Doolittle, who no longer had to stretch their escort fighters to cover the bomber formations of both air forces.[39] The Eighth sent 1,000 bombers to the Berlin area: 368 B-24s bombed targets in the vicinity of the city, and 560 B-17s, using visual bombing techniques, released 1,371 tons of bombs, 20 percent of them incendiaries, on the military and civilian government area in the center of the city. This was the ninth release since March 6 by the Eighth of 750 or more tons on the heart of the city.[40]

The idea of reprisal raids for the V-1, once started, gained a life of its own. By June 27, USSTAF developed Operation SHATTER, which proposed to bomb 100 or more German cities in a single day in order to demonstrate to the German people (1) their vulnerability, (2) their defenselessness, (3) the full scope of Allied air power, (4) the fact that no city in Germany was too insignificant a target, and (5) the decline of the Luftwaffe. The authors of this plan, however, did not wish the attack to be tarred with the brush of terror bombing. They suggested striking utilities, transportation networks, government buildings, or minor industries.[41]

Churchill raised the subject of reprisal raids at his Chiefs of Staff meeting on July 1, suggesting that the British announce their intention to flatten lesser German cities in turn if V-1 attacks continued. The British Chiefs agreed to postpone action to allow for a thorough study. In the meantime, Churchill took up the policy with Bedell Smith, who approved it, and Tedder, who considered it ineffective and "wickedly uneconomical."[42] At the British Chiefs of Staff meeting on July 3, Portal spoke against retaliatory bombing, warning that it gave "invaluable proof" to the Germans that their V-1 policy had succeeded and amounted to entering into negotiations with the enemy. The Germans would not alter their plans for the sake of unimportant towns, and such bombing would divert resources from more important communications and oil targets. The other Chiefs agreed to further study.[43]

At his War Cabinet meeting that evening Churchill ordered his Chiefs to take up the matter the next day. Portal presented further arguments against the idea. Fearing that the Germans might resort to counter measures, such as murdering downed air crews from British reprisal raids, he recommended adding V-1 attacks to the list of war crimes for which the Nazis would be held accountable after the war. "We could not hope to keep pace with the Germans in a campaign of reprisals," he concluded. The British Chiefs agreed to prepare a report on all aspects of retaliatory bombing, including the use of poison gas.[44] The report, prepared by the Air Staff and the Ministry of Economic Warfare, took twenty-four hours and reflected Portal's views. "No threat," he reasoned, "is likely to deter Hitler in his present fix. Indeed it may well encourage him to order more F.B.'s [flying bombs] and make still further efforts to increase the scale of attack." A threat to bomb the towns (1) implied a guarantee not to bomb them if Hitler stopped his V-1 campaign and (2) opened the door to the Germans on negotiations over other aspects of bombing. Portal acknowledged, "Actually, London with its vast production, its communications centres, and the seat of Government is (under the conditions prevailing in the present war) a perfectly legitimate target for the sort of 'browning' [night nuisance] attacks which we are making by instruments on Berlin."[45] The final report repeated Portal's arguments recommending rejection of the policy.[46] This rejection did not end the matter. On July 5, the British Chiefs of Staff agreed "that the time might well come in the not too distant future when an all-out attack by every means at our disposal on German civilian morale might be decisive." The British Chiefs recommended to Churchill "that the method by which such an attack would be carried out should be examined and all possible preparations made."[47]

For the next month a working committee with Air Staff, Foreign Office, Ministry of Economic Warfare, and USSTAF representatives met to determine the ideal approach to conducting a morale attack. On July 22, the committee issued a preliminary report and concluded that the object of any morale attack was "to influence the minds of the German authorities in such a way that they prefer organized surrender to continued resistance." Until final military defeat was imminent, the Allies should continue the bomber offensive against economic and military targets. Any assault should be coordinated with Allied propaganda policy and directed against the High Command, the army, and the civilian population. Because of its importance as a center of population, industry, communications, and administration, Berlin was selected as the target of the committee's campaign. The results of such bombing—the disruption of governmental services and communications at a critical juncture, as well as the demoralization of minor civil servants—would lead to an overall breakdown of public morale. Berlin had the operational advantage of being free of weather restrictions (its size made it easy to locate on radar scopes), and it could be attacked on short notice because both air forces knew the route to and the defenses of the city. The committee proposed to deliver 20,000 tons of bombs in a four-day and three-night round-the-clock blitz of the administrative center of Berlin.[48] According to the British, Spaatz was in "general agreement" with the recommendations, but preferred "that no reference should be made in it to the concurrence of his unofficial representative at the meeting which discussed it."[49]

Spaatz's reasons for withholding "official" concurrence were not clear. Apparently, the plan's focus on population bombing troubled him. On July 21, after receiving advance notice of the morale committee's report, he discussed the issue with Eisenhower, who stated, "We will continue precision bombing and not be deflected to morale bombing."[50] Yet on the same day, Spaatz's Deputy for Operations, Maj. Gen. Frederick L. Anderson, issued a USSTAF policy directive to both the Eighth and Fifteenth Air Forces. Noting Spaatz's oft reiterated and continuing intention to bomb precision targets, Anderson categorically denied any intention to area-bomb. But having denied the intention, Anderson proceeded to authorize the practice: "We will conduct bombing attacks through the overcast where it is impossible to get precision targets. Such attacks will include German marshalling yards whether or not they are located in German cities."[51] As Anderson and Spaatz well knew, bombs dropped on targets in cities using overcast bombing techniques would cause great collateral damage. Apparently, it was acceptable to attack German civilians if they lived in cities with military targets, but not acceptable to make German civilians targets in and of themselves.

In fact, thanks to four missions against Munich, which bombed through overcast and carried large percentages of incendiaries, Eighth Air Force records showed a wartime high for tonnage dropped on "towns & cities" of 9,886 tons in July 1944.[52] Anderson and others in USSTAF did not regard this policy as hypocritical. They knew they had not aimed these raids at civilians, but rather at military targets. They judged themselves by their motives rather than their results.

The committee's final draft, submitted to the British Chiefs of Staff on August 3, placed even greater emphasis on population bombing and gave the plan of attack on German civilian morale a code name—THUNDERCLAP.[53] The operational details called for 2,000 Eighth Air Force bombers to drop 5,000 tons, under visual conditions, on a $2^1/_2$ square-mile area of central Berlin, estimated to contain a daytime population of 375,000. A bomb density of 2,000 tons per square mile would produce approximately 137,500 dead and 137,500 seriously injured. If necessary, the Fifteenth Air Force could participate, and Bomber Command could follow up with a night incendiary raid.[54]

The plan continued to percolate through the AAF and RAF staffs. Kuter questioned it, writing to Anderson, "Since any such attack will feature U.S.A.A.F. units in the limelight, we should consider whether the recent buzz bomb attacks have not instilled in the British Government a desire for retaliation in which American air units will be called upon to share with the R.A.F. Bomber Command the onus for the more critical features of night area bombing." Kuter reaffirmed the AAF's policy of attacking military targets. "Our entire target policy has been founded on the fact that it was uneconomical to bomb any except military objectives and the German productive capacity. The bombing of civilian targets in Germany cannot be expected to have similar effects to those which might be expected in a democratic country where the people are still able to influence national will." Kuter concluded: "It is contrary to our national ideals to wage war against civilians."

Ironically, a war plan Kuter had helped to author three years earlier called for the very action he now questioned. AWPD/1 had provided for a massive strategic bombing campaign against Germany and contained specific suggestions on possible target systems. It listed four lines of action whose accomplishment would fulfill the air mission in Europe, including "undermining of German morale by air attack of civil concentrations." In discussing that action AWPD/1 stated:

> Timeliness of attack is most important in the conduct of air operations directly against civil morale. If the morale of the people is already low because of sus-

tained suffering and deprivation and because the people are losing faith in the ability of the armed forces to win a favorable decision, then heavy and sustained bombing of cities may crash that morale entirely. However, if these conditions do not exist, then area bombing of cities may actually stiffen the resistance of the population, especially if the attacks are weak and sporadic. . . . It is believed that the entire bombing effort might be applied to this purpose when it becomes apparent that the proper psychological conditions exist.

In one of its annexes AWPD/1 spoke of Berlin's role in the anticipated air war. Immediately after strategic bombing had heavily and visibly damaged its economic targets, "or immediately after some major set-back of the German ground forces, it may become highly profitable to deliver a large scale all-out attack on the civil population of Berlin. In this event any or all of the bombardment forces may be diverted for this mission."[55]

Spaatz, as Chief of the AAF Staff, Arnold, as Commanding General of the AAF, Army Chief of Staff Marshall, Secretary of War Stimson, and President Roosevelt had all endorsed AWPD/1 before the Japanese attack on Pearl Harbor. Kuter and Spaatz may have objected less to the concept of a campaign or mission against morale then to the timing of THUNDERCLAP.

In any case, like any good staff officer, Kuter began to prepare a contingency plan for the remote possibility that the AAF, "even though we are strongly opposed at this time to such methods," might participate in such an operation. Kuter selected a dozen smaller cities, "ancient, compact, historic, wide-spread and of as much industrial importance as possible." The AAF would warn the cities that one of them would be destroyed (to cause panic in all twelve) and finally all forces would deliver a concentrated attack on the selected city.[56] Arnold may never have seen this plan, but he objected strongly when the British proposal to attack civilian morale reached his desk. He preferred not to direct the attack solely at Berlin or the German people. He suggested a six-day-long series of sweeps by all available fighters and heavy bombers over all of Germany.[57]

On August 3, the Air Staff presented THUNDERCLAP to the British Chiefs, who suggested that the War Cabinet's Joint Planning Staff prepare an additional study regarding a possible assault on the Nazi machinery of repression, particularly the S.S. and the Gestapo. This attack would occur in coordination with, but not at the same time as, THUNDERCLAP in order to weaken Nazi control of the people.[58] An Air Staff review of a draft of this plan rejected the bombing of security forces, reiterated the virtues of bombing Berlin, and produced a blood-curdling analysis of the advantages of THUNDERCLAP, noting: "A spectacular and final object lesson to the German people on the consequences of universal aggression would be of continuing value in the post-war period. Again, the total devastation of the centre of a vast city such as Berlin would offer incontrovertible proof to all peoples of the power of a modern air force." The Air Staff suggested "that such a proof would appreciably ease the task of policing the occupied areas largely by means of Air Forces. Moreover, it would convince our

Russian allies and the Neutrals of the effectiveness of Anglo-American air power." The analysis concluded, "When allied forces had occasion to occupy, or neutral representatives to visit Berlin, they would be presented with a long continuing memorial to the effects which strategical bombing had produced in this war and could produce at any time again."[59]

The final plan of attack on the German government went forward on August 17. The Joint Planning Staff, because of the wide dispersion of targets and doubts as to their exact location, did not predict that the scheme was "likely to achieve any worthwhile degree of success."[60] The RAF Air Staff had additional concerns: The German government was not vulnerable; the selected small targets required visual bombing; and the RAF had insufficient intelligence. In addition, raids on complexes with concentration camps would produce casualties among the "internees."[61] Churchill agreed that the plan was impractical. He suggested instead drawing up a short list of war criminals, 50 to 100 high ranking Nazis, who would be executed if they fell into Allied hands. Publishing such a list, he speculated, would open a gap between those named and the people. He observed, "At the present moment, none of the German leaders has any interest but fighting to the last man, hoping he will be that last man. It is very important to show the German people that they are not on the same footing as Hitler, Goering, Himmler and other monsters who will infallibly be destroyed."[62]

Later in August, SHAEF Headquarters began to discuss THUNDERCLAP.[63] On August 24, at the Allied Air Commanders' meeting, Harris suggested that the Allies threaten in an ultimatum to the Germans to destroy certain towns if any V-2 rockets were fired into London.[64] The suggestion was referred to the RAF Air Staff which quietly buried it. Spaatz gave Eisenhower his opinion of THUNDERCLAP, "I am opposed to this operation as now planned. We are prepared to participate in an operation against Berlin, but in doing so will select targets for attack of military importance." Spaatz added, "U.S. Bombing Policy, as you know, has been directed against precision military objectives, and not morale."[65] Eisenhower, in his endorsement of Spaatz's letter, noted that the operation would occur only under a limited set of conditions. He noted that although he had always insisted that USSTAF bomb precision targets he was "always prepared to take part in anything that gives real promise to ending the war quickly." Eisenhower promised Spaatz, "The policies under which you are now operating will be unchanged unless in my opinion an opportunity arises where a sudden and devastating blow may have an incalculable result."[66]

Spaatz expressed stronger views to Arnold, who, unlike Eisenhower, did not require his subordinates to eschew inter-Allied bickering:

> I have been subjected to some pressure on the part of the Air Ministry to join hands with them in morale bombing. I discussed this matter previously with [Robert] Lovett when he was here and have maintained a firm position that our bombing will continue to be precision bombing against military objective [sic].

While admitting that a case could be made for bombing Berlin, Spaatz stated flatly, "I personally believe that any deviation from our present policy, even for an exceptional case, will be unfortunate. There is no doubt in my mind that the RAF want very much to have the U.S. Air Forces tarred with the morale bombing aftermath, which we feel will be terrific."[67] THUNDERCLAP'S prediction of 137,500 dead and an equal number seriously wounded as a result of American bombing was apparently too much for him.

Eisenhower had the last word. On September 9, he asked Spaatz to make sure Doolittle would be ready to bomb Berlin at a moment's notice. Spaatz complied, instructing the Eighth to drop plans to hit military objectives and to be ready to drop bombs "indiscriminately" on the city when Eisenhower gave the order.[68] Eisenhower may have been holding THUNDERCLAP as a last card to play in the faltering drive across France. Only the last-gasp Operation MARKET-GARDEN paratroop drop in Holland, scheduled for mid-September, seemed to offer hope of a quick breakthrough. Had the paratroopers succeeded in establishing a bridgehead over the Rhine, the moment for launching THUNDERCLAP might have arrived. Instead, MARKET-GARDEN proved a costly failure.

Ironically, the British and the Americans may have missed their opportunity. One can only speculate on the results of an antimorale raid coming on the heels of the July 20 assassination attempt on Hitler. For a brief instant before Hitler savagely and sadistically retaliated against the plotters, confusion reigned. If nothing else, a raid at that time would have further roiled an already boiling pot. The Allied breakout from the Normandy beachhead, which would have occurred at approximately the same time, might have added the final push. Talk of THUNDERCLAP subsided with the establishment of a stalemate on the Western Front in September 1944 but would be resurrected under a different set of circumstances four months later.

THUNDERCLAP and its planning illustrated how confident air power leaders still were in the bomber fleet as an effective striking force. In the period between the two world wars, Western air power experts and general public alike subscribed to the view that a massive strategic bombing attack, delivered in a sudden stroke at the beginning of hostilities, might quickly end a war between major powers. This so-called bolt from the blue was intended to totally disrupt daily life and inflict such horrific casualties on civilians as to compel the recipient power to capitulate. Yet, long after Chinese, British, and, especially, German civilians had demonstrated a capacity to withstand the heaviest of aerial bombardments, Allied air planners still seriously proposed a back-breaking, seventy-two-hour operation of THUNDERCLAP's magnitude. The estimated casualty figures were more akin to those predicted in 1935 by the RAF Air Staff—150,000 casualties in the first week of the bombing of London[69]—than those to be expected in 1944. Even the operation's code name evoked the image of the prewar bolt-from-the-blue mentality.

Strategic Bombing in the Summer of 1944

Following the successful breakthrough at St. Lô, described later in Chapter 13, the Allies advanced spectacularly through France. They pushed a defeated, disorganized foe before them, recapturing Paris on August 25 and taking most of the great port of Antwerp on September 4. A week later an armored reconnaissance squadron crossed the 1939 German border. By that time, however, the Allied armies had literally run out of gas as they forged ahead of their supply lines. This enforced halt at the German border, combined with the frantic but successful effort of the *Wehrmacht* to cobble together a solid defensive line, turned a war of movement back into a war of position.

Once the ground forces established themselves on the Continent, Spaatz hoped to return his command to what he considered its primary task—the strategic bombardment of Germany. In June 1944, the Eighth Air Force conducted only four missions over German industrial targets. On June 18 and 20, it attacked oil targets, losing 50 heavy bombers and writing off 4 more. On June 21, the Eighth lost an additional 45 heavy bombers in a raid on the center of Berlin. On June 29, Doolittle's bombers again attacked oil targets. Nevertheless, of the 320 heavy bombers lost by the Eighth in combat in June, at least 55 percent fell in action against CROSSBOW sites or in missions against airfields, bridges, and other tactical targets in France.[70] For the first time, losses of heavy bombers to antiaircraft artillery exceeded those lost to Luftwaffe fighters.[71] That fact indicated three features of June operations: the German transfer of hundreds of fighters to ground-support roles; the preponderant number of missions flown by the Eighth against tactical targets defended, if at all, solely by flak; and the increasing efficiency and number of expanded radar-directed German antiaircraft artillery batteries. In January 1944, flak had accounted for only 27 bomber losses;[72] in June, the Eighth lost 2½ bombers (201) to flak for each one lost to enemy fighters (80).

Each month from June 1944, in the case of the Eighth Air Force, and July, in the case of the Fifteenth, until the end of the war in May 1945, USSTAF lost more bombers to flak than to enemy fighters. From September 1944 to May 1945, the Eighth lost 511 bombers to fighters and 1,263 to flak.[73] During the same period the Fifteenth lost 33 B-17s and B-24s to fighters and 681 to flak.[74]

The effectiveness of German antiaircraft stemmed, in part, from a reorganization and vast expansion of the Reich's flak defenses ordered by Hitler in response to RAF raids in 1943.[75] From August 1943 to June 1944, personnel devoted to the antiaircraft reorganization doubled, to 300,000, including 75,000 secondary school students, 45,000 Soviet POW volunteers, and 15,000 women.[76] This increase in personnel enabled the Germans to field larger numbers of heavier antiaircraft guns. These heavier 135mm weapons could place their shells far higher than 88mm antiaircraft guns. Large-caliber weapons eliminated much of the relative immunity to flak that the higher flying B-17 had enjoyed over the B-24, whose optimal performance altitude was 3,000 to 5,000 feet lower.

German countermeasures consumed vast quantities of manpower and matériel sorely needed elsewhere. The thousands of high-velocity artillery pieces and the thousands of tons of ammunition they either consumed or kept idle in reserve would have greatly aided hard-pressed German defenders on the Eastern Front in their efforts to halt the Soviet advance. Because strategic bombing raids were restricted by weather conditions and shifting priorities, German flak forces were spread thin to defend many areas. Yet, most defensive flak forces fought only a few days a month, further accentuating the drain they imposed on the Reich's economy with long periods of enforced idleness that tied up needed resources.

Moreover, by October 1944 the Germans, unknown to the AAF, had developed the ability to track the bombers carrying H2X radar. This ability greatly aided their range computations.[77] Even such missions as the November 25, 1944, attack by the Eighth Air Force on the heavily defended Leuna oil plant, in which 766 bombers dropped their explosive cargoes through thick clouds and suffered 209 (27 percent) aircraft damaged by flak,[78] did not alert the AAF to its new vulnerability. A visual attack on October 7 by 142 B-17s of the 1st Bombardment Division on another oil target, Politz, near Stettin, left only 19 unscathed and lost 17, with 30 heavily damaged and 76 slightly damaged. The lead ships, equipped with H2X, suffered particularly heavy damage.[79] All this, however, lay in the future. At the end of June 1944, Spaatz still pressed to have his planes released for missions over Germany.

In July, after Spaatz gained Eisenhower's agreement that the days offering visual conditions over Germany ought to be used for bombing,[80] the Eighth sent missions into Germany twelve times. So quickly did the weather change over central Europe that one-half of those missions employed H2X radar bombing over the target. Four of the missions struck oil targets, while the others attacked aircraft production, ball-bearing plants, and the experimental rocket station at Peenemunde.[81] Of the 352 bombers lost by the Eighth in July, strategic missions accounted for at least 212 lost and 35 written off,[82] 70 percent of the month's losses. The Fifteenth sent out fifteen strategic missions, thirteen of them directed all or in part against Axis oil targets. It lost 196 heavy bombers in June and 317 more in July, the costliest month in its history. The Fifteenth's losses reflected how effectively antiaircraft artillery defenses were being employed by the Germans at Ploesti and other oil targets. Given the difference in aircraft on hand between the Fifteenth (1,407 heavy bombers) and the Eighth (3,492 heavy bombers) in July 1944,[83] Twining's forces suffered casualties at more than twice the rate of Doolittle's. The figures demonstrate the return of both air forces to the Combined Bomber Offensive.

Despite such heavy casualties during their raids of June and July, efforts of the Eighth and Fifteenth further aggravated Germany's critically low oil supply.

A German holding an antiaircraft range finder in the field.

Ultra tracked Allied progress against Germany, particularly this most vulnerable sector of its war economy. On July 9, Ultra deciphered a circular from Goering to his field commanders, which read in part, "The deep inroads made into the supply of aircraft fuel demand the most stringent reduction in flying. Drastic economy is absolutely essential.[84] Another intercept of July 29 gave the results of attacks on Merseburg, the single largest synthetic oil plant: "Heaviest attacks so far; heavy damage—works provisionally 100 percent out of action."[85]

The American breaking of Japanese ciphers supplied more information. In August, three confidential telegrams from the Japanese ambassador in Berlin to Tokyo gave new information on the effect of Allied bombing. The ambassador reported confidential statements made by Speer that presented as rosy a picture as possible but could not conceal the damage done by the strategic bombing offensive. Speer stated that, overall, the bombing had checked the rise of the production curve. It had not to caused production in the aggregate to fall. The attacks on oil installations were, however, another matter. "For the first time," Speer continued, *"wehrwirtshaftlich* [war economy] raids, which might deal a really fatal blow to Germany, had begun." The oil offensive "was the problem to which they attached the greatest importance at the moment," and the Germans intended to strain every nerve to restore the situation. Speer then lied to the Japanese ambassador, telling him that Allied claims of 50 percent destruction of German oil supplies overstated the case. After observing that only the regaining of air superiority could combat Allied heavy bombers, he offered wildly inflated production figures for single- and twin-engine fighters, claiming production of

Germans preparing to fire 88mm antiaircraft artillery.

4,500 in July and predicted 6,500 to 7,000 a month by the end of the year. Those totals were more than double the actual production achieved. Provided manpower and oil stocks did not evaporate, Speer hoped to free Germany from the bomber threat and to increase production of oil.[86] This intercept must have confirmed Spaatz's resolve to continue the oil offensive and the counterair campaign.

For USSTAF, August and the first part of September brought no change in routine. The Eighth attacked the CROSSBOW system; aided the ground forces by striking tactical targets; and (most important, from Spaatz's point of view) launched ten missions into Germany, seven of them strikes against portions of the oil industry.[87] The Fifteenth Air Force flew thirteen strategic missions against Balkan and German oil targets.[88] On August 24, the two air forces coordinated their efforts in combined raids on synthetic oil plants in Germany; on the same day, all oil production ceased at Ploesti, which the Soviets occupied a few days later. From April through August 1944, the Fifteenth expended 13,649 tons of bombs and lost 350 heavy bombers solely against Ploesti.[89] A warning from the British Joint Intelligence Committee on August 7 had helped to spur Spaatz to maximum effort against oil. A vast program was being instituted by the Germans to repair the oil plants as rapidly as possible.[90] Henceforth, the oil campaign became a race between the Allied bombers to destroy and German labor to repair. For the month of August, the Eighth lost 331 bombers in combat, more than 70 percent of them (238) to antiaircraft artillery. The Fifteenth, whose total bomber force was less than half that of the Eighth, lost 254 heavy bombers, 112 of them to flak and 91 to enemy fighters.[91]

These oil attacks as had those in July reduced Speer to a state of frustration. He recalled, "Again and again I had explained to him [Hitler] that it would be pointless to have tanks if we could not produce enough fuel." Speer added that, even as he attempted to cope with the oil bombings, "I was aghast at the incomprehension of our leadership." He implored Hitler to reserve a significantly larger part of the fighter-plane production for the home front and "to give sufficient high priority to protecting the home hydrogenation plants by fighter planes so that in August and September at least partial production will be possible." At the end of July, Speer obtained from Hitler and Goering a promise to set aside a force of 2,000 fighter planes to be available by the first of September,[92] and he secured authorization to have his subordinate, Edmund Geilenberg, placed in charge of restoring fuel production. Within two months Geilenberg had 150,000 workers, many of them slave laborers, assigned to rebuilding the synthetic plants. By late autumn he had 350,000 workers, many diverted from essential armaments production, assigned to restoring oil production.[93] This diversion, together with the huge antiaircraft organization, created another drain on the German war effort directly attributable to strategic bombing.

None of Speer's and Geilenberg's efforts could prevent a serious decline in Germany's oil situation. In August the Fischer-Tropsch process and the hydro-

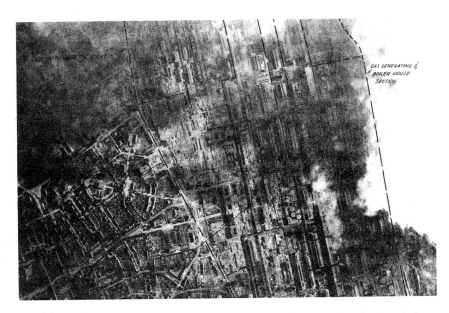

GAS GENERATING &
BOILER HOUSE
SECTION

Overhead view of the Merseburg synthetic oil refinery *(above)* showing bomb damage after an Eighth Air Force strike, July 1944. A dark plume *(below)* rises above the lighter colored smoke generated by German defenders to conceal the Merseburg works during the raid.

genation synthetic fuel plants, which produced high-octane distillates, delivered 47,000 tons of aviation fuel, 13.5 percent of April's production. Imported oil had fallen to 11,000 tons, a mere 10.6 percent of April's figures. ULTRA described fuel shortages cutting into the Luftwaffe's operations on the Eastern Front. On August 10, air units withdrawing from France were ordered to evacuate fuel stocks down to the "last drop." Five days later, the Luftwaffe's high command ordered *Luftflotte* 3 (or the 3d air fleet) in France to curtail operations in order to release fuel for training 120 crews per month for the west or to accept a lower training fuel allocation sufficient for 40 crews per month.[94] From all sources the Germans garnered 345,000 tons of finished oil products, 42.6 percent of April's total.[95] This decline was attributable solely to USSTAF's oil bombing campaign. Attacks on the hydrogenation plants disrupted other parts of the German chemical industry. These plants produced methanol and nitrogen, key components in synthetic rubber and explosives. The Germans had no natural source for either substance and could not easily substitute for them. Speer morosely recorded, "From October 1944 on, our explosives consisted of 20 percent rock salt, which reduced their effectiveness correspondingly."[96]

Problems of the American Strategic Air Forces

During the summer of 1944, Spaatz did not spend all of his time attending Air Commanders' Meetings or justifying the need for strategic bombing of Germany. He spent much of his time and effort in somewhat more mundane administrative concerns. Personnel considerations topped the list. Although a complete study of the Eighth Air Force's personnel difficulties would fill a large volume, Spaatz expended considerable energy on three interrelated problems: crew morale, crew replacements, and internment of crews in foreign countries.

As the AAF official history admits, "Low morale among air crews, particularly in the Eighth Air Force, was a nagging problem during the middle of 1944."[97] The ground crews, who maintained, serviced, and repaired aircraft, also suffered from poor morale brought about by an entirely different set of circumstances. Aside from matters that soldiers have grumbled about since the profession of arms began, such as food, boredom, and the general incomprehensibility of most actions or decisions by the powers that be, AAF ground and air crews in Europe fought two different types of wars. The ground crews did not rotate back to the United States after a set period; they stayed with their units throughout the war. Added to the certainty of no home leave—although leave spent in England was not unpleasant—were primitive working conditions and long hours.

Britain was as civilized and developed a country as any in which the AAF worked in 1944. Even so, the Eighth's bomber and fighter fields, for the most part, offered few hangars and covered working spaces. In periods of heavy operations in wintertime, the ground crews, who worked during the night and in the early morning, suffered greatly from the cold and damp. Italy offered even fewer amenities or diversions; its weather was certainly harsher than that of England. During the summer, the ground crews had to work harder and harder in response to dramatically increasing numbers of missions. Of course, they did not risk their lives or suffer to the same extent as those in the infantry or on the front lines. However, they were exposed to the rigors of the flight line, where boring and dangerous conditions steadily took their toll. As Eaker noted to Arnold in a summary of operations, dated June 1, "Those [ground crews] who have been in the theater approaching two years are definitely weary and not as keen as they were and their work falls off."[98]

The air crews fought a private war, the horizons of which extended little beyond themselves or their planes. Throughout the summer the Eighth Air Force's percentage of aircraft lost per sortie rate declined. The rate dropped from 3.6 percent in April to 2.2 percent in May, 1.1 in June, when the Eighth flew only four strategic missions, and 1.5 percent in both July and August. The lower loss rates greatly increased an air crew's chances of completing its tour of duty. Unfortunately, the apprehension level of the crews did not decline. Many still seemed to react as they had when loss rates were higher. The lengthening of the combat tour in February 1944 from twenty-five to thirty missions dealt a blow to everyone's morale. Even at 1.5 percent loss per sortie for thirty missions, a crew member stood a 36 percent chance of not surviving. With the summer came increased numbers of missions and the opportunity for some crews to finish their required tour of thirty missions in as little as sixty-two days.[99] The Eighth retained some crews for more than thirty missions. On July 1, for example, 117 crews, almost 4 percent of the crews on hand, had thirty missions.[100] Eighth Air Force reports identified the causes of poor morale as the lack of understanding of the difficulties of combat crews by their superior officers, inadequate fighter escort on some missions, the seemingly elastic limit on combat tours, and too frequent missions.[101]

The air crew rotation policy instituted by Spaatz and Doolittle in the spring of 1944 dampened spirits further. Before its imposition, air crews completing their combat tours returned to the United States. and, in practice, flew no more combat missions. However, heavy losses compelled Spaatz and Doolittle to discontinue the permanent release of at least some trained crews that had finished their initial tours. They were obliged to return to Europe for another tour of duty after a month's furlough of rest and recreation in the United States. They as well as crews already into their first tour who could easily picture themselves in the same situation naturally felt aggrieved. Arnold, apparently, wished to halt any furloughs. The low morale of the crews returning to the United States was obvious and did nothing for the AAF's public image. The ideal solution to the problem—lack of trained manpower—would have been a replacement pipeline full of crews—a goal the AAF never managed to achieve.

In fact, at least as seen from AAF Headquarters in Washington, USSTAF's furlough scheme threatened to upset the carefully crafted training program for

Eighth Air Force ground crews servicing a P-38. They worked unprotected from the elements, often at night.

air crew replacements. In a letter dated June 21, Lt. Gen. Barney M. Giles, Deputy Commanding General, AAF, and Chief of the AAF Staff, informed Spaatz that "General Arnold had contended successfully that every crew going to the wars is entitled to an even chance at surviving its tour . . . it has . . . been necessary that we train two crews for every one you lose."[102] Once Spaatz's forces achieved their goal of two crews per heavy bomber, the replacement and force build-up flow would of necessity slow.

The two-crew-per-bomber policy had become the foundation of AAF crew training. From his office in the Pentagon, where he poured over the figures detailing the ebb and flow of personnel through training, Giles attempted to convey to Spaatz the importance that AAF Headquarters had attached to continuing a proven system. He noted that Spaatz's retention of crews in Europe threatened to cause backlogs and delays throughout the replacement pipeline and that

> Any change in what is now a smooth machine would not be good. As you can
> see, a major leave and furlough policy in our four largest air forces would force
> a considerable change and a downward revision in our crew training which
> might not be smart until we see the final victory more immediately ahead than
> we now see it.

Giles added the hope "that having built the track we can keep the program

447

running on it without any further hitches until we get you up to strength when, I am convinced, we should return to the old rotation system.[103]

A month later Spaatz replied that he, too, wished to return to a straight rotation policy, which he estimated would occur on August 1, the date the Eighth would reach its authorized strength of two crews per aircraft. But he also wished to retain the right to return, temporarily, for rest and recuperation certain key personnel such as group and squadron commanders, lead pilots, bombardiers, and navigators.[104] The Eighth reached its goal of double crews in July. The Fifteenth, which had a higher casualty rate, had only one and one-half crews per plane on July 31.[105]

The number of Eighth Air Force crews interned as a result of crashing or landing in neutral countries jumped from eighteen in May to thirty-eight in June and forty-one in July.[106] Although these crews and planes amounted to only a tiny fraction of the totals sent out, Arnold received the statistics with alarm, especially after he read reports of interviews with interned crews conducted by U.S. diplomatic personnel.

The 2d Bombardment Division seemed particularly prone to this problem, in part because the B-24's longer range, as compared with the B-17's, allowed it to fly deeper penetration missions. On deep missions a crew in a damaged plane might be more likely to land in neutral territory than to chance a long, dangerous return trip to Britain. In June, three-quarters of the crews interned belonged to the 2d Bombardment Division (28 of 38); in July about 40 percent of interned crews belonged to the 2d Division (15 of 41). During the June 20 raid on Politz, an oil target in Poland, conducted by 358 2d Division B-24s, an eye-popping 20 bombers landed in Sweden. The next day, the fourth in a row in which the Eighth launched more than 1,100 bombers, 14 more bombers (7 from the 2d Division) on missions to the Berlin area landed in Sweden.[107]

In mid-July, Spaatz suggested to Arnold that battle-experienced, intelligent, senior USSTAF air officers join the diplomatic representatives in Sweden and Switzerland to interview the crews and to evaluate and investigate the reasons for their landings from a more professional perspective.[108] On July 27, Arnold sent a message to Spaatz in which he noted the increasing number of aircraft making landings in neutral countries "without indication of serious battle damage or mechanical failure, or shortage of fuel." Then he noted diplomatic reports confirming "the fact that the landings were intentional evasions of further combat service." Finally, Arnold insisted, "It is plainly evident that measures must be taken immediately against the development of such a state of mind among [other] flyers and crews now engaged in extremely active operations."[109] Arnold emphasized "that great care be taken not to hold combat crews in the theater until war weariness provokes an uncontrollable urge to grasp release by the action indicated." He further required Spaatz to return all crews over USSTAF's authorized strength and to use green crews to the maximum extent. Arnold cautioned that "individuals or crews who appear near the breaking point should also be returned for reconditioning."[110]

On July 29, Spaatz strongly defended his crews to Arnold. Speaking for himself and Eaker, he noted, "We resent the implication that these crews are cowards, are low in morale or lack the will to fight. Such is a base slander against the most courageous group of fighting men in this war."[111] He pointed out that the internees amounted to only a tiny fraction among crews dispatched and that some groups had persevered despite 60 percent casualties. He observed that the morale of the crews depended to some extent on the morale of their commanding officers, many of whom held ranks inferior to their responsibilities. He suggested that several of his wing commanders be promoted to brigadier general, and he repeated his desire to have USSTAF officers assigned to diplomatic staffs. He stressed that "the most recent program for sending war weary crews back to the US should meet the combat fatigue situation, and you can rest assured that we will not maintain combat crews in operations when they approach the breaking point, provided you continue to send replacement crews. . . ."[112] Spaatz did acknowledge, however, that "in the past some crews have undoubtedly been employed who were very tired, overstrained and near the breaking point. This has been done because of crew shortages, the importance of the battle and in a desire to put forth maximum effort in destroying the German Air Force before launching OVERLORD." Spaatz argued that the employment of overtired crews "was inevitable in the initial application of our vastly expanding air forces. It was by these means that the necessary air supremacy has been established which has enabled the American Air Forces to get the situation in hand in the European Theater."[113]

This response did not placate Arnold, who sent Lt. Col. James W. Wilson from Headquarters, AAF, to the European Theater of Operations to investigate and to report back to him. Wilson arrived in London on August 26, carrying a set of confidential personnel instructions and an equally confidential letter from Arnold to Spaatz. In it Arnold wrote that he did not blame Spaatz for resenting the implied slander or for defending his troops. "Nevertheless," he continued,

> I am concerned lest we fail to note any incipient weaknesses that may not be apparent, but whose existence may be indicated by reports even by unskilled observers or constitutional faultfinders. For your information, these unfortunate attitudes are reputed to include, beyond the normal griping, lack of respect (amounting to near hatred) for certain very senior leaders; disgust with the influence of political expedients on tactical and strategical employment; lack of desire to kill Germans; lack of understanding as to the political necessity for fighting the war; general personal lassitude with consequent lack of patriotic enthusiasm for their jobs. We must not let our aversion to believing them influence our thinking or our determination to ferret out facts if early knowledge of even the faintest taint would enable us to take efficacious preventative measures.[114]

449

Arnold assured Spaatz that Wilson came neither as an "inspector" nor as a "spy" but merely to "clarify a situation that I fear has become clouded due to many rumors and reports."[115]

In his instructions to Wilson, which Wilson handed over to Spaatz, Arnold revealed that, in addition to diplomatic reports, reports from a flight surgeon recently on duty with the Eighth indicated "a possible deterioration of combat crew morale." Arnold said, "If these reports are essentially correct, immediate action must be taken to prevent serious reductions in the fighting efficiency of air crews in the European Theater of Operations." Arnold instructed Wilson to "mingle with combat crewmen of all grades in tactical units" to determine for himself their attitudes and then to submit to him and Spaatz a report with recommendations.[116]

In mid-September, Wilson, who claimed to have talked to more than a thousand crew members, reported to Arnold that morale, after a drop-off in July,[117] had recently improved considerably. "Not only were the airmen confident of their airplanes, their methods, and themselves, but they felt sure they were doing more to win the war than either the ground forces or the RAF." Wilson's informal investigation, plus other investigations conducted on Arnold's behalf, and the findings of specially detailed USSTAF officers who interviewed the interned crews convinced Arnold and Spaatz that the morale problem had been greatly exaggerated.[118]

The advance of the ground forces to the western borders of Germany virtually ended the internment controversy. Once crews could land safely in France, instead of farther away in England, the attractiveness of Sweden and Switzerland

Lt. Gen. Carl A. Spaatz visiting a crew replacement center, England, June 12, 1944.

450

diminished. Later, in the winter of 1944–1945, the Soviet advance to the eastern borders of Germany allowed crews whose planes were damaged in deep missions to Berlin and beyond to land in Soviet-occupied territory instead of Sweden.

Of all the bombing by USSTAF during the summer of 1944, only the strategic bombing of oil, with its side effects on the German chemical industry, hastened eventual Allied victory. CROSSBOW bombing did little more than crater the Pas-de-Calais district. Nor would morale bombing, given the blows subsequently withstood by the German populace, have furthered the Allied cause effectively.

For Spaatz and the U.S. Strategic Air Forces in Europe, the summer of 1944 represented a season-long fight to prevent the weakening of the strategic bomber offensive with the diversion of the heavy-bomber effort to other important, but less crucial, tasks. Spaatz succeeded, by and large, in fending off all but the most necessary distractions from the main strategic effort. After establishing the dramatic potential of the oil plan in the May 1944 raids, he managed to pry out of Eisenhower enough freedom of action to continue and steadily increase in scale the assault on the life's blood of the German military machine. Finally, Spaatz showed once again his flexibility and common sense by, on the one hand, rejecting such extreme air power proposals as terror-bombing and, on the other, sending his heavy bombers into direct support of ground troops (discussed in the next chapter), an action not contemplated by prewar bombing enthusiasts.

Chapter 13

Summer 1944:
Heavy Bombers in
Close Air Support
(July–August 1944)

Technically viewed, the bombing was good.[1]

—*AAF official history on* COBRA, *1951.*

Though the results were not what we expected, it never occurred to us that we could fail after the use of such mass aircraft.[2]

—*After-action questionnaire of U.S. 9th Infantry Division on results of* COBRA, *1944*

In July and August 1944, the Allied strategic bombers departed from their customary tasks of attacking vital military or political targets and engaging in counterair and interdiction campaigns to directly assist the Allied ground forces on the battlefield. The Allied ground forces, bogged down in the excellent defensive terrain of Normandy, required heavy-bomber assaults in addition to those planned for D-day. This foray into large-scale close air support presented unique and unanticipated command, control, and technical problems to the Eighth Air Force and Bomber Command as they sought to fulfill obligations for which they lacked methods and training. These close air support missions were, of course, diversions from the strategic effort. Not all Allied airmen agreed with the necessity of heavy bombers in close air support. Tedder, for instance, believed that Leigh-Mallory had oversold the army on the need for air support. But Spaatz, although he might have preferred to attack targets in Germany, assented, without coercion by Eisenhower or Tedder, to all requests to aid the ground forces. The complex interplay between the command and control of the bombers, the technical difficulties associated with heavy-bomber strikes close to friendly troops, and the effects of conflicts among air leaders on the entire equation are the themes of this chapter.

Initial Attempts at Ground Support

Although the Allied air forces had cut the Luftwaffe at the front to bits, the Allied ground forces, under the overall command of Gen. Montgomery's 21 Army Group, encountered stiff resistance. The Germans kept the Allies on their relatively cramped beachhead. On the Allied left flank, the British 2d Army could not take the city of Caen or break into the clear area beyond the River Orne. On the Allied right the U.S. First Army, under Lt. Gen. Omar N. Bradley, found itself enmeshed in the *bocage,* or hedgerow country. Hedgerows, earthen dikes four feet high covered with tangled vegetation, provided perfect static defensive positions that slowed the American advance to a crawl.[3] From the air, however, the *bocage* appeared insignificant.

Allied airmen found the failure of the ground forces to expand the beachhead rapidly in the face of determined enemy resistance frustrating. On June 14, at the Daily Air Commanders' Meeting at Stanmore, Air Marshal "Mary" Coningham announced that his own information on the situation at the front did not jibe with that supplied by the army. He described the situation as "near crisis."[4] To bolster morale, the airmen decided to put in an especially heavy mission near the front line, and Air Chief Marshal Tedder, Deputy Supreme Commander of the Allied Expeditionary Force, canceled an Eighth Air Force mission over Berlin scheduled for the next day.[5] Later on June 14, Tedder, who had attended the air meeting, persuaded Eisenhower to fly to the front with him to get a firsthand opinion of affairs there.

At this point the confused Allied air command situation once again became a problem. Leigh-Mallory, Commander in Chief of the Allied Expeditionary Air Force, commanded all air directly assigned to Eisenhower: the British 2d Tactical Air Force and the American Ninth (Tactical) Air Force. Spaatz and Harris, although controlled by Eisenhower, through Tedder, had the task, independent of Eisenhower, of conducting the Combined Bomber Offensive against Germany. Furthermore, Harris and Spaatz not only questioned Leigh-Mallory's competence to conduct heavy-bomber operations but denied his claims that his position gave him operational command of all air power working with Eisenhower. As a result, the two heavy-bomber commanders had refused to allow their organizations to come under Leigh-Mallory's hand. This led Eisenhower to appoint Tedder, his preferred choice for overall air commander, as overall coordinator between the tactical and strategic air forces. To further confuse the situation, Leigh-Mallory, in the few days immediately before and after the assault phase of the invasion, had actually been given operational control of the heavy bombers by Eisenhower in order to ensure their full integration into the vital air operations of that phase of the invasion. As a result, he may have assumed he would again receive such control in other times of crisis.

The next link down the chain of command had more problems. Leigh-Mallory's AEAF Headquarters, supposedly a combined U.S.-British headquarters, was really a house divided between its British and American components. The AAF official history succinctly stated the American view of the AEAF by calling it "possibly the least successful venture of the entire war with a combined Anglo-American command."[6] The British component in AEAF Headquarters outnumbered the American component two to one at the general officer's rank. Leigh-Mallory had annoyed the Americans by taking care that for each combined section of the headquarters the senior British officer outranked his American counterpart.

On several occasions Spaatz had to restrain the strong-willed Deputy Commander of the AEAF, Maj. Gen. Hoyt S. Vandenberg, whom he had brought in to replace an ineffectual predecessor, from complaining too bitterly and vociferously about Leigh-Mallory and his actions, one of which involved procedures in AEAF War/Operations Room actions.[7] Leigh-Mallory disliked the combined operation of the AEAF War/Operations Room and ruled that it be run entirely by British personnel using British methods. On June 6, the AEAF War/Operations Room posted no information on the progress at the American beaches until long after 5:00 P.M. As Vandenberg recorded in his diary, "I asked for an explanation and pointed out quite forcibly that, in my opinion, the whole proceeding from an informational point of view was entirely inexcusable." Vandenberg pointed out that "all three British beaches had clearly defined information as to the approximate position of the front lines, but . . . there was not a single mark on either of the American beaches."[8] Vandenberg "stormed" from the War/Operations Room and drove to Leigh-Mallory's headquarters to demand remedial action.

The next day Vandenberg asked Spaatz whether he "should open up the fight." Spaatz replied that "the time was not ripe." But Spaatz and Doolittle, Commander of the Eighth Air Force, suggested that Vandenberg inform Leigh-Mallory that the Eighth "was very displeased with the manner in which their operations were being presented and that, as far as General Spaatz was concerned, he felt strongly that the whole picture was so confused by the various presentations that an accurate analysis and the proper action to take was, as a result, impossible."[9] Spaatz particularly objected to Leigh-Mallory's Daily Air Commanders' Meetings, not only because they confused many issues but because they dragged on interminably and produced, in his opinion, little of import.[10]

Nor did Leigh-Mallory and his chief Commonwealth subordinate, Coningham, work together well. Coningham, although less aloof and stiff than Leigh-Mallory, had no greater knack than his superior for getting along with his fellow

RAF Operations Room. Deep underground, its walls were lined with huge maps, charts, and blackboards.

officers. Coningham seldom took the time to conceal his contempt for anyone who failed to appreciate his brilliance and his ideas concerning air-ground cooperation.[11] Coningham may have been the prime advocate of improved air-ground cooperation, but his venomous view of Montgomery led him to violate a prime tenet of his own creed—the ground commander and the air commander should site their headquarters at the same place in order to provide the swiftest communications and maximum cooperation between the two combat forces. Claiming that the beachhead could not yet provide the sophisticated communications network he needed to control his forces, Coningham stayed at his own headquarters, designated AEAF, HQ (Advanced), at Uxbridge in England, while Montgomery set up headquarters on the beachhead.[12]

As Commander, AEAF, HQ (Advanced), Coningham had day-to-day control of the tactical air forces, both the British 2d Tactical Air Force and the U.S. Ninth Air Force, and directed their efforts to assist the ground troops. Plans called for the dissolution of AEAF, HQ (Advanced), when the beachhead expanded enough to allow the separation of the British and American forces into different army groups, whereupon each air force would cooperate with the army group composed of its nation's ground forces. This arrangement never functioned smoothly because Leigh-Mallory refused to accept it, because Montgomery did his best to ignore Coningham,[13] and because the Commander of the Ninth Air Force, Lt. Gen. Lewis H. Brereton, asserted his independence whenever possible.

456

After the meeting on June 14, Leigh-Mallory, who still had nominal control of targeting for the heavy bombers, on his own initiative flew to Normandy to consult with Montgomery. Montgomery, a less than enthusiastic host, still resented Leigh-Mallory for refusing five days earlier to allow the 1st British Airborne Division to conduct a drop just beyond Caen in order to surround the city and hasten its fall. In fact, Montgomery had just denounced Leigh-Mallory in a scathing letter to his own Chief of Staff, Maj. Gen. Francis (Freddie) de Guingand:

> The real point is that LM [Leigh-Mallory] sitting in his office cannot possibly know the local battle form over here; and therefore he must not refuse my demands unless he first comes over to see me; he could fly here in a Mosquito in $\frac{1}{2}$ hour, talk for an hour, and be back in England in $\frac{1}{2}$ hour. Obviously he is a gutless bugger, who refuses to take a chance and plays for safety on all occasions. I have no use for him.[14]

When Leigh-Mallory offered to employ the whole of Bomber Command, USSTAF, and the AEAF "to blast out the Eighth [2d] Army from in front of Caen," however, Montgomery readily agreed with his suggestion.[15] Leigh-Mallory returned to England, promising to send part of his staff to the beachhead the next day to firm up a plan with officers of the British 2d Army.[16]

Leigh-Mallory's blithe offer of the entire strength of Allied air power brought the frustration of Coningham and Spaatz to the fore. Early in the morning both men had heard of the proposal. Spaatz undoubtedly heard from Vandenberg, whose American second-in-command, Brig. Gen. Frederic H. Smith, Jr., had more or less forced his presence into Leigh-Mallory's conference with Montgomery. At 2:00 A.M. on June 15, Smith had roused Vandenberg to tell him of matters afoot. They agreed that such a "use contemplated was not proper."[17] Vandenberg directed Smith to keep the number of planes involved to a minimum.

Coningham, who had left his headquarters for dinner on June 14, claimed that he had never been informed, but Leigh-Mallory indicated in his diary that he spoke to Coningham's deputy, Air Vice-Marshal Stephen Strafford and explained the plan to him in detail.[18] It seems unlikely that Coningham's deputy would have neglected to inform his chief of such an important impending operation at the first opportunity. Leigh-Mallory's plan incensed Coningham because it had cut him out of the decision-making process. As Commander of AEAF (Advanced), the major tactical air operational headquarters, Coningham insisted that he, not Leigh-Mallory, should negotiate with Montgomery. Spaatz, too, objected to what he considered Leigh-Mallory's usurpation of his prerogative concerning command of the heavy bombers.

Early on June 15 at the Daily Air Commanders' Meeting, Leigh-Mallory discussed the possibility of air assistance to the army to break up the "stalemate" in front of Caen. Opposition was immediate. A guest at the meeting, General

Henry H. Arnold, Commanding General, AAF, had come to London to attend meetings of the Combined Chiefs of Staff and to inspect the beachhead; he spoke up and "expressed the hope that" this was not going to be "another Cassino,"[19] where a heavy-bomber attack had reduced its target to rubble, and ironically provided the enemey a far better defensive position.

Even as Leigh-Mallory addressed the Daily Air Commanders' Meeting, Tedder and Eisenhower flew to the beachhead to check on the extent of the "crisis" for themselves. They met Coningham, who, in Tedder's words, "happened to be in Normandy,"[20] and drove to Montgomery's headquarters. Montgomery, however, was not there, and rather than cool their heels until he returned, they continued on to Lt. Gen. Miles Dempsey's British 2d Army Headquarters. There they found a joint air force-army planning session, consisting of part of Leigh-Mallory's AEAF staff and some of the 2d Army staff, in progress. Leigh-Mallory had sent his ubiquitous civilian scientific adviser, Professor Solly Zuckerman, who had concocted another of his mathematically based bombing schemes, this time involving close support of front-line troops by heavy bombers, and some of the AEAF military staff to draw up a bomb line with Dempsey and the 2d Army staff.

Tedder, flanked by Coningham and Air Vice-Marshal Harry Broadhurst, marched into this cabal and broke it up. Tedder claimed in his memoirs that he did so because neither Spaatz nor Coningham was represented at the meeting.[21] This disingenuous explanation does not accord with the facts. Coningham was aware of the meeting, having informed Tedder of it the night before,[22] and could have sent representatives had he wished. Nor was Coningham's presence in Normandy a coincidence. Similarly Spaatz, although not formally represented, not only knew of the meeting from Vandenberg, but could count on accurate reports from the two American general officers present at the session, Brig. Gens. Frederic H. Smith and David M. Schlatter, Ninth Air Force Deputy Chief of Staff, Operations, who would, he knew, voice their opposition to the "misuse" of American heavy bombers.[23]

Tedder stopped the meeting because Leigh-Mallory had violated military protocol in bypassing Coningham.[24] When Tedder and Eisenhower caught up with Montgomery later in the day, they made clear to him that his counterpart in the air chain of command was Coningham, not Leigh-Mallory. Tedder also made it clear to Dempsey that Air Vice-Marshal Broadhurst was his opposite number.[25] "Montgomery," stated Tedder, "seemed relieved to have this confirmation."[26] Given Montgomery's attitude toward Coningham, the extent of his "relief" is questionable. Tedder's efforts, however, did end this first attempt to divert the heavy bombers. Leigh-Mallory, for his part, took Tedder's actions as a personal rebuff and had to be dissuaded from resigning.[27]

On the evening of June 15, after his return from Normandy, Eisenhower met with Spaatz. Apparently, to ease by the logjam on the ground and perhaps to

British 2d Army
Commander Lt. Gen. Miles
Dempsey and Air Com-
modore Archibald Boyle.

Imperial War Mueuml

chide Spaatz gently for his adamant opposition to the use of heavy bombers in
direct close support of the ground forces, Eisenhower brought up the subject of
"the necessity for exercising full imagination in the employment of forces."[28]
Spaatz did not apply this gentle hint to himself. In his diary he recorded after the
meeting:

> Later developments indicate that complete lack of imagination exists in the
> minds of Army command, particularly Leigh-Mallory and Montgomery, who
> visualize best use of tremendous air potential lies in plowing up several square
> miles of terrain in front of the ground forces to obtain a few miles of advance.
> Our forces now are far superior to [the] Germans opposing us, both in men and
> material. The only thing necessary to move forward is sufficient guts on the
> part of the ground commanders.[29]

Two days afterwards, Spaatz suggested to Tedder that the strategic bombers
be allowed to resume a full-scale campaign against Germany, save for a force
held back to act as a "fire brigade" for the ground forces.[30] For his part, Leigh-
Mallory simply could not understand Spaatz's continuing insistence on strategic
bombing. Near the end of June he noted in his campaign diary, "The Americans
are a strange lot. They are still obsessed with the notion that to bomb Germany
in daylight is the proper course."[31]

Although Spaatz managed to avoid a diversion to morale bombing, he could not ignore the demands of the ground forces for any tactical bombing that might help them break out of the beachhead. During July and August he committed the Eighth's heavy bombers four times in close support of ground attacks—three times for Montgomery and one time for Bradley.

By the end of June, Allied air leaders had begun to question the progress of the ground forces in Normandy. Montgomery's seemed particularly slow paced. "I am feeling," Leigh-Mallory remarked, "slightly frustrated and have the distinct feeling that the Army is becoming more and more sealed in."[32] On July 1, he noted, "The Army I can only describe as stagnant."[33] Coningham also criticized the army's slow progress. Portal and Tedder agreed that the problem was Montgomery, who could neither be removed nor moved to action.[34] Eisenhower's complaints about him to Churchill resulted in a four-hour argument between the Prime Minister, who was no fan of Montgomery, and the Chief of the Imperial General Staff, General Alan Brooke, a staunch supporter.[35] For his part, Montgomery maintained that he had not received vigorous enough air support.[36]

To Leigh-Mallory the best way to break the army free was to give it as much air support as possible. "I have always taken the view," he stated in his usual assertive way, "that the Army must be given all the air support it desires." Then he described his frustrations:

> What I have been up against more or less since D-Day is the school of thought which takes the view that air support given to the Army should be the minimum rather than the maximum, on the principle that if you give the Army an inch it will take a mile. This school of thought urges as a principle that really heavy Air Forces should not be employed on the battlefront, but elsewhere beyond and outside it. I maintain, and have always, that heavy bombers can produce a concentration of high explosive infinitely greater than any which can be produced by any other means.[37]

To prove his point, Leigh-Mallory arranged for Bomber Command and the Eighth to aid Montgomery's lunge forward on July 8. Tedder warned Leigh-Mallory "that he was in danger of leading the Army up the garden path by his sweeping assurances of help." Tedder was convinced that neither the army nor Leigh-Mallory fully understood the limitations of air support on the battlefield or the role of air power outside the battle area.[38]

During the night of July 7–8, Bomber Command dropped 6,000 half-ton bombs directly on northern Caen[39] and on targets 6,000 yards beyond the British front lines, with negligible damage to the Germans. The raid devastated about $2^1/_2$ square miles, leaving practically contiguous craters, none of which measured less than 20 feet across, that blocked all the roads to Caen save one.[40] The Eighth bombed bridges and tunnels beyond the German lines. The bombing, according to Zuckerman, who observed and prepared a detailed report on it soon after it occurred, did not result in any Allied casualties but neither did it demoralize or materially affect the Germans.[41]

Zuckerman concluded that a great deal of French property was unnecessarily destroyed, and he expressed some doubt as to whether the batteries and other strong points listed by the British 2d Army were even in the target area. He suggested, in future, bombing closer to the troops or on the flanks of an attack and more careful planning.[42] Tedder, examining Zuckerman's report a few days later, said he had "never read a more demoralizing document" and refused to circulate it.[43] He probably feared that it might damage air-ground relations.

Montgomery's next attack, Operation GOODWOOD, seemed to offer more toward a breaking through. Although cautious with subordinates, to whom he spoke merely of killing Germans and improving positions, Montgomery told Eisenhower that the operation might have "far reaching results." On July 14, he informed Tedder that the plan "promises to be decisive."[44] This prospect delighted the airmen. Tedder, noting the agreement of the senior airmen, proclaimed the operation "a brilliant stroke which will knock loose our present shackles. Every plane available will be ready for such a purpose."[45] Leigh-Mallory hoped that at long last his moment had come. After the affair of mid-June he had

> decided to sit tight for I felt quite sure that the plum would fall ripely into my hand. Now, as the result of my talks in France yesterday and the day before, I feel sure that it has. The policy of double-dealing, the effect of which has been to deny the Army what it wanted in the field, has failed.[46]

Leigh-Mallory and Montgomery agreed to cut out Coningham and to deal directly with each other. Leigh-Mallory intended to move his mobile headquarters caravan into Montgomery's 21 Army Group Headquarters and take charge of the tactical air battle. He gleefully recorded, "This means I am going to put Air Marshal Coningham where he ought to be, in charge of one branch of the General Air Forces, and I am going to take command of their dispositions myself. If he does not like the situation, he will have to clear out." As for Tedder, if he objected, "then he or I will go. My mind is now fully made up. Either I am to be allowed to direct, if necessary, the whole air forces available to the full and immediate support of the Army or I shall resign on that issue."[47]

On July 11, Leigh-Mallory blithely went to see Portal and informed him of his intentions to restructure the air command in Normandy. Portal appeared "somewhat startled." He appeared "still more startled when I said that I did not intend to inform Tedder that I was going to see the Supreme Commander-in-Chief, but would tell him after I had done so." Leigh-Mallory explained that, in his view, "Tedder had not been open with me over the role which Coningham should play in his estimation, and that, in any case, I was perfectly entitled to go direct to Ike."

Leigh-Mallory did go to see Eisenhower and outlined his ideas on taking a larger share in directing the battle and putting Coningham in his place. The Supreme Commander seemed agreeable but apparently did not commit himself. Then Leigh-Mallory bearded the lion in his den—he saw Tedder. They engaged in "some very plain speaking." Leigh-Mallory complained that Tedder did everything through Coningham. Tedder replied that Eisenhower had delegated the authority to control air to him.[48] If Leigh-Mallory insisted on taking control of the tactical battle and interfering with Coningham and Brereton, Tedder threatened to take away from him all voice in the employment of heavy bombers. Portal sided with Tedder.[49] The situation remained unresolved until after Operation GOODWOOD.

On July 18, Bomber Command and the Eighth Air Force provided direct support for the next British assault. At dawn Bomber Command dropped 6,000 half-ton bombs and 9,600 500-pound bombs on three target areas. At 7:00 A.M. medium bombers of the Ninth Air Force swept over the field, but many could not drop their bombs through the clouds of smoke and dirt left behind by Bomber Command. Then, at 8:30 A.M., the B-24s of the Eighth's 2d Bombardment Division, 570 strong, dropped almost 13,000 100-pound and 76,000 20-pound fragmentation bombs (1,410 tons in all) on a key tactical feature, Bourguebus Ridge. In all, 4,500 Allied aircraft beset the Germans. Once again, bombing did not completely clear the way for the ground forces.

Bomber Command struck first in the remarkably clear morning, hitting most of its targets squarely. Even four months later a British Bombing Analysis Unit reported that one area "resembled the surface of the moon." It found the rusting remains of an entire *Panzer* company—fifteen tanks and twelve half-tracks—none of which had been hit with shells or mortars. Only a few of the B-24s' fragmentation weapons fell on their targets; most scattered over the countryside. In the ensuing ground assault, Allied troops encountered particularly stiff resistance in the American target areas.[50] Bomb bursts had cratered the terrain, hindering the advance of some units, and had failed to knock out all of the entrenched German tanks and antitank guns. Furthermore, the Germans, anticipating the attack, had prepared deep defenses, many of which had not come under fire. Operation GOODWOOD, like its predecessors, soon ground to a bloody halt.[51]

It was no fluke that the British heavy bombers were more accurate than the American heavy bombers. As illogical as it seemed, British night tactics produced more precise bombing than American daylight tactics. The Americans flew compact formations in which only the lead bombardier made full use of his accurate Norden Visual Bombsight (M-9). This practice produced closely grouped bomb patterns and many missed targets. When several groups bombed a target, as they usually did, however, some of the bomb patterns landed directly where they should have. Because Bomber Command could not fly formations at night, each bombardier made all bombsight corrections.

Moreover, whereas the Eighth used radar only in its lead planes, almost all British bombers carried radar and crews trained in more accurate radar bombing. In addition, by the summer of 1944, Bomber Command was employing a "master bomber" or airborne air controller who stayed over the target for an entire mission and adjusted the bombing as it occurred. For the last year of the war, Bomber Command, plane for plane, not only delivered more tonnage but delivered it more effectively.[52] Of course, if the British had had to fly their lightly armed bombers in formation, in daylight, without escort from their short-ranged Spitfires, the analysis of bomb plots might well have tilted toward the Americans.

The failure of Montgomery's much ballyhooed attack led to a round of recriminations among top Allied leaders. The airmen, in particular, expressed keen disappointment. The normally unflappable Tedder began to agitate for Montgomery's dismissal and wrote to his old friend, Lord Trenchard, the founder of the RAF, that he and Eisenhower had been "had for suckers" by Montgomery.[53] At a high-level SHAEF staff meeting on July 21, Tedder asked Bedell Smith when the army would get to the V-1 launch sites in the Pas-de-Calais region of France. When Bedell Smith replied it would not be soon, Tedder sarcastically remarked, "Then we must change our leaders for men who will get us there."[54] Leigh-Mallory felt "bitterly disappointed, for it does not seem to me that the breakthrough which we produced has been exploited and pressed to a conclusion."[55] Eisenhower fumed as well. He acidly noted that the air forces had dropped a thousand tons of bombs for each mile of Montgomery's advance and wondered whether the Allies could afford to move through all of France at such a cost.[56]

Operation COBRA

The Eighth's next and last ground support mission in July proved to be both its most effective and its most controversial, because some of its bombs dropped short of the intended target area, landed among American troops, killed over one hundred of them and wounded hundreds more. This mission, flown in support of Lt. Gen. Omar N. Bradley's Operation COBRA, greatly assisted the ground forces in their attack, which eventually penetrated the German main line of resistance and produced the opportunity for the long-awaited Allied breakout from the Normandy beachhead.

The plan for COBRA came almost solely from Bradley, who first expounded it, and his chief subordinate, who would execute it, Maj. Gen. J. Lawton "Lightning Joe" Collins, at that time Commander of the U.S. VII Army Corps. Bradley had decided on the plan's outline by July 10,[57] and he presented it to his staff and to his corps commanders on July 12. COBRA differed from the usual pattern of American offensives. First, once the U.S. First Army reached the part of the road between St. Lô and Périers, where the offensive was to start, Collins would use his combat-experienced reserve of two U.S. armored divisions, the 2d and 3d—both organized according to an early wartime table of organization and equipment which gave them greater numbers of tanks than the typical U.S. armored division—and the fully motorized 1st Infantry Division to launch a narrow and concentrated attack on the German front line. As Russell F. Weigley, in his study of the campaign in France and Germany, has made clear, their concentration on a narrow front departed from the wide-front operations usually conducted by U.S. ground forces.[58] Bradley meant to conduct a battle to pierce enemy lines rather than to continue the attritional struggles of the earlier phases of the campaign. ULTRA intercepts helped to fuel Bradley's determination. The two enemy units opposite him, *II Parachute Corps* and *LXXXIV Corps*, reported heavy losses before July 10 and continuing heavy losses during the next two weeks. The senior German officers on the scene expected a breakthrough at any moment.[59]

Second, Bradley insisted that a heavy aerial bombardment immediately precede the beginning of COBRA. From its inception, Bradley intended that the air bombardment include the use of heavy bombers. As Bradley described it, "Realizing the great power we had in our Air Force, I wanted to secure someplace where we could use a great mass of power to virtually wipe out some German division opposing part of our line and then punch a hole through."

Bradley chose the straight stretch of road running from St. Lô through Périers to Lossay, having determined[60] that it could support the large force he intended to deploy. The air bombardment, in Bradley's mind, offset the lack of artillery firepower available. He told his chief of artillery, Brig. Gen. Charles E. Hart, that if he had had ten times the number of guns, he might have dispensed with air support.[61] Lack of artillery ammunition, at least as much as lack of artillery pieces, prevented an extensive gunfire bombardment. The Allied supply situation, restricted to what could come in over the original landing beaches, did not allow for a surfeit of shells. Bradley also wanted the "blast effect" of the bombs, which, with their thin metal casings, greatly exceeded the blast effect of artillery shells of similar weight.[62]

Because Bradley himself had originated the idea of employing heavy bombers, he had several preconceived notions about how they should be used. He required that the air bombardment fall into a rectangular area approximately 4 miles long and 1¾ miles deep, 7,000 yards by 2,500 yards.[63] The area covered the entire front of his initial attack. He also required that only 100-pound fragmentation bombs be dropped[64] to prevent excessive cratering that would hamper the advance of the infantry and, more important, the mechanized forces. He planned to withdraw his troops 800 yards from the front line.[65] A withdrawal of only 800 yards cut the safety margin exceedingly fine, but Bradley wished to avoid placing his troops too far away to follow up the attack without delay and letting the Germans reoccupy the conceded space, which would, in turn, force his men to fight through an enlarged defensive position. Bradley also wanted the air bombardment conducted rapidly; if it stretched out over several hours, it would lose its shock effect.

Bradley recognized that the airmen would prefer to approach the target box at a right angle to the front, flying from north to south, first crossing over the American lines and then dropping their bombs on the Germans to minimize exposure to antiaircraft fire. Bradley, however, wished the bombers to fly parallel to the front (along German lines) rather than perpendicular to it, in order to provide a greater security margin for his troops. The bombers could attack from east to west, during the morning, putting the sun in the eyes of the antiaircraft gunners, or reverse the course of attack in the afternoon.[66]

Bradley had picked the St. Lô–Périers road as the battle's start line because it was straight, paralleled the front immediately behind or on the German front line, and would serve as a clear and unmistakable aiming point for the air forces. The entire target box fell just to the south of the road.[67] As Bradley stated in his 1951 memoirs, "Indeed it was the thought of saturation bombing that attracted me to the Périers road. Easily recognizable from the air, the road described a long straight line that would separate our position from that of the Germans. *The bombers, I reasoned, could fly parallel to it without danger of mistaking our front*" [emphasis added].[68]

Given the key role allotted to air power in the attack, it is puzzling why Bradley waited until July 19 to fully inform the Allied air commanders of his scheme and their place in it. He merely said that he did not approach them until he had finished his plans and obtained Montgomery's approval on July 18.[69] On July 19, Bradley, flew from his headquarters in Normandy with his tactical air commander, Maj. Gen. Elwood R. (Pete) Quesada, Commander of the IX Tactical Air Command, to Leigh-Mallory's headquarters at Stanmore. There they found arrayed the full panoply of Allied air leadership—Tedder, Leigh-Mallory, and Spaatz—accompanied by Vandenberg, Brereton, Doolittle, Coningham, and lesser lights.[70] In his memoirs Bradley glossed over the differences between himself and the air chiefs. He baldly stated:

> Air's enthusiasm for COBRA almost exceeded that of our troops on the ground, for air welcomed the St. Lô carpet attack as an unrivaled opportunity to test the feasibility of saturation bombing. Leigh-Mallory proposed a heavier concentration of bombers than the Allies had ever before put into the air.[71]

Bradley left the meeting with a commitment for 1,500 heavy bombers, almost 900 medium bombers, and 350 fighter bombers.[72]

Bradley's description masked the serious differences he had had with the other airmen in attendance, who had initially insisted on a safety zone of 3,000 yards to separate his troops from the bombing. They agreed to reduce the safety zone to 1,500 yards, which still did not satisfy him. In the end he agreed to withdraw the troops only 1,200 yards. The heavy bombers, however, would not strike the front edge of the target box and would thereby add 250 yards to their

Maj. Gen. Elwood R. "Pete" Quesada, Commanding General, IX Tactical Air Command.

safety zone. Fighter-bombers would cover those 250 yards with their own more accurate and easily deliverable ordnance.[73] Leigh-Mallory even attempted to gain the participation of Bomber Command, but Bradley and Vandenberg both vetoed his idea. Bomber Command was equipped to drop only large bombs whose craters might retard the advance.[74]

At the meeting, Quesada and Bradley insisted that the bombers fly parallel to the front,[75] When some of the airmen present agreed with them, they apparently assumed that all of the airmen present agreed with them. In this they were mistaken. They had unknowingly run afoul of the air command system, which at that moment was suffering from tangled lines of authority and was riven with even greater personal animosity than usual.

On the American side of the house several principals were involved in a game of musical chairs. Two days before the July 19 meeting Eisenhower and Spaatz had accepted Marshall's recommendation that Brereton vacate his post as Commander of the Ninth Air Force to assume command of Combined Airborne Headquarters, which consisted of all British and American airborne divisions in the theater (a force of three divisions), plus separate troops, the IX Troop Carrier Command, and RAF transport and troop carrier formations. This conglomeration became the First Allied Airborne Army in August 1944.[76]

Meanwhile, Vandenberg, whom Spaatz and Eisenhower had originally wanted for the airborne command but whom Marshall refused to promote,[77]

466

would move over to command the Ninth. The Ninth's Deputy Commander, Maj. Gen. Ralph Royce (another member of Spaatz's West Point Class of 1914), would take over Vandenberg's old post as Deputy Commander in Chief, AEAF. Although the principals had learned of these moves, the War Department and Marshall had not yet approved them. This left most of the American tactical air high command in a state of flux. If his diary is a reliable guide, Vandenberg spent a considerable amount of time during this period stewing over the "Royce-Brereton-Vandenberg triangle."[78] Quesada apparently continued, blissfully unaware of his superior's command changes until later.

Brereton may well have been "kicked upstairs"—at least, Bradley thought so.[79] He said of Brereton, "Ike knew Brereton was not pulling his weight. I had told Ike he was hard to do business with. Brereton never seemed interested in the job, would never throw himself into it."[80] Brereton had committed two of the worst sins possible for an air commander with a ground support mission. He had not established a good working relationship with nor set up his headquarters directly alongside his counterpart in the ground forces. Apparently, after he set up his own plush headquarters in Normandy, he hardly ever went to see Bradley in the field, only a mile away.[81] Unlike Coningham, who also had a less-than-exemplary relationship with his counterpart in the ground forces, Brereton had neither the patina of past success nor the support of his superiors in the air chain of command. His aspirations for independence and his support of the transportation plan had probably irritated Spaatz. In the somewhat feudal and definitely hierarchical nature of the military establishment there was no indication that Brereton was a "Spaatz man." Conversely, Vandenberg had formed strong ties to the Arnold-Spaatz section of the Army Air Forces.

As the American generals sorted out their new positions, the British air marshals engaged in a brouhaha of their own, revolving around their respective views of Montgomery. Coningham was still hostile toward him, Tedder, as discussed earlier, had taken up the warpath against him for his supposed lack of vigor and success and had continued the campaign for his relief. Leigh-Mallory, marching to his own drum, had alienated Portal, Tedder, and SHAEF Headquarters staff by literally moving in with Montgomery. In his Command Diary, on July 19, Tedder noted:

> Montgomery will not deal with Coningham, but only with L-M [Leigh-Mallory]. This entails Broadhurst, Coningham's subordinate, dealing *direct* with L-M. . . . L-M has even moved his own personal caravan . . . with Monty. L-M seems to be cashing in on the discomfiture of his own subordinate.[82]

This finished Leigh-Mallory as far as Tedder was concerned.

In his postwar memoirs Tedder proceeded directly from the end of GOOD-WOOD to the air command situation. GOODWOOD's failure allowed him to squelch Leigh-Mallory's ambition to take a more active role.

Field Marshal Bernard
L. Montgomery, General
Officer Commanding, 21
Army Group, Northwest
Europe, 1944–1945.

Imperial War Mueum

> My immediate problem was to place on a more solid footing the arrangements
> for control of our Air Forces. Leigh-Mallory, though earnest, zealous, and brave,
> did not inspire confidence as Commander of the Allied Expeditionary Air
> Forces. It seemed to me that he was insufficiently firm in explaining to the Army
> authorities the limitations of air-power in direct support of the ground battle.[83]

Montgomery meanwhile had developed a greater appreciation for Leigh-Mallory's qualities. He wrote to a friend at the War Office in London, "We must definitely keep Leigh-Mallory as Air Commander-in-Chief. He is the only airman who is out to help us with the land battle and has no jealous reactions."[84] In the eyes of most of the top Allied airmen, Montgomery's support could only have been the kiss of death.

At this point Tedder decided to eliminate or greatly reduce Headquarters, AEAF. He had already removed CROSSBOW from AEAF's purview and had informed Leigh-Mallory that if he, Leigh-Mallory, wished to move forward to direct the tactical battle at the expense of Coningham, then he, Tedder, would resume total direction of the strategic air forces. "I could not help feeling," wrote Tedder in 1966, "that Leigh-Mallory's large assurances to Montgomery encouraged the unhealthy tendency of the Army to rely on air-power for support of a kind which it could not confer."[85]

Bradley, and probably Quesada, could have had little idea of the quagmire into which they had stepped. Leigh-Mallory's enthusiastic support for COBRA at

468

the meeting of July 19 must have left the impression that he would ensure the adherence of the other airmen. After all, when Bradley gave an order to his subordinates or agreed to an operation on their behalf, he very naturally assumed that they would follow his lead once a decision was made, even if they had previously expressed disagreement. Bradley had, of course, heard the protests of Vandenberg and Brig. Gen. Orvil A. Anderson, Doolittle's operations officer, that the big bombers could not fly parallel to the front, but he had also heard Leigh-Mallory dismiss these objections.[86] With good reason, then, Bradley assumed that the airmen had accepted his strictures and he returned to the Continent jubilant at the extent of the air commitment. He and the Air Chiefs had set the date for COBRA for the morning of July 21, less than thirty-six hours away.[87]

The Air Chiefs had also completed the air command arrangements for COBRA, a bizarre mishmash that excluded USSTAF and the Eighth Air Force from most command decisions and left the heavy bombers subject to the orders of men who understood little of the technical difficulties involved in their operation. Tedder, who had approved the mission in the first place, would provide top-level supervision; Leigh-Mallory would set the time and date of the operation; Brereton would plan the bomber attack; and Quesada would coordinate the air attack with the ground forces.[88]

Inclement weather forced the postponement of COBRA from July 21 to July 24. This postponement gave the Eighth the chance to send a 1,100-bomber raid against German aircraft production plants on July 21 and a 280-bomber attack on French airfields on July 23. On the evening of July 23, AEAF's meteorologists predicted that the weather on the next day would be suitable for COBRA. USSTAF's weathermen had a different forecast. They predicted heavy to moderate clouds for July 24 and better conditions for July 25 in the St. Lô area. They foresaw good bombing weather over Berlin and central Germany on July 24.

At 9:30 P.M. on July 23, Spaatz's Deputy for Operations, Maj. Gen. Frederick L. Anderson, called Leigh-Mallory for an immediate decision as to the target because the Eighth needed to know which bombs to load, 500-pound general-purpose bombs and incendiaries for Berlin or fragmentation bombs for St. Lô. Leigh-Mallory, relying on his own forecasts, set the starting time for COBRA's air bombardment at 10:00 A.M. On the morning of July 24, AEAF's meteorologists revised their estimates and called for slowly breaking clouds from 11:00 A.M. to 1:00 P.M. Therefore, at 6:30 A.M. Leigh-Mallory delayed the attack for two hours, rescheduling it for 12 noon.[89] Despite the unease of their own Eighth Air Force weathermen, 1,586 B-17s and B-24s left their bases to participate in COBRA. Leigh-Mallory flew to Bradley's headquarters. Vandenberg and Smith flew forward as well. They saw little; except for a brief period when the clouds thinned somewhat, the skies stayed heavily overcast with a ceiling of only 5,000 feet. Leigh-Mallory had no choice but to call off the mission and reschedule it for the next day.

Unfortunately, the timing of this decision—he waited until the last moment to cancel—revealed Leigh-Mallory's unfamiliarity with the handling of heavy bombers and reflected unfavorably on his ability to command such formations. The cancellation caused tragedy and confusion. Incredibly, the ground forces had no direct communications link to the bombers in the air. Quesada passed Leigh-Mallory's halt order back to Stanmore by radio-telephone, where its receipt produced immediate consternation in the Daily Air Commanders' Meeting, which had convened, as usual, at 11:00 A.M. Tedder, Spaatz, Harris, Doolittle, and Eaker (who had come up from the Mediterranean for his and Spaatz's end-of-the-month meeting) were nonplussed. Doolittle said that the bombers were only seven minutes from their targets and could not be recalled now. He assumed that the planes would return fully loaded if they could not bomb visually. Spaatz wanted to know who had set the attack for noon, when the Eighth's weathermen had predicted solid overcast at that time, with a chance of some clearing only at 2:00 P.M. Bradley, he said, had indicated that he could wait until 3:00 P.M. for the bombing to start. "Why," asked Spaatz, "had the earlier time been selected?"[90] No one present could answer him.

Over St. Lô the first of the Eighth's three bombardment divisions made no attack because of poor visibility. In the second bombardment division to pass, one group (35 bombers), after making three runs to identify its target, released its bombs. The third bombardment division to arrive over the target box found weather conditions slightly improved, and 317 bombers loosed their loads, 550 tons of high explosives and 135 tons of fragmentation bombs, before finally receiving the recall order.[91] All the heavy bombers had approached and bombed at a right angle, or perpendicular, to the front line. Some had dropped short, directly onto their own troops. They killed 25 men and wounded 131 more of the 30th Division.

The performance enraged Bradley. Thanks to the confusion caused by bombing after the cancellation of the air phase of COBRA and some indecision as to whether the ground phase was also postponed, his troops had to fight hand-to-hand to regain the start line.[92] The German LXXXIV Corps defending St. Lô optimistically (and prematurely) reported that it had shot the American offensive into the ground with a great expenditure of artillery ammunition.[93]

Bradley could scarcely believe that the bombers had not struck parallel to the front. At his command post he found Leigh-Mallory equally upset. "But what worries me more than anything else," Bradley told Leigh-Mallory, "is the fact that those heavies came in over our heads instead of parallel to the Périers road. I left Stanmore with a clear understanding that they would fly parallel to the road."[94] Vandenberg and Brig. Gen. Frederic H. Smith, his deputy, attempted to explain to Bradley, Leigh-Mallory, and Quesada why the mission could not be carried out as planned—to little effect. Bradley did not even mention them in his memoirs, but Vandenberg noted sourly in his diary, "General Bradley gave the appearance of having very little idea as to the cloud conditions required for heavy bombardment, a situation we attempted to remedy."[95] Before leaving Bradley's headquarters, Leigh-Mallory promised to check on the bombers' direction of attack.

Leaving an incensed Bradley behind, Vandenberg flew back to England where he found a message to call an irate Spaatz. Spaatz demanded to know why the mission had not been set up for Tuesday, July 25, "when his weather people had given a much brighter forecast for that day than they had for Monday."[96] Vandenberg replied that his forecasters had predicted no better weather for Tuesday than for Monday, and besides, he himself had observed that, as the Eighth's meteorologists had predicted, the weather had not broken that afternoon. Spaatz responded that if the COBRA mission was on for Tuesday and if there was any difference of opinion between the two groups of meteorologists, he should be informed at once. By 9:00 P.M. that evening Vandenberg informed Spaatz that all of the meteorologists had agreed on 10:00 A.M. for the next day's mission over St. Lô.[97] What irked Spaatz was not the bombing short, but the waste of effort for 1,600 of his bombers. The late decision to cancel had cost him a day of visual bombing conditions over Berlin and central Germany.[98]

Vandenberg's busy evening continued. He talked to Eighth Air Force Headquarters and, after some argument, informed it of Leigh-Mallory's desire for bombing parallel to the road. Eighth Air Force Headquarters replied that as long as Bradley required that the bombers attack in as little time as possible, they could not fly parallel. Funneling more than 1,500 bombers through the short side of the target box would take 2½ hours, if it could be done at all. Soon afterward, Maj. Gen. Frederick L. Anderson of USSTAF called Vandenberg. He, too, emphasized that "the time factor" controlled their direction of attack. He suggested that Bradley might want to extend the time allowed. Before Vandenberg could pass this message on to Leigh-Mallory, Leigh-Mallory informed him that he had just spoken to Bradley and that Bradley could not accept a lengthier attack and, therefore, "had decided to accept the additional risk of perpendicular to the road bombing."[99]

Bradley had accepted the alternative with extreme reluctance. Later he expressed his feelings about having been coerced:

> I was shocked and angered by air's reply, for to me it represented a serious breach of good faith planning. . . . Had I known of air's intent to chance the perpendicular approach, I would never have consented to its plan.

What clinched the decision for Bradley was Leigh-Mallory's latest weather forecast, which noted that a low-pressure area would move into the St. Lô area in the afternoon of July 25, carrying with it several days of bad weather. In addition, at an earlier command conference he and his subordinates had decided to wait only one or two more days for air support. Bradley would have pulled his troops farther back had he known in advance of the bombers' approach route.[100]

The status of the enemy troops facing his attack added to Bradley's anxiety. Signal intelligence decrypts from July 14 and 21 revealed that the German *LXXXIV Corps* and *II Parachute Corps* had reported serious disorganization as a result of earlier American attacks and were unsure that they could continue a successful defense. Further messages on July 22, 24, and 25 detailed the steadily depreciating combat value of *II Parachute Corps*.[101] An extraordinary opportunity beckoned if only Bradley's forces could go forward, and the blow could not be long delayed. A more ominous signal, which indicated that the Germans might have begun to realize their vulnerability to Bradley's forces in this section of the beachhead, dated late July 22, decrypted 8:18 A.M. July 23, from the German *Seventh Army* Luftwaffe liaison, urgently requested reconnaissance of powerful new U.S. forces with tanks (Patton's Third Army) opposite the *17th SS Panzer Grenadier Division*.[102] (See Map 14, Operation COBRA Area, Night of July 24–25, 1944.)

On the morning of July 25, at about 10:00 A.M., Eighth Air Force mission no. 494 began its bomb drop. In an effort equaling the previous day's, the Eighth dispatched 1,581 B-17s and B-24s. Unlike the day before, 1,503 of the heavies released their high-explosive cargo and sent it hurtling toward the front line. Over 3,300 tons of explosives plus 870 tons dropped by the medium bombers and fighter-bombers crashed into the greatly understrength German *Panzer Lehr Division*, killing 1,000 of its men, destroying three of its battalion command posts, knocking out all but a dozen of its armored fighting vehicles, and wiping out an attached parachute regiment.[103] Lt. Gen. Fritz Bayerlein, the division's commander, described the Normandy scene in a postwar interrogation. "It was hell. . . . The planes kept coming overhead like a conveyor belt, and the bomb carpets came down. . . . My front lines looked like a landscape on the moon, and at least seventy percent of my personnel were out of action—dead, wounded, crazed or numb."[104] At 10:00 A.M. Bayerlein reported to his superiors that the air bombardment heralded an American breakthrough attempt. He urgently requested the Luftwaffe's assistance.[105]

Despite this punishing blow and the artillery barrage that followed it, the well-disciplined and -trained German survivors, in a last-gasp effort, managed to prevent the American breakthrough for one more day. By the night of July 25, the American assault had advanced only a mile south of the Périers road, still within the target box. The general gloom and disappointment that surrounded the first day's action did not affect General Collins. He sensed that the attack had broken through the German lines. Signal intelligence on the Germans' weakened state even before the offensive, which Bradley undoubtedly shared with Collins, and the early morning decryption of Bayerlein's plea for help must have confirmed his feelings. ULTRA also intercepted a message dated before dawn on July 26 in which *LXXXIV Corps* reported a shortage of 88mm antitank ammunition, heavy casualties, and a deteriorating situation.[106] On the evening of July 25, Collins summoned his armor to the front with orders to push through

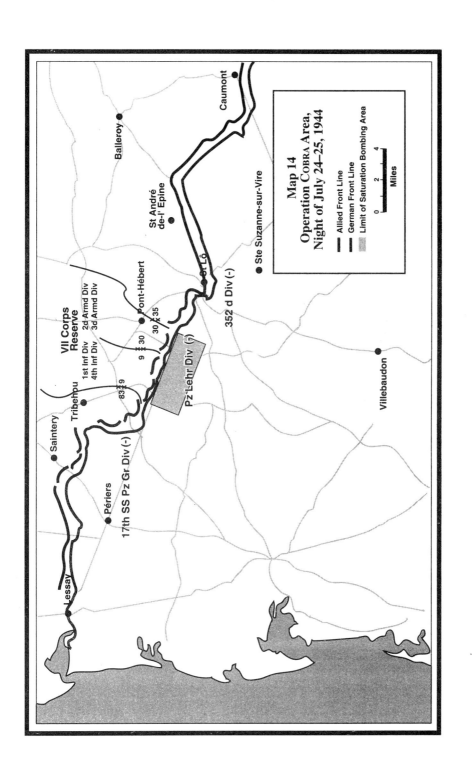

Map 14
Operation COBRA Area,
Night of July 24–25, 1944

Allied Front Line
German Front Line
Limit of Saturation Bombing Area

0   2   4
Miles

Caumont

Balleroy

St André
de-l' Epine

Ste Suzanne-sur-Vire

St Lô

Pont-Hébert

352 d Div (-)

VII Corps
Reserve

2d Armd Div
3d Armd Div

1st Inf Div
4th Inf Div

30 X 35

9   30

83   9

Pz 'Lehr Div (?)

Saintery

Tribehou

17th SS Pz Gr Div (-)

Périers

Villebaudon

Lessay

the last German defenders and exploit the breakthrough.[107] The German forces in Normandy, bled white by seven weeks of attrition, their attention focused on the Caen sector by Montgomery's repeated attacks, and their mobility curtailed by Allied control of the air, did not react quickly or forcefully enough to Bradley's offensive. On July 26, Collins's troops burst through the thin screen of Germans opposing them, and, thanks to the ingeniously simple idea of welding iron shears to the front of each tank, which gave them a tactical advantage over the road-bound Germans, the Americans plowed through the hedgerows into the clear terrain beyond. The race through France to the German border had begun.

On the afternoon of July 25, however, the long-awaited breakthrough seemed as far away as ever. In addition to the surprisingly stout German defense, more short bombings had shaken the advancing troops. Although in retrospect it was evident that the air bombardment had accomplished its goal of wrecking the German defenses, Americans on the spot were naturally more inclined to dwell on their own losses. Once again, the 30th Infantry Division bore the brunt of friendly fire. A unit of the 9th Infantry Division also suffered heavily. Short bombs killed 111 Americans, including Lt. Gen. Leslie J. McNair, the highest-ranking Allied officer to die in the campaign, and wounded 490 more.[108] Ironically, McNair, in his previous assignment as head of the Army Ground Forces, had been one of the harshest critics of the AAF's lack of training in close air support. Other GIs suffered from combat fatigue or, to use the more vivid World War I term, shell shock. As a direct result of the July 25 bombings, the 30th Infantry Division reported 164 cases of combat exhaustion.[109] Eisenhower, who had come to Bradley's headquarters to observe the first day of the offensive, was more dismayed by the short bombing than Bradley and said of the heavy bombers' performance, "I don't believe they can be used in support of ground forces. That's a job for artillery. I gave them a green light this time. But I promise you it's the last."[110]

Bombs from between thirty-five and sixty heavy bombers and forty-two medium bombers fell within American lines,[111] all as a result of human error.[112] The bombers were working under what were for them unusual conditions. They had planned to bomb at 15,000 to 16,000 feet, but cloud cover over St. Lô forced them to recompute their sights while airborne and to bomb at 12,000 feet. In descending to the lower altitude, formations loosened up, as nervous pilots sought air space in congested areas over the target. Elongated bomb patterns resulted as the groups followed standard procedure and released their bombs when the lead plane dropped its bombs. On the ground, a prevailing wind from the south quickly dissipated the smoke from the marking shells fired by American artillery. This smoke soon mixed with the clouds from the attack and drifted back toward the American lines, masking any aiming points.[113] The all-important St. Lô–Périers road, visible on the map, like much else in Normandy, proved less prominent from the air. Years later Quesada berated himself:

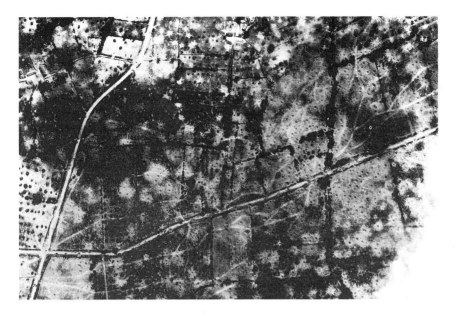

The shattered aftermath of Operation COBRA near St. Lô, France, July 26, 1944.

Now, everybody made a mistake, including Pete Quesada, in thinking that the St. Lô road was a good and visible demarcation point that anybody could see, and it turned out not to be so. The St. Lô road was . . . rather obscure . . . and I have always condemned myself . . . [for] not having flown over this road myself and looked at it.[114]

In fact, many bombardiers, well aware of the first day's tragedy, took great pains not to bomb short on the second day. One-half of the 1st Bombardment Division, approximately 150 to 200 bombers, delivered their loads beyond the target. Unfortunately, 2 to 4 percent of the bombers dropped short. One bombardier had trouble with his bombsight and recomputed visually, with poor results; another failed to identify vital landmarks properly; and a command pilot failed to observe the order to drop by bomb group, ordering "bombs away" when his wing leader, several hundred yards ahead of the pilot's formation, dropped his bombs.[115]

The next day Spaatz talked to Doolittle, Eisenhower, and Bradley. In summarizing the operation, Spaatz made four main points:

1. Short bombing, like short rounds from supporting artillery fire, was an unavoidable fact of life.

2. The mass of bombs dropped on St. Lô had so demoralized the enemy that the demoralized U.S. troops had still succeeded in achieving a breakthrough.

3. Because of their striking power and potential for tremendous damage, masses of heavy bombers should not be routed over friendly troops.

4. All our bombing experience shows that lateral error is greater than range error. To achieve the foregoing, the Air Commander himself must determine what weight of effort can be placed in any area selected by the Army Commander and must have the power to decide whether or not an area can be attacked at all.[116]

Spaatz's problem with lateral dispersion, also known as drift, raised an issue seldom discussed in other analyses of COBRA. That was perhaps for two reasons: (1) either the strategic airmen had become so accustomed to analyzing bomb plots that they regarded it as a given and subconsciously assumed that everyone understood, or (2) the airmen believed it to be so technical that they could not possibly explain it to an outsider. In a perpendicular approach, if a plane released bombs at the proper time, its forward momentum would be imparted to its bombs and would carry them beyond friendly lines, even if they veered off a straight course. A parallel approach did not have that advantage. Even if a heavy bomber released its bombs at the correct time, side-to-side error, which was much harder to calculate and compensate for than forward momentum, would almost certainly carry bombs into friendly forces.

Furthermore, if bombers on a parallel approach entered the target zone at an angle different from the briefed approach, any under- or over-shooting of the target could again put strings of bombs into friendly troops. In any attempt to send 1,500 bombers through a two-and-one-half-mile-wide parallel approach, congestion would invariably put many groups on the wrong approach angle. A parallel approach for COBRA would force the bombers to form a column two groups wide, extending all the way back to Holland, and take several hours to funnel over the target. Although lateral dispersion caused no attributable casualties, the AAF official history does note that for COBRA "spillage to the east and west of their targets" occurred for several of the formations, all of which flew from north to south.[117]

The Eighth's standard operating procedure added to the possibility of lateral dispersion. Although, by this stage in the war, most heavy bombers carried the improved Norden bombsight (M-9), capable of very high accuracy in well-trained hands, only the lead bombardier in each formation, usually the group or wing in 1944, used his bombsight to correct both for drift (side-to-side accuracy) and for range or rate (front-to-back accuracy). The remaining bombardiers in the formation corrected for range only and released their bombs when they saw the lead plane release its bombs. Most of the bombardiers in a formation did not correct for drift.

This procedure was obviously not ideal for maximum bombing efficiency but had been adopted for safety's sake. By 1944 the bombardier was actually able to take over control of his aircraft from the pilot when he adjusted his sight and allowed the bombsight, through its electrical connection with the automatic pilot, to adjust course. In a formation, kept tight to maximize each aircraft's defensive power and the compactness of its bomb patterns, the danger of midair collision would have greatly increased had each bombadier maneuvered independently to correct his aim. Hence, only the formation's lead bombardier made the necessary corrections; the others conformed to his movements.[118] It was hardly likely that the Eighth could or would change this practice for a single mission with only a few days' notice.

If timing and lateral dispersion problems necessitated a perpendicular approach, why, then, did Spaatz recommend parallel bombing for future support missions requiring heavy-bomber participation? He did so to avoid psychological damage to the assault troops. The day after the COBRA bombardment, Spaatz recorded in his Command Diary,

> If by any chance a gross error in the leading formations causes bombs to fall among our troops, the psychological effect of succeeding waves of bombing becomes terrific since, if one of our formations errs, in the minds of the soldiers on the ground the same error may be made by others, and their worry and anxiety builds up to tremendous proportion.[119]

Lt. Gen. Carl A. Spaatz alighting from his B-17 at an Eighth Air Force B-24 base to confer with his air crews. He visited immediately before and after combat operations whenever possible.

Parallel bombing would reduce the number of planes passing over the troops.

Spaatz also recommended selecting more aiming points to reduce the concentration of planes and potential errors at a single point—a 1,500-yard safety margin simply did not suffice. Finally, Spaatz conceded to the ground commander, Bradley, the right to suggest the target area, but he reserved to the air commander the right to determine the weight of effort placed on any specific point and "the power to decide whether or not an area can be attacked at all."[120] As Spaatz well knew, he and Doolittle had had too little voice in determining either the time of the attack or its feasibility under prevailing weather conditions.

Although Spaatz had defended the work of the Eighth to Eisenhower and Bradley, the performance of the 2d Bombardment Division, made up entirely of B-24s, apparently had not pleased him. In contrast to American ground force leaders like Bradley, Patton, and even Eisenhower, who openly relieved several division commanders and lesser officers promptly, if not too promptly, for inadequate performance, Spaatz did not deal harshly with his subordinate commanders. If they failed the test of combat, he quietly sent them to other posts. This seems to have been the fate of the commanding general of the 2d Bombardment Division, Maj. Gen. James P. Hodges.

In mid-August the Eighth reorganized. It reduced VIII Fighter Command to a paper organization and assigned its fighter groups directly to the three bombardment divisions, which became air divisions. This reorganization enabled the same bomber and fighter formations to operate together for extended periods and thus ensured close cooperation between them, with the goal of reducing the number of occasions on which either type of aircraft would miss an all-important air rendezvous. Bombers without constant escort still proved easy marks for the Luftwaffe.

As part of the reorganization, Maj. Gen. William E. Kepner, who had a reputation as a troubleshooter, took over Hodges's bombardment division. Within twenty days of COBRA, Hodges found himself in Washington as Assistant Chief of the Air Staff, Intelligence, Headquarters, AAF. He never held another combat command and retired in 1951 still a major general. This reassignment had been in the works before COBRA. On the day of the bombing, Hodges attended a luncheon given by Spaatz's Chief of Intelligence, Brig. Gen. George C. McDonald, where he met the top British intelligence officers and was processed into the "real Blackmarket Intelligence business."[121] Hodges's new post was, apparently, not highly regarded. His predecessor as Assistant Chief of the Air Staff, Intelligence, Brig. Gen. Thomas D. White, upon leaving the assignment, pungently commented to McDonald, "I never have had an unhappier job tho' few people know it; A-2 will forever suck the hind tit [sic] in the AAF."[122]

From January 1944 through July 1944, the 2d Bombardment Division's bombing accuracy had fallen far behind that of the 1st Division's and, for five of those seven months, behind the 3d Division's as well.[123] In the Eighth, the B-24 was considered inferior to the B-17, mostly because of its lower effective combat air ceiling and poor center of gravity, caused by many modifications, which made it more prone to flak losses and more difficult for pilots to operate. However, it had performed well for the Fifteenth Air Force.[124] The aircraft's capabilities did not account for the poor achievements of Hodges's units.

The 2d Division did badly during COBRA, leading the mission on both July 24 and 25. Its lead bombers had the easiest time because the smoke of previous groups did not obscure their aiming points and targets and because enemy flak had not had time to find its range and adjust for atmospheric conditions. On July 25, thirteen of the 2d's forty-five squadrons bombing dropped short of the target area; two of those dropped 2,800 to 3,000 yards short, among the American troops. In the 3d Division, which followed, six out of thirty-six squadrons bombed short, with one of those—the 100th Bomb Group—dropping bombs into the American lines.

In the 1st Division, only one squadron bombed short of the target area, by a mere 100 yards, and five groups withheld their cargoes and hit alternate targets because they could not identify their aiming points. One-half of the 1st Division bombed beyond the target area; obviously, its bombardiers had taken to heart the briefings concerning the proximity of U.S. troops to the target box.[125]

After Hodges left the 2d Division, its bombing accuracy improved to equal or surpass that of the other divisions. In January, February, and March 1945, it significantly outdistanced them.[126]

As the breakthrough progressed and the troops and commanders had a chance to assess the damage inflicted on the Germans, emotions cooled. By July 28, Bradley wrote to Eisenhower: "This operation could not have been the success it has been without such close cooperation of the Air. In the first place the bombardment we gave them last Tuesday was apparently highly successful, even though we did suffer many casualties ourselves."[127]

Later Missions in Support of Ground Operations

Montgomery requested another heavy-bomber mission for early August to assist an offensive by his newly established 1st Canadian Army. On August 5, Spaatz and Vandenberg[128] met with other air leaders, including Tedder and Leigh-Mallory and,[129] after a five-hour session, they agreed to supply the American and British heavy bombers.

At 10:00 P.M. on August 7, Leigh-Mallory once again tried to make last-minute changes in operational plans. He called Spaatz and informed him that the AAF's bombing effort over two of the aiming points needed augmentation because he had already requested Harris and Bomber Command to give additional support for those two areas. Spaatz, apparently incensed at another example of Leigh-Mallory's penchant for interference and inability to let well enough alone, immediately called Tedder and gained his agreement that if the attack needed more weight, the Americans themselves would supply it. Spaatz was seeking to avoid the confusion that was very likely to result if the two Allied bomber forces attacked the same pinpoint targets. Then Spaatz called Leigh-Mallory back and obtained his agreement to place more American bombers over the aiming points in question.[130] The next day the Eighth dispatched 678 bombers to follow up the initial bombardment of 637 RAF aircraft.[131] The 2d Bombardment Division did not participate in this attack.

This combined attack incorporated several lessons learned from the St. Lô and earlier air bombardments. Bomber Command did not bomb directly ahead of the troops. Instead, it delivered large bombs, with their accompanying cratering effect, on both flanks of the assaulting Canadians in order to seal off lateral movement by German reinforcements. Also, the RAF, departing from its practice in earlier close support missions, attacked at night, when the Canadians began their own assault, penetrating the first two German lines and gaining five kilometers. Ground mist in the morning delayed further attacks, which allowed the Germans to counterattack. Nevertheless, Lt. Gen. G. C. Simonds, Commander of the 2d Canadian Corps, committed two inexperienced armored divisions, the 4th Canadian and the 1st Polish, to exploit the attack.[132]

At 1:00 P.M. on August 8, the Eighth Air Force arrived to bomb its targets. Scouting planes had preceded it to check weather conditions and the state of the target areas, which were marked by smoke shells and flares. As planned, the bombers flew parallel to the lines of the attacking troops, a tactic forcing a long flight over enemy territory and, of course, magnifying the usual problems of operating in congested air space. After the troops had withdrawn only 1,500 yards—the Canadians, like Bradley, apparently were willing to chance casualties rather than give up too much ground and momentum—the American heavy bombers delivered their attacks flying north to south.

The bombardment struck its targets in turn, in the manner of a creeping barrage. The bombers flew straight and level down forty miles of the German lines and received intense heavy flak for the entire distance. The 681 attackers lost 7 bombers, wrote off 4 more as not repairable, and had 107 with major damage and 187 with minor damage. They dropped 1,275 tons of bombs. Two of their four aiming points were well covered. Clouds of dust prevented the bombing of one point and allowed only 30 percent of the bombers to drop on the other.[133]

Two 12-plane formations, unfortunately, bombed short, killing 65 and wounding 265 Canadians and Poles in areas packed with unsuspecting members of the 1st Polish Armored Division and the 3d Canadian Infantry Division, many of them sitting in their vehicles moving or waiting to move up to the front. Some of the bombs fell on the tactical headquarters of the Canadian division, wounding its commander, Maj. Gen. R.F.L. Kellor, and forcing his evacuation.[134] The discomfiture caused by the shorts, the 5-minute safety delay between the bombardment and the renewal of the ground assault, the 1,500-yard safety margin, and the two divisions' inexperience caused the attack to bog down. It halted on August 9 after gaining 13 kilometers.[135]

AAF after-action reports revealed the near impossibility of preventing such short bombing. In one bomb group an antiaircraft round hit the lead plane just after it had decided to bypass the primary target, which was obscured by smoke. The round caused a fire in the bomb bay. The pilot, fearing for the lives of himself and his crew, salvoed his bomb load. The rest of the formation followed his lead. Their bombs landed in the friendly city of Caen.

In a second instance, the lead bombardier and pilot, confused by a course change to avoid intense flak, performed "exceedingly poorly," misidentifying their targets and dropping the formation's bombs just to the south of Caen.[136] Such errors were inevitable on any large mission. The only way to keep them from adversely affecting the friendly assault troops was to bomb so far behind the enemy front line that any direct advantage the troops might gain was eliminated.

The next day Spaatz flew to the Continent. At Heston Airfield, just before taking off, he encountered Eisenhower, who had just come from Normandy to review the paratroops of the 82d and 101st Divisions. They discussed the use of heavy bombers in close support. After describing what he had learned so far, much of it based on an extensive report from Doolittle on operations of July 24 and 25, Spaatz incorrectly noted that most of the gross bombing errors were the result of enemy antiaircraft fire or the actions of enemy aircraft. Eisenhower suggested that Spaatz visit Montgomery, who, after the previous day's short bombing, had apparently developed misgivings about the employment of heavy bombers in close support. Before they parted Spaatz told Eisenhower that, in his opinion, "the only significant breakthrough obtained had been through the use of heavy bombardment [aircraft]."[137]

Once on the Continent, Spaatz visited, in order, Bradley, Patton, and Montgomery. The first two praised the cooperation of the tactical air forces, which had helped the speed and success of their advances. Spaatz found Montgomery singing a tune slightly different from the one Eisenhower had heard. Montgomery apparently told Spaatz that "the breakthrough of the Army was made possible by heavy bombardment," and that "to have attempted such a breakthrough without such preparation would have cost him 10,000 men."[138] Montgomery had certainly not sworn off using heavy bombers.

Five days later, on August 14, a daylight Bomber Command bombardment preceded another 1st Canadian Army lunge toward Falaise. This time the RAF dropped short, causing 400 Commonwealth casualties, including 65 killed and 91 missing, many blown to bits. A recent history of the RAF explained why:

> It appeared that someone had omitted to inform Bomber Command that the Army's standard color for marking its positions was yellow; this was Bomber Command's target-indicating colour, and 77 aircraft which had gone astray

proceeded to bomb on yellow marks—(the more the troops burnt yellow flares to show their position the more the errant aircraft bombed them).[139]

Once again the Poles suffered along with the Canadians. Ironically forty-four of the bomber crews dropping short were Canadian. The RAF, adding insult to injury, almost killed one of its own in a concentration of short bombs—Air Marshal Coningham—and a Canadian corps commander.[140]

Allied heavy bombers did not fly another close support mission until November 16, 1944, when they participated in the preliminary bombardment of Operation QUEEN, a U.S. First Army offensive in the Huertgen Forest region near Aachen. Their overall performance in close support during the campaign in northwestern Europe indicates that heavy bombers were not entirely suitable weapons. They did not belong on the tactical battlefield unless all other ground or tactical air firepower available was insufficient. A flyswatter and a sledge-hammer can both kill flies, but the ease of use of the former made it far easier to control and more effective than the sound and force of the latter. In three out of four cases, close support of the ground troops, although spectacular, achieved little for effort involved. The ground troops did not achieve a breakthrough. In the fourth case, at St. Lô, the heavy bombers expedited the success of a massive ground offensive by undercutting German resistance and probably saved American lives.

The attacks in support of Montgomery, who faced the bulk of the Germans' high-quality armored formations, could do little because he did not have the preponderance of strength necessary to overwhelm the troops facing him. Sheer weight of fire cannot make up for lack of manpower against a first-class opponent. The *Panzer Lehr Division* held on for one more day despite its drenching from the air. If the Germans had had reserves available, they might well have delayed the breakthrough for days. The decisive factors in the St. Lô breakthrough were Bradley's massing of four divisions on a single division front and the Germans' total lack of reserves to respond. This blow would have succeeded in any case, but the heavy-bomber attack helped the assault to penetrate the German lines more quickly and with fewer American casualties.

Chapter 14

Stalemate on the
German Frontier
(September 11–December 15, 1944)

There is no conclusive evidence of any intention of the Germans to quit.[1]

—Spaatz to Arnold, September 24, 1944

To what extent the ground forces can advance during the ensuing late fall and winter months is anyone's guess. However, it is my prediction that unless the weather is extremely unusual, the ground advances will be very limited until the good weather of spring again permits the overwhelming air cover to which they have become accustomed. Barring a disintegration within Germany itself or the benefit of a spell of good weather in October or November, I foresee a repetition of the winter in Africa and last winter in Italy.[2]

—Spaatz to Lovett, October 1, 1944.

From the middle of September through the middle of December 1944, the U.S.-British ground forces engaged in a series of sanguinary battles from the Swiss border to the North Sea. As the Allied armies inched forward against the stout resistance of hastily created or largely reconstituted German divisions, Allied air power continued to dominate the skies over the battle lines and above Hitler's truncated empire.

In September, at a high-level Anglo-American conference in Quebec, code-named OCTAGON, Roosevelt, Churchill, and the Combined Chiefs of Staff, in the midst of discussion concerning strategy and coming operations in the Pacific and Europe, resolved the air command tangle in the European Theater of Operations by abolishing the AEAF and removing, over Spaatz's and Eisenhower's objections, Bomber Command and USSTAF from Eisenhower's direct control. Within the European Theater, Spaatz and his fellow Allied airmen faced, as usual, the task of setting strategic bombing priorities in the light of changing perceptions of remaining German military and economic strength. In addition, Spaatz had to balance the requirements of the strategic bombing campaign with the needs and exigencies of the ground situation. Finally, just as the Allied armies confronted recovered and effective opponents, Spaatz feared a revival of the Luftwaffe, which had begun to deploy the deadly new jet, the Me 262.

A controversial phase of the AAF's strategic bombing effort in Europe began in the autumn of 1944. Strong advocates of U.S. strategic bombing, such as former strategic bomber commander Maj. Gen. Haywood S. Hansell, have pointed to the four months from mid-September to mid-January as the time when the bombing offensive fatally weakened Germany "before a single Allied soldier set foot on German soil," catastrophically injured selected German economic and industrial systems, and completed the remaining original strategic objectives of AWPD/1.[3] Academic critics of the bombing offensive have detected an effort "adrift among conflicting visions of the road to victory"[4] and an AAF reversion "from its selective bombing doctrine to the Douhetian principles of mass attack and terror."[5] None of those views completely encompassed the reality of the bombing effort, yet all described, with varying degrees of objectivity, important aspects of the state of strategic bombing in Europe in the last quarter of 1944.

This chapter and the one that follows show how the bombing of railroad marshaling yards could simultaneously be a euphemism for area bombing and a killing blow to the German war economy; how bomber leaders constantly shifted bombing priorities, yet continued to strangle both oil production and transportation; and how precision bombing became a jackhammer reducing German cities to rubble, instead of a scalpel cutting the heart out of German industry.

The Removal of the Strategic Air Forces from SHAEF's Control

In late August 1944, Spaatz visited Eaker in the Mediterranean primarily to discuss the fate of the XII Tactical Air Command (XII TAC), which had accompanied Lt. Gen. Jacob L. Devers's 6th Army Group in its invasion of southern France (Operation ANVIL/DRAGOON) and in its advance to the north. When Devers's and Eisenhower's troops made contact with each other, they would all come under Eisenhower's control. Until then, Eaker and Spaatz agreed that Vandenberg, Commander of the Ninth Air Force, and Lt. Gen. John K. Cannon, Commander of the Twelfth Air Force, would coordinate the activities of XII Tactical Air Command, through a REDLINE cable link already established between the two headquarters.6 Afterward, XII TAC would come under the operational and administrative control of the Ninth Air Force.7

Spaatz and Eaker used the occasion to pass on to Arnold, for his use at the coming conference at Quebec, their views of the air command arrangements in the European Theater of Operations. After declaring that the current AAF organization was "the most satisfactory" likely to be attained, they went on to condemn the AEAF. Each army group, they added, needed its own air force, and those air forces required no more controls between them than did the army groups. Just as no intervening headquarters existed between Eisenhower, who would formally assume command of all ground forces on September 1, and his army group commanders, none should exist between Eisenhower and his air forces.8

On the afternoon of his return from the Mediterranean on August 30, Spaatz discussed with Eisenhower the organization of the U.S. Army Air Forces in the ETO. The next morning he held further discussions on the subject with Tedder and again with Eisenhower. That afternoon he met with Ambassador Winant and RAF Chief of Staff Charles Portal. All agreed that the AEAF ought to be disbanded. Spaatz cheerfully informed Robert Lovett, Assistant Secretary of War for Air, "In general, it is our desire to eliminate the Allied Expeditionary Air Force as soon as possible and I believe this will be accomplished. That headquarters has been a cause for disagreement since its inception."9

In his meeting with Spaatz, Portal not only had indicated a willingness to dispense with the AEAF but also had raised the issue of the changing command arrangements between Eisenhower and the strategic air forces. Because OVERLORD had obviously succeeded, Portal wished to invoke the provision, previously agreed upon by the CCS, of preinvasion air agreements that called for the independence of Bomber Command and USSTAF sometime after the establishment of the Western Allies on the Continent.10 Instead of supporting this move, as might have been expected, Spaatz opposed it.

Spaatz assumed that Portal intended "to attempt to obtain a decision for the return of the strategic forces to the status existent January 1, 1944,"11 and he had no wish that Portal resume his role as chief interlocutor of the Combined Bomber Offensive. Before OVERLORD, Spaatz had strenuously objected to several of Portal's actions, especially his refusal to authorize the bombing of the Ploesti oil facilities. In the months since then, Spaatz had become accustomed to serving under Eisenhower's congenial hand and had no wish to exchange an American master for a British one. Spaatz warned Arnold that "under no conditions should RAF Bomber Command be consolidated with the U.S. Strategic Air Forces." He foresaw continued heavy losses for the RAF if it flew at night or, if it operated by day, extensive disruption of his own fighters covering it. Spaatz realized that Bomber Command would not accept an overall American strategic bombing commander; as for USSTAF, he added, "It may not be fully appreciated by you how strongly our American Air Force personnel feel about serving under British Command."[12] Instead, Spaatz suggested to Portal that Eisenhower have both operational control and direct command of the heavy bombers.[13]

Spaatz preferred a slight modification of the current status of command relations. He had completely turned Eisenhower, with whom he worked extremely well, against the reversion to Portal's control of the strategic air forces on September 1.[14] Neither saw any need for a change in arrangements.

At Spaatz's urging, Eisenhower detailed their objections in messages to both Marshall and Arnold. Emphasizing that he "would regard any change as a serious mistake," Eisenhower told Marshall that he needed to retain control of the strategic forces in order to concentrate the greatest possible strength for the "penetration" of Germany. So far, there had been no disputes between his headquarters and the British Chiefs of Staff concerning the bombers. Moreover, strategic priorities and bombing missions needed to be carefully coordinated with the ground battle by planners in his own headquarters. To facilitate such coordination, Spaatz, on September 1, had moved his headquarters to the Continent, next to Eisenhower's. Air Chief Marshal Harris, head of Bomber Command, had sent his own liaison officers. Thus, Eisenhower urged, USSTAF should stay under his control. Reversion of Bomber Command to Portal's direction would make it difficult to coordinate the two strategic commands—one under Portal and one under Spaatz.[15]

On September 3, Eisenhower told Arnold, "All of us are striving to keep the heavies on normal tasks but emergency use in battle must be assured by continuation of the command system."[16] Arnold replied,

> With regard to the Strategic Air Force command situation, I agree *wholeheartedly* [emphasis in original] with the view expressed in your recent cables that the control now vested in your headquarters should not be changed to revert to Chief of Air Staff but instead that all strategic air forces should be placed under your command.[17]

At the Second Quebec Conference, September 12–17, 1944, Arnold, however, "flopped over" on the issue of independence for the heavy bombers.[18] During the conference, which dealt mainly with European occupation policy and the war against Japan, Portal gained Arnold's consent and the approval of the CCS to detach the strategic air forces from Eisenhower's control. This air issue had meant more to Portal than to any of the other Chiefs. By bringing Harris, who, like Spaatz, had enjoyed comparative freedom under Eisenhower's lenient yoke, back under the control of the Air Ministry, Portal hoped to rein him in.[19]

In August, Harris had obtained Tedder's and Eisenhower's permission to mount twelve area attacks on German cities when his forces were not required elsewhere. In a single attack on Königsberg on the night of August 29–30, for example, only 175 Lancaster heavy bombers left 134,000 people homeless.[20] Portal and the Air Staff, however, disapproved of such attacks. They had at last seized on the oil plan with the enthusiasm only a convert can generate[21] and hoped to redirect Harris's efforts toward the synthetic plants and refineries.[22] Ironically, Harris, who for the first time actually subordinated himself to another commander, operated with more freedom after the command change from Eisenhower to the Air Ministry than before.[23] He happily stepped up his program to area bomb German cities.[24] At Quebec, Portal apparently wanted so badly to control Harris that he was willing to pull Bomber Command out from under Eisenhower and leave USSTAF under SHAEF if the Americans refused to cooperate.[25]

Arnold and Marshall initially resisted Portal's suggestions, but the next day, September 13, the British and American Chiefs agreed to the substance of his new command arrangements.[26] The CCS directive to Spaatz and Air Marshal Norman Bottomley, Deputy Chief of Staff for Operations, RAF, announced the new command structure and specified certain target priorities. The CCS vested joint executive responsibility for the control of strategic bomber forces in Europe in the Chief of Staff, RAF, and the Commander, AAF, who in turn, designated Bottomley and Spaatz as their representatives for the purpose of providing control and local coordination through consultation. The directive required support of the ground and naval forces and charged Spaatz and Bottomley with the task of coordinating their actions with the theater tactical air forces. After accepting current target priorities, it added six further objectives:

1. Counter air force action consisting of policing current production facilities;

2. Direct support of land and naval forces whenever the Supreme Commanders called for it;

3. The bombing of important industrial areas when weather made other targets impractical, and the use of blind bombing techniques if necessary;

4. Attacks in support of the Soviet armies, when authorized by the CCS;

5. Continued support for British Special Operations Executive/American Office of Strategic Services* operations; and

6. Targets of opportunity, such as the German fleet or submarines.[27]

These objectives reflected particularly the concerns of the Combined Chiefs. The first three points were already part of current directives to the bomber forces. Before accepting the change, both the American and British Chiefs had ensured that the heavy bombers would be available for other purposes if needed. Point 3 authorized RAF area bombing, while point 4, inserted at the behest of the British,[28] introduced an entirely new consideration, of little importance until January and February 1945.

---

* The British Special Operations Executive (SOE) and the American Office of Strategic Services (OSS) were Allied intelligence organizations heavily involved with resistance movements in German-occupied Europe. They also engaged in other types of covert intelligence operations directed against the Germans.

Why did Arnold revise his stance on the issue of command change for the strategic air forces? In a letter to Spaatz shortly after the directive was issued, Arnold wrote that he "found it expedient to agree to having the responsibility for the direction of the U.S. Strategic Air Forces vested in me." The reason, he implied, was that Portal had formulated a plan to equalize the RAF and the AAF by making them co-directors of the Combined Bomber Offensive.[29] A few days later, in an "Eyes Only" letter to Spaatz, Arnold explained further,

> I went to Quebec with a firm conviction that we should not change the control of the Strategic Air Forces RAF and AAF, but after I went into the matter more thoroughly and saw that there was no control lost by the United States Higher Command and that provisions could be made for General Eisenhower to get strategic bombing missions upon request, I flopped over. In my opinion the advantages of having you as my representative determine the targets and objectives for the Strategic Air Force on a co-equal status with Portal give us a position in the scheme of things that we have never had before.[30]

When Spaatz and Eisenhower first learned of the CCS's decision, they were not happy.[31] Their initial surprise soon passed and, although Eisenhower termed the new structure a "poor arrangement,"[32] both he and Spaatz had no qualms about the decision. Both men admitted that their personal and official relationships were so close that Eisenhower would get "just as much support from the Strategic Air Forces under this arrangement as he did before."[33]

The Quebec Conference also approved the demise of the AEAF. On September 14, Eisenhower had agreed with Arnold "that under the present circumstances we can get along without Leigh-Mallory's headquarters."[34] Within a few days, Eisenhower received formal notification of Leigh-Mallory's transfer to the Allied Air Forces in South East Asia. The idea for this posting had come from Admiral Lord Louis Mountbatten, the Allied Commander in Chief, South East Asia Command (SEAC).[35] Mountbatten had worked closely with Leigh-Mallory in 1942 on the planning and conduct of the ill-fated Dieppe raid. Portal wholeheartedly embraced the idea (it offered a face-saving method of removing a difficult personality from northwest Europe) and presented it to Arnold. Arnold, who felt that the Air Commander's post in SEAC ought to be awarded to an American officer since the AAF supplied the majority of the theater's aircraft, was quite irritated, but nonchalantly suggested that Leigh-Mallory be assigned, instead, to one of the British military missions in the United States. It is hard to imagine a less congenial placement for the ethnocentric commander of the AEAF. With feigned indifference, Arnold protested to Eisenhower that Leigh-Mallory's disposition was an internal RAF matter, noting that a suitable assignment for one of over twenty Air Chief Marshals and Marshals of the Royal Air Force on the RAF's active rolls was not an insuperable problem.[36]

Since the Second Quebec Conference agreed to intensify operations in Burma and since the British supplied most of the naval and ground forces in that

Air Marshal James M.
Robb, RAF, Chief of Staff
(Air), SHAEF, 1945.

Imperial War Museum

theater, Mountbatten's request for Leigh-Mallory outweighed Arnold's desire to see the post go to an American. Because Leigh-Mallory had become heavily involved in air operations surrounding Operation MARKET-GARDEN, the Allied paratroop drop designed to seize a series of bridges and break through across the Rhine, Eisenhower delayed his release until October 15.[37] On that date the AEAF ceased to exist.*

Coningham became responsible for the administration of his 2d Tactical Air Force, while administrative control of the Ninth Air Force remained with Spaatz. Eisenhower created a new position within his own headquarters, Chief of Staff (Air), and designated Air Vice-Marshal James M. Robb, Spaatz's Deputy Commander from the Northwest African Air Forces, to fill it. Robb would take over the AEAF's operational functions. To Tedder fell the tasks of coordinating the Allied tactical air forces and presenting Eisenhower's requirements for strategic bombing to the strategic bomber commanders.[38] Robb's large and predominately British staff, although less controversial than the AEAF, proved no more effective at handling operations or at suppressing national jeal-

---

* En route to India, the plane carrying Leigh-Mallory, his wife, and his staff became lost in the mountains thirty miles from Grenoble, France, and crashed, killing all aboard. Seven months later, a French farmer discovered the wreckage, solving the mystery of the air marshal's disappearance. Air Chief Marshal Keith Park replaced Leigh-Mallory in SEAC.

ousies.[39] Nonetheless, the final form of Allied air command in Europe had been established. (See Chart 7, System of Control of Strategic Air Forces.)

The new format made no difference to the congenial relationship already established between Spaatz, Tedder, and Eisenhower. As Eisenhower moved SHAEF to Granville, Normandy, thence to Paris, and finally to Reims, Spaatz, after momentarily deciding in the first flush of command change that his presence might be more useful in London,[40] marched in lockstep, keeping his personal headquarters next to the Supreme Commander's. On October 1, Spaatz informed Lovett, "We have moved an advance headquarters of USSTAF to the vicinity of Paris and very close to Eisenhower's main headquarters. . . . I expect to spend practically all of my time here in order to be close to Eisenhower."[41] Spaatz left Maj. Gen. Frederick L. Anderson in London to ensure coordination of operations. This propinquity facilitated Spaatz's administrative control of the large AAF contingent in France and maintained short and speedy lines of coordination between the strategic air forces and the Supreme Commander.

Strategic Target Selection in the Autumn of 1944

One of the chief contributions Spaatz made to the conduct of the war during the late summer and autumn of 1944 was the setting of target priorities for the U.S. Eighth and Fifteenth Strategic Air Forces. He insisted on the primacy of oil targets with the same tenacity that Harris displayed in his embrace of area bombing.

On September 1, Spaatz issued a new set of target priorities reflecting his and USSTAF's assessment of the German military and economic situation. Four factors influenced his judgment: (1) the success of the oil attacks, (2) the dispersal of the German aircraft industry, (3) the acute shortage of trained German pilots, and (4) the German losses in men and matériel to the Anglo-American forces in France and to the Soviets during its summer offensive, which alone had destroyed twenty-five German divisions.

From these factors, Spaatz drew three conclusions:

1. The Luftwaffe, the German ground forces, and the German economy all faced imminent collapse from lack of fuel.
2. Pilot and aviation fuel shortages, not lack of aircraft, would severely limit Luftwaffe operations in the future.
3. The Germans lacked sufficient military equipment to reequip battered formations and to equip newly raised units.

Therefore, to take advantage of the few remaining summer days, Spaatz issued instructions to Doolittle and Twining to intensify their attacks on oil targets, to confine any attacks on the German aircraft production industries to those manufacturing components for rockets and jet fighters, to devote excess effort to the

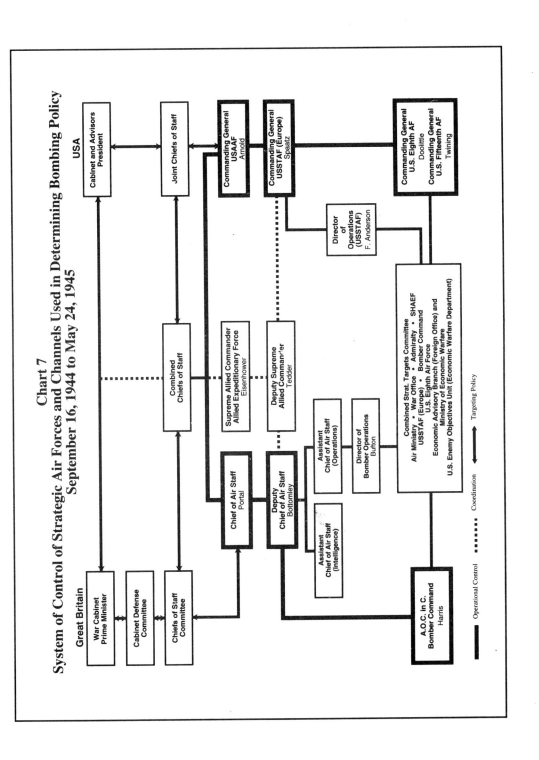

Chart 7
System of Control of Strategic Air Forces and Channels Used in Determining Bombing Policy
September 16, 1944 to May 24, 1945

Great Britain

War Cabinet
Prime Minister

Cabinet Defense
Committee

Chiefs of Staff
Committee

Chief of Air Staff
Portal

Deputy
Chief of Air Staff
Bottomley

Assistant
Chief of Air Staff
(Operations)

Assistant
Chief of Air Staff
(Intelligence)

Director of
Bomber Operations
Bufton

A.O.C. in C.
Bomber Command
Harris

USA

Cabinet and Advisors
President

Joint Chiefs of Staff

Commanding General
USAAF
Arnold

Commanding General
USSTAF (Europe)
Spaatz

Commanding General
U.S. Eighth AF
Doolittle
Commanding General
U.S. Fifteenth AF
Twining

Director
of
Operations
(USSTAF)
F. Anderson

Combined
Chiefs of Staff

Supreme Allied Commander
Allied Expeditionary Force
Eisenhower

Deputy Supreme
Allied Commander
Tedder

Combined Strat. Targets Committee
Air Ministry • War Office • Admiralty • SHAEF
USSTAF (Europe) • U.S. Eighth Air Force • Bomber Command
Economic Advisory Branch (Foreign Office) and
Ministry of Economic Warfare
U.S. Enemy Objectives Unit (Economic Warfare Department)

Operational Control

Coordination

Targeting Policy

destruction of, in order of priority, ordnance depots, armored fighting vehicle production, and motor transport production, and, finally if weather "or other considerations" made these targets "impracticable," to employ bombing-through-clouds techniques or other methods to strike transportation targets.[42]

Aside from its emphasis on oil, to which all of his post-D-day directives gave primacy, this memo signaled Spaatz's diminishing sense of urgency regarding the Luftwaffe and increased interest in an antiordnance/military equipment campaign already started on a small scale in August. The memo also indicated his willingness to employ his force during bad weather over Germany, even though it was dependent on inaccurate H2X radar. This method, as Spaatz well knew, performed best over built-up areas (cities) but had little ability to pick out individual targets (marshaling yards, etc).[43] H2X accuracy improved greatly if any part of a bomb run could be done visually. Moreover, transportation sites offered a good subsidiary system when bomb groups that were unable to hit their primary target often found that openings in the clouds presented them with targets of opportunity, such as marshaling yards. Nonetheless, Spaatz had no qualms about any incidental damage that bombs falling short would cause among German civilians.

Within days of the September 1 directive, Air Marshal Bottomley discussed new priorities with Spaatz and Tedder. By that time German defenses had visibly stiffened, taking the edge off some of the optimism in Allied command circles. The day before they received the Quebec directive, September 13, 1944, the three agreed to a new scheme for new circumstances. In this scheme, Spaatz assented to a rearrangement of his just-issued priorities. Oil retained top priority. ULTRA intercepts continued to confirm the injury inflicted by the oil offensive. A September 7 decryption revealed an order calling for qualified volunteers from other branches of the Luftwaffe to join the fighter arm in order to conserve on training fuel. A September 11 decryption uncovered Goering's order of September 1 restricting flights to a bare minimum to ensure that every possible drop went to operational training.[44]

German rail and water transportation systems, particularly those located in the Ruhr and Saar and leading from those regions to the front, would be the targets of the strategic air forces, which would carry out attacks progressively deeper into Germany. The tactical air forces would deal with transportation targets closest to the battlefront. Motor transport, armored fighting vehicles, and ordnance plants and depots would have the same priority as transportation systems. The Luftwaffe would receive any residual effort. This new schedule, which served as a basis for a more formal directive issued in accordance with the instructions from Quebec, meant that Tedder had succeeded in upgrading to second priority his own preferred target system, that of transportation.[45]

On September 25, Bottomley issued a "Directive for the Control of Strategic Bomber Forces in Europe," to Arthur Harris.[46] Spaatz had agreed to this directive, later designated "Strategic Bombing Directive No. 1," two days earlier.[47]

Air Marshal Norman H. Bottomley, Deputy Chief of the Air Staff, RAF, 1943.

Imperial War Museum

Bottomley's directive conformed, for the most part, to his previous discussion with Tedder and Spaatz, but one item reappeared. Referring to important industrial areas, the document stated, "When weather or tactical conditions are unsuitable for operations against specific primary objectives, attacks should be delivered on important industrial areas, using blind bombing techniques as necessary." Area bombing simply would not disappear. Given the tenor of the times, no one could have justified keeping idle the heavy-bomber fleets, on which so much national treasure and energy had been heaped, merely because cloud cover or darkness necessitated their use against built-up areas rather than specific targets.

Bottomley's directive also provided for the periodic issuance of a separate list of strategic targets. The list would specify the targets best calculated to achieve the goals of the bomber offensive and would set relative priorities among them. The directive further noted that the priorities within the list would "be adjusted in . . . accordance with the situation." Interestingly enough, the first list lumped attacks on the German rail transport system in a secondary category with missions against the Luftwaffe. Both types of attack would occur "from time to time." In the meantime, oil targets retained first priority; second priority went to ordnance, tanks and motor transport depots, tank assembly plants, and motor transport assembly plants, in that order.[48] Apparently the Allied air leaders felt that the immediate denial of tactical equipment to the German ground forces would still pay a greater dividend than a protracted series of strategic attacks on transport. This view, which emphasized short-term results, mirrored the hopes still prevalent that the Germans would collapse with one more good push. Eisenhower's headquarters in particular placed the highest priority on the *Wehrmacht*'s major ordnance depots.[49]

Within a week this optimism had evaporated. The Allied air leaders began to search for new ways to employ their forces. At one of the last of Leigh-Mallory's Daily Air Commanders' Meetings, on September 29, held at Versailles, Air Marshal Coningham suggested "that it might be a matter of months before the Army would make any considerable move into Germany, and that the only hope of a quick finish to the war was from a collapse inside Germany."[50] In view of that prospect, which might allow the Germans time to raise a large force of jets and to improve their antiaircraft defenses, he pressed for an immediate, concentrated attack to cripple either German morale or the jet aircraft industry. He was seconding a proposition Spaatz had voiced moments earlier—that, with three or four continuous days of good weather predicted for October, an all-out effort might prove profitable. Leigh-Mallory agreed, pointing out that the tactical bomb line already in effect provided an ideal basis for a division of labor between the tactical and strategic forces. Spaatz then clarified his proposal, indicating that he envisaged an all-out attack by the combined strategic and tactical forces outside the tactical area. Such an attack "was bound to have considerable effect on morale, especially if kept up for two or three days."[51]

Bottomley attempted to throw cold water on the whole idea. The inhabitants of 100 smaller cities in Germany made up only 10 percent of the population—not enough, in his opinion, to influence the German High Command. The Chiefs of Staff, he continued, had already approved THUNDERCLAP (a maximum-force, combined strike by USSTAF and Bomber Command on Berlin) for implementation when German morale showed signs of cracking. Until then, the German war effort ought to remain the primary target. Besides, any all-out attack would have maximum impact if tightly focused on a single objective, such as transportation in a single region. To defuse the effort over a wide area against something as amorphous as morale would have little long-term benefit. Bottomley concluded by requesting that the air forces place priority on the transportation network of the Saar and Ruhr industrial regions in support of the ground effort that Eisenhower intended to direct against them.[52] The meeting ended with no agreement on any all-out massive attack. Soon afterward, however, both the Air Ministry and USSTAF began to formulate plans[53] for widespread maximum-force attacks against Germany (code-named HURRICANES I and II).

Spaatz strongly supported the HURRICANE plans. On October 1 he wrote to Lovett:

> I have urged and started the development of a plan for the full-out beating up of Germany with all the Air Forces at our disposal, if and when we have a proper weather break.

He did not know whether such an operation could be decisive, but, he wrote, *"To my mind it represents the only means of terminating the war this year with our forces"* [emphasis added].[54]

Spaatz believed that the plans were a necessary gamble. How much to wager remained a question. As he explained to Arnold on October 4, oil remained the overriding priority, but, he went on, "I must emphasize that the war with Germany is not over and with the stagnation of the ground front, it may be up to Air to force Germany out of the war." Spaatz then described the HURRICANE plans, both of which had RAF approval.

HURRICANE I concentrated Bomber Command and the Eighth Air Force, plus portions of the theater's tactical air forces, against targets in western Germany, primarily the Ruhr area. This event was to be closely tied with the maneuver of the ground forces. The attack was to be all-out, except when weather permitted attack on high-priority oil targets throughout Germany.

HURRICANE II required good weather over all of Germany and involved a concentration of all U.S. and British air forces from the Mediterranean and Britain over Germany. This force was to attack targets in the following priority: (1) oil; (2) ordnance depots; (3) motor transport depots and armored force vehicle depots; and (4) transportation. The Allies would be hitting something almost everywhere they could reach. Both plans kept oil targets foremost.[55] Spaatz would not loosen his grip on oil, the life's blood of the Nazi military machine. As he had told Doolittle and Twining the previous day, "Failure to maintain this primary aim will result in immediate increase in fighting effectiveness of enemy ground forces and offensive operations by the GAF."[56]

After meetings on October 3 between Bottomley for the Air Ministry, Tedder and Robb for SHAEF, and Anderson and Spaatz for USSTAF, the airmen set October 7 as the tentative date for HURRICANE II.[57] Given the relative quiet in ground operations, the more strategically oriented HURRICANE II seemed a better choice than HURRICANE I, which limited itself to the Ruhr and was meant to assist a ground offensive. Arnold concurred with the HURRICANE II plan to emphasize oil targets, but wanted attacks on "everything of military importance," to impress all sections of Germany with Allied air power's "overwhelming superiority and destructive power." Arnold explicitly added, "I will not condone attacks on purely civilian objectives."[58]

Neither HURRICANE plan was ever executed. Despite forecasts of a stretch of clear days during the first two weeks of October, prolonged good weather never materialized. Instead, USSTAF took advantage of the few clear days to strike the vital oil plants again. By mid-October the opportunity, improbable and fleeting as it was, had passed.

Near the end of October the Allies again reviewed their strategic priorities for air. This review, caused by the stagnation of the front on one hand and Marshall's hope for a quick end to the war on the other, produced a new directive. Revision in the face of changing circumstances does not seem remarkable;

what was remarkable was Marshall's optimism, which he maintained even after an extensive visit to the Western Front in early October. As late as October 20, he reported to Eisenhower that the U.S. Chiefs of Staff contemplated issuing "at an early date" a directive for a supreme effort to end the war in Europe by January 1. Such a decision, said Marshall, would require the employment of the strategic air forces in an almost exclusively tactical manner.[59] In response to Marshall's request for frank comment, Eisenhower mentioned his logistical difficulties but also volunteered that more infantry and supplies might produce a quicker conclusion.

In the same message Eisenhower supported strategic use of the heavy bombers. Poor weather prevented them from flying in direct support of the ground forces. Also, noted Eisenhower, "We know in these conditions our best bet has been to keep hammering constantly at the enemy's oil."[60] The British Chiefs of Staff also discounted the chances of ending the war before the start of the year. The Air Staff, in particular, objected to diverting the heavy bombers from oil targets, which, if freed from attack, would rapidly regain much higher production levels. Consequently, the British asked Marshall to shelve the directive, which he did on November 1.[61]

The bombing results of September and October had shown the inconclusiveness of the campaign against ordnance, tanks, and motor transport. Oil targets had absorbed most of the visual bombing days, and USSTAF had employed blind bombing techniques for part of most raids against military equipment targets. This produced less accurate bombing. Meanwhile, the German front-line troops showed no equipment shortages attributable to the bombing, and postwar analysis revealed no major effects. By the end of October, the Allies were ready to try different target systems.[62]

The British Air Staff, for its part, wanted a new directive that would enable it to get better control over Harris. Since the CCS directive of September 14 placing him again under Portal, Harris had proceeded on his own course as he continued to do at least until the beginning of 1945. During the last three months of 1944, Bomber Command dropped 53 percent of its bombs on cities, 15 percent on railways and canals, 18 percent on miscellaneous targets, and only 14 percent on oil targets.[63] Harris, who enjoyed personal access to Churchill and great prestige from Bomber Command's status as both the largest component of the RAF and the most successful punisher of the Germans, rebuffed Portal's repeated attempts to have him concentrate on oil targets. By late January 1945 the dispute between Harris and Portal over oil targeting culminated in a threat by Harris to resign. Although Portal had the authority to accept Harris's resignation, he chose not to. Removing him would have been difficult to justify to Churchill and the British populace, who regarded Harris as a war hero. However, in declining Harris's gesture, Portal lost any sanction he might have held. Consequently, Harris persisted in flouting Portal's authority until the end of the war. In any case, Bomber Command had delivered only 6 percent of its bombs against oil targets in October,[64] a figure Portal and Bottomley wanted greatly increased.

Portal also solicited Tedder's views on new instructions for the heavy bombers.[65] Tedder replied on October 25 with a tightly reasoned brief favoring transportation as the primary target system. After referring to the current operations of the strategic and tactical air forces, he continued, "I am not satisfied that on these lines, we are using our air power effectively. The various types of operations should fit into one comprehensive pattern, whereas I feel that at present they are more like a patchwork quilt."[66] Tedder believed that the one common factor underlying the entire German war effort, from political control to troop supply, was communications. He argued, "Our primary air objective should be the enemy's communications. Road, water and rail are interdependent and complementary, and our Air operations should play on that fact. The present oil plan is the key to movement by road or air, and, moreover, directly affects operations in the battle area."[67]

Tedder had integrated the oil plan into his own, adding two factors that he believed would make his antitransportation system effort even more telling than the one that had preceded OVERLORD. First, all loss of transport traffic would be a dead loss to the German war effort. In France, the *Wehrmacht* required only 20 percent of all rail traffic, with much of the remainder going to support the French economy. In Germany, any loss of transportation would eventually produce a shortage or delay in the German war effort. In Germany, bombed-out transport lines could be replaced only at the cost of other vital programs, whereas, in France the *Wehrmacht* could use a large portion of the 80 percent of remaining capacity to replace bombed-out capacity.

Second, noted Tedder, "In FRANCE and BELGIUM the programme of attacks on rail centres was severely limited, both as regards selection of targets and as regards weather conditions, by the need to avoid civilian casualties; no such limitations affect attacks on German rail centres."[68] Tedder had concluded that by concentrating heavy bombers over marshaling yards, oil targets, the canal system, and "centres of population" in the Ruhr, and backing up that concentration with the tactical air forces' operations against trains, rail embankments, and selected bridges, the Allies "would rapidly produce a state of chaos which would vitally affect not only the immediate battle on the West Wall, but also the whole German war effort."[69]

British intelligence buttressed Tedder's arguments. As early as July 1944 the British Joint Intelligence Committee detected diversion of essential war freight from the overstrained railroads to the inland water transport system. By the end of August the Allies perceived an overall weakening of the German transport system demonstrated by more diversion to water transport and delay in the delivery of war production materials. Intelligence from high-grade intercepts in October revealed a worsening situation. An October 10 decryption of an October 2 message from the Japanese naval attaché reported gradually increasing havoc

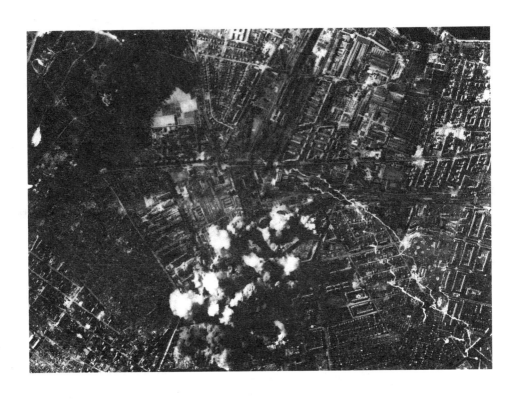

The Reich Besieged. The cumulative effect of strategic bombing was evident by late 1944. *Clockwise from above*: Eighth Air Force bombs struck the Tegel tank works and a nearby gas plant *(above, left)* in Berlin, October 6, 1944. A tangle of wagons, twisted track, and craters *(above, right)* mark the marshaling yard at Limburg after a Ninth Air Force raid. "Wheels Must Roll for Victory!" is the exhortation *(below)* amid the ruin of a rail terminus late in the war. River transport suffered the loss of countless barges and tugs *(opposite, below)*, as this scene near Mainz attests. The Magdeburg synthetic oil plant *(opposite, above)* shows the effects of repeated American attacks by early 1945.

on the lines of communications and confusion in the transport of coal and munitions from the Rhineland. A particularly telling decryption on October 24 of a four-day-old message from Hitler's headquarters quoted a Speer report that destruction of traffic installations and lack of power had brought from thirty to thirty-five percent of all armament factories to a standstill.[70] Lack of power meant lack of coal to fire generating plants, a sign of serious, if not catastrophic, rail disruption. This intercept can only have convinced the Allied air leaders both of the efficacy of transportation bombing and of the diminishing capacity of the Germans to absorb more of it.

After a meeting on October 28 at SHAEF in Paris, at which the possible contributions both the strategic and the tactical air forces could make in assisting the ground forces were thoroughly analyzed, Spaatz and Bottomley issued a new directive, Strategic Directive No. 2. It deleted the military equipment targets not specifically requested by the ground forces. This deletion left only two target systems: the petroleum industry and lines of communication, the latter with second priority. Spaatz and the British Air Staff had maintained top priority for oil targets but had also seen the advantages of Tedder's campaign against communications.[71]

Meanwhile, Harris had an escape clause as wide as an *autobahn*. Strategic Directive No. 2 authorized the bombing of "Important Industrial Areas"—that useful euphemism for area bombing—whenever weather or tactical conditions were unsuitable for the two main objectives. Bottomley modified the clause slightly by adding language requiring these alternative attacks to contribute, as far as possible, to the destruction of the oil and transport systems. He also wrote a cover letter to Harris emphasizing the importance of oil—to little avail. Harris believed in neither oil nor communication targets. He dryly annotated his copy of Bottomley's letter, "Here we go around the Mulberry bush."[72] In November, however, Harris did increase petroleum strikes to 24.6 percent of his total effort, a figure not far from the Fifteenth's 28.4 percent. In November the Eighth Air Force dropped 39 percent of its bomb tonnage on oil targets.[73] This directive remained in effect until it was replaced by Strategic Directive No. 3, issued on January 12, 1945.

Operations

The changes in strategic priorities, none of which displaced the oil campaign from its position as the target system of highest priority, had less effect on the operations of USSTAF during the autumn of 1944 than the advances of the ground forces, the severity of the weather, and the resurgence of the Luftwaffe. Constantly increasing numbers of enemy operational jet and conventional fighter aircraft available from September onward constituted, in Spaatz's eyes, the greatest potential threat to the success of a continued Allied strategic bomber offensive against Germany.

The advance of the Allied ground forces across France in the summer of 1944 had greatly complicated the Luftwaffe's defense problems. Whatever advantage accrued to Germany's hard-pressed aerial defenders from the forced concentration of almost all of their resources into Germany proper did not offset the disadvantages occasioned by the destruction of most of their early warning network in the occupied countries or the denial of sufficient territory in which to conduct a defense in depth. The heretofore relatively efficient German night-fighter force probably suffered a greater decline in operational ability because of these factors than the day force. In May and June, when Bomber Command devoted a great part of its strength to 25,000 night sorties over France in support of OVERLORD, the night fighters shot down 265 British heavy bombers. In September and October, when Bomber Command flew more than 16,000 night sorties against targets in Germany, the British credited only 36 losses to enemy night fighters.[74]

As Allied ground forces advanced they disorganized the Luftwaffe's fighter defenses, but when they were halted at the German border they stretched the Allied bomber effort in two ways. (See Map 15, Front Lines, 1944–1945.) The inability of the Allied logistics system to keep pace with the rapid advance of its armies led to the diversion of an entire B-24 combat wing, composed of four combat groups (approximately 200 bombers), to the task of ferrying supplies to the forward troops; and the scarity of supplies led Eisenhower to limit the broad-based advance of his forces in favor of a single narrow thrust. After some hesitation between alternatives offered by Montgomery, who championed an airborne thrust across Holland to the Rhine, and Bradley, who advocated an attack through the Saar to the Rhine, Eisenhower settled on Montgomery's proposal, code-named Operation MARKET-GARDEN. In its planning and execution, Montgomery's airborne operation tied up the theater's air transport craft, making them unavailable to the ground forces throughout the theater, and it diverted the Eighth Air Force from strategic targets in Germany.[75]

From August 29 to September 30, USSTAF directed the Eighth Air Force to conduct cargo trucking operations to assist the Allied armies in France. Starting with a small force of fewer than 30 aircraft on August 29, the operation grew to 200 by September 8. Eventually 225 B-24s made the daily trek from supply sources in England to the Continent. In the first ten days the planes carried 1,383 tons of supplies, mostly medicine and food, to Orleans/Briey Airfield, seventy miles south of Paris. When loading, unloading, and flying went smoothly, many planes made two trips a day.[76]

After a three-day pause for reorganization, the second phase of the operation began on September 12. This time the bombers carried mostly 80-octane gasoline for the forward armored units. They had a commitment, never attained, to deliver 354,000 gallons of gasoline a day. On September 14, the B-24s began to land at Chartres, 50 miles to the southwest of Paris. Eight days later, the Eighth continued to deliver gasoline to three airfields: Chartres, St. Dizier (120 miles

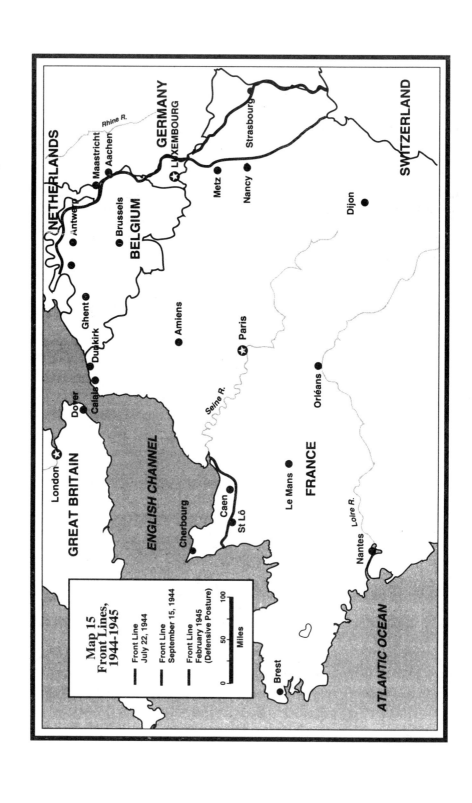

Map 15
Front Lines,
1944-1945

Front Line
July 22, 1944

Front Line
September 15, 1944

Front Line
February 1945
(Defensive Posture)

Miles

0   50   100

GREAT BRITAIN

London

ENGLISH CHANNEL

Dover

Calais

Dunkirk

Ghent

Antwerp

Brussels

BELGIUM

NETHERLANDS

Maastricht

Aachen

Rhine R.

GERMANY

LUXEMBOURG

Metz

Nancy

Strasbourg

SWITZERLAND

Dijon

Amiens

Paris

Seine R.

Orléans

Cherbourg

Caen

St Lô

Le Mans

FRANCE

Loire R.

Nantes

Brest

ATLANTIC OCEAN

east of Paris), and Florennes, Belgium (140 miles northeast of Paris). During this second phase, despite missing three days because of weather, the ferry service delivered 8,226 tons of gasoline (2,703,255 gallons/169,000 per day) and 244 tons of other supplies.[77] Spaatz considered the diversion sound; he merely wished that the army had called on him before it had come to a halt.[78]

Operation MARKET-GARDEN, a three-division airborne assault conducted by the First Allied Airborne Army operating under the command of Montgomery's 21 Army Group, was part of the Allies' bold attempt to break through the German lines in Holland and into Germany itself. At the very least the Allies hoped to cut off the German *Fifteenth Army* in Holland, turn Germany's border defenses, and position 21 Army Group around the north flank of the Ruhr.[79] The operation achieved none of these goals. As the official U.S. Army history stated, "By the merciless logic of war, MARKET-GARDEN was a failure."[80]

Two features of the operation impinged on the strategic air forces: the locking up of the theater's air transport assets and the diversion of the strategic effort to the direct support of the ground forces. In the first four days of the operation, September 17–20, the Eighth committed both its bombers and its fighters. General Doolittle, a few days after the close of the affair, estimated that "MARKET cost four (4) major and two (2) minor heavy bomber missions in September."[81] On September 17, 875 of the Eighth's heavy bombers dropped fragmentation bombs in support of MARKET-GARDEN, while another 703 of its fighters strafed enemy antiaircraft positions, for a loss of 2 bombers and 14 fighters. On September 18, 254 B-24s dropped supplies for the paratroops. That mission lost 8 bombers to flak, and about half of the remainder received battle damage. Its 575 fighter escorts lost 20 aircraft and wrote off 9 more upon return to base, all to flak.[82]

At the Daily Air Commanders' Meeting on September 19, Doolittle complained that because the involvement of all of his fighters in support of the troops prevented the use of heavy bombers elsewhere, "he hoped that it [MARKET-GARDEN] would not be extended beyond the four days, as in addition to preventing heavy bomber operations, it was proving very expensive in fighters."[83] The Eighth continued its commitment to the ground offensive until September 26, during which time it limited those bombers not involved in the operation to shallow penetrations into western Germany. It bombed marshaling yards, airfields, and military equipment targets but no major oil targets.[84]

In addition to the diversions caused by MARKET-GARDEN, weather greatly affected the operations of USSTAF in the autumn of 1944. In mid-December, Spaatz ruefully commented in a letter to Lovett, "We have been facing unusual handicaps from weather in our operations."[85] On the same day, he wrote to Arnold, "Weather is, of course, the serious handicap in any operation at this time of year. Practically all of our bombing for the last two months has been PFF [blind bombing]. The amount of rainfall exceeds, in the opinion of experts to whom we have talked, any experienced for the last thirty years."[86]

Spaatz did not exaggerate the problem. The AAF official history noted that in the last quarter of 1944, 80 percent of the Eighth's and 70 percent of the Fifteenth's missions employed, at least in part, blind-bombing devices.[87] An Eighth Air Force Operational Analysis Section report on the bombing accuracy for the period September 1 to December 31, 1944, graphically depicted the effects of weather on operational performance. Of the seventy-three days in the period in which the Eighth conducted heavy-bomber operations, visual means could be used on only twenty-six days. Only 14 percent of the Eighth's bombing was done by visual means under good visibility. Even in good visibility (no cloud cover, no German smoke screens, or haze), high altitude and smoke from preceding bombing meant that only 30 percent of the bombs landed within 1,000 feet of their aiming point. Thirty-five percent of the bombing employed H2X through complete cloud cover. The possibility that bombs would land within 1,000 feet of an aiming point was 150 times greater with good visibility than with H2X through 100 percent cloud cover.[88]

Even for visual targets, bombing accuracy in the fourth quarter of the year fell a dramatic 40 percent—a drop that the report attributed to more heavily defended targets, longer missions, and poor flying conditions. More flak at the target meant increased altitudes and decreased accuracy. Table 5 shows the abysmal results obtained for 58 percent of the bombing employing H2X. An official postwar survey admitted, "It cannot be said that this equipment [H2X] was in any sense a precision bombing instrument."[89]

The German synthetic oil industry, particularly, benefited from cloud cover and man-made smoke screens. Large-scale visual attacks on September 11, 12, and 13 brought the production of aviation fuel to a virtual halt from September 11 to 19.[90] For the month, the fourteen chief hydrogenation plants produced only 5,300 tons, one-thirtieth of their May 1944 production.[91] In October, however, the Eighth dropped more tonnage on military equipment targets than on oil targets. It also conducted only three oil raids using completely visual means. As a result, German aviation gas production tripled to 16,400 tons. In November, the Eighth did not have a single completely visual attack on an oil targets. Although it devoted 39 percent of its bombing effort (16,147 tons) aided by 32 percent of the Fifteenth's efforts (4,837 tons) and 24 percent of Bomber Command's (13,060 tons), German aviation gasoline production doubled again to 35,400 tons.

In December, the Eighth Air Force diverted much of its energy to helping the ground forces repel the German Ardennes counteroffensive at the Battle of the Bulge. Hitler's last gamble to win the war on the Western Front, which began December 16, was initially successful but within two weeks it had been contained by the Allies. Communications bombing and tactical support for the Battle of the Bulge lowered the Eighth's capacity to bomb oil targets. Consequently, the Eighth delivered only 2,940 tons of bombs, only 7.2 percent of its

Table 5
The Relationship between H2X Bombing Accuracy and Cloud Cover
September 1–December 31, 1944

Estimated Percentage of Bombs within Standard Distances around Assigned Aiming Point						
Reported Cloud Cover	1,000 Feet	¹/₂ Mile	1 Mile	3 Miles	5 Miles	Percentage of Total Eighth Air Force
10/10	0.2	1.2	5.6	39.8	58.5	35
8-9/10	1.0	7.3	22.5	67.4	82.0	15
6-7/10	2.0	12.5	36.5	84.0	90.5	5
4-5/10	4.4	22.8	48.5	89.1	96.0	3

Based on Eighth Air Force Operations Analysis Section, "Report on Bombing Accuracy, Eighth Air Force, 1 September to 31 December 1944," April 20, 1945, Spaatz Papers, Subject File 1929–1945.

total monthly tonnage, on oil targets. The Fifteenth, however, picked up the slack, employing 43.5 percent of its total effort and dropping 6,939 tons on oil targets. Bomber Command, with its ability to drop heavier bombs than the AAF, delivered the most punishing single blow in a night attack, December 6–7, on Leuna-Merseburg. This attack, combined with two Eighth Air Force raids, stopped all production at Leuna for December, the chief reason German aviation gasoline production declined to 23,400 tons in that month.[92]

Despite diversions and weather, the offensive against oil targets in the fall of 1944 kept the total of oil production from all sources in Germany to only one-third of production in January 1944.[93] (See Chart 8, Total German Synthetic Fuel Production, 1940–1945.)

The oil plants required repeated attacks in part because of the Germans' repair efforts and in part because of the low accuracy of the bombing. Out of every 100 bombs dropped on oil plants, 87 missed the target completely, 8 landed in open spaces inside the plant causing no damage, 2 landed on the plant, but failed to explode, 1 hit pipelines or other utilities causing repairable damage, and 2 hit buildings and important equipment.[94]

505

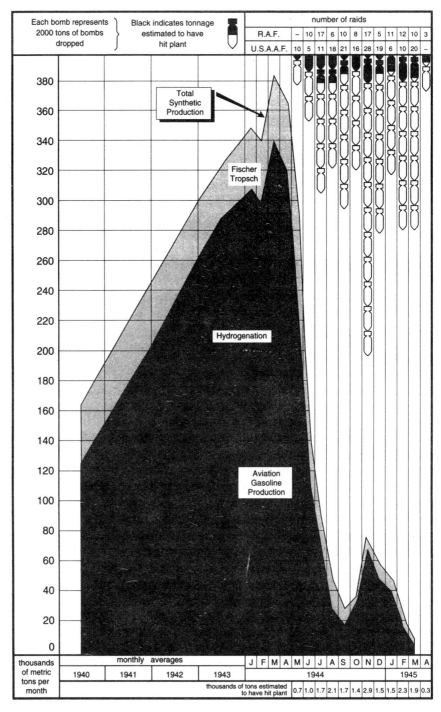

Chart 8
Total German Synthetic Fuel Production, 1940–1945

These figures emphasize the vital importance of visual bombing; postwar data indicate that full visual bombing of the oil plants scored five times as many hits as full-instrument attacks.[95]

In the last third of the year the Eighth devoted increasing attention to rail installations, tracks, marshaling yards, and stations—components of the marshaling yard target complex.[96] The Eighth delivered the bulk of its bombs nonvisually, which meant that the area around the target, invariably a city, was drenched. In September, the Eighth released 13,053 tons of bombs (33 percent visual sighting, 32 percent of monthly total) on marshaling yards, exceeding the total of the previous three months, in which it had assisted the ground troops and bombed CROSSBOW targets. The figure went up in October to 18,844 tons (5 percent visual sighting, 43 percent of monthly total), fell in November to only 11,829 tons (14 percent visual sighting, 29 percent of monthly total) when the Eighth rained bombs on the oil industry, and rose in December to 22,921 tons (30 percent visual sighting, 55 percent of monthly total) when the Eighth aided the ground forces against the German Ardennes counteroffensive by pummeling enemy transport lines feeding the attack.[97]

This deluge of bombs played havoc with the German rail system or *Reichsbahn*. The *Reichsbahn* and, to a lesser extent, the German river and canal transport system, like the bloodstream carrying oxygen, carried coal to German industry. Without coal, all war production would grind to a halt, as the factories and power plants consumed the last of their stockpiles. The *Reichsbahn* also transported other raw materials and finished and semifinished assemblies from subcontractors to factories, while hauling completed arms and munitions to military depots. Troop trains and military supply trains had the highest priority, followed by coal trains. All other traffic, including essential war production traffic, would be cut back in favor of the highest-priority trains. In striking the marshaling yards and canals, the Eighth tightened the same deadly tourniquet around the artery supplying coal to the German war economy as it had around the synthetic oil plants feeding the German military machine.

If the oil campaign was Spaatz's contribution to winning the war, the transportation campaign was Tedder's. Tedder was fortunate that Spaatz willingly aided him because Harris continued his area bombing campaign. Spaatz had sound technical reasons for striking marshaling yards. The terrible weather of the fall of 1944 compelled his forces to bomb blind, which meant bombing targets that could be picked up on H2X. As mentioned earlier, the Germans had located synthetic oil plants away from cities. Although large, these facilities were not large enough to give a consistently identifiable return on H2X radar. They had to be bombed by visual means in order to achieve a reasonable return on the effort invested to get to them. Bombs that missed the synthetic plants usually fell in open country where they did little harm. However, H2X had no trouble locating cities and the marshaling yards within them and, given any break in the clouds, the yards would be well hit. But therein lay the tragic conundrum of the strategic bombing campaign: a well-hit marshaling yard meant a well-hit city, with block upon block of residential areas gutted, families left homeless, small businesses smashed, and workers and others—including women and children—blown to bits or, more likely, burned or crushed by the hundreds, if not the thousands.*

Eighth Air Force policy increased the likelihood of area bombing. On October 29, 1944, a memorandum defining standard procedure for operations set the policy for attack on secondary and last-resort targets:

> 1. No towns or cities in Germany will be attacked as secondary or last resort targets, targets of opportunity, or otherwise, unless such towns contain or have immediately adjacent to them, one (1) or more military objectives. Military objectives include railway lines; junctions; marshalling yards; railway or road bridges, or other communications networks; any industrial plant; and such obvious military objectives as oil storage tanks, military camps and barracks, troop concentrations, motor transport or AFV parks, ordnance or supply depots, ammunition depots; airfields; etc.

> 2. Combat crews will be briefed before each mission to insure that no targets other than military objectives in Germany are attacked.

> 3. It has been determined that towns and cities large enough to produce an identifiable return on the H2X scope generally contain a large proportion of the military objectives listed above. These centers, therefore, may be attacked as secondary or last resort targets by through-the-overcast bombing technique.[98]

Almost every city or town in Germany with a population exceeding 50,000 met the foregoing criteria. This policy made it open season for bombing Germany's major cities in any weather. Those cities fortunate enough not to show up on H2X could still be bombed by visual or visually assisted means. If the AAF did not actually abandoned its precision techniques for area and terror bombing in this memo, it came perilously close.

On September 5, the Eighth began to inflict the death-of-a-thousand-cuts on the German transportation system (see Map 16, Greater German Transport Network) with a raid of 218 B-24s dropping, by visual means, 463 tons on the Karlsruhe marshaling yards. Escorting and sweeping fighters strafed transportation targets and claimed 192 aircraft destroyed on the ground.[99] In attacks mounted on October 14, 15, 17, and 18, the Eighth bombed Cologne, employing for the most part H2X radar and in one the far more accurate Gee-H radar/ground beacon system. These raids, plus raids on Hamm and RAF raids on Duisburg and

---

* Everyone in Germany had heard, in one form or another, of the old grandfather who had gone into city X with five coffins for his son, daughter-in-law, and their three children, killed in an Allied bombing raid, only to return with the remains of all in a single bucket.

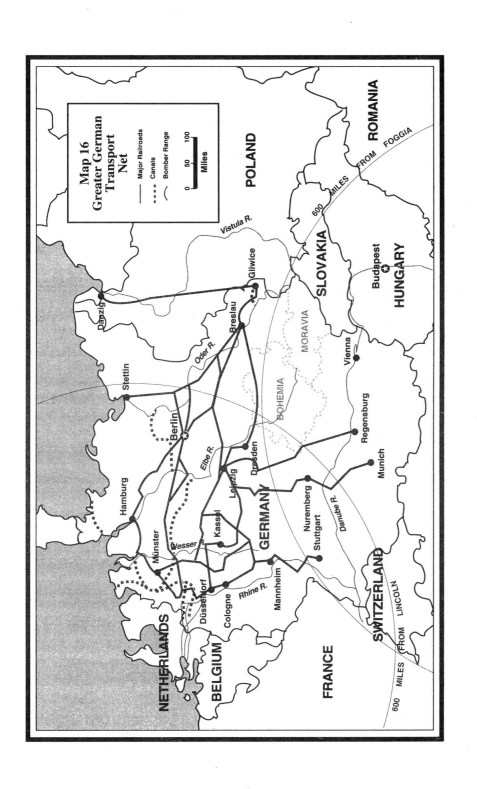

Map 16
Greater German
Transport
Net

Major Railroads
Canals
Bomber Range

0   50   100
Miles

Wedau on October 14, almost shut down the coal railroad gateways leading from the Ruhr. They temporarily cut coal traffic by 80 percent. The October 14 strike by U.S. planes at Cologne not only damaged the yards but by a stroke of extraordinary chance set off the demolition charges affixed to the Cologne-Mulheimer Bridge. The 13,000-ton suspension span, roadway intact, collapsed into the Rhine River, blocking navigation. Only unusually high water later in the winter allowed a few days of traffic to float over the wreckage.[100] On October 29, ULTRA revealed this debacle to the Allies.[101] By the end of October, as a result of Allied bombing, Germany's three most important western waterways had ceased to function at the time of their highest use before the winter freeze drastically lowered their efficiency.

The *Reichsbahn* had great reserves: rolling stock and locomotives looted from all of Europe; an abundance of trackage for alternate routes; and well-trained, relatively numerous repair crews. All this did not suffice. By the first week of November, 50,000 "workers" from Holland reinforced repair crews. By mid-November the Germans committed 161,000 workers, 95,000 of them in the Ruhr. Marshaling yards had top priority. On November 29, Hitler allowed Speer to send 150,000 laborers, taken from all sections of the country, including some engaged in fortification work, to the Ruhr. But enormous inputs of unskilled labor could not substitute for exhausted trained crews. Repairs to constantly bombed yards consumed spare parts, signals, switches, and rails. Bombs churned up the earth, making it unable to support the rails and flattened the switching humps, dramatically decreasing the yards' ability to marshal cars into proper trains.[102]

Unable to use wrecked or unrepaired telecommunications equipment, *Reichsbahn* and German industrial managers made fatal recourse to their code machines. By November 1944 the British Government Code and Cypher School—the ULTRA organization—had broken two *Reichsbahn* Enigma keys (code-named BLUNDERBUSS and CULVERIN) for Germany and the west and some armament industry *Geheimschreiber* settings (FISH).* A November 8 decryption called for more use of waterways. Other decryptions spoke of increased antiaircraft defenses for traffic installations, and a January 1 decryption stated that fighter-bomber attacks (from the Ninth Air Force) in the area between the Moselle and the Saarland had ruined weeks of repair work, eliminated telephone facilities, and made it impossible to reroute trains.[103]

This cumulative destruction of the yards took its toll on the economy. Items of military necessity, troop and vital supply trains, could get through on a single track, which could be opened in a few hours or days. Even so, point-to-point travel times in Germany lengthened. But one through line did not a functioning

---

* The *Geheimschreiber* was a more advanced machine than the Enigma and was used for Hitler's and other high-ranking officials' traffic.

marshaling yard make. Raid after raid, repair after repair, each not quite as good as the last, reduced the capacity of the yards in an ever-descending spiral, dooming the German war economy. The thousands of separate items needed for production, not to mention coal, piled up at the factories and shaft heads or lay idle in marshaling yards or sidings, as the trains to haul them could no longer be put together. By November the *Reichsbahn* got a chilling glimpse of its future. It could not even keep its own fireboxes full. Instead of the normal twenty-day supply of hard coal, the system's supply stood at eleven days on November 5, ten days on November 11, nine on November 18, eight on November 20, six days on December 1, and five days on December 12. The east suffered as badly as the west, and in the south, cut off from the Ruhr by shattered rail lines, empty bins testified to a complete coal famine.[104]

When the *Reichsbahn* resorted to brown coal for its fuel, locomotive power dropped, repair intervals tripled, and a much larger smoke cloud made the engines easier targets for roving Allied fighter-bombers and fighters. Reduced to a hand-to-mouth fuel situation in one of the greatest coal producing countries in the world, and unable to marshal necessary trains, the *Reichsbahn* imposed further embargoes on cargo. In the western areas, only coal and *Wehrmacht* troop and supply shipments were allowed; not even food or armament production trains could be placed.* The railroads even refused a plea from the Ministry of Food and Agriculture for additional car space for the harvest.[105] Clearly, the economic life of Germany was ebbing away. Yet, like the *Wehrmacht* and the Luftwaffe, the *Reichsbahn* was capable of one last effort, which Hitler demanded and squandered in his futile Ardennes counteroffensive.

The Resurgence of the Luftwaffe

Spaatz's chief concern during the fall of 1944 was a possible resurgence in the effectiveness of the Luftwaffe's fighter force. September 1944, the month in which Germany produced its wartime high of 3,375 fighter aircraft (thanks to high priorities given fighter production and to a thorough dispersal program for the fighter assembly plants), gave indications that such a resurgence could occur. On September 11 and 12, large numbers of Luftwaffe fighters opposed Eighth Air Force missions directed against important oil hydrogenation plants for the first time since the oil strikes in May 1944. The Eighth lost 75 heavy bombers on those two missions.[106]

On September 27, when the Eighth hit industrial and transportation targets, the Luftwaffe demonstrated its still deadly effectiveness against unescorted bomber formations. Using newly developed tactics based on the development of

---

* In railroad terminology placing is the assembly and ordering of cars within a train. Normally, placing occurs only in a marshaling yard.

the *Sturmgruppe* (literally storm group, a special bomber assault unit consisting of heavily armored FW 190 fighters equipped with rapid-firing 30mm cannons), the Luftwaffe pounced on the 445th Bomb Group, whose 37 B-24s had wandered out from under the protective umbrella of its escort. In the three minutes between the bombers' plea for help and the arrival of the 361st Fighter Group's P-51s, *Sturmgruppe II/JG4's* 48 aircraft disrupted the formation and shot down 26 bombers; 2 more badly damaged bombers crashed in France. This was the largest loss by a single group during a mission ever experienced by the Eighth. The other 1,155 bombers dispatched lost only 2 bombers to enemy action.

The *Sturmgruppe's* heavily armed and armored planes proved a double-edged weapon. Additional weight severely hampered their maneuverability. The nimble Mustang P-51s of a single squadron of the 361st probably saved the remainder of the 445th; they certainly avenged their comrades. They intercepted the *Sturmgruppe* and its escort of Bf 109s, shooting down 18 fighters—the Eighth Air Force record for kills by a single squadron in a single day.[107]

This increase in Luftwaffe activity did not go unremarked by Spaatz or Arnold. On September 3, Maj. Gen. Frederick L. Anderson, with Spaatz's approval, warned Arnold of USSTAF's concern over the progress of the Germans in fielding their new jet fighter, the Me 262. Anderson described the attacks the AAF in Europe planned to make on the enemy's jet airframe, engine, and fuel-manufacturing facilities, and on the experimental and training airfields. Two of USSTAF's greatest worries were (1) the Germans' obvious intention to use their jets against Allied photographic reconnaissance aircraft and (2) the small, dispersed underground sites where the jets themselves were assembled. Anderson requested the earliest possible deployment of the American jet fighter, the P-80.[108] Arnold replied that the AAF in the United States was working hard to meet Spaatz's requirements. New, more effective P-51s and P-47s had gone into production, and so would the P-80 when its development was finished. Arnold also promised to send the latest bombing-through-overcast radar devices as they became available.[109]

The terrible losses absorbed by the 445th had a sobering effect on the heavy-bomber commanders. Although the Luftwaffe never duplicated the September 27 feat, the Americans had to assume that it would. On September 28, Doolittle wrote to Spaatz. He cited a gradual increase in the strength and aggressiveness of the Luftwaffe as a reason periodically to give "first priority to the conduct of winter air operations on the German Air Force-in-being to insure that their aircraft productive capacity does not get out of hand." Doolittle added, "It is inexpedient for us to permit them to build up their force to a point where, even though we fly the maximum number of our limited escort fighters on every deep penetration bomber mission, they are able, in their periodic attacks, to take a serious toll of bombers."[110]

Three weeks later, a still worried Doolittle described the new *Sturmgruppe* tactics:

The Germans have developed a "line abreast" method of attack and it has proved so effective that they are now using it almost to the exclusion of other forms of attack. The concentrated fire from "line abreast" attacks has greatly reduced the effectiveness of the defensive fire of our bombers. Once a 'line abreast' attack is launched, it is practically impossible to break up that particular attack unless our fighters are in a position between the bombers and the attacking enemy. Split-second timing is necessary and we do not have enough fighters to give close cover to all of our bombers.[111]

Doolittle pleaded for the forward deployment of a new and more effective Allied radar. He informed Spaatz that microwave early warning radar (MEW) should come forward to Luxembourg where, with its 250-mile range, it could observe enemy fighter formations as they formed up, direct and control friendly fighters, pinpoint bomber forces and direct them to the vicinity of their targets in overcast, and help Allied aircraft locate home or emergency fields in very bad weather. "It is my personal opinion," added Doolittle, "and that of our fighter controllers, that with our M.E.W. located on the Continent, operated by the Eighth Air Force and tied in with this headquarters by adequate communications, the effectiveness of Eighth Air Force fighters will be increased at least 50%."[112]

Spaatz shared Doolittle's feeling of alarm, but he focused on potential and actual German technical advances. At the beginning of October he wrote to Lovett, "The Luftwaffe has raised its head a bit in the past week or so by means of jet propelled or rocket planes that are now able to carry on reconnaissance which was denied to them prior to D-Day and up until quite recently."[113] At about the same time he wrote to Arnold expressing a more pessimistic outlook: "There is every chance, I think, that the Germans may be using proximity fuzes* or an improved type of radar control for their flak. We can't prove this yet and our increased flak losses may be due simply to the fact that they are concentrating all their available flak in a smaller area." Spaatz also expressed concern about German jet aircraft: "The Hun has still got a lot of fight left in him, even in the air, and we must concentrate to kill him off if possible before he can develop these new threats against us."[114]

---

* The proximity, or variable time (VT), fuze was an "influence" fuze. The fuze contained a miniature wet-cell battery and a five-tube two-way radio activated by the impact of the firing artillery piece. It transmitted a 140-foot doughnut-shaped signal, which, in proximity to aircraft or the ground, reflected back to the fuze, triggering an electric impulse that detonated the shell. Although it was difficult to manufacture, and, as a consequence, had a high dud rate, it was the most effective antiaircraft fuze of the war. It eliminated the extremely difficult problem of fuze setting for larger antiaircraft artillery guns, increasing the effect of antiaircraft fire by approximately 300 percent. The shell was developed in strict secrecy and first employed by the U.S. Navy in the Pacific. The V-1 campaign in the summer of 1944 prompted its use in England. Not until mid-December 1944 did the Americans employ it on the European continent. See Frank E. Comparato, *Age of the Great Guns: Cannon Kings and Cannoneers who Forged the Firepower of Artillery* (Harrisburg, Pa.: Stackpole, 1965), pp. 265–267, for a more detailed description of the fuze and its effectiveness.

RAF Air Intelligence added to Spaatz's unease. On October 1, AI estimated, correctly, that in September the Germans had reached a new monthly high in single-engine fighter plane production and predicted, incorrectly, that the upward trend would continue. AI assessed the current Luftwaffe single-engine fighter strength at 2,000 and guessed that it could rise to 2,500 in six months. An October 3 ULTRA decryption showed a Luftwaffe reorganization shifting fighter forces back to the defense of the Reich. Six days later, signal intelligence disclosed Goering's orders reducing close support fighters in the west by 150 aircraft and adding that number to strategic defense.[115]

On October 4, Spaatz, in an "Eyes Only" letter to Arnold, showed that the shock of the attack on the 445th Bombardment Group had abated. After noting that recent losses were "not unduly high," he said, "I am reasonably sure that, at the present time, the Germans have no new weapons that are causing our losses, although I am not overlooking the possibility of proximity fuzes, and better ammunition and sights for their fighters."[116] Nevertheless, Spaatz retained enough concern that he authorized the Fifteenth Air Force to abandon temporarily the oil campaign if it felt the need to defend itself by attacking airfields and aircraft production.[117]

After approving the forward move of the theater's only microwave early warning radar set, Spaatz sought to enhance intelligence operations. On October 20, he asked Portal to move the RAF "Y" Service tactical radio interception unit from England to the Continent, arguing, "In as much as the German defensive measures appear to be increasing in capacity and efficiency, it is of vital importance to the successful continuation of our daylight bombing operations that we obtain . . . every possible means to improve the efficiency of our fighter coverage."[118] The same day Spaatz wrote to Air Vice-Marshal Robb, head of SHAEF's air section, "The increasing efficiency of German Air Force operations against our penetration necessitates that every means be taken to improve the efficiency of our own fighter operations in their protection of the bombers." Thereupon, Spaatz requested improved voice and teletype circuits to enable better communications linking Eighth Air Force Headquarters, Ninth Air Force Advanced Headquarters, the MEW set in Luxembourg, and the "Y" Service unit moving to the Continent.[119]

Additional signal intelligence may have heightened Spaatz's concern. In mid-October RAF Air Intelligence informed the British Joint Intelligence Committee that the Germans had enough fuel for advanced fighter training and maximum deployment for defense of the Reich. AI added that front-line fighter strength had risen 25 percent from August 1 and would continue to increase. From this data AI concluded that the Luftwaffe, in conjunction with its jet and rocket aircraft, might secure some degree of air superiority over Germany, thereby enabling it to protect vital war industries during the upcoming winter.[120] On October 17, a signal from *Luftflotte Reich*, decrypted by Bletchley Park the

514

next day, gave close-support forces the main task of engaging Allied air forces in the rear of the operational area and over the population working on the West Wall (German border fortifications). They would undertake ground support only in critical situations. An October 26 decryption of an October 18 message unambiguously set the Luftwaffe's main task as the strategic defense of the Fatherland and warned of impending transfers of additional ground support fighters to air defense.[121] None of this could have added to Spaatz's peace of mind.

Spaatz visited Bradley at his headquarters on October 21. After being briefed on the 12th Army Group's plans for an attack on November 10, Spaatz told Bradley of his concern about the German air buildup. Spaatz feared that daylight bombing into Germany would become very expensive and that the strategic air force might have to lose "about 40,000 crew members" in order to maintain present air superiority. Spaatz added that it was essential for the army to press forward to the Rhine in order to obtain advanced airfields that would enable the Ninth to move forward and the Eighth to send its fighters into the continental fields vacated by the Ninth. Such a move would almost double the effectiveness of his fighters, Spaatz declared. Bradley replied that if good flying weather appeared likely, he could advance the date of his attack to November 5. Spaatz responded that the strategic air forces were prepared to lay down a barrage wherever Bradley requested it, weather permitting. In any case, Spaatz promised to aid Bradley's attack by operating the Eighth's fighters just to the east of the Rhine to enable the Ninth's fighters to concentrate on Bradley's immediate front.[122] If nothing else, this interchange between Bradley and Spaatz demonstrated more integration and interdependence between the ground and strategic air efforts than is usually conceded by the proponents of either effort.

This conversation probably had little influence on Bradley's plans; he made no mention of it in his memoirs. The U.S. Army official history does note, however, that one reason Eisenhower and his advisers [Spaatz?] wished to avoid a halt in operations in November was that they feared such a pause might give the Germans the chance to increase jet fighter production and discover the proximity fuze "which might blast Allied bombers from the skies."[123]

The weather, as Spaatz anticipated, did not cooperate. Patton's Third Army began its attack toward Metz on November 8. Hodges's First Army, which had included a massive air bombardment as a prelude to its attack, postponed action from November 10 to November 16 because the heavy bombers could not fly until then. This attack, code-named Operation QUEEN, far exceeded the St. Lô/COBRA attack in technical efficiency. Unfortunately, its ultimate effectiveness came nowhere close to the proficiency of its predecessor in Normandy. In its preparations and execution QUEEN showed how far the Eighth Air Force had come in its ground support role. Instead of only a few days' preparation, Doolittle rehearsed his forces thoroughly for the assault. On November 7 he conducted a full-scale "experimental" practice attack on a target in England to test safety measures. He also insisted that he have more input into advance planning; if he had only short notice, the Army "must expect the hazards incidental to support from heavy bombers."[124]

Unlike earlier bomber-support attacks, Queen employed elaborate measures to mark the front lines. In addition to sixty-four 90mm antiaircraft artillery pieces that fired colored shells, giant ground-marking panels laid out by the troops, and a string of barrage balloons, the Eighth set up a series of radio and radar beacons close to the line. The planes would bomb no closer than 3,600 yards from the troops, well over twice the margin used in the St. Lô attack.[125]

On the morning of November 16, a total of 1,191 Eighth Air Force heavy bombers dropped their fragmentation bombs through overcast, killing only one American soldier and wounding only three with short bombs. An additional 1,188 Bomber Command aircraft bombed and cratered areas flanking the assault in the hope of preventing enemy reinforcement. Unfortunately, this attack, World War II's largest air attack in direct support of ground troops, did not produce results commensurate with efforts. Because of the large safety zone, most bombs fell beyond the German main line of resistance, striking artillery positions and fortuitously cutting up a German infantry division caught in the open while relieving a front-line unit. After a few hours, enemy resistance stiffened. Subsequent fighting produced no spectacular breakthrough, only more dogged attritional warfare. The air commanders blamed the large safety zone for poor results, because it prevented a rapid follow-up by the ground forces.[126] Spaatz commented to Arnold: "As a result of these operations, it has very definitely been established that unless there is a quick follow up of the bombardment by ground troops, the enemy recovers from the shock and the effect of the bombing is vitiated."[127]

Other factors prevented this attack from achieving the tremendous results of the St. Lô breakthrough. First, the U.S. ground forces did not launch so highly concentrated an attack as in Normandy. Second, the Germans—in contrast to their attenuated situation in France—had adequate reserves, which allowed them to seal any break in their lines before it became critical. Even if Queen had severely damaged the front-line troops, it would have made no lasting break.

At the beginning of December the Allies seriously considered diverting more strategic effort to the direct support of their bogged-down ground troops to achieve an immediate end to hostilities. Why bomb strategic targets when the war might be over in sixty days? On December 5, the air commanders and Eisenhower met at Versailles "to devise some means of using the strategic air forces in such a way as to bring about an early decision on the Western Front."[128]

After opening the meeting by acknowledging the stalemated position of the ground forces and the pressure from the CCS to end the war quickly, Tedder suggested possible solutions: (1) conducting another Queen-type operation or (2) providing continuous close support by heavy bombers over a long period of time. By limiting the airmen to these two options, Tedder hoped that Eisenhower would understand what extended heavy-bomber support would cost him in terms of damage not inflicted on the interior of Germany. Spaatz spoke up immediately. He could deliver 40,000 to 50,000 tons of bombs per month. Of that total, 10,000 tons of bombs were needed to keep German production down at ten oil facilities, which, if they could continue operating uninterrupted for a month, might bring forth 400,000 tons of all types of fuel. In addition, Spaatz suggested that the antitransportation attacks had begun to show results and should continue to receive "some effort." As for the Luftwaffe, it could be limited by air battle alone without Allied recourse to bombing. Hence perhaps 30,000 tons of bombs were left for tactical support.[129]

After Spaatz's recitation, Tedder skillfully guided the meeting toward the conclusion that he and most of the other airmen supported: the strategic air forces should mount QUEEN-like operations when required, but should also persevere with the strategic bomber offensive. From Coningham and Quesada Tedder extracted agreement that heavy-bomber carpet bombing would not materially assist the tactical air forces at present. Tedder also gained from Doolittle and Harris agreement that QUEEN-like operations would be the most effective type of ground support operation for the heavy bombers. Doolittle noted that the Eighth had begun to train strategic air support parties and planned to have an airborne air controller to assist in future operations.[130]

The airmen emphasized to Eisenhower that they thought QUEEN-like operations would be most effective only if they supported troops actually moving forward. Repeated and continued bombings of targets such as villages and towns immediately behind the front lines would accomplish virtually nothing. Eisenhower agreed and closed by paying the air forces a compliment: "It was impossible to convince the Army that the battle of St. Lô had not been won as a result of the direct support given by the 8th Air Force."[131]

The next day, Spaatz flew to Patton's headquarters and offered him the direct support of the heavy bombers during the attack on the Siegfried Line in a week or ten days. Because Patton's attack would occur at the boundary between Devers's 6th Army Group and Bradley's 12th Army Group, Spaatz also visited Devers on December 7 and Bradley on December 8.[132] However, the German Ardennes counteroffensive caused the hurried shelving of this initiative.

As the Eighth prepared for QUEEN and possible ground-support missions, Spaatz fretted over the Luftwaffe, which now had far more fighter aircraft than ever before. From the all-time high of 3,375 fighters in September, production fell off only slightly to 2,975 machines in October and to 2,995 and 2,630 in the last two months of the year.[133] If the Luftwaffe had possessed the fuel necessary to train its pilots properly and to oppose all raids in strength, this formidable force might have fulfilled the hopes of its masters. Despite their severe losses in the quarter ending December 31, 1944, the Germans placed 4,219 more aircraft into service than they lost, 90 percent of them fighters.[134]

The Germans were at cross-purposes about how to deploy this force. Maj. Gen. Adolph Galland, the Luftwaffe day-fighter commandant, and Speer hoped to use it to defend Germany from the Allied heavy bombers. On October 5, Speer concluded a report to Hitler on the oil situation with this recommendation: "Raise the effective fighting capacity of the German fighter force to such a height as is absolutely possible, to add all available machines to its strength, and then concentrate this fighter force for the protection of the home armaments and war production."[135]

In the meantime, Galland, according to his postwar interrogations, succeeded in convincing Goering and the Luftwaffe General Staff that the fighter forces needed a period of rest and rehabilitation before being returned to combat.[136] Alternatively, Hitler may have decided at that point to allow the conservation of fighters in order to save them for his planned counteroffensive. In any case, probably unaware of Hitler's plans, Galland confidently began to implement his own scheme. He stripped Italy and Austria of German fighters, increased the number of planes per group to 68, made sure that each group received fifteen hours (a pitiful amount) of special training in air defense, and reorganized the command structure to reflect the actual basing of his aircraft. By early November he claimed a strength of 3,000 aircraft, 2,500 of them operational.[137] The Eighth and Ninth Air Forces had a paper strength of 4,204 fighters,[138] with a high serviceability rate, and the British could add 2,000 more fighter aircraft. Galland claimed that he had achieved a satisfactory resolution to fighter leadership personnel problems and, although he admitted that fuel shortages hampered training, he maintained that all formations had had enough time to complete their courses.

Galland planned to use this rejuvenated force in a series of "Big Blows" against the Eighth Air Force. The first interception would consist of 1,000 fighters, 300 to 400 of which would refuel and attack again. A further 80 to 100 night fighters would pick off cripples headed for Sweden or Switzerland.[139] Under Galland's direction, the fighter force carefully practiced the tactics required for such a large-scale operation and awaited the combination of a clear day and a deep bomber penetration to put their preparations into practice.[140] With all in readiness by November 12, Galland hoped to shoot down 500 bombers in a single day. He expected to lose an equal number of fighters and 150 pilots. This effort, he thought, would force the Americans to resume bombing the aircraft industry (instead of oil targets) and perhaps give the Germans the chance to hold the Soviets while making a separate peace with the Anglo-American Allies.[141]

The weather in mid-November never provided the clear day both the AAF and the Luftwaffe hoped for. In late November Galland received orders to transfer fighters to the Western Front, ostensibly to defend against a coming Allied attack, but, as he subsequently realized, in reality to assist the counteroffensive.[142] Once engaged in the Battle of the Bulge, the pilots, without even minimal training in ground support, and their machines rapidly succumbed to the massive air power the Allies applied to halt the attack. One of Germany's last hopes to protect its industry—a slim hope, given the poor performance of its pilots—went down in flames as the fighter arm dissipated itself in vain attempts to assist the German ground forces. During the Battle of the Bulge the Germans lost hundreds of fighters in air-to-air combat and hundreds more in ground attacks, including more than 200 on a spectacular but ineffective New Year's Day raid on Allied airfields.

No full-scale Big Blow was ever launched; but the tactics and control techniques developed in case it was must have aided the Luftwaffe in fielding its three largest interceptions of the war. On November 2, 21, and 26 at least 500 German fighters arose to defend their Fatherland. These interceptions evoked both consternation and relief within USSTAF and the Eighth—consternation because such large forces could be marshaled and relief because they were ineffective. In the entire month of November the AAF credited German fighters with the destruction of only 50 heavy bombers, a far cry from the 314 bombers shot down by enemy fighters in April.[143] What is more, the Luftwaffe paid a heavy price. Even if the claims of the bomber gunners were invariably inflated, American fighters, most of whose kills were recorded by gunsight cameras, knocked down 102 enemy fighters on November 2, 68 on November 21, and 114 on November 26.[144]

Yet, the large-scale German interception on November 2 sent a shiver through USSTAF. Three days later Spaatz wrote a long letter to Arnold explaining his current thinking on the situation. "For some months we have been carefully weighing the build up of the German fighter force," reported Spaatz. Showing that he had grasped at least the outline of Galland's Big Blow, Spaatz continued:

> It has been increasingly evident that the GAF was being processed to become a major threat to our deep penetrations, in daylight, into Germany. The operations last Thursday, at which time the GAF hit our penetration with a well laid plan, and in strength, resulted in an outstanding aerial victory for our forces. However, this victory was attained because of almost perfect fighter cover and because of a fortunate chain of circumstances which contributed to the decisive outcome.[145]

Spaatz described four factors in the Luftwaffe's resurgence: conversion of its remaining bomber pilots to fighter pilots, all-out expansion of the entire fighter force, the highest-priority development and production of jet aircraft, and perhaps most important, the continuation of a conservation policy. Spaatz noted that the enemy met his critical oil shortage by not operating during the increasing periods of poor weather or against shallow penetrations or well-escorted bomber missions. "Thus," Spaatz informed Arnold, "it is possible that during our deep penetrations we can be hit in force now, and this possibility is con-

General Dwight D. Eisenhower, Supreme Allied Commander, and his two leading ground commanders, Lt. Gen. Jacob L. Devers *(left)***, Commanding General, 6th Army Group, and Lt. Gen. Omar N. Bradley** *(right)***, Commanding General, 12th Army Group, November 1944.**

stantly increasing with the resurgence of the GAF during the winter. This is a point of serious concern and may have a major effect on the war should it last throughout the spring."[146]

Spaatz went on to discuss the countermeasures necessary to avert the threat. In his opinion the Eighth had too few fighters; with the influx of new bomber groups in the spring and summer there was only one fighter to protect every two bombers. This shortage posed a serious problem because it offered Spaatz only two options: reducing the number of bombers sent on deep missions to a number which the fighters could adequately cover, or sending out the maximum number of bombers on each mission, knowing full well that a massive German attack might overwhelm both a thinly spread escort and its flock. Spaatz regarded the first alternative as unacceptable because winter weather limited the number of good bombing days to a handful. With key targets protected by weather, flak, and smoke screens, the only way to obtain a reasonable assurance of destruction was by concentrating the maximum force on each target. Having decided to risk

**Lt. Gens. Carl A. Spaatz, George S. Patton, and James H. Doolittle; Maj. Gen. Hoyt
S. Vandenberg, Commanding General, Ninth Air Force; and Brig. Gen. O. P.
Weyland, Commanding General, XIX Air Support Command, autumn 1944.**

the second alternative, Spaatz strove to limit the Germans' opportunities for
attack. Microwave early warning radar and "Y" signal intercepts helped, but, as
he told Arnold, "a permanent movement of the Eighth Air Force fighters from
the U.K. to the Belgium-Holland area is the only real answer to increasing our
escort fighter density."[147] Such a move could not occur until the British 2d
Tactical Air Force moved forward and vacated its present fields, more communications equipment arrived to supplement the already overloaded equipment on
the Continent, and Montgomery succeeded in opening Antwerp.[148]

In the meantime, the Americans took countermeasures. On November 27, the
Eighth sent two forces into Germany. The first, made up of 515 heavy bombers
escorted by 241 fighters, bombed marshaling yards in southwest Germany. The
second force, composed of 460 fighter bombers, headed for four oil centers in
northern and central Germany. Using radio deception methods to trick the
Germans into mistaking fighter formations for heavy bombers and aided by both
heavy overcast (which prevented ground observers from identifying the aircraft)
and newly deployed very high frequency radar jammers (which partially blinded
the German ground controllers), this force, vectored to the German fighter rendezvous areas by the newly positioned MEW radar, provoked strong German
reaction. In the ensuing fighter melee the Americans claimed to have downed 98
enemy fighters, against a loss of 12 of their own.[149] As Spaatz observed to

521

General Giles, Chief of the Air Staff, two weeks later, "Our war is becoming a radar war. We depend heavily on the operational capabilities of a small number of radar sets of extraordinary performance." As H2X had increased the bombers' effectiveness in the first half of 1944, the three MEW sets in the theater were largely responsible, Spaatz said, "for the superiority of our fighters over Germany. We are therefore willing to pay the high price of the introduction of new and complicated apparatus because the return is proportionately high."[150]

Arnold, too, felt the growing threat of the Luftwaffe. In his reply to Spaatz's letter of November 5, he agreed on the urgency of getting the Eighth's fighters to the Continent. He displayed a more open attitude than Spaatz did toward the possibility of changing priorities such as increasing night bombing, sacrificing heavy bomber effort in favor of more fighter sweeps, or creating a strategic fighter force to conduct additional fighter sweeps. Arnold closed on a hopeful note: "The staggering losses you have inflicted in the past few days suggest that numerical increases in aircraft may not reflect the true position of the GAF."[151]

Another letter from AAF Headquarters in Washington, this time from General Giles, further explained the attitude prevalent there. He admitted AAF Headquarters' concern over the growing strength of the Luftwaffe and mentioned alternatives studied and rejected, including a suggestion for 500 additional fighters. "If we are to hit the Germans low with the fighters and high with the bombers," wrote Giles, "it will have to be done with the means we know we possess." Giles also seconded Spaatz's desire to get the fighters to the Continent and supported the maximum use of heavy bombers. Finally, he expressed concern about the accuracy of the Eighth's blind bombing.[152]

At USSTAF, examination of November's operations restored a certain amount of optimism. Spaatz wrote to Washington, "In spite of the buildup of strength, his [the enemy's] overall effectiveness has not increased. In recent operations, when he has come up to fight, we have destroyed as much as 25% of his forces. . . . "[153] If Spaatz's airmen could only get a break in the weather, they could destroy the German fighter force and free the escorts to return to a purely offensive role. "In the meantime," he assured Lovett, "our motto is—the maximum tonnage of bombs on Germany that the weather will permit."[154]

Three days after his letter, three German armies plus supporting troops stormed through the surprised American defenders in Belgium's Ardennes Forest region and began to drive for the Meuse River and Antwerp. If they succeeded they would split the American and British army groups and possibly crush each separately. The Luftwaffe supported this offensive with all its capabilities. Spaatz and the other Allied airmen finally had the chance they had sought to destroy the Luftwaffe.

Arnold and the Public Image of the AAF

The goal of winning the war dominated the thoughts and actions of both Arnold and Spaatz. Nonetheless, the two also worked toward the fulfillment of another goal, the independence of the Air Force within the U.S. military establishment. Toward this end, USSTAF had to present itself to the public and to its elected representatives in the U.S. Congress in the best possible light—hence, Arnold's and Spaatz's concern with the amount, quality, and type of press coverage for the AAF.

Naturally, Arnold in Washington felt the need for a good press more acutely than Spaatz in Europe. Arnold dealt daily with the heads of the services, congressional committees, the British Chiefs of Staff, the civilian politicians in charge of the War Department, and, occasionally, the President—all in a goldfish-bowl atmosphere. As a result, he could assess the position of the AAF in the hierarchy and its future prospects with a precision unobtainable elsewhere. The AAF's position depended not only on its actual performance but on its perceived performance as well. Arnold, with his hand so close to the nation's pulse, at least with regard to air matters, invariably pressed his air force commanders for favorable news items to convince the public of the AAF's importance to the war effort. Spaatz, concerned as he was with the operation and administration of the AAF's three largest numbered air forces, felt the pressure from Washington on public relations and reacted to it.

The invasion of France caused an abrupt decline in the amount of press coverage devoted to the AAF in Europe. Heretofore, the AAF, as the only all-American force in the ETO directly engaged in combat with the Nazis, had enjoyed front-page coverage of its operations. Indeed, press attention further focused on it because censorship and restrictions concerning the ground forces' state of preinvasion preparations actively diverted attention from other U.S. forces. After D-day the situation reversed itself. On June 8, Chief of the Air Staff Giles wrote Spaatz, "We all appreciate your innumerable current problems and your magnificent participation in the invasion. However, the newspapers here are pressing us for some special material which I should like to have you get together for us at the earliest practicable moment." Giles asked for a brief, colorful overview of the air forces in action, with special stories on troop-carrier and heavy-bomber operations. In a penciled note he requested stories on the fighters, too.[155]

The breakout from Normandy and the drive to the Siegfried Line kept the ground forces on the front pages. In late September, Arnold wrote Spaatz, "I am extremely concerned over current press releases stressing remarkable achievements of Ground Force commanders such as Hodges, Patton, and Patch in speeding the war to an early and successful end with armor, mobile infantry, and artillery occupying the spotlight." Instead Arnold wanted to see balanced narration of battles and offensives, with the effects of an action upon the outcome being described in true relation to the overall success, one would imagine that air power played a relatively small part in the liberation of the occupied countries and the defeat of the German airmen therein. However, you must apply pressure in Europe while I apply it here, to the end that our press releases more nearly picture in proper balance the relative contribution of ground, sea and air forces in our approach toward a complete victory over our enemies.

Next, Arnold expressed his view on the necessity of a favorable public opinion for air power. "I consider the whole subject of realistic reorientation of the public's concept of the effects of air power upon the outcome of the war so important that I will scour the country to provide you with the men most capable of putting into words the achievements of the Army Air Forces."[156] Finally, Arnold wanted Spaatz to emphasize that USSTAF was no longer under Eisenhower's control so that the public would know that the strategic air offensive was playing an independent role in Europe.

Spaatz, who had appeared on the D-day cover of *Time* magazine, must at first have wondered what more Arnold could want. In his reply, prepared by Anderson, Spaatz shared Arnold's "concern over the inadequate attention given to air operations in press and radio accounts of the war in Europe and other theaters."[157] After describing various measures taken to remedy the situation, Spaatz noted, "In case of a stalemate on the ground, our operations should become top news once more." He then asked for twelve additional public relations officers for the Ninth Air Force. He also wrote that he had asked Doolittle and Vandenberg "to redouble their efforts to help us achieve the results you want."

In November, Arnold escalated his criticism of Spaatz's public relations effort. Having just gained Marshall's permission to establish the AAF Office of Information Services[158] to issue press releases, he groused to Spaatz, "I am increasingly concerned about the display given accomplishments of the Air Forces in your area by the American newspapers. Since these stories originate in the theater, the primary reason for the monotonous presentations must be over there."[159] In typical fashion Arnold informed Spaatz of his intention to send an officer, Col. Rex Smith, Chief of the AAF Office of Information Services, out "for a complete study of this situation for such remedial recommendations as are necessary." Arnold expressed his opinion in no uncertain terms: "I consider this problem of the highest priority in the Air Forces now."[160]

Arnold passed the word informally, too. On the previous day, he had asked Brig. Gen. George C. McDonald, Spaatz's Chief of Intelligence, who had come to Washington to attempt to justify a large increase in USSTAF's intelligence staff, to convey his concern. McDonald recorded that Arnold told him that at the present time one had to turn to the inside pages of the newspapers to find any mention of the Air Forces. He stated that among the hundreds of thousands of Air Force personnel under General Spaatz, someone should be able to glamorize the stories of the Air Force and give them freshness, interest and vitality. He pointed out that on the front page, bold head-lines would appear that a certain town of three hundred inhabitants, that no one had ever heard of, was captured by General Patton's troops while the tremendous contributions of the Air Forces are found on the seventh page of the New York Times. General Arnold stated that he had been informed that the fault lay on the other side and that General Spaatz would have to correct it within his command, that he would not do the necessary [work] over here—it would have to begin with USSTAF and its commands.[161]

On November 30, Spaatz received yet another letter from Arnold, delivered by Colonel Smith, which elaborated on Arnold's demands for improved public relations:

> As you are no doubt aware, my concern is that through proper presentation to the press the American people be given the facts necessary to a correct evaluation of the part air power has played in the war, to the end that the United States should not make the mistake of allowing through lack of knowledge the tearing down in postwar years of what has cost us so much blood and sweat to build up.[162]

Like all the professional soldiers of his generation, Arnold had never forgotten the pell-mell demobilization of the U.S. armed forces that had followed World War I.

Smith, on the first leg of a trip to all the combat theaters where the AAF operated, brought with him a list of fifty points applicable to the writing of communiques and press releases. Arnold wanted the list distributed to all AAF public relations officers (PROs) and told Spaatz, "I feel your personal attention is needed in insuring that the point of view is adequately presented to each PRO." As a parting shot Arnold observed, "I trust that with all of us approaching the vital question of public relations along more or less the same lines, we may regain with the American public the position which we now only hold in the minds of our enemies."[163]

By December 9 Spaatz had reorganized his public relations effort, installing Col. Hal Bowman, whom he had described as a fine officer with a first-class combat record, as a new Deputy Chief of Staff with the primary function of representing USSTAF to the press.[164] Spaatz told Vandenberg to make a similar appointment.[165] By the end of the month, with matters apparently satisfactorily in hand, USSTAF passed Rex Smith on to Ira Eaker in the Mediterranean.[166]

By then the Battle of the Bulge had thoroughly tested the new public relations organization, and had graphically demonstrated once again the importance of air power. The American papers practically tumbled over one another praising the AAF's efforts to stem the German tide.

Conclusions

The last third of 1944 was for Spaatz, USSTAF, and all of the Allied forces in the European Theater of Operations a time of frustration. The goal of defeating the Third Reich, which had seemed tantalizingly close in the beginning of September, receded as the ground forces halted on the German border and an exceptionally wet autumn severely hampered operations both on the land and in the air. True, the sun refused to shine on either side, but it cannot be denied that this situation favored the German land forces, the Luftwaffe, and the battered oil plants more than the Allies. What the Allied leaders did not fully appreciate was that the still-imposing facade of the Nazi state was hiding a gutted, bombed-out building. Once they toppled the wall, which would still take some doing, nothing of consequence would remain.

Despite Spaatz's success in keeping oil the top priority, German oil production increased throughout the last third of the year, but remained a mere fraction of what it was before the campaign began. Spaatz's fears that the Luftwaffe's relative inactivity in September and October, coupled with high fighter-plane production and the introduction of jet fighter aircraft, presaged a resurgence in its effectiveness, proved exaggerated. USSTAF bomber casualties decreased dramatically in the fourth quarter of the year, especially in view of the fact that the size of its total bomber force had more than doubled from January to December. (See Table 6, USSTAF Bomber Losses by Quarter, 1944–1945.)

The table shows that during the latter half of the year German fighter aircraft effectiveness declined and Allied losses from antiaircraft fire increased. Both results were to some extent the fault of the oil offensive, which had reduced the fuel available to German fighters for training and operations while exposing USSTAF's bombers to extremely heavy concentrations of antiaircraft guns. The Leuna-Merseburg oil complex, for example, had heavier flak defenses than Berlin.[167] In addition, the table, to some extent, demonstrates the often unsung contributions of the Fifteenth Air Force. Throughout 1944 the Fifteenth Air Force had only half as many bombers assigned to it as the Eighth Air Force. Thus, its losses suffered in the last six months of 1944 stand out dramatically. In fact, during the period covered by this chapter, the Fifteenth was suffering almost twice the rate of casualties as the Eighth.[168] The Fifteenth's lower-flying B-24s paid in blood for the range that enabled them to fly from Italy to the Reich's synthetic oil facilities.

By mid-September 1944 U.S. air power in Europe far exceeded the strength envisaged for it in AAF prewar planning. Air War Plans Division/1 (AWPD/1) of July 1941 had called for 44 heavy-bombardment groups (2,992 aircraft), 10 medium-bombardment groups (850 planes), and 16 fighter groups (2,080 aircraft) to operate against Germany from Britain and the Near East. By August 31, 1944, the AAF in the European and Mediterranean Theaters of Operations

526

Table 6
USSTAF Bomber Losses by Quarter, 1944–1945
(Combined Eighth and Fifteenth Air Forces)

Year	Total	Anti- Aircraft	Enemy Aircraft	Other Unknown
Eighth AF **Losses**				
1944				
1 Qtr.	819	220	487	112
2 Qtr.	1,116	389	637	90
3 Qtr.	1,057	646	278	133
4 Qtr.	505	332	114	59
1945	973	624	199	150
Total	4,470	2,211	1,715	544
Fifteenth AF **Losses**				
1944				
1 Qtr.	267	40	168	59
2 Qtr.	565	251	243	74
3 Qtr.	665	353	182	120
4 Qtr.	477	289	19	169
1945	481	321	7	153
Total	2,455	1,254	626	575
USSTAF **Losses**				
1944				
1 Qtr.	2,086	260	655	171
2 Qtr.	1,681	640	877	164
3 Qtr.	1,722	999	470	253
4 Qtr.	982	621	133	228
1945	1,454	945	206	303
Total	6,925	3,465	2,341	1,119

Compiled from AAF *Statistical Digest, World War II*, pp. 255–256, Tables 159 and 160.

possessed 62 heavy-bombardment groups (4,980 planes), 18 medium-bombardment groups (1,513 planes), and 45 fighter groups (4,969 planes), almost twice the force outlined by AWPD/1.[169] British Bomber Command added 1,871 more heavy bombers and the British 2d Tactical Air Force supplied 293 medium bombers and 999 fighters.[170] Against this enormous force, the Luftwaffe command on the Western Front mustered 431 fighter aircraft.[171]

In addition to their numerical advantage, the Allied strategic air forces had gained control of their own operations. They ended the CROSSBOW campaign and succeeded in temporarily bombing out all production of aviation fuel. The stage seemed set for the rapid extinction of the German economy. Yet, althouth it had begun to stumble, it continued to function at least until the beginning of 1945. As General Hansell put it, the strategic bombing offensive "fatally weakened" Germany in the fall of 1944. The bombing of oil, with its side effects on the explosives and synthetic rubber industries, and of transportation, with its disruption of coal, ball bearings, and semifinished goods distribution, wreaked havoc on the German military machine and economy. Precision bombing had wrecked the oil plants in the summer 1944, but blind bombing in the autumn, although allowing a slight increase in production, kept the plants suppressed. Similarly, the blind bombing of cities containing marshaling yards dealt a body blow to the German rail system. Instead of being a quick, surgical means of destroying enemy war industry and morale, strategic bombing had developed into a weapon of attrition which bludgeoned Germany into submission.

Several factors contributed to the failure of strategic bombing to end the war more quickly. The Combined Bomber Offensive was embraced in name only. Harris, following his strategy of area bombing, refused to cooperate even with his own Air Staff, thereby shortchanging the oil and transportation campaigns alike. Bomber Command's heavy bombs inflicted more damage than the lighter American bombs; more heavy bombs dropped on oil targets would have significantly increased the total damage to the synthetic petroleum industry. Harris's stratagem of area bombing of cities, merely because they appeared on his list of sixty-three cities suitable for bombing, wreaked great damage but did not necessarily contribute to a coherent anti-transportation campaign. The weather allowed only a few days of visual bombing, which the Eighth used to bomb oil targets; 70 to 80 percent of USSTAF's effort involved radar assistance.

Under pressure from Arnold, Spaatz had to put more bombers into the air and use his increased bombing capacity to the fullest. After devoting the maximum of his resources that conditions allowed against oil plants, Spaatz had to find targets for the rest of the bomblift. He wavered between ordnance and motor vehicles, which were targets requested by the ground forces, and transportation, the system advocated by Tedder. After considering such schemes as the HURRICANE morale sweeps throughout Germany, Spaatz finally chose transportation. No other system could absorb the force he had available, and signal intelligence revealed its vulnerability. The H2X radars in his heavy bombers could at least pick out the cities that contained marshaling yards, and his fighters, when they descended to ground level, could certainly follow the roads and rails, shooting up any vehicles they encountered.

The decision to bomb transportation, concurred in by Spaatz, Tedder, Bottomley, and, through him, Portal, would eventually result in the complete disruption of German economic life. It would also firmly affix to the concept of daylight strategic bombing the stigma of the wanton destruction of German cities and the callous slaughter of thousands of German noncombatants.

Chapter 15

Victory:
(December 16, 1944–May 9, 1945)

In my opinion, Germany has been more completely
destroyed than any nation since Carthage. I believe from
now on that increasing evidence will become available to
the public as to the effect of the strategic bombing on
German War capacity.[1]

—Spaatz to Lovett, May 2, 1945

From December 16, 1944, when the Germans opened their counteroffensive
in the Ardennes, to May 9, 1945, when the Germans surrendered to the Soviets
in Berlin, Spaatz continued to direct the forces under his command toward the
goal of victory. His twofold mission remained as defined at the Casablanca
Conference in January 1943: the support of the Allied ground forces, when
required, and the strategic bombing of Germany to bring about "the progressive
destruction and dislocation of the German military, industrial and economic system and the undermining of the morale of the German people to a point where
their capacity for armed resistance is fatally weakened."[2] Until mid-January
1945, Spaatz concentrated on ground support in order to help defeat the last
major German offensive on the Western Front. After mid-January, he oversaw
the culmination of the American portion of the Combined Bomber Offensive,
which brought German industry to a standstill and witnessed the most controversial bombing raid in the European war, the bombing of Dresden.

The Battle of the Bulge

On the morning of December 16, 1944, three German armies, the *Seventh
Army*, the *Fifth Panzer* and *Sixth SS Panzer Armies*, began the Ardennes counteroffensive. German commando units, some dressed in Allied uniforms, spread

confusion behind Allied lines. The Germans had deliberately waited for a period of severe weather to shield them from overwhelming Allied superiority in the air. Carefully husbanded fuel, enough for only a few days of operations, allowed the German armies to advance and the Luftwaffe to fly. When the weather cleared, the Luftwaffe employed the last of its muscle to aid the ground troops and defend them from Allied air power.

The surprise and confusion among American front-line troops was echoed at Allied Headquarters in Paris, where wild rumors concerning Germans in Allied uniforms circulated. Spaatz directed that all units under his control tighten security against sabotage. His Deputy for Administration, Maj. Gen. Hugh Knerr, even suggested that a restricted zone of blocked-off streets, sentry boxes, and pillboxes be set up around the USSTAF Headquarters complex in Paris.[3] Apparently this scheme was not carried out. As Spaatz later admitted to Arnold, "The offensive undertaken by the Germans on December 16th undoubtedly caught us off balance."[4]

Spaatz responded decisively to the need of the Allied ground forces for additional air support. He directed two of the Eighth's fighter groups to move immediately to the Continent, if they could find proper air fields, and place themselves under Vandenberg's operational control. Spaatz also designated the Eighth's 2d Air Division, which had begun to specialize in Gee-H radar bombing, to act as a fire brigade that Vandenberg could call directly, without first contacting USSTAF or SHAEF. Gee-H, with a range of 300 miles, employed an airborne transmitter and two ground beacons to fix a target's position; it had a bombing accuracy much superior to H2X alone.[5] The remaining two-thirds of the heavy-bomber force would attack targets west of the Rhine, even if they obtained only temporary results, until the emergency ended.[6]

Despite vile weather, which included thick ground fog in England that made bomber takeoffs and landings extremely treacherous, the Eighth sent out missions on December 18 and 19. On December 18, only 411 of 985 bombers bombed their targets; all used radar. The next day, 312 heavy bombers bombed tactical targets behind German lines; again, all of them employed radar—H2X for most of the targets and Gee-H for eight targets. On December 23, the Allies received help from the east—not the start of the Soviet winter offensive, but an area of high pressure, called by meteorologists a "Russian high," which cleared away the clouds, providing five days of flying weather. The next day the Eighth put up every bomber that could fly—2,046—and dropped 5,052 tons of bombs, all visually, on airfields and communications centers in western Germany, its largest single-day totals of the war.[7] For the first four days of clear weather the Luftwaffe vainly sought to keep the Allied air forces from scourging the *Wehrmacht's* supply lines and railheads. The Eighth's fighters alone claimed 160 German aircraft, a figure added to the 69 claimed on December 23. The Eighth's losses for December 24 to December 28 amounted to 21 bombers and 25 fighters, while it dispatched 4,535 bomber sorties and released 11,245 tons of ordnance.[8] On December 26, at a high-level staff meeting at SHAEF in Paris, Spaatz urged the ground forces to follow up the air attack as soon as possible, saying, "The Hun can't take the pounding we have been giving him in the midriff indefinitely."[9] The whirlwind of bombs continued to fall. Between December 16 and January 4, the Eighth and Ninth Air Forces dropped 35,747 tons on tactical targets.[10] For the month of January the Eighth flattened marshaling yards and communications centers west and east of the Rhine with 24,496 tons of high explosives and incendiaries.[11]

The good flying days of the Russian high enabled the Eighth and Ninth Air Forces to bomb airfields, communication centers, supply dumps, and enemy troops so fiercely that the German attack lost much of its mobility. The lack of mobility would soon contribute to supply shortages among German front-line troops. Allied ground forces halted the Germans five miles short of the Meuse River on December 24, and by December 26 the Americans had relieved the surrounded U.S. 101st Airborne Division defending the key road junction at Bastogne. Allied bombing began to take an increasing toll; on December 27 a German unit reported that Allied heavy bombers had left the key crossroads of St. Vith impassable.[12] In the meantime, on December 22, Patton's Third Army had begun a counterattack along the southern flank of the Bulge and made steady progress. Although much stubborn defensive fighting on the ground lay ahead as the Allies reduced the Bulge, the German attack had crested and had begun to recede. The crisis passed. The defenders on the ground stopped the offensive, but air eased their task by strangling the enemy's supply lines. The AAF official history put the claims of the Eighth and Ninth Air Forces for destruction in the period of the Bulge (December 16, 1944, through January 31, 1945) at 11,378 motor transport vehicles, 1,161 tanks and armored fighting vehicles, 507 locomotives, 6,266 railroad cars, 472 gun positions, 974 rail cuts, 421 road cuts, and 36 bridges.[13]

The British Government Code and Cypher School (GC and CS), which decrypted the German Enigma codes and supplied high-grade signal intelligence (ULTRA), provided information beyond price. The Allied leadership had continuous access to copious and immediate high-grade signal intelligence. Never before in the history of warfare have one side's moves been known so quickly and accurately to the other. In effect, Allied generals almost sat in their enemies' command posts. They knew the daily attack plans, ration strength, and supply status of every large German unit. They knew when and where the German spearheads ran short of fuel and ammunition. And they knew German appreciations of Allied actions.[14] *Wehrmacht* and Luftwaffe signals were an open book to their foes.

On December 18, within six hours of its dispatch, Allied airmen knew of the Germans' intention to give fighter cover against Allied fighter-bombers and heavy bombers attacking the *Wehrmacht* spearheads. Four days later the Allies learned of orders to have the fighters engage four-engine bombers; a subsequent

The Battle of the Bulge. The flight line *(above)* at a P-51 base in England, winter, 1944–1945; an Eighth Air Force fighter *(below)* taking on a German locomotive, January 1945. Wide-ranging and persistent attacks on *Reichsbahn* rolling stock added to the enemy's difficulties during its last large-scale offensive effort in the west.

message revealed heavy losses. By December 26, decryptions betrayed the Luftwaffe's intention to suspend its policy of attacking heavy bombers and to switch to the defense of German spearheads and thrust lines. On December 24, RAF Air Intelligence (AI) concluded from its analysis of operational signal intelligence that the Luftwaffe had committed all available forces to a do-or-die effort in which it had suffered heavy losses and that if its current scale of activity continued, its efficiency might rapidly decline. Three days later AI observed that Luftwaffe forces supporting the offensive had so lost in serviceability and strength that they could no longer carry on without a period of bad weather for recuperation.[15]

At the end of December, Spaatz visited Bradley's and Patton's headquarters. He and Bradley discussed the nature and extent of the strategic air forces' commitment to halting the German attack. Bradley expressed satisfaction and wanted more massive raids and bombing of communications centers behind German lines.[16] They both agreed to play down several incidents in which bombs fell short, one of which was the bombing of the U.S. 4th Armored Division Headquarters, and the shooting down of many Allied planes by friendly fire.[17] By not emphasizing those incidents, they apparently hoped to defuse hard feelings in both branches of the service.

The Luftwaffe's increased effort in ground support during the battle had prompted Allied ground troops to fire at all overhead aircraft. On Janaury 1, as Spaatz flew to Hodges's headquarters in Liege, his own plane came under heavy, but fortunately inaccurate, antiaircraft fire from Patton's troops.

Spaatz found that Hodges, too, wanted to continue hitting communications centers and marshaling yards in preference to carpet bombing in front of the troops. Spaatz left Liege with the impression that the strain of the offensive had begun to tell on Hodges. Spaatz commented in his Command Diary, "Hodges and staff did not make a very good impression and seem to lack aggressiveness."[18] Bradley recorded a similar thought.[19] In his meetings with the generals, Spaatz had urged them to attack immediately, while the Germans still reeled under the full weight of nine days of successfully applied Allied air power.[20]

On New Year's Day, Spaatz saw firsthand the work of the Luftwaffe. That morning a force of more than 800 German fighters, employing strict radio silence, had swept over sixteen Allied airfields in Belgium and Holland. They destroyed 196 airplanes, 36 of them American, but suffered catastrophic losses, mostly as a result of Allied antiaircraft fire and their own poor training. Galland, the German fighter chief, reported 220 planes lost, many of them piloted by irreplaceable instructor pilots and veteran squadron leaders.[21] That afternoon, Spaatz landed at two of the attacked fields; he observed no damage at either.

The next day, he returned to Paris where he discussed his trip with Bedell Smith, Eisenhower's Chief of Staff, who agreed that the ground forces ought to move forward immediately. That evening, Spaatz had Air Marshal Robb, SHAEF Deputy Chief of Staff for Air, to dinner. Robb recruited Spaatz into a scheme, apparently hatched in Eisenhower's headquarters and in the British Chiefs of Staff, to bring British Field Marshal Harold R.L.G. Alexander, Allied Commander in Chief in the Mediterranean, into the European Theater as Commander of the Allied Ground Forces under Eisenhower. Spaatz's agreement, based on his knowledge of Alexander, his disapproval of Montgomery, and his recent unsatisfactory trip to the front, reflected his frustration with the ground situation.[22]

Eisenhower himself waffled on the issue. On January 3, after talking to Churchill and the British Chief of the Imperial General Staff, Field Marshal Alan Brooke, he appeared to be receptive to the idea, but Marshall, the U.S. Army Chief of Staff, vehemently opposed it. At the end of the month, when the two men met in southern France before the meetings of the CCS at Malta and of Churchill-Stalin-Roosevelt at Yalta, Marshall told Eisenhower that he would resign rather than accept a British ground commander. Given the now dominant position of the Americans in the Anglo-American coalition, Marshall's opposition decided the matter. At the subsequent Malta/Yalta meetings, however, the Americans did agree that Tedder and Alexander should exchange positions in mid-March. But by then the military situation had so changed that Churchill and Brooke accepted Eisenhower's decision to leave Tedder and Alexander in place.[23] If Tedder had gone to the Mediterranean, Eisenhower wanted Spaatz as his air commander in chief.[24]

The Battle of the Bulge, an important chapter in the annals of U.S. ground forces, also had an important effect on the U.S. strategic bombing effort. First, as a result of the battle, the Germans suffered heavy losses of conventional propeller-driven fighters. In the first three weeks of the Ardennes counteroffensive, the Americans alone claimed more than 600 German aircraft destroyed.[25] These losses, combined with a massive transfer of aircraft to the Eastern Front to oppose the Soviets' winter offensive, which began on January 12, relegated the Western Front to the status of a secondary air theater for the Luftwaffe. In addition, the Luftwaffe imposed a strict conservation policy on its remaining planes, forbidding them to fly over enemy territory or to engage heavy bombers in any but the most favorable circumstances.[26] Luftwaffe inactivity gave the Eighth and Fifteenth Air Forces even greater operational freedom.

Second, the Battle of the Bulge diverted the Eighth Air Force from strategic operations. Between December 16, 1944, and January 8, 1945, the Eighth flew only one strategic mission—on December 31, one-third of the force attacked oil targets deep in Germany. Fortunately, the Fifteenth Air Force picked up much of the slack; from December 17 through January 8, it made eleven attacks on German and Austrian oil targets.[27] Nonetheless, strategic targets in central Germany gained some respite.

Third, the Battle of the Bulge delivered the coup de grace to the *Reichsbahn*. The previous autumn's bombing had exhausted the repair crews and all stores of spare parts and repair material. The system had already begun to falter, but the

Battle of the Bulge opened an unstaunchable wound. The *Reichsbahn* strained every nerve and used every expedient to keep the troop and supply trains flowing to the offensive. The priority given the *Wehrmacht* drained the entire system. Thousands of cars were lost and even more mired in the huge backlogs created by poor coordination due to attacks on marshaling yards and disruption of telecommunications. By the end of the offensive, car placings (the forming of incoming rail cars into separate outgoing trains) in Germany stood at only one-third of what they had been during the same period in 1944. The *Reichsbahn Direktorate* of Essen and Cologne, the main shipping points of hard coal and brown coal respectively, fell to 39 percent and 16 percent of normal.[28] Trains cluttered yards and sidings. By Christmas, 1,100 trains and 75,000 to 100,000 cars stood idle.[29] That number rose to 1,994 by January 18. This situation contributed to ballooning car turnaround times up from six and a half days per car in November 1943 to twenty days by January 1945. At times, even the highest-priority "Blitz" shipments were idled.[30] Conditions were so bad that the *Reichsbahn* even resorted to the self-defeating expedient of purposely derailing trains to clear the tracks. On January 19, the system embargoed all freight everywhere excepting *Wehrmacht* and coal traffic. The resulting elimination of all piece-goods traffic sounded the death knell for any coordinated industrial effort.[31]

The paralysis of the transportation system spread quickly to the industrial network. The disruption caused by the Ardennes air attacks shut down three major power plants in the Ruhr for lack of coal. Transmission lines downed by air attacks broke the region into power islands, halting production at plants that lacked their own generating facilities. Delivery of iron ore to the Ruhr's smelters plummeted by 80 percent in December, raw iron production sagged by 71 percent the same month, raw steel slid by 66 percent in January, and rolling mill activity collapsed to 20 percent of the average during the third quarter of 1943. In central Germany the factories slowed. At the Krupp-Gruson Werke, shell and gun forgings shops closed from the lack of natural gas because the local utility company had no coal. Tank production declined from 114 in October to 65 in January for lack of parts. In December 1944, the ball-bearing industry collapsed, the victim of its own dispersion, which had made it extremely vulnerable to transportation disruption.[32]

Production of weapons tumbled. Thanks to the heavy issue of weapons to the *Volkssturm,* or people's militia, and to the units involved in the Ardennes offensive, which were not replaced by the factories and the rail lines, by January 1945 *Wehrmacht* stocks of K-98 rifles went from ten to three days' supply; stocks of Type 44 assault rifles dropped from four months' to three weeks' supply; and stocks of the 88mm antitank gun declined from one month's to two weeks' supply. Supplies to combat units fell by 11 percent compared with December.[33]

The Allies, however, did not fully appreciate the magnitude of the disaster inflicted by their transportation bombing. For instance, they did not decrypt the large commercial traffic of 20,000 weekly messages. Not until late February did a report commissioned by Bottomley demonstrate the value of this traffic, which contained a plethora of information on the German coal famine. On February 28, Spaatz and Portal received a fresh commercial intercept detailing the increase in unshipped coal tonnage at the mines and the closings of plants because of transport disorganization.[34]

Higher level GC and CS interceptions partially filled in the picture. In mid-January, German *Army Group G* reported the condition of the rail system as "very strained" in the Mainz area, "strained" at Cologne, "extremely strained" in the Saarbrucken district, and "unsatisfactory" in the Karlsruhe district. On January 28, the Armaments Ministry complained of plant closings from the lack of coal. In a February 3 decryption, the Japanese naval attaché spoke of the Germans' inability to move commodities such as coal from their production points, which adversely affected various war supplies. RAF Air Intelligence collected, by the beginning of February, massive evidence of coal shortages from signals sent by local armaments production coordinators. By February 8, the British Joint Intelligence Committee (JIC) suggested that halting all coal shipments from the Ruhr would stop rail transport and have "effects as important as oil."[35] It made little difference; by February coherent economic activity in Germany had ceased.[36]

As for ammunition, a January 18 decryption of a January 10 message divulged a general ammunition shortage due to raw material shortages and production and transportation difficulties. Another decryption two days later advised that, in certain cases, even worthwhile artillery targets would have to be passed over. On March 2, a decryption revealed an order limiting expenditure of 88mm flak ammunition to exceptional circumstances because of serious supply deficiencies.

Understandably, the Allies did not consider the woes of their opponents so much as they did their own difficulties. Hence, the counteroffensive stimulated unjustified pessimism within the higher echelons of the Allied command. Allied commanders had not lost their faith in ultimate victory, but they now perceived the road to victory as steeper than they had previously thought.

The Battle of the Bulge brought about a reappraisal of long-range goals in USSTAF. Two weeks after the offensive started, Arnold, reflecting the thinking in Washington, wrote to Spaatz, "General Marshall . . . has been pressing in Washington for any and every plan to bring increased effort against the German forces. . . . Periods of about *sixty days* have been discussed" [emphasis in original].[37] Arnold went on to state that he could not view "with complacency" estimates that the war in Europe would not end until the summer of 1945.

In Paris, meanwhile, Spaatz and USSTAF had adopted a somewhat longer perspective. By the end of 1944, they foresaw a war of several more months duration if strategic air power did not return to the oil campaign and if German jet production continued unabated. The specter of hundreds of twin-jet-engine

Bomb damage from Ninth Air Force P-47s to a rail yard near Cologne, Germany.

Me 262s, each armed with four 30mm cannons, launched against the slower American escort fighters and lumbering heavy bombers haunted Spaatz's calculations.

A particularly hair-raising report from his chief of intelligence, Brig. Gen. George C. McDonald, greatly impressed Spaatz when it crossed his desk on January 3, 1945. This report, titled "Allied Air Supremacy and German Jet Planes," opened by stating dramatically,

> Maintenance of Allied Air Supremacy over Europe in 1945 is confronted by a serious threat. This threat menaces both continuance of our Strategic bombardment and the superiority, both offensively and defensively, of the fighter bomber cover under which our troops fight. This threat is the opposition of a large and increasing German jet plane fighter force, sustained by rapidly expanding capacity for . . . production. . . .[38]

McDonald expressed little doubt of the Germans' ability to have, at the most conservative estimate, 300 to 400 jets available for daily use by July 1, 1945, provided "they are given time and freedom from counter-measures." Because the jets did not run on high-octane aviation fuel but on kerosene and other lesser-quality fuels, the bombing of oil facilities could not immobilize them as it had conventional fighters. Although Allied bombing had halted at least 80 percent of production at the large and complex hydrogenation and Fischer-Tropsch process synthetic plants, which produced aviation and other high-quality fuels, synthetic plants producing low-grade benzoil were more numerous, more widely scattered, smaller, and less complex. Their production had only fallen by half, as had the domestic refining of crude oil. In all, German production of finished oil products declined from 900,000 tons in January 1944 to 303,000 tons in December.[39] But a small amount of almost any type of fuel would suffice for the Me 262. According to the report, this situation left the Allies two options: (1) either ignore the threat of the jets and gamble on the war's ending before July 1 or (2) initiate immediate countermeasures at considerable cost to the current bombing effort.

Given the lowered expectations prevalent in the Allied High Command at the turn of the year, McDonald's report recommended bombing the jet-engine plants and the airfields associated with jet testing, training, and operation. McDonald pointed to the successful dispersal and underground placement of German jet assembly plants, and warned that since the same treatment of jet engine plants was surely imminent, bombing had to begin immediately, not in three months' time.[40] He noted, "The question is not so much whether we can afford to initiate counter measures against jet development as whether we can afford not to. Such a program will be expensive for us in the dearest of all our resources which is visual bombing weather." McDonald realized that his suggestion meant the diversion of substantial bomb tonnage from other strategic targets, but he added:

> Failure to take every possible precaution to neutralize this threat now may gravely compromise the capabilities of our entire bombardment effort within a few months. What is more, Allied troops have never fought successfully under anything less than overwhelming air superiority. The German jet program is capable of reversing that superiority by mid-summer.[41]

Finally, McDonald cautioned that "the Strategic Air Forces cannot be responsible for the maintenance of Allied Aerial Supremacy over Europe unless they are given sufficient freedom from other demands to allocate the necessary proportion of visual strategic bombing against German jet development," and he requested a new directive making the priority of jet targets equal to that of oil.[42]

This report had an almost galvanic effect on Spaatz, who, with Doolittle, visited Eisenhower on January 5 to recount their worries about the jets, and to request permission to begin bombing "in the near future." They had estimated that 10,000 tons of visual bombing would set back the German program three months, which was "absolutely necessary to enable our own jet production to catch up." In addition, they emphasized the reported buildups in the Germans' production of oil, construction of submarines, and manufacture of armored fighting vehicles.[43]

As mentioned, the concentration of the Eighth Air Force on tactical bombing related to the Battle of the Bulge had slightly eased the pressure on Germany's oil industry. Also, early in 1945, new mass-produced, faster, snorkle-breathing U-boats had begun to enter service. These new submarines might allow the Nazis to successfully reopen the Battle of the Atlantic, jeopardizing the Allies' supply lines from the United States. The Allies had also completely lost their capability to decipher U-boat signals;[44] a change in German code procedure had deprived the Allied navies of much of their knowledge of the location and intentions of the enemy. This loss accounted in part for the panic in Allied naval circles that led to pressure on the airmen to bomb submarine construction yards. As for tanks, intelligence indicated that, upon manufacture, they reached the front in less than a month. The Germans had suffered severe tank losses in the Bulge, and the anticipated Soviet winter offensive would cause more; thus a campaign against tank plants was essential in order to hamper the Germans' ability to replace losses. All these factors, Spaatz and Doolittle told Eisenhower, meant that the Eighth should return to strategic targeting at once. Eisenhower disagreed; the critical battle situation, he insisted, still required all the strategic bomber help that Spaatz could spare.[45]

Spaatz, however, did not give up. Latest intelligence, he said, had shown that the Germans would produce more oil than their minimum requirements in January, if unmolested by the Eighth. He probably expressed the general feeling in USSTAF that continuing to bomb marshaling yards and other tactical targets west of the Rhine would only lengthen the war[46] by relieving German industry of the pressure of strategic bombardment.

On January 6, with Bedell Smith's support, Spaatz gained Eisenhower's permission for two-thirds of the bomber force to resume oil attacks as a top priority, followed by tank plants and jet production, if necessary.[47] The other third of his force, the Gee-H-equipped 2d Air Division, would assist the ground forces. Three days later, on January 9, Spaatz gained Smith's consent to bomb enemy jet production at the same priority visual bombing level as oil.[48]

Spaatz's concern about over commitment to tactical bombing reached the newly constructed Pentagon in Washington. In a pair of "Eyes Only" letters to Arnold, both dated January 7, Spaatz expressed the general pessimism and fear of German jets prevalent within USSTAF. In one letter he wrote: "Our estimate of the situation concerning the whole German war proposition does not lead up to the conclusion that German strength will crack in the near future." As for oil, Spaatz's intelligence estimates indicated that the Germans could operate along defensive lines if they practiced the strictest economy. He predicted German resistance to the bitter end and concluded: "Unless our ground armies succeed in obtaining a significant victory over German ground armies west of the Rhine in the reasonably near future, it will be necessary to reorient ourselves and prepare for a long, drawn out war."[49]

In the second letter, Spaatz addressed Arnold's fear of the growth of the Germans' conventional fighter force. Arnold had even suggested that the CCS might find it necessary "to revise current directives and to consider seriously the issuance of an overriding directive aimed at reconquest of the Luftwaffe."[50] Spaatz replied, "All of us here feel, however, that the distinct threat is from the German jet fighter rather than a buildup in strength of the [Bf] 109s and [FW] 190s. All past experience shows that our fighter force can amply take care of any buildup of 109s and 190s."[51]

At a SHAEF meeting on January 9, Spaatz noted that the Bulge had kept bombing concentrated in the battle area, allowing unhampered jet aircraft construction. His revised intelligence estimates showed greater-than-expected growth of jet production and predicted that the Germans might have 300 to 400 jets in operation by April. Jet assembly factories would have to be dealt with very soon in order to push back production three months.[52] A day later Spaatz sent one of the theater's experts on German and British jets back to Washington to brief Arnold. In his cover letter, Spaatz reiterated, "The jet airplane represents a very grave danger to us and could cause great trouble if employed in the proper manner."[53]

On January 11 at the Weekly Air Commanders' Conference, Spaatz, Anderson, and Doolittle reviewed the strategic bombing situation. "From the strategic point of view," lamented Anderson, "the picture is very sad!" The strategic air forces "were paying a tremendous price by concentrating on helping ground forces." Now oil, ball bearings, aircraft factories, and submarine yards would all have to be hit again. Doolittle backed up Anderson "100% or possibly even more." Unless the bombing of strategic targets resumed at once, German jets would prevent deep-penetration raids after July. Spaatz took note of Eisenhower's agreement to release two-thirds of the Eighth to attack oil and jets. Then he suggested specific U-boat targets as well as armored fighting vehicles.[54] Support for hitting the vehicle plants had originated in Eisenhower's headquarters[55] and reflected the needs of the ground forces. Spaatz probably added them as part of his agreement with Eisenhower allowing USSTAF partial resumption of the strategic offensive.

"Directive No. 3 for the Strategic Air Forces in Europe," agreed upon by Spaatz and Bottomley on January 12 and issued January 16, formalized the new strategic priorities. In his cover letter to Arnold, Spaatz stated simply, "A new directive is necessary at this time since we have recently had to revise our estimate of V-Day [Victory Day in Europe], and consequently must include the attack of target systems with a longer range application."[56] After retaining oil, transportation, and important industrial areas as priority targets, it added both the authorization to employ "the necessary amount of strategic effort" required to neutralize jets and the instruction that the U-boat organization "will be attacked whenever possible by marginal effort or incidental to operations covered by the proceeding priorities."[57] In this case, the marginal effort would provide a substantial number of bombs for submarines because missions diverting from visual targets could obtain excellent H2X resolution from coastal targets. The Air Staff in Washington found the directive "a very much too conservative approach to the problem." They asked Spaatz to consider raising the priority of U-boats and ground support.[58] Portal, who did not agree that jets constituted a threat because he did not believe that the war would drag on, accepted the directive as temporary. He hoped to revise it during the CCS meetings at the end of January.[59]

THUNDERCLAP and Dresden

Even as Spaatz and Bottomley issued Directive No. 3, events had begun to overtake it. The Soviets opened their winter offensive on January 12. Overwhelming the German defenders, they drove hundreds of thousands of German refugees before them, conquered the Silesian industrial area (Germany's last intact, unbombed production base, which also included large coal deposits), and reached the Oder River, forty-five miles east of Berlin, by January 31. As the Red offensive steamrolled forward, the Western Allies prepared to renew their own offensive. In the meantime, the Soviet and Anglo-American high commands and political leadership finished plans for a series of American, Anglo-American, and Tripartite conferences at Marseilles, Malta, and Yalta. The conjunction of these events produced an aberration in strategic priorities that led directly to the bombing of Dresden and the loss of at least 35,000 lives.

One impetus behind the Allies' decision to bomb cities in eastern Germany, including Dresden, stemmed from a desire on the part of the British and Americans to support the Soviet offensive by knocking out transportation centers serving the German Eastern Front, in order to prevent the rapid shifting of forces among sectors along it and the transfer of troops from the west to the east. Berlin, as the administrative center of the nation and the nerve center and transportation nexus for a large section of the Eastern Front, would be an obvious target of any effort to assist the Soviets' drive. Accordingly, on January 16 Spaatz's chief of staff ordered Doolittle to take a new look at Operation THUNDERCLAP and begin planning its execution.[60]

As mentioned in Chapter 12, the Allies first conceived of THUNDERCLAP as a combined Bomber Command-USSTAF daylight mission on Berlin in response to the German V-1 offensive during the summer of 1944. Because of opposition from Spaatz and others, it had been planned but not carried out. By early September 1944, USSTAF planners had filed it away for reconsideration when the situation in Germany deteriorated to the extent that one large blow on Berlin might shock its government into surrender. With the Germans' Ardennes counteroffensive turned back and the Soviets' shattering of the front in the east, Spaatz must have believed that the crucial moment might come soon.

The British, too, began to consider THUNDERCLAP. On January 22, Air Commodore Sidney O. Bufton, Director of Bomber Operations and Chairman of the Combined Strategic Targeting Committee (a combined USSTAF and British Air Staff agency that selected specific strategic targets and ranked them for bombing by the strategic air forces) suggested to Air Marshal Bottomley the launching of THUNDERCLAP while the Soviet offensive was in full stride.[61] He feared that the psychological moment would pass if it was not implemented before the Soviets' momentum slowed.[62] The Assistant Chief of the Air Staff for Operations, agreed, noting, "The German radio has recently shown signs of hysteria in broadcasts to the people, and a heavy air attack on the capital and other big towns now might well ruin already shaky morale."[63]

THUNDERCLAP soon gained adherents on the British JIC, which, while discounting its effects on morale, suggested that it be adopted directly to assist the Soviet offensive. In a detailed examination of its possible repercussions, the JIC, on January 25, 1945, observed that it would "create great confusion, interfere with the orderly movement of troops to the front and hamper the German military and administrative machine."[64] The committee suggested that attacks on Berlin might have a "political value in demonstrating to the Russians, in the best way open to us, a desire on the part of the British and Americans to assist them in the present battle."[65]

Also on January 25, Harris and Spaatz both received notice that the time for THUNDERCLAP had come. Bottomley, after perusing the JIC's findings, telephoned Harris to discuss them. Harris suggested supplementing the main attack on Berlin with strikes against Chemnitz, Leipzig, and Dresden because these cities, like Berlin, would have had their vital communication links stretched thin by refugees from the east. They had also been relatively untouched by Harris's area bombing campaign. Bottomley and Harris agreed that Spaatz must be consulted. Meanwhile in Paris, at the Weekly Allied Air Commanders' Conference, the airmen examined the possible uses "of the Heavies in the new military situation." At the end of their discussion Tedder asked whether the time had come to stage Operation THUNDERCLAP; presumably, he had either read the JIC report or had heard about it from Bufton directly. Spaatz agreed, saying that he "felt that this operation should be held in instant readiness, but not ordered until the Russians were either on the Oder in strength, or across it." Tedder accepted Spaatz's recommendation.[66]

Spaatz's consent to THUNDERCLAP did not mean his wholehearted adoption of terror-bombing. As will be seen, he did not believe that THUNDERCLAP would end the war, although he did feel that a big raid on Berlin would demonstrate solidarity with the Soviets and disrupt the city's capability to aid the defense of the Eastern Front. Spaatz was following events there closely. The day before the Air Commanders' meeting he had told a SHAEF meeting, "I don't think we are paying nearly enough attention to what is happening in the East. We are using the wrong end of the telescope."[67]

On the evening of January 25, the Prime Minister jumped into the question of bombing cities in eastern Germany. Part of his concern may have sprung from a British Joint Intelligence Subcommittee report, prepared for him alone, on "German Strategy and Capacity to Resist." The document predicted that Germany might collapse by mid-April if the Soviet offensive overran them at their eastern defenses before they could consolidate. Alternatively, the Germans might hold out until November if they could stop the Soviets from conquering Silesia.[68] Any help given the Russians on the Eastern Front would shorten the conflict. Churchill asked the Secretary of War for Air, Archibald Sinclair, what plans the RAF had made for "blasting the Germans in their retreat from Breslau."[69] Sinclair passed Churchill's inquiry to Portal. Portal, hard at work preparing for the coming Malta and Yalta meetings, replied cautiously that oil, subject to the demands of the jet assembly factories and submarine yards, should continue to have top priority. However, he reluctantly allowed that the Allies should use the "available effort in one big attack on Berlin and attacks on Dresden, Leipzig, Chemnitz, or any other cities where a severe blitz will not only cause confusion in the evacuation from the east but will hamper the movement of troops from the west."[70] Portal further recommended that the CCS, Spaatz, and Tedder all have a chance to approve the new suggestion.

Portal's reply failed to assuage the Prime Minister, who shot back:

> I did not ask you last night about plans for harrying the German retreat from Breslau. On the contrary, I asked whether Berlin, and no doubt other large cities in East Germany, should not now be considered attractive targets. I am glad that this is under 'examination.' Pray report to me tomorrow what is going to be done.[71]

This sarcastic missive prodded Bottomley, who had begun to act as Chief of the Air Staff because of Portal's scheduled departure for the Mediterranean, to write to Harris, enclosing the JIC report and informing him of Portal's and Churchill's desires. "I am therefore to request that subject to the qualifications stated above, and as soon as moon and weather conditions allow, you will undertake such attacks with the particular object of exploiting the confused conditions which are likely to exist in the above mentioned cities during the successful Russian advance."[72] Bottomley issued this unequivocal order before consulting with either Spaatz or the CCS. He also informed Churchill that operations against cities in eastern Germany would begin as soon as conditions permitted (the moon would not allow deep penetrations until February 3 or 4).[73]

The next day, January 28, Spaatz flew to England to celebrate the third anniversary of the Eighth's formation. He lunched with Bottomley, at which time the two no doubt discussed bombing policy. Spaatz may also have spoken to Portal before the latter left for the Malta conference.[74] Spaatz did not agree to bomb any cities in eastern Germany except Berlin. He verbally gave to Doolittle the following priorities: (1) oil (visual), (2) Berlin (visual or blind), (3) the Ruhr, (4) Munich, and (5) Hamburg. Spaatz further ordered the Eighth's fighters (1) to cover the bombers, (2) to strafe oil targets, and (3) to interrupt "traffic from West to East toward Berlin and Dresden."[75] This verbal order implies that although Spaatz was sympathetic to the desire to help the Soviets, by limiting, if possible, German west to east military movement, he rejected the bombing of cities merely to produce more refugees.* This order clarified a previous one given to Doolittle on January 24, that stated, "Anticipating that the enemy will attempt to reinforce the Russian Front by rail movement of units which have been engaged recently on the Western Front, it is desired that your fighters be used until further notice to assist in an interdiction program by strafing rail lines."[76] Also on January 28, Spaatz's headquarters delivered THUNDERCLAP's plan to the Eighth Air Force. Among the primary aiming points were the Air Ministry, Gestapo headquarters, and the Alexanderplatz railway station, all in the governmental and administrative center of Berlin. At this point USSTAF still envisaged full implementation of the plan, including a follow-up raid by the RAF on the night after the American bombing.[77] After meeting with Spaatz, Bottomley visited Tedder in Paris. According to Tedder they agreed to maintain oil as top priority when visual conditions existed, with first Berlin, then Leipzig, and, finally, Dresden as the next targets.[78]

In the meantime Spaatz had already put in train a large operation over Berlin. He insisted, however, that this attack have specific aiming points such as "industrial plants, Administrative Headquarters or, possibly, railway stations."[79] Thus, he confirmed the AAF's policy of at least attempting to hit strategic targets rather than resorting to intentional area bombing.

On January 31, Bottomley radioed the results of his meeting with Spaatz to Portal in Malta.[80] The next day Spaatz read the same message at the Weekly Allied Air Commanders' Conference, where no one present questioned it.[81] According to an intelligence briefing at the same conference, the German *Sixth S.S. Panzer Army* had left the Bulge in the west and was presumed headed toward the Eastern Front. In the message, Bottomley, after noting first priority to the main synthetic oil plants, stated, "Next in order of priority for Air Forces operating in the UK is attack of Berlin, Leipzig, Dresden and associated cities where heavy attack will cause great confusion in civilian evacuation from the east and hamper movement of reinforcements from other fronts."[82]

Like all the agreements between Spaatz and Bottomley since September 1944, this one on bombing priorities did not mean that Spaatz accepted every word as policy for USSTAF. Rather, it represented the usual compromise according to

---

* I have found no records in Spaatz's, Doolittle's, or the Eighth Air Force's files indicating a desire to bomb for the sake of producing "refugees."

Maj. Gen. Laurence S.
Kuter, Assistant Chief of
Staff for Plans, U.S. Army
Air Forces, 1945.

capabilities as described in prior directives. The Eighth would attempt to bomb strategic targets in Berlin, either visually or with blind-bombing techniques, while its fighters, after flying escort, would descend to the deck and harass west-to-east rail traffic. Spaatz had agreed only to continue long-standing procedures. As for the RAF, it also continued its long-standing policy of night area bombing.

Even as Spaatz agreed to this new directive, the subject of strategic air targets became one of the topics of discussion at the Malta and Yalta conferences between the Allies fighting Germany. A severe heart attack in early January had temporarily removed Arnold from AAF affairs, thus depriving Marshall of his most trusted and influential air power adviser and leaving the AAF scrambling to fill the leadership void he had opened. Arnold's absence also handicapped the AAF at the Malta/Yalta Conferences. Maj. Gen. Laurence S. Kuter, who attended for him, simply did not have the rank or prestige in those meetings that would have been accorded to Arnold as a matter of course. Kuter wrote to Arnold from Malta, "Without you we are just tolerated from bottom to *top*" [emphasis in original].[83] The AAF at this point had one five-star general, Arnold, but no four-star generals. Whoever headed its delegation would have had at least a two-grade disadvantage compared with the other chiefs, and Kuter had a three-star disadvantage.

Parenthetically, the AAF delegation's lack of stature at the conferences gave Spaatz the chance to strengthen his own role in its internal deliberations. At the Second Quebec Conference he had learned of events only after they had taken

547

place. Spaatz in this case had his own representation within the AAF delegation. On January 27, he sent Maj. Gen. Frederick L. Anderson, his Deputy for Operations, to Malta. Spaatz ensured that Anderson went equipped with briefs presenting USSTAF's views on the employment of U.S. air power in Europe and the Mediterranean. Backed by Eisenhower, Spaatz wanted the Twelfth Air Force transferred to the European Theater. He also instructed Anderson to emphasize the German jet airplane problem in discussions with the CCS.[84] Kuter, who had some doubt as to the legitimacy of Anderson's presence, accepted him into his own delegation.[85]

Events at the Malta Conference reinforced Spaatz's determination to bomb Berlin. General Giles, acting AAF Commander in Arnold's absence, observed in a telegram to Kuter in Malta on January 31, "Indications are that pandemonium reigns in Berlin as a result Soviet advances in the East suggest that you propose action to have all available day and night heavy bomber aircraft directed against Berlin for the next few days with a view towards accentuating this condition."[86] Kuter replied that the Allies had scheduled the operation to begin as soon as weather permitted.[87]

Meanwhile, General Marshall was expressing views on air power contrary to Arnold's. At the first Malta CCS meeting on January 30, Marshall suggested skip-bombing the entrances of underground German manufacturing plants. The airmen present discouraged the idea. Next, he reportedly expressed "his desire to see attacks over all of Germany, by fighters, in accordance with [what] he called the 'Quesada plan,' which he said had been turned down by his air advisers in Washington—and he still didn't know why."[88]

Outside the formal meetings he indicated his desire to bomb Berlin and other cities—without offending the Soviets.[89] Anderson took advantage of these informal discussions to tell Marshall of USSTAF's upcoming plans and pointed out that USSTAF had already rejected the Quesada plan in favor of its own Operation CLARION,[90] a revision of the HURRICANE plan for a mass air assault on lesser communication points throughout Germany.

The Quesada plan, named for its originator, Maj. Gen. Elwood "Pete" Quesada, Commander of the IX Air Support Command, called for the establishment of a force of 500 fighter-bombers controlled by the strategic air forces to bomb and strafe strategic targets and communications far beyond the tactical air force zone immediately on or behind German lines. Quesada had persuaded the Assistant Secretary of War for Air, Robert A. Lovett, to adopt this plan as his own and to campaign vigorously for its acceptance. It was one of, perhaps, the few instances in World War II in which a civilian War Department leader, Lovett, actually supported and advocated an operational plan to the military hierarchy. Lovett called the plan Jeb Stuart, after the Confederate Cavalry leader, and submitted it to Arnold on January 9, 1945.[91]

The plan had a cool reception in AAF Headquarters. The Air Staff noted that the allocation of an additional 500 aircraft plus support troops was "not within our current AAF capabilities." Kuter, speaking for the Air Staff, recommended forwarding the proposal to Spaatz without comment.[92] Because the plan provided no new forces, Spaatz turned it down.[93] He hoped, instead, to implement CLARION. By attacking numerous unbombed transportation/ communications targets in small towns throughout Germany, CLARION sought to demonstrate the might of Allied air power to millions of Germans who had not yet witnessed it, to overwhelm *Reichsbahn* repair crews, and to damage the infrastructure of the transport system. According to Anderson, his exposition of USSTAF's plans, including its rejection of the Jeb Stuart plan, "greatly reassured" Marshall.[94]

Marshall and Anderson also discussed Bottomley's message giving Berlin, Leipzig, and Dresden a priority second only to oil targets. Marshall emphasized that the Soviets must receive notification through current liaison channels (i.e., the U.S. Military Mission in Moscow). He also suggested that, in addition to the attacks on Berlin and other eastern cities, "attacks on Munich would probably be of great benefit because [they] would show the people that are being evacuated to Munich that there is no hope."[95] His suggestion may have come from intelligence reports indicating the evacuation of people and government offices from Berlin to Munich. Although his suggestion did not necessarily imply that Marshall supported indiscriminant bombing of civilians, it certainly indicated his willingness to demoralize the population in general and the Nazi leadership in particular.

The next day Spaatz ordered Twining to attack Munich when weather and other priorities permitted, observing that the city was valuable not only as a communications target but also as a future destination in "Some evacuation [that] may take place from Berlin and Eastern Germany . . . as result of Russian advance."[96] Spaatz also confirmed that the Soviet General Staff had been notified of the Berlin mission.[97] Weather and concentration on oil and on transportation prevented the Fifteenth from carrying out this order. Not until March 24 did the Fifteenth bomb Munich, and then under strategic circumstances much different from those at the beginning of February.

In the message to Twining, Spaatz further noted that the January 31 revision of target priorities represented the usual division of labor between Bomber Command and USSTAF. Spaatz explained that the Eighth would attack Berlin, while Bomber Command had plans "to attack other large communications targets such as Leipzig and Dresden."[98]

The upcoming mission to Berlin, although not THUNDERCLAP (because it was not a combined RAF-AAF round-the-clock attack intended to kill or injure up to 275,000 persons), was out of the ordinary. Doolittle informed Spaatz that he was prepared to undertake THUNDERCLAP, but he vehemently objected to the targets in the center of the city that USSTAF had instructed him to hit: "There are no basically important strictly military targets in the designated area." Doolittle pointed out that to bomb the center of the city accurately he would have to bomb visually and take his forces over almost all the 300 heavy guns defending the city and risk heavy casualties to his low-flying B-24s. He also questioned the effectiveness of THUNDERCLAP or any bombing attack aimed at morale. In his opinion, the people of Berlin would have plenty of warning to take shelter, and "the chances of terrorizing into submission, by merely an increased concentration of bombing, a people who have been subjected to intense bombing for four years is extremely remote." Finally, Doolittle appealed to Spaatz saying, "We will, in what may be one of our last and best remembered operations regardless of its effectiveness, violate the basic American principle of precision bombing of targets of strictly military significance for which our tactics were designed and our crews trained and indoctrinated." He recommended to Spaatz that that area bombing be left to the RAF and that the AAF confine itself to picking precision military targets to assure an effective mission with a minimum of loss.[99] Doolittle felt that the raid definitely went over the line separating incidental damage caused by an attack on military targets and area bombing.

Spaatz sent Doolittle a somewhat ambiguous reply. He did not even mention THUNDERCLAP; instead, he restated his target priorities. Visual attacks on synthetic oil plants, especially those in the Leipzig area, had first priority. He anticipated that any bombing of Berlin would not be visual, but that city "at this time" had a priority second only to oil. In closing, Spaatz observed, "With that in mind, anticipate that you will hit Berlin whenever conditions do not repeat not [sic] indicate possibility of visual bombing of oil targets but do permit operations to Berlin."[100]

On February 2, bad weather forced the Eighth to postpone the Berlin mission by twenty-four hours. Weather forecasts indicated marginal weather with only a chance for a shallow penetration the next day. That evening Spaatz's headquarters called the Eighth and insisted on a Berlin mission. The Eighth's planners drew up two plans: Plan A, a raid by all bomb divisions on Berlin's industrial areas of Spandau, Tegel, and Seimenstadt; and Plan B, raids on oil and transportation targets in western and central Germany, if weather proved too inclement for a deep penetration. The weather deteriorated, ruling out visuals for most of Germany. At USSTAF's insistence the Eighth drew up two more plans: Plan C, "a Berlin attack by all B.D.s [Bombardment Divisions] on the heart of the 'official' city, east of the Tiergarten"; and Plan D, "a similar attack on Dresden."[101] At the same time, Spaatz recommended to Doolittle that his combat camera unit send still and motion picture cameramen on the raid and that he offer a "flight to any qualified correspondents quickly available." Spaatz further recommended that flash news summaries and mission communiques "stress effort to disrupt reinforcement of Eastern Front and increase administrative confusion."[102] This language indicated that he did not intend to carry out THUNDERCLAP. Instead, he wished to emphasize the practical aspects of the raid. Pressure from AAF Headquarters and Marshall must have added to his desire to punish the German capital posthaste.

Doolittle complied, sending four combat cameramen with two groups and a

BBC correspondent with a third. Six more combat cameramen covered the ground activities at three bases. In addition, the Eighth made plans to develop the film quickly and to title it "Inter-Allied Cooperation: Eighth Air Force Strategic Heavies Tactically Bomb Berlin for Soviets." Once the film was developed, the Eighth would rush it to the Combat Camera Unit Headquarters in New York City and offer prints for the newsreels in London. The Eighth even went so far as to take sound film of the target officer, the bomber controller, and the fighter controller briefing Doolittle.[103]

Before he received press recommendations, Doolittle double-checked Spaatz's priorities, informing him via REDLINE that the uncertain weather might allow an attack on Berlin but bad weather at home bases might divert the whole force to the Continent on its return. Then he noted a bare chance of visual conditions over oil targets with an alternative shallow penetration on transportation if all else failed. Almost desperately he asked, "Is Berlin still open to air attack? Do you want priority oil targets hit in preference to Berlin if they definitely become visual? Do you want center of city hit or definitely military targets, such as Spandau, on the Western outskirts?"[104] Spaatz replied by phone annotating his copy of the message, "Told Doolittle to hit oil if visual assured; otherwise, Berlin—center of the city."[105]

Spaatz's answer clearly demonstrates his and the AAF's order of importance in targeting: vital military targets, such as oil, first. He and Doolittle apparently disagreed over what constituted a "definitely military target." From his position close to Eisenhower's headquarters and as chief American airman in Europe, Spaatz would naturally take a more expansive view of military targets than Doolittle, who concentrated solely on operations. To Spaatz, a demonstration of support for the Russians and the disruption of government and rail yards in Berlin were justifiable goals. Doolittle thought the raid would tarnish the AAF's reputation and expose his crews to too much danger for too little return. Spaatz thought it would show the ability of the AAF to cooperate at the highest levels of the alliance while remaining independent. In any case, the raid pushed the definition of military target to the limit, since Spaatz anticipated a nonvisual attack and therefore knew the raid would be wildly inaccurate. Nonetheless, it would seem that Spaatz hoped—albeit faintly—that a heavy raid on Berlin just might crack the morale of the German High Command and produce a surrender. In fact, he admitted at least that much when he acknowledged in 1969 that, "We never had as our target, in foreign [German occupied?] Europe, anything except a military target—except Berlin."[106]

On February 3, 1945, heavy bombers of Eighth Air Force mission No. 817 left their fields and turned to the East, toward Germany. What was their mission? To give incidental aid to the Russians, assuredly yes. To comply with suggestions from Washington and from the Chief of Staff, also yes. But Doolittle's and Spaatz's reactions indicate an additional goal. The mission is unique among the approximately eight hundred Eighth Air Force missions flown under USSTAF's command, for the nature and vehemence of Doolittle's objection to his targets. Eleven days later, for instance, Doolittle made no objection whatsoever to hitting the marshaling yards in Dresden. Nor did he object to hitting the three rail yards in Berlin on February 26. But the whole tenor of his communications with Spaatz shows his perception that this was a terror raid as suggested by THUNDERCLAP.

Likewise, Spaatz's direct orders to "hit the center of the city" are unique. He knew that bombing rail yards meant bombing city centers. He often ordered raids on transportation and other targets within cities, but in no other instance did he specify it explicitly as he did for this mission. On January 16, four days after the start of the Societ offensive, he had THUNDERCLAP delivered to the Eighth Air Force. On January 25, he agreed with Tedder to have the plan ready for instant implementation. On January 30 and February 2, he insisted that Doolittle bomb the THUNDERCLAP targets. It is a reasonable surmise that Spaatz hoped that THUNDERCLAP might succeed.

But Spaatz the air force commander with three years of combat experience differed greatly from Spaatz the Washington planning officer of 1941, who had approved of the morale bombing of Berlin in Air War Plan No. 1 (AWPD/1). By February 1945, airmen such as Harris had repeatedly had to backtrack from assurances about the effectiveness of bombing. If Spaatz were to espouse THUNDERCLAP publicly (it seems never to have been mentioned in the press accounts of the time), he and air power would lose prestige if the operation failed. Apparently, Spaatz judged the chances of the operation's success as low—too low for advance publicity, but high enough to risk the effort of one raid, which he was under pressure to fly in any case. To Spaatz, a man famous at the poker table for his affinity to drawing to an inside straight, the gamble seemed worth it.

The Eighth struck Berlin with more than 1,000 B-17s. Of these, 932, employing mostly visual methods but hampered by the need for violent evasive action to avoid intense flak, dropped 2,279 tons of bombs (250 tons of them incendiaries), losing 23 of their number to flak and none to German fighters. The 1st Air Division, which led the attack, bombed visually. The following 3d Air Division bombed visually with H2X assisting. Post attack photo reconnaissance showed severe damage to the Anhalter rail station and moderate damage to Tempelhof marshaling yard and the Schlesischer rail station (secondary aiming points on the THUNDERCLAP target list). In the center of the city, industrial and residential property suffered severe damage, while government offices along the Wilhelmstrasse, including the Air Ministry, Reich Chancellory, Foreign Office, and Gestapo headquarters (primary aiming points on the THUNDERCLAP target list), received numerous hits.[107] Many bombs missed their aiming points and fell into residential areas of the city.[108] For the tenth and last time the Eighth had bombed the civil and military government area of Berlin.[109] But Doolittle employed only his B-17s; the more vulnerable B-24s, in keeping with Spaatz's verbal directive to send at least 400 bombers against oil whenever possible, went to bomb the Magdeburg synthetic oil plant. Of the 434 B-24s dispatched, 116 bombed the oil plant. Most of the rest bombed the Magdeburg marshaling yard using H2X, when clouds obscured the primary target.

The Germans, in accordance with their standard policy, declared the Berlin raid a terror-bombing attack, and stories in their own and neutral presses claimed 20,000 dead.[110] In this instance the German government and propaganda organs had been hit where they hurt. The AAF official history uncritically accepts a figure of 25,000.[111] Recent figures based on records of the Berlin City Archives and the *Bundesarchiv* indicated losses of 2,893 dead, 729 seriously injured, 1,205 slightly injured, and 120,000 left homeless.[112] Given the relative accuracy of the visual bombing employed and the sparing use of fire bombs by the Eighth on this mission, the lower figures were probably closer to the truth. This mission, unusual because of its accuracy and low volume of fire bombs, apparently struck its assigned targets—rail junctions and the center of government. But the heavy damage inflicted on residential areas showed that, even under favorable conditions, AAF precision attacks on city areas had considerable "spillage" into the civilian population. After-attack reports show that some groups managed to miss the 883 square miles of Berlin altogether.[113] The Berlin Chamber of Commerce called this raid the worst yet experienced and cited heavy damage to the southwestern and southeastern business sections, which caused a significant drop in industrial production.[114]

That this mission greatly aggravated the calamitous situation in Berlin cannot be doubted. There was no proof one way or the other, however, that it significantly delayed rail movement or added to the administrative confusion of the capital. To the world the AAF emphasized both the "direct tactical aid" given to Marshal Zhukov's advancing armies and the damage to rail stations and government buildings.[115] The *New York Times* reported: "The raid was designed to fan the flames of German civilian discontent, but even more important, to snarl the enemy's administrative machinery, disrupt his communications and disorganize his control of the Reich's military forces pouring eastward to man the Oder River line."[116]

Berlin remained centered in the Eighth's sights. On February 5, Spaatz told his staff that Berlin retained its priority after oil and before transportation.[117] Later in the day, he received word from Anderson at Yalta that the Soviets had formally requested air attacks against Berlin and Leipzig.[118] Spaatz replied, "All out effort will be placed against targets mentioned whenever weather conditions permit."[119] In response to Marshall's request the Eighth planned a raid by all three air divisions on the center of Munich on February 5, but it was canceled because of weather. On February 6, weather again caused the cancellation of a trip to Berlin.[120]

That same day Spaatz replied to Arnold's pessimistic note of January 14, informing him of the plans for CLARION, which he hoped would paralyze all traffic in Germany. He rejected the Jeb Stuart plan but noted, "For the past two

Fratricide over Berlin. The death of a B-17 by friendly bombers, February 3, 1945. The low squadron has strayed beneath the lead squadron, directly into the path of its just-released bombs. No parachutes were sighted as the pictured aircraft, whose left stabilizer was struck and sheared off, plunged to the ground.

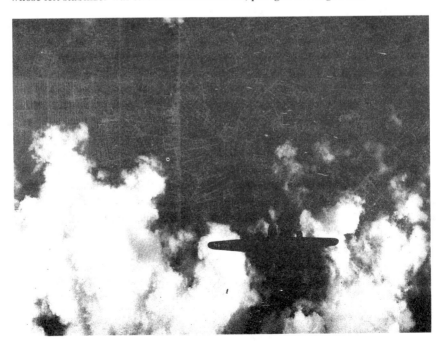

weeks we have been using the returning escort fighters in a Jeb Stuart role with the intention of preventing rapid movement of German troops from the Western to the Eastern front by strafing rail traffic." As for Jeb Stuart, THUNDERCLAP, and CLARION, Spaatz observed, "Your comment on the decisiveness of results achieved by air power leads me to believe you might be following the chimera of the one air operation which will end the war." Spaatz no longer believed such an animal existed. He spoke of the difficulty of exploiting and measuring the results of air operations. Only in the aggregate could one see that Allied air power had badly damaged the German economy and denied oil to the German military.[121]

On February 6, the Eighth attempted to attack oil targets only to find clouds over the synthetic plants, which meant that more than 1,300 bombers hit either secondary targets or targets of opportunity. On February 9, another 1,300-plane mission against the same targets was thwarted by the weather. Secondary targets were again bombed. On February 13, USSTAF called the Eighth to report that the weather would be "beautiful" over Dresden and Chemnitz. The Eighth drew up three plans: Plan A, for a short mission over western Germany in case of marginal weather; Plan B, for the 1st and 3d Air Divisions to bomb Dresden and the 2d Division to bomb Chemnitz (after these cities' names, the planners noted, "Beat'em up"); and Plan C, for the 1st and 3d Air Divisions to bomb Dresden and the 2d Division, in case it could not climb over the clouds to eastern Germany, to bomb transport and jet targets in central Germany.[122] After postponing the attack for twenty-four hours because of the weather, 1,377 B-17s and B-24s set out on February 14 to bomb marshaling yards in Dresden and Chemnitz and to bomb the oil plant in Magdeburg. The 340 B-24s of the 2d Air Division that were redirected from Plan C because of the possibilty of visual oil bombing and sent against synthetic plants found bad weather and diverted to Magdeburg's marshaling yards, where they dropped 811 tons of bombs (215 tons of them fire bombs) by H2X; the 294 B-17s of the 3d Air Division that were diverted from Plan C because of the heavy RAF raid on Dresden the previous night, employing H2X, dropped 718 tons of bombs (228 tons of fire bombs) on the Chemnitz yards; and 311 B-17s of the 1st Air Division, using visually assisted H2X, dropped 771 tons of bombs (including 294 tons of incendiary bombs) on the Dresden marshaling yards.[123]

But several eyewitnesses in Dresden never even noticed the American bombs.[124] Some of the city's inhabitants failed to pay much attention to this mission because on the previous night, February 13–14, 796 Lancaster heavy bombers of Bomber Command, in a two-wave attack, had released 2,646 tons of bombs, including 1,181 tons of incendiaries, into the very heart of the city. Much of Dresden's antiaircraft defense, including almost all the heavy guns capable of reaching high altitudes, had left to serve as antitank units on the Eastern Front or to supplement flak defenses at points hit more often by the Allies. Thus, British and American raids met no opposition. The British, in particular, benefited from the lack of interference because their airborne controller could bring his planes in undisturbed and direct them to drop their cargoes in a newly developed fan-shaped pattern that maximized the coverage and effect of incendiary bombs. The RAF conducted a technically perfect fire-raising attack on the city.[125]

Several factors had to combine to create the phenomenon of a fire storm. Weather had to be favorable—dry with low humidity. Many large fires had to be started in a short time. The built-up city area had to be blanketed with a bomb mix, that included large percentages of incendiaries and high explosives. The large percentage of incendiary bombs made it impossible for individual efforts to stop the fires, while high-explosive bombs drove the populace and most fire guards into shelters, discouraged fire fighters, smashed water-main networks, created road blocks, broke windows, and opened up buildings and holed roofs. Unlike a large fire, which starts at a single point and spreads by easy stages over the course of several hours, a fire storm's huge blaze starts with incredible rapidity. Within twenty minutes after the first attack wave struck Hamburg (in July 1943), two out of three buildings in a four-and-one-half square-mile area were ablaze. This quick buildup made fire fighting impossible. As flames broke through the roofs, a column of super-heated air shot up from the burning area to a height exceeding 13,000 feet and sucked in cooler air at its base, creating a street-level draft measured at thirty-three miles per hour. (To panicked individuals at ground level this wind blowing directly toward the maelstrom would have seemed even fiercer.) The resultant gale carried burning material and sparks down the streets and heated all combustibles in the area to the ignition point. Thus, the fire spread toward its center and was, eventually, self-limiting.

Seventy percent of the deaths in the fire storm came as a result of carbon-monoxide poisoning. The fire consumed the free oxygen in the area and replaced it with the products of combustion, one of which, carbon monoxide, seeped into basement bomb shelters killing the occupants painlessly and silently. To avoid death people had to leave their shelters before the fire became too intense, brave the fires along the streets, and face the bombs still coming down. This prospect made it difficult for the authorities to convince people of the danger they risked if they stayed too long in the shelters.[126]

By early morning on February 14, Ash Wednesday, a fire storm engulfed the middle of Dresden causing staggering loss of life. Estimates of the death toll range from a low of 35,000, now accepted as the best guess, to a high of 250,000. No one will ever know the exact figure with certainty, because Silesian refugees, evacuees from other bombed cities, slave laborers, and other displaced persons had jammed into the almost untouched city. Few of the city's residents and recent arrivals had ever experienced a major bombing. They had little idea of how to protect themselves.[127]

The 311 American B-17s, which for this mission carried approximately the same percentage of fire bombs as the Lancasters, attacked shortly after 12:00

557

P.M. After releasing 771 tons of ordnance, they reported a low-lying haze of smoke that prevented observation of their bombs' fall. Nevertheless, immediate post-raid analysis of strike photos taken by the attacking bombers, indicated "that the majority of the bombs dropped fell into heavily built-up areas of the city," and stated, "damage to the city should be severe."[128] The next day, at an Allied Air Commanders' Conference, Doolittle reported that "the fires lit by Bomber Command the previous night had been re-kindled," and he noted with "greatest reticence" that the smoke had risen to 15,000 feet.[129] That same day, 210 B-17s unable to bomb their primary target, the synthetic oil plant at Ruhland, diverted to their secondary target, Dresden. Using H2X, they dropped 461 tons of bombs, all high explosives, on the stricken city.[130] In all, the planes under Spaatz's command had flown 521 heavy-bomber sorties and had dropped 1,232 tons of bombs on Dresden. Their bombs mattered little, for the RAF had already virtually leveled the city. As a result of these raids the AAF official history, relying, in part, on immediate postmission aerial photography, stated, "If casualties were exceptionally high and damage to residential areas great, it was also evident that the city's industrial and transportation establishments had been blotted out."[131]

The Dresden raids, like earlier missions against Berlin, evoked bitter accusations of terror bombing from the German propaganda machine and strong reaction in the neutral press. A February 17 broadcast by the German Overseas Service in English for North America awarded Spaatz the "Order of the White Feather" for "acts of exceptional cowardice in bombing German cities filled with pitiful refugees."[132]

This time, however, the American press joined in the uproar. On February 16, Air Commodore C. M. Grierson of the SHAEF Air Staff held a background press conference. He spoke only for the SHAEF Air Staff Section, but the nature of the conference, which dealt with strategic bombing policy, gave some reporters the impression that he represented Spaatz and Harris as well. After touching on oil and communications bombing, Grierson, an RAF intelligence officer before his posting to SHAEF, discussed the use of heavy bombers against centers of population. He noted that large raids on population centers always led the Germans to bring in numerous trainloads of extra supplies and to evacuate the homeless. That type of relief relied, stated Grierson,

> on rapid and sound communication between the big cities and the whole of the interior of Germany itself, so that the destruction of not only communications centres, but also of towns where the relief comes from and where the evacuees go to, are very definitely operations which contribute greatly toward the break up of the German economic system.

When Grierson was asked about the attack on Dresden and other points ahead of the Russian front he responded, "I should say the reasons for the attack are probably at least twofold. First of all they are centres to which evacuees are being moved. They are centres of communication through which traffic is moving across to the Russian front, and from the Western front to the East." When asked for further cities on the list he replied, "I cannot give the list offhand. I think all those places through which the communications passed from West to East and those from North to South, and then the obvious centres of evacuation of population and probably emergency food storage." When asked whether the aim of the Dresden attack was "to cause confusion among refugees or to blast communications carrying military supplies," Grierson answered, "Primarily communications to prevent them moving military supplies. To stop movement in all directions if possible—movement of everything."[133]

In response to other questions, the air commodore said that "further bombing attacks of German cities which are incidental and complementary to the communications attacks must have an affect on her [*sic*] internal economic system and what morale there is left to have any effect on." Finally, Grierson implied that the Allies hoped to stop coal from leaving the Ruhr for, among other reasons, the purpose of increasing civilian suffering.[134]

Grierson had denied that the attack on Dresden was terror bombing. He had outlined a program aimed primarily on causing confusion and lowering morale by bombing civilian evacuees, chivying them from point to point, and denying them comfort, food, and heating supplies. Although he denied that the Allies had begun a terror-bombing campaign, he implied that the bombing of eastern German cities was mainly intended to produce hordes of refugees and to increase civilian suffering.

An Associated Press correspondent at the briefing, Howard Cowan, sent a slightly embellished account of Grierson's remarks to SHAEF's censor who, instead of passing the story on to USSTAF's censor because it dealt with strategic bombing policy, allowed it to go forward.[135] On February 18, the *Washington Star* and other papers across the nation gave the story front-page treatment, much to the dismay of Arnold, who, along with Marshall and Secretary of War Henry L. Stimson, promptly asked Spaatz for an explanation. Three days after the story's release, Kuter, who had returned to Washington, observed, "The Cowan story has given us a heavy set-back in the American Press on the question of precision bombing and the basic principle of the employment of the American Strategic Air Forces."[136]

Cowan had written:

> The Allied Air Commanders have made the long awaited decision to adopt deliberate terror bombing of the great German population centers as a ruthless expedient to hasten Hitler's doom. . . . Their avowed purpose will be creating more confusion in the German traffic tangle and sapping German morale.

Cowan went on to describe Grierson's remarks pertaining to the strains placed on the German transportation system by the relief work associated with cities either bombed out or jammed with civilians fleeing the Soviet advance from the east.[137]

The series of queries and responses that this story initiated between Washington and Paris followed on the heels of a preliminary exchange between Kuter and Spaatz. On February 13, Kuter, visiting Eaker at the latter's headquarters, read, he claimed for the first time, Bottomley's January 31 directive. There can be little doubt that Kuter had already seen the new directive at Yalta.[138] Apparently Eaker's opposition to city bombing led Kuter to reexamine his own views. He felt that the directive varied too far from Directive No. 3, which the CCS had tacitly agreed to at Malta. He complained in a cable to Spaatz that the "insertion of what can be read as indiscriminate bombing of German cities is priority second only to synthetic oil plants." This, said Kuter, would divert too much strength from the effort devoted to submarines, violating the informal agreements reached in Malta between the Army, the AAF, and the Navy on the amount of air effort to be expended on the submersibles. Kuter added that unless intelligence showed that the bombing of German cities would have a dramatic effect on ultimate victory "we are not keeping good faith with the US JCS." He therefore requested the data supporting the decision to add east German cities to bombing priorities. Kuter did not, however, ask that the January 31 directive be rescinded. "It is understood," he said, "that my questioning of your directive in General Arnold's name does not interfere with current execution of your directive."[139]

Giles, who had received an information copy of the cable, told Kuter that AAF Headquarters had no information "as to the basis of decision to attack German cities on a continuous number two priority." Giles also noted that AAF Headquarters considered the cities as targets of opportunity that should not retain second priority.[140]

In his reply to Kuter and Giles on February 14, Spaatz detailed his thoughts on the Bottomley directive and defined current USSTAF strategic policy. He maintained that Bottomley's directive referred only to Bomber Command, and differed in detail from his own instructions to USSTAF, which were intended to be temporary. He had based them on "the premise that the Russian offensive and the maintenance of same was [sic] of primary strategical importance." His most important contribution to the Soviets' winter offensive, he said, was the continued bombing of oil production facilities. His second most important was the attacking of

> transportation in major cities feeding the Russian front and concomitant disruption of administration particularly in such centers as Berlin. That these were important contributions to Allied solidarity is evidenced by the Russian reaction to this program and the fact that they themselves requested attacks on Berlin and Leipzig.[141]

Spaatz refuted Kuter's imputation of bad faith with the JCS:

> This program was concurred in by Gen. Marshall and he suggested its extension to include attacks on Munich. My directive at that time specified that

attacks would be made on Berlin when overcast conditions prevented visual attacks on oil. This has since been expanded to include attacks against Dresden, Leipzig and Munich, of which Dresden had this date been attacked. *Since these attacks are primarily aimed at transportation,* [emphasis added] it represents no change in priority but merely a change in emphasis from the battle in the West to the battle in the East.

As for submarines, Spaatz stated, "It is not considered that this situation has any influence on the amount of effort which will be placed on the submarine system under current directive since attacks are influenced almost entirely by weather areas."[142]

Giles and Arnold, who did not know exactly how Spaatz's instructions differed from Bottomley's directive, accepted Spaatz's answer on faith. Speaking for himself and Arnold, Giles stated that Spaatz's views, as expressed in the cable of February 14, were acceptable: "Providing that not involved are instructions or implications for promiscuous bombing of German cities for the purpose of causing civilian confusion. It has always been our view that the communications objectives in large cities were to be attacked under existing priorities as stated in directive number 3."[143]

This cable had hardly left Giles's desk when Cowan's front-page story hit the streets of America. Arnold radioed another message to Spaatz: "Complete clarification has become essential to resolve my now existing confusion as to directives and priorities under which the Strategic Air Forces are presently operating." Arnold requested urgent transmission of the text of USSTAF's current operating directive along with any comments Spaatz cared to make.[144]

Both Giles's and Arnold's cables arrived in Paris after Spaatz had left for the Mediterranean to confer, as he did periodically, with Eaker. Because the situation required speedy response, Frederick Anderson, speaking for Spaatz, replied to the worried communications from the Pentagon.[145] To Giles, who passed the messages on to Arnold, Anderson rejoined, "It has always been my policy that civilian populations are not suitable military objectives." Anderson went on to explain the differences between Bottomley's directives and Spaatz's: "Although in general parallel in priorities and issued after mutual consultation, [they] often reflect the difference in capabilities of the two forces. On this occasion, I did not issue a complete new Directive since it was necessary only to change emphasis within the Priorities of Directive Number Three." Finally, Anderson observed that "such changes within the broad framework of formal Directives are almost a daily occurrence to keep abreast of the changing situation."[146] Anderson next paraphrased for Giles the current directive to the Eighth Air Force dated January 30, 1945. It differed little from Spaatz's verbal orders to Doolittle on January 28. Visual attacks on oil had first priority, bombing attacks (probably through overcast) on Berlin had second priority, and attacks on the Cologne-Ruhr-Kassel area had third priority. "With above in mind," stated Spaatz's directive to Doolittle, "anticipate you will hit Berlin whenever weather conditions do not indicate possibility of visual bombing of oil targets but do permit operations to Berlin."[147]

In his cables to Giles and then to Arnold, Anderson justified Berlin as a target on several grounds. The city served as a focal point in the supply and defense against the Red Army's attack and as a suspected transshipment point for the *Sixth S.S. Panzer Army*.[148] Furthermore, Berlin's position as a center of communications, administration, and industry required some effort. Such effort would force the Luftwaffe into the air to fight; require the Luftwaffe to station fighters close to the city, thus removing them from the Western Front; and contain a large flak defense that, if left alone, would disperse to defend other targets.[149]

Anderson told Washington that USSTAF still operated according to Directive No. 3 but added, "I believe that the power of the Russian advance is the greatest strategic factor at the present time in this war and as the situation dictates, I believe it should be strongly supported."[150] These answers satisfied Arnold. On February 19, he informed Spaatz that the two messages so far received had "resolved all open questions. It is now understood that you are proceeding along lines consistent with Directive No. Three."[151]

Anderson next turned to limiting any public relations damage done by Cowan's story. After discussions with Eisenhower, they agreed not to stir up already muddy waters by issuing an official statement denying the story, which would only keep it alive.[152] With Virgil Pinkley, European manager of United Press, Anderson reviewed USSTAF's position on bombing. Col. Max Boyd, USSTAF's chief public relations officer, also told several reporters that there had been no change in policy, only "a shift of emphasis from West to East to weaken German defenses against the Russian Offensive." In these talks USSTAF acknowledged that "attacks against targets in populous centers always have and always will endanger civilian lives" but emphasized that the AAF would continue to improve its technique to obtain the greatest possible concentration of bombs directly on military targets selected for attack.[153]

Spaatz summarized the whole affair in a letter to Robert Lovett on February 21:

> As you know, our strategic policy directives and the Air Ministry directives to R.A.F. Bomber Command parallel except that the technique of the R.A.F. operation requires the accomplishment of the same results by the use of area bombing. Our policy, of course, has remained unchanged. The technique of setting up on the transportation system in our recent raid on Berlin was the same as that used in our raids on the same city throughout last year. If there is a point of difference, it is merely in effectiveness since the strike was unusually good. The SHAEF officer giving out the interview was not authorized to talk concerning strategic air bombing policies and did not present General Eisenhower's or my views.[154]

In the years since the bombing of Dresden, several questions have recurred, four of which definitely touch on Spaatz's decisions or responsibilities:

1. *Who ordered the bombing of Dresden?* Although the Joint Intelligence Committee, the British Air Staff, Tedder, and Spaatz had all begun to consider aiding the Soviet offensive, Churchill must bear the responsibility for shifting the heavy-bomber effort to the Eastern Front. He prodded the RAF to place east German cities at the top of its priority list. Harris was the first to suggest Dresden in this connection. Spaatz, as the chief American official involved in setting priorities for the U.S. strategic air forces, accepted the change of targeting locale proposed by the British and ordered attacks on Berlin, Dresden, Munich, and associated cities.

2. *Did the Soviets request the bombing of Dresden?* No, the Soviets never specifically asked for it. They were aware from the Tripartite negotiations at Yalta, however, that the British and the Americans had reserved the right to bomb it whenever they chose.[155] In addition, at Yalta the Soviets requested "an action on communications [to] hinder the enemy from carrying out the shifting of his troops to the East from the Western Front, from Norway, and from Italy, in particular, to paralyze Berlin and Leipzig."[156] Spaatz, in accordance with previous agreements, notified the Soviets twenty-four hours before the February 13 mission and twenty-four hours prior to the February 14 mission of his intention to attack Dresden.[157] At no time did the Soviets express a wish to halt the bombing of Dresden.

3. *Was Dresden a legitimate military target?* Dresden, as the seventh-largest city in Germany, possessed many small workshops, factories, and perhaps 50,000 workers employed in the arms industry;[158] none of these alone had attracted the interest of Allied targeting officers. In February 1945, however, Dresden's position as a communications center became all important once the Soviets neutralized Breslau. It then became a communications linchpin of the southern part of the Eastern Front. The main rail lines from Leipzig and Berlin joined just outside the city, while the chief rail line to Prague and to Hungary and a main line due east to Breslau radiated from within the city. If the Allies could significantly retard or halt communications through Dresden, the German effort against the Soviets in that sector would weaken, perhaps fatally. Dresden's importance as a communications center made it a legitimate military target.

4. *Did the Allied air attacks on Dresden deviate from established bombing policy?* They did not. The RAF employed a main-force attack, as it had often done before, which started a fire storm—the intended, but seldom achieved, result of all main-force attacks on city areas. As a matter of policy, the RAF routinely bombed city areas in order, as the RAF official historians state, "to dislocate the German war economy by the destruction of what were regarded as profitable targets in it, namely the residential centres of the industrial population."[159] Harris, Bomber Command's chief, believed absolutely in area bombing and kept a list of sixty-three German cities he meant to destroy. Two weeks after Dresden,

in reference to a main force attack on Pforzheim, the RAF's last area attack of the war, Harris, according to the minutes of an Allied Air Commanders' Conference, boasted to his fellow air commanders "the whole place has been burned out. This attack had been what was popularly known as a deliberate terror attack." Harris said that he knew "that in certain quarters, the value of these area attacks was disputed. Pforzheim was a town which contained innumerable small workshops for the manufacture of precision instruments. This attack must have destroyed the 'home-work' of the population and their equipment." Harris finished by noting, "Bomber Command had now destroyed 63 German towns in this fashion."[160] Of the 389 main-force attacks and 482,437 tons of bombs the RAF sent against German towns, Dresden had received only a single raid and 2,978 tons of bombs. In comparison, the RAF subjected Berlin to 24 main-force attacks (49,400 tons of bombs) and Essen to 28 such attacks (39,907 tons of bombs).[161]

Nor did the American attack on Dresden deviate from established AAF policy. Long after the war, in 1969, Spaatz succinctly stated his and USSTAF's reasoning during this period, "When the Dresden operation came down, we bombed the military targets . . . some marshaling yards. This is what we did. Now maybe some of the bombs fell on Dresden, but the target was a military target." Only one-third of the Eighth Air Force, carrying a high but not unusual percentage of incendiary bombs, attacked Dresden. As usual, when confronted with less-than-adequate visual conditions, the Eighth resorted to H2X to make its drops, which, assuming 30 to 50 percent cloud cover and standard accuracy, meant that only 30 percent of the bombs fell within half a mile of aiming points.[162] Following standard procedures, the B-17s had aimed for Dresden's marshaling yards located in the center of the city, and therefore dropped a good many bombs on the already devastated residential area. The Dresden raid was business as usual for the Eighth Air Force in the winter of 1944–1945.

U.S. Bombing Policy during the Winter of 1944–1945

The Dresden mission, however, did highlight USSTAF's use of incendiary bombs and blind-bombing techniques over major German towns and cities. The U.S. Strategic Air Forces in Europe freely employed both over German cities but rarely over cities in German-occupied Europe. One week after Dresden and after the Cowan story as well, Frederick Anderson informed the RAF Director of Bomber Operations, "It is the policy of the U.S. Strategic Air Forces in Europe to limit attacks to military objectives and to use precision bombing techniques. When weather conditions preclude visual bombing, military objectives in Germany proper suitable for 'bombing through overcast' technique are selected for attack." Then Anderson differentiated between Germany proper and German-occupied territory: "Under normal conditions it is not our policy to attack targets in enemy occupied territory unless the target can be identified by visual means."[163]

564

The weather of central Europe forced the Americans to develop a technological alternative to precision daylight bombing, which, except for fairly accurate short-range systems such as Gee-H and Oboe, meant H2X. H2X was, of course, inaccurate and fit only for locating large cities. Without H2X the Eighth Air Force could operate for only a handful of days in the fall and winter. During the fourth quarter of 1944, Berlin had only seven days of visual (less than 50 percent cloud cover) bombing weather; Munich, southern Germany, and southern Austria had five days; and central and western Germany had only three days of visual weather. Adding days of visually assisted weather (50 percent to 80 percent cloud cover or more than 80 percent with large local breaks in the clouds) doubled these numbers.[164] The AAF could not justify a force of 2,000 bombers if it flew only once or twice a month. Hence, inaccurate radar missions went out as often as weather permitted safe takeoff, landing, and travel to the target. Spaatz took pride in the ability of his force to fly in foul weather. In mid-March, he noted proudly to both Arnold and Marshall that the Eighth had become an all-weather force. To Marshall he wrote, "It has been my constant aim to develop an all-weather air force capable of placing its impact on the enemy every day of the year. Progress in this field has developed at an outstanding rate and the crews flying the missions have kept pace with the developments in admirable fashion."[165] Similarly, he informed Arnold, "Both fighters and bombers operate in weather which was never conceived to be suitable for combat operations, and, as a result, we have been able to maintain approximately five times the pressure on the enemy that would have been possible if we were restricted to visual bombing."[166]

In its use of incendiary bombs, the Eighth Air Force again demonstrated a policy of greater harshness toward German cities than targets in occupied territory. The standard American incendiary bomb from January 1944 on was the four-pound magnesium, thermite-filled, incendiary M50A1, dropped in 500-pound clusters. On ignition, it burned for six to eight minutes at a temperature of 2,300 degrees Fahrenheit.[167] These incendiary bombs had no blast or fragmentation effects, consequently they were useless against personnel or hardened structures, such as concrete fortifications. Nor could they significantly damage field fortifications, marshaling yards, or, in the opinion of the Eighth Air Force, major industrial facilities. The Eighth did not even employ fire bombs against oil targets, which postwar studies indicate could well have suffered worse damage if a higher percentage had been included in the mix of bombs dropped on them.[168] Incendiary bombs had one function—the destruction of soft targets, that is, houses, commercial buildings, and administrative/governmental offices.

In March 1945, the Eighth Air Force conducted a bombing campaign against German military bases, including barracks *(Kasernes)*, the closest military equivalent to the civilian structures just mentioned. This campaign indicated the Eighth's desired mix of bombs to achieve maximum damage on soft targets, a shade under 40 percent of total tonnage of fire bombs and 60 percent of total tonnage of high explosives.[169] On February 14, the Eighth dropped 40 percent

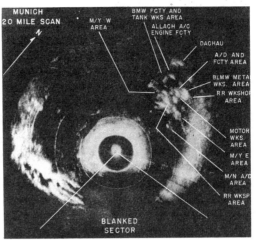

MUNICH
20 MILE SCAN

N

M/Y W
AREA

BMW FCTY AND
TANK WKS AREA

ALLACH A/C
ENGINE FCTY

DACHAU

A/D AND
FCTY AREA

BLMW METAL
WKS. AREA

RR WKSHOP
AREA

MOTOR
WKS.
AREA

M/Y E
AREA

M/N A/D
AREA

RR WKSP
AREA

BLANKED
SECTOR

Cities in Crisis. The Eighth Air Force attacked military objectives located well inside populated areas. *Clockwise from above*: Before and after photographs of the Tiergarten in Berlin show the damage to residential sections of the city. Incendiary and high-explosive ordnance *(right)* descend toward the cloud cover over Berlin, February 26, 1945. The roof of the Potsdam railroad station *(opposite, below)* collapsed under bombardment that same day. The shadow of a B-24 Liberator *(opposite, left, above)* races along the tracks leading into Munich's main railroad station. The twin towers of the city's famed *Frauenkirche* are on the horizon. Munich is laid out on the H2X radar screen *(opposite, right, above)* of a Fifteenth Air Force bomber.

of total tonnage in fire bombs on Dresden, as did the RAF, whose policy and operational techniques called for the greatest possible damage to city areas.

Examination of the Eighth's attacks on Berlin from March 1944 to March 1945 and of those in France during May and June 1944 show a dramatic contrast in their use of incendiaries. In May 1944, the Eighth's heavy bombers dropped 19,854 tons on France, 745 of them incendiaries.[170] Of these, 685 tons hit German-occupied military airfields, targets by their very nature located at some distance from city areas. In June 1944, 44,209 tons of the Eighth's bombs fell on France, only 103 tons of them incendiaries (dropped mostly on airfields).[171] Given Churchill's pressure to limit civilian casualties and destruction in occupied countries and the Eighth's policy of employing only visual bombing techniques over occupied territory, these figures seem to demonstrate the Eighth's desire and ability to limit damage as much as possible to purely military targets.

The bombing of Berlin showed the other side of the coin. From March 4, 1944, to March 18, 1945, the Eighth sent fifteen major missions of at least 700 tons of bombs each, and four minor missions over Berlin. These missions lost 264 aircraft and placed 21,733 tons on the city, including 8,089 tons of incendiaries or 37 percent of the total, a figure very close to the optimum for maximum destruction of soft targets. Of the four major raids with the least number of incendiaries (less than 20 percent apiece), three including the February 3, 1945, raid used visual bombing methods. More than 90 percent of all bombs fell on three targets: military and civil government areas (12,440 tons, 4,475 tons incendiary), railroad stations (5,259 tons, 2,494 tons incendiary), and industrial targets (2,410 tons, 937 tons incendiary).[172] Those were legitimate military targets and served as aiming points for the Eighth's bombardiers. Berlin's size and the location of its targets, mostly in the heart of the city, meant that every bomb missing a target hit housing or other nonmilitary targets.

On February 26, 1945, all three air divisions of the Eighth—1,135 heavy bombers—attacked three railroad stations with 2,778 tons of bombs, 44 percent of them fire bombs. The Schlesischer, Alexanderplatz, and Berlin-North stations were all located within two miles of the center of Berlin. Using H2X through complete overcast, the mission started large fires and killed many civilians. RAF Mosquito night-intruder bombers attacking twelve hours later reported fires still burning.[173] After the February 26 mission, with its 500,000 fire bomblets, the typical Berliner, with reason, would have been hard put to distinguish between RAF area bombing and AAF precision bombing.

A further look at Eighth Air Force operations has revealed two egregious examples of the gap between bombing practice and stated bombing policy: the target categories "city areas" and "marshaling yards." The two most cited Eighth Air Force statistical summaries that cover the entire war do not list a target category "city areas" or "towns and cities."[174] Both summaries were prepared from the same set of data within a month of the end of the war in Europe.

Monthly statistical summaries of the Eighth's operations prepared during the war, almost contemporaneously with the events they recorded, tell a different story. The Eighth Air Force Monthly Statistical Summary of Operations, generated at the end of each month from May 1944 to April 1945, listed a "city areas" target category. For calendar year 1944, the summary reported that the Eighth dropped 43,611 tons on "city areas."[175] Nor did these reports make any bones about their targets. The report for the May 8, 1944, Berlin raid baldly states, "Berlin city area attacked. Bombing raid done through 10/10 undercast on PFF markers. Believed that the center of Berlin was well hit."[176] After reaching a high of 9,886 tons (41 percent incendiaries) in July 1944, when the Eighth conducted a series of H2X raids on Munich, the monthly "city area" totals steadily declined to 383 tons in December.

A summary in a working paper from a USSTAF file, "Review of Bombing Results," shows a similar dichotomy according to time period. From January 1944 through January 1945, the Eighth dropped 45,036 tons on "towns and cities."[177] From February 1945 through the end of the war, this summary showed not a single ton of bombs falling on a city area. Unless the Eighth had developed a perfect technique for bombing through overcast, such a result was simply impossible. Obviously, the word had come down to deemphasize reports on civilian damage. For instance, when Anderson cabled Arnold about USSTAF's press policy on the Dresden controversy in February 1945, he noted, "Public relations officers have been advised to take exceptional care that the military nature of targets attacked in the future be specified and emphasized in all cases. As in the past the statement that an attack was made on such and such a city will be avoided; specific targets will be described."[178]

The U.S. Strategic Bombing Survey, although not explicitly listing a target category such as cities or towns, had an interesting definition of "industrial areas." The survey placed three types of targets in "industrial areas": (1) cities, towns, and urban areas; (2) public utilities (electric, gas, water, and telephone companies); and (3) government buildings. Given that definition the survey even managed to describe RAF area raids as strikes against "industrial targets."[179]

The target category "marshaling yards" received more of the Eighth's bomb tonnage than any other, somewhere between 175,000 and 200,000 tons of bombs.[180] At least 25 percent of all the Eighth Air Force bombs dropped over Europe fell on "marshaling yards." One-third of the American incendiary bombs dropped over Germany fell on the same system. As a matter of directive and policy for most of the period between September 1944 and April 1945, the same period in which the Eighth delivered 90 percent of the total tonnage dropped on the system, marshaling yards had the highest nonvisual bombing priority. During that period the Eighth Air Force dropped 168,038 tons of bombs, 70 percent (117,816 tons) blind and 30 percent (50,222 tons) visually.[181] Postwar research showed that only 2 percent of bombs dropped by nonvisual means landed within 1,000 feet of their aiming points.[182] Rail yards as such, however, were poor targets for incendiaries. If the fire bombs landed directly on or near rail cars, they destroyed or damaged them; otherwise, they could do little harm to the heavy equipment or trackage. The Eighth realized this. Of the 9,042 tons of bombs dropped on French rail yards, mostly during the pre-OVERLORD transportation bombing phase, when the Americans took scrupulous care to avoid French civilian casualties, 90 percent were visually sighted and only 33 tons were incendiaries.[183] Even over Germany itself, during Operation CLARION, when the Eighth bombed dozens of small yards and junctions in lesser German towns, it dropped, over a two-day period of visual conditions, 7,164 tons of bombs in all, but less than 3 tons of fire bombs.[184]

In contrast, using H2X, the Eighth pummeled marshaling yards and rail stations in large German cities with high percentages of incendiary bombs. For example, rail targets in at least four major cities garnered the following percentages of fire bombs out of all bombs dropped on them: Cologne, 27 percent; Nuremberg, 30 percent; Berlin, 37 percent; and Munich, 41 percent.[185] "Marshaling yards" undoubtedly served as a euphemism for city areas. Because the yards themselves were not good targets for incendiaries, the prime purpose in employing such weapons was to take advantage of the known inaccuracy of H2X bombing in order to maximize the destruction of warehouses, commercial buildings, and residences in the general vicinity of the target. Large numbers of planes scattering their bombs around their mostly unseen and unverifiable aiming points surely would cause great collateral damage to any soft structures located nearby.

The AAF never officially acknowledged that it had bombed German city areas as a matter of policy. Analysis of the Eighth's bombardment policy, of its employment of incendiary bombs, and of its targeting of "city areas" and "marshaling yards" clearly reveals that, despite denials, it did engage in the deliberate bombing of German population centers. There were only two discernible, but important, differences between the AAF's practice and the RAF's admitted policy. First, unlike RAF Bomber Command, under the direction of Harris, the AAF did not consider city areas its chief and preferred target. Whereas Harris repeatedly and sarcastically scoffed at any other target system as a "panacea," the AAF preferred to bomb oil and other recognizable and identifiable target systems whenever visual methods would allow. Spaatz correctly believed that the bombing of crucial oil and transportation targets would end the war sooner, with less loss of life, than area bombing. Second, the AAF in Europe never developed, trained for, or employed the specialized fire-raising techniques used by Bomber Command. To do so would have openly acknowledged a city area bombing policy. Under nonvisual bombing conditions (night or heavy overcast), however, the points of attack and the bomb loadings of the RAF and the AAF were virtually indistinguishable, as were their results.

Yet American air commanders were neither fools nor hypocrites. Michael S. Sherry far overstates the case when he brands them technological fanatics and speaks of the "evil of American bombing." His pairing them with Adolf Eichmann, the Nazi S.S. officer responsible for the deaths of millions of Jews because they, like Eichmann, seemed to personify the "banality of evil" and were neither frenzied nor hateful seems particularly overblown.[186] The Germans could have stopped the bombing by surrender. The victims of the Holocaust could not stop the slaughter by any means, and their numbers of casualties were vastly greater than the numbers of casualties inflicted by Allied bombing—even if the two types of death are comparable in other respects, which they are not. The contradiction of American bombing was that although the target category "marshaling yards" served as a euphemism for area bombing, the bombardment of marshaling yards also broke the back of the German war economy. It was the bombing of the yards, not the paralysis of the inland waterway system or the destruction of rolling stock and locomotives, that disrupted the vital car placings, severing the coal/transport nexus, shattering the geographic division of labor, and toppling the production edifice built by Speer.[187]

Operations to the End of the War

On February 21, 1945, Allied weather forecasters predicted clear skies over much of Germany for the next day, whereupon Allied air leaders, at the request of Eisenhower's headquarters,[188] scheduled Operation CLARION for execution on February 22. CLARION, a descendant of the HURRICANE plans of autumn 1944, called for attacks by all available Allied strategic and tactical air power on German rail and water communications in the hope of disrupting the Germans' economic life and front-line tactical situation. By attacking numerous unbombed targets near small cities and towns, the Allies also hoped to provide millions of Germans with proof of Allied air superiority. British and American fighters and bombers would spread out all over Germany blasting transport targets such as grade crossings, stations, barges, docks, signals, tracks, bridges, and marshaling yards. The plan purposely selected targets near small towns heretofore untouched by the war and therefore not likely to have strong antiaircraft defenses. To heighten their accuracy, the Eighth's and Fifteenth's heavy bombers came in at unusually low altitudes. Some of them bombed from 6,000 feet, while the Ninth's medium bombers buzzed up and down the rail lines destroying locomotives and disrupting traffic. More than 3,500 heavy bombers and 4,900 fighters took part. The bombers attacked 219 transportation targets, while the fighters destroyed or damaged 594 locomotives and 3,803 rail cars.[189]

Eisenhower's headquarters had requested CLARION in order to assist an offensive by Lt. Gen. William G. Simpson's U.S. Ninth Army, scheduled to begin the night of February 22–23. The Ninth meant to stage an assault crossing of the Ruhr River, clear the Cologne plain, seize Cologne itself, and close up to the Rhine, all of which he accomplished by March 7. Spaatz had been itching for months to go ahead with CLARION. As discussed in the previous chapter, he had hoped to carry out HURRICANE in October, but the weather had proved unsuitable. On February 1, at the Allied Air Commanders' Conference, he had pressed for immediate execution of CLARION.[190] On February 2, Anderson had presented CLARION to Marshall at Malta as USSTAF's alternative to the Jeb Stuart plan.[191] The same day Spaatz informed Twining and Eaker of his intention to order CLARION when conditions allowed it. When Twining objected to the special tactics called for in the plan but not the concept behind it,[192] Spaatz accommodated him with some slight modifications to provide more safety for the heavy bombers. On February 5, Spaatz told Arnold that CLARION was cocked and primed, although he also noted that he no longer expected any single air operation to win the war.[193]

The results of CLARION justified Spaatz's caution. The operation, which took place on February 22–23, failed to achieve its lofty goals. It did not precipitate a crisis among the railway workers, overwhelm the Reichsbahn's repair facilities, disrupt the railways enough to affect the front-line troops immediately, or drive home the war to the German people. CLARION did, however, destroy a considerable amount of rolling stock and lowered the throughput capacity of several main rail lines for the duration of the war. The operation added further strain and attrition to a system already collapsing from the cumulative effects of the destruction being rained upon it.[194] Although Anderson probably spoke for all of USSTAF when, a month later, he proclaimed it "singularly effective,"[195] neither USSTAF nor the rest of the Allied airmen repeated the operation—first, because it required a special set of weather conditions and, second, because it required all Allied air forces to give up their primary missions to concentrate on a special project with unquantifiable results.

CLARION did provide a side benefit for the AAF, however—the opportunity for USSTAF to stage a press blitz to counteract the reporting of the Dresden bombing. USSTAF had a United Press correspondent at Eighth Air Force to cover the planning; briefed the press in London and Paris; sent a planeload of reporters to front-line fields to cover the story; sent its own combat camera crews out to get movie and still footage of the operation, which it promptly released; and gained a fifteen-minute news spot on the domestic U.S. National Broadcasting Company network.[196]

Each day from February 19 through March 4 the Eighth sent out more than 1,000 heavy bombers. With the exception of CLARION, which consumed two precious days of visual bombing, the rest of the attacks—including a massive one on Berlin (February 26) and others on the communications centers at Munich (February 25), Leipzig (February 27), Halle (February 27), and Chemnitz (March 3)—used combinations of mostly radar and some visual bombing.[197] In February the Luftwaffe mounted only one interception of more than 100 planes, for the February 9 attack on oil plants; otherwise, it offered only feeble resistance because most of its fighter effort was devoted to the hard-pressed Eastern Front. ULTRA intercepts showed that by the end of January the Luftwaffe had transferred 800 single-engine fighters to the east.[198] Nonetheless, Allied intelligence noted darkly that German jets had begun to attack in numbers and formations, indicating that problems in their deployment and tactics may have been solved.[199] February repeated the pattern of January when the Luftwaffe, heavily committed to the Battle of the Bulge and the Soviet offensive, had, for the most part, failed to oppose strategic bombing missions. Of course, in January, 75 percent of the Eighth's bomber effort went for tactical targets to aid the ground forces rather than to dislocate Germany's economy.[200]

The Eighth lost 314 bombers (49 to fighters) in January 1945 and another 227 bombers (14 to fighters) in February.[201] The Fifteenth did not lose a single bomber to fighters in either month, although overall it suffered heavy bomber losses (88 in January and 147 in February).[202] USSTAF lost large numbers of bombers to flak when it attacked targets defended by men and matériel released from other parts of Hitler's shrinking domain. The 24 bombers lost to flak over Berlin on February 3 amounted to almost 15 percent of the month's total lost to antiaircraft fire. Even as Germany fell from the precipice, its defenses still functioned.

In February, freed from the support requirements imposed by the Battle of the Bulge, the Eighth renewed its all-out war on Germany's economy. It fielded missions on twenty days in February, as did the Fifteenth. These raids, plus those of Bomber Command, lowered German Bergius and Fischer-Tropsch process oil production from 37,000 to 13,000 tons a month, less than 4 percent of January's 1944 figure.[203] For the month, USSTAF dropped more than 74,400 tons, including some 54,000 tons on transportation targets, while Bomber Command added another 45,900.[204] The German economy, gravely weakened by the loss of Silesian industry and coal, Hungarian natural oil, and Polish synthetic oil, and with its railcars creaking to a halt, collapsed under this rain of bombs. "By the end of February," stated the AAF official history, "Nazi Germany was no longer an industrial nation."[205]

In March the twin titans of USSTAF and Bomber Command piled Ossa on Pelion, ranging over all parts of Germany. They dropped a wartime monthly high of almost 170,000 tons of death and destruction on the nearly prostrate Germans; USSTAF contributed 102,000 tons to that total.[206] The Soviet army paused in its offensive, except in Hungary and East Prussia, to establish supply lines and organize the large territory they had taken from the Germans. The Western Allies drove the Nazis from the Rhineland and the Palatinate. After capturing the Ludendorff Bridge across the Rhine at Remagen on March 7, the Americans rapidly built up a strong bridgehead. In the last week of March, Montgomery's 21 Army Group crossed the Rhine, while Bradley's 12th Army Group and Devers's 6th Army Group broke out of their Rhine bridgeheads.

By April 1, Montgomery's and Bradley's troops linked up at Lippstadt, surrounding the Ruhr and pocketing an entire German army group. This group surrendered on April 18, yielding 317,000 prisoners of war. In the meantime the Allies had continued their drive east to the River Elbe, which they reached also on April 18. The Soviets renewed their offensive on April 16. They surrounded

Berlin on April 25; after grim house-to-house fighting, they completely occupied the city on May 2. German forces in Italy surrendered the same day. Hitler, who had refused to leave his air-raid shelter in the Nazi capital, committed suicide on April 30, issuing orders for counterattacks and scorched-earth resistance until the last. At 2:42 A.M. on May 7, at Reims, France, the Germans capitulated, effective 11:01 P.M., May 8, to Eisenhower. At 2:00 A.M., May 9, in Berlin, the Germans surrendered to the Soviets.

For most of the last ten hectic weeks of the war, business at USSTAF continued as usual. The German Me 262 jet continued to trouble the American air command. During March the Luftwaffe seldom sent up its piston-driven aircraft to contest the Eighth's strategic raids. Those Bf 109s and FW 190s that had fuel used it in ground-support roles, especially on the Eastern Front. The Me 262s, perhaps no more than fifty at any one time, showed "considerable improvement" in their tactics and organization.[207] The number of Eighth Air Force bombers lost to enemy fighters rose from fourteen in February to sixty-three in March[208]—the greatest number of bombers lost to fighters in six months. This situation caused concern but fell far short of the monthly totals suffered by a smaller Eighth Air Force in the first six months of 1944. The Fifteenth lost seven bombers to fighters in March—the only bombers it lost to enemy aircraft for all of 1945.[209]

On March 11, Spaatz wrote to Giles that because the American jet, the P-80, would not become operational until autumn 1945, the German's "technical advantage must be countered by overwhelming numbers of conventional fighters manned by pilots trained to both outthink and outshoot [the enemy]. . . ." Spaatz added, "There is little doubt that part, if not all of this force, will be committed to the task of countering our strategic operations as soon as suitable tactics have been developed."[210]

A week later, March 18, Me 262s shot down at least six bombers. The next day, March 19, they made a concentrated attack on another bomber formation, causing Anderson to tell Spaatz, "A touch of the Hun's old cunning and aggressive spirit was apparent today."[211] In addition, the Americans spotted at least one formation of thirty-six jets, the largest seen up to that time. Allied intelligence remarked that the formation "betokened a much more advanced state of development than previous reaction seemed to indicate."[212] At the Air Commanders' Conference on March 21, Doolittle informed the assembled airmen that "the threat which they had been anticipating had now materialized. Jets were now attacking in formations as large as 36 aircraft and were using more effective tactics." He also spoke of new tactics employed by the Germans: "Besides attacking the bombers, they were attacking the fighter escort immediately on penetration in the hope of making them drop their tanks. "The time had come," he said, "for an all-out operation against the G.A.F. by both the Tactical and Strategic Air Forces."[213] According to Doolittle, a massive two-day operation to "posthole" jet airfield runways and to drop fragmentation bombs on dispersal areas would reduce the Luftwaffe to a point at which USSTAF's fighters could engage in offensive operations rather than tie themselves to bomber escort. Bottomley expressed some doubt about the necessity of such an operation, but Tedder recommended antiair strikes as soon as the air forces finished their commitments to support both Montgomery's assault crossing of the Rhine and the massive paratroop drop planned to assist it.[214]

In the last week of March the Eighth attacked the German jet airfields, achieving some success. Nevertheless, Doolittle reported at the next Allied Air Commanders' Conference that "the jet strength of the G.A.F. was increasing uncomfortably."[215] A discussion of bomber priorities followed. Doolittle reiterated that the Eighth's losses to fighters had risen sharply since an "all-time" low in February. At the end, Tedder summed up the feeling of the airmen present, including Spaatz, "that more effort should be directed against the G.A.F. to provide greater immunity to the Eighth Air Force, the Army, and supply aircraft."[216] As Tedder apparently realized, the Allies had such overwhelming superiority they could easily spare more effort to extinguish the Luftwaffe completely.

Spaatz did not spend all of March worrying about the Luftwaffe's relatively feeble efforts. Other events gave him the opportunity to play the diplomat. During CLARION and again in early March, AAF units accidentally bombed Switzerland. An attack on February 22 on Schaffhausen which killed sixteen persons, and the attacks of March 4 on the Basel marshaling yards (fortunately, only nine heavy bombers dropped 21.5 tons by visual means) and on the "industrial area" of Zurich (heavy bombers using H2X dropped 12.7 tons of bombs) naturally created a furor. The February 22 attack had provoked Marshall to cable Eisenhower, "Will you please have someone look into this and let me know what can be done toward preventing recurrence of these incidents?"[217] The March bombing incidents elicited a stronger response from Marshall, who cabled Spaatz directly: "The successive bombing of Swiss territory now demands more than expressions of regret." He ordered Spaatz to leave immediately for Geneva and to present to the appropriate Swiss officials information as to the cause of the incidents, Spaatz's plans for corrective action, and "a formal apology." Marshall further requested that Spaatz undertake the mission in "maximum secrecy" with "no publicity."[218]

This message reached Spaatz on March 6. By March 8, in Bern and in the company of U.S. Minister to Switzerland Leland Harrison, Spaatz extended official and personal regrets to the Swiss Foreign Minister, the Minister of War, the Commander in Chief of the Swiss army, and the Chief of the Swiss Air Corps. He briefly explained the difficulties of winter bomber operations, emphasizing the prohibition, previously agreed to by the Allies, against bombing within 50 miles of the Swiss border.[219]

He promised to set up two zones: one from 150 to 50 miles outside Switzerland within which he would forbid attacks without positive identification, and the other within 50 miles of the Swiss border, where no attacks could be made without his express permission. All this appeased the Swiss. In keeping

Ruin and Risk. Amid the destruction of the Reich, the Germans could mount a sometimes effective defense against the Allies' aerial onslaught. *Clockwise from above*: Fifteenth Air Force raids flattened large fuel storage tanks at Torgau. The Fieseler aircraft plant *(opposite, above)* is a nearly complete wreck as an Allied soldier tours the works after war's end. Marshaling yards at Eleinberg *(opposite, middle)* show heavy cratering in a photographic survey taken in May 1945. The alarming successes of Me 262 fighters against American bombers and fighters in March 1945 led to heavy raids on jet assembly plants and airfields. An assembly line for the Messerschmitt wonder weapon *(opposite, below)* in a wooded area near Obertraubling in Bavaria was struck by the Fifteenth Air Force late in the war. A B-24 Liberator *(below)*, severed by German flak, tumbles across the sky during a raid on submarine construction yards in Kiel, April 12, 1945, barely three weeks before all German resistance collapsed.

General Carl A. Spaatz, Lt. Gen. James H. Doolittle, and the crews of the 303d Bomb Group discussing the results of a raid on the oil refinery at Halle, Germany, March 31, 1945.

with their neutrality, they agreed to keep the forbidden zones strictly confidential in order to keep the Germans from moving additional tempting targets close to the Swiss borders. The Swiss, for the purposes of domestic public opinion, issued a communiqué after Spaatz's departure describing the visit in general terms. To Marshall, Spaatz reported, "It seems evident to me that with the present restrictions which have been established, plus the fact that the importance of these incidents has been most forcibly impressed on our Air Forces, there should be little danger of any recurrence of any such violations of Swiss sovereignty."[220] Spaatz's visit satisfied Marshall.[221] Both men went back to fighting the war.

Four days after his return from Bern, Spaatz received official word of his nomination as a full four-star general with date of rank from March 11, making him senior, by one day, to Bradley. The news found him seated at the poker table in his headquarters near Paris. Eisenhower's naval aide, Captain Butcher, described Spaatz's reaction. First, he ordered champagne for the house; then he growled, "Come on and deal."[222]

Arnold had long sought Spaatz's promotion. In September 1944, he had asked Eisenhower to recommend Spaatz for a fourth star.[223] Eisenhower turned Arnold down, writing, "I can start off by saying that in my opinion there is no better all-round air officer than Spaatz. His common sense, loyalty, technical knowledge and complete readiness to cooperate are unexcelled and I wouldn't trade him for any other field commander of the Air Forces that I know."[224] Eisenhower believed that only the top American officer in a theater should hold four-star rank; otherwise the grade would become "spread too far."

Eisenhower's promotion to the newly created five-star rank, General of the Army, on December 16, 1944, however, eased his objections to additional four-star officers. On December 21, he asked Marshall to ask the President to propose Bradley and Spaatz for promotion.[225] Congress, however, had adjourned. Confirmation of any nominations would have to wait. Eisenhower repeated his requests on January 12 and 14.[226] At Marseilles on January 28, he consulted with Marshall, who, about to depart for the conferences at Malta and Yalta, agreed to nominate Bradley and Spaatz when the time came. He would not make any recommendations to the President, however, until he had decided on what other four-star promotions to send forward.[227]

The same day, Eisenhower told Kuter, "no one could tell him that Tooey Spaatz was not the best operational air man in the world." Kuter passed the assessment along to Arnold, saying that Eisenhower "then qualified his statement by saying Tooey was not a paper man, couldn't write what he wanted, and couldn't conduct himself adequately at a conference, but he had the utmost respect from everybody, ground and air, in the Theater." Kuter also reported Eisenhower's view that Spaatz's decisions were "sound and he knew exactly what he was doing."[228]

Eventually, Marshall sent his recommendations to Roosevelt. Shortly thereafter, Congress approved them. Spaatz became the fourth most senior officer in the Army Air Forces. He ranked below Arnold, a five-star general, and two other four-star officers—Joseph T. McNarney, Deputy Supreme Commander in the Mediterranean, who had served as Marshall's deputy; and George C. Kenney, MacArthur's air commander. McNarney and Kenney achieved their four-star rank five days and two days, respectively, before Spaatz's elevation to full general.

The Eighth operated bombers on twenty-six days in March, dispatching 1,000 or more bombers on twenty of them.[229] On March 15, the Eighth flew a special mission at the request of the Manhattan Project, the code name for the American atomic bomb program. Intelligence available to the project indicated that the Germans were engaged in manufacturing thorium and uranium at Oranienburg, a town fifteen miles north of Berlin. Because this town was in the projected Soviet zone of occupation and would not therefore be open for exploitation by western scientists, the head of the Manhattan Project, Maj. Gen. Leslie R. Groves, asked Spaatz to bomb it. The Eighth sent 675 bombers with more than 1,400 tons of ordnance against it. Covering the true purpose of its mission by attacking the headquarters of the German army in nearby Zossen, the Eighth unleashed 672 additional bombers. Both missions succeeded in damaging their targets. All above-ground structures of the uranium plant were destroyed and the attack at Zossen incapacitated the Chief of the German General Staff, General Heinz Guderian.[230]

The Eighth maintained its plans of operation, encountering no substantial interference. On March 15, Doolittle reported that only a deficiency of maintenance personnel limited his operations, not the Luftwaffe.[231] As the Allied airmen watched the German economy wither under their assaults, they shifted their operations to targets not yet bombed to complete devastation. On March 13, Spaatz observed to Marshall, "There is much evidence that the German railroad system is becoming more and more demoralized, and that their [sic] oil position has almost reached the starvation point."[232] The Allies' land advances in the west and the east, their violations of Swiss territory, and their discovery that the Germans had begun to shift large numbers of POWs still in their hands to the south, forced the Eighth in early March to close "the era of unrestricted strafing," much to the relief of American fighter pilots, who had suffered most of their casualties from light flak on low-level missions. They would now fly specific strafing missions instead of free-lancing.[233]

By midmonth, Spaatz informed Washington of a change in priorities: "We have our strategic program well in hand and are shifting the emphasis of our attacks closer to the Ground Forces, first to help them across the Rhine and then to exploit the crossing."[234] At the beginning of April, with the end of German resistance clearly in view, Spaatz cautioned his forces against making any mistakes, such as shooting down Allied planes or dropping bombs in the wrong places; American and Soviet fighters had engaged in a dogfight on March 18 with a loss of six Soviet aircraft.[235] "Incidents do not get severe criticism when the war is intense," remarked Spaatz, "but as soon as the war is about knocked over . . . a small mistake is magnified."[236]

While Spaatz worried about peacetime reactions to what he regarded as small mistakes, political leaders concerned themselves with reactions to possible major blunders. On March 28, Churchill, in a note to Portal, questioned the need for continued area bombing:

> The moment has come when the question of bombing German cities simply for the sake of increasing the terror, though under other pretexts should be reviewed. Otherwise we shall come into control of an utterly ruined land. The destruction of Dresden remains a serious query against the conduct of Allied bombing. I am of the opinion that military objectives must henceforward be more strictly studied in our own interests rather than that of the enemy. The Foreign Secretary has spoken to me on this subject, and I feel the need for more precise concentration upon military objectives such as oil and communications behind the immediate battle-zone, rather than on mere acts of terror and wanton destruction, however impressive.[237]

This minute, with its implication that the airmen were running amok, rocked Portal, who found it unacceptable.[238] Given Churchill's support of Harris's methods throughout the war and his bullying of the Air Staff into bombing east German cities, one of which, he was specifically informed would be Dresden, the minute seemed at best churlish and at worst an attempt to shift the entire responsibility for the policy of area bombing from civilian to military leadership. Portal suggested that Churchill withdraw the minute.[239]

Portal also asked Bottomley to obtain Harris's comments immediately. Bottomley wrote of Churchill's note to Harris, "I am sure you will agree that [it] misinterprets the purpose of our attacks on industrial areas in the past, and appears to ignore the aim given by the Combined Chiefs of Staff in their directives which have been blessed by the Heads of Government."[240]

Harris, after three years of implementing official policy, erupted in anger. He termed Churchill's note "abusive" and "an insult both to the bombing policy of the Air Ministry and to the manner in which that policy has been executed by Bomber Command." As for Dresden, Harris commented,

> The feeling, such as there is, over Dresden, could be easily explained by any psychiatrist. It is connected with German bands and Dresden shepherdesses. Actually, Dresden was a mass of munitions works, an intact government centre, and a key transportation point to the East. It is none of those things now.

Not satisfied with that observation, Harris argued that area bombing ought to continue precisely because the Germans no longer had the ability to recover from it, adding:

> I therefore assume that the view under consideration is something like this: no doubt in the past we were justified in attacking German cities. But to do so was always repugnant and now that the Germans are beaten anyway we can properly abstain from proceeding with these attacks.

He also said that he could never agree to such reasoning:

> Attacks on cities like any other act of war are intolerable unless they are strategically justified. But they are strategically justified in so far as they tend to shorten the war and so preserve the lives of Allied soldiers. To my mind, we have absolutely no right to give them up unless it is certain that they will not have that effect.

Harris then paraphrased Bismarck, "I do not personally regard the whole of the remaining cities of Germany as worth the bones of one British Grenadier." Besides, he pointed out, technical factors, such as a shortage of high-explosive bombs but ample supplies of incendiaries also meant either continuing area bombing or standing down the entire force. Finally, Harris mentioned Japan. "Are we going to bomb their cities flat" to help the army? Or are we going to bomb only their outlying factories, largely underground by the time we get going, and subsequently invade at the cost of 3 to 6 million casualties?"[241]

On March 30, Churchill withdrew the original minute, substituting on April 1 a much milder one that merely requested the Air Staff to investigate whether "our attacks do more harm to ourselves in the long run than they do to the enemy's immediate war effort."[242] On April 4, Portal replied that "at this advanced stage of the war no great or immediate additional advantage can be expected from the attack of the remaining industrial centres of Germany."[243] The Air Staff, however, did reserve the right to use area bombing to assist the advance of the Allied armies or to meet any stiffened German resistance. The Air Staff recommended no change in current strategic directives. USSTAF's comment on the British discontinuation of area bombing revealed the contradictions in its own policies: "The U.S. Strategic Air Forces in Europe have not at any time had a policy of making area bombing attacks upon German cities. Even our attacks against the Berlin area were always directed against military objectives." However, USSTAF acknowledged that "our Pathfinder [H2X] attacks against communications centers have often resulted in an area type of bombing because of the inaccuracy of this type of bombing."[244]

By the beginning of April, the question of continuing to engage in area bombing or, indeed, of even going on with the strategic bomber offensive had become moot. The Allied airmen could scarcely find a strategic target in the detritus of the Nazi state that justified the expense of attack.

By April 5, USSTAF acknowledged that, except for U-boat yards, all targets "should now be regarded as tactical targets." Of the tactical targets, USSTAF accorded first priority to the Luftwaffe and second priority to communications centers in central and southern Germany.[245] This change in emphasis did not affect the pace of operations: USSTAF heavy bombers flew on nineteen of the first twenty-five days of the month, dropping 46,628 tons of bombs mostly on marshaling yards (17,006 tons, less than 10 percent incendiaries), airfields (8,597 tons), and in ground support (10,885 tons).[246]

On April 10, Tedder, noting that the strategic air forces had agreed that their primary objective was now direct support of the land campaign, requested Spaatz to put full effort on enemy rail communications, especially those in central Germany.[247] Apparently Tedder and Eisenhower hoped to prevent effective north-to-south as well as west-to-east transfers of German men and matériel. Spaatz ordered Doolittle to give enemy communications top priority and push airfield bombing back a notch. Spaatz added hopefully, "Wherever suitable, Clarion low altitude, small formation technique should be used to obtain maximum effectiveness."[248]

At last, on April 12, Spaatz and Bottomley, after consulting Tedder, agreed on a final directive, Strategic Directive No. 4, which brought the strategic air war in Europe to a close. The top priority mission of the strategic air forces was "to give direct assistance to the land campaign." Operations to support the Soviet armies would occur only if directly requested by the Soviet High Command. Second priority went to oil supplies, particularly gasoline in storage depots, enemy lines of communications, and "such other missions as may be requested by the Supreme Commanders." The directive next allowed policing attacks against the Luftwaffe and provided that the marginal effort would remain concentrated on U-boats. The area bombing catchall category "Important Industrial Areas" disappeared, as did the requirement to support clandestine intelligence activities.[249]

War's End. *Top to bottom*: General Henry H. Arnold, General Carl A. Spaatz, and Lt. Gen. Hoyt S. Vandenberg celebrate victory at decoration ceremonies in Luxembourg on April 7, 1945; General Eisenhower and Prime Minister Churchill share a joke in the final days of the conflict; and General Carl A. Spaatz, Commanding General, U.S. Strategic Air Forces in Europe, and General Jean de Lattre de Tassigny, Commanding General, First French Army, sign the German surrender to the Soviet Union in Berlin as observers for their countries, early on the morning of May 9, 1945.

Four days later, Spaatz formally signaled the end of the strategic effort to Doolittle and Twining:

> The advances of the Ground Forces have brought to a close the Strategic Air War waged by the United States Strategic Air Forces and the Royal Air Force Bomber Command. It has been won with a decisiveness becoming increasingly evident as our armies overrun Germany. From now on, our Strategic Air Forces must operate with our Tactical Air Forces in close cooperation with our armies.[250]

On April 25, 1945, the Eighth Air Force sent out its last European bombardment mission. Mission no. 968 dispatched 589 B-17s and B-24s, 554 of which, using visual methods, unloaded 1,386 tons on the Skoda arms plant and airfields at Pilsen, Czechoslovakia, and on marshaling yards at Salzburg, Bad Reichenhall, and Hallein. The B-17s attacking Pilsen lost 6 bombers to enemy action and wrote off 4 more as not repairable.[251] The same day the Fifteenth sent 519 heavy bombers to Linz, losing 15. On April 26, the Fifteenth dispatched the last U.S. heavy-bomber mission over greater Germany to bomb targets near Klagenfurt in the Austrian Alps.

The AAF in Europe and Spaatz had fought their way down a long, hard road from the tentative publicity mission on July 4, 1942, and the first heavy-bomber mission over the Rouen marshaling yards on August 17, 1942. The Luftwaffe had countered their operations until the very last. The Eighth lost 266 bombers (63 to fighters) in March 1945 and 190 more (72 to fighters) in April,[252] while the Fifteenth lost 149 bombers (7 to fighters) in March and 83 (none to fighters) in April.[253] As late as April 10, when the Eighth made its last raid on the Berlin area, German jets shot down 10 bombers, their highest single day's toll.[254]

The war in Europe had not yet ended for Spaatz. After witnessing the German surrender to the British and Americans at Reims on May 7, at Eisenhower's behest, he accompanied Tedder to Berlin for the German surrender to the Soviets. The C-47 carrying Tedder, Spaatz, French General Jean de Lattre de Tassigny, their assistants, and press representatives, left Reims airfield at 8:25 A.M. on May 8 and landed first at an ex-Luftwaffe field held by the Americans at Stendal, near the Elbe River. For an hour they poked about the field littered with about 150 derelict German planes in various stages of disrepair. When the Soviet fighter escort arrived, they flew on to Berlin. A half-hour later, they arrived over Berlin; the city was cloaked in haze and smoke from still-smoldering buildings. The destruction, they testified, was awesome.[255]

After reviewing a Soviet honor guard at Tempelhof airfield, they boarded confiscated German automobiles and drove through the outskirts of the city to Karlshorst, a suburb in the northeast. Their route led through numerous former German roadblocks. The Soviets, afraid of snipers, had cleared all Germans from the area. For the most part the company rode in deathly silence.

Once they arrived, most of the party sat while Tedder, Soviet Marshal

Zhukov, and other Soviet functionaries debated armistice terms. Tedder had brought a draft instrument of surrender similar to the one signed at Reims. For the next twelve hours, the Soviets tediously contested every outstanding issue with Tedder. At first, they refused to allow either Spaatz or de Lattre de Tassigny to sign but eventually relented. At 11:00 P.M., the Soviets presented the terms to the German plenipotentiaries, headed by Field Marshal Keitel, who signed after some momentary and pointless haggling.[256]

Pandemonium broke loose as Soviet photographers practically mobbed the participants. After the signing, the Germans departed, while the Soviets laid out a banquet, with bottles of champagne, red wine, white wine, brandy, and vodka beside each plate. Toast followed toast, shots of vodka followed shots of vodka. Several celebrants succumbed to alcohol; one of these was Butcher, who afterwards couldn't even remember the next few hours. Later that morning, at Tedder's request, the party returned to Tempelhof directly through the heart of Berlin so that they could take a fuller measure of the German defeat. Then they returned to Reims. Spaatz had finished his part in the war against Germany.

Chapter 16

An Assessment

In the final phase of the war, when air superiority had been achieved, the potential of the strategic air offensive was greater than its achievement. This was primarily due to the difficulty of obtaining a unified and concentrated policy through the channels of divided command and in the conditions of divided opinion.[1]

—Official British history of the bomber offensive, 1961

Of all the accomplishments of the air forces, the attainment of air supremacy was the most significant, for it made possible the invasions of the continent and gave the heavy bombers their opportunity to wreck the industries of the Reich.[2]

—Official AAF history of World War II, 1951

Because of Spaatz's close wartime association with strategic bombing, any assessment of his role in the air war in Europe of necessity becomes an analysis of the Anglo-American strategic bombing campaign against Germany. The bald facts concerning that offensive have remained undisputed for over forty years. The heavy bombers of the Eighth and Fifteenth Air Forces flew 488,065 sorties, their fighters an additional 350,864. The two air forces dropped 1,005,729 tons of bombs, 28 percent of them on marshaling yards, 13 percent of them (133,807) on oil targets, 18 percent on aircraft targets, and the remaining 41 percent on lower priority targets. They claimed 15,426 German aircraft destroyed in the air, 8,435 by heavy bombers, and lost 8,759 heavy bombers and 3,546 fighters.[3] The AAF in the European and Mediterranean Theaters lost 35,844 men dead, 13,727 wounded, 33,414 captured or interned, and 5,958 missing. U.S. Navy and Marine battle dead for all theaters totaled 36,950 and 19,733 respectively.[4] The British Royal Air Force Bomber Command dropped an additional 1,047,412 tons of bombs[5] and lost 8,325 bombers and 55,573 personnel.[6] Given the comparable quality of the manpower involved, Bomber Command's dead exceeded the number of British Empire officers killed in World War I by 40 percent.[7] From October 1939 through May 1945, the RAF and the two U.S. strategic air forces dropped 543,054 tons of bombs (31 percent of them incendiaries) in raids specifically directed against the sixty-one German cities with populations exceeding 100,000. The strategic bombing campaign, at a minimum, killed 250,000 people and left 7,500,000 homeless.[8] Tactical Allied bombing in Germany added 55,000 more dead and 360,000 wounded.[9] Allied air power destroyed 3,600,000 dwelling units, 20 percent of the German total. Overall, Anglo-American air power in Europe dropped 2,700,000 tons of bombs, flew 1,440,000 bomber sorties and 2,680,000 fighter sorties, and reached peaks of 1,300,000 men and 28,000 aircraft in combat commands.[10]

Spaatz drove home a strategic air offensive that had faltered from lack of resources. From January 1, 1944, through May 8, 1945, he wielded a weapon of frightful power. That a single modern strategic multiple warhead missile, or a nuclear missile submarine, or a strategic bomber can each carry several times the one megaton dropped by USSTAF in no way diminishes the issues raised by Spaatz's direction of the U.S. strategic bomber offensive. He more than any other person must bear the responsibility and consequences for the application of U.S. strategic air power to Germany.

Some analysts have criticized the selection of targets. Maj. Gen. Haywood S. Hansell, Jr., one of the AAF's chief strategic and targeting planners, who participated in both AWPD/1 and AWPD/42 and led a B-29 bomber command against Japan, has faulted the failure to bomb the eight grinding-wheel manufacturing plants* and electric power generation network.[11] The United States Strategic Bombing Survey suggested that an investment of 12,000 to 15,000 tons per month on German transportation targets beginning in February 1944 instead of September 1944 would have caused the German war economy to collapse months earlier, in time for the effect of that collapse to be fully felt by the troops at the front. Although such arguments presuppose more detailed intelligence and more accurate intelligence evaluation than were available, their proponents were correct in concluding that the strategic bombing effort could have been employed more efficiently, but only if Spaatz had been free to operate in a vacuum, with no necessity to respond to the bureaucratic, institutional, and operational forces surrounding him.

From March through July 1944, the needs of OVERLORD and the beachhead undermined USSTAF's ability to conduct unfettered strategic bombing. Once Spaatz and Doolittle had obtained a measure of air superiority through their aggressive use of long-range escort fighters, the all-consuming bureaucratic bat-

---

* The loss of abrasive grinding wheels would have crippled the German armaments industry by denying it the ability to machine metal castings such as gun barrels, shells, and crankshafts.

tle between the oil and transportation plans began. Having committed himself to the oil plan, Spaatz could hardly shift gears by pointing to other target systems even more likely to bring the Nazis to heel without appearing fickle or foolish. CROSSBOW bombing, a requirement imposed on the strategic bombers by British domestic political considerations, was by far the biggest waste of blood, aircraft, and bombs of the entire strategic campaign.

In the summer of 1944, USSTAF crushed the German oil industry and, by September 14, was able to bomb where it willed, but nature robbed the strategic bombing campaign of its opportunity. Four months of bad weather did not provide enough days of visual bombing to strike and restrike, if necessary, the oil plants, let alone other target systems requiring precise bombing. Bad weather forced Spaatz to condone transportation attacks on major urban marshaling yards which razed the yards and the towns, strangled the *Reichsbahn* in its own rolling stock, and wrecked the German war economy. By the end of January 1945 no new industrial target system would have made a significant difference.

On the basis of performance, the American strategic bombing campaign fulfilled three-quarters of the Casablanca directive: it brought about "the progressive destruction and dislocation of the German military, industrial, and economic system;" it did not, however, undermine the morale of the German people. The oil campaign of the summer of 1944 was the fulfillment of the prewar doctrines of precision bombardment. American strategic bombers selected an indispensable military target system (oil shortages had a far greater effect on German armed forces than on German industry), attacked it by visual means, and brought aviation gasoline production to a virtual halt by September 1944. That was what American heavy bombers were supposed to do.

The transportation campaign demonstrated the triumph of wartime necessity over prewar theory. Spaatz had produced an almost all-weather force of limited accuracy. The constant cloud cover during the autumn of 1944 negated any hope of consistent precision bombing—hence the selection of the marshaling yards, a target system of more economic than military importance. Any significant breakdown of the German wartime economy would eventually have dramatic consequences at the front line. Employing bombing-through-clouds techniques, often partially assisted by visual means, USSTAF bombed out the marshaling yards, wrecked the coal transportation nexus, and brought German industry to its knees.

The U.S. strategic bombing effort inflicted severe, if not fatal, damage to the German military and German war economy. Independently, the effort did not defeat Germany, as air power advocates had hoped. The slow buildup of forces, thanks in part to the bottleneck in Anglo-American shipping availability, the diversion of strength to the Pacific and the Mediterranean, operational difficulties, intelligence errors that led to overestimation of damage inflicted, and debates concerning targeting prevented the most efficient application of air power to crucial sectors of the German war economy. However, what the bombing did accomplish was substantial in contributing to Germany's defeat. The

Anglo-American bombing offensive brought the war to the German people long before their armies were forced back onto German soil. In a war in which the effort of civilian workers on the production lines was as essential to victory as the fighting of soldiers on the front lines, the very existence of the strategic bombing offensive encouraged U.S. and British civilians and inflicted pain and suffering on the enemy. The British may have devoted 40 to 50 percent of their total war production to the air forces; the U.S. expended up to 35 percent; and the Germans up to 40 percent. German war production increased throughout the war, reaching its peak in the third quarter of 1944. Strategic air bombardment undoubtedly kept that increase from going higher still. It forced the dispersion of factories and the building of underground facilities, made German production more vulnerable to transportation disruption, lowered production by forcing smaller, more labor-intensive production units which denied the Germans the manufacturing economies of scale available to their enemies, disorganized workers' lives, and probably lowered their productivity. In ways great and small— and utterly incalculable—strategic bombing made German war production less efficient and less effective than it would have been if the bombers had not flown night after night and day after day.

Strategic bombing also forced the Germans into an enormous defense and reconstruction effort, diverting their aircraft manufacture almost exclusively into fighter and interceptor production. The bombing of oil not only limited mobility but, as a side effect, also greatly reduced nitrogen production, hampering the manufacture of explosives and fertilizers. By 1944 Germany had two million soldiers, civilians, and prisoners of war engaged in ground antiaircraft defense, more than the total number of workers in its aircraft industry. An additional million workers were engaged in repair and rebuilding; the oil industry alone absorbed a quarter of a million. Speer estimated that 30 percent of total gun output and 20 percent of heavy ammunition output was intended for air defense, a significant loss to the ground forces of high velocity weapons suitable for anti-tank defense. Speer further estimated that 50 percent of electrotechnical production and one-third of the optical industry was devoted to radar and signals equipment for the antiaircraft effort, further starving the front lines of essential communications equipment.[12]

The Allied strategic bombing effort could not reasonably have been expected to do more. It vindicated the treasure expended on it. If in the final analysis it accomplished its ends more by brute force than by elegant precision, the fault lay in the unrealistic assumptions of prewar doctrine as to wartime accuracy, European weather, and radar technology. The AAF was fortunate that the great mass of bombers that arrived in Europe in 1944 were accompanied by large numbers of long-range escort fighters. If production, shipping, and manpower had allowed those bombers to arrive six months earlier, they might well have been impaled on the German air defense system.

Strategic bombing did not achieve the last task imposed by the Casablanca

590

directive: undermining "the morale of the German people to a point where their capacity for armed resistance" was fatally weakened. In its pursuit of that goal, chiefly by means of city or area bombing, Allied strategic bombing raised questions of moral and ethical significance. During the war, area bombing was questioned on the floor of Parliament, first by the bishop of Chichester in February 1944, and then by Richard Stokes in March 1945. Twenty-five years ago David Irving resurrected the ghosts of Dresden. One recent critic has written of the "evil of American bombing," calling it a "sin of a peculiarly modern kind because it seemed so inadvertent, seemed to have involved so little choice."[13] Another has noted, "The most important factor moving the AAF toward Douhetian war was the attitude of the country's top civilian and military leaders," specifically blaming Arnold, Marshall, Eisenhower, Lovett, Stimson, and Roosevelt, but not Spaatz, as responsible for the shift to area bombing.[14] These critics and many others have recoiled at a policy that resulted in the death of more than 300,000 persons.

It was the RAF that conducted most of the area bombing and, like the AAF, the RAF resorted to it because weaknesses in its operational technique left it no choice. Bomber Command persisted in area bombing after it had developed an accuracy surpassing even visual bombing, as practiced by USSTAF. To belabor the enemy with the only weapon available was one thing, but to continue to use it when better means were at hand delayed the end of the war and needlessly killed tens of thousands. If the RAF earned any blame for its conduct of the air war, it was for its area bombing conducted after June 1944.

In the autumn of 1944 and the following winter, the AAF also turned to city bombing, ostensibly to destroy the rail yards. Lowering of morale, although seldom mentioned, was almost certainly an added and hoped-for consequence. In contrast to RAF bombing, AAF nonvisual bombing never became particularly accurate. Arnold, Lovett, Spaatz, Eisenhower, and Marshall knew that bombing-through-overcast techniques produced wildly imprecise results. If Stimson and Roosevelt did not know, it was because they did not ask. However wrong it may have been, the AAF's area bombing hastened the war's end.

The RAF killed its hundreds of thousands, the AAF its tens of thousands. But opprobrium cannot be added up in a ledger book with exact amounts entered in each account. To whom should one assign the guilt for the 125,000 German civilians killed during the Russian storming of Berlin?[15] How should one weigh the murder of 325,000 Jews by the SS at the Treblinka death camp between July 28 and September 21, 1942?[16] To those who accepted the truism that two wrongs never make a right, then nothing can excuse the area bombing of the Allied strategic campaign no matter how evil the German state. At the other extreme, those who believed that any means justified the end find nothing abhorrent in area bombing. Between those opinions lies a vast middle ground. Area bombing cannot be examined as a separate, unique phenomenon judged only by numbers of missions flown and bombs dropped versus people killed. A more valid yardstick would be the extent to which the action contributed to ending the war as quickly as possible with minimum loss of life.

Placed in the context of the entire war against the European Axis, area bombing caused more civilian casualties than any other type of warfare employed by the British and American Allies, but area bombing—the bombing of rail yards is an exception—did not decisively influence the war's outcome. Hence area bombing failed on both military and humanitarian grounds: it did not shorten the war and it took lives unnecessarily.

For three years Spaatz commanded AAF units that were either destined for or serving in the war against the European Axis. From the start, on his assumption of command of the Eighth Air Force on May 10, 1942, almost until the German surrender in Berlin on May 9, 1945, his responsibilities grew. From the command of an incompletely trained force of five groups, his authority increased until he controlled, in one way or another, an armada of four air forces made up of 135 groups, including 61 heavy-bomber groups and 42 fighter groups. On February 1, 1945, Eisenhower rated Spaatz and Bradley equally as the two American general officers in the Combined European and Mediterranean Theaters of Operation who had rendered the most valuable service in the war against the Germans. Of Spaatz, he commented, "Experienced and able air leader; loyal and cooperative; modest and selfless; always reliable."[17] Bradley prepared a similar list on December 1, 1944; he ranked Spaatz second, after Bedell Smith.[18] Spaatz's subordinates appreciated him as well. Years after the war Doolittle observed,

> I suppose if it were possible for one man to love another man, I love Gen. Spaatz. I guess it's . . . better . . . [to say] that I idolize Gen. Spaatz. He is perhaps the only man that I have ever been closely associated with whom I have never known to make a bad decision."

According to Doolittle, it was soundness of judgment that earned Spaatz Eisenhower's trust.[19]

Spaatz must be ranked as one of the premier airmen of World War II with Harris and Tedder. Spaatz commanded the largest heavy-bomber force of all time at the same time he had de facto control over two large tactical air forces. No other airman of the war had so vast an operational responsibility. His combined force was three times larger than that commanded by Harris, the British strategic bomber commander. Like Harris, Spaatz eventually resorted to a type of area bombing, but never with the unseemly relish of his British counterpart. Spaatz's effort was directed at a particular target system, rail yards, unlike Harris's which was aimed at the broad target category of industrial areas. Although Spaatz was more cooperative with his superiors than Harris, he did not gain the amount of respect and admiration from the air crews that Harris did—probably because he eschewed the limelight. No government-sponsored press campaign extolled his efforts at the head of his command. Spaatz did not have the depth of strategic vision or the intellectual bent of Tedder, but he proved a good coalition soldier, and his advocacy of oil was as great a factor in Germany's defeat as Tedder's advocacy of transportation.

Coningham, Leigh-Mallory, and Eaker must rank below Spaatz. None of them commanded a force of comparable size. The first two were far too parochial in their views, and their difficult personalities did not fit them for larger roles. Eaker had abilities different from but equal to Spaatz's. He was more outgoing, articulate, and technologically interested in his trade. Eaker made an excellent coalition soldier, cooperating loyally with Wilson and Slessor in the Mediterranean. From November 1942 to December 1943, no one could have done better than, and few as well as, he did as commander of the Eighth Air Force. Eaker was almost as close to Arnold as Spaatz was. What he didn't have was Spaatz's luck. Eaker was the right man at the right place at the wrong time. He lacked the bombers and crews, long-range escort fighters, drop tanks, and H2X radar sets his successor had in abundance. Spaatz would have done no better and would have suffered the same inevitable defeat over Schweinfurt, but he probably would have outlasted Eaker, by virtue of his stronger relationship with Arnold, by about two months—long enough to get to Big Week and to stay in command for the rest of the war. Ira Eaker knew his business, but in some indefinable way he lacked Spaatz's "fire in the gut" and the ability to extract the last ounce of effort from his force or to stand up to Arnold.

By the time the United States entered World War II, Spaatz had a set of fixed character traits, firm beliefs, and over three decades' experience as a military aviator, all of which greatly influenced his subsequent career. He was a drinker and gambler before and during the war. His personal correspondence is heavily laced with liquor bills and gambling checks. Like Churchill, he apparently had a large capacity for alcohol. There is no evidence whatsoever, however, of errors in judgment or decorum attributable to indulgence in spirits. Nor were there any whispers of overindulgence, such as those that plagued Ulysses S. Grant before and after the Battle of Shiloh. Spaatz's gambling for relatively high stakes had no effect on the conduct of his command. (He seems to have broken even over the long term.)

Spaatz had a quick mind and did not suffer fools gladly. He was taciturn and shy in public. As a result, he abhorred staff meetings and the day-to-day minutiae of a vast headquarters. He surrounded himself with men he knew and trusted who screened out unimportant details and kept them from reaching his desk. This distaste for staff routine dovetailed neatly with the ways he relaxed—playing cards, darts, and guitar in his headquarters' houses.

Spaatz's methods left him open to charges of cronyism. Many key members of his headquarters/household were World War I retreads; some had even trained under him at Issoudun. His chief of staff, Edward P. Curtis, and his director of intelligence, George C. McDonald, had both been fighter pilots in World War I. Each had several credited victories for shooting down German planes. Spaatz fought to obtain high rank for those men and others such as

Doolittle, Vandenberg, and Norstad. He did much for his friends, but he also chose wisely. Spaatz naturally promoted people he knew well, but he also knew them to be competent and capable of handling greater responsibility.

Similarly, Spaatz benefited from his close personal relationship with Arnold. In the small prewar Air Corps, they served together several times; chance and personal chemistry made them friends. In those years Arnold had the opportunity to gauge Spaatz's operational competence, reliability, loyalty, and dedication to the cause of air autonomy. Consequently, as Arnold rose in position, he gave Spaatz increasing responsibility. Spaatz was Arnold's favorite. Arnold repeatedly placed him in positions, such as Air Corps Plans Section Chief, Special Observer to England, and Chief of the Air Staff, which challenged him and gave him the chance to prepare for the coming war as well as to advance his career. Without Arnold, Spaatz would not have been in the right place at the right time. Arnold deserves full credit for having the judgment and foresight to back Spaatz, but Spaatz deserves equal credit for the manner in which he fulfilled Arnold's expectations. One need only to look at the way Arnold treated his other favorite, Ira Eaker, to realize that he valued achievement over friendship. If Spaatz had failed to perform, Arnold would surely have put him aside, too.

Spaatz, strengthened by Arnold's abiding friendship and support, was able to resist the demands of the British, the ground forces, transportation plan advocates, and others to divert his resources from daylight strategic bombing and autonomy for the AAF. Their relationship eased Spaatz's administrative tasks. Although Arnold on occasion might gibe at his handling of men and matériel, each had faith that the other was doing his utmost and was doing it competently. Spaatz was lucky to have Arnold's friendship and to return to Britain when supplies had begun to arrive in abundance. Good luck, however, was also the residue of skill. Without character and ability Spaatz could scarcely have performed so well in his climb to the heights.

At the beginning of the war, Spaatz, as did many senior Army Air Force officers, espoused particular doctrines associated with daylight precision bombing and advocated the creation of U.S. military aviation as an independent service equal to the Army and the Navy. These views, which did not change, colored most of his wartime decisions. His years of experience with mossbacked ground force and naval officers and his own ignorance of and antipathy toward ground matters gave him little appreciation of military problems other than those dealing directly with air. Spaatz did poorly at Leavenworth; the curriculum of its Command and General Staff School concentrated almost solely on ground problems.

Spaatz's judgment was not infallible. Passionate beliefs in the doctrine of precision bombing and in the independence of air power served him well in the great strategic debates revolving around air power, but they limited his ability to judge questions affecting the combined roles of all the services. He opposed the North African invasion because it weakened and delayed the strategic offensive

594

against Germany. He shared an unwarranted optimism with Eisenhower and Eisenhower's staff as to the feasibility of an invasion of France in 1942 or 1943. Given the poor initial performance of U.S. forces in French North Africa and the far greater resources that would have been available to the German defenders, such an invasion could only have resulted in disaster—as the British, based on their intelligence, argued. Even in mid-1943 Spaatz so overrated the effectiveness of his bombers that he boasted to Arnold that he could defeat Germany if only he could consistently get 200 heavy bombers airborne for each mission. Two years later, six or seven times that number could still not bring about Germany's fall without the help of a tremendous ground campaign.

Spaatz's appreciation of OVERLORD was flawed as well. As an airman he doubted that the resources and matériel expended on it justified its cost. He mistrusted the ground forces' fighting capacity—without the support of facts. Similarly, in the operations before the Normandy breakout, he and the other airmen failed to understand fully the problems faced by the Army. Their criticisms and constant prodding for action did them little credit. Spaatz's suggestion to U.S. Ambassor to Britain John G. Winant, in February 1944, of a thrust through Norway and Sweden might have brought his heavy bombers closer to Germany, but it still left the ground forces a sea away. Spaatz's earlier suggestion to Hopkins, in November 1943, to seize northern Italy would have advanced the bombers but would have left the ground forces confronted with the difficulties of mounting a major campaign across the Alps.

Although Spaatz could not view strategy broadly because of his ignorance of geopolitics and his dismissal of the ground forces' perspective, he could, because of his expertise, bring great insight to the selection of bombing targets. The issue of the transportation plan versus the oil plan was such a complex skein of conflicting priorities and personalities that it defied a simple answer. Spaatz was undoubtedly correct in his contentions that the heavy-bomber offensive would gain air superiority over western Europe by defeating the Luftwaffe over Germany and that the Luftwaffe would only fight to defend vital targets within Germany.

It does not follow from those contentions, however, that an attack directed against German tactical mobility in France was unnecessary or required no assistance from the heavy bombers. The transportation plan in its original form, which required massive air strikes from both Bomber Command and the Eighth Air Force, would probably have damaged the French railway system enough to seriously delay German reinforcements bound for Normandy. But the plan could not guarantee air superiority, and it implied that U.S. heavy bombers would serve under a British commander who did not sufficiently value strategic bombardment. Predictably, Spaatz rejected it out of hand. Even if his and Leigh-Mallory's personalities had meshed perfectly, he would have fought the plan because of its mishandling of strategic bombers and stifling of AAF pretensions to autonomy. Spaatz's fight against the transportation plan delayed its imposition and resulted in its modification. As a result, attritional air battles over Germany were ensured and an effective bridge-busting campaign was launched, which, even the transportation plan's supporters admitted, added to its success.

The oil plan, as all observers recognized, was Spaatz's finest moment. It ruined the Luftwaffe as a viable air force and dashed the weapon of mobility from the hands of the German ground forces. He selected a compact, crucial, vulnerable system of targets and pursued it relentlessly. Unfortunately, the oil campaign was only one of two such efforts mounted by the strategic bomber forces; Harris pursued his area bombing of German cities with equal tenacity.

Spaatz's experiences in training and operations made him an excellent combat commander. Building on the foundation prepared by Eaker, Spaatz established the Eighth Air Force in Britain. He did not commit it to action until he was sure that he had at least trained it adequately, building on the little it had been given in the States. Similarly, in North Africa, he set up the Northwest African Training Command to bring his crews closer to the standards of his Allies and opponents. Yet his insistence on thorough training for and maximum performance by his air crews led directly to the ultimate irony of the strategic campaign.

Given the technology available to him, Spaatz helped to produce a nearly all-weather force. He used the most modern radar, employed electronic counter-measures, took full advantage of ULTRA, and pushed his commanders and their men and machines to their limits in order to exploit all the force available to him. Once he had created this available force, it had to be employed. Spaatz, who violently objected to the killing of French civilians, sanctioned the bombing of transportation centers in eastern Germany, the smashing of rail stations in Berlin, and the demolition of marshaling yards in numerous German cities. He did not relish destruction for destruction's sake; rather he faced the problem of how to wield an expanding force of limited accuracy against an opponent who had large reserves of manpower (slave labor, women, and domestic servants) and machine tools (most German industry worked single shifts for much of the war and had ample stocks of machine tools on hand) without causing excessive or unnecessary collateral damage. To Spaatz, to most of his fellow soldiers, to his government, and to the people his government represented it was better to err on the side of excessive force by pulverizing the Reich, than to leave it the strength to resist and to kill more Allied soldiers. In the merciless logic of total war, Spaatz decided correctly.

Without Spaatz and his insistence on the oil plan and his devastating campaign against the Luftwaffe before the Normandy invasion, the Allies would still have defeated Nazi Germany. With Spaatz, the Allies defeated Hitler and his henchmen months earlier than they otherwise might have. Each day beyond May 8 would have seen the ovens of the Third Reich still operating and the combatants of both sides still suffering in battle lines throughout Europe. That the war in Europe ended when it did is reason enough to place Spaatz in the front rank of the Allied leaders of World War II.

★　　★　　★　　★

Although Spaatz's war in Europe ended with the German surrender in Berlin, his service to his country continued. On July 29, 1945, he arrived on the island of Guam to assume command of the U.S. Strategic Air Forces in the Pacific, which included the Mariana Islands-based Twentieth Air Force, under Lt. Gen. Nathan F. Twining, and the Eighth Air Force, still under Lt. Gen. James H. Doolittle and soon to be based on the island of Okinawa. After receiving authorization from President Harry S. Truman and General George C. Marshall, Spaatz ordered the dropping of atomic bombs on Hiroshima and Nagasaki. Three weeks later, on September 1, 1945, Spaatz stood on the deck of the USS *Missouri* to witness the surrender of the last of the Axis powers. He was the only U.S. military officer to attend all three surrenders, the first in Reims, the second in Berlin, and the third in Tokyo Bay. After the war, Spaatz succeeded General Henry H. Arnold as Commanding General, U.S. Army Air Forces. From that post he directed the AAF's campaign to separate itself from the Army. When the U.S. Air Force was established by Congress in September 1947, Spaatz became its first Chief of Staff. He retired in April 1948. Shortly thereafter, he became a columnist on military matters for *Newsweek* magazine. He worked for *Newsweek* until 1961, when, at the age of seventy, he retired again. Spaatz died on July 14, 1974. He is buried at the U.S. Air Force Academy, whose site he helped to select, in Colorado Springs, Colorado.

Statistical Appendices

Source for all Statistical Appendices: *Army Air Forces Statistical Digest, World War II* (Washington, D.C.: Office of Statistical Control, 1945).

Appendix 1

Aviation Personnel in the Army
(Percent of Total Army Strength)

Year	Number	Percent of Total
1912 (1 Nov)	51	0.1
1913 (30 Sep)	114	0.1
1914	122	0.1
1915	208	0.2
1916	311	0.3
1917 (6 Apr)	1,218	0.6
1918 (11 Nov)	195,023	25.3
1919	25,603	2.7
1920	9,050	4.5
1921	11,649	5.1
1922	9,642	6.5
1923	9,441	7.2
1924	10,547	7.4
1925	9,670	7.1
1926	9,674	7.2
1927	10,008	7.5
1928	10,549	7.8
1929	12,131	7.8
1930	13,531	9.8
1931	14,780	10.6
1932	15,028	11.2
1933	15,099	11.1
1934	15,861	11.5
1935	16,427	11.7
1936	17,233	10.3
1937	19,147	10.7
1938	21,089	11.5
1939	23,455	12.4
1940	51,165	19.1
1941	152,125	10.4
1942	764,415	24.9
1943	2,197,114	31.4
1944	2,372,292	29.7
1945	2,282,259	24.1

Appendix 2

Direct Cash Appropriations and Expenditures
Fiscal Years 1899 to 1946

Year	Direct Cash Appropriations*	Expenditures[†]
1899	50,000[‡]	
1909	30,000[§]	
1912	125,000	
1913	100,000	
1914	175,000	
1915	200,000	
1916	801,000	
1917	18,681,666	
1918	735,000,000	
1919	952,304,758	
1920	28,123,503	
1921	35,124,300	30,913,798
1922	25,648,333	23,095,257
1923	13,060,000	18,141,688
1924	12,626,000	11,015,365
1925	13,476,619	11,680,955
1926	15,911,191	14,900,264
1927	15,256,694	16,759,286
1928	21,117,494	19,437,722
1929	28,911,431	23,261,643
1930	34,910,059	28,051,563
1931	38,945,968	38,651,204
1932	31,850,892	33,046,254
1933	25,673,236	21,929,302
1934	31,037,769	17,372,277
1935	27,917,702	20,337,871
1936	45,600,444	32,026,622
1937	59,619,694	41,055,082
1938	58,851,266	50,875,129
1939	71,099,532	83,164,156
1940	186,562,847	108,169,717
1941	2,173,608,961	605,409,021
1942	23,049,935,463	2,554,863,420
1943	11,317,416,790	9,391,855,445
1944	23,655,998,000	13,087,279,848
1945	1,610,717,000	11,357,390,523
1946	517,100	1,349,030,427[#]
Grand Total	$64,336,985,712	$38,989,713,839

*Includes appropriations for salaries, Office, Chief of Air Corps.

[†]Expenditures for Jul 1920–Aug 1946, data unavailable for 1899–Jun 1920.

[‡]Allotted to Dr. S. P. Langley for experiments in aerodynamics.

[§]Allotted to pay for Wright airplane which completed tests in 1909.

[#]Expenditures for July and August only.

Appendix 3

Combat Groups Overseas
December 1941 to August 1945

	European Theater of Operations						Mediterranean Theater of Operations					
	Heavy Bomb	Med/Lt Bomb	Fighter	Troop Carrier	Recon	Total	Heavy Bomb	Med/Lt Bomb	Fighter	Troop Carrier	Recon	Total
1941 Dec	-	-	-	-	-	-	-	-	-	-	-	-
1942 Jan	-	-	-	-	-	-	-	-	-	-	-	-
Feb	-	-	-	-	-	-	1	-	-	-	-	1
Mar	-	-	-	-	-	-	1	-	1	-	-	2
Apr	-	-	-	-	-	-	1	-	1	-	-	2
May	-	-	-	-	-	-	1	-	-	-	-	1
Jun	1	-	-	1	-	2	1	-	-	-	-	1
Jul	2	-	2	1	-	5	2	1	1	-	-	4
Aug	9	-	$3\frac{2}{3}$	2	-	$14\frac{2}{3}$	2	1	1	-	-	4
Sep	9	-	$4\frac{2}{3}$	3	$1\frac{1}{4}$	$17\frac{11}{12}$	2	1	1	-	-	4
Oct	9	4	$8\frac{2}{3}$	-	$1\frac{1}{2}$	$23\frac{1}{6}$	2	1	$2\frac{3}{4}$	3	-	$8\frac{3}{4}$
Nov	7	1	5	$\frac{1}{2}$	$1\frac{3}{4}$	$15\frac{1}{4}$	4	5	$7\frac{5}{12}$	4	1	$21\frac{5}{12}$
Dec	6	1	5	$\frac{1}{2}$	$1\frac{1}{2}$	14	$4\frac{3}{4}$	6	$8\frac{1}{4}$	4	$1\frac{1}{4}$	$24\frac{1}{2}$
1943 Jan	7	1	3	$\frac{1}{2}$	$1\frac{1}{4}$	$12\frac{3}{4}$	5	6	$12\frac{3}{4}$	4	$1\frac{1}{2}$	$29\frac{1}{4}$
Feb	7	1	3	$\frac{1}{2}$	$1\frac{1}{4}$	$12\frac{3}{4}$	5	8	13	4	$1\frac{1}{2}$	$31\frac{1}{2}$
Mar	7	1	3	$\frac{1}{2}$	$1\frac{1}{4}$	$12\frac{3}{4}$	5	8	13	4	$1\frac{1}{2}$	$31\frac{1}{2}$
Apr	12	1	3	$\frac{1}{2}$	$1\frac{1}{4}$	$17\frac{3}{4}$	$5\frac{3}{4}$	8	13	4	$1\frac{3}{4}$	$32\frac{1}{2}$
May	14	1	3	$\frac{1}{2}$	$1\frac{1}{2}$	20	6	8	$14\frac{1}{3}$	7	$1\frac{1}{2}$	$36\frac{5}{6}$
Jun	16	3	5	$\frac{1}{2}$	$1\frac{1}{3}$	$26\frac{1}{6}$	8	8	14	7	2	39
Jul	16	4	6	$\frac{1}{2}$	$1\frac{1}{3}$	$28\frac{1}{6}$	9	8	14	7	$2\frac{1}{6}$	$40\frac{1}{6}$
Aug	17	4	7	$\frac{1}{2}$	2	$30\frac{1}{2}$	9	8	14	7	2	40
Sep	20	4	9	$\frac{1}{2}$	2	$35\frac{1}{2}$	6	8	14	7	2	37
Oct	$20\frac{1}{3}$	4	11	$1\frac{1}{2}$	2	$38\frac{5}{6}$	6	8	14	7	$2\frac{1}{6}$	$37\frac{1}{6}$
Nov	$22\frac{1}{2}$	4	12	2	$1\frac{1}{3}$	$41\frac{5}{6}$	6	8	14	7	$2\frac{5}{12}$	$37\frac{5}{12}$
Dec	26	4	17	$2\frac{1}{2}$	$1\frac{3}{4}$	$51\frac{1}{4}$	$7\frac{1}{2}$	8	14	7	2	$38\frac{1}{2}$
1944 Jan	$28\frac{3}{4}$	4	$19\frac{1}{4}$	4	3	59	$3\frac{1}{4}$	8	$14\frac{1}{4}$	7	3	$45\frac{1}{2}$
Feb	31	8	21	$9\frac{1}{2}$	3	$72\frac{1}{2}$	17	7	13	3	3	43
Mar	33	10	25	$13\frac{1}{2}$	3	$84\frac{1}{2}$	20	7	13	3	3	46
Apr	39	11	32	14	3	99	21	7	13	3	2	46
May	41	11	33	14	3	102	21	7	13	3	2	46
Jun	41	11	33	14	3	102	21	7	13	3	2	46
Jul	41	11	33	14	3	103	21	7	13	3	2	46
Aug	41	11	33	14	4	103	21	7	13	3	2	46
Sep	41	11	32	14	4	103	21	7	13	3	2	46
Oct	41	11	33	14	5	104	21	7	12	3	2	45
Nov	41	13	33	14	5	106	21	5	12	3	2	43
Dec	40	13	33	14	5	105	21	5	12	3	2	43
1945 Jan	40	13	33	14	5	105	21	4	12	3	2	42
Feb	40	13	35	14	5	107	21	4	10	3	2	40
Mar	40	13	35	14	6	108	21	4	10	3	2	40
Apr	40	13	35	15	6	109	19	4	10	3	2	38
May	28	13	35	12	6	94	13	4	10	1	2	30
Jun	15	13	35	12	6	81	6	3	10	1	2	22
Jul	7	9	35	6	6	63	5	-	10	1	2	18
Aug	7	8	33	4	4	56	5	-	5	1	2	13

Pacific Ocean Area						Far East Air Forces					
Heavy Bomb	Med/Lt Bomb	Fighter	Troop Carrier	Recon	Total	Heavy Bomb	Med/Lt Bomb	Fighter	Troop Carrier	Recon	Total
2	-	3	-	2	5	-	1	-	-	-	1
2	-	3	-	-	5	1	-	1	-	-	2
2	-	3	-	-	5	1	-	2	-	-	3
2	-	3	-	-	5	2	3	3	-	-	8
2	-	3	-	-	5	2	3	3	-	-	8
2	-	3	-	-	5	2	3	3	-	-	8
2	-	3	-	-	5	2	3	3	-	-	8
1	-	3	-	-	4	3	3	3	-	-	9
2	-	3	-	-	5	3	3	3	-	-	9
2	-	3	-	-	5	3	3	3	-	-	9
$1\frac{1}{2}$	-	3	-	-	$4\frac{1}{2}$	$4\frac{1}{2}$	3	3	-	-	$10\frac{1}{2}$
$1\frac{1}{2}$	-	3	-	-	$4\frac{1}{2}$	$4\frac{1}{2}$	3	3	1	-	$11\frac{1}{2}$
1	-	$2\frac{5}{8}$	-	-	$3\frac{5}{8}$	4	3	$4\frac{1}{8}$	1	$\frac{1}{2}$	$12\frac{5}{8}$
1	-	$2\frac{3}{4}$	-	-	$3\frac{3}{4}$	4	3	4	2	$\frac{1}{2}$	$13\frac{1}{2}$
1	-	$2\frac{1}{4}$	-	-	$3\frac{1}{4}$	4	3	$4\frac{3}{4}$	2	$\frac{1}{2}$	$14\frac{1}{4}$
2	-	$2\frac{1}{4}$	-	-	$4\frac{1}{4}$	3	$3\frac{1}{2}$	5	2	$\frac{1}{2}$	14
$1\frac{1}{2}$	-	$2\frac{1}{4}$	-	-	$3\frac{3}{4}$	$4\frac{1}{2}$	$3\frac{1}{2}$	5	2	$\frac{3}{4}$	$15\frac{3}{4}$
1	-	$2\frac{1}{4}$	-	-	$3\frac{1}{4}$	5	5	5	2	$\frac{1}{2}$	$17\frac{1}{2}$
1	-	$2\frac{1}{4}$	-	-	$3\frac{1}{4}$	5	5	5	$3\frac{1}{2}$	$\frac{1}{2}$	19
1	-	2	-	-	3	5	5	7	$3\frac{1}{2}$	$\frac{1}{2}$	21
1	-	2	-	-	3	5	5	$7\frac{1}{12}$	5	$\frac{1}{3}$	$22\frac{5}{12}$
1	-	2	-	-	3	5	5	7	5	$\frac{1}{3}$	$22\frac{1}{3}$
2	1	2	-	-	5	5	5	7	5	1	23
2	1	2	-	-	5	5	6	7	5	$1\frac{1}{3}$	$24\frac{1}{3}$
2	1	2	-	-	5	5	6	8	5	$2\frac{2}{3}$	$26\frac{2}{3}$
2	1	2	-	-	5	6	5	8	5	3	27
2	1	2	-	-	5	6	6	8	5	3	28
2	1	2	-	-	5	6	6	8	5	3	28
2	1	3	-	-	6	6	6	8	5	3	28
2	1	3	-	-	6	6	6	8	5	3	28
3	1	3	-	-	7	6	6	8	5	3	28
3	1	3	-	-	7	6	6	8	5	3	28
3	1	3	-	-	7	6	6	6	5	3	28
3	1	3	-	-	7	6	6	8	5	3	28
3	1	3	-	-	7	6	6	8	6	3	29
3	1	3	-	-	7	6	6	8	7	3	30
3	1	3	-	-	7	6	6	8	7	3	30
3	1	3	-	-	7	6	6	8	7	3	30
3	1	3	1	-	8	6	6	8	7	3	30
3	1	3	1	-	8	6	6	8	7	3	30
3	1	3	1	-	8	6	6	8	7	3	30
3	2	3	1	-	9	6	6	8	7	3	30
3	2	3	1	-	9	6	6	8	7	3	30
3	2	-	1	-	6	6	6	8	7	3	30
3	2	-	-	-	5	6	6	8	7	3	30

Combat Groups Overseas
December 1941 to August 1945

	China and India-Burma						Alaska					
	Heavy Bomb	Med/Lt Bomb	Fighter	Troop Carrier	Recon	Total	Heavy Bomb	Med/Lt Bomb	Fighter	Troop Carrier	Recon	Total
1941 Dec	-	-	1	-	-	1	-	-	-	-	-	-
1942 Jan	-	-	1	-	-	1	-	-	-	-	-	-
Feb	-	-	1	-	-	1	-	-	-	-	-	-
Mar	-	-	1	-	-	1	-	-	-	-	-	-
Apr	-	-	1	-	-	1	-	-	-	-	-	-
May	-	-	2	-	-	2	-	-	-	-	-	-
Jun	1	-	2	-	-	3	-	-	-	-	-	-
Jul	1	-	2	-	-	3	-	-	-	-	-	-
Aug	1	-	2	-	-	3	-	$\frac{1}{4}$	-	-	-	$\frac{1}{4}$
Sep	1	1	2	-	-	4	-	$\frac{1}{4}$	1	-	-	$1\frac{1}{4}$
Oct	1	1	2	-	-	4	-	$\frac{1}{4}$	1	-	-	$1\frac{1}{4}$
Nov	1	1	2	-	-	4	-	$\frac{1}{4}$	1	-	-	$1\frac{1}{4}$
Dec	1	1	2	-	-	4	$\frac{3}{4}$	$\frac{3}{4}$	1	-	-	$2\frac{1}{2}$
1943 Jan	1	1	2	-	-	4	$\frac{3}{4}$	$\frac{3}{4}$	1	-	-	$2\frac{1}{2}$
Feb	2	1	2	-	-	5	$\frac{3}{4}$	$\frac{3}{4}$	1	-	-	$2\frac{1}{2}$
Mar	2	1	2	-	-	5	$\frac{3}{4}$	$\frac{3}{4}$	1	-	-	$2\frac{1}{2}$
Apr	2	1	2	-	$\frac{1}{4}$	$5\frac{1}{4}$	$\frac{3}{4}$	$\frac{3}{4}$	1	-	$\frac{1}{4}$	$2\frac{3}{4}$
May	2	1	2	-	$\frac{1}{4}$	$5\frac{1}{4}$	$\frac{3}{4}$	$\frac{3}{4}$	1	-	$\frac{1}{4}$	$2\frac{3}{4}$
Jun	2	1	3	-	$\frac{2}{3}$	$6\frac{2}{3}$	$\frac{3}{4}$	$\frac{3}{4}$	1	-	-	$2\frac{1}{2}$
Jul	2	1	3	-	$\frac{2}{3}$	$6\frac{2}{3}$	$\frac{3}{4}$	$\frac{3}{4}$	$1\frac{1}{2}$	-	-	3
Aug	2	1	4	-	$\frac{1}{3}$	$7\frac{1}{3}$	$\frac{3}{4}$	$\frac{3}{4}$	$1\frac{2}{3}$	-	-	$3\frac{1}{6}$
Sep	2	1	4	-	$\frac{1}{3}$	$7\frac{1}{3}$	$\frac{1}{4}$	$\frac{1}{4}$	1	-	-	$1\frac{1}{2}$
Oct	2	1	4	-	$\frac{1}{2}$	$7\frac{1}{2}$	$\frac{1}{4}$	$\frac{1}{4}$	1	-	-	$1\frac{1}{2}$
Nov	2	1	4	$\frac{1}{2}$	1	$8\frac{1}{2}$	-	1	-	-	-	-
Dec	2	1	4	$\frac{3}{4}$	$\frac{1}{2}$	$8\frac{1}{4}$	-	1	-	-	-	1
1944 Jan	2	1	4	1	-	8	$\frac{1}{2}$	$\frac{1}{2}$	1	-	-	2
Feb	2	1	4	1	1	9	$\frac{1}{2}$	$\frac{1}{2}$	1	-	-	2
Mar	2	1	4	1	1	9	$\frac{1}{2}$	$\frac{1}{2}$	1	-	-	2
Apr	2	2	6	1	1	12	$\frac{1}{2}$	$\frac{1}{2}$	1	-	-	2
May	2	2	6	2	1	13	$\frac{1}{2}$	$\frac{1}{2}$	1	-	-	2
Jun	2	2	6	3	1	14	$\frac{1}{2}$	$\frac{1}{2}$	1	-	-	2
Jul	2	2	6	3	1	14	$\frac{1}{2}$	$\frac{1}{2}$	1	-	-	2
Aug	2	2	6	4	1	15	$\frac{1}{2}$	$\frac{1}{2}$	1	-	-	2
Sep	2	2	6	4	1	15	$\frac{1}{2}$	$\frac{1}{2}$	1	-	-	2
Oct	2	2	6	4	1	15	$\frac{1}{2}$	$\frac{1}{2}$	1	-	-	2
Nov	2	2	6	6	1	17	$\frac{1}{2}$	$\frac{1}{2}$	1	-	-	2
Dec	2	2	6	6	1	17	$\frac{1}{2}$	$\frac{1}{2}$	1	-	-	2
1945 Jan	2	2	6	6	1	17	$\frac{1}{2}$	$\frac{1}{2}$	1	-	-	2
Feb	2	2	6	6	1	17	$\frac{1}{2}$	$\frac{1}{2}$	1	-	-	2
Mar	2	2	6	6	1	17	$\frac{1}{2}$	$\frac{1}{2}$	1	-	-	2
Apr	2	2	6	6	1	17	$\frac{1}{2}$	$\frac{1}{2}$	1	-	-	2
May	2	2	6	6	1	17	$\frac{1}{2}$	$\frac{1}{2}$	1	-	-	2
Jun	2	2	6	6	1	17	1	-	1	-	-	2
Jul	2	2	6	6	1	17	1	-	1	-	-	2
Aug	2	2	6	6	1	17	1	-	1	-	-	2

Twentieth Air Force						Latin America and Atlantic Bases					
Heavy Bomb	Med/Lt Bomb	Fighter	Troop Carrier	Recon	Total	Heavy Bomb	Med/Lt Bomb	Fighter	Troop Carrier	Recon	Total
-	-	-	-	-	-	3	1	5	-	1	10
-	-	-	-	-	-	3	1	5	-	1	10
-	-	-	-	-	-	3	1	5	-	1	10
-	-	-	-	-	-	3	1	5	-	1	10
-	-	-	-	-	-	3	1	5	-	1	10
-	-	-	-	-	-	$3\frac{1}{4}$	1	5	-	1	$10\frac{1}{4}$
-	-	-	-	-	-	$3\frac{1}{4}$	1	5	-	1	$10\frac{1}{4}$
-	-	-	-	-	-	$3\frac{1}{4}$	1	5	-	1	$10\frac{1}{4}$
-	-	-	-	-	-	$3\frac{1}{4}$	1	5	-	1	$10\frac{1}{4}$
-	-	-	-	-	-	$3\frac{1}{4}$	1	5	-	1	$10\frac{1}{4}$
-	-	-	-	-	-	$2\frac{1}{4}$	1	5	-	1	$9\frac{1}{4}$
-	-	-	-	-	-	$2\frac{1}{4}$	1	4	-	1	$8\frac{1}{4}$
-	-	-	-	-	-	2	1	4	-	1	8
-	-	-	-	-	-	2	1	4	-	1	8
-	-	-	-	-	-	2	1	4	-	1	8
-	-	-	-	-	-	2	1	4	-	1	8
-	-	-	-	-	-	2	1	5	-	1	9
-	-	-	-	-	-	1	1	4	-	$1\frac{1}{2}$	$7\frac{1}{2}$
-	-	-	-	-	-	1	1	4	-	1	7
-	-	-	-	-	-	1	1	4	-	1	7
-	-	-	-	-	-	1	1	4	-	1	7
-	-	-	-	-	-	1	1	4	-	1	7
-	-	-	-	-	-	1	1	4	-	-	6
-	-	-	-	-	-	1	1	3	-	-	5
-	-	-	-	-	-	1	1	3	-	-	5
-	-	-	-	-	-	-	1	$\frac{1}{2}$	-	-	$1\frac{1}{2}$
-	-	-	-	-	-	-	-	1	-	-	1
-	-	-	-	-	-	-	-	-	-	-	-
-	-	-	-	-	-	-	-	-	-	-	-
4	-	-	-	-	4	-	-	-	-	-	-
4	-	-	-	-	4	-	-	-	-	-	-
4	-	-	-	-	4	-	-	-	-	-	-
4	-	-	-	-	4	-	-	-	-	-	-
4	-	-	-	-	4	-	-	-	-	-	-
8	-	-	-	-	8	-	-	-	-	-	-
8	-	-	-	-	8	-	-	-	-	-	-
10	-	-	-	-	10	-	-	-	-	-	-
12	1	-	-	-	13	-	-	-	-	-	-
14	1	-	-	-	15	-	-	-	-	-	-
16	2	-	-	-	18	-	-	-	-	-	-
16	4	-	-	-	20	-	-	-	-	-	-
18	4	-	-	-	22	-	-	-	-	-	-
18	4	-	-	-	22	-	-	-	-	-	-
21	8	-	-	-	29	-	-	-	-	-	-
23	8	1	-	-	32	-	-	-	-	-	-

Appendix 4

Total Battle Casualties in Theaters against Germany
December 1941 to August 1945

	Officers				Enlisted Personnel				Total Personnel			
	Died	Wounded*	Missing†	Total	Died	Wounded*	Missing†	Total	Died	Wounded*	Missing†	Total
1941 Dec	-	1	-	1	-	-	-	-	-	1	-	1
1942 Jan	18	5	-	23	20	17	3	40	38	22	3	63
Feb	9	4	9	22	20	12	5	37	29	16	14	59
Mar	-	-	-	-	-	-	1	1	-	-	1	1
Apr	4	-	-	4	-	1	2	3	4	1	2	7
May	2	-	1	3	1	-	5	6	3	-	6	9
Jun	1	-	5	6	1	1	4	6	2	1	9	12
Jul	18	-	3	21	17	2	1	20	35	2	4	41
Aug	24	1	4	29	13	1	-	14	37	2	4	43
Sep	18	6	14	38	18	9	12	39	36	15	26	77
Oct	40	6	11	57	37	33	15	85	77	39	26	142
Nov	66	22	27	115	68	49	18	135	134	71	45	250
Dec	98	27	34	159	86	37	36	159	184	64	70	318
Total 1942	298	71	108	477	281	162	102	545	579	233	210	1,022
1943 Jan	234	78	78	390	284	178	105	567	518	256	183	957
Feb	226	51	122	399	272	180	208	660	498	231	330	1,059
Mar	133	56	63	252	142	88	56	286	275	144	119	538
Apr	161	59	157	377	180	110	136	426	341	169	293	803
May	245	98	170	513	330	156	192	678	575	254	362	1,191
Jun	211	56	211	478	325	143	221	689	536	199	432	1,167
Jul	454	127	304	885	544	256	397	1,197	998	383	701	2,082
Aug	395	73	452	920	549	176	590	1,315	944	249	1,042	2,235
Sep	233	74	231	538	278	136	338	752	511	210	569	1,290
Oct	343	73	527	943	510	166	759	1,435	853	239	1,286	2,378
Nov	267	71	293	631	1,091	269	357	1,717	1,358	340	650	2,348
Dec	277	71	504	852	413	252	605	1,270	690	323	1,109	2,122
Total 1943	3,179	887	3,112	7,178	4,918	2,110	3,964	10,992	8,097	2,997	7,076	18,170
1944 Jan	474	114	655	1,243	633	257	851	1,741	1,107	371	1,506	2,984
Feb	626	136	1,111	1,873	792	370	1,618	2,780	1,418	506	2,729	4,653
Mar	639	168	1,125	1,932	874	360	1,578	2,812	1,513	528	2,703	4,744
Apr	792	260	1,780	2,832	1,441	464	2,482	4,387	2,233	724	4,262	7,219
May	790	306	1,455	2,551	1,146	561	1,830	3,537	1,936	867	3,285	6,088
Jun	1,155	485	1,434	3,074	1,191	528	1,718	3,437	2,346	1,013	3,152	6,511
Jul	996	375	1,515	2,886	1,206	543	2,014	3,763	2,202	918	3,529	6,649
Aug	851	373	1,485	2,709	791	460	1,893	3,144	1,642	833	3,378	5,853
Sep	615	314	1,365	2,294	647	422	1,499	2,568	1,262	736	2,864	4,862
Oct	411	183	923	1,517	456	268	1,157	1,881	867	451	2,080	3,398
Nov	555	183	1,116	1,854	525	322	1,304	2,151	1,080	505	2,420	4,005
Dec	476	245	1,344	2,065	479	372	1,544	2,395	955	617	2,888	4,460
Total 1944	8,380	3,142	15,308	26,830	10,181	4,927	19,488	34,596	18,561	8,069	34,796	61,426
1945 Jan	349	219	659	1,227	337	309	806	1,452	686	528	1,465	2,679
Feb	278	186	1,089	1,553	299	261	1,318	1,878	577	667	2,407	3,431
Mar	522	318	1,264	2,104	417	308	1,544	2,269	939	626	2,808	4,373
Apr	289	127	777	1,193	252	218	918	1,388	541	345	1,695	2,581
May	3	3	18	24	3	1	17	21	6	4	35	45
Jun	4	1	3	8	1	-	-	1	5	1	3	9
Jul	1	-	-	1	1	1	-	2	2	1	-	3
Aug	-	-	-	-	-	-	-	-	-	-	-	-
Total 1945	1,446	854	3,810	6,110	1,310	1,098	4,603	7,011	2,756	1,952	8,413	13,121
Date unknown	38	33	277	348	68	75	134	477	106	108	611	825
Grand Total	13,341	4,988	22,615	40,944	16,758	8,372	28,491	53,621	30,099	13,360	51,106	94,565

*Wounded and evacuated.
†Missing, interned, and captured.

Appendix 5

Total Battle Casualties in European Theater of Operations
December 1941 to August 1945

	Officers				Enlisted Personnel				Total Personnel			
	Died	Wounded*	Missing†	Total	Died	Wounded*	Missing†	Total	Died	Wounded*	Missing†	Total
1941 Dec	-	-	-	-	-	-	-	-	-	-	-	-
1942 Jan	11	1	-	12	19	8	3	30	30	9	3	42
Feb	7	1	4	12	19	7	5	31	26	8	9	43
Mar	-	-	-	-	-	-	1	1	-	-	1	1
Apr	4	-	-	4	-	1	2	3	4	1	2	7
May	1	1	1	1	-	-	4	4	1	-	4	5
Jun	1	-	-	1	1	1	1	3	2	1	1	4
Jul	5	-	3	8	4	1	1	6	9	1	4	14
Aug	18	1	2	21	-	1	-	1	18	2	2	22
Sep	13	3	7	23	10	8	10	28	23	11	17	51
Oct	29	1	8	38	21	20	11	52	50	21	19	90
Nov	38	17	18	73	33	25	10	68	71	42	28	141
Dec	38	17	26	81	38	23	24	85	76	40	50	166
Total 1942	165	41	68	274	145	95	72	312	310	136	140	586
1943 Jan	142	33	40	215	182	107	82	371	324	140	122	586
Feb	151	29	56	236	213	107	132	452	364	136	188	688
Mar	66	23	28	117	90	54	34	178	156	77	62	295
Apr	35	7	105	147	79	26	101	206	114	33	206	353
May	151	47	152	350	265	90	177	532	416	137	329	882
Jun	153	33	191	377	284	83	212	579	437	116	403	956
Jul	201	49	239	489	304	114	331	749	505	163	570	1,238
Aug	130	39	317	486	234	92	407	733	364	131	724	1,219
Sep	139	45	182	366	190	67	280	537	329	112	462	903
Oct	256	49	476	781	414	114	709	1,237	670	163	1,185	2,018
Nov	180	51	246	477	261	112	288	661	441	163	534	1,138
Dec	204	52	420	676	313	181	531	1,025	517	233	951	1,701
Total 1943	1,808	457	2,452	4,717	2,829	1,147	3,284	7,260	4,637	1,604	5,736	11,977
1944 Jan	329	72	522	923	467	189	675	1,331	796	261	1,197	2,254
Feb	468	102	812	1,382	587	268	1,223	2,078	1,055	370	2,035	3,460
Mar	452	126	985	1,563	576	203	1,403	2,182	1,028	329	2,388	3,745
Apr	525	187	1,303	2,015	688	332	1,793	2,813	1,213	519	3,096	4,828
May	540	174	1,034	1,748	795	290	1,283	2,368	1,335	464	2,317	4,116
Jun	908	379	943	2,230	835	401	1,077	2,313	1,743	780	2,020	4,543
Jul	642	228	920	1,790	738	296	1,013	2,047	1,380	524	1,933	3,837
Aug	606	225	925	1,756	536	284	1,034	1,854	1,142	509	1,959	3,610
Sep	525	250	1,080	1,855	556	303	1,074	1,933	1,081	553	2,154	3,788
Oct	286	102	535	923	293	162	639	1,094	579	264	1,174	2,017
Nov	410	114	760	1,284	385	206	850	1,441	795	320	1,610	2,725
Dec	365	150	810	1,325	333	224	788	1,345	698	374	1,598	2,670
Total 1944	6,056	2,109	10,629	18,794	6,789	3,158	12,852	22,799	12,845	5,267	23,481	41,593
1945 Jan	263	167	457	887	270	234	541	1,045	533	401	998	1,932
Feb	180	104	646	930	197	155	731	1,083	377	259	1,377	2,013
Mar	429	256	811	1,496	331	224	892	1,447	760	480	1,703	2,943
Apr	201	75	547	823	161	127	655	943	362	202	1,202	1,766
May	2	3	10	15	3	1	10	14	5	4	20	29
Jun	3	-	-	3	1	-	-	1	4	-	-	4
Jul	-	-	-	-	-	-	-	-	-	-	-	-
Aug	-	-	-	-	-	-	-	-	-	-	-	-
Total 1945	1,078	605	2,471	4,154	963	741	2,829	4,533	2,041	1,346	5,300	8,687
Date unknown	18	24	209	251	25	36	255	316	43	60	464	567
Grand Total	9,125	3,236	15,829	28,190	10,751	5,177	19,292	35,220	19,876	8,413	35,121	63,410

*Wounded and evacuated.
†Missing, interned, and captured.

Appendix 6

Total Battle Casualties in Mediterranean Theater of Operations
December 1941 to August 1945

	Officers				Enlisted Personnel				Total Personnel			
	Died	Wounded*	Missing†	Total	Died	Wounded*	Missing†	Total	Died	Wounded*	Missing†	Total
1941 Dec	-	1	-	1	-	-	-	-	-	1	-	1
1942 Jan	7	4	-	11	1	9	-	10	8	13	-	21
Feb	2	3	5	10	1	5	-	6	3	8	5	16
Mar	-	-	-	-	-	-	-	-	-	-	-	-
Apr	-	-	-	-	-	-	-	-	-	-	-	-
May	1	-	1	2	1	-	1	2	2	-	2	4
Jun	-	-	5	5	-	-	3	3	-	-	8	8
Jul	13	-	-	13	13	1	-	14	26	1	-	27
Aug	6	-	2	8	13	-	-	13	19	-	2	21
Sep	5	3	7	15	8	1	2	11	13	4	9	26
Oct	11	5	3	19	16	13	4	33	27	18	7	52
Nov	28	5	9	42	35	24	8	67	63	29	17	109
Dec	60	10	8	78	48	14	12	74	108	24	20	152
Total 1942	133	30	40	203	136	67	30	233	269	97	70	436
1943 Jan	92	45	38	175	102	71	23	196	194	116	61	371
Feb	75	22	66	163	59	73	76	208	134	95	142	371
Mar	67	33	35	135	52	34	22	108	119	67	57	243
Apr	126	52	52	230	101	84	35	220	227	136	87	450
May	94	51	18	163	65	66	15	146	159	117	33	309
Jun	58	23	20	131	41	60	9	110	99	83	29	211
Jul	253	78	65	396	240	142	66	448	493	220	131	844
Aug	265	34	135	434	315	84	183	582	580	118	318	1,016
Sep	94	29	49	172	88	69	58	215	182	98	137	387
Oct	87	24	51	162	96	52	50	198	183	76	101	360
Nov	87	20	47	154	830	157	69	1,056	917	177	116	1,210
Dec	73	19	84	176	100	71	74	245	173	90	158	421
Total 1943	1,371	430	660	2,461	2,089	963	680	3,732	3,460	1,393	1,340	6,193
1944 Jan	145	42	133	320	166	68	176	410	311	110	309	730
Feb	158	34	299	491	205	102	395	702	363	136	694	1,193
Mar	187	42	140	369	298	157	175	630	485	199	315	999
Apr	267	73	477	817	753	132	689	1,574	1,020	205	1,166	2,391
May	250	132	421	803	351	271	547	1,169	601	403	968	1,972
Jun	247	106	491	844	356	127	641	1,124	603	233	1,132	1,968
Jul	354	117	595	1,096	468	247	1,001	1,716	822	394	1,596	2,812
Aug	245	148	560	933	255	176	859	1,290	500	324	1,419	2,243
Sep	90	64	285	439	91	119	425	635	181	183	710	1,074
Oct	125	81	388	594	163	106	518	787	288	187	906	1,381
Nov	145	69	356	570	140	116	454	710	285	185	810	1,280
Dec	111	95	534	740	146	148	756	1,050	257	243	1,290	1,790
Total 1944	2,324	1,033	4,679	8,036	3,392	1,769	6,636	11,797	5,716	2,802	11,315	19,833
1945 Jan	86	52	202	340	67	75	265	407	153	127	467	747
Feb	98	82	443	623	102	106	587	795	200	188	1,530	1,418
Mar	93	62	453	608	86	84	652	822	179	146	1,105	1,430
Apr	88	52	230	370	91	91	263	445	179	143	493	815
May	1	-	8	9	-	-	7	7	1	-	15	16
Jun	1	1	3	5	-	-	-	-	1	1	3	5
Jul	1	-	-	1	1	1	-	2	2	1	-	3
Aug	-	-	-	-	-	-	-	-	-	-	-	-
Total 1945	368	249	1,339	1,956	347	357	1,774	2,478	715	606	3,113	4,434
Date unknown	20	9	68	97	43	39	79	161	63	48	147	258
Grand Total	4,216	1,752	6,784	12,754	6,007	3,195	9,199	18,401	10,223	4,944	15,985	31,155

*Wounded and evacuated.
†Missing, interned, and captured.

Appendix 7

Heavy Bomber and Day Fighter Crew Losses*
June 1943 to August 1945

	1943							1944		
	Jun	Jul	Aug	Sep	Oct	Nov	Dec	Jan	Feb	Mar

Heavy Bomber Crew Losses
European Theater of Operations

	Jun	Jul	Aug	Sep	Oct	Nov	Dec	Jan	Feb	Mar
Combat and Accident Losses	87	114	103	83	186	87	131	248	264	308
Retirements	-	-	-	24	19	10	17	46	98	167
Other Losses	86	9	(26)	10	6	(27)	(22)	35	48	156
Total Losses	173	123	77	117	211	70	126	329	410	631

Mediterranean Theater of Operations

	Jun	Jul	Aug	Sep	Oct	Nov	Dec	Jan	Feb	Mar
Combat and Accident Losses	9	32	84	24	13	22	33	34	109	71
Retirements	-	-	-	46	45	12	21	41	43	25
Other Losses	21	17	(19)	3	(5)	(17)	(11)	5	14	(11)
Total Losses	30	49	65	73	53	17	43	80	166	85

All Theaters

	Jun	Jul	Aug	Sep	Oct	Nov	Dec	Jan	Feb	Mar
Combat and Accident Losses	110	172	206	128	217	135	194	309	378	400
Retirements	-	-	4	78	89	37	48	103	188	238
Other Losses	141	61	(37)	45	(1)	(41)	(55)	53	56	150
Total Losses	251	233	173	251	305	131	187	465	622	788

Day Fighter Crew Losses
European Theater of Operations

	Jun	Jul	Aug	Sep	Oct	Nov	Dec	Jan	Feb	Mar
Combat and Accident Losses	9	17	10	13	12	37	53	85	105	192
Retirements	-	-	-	2	2	3	-	-	4	3
Other Losses	1	-	(6)	(19)	21	10	101	33	(52)	24
Total Losses	10	17	4	(4)	35	50	154	118	57	219

Mediterranean Theater of Operations

	Jun	Jul	Aug	Sep	Oct	Nov	Dec	Jan	Feb	Mar
Combat and Accident Losses	52	74	93	50	12	12	54	72	61	47
Retirements	-	35	-	156	75	49	90	90	80	57
Other Losses	78	136	91	(25)	(18)	(54)	2	(6)	7	(10)
Total Losses	130	245	184	181	69	7	146	156	148	94

All Theaters

	Jun	Jul	Aug	Sep	Oct	Nov	Dec	Jan	Feb	Mar
Combat and Accident Losses	76	135	158	112	64	94	137	211	196	274
Retirements	-	48	-	182	125	101	155	174	167	197
Other Losses	162	227	59	28	48	2	174	(59)	(26)	91
Total Losses	238	410	217	322	237	197	466	326	337	562

*Figures in parentheses indicate the excess over losses of gains resulting from formation of additional crews out of personnel returned from missing, reclassified from ground to air duties, and received from the U.S. as individuals rather than as crew members.

Heavy Bomber and Day Fighter Crew Losses*
June 1943 to August 1945

	1944								
	Apr	May	Jun	Jul	Aug	Sep	Oct	Nov	Dec

Heavy Bomber Crew Losses
European Theater of Operations

	Apr	May	Jun	Jul	Aug	Sep	Oct	Nov	Dec
Combat and Accident Losses	371	308	239	302	203	274	130	211	119
Retirements	167	191	257	342	451	347	410	410	347
Other Losses	124	45	(59)	35	87	60	(8)	(30)	(4)
Total Losses	662	544	437	679	741	681	532	591	462

Mediterranean Theater of Operations

	Apr	May	Jun	Jul	Aug	Sep	Oct	Nov	Dec
Combat and Accident Losses	183	169	175	255	149	55	111	84	151
Retirements	20	52	89	206	366	216	131	218	107
Other Losses	(22)	42	122	(9)	7	(7)	(1)	1	22
Total Losses	181	263	386	452	522	264	241	303	280

All Theaters

	Apr	May	Jun	Jul	Aug	Sep	Oct	Nov	Dec
Combat and Accident Losses	589	500	438	571	367	347	276	316	290
Retirements	220	274	380	640	850	590	602	677	533
Other Losses	114	93	78	31	81	88	4	(20)	23
Total Losses	923	867	896	1,242	1,298	1,025	882	973	846

Day Fighter Crew Losses
European Theater of Operations

	Apr	May	Jun	Jul	Aug	Sep	Oct	Nov	Dec
Combat and Accident Losses	207	245	458	297	385	191	144	246	246
Retirements	58	47	43	66	118	319	353	340	221
Other Losses	(7)	(21)	(66)	(9)	224	106	(63)	76	125
Total Losses	258	271	435	354	727	616	434	662	592

Mediterranean Theater of Operations

	Apr	May	Jun	Jul	Aug	Sep	Oct	Nov	Dec
Combat and Accident Losses	85	123	137	104	113	86	61	85	72
Retirements	119	112	90	138	150	87	60	124	76
Other Losses	(45)	1	(25)	116	16	44	6	28	26
Total Losses	159	236	202	358	279	217	127	237	174

All Theaters

	Apr	May	Jun	Jul	Aug	Sep	Oct	Nov	Dec
Combat and Accident Losses	338	403	628	440	536	317	283	396	399
Retirements	276	242	188	260	373	527	582	552	370
Other Losses	(123)	29	(109)	106	209	197	43	53	121
Total Losses	491	674	707	806	1,118	1,041	908	1,001	890

*Figures in parentheses indicate the excess over losses of gains resulting from formation of additional crews out of personnel returned from missing, reclassified from ground to air duties, and received from the U.S. as individuals rather than as crew members.

	1945							1943	1944	1945	Total
Jan	Feb	Mar	Apr	May	Jun	Jul	Aug	(Jun-Dec)		(Jan-Aug)	
157	101	167	150	6	6	3	-	791	2,977	590	4,358
420	379	597	690	-	-	-	-	70	3,233	2,086	5,389
(63)	(23)	(103)	(13)	28	(53)	32	4	36	489	(191)	334
514	457	661	827	34	(47)	35	4	897	6,699	2,485	10,081
37	85	93	46	(7)	2	-	1	217	1,546	257	2,020
55	126	196	426	50	-	-	-	124	1,514	853	2,491
12	48	12	35	(63)	26	(7)	7	(11)	163	70	222
104	259	301	507	(20)	28	(7)	8	330	3,223	1,180	4,733
217	201	279	208	17	31	29	10	1,162	4,781	992	6,935
550	572	890	1,237	179	103	108	144	256	5,295	3,783	9,334
(39)	27	(99)	31	(37)	(36)	40	16	113	751	(97)	767
728	800	1,070	1,476	159	98	177	170	1,531	10,827	4,678	17,036
190	232	267	230	23	15	22	(1)	151	2,801	978	3,930
219	162	212	307	488	-	-	-	7	1,572	1,388	2,967
23	57	41	47	23	36	(24)	9	108	370	212	690
432	451	520	584	534	51	(2)	8	266	4,743	2,578	7,587
56	69	83	83	(11)	10	5	3	347	1,046	298	1,691
60	79	80	141	96	13	-	-	405	1,183	469	2,057
21	13	3	19	17	25	7	(27)	210	158	78	446
137	161	166	243	102	48	12	(24)	962	2,387	845	4,194
322	353	456	388	71	117	114	65	776	4,421	1,886	7,083
372	302	391	560	736	236	200	216	611	3,908	3,013	7,532
150	118	91	144	100	124	49	73	700	532	849	2,081
844	773	938	1,092	907	477	363	354	2,087	8,861	5,748	16,696

Appendix 8

Aircraft in all Theaters against Germany
June 1942 to August 1945

	1942							1943
	Jun	Jul	Aug	Sep	Oct	Nov	Dec	Jan
Combat Airplanes								
1st Line	17	369	567	613	1,060	1,426	1,744	1,905
2nd Line	9	24	25	25	29	32	36	30
Total	26	393	592	638	1,089	1,458	1,780	1,935
Heavy Bombers								
1st Line	17	86	160	241	361	368	368	413
B-17	-	54	114	155	245	244	246	293
B-24	17	32	46	86	116	124	122	120
2nd Line	-	-	1	1	1	1	1	1
Total	17	86	161	242	362	369	369	414
Medium Bombers								
1st Line	-	-	50	56	105	116	179	212
B-25	-	-	50	55	77	92	104	125
B-26	-	-	-	1	28	24	75	87
2nd Line	-	-	-	-	-	-	-	-
Total	-	-	50	56	105	116	179	212
Light Bombers								
1st Line	-	-	-	9	18	33	40	43
A-20	-	-	-	9	18	33	40	43
A-26	-	-	-	-	-	-	-	-
2nd Line	9	24	24	24	24	23	19	15
Total	9	24	24	33	42	56	59	58
Fighters								
1st Line	-	283	355	294	556	884	1,058	1,117
P-38	-	80	131	133	184	253	302	293
P-39	-	-	-	-	177	251	210	177
P-40	-	44	60	59	72	190	259	366
P-47	-	-	-	-	-	-	88	120
P-51	-	-	-	-	-	-	-	-
Night Fighters	-	-	-	-	-	-	-	-
Other	-	159	164	102	123	190	199	161
2nd Line	-	-	-	-	-	-	-	-
Total	-	283	355	294	556	884	1,058	1,117
Reconnaissance								
1st Line	-	-	2	13	20	25	99	120
F-4, F-5	-	-	2	13	20	21	36	33
F-6	-	-	-	-	-	-	-	10
F-7	-	-	-	-	-	-	-	-
F-8	-	-	-	-	-	-	-	-
Other	-	-	-	-	-	4	63	77
2nd Line	-	-	-	-	4	8	16	14
Total	-	-	2	13	24	33	115	134
Grand Total*	26	445	692	762	1,286	1,690	2,065	2,245

*Includes other aircraft not shown (transports, trainers, and communications aircraft.)

					1943					
Feb	Mar	Apr	May	Jun	Jul	Aug	Sep	Oct	Nov	Dec
2,416	2,888	3,682	4,522	5,107	5,283	5,277	5,371	5,532	6,273	7,003
29	30	50	74	105	120	133	166	184	198	235
2,445	2,918	3,732	4,596	5,212	5,403	5,410	5,537	5,716	6,471	7,238
462	557	891	1,028	1,295	1,388	1,348	1,448	1,520	843	2,167
328	396	697	828	1,052	1,134	1,124	1,148	1,205	1,434	1,591
134	161	194	200	243	254	224	300	315	409	576
1	1	1	14	13	13	13	41	34	112	96
463	558	892	1,042	1,308	1,401	1,361	1,489	1,554	1,955	2,263
250	317	424	722	1,051	1,152	1,161	1,121	984	1,037	1,074
161	232	236	369	438	423	399	360	252	341	378
89	85	188	353	613	729	762	761	732	696	696
-	-	-	-	-	-	-	1	1	14	10
250	317	424	722	1,051	1,152	1,161	1,122	985	1,051	1,084
62	101	157	165	166	155	137	126	116	112	134
62	101	157	165	166	155	137	126	116	112	134
-	-	-	-	-	-	-	-	-	-	-
14	13	32	37	37	37	31	29	28	33	33
76	114	189	202	203	192	168	155	144	145	167
1,457	1,797	2,022	2,443	2,394	2,366	2,407	2,451	2,744	3,042	3,392
336	472	558	567	516	450	374	389	372	441	596
180	224	294	359	350	333	393	259	251	232	241
571	649	668	733	717	690	625	579	491	456	432
176	203	263	307	341	421	653	811	1,084	1,320	1,514
-	51	89	298	290	260	231	221	322	369	399
-	-	-	-	-	23	43	43	39	42	45
194	198	150	179	180	189	188	149	185	182	165
-	-	-	4	19	20	7	8	31	35	64
1,457	1,797	2,022	2,447	2,413	2,386	2,414	2,459	2,775	3,077	3,456
185	116	188	164	201	222	224	225	168	239	236
54	53	47	46	48	73	71	72	69	108	127
35	20	27	27	27	24	40	44	22	42	52
-	-	-	-	-	-	-	-	-	-	-
-	-	-	-	-	-	-	-	1	1	1
96	43	114	91	126	125	113	109	76	88	56
14	16	17	19	36	50	82	87	90	4	32
199	132	205	183	237	272	306	312	258	243	268
2,758	3,291	4,101	5,263	5,928	6,099	6,152	6,354	6,582	7,395	8,237

Appendix 8 (continued)

Aircraft in all Theaters against Germany
June 1942 to August 1945

	1944								
	Jan	Feb	Mar	Apr	May	Jun	Jul	Aug	Sep
Combat Airplanes									
1st Line	8,267	9,413	10,910	11,593	11,844	11,522	12,538	12,493	12,692
2nd Line	216	206	431	469	954	907	868	1,206	1,257
Total	8,483	9,619	11,341	12,062	12,798	12,429	13,406	13,699	13,949
Heavy Bombers									
1st Line	2,608	2,842	3,524	3,900	4,347	4,226	4,605	4,880	4,995
B-17	1,650	1,701	1,884	1,860	1,863	1,786	2,011	2,195	2,334
B-24	958	1,141	1,640	2,040	2,484	2,440	2,594	2,685	2,661
2nd Line	64	57	63	122	289	266	294	353	384
Total	2,672	2,899	3,587	4,022	4,636	4,492	4,899	5,233	5,379
Medium Bombers									
1st Line	1,217	1,385	1,491	1,640	1,561	1,471	1,604	1,563	1,569
B-25	403	395	361	453	465	395	440	438	463
B-26	814	990	1,130	1,187	1,096	1,076	1,164	1,125	1,106
2nd Line	10	17	100	101	237	278	230	271	203
Total	1,227	1,402	1,591	1,741	1,798	1,749	1,834	1,834	1,772
Light Bombers									
1st Line	150	247	410	444	488	501	541	531	617
A-20	150	247	410	444	488	501	541	514	549
A-26	-	-	-	-	-	-	-	17	68
2nd Line	34	42	47	49	58	56	61	80	75
Total	184	289	457	493	546	557	602	611	692
Fighters									
1st Line	4,033	4,665	5,179	5,260	4,969	4,844	5,277	4,969	4,844
P-38	809	893	1,048	1,063	1,050	905	842	643	678
P-39	248	366	375	336	293	244	241	175	-
P-40	391	328	298	274	181	139	103	-	-
P-47	1,696	2,009	2,288	2,335	2,241	2,176	2,355	2,465	2,457
P-51	659	819	989	1,175	1,132	1,284	1,642	1,588	1,616
Night Fighters	50	51	47	46	66	90	94	98	93
Other	180	199	134	31	6	6	-	-	-
2nd Line	78	65	166	155	326	258	258	475	572
Total	4,111	4,730	5,345	5,415	5,295	5,102	5,535	5,444	5,416
Reconnaissance									
1st Line	259	274	306	349	479	480	511	550	667
F-4, F-5	128	149	160	174	196	218	234	242	288
F-6	71	76	101	119	205	192	177	195	265
F-7	-	-	1	1	-	-	-	-	-
F-8	1	1	6	16	28	36	65	67	65
Other	59	48	38	39	50	34	35	46	49
2nd Line	30	25	55	42	44	49	25	27	23
Total	289	299	361	391	523	529	536	577	690
Grand Total*	9,644	10,897	13,163	14,169	15,461	15,210	16,485	16,913	17,027

*Includes other aircraft not shown (transports, trainers, and communications aircraft.)

	1944						1945				
	Oct	Nov	Dec	Jan	Feb	Mar	Apr	May	Jun	Jul	Aug
	13,030	13,174	12,707	12,612	12,889	13,242	13,378	12,292	9,301	6,914	6,004
	1,469	1,511	1,554	1,523	1,517	1,443	1,467	1,246	1,077	1,381	1,127
	14,499	14,685	14,261	14,135	14,406	14,685	14,845	13,538	10,378	8,295	7,131
	5,054	4,894	1,460	4,727	4,899	5,072	4,925	4,047	1,854	1,189	1,135
	2,619	2,599	2,677	2,663	2,790	2,891	2,788	2,517	1,604	1,164	1,123
	2,435	2,295	2,134	2,064	2,109	2,181	2,137	1,530	250	25	12
	575	614	631	607	644	590	634	473	419	270	70
	5,629	5,508	5,442	5,334	5,543	5,662	5,559	4,520	2,273	1,459	1,205
	1,533	1,507	1,395	1,363	1,376	1,297	1,220	1,177	951	720	715
	436	402	375	397	423	414	393	367	217	3	1
	1,097	1,105	1,020	966	953	883	827	810	734	717	714
	215	219	222	216	194	195	224	227	157	151	128
	1,748	1,726	1,617	1,579	1,570	1,492	1,444	1,404	1,108	871	843
	648	802	782	791	827	889	977	942	802	564	378
	517	490	459	439	420	395	358	315	308	297	295
	131	312	323	352	407	494	619	627	494	267	83
	71	66	63	71	70	74	92	111	77	59	52
	719	868	845	862	897	963	1,069	1,053	879	623	430
	5,053	5,203	4,955	5,002	5,079	5,268	1,284	5,423	5,099	3,924	3,381
	684	661	575	562	570	625	579	555	518	311	182
	-	-	-	-	-	-	-	-	-	-	-
	2,477	2,435	2,244	2,285	2,319	2,283	2,355	2,292	2,183	1,829	1,749
	1,796	2,019	2,039	2,053	2,086	2,228	2,455	2,427	2,279	1,670	1,368
	96	88	97	102	104	132	145	148	117	114	82
	-	-	-	-	-	-	-	-	-	-	-
	588	594	619	612	589	538	469	417	406	834	747
	5,641	5,797	5,574	5,614	5,668	5,806	6,003	5,840	5,505	4,758	4,128
	742	768	764	729	708	716	722	703	595	517	395
	307	346	352	332	317	330	338	318	285	228	135
	317	309	296	270	255	248	259	254	247	242	216
	-	-	-	-	-	-	-	-	-	-	-
	63	57	65	79	82	89	78	78	12	6	-
	55	56	51	48	54	49	47	53	51	41	44
	20	18	19	17	20	46	48	18	18	67	130
	762	786	783	746	728	762	770	721	613	584	525
	17,999	18,134	17,787	17,575	17,906	18,367	18,736	17,061	13,568	10,854	9,329

Appendix 9

Aircraft in the European Theater of Operations
June 1942 to August 1945

				1942				1943
	Jun	Jul	Aug	Sep	Oct	Nov	Dec	Jan
Combat Airplanes								
1st Line	-	283	401	445	879	840	823	739
2nd Line	9	24	24	24	28	19	24	24
Total	9	307	425	469	907	859	847	763
Heavy Bombers								
1st Line	-	44	104	178	296	247	219	214
B-17	-	44	104	144	234	180	178	175
B-24	-	-	-	34	62	67	41	39
2nd Line	-	-	-	-	-	-	-	-
Total	-	44	104	178	296	247	219	214
Medium Bombers								
1st Line	-	-	-	10	61	44	29	19
B-25	-	-	-	9	33	34	23	13
B-26	-	-	-	1	28	10	6	6
2nd Line	-	-	-	-	-	-	-	-
Total	-	-	-	10	61	44	29	19
Light Bombers								
1st Line	-	-	-	9	18	33	8	6
A-20	-	-	-	9	18	33	8	6
A-26	-	-	-	-	-	-	-	-
2nd Line	9	24	24	24	24	11	8	10
Total	9	24	24	33	42	44	16	16
Fighters								
1st Line	-	239	295	235	484	495	516	458
P-38	-	80	131	133	184	138	168	163
P-39	-	-	-	-	177	251	177	102
P-40	-	-	-	-	-	-	-	-
P-47	-	-	-	-	-	-	88	120
P-51	-	-	-	-	-	-	-	-
Night Fighters	-	-	-	-	-	-	-	-
Other	-	159	164	102	123	106	83	73
2nd Line	-	-	-	-	-	-	-	-
Total	-	239	295	235	484	495	516	458
Reconnaissance								
1st Line	-	-	2	13	20	21	51	42
F-4, F-5	-	-	2	13	20	21	15	18
F-6	-	-	-	-	-	-	-	10
F-8	-	-	-	-	-	-	-	-
Other	-	-	-	-	-	-	36	14
2nd Line	-	-	-	-	4	8	16	14
Total	-	-	2	13	24	29	67	56
Grand Total*	9	359	520	588	1,100	932	944	860

*Includes other aircraft not shown (transports, trainers, and communications aircraft.)

1943

Feb	Mar	Apr	May	Jun	Jul	Aug	Sep	Oct	Nov	Dec
781	718	1,047	1,213	1,613	1,826	2,177	2,485	2,936	3,708	4,111
24	11	29	47	58	69	98	134	127	127	131
805	729	1,076	1,260	1,671	1,895	2,275	2,619	3,063	3,835	4,242
255	303	590	692	834	844	895	931	1,104	1,460	1,610
186	229	502	599	783	820	786	835	907	1,166	1,302
69	74	88	93	51	24	109	96	197	294	308
-	-	-	13	12	12	12	40	34	94	76
255	303	590	705	846	856	907	971	1,138	1,554	1,686
17	18	54	121	336	450	493	484	479	467	443
4	1	1	1	1	1	1	-	-	-	-
13	17	53	120	335	449	492	484	479	467	443
-	-	-	-	-	-	-	1	1	1	1
17	18	54	121	336	450	493	485	480	468	444
6	2	-	-	-	-	-	-	-	8	25
6	2	-	-	-	-	-	-	-	8	25
-	-	-	-	-	-	-	-	-	-	-
10	9	28	33	33	33	31	29	28	28	28
16	11	28	33	33	33	31	29	28	36	53
432	358	297	332	346	426	668	939	1,270	1,621	1,862
100	56	25	16	2	2	12	93	105	188	380
56	22	9	9	3	3	3	1	1	1	1
15	15	-	-	-	-	-	-	-	-	-
176	203	263	307	341	421	653	811	1,005	1,201	1,215
-	-	-	-	-	-	-	34	159	231	266
-	-	-	-	-	-	-	-	-	-	-
85	62	-	-	-	-	-	-	-	-	-
-	-	-	-	-	-	-	4	4	4	4
432	358	297	332	346	426	668	943	1,274	1,625	1,866
71	37	106	68	97	106	121	131	83	152	171
19	19	17	17	11	21	20	20	20	56	79
35	-	-	-	-	-	18	24	3	23	36
-	-	-	-	-	-	-	-	-	-	-
17	18	89	51	86	85	83	87	60	73	56
14	2	1	1	13	24	55	60	60	-	22
85	39	107	69	110	130	176	191	143	152	193
903	873	1,211	1,420	1,841	2,069	2,452	2,827	3,310	4,152	4,618

Appendix 9 (continued)

Aircraft in the European Theater of Operations
June 1942 to August 1945

	1944								
	Jan	Feb	Mar	Apr	May	Jun	Jul	Aug	Sep
Combat Airplanes									
1st Line	5,035	5,952	7,035	7,700	7,834	7,505	8,423	8,605	8,735
2nd Line	98	93	136	175	517	460	473	609	637
Total	5,133	6,045	7,171	7,875	8,351	7,965	8,896	9,214	9,372
Heavy Bombers									
1st Line	1,774	1,965	2,259	2,562	2,937	2,929	3,304	3,435	3,398
B-17	1,341	1,412	1,487	1,492	1,502	1,471	1,695	1,829	1,927
B-24	433	553	772	1,070	1,435	1,458	1,609	1,606	1,471
2nd Line	43	33	36	85	200	171	188	227	261
Total	1,817	1,998	2,295	2,647	3,137	3,100	3,492	3,662	3,659
Medium Bombers									
1st Line	506	670	837	866	788	804	853	850	843
B-25	-	-	-	-	-	-	-	-	-
B-26	506	670	837	866	788	804	853	850	843
2nd Line	1	1	1	12	58	41	39	65	33
Total	507	671	838	878	846	845	892	915	876
Light Bombers									
1st Line	40	121	289	331	385	387	430	436	508
A-20	40	121	289	331	385	387	430	419	440
A-26	-	-	-	-	-	-	-	17	68
2nd Line	29	37	35	35	40	39	43	46	44
Total	69	158	324	366	425	426	473	482	552
Fighters									
1st Line	2,528	2,998	3,419	3,685	3,382	3,046	3,480	3,470	3,470
P-38	637	669	707	750	673	568	584	477	379
P-39	-	-	-	-	-	-	-	-	-
P-40	-	-	-	-	-	-	-	-	-
P-47	1,348	1,630	1,920	1,985	1,870	1,632	1,706	1,768	1,840
P-51	543	699	792	950	819	803	1,143	1,177	1,203
Night Fighters	-	-	-	-	20	43	47	48	48
Other	-	-	-	-	-	-	-	-	-
2nd Line	4	4	21	12	188	173	191	258	289
Total	2,532	3,002	3,440	3,697	3,570	3,219	3,671	3,728	3,759
Reconnaissance									
1st Line	187	198	231	256	342	339	356	414	516
F-4, F-5	79	97	118	117	115	134	131	156	184
F-6	50	53	71	87	152	138	128	153	222
F-8	-	-	5	15	27	35	64	67	65
Other	21	18	43	31	31	36	12	13	10
2nd Line	58	48	37	37	48	32	33	38	45
Total	208	216	274	287	373	375	368	427	526
Grand Total*	5,685	6,917	8,562	9,645	10,637	10,343	11,091	11,835	11,951

*Includes other aircraft not shown (transports, trainers, and communications aircraft.)

	1944			1945							
Oct	Nov	Dec	Jan	Feb	Mar	Apr	May	Jun	Jul	Aug
9,165	9,620	9,210	8,948	9,323	9,525	9,776	9,053	7,238	6,046	5,634
750	798	860	850	887	872	897	743	536	447	427
9.915	10,418	10,070	9,798	10,210	10,397	10,673	9,796	7,774	6,493	6,061
3,473	3,444	3,351	3,202	3,335	3,412	3,332	2,707	1,306	811	792
2,143	2,123	2,168	2,125	2,269	2,367	2,291	1,988	1,147	787	780
1,330	1,321	1,183	1,077	1,066	1,045	1,041	719	159	24	12
345	351	355	332	367	349	356	251	136	49	36
3,818	3,795	3,706	3,534	3,702	3,761	3,688	2,958	1,442	860	828
818	1,012	998	952	943	873	821	810	734	717	714
-	-	-	-	-	-	-	-	-	-	-
818	1,012	998	952	943	873	821	810	734	717	714
44	45	47	41	45	49	87	90	27	29	37
862	1,057	1,045	993	988	922	908	900	761	746	751
550	710	692	663	657	718	809	804	775	556	378
419	398	371	359	344	327	320	315	308	297	295
131	312	321	304	313	391	489	489	467	259	83
39	37	35	44	42	42	38	33	28	27	26
589	747	727	707	699	760	847	837	803	583	404
3,721	3,843	3,585	3,550	3,821	3,951	4,250	4,186	3,960	3,529	3,368
356	322	257	257	239	250	244	234	202	195	176
-	-	-	-	-	-	-	-	-	-	-
-	-	-	-	-	-	-	-	-	-	-
1,942	1,890	1,735	1,735	1,959	1,931	2,057	2,012	1,942	1,789	1,749
1,366	1,579	1,548	1,515	1,576	1,694	1,867	1,846	1,728	1,459	1,361
57	52	45	43	47	76	82	94	88	86	82
-	-	-	-	-	-	-	-	-	-	-
319	361	417	424	424	407	392	358	339	331	319
4,040	4,204	4,002	3,974	4,245	4,358	4,642	4,544	4,299	3,860	3,687
603	611	584	581	567	571	564	546	463	433	382
186	193	179	191	183	194	188	167	153	144	135
304	308	292	266	251	244	254	250	247	242	216
63	57	65	79	82	89	78	78	12	6	-
3	4	6	9	9	25	24	11	6	11	9
50	53	48	45	51	44	44	51	51	41	31
606	615	590	590	576	596	588	557	469	444	391
12,858	13,427	13,126	12,598	13,116	13,518	13,927	12,819	10,500	8,674	7,993

Appendix 10

Aircraft in the Mediterranean Theater of Operations
June 1942 to August 1945

	1942							1943
	Jun	Jul	Aug	Sep	Oct	Nov	Dec	Jan
Combat Airplanes								
1st Line	17	86	166	168	181	586	921	1,166
2nd Line	-	-	1	1	1	13	12	6
Total	17	86	167	169	182	599	933	1,172
Heavy Bombers								
1st Line	17	42	56	63	65	121	149	199
B-17	-	10	10	11	11	64	68	118
B-24	17	32	46	52	54	57	81	81
2nd Line	-	-	1	1	1	1	1	1
Total	17	42	57	64	66	122	150	200
Medium Bombers								
1st Line	-	-	50	46	44	72	150	193
B-25	-	-	50	46	44	58	81	112
B-26	-	-	-	-	-	14	69	81
2nd Line	-	-	-	-	-	-	-	-
Total	-	-	50	46	44	72	150	193
Light Bombers								
1st Line	-	-	-	-	-	-	32	37
A-20	-	-	-	-	-	-	32	37
A-26	-	-	-	-	-	-	-	-
2nd Line	-	-	-	-	-	12	11	5
Total	-	-	-	-	-	12	43	42
Fighters								
1st Line	-	44	60	59	72	389	542	659
P-38	-	-	-	-	-	115	134	130
P-39	-	-	-	-	-	-	33	75
P-40	-	44	60	59	72	190	259	366
P-47	-	-	-	-	-	-	-	-
P-51	-	-	-	-	-	-	-	-
Night Fighters	-	-	-	-	-	-	-	-
Other	-	-	-	-	-	84	116	88
2nd Line	-	-	-	-	-	-	-	-
Total	-	44	60	59	72	389	542	659
Reconnaissance								
1st Line	-	-	-	-	-	4	48	78
F-4, F-5	-	-	-	-	-	-	21	15
F-6	-	-	-	-	-	-	-	-
F-7	-	-	-	-	-	-	-	-
F-8	-	-	-	-	-	-	-	-
Other	-	-	-	-	-	4	27	63
2nd Line	-	-	-	-	-	-	-	-
Total	-	-	-	-	-	4	48	78
Grand Total*	17	86	172	174	186	758	1,121	1,385

*Includes other aircraft not shown (transports, trainers, and communications aircraft.)

Feb	Mar	Apr	May	Jun	Jul	Aug	Sep	Oct	Nov	Dec
1,635	2,170	2,635	3,309	3,494	3,457	3,100	2,886	2,496	2,565	2,892
5	19	21	27	47	51	35	32	57	71	104
1,640	2,189	2,656	3,336	3,541	3,508	3,135	2,918	2,653	2,636	2,996
207	254	301	336	461	544	453	517	416	383	557
142	167	195	229	269	314	338	313	298	268	289
65	87	106	107	192	230	115	204	118	115	268
1	1	1	1	1	1	1	1	-	18	20
208	255	302	337	462	545	454	518	416	401	577
233	299	370	601	715	702	668	637	505	570	631
157	231	235	368	437	422	398	360	252	341	378
76	68	135	233	278	280	270	277	253	229	253
-	-	-	-	-	-	-	-	-	13	9
233	299	370	601	715	702	668	637	505	583	640
56	99	157	165	166	155	137	126	116	104	109
56	99	157	165	166	155	137	126	116	104	109
-	-	-	-	-	-	-	-	-	-	-
4	4	4	4	4	4	-	-	-	5	5
60	103	161	169	170	159	137	126	116	109	114
1,025	1,439	1,725	2,111	2,048	1,940	1,739	1,512	1,474	1,421	1,530
236	416	533	551	514	448	362	296	267	253	216
124	202	285	350	347	330	290	258	250	231	240
556	634	668	733	717	690	625	579	491	456	432
-	-	-	-	-	-	-	-	79	119	299
-	51	89	298	290	260	231	187	163	138	133
-	-	-	-	-	23	43	43	39	42	45
109	136	150	179	180	189	188	149	185	182	165
-	-	-	4	19	20	7	4	27	31	60
1,025	1,439	1,725	2,115	2,067	1,960	1,746	1,516	1,501	1,452	1,590
114	79	82	96	104	116	103	94	85	87	65
35	34	30	29	37	52	51	52	49	52	48
-	20	27	27	27	24	22	20	19	19	16
-	-	-	-	-	-	-	-	-	-	-
-	-	-	-	-	-	-	-	1	1	1
79	25	25	40	40	40	30	22	16	15	-
-	14	16	18	23	26	27	27	30	4	10
114	93	98	114	127	142	130	121	115	91	75
1,855	2,418	2,890	3,843	4,087	4,030	3,700	3,527	3,272	3,243	3,619

Appendix 10 (continued)

Aircraft in the Mediterranean Theater of Operations
June 1942 to August 1945

	Jan	Feb	Mar	Apr	May	Jun	Jul	Aug	Sep
Combat Airplanes									
1st Line	3,232	3,461	3,875	3,893	4,010	4,017	4,115	3,888	3,957
2nd Line	118	113	295	294	437	447	395	597	620
Total	3,350	3,574	4,170	4,187	4,447	4,464	4,510	4,485	4,577
Heavy Bombers									
1st Line	834	877	1,265	1,338	1,410	1,297	1,301	1,445	1,597
B-17	309	289	397	368	361	315	316	366	407
B-24	525	588	868	970	1,049	982	985	1,079	1,190
2nd Line	21	24	27	37	89	95	106	126	123
Total	855	901	1,292	1,375	1,499	1,392	1,407	1,571	1,720
Medium Bombers									
1st Line	711	715	654	774	773	667	751	713	726
B-25	403	395	361	453	465	395	440	438	463
B-26	308	320	293	321	308	272	311	275	263
2nd Line	9	16	99	89	179	237	191	206	170
Total	720	731	753	863	952	904	942	919	896
Light Bombers									
1st Line	110	126	121	113	103	114	111	95	109
A-20	110	126	121	113	103	114	111	95	109
A-26	-	-	-	-	-	-	-	-	-
2nd Line	5	5	12	14	18	17	18	34	31
Total	115	131	133	127	121	131	129	129	140
Fighters									
1st Line	1,505	1,667	1,760	1,575	1,587	1,798	1,797	1,499	1,374
P-38	172	224	341	313	377	337	258	166	299
P-39	248	366	375	336	293	244	241	175	-
P-40	391	328	298	274	181	139	103	-	-
P-47	348	379	368	350	371	544	649	697	617
P-51	116	120	197	225	313	481	499	411	413
Night Fighters	50	51	47	46	46	47	47	50	45
Other	180	199	134	31	6	6	-	-	-
2nd Line	74	61	145	143	138	85	67	217	283
Total	1,579	1,728	1,905	1,718	1,725	1,883	1,764	1,716	1,657
Reconnaissance									
1st Line	72	76	75	93	137	141	155	136	151
F-4, F-5	49	52	42	57	81	84	103	86	104
F-6	21	23	30	32	53	54	49	42	43
F-7	-	-	1	1	-	-	-	-	-
F-8	1	1	1	1	1	1	1	-	-
Other	1	-	1	2	2	2	2	8	4
2nd Line	9	7	12	11	13	13	13	14	13
Total	81	83	87	104	150	154	168	150	164
Grand Total*	3,959	3,980	4,601	4,524	4,824	4,867	5,394	5,078	5,076

*Includes other aircraft not shown (transports, trainers, and communications aircraft.)

	1944			1945						
Oct	Nov	Dec	Jan	Feb	Mar	Apr	May	Jun	Jul	Aug
3,865	3,554	3,497	3,664	3,566	3,717	3,602	3,239	2,063	868	370
719	713	694	673	630	571	570	503	541	934	700
4,584	4,267	4,191	4,337	4,196	4,288	4,172	3,742	2,604	1,802	1,070
1,581	1,450	1,460	1,525	1,564	1,660	1,593	1,340	548	378	343
476	476	509	538	521	524	497	529	457	377	343
1,105	974	951	987	1,043	1,136	1,096	811	91	1	-
230	263	276	275	277	241	278	222	283	221	34
1,811	1,713	1,736	1,800	1,841	1,901	1,871	1,562	831	599	377
715	495	397	411	433	424	399	367	217	3	1
436	402	375	397	423	414	393	367	217	3	1
279	93	22	14	10	10	6	-	-	-	-
171	174	175	175	149	146	137	137	130	122	91
886	669	572	586	582	570	536	504	347	125	92
98	92	90	128	170	171	168	138	27	8	-
98	92	88	80	76	68	38	-	-	-	-
-	-	2	48	94	103	130	138	27	8	-
32	29	28	27	28	32	54	78	49	32	26
130	121	118	155	198	203	222	216	76	40	26
1,332	1,360	1,370	1,452	1,258	1,317	1,284	1,237	1,139	395	13
328	339	318	305	331	375	335	321	316	116	6
-	-	-	-	-	-	-	1	2	-	-
-	-	-	-	-	-	-	-	-	-	-
535	545	509	550	360	352	298	280	241	40	-
430	440	491	538	510	534	588	581	551	211	7
39	36	52	59	57	56	63	54	29	28	-
-	-	-	-	-	-	-	-	-	-	-
269	233	202	188	165	131	77	59	67	503	428
1,601	1,593	1,572	1,640	1,423	1,448	1,361	1,296	1,206	898	441
139	157	180	148	141	145	158	157	132	84	13
121	153	173	141	134	136	150	151	132	84	-
13	1	4	4	4	4	5	4	-	-	-
-	-	-	-	-	-	-	-	-	-	-
5	3	3	3	3	5	3	2	-	-	13
17	14	13	8	11	21	24	7	12	56	121
156	171	193	156	152	166	182	164	144	140	134
5,101	4,707	4,661	4,977	4,790	4,849	4,809	4,242	3,068	2,180	1,336

Appendix 11

Aircraft Losses*
December 1941 to August 1945

Heavy Bombers

| | 1941 | 1942 | | | | | | | |
	Dec	Jan	Feb	Mar	Apr	May	Jun	Jul	Aug
European Theater of Operations									
1st Line Losses†	-	-	-	-	-	-	-	-	2
2d Line Losses	-	-	-	-	-	-	-	-	-
Dropped to 2d Line	-	-	-	-	-	-	-	-	-
Total Losses	-	-	-	-	-	-	-	-	2
Mediterranean Theater of Operations									
1st Line Losses†	-	-	-	-	-	-	5	4	4
2d Line Losses	-	-	-	-	-	-	-	-	-
Dropped to 2d Line	-	-	-	-	-	-	-	-	-
Total Losses	-	-	-	-	-	-	5	4	4
Total Bomber Losses Against Germany	-	-	-	-	-	-	5	4	6
Total Bomber Losses All Theaters	29	15	22	9	4	11	19	15	29

Fighters

	Dec	Jan	Feb	Mar	Apr	May	Jun	Jul	Aug
European Theater of Operations									
1st Line Losses†	-	-	-	-	-	-	-	-	15
2d Line Losses	-	-	-	-	-	-	-	-	-
Dropped to 2d Line	-	-	-	-	-	-	-	-	-
Total Losses	-	-	-	-	-	-	-	-	15
Mediterranean Theater of Operations									
1st Line Losses†	-	-	-	-	-	-	-	-	6
2d Line Losses	-	-	-	-	-	-	-	-	-
Dropped to 2d Line	-	-	-	-	-	-	-	-	-
Total Losses	-	-	-	-	-	-	-	-	6
Total Fighter Losses Against Germany	-	-	-	-	-	-	-	-	21
Total Fighter Losses All Theaters	310	7	80	141	65	99	83	49	82

*Figures in parentheses, for "Losses," indicate the excess of gains from salvage over losses; for "Dropped to 2d Line," indicate net gains from 2d to 1st line.
†Combat and Accident

1942				1943												1944	
Sep	Oct	Nov	Dec	Jan	Feb	Mar	Apr	May	Jun	Jul	Aug	Sep	Oct	Nov	Dec	Jan	Feb
3	12	13	20	20	38	24	30	77	95	118	137	111	214	112	207	264	315
-	-	-	-	-	-	-	-	-	1	-	-	-	1	-	-	3	-
-	-	-	-	-	-	-	-	-	-	-	-	28	-	-	-	-	-
3	12	13	20	20	38	24	30	77	96	118	137	111	215	112	207	267	315
8	5	6	5	11	26	2	13	18	10	30	87	26	59	29	38	60	137
-	-	-	-	-	-	-	-	-	-	-	-	-	2	1	-	-	2
-	-	-	-	-	-	-	-	-	-	-	-	-	-	18	2	1	4
8	5	6	5	11	26	2	13	18	10	30	87	26	61	30	38	60	137
11	17	19	25	31	64	27	43	95	106	148	224	137	276	142	245	327	457
30	29	38	41	59	80	50	77	120	125	190	256	165	315	182	278	370	477
6	7	6	34	11	15	10	19	16	12	18	23	27	30	62	58	110	129
-	-	-	-	-	-	-	-	-	-	-	-	-	-	-	-	1	-
-	-	-	-	-	-	-	-	-	-	-	-	5	-	-	-	-	-
6	7	6	34	11	15	10	19	16	12	18	23	27	30	62	58	111	129
3	5	33	91	129	100	70	177	147	106	170	216	214	149	85	115	150	175
-	-	-	-	-	-	-	-	-	-	-	-	-	11	-	-	-	3
-	-	-	-	-	-	-	-	-	-	-	-	-	-	24	1	2	5
3	5	33	91	129	100	70	177	147	106	170	216	214	160	85	115	150	178
9	12	39	127	140	115	80	196	163	118	188	239	241	190	147	173	261	307
89	75	146	169	212	169	150	307	261	198	304	365	367	300	279	328	393	413

Appendix 11 (continued)

Aircraft Losses*
December 1941 to August 1945

Heavy Bombers

	1944									
	Mar	Apr	May	Jun	Jul	Aug	Sep	Oct	Nov	Dec
European Theater of Operations										
1st Line Losses†	325	467	414	422	382	331	399	209	235	186
2d Line Losses	-	2	3	3	9	9	9	12	12	10
Dropped to 2d Line	5	101	152	19	34	41	43	98	23	26
Total Losses	325	469	417	425	391	340	408	221	247	196
Mediterranean Theater of Operations										
1st Line Losses†	99	211	199	219	329	273	112	170	152	221
2d Line Losses	-	3	3	3	3	3	8	7	1	177
Dropped to 2d Line	4	15	60	37	37	28	6	114	35	(3)
Total Losses	99	214	202	222	332	276	120	177	153	225
Total Bomber Losses Against Germany	424	683	619	647	723	616	528	398	400	421
Total Bomber Losses All Theaters	466	737	654	690	767	661	563	474	545	494

Fighters

	Mar	Apr	May	Jun	Jul	Aug	Sep	Oct	Nov	Dec
European Theater of Operations										
1st Line Losses†	229	358	475	674	444	613	400	499	363	464
2d Line Losses	3	-	-	24	25	14	18	18	19	17
Dropped to 2d Line	20	5	176	9	43	54	52	43	30	74
Total Losses	232	358	475	698	469	627	418	517	382	481
Mediterranean Theater of Operations										
1st Line Losses†	99	161	256	236	201	272	167	125	168	140
2d Line Losses	2	1	17	22	2	6	14	1	12	1
Dropped to 2d Line	38	15	95	9	7	168	65	4	4	1
Total Losses	101	162	273	258	203	278	181	126	180	141
Total Fighter Losses Against Germany	333	420	748	956	672	905	599	643	562	622
Total Fighter Losses All Theaters	496	646	840	1147	808	1100	793	855	922	987

---

*Figures in parentheses, for "Losses," indicate the excess of gains from salvage over losses; for "Dropped to 2d Line," indicate net gains from 2d to 1st line.
†Combat and Accident

	1945							Total 1941 (Dec)	Total 1942 (Jan-Aug)	Total 1943	Total 1944	Total 1945	Grand Total
Jan	Feb	Mar	Apr	May	Jun	Jul	Aug	(Dec)	(Jan-Aug)				
343	220	304	216	49	(25)	3	-	-	50	1,183	3,949	1,110	6,292
22	2	5	5	111	56	16	-	-	-	2	72	226	300
5	34	(5)	17	8	2	-	4	-	-	28	542	65	635
365	222	309	221	160	31	19	9	-	50	1,185	4,021	1,336	6,592
119	158	169	107	42	10	(1)	4	-	37	349	2,180	608	3,174
4	9	3	36	27	30	28	36	-	-	3	37	346	386
22	5	25	29	81	(23)	90	(26)	-	-	20	363	178	561
128	161	205	134	72	38	35	181	-	37	352	2,217	954	3,560
393	383	514	355	232	69	54	190	-	87	1,532	6,238	2,290	10,152
569	398	586	424	351	171	128	294	29	262	1,897	6,898	2,921	12,007
396	391	509	433	112	70	55	31	-	68	301	4,758	1,997	7,124
21	22	21	21	30	19	19	5	-	-	-	139	158	297
28	35	10	7	6	1	10	(7)	-	-	5	506	90	601
417	413	530	454	142	89	74	36	-	68	301	4,897	2,155	7,421
104	130	128	151	36	35	12	10	-	138	1,678	2,150	606	4,572
1	28	30	63	15	22	15	269	-	-	11	81	443	535
2	6	1	12	7	11	421	245	-	-	25	413	705	1,143
105	158	158	214	51	57	27	279	-	138	1,689	2,231	1,049	5,107
522	571	688	668	193	146	101	315	-	206	1,990	7,128	3,204	12,528
836	802	937	964	466	525	391	630	310	1,085	3,240	9,400	5,551	19,586

Appendix 12

Combat Sorties Flown, Europe
December 1941 to August 1945

	ETO	MTO	Total
1941 Dec	-	-	-
1942 Jan	-	-	-
Feb	-	-	-
Mar	-	-	-
Apr	-	-	-
May	-	-	-
Jun	-	70	70
Jul	-	166	166
Aug	324	255	579
Sep	423	576	999
Oct	534	1,519	2,053
Nov	629	2,544	3,173
Dec	543	2,166	2,709
Total 1942	2,453	7,296	9,749
1943 Jan	767	4,330	5,097
Feb	976	3,362	4,338
Mar	1,564	6,478	8,042
Apr	989	12,963	13,952
May	3,915	12,724	16,639
Jun	4,104	13,248	17,352
Jul	5,531	24,370	29,901
Aug	5,826	21,532	27,358
Sep	9,294	20,659	29,953
Oct	7,463	14,124	21,587
Nov	9,624	15,856	25,480
Dec	13,876	19,948	33,824
Total 1943	63,929	169,594	233,523
1944 Jan	15,183	28,992	44,175
Feb	24,425	20,568	44,913
Mar	31,950	24,798	56,748
Apr	43,434	30,645	74,079
May	67,979	42,539	110,518
Jun	96,096	33,947	130,043
Jul	74,878	33,987	108,865
Aug	77,976	37,968	115,944
Sep	57,384	26,359	83,743
Oct	52,596	22,607	75,203
Nov	52,299	26,055	78,354
Dec	61,089	28,347	89,436
Total 1944	655,289	356,812	1,012,101
1945 Jan	47,477	16,914	64,491
Feb	68,365	31,348	99,713
Mar	111,472	35,408	146,880
Apr	79,402	41,495	120,897
May	5,565	646	6,211
Jun	-	-	-
Jul	-	-	-
Aug	-	-	-
Total 1945	312,381	125,811	438,192
Grand Total	1,034,052	659,513	1,693,565

Appendix 13

Combat Sorties Flown in the European Theater of Operations
August 1942 to May 1945

	Heavy Bomber		Med/Lt Bomber		Fighter		Total	
	Airborne	Effective	Airborne	Effective	Airborne	Effective	Airborne	Effective
1942 Aug	114	76	-	-	210	200	324	276
Sep	183	99	-	-	240	230	423	329
Oct	284	143	-	-	250	240	534	383
Nov	519	271	-	-	110	100	629	371
Dec	353	165	-	-	190	180	543	345
Total 1942	1,453	754	-	-	1,000	950	2,453	1,704
1943 Jan	338	220	-	-	429	422	767	642
Feb	526	313	-	-	450	435	976	748
Mar	956	823	-	-	608	584	1,564	1,407
Apr	449	349	-	-	540	510	989	859
May	1,672	1,471	23	23	2,220	2,109	3,915	3,603
Jun	2,107	1,268	-	-	1,997	1,879	4,104	3,147
Jul	2,829	1,743	416	416	2,286	2,133	5,531	4,292
Aug	2,265	1,850	1,297	904	2,264	2,017	5,826	4,771
Sep	3,259	2,457	2,611	1,808	3,424	2,987	9,294	7,252
Oct	2,831	2,117	1,236	521	3,396	2,888	7,463	5,526
Nov	4,157	2,581	1,562	867	3,905	3,436	9,624	6,884
Dec	5,973	4,937	2,162	994	5,741	5,101	13,876	11,032
Total 1943	27,362	20,129	9,307	5,533	27,260	24,501	63,929	50,163
1944 Jan	6,367	5,027	1,649	1,050	7,167	6,464	15,183	12,541
Feb	9,884	7,512	3,862	2,373	10,679	9,703	24,425	19,588
Mar	11,590	8,773	4,099	3,025	16,261	14,613	31,950	26,411
Apr	14,464	9,945	7,416	5,332	21,554	19,216	43,434	34,493
May	19,825	13,975	11,944	8,523	36,210	32,860	67,979	55,358
Jun	28,925	22,713	11,711	8,908	55,460	50,748	96,096	82,369
Jul	23,917	18,864	8,008	5,839	42,953	39,923	74,878	64,626
Aug	22,967	18,964	9,182	6,588	45,827	42,409	77,976	67,961
Sep	18,268	15,617	5,431	3,379	33,685	30,397	57,384	49,393
Oct	19,082	17,058	3,633	1,800	29,881	27,132	52,596	45,990
Nov	17,003	15,245	5,176	3,224	30,120	27,871	52,299	46,340
Dec	18,252	16,424	7,350	4,881	35,487	33,242	61,089	54,547
Total 1944	210,544	170,117	79,461	54,922	365,284	334,578	655,289	559,617
1945 Jan	16,702	14,750	4,457	2,998	26,418	24,561	47,577	42,309
Feb	22,884	19,933	9,255	7,902	36,226	34,515	68,365	62,350
Mar	31,169	28,804	17,461	15,792	62,842	60,199	111,472	104,795
Apr	20,514	18,180	10,832	9,209	48,056	45,453	79,402	72,842
May	2,276	2,254	278	167	3,011	2,557	5,565	4,978
Total 1945	93,545	83,921	42,283	36,068	176,553	167,285	312,381	287,274
Grand Total	332,904	274,921	131,051	96,523	570,097	527,314	1,034,052	898,758

Appendix 14

Combat Sorties Flown in the Mediterranean Theater of Operations
June 1942 to May 1945

	Heavy Bomber		Med/Lt Bomber		Fighter		Total	
	Airborne	Effective*	Airborne	Effective*	Airborne	Effective*	Airborne	Effective*
42 Jun	70		-		-		70	
Jul	166		-		-		166	
Aug	180		71		4		255	
Sep	217		73		286		576	
Oct	280		299		940		1,519	
Nov	513		351		1,680		2,544	
Dec	482		244		1,440		2,166	
Total 1942	1,908		1,038		4,350		7,296	
43 Jan	739	622	891	771	2,700	2,452	4,330	3,845
Feb	734	585	607	503	2,021	1,755	3,362	2,843
Mar	835	720	1,134	931	4,509	4,079	6,478	5,730
Apr	1,586	1,359	2,404	2,089	8,973	8,372	12,963	11,820
May	2,152	1,890	2,283	2,099	8,289	7,653	12,724	11,642
Jun	2,065	1,944	2,656	2,476	8,527	7,974	13,248	12,394
Jul	3,242	2,860	4,784	4,579	16,344	15,660	24,370	23,099
Aug	2,298	2,097	4,563	4,337	14,671	14,074	21,532	20,508
Sep	2,909	2,339	5,429	5,011	12,321	11,771	20,659	19,121
Oct	2,005	1,427	3,259	2,791	8,860	8,146	14,124	12,364
Nov	1,785	1,069	3,358	2,633	10,713	9,717	15,856	13,419
Dec	2,039	1,606	3,644	2,986	14,265	13,041	19,948	17,633
Total 1943	22,389	18,518	35,012	31,206	112,193	104,694	169,594	154,418
44 Jan	4,720	3,811	4,933	4,248	19,339	18,230	28,992	26,289
Feb	3,981	2,380	4,065	2,804	12,522	11,468	20,568	16,652
Mar	5,996	4,202	4,141	3,437	14,661	13,413	24,798	21,052
Apr	10,182	8,084	4,153	3,390	16,310	14,908	30,645	26,382
May	14,432	11,584	7,028	5,787	21,079	19,652	42,539	37,023
Jun	11,761	10,001	5,420	4,777	16,766	15,568	33,947	30,346
Jul	12,642	10,825	5,295	4,447	16,050	14,768	33,987	30,040
Aug	12,194	10,760	6,802	5,661	18,972	17,538	37,968	33,959
Sep	10,056	8,509	5,002	4,152	11,301	10,467	26,359	23,128
Oct	9,567	6,037	3,477	2,382	9,563	8,601	22,607	17,020
Nov	9,259	6,955	4,811	3,623	11,985	10,776	26,055	21,354
Dec	10,050	7,235	3,317	2,522	14,980	13,605	28,347	23,362
Total 1944	114,840	90,383	58,444	47,230	183,528	168,994	356,812	306,607
45 Jan	4,002	2,918	2,947	2,202	9,965	9,219	16,914	14,339
Feb	13,444	10,748	3,998	2,961	13,906	12,433	31,348	26,142
Mar	14,939	12,737	4,971	4,056	15,498	14,583	35,408	31,376
Apr	15,846	11,771	6,752	5,560	18,897	17,567	41,495	34,898
May	42	36	59	51	545	502	646	589
Total 1945	48,273	38,210	18,727	14,830	58,811	54,304	125,811	107,344
Grand Total	187,410	147,111	113,221	93,266	358,882	327,992	659,513	568,369

*Effective sortie figures are for Jan 1943 to May 1945.

Appendix 15

Fighter Sorties Flown against Germany
January 1943 to May 1945

	European Theater of Operations					Mediterranean Theater of Operations				
	Escort	Bombing, Strafing	Recon	Other*	Total	Escort	Bombing, Strafing	Recon	Other*	Total
1943										
Jan	-	-	-	429	429	1,352	286	186	876	2,700
Feb	-	-	-	450	450	1,093	350	312	266	2,021
Mar	-	-	-	608	608	2,238	505	68	1,698	4,509
Apr	8	-	8	524	540	3,433	2,063	388	3,089	8,973
May	384	-	-	1,836	2,220	2,889	2,393	204	2,803	8,289
Jun	169	-	-	1,828	1,997	3,769	1,770	94	2,894	8,527
Jul	607	-	-	1,679	2,286	6,232	3,916	353	5,843	16,344
Aug	1,578	-	-	686	2,264	4,486	4,011	521	5,653	14,671
Sep	2,167	-	-	1,257	3,424	2,493	4,491	210	5,127	12,321
Oct	2,890	-	-	506	3,396	2,241	3,951	151	2,517	8,860
Nov	2,638	105	2	1,160	3,905	3,036	4,161	334	3,182	10,713
Dec	5,095	89	57	500	5,741	3,713	6,157	291	4,104	14,265
Total	15,536	194	67	11,463	27,260	36,975	34,054	3,112	38,052	112,193
1944										
Jan	6,080	201	-	886	7,167	4,526	6,359	-	8,454	19,339
Feb	10,295	83	-	301	10,679	2,628	4,014	-	5,880	12,522
Mar	14,659	887	-	715	16,261	4,487	4,037	-	6,137	14,661
Apr	14,072	3,803	-	3,679	21,554	6,050	6,844	-	3,416	16,310
May	26,091	6,405	-	3,714	36,210	6,746	11,759	-	2,574	21,079
Jun	27,970	11,320	-	16,170	55,460	5,862	8,232	-	2,672	16,766
Jul	20,577	9,098	-	13,278	42,953	8,235	5,223	-	2,592	16,050
Aug	23,793	4,524	-	17,510	45,827	7,887	6,461	-	4,624	18,972
Sep	13,531	11,056	-	9,098	33,685	4,513	4,164	-	2,624	11,301
Oct	15,659	11,731	-	2,491	29,881	4,003	4,583	-	977	9,563
Nov	19,082	7,542	-	3,496	30,120	4,270	6,822	-	893	11,985
Dec	15,723	12,940	-	6,824	35,487	6,141	7,988	-	851	14,980
Total	207,532	79,590	-	78,162	365,284	65,348	76,486	-	41,694	183,528
1945										
Jan	10,898	9,878	4,473	1,169	26,418	2,311	7,402	1	251	9,965
Feb	13,261	13,906	8,410	649	36,226	6,658	6,868	-	380	13,906
Mar	19,853	37,311	452	5,226	62,842	-	15,062	4	432	15,498
Apr	16,654	25,420	4,452	1,530	48,056	5,340	11,749	1,400	408	18,897
May	168	729	362	1,752	3,011	-	332	176	37	545
Total	60,834	87,244	18,149	10,326	176,553	14,309	41,413	1,581	1,508	58,811
Grand Total	283,902	167,028	18,216	99,951	569,097	116,632	151,953	4,693	81,254	354,532

*Includes patrol, interception, sweep, and sea-search sorties.

Appendix 16
Bombs Dropped against Germany
1943 to 1945

	1943	1944	1945 (Jan–Aug)	Total
High Explosive				
4,500 lb	-	-	158	158
2,000 lb	2,322	32,104	14,149	48,575
1,000 lb	36,548	350,755	177,666	564,969
600 lb	712	-	-	712
550 lb (Russian)	-	1,645	-	1,645
500 lb	296,093	1,865,398	928,425	3,089,916
350 lb	-	-	12	12
250 lb	108,464	711,293	235,532	1,055,289
160 lb	79	-	-	79
100 lb	61,905	945,636	512,668	1,520,209
40 lb	2,707	-	-	2,707
Total	508,830	3,906,831	1,868,610	6,284,271
Individual Fragmentation				
260 lb	-	116,955	81,803	198,758
90 lb	-	1,696	-	1,696
85 lb	-	290	-	290
30 lb	5,435	-	-	5,435
Total	5,435	118,941	81,803	206,179
Fragmentation Cluster				
540 lb	-	306	3,670	3,976
480-400 lb	-	991	1,893	2,884
360 lb	-	4	3,275	3,279
180 lb	5	2	-	7
120 lb	127,378	429,667	199,259	756,304
96 lb	-	200	300	500
69 lb (Parachute)	-	1,960	19	1,979
Total	127,383	433,130	208,416	768,929
Individual Incendiary				
500 lb	2,546	12,578	18,781	33,905
360 lb	-	-	91	91
250 lb	-	-	93	93
250 lb (British)	9,410	2,202	-	11,612
200 lb (British)	350	-	34,881	350
100 lb	145,519	625,994	11,777	806,394
100 lb (White Phosphorous)	7	3,475	-	15,259
67 lb	756	-	-	756
4 lb	512	-	-	512
Total	159,100	644,249	65,623	868,972
Incendiary Cluster				
512 lb	-	1,283	-	1,283
500 lb	335	360	-	695
480 lb	-	475	363	838
440 lb	-	158,536	108,487	267,023
136 lb	748	126	-	874
Total	1,083	160,780	108,850	270,713
Class C-Fire				
165-150 gal	-	727	699	1,426
110-100 gal	-	3,271	3,522	6,793
75 gal	-	722	3,249	3,971
50 gal	-	-	10	10
Total	-	4,720	7,480	12,200
Armor-Piercing				
1,600 lb	-	1,122	-	1,122
500 lb	-	-	4	4
Total	-	1,122	4	1,126
Semi-Armor Piercing				
1,000 lb	-	11,633	4,587	16,220
500 lb	-	20,934	9,981	30,915
Total	-	32,567	14,568	47,135

Appendix 17

Tons of Bombs Dropped
December 1941 to August 1945

	ETO	MTO	Total Against Germany	Total Against Japan	Total Against Germany and Japan
1941 Dec	-	-	-	36	36
1942 Jan	-	-	-	20	20
Feb	-	-	-	47	47
Mar	-	-	-	68	68
Apr	-	-	-	128	128
May	-	-	-	184	184
Jun	115	-	115	295	410
Jul	357	-	357	299	656
Aug	135	414	549	409	958
Sep	215	482	697	459	1,156
Oct	334	771	1,105	564	1,669
Nov	612	1,195	1,807	752	2,559
Dec	417	1,076	1,493	855	2,348
Total 1942	1,713	4,410	6,123	4,080	10,203
1943 Jan	739	1,983	2,722	859	3,581
Feb	705	1,719	2,424	1,147	3,571
Mar	1,530	2,773	4,303	1,644	5,947
Apr	1,130	5,053	6,183	2,033	8,216
May	2,688	7,297	9,985	2,344	12,329
Jun	2,468	8,596	11,064	1,845	12,909
Jul	4,366	13,846	18,212	4,041	22,253
Aug	5,072	12,584	17,656	4,333	21,989
Sep	8,519	13,942	22,461	4,212	26,673
Oct	6,015	7,625	13,640	5,013	18,653
Nov	8,309	9,480	17,789	5,921	23,710
Dec	14,114	13,564	27,678	11,291	38,969
Total 1943	55,655	98,462	154,117	44,683	198,800
1944 Jan	14,015	19,097	33,112	7,885	40,997
Feb	22,566	11,595	34,161	9,912	44,073
Mar	26,539	17,440	43,979	12,255	56,234
Apr	38,540	29,856	68,396	13,537	81,933
May	56,874	46,075	102,949	14,715	117,664
Jun	85,648	36,287	121,935	10,499	132,434
Jul	63,062	41,769	104,831	10,034	114,865
Aug	67,766	40,280	108,046	9,458	117,504
Sep	52,175	29,285	81,460	12,849	94,309
Oct	52,860	22,108	74,968	12,329	87,297
Nov	51,413	26,695	78,108	15,025	93,133
Dec	60,501	26,506	87,007	18,528	105,535
Total 1944	591,959	346,993	938,952	147,026	1,085,978
1945 Jan	54,474	14,539	69,013	19,335	88,348
Feb	80,348	32,661	113,009	23,919	136,928
Mar	118,003	41,120	159,123	41,088	200,211
Apr	69,242	44,365	113,607	44,007	157,614
May	368	151	519	47,180	47,699
Jun	-	-	-	50,893	50,893
Jul	-	-	-	53,665	53,665
Aug	-	-	-	26,869	26,869
Total 1945	322,435	132,836	455,271	306,956	762,227
Grand Total	971,762	582,701	1,554,463	502,781	2,057,244

Appendix 18

Tons of Bombs Dropped on German Targets
1942 to 1945

	1942 (Jun-Dec)			1943		
	ETO	MTO	Total	ETO	MTO	Total
Heavy Bombers						
Albania	-	-	-	-	91	91
Austria	-	-	-	-	665	665
Bulgaria	-	-	-	-	347	347
Czechoslovakia	-	-	-	-	-	-
Denmark	-	-	-	-	-	-
France	1,624	-	1,624	14,237	924	15,161
Germany	-	-	-	27,598	1,453	29,051
Greece	-	-	-	-	1,293	1,293
Hungary	-	-	-	-	-	-
Italy	-	-	-	-	23,795	23,795
Low Countries	36	-	36	767	-	767
North Africa	-	3,251	3,251	-	19,517	19,517
Norway	-	-	-	1,497	-	1,497
Poland	-	-	-	-	-	-
Rumania	-	-	-	-	1,382	1,382
Yugoslavia	-	-	-	-	1,018	1,018
Other*	53	-	53	3,353	-	3,353
Total	1,713	3,251	4,964	47,452	50,485	97,937
Medium/Light Bombers and Fighters						
Albania	-	-	-	-	-	-
Austria	-	-	-	-	-	-
Bulgaria	-	-	-	-	-	-
Czechoslovakia	-	-	-	-	-	-
Denmark	-	-	-	-	-	-
France	-	-	-	8,203	-	8,203
Germany	-	-	-	-	-	-
Greece	-	-	-	-	-	-
Hungary	-	-	-	-	-	-
Italy	-	-	-	-	22,653	22,653
Low Countries	-	-	-	-	-	-
North Africa	-	1,159	1,159	-	25,324	25,324
Norway	-	-	-	-	-	-
Poland	-	-	-	-	-	-
Rumania	-	-	-	-	-	-
Yugoslavia	-	-	-	-	-	-
Other*	-	-	-	-	-	-
Total	-	1,159	1,159	8,203	47,977	56,180
All Types						
Albania	-	-	-	-	91	91
Austria	-	-	-	-	665	665
Bulgaria	-	-	-	-	347	347
Czechoslovakia	-	-	-	-	-	-
Denmark	-	-	-	-	-	-
France	1,624	-	1,624	22,440	924	23,364
Germany	-	-	-	27,598	1,453	29,051
Greece	-	-	-	-	1,293	1,293
Hungary	-	-	-	-	-	-
Italy	-	-	-	-	46,448	46,448
Low Countries	36	-	36	767	-	767
North Africa	-	4,410	4,410	-	44,841	44,841
Norway	-	-	-	1,497	-	1,497
Poland	-	-	-	-	-	-
Rumania	-	-	-	-	1,382	1,382
Yugoslavia	-	-	-	-	1,018	1,018
Other*	53	-	53	3,353	-	3,353
Total	1,713	4,410	6,123	55,655	98,462	154,117

*Includes tonnage jettisoned.

	1944			1945 (Jan-May)			Grand Total	
ETO	MTO	Total	ETO	MTO	Total	ETO	MTO	Total
-	280	280	-	-	-	-	371	371
-	34,552	34,552	400	38,566	38,966	400	73,783	74,183
-	2,253	2,253	-	-	-	-	2,600	2,600
796	8,193	8,989	3,564	2,246	5,810	4,360	10,439	14,799
60	-	60	-	-	-	60	-	60
119,460	18,186	137,646	7,628	-	7,628	142,949	19,110	162,059
295,470	23,849	319,319	198,661	10,612	209,273	521,729	35,914	557,643
-	1,932	1,932	-	-	-	-	3,225	3,225
364	19,250	19,614	-	2,614	2,614	364	21,864	22,228
-	61,917	61,917	-	27,029	27,029	-	112,741	112,741
12,312	-	12,312	1,035	-	1,035	14,150	-	14,150
-	-	-	-	-	-	-	22,768	22,768
-	-	-	-	-	-	1,497	-	1,497
316	1,144	1,460	-	-	-	316	1,144	1,460
287	24,746	25,033	-	-	-	287	26,128	26,415
-	17,519	17,519	-	3,503	3,503	-	22,040	22,040
17,100	23,619	40,719	8,101	6,329	14,430	28,607	29,948	58,555
446,165	237,440	683,605	219,389	90,899	310,288	714,719	382,075	1,096,794
-	-	-	-	-	-	-	-	-
-	-	-	-	1,843	1,843	-	1,843	1,843
-	-	-	-	-	-	-	-	-
-	-	-	-	-	-	-	-	-
143,056	4,976	148,032	21,357	-	21,357	4,976	-	177,592
1,369	-	1,369	81,689	500	82,189	83,058	500	83,558
-	-	-	-	-	-	-	-	-
-	-	-	-	-	-	-	-	-
-	104,577	104,577	-	36,341	36,341	-	163,571	163,571
1,369	-	1,369	-	-	-	1,369	-	1,369
-	-	-	-	-	-	-	26,483	26,483
-	-	-	-	-	-	-	-	-
-	-	-	-	-	-	-	-	-
-	-	-	-	2,000	2,000	-	2,000	2,000
-	-	-	-	1,253	1,253	-	1,253	1,253
145,794	109,533	255,347	103,046	41,937	144,983	257,043	200,626	457,669
-	280	280	-	-	-	-	371	371
-	34,552	34,552	400	40,409	40,809	400	75,626	76,026
-	2,253	2,253	-	-	-	-	2,600	2,600
796	8,193	8,989	3,564	2,246	5,810	4,360	10,439	14,799
60	-	60	-	-	-	60	-	60
262,516	23,162	285,678	28,985	-	28,985	315,565	24,086	339,651
296,839	23,849	320,688	280,350	11,112	291,462	604,787	36,414	641,201
-	1,932	1,932	-	-	-	-	3,225	3,225
364	19,250	19,614	-	2,614	2,614	364	21,864	22,228
-	166,494	166,494	-	63,370	63,370	-	276,312	276,312
13,681	-	13,681	1,035	-	1,035	15,519	-	15,519
-	-	-	-	-	-	-	49,251	49,251
-	-	-	-	-	-	1,497	-	1,497
316	1,144	1,460	-	-	-	316	1,144	1,460
287	24,746	25,033	-	-	-	287	26,128	26,415
-	17,519	17,519	-	5,503	5,503	-	24,040	24,040
17,100	23,619	40,719	8,101	7,582	15,683	28,607	31,201	59,808
591,959	346,993	938,952	322,435	132,836	455,271	971,762	582,701	1,554,463

Tons of Bombs Dropped by Heavy Bombers on Germany
June 1942 to May 1945

Target	1942 (Jun-Dec)	1943	1944	1945 (Jan-May)	Grand Total
European Theater of Operations					
Marshaling Yards	154	5,348	89,884	100,224	195,610
Oil Installations	-	238	52,622	15,250	68,110
Airdromes and Airfields	543	5,513	57,810	18,825	82,691
Railroads, Roads and Bridges	-	-	17,328	13,229	30,557
Military Installations	-	1,745	45,879	15,284	62,908
Other Specific Industries	78	7,030	32,658	13,726	53,492
Aircraft Factories	149	5,090	36,726	2,472	44,437
Ground Cooperation	-	-	25,647	11,311	36,958
City Areas	-	-	42,603	4,217	46,820
Ship Yards, Sub Pens	736	18,072	6,973	8,646	34,427
Other Communications	-	-	21,937	3,516	25,453
Miscellaneous	-	3,333	-	4,588	7,921
Jettisoned and unidentified	53	1,083	16,098	8,101	25,335
Total	1,713	47,452	446,165	219,389	714,719
Mediterranean Theater of Operations					
Marshaling Yards	-	16,565	64,834	38,298	119,697
Oil Installations	-	-	46,769	11,312	58,081
Airdromes and Airfields	-	8,215	23,002	3,819	35,036
Railroads, Roads and Bridges	-	1,610	24,399	14,003	40,012
Military Installations	-	-	2,683	4,580	7,263
Other Specific Industries	-	1,558	12,064	3,012	16,634
Aircraft Factories	-	1,281	13,045	-	14,326
Ground Cooperation	-	36	12,073	8,039	20,148
City Areas	-	749	-	46	795
Ship Yards, Sub Pens	-	-	2,216	-	2,216
Other Communications	-	775	8,929	1,461	11,165
Miscellaneous	3,251	19,696	3,807	-	26,754
Jettisoned and unidentified	-	-	23,619	6,329	29,948
Total	3,251	50,485	237,440	90,899	382,075
European and Mediterranean Theaters of Operations					
Marshaling Yards	154	21,913	154,718	138,522	315,307
Oil Installations	-	238	99,391	26,562	126,191
Airdromes and Airfields	543	13,728	80,812	22,644	117,727
Railroads, Roads and Bridges	-	1,610	41,727	27,232	70,569
Military Installations	-	1,745	48,562	19,864	70,171
Other Specific Industries	78	8,588	44,722	16,738	70,126
Aircraft Factories	149	6,371	49,771	2,472	58,763
Ground Cooperation	-	36	37,720	19,350	57,106
City Areas	-	749	42,603	4,263	47,615
Ship Yards, Sub Pens	736	18,072	9,189	8,646	36,643
Other Communications	-	775	30,866	4,977	36,618
Miscellaneous	3,251	23,029	3,807	4,588	34,675
Jettisoned and unidentified	53	1,083	39,717	14,430	55,283
Total	4,964	97,937	683,605	310,288	1,096,794

Appendix 20

Tons of Bombs Dropped in the European Theater of Operations
August 1942 to May 1945

	Heavy Bomber			Med/Lt Bomber			Fighter			All Types		
	HE*	Incendiary	Total	HE*	Incendiary	Total	HE*	Incendiary	Total	HE*	Incendiary	Total
1942												
Aug	135	-	135	-	-	-	-	-	-	135	-	135
Sep	215	-	215	-	-	-	-	-	-	215	-	215
Oct	334	-	334	-	-	-	-	-	-	334	-	334
Nov	612	-	612	-	-	-	-	-	-	612	-	612
Dec	417	-	417	-	-	-	-	-	-	417	-	417
Total	1,713	-	1,713	-	-	-	-	-	-	1,713	-	1,713
1943												
Jan	739	-	739	-	-	-	-	-	-	739	-	739
Feb	705	-	705	-	-	-	-	-	-	705	-	705
Mar	1,530	-	1,530	-	-	-	-	-	-	1,530	-	1,530
Apr	1,130	-	1,130	-	-	-	-	-	-	1,130	-	1,130
May	2,654	23	2,677	-	-	11	-	-	-	2,665	23	2,688
Jun	2,468	-	2,468	-	-	-	-	-	-	2,468	-	2,468
Jul	3,504	599	4,103	258	5	263	-	-	-	3,762	604	4,366
Aug	3,453	326	3,779	1,284	9	1,293	-	-	-	4,737	335	5,072
Sep	5,515	228	5,743	2,764	12	2,776	-	-	-	8,279	240	8,519
Oct	4,290	843	5,133	882	-	882	-	-	-	5,172	843	6,015
Nov	5,072	1,796	6,868	1,424	-	1,424	17	-	17	6,513	1,796	8,309
Dec	9,419	3,158	12,577	1,530	-	1,530	7	-	7	10,956	3,158	14,114
Total	40,479	6,973	47,452	8,153	26	8,179	24	-	24	48,656	6,999	55,655
1944												
Jan	9,651	2,746	12,397	1,579	-	1,579	39	-	39	11,269	2,746	14,015
Feb	16,670	2,476	19,146	3,397	-	3,397	23	-	23	20,090	2,476	22,566
Mar	16,357	4,989	21,346	4,998	64	5,062	131	-	131	21,486	5,053	26,539
Apr	22,829	4,747	27,576	9,372	103	9,475	1,489	-	1,489	33,690	4,850	38,540
May	33,123	4,906	38,029	15,120	36	15,156	3,684	5	3,689	51,927	4,947	56,874
Jun	58,396	1,229	59,625	15,677	24	15,701	10,321	1	10,322	84,394	1,254	85,648
Jul	39,483	7,122	46,605	9,873	10	9,883	6,567	7	6,574	55,923	7,139	63,062
Aug	43,987	5,318	49,305	10,648	68	10,716	7,721	24	7,745	62,356	5,410	67,766
Sep	34,852	7,310	42,162	5,712	-	5,712	4,300	1	4,301	44,864	7,311	52,175
Oct	33,360	11,727	45,087	3,101	-	3,101	4,574	98	4,672	41,035	11,825	52,860
Nov	41,210	608	41,818	5,436	-	5,436	4,019	140	4,159	50,665	748	51,413
Dec	39,181	3,888	43,069	8,359	46	8,405	8,726	301	9,027	56,266	4,235	60,501
Total	389,099	57,066	446,165	93,272	351	93,623	51,594	577	52,171	533,965	57,994	591,959
1945												
Jan	39,382	2,731	42,113	5,094	14	5,108	6,941	312	7,253	51,417	3,057	54,474
Feb	47,554	7,446	55,000	13,554	334	13,888	10,955	505	11,460	72,063	8,285	80,348
Mar	64,323	11,000	75,323	24,956	2,452	27,408	13,337	1,935	15,272	102,616	15,387	118,003
Apr	41,591	5,362	46,953	14,528	1,152	15,680	5,689	920	6,609	61,808	7,434	69,242
May	-	-	-	301	-	301	67	-	67	368	-	368
Total	192,850	26,539	219,389	58,433	3,952	62,385	36,989	3,672	40,661	288,272	34,163	322,435
Grand Total	624,141	90,578	714,719	159,858	4,329	164,187	88,607	4,249	92,856	872,606	99,156	971,762

*High Explosive.

Tons of Bombs Dropped in the Mediterranean Theater of Operations
June 1942 to May 1945

	Heavy Bomber			Med/Lt Bomber			Fighter			All Types		
	HE*	Incendiary	Total	HE*	Incendiary	Total	HE*	Incendiary	Total	HE*	Incendiary	Total
1942												
Jun	115	-	115	-	-	-	-	-	-	115	-	115
Jul	357	-	357	-	-	-	-	-	-	357	-	357
Aug	346	-	346	68	-	68	-	-	-	414	-	414
Sep	411	-	411	71	-	71	-	-	-	482	-	482
Oct	424	-	424	297	-	297	50	-	50	771	-	771
Nov	815	-	815	329	-	329	51	-	51	1,195	-	1,195
Dec	783	-	783	212	-	212	81	-	81	1,076	-	1,076
Total	3,251	-	3,251	977	-	977	182	-	182	4,410	-	4,410
1943												
Jan	1,354	-	1,354	586	2	588	41	-	41	1,981	2	1,983
Feb	1,221	-	1,221	488	-	488	10	-	10	1,719	-	1,719
Mar	1,557	-	1,557	1,162	-	1,162	54	-	54	2,773	-	2,773
Apr	2,777	-	2,777	1,935	-	1,935	341	-	341	5,053	-	5,053
May	4,305	-	4,305	2,334	1	2,335	656	1	657	7,295	2	7,297
Jun	4,732	-	4,732	3,030	-	3,030	834	-	834	8,596	-	8,596
Jul	6,883	-	6,883	5,680	-	5,680	1,283	-	1,283	13,846	-	13,846
Aug	5,047	-	5,047	5,948	-	5,948	1,589	-	1,589	12,584	-	12,584
Sep	5,256	27	5,283	7,171	-	7,171	1,488	-	1,488	13,915	27	13,942
Oct	4,180	2	4,182	2,365	-	2,365	1,078	-	1,078	7,623	2	7,625
Nov	5,392	-	5,392	2,921	-	2,921	1,167	-	1,167	9,480	-	9,480
Dec	7,752	-	7,752	3,895	-	3,895	1,917	-	1,917	13,564	-	13,564
Total	50,456	29	50,485	37,515	3	37,518	10,458	1	10,459	98,429	33	98,462
1944												
Jan	11,051	-	11,051	5,947	8	5,955	2,079	12	2,091	19,077	20	19,097
Feb	6,611	136	6,747	3,278	-	3,278	1,569	1	1,570	11,458	137	11,595
Mar	9,842	534	10,376	5,457	-	5,457	1,589	18	1,607	16,888	552	17,440
Apr	20,657	599	21,256	5,599	-	5,599	2,822	179	3,001	29,078	778	29,856
May	29,606	749	30,355	9,908	34	9,942	5,686	92	5,778	45,200	875	46,075
Jun	23,637	829	24,466	7,842	43	7,885	3,926	10	3,936	35,405	882	36,287
Jul	30,621	1,562	32,183	7,038	91	7,129	2,454	3	2,457	40,113	1,656	41,769
Aug	27,660	179	27,839	9,348	67	9,415	2,954	72	3,026	39,962	318	40,280
Sep	20,645	211	20,856	6,473	50	6,523	1,900	6	1,906	29,018	267	29,285
Oct	15,712	545	16,257	4,081	48	4,129	1,710	12	1,722	21,503	605	22,108
Nov	16,153	1,144	17,297	6,119	7	6,126	3,255	17	3,272	25,527	1,168	26,695
Dec	18,308	449	18,757	4,091	38	4,129	3,613	7	3,620	26,012	494	26,506
Total	230,503	6,937	237,440	75,181	386	75,567	33,557	429	33,986	339,241	7,752	346,993
1945												
Jan	6,784	-	6,784	3,738	57	3,795	3,836	124	3,960	14,358	181	14,539
Feb	24,417	91	24,508	4,789	154	4,943	3,054	156	3,210	32,260	401	32,661
Mar	30,265	-	30,265	6,895	152	7,047	3,621	187	3,808	40,781	339	41,120
Apr	29,181	77	29,258	9,242	104	9,346	5,334	427	5,761	43,757	608	44,365
May	84	-	84	4	-	4	39	24	63	127	24	151
Total	90,731	168	90,899	24,668	467	25,135	15,884	918	16,802	131,283	1,553	132,836
Grand Total	374,941	7,134	382,075	138,341	856	139,197	60,081	1,348	61,429	573,363	9,338	582,701

*High Explosive.

Appendix 22
Combat Losses by Theater
January 1942 to 1945

	ETO	MTO	Total Against Germany	Total Against Japan	Total Against Germany and Japan
1942 Jan	-	-	-	5	5
Feb	-	-	-	46	46
Mar	-	-	-	12	12
Apr	-	-	-	4	4
May	-	-	-	50	50
Jun	-	5	5	47	52
Jul	-	3	3	25	28
Aug	8	6	14	28	42
Sep	2	6	8	30	38
Oct	11	6	17	16	33
Nov	17	18	35	57	92
Dec	17	42	59	21	80
Total 1942	55	86	141	341	482
1943 Jan	21	112	133	27	160
Feb	24	86	110	25	135
Mar	22	83	105	24	129
Apr	34	168	202	40	242
May	92	157	249	37	286
Jun	98	117	215	59	274
Jul	134	256	390	107	497
Aug	135	283	418	86	504
Sep	118	163	281	77	358
Oct	201	120	321	95	416
Nov	160	87	247	122	369
Dec	222	135	357	120	477
Total 1943	1,261	1,767	3,028	819	3,847
1944 Jan	277	221	498	145	643
Feb	393	268	661	114	775
Mar	551	202	753	138	891
Apr	732	311	1,043	127	1,170
May	761	387	1,148	97	1,245
Jun	904	419	1,323	134	1,457
Jul	712	473	1,185	109	1,294
Aug	968	487	1,455	103	1,558
Sep	758	233	991	112	1,103
Oct	552	263	815	148	963
Nov	538	281	819	235	1,054
Dec	603	324	927	209	1,136
Total 1944	7,749	3,869	11,618	1,671	13,289
1945 Jan	646	189	835	249	1,084
Feb	580	273	853	190	1,043
Mar	774	284	1,058	208	1,266
Apr	579	246	825	242	1,067
May	43	17	60	256	316
Jun	-	-	-	216	216
Jul	-	-	-	194	194
Aug	-	-	-	144	144
Total 1945	2,622	1,009	3,631	1,699	5,330
Grand Total	11,687	6,731	18,418	4,530	22,948

Appendix 23

Combat Losses in the European Theater of Operations
August 1942 to May 1945

	Heavy Bomber				Med/Lt Bomber				Fighter				All Types			
	Aircraft	AA	Other	Total	Aircraft	AA	Other	Total	Aircraft	AA	Other	Total	Aircraft	AA	Other	Total
42																
ug	-	-	-	-	-	-	-	-	8	-	-	8	8	-	-	8
p	2	-	-	2	-	-	-	-	-	-	-	-	2	-	-	2
ct	8	-	2	10	-	-	-	-	1	-	-	1	9	-	2	11
ov	10	-	3	13	2	-	1	3	1	-	-	1	13	-	4	17
c	17	-	-	17	-	-	-	-	-	-	-	-	17	-	-	17
Total	37	-	5	42	2	-	1	3	10	-	-	10	49	-	6	55
43																
n	18	-	-	18	-	-	-	-	3	-	-	3	21	-	-	21
b	21	-	2	23	-	-	-	-	1	-	-	1	22	-	2	24
ar	18	-	3	21	-	-	-	-	1	-	-	1	19	-	3	22
pr	28	1	-	29	-	-	-	-	5	-	-	5	33	1	-	34
ay	48	13	8	69	1	8	2	11	9	-	3	12	58	21	13	92
n	78	12	-	90	-	-	-	-	8	-	-	8	86	12	-	98
l	79	29	10	118	1	1	-	2	14	-	-	14	94	30	10	134
ug	87	20	10	117	6	-	2	8	7	-	3	10	100	20	15	135
p	46	25	27	98	4	2	2	8	10	-	2	12	60	27	31	118
ct	139	38	9	186	-	-	1	1	13	-	1	14	152	38	11	201
ov	53	25	17	95	3	7	1	11	53	1	-	54	109	33	18	160
ec	85	65	22	172	1	5	-	6	37	-	7	44	123	70	29	222
Total	700	228	108	1,036	16	23	8	47	161	1	16	178	877	252	132	1,261
44																
n	139	27	37	203	1	2	2	5	57	6	6	69	197	35	45	277
b	170	81	20	271	4	14	1	19	69	13	21	103	243	108	42	393
ar	178	112	55	345	2	9	4	15	54	46	91	191	234	167	150	551
pr	314	105	1	420	1	25	6	32	201	60	19	280	516	190	26	732
ay	211	122	43	376	10	28	7	45	176	98	66	340	397	248	116	761
n	112	162	46	320	25	12	7	44	147	226	167	540	284	400	220	904
l	80	201	71	352	5	23	6	34	65	153	108	326	150	377	185	712
ug	61	238	32	331	2	75	14	91	100	294	152	546	163	607	198	968
p	137	207	30	374	-	25	2	27	104	190	63	357	241	422	95	758
ct	36	112	29	177	-	24	2	26	99	198	52	349	135	334	83	552
ov	50	146	13	209	1	18	12	31	80	164	54	298	131	328	79	538
ec	28	74	17	119	42	48	28	118	141	163	62	366	211	285	107	603
Total	1,516	1,587	394	3,497	93	303	91	487	1,293	1,611	861	3,765	2,902	3,501	1,346	7,749
45																
n	49	222	43	314	-	28	30	58	72	162	40	274	121	412	113	646
b	14	157	25	196	4	68	13	85	38	208	53	299	56	433	91	580
ar	63	164	39	266	5	52	32	89	76	244	99	419	144	460	170	774
pr	72	77	41	190	11	18	17	46	36	207	100	343	119	302	158	579
ay	1	4	2	7	-	-	-	-	5	16	15	36	6	20	17	43
Total	199	624	150	973	20	166	92	278	227	837	307	1,371	446	1,627	549	2,622
Grand Total	2,452	2,439	657	5,548	131	492	192	815	1,691	2,449	1,184	5,324	4,274	5,380	2,033	11,687

Appendix 24

Combat Losses in the Mediterranean Theater of Operations
June 1942 to May 1945

	Heavy Bomber				Med/Lt Bomber				Fighter				All Types			
	Aircraft	AA	Other	Total	Aircraft	AA	Other	Total	Aircraft	AA	Other	Total	Aircraft	AA	Other	Total
1942																
Jun	4	-	1	5	-	-	-	-	-	-	-	-	4	-	1	5
Jul	3	-	-	3	-	-	-	-	-	-	-	-	3	-	-	3
Aug	1	-	-	1	1	-	1	2	3	-	-	3	5	-	1	6
Sep	-	-	-	-	6	-	-	6	-	-	-	-	6	-	-	6
Oct	1	-	-	1	2	-	-	2	3	-	-	3	6	-	-	6
Nov	1	2	-	3	-	1	-	1	10	4	-	14	11	7	-	18
Dec	2	2	-	4	-	4	-	4	30	4	-	34	32	10	-	42
Total	12	4	1	17	9	5	1	15	46	8	-	54	67	17	2	86
1943																
Jan	11	-	-	11	11	1	1	13	78	6	4	88	100	7	5	112
Feb	6	-	-	6	14	10	4	28	40	10	2	52	60	20	6	86
Mar	2	-	-	2	8	5	-	13	55	7	6	68	65	12	6	83
Apr	11	2	-	13	24	10	5	39	109	4	3	116	144	16	8	168
May	12	4	-	16	18	3	4	25	89	16	11	116	119	23	15	157
Jun	8	2	-	10	18	2	6	26	58	3	20	81	84	7	26	117
Jul	16	9	5	30	49	22	2	73	112	12	29	153	177	43	36	256
Aug	41	31	13	85	27	12	2	41	113	17	27	157	181	60	42	283
Sep	15	1	4	20	32	6	17	55	56	5	27	88	103	12	48	163
Oct	32	2	3	37	22	1	10	33	32	6	12	50	86	9	25	120
Nov	25	1	2	28	9	4	7	20	18	15	6	39	52	20	15	87
Dec	30	3	3	36	7	4	8	19	56	14	10	80	93	21	21	135
Total	209	55	30	294	239	80	66	385	816	115	157	1,088	1,264	250	253	1,767
1944																
Jan	20	10	24	54	28	15	7	50	70	17	30	117	118	42	61	221
Feb	106	11	11	128	12	19	5	36	57	25	22	104	175	55	38	268
Mar	42	19	24	85	8	13	7	28	38	9	42	89	88	41	73	202
Apr	105	65	24	194	10	2	-	12	38	17	50	105	153	84	74	311
May	50	107	18	175	-	23	9	32	52	59	69	180	102	189	96	387
Jun	85	79	32	196	9	12	1	22	67	70	64	201	161	161	97	419
Jul	94	170	53	317	4	10	7	21	43	42	50	135	141	222	110	473
Aug	91	112	51	254	3	20	13	36	39	54	104	197	133	186	168	487
Sep	7	71	16	94	8	12	2	22	18	55	44	117	33	138	62	233
Oct	-	110	30	140	4	18	3	25	2	55	41	98	6	183	74	263
Nov	1	69	62	132	12	14	3	29	10	54	56	120	23	137	121	281
Dec	18	110	77	205	3	5	3	11	7	36	65	108	28	151	145	324
Total	619	933	422	1,974	101	163	60	324	441	493	637	1,571	1,161	1,589	1,119	3,869
1945																
Jan	-	46	42	88	2	9	9	20	-	33	48	81	2	88	99	189
Feb	-	108	39	147	-	14	5	19	4	44	59	107	4	166	103	273
Mar	7	93	49	149	1	21	3	25	13	56	41	110	21	170	93	284
Apr	-	65	18	83	-	14	6	20	7	72	64	143	7	151	88	246
May	-	9	5	14	-	-	-	-	-	1	2	3	-	10	7	17
Total	7	321	153	481	3	58	23	84	24	206	214	444	34	585	390	1,009
Grand Total	847	1,313	606	2,766	352	306	150	808	1,327	822	1,008	3,157	2,526	2,441	1,764	6,731

Appendix 25

Enemy Aircraft Destroyed
February 1942 to August 1945

	ETO	MTO	Total
1942 Feb	-	-	-
Mar	-	-	-
Apr	-	-	-
May	-	-	-
Jun	-	-	-
Jul	-	2	2
Aug	3	-	3
Sep	16	1	17
Oct	49	43	92
Nov	47	36	83
Dec	54	76	130
Total 1942	169	158	327
1943 Jan	50	194	244
Feb	74	143	217
Mar	142	211	353
Apr	150	523	673
May	380	350	730
Jun	311	267	578
Jul	575	313	888
Aug	457	602	1,059
Sep	303	483	786
Oct	870	290	1,160
Nov	222	175	397
Dec	331	189	520
Total 1943	3,865	3,740	7,605
1944 Jan	795	320	1,115
Feb	741	377	1,118
Mar	910	307	1,217
Apr	1,291	958	2,249
May	1,220	532	1,752
Jun	663	562	1,225
Jul	661	872	1,533
Aug	1,013	598	1,611
Sep	1,091	251	1,342
Oct	353	259	612
Nov	702	86	788
Dec	985	117	1,102
Total 1944	10,425	5,239	15,664
1945 Jan	465	8	473
Feb	460	28	488
Mar	750	145	895
Apr	4,257	110	4,367
May	28	-	28
Jun	-	-	-
Jul	-	-	-
Aug	-	-	-
Total 1945	5,960	291	6,251
Grand Total	20,419	9,497	29,916

Appendix 26

Enemy Aircraft Destroyed in the European Theater of Operations
August 1942 to May 1945

	By Heavy Bombers			By Med\Lt Bombers			By Fighters			By All Types		
	Air	Ground	Total	Air	Ground	Total	Air	Ground	Total	Air	Ground	Total
1942 Aug	2	-	2	-	-	-	1	-	1	3	-	3
Sep	16	-	16	-	-	-	-	-	-	16	-	16
Oct	44	-	44	-	-	-	5	-	5	49	-	49
Nov	47	-	47	-	-	-	-	-	-	47	-	47
Dec	53	-	53	-	-	-	1	-	1	54	-	54
Total 1942	162	-	162	-	-	-	7	-	7	169	-	169
1943 Jan	45	-	45	-	-	-	5	-	5	50	-	50
Feb	72	-	72	-	-	-	2	-	2	74	-	74
Mar	142	-	142	-	-	-	-	-	-	142	-	142
Apr	146	-	146	-	-	-	4	-	4	150	-	150
May	372	-	372	-	-	-	8	-	8	380	-	380
Jun	293	-	293	-	-	-	18	-	18	311	-	311
Jul	527	-	527	6	-	6	42	-	42	575	-	575
Aug	401	-	401	3	-	3	53	-	53	457	-	457
Sep	255	-	255	10	-	10	38	-	38	303	-	303
Oct	791	-	791	3	-	3	76	-	76	870	-	870
Nov	106	-	106	11	-	11	105	-	105	222	-	222
Dec	231	-	231	-	-	-	100	-	100	331	-	331
Total 1943	3,381	-	3,381	33	-	33	451	-	451	3,865	-	3,865
1944 Jan	582	-	582	10	-	10	203	-	203	795	-	795
Feb	397	-	397	2	-	2	341	1	342	740	1	741
Mar	363	-	363	2	-	2	469	76	545	834	76	910
Apr	346	-	346	-	-	-	418	527	945	764	527	1,291
May	380	-	380	2	-	2	596	242	838	978	242	1,220
Jun	42	-	42	3	-	3	470	148	618	515	148	663
Jul	98	-	98	3	-	3	407	153	560	508	153	661
Aug	23	-	23	2	-	2	551	437	988	576	437	1,013
Sep	65	-	65	-	-	-	586	440	1,026	651	440	1,091
Oct	12	-	12	-	-	-	202	139	341	214	139	353
Nov	29	-	29	-	-	-	492	181	673	521	181	702
Dec	61	-	61	26	-	26	867	31	898	954	31	985
Total 1944	2,398	-	2,398	50	-	50	5,602	2,375	7,977	8,050	2,375	10,425
1945 Jan	41	-	41	-	-	-	337	87	424	378	87	465
Feb	1	-	1	1	-	1	163	295	458	165	295	460
Mar	23	-	23	11	-	11	395	321	716	429	321	750
Apr	92	-	92	8	-	8	454	3,703	4,157	554	3,703	4,257
May	-	-	-	-	-	-	13	15	28	13	15	28
Total 1945	157	-	157	20	-	20	1,362	4,421	5,783	1,539	4,421	5,960
Grand Total	6,098	-	6,098	103	-	103	7,422	6,796	14,218	13,623	6,796	20,419

Appendix 27

Enemy Aircraft Destroyed in the Mediterranean Theater of Operations
July 1942 to May 1945

	By Heavy Bombers			By Med\Lt Bombers			By Fighters			By All Types		
	Air	Ground	Total	Air	Ground	Total	Air	Ground	Total	Air	Ground	Total
1942 Jul	2	-	2	-	-	-	-	-	-	2	-	2
Aug	-	-	-	-	-	-	-	-	-	-	-	-
Sep	1	-	1	-	-	-	-	-	-	1	-	1
Oct	8	-	8	3	10	13	22	-	22	33	10	43
Nov	6	5	11	-	-	-	16	9	25	22	14	36
Dec	19	1	20	3	8	11	43	2	45	65	11	76
Total 1942	36	6	42	6	18	24	81	11	92	123	35	158
1943 Jan	74	-	74	33	30	63	56	1	57	163	31	194
Feb	47	-	47	33	6	39	57	-	57	137	6	143
Mar	63	12	75	21	12	33	103	-	103	187	24	211
Apr	75	100	175	27	2	29	319	-	319	421	102	523
May	107	7	114	30	41	71	132	33	165	269	81	350
Jun	81	17	98	37	5	42	115	12	127	233	34	267
Jul	89	49	138	36	14	50	125	-	125	250	63	313
Aug	308	-	308	114	-	114	117	63	180	539	63	602
Sep	124	42	166	88	90	178	102	37	139	314	169	483
Oct	64	53	117	25	42	67	81	25	106	170	120	290
Nov	84	22	106	9	33	42	21	6	27	114	61	175
Dec	128	3	131	1	3	4	42	12	54	171	18	189
Total 1943	1,244	305	1,549	454	278	732	1,270	189	1,459	2,968	772	3,740
1944 Jan	135	-	135	15	-	15	170	-	170	320	-	320
Feb	230	19	249	14	-	14	111	3	114	355	22	377
Mar	105	74	179	2	6	8	103	17	120	210	97	307
Apr	429	202	631	-	-	-	224	103	327	653	305	958
May	242	38	280	-	-	-	190	62	252	432	100	532
Jun	226	20	246	-	-	-	285	31	316	511	51	562
Jul	336	39	375	1	-	1	376	120	496	713	159	872
Aug	122	44	166	-	4	4	151	277	428	273	325	598
Sep	13	5	18	-	-	-	18	215	233	31	220	251
Oct	-	-	-	2	-	2	60	197	257	62	197	259
Nov	3	10	13	7	-	7	34	32	66	44	42	86
Dec	48	-	48	3	-	3	38	28	66	89	28	117
Total 1944	1,889	451	2,340	44	10	54	1,760	1,085	2,845	3,693	1,546	5,239
1945 Jan	-	-	-	-	-	-	8	-	8	8	-	8
Feb	-	-	-	1	-	1	8	19	27	9	19	28
Mar	9	8	17	5	-	5	105	18	123	119	26	145
Apr	-	-	-	-	-	-	68	42	110	68	42	110
May	-	-	-	-	-	-	-	-	-	-	-	-
Total 1945	9	8	17	6	-	6	189	79	268	204	87	291
Grand Total	3,178	770	3,948	510	306	816	3,300	1,364	4,664	7,003	2,494	9,497

Gasoline Consumption in the European Theater of Operations
August 1942 to May 1945
(thousands of gallons)

	Heavy Bomber	Med/Lt Bomber	Fighter	Total
1942 Aug	274	-	21	295
Sep	439	-	25	464
Oct	710	-	26	736
Nov	1,303	-	11	1,314
Dec	876	-	20	896
Total 1942	3,602	-	103	3,705
1943 Jan	1,234	-	29	1,263
Feb	1,318	9	60	1,387
Mar	2,035	17	67	2,119
Apr	1,872	34	164	2,070
May	4,528	19	752	5,299
Jun	4,930	-	697	5,627
Jul	8,780	368	809	9,957
Aug	5,656	1,320	951	7,927
Sep	8,181	1,747	1,367	11,295
Oct	8,678	942	1,476	11,096
Nov	9,531	1,113	1,802	12,446
Dec	13,266	1,381	2,384	17,031
Total 1943	70,009	6,950	10,558	87,517
1944 Jan	13,993	1,153	3,208	18,354
Feb	19,641	2,470	4,390	26,501
Mar	26,284	3,015	6,674	35,973
Apr	31,019	4,394	9,950	45,363
May	51,036	7,331	15,641	74,008
Jun	57,205	6,848	17,288	81,341
Jul	58,636	5,950	15,115	79,701
Aug	57,230	5,977	14,744	77,951
Sep	47,627	4,852	12,275	64,754
Oct	53,786	3,289	11,370	68,445
Nov	44,283	3,983	10,816	59,082
Dec	38,693	4,826	10,374	53,893
Total 1944	499,433	54,088	131,845	685,366
1945 Jan	43,757	3,630	8,061	55,448
Feb	60,162	6,379	11,757	78,298
Mar	77,497	12,372	20,156	110,025
Apr	62,536	11,213	18,020	91,769
May	29,589	5,725	7,970	43,284
Total 1945	273,541	39,319	65,964	378,824
Grand Total	846,585	100,357	208,470	1,155,412

Appendix 29

Gasoline Consumption in the Mediterranean Theater of Operations
June 1942 to May 1945
(thousands of gallons)

	Heavy Bomber	Med/Lt Bomber	Fighter	Total
1942 Jun	13	-	-	13
Jul	31	-	-	31
Aug	34	40	-	74
Sep	42	44	4	90
Oct	52	173	12	237
Nov	390	211	300	901
Dec	386	148	295	829
Total 1942	948	616	611	2,175
1943 Jan	1,237	656	834	2,727
Feb	1,067	390	500	1,957
Mar	1,011	631	937	2,579
Apr	2,335	1,342	1,599	5,276
May	3,509	1,741	2,425	7,675
Jun	3,028	2,116	2,608	7,752
Jul	5,955	4,376	4,050	14,381
Aug	4,205	3,550	3,645	11,400
Sep	5,051	4,419	3,221	12,691
Oct	3,221	2,953	2,067	8,241
Nov	2,712	2,205	2,137	7,054
Dec	3,046	2,279	2,211	7,536
Total 1943	36,377	26,658	26,234	89,269
1944 Jan	7,193	3,004	3,200	13,397
Feb	5,905	2,360	2,170	10,435
Mar	9,954	2,795	2,911	15,660
Apr	18,598	3,019	4,518	26,135
May	27,015	4,299	5,434	36,748
Jun	26,147	4,744	5,568	36,459
Jul	29,373	4,573	5,989	39,935
Aug	30,621	5,031	7,199	42,851
Sep	25,244	4,239	4,748	34,231
Oct	22,570	2,934	3,884	29,388
Nov	23,864	3,447	4,598	31,909
Dec	23,550	2,321	5,316	31,187
Total 1944	250,034	42,766	55,535	348,335
1945 Jan	12,724	1,976	3,941	18,641
Feb	32,574	2,774	4,990	40,338
Mar	37,657	3,170	6,664	47,491
Apr	37,533	3,361	7,188	48,082
May	8,481	1,271	1,746	11,498
Total 1945	128,969	12,552	24,529	166,050
Grand Total	416,328	82,592	106,909	605,829

Appendix 30

Expenditures from Direct Appropriations by Major Project
July 1942 to August 1945
(thousands of dollars; figures in parenthesis are negative)

	Procurement					
	Aircraft and Spares	Missiles	Balloons	Gliders	Aircraft Modification	Night Sight Systems
1942 Jul	254,240	-	-	707	1,363	85
Aug	436,098	-	-	4,637	1,483	31
Sep	398,330	-	-	2,367	4,851	153
Oct	445,727	-	-	7,470	3,449	52
Nov	208,225	-	-	4,014	2,554	(15)
Dec	432,132	-	-	15,151	10,220	194
Total 1942	2,174,752	-	-	34,346	23,920	500
1943 Jan	824,772	-	-	17,696	5,210	73
Feb	671,574	-	-	10,670	4,086	55
Mar	791,800	-	-	16,092	8,835	64
Apr	558,878	-	-	8,409	6,551	(29)
May	686,222	-	-	13,897	5,571	10
Jun	1,192,623	-	15,061	18,245	3,161	1,786
Jul	659,938	-	809	13,694	2,367	47
Aug	744,523	-	7,557	12,698	3,023	(13)
Sep	737,753	-	4,815	13,542	3,327	89
Oct	786,339	-	6,459	10,215	4,525	76
Nov	832,252	-	3,499	16,554	2,079	175
Dec	880,520	-	2,573	13,936	2,637	172
Total 1943	9,367,194	-	40,773	165,648	51,372	2,505
1944 Jan	789,342	-	2,963	14,521	5,834	485
Feb	692,131	-	1,431	12,641	9,782	175
Mar	966,739	-	461	13,563	15,565	55
Apr	814,996	-	871	10,482	14,724	(49)
May	797,798	-	437	7,670	18,775	64
Jun	658,013	-	236	8,504	17,358	90
Jul	734,034	-	15	4,900	12,509	63
Aug	840,857	-	10	3,385	17,989	21
Sep	750,219	-	110	2,638	17,628	56
Oct	465,547	-	3	(4,897)	11,075	35
Nov	584,190	-	50	4,600	17,498	27
Dec	475,712	-	(4)	3,824	18,696	29
Total 1944	8,569,578	-	6,583	81,831	177,433	1,051
1945 Jan	541,021	-	(2)	4,884	15,521	25
Feb	576,630	4,360	(3)	8,001	13,436	6
Mar	852,592	2,000	1	8,359	14,655	8
Apr	660,795	1,470	(1)	9,233	13,611	14
May	728,663	1,362	-	11,364	10,636	22
Jun	516,397	1,951	-	9,565	13,057	35
Jul	548,870	2,844	-	10,761	9,584	28
Aug	425,362	1,084	-	11,881	7,546	8
Total 1945	4,850,330	15,071	(5)	74,048	98,046	146
Grand Total	$24,961,854	$15,071	$47,351	$355,873	$350,771	$4,202

Appendix 30 (continued)

Expenditures from Direct Appropriations by Major Project
July 1942 to August 1945
(thousands of dollars; figures in parenthesis are negative)

	Procurement					
	Aircraft Maintenance	Aircraft Fuel/Oil	Ind/Org* Equipment	Miscellaneous Equipment	Photographic Equipment	Maps/ Mapping
1942 Jul	8,710	6,509	25,148	12,386	751	250
Aug	10,360	4,552	31,581	14,271	1,200	15
Sep	13,456	8,009	43,403	16,289	1,925	143
Oct	15,065	7,723	56,681	14,842	2,352	925
Nov	43,948	5,624	33,843	4,184	1,491	80
Dec	21,716	9,633	61,364	10,057	554	1,192
Total 1942	113,255	42,050	252,020	72,029	8,273	2,605
1943 Jan	20,508	8,993	53,843	4,223	3,807	199
Feb	20,552	7,926	41,797	4,139	1,402	565
Mar	45,480	39,257	27,092	47,881	2,985	218
Apr	23,718	9,321	47,931	3,631	2,937	1,118
May	32,371	9,365	78,006	6,180	655	13
Jun	57,144	31,180	84,942	13,855	3,611	(505)
Jul	36,075	33,894	71,023	23,418	958	2,322
Aug	37,876	21,154	53,385	15,398	1,087	242
Sep	49,714	89,572	49,377	13,584	1,258	197
Oct	40,161	30,607	41,365	10,960	1,618	773
Nov	37,051	29,123	45,889	10,584	1,321	923
Dec	51,917	22,428	35,624	8,623	1,519	539
Total 1943	452,567	332,820	630,275	162,476	23,158	6,604
1944 Jan	50,591	32,499	63,145	(2,715)	1,322	836
Feb	49,724	30,984	55,566	7,463	1,143	527
Mar	55,510	34,628	46,629	6,483	1,745	598
Apr	51,230	29,543	36,596	7,131	1,614	602
May	54,755	47,306	35,794	7,294	1,677	824
Jun	63,448	86,563	34,604	3,458	971	594
Jul	47,089	47,325	26,158	4,545	1,636	1,098
Aug	42,726	36,416	29,981	5,565	2,773	598
Sep	41,023	23,736	26,564	9,647	2,434	786
Oct	42,682	(28,958)	26,563	5,712	2,706	1,327
Nov	33,760	20,780	25,163	4,552	2,505	594
Dec	29,664	37,443	19,998	4,584	2,882	648
Total 1944	562,202	398,265	426,751	63,719	23,408	9,032
1945 Jan	34,787	52,351	21,232	5,845	2,143	674
Feb	35,742	44,602	20,988	8,075	1,742	134
Mar	40,553	82,495	26,396	7,840	2,774	541
Apr	36,130	66,681	26,358	8,280	2,279	538
May	29,604	46,508	29,214	7,649	2,239	570
Jun	27,913	58,138	27,179	7,020	1,890	547
Jul	27,984	65,151	26,975	6,505	1,215	637
Aug	15,964	48,612	27,005	8,663	1,064	270
Total 1945	248,677	464,538	205,347	59,877	15,346	3,911
Grand Total	$1,376,701	$1,237,673	$1,514,393	$358,101	$70,185	$22,152

*Individual and organizational equipment.

		Procurement			Non-procurement	Grand Total
Other Requirements	R&D	Test Equipment	Advance* Payments	Total		
-	2,422	3,051	-	315,622	31,967	347,589
437	2,784	2,580	-	510,029	36,636	546,665
22,466	4,439	3,567	-	519,398	42,868	562,266
3,277	4,572	1,964	-	564,094	40,194	604,288
959	2,733	3,667	-	311,307	42,485	353,793
(3,362)	5,282	901	-	565,034	50,682	615,716
23,772	22,232	15,730	-	2,785,484	244,832	3,030,316
3,573	18,320	1,165	-	962,382	1,882	964,264
18,694	6,257	1,765	-	789,482	103,863	893,345
52,364	6,081	876	-	1,039,025	88,103	1,127,128
29,622	4,068	169	-	696,324	110,959	807,283
33,121	5,302	889	-	871,602	86,496	958,098
29,785	8,665	1,553	-	1,461,107	150,311	1,611,418
22,749	6,393	(238)	-	873,449	118,729	992,178
36,481	14,497	1,139	-	949,047	102,426	1,051,473
30,831	9,383	467	-	1,003,909	105,653	1,109,562
36,870	5,192	880	-	976,040	114,925	1,090,965
37,562	58	1,142	-	1,018,212	107,564	1,125,776
40,468	8,152	2,020	-	1,071,128	98,196	1,169,324
372,120	92,368	11,827	-	11,711,707	1,189,107	12,900,814
50,117	11,842	1,638	-	1,022,420	90,042	1,112,462
33,692	9,812	1,581	-	906,652	104,549	1,011,201
26,078	6,694	1,217	-	1,175,965	191,292	1,277,257
15,070	10,286	1,112	-	994,208	92,016	1,086,224
6,391	6,571	1,010	-	986,366	94,811	1,081,177
5,072	10,047	(1,024)	-	887,934	91,745	979,679
1,991	8,117	877	-	890,357	88,365	978,722
3,436	10,584	3,485	-	997,826	100,785	1,098,611
5,671	8,912	4,345	-	893,769	94,055	987,824
6,727	9,226	3,222	350,829	891,799	78,473	970,272
3,928	7,269	1,920	157,218	864,054	92,054	956,108
36	7,554	1,680	330,658	803,394	83,435	886,829
158,209	106,914	21,063	708,705	11,314,744	1,111,622	12,426,366
1,956	9,486	1,407	104,416	795,746	90,355	886,101
2,575	8,155	2,078	69,638	796,159	87,440	883,599
9,649	9,394	662	(50,900)	1,007,019	98,338	1,105,357
3,160	7,830	592	(27,444)	809,526	87,114	896,640
9,506	10,287	342	(31,831)	856,135	95,052	951,187
2,613	9,800	304	(31,862)	644,547	111,590	756,137
6,091	9,205	479	(52,688)	663,641	89,314	752,955
1,021	8,625	510	(63,006)	494,609	101,467	596,076
36,571	72,782	6,374	(83,677)	6,067,382	760,670	6,828,052
$590,672	$294,296	$54,994	$625,028	$31,879,317	$3,306,231	$35,185,548

*Advance payments less recoupments. Advance payments to contractors were charged directly to individual projects prior to 1 October 1944.

Notes

Notes

Introduction

1. Tables, Army Air Forces, Management Control, Office, Director of Statistical Control, "Airplanes in U.S. Army Air Forces," April 29, 1942, and "U.S Army Air Forces Strength," April 29, 1942, Papers of Henry H. Arnold, Library of Congress, Manuscript Division, Official File 1932–1946, folder: AF Strength, box 40.

Part One
Carrying the Flame
From West Point to London

Chapter 1
Spaatz's Early Career

1. Frank Freidel, *Over There: The Story of America's First Great Overseas Crusade* (New York: Bramhall House, 1964), p. 152.

2. Interview, Gen. Carl A. Spaatz by Donald Shaughnessey, Washington, D. C., 1959–1960, Arnold Oral History Project, Columbia University, New York, N.Y., p. 2.

3. David R. Mets, unpublished book-length manuscript biography of Carl A. Spaatz, prepared from original sources and extensive interviews with Spaatz's family and acquaintances, pp. 1–16, hereafter cited as Mets, "Spaatz Biography." This study has the most complete information on Spaatz's early life found anywhere. The study emphasizes Spaatz's pre-World War II career and contains much useful information. For the published version of this work, see David R. Mets, *Master of Airpower: General Carl A. Spaatz* (Novato, Calif.: Presidio Press for the Air Force Historical Foundation/Aerospace Education Foundation, 1988).

4. David R. Mets, "Carl A. Spaatz: A Model for Leadership," paper presented at the joint American Military Institute-Air Historical Foundation meeting, Bolling AFB, Washington, D.C., April 1984, p. 3.

5. Ibid.

6. USMA, *The Howitzer 1914* (West Point: USMA, 1914), p. 84.

7. Walter T. Bonney, *The Heritage of Kitty Hawk* (New York: W.W. Norton, 1962), p. 119.

8. Interview, Gen. Carl A. Spaatz by Arthur Goldberg, May 1965, USAF Oral History Collection, AFHRC file no. D239.0512–755, p.2.

9. Minutes, Conference with Gen. Carl Spaatz and the Gillem Board, October 18, 1945, Papers of Carl A. Spaatz, Library of Congress, Manuscript Division, Diary File. Hereafter referred to as Spaatz Papers, Diary.

10. Interview, Spaatz by Shaughnessey, 1959–1960, p. 9.

11. Memo, Brig. Gen. Carl A. Spaatz, Chief of the Air Staff, to Maj. James H. Higgs, September 11, 1941, Spaatz Papers, Diary. This memo was an official biography approved by Spaatz.

12. Entries for May 5 to November 15, 1917, Spaatz Papers, Notebooks.

13. Maurer Maurer, ed., *The U.S. Air Service in World War I* (Washington, D.C.: AF/CHO, GPO, 1978), p. 97. This citation is from the Official Final Report of the Aviation Section, completed at the end of the war and printed in full in this volume.

14. Ibid.

15. Ibid.

16. Freidel, *Over There*, p. 153.

17. Maurer, *The Air Service in World War I*, pp. 106, 112–113.

18. U.S. Army Air Service, American Expeditionary Forces ("Gorrell History"), Series J, vol. 9, "The Third Aviation Instruction Center, Issoudun, France," p. 202. from microfilm copy at the Air Force Historical Research Center (AFHRC), Maxwell AFB, Ala. Cited in prepublication manuscript biography of Carl A. Spaatz by David Mets.

19. Report of the Secretary of War, 1919 (Washington, D.C.: GPO, 1919), p. 13.

20. Interview, 1st Lt. Charles R. D'Olive, interviewer unknown, June 16, 1969, New York, N.Y., Columbia University Oral History Research Office, AFHRC file no. K239.0512–612.

21. Interview, Spaatz by Shaughnessey, 1959–1960, p. 12.

22. War Department General Order No. 123, December 11, 1918.

23. Spaatz's Personal Notebooks, Spaatz Papers, Notebooks. Spaatz noted that he left Issoudun on August 30 and returned September 27.

24. Maurer, *The Air Service in World War I*, vol. 3, p. 523, contains a copy of Spaatz's after-action report.

25. Edwin I. James, "Pershing's Airmen All American Now," *New York Times*, September 30, 1918, p. 2. The story's dateline is September 28, 1918.

26. Msg J–205, Mitchell to Spatz, September 26, 1918, Spaatz Papers, Diary.

27. Interview, Spaatz by Shaughnessey, 1959–1960, p. 13.

28. Dewitt S. Copp, *A Few Great Captains: The Men and Events That Shaped the Development of U.S. Air Power* (Garden City, N.Y.: Doubleday, 1980), p. 24.

29. Ibid., pp. 22–23.

30. Thomas H. Greer, *The Development of Air Doctrine in the Army Air Arm, 1917–1941*, USAF Historical Study No. 89, (Maxwell AFB, Ala.: Air University Press, 1955), pp. 14–15.

31. Interview, Spaatz by Shaughnessey, 1959–1960, p. 24. In the interview Spaatz gives the year of the hearings as 1917, but from the context of his remarks he seems to be referring to the hearings of 1919.

32. Ibid., p. 13.

33. Report of the Secretary of War, Chief of Staff's Report, 1932, pp. 64–70. This contains an excellent discussion of the official Army

34. Maurer Maurer, *Aviation in the U.S. Army, 1919–1939* (Washington, D.C.: AF/CHO, GPO, 1987), pp. 52–55, 205.

35. Compiled from Reports of the Chief of the Air Corps, 1921–1938.

36. Compiled from the Reports of the Secretary of War, 1923–1935.

37. Annual Report of the Chief of the Air Corps, 1930.

38. Annual Report of the Chief of the Air Corps, 1924.

39. Ibid. In 1986, 65 percent of Air Force officers were captains and lieutenants.

40. Numbers of reserve officers used by each branch were compiled from the statistical sections of the Annual Reports of the Secretary of War, 1922–1935.

41. Annual Report of the Secretary of War, Report of the Assistant Secretary of War for Air, 1930, p. 59.

42. Compiled from Annual Reports of the Secretary of War, 1924–1933.

43. See, for example, the Annual Report of the Chief of the Air Service, 1924, pp. 31–35.

44. Report of the Surgeon General of the U.S. Army, 1937 (Washington, D.C.: GPO, 1937), pp. 73–74.

45. Maurer, *Aviation in the U.S. Army*, p. 477. Maurer bases his figures on those submitted to the Baker Board.

46. See James P. Tate, "The Army and Its Air Corps: A Study in the Evolution of Army Policy Towards Aviation, 1919–1941," unpublished Ph. D. dissertation, University of Indiana, 1976, for a thorough discussion of the air arm's position in the interwar years. In particular see pp. 90, 130–133, 152–156 for examples of budget deliberations concerning the various administrations' attitudes toward the military aviation budget.

47. Ltr, Office, Director of Air Service to Maj. Carl Spatz, Western Department, subj: Commendatory Letter, December 29, 1919, Spaatz Papers, Diary.

48. Mets, "Spaatz Biography," pp. 79–81.

49. Entry for October 26, 1919, Spaatz Papers, Notebooks.

50. War Department Special Orders 95-0, para. 110, April 23, 1919. The other five recipients were Brig. Gen. William Mitchell, Lt. Col. Lewis H. Brereton, Lt. Col. John N. Reynolds, Maj. Melvin A. Hall, and Capt. Reed M. Chambers. Before America's entry into World War I, twenty-four men, including Brereton, had earned the Military Aviator rating for pioneering air efforts. The National Defense Act of

1920, however, abolished the rating except for the six men who had earned it for distinguished service in France.

51. Entry for May 10, 1925, Spaatz Papers, Diary.

52. Copp, *Great Captains*, pp. 29–30.

53. Wesley Frank Craven and James Lea Cate, eds., *The Army Air Forces in World War II*, vol. 1: *Plans & Early Operations, January 1939 to August 1942* (Chicago: University of Chicago Press, 1948), p. 26.

54. Ltr, Adjutant General, War Department to Maj. Carl Spatz, subj: Reprimand, August 6, 1925, Spaatz Papers, Diary.

55. Entries for October–November 1924, Spaatz Papers, Diary.

56. Alfred F. Hurley, *Billy Mitchell: Crusader for Air Power* (New York: Franklin Watts, 1964), p. 81. Mitchell had another reason for frequent visits to Detroit—the woman who became his second wife also lived there.

57. Ltr, Brig. Gen. William Mitchell to Maj. Gen. Mason N. Patrick, August 3, 1922, Spaatz Papers, Diary.

58. Ltr, Mitchell to Spatz, June 1, 1923, Spaatz Papers, Diary.

59. Ltr, Spatz to Mitchell, June 24, 1923, Spaatz Papers, Diary.

60. Greer, *Development of Air Doctrine*, p. 9.

61. Ibid., p. 31.

62. Ibid., pp. 30–40.

63. Ibid., p. 37, citing ltr, Spatz to Chief of the Air Service, February 7, 1922.

64. Ltr, Spatz to Capt. B. V. Baucom (Chief of Pursuit Training), Kelly Field, Tex., February 6, 1923, Spaatz Papers, Diary.

65. Ltr, Spatz to 1st Lt. H. W. Cook, Air Corps Tactical School (ACTS), Langley Field, Va., February 13, 1923, Spaatz Papers, Diary.

66. Ltr, Spatz to Maj. L. H. Brereton, Kelly Field, Tex., April 19, 1923, Spaatz Papers, Diary.

67. Ltr, Spatz to Capt. B. V. Baucom, Kelly Field, San Antonio, Tex., March 14, 1924, Spaatz Papers, Diary.

68. Entry for May 11, 1925, Spaatz Papers, Diary.

69. Entry for June 30, 1925, Spaatz Papers, Diary.

70. U.S. Congress, House, *Select Committee of Inquiry into Operations of the United Air Services,* Hearings, 68th Cong., 2d Sess., 1925, part 3, p. 2246.

71. Burke Davis, *The Billy Mitchell Affair* (New York: Random House, 1967), pp. 251–253.

72. Testimony of Maj. Carl Spatz, Air Service, U.S. Army, Court-Martial of Col. William Mitchell, November 9, 1925, pp. 382–428, Modern Military Field Branch, National Archives and Records Administration's (NARA) Washington National Records Center, Suitland, Md.

73. Interview, Spaatz by Shaughnessey, 1959–1960, p. 27.

74. Interview, Ruth Spaatz by James C. Hasdorff, Washington, D. C., March 3, 1981, USAF Oral History Collection, AFHRC file no. K239.0512–1266, p. 17.

75. James Parton, *"Air Force Spoken Here": General Ira Eaker and the Command of the Air* (Bethesda, Md.: Adler & Adler, 1986), p. 71. See pp. 68–77 of this work for a good description of the *Question Mark* episode.

76. Interview, Ruth Spaatz by Hasdorff, pp. 46-47.

77. Copp, *Great Captains*, p. 84.

78. Ltr, W. Ward Smith to Lt. Gen. Eaker, April 24, 1943, Library of Congress, Manuscript Division, Papers of Ira C. Eaker, Correspondence, Box 6. Smith had been part of the *Question Mark* ground team. In this letter to his old friend Eaker, he used extracts of letters written to his son during the flight to recall past events.

79. Ltr, Adjutant General, War Department, to Maj. Carl Spatz, subj: Distinguished Flying Cross, March 6, 1929, Spaatz Papers, Diary.

80. Ltr, Comptroller General of the United States to Maj. M. T. Comagys through Chief of Finance, War Department, May 4, 1929, Spaatz Papers, Diary.

81. Maurer, *Aviation in the U.S. Army*, p. 265. Maurer's book (pp. 260–265) contains one of the best overall accounts of the *Question Mark* flight.

82. Ltr, Spatz to Arnold, February 5, 1935, Spaatz Papers, Diary, Personal.

83. Mets, "Spaatz Biography," pp. 174–175.

84. See Greer, *The Development of Air Doctrine,* pp. 46–47, for a discussion of the development of these planes.

85. Ibid., pp. 58–66.

86. Ibid., p. 61.

87. For a thorough examination of the impact of Douhet and Mitchell on the ACTS, the font of Air Corps bomber doctrine, see the unpublished Ph.D. dissertation by Raymond Richard Flugel, "United States Air Power Doctrine: A Study of the Influence of William Mitchell and Giulio Douhet at the Air Corps Tactical School, 1921–1935" (University of Oklahoma, 1965). This work shows how Douhet's thought influenced Mitchell's ideas and how the ACTS,

through Mitchell, adopted them almost *in toto.*

88. Greer, *The Development of Air Doctrine,* pp. 47–55.

89. This is a rough paraphrase of a more detailed list found in Craven and Cate, *Plans & Early Operations,* pp. 51–52.

90. John Terraine, *A Time for Courage: The Royal Air Force in the European War, 1939–1945* (New York: Macmillan, 1985), p. 13.

91. Greer, *The Development of Air Doctrine,* p. 60.

92. Interview, Spaatz by Shaughnessey, 1959–1960, p. 48.

93. Ibid. p. 77.

94. For a sympathetic biography of Eaker, see Parton, *"Air Force Spoken Here": General Ira Eaker and the Command of the Air.* Parton served as Eaker's personal aide during the war and supplied many firsthand anecdotes.

Chapter 2
Prewar Planning

1. Entry for August 28, 1940, Battle of Britain Diary, Spaatz Papers, Notebooks. Spaatz kept a handwritten notebook of his experiences and observations in Britain in the summer of 1940. All subsequent references to this portion of Spaatz's Diary refer to the handwritten notebook not the retyped pages inserted in his "Diary File."

2. Mark S. Watson, *United States Army in World War II,* subseries: The War Department, *Chief of Staff: Pre-War Plans and Preparations* (Washington, D.C.: OCMH, GPO, 1950), pp. 132–136.

3. Ibid., pp. 136–143.

4. Ibid., p. 127.

5. Ibid., p. 279.

6. Phillip S. Meilinger, "Hoyt S. Vandenberg: The Life of a General," unpublished Ph.D. dissertation, University of Michigan, 1985, pp. 42–44. Vandenberg joined the Plans Section in April 1939 and worked closely with Spaatz throughout the period. The two founded a solid professional relationship that earned Vandenberg Spaatz's support throughout the remainder of their careers.

7. Watson, *Pre-War Plans ,* pp. 142–143.

8. Irving Brinton Holley, Jr., *United States Army in World War II,* subseries: *Special Studies, Buying Aircraft: Materiel Procurement for the Army Air Forces* (Washington, D.C.: OCMH, 1964), pp. 200–201.

9. Ibid., pp. 180, 202.

10. Craven and Cate, *Plans & Early Operations,* pp. 128–129.

11. Interview, Spaatz by Shaughnessey, 1959–1960, p. 44.

12. Memo, Chief, Plans Division, to Chief of the Air Corps, March 4, 1941, Spaatz Papers, Diary.

13. Ltr, Spaatz to Arnold, August 27, 1940, Spaatz Papers, Diary.

14. Msg 2132, Air Attaché Washington to Air Ministry, February 13, 1940, AIR 2/7172, Public Records Office, Kew, Great Britain. Hereafter referred to as PRO AIR 2/7172.

15. Minute 2, Chief of the RAF Air Staff to Director of Plans and Director of Intelligence, February 7, 1940, PRO AIR 2/7172. This minute was signed by the Deputy Chief of the Air Staff.

16. Msg 291, Lord Lothian to the Secretary of State for Air, March 1, 1940, PRO AIR 2/7172.

17. Minute 12, Chief of the Air Staff to Secretary of State for Air, March 11, 1940, PRO AIR 2/7234.

18. Msg S.5004/T.W.1, Air Ministry (T.W.1). to Bomber, Fighter, and Coastal Commands, June 8, 1940, PRO AIR 2/7234. This message applied the restrictions specifically to Spaatz's mission. See also minute 20 (S.3871), A.C.A.S.(T) to D.C.A.S., April 14, 1940, PRO AIR 2/7234, which set the general disclosure policy.

19. Memo, Brig. Gen. B. K. Yount, Assistant Chief of the Air Corps, to Assistant Chief of Staff, G–2, subj: Special Instructions for Lieutenant Colonel Grandison Gardner, Air Corps, and Major Franklin O. Carroll, Air Corps, Designated as Assistant Military Attachés for Air to England, AFHRC file no. 168.7016–13, Papers of Grandison Gardner.

20. Rpt 25,712–W, Military Attaché, Paris, subj: Partial Report of Visit of Lieutenant-Colonel Grandison Gardner and Major Franklin O. Carroll to England, May 24, 1940, AFHRC file no. 168.7016, AF/CHO microfilm reel A 1862.

21. Rpt A.I.1.(f), W. Grandon to Capt. Bateman, subj: Visits of American Officers, May 11, 1940, PRO AIR 2/7172.

22. Index Listing, name index to correspon-

dence of the Military Intelligence Division of the War Department General Staff, 1917–1941, NARA, Microfilm Project M1194, reel 219, citing memo, G–2 to ND, May 16, 1940, MID file no. 2610-191.

23. Ltr, Ref A.M.2223, Col. Martin F. Scanlon to Air Commod. A. R. Boyle, Director of Intelligence, RAF Staff, May 17, 1940, PRO AIR 2/7234.

24. Entries for June 1, 3, 1940, Battle of Britain Diary, Spaatz Papers, Notebooks. After a hiatus of sixteen years Spaatz resumed his personal notebook/diary, presumably to refresh his memory for subsequent reports. There is no indication that he kept these notes from any desire to preserve "history."

25. Entries for June 2, 3, 1940, Battle of Britain Diary, Spaatz Papers, Notebooks.

26. Rpt S.5004, Flt. Lt. W.E.N. Growdon, Report by the Escorting Officer on the Visits of Major McDonald, Colonel Spaatz and Captain Kelsy to Royal Air Force Units, June 24, 1940, PRO AIR 2/7234.

27. Minute, Director of Intelligence to Director of Plans, June 13, 1940, PRO AIR 2/7250.

28. Watson, *Pre-War Plans*, pp. 92–93. Capt. Royal E. Ingersoll visited London for private and "purely exploratory" talks about naval cooperation against Japan.

29. Ibid., pp. 106–107.

30. Richard M. Leighton and Robert W. Coakley, *United States Army in World War II*, subseries: *The War Department, Global Logistics and Strategy, 1940–1943* (Washington, D.C.: OCMH, GPO, 1955), pp. 32–33. This work includes a discussion on the legal twists of the transfer and on the extent to which the equipment transferred was surplus to U.S. needs.

31. J.R.M. Butler, *Grand Strategy*, vol. 2: *September 1939–June 1941* (London: HMSO, 1957), p. 243.

32. Minute, Director of Intelligence to Director of Plans, June 13, 1940, PRO AIR 2/7230. See also memo, subj: Gen. Spaatz's Visit to the Air Ministry, June 1940, n.d. [ca. 1944], Spaatz Papers, Subject File 1929–1945, and memo, subj: Anglo-American Air Collaboration, Air Ministry, Air Historical Branch, n.d. [ca. 1944], Spaatz Papers, Subject File 1929–1945. The Air Ministry prepared these documents on air collaboration in response to a request for information on Spaatz's 1944–1945 command, the U.S. Strategic Air Forces in Europe, from the official historian, Dr. Bruce Hopper.

33. Minute, Director of Plans (Slessor) to Deputy Director of Plans, June 17, 1940, PRO AIR 2/7250. Slessor postscripted this minute with the following admonition, "This should be kept very confidential and discussed with no one but MacDonald personally."

34. Minute, Plans 2 [Deputy Director of Plans] to Director of Plans, June 15, 1940, PRO AIR 2/7250. See also memo, subj: Gen. Spaatz's Visit to the Air Ministry, June 1940, n.d. [ca. 1944], Spaatz Papers; Subject File 1929–1945, and memo, subj: Anglo-American Air Collaboration, Air Ministry Air Historical Branch, n.d. [ca. 1944], Spaatz Papers, Subject File 1929–1945.

35. Msg 1019, Lord Lothian to Foreign Office, PRO PREM 3/457.

36. Minute, Director of Plans to Air Staff Directors, June 20, 1940, PRO AIR 2/7250.

37. Minutes, Foreign Minister to the Prime Minister, June 27, 1940, PRO PREM 3/457.

38. Msgs 1331, Foreign Office to Lord Lothian, June 30, 1940, and 1201, Lord Lothian to the Foreign Office, July 2, 1940, PRO PREM 3/457.

39. Watson, *Pre-War Plans*, pp. 113–115.

40. MID correspondence name index, citing memo, G–2 to Adjutant General, July 3, 1940, MID file no. 2345.872. Spaatz requested an extension in view of "expected air operations."

41. Minute 2, Wing Commander C. R. Porr, A.I.1(f) to Air Commod. A. R. Boyle, Director of Intelligence, June 24, 1940, PRO AIR 2/7251.

42. Minute 3 and postscript, Director of Plans to Vice Chief of the Air Staff, June 28, 1940, and July 3, 1940, PRO AIR 2/7251.

43. Minute 5 (S.5185), A.C.A.S.(G), Air Commodore Richard Peck, to A.I.1.(f), July 3, 1940, PRO AIR 2/7251.

44. Entry for July 16, 1940, Battle of Britain Diary, Spaatz Papers, Notebooks.

45. Ibid.

46. Charles Webster and Noble Frankland, *The Strategic Air Offensive Against Germany, 1939–1945*, vol. 1: *Preparation* (London: HMSO, 1961), pp. 147–150.

47. Ltr, Spaatz to Arnold, July 31, 1940, Spaatz Papers, Diary.

48. John Slessor, *The Central Blue: The Autobiography of Sir John Slessor, Marshal of the Royal Air Force* (New York: Frederick A. Praeger, 1957), pp. 314–316. Slessor personally escorted Donovan to a number of British bases. See Corey Ford, *Donovan of O.S.S.* (Boston: Little, 1970), pp. 90–94, for more on Donovan's visit.

49. Entry for August 2, 1940, Battle of

Britain Diary, Spaatz Papers, Notebooks.

50. Ltr, William Donovan to Chief of the RAF Air Staff, Air Chief Marshal Sir Cyril Newall, August 27, 1940, PRO AIR 8/368.

51. Ibid.

52. Report by Squadron Leader M. Tod, Escorting Officer to Col. Carl Spaatz and Lt. Col. F.O'D. Hunter (Assistant Air Attachés) on a visit to No. 12 Fighter Group, August 17, 1940, PRO AIR 2/7251.

53. Rpt 41532, MA London, subj: Organization Headquarters Fighter Group, August 21, 1940, AFHRC file no. 170.2278–1, AF/CHO microfilm reel B 1753, frames 1277–1282.

54. Lincoln Barnett, "General Spaatz, America's No. 1 Airman in Africa," *Life*, April 19, 1943, p. 76.

55. Ltr, Spaatz to Arnold, July 31, 1940, Spaatz Papers, Diary.

56. Entry for August 19, 1940, Battle of Britain Diary, Spaatz Papers, Notebooks.

57. Entry for August 27, 1940, Battle of Britain Diary, Spaatz Papers, Notebooks.

58. Entry for July 7, 1940, Battle of Britain Diary, Spaatz Papers, Notebooks. Spaatz noted a "deeply rooted" jealousy between the RAF and the British Army. He felt that the soldiers had failed to appreciate the help given to them by the RAF in the skies over Dunkirk and were incensed over what they considered lack of support. As a consequence, the Army apparently wanted more control over RAF-Army coordination aircraft. Spaatz suspected that if the British Army had been properly equipped with antiaircraft weapons, it might have been a different story. Like the Air Corps, the RAF at this time had neglected to develop effective close air support doctrine.

59. Entry for August 27, 1940, Battle of Britain Diary, Spaatz Papers, Notebooks.

60. Entry for August 30, 1940, Battle of Britain Diary, Spaatz Papers, Notebooks.

61. Entry for September 8, 1940, Battle of Britain Diary, Spaatz Papers, Notebooks.

62. Drew Middleton, *The Sky Suspended* (New York: Longman's Green, 1960), pp. 156–157. Four years later when Middleton reminded Spaatz of the statement, Spaatz commented, "Goes to show you that colonels are mighty smart fellows—sometimes."

63. Entry for September 12, 1940, Battle of Britain Diary, Spaatz Papers, Notebooks.

64. Ltr, Spaatz to Arnold, August 27, 1940, Spaatz Papers, Diary.

65. Slessor, *The Central Blue*, p. 316.

66. Craven and Cate, *Plans & Early Operations*, pp. 104–116. See also Watson, *Pre-War Plans*, pp. 278–279.

67. Watson, *Pre-War Plans*, p. 289.

68. Ibid., pp. 289–290.

69. Ibid., pp. 291–293.

70. Craven and Cate, *Plans & Early Operations*, pp. 136–137.

71. Watson, *Pre-War Plans*, pp. 371–373.

72. Craven and Cate, *Plans & Early Operations*, p. 137.

73. Ibid., p. 138.

74. Watson, *Pre-War Plans*, pp. 379–382.

75. Memo, Brig. Gen. Carl Spaatz to Chief of the Air Corps, March 4, 1941, Spaatz Papers, Diary.

76. Memo, Chief of Air Corps to Chief of Staff, March [3–5], 1941, Spaatz Papers, Diary.

77. Watson, *Pre-War Plans*, pp. 382–383.

78. See the complete text of the President's letter given in Joint Board Document No. 355 (Serial 707), subj: Joint Board Estimate of United States Overall Production Requirements, pp. 1–2, AFHRC file no. 145.81–23.

79. Memo to the Chief of the Air Staff, subj: Notes on Preparation of AWPD/1, November 19, 1941, Spaatz Papers, Diary.

80. Copy of AWPD/1, Spaatz Papers, Subject File 1929–1945.

81. I. B. Holley, Jr., "Of Saber Charges, Escort Fighters, and Spacecraft," *Air University Review* XXXIV, No. 6 (September–October 1983): 9.

82. Memo, Chief of Plans Division to Executive, subj: Disapproval of Change Order, March 10, 1941, AFHRC file no. 145.91–506, January 1937–September 1941, Pursuit Aircraft, AF/CHO reel A 1422, frames 1586–1587. At some point in the preparation or publication of Holley's article, the reel frame numbers were misprinted 1386–1387.

83. For a discussion of the relationship between a change order and procurement see Benjamin S. Kelsey, *The Dragon's Teeth* (Washington, D.C.: Smithsonian Institution Press, 1982), pp. 119–122.

84. Memo, Major Vandenberg to General Spaatz, subj: Disapproval of Change Order, March 4, 1941, AFHRC file no. 145.91–506, AF/CHO microfilm reel A 1422, frame 1588.

85. Ibid.

86. Bernard Boylan, *Development of the Long-Range Escort Fighter*, USAF Historical Study No. 136 (Maxwell AFB, Ala.: Air University, 1956), pp. 50–53.

87. AWPD/1, tab 4, AFHRC file no. 145.81–23. James Lea Cate, "The Air Corps Prepares for War, 1939–1941," chapter 4 in Craven and Cate, *Plans & Early Operations*, pp. 148–149,

682

presents AWPD/1's escort recommendations in very favorable light. If one did not know that the escort fighter called for in the plan was in reality a convoy defender, one would probably receive the impression, from Cate, that the framers of AWPD/1 had accurately foreseen the consequences of the AAF's lack of suitable escorts and had suggested the proper remedy.

88. Memo, Maj. Gen. Henry H. Arnold, Chief of the Air Corps, to Col. Ira C. Eaker, subj: Additional Instructions on Trip to England, August 22, 1941, AFHRC file no. 168.04–6, AF/CHO microfilm reel A 1593, frame 570. In this memo Arnold indicated his intention to call a board to "critically analyze the whole pursuit picture."

89. Memo, Arnold to Eaker, subj: Letter of Instructions, August 20, 1941, AFHRC file no. 168.04–6 AF/CHO microfilm reel A 1593, frame 571.

90. Memo, Arnold to Eaker, subj: Additional Instructions on Trip to England, August 22, 1941, AFHRC file no. 168.04–6 AF/CHO microfilm reel A 1593, frame 570.

91. Webster and Frankland, *The Strategic Air Offensive*, vol. 1, pp. 236–239.

92. Ibid., p. 239, citing memo, Portal to Churchill, May 27, 1941.

93. Rpt, Col. Ira C. Eaker to Chief of the Army Air Forces, subj: Report on Trip to England, n.d.

[Mid-October 1941], Section III, Fighter Development for the Future, p. 24, AFHRC file no. 168.04–6, AF/CHO microfilm reel A 1593. The itinerary of Eaker's trip, included in his final report, places his conversation with Portal on September 28.

94. Ibid., p. 23.

95. Report of a Board of Officers, Appointed to Make Recommendations with Respect to the Future Development of Pursuit Aircraft, Its Accessory Equipment and Operational Employment, to the Chief of the Army Air Forces, Washington, D.C., October 27, 1941, pp. 18, 46, AFHRC file no. 168.15–5, AF/CHO microfilm reel A 1611, frames 324 and 358.

96. Ibid., p. 16.

97. Ibid., pp. 46–47, 49.

98. Ltr, Spaatz to Arnold, November 7, 1933, Spaatz Papers, Diary.

99. F. G. Swanborough, *United States Military Aircraft Since 1909* (New York: Putnam, 1963), pp. 360–367.

100. U.S. War Department, Office of Statistical Control, *Army Air Forces Statistical Digest, World War II* (Washington, D.C.: GPO, 1945), table 82, p. 134.

101. See Kelsey, *Dragon's Teeth*, pp. 110–112, for a discussion of how Air Corps procurement policy in the 1930s may have encouraged "conservative" designs.

Chapter 3
Spaatz Commands the Eighth Air Force

1. Beirne Lay, Jr., and Sy Bartlett, *Twelve O'Clock High!* (New York: Ballantine Books, 1965), p. 64. Both Lay and Bartlett were in England with the Eighth Air Force in late 1942—Bartlett, a Hollywood screen writer, as one of Spaatz's personal aides, and Lay as unofficial historian and public relations man. "Pritchard" was an amalgam of Spaatz and Eaker, although in this case he seems mostly Spaatz. Spaatz would never have uttered the words placed in Pritchard's mouth, but it was not unlikely that he thought them.

2. Dewitt S. Copp, *Forged in Fire: The Strategy and Decisions in the Air War Over Europe, 1940–1945* (Garden City: Doubleday & Co., 1982), p. 200.

3. Ltr, Spaatz to Maj. Gen. B. D. Foulois, February 29, 1932, Spaatz Papers, Diary.

4. Notes, [Air Staff] Staff Meeting, December 7, 1941, AFHRC file no. 168.15, AF/CHO microfilm reel A 1611, frame 170.

5. Interview, Gen. Lauris Norstad by Hugh N. Ahmann, February–October 1979, USAF Oral History Collection, AFHRC file no. K239.0512–1116, pp. 501–502.

6. Maurice Matloff and Edwin M. Snell, *United States Army in World War II*, subseries: *The War Department, Strategic Planning for Coalition Warfare, 1941–1942* (Washington, D.C.: OCMH, GPO, 1953), pp. 114–119.

7. Ibid., pp. 102–105.

8. Ibid., pp. 175–176.

9. Alfred D. Chandler, *The Papers of Dwight David Eisenhower: The War Years* (Baltimore: Johns Hopkins Press, 1970) vol. 1, memo to the Chief of Staff, February 1942, item 160, pp. 145–148; and memo to the Chief of Staff, February 28, 1942, item 162, pp. 149–155. Item 160 did not have a complete date. The editors place it after February 16, the date Eisenhower assumed the post of Chief of the War Plans Division.

10. Ray S. Cline, *United States Army in World War II*, subseries: *The War Department, Washington Command Post: The Operations Division* (Washington, D.C.: OCMH, GPO, 1951), pp. 154–155.

11. Ibid., pp. 156–157.

12. D.O. (42) 10th Meeting, War Cabinet Minutes, Defense Committee (Operations), Meeting of 10:00 P.M. 14th April 1942, minute recorded on April 15, 1942, PRO PREM 3/333/6. This minute contains the views of Marshall, Hopkins, Churchill, and the British Chiefs of Staff.

13. Cline, *Washington Command Post*, p. 151.

14. Warren F. Kimball, ed., *Churchill and Roosevelt: The Complete Correspondence*, vol. 1: *Alliance Emerging* (Princeton, N.J.: Princeton University Press, 1984), p. 393.

15. Wesley F. Craven and James L. Cate, *The Army Air Forces in World War II*, vol. 2: *Europe: Torch to Pointblank, August 1942 to December 1943* (Chicago: University of Chicago Press, 1949), p. 29.

16. Memoirs of Richard D'O. Hughes, chap. 8 "1941–1945," pp. 13–16. Unpublished manuscript memoirs in the possession of Professor W.W. Rostow, University of Texas at Austin.

17. Entry for May 10, 1942, Command Diary, Spaatz Papers, Diary.

18. Ibid.

19. Entry for May 14, 1942, Command Diary, Spaatz Papers, Diary.

20. Ibid.

21. Ibid.

22. Entry for May 15, 1942, Command Diary, Spaatz Papers, Diary.

23. Entry for May 16, 1942, Command Diary, Spaatz Papers, Diary.

24. Ibid.

25. Craven and Cate, *Plans & Early Operations*, pp. 623–624.

26. Ibid., p. 624.

27. For the ability of the British to read Luftwaffe codes, see F. W. Winterbotham, *The Ultra Secret* (New York: Dell, 1982), pp. 67–86.

28. Williamson Murray, *Strategy for Defeat: The Luftwaffe, 1933–1945* (Maxwell AFB, Ala.: Air University Press, 1983), pp. 134, 138. On p. 134 Murray notes that in September 1942, German night defenses had 345 aircraft assigned. On p. 138 he gives the combat strength of the Luftwaffe at 4,942 aircraft. British Air Ministry, *The Rise and Fall of the German Air Force, 1933–1945*, (New York: St. Martin's Press, 1983), p. 209, gives a first-line strength of 3,960

on December 31, 1942, of which 1,755 were single- or twin-engine fighters. This work was compiled from British Intelligence sources and immediate postwar investigations.

29. Webster and Frankland, *The Strategic Air Offensive*, vol. 1, p. 490.

30. Entry for May 21, 1942, Command Diary, Spaatz Papers, Diary.

31. Entry for May 22, 1942, Command Diary, Spaatz Papers, Diary.

32. Ibid. This is probably a reference to a letter from Eaker to Col. Asa N. Duncan, [Chief of Staff, 8th Air Force], May 10, 1942, AFHRC File: Brig. Gen. Eaker's Miscellaneous Papers. Eaker discusses the problems involved in basing U.S. fighter units.

33. British Air Ministry, Air Historical Branch, RAF Narrative, "Anglo-American Collaboration in the Air War over North West Europe," p. 53.

34. Ibid., p. 80.

35. Ibid., p. 131.

36. Ltr, Eaker to Duncan, May 10, 1942, AFHRC File: Brig. Gen. Eaker's Miscellaneous Papers.

37. Msg W.799, Air Ministry Whitehall (Slessor) to RAFDEL (Evill) Washington, D.C., May 9, 1942, PRO AIR 8/1052; and msg WX–2893, RAFDEL (Evill) to Air Ministry Whitehall (Slessor), May 11, 1942, PRO AIR 8/1052.

38. British Air Ministry, Air Hisorical Branch, RAF Narrative, "Anglo-American Collaboration," pp. 135–136.

39. Ibid., pp. 149–150.

40. Entries for May 23–26, 1942, Command Diary, Spaatz Papers, Diary.

41. Entries for May 29–31, 1942, Command Diary, Spaatz Papers, Diary.

42. Entries for May 31, June 1, 1942, Command Diary, Spaatz Papers, Diary.

43. Entry for June 1, 1942, Command Diary, Spaatz Papers, Diary.

44. Entry for June 11, 1942, Command Diary, Spaatz Papers, Diary.

45. Entries for June 12–18, 1942, Command Diary, Spaatz Papers, Diary.

46. Entry for June 19, 1942, Command Diary, Spaatz Papers, Diary.

47. Entry for June 20, 1942, Command Diary, Spaatz Papers, Diary.

48. Ltr, Spaatz to Arnold, July 5, 1942, Spaatz Papers, Diary.

49. Kay Summersby Morgan, *Past Forgetting* (New York: Simon and Schuster, 1975), p. 33.

50. Entry for June 23, 1942, Command Diary, Spaatz Papers, Diary.

51. Ibid., entries for June 24 and 25, 1942.

52. Craven and Cate, *Plans & Early Operations*, p. 628.

53. Ibid.

54. Ibid.

55. British Air Ministry, Air Historical Branch, RAF Narrative, "The RAF in the Bombing Offensive Against Germany," vol. 4: "A Period of Expansion and Experiment, March 1942–January 1943," p. 337.

56. Ltr, Arnold to Maj. Gen. D. D. Eisenhower, Commanding General, ETO, June 22, 1942, Arnold Papers, Letters to Commanders in the Field, box 38. Arnold apparently gave Spaatz verbal instructions, saving the detailed policy for Eisenhower who, as theater commander, was ultimately responsible for it.

57. Entry for June 22, 1942, Command Diary, Spaatz Papers, Diary.

58. Entry for June 23, 1942, Command Diary, Spaatz Papers, Diary.

59. Ibid.

60. Entry for July 15, 1942, Command Diary, Spaatz Papers, Diary.

61. Entry for October 22, 1942, Command Diary, Spaatz Papers, Diary.

62. John MacCormac, "British-U.S. Rift on Planes Holding Up Air Offensive," *New York Times,* August 8, 1942.

63. Raymond Daniell, "Joint Attack on Germany Near," *New York Times,* August 11, 1942.

64. Craven and Cate, *Plans & Early Operations*, p. 657.

65. Entries for August 11, 13, 18, 19, 21, 1942, Command Diary, Spaatz Papers, Diary.

66. Ibid.

67. British Air Ministry, Air Historical Branch, RAF Narrative, "Anglo-American Cooperation," pp. 161–162.

68. See entry for August 20, 1942, Command Diary, Spaatz Papers, Diary, for Spaatz's draft. See Craven and Cate, *Plans & Early Operations*, pp. 608–611, for final text and discussion.

69. British Air Ministry, Air Historical Branch, RAF Narrative, "The RAF in the Bombing Offensive Against Germany," vol. 4: "A Period of Expansion and Experiment, March 1942–January 1943," p. 337.

70. Webster and Frankland, *The Strategic Air Offensive*, vol. 1, pp. 358–359.

71. Copp, *Forged in Fire*, p. 259.

72. Entry for July 11, 1942, Command Diary, Spaatz Papers, Diary.

73. Entry for June 26, 1942, Command Diary, Spaatz Papers, Diary.

74. Chandler, *Eisenhower's Papers*, vol. 1,

item 354; ltr, Eisenhower to Arnold, June 26, 1942, pp. 362–363.

75. Interview, Gen. Carl A. Spaatz by Bruce C. Hopper, London, England, June 27, 1945, Spaatz Papers, Subject File 1929–1945, p. 4.

76. Entry for June 26, 1942, Command Diary, Spaatz Papers, Diary.

77. Webster and Frankland, *The Strategic Air Offensive,* vol. 1, pp. 403–404.

78. British Air Ministry, Air Historical Branch, RAF Narrative, "The RAF in the Bombing Offensive Against Germany," vol. 3: "Area Bombing and the Makeshift Force, June 1941–February 1942,"

79. Charles Webster and Noble Frankland, *The Strategic Air Offensive Against Germany 1939–1945*, vol. 4: *Annexes and Appendices* (London: HMSO, 1961), pp. 4–6.

80. Ibid., pp. 135–140 and 143–147.

81. Webster and Frankland, *The Strategic Air Offensive*, vol. 1, pp. 178–180 and 247–248. For a more caustic description of the reports see Max Hastings, *Bomber Command: The Myths and Reality of the Strategic Bombing Offensive, 1939–1945* (New York: Dial, 1979), pp. 108–110.

82. Terraine, *A Time for Courage*, p. 468. For a negative judgment of Harris, see Charles Messenger, *"Bomber" Harris and the Strategic Bombing Offensive, 1939–1945* (New York: St. Martin's Press, 1984).

83. Hastings, *Bomber Command*, p. 135.

84. Webster and Frankland, *The Strategic Air Offensive*, vol. 1, pp. 340, 464.

85. Craven and Cate, *Plans & Early Operations*, p. 655.

86. Memo, HQ VIII Bomber Command to Commanding Officer, 1st Provisional Wing, subj: Inferior Performance, August 2, 1942, Eaker Papers, box 1.

87. Ltrs, Arnold to Spaatz, July 16, August 9, 1942, Spaatz Papers, Diary.

88. "Air Battle Feats Praised by Arnold," *New York Times,* August 16, 1942, pp. 1, 37.

89. Memo, Air Staff Bomber Operations to DDAT, January 6, 1942, PRO AIR 20/4808.

90. Peter Masefield, "America's Share in Air Offensive: Pooling Men and Machines," *Sunday Times,* August 16, 1942, p. 5.

91. Eaker, Diary Notes, August 2, 1942, part 1: February 4, 1942–July 31, 1944, Eaker Papers, box 1. At this time Spaatz and Eaker agreed that as a matter of policy no observers would be allowed to ride on bomber missions unless qualified as gunners. Eaker further noted that Spaatz, in fact, intended to visit the 97th Bomb Heavy Group in order to get some gunnery practice.

92. Eaker, Diary Notes, August 5, 1942, Eaker Papers, box 1.

93. Ronald Lewin, *Ultra Goes to War: The First Account of World War II's Greatest Secret Based on Official Documents* (New York: McGraw-Hill, 1978), p. 240.

94. Copp, *Forged in Fire*, p. 286.

95. Hughes, "Memoirs," chap. 8, p. 24.

96. Craven and Cate, *Plans & Early Operations*, p. 662.

97. Memo, Arnold to Roosevelt, subj: Reply to Peter Masefield's Criticism of Flying Fortresses and Liberators, August 19, 1942, Arnold Papers, box 45.

98. Ltr, Arnold to Spaatz, August 19, 1942, Spaatz Papers, Diary.

99. Ltr, Spaatz to Arnold, n.d. [August 21, 1942], Arnold Papers, box 49.

100. Ltr, Spaatz to Arnold, August 21, 1942, Spaatz Papers, Diary. This letter was written before Spaatz learned of the results of the fourth raid.

101. Ltrs, Arnold to Spaatz, July 30, August 9, 1942, Spaatz Papers, Diary.

102. Ltr, Spaatz to Arnold, August 11, 1942, Spaatz Papers, Diary.

103. Ltr, Spaatz to Arnold, August 14, 1942, Spaatz Papers, Diary.

104. Ltr, Arnold to Spaatz, September 2, 1942, Spaatz Papers, Diary.

105. Ltr, Arnold to Spaatz, September 15, 1942, Spaatz Papers, Diary.

106. Ibid., Spaatz's diary lists several evenings spent with correspondents and gives details of the plane crash.

107. Entry for August 20, 1942, Command Diary, Spaatz Papers, Diary. See also Chandler, *Eisenhower's Papers*, vol. 1, item 440, msg 1324, Eisenhower to Marshall, August 20, 1942, pp. 483–484.

108. All statistics are compiled from Roger A. Freeman, *Mighty Eighth War Diary* (London: Jane's Publishing Inc., 1981), pp. 9–27.

109. *AAF Statistical Digest, World War II*, table 89, p. 157.

110. Msg AGWAR R–2408, Arnold to Spaatz, October 25, 1942, Spaatz Papers, Eighth Air Force File.

111. United States Strategic Bombing Survey (USSBS), Military Analysis Division, *Weather Factors in Combat Bombardment Operations in the European Theater* (Washington, D.C.: GPO, January 1947), vol. 62, p. 2.

112. Memo, Eighth Air Force Bomber Command to CG, Eighth Air Force, subj: Accuracy of Bombardment—4 Missions, August 27, 1942, Eaker Papers, box 1.

113. Memo, CG, Eighth Air Force Bomber Command, to CG, Eighth Air Force, subj: Night Bombing, October 8, 1942, Eaker Papers, box 1.

114. Ltr, CG, Eighth Bomber Command, to CG, AAF, October 20, 1942, Eaker Papers, box 1.

115. Interview, Brig. Gen. Alfred R. Maxwell by Bruce C. Hopper, London, England, June 22, 1945, Spaatz Papers, Subject File 1929–1945, pp. 21–22.

116. Ibid., p. 22.

117. Ibid; interview, Spaatz by Hopper, June 27, 1945, p. 7.

118. Ibid., p. 8.

119. Interview, Gen. Laurence S. Kuter by Thomas A. Sturm and Hugh N. Ahmann, September 30–October 3, 1974, USAF Oral History Collection, AFHRC file no. K239.0512–810, p. 284. For a physical description of Park House and an account of a typical evening there, see Maj. Gen. L. S. Kuter, "Notes on Trip to England, France, and Italy, May 28–June 21, 1944," n.d. [summer 1944], pp. 3–5, AFHRC file no. K105.5–175.

120. Wayne Thompson, ed., *Air Leadership: Proceedings of a Conference at Bolling Air Force Base, April 13–14, 1984* (Washington, D.C.: AF/CHO, GPO, 1986), p. 42.

121. Robert H. Ferrell, ed., *The Eisenhower Diaries* (New York: W. W. Norton, 1981), pp. 94–95, entry for June 11, 1943.

122. Winston S. Churchill, *The Second World War*, vol. 4: *The Hinge of Fate* (Boston: Houghton Mifflin, 1950), pp. 432–433.

123. Matloff and Snell, *Strategic Planning for Coalition Warfare, 1941–1942*, p. 276.

124. Ibid., p. 273.

125. Ibid., p. 278.

126. Entry for July 19, 1942, Command Diary, Spaatz Papers, Diary. A complete draft of Spaatz's "Air Plan to Support the Attack and Occupation of Cherbourg Peninsula" can be found in his Diary file.

127. Entry for July 21, 1942, Command Diary, Spaatz Papers, Diary.

128. COS(42) 75th Meeting (O), July 18, 1942, Minutes, July 20, 1942, PRO PREM 3/333/9.

129. Ltr, Arnold to Spaatz, July 30, 1942, Spaatz Papers, Diary.

130. Ltr, Spaatz to Arnold, August 11, 1942, Spaatz Papers, Diary.

131. Ibid.

132. Chandler, *Eisenhower's Papers*, vol.1, item 425, msg 1127, Eisenhower to Marshall, August 13, 1942, pp. 464–465.

686

133. Craven and Cate, *Torch to Pointblank*, p. 52.

134. Ibid.

135. Ibid., p. 21, citing Minutes, CG, Eighth Air Force Commanders' Meeting, November 10, 1942.

136. Chandler, *Eisenhower's Papers*, vol. 1, p. 550, note 1.

137. Ibid.

138. Msg, Arnold to Eisenhower, September 10, 1942, Spaatz Papers, Diary.

139. Draft msg, September 10, 1942, Spaatz Papers, Diary.

140. Chandler, *Eisenhower's Papers*, vol. 1, item 492, msg 2028, Eisenhower to Marshall, September 10, 1942, p. 550.

141. Ltr, Spaatz to Arnold, August 21, 1942, Spaatz Papers, Diary.

142. Ltr, Spaatz to Arnold, August 24, 1942, Spaatz Papers, Diary.

143. Ltr, Arnold to Spaatz, July 30, 1942; ltrs, Spaatz to Arnold, August 24, 27, 1942, Spaatz Papers, Diary.

144. Craven and Cate, *Torch to Pointblank*, p. 277, citing memo from the President to Marshall.

145. Entry for August 26, 1945, Command Diary, Spaatz Papers, Diary.

146. Ltr, Spaatz to Arnold, August 27, 1942, Spaatz Papers, Diary.

147. Ltr, Arnold to Spaatz, September 3, 1942, Spaatz Papers, Diary.

148. Memo, Arnold to Hopkins, subj: Plans for Operation Against the Enemy, September 3, 1942, Arnold Papers, box 43.

149. Craven and Cate, *Torch to Pointblank*, pp. 277–279.

150. Ibid., p. 290.

151. Ibid., pp. 290–295.

152. Ltr, Stratemeyer [AAF Chief of Staff] to Spaatz, August 25, 1942, Spaatz Papers, Diary.

153. Chandler, *Eisenhower's Papers*, vol. 1, item 485, msg 1812, Eisenhower to Marshall, September 5, 1942, pp. 543–544.

154. Ibid., p. 544, text given in note to item 485.

155. Memo, Eisenhower to Spaatz, October 13, 1942, Spaatz Papers, Diary. See also Command Diary, entry for September 25, 1942.

156. Entry for October 15, 1942, Command Diary, Spaatz Papers, Diary.

157. Ltr, Arnold to Spaatz, September 3, 1942, Spaatz Papers, Diary.

158. Ltr, Stratemeyer to Spaatz, September 17, 1942, Spaatz Papers, Diary.

159. Ltr, Spaatz to Stratemeyer, September 25, 1942, Spaatz Papers, Diary.

160. See Craven and Cate, *Torch to Pointblank*, pp. 633–634, for a brief discussion on this problem.

161. Chandler, *Eisenhower's Papers*, vol. 1, item 530, pp. 587–589, msg 2867, Eisenhower to Marshall, September 29, 1942, pp. 587–589. This cable is a substantial revision of a draft cable given to Eisenhower by Spaatz. Eisenhower's support of AWPD/42 was hardly the ringing endorsement the AAF would have liked him to accept. Apparently Spaatz's draft came directly from Arnold; Spaatz's diary contains a copy of the draft.

162. Ibid., item 538, ltr, Eisenhower to Marshall, October 7, 1942, pp. 598–601.

163. Digest of a conversation between General Eisenhower and General Spaatz, WIDEWINGS, October 29, 1942, Spaatz Papers, Diary.

164. Ibid.

165. Ltr, Stratemeyer to Spaatz, November 13, 1942, Spaatz Papers, Diary.

166. Ltr, Arnold to Spaatz, November 15, 1942, Spaatz Papers, Diary.

167. Ltr, Arnold to Eisenhower, November 15, 1942, cited in "Notes and Extracts from Spaatz Diaries—1942," Spaatz Papers, USSTAF File.

168. Ltr, Stratemeyer to Spaatz, November 20, 1942, Spaatz Papers, Diary.

169. Entry for November 23, 1942, Command Diary, Spaatz Papers, Diary.

170. Ibid.

Part Two

Tempering the Blade
The North African Campaign

Chapter 4

The Race for Tunisia

1. British Air Ministry, Air Historical Branch, RAF Narrative, "The North African Campaign, November 1942–May 1943," p. 202.

2. Craven and Cate, *Torch to Pointblank*, p. 54, citing October 30, 1942, meeting between Doolittle and Spaatz.

3. James L. Cash, "The Employment of Air Power in the North African Campaign," October 9, 1951, p. 80, AFHRC file no. K612.549–1, citing General of the Army Dwight D. Eisenhower's Report to the CCS on Operations in the Mediterranean Area, 1942–1944 (part 1, Northwest African Campaign, 1942–43), pp. 54–55. Cash's work consists of a compilation of extracts of key documents from the campaign.

4. Ibid.

5. Memo, Air Plan to Support the Attack and Occupation of Cherbourg Peninsula, n.d. [ca. July 19, 1942], Spaatz Papers, Diary.

6. George F. Howe, *United States Army in World War II*, subseries: *The Mediterranean Theater of Operations, Northwest Africa: Seizing the Initiative in the West* (Washington, D.C.: OCMH, GPO, 1957), pp. 36–37. The three invasion force commanders reported directly to Eisenhower. No overall ground commander existed.

7. Craven and Cate, *Torch to Pointblank*, p. 54.

8. Interview, Lt. Gen. James H. Doolittle by Lt. Col. Robert M. Burch, Maj. Ronald R. Fogelman, and Capt. James P. Tate, September 26, 1970, USAF Oral History Collection, AFHRC file no. K239.0512–0793, p. 49.

9. Doolittle badly needs a good biography. The current works on him range in quality from execrable to acceptable. The most useful biography is Lowell Thomas and Edward Jablonski, *Doolittle: A Biography* (Garden City, N.Y.: Doubleday, 1976). Also see, Quentin Reynolds, *The Amazing Mr. Doolittle* (New York: Appleton-Century-Cross, 1953); and Carroll V. Glines, *Jimmy Doolittle, Daredevil Aviator and Scientist* (New York: Macmillan, 1972).

10. Dwight D. Eisenhower, *Crusade in Europe* (Garden City, N.Y.: Doubleday, 1948), p. 122. In the same paragraph Eisenhower noted that Doolittle later "became one of our really fine commanders."

11. Interview, Doolittle by Burch, Fogelman, and Tate, September 26, 1970, pp. 42–43.

12. Craven and Cate, *Torch to Pointblank*, p. 51.

13. Msgs 2161, Eisenhower to Marshall, September 13, 1942, and 2181, Eisenhower to Marshall, September 14, 1942, Eisenhower Pre-Presidential Papers, Eisenhower Presidential Library, Abilene, Kan.

14. Msg, Marshall to Eisenhower, September 14, 1942, Verifax 240.7, item 2535, Papers of George C. Marshall, George C. Marshall Foundation, Lexington, Va. This is Marshall's hand-written draft; the official cable can be located in the National Archives as item no. 744, CM-OUT 4695, September 14, 1942, OPD TS Message File.

15. Msg, Marshall to Eisenhower, September 26, 1942, Marshall Papers, folder 43, box 66. This message bears Marshall's hand-written and initialed note, "Not used Gen Clarke will take by hand. GCM."

16. Richard M. Leighton and Robert W. Coakley, *United States Army in World War II*, subseries: *The War Department, Global Logistics and Strategy, 1940–1943* (Washington, D.C.: OCMH, GPO, 1954), pp. 437–438.

17. Air Marshal William Welsh, "Report on Operation 'Torch'," n.d. [early 1943], para. 30, p. 9. PRO AIR 2/8805. This report covers Welsh's entire term as commander of the EAC and should be used with care, as it does not mention many RAF errors while being critical of the Americans and the British army.

18. Rpt, "Operation 'TORCH'—Lessons Learnt, Report of Investigation Carried Out in North Africa by Wing Commander Broad," February 19, 1943, PRO AIR 20/4521.

19. Arthur Tedder, *With Prejudice: The War Memoirs of Marshal of the Royal Air Force Lord Tedder* (Boston: Little, Brown, 1966), p. 381.

20. Craven and Cate, *Torch to Pointblank*, p. 127.

21. WDTR 440–15, Fundamental Principles for the Employment of the Air Service, January 26, 1926, sec. 1, vol. 1, paras. 3 and 4a.

22. Ibid., sec. 4, para. 16g.

23. WDTR 440-15, Employment of the Air Forces of the Army, October 15, 1935, sec. 3, para. 6f.

24. Robert Frank Futrell, *Ideas, Concepts, Doctrine: A History of Basic Thinking in the United States Air Force, 1907–1964* (Maxwell AFB, Ala.: Air University, 1971), pp. 49–51.

25. WDFM 1–5, Employment of Aviation of the Army, April 15, 1940, sec. 2, para. 18b.

26. Ibid., sec. 4, paras. 26a & b.

27. Memo, Arnold to Spaatz, subj: Lack of Coordination between Ground and Air in the Carolinas and Louisiana Maneuvers, November 28, 1941, Arnold Papers, folder: Maneuvers, box 44.

28. Ibid.

29. Craven and Cate, *Torch to Pointblank*, p. 137.

30. FM 31–35, "Aviation in Support of Ground Forces," April 9, 1942, chap. 2, sec. 1, para. 6.

31. Ibid.

32. Ibid, chap. 2, sec. 1, para. 10.

33. Ibid, chap. 2, sec. 3, para. 31. See Craven and Cate, *Torch to Pointblank*, p. 137.

34. Futrell, *Ideas, Concepts, Doctrine*, p. 66.

35. Kent Roberts Greenfield, *Army Ground Forces and the Air-Ground Battle Team: Including Light Aviation,* Historical Study No. 35 (Ft. Monroe, Va.: Air Ground Forces, 1948), pp. 11–12.

36. Memo, Marshall to Arnold, July 10, 1942, and memo, Arnold to Marshall, subj: Air-Ground Support of Armored Forces, July 20, 1942, Arnold Papers, folder: Support of Armored Forces, box 42.

37. Ltrs, Devers to Arnold, September 5, 1942, Arnold to Devers, September 23, 1942. Arnold Papers, folder: Support of Armored Forces, box 42.

38. Ltr, McNair to Arnold, December 30, 1942, Arnold Papers, folder: Air-Ground Support, box 42.

39. "Talk by Air Vice Marshal Sir A. Coningham, to Assembled British and American General and Senior Officers at the End of the Second Day of the Army Exercise," February 16, 1943, paras. 6–7.

40. British Air Ministry, Air Historical Branch, RAF Narrative, "The North African Campaign," p. 202.

41. I.S.O. Playfair and C.J.C. Molony, *The Mediterranean and the Middle East*, vol. 4: *The Destruction of the Axis Forces in Africa* (London: HMSO, 1966), p. 182. See also Lt. Gen. Anderson's dispatch, "Operations in North West Africa from 8th November 1942 to 13th May 1943," Supplement to the *London Gazette*, November 5, 1946, p. 5454. Anderson completed the dispatch on June 7, 1943, but the War Office did not publish it until after the war. A note to the dispatch added by the War Office admits the scarcity of light antiaircraft weapons.

42. British Air Ministry, Air Historical Branch, RAF Narrative, "The North African Campaign," pp. 202–204.

43. Welsh, "Operation Torch," paras. 61–62, pp. 21–22. See also, ltr, JR/145 Air Marshal Sir James Robb to Air Commodore T. N. McEvoy, Air Ministry, July 22, 1946, Papers of James Robb, RAF Museum, Hendon, England.

44. Howe, *Northwest Africa*, pp. 278–279, 292. See also Anderson, dispatch, p. 5452.

45. Ltr, AC/1623/Org., Air Commodore in Charge of Administration, EAC, to Col. Zane, Twelfth Air Force, subj: Maintenance of Air Forces in the Forward Area, December 8, 1942, PRO AIR 23/6561.

46. Welsh, "Operation Torch," p. 27. Tedder, *With Prejudice*, p. 370 says that Eisenhower assured him that the forward AAF units were under Welsh's "operational control," but this seems to overstate the strength of Welsh's position.

47. Howe, *Northwest Africa*, p. 294; Playfair, *The Destruction of the Axis Forces in Africa*, p. 183.

48. Playfair, *The Destruction of the Axis Forces in Africa*, p. 171; F. H. Hinsley, *British Intelligence in the Second World War: Its Influence on Strategy and Operations*, vol. 2 (New York: Cambridge University Press, 1983), vol. 2 pp. 487–488.

49. Anderson, dispatch, p. 5454. At this point in the dispatch the War Office weakened Anderson's excuses by noting, "By the standards of later campaigns this enemy air activity was not on a serious scale. Its moral effect at the time, however, was increased by the inexperience of the troops and by the scarcity of light A.A. weapons."

50. British Air Ministry, Air Historical Branch, RAF Narrative, "The North African Campaign," p. 76.

51. Ltr, JR/145, Air Marshal Robb to Air Commodore McEvoy, July 22, 1946, Robb Papers.

52. Telephone msg, Eisenhower to Spaatz,

November 13, 1942, Spaatz Papers, Diary.

53. Hinsley, *British Intelligence*, vol. 2, pp. 465–466, 487–489.

54. Ibid., pp. 489–490

55. Ltr, Spaatz to Arnold, November 23, 1942, Spaatz Papers, Diary.

56. Ibid.

57. Chandler, *Eisenhower's Papers*, vol. 2, ltr, Eisenhower to Arnold, November 21, 1942, item 654, pp. 750–752.

58. Msg, Spaatz to Arnold, November 24, 1942, Spaatz Papers, Diary.

59. Chandler, *Eisenhower's Papers*, vol. 2, item 684, Msg, Eisenhower to Gen. H. L. Ismay, December 3, 1942, pp. 790–791.

60. Ltr, Spaatz to Stratemeyer, December 9, 1942, Spaatz Papers, Diary.

61. Entry for December 2, 1942, Command Diary, Spaatz Papers, Diary.

62. Ibid. See also Craven and Cate, *Torch to Pointblank*, p. 108.

63. Entry for December 2, 1942, Command Diary, Spaatz Papers, Diary.

64. Entry for December 3, 1942, Command Diary, Spaatz Papers, Diary.

65. Rpt, "Notes on Decisions Taken as Result of Policy Laid Down at Commander in Chief's Conference, 3rd December 1942," PRO AIR 23/6558.

66. Meeting of [AFHQ] Air Staff, December 8, 1942, Spaatz Papers, Diary. See also Winterbotham, *The Ultra Secret*, p. 146. For McDonald's transfer, see ltr, Spaatz to Eaker, December 9, 1942, Spaatz Papers, Diary.

67. Chandler, *Eisenhower's Papers*, vol. 2, item 685, Msg, Eisenhower to Combined Chiefs of Staff, December 3, 1942, pp. 791–793.

68. British Air Ministry, Air Historical Branch, RAF Narrative, "The North African Campaign," p. 77, cites Command Post 1st Army Situation Report on December 3, dated December 4, 1942.

69. Ibid.

70. Alfred M. Beck, Abe Bortz, Charles W. Lynch, Lida Mayo, and Ralph F. Weld, *United States Army in World War II*, subseries: *The Technical Services, The Corps of Engineers: The War Against Germany* (Washington, D.C.: CMH, GPO, 1985), p. 86.

71. Ibid., p. 87.

72. Entries for December 3–23, 1942, Command Diary, Spaatz Papers, Diary.

73. British Air Ministry, Air Historical Branch, RAF Narrative, "The North African Campaign," p. 82.

74. Howe, *Northwest Africa*, appendix B, table 9, p. 682.

75. Playfair, *The Destruction of the Axis Forces in Africa*, citing the Italian official naval historian, p. 210.

76. Ibid.

77. Ibid., p. 190.

78. Craven and Cate, *Torch to Pointblank*, p. 108.

79. Chandler, *Eisenhower's Papers*, vol. 2, item 705, Memo for the record dictated by Eisenhower to Capt. Harry Butcher, December 10, 1942, pp. 823–825. This memo appears in a truncated version in Harry C. Butcher, *My Three Years with Eisenhower: The Personal Diary of Harry C. Butcher, USNR Naval Aide to General Eisenhower, 1942–1945*, (New York: Simon and Schuster, 1946), p. 220. See Tedder, *With Prejudice*, pp. 372–373, for Tedder's description of events.

80. See Tedder, *With Prejudice*, for Tedder's early career.

81. Arthur Tedder, "Air, Land and Sea Warfare," *Royal United Services Institute Journal* XCI (February 1946), p. 64.

82. Tedder, *With Prejudice*, pp. 380–383.

83. Ibid., p. 382.

84. Memo, Brig. Gen. H. A. Craig to CINC, AFHQ [Eisenhower], December 23, 1942, Spaatz Papers, Diary.

85. Sir Arthur Coningham, "The Development of Tactical Air Forces," a lecture delivered on February 20, 1946, *Royal United Services Institute Journal* XCI (May 1946), p. 213.

86. Shelford Bidwell and Dominick Graham, *Firepower: British Army Weapons and Theories of War, 1904–1945* (London: George Allen & Unwin, 1982), p. 275.

87. Ibid., p. 263

88. Ibid., p. 264

89. Ibid., pp. 264–265.

90. I.S.O. Playfair, F. C. Flynn, C.J.C. Molony, and S. E. Toomer, *The Mediterranean and Middle East*, II: *The Germans Come to the Help of Their Ally (1941)* (London: HMSO, 1956), pp. 294–295. This work supplied the chronology for Coningham's efforts after his assumption of command.

91. Ibid., pp. 268–269.

92. Speech, Coningham to Senior Officers, Tripoli, February 16, 1943, PRO AIR 20/5533.

93. "Report on Visit of Air Marshal Sir Trafford Leigh-Mallory to North West Africa, March/April, 1943," April 1943, part 2, pp. 4, 6–7, paras. 21–22 and 34–44, PRO AIR 20/4521. Leigh-Mallory's sole purpose in visiting North Africa was to examine the tactical air command and control arrangements and their applicability to the cross-channel invasion. His

exposition of the scheme he found in operation in the WDAF should be considered authoritative.

94. Coningham, "The Development of Tactical Air Forces," p. 215.

95. Chandler, *Eisenhower's Papers*, vol. 2, item 743, Msg 3486, Eisenhower to Marshall, December 29, 1942, p. 874.

96. Ibid.

97. Ibid.

98. Ibid., msg 3626, Eisenhower to Marshall,

December 29, 1942, item 746, p. 878.

99. Tedder, *With Prejudice*, p. 385.

100. Craven and Cate, *Torch to Pointblank*, p. 109.

101. Ibid.

102. Entries for January 1, 3, 18, 20, 1943, Command Diary, Spaatz Papers, Diary.

103. Memo, Sanders to Eisenhower, subj: Problems Connected with the Development of Allied Air Power in the North African Theater, November 30, 1942, PRO AIR 23/6561.

Chapter 5
Failure and Reorganization

1. Tedder, "Air, Land and Sea Warfare," *Journal of the Royal United Services Institute*, p. 65.

2. Maurice Matloff, *United States Army in World War II*, subseries: *The War Department, Strategic Planning for Coalition Warfare, 1943–1944* (Washington, D.C.: GPO, 1959), p. 28, citing Combined Chiefs of Staff Document CCS 155/1, January 19, 1943.

3. Ibid., citing CCS 166/1/D, January 21, 1943, "The Bomber Offensive from the United Kingdom."

4. Entry for February 23, 1943, Command Diary, Spaatz Papers, Diary.

5. Craven and Cate, *Torch to Pointblank*, pp. 114, 162–163.

6. Msg C–150, Churchill to Roosevelt, September 16, 1942, in Kimball, *Churchill & Roosevelt: The Complete Correspondence*, vol. 1, pp. 597–598.

7. Minute, Portal to Churchill, October 13, 1942, PRO AIR 8/711.

8. Minute, Portal to the Secretary of State for Air [Archibald M. S. Sinclair], September 27, 1942, PRO AIR 8/711.

9. Minute, Slessor to Portal, September 26, 1942, PRO AIR 8/711.

10. Msg T.1345/2, Churchill to Hopkins, October 16, 1942, PRO AIR 8/711.

11. Note on Air Policy, W. S. Churchill, October 22, 1942, PRO AIR 8/711.

12. Minute, Sinclair to Churchill, October 23, 1942, PRO AIR 8/711.

13. Minute, Churchill to Portal and Sinclair, October 26, 1942, PRO AIR 8/711.

14. Minute, Sinclair to Churchill, October 28, 1942, PRO AIR 8/711.

15. Minute, Portal to Churchill, November 7,

1942, PRO AIR 8/711.

16. Msg 408, Air Ministry [Portal] to RAF Delegation [Slessor], November 21, 1942, PRO AIR 8/711.

17. W.P. (42) 580, note by the Prime Minister and Minister of Defence, subj: Air Policy, December 16, 1942, PRO PREM 3/452/1.

18. Ibid.

19. Leighton and Coakley, *Global Logistics*, pp. 677–679.

20. W.P. (42) 616, note by the Secretary of State for Air, subj: Air Policy, December 29, 1942, PRO PREM 3/452/1.

21. Note by the Secretary of State for Air, subj: The Bombing Policy of the USAAF., n.d. [January 9, 1943], PRO AIR 8/711.

22. Minute 26/3, Churchill to Sinclair, January 10, 1943, PRO PREM 3/452/1.

23. Documents CCS 135, memo by the U.S. Chiefs of Staff, subj: Basic Strategic Concept for 1943, December 26, 1942; CCS 135/1, memo by the British Chiefs of Staff, subj: Basic Strategic Concept for 1943—The European Theater, January 2, 1943; and CCS 135/2, subj: American-British Strategy in 1943, January 3, 1943, published in Department of State, *Foreign Relations of the United States: Conferences at Washington, 1941–1942 and Casablanca, 1943* (Washington, D.C.: GPO, 1968), pp. 735–752 (hereafter referred to as *FRUS*).

24. CCS 135, subj: Basic Strategic Concept for 1943, *FRUS: Washington-Casablanca*, p. 737.

25. CCS 135/2, subj: American-British Strategy, January 3, 1943, *FRUS: Cairo-Teheran*, pp. 746–747.

26. Parton, *"Air Force Spoken Here,"* pp.

217–220.

27. Papers given to the Prime Minister by General Eaker (January 20, 1943), PRO PREM 3/452/1.

28. Churchill, *The Hinge of Fate*, p. 679.

29. Parton, *"Air Force Spoken Here,"* pp. 221–222.

30. Craven and Cate, *Torch to Pointblank*, p. 843.

31. Elliott Roosevelt, *As He Saw It* (New York: Duell, Sloan, and Pearce, 1946), pp. 100–102.

32. Memo, Arnold to Stratemeyer, subj: Bombing of Germany by U.S. Bombers from England, February 26, 1943, Arnold Papers, box 49.

33. Entry for January 19, 1943, Command Diary, Spaatz Papers, Diary.

34. Interview, Spaatz by Shaughnessey, 1959–1060, pp. 66–67.

35. Memo, Arnold to Stratemeyer, subj: Bombing of Germany by U.S. Bombers from England, February 26, 1943, Arnold Papers, box 49.

36. CCS 166/1/D, memo by the Combined Chiefs of Staff, subj: The Bomber Offensive from the United Kingdom, January 21, 1943, published in *FRUS: Washington-Casablanca*, pp. 781–782.

37. General Order No. 1, Headquarters Allied Air Force, January 7, 1943, Spaatz Papers, Diary.

38. Entry for January 17, 1943, Command Diary, Spaatz Papers, Diary. This entry makes clear that the commander of XII ASC, not the commander of II Corps, would control air decisions.

39. Butcher, *My Three Years with Eisenhower*, pp. 229–230.

40. Patton has been the subject of numerous biographies. One of the most illuminating publications on his military thought and actions is Martin Blumenson, *The Patton Papers* (Boston: Houghton Mifflin, 1972–1974), in two volumes. These volumes are mostly in Patton's own words and they admirably reveal his military actions and philosophy. For the general's personal side, see Ladislas Farago, *Patton: Ordeal and Triumph* (New York: Ivan Obolensky, Inc., 1963), and Martin Blumenson, *Patton: The Man Behind the Legend 1885–1945* (New York: William Morrow, 1985).

41. Howe, *Northwest Africa*, p. 447.

42. L[ucian] K. Truscott, *Command Missions: A Personal Story* (New York: E. P. Dutton, 1954), pp. 144–145. In contrast to the proliferation of material on Patton, almost noth-

ing has been written on Fredendall's character or personality. Truscott, who served as Eisenhower's representative at the front, had ample opportunity to observe Fredendall for his entire tour as commander of II Corps and to form a firsthand opinion.

43. Chandler, *Eisenhower's Papers*, vol. 2, notes for Commander Butcher, December 10, 1942, item 705, p. 824.

44. Ibid., note 5, p. 938.

45. Ibid., msg from Eisenhower to Fredendall, February 4, 1943, item 808, pp. 939–941.

46. XII ASC Report of Operations, April 9, 1943, p. 23, NARA Record Group (RG) 337, Army Ground Forces Central Decimal File, file no. 319.1/83, box 245.

47. Ltr, Doolittle to Air Commander in Chief, Allied Air Forces [Spaatz], January 20, 1943, Papers of James H. Doolittle, Library of Congress, Manuscript Division, box 19.

48. Entry for January 21, 1943, Command Diary, Spaatz Papers, Diary. Craig had also developed a raging case of pneumonia that incapacitated him, making his replacement inevitable. The change of assignment certainly did Craig's career no harm; he continued to receive excellent staff assignments and retired as a three-star general.

49. Ltr, Doolittle to Spaatz, January 23, 1943, Doolittle Papers, box 19.

50. Rpt, CG XII ASC [Williams] to CG, NATO [Eisenhower], subj: "Report of Operations," April 9, 1943, p. 3, NARA, RG 337, AGF Central File, 319.1/83, box 245.

51. Truscott, *Command Missions*, p. 144.

52. Harry Butcher, "Manuscript of Butcher Diary," pp. 168 and 197, Eisenhower Presidential Library, Abilene, Kans. This is the complete draft of the published Butcher Diary and contains many passages deleted from the published version because of security or personal considerations.

53. Truscott, *Command Missions*, p. 144.

54. British Air Ministry, Air Historical Branch, RAF Narrative, "The North African Campaign," pp. 204–205.

55. Playfair, *The Destruction of Axis Forces in Africa*, pp. 308–309.

56. Howe, *Northwest Africa*, pp. 379, 381.

57. Ibid., p. 396; Entry for February 6, 1943, Command Diary, Spaatz Papers, Diary.

58. Howe, *Northwest Africa*, pp. 139–140.

59. Entry for January 21, 1943, Command Diary, Spaatz Papers, Diary.

60. Chandler, *Eisenhower's Papers*, vol. 2, item 767, Memo of Conference at Advanced

Allied Air Force Headquarters, January 21, 1943, p. 918.

61. Ibid., p. 919.

62. Ibid., msg, Eisenhower to Russell Peter Hartle, item 770, pp. 904–905.

63. Entries for January 21, 22, 1943, Command Diary, Spaatz Papers, Diary.

64. Entries for January 27–30, 1943, Command Diary, Spaatz Papers, Diary.

65. Entry for February 5, 1943, Command Diary, Spaatz Papers, Diary.

66. Howe, *Northwest Africa*, p. 399.

67. Ibid.

68. Entry for February 5, 1943, Command Diary, Spaatz Papers, Diary.

69. Ibid.

70. Entry for January 17, 1943, Command Diary, Spaatz Papers, Diary.

71. Entry for February 6, 1943, Command Diary, Spaatz Papers, Diary. In addition, see Eisenhower, *Crusade in Europe*, p. 141: "It was the only time during the war that I ever saw a divisional or higher headquarters so concerned over its own safety that it dug itself underground shelters."

72. Ltr, Spaatz to Arnold, February 8, 1943, Spaatz Papers, Diary.

73. Ltr, Spaatz to Stratemeyer, February 8, 1943, Spaatz Papers, Diary.

74. Craven and Cate, *Torch to Pointblank*, p.

161, citing a manuscript by S/Ldr J. N. White, "Evolution of Air Command in the Mediterranean," November 13, 1944.

75. Ibid., pp. 161–165.

76. Ibid., p. 163.

77. Entry for February 17, 1943, Command Diary, Spaatz Papers, Diary.

78. Craven and Cate, *Torch to Pointblank*, p. 157.

79. Playfair, *The Destruction of Axis Forces in Africa*, p. 311.

80. Command Diary, entry for February 23, 1943, Spaatz Papers, Diary.

81. Entries from "Casablanca Notes," January 4, 5, 1943, Spaatz Papers, Subject File 1929–1945.

82. Playfair, *The Destruction of the Axis Forces in Africa*, p. 291.

83. XII ASC, "Operations Report," April 9, 1943, p. 6, NARA, RG 337, Army Ground Forces Central File 319.1/83, box 245.

84. Playfair, *The Destruction of Axis Forces in Africa*, p. 302. Playfair has the best account of air actions during the period, better than either American official history. For a good popular account of the action, see Martin Blumenson, *Kasserine Pass* (Boston: Houghton Mifflin, 1967).

85. Chandler, *Eisenhower's Papers*, vol. 2, Memo, February 25, 1943, item 843, p. 992.

Chapter 6
The Collapse of the Axis Bridgehead

1. Chandler, *Eisenhower's Papers*, vol. 2, item 962, ltr, Eisenhower to Arnold, May 2, 1943, p. 1107.

2. Hinsley, *British Intelligence*, vol. 2, p. 607.

3. Entry for March 1, 1943, Command Diary, Spaatz Papers, Diary.

4. Entry for March 2, 1943, Command Diary, Spaatz Papers, Diary.

5. Ltr, Spaatz to Arnold, March 7, 1943, Spaatz Papers, Diary.

6. Craven and Cate, *Torch to Pointblank*, p. 169–170.

7. Entry for March 3, 1943, Command Diary, Spaatz Papers, Diary.

8. Rpt, Maj. Gen. Lloyd R. Fredendall, subj: Notes on Recent Operations on the Tunisian Front, March 10, 1943, Fredendall Papers, Eisenhower Presidential Library, Abilene, Kans.

9. Entry for March 3, 1943, Command Diary, Spaatz Papers, Diary.

10. Craven and Cate, *Torch to Pointblank*, p. 130.

11. Ibid., p. 131; ltr, Spaatz to Stratemeyer, March 26, 1943, Spaatz Papers, Diary.

12. Report on Morale (United States Army Air Force Personnel), Col. Everett Cook to CG, NAAF [Spaatz], April 20, 1943, Spaatz Papers, Diary.

13. Staff Meeting, March 4, 1943, and Conference Notes, March 5, 1943, Spaatz Papers, Diary.

14. Martin R. R. Goldman, "Morale in the AAF in World War II," USAF Historical Study No. 78, (USAF Historical Division, Air University, Maxwell AFB, Ala., 1953), p. 44, citing rpt, Maj. Robert B. Nelson, Jr., to Air Surgeon, AAF, subj: Morale of Flying

Personnel. May 20, 1943, folder: Morale and Welfare November 23, 1942–December 30, 1943, AGO 330.11A. Goldman provides some intriguing details but little insight into AAF morale.

15. Ibid., p. 30. This did not completely solve the food situation. A postwar USAF study noted that overall food quality, not just British rations, was prevented from "developing into a disturbing problem" only by the advance into Italy, which increased the supply of fresh meat and dairy products as well as providing the benefits of improved and relatively abundant refrigeration of fresh produce and meats.

16. Ibid., p. 59, which reported that movie showings were "easily the most consistently popular form of diversion in all theaters [of operation], and the one credited with doing the most good for morale."

17. Report on Morale, Col. Cook to Spaatz, April 20, 1943, Spaatz Papers, Diary.

18. Beck et al., *Corps of Engineers: War Against Germany*, p. 89.

19. Ltr, Spaatz to Stratemeyer, March 26, 1943, Spaatz Papers, Diary.

20. Chandler, *Eisenhower's Papers*, vol. 2, item 986, ltr, Eisenhower to Spaatz, May 12, 1943, pp. 1125–1126.

21. Ltr, Spaatz to Arnold, March 7, 1943, Spaatz Papers, Diary.

22. Hinsley, *British Intelligence*, vol. 2, p. 576.

23. Conference Notes, March 17, 1943, Spaatz Papers, Diary.

24. Hinsley, *British Intelligence*, vol. 2, p. 575.

25. Ibid., p. 574.

26. Ibid., p. 607.

27. Ibid., pp. 607–608.

28. Ibid., p. 607.

29. Craven and Cate, *Torch to Pointblank*, p. 189.

30. Entries for January 16, 18, 1943, Command Diary, Spaatz Papers, Diary.

31. Craven and Cate, *Torch to Pointblank*, p. 189.

32. Staff Meeting, March 4, 1943, Spaatz Papers, Diary.

33. Entry for March 20, 1943, Command Diary, Spaatz Papers.

34. Conference Notes, April 2, 1943, Command Diary, Spaatz Papers, Diary.

35. Hinsley, *British Intelligence*, vol. 2, p. 607.

36. Conference Notes, April 2, 1943, Spaatz Papers, Diary.

37. Craven and Cate, *Torch to Pointblank*,

pp. 189–190.

38. Ltr, Spaatz to Eaker, April 8, 1943, Spaatz Papers, Diary.

39. Hinsley, *British Intelligence*, vol. 2, pp. 608–609.

40. National Security Agency Special Research History no. 13 (SRH–013), "ULTRA History of US Strategic Air Force Europe vs. German Air Forces," June 6, 1945, AF/CHO, p. 62.

41. Hinsley, *British Intelligence*, vol. 2, p. 609.

42. Ibid.

43. Ibid.

44. Craven and Cate, *Torch to Pointblank*, p. 196.

45. Hinsley, *British Intelligence*, vol. 2, p. 614.

46. *AAF Statistical Digest, World War II*, table 120, p. 222.

47. Ibid., table 102, p. 189.

48. Craven and Cate, *Torch to Pointblank*, p. 194. After the first month of the campaign the Twelfth Air Force did not operate B-24s which, because of their superior range, became the exclusive province of the Ninth Air Force.

49. Ltr, Spaatz to Arnold, May 24, 1943, Spaatz Papers, Diary.

50. Ltr, Spaatz to Arnold, February 8, 1943, Spaatz Papers, Diary.

51. Craven and Cate, *Torch to Pointblank*, p. 184; *United States Army in World War II*, subseries: *The Pictorial Record, The War Against Germany and Italy: Mediterranean and Adjacent Areas* (Washington, D.C.: OCMH, GPO, 1951), p. 164.

52. See Margaret Bourke-White, "Bourke-White Goes Bombing," *Life*, March 1, 1943. Bourke-White flew on a raid over an Axis airfield on January 22, 1943. She credits Doolittle with giving her permission, and probably consulted Spaatz, a friend of hers, as well.

53. "The Plotters of Souk-el-Spaatz," *Time*, March 22, 1943.

54. Ltr, Arnold to Spaatz, April 10, 1943, Spaatz Papers, Diary.

55. Ibid.

56. Ltr, Spaatz to Arnold, April 21, 1943, Command Diary, Spaatz Papers, Diary.

57. Ltr, Spaatz to Stratemeyer, March 26, 1943, Command Diary, Spaatz Papers, Diary.

58. Interview, Kuter by Sturm and Ahmann, September 30–October 3, 1974, p. 305.

59. Entry for February 23, 1943, Spaatz Papers, Command Diary, Spaatz Papers, Diary.

60. Entries for March 31, April 13, 27, 1943, Command Diary, Spaatz Papers, Diary.

61. Butcher, *My Three Years with Eisenhower*, p. 287.

62. Richard H. Kohn and Joseph P. Harahan, eds., *Air Superiority in World War II and Korea*, series: *USAF Warrior Studies* (Washington, D.C.: AF/CHO, GPO, 1983), pp. 56-60.

63. Ltr, Spaatz to Arnold, May 24, 1943, Spaatz Papers, Diary.

64. Solly Zuckerman, *From Apes to Warlords* (New York: Harper & Row, 1978), p. 204.

65. Carlo D'Este, *Decision in Normandy* (New York: E. P. Dutton, 1983), pp. 218–219.

66. Nigel Hamilton, *Master of the Battlefield: Monty's War Years 1942–1944* (New York: McGraw-Hill, 1983), pp. 199–200. Hamilton even goes to the absurd length of crediting Broadhurst with the development of British air support theory—a gross misinterpretation of actuality.

67. Msg, A188, AOC, NATAF to XII ASC, March 17, 1943, Spaatz Papers, Diary.

68. Memo, HQ, XII ASC to OIC, NATAF, March 23, 1943, Command Diary, Spaatz Papers, Diary.

69. Entries for March 25, April 14, 1943, Command Diary, Spaatz Papers, Diary.

70. VIII Air Support Command, "Air Operations in Support of Ground Forces in Northwest Africa (March 15–April 5, 1943)," observers rpt, U.S. Army Military History Institute, Carlisle, Pa.

71. Ltr, Spaatz to Stratemeyer, February 8, 1943, Spaatz Papers, Diary.

72. Entry for March 13, 1943, Command Diary, Spaatz Papers, Diary.

73. Entries for March 30, April 10, 1943, Command Diary, Spaatz Papers, Diary.

74. Rpt, CG, XII ASC [Williams] to CG, NATO (North African Theater of Operations) [Eisenhower], subj: "Report of Operations," April 9, 1943, p. 8, NARA, RG 337, AGF Central File 319.1/83, box 245.

75. Report of the Northwest African Tactical Air Force on Operations, February 18–May 11, 1943, n.d. [May 1943], p. 20, PRO AIR 20/5535.

76. Omar N. Bradley, *A Soldier's Story* (New York: Henry Holt, 1951), p. 62; Omar N. Bradley and Clay Blair, *A General's Life* (New York: Simon and Schuster, 1983), p. 147.

77. Blumenson, *The Patton Papers*, vol. 2, p. 205.

78. Entries for March 24, 25, 1943, Command Diary, Spaatz Papers, Diary.

79. Howe, *Northwest Africa*, p. 562; NATAF Final Report, p. 24. PRO AIR 20/5535.

80. NATAF Final Report, p. 24, PRO AIR 20/5535.

81. Msg, SPEC 40 NATAF to NAAF [Spaatz], April 2, 1943, Spaatz Papers, Diary. This message cites the text of Patton's message.

82. Ibid.

83. Ltr, Coningham to AVM H.E.P. Wigglesworth, Deputy Commander, Mediterranean Air Command, April 5, 1943, PRO AIR 23/7439.

84. Tedder, *With Prejudice*, pp. 410–411.

85. Entry for April 2, 1943, Command Diary, Spaatz Papers, Diary.

86. Entry for April 3, 1943, Command Diary, Spaatz Papers, Diary.

87. Ibid.

88. Tedder, *With Prejudice*, p. 411.

89. NATAF Final Report, p. 24, PRO AIR 20/5535.

90. Entry for April 4, 1943, Command Diary, Spaatz Papers, Diary.

91. Ibid.

92. Blumenson, *The Patton Papers*, vol. 2, pp. 208–209.

93. Ltr, Coningham to Wigglesworth, April 5, 1943, PRO AIR 23/7439.

94. Msg SPEC–46, NATAF to NAAF, April 5, 1943, Spaatz Papers, Diary.

95. Interview, Maj. Gen. Edward P. Curtis by James C. Hasdorff, November 22–23, 1975, USAF Oral History Collection, AFHRC file no. K239.0512–875, p. 55.

96. Chandler, *Eisenhower's Papers*, vol. 2, item 927, msg, Eisenhower to Marshall, April 5, 1943, p. 1071.

97. Entry for April 5, 1943, Command Diary, Spaatz Papers, Diary.

98. Chandler, *Eisenhower's Papers*, vol. 2, item 928, msg, Eisenhower to Patton, April 5, 1943, pp. 1072–1073.

99. Blumenson, *The Patton Papers*, vol. 2, p. 210.

100. Howe, *Northwest Africa*, pp. 586–587.

101. Ibid., p. 590.

102. Entry for April 8, 1943, Command Diary, Spaatz Papers, Diary.

103. Craven and Cate, *Torch to Pointblank*, pp. 198–199.

104. Entry for April 20, 1943, Command Diary, Spaatz Papers, Diary.

105. NATAF Final Report, p. 28. PRO AIR 20/5535.

106. Playfair, *The Destruction of Axis Forces in Africa*, p. 447.

107. Report on Air Operations by No. 242 Group R.A.F. in Support of 1st Army Tunisia, 1943, n.d. [ca. May 1943], p. 13, PRO AIR 23/7434.

108. Ibid., p. 11.

109. Entry for April 29, 1943, Command Diary, Spaatz Papers, Diary.

110. Msg, Spaatz to Eisenhower, May 1, 1943, Spaatz Papers, Diary.

111. Ibid.

112. Entry for May 4, 1943, Command Diary, Spaatz Papers, Diary.

113. Msg, Spaatz to Eisenhower, May 1, 1943, Spaatz Papers, Diary; ltr, Stratemeyer to Arnold, May 7, 1943, Spaatz Papers, Diary.

114. Ibid.

115. Entry for May 12, 1943, Command Diary, Spaatz Papers, Diary; Tedder, *With Prejudice*, p. 399.

116. Ltr, Spaatz to Arnold, May 24, 1943, Spaatz Papers, Diary.

117. Ltr, Spaatz to Arnold, March 7, 1943, Spaatz Papers, Diary.

118. Ibid.

119. Ltr, Arnold to Spaatz, May 6, 1943, folder: North African Operations, Arnold Papers, box 39; memo, Brig. Gen. T. J. Hanley, Deputy Chief of the Air Staff, to all Assistant Chiefs of the Air Staff, subj: Air Operations in North Africa, April 20, 1943, Decimal File 370.2 Africa (16), Arnold Papers, box 104.

120. "The Plotters of Souk-el-Spaatz," (cover), *Time*, March 22, 1943, p. 22.

121. Pamphlet, Bernard L. Montgomery, "Some Notes on High Command in War," p. 2, NARA, RG 165, OPD File 384, case 39, box 1305.

122. Talk by Air Vice Marshal Sir A. Coningham, February 16, 1943, Tripoli, PRO AIR 20/5535.

123. Ltr, Spaatz to Arnold, February 19, 1943, AF/CHO microfilm reel A 1657A, frames 965–966.

124. Memo for the Chief of Staff from the Assistant Secretary of War, April 18, 1943, NARA, RG 165, OPD–384, box 1305.

125. Memo for the Assistant Chief of Staff, Operations Division from Col. H. J. Matchett, Acting Assistant Chief of Staff, G–3, subj: General Montgomery's Notes on "High Command in War," April 24, 1943, NARA, RG 165, G–3 (370.6-384).

126. Memo for the Chief of Staff from Brig. Gen. J. E. Hull, Acting Assistant Chief of Staff, OPD, April 29, 1943, NARA, RG 165, G–3 (370.6-384).

127. Memo for General [John E.] Hull, Acting Assistant Chief of Staff, OPD, from Col. S. E. Anderson, subj: Revision of Training Literature, May 8, 1943, NARA, RG 165, OPD-384, Case 39, box 1305. Colonel Anderson attempted to eliminate AGF coordination by insisting that input to revisions of an AAF manual need come only from the AAF. Brig. Gen.

Hull overruled him, noting that revisions need not be unanimous. Anderson later gained much experience in air-ground cooperation as the commander of IX Bomber Command, a unit of medium bombers assigned to assist Lt. Gen. Omar Bradley's 12th Army Group during the campaign in northwestern Europe.

128. Memo for the Chief of Staff from Lt. Gen. Ben Lear, Commanding General, AGF, subj: General Montgomery's Notes on "High Command in War," May 17, 1943, NARA, RG 165, G–3 (370.6–384).

129. Memo for the Assistant Chief of Staff, G–3, from the Acting Chief of Staff, subj: Revision of Training Literature, May 31, 1943, NARA, RG 165, G–3 (370.6–384).

130. War Department Field Manual 100–20, Field Service Regulations, Command and Employment of Air Power (Washington, D.C.: GPO, July 21, 1943), sec. I, para. 1–3, pp. 1–2.

131. Memo for the record attached to memo for the Adjutant General from Brig. Gen. Ray E. Porter, Assistant Chief of Staff, G–3, subj: Publication of FM 100–20, Field Service Regulations, Command and Employment of Air Power, June 30, 1943, NARA, RG 165, G–3 (370.6–834).

132. Memo for Col. Nelson, G–3, from Col. J. B. Burwell, G–3, June 24, 1943, NARA, RG 165, G–3 (370.6–384).

133. See entry for February 6, 1943, Command Diary, for mention of Spaatz's discussion with Porter. See ltr, Stratemeyer to Arnold, May 7, 1943, for a connection to Stratemeyer, and ltr, Kuter to Spaatz, May 25, 1943, all sources in Spaatz Papers, Diary.

134. WDFM 100–20, "Command and Employment of Air Power," (Washington, D.C.: GPO, July 21, 1943), chap. 1, sec. 1, para. 2.

135. Ibid., chap. 1, sec. 1, para. 3.

136. Ibid., chap. 2, sec. 3, para. 15.

137. Ibid., chap. 2, sec. 3, par. 16, subpar. b.

138. WDFM 31–35, April 9, 1942, chap. 2, sec. 1, para. 6.

139. WDFM 100–20, chap. 1, sec. 1, para. 3.

140. Ibid., chap. 2, sec. 2, para. 12.

141. Ltr, Kuter to Spaatz, May 25, 1943, Spaatz Papers, Diary.

142. Ibid., ltr, Arnold to Spaatz, June 28, 1943.

143. Ltr, Kuter to Col. Glen Martin, Special Consultant to the Secretary of the Air Force, November 22, 1950, AF/CHO, "The Kuter Report."

144. WDFM 100–20, chap. 1, sec. 1, para. 1.

145. WDFM 100–20, chap. 2, sec. 3, para. 16, subpara. b.

146. 384 (S)–GNGCT (5–6–43), Memo for the Chief of Staff from Lt. Gen. Ben Lear, Commanding General, Army Ground Forces, subj: "General Montgomery's Notes on 'High Command' in War," May 17, 1943, NARA, RG 165, Records of the War Department General and Special Staffs, G–3 370.6–384.

147. Greenfield, "Army Ground Forces and the Air-Ground Battle Team," pp. 48–50.

148. FM 1–5, January 18, 1943, chap. 2, sec. 3, para. 26. Also see chap. 4, sec. 3, para. 57.

149. Ibid., chap. 5, sec. 2, par. 63, subpar. b.

150. Ibid., chap. 3, sec. 6, para. 30.

151. Ibid., chap. 5, sec. 1, par. 58, subpar. c.

152. Ibid., subparas. d and e.

153. Rpt, Maj. Gen. W. H. Walker to CG, AGF, subj: Report of Visit to North African Theater of Operations, June 12, 1943, NARA, RG 337, AGF File 315.1, box 242.

154. Ltr, Brig. Gen. Paul M. Robinett to Marshall, December 8, 1942, Arnold Papers, folder: Air-Ground Support, box 42.

155. Greenfield, "Army Ground Forces and the Air-Ground Battle Team," p. 77, citing statements by Kern, May 13, 1943, and Ryder, June 18–19, 1943.

156. Ltr, Kuter to Coningham, June 26, 1943, AIR PRO 23/7439.

157. Ltr, Spaatz to Arnold, May 24, 1943, Spaatz Papers, Diary.

158. Interview, Spaatz by Goldberg, May 19, 1965, p. 25.

159. Rpt, HQ XII ASC to CG, NATO, subj: "Report of Operations," April 9, 1943, NARA, RG 337, Army Ground Forces Central Files, file 319.1/83, box 245.

160. Ltr, Kuter to Col. Glen Martin, Special Consultant to the Secretary of the Air Force, November 22, 1950, AF/CHO, "The Kuter Report."

161. Ltr, Spaatz to CG, AAF, subj: Employment of Support Aviation, May 27, 1943, Spaatz Papers, Diary.

162. Greenfield, "Army Ground Forces and the Air-Ground Battle Team," pp. 42–43. Some divisions were double- or triple-counted in these totals; the Army did not have 104 divisions in the United States on that date.

163. Memo for Asst. C/S, A–1, NAAF, from Deputy AC/S, A–1, June 1, 1943, Spaatz Papers, Diary. These figures include the last day of May 1943 and therefore slightly overstate total casualties.

164. *AAF Statistical Digest, World War II,* table 160, p. 256. These figures include the losses of the Ninth Air Force as well.

Part Three
Mediterranean Interlude
From Pantelleria to London

Chapter 7
Pantelleria and Sicily

1. Ltr, Spaatz to Henry [Berliner ?], June 18, 1943, Spaatz Papers, Diary.

2. Blumenson, *The Patton Papers,* vol.2, p. 314.

3. Craven and Cate, *Torch to Pointblank,* pp. 419–422.

4. Ibid.

5. Albert N. Garland and Howard McGaw Smyth, *United States Army in World War II,* subseries: *The Mediterranean Theater of Operations, Sicily and the Surrender of Italy* (Washington, D.C.: OCMH, GPO, 1965), pp. 70, 73.

6. Ibid., p. 419. See also msg 1409 for Marshall from Eisenhower, February 17, 1943,

PRO AIR 23/5485.

7. Craven and Cate, *Torch to Pointblank,* p. 423.

8. Ibid.

9. Chandler, *Eisenhower's Papers,* vol.2, item 982, msg NAF–219, Eisenhower to Combined Chiefs of Staff, May 11, 1943, p. 1122.

10. Ibid., item 992, msg, Eisenhower to Marshall, May 13, 1943, p. 1130.

11. Craven and Cate, *Torch to Pointblank,* p. 424.

12. Ibid., p. 425.

13. Entry for May 16, 1943, Command

Diary, Spaatz Papers, Diary.

14. Zuckerman, *Apes to Warlords*, p. 183.

15. Entry for May 17, 1943, Command Diary, Spaatz Papers, Diary.

16. Craven and Cate, *Torch to Pointblank*, p. 425.

17. Entries for May 17, 18, 19, 1943, Command Diary, Spaatz Papers, Diary.

18. Entry for May 19, 1943, Command Diary, Spaatz Papers, Diary.

19. Entry for May 20, 1943, Command Diary, Spaatz Papers, Diary.

20. Ibid.

21. Eisenhower, *Crusade in Europe*, p. 165; Butcher, *My Three Years with Eisenhower*, pp. 329–330.

22. Chandler, *Eisenhower's Papers*, vol. 2, item 1091, memo for Personal Record, July 1, 1943, p. 1231.

23. Entry for May 22, 1943, Command Diary, Spaatz Papers, Diary.

24. Entry for May 23, 1943, Command Diary, Spaatz Papers, Diary.

25. Chandler, *Eisenhower's Papers*, vol. 2, item 1020, msg, Eisenhower to Marshall, May 25, 1943, p. 1154.

26. Ibid., item 1091, memo for the Personal Record, July 1, 1943, p. 1231.

27. Zuckerman, *Apes to Warlords*, pp. 173–174.

28. Ibid., pp. 184–185.

29. Ibid., p. 186.

30. Operation CORKSCREW, Minutes of Meeting on May 28, 1943, Spaatz Papers, Diary.

31. Zuckerman, *Apes to Warlords*, p. 185.

32. Ibid., p. 187.

33. Ibid.

34. Entry for May 28, 1943, Command Diary, Spaatz Papers, Diary.

35. Entry for June 6, 1943, Command Diary, Spaatz Papers, Diary.

36. Ibid.

37. Craven and Cate, *Torch to Pointblank*, pp. 425–426.

38. Entry for June 6, 1943, Command Diary, Spaatz Papers, Diary.

39. Entry for June 8, 1943, Command Diary, Spaatz Papers, Diary. See also Zuckerman, *Apes to Warlords*, pp. 189–192.

40. Entry for June 8, 1943, Command Diary, Spaatz Papers, Diary.

41. Zuckerman, *Apes to Warlords*, p. 190.

42. Ibid., p. 188.

43. Entry for June 8, 1943, Command Diary, Spaatz Papers, Diary.

44. Chandler, *Eisenhower's Papers*, vol. 2, item 1046, msg, Eisenhower to Marshall, June 9, 1943, p. 1181.

45. Entry for June 8, 1943, Command Diary, Spaatz Papers, Diary.

46. Entry for June 9, 1943, Command Diary, Spaatz Papers, Diary.

47. Ibid.

48. Ibid.

49. Chandler, *Eisenhower's Papers*, vol. 2, item 1075, msg, Eisenhower to Marshall, June 26, 1943, p. 1212.

50. Craven and Cate, *Torch to Pointblank*, p. 424.

51. Entry for June 9, 1943, Command Diary, Spaatz Papers, Diary.

52. Entry for June 11, 1943, Command Diary, Spaatz Papers, Diary.

53. Craven and Cate, *Torch to Pointblank*, p. 429, citing *Times* [London], June 15, 1943.

54. Garland and Smyth, *Sicily and the Surrender of Italy*, pp. 71–72.

55. Ibid.

56. Msg, Spaatz and Lovett to Arnold, June 11, 1943, Spaatz Papers, Diary.

57. Msg, Spaatz to Mediterranean Air Command [Tedder ?], July 1, 1943, Spaatz Papers, Diary.

58. Entry for June 12, 1943, Command Diary, Spaatz Papers, Diary.

59. Ltr, Spaatz to Henry [Berliner?], June 18, 1943, Spaatz Papers, Diary.

60. Memo, Spaatz to Tedder, "Interim Statement of Operation CORKSCREW," June 20, 1943, Spaatz Papers, Diary.

61. Zuckerman, *Apes to Warlords*, p. 195.

62. CCS Memorandum of Information No. 143, "Pantelleria Operations," p. 13, PRO PREM 3/228/4.

63. Zuckerman, *Apes to Warlords*, p. 194.

64. Craven and Cate, *Torch to Pointblank*, p. 433.

65. Ltr, Allied Force Headquarters from Maj. Gen. W. L. Clutterbuck, June 13, 1943, PRO AIR 23/3305.

66. Hamilton, *Master of the Battlefield*, p. 287.

67. Craven and Cate, *Torch to Pointblank*, p. 432.

68. Hamilton, *Master of the Battlefield*, pp. 245–272. See also Bernard L. Montgomery, *The Memoirs of Field-Marshal the Viscount Montgomery of Alamein, K.G.* (New York: World Publishing, 1958), pp. 153–164.

69. Craven and Cate, *Torch to Pointblank*, p. 443.

70. Ibid., p. 444.

71. C.J.C. Molony, F. C. Flynn, H. L. Davies, and T. P. Gleave, *The Mediterranean and*

Middle East, vol. 5, *The Campaign in Sicily 1943 and the Campaign in Italy 3rd September 1943 to 31st March 1944* (London: HMSO, 1973), pp. 32–33.

72. Craven and Cate, *Torch to Pointblank*, p. 445

73. Ibid. For a thorough discussion of Axis air strength at the time of the invasion, see Hinsley, *British Intelligence*, vol. 3, part 1, pp. 80–81.

74. Ibid., p. 83.

75. Entry for June 18, 1943, Command Diary, Spaatz Papers, Diary.

76. Ltr, Spaatz to Arnold, June 24, 1943, Spaatz Papers, Diary.

77. Hinsley, *British Intelligence*, vol. 3, part 1, pp. 82–84.

78. Ibid., p. 84.

79. Ibid., p. 82.

80. Entry for May 13, 1943, Command Diary, Spaatz Papers, Diary.

81. Entry for May 24, 1943, Command Diary, Spaatz Papers, Diary.

82. Blumenson, *The Patton Papers*, vol. 2, p. 254.

83. Entry for May 22, 1943, Command Diary, Spaatz Papers, Diary.

84. Notes, Spaatz-Cannon conference, May 24, 1943, Spaatz Papers, Diary.

85. Msg, SPEC–120, Coningham to Spaatz, June 3, 1943, Spaatz Papers, Diary.

86. Ltr, Spaatz to Arnold, June 24, 1943, Spaatz Papers, Diary.

87. Greenfield, "Army Ground Forces and the Air-Ground Battle Team," p. 77, citing a statement by Lucas on July 21, 1943.

88. Molony, *The Campaign in Sicily and Italy*, p. 173.

89. Garland and Smyth, *Sicily and the Surrender of Italy*, pp. 175–182. This official history gives a full and balanced account of this tragedy. It concludes that no one in particular but everyone in general was responsible. See also memo, Maj. Gen. M. B. Ridgway, subj: Reported Loss of Transport Planes and Personnel Due to Friendly Fire, August 2, 1943, Arnold Papers, folder: Air Support of Armored Forces [misfiled?], box 42.

90. Craven and Cate, *Torch to Pointblank*, p. 454.

91. Chandler, *Eisenhower's Papers*, vol. 2, item 1115, msg, Eisenhower to Patton, July 12, 1943, p. 1255. Spaatz's copy is in his diary.

92. Ltr, Spaatz to Arnold, July 14, 1943, Spaatz Papers, Diary.

93. 1st and 2nd endorsements of report by Commanding General, Northwest African Troop Carrier Command, July 20, 1943, Spaatz Papers, Diary.

94. Ltr, Spaatz to Arnold, May 24, 1943, Spaatz Papers, Diary.

95. Entry for June 1, 1943, Command Diary, Spaatz Papers, Diary.

96. Entry for June 21, 1943, Command Diary, Spaatz Papers, Diary.

97. Conference notes, July 5, 1943, Spaatz Papers, Diary.

98. Entry for August 4, 1943, Command Diary, Spaatz Papers, Diary.

99. Entries for August 13, 15, 1943, Command Diary, Spaatz Papers, Diary.

100. Ibid.

101. Entry for August 3, 1943, Command Diary, Spaatz Papers, Diary.

102. U.S. Congress, Senate, Sen. Richard B. Russell Presenting the Conclusions of the Special Committee to Visit the War Theaters, 74th Cong., 1st Sess., October 11, 1943, *Congressional Record*, pp. 8189–8190.

103. Ltr, Spaatz to Arnold, May 24, 1943, Spaatz Papers, Diary.

104. Entry for May 13, 1943, Command Diary, Spaatz Papers, Diary.

105. Entry for May 24, 1943, Command Diary, Spaatz Papers, Diary.

106. Entries for June 1, 6, 12, 21, 1943, Command Diary, Spaatz Papers, Diary.

107. Entry for June 27, 1943, Command Diary, Spaatz Papers, Diary.

108. Entry for July 12, 1943, Command Diary, Spaatz Papers, Diary.

109. Entry for July 13, 1943, Command Diary, Spaatz Papers, Diary.

110. REDLINE msg JC–6–CS, Spaatz to Cannon, August 7, 1943, Spaatz Papers, Cables.

111. REDLINE msg CS–1–JC, Cannon to Spaatz, August 7, 1943, Spaatz Papers, Cables.

112. Butcher, *My Three Years with Eisenhower*, p. 365.

113. Chandler, *Eisenhower's Papers*, vol. 2, item 1121, msg 140, Eisenhower to Marshall, July 18, 1943, pp. 1263–1264.

114. Ibid., see footnote 2 to item 1121, p. 1265. See also msg, Eisenhower to Marshall, July 26, 1943, Spaatz Papers, Diary.

115. Entry for August 4, 1943, Command Diary, Spaatz Papers, Diary.

116. Entry for August 9, 1943, Command Diary, Spaatz Papers, Diary.

117. Slessor, *The Central Blue*, p. 557.

118. Samuel Eliot Morison, *History of United States Naval Operations in World War II*, vol. 9: *Sicily-Salerno-Anzio: January 1943–June 1944* (Boston: Little, Brown, 1954), pp. 215–216.

119. For criticism of the Allied response to the evacuation, see S. W. Roskill, *The War at Sea 1939–1945*, vol. 3, part 1, *The Offensive 1st June 1943–31st May 1944* (London: HMSO, 1960), pp. 147–150; Garland and Smyth, *Sicily and the Surrender of Italy*, pp. 411–412.

120. Molony, *The Campaign in Sicily and Italy*, p. 184.

121. Roskill, *The War at Sea*, vol. 3, part 1, p. 148. For this account of the evacuation Roskill appears to have examined Coningham's papers.

122. Garland and Smyth, *Sicily and the Surrender of Italy*, p. 412.

123. Roskill, *The War at Sea*, vol. 3, part 1, pp. 148–149.

124. Coningham, "The Development of Tactical Air Forces," *RUSI Journal* XCI (May 1946), p. 216.

125. Entry for August 9, 1943, Command Diary, Spaatz Papers, Diary.

126. Entries for August 11–17, 1943, Command Diary, Spaatz Papers, Diary.

127. Entry for August 4, 1943, Command Diary, Spaatz Papers, Diary.

128. Garland and Smyth, *Sicily and the Surrender of Italy*, pp. 411–412; Roskill, *The War at Sea*, vol. 3, part 1, pp. 147–150.

Chapter 8

Salerno and London

1. Ltr, Spaatz to Eaker, September 18, 1944, Spaatz Papers, Diary.

2. Craven and Cate, *Torch to Pointblank*, p. 544.

3. Chandler, *Eisenhower's Papers*, vol. 3, item 1257, msg 476, Eisenhower to CCS, September 15, 1943, pp. 1424–1425.

4. Craven and Cate, *Torch to Pointblank*, p. 538.

5. Morison, *Sicily-Salerno-Anzio*, p. 280. Morison's figures are for the entire operation not just the counterattack period. He does not state just how many of the 11,000 tons of naval shellfire fell from September 12–15 as opposed to the preliminary assault and follow up naval bombardments. Nonetheless naval gunfire was, in most cases, more accurate than an attack and of comparable weight in the aggregate.

6. Ltr, Alexander to Spaatz, September 17, 1943, Spaatz Papers, Diary.

7. Chandler, *Eisenhower's Papers*, vol. 3, item 1262, msg, Eisenhower to McNarney, September 16, 1943, pp. 1428–1430.

8. Ibid., item 1253, msg, Eisenhower to Marshall, September 14, 1943, pp. 1416–1417. See also ltr, Spaatz to Arnold, September 15, 1943, Spaatz Papers, Diary.

9. Ltr, Spaatz to Arnold, July 30, 1943, Spaatz Papers, Diary.

10. Msg, Eisenhower to Marshall, August 1, 1943, Spaatz Papers, Diary.

11. Msg A–2143, Spaatz to Eisenhower, August 27, 1943, Spaatz Papers, Diary; ltr, Spaatz to Arnold, September 15, 1943, Spaatz Papers, Diary.

12. Chandler, *Eisenhower's Papers*, vol. 3, item 1253, msg 470, Eisenhower to Marshall, September 14, 1943, pp. 1416–1417.

13. Wesley Frank Craven and James Lea Cate, *The Army Air Forces in World War II*, vol. 6: *Men and Planes* (Chicago: University of Chicago Press, 1955), pp. 516–522.

14. Msg AV–417, Spaatz to Arnold (Eyes Only), August 17, 1943, Spaatz Papers, Cables.

15. *Time*, September 20, 1943, pp. 66, 68.

16. Ltr, Arnold to Spaatz, September 10, 1943, Spaatz Papers, Diary.

17. Msg JC–99–CS, Spaatz to Cannon, September 18, 1943, Spaatz Papers, Cables.

18. See Alan M. Osur, *Blacks in the Army Air Forces During World War II: The Problem of Race Relations* (Washington, D.C.: AF/CHO, GPO, 1977), pp. 48–50. Osur identifies this officer as Col. Momyer.

19. Rpt, Maj. Gen. Edwin J. House, Commanding General, XII ASC, to Maj. Gen. John K. Cannon, Deputy Commander, NATAF, subj: Combat Efficiency of the 99th Fighter Squadron, September 16, 1943, Spaatz Papers, Diary.

20. 1st endorsement, Maj. Gen. John K. Cannon, Deputy Commander, NATAF, to Lt. Gen. Carl A. Spaatz, Commanding General, NAAF, September 18, 1943, Spaatz Papers, Diary.

21. Entry for June 4, 1943, Command Diary, Spaatz Papers, Diary.

22. 2nd endorsement, Lt. Gen. Carl Spaatz, CG, NAAF, to Gen. H. H. Arnold, CG, AAF, September 19, 1943, Spaatz Papers, Diary.

23. Osur, *Blacks in the AAF*, p. 50.

24. Minutes, Conference with General Carl Spaatz and the Gillem Board, 1,000 Hours, October 18, 1945, Spaatz Papers, Diary.

25. Interview, Curtis by Hasdorff, November 22–23, 1975, pp. 82–83.

26. Routing slip, Headquarters U.S. Air Forces Rest Camps AAFSC/MTO, May 19, 1944, AFHRC file no. 632.217.

27. Chandler, *Eisenhower's Papers*, vol. 2, item 992, msg, Eisenhower to Marshall, May 12, 1943, pp. 1129–1131.

28. Craven and Cate, *Torch to Pointblank*, pp. 477–483.

29. Ibid.

30. Ronald Schaffer, *Wings of Judgement: American Bombing in World War II* (New York: Oxford University Press, 1985), p. 46.

31. Molony, *The Campaign in Sicily and Italy*, p. 172.

32. Ibid.

33. JCS memo, Deane to Arnold, subj: Bombing Objectives, June 10, 1943, Spaatz Papers, Diary.

34. Entry for June 1, 1943, Command Diary, Spaatz Papers, Diary. This presentation made little impression on Alan Brooke, who did not mention it in his own account of the day. See Arthur Bryant, *The Turn of the Tide, A History of the War Years: Based on the Diaries of Field Marshal Lord Alan Brooke, 1939–1943* (Garden City, N.Y.: Doubleday, 1957), p. 523.

35. Entry for June 14, 1943, Command Diary, Spaatz Papers, Diary.

36. Ltr, Spaatz to Lyle G. Wilson, May 8, 1943, Spaatz Papers, Diary.

37. Matloff, *Strategic Planning for Coalition Warfare 1943–1944*, p. 151.

38. Ltr, Spaatz to Arnold, July 27, 1943, AFHRC file no. 168.491, AF/CHO microfilm reel A 1657A, frame 1015.

39. Craven and Cate, *Torch to Pointblank*, pp. 483, 684.

40. Ltr, Spaatz to Lovett, August 20, 1943, Spaatz Papers, Diary.

41. Ltr, Spaatz to Arnold, June 24, 1943, Spaatz Papers, Diary.

42. Ltr, Spaatz to Arnold, July 14, 1943, Spaatz Papers, Diary.

43. Msg, Marcus 914 RAFDEL to Air Ministry (personal for CAS), July 23, 1943, PRO AIR 20/1011.

44. Msg, Welsh 78, Air Ministry [Portal] to RAFDEL [Welsh], July 26, 1943, PRO AIR 20/1011.

45. See note by the Air Staff, Welsh to Arnold, July 31, 1943, Arnold Papers, box 274.

46. Msg, Marcus 133, Welsh to Portal, August 2, 1943, PRO AIR 20/1011.

47. Ltr, Arnold to Spaatz, August 20, 1943, Spaatz Papers, Diary. See Craven and Cate, *Torch to Pointblank*, p. 495.

48. Craven and Cate, *Torch to Pointblank*, pp. 494–496; Chandler, *Eisenhower's Papers*, vol. 2, item 1145, msg NAF–303, Eisenhower to CCS, pp. 1296–1297.

49. Craven and Cate, *Torch to Pointblank*, pp. 495, 716–717.

50. Ibid., p. 495.

51. Butcher, *My Three Years with Eisenhower*, pp. 379–380, 393, 398.

52. Chandler, *Eisenhower's Papers*, vol. 2, notes to item 1231, p. 1232.

53. CCS 303/3, August 17, 1943.

54. Minutes, CCS 101st Meeting, August 14, 1943.

55. Ltr, Arnold to Spaatz, August 20, 1943, Spaatz Papers, Diary.

56. Msg. A–2143, Spaatz to Eisenhower, August 27, 1943, Spaatz Papers, Diary; msg 6256, Eisenhower to Spaatz, August 26, 1943, Spaatz Papers, Diary.

57. Chandler, *Eisenhower's Papers*, vol. 3, item 1265, msg 497, Eisenhower to Marshall, September 18, 1943, pp. 1434–1435.

58. For Arnold's plan see CCS 217/1 "Plan to Assure the Most Effective Exploitation of the Combined Bomber Offensive," October 19, 1943. See also Craven and Cate, *Torch to Pointblank*, pp. 564–565, for the course of negotiations. Msg JSM–1276, Britman, Washington to Air Ministry, October 23, 1943, PRO AIR 20/4419, contained the British side of the decision.

59. Msg R–4757/698 (FAN 254), CCS to Eisenhower, October 23, 1943, PRO AIR 20/1011.

60. Memo, Somervell to Spaatz, October 30, 1943, msg 3787, Eisenhower [Spaatz] to Arnold, October 30, 1943; msg 1420, Arnold to Eisenhower for Spaatz, October 31, 1943, all sources in Spaatz Papers, Diary.

61. Msg W–840, Portal to Welsh, AIR PRO 20/1011.

62. Minute, Assistant Chief of the Air Staff (Ops.) to the Chief of the Air Staff, October 25, 1943, AIR PRO 20/1011.

63. Msg OZ–3387 (COS [W] 908), British Chiefs of Staff to Britman, Washington, PRO AIR 20/4419.

64. Minute D.191/3, Churchill to Chiefs of Staff and Portal, PRO AIR 20/1011.

65. Msg JSM 1290, from Joint Staff Mission, Washington, to War Cabinet Office, London, October 29, 1943, PRO AIR 20/4419.

66. See JCS memo to the President (aboard the U.S.S. *Iowa*), November 17, 1943, and CCS 400 "Integrated Command of U.S. Strategic Air Forces in the European—Mediterranean Area,"

November 18, 1943, *FRUS: Cairo-Teheran*, pp. 203–209 plus organization charts, and pp. 228–232.

67. Msg, Marcus 133, Welsh to Portal, August 2, 1943, PRO AIR 20/1011.

68. Arnold's "Trip to England" Notebook, August 31–September 8, 1943, Arnold Papers, Journals File, box 271.

69. List of 23 points for Gen. Arnold's personal action resulting from trip to England, September 6, [1943], HQ Eighth Air Force, Office of the Assistant Chief of Staff, A–2, Arnold Papers, Official File, box 49.

70. Robert E. Sherwood, *Roosevelt and Hopkins: An Intimate History* (New York: Harper & Brothers, rev. ed., 1950), p. 764, citing memo, Hopkins to FDR, October 4, 1943.

71. Copp, *Forged in Fire*, p. 445.

72. Memo, JCS to the President, November 17, 1943, *FRUS: Cairo-Teheran*, pp. 203–209.

73. CCS 400, November 18, 1943, *FRUS: Cairo-Teheren*, pp. 228–232.

74. For British arguments against setting up a Supreme Strategic Bombing Commander, see CCS 400/1 "Control of Strategic Air Forces in Northwest Europe and the Mediterranean," memo by the British Chiefs of Staff, Cairo, November 26, 1943, *FRUS: Cairo-Teheran*, pp. 432–435. See also Craven and Cate, *Torch to Pointblank*, p. 748.

75. Butcher, *My Three Years with Eisenhower*, pp. 446–448.

76. Ibid.

77. Churchill-Marshall Dinner Meeting, November 23, 1943, and meeting of the CCS with Roosevelt and Churchill, November 24, 1943, *FRUS: Cairo-Teheran*, pp. 326, 334.

78. Sherwood, *Roosevelt and Hopkins*, p. 803. See Matloff, *Strategic Planning 1943–44*, p. 381, for a concise analysis of this decision.

79. Minutes, CCS 134th meeting, December 4, 1943, and Minutes, CCS 138th meeting, December 7, 1943, *FRUS: Cairo-Teheran*, pp. 681–686 and 756–757.

80. CCS 400/2 "Control of Strategic Air Forces in Northwest Europe and in the Mediterranean," December 4, 1943, *FRUS: Cairo-Teheren*, pp. 787–789.

81. Minutes, CCS 138th Meeting, December 7, 1943, *FRUS: Cairo-Teheren*, p. 757.

82. Minutes, CCS 134th Meeting, December 4, 1943, *FRUS: Cairo-Teheren*, p. 685.

83. Arnold, *Global Mission*, p. 445. See also Trip to England, August 31, 1943–September 8, 1943, Arnold Papers, Journals, box 271.

84. Arnold, Global Mission, p. 450.

85. Ibid., pp. 472–473.

86. Trip to Sextant, November 11, 1943–December 15, 1943, Arnold Papers, Journals, box 272. This is Arnold's diary of the trip and contains much valuable information. See also Copp, *Forged in Fire*, p. 447.

87. Entry for December 8, 1943, Command Diary, Spaatz Papers, Diary.

88. Butcher, *My Three Years with Eisenhower*, p. 455; Eisenhower, *Crusade in Europe*, p. 217. Both authors give the strong impression that Eisenhower merely approved of Spaatz's appointment and did not propose it.

89. Trip to Sextant, Arnold Papers, Journals, box 272.

90. [Memo for the Record], "Principle Points Discussed with General Arnold," n.d. [ca. December 8, 1943], Spaatz Papers, Diary.

91. Ibid.

92. Ibid.

93. Chandler, *Eisenhower's Papers*, vol. 3, item 1428, msg W–8550, Eisenhower to Marshall, December 25, 1943, pp. 1611–1612.

94. Butcher, *My Three Years with Eisenhower*, p. 455.

95. Ibid., p. 456.

96. Chandler, *Eisenhower's Papers*, vol. 3, item 1428, msg W–8550, Eisenhower to Marshall, December 25, 1943, pp. 1611–1612.

97. Entry for December 9, 1943, Command Diary, Spaatz Papers, Diary.

98. Ibid.

99. See ltrs, Arnold to Eaker, June 15, 1943; July 7, 1943; August 1, 1943; Arnold Papers, File BC to GB, box 49, and msg R–3550, Arnold to Eaker, Eaker Papers, box 16.

100. Memo, Notes on Strategic Bombardment Conference, Gibraltar, November 8, 9, 10, 1943, by Col. George C. McDonald, Spaatz Papers, Diary.

101. Msg W–4779 (MC OUT 2784), Spaatz and Eaker to Arnold, November 9, 1943, Spaatz Papers, Diary.

102. Ltr, AM W. L. Welch, Head, RAF Delegation in Washington, to Arnold, December 14, 1943, AF/CHO microfilm reel 34163, frames 1260–1261. This letter contains the text of Portal's message to Arnold and is found in a microfilm copy of the Papers of Gen. Lawrence Kuter. The originals are part of the manuscript collections of the U.S. Air Force Academy at Colorado Springs. See Parton, *"Air Force Spoken Here,"* pp. 329–346. Parton, who examined many of the same sources, reaches some different conclusions in his defense of Eaker during this period.

103. Msg R–7075, Arnold to Eaker, December 18, 1943, Eaker Papers, box 16.

702

104. Interview, Lt. Gen. Ira C. Eaker by Arthur K. Marmor, January 1966, USAF Oral History Collection, AFHRC file no. K239–0512.626, p. 13.

105. Ltr, Eaker to Fechet, December 22, 1943, Eaker Papers, box 7.

106. Msg, Eaker to Arnold, December 19, 1943, Eaker Papers, box 16.

107. For the text of Eaker's message to Spaatz, see msg AF–434, Spaatz to Arnold, December 19, 1943, Spaatz Papers, Diary.

108. Ltr, Welsh to Arnold, December 20, 1943, AF/CHO microfilm reel 34163, frames 1262–1263. This letter contains the text of Portal's message to Arnold; the original is from the Kuter Papers at the Air Force Academy.

109. Ibid.

110. Msg R–7136, Arnold to Devers, December 20, 1943, Eaker Papers, box 16. The attribution to Kuter can be found in Copp, *Forged in Fire*, p. 450. For an example of Kuter's criticisms of Eaker's performance, see memo, Kuter to Arnold, October 26, 1943, AF/CHO microfilm reel B 5046, frame 1825. In the memo Kuter says with regard to the bombing record of the Eighth from April 1 to October 20, "Only a *very small weight* of bombers has been utilized against the *primary targets in Pointblank*, and fewer against the type targets now recommended by the Committee of Target Analysts in the USA, namely, Fighter Aircraft, Ball Bearings, and Grinding Wheels" [emphasis in the original].

111. Ltr, Arnold to Welsh, December 27, 1943, AF/CHO microfilm reel 34163, frame 1266, Kuter Papers, Air Force Academy.

112. Msg A–4989, Arnold to Eaker, December 21, 1943, Eaker Papers, box 16.

113. Msg AF–434, Spaatz to Arnold, December 19, 1943, Spaatz Papers, Diary.

114. Entry for December 23, 1943, Command Diary, Spaatz Papers, Diary.

115. Entry for December 9, 1943, Command Diary, Spaatz Papers, Diary.

116. Interview, Spaatz by Shaughnessey, 1959–1960, pp. 65–66.

117. Entry for December 23, 1943, Command Diary, Spaatz Papers, Diary.

118. Ibid.

119. Forrest Pogue, *George C. Marshall: Organizer of Victory 1943–1945* (New York: Viking, 1973), pp. 324–325.

120. Msg 5585, Marshall to Eisenhower, [received] December 24, 1943, D. D. Eisenhower Pre-Presidential Papers, Official Cable File, Eisenhower Library, Abilene, Kans.

121. Entry for December 25, 1943, Command Diary, Spaatz Papers, Diary.

122. Chandler, *Eisenhower's Papers*, vol. 3, item 1428, msg W–8550, Eisenhower to Marshall, December 25, 1943, pp. 1611–1615.

123. Ibid., vol. 3, item 1429, msg 19181, Eisenhower to Eaker, December 25, 1943, pp. 1615–1616.

124. Entry for December 26, 1943, Command Diary, Spaatz Papers, Diary.

125. Ibid.

126. Interview, Spaatz by Shaughnessey, 1959–1960, p. 63.

127. Ibid., p. 65.

128. Interview, Gen. Carl A. Spaatz by the U.S. Air Force Academy Department of History, September 27, 1968, p. 18.

129. Ibid.

130. Craven and Cate, *Torch to Pointblank*, p. 750.

131. Ltr, Arnold to Spaatz, n.d. [late February 1944], AFHRC file no. 168.491, AF/CHO microfilm reel A 1657, frames 1082–1085. Spaatz received this letter on March 1 and returned his copy, one of only two made, with his reply. A copy of Spaatz's copy, with Spaatz's penciled notations faithfully transcribed, found its way into AAF files and thence to microfilm.

132. Chandler, *Eisenhower's Papers*, vol. 3. The following cables and the footnotes to them contain discussion of Marshall's replies to Eisenhower: item 1428, msg W–8550, December 25, 1943; item 1440, msg W–8678, December 27, 1943; item 1445, msg W–8710, December 28, 1943; and item 1449, December 29, 1943, pp. 1611–1614, 1622–1624, 1626–1628, and 1630–1631.

133. British Air Ministry, Air Historical Branch, RAF Narrative, "The North African Campaign," pp. 152–153.

Part Four
The Point of the Blade
Strategic Bombing and
the Cross-Channel Invasion

1. USSBS, Aircraft Division, Industry Report, vol. 4, 2d ed. (Washington, D.C.: GPO, 1947), p. 5.

2. Charles Webster and Noble Frankland, *The Strategic Air Offensive Against Germany, 1939–1945*, vol. 2: *Endeavor* (London: HMSO, 1961), p. 83.

3. Msg K–3189, Spaatz to Arnold, January 19, 1944, Spaatz Papers, Diary.

4. Craven and Cate, *Torch to Pointblank*, pp. 364–365.

5. Ibid., pp. 356–357.

Chapter 9
The Luftwaffe Engaged

1. Ltr, Spaatz to Arnold, January 10, 1944, Spaatz Papers, Eighth Air Force File, 1942–1945.

2. Msg 9524, Arnold to Spaatz, January 31, 1944, Spaatz Papers, Diary.

3. Craven and Cate, *Torch to Pointblank*, pp. 705–706.

4. Ibid.

5. Freeman, *Mighty Eighth War Diary*, p. 126.

6. Ibid., pp. 704, 729.

7. *FRUS: Cairo-Tehran*, 133d meeting of the CCS., p. 685.

8. Carrier Sheet, subj: "Loss Rate By Combat Crew Experience," Lt. Col. H. Fay to Col. E. Cook, Deputy Chief of Staff USSTAF, January 10, 1944, Spaatz Papers, Diary.

9. Memo for the Chief of Staff from Arnold, subj: Army Air Forces Heavy Bomber Crew Loss Rates in Eighth Air Force in U.K., December 27, 1943, Arnold Papers, Operations folder: box 44.

10. Craven and Cate, *Torch to Pointblank*, p. 705.

11. Ibid., p. 639.

12. Murray, *Strategy for Defeat* , p. 234.

13. Wesley Frank Craven and James Lea Cate, *The Army Air Forces in World War II*, vol. 3, *Europe: Argument to V-E Day, January 1944 to May 1945* (Chicago: University of Chicago Press, 1951), p. 26.

14. See Murray Green, "The Pen and the Sword," in John L. Frisbee, ed., *The Makers of the United States Air Force* (Washington, D.C.: AF/CHO, GPO, 1987) pp. 99–126 for a short biography of Hugh Knerr.

15. Craven and Cate, *Torch to Pointblank*, pp. 755–756. See also Command Diary, entry for December 30, 1943, and conference notes, December 31, 1943, Spaatz Papers, Diary.

16. Ltr, Spaatz to Arnold, March 18, 1944, Spaatz Papers, Diary.

17. Msg, Smith to Eisenhower, January 1, 1944, Spaatz Papers, Diary.

18. Entry for January 1, 1944, Command Diary, Spaatz Papers.

19. Sir Frederick Morgan, *Overture to Overlord* (Garden City, N.Y.: Doubleday, 1950), p. 257.

20. Osur, *Blacks in the Army Air Forces*, p. 100, citing ltr, Eaker to Osur, December 5, 1974.

21. Ibid., pp. 100–102.

22. Mattie E. Treadwell, *United States Army in World War II*, subseries: *Special Studies: The Woman's Army Corps* (Washington, D.C.: OCMH, GPO, 1954), p. 384.

23. Entry for January 3, 1944, Command Dairy, Spaatz Papers, Diary.

24. Craven and Cate, *Argument to V-E Day*, p. 21.

25. Memo, Spaatz to CG, AAF [Arnold], subj: H2X Pathfinders for the Strategic Air Forces, January 14, 1944, Spaatz Papers, Diary.

26. Ltr, Arnold to Spaatz, January 5, 1944, Spaatz Papers, Diary.

27. Ltr, Spaatz to Arnold, January 10, 1944, Spaatz Papers, Eighth Air Force File, 1942–1945.

28. Memo, Spaatz to CG/AAF, January 14, 1944, Spaatz Papers, Eighth Air Force File, 1942–1945.

29. Minutes of Commanders' Meeting,

September 10, 1943, Eaker Papers, box 20.

30. FM 100–20, chap. 2, sec. 2, para. 13, p. 9.

31. Ibid., para. 12, p. 8.

32. Ibid., sec. 3, para. 16, p. 10.

33. Memo to General Marshall, from Arnold, subj: CCS Air Plan for the Defeat of Germany, November 3, 1943, Arnold Papers, folder: JCS, box 43.

34. W. W. Rostow, *Pre-Invasion Bombing Strategy: General Eisenhower's Decision of March 25, 1944* (Austin: University of Texas Press, 1981), pp. 17–18.

35. Entry for January 4, 1944, Command Diary, Spaatz Papers, Diary.

36. Entries for May 10, 14, 15, 16, 1942, Command Diary, Spaatz Papers, Diary.

37. Entries for January 6, 8, 1944, Command Diary, Spaatz Papers, Diary.

38. Memo, Spaatz to CG, Eighth Air Force, subj: Operational Directive, n.d. [January 11, 1944], Spaatz Papers, Subject File 1929–1945.

39. Msg K–3214, Spaatz to Arnold, January 21, 1944, Spaatz Papers, Diary.

40. Ltr, Spaatz to Arnold, January 23, 1944, Spaatz Papers, Diary.

41. Ibid.

42. Ltr, Spaatz to Lovett, January 23, 1944, Spaatz Papers, Diary.

43. Entry for January 22, 1944, Command Diary, Spaatz Papers, Diary.

44. Ibid.

45. Murray, *Strategy for Defeat*, chart, p. 234.

46. Stephen L. McFarland, "The Evolution of the American Strategic Fighter in Europe 1942–44," *The Journal of Strategic Studies* X (June 1987), pp. 193–194; interview, Lt. Gen. Barney M. Giles by James C. Hasdorff, November 20–21 1974, USAF Oral History Collection, AFHRC file no. K239.0512–814, pp. 98–99; Benjamin S. Kelsey, *The Dragon's Teeth* , p. 68.

47. For a sketch of Kepner's life see Paul F. Henry, "William E. Kepner: All the Way to Berlin," in Frisbee, *Makers of the USAF,* pp. 151–176.

48. Interview, Maj. Gen. William E. Kepner by Bruce Hopper, July 15, 1944, VII F.C. HQ, Spaatz Papers, Subject File 1929–1945.

49. Hinsley, *British Intelligence,* vol. 3, part 2, p. 317.

50. Craven and Cate, *Argument to V-E Day,* pp. 22–24.

51. Freeman, *Mighty Eighth War Diary,* p. 165. Freeman also notes three additional B–17s written off as a result of battle damage.

52. Ibid. See also notes of "Information Available Regarding Heavy Bomber Mission 11 January," n.d. [mid-January] Spaatz Papers, Diary.

53. Record, telephone conference, January 12 [13?], 1944, 1800 hrs British time, Spaatz Papers, Diary.

54. Ltr, Arnold to Spaatz, January 24, 1944, AFHRC file no. 168.491, AF/CHO microfim reel A 1657A, frames 1064–1065.

55. Msg K–3214, Spaatz to Arnold, January 21, 1944, Spaatz Papers, Diary.

56. Ltr, Spaatz to Lovett, January 23, 1944, Spaatz Papers, Diary.

57. Craven and Cate, *Argument to V-E Day,* pp. 24–25; Carter and Mueller, *Combat Chronology 1941–1945,* pp. 263–264.

58. Msg AX–621, Air Ministry to USSTAF, February 17, 1944, Spaatz Papers, Diary.

59. Peter Wykeham, *Fighter Comand; A Study of Air Defence, 1914–1960* (London: Putnam, 1960), pp. 242–243.

60. Terraine, *A Time for Courage,* p. 196.

61. Denis Richards, *Royal Air Force, 1939–1945,* vol. 1, *The Fight at Odds* (London: HMSO, 1953), p. 194.

62. British Air Ministry, Air Historical Branch, RAF Narrative, "The Liberation of North West Europe," vol. 1, "The Planning and Preparation of the Allied Expeditionary Air Force for the Landings in Normandy," pp. 33–35. The narrative by the RAF Historical Section was prepared exclusively from original security-classified documentation. The bulk of its documentation comes from the Papers of Air Chief Marshal Leigh-Mallory, which have since found their way from the Air Ministry to the Public Records Office. It is probably the best, if not the only, history of the AEAF and presents the views of Leigh-Mallory clearly and accurately.

63. Terraine, *A Time for Courage,* p. 196.

64. Russell F. Weigley, *Eisenhower's Lieutenants: The Campaigns of France and Germany, 1944–1945* (Bloomington: Indiana University Press, 1981), p. 59.

65. E. J. Kingston-McCloughry, *The Direction of War: A Critique of the Political Direction and High Command in War* (London: Jonathan Cape, 1955), p. 121.

66. Terraine, *A Time for Courage,* p. 196.

67. Weigley, *Eisenhower's Lieutenants,* p. 59.

68. Numerous entries in Vandenberg's diaries, Papers of Hoyt S. Vandenberg, Library of Congress, Manuscript Division; interview, Gen. Frederic H. Smith by James C. Hasdorff and Brig. Gen. Noel F. Parrish, USAF Oral

History Collection, June 7–8, 1976, AFHRC file no. K 239.0512–903.

69. For Coningham's difficulties with Leigh-Mallory, see D'Este, *Decision in Normandy*, pp. 214, 222–225. For an example of Leigh-Mallory's treatment of Brereton, see Lewis H. Brereton, *The Brereton Diaries* (New York: William Morrow, 1946), p. 228, entry for December 10, 1943.

70. Kingston-McCloughry, *The Direction of War*, p. 120.

71. Weigley, *Eisenhower's Lieutenants*, pp. 58–59.

72. D'Este, *Decision in Normandy*, p. 210.

73. Ltr, Maj. Gen. William O. Butler, USAAF Branch, HQ COSSAC, to Maj. Gen. Barney M. Giles, Chief of Air Staff, 13 November 1943. AFHRC file no. 168. 491, AF/CHO microfilm reel A 1657, frame 530.

74. Entry for February 15, 1944, Command Diary, Spaatz Papers, Diary.

75. Weigley, *Eisenhower's Lieutenants*, p. 59.

76. British Air Ministry, Air Historical Branch, RAF Narrative, "The Liberation of North West Europe," vol. 1, " AEAF Planning and Preparation," pp. 25–27.

77. Entry for January 3, 1944, Command Diary, Spaatz Papers, Diary.

78. Charles Webster and Noble Frankland, *The Strategic Air Offensive Against Germany 1939–1945*, vol. 3, *Victory* (London; HMSO, 1961), p. 16.

79. Msg W–9378/8965, Morgan to Eisenhower, January 9, 1944, Spaatz Papers, Diary. See note at bottom of copy in Spaatz's diary, which gives his comments to Butler.

80. Msg R–8127, Marshall to Spaatz and Morgan, January 15, 1944, Spaatz Papers, Diary.

81. Chandler, *Eisenhower's Papers*, vol. 3, item 1423, msg, Eisenhower to Marshall, December 17, 1943, pp. 1604–1607.

82. Ibid., item 1470, msg, Eisenhower to Marshall, January 31, 1944, pp. 1648–1649.

83. Ibid.

84. Ibid.

85. Ibid., item 1472, msg 6490, Eisenhower to Smith, January 5, 1944, pp. 1651–1652.

86. Ltr, Arnold to Eisenhower, January 17, 1944, Arnold Papers, Correspondence.

87. Conference notes, Spaatz, Eaker, Giles, January 9, 1944, Spaatz Papers, Diary.

88. Entry for January 17, 1944, Command Diary, Spaatz Papers, Diary.

89. Ibid.

90. Entry for January 22, 1944, Command Diary, Spaatz Papers, Diary.

91. Entry for January 24, 1944, Command Diary, Spaatz Papers, Diary.

92. Msg K–3189, Spaatz to Arnold, January 19, 1944, Command Diary, Spaatz Papers, Diary.

93. Ibid. See notes on Eisenhower's corrections on copy in Spaatz's files.

94. Entry for June 20, 1944, Command Diary, Spaatz Papers, Diary.

95. Entry for January 21, 1944, Command Diary, Spaatz Papers, Diary.

96. Entry for January 20, 1944, Command Diary, Spaatz Papers, Diary.

97. Entry for January 24, 1944, Command Diary, Spaatz Papers, Diary.

98. Ltr, Spaatz to Arnold, February 1, 1944, Spaatz Papers, Diary. Margin notes on this document indicate Spaatz did not send it to Arnold, but instead retained it for his own files.

99. Memo, to General Spaatz, subj: "Conference at Air Chief Marshal Leigh-Mallory's Headquarters," from F. L. Anderson, February 4, 1944, Spaatz Papers, Diary.

100. Ltr, Portal to Spaatz, February 15, 1944, Spaatz Papers, Diary.

101. Ibid.

102. Craven and Cate, *Argument to V-E Day*, p. 109.

103. Conference notes, February 19, 1944, Spaatz Papers, Diary.

104. Ibid.

105. Msg IE–129 CS [Redline], Spaatz to Eaker, February 19, 1944, Spaatz Papers, Cables File.

106. Craven and Cate, *Argument to V-E Day*, p. 32.

107. Ibid., p. 31. See also ltr, Spaatz to Arnold, January 23, 1944, Spaatz Papers, Diary; interview, Col. R. D. Hughes by Bruce C. Hopper, London, March 20, 1944, p. 1, Spaatz Papers, Subject File 1929–1945; Hughes stated, "We were all resigned to losing 150–200 heavies on the first initial show."

108. Msg. Spaatz to Eaker, February 19, 1944, Spaatz Papers, Diary. The message was cancelled by Spaatz before transmission to Eaker.

109. Entry for February 19, 1944, Command Diary, Spaatz Papers, Diary.

110. Craven and Cate, *Argument to V-E Day*, p. 32.

111. Ibid.

112. Bernard Boylan, *Development of the Long-Range Escort Fighter* (USAF Historical Study No. 139 K101–136, 1955), p. 180.

113. Roger Freeman, *Mighty Eighth War*

706

Diary (London: Jane's, 1981), pp. 183, 297. Also see Kelsey, *Dragon's Teeth*, pp. 134–135. Kelsey made the first P-38 test flight, served as the project officer for the P-38's development, and in 1943–1944 commanded the Eighth Air Forces Operational Engineering Section. In his view, the performance of P-38s in Europe was hampered by their pilot's poor opinion of their performance an opinion, not shared by P-38 pilots in other theaters of operation.

114. Interview, Williamson by Hopper, June 14, 1944.

115. Ibid.

116. Haywood S. Hansell, *The Air Plan That Defeated Hitler* (Atlanta: Higgins-McArthur/Longino and Porter, 1972), p. 181.

117. Craven and Cate, *Argument to V-E Day*, p. 34.

118. Interview, Williamson by Hopper, June 14, 1944.

119. Ibid.

120. Compiled from Bomb Group Mission reports found in Freeman, *Mighty Eighth War Diary*, pp. 183 188.

121. Murray, *Strategy for Defeat*, p. 242; Craven and Cate, *Argument to V-E*, p. 43.

122. Combined Operational Planning Committee, "Third Periodic Report on Enemy Daylight Fighter Defenses and Interception Tactics, Period 15 February 1944–2 March 1944," March 26, 1944, Spaatz Papers, Subject File 1929–1945.

123. Murray, *Strategy for Defeat*, p. 242.

124. Ibid., p. 234.

125. Craven and Cate, *Argument to V-E Day*, p. 45.

126. British Air Ministry, Air Historical Branch, RAF Narrative, "The RAF in the Bombing Offensive Against Germany," vol. 5, "The Full Offensive, February 1943–February 1944," p. 164.

127. Ibid., p. 165.

128. Ibid.

129. Craven and Cate, *Argument to V-E Day*, pp. 45–47; Murray, *Strategy for Defeat*, pp. 253–255.

130. Craven and Cate, *Argument to V-E Day*, pp. 43–44.

131. Ltr, Spaatz to Arnold, n.d. [early March 1944], Spaatz Papers, Diary.

132. Ibid.

133. Ibid.

134. Ibid.

135. Interview, Hughes by Hopper, March 20, 1944.

136. Ibid.

137. Webster and Frankland, *The Strategic*

Air Offensive, vol. 3, p. 23.

138. Butcher, *My Three Years with Eisenhower*, p. 447.

139. Interview, Gen. Carl A. Spaatz by the Air Force Academy Department of History, September 27, 1968, p. 17.

140. Entry for February 10, 1944, Command Diary, Spaatz Papers, Diary.

141. Ibid.

142. Conference notes, April 10, 1944, Spaatz Papers, Diary.

143. Ibid.

144. Webster and Frankland, *The Strategic Air Offensive*, vol. 3, pp. 24–25.

145. Max Hastings, *Bomber Command* (New York: Dial, 1980), pp. 263–268; Murray, *Strategy for Defeat*, pp. 216–222.

146. Murray, *Strategy for Defeat*, p. 220.

147. Webster and Frankland, *The Strategic Air Offensive*, vol. 3, p. 27.

148. Zuckerman, *Apes to Warlords*, pp. 216–220.

149. AEAF/MS 22007/Air Ops., "'OVERLORD' Employment of Bomber Forces in Relation to the Outline Plans," February 12, 1944, Spaatz Papers, Diary.

150. Rostow, *Pre-Invasion Bombing Strategy*, pp. 46–47 and 50. See also Arthur Tedder, *With Prejudice*, p. 489.

151. Memo, Assistant Director of Intelligence, USSTAF [Hughes] to Deputy Commander for Operations, "Planning Conference at Norfolk House," January 25, 1944, Spaatz Papers, Diary.

152. Draft msg, Spaatz to Arnold, February 7, 1944, Spaatz Papers, Diary.

153. Ibid.

154. Memo, Assistant Director of Intelligence, USSTAF [Hughes] to CG, USSTAF [Spaatz], subject "Conference Held at AEAF Headquarters, Stanmore 15 February 1944," February 15, 1944, Spaatz Papers, Diary.

155. AEAF/MS 22007/Air Ops., February 12, 1944, p. 1.

156. Memo, Hughes to Spaatz, February 15, 1944, Spaatz Papers, Diary.

157. Ibid.

158. Zuckerman, *Apes to Warlords*, p. 235.

159. Memo, Hughes to Spaatz, February 15, 1944, Spaatz Papers, Diary.

160. Ibid.

161. Ibid.

162. Entry for February 15, 1944, Command Diary, Spaatz Papers, Diary.

163. Chandler, *Eisenhower's Papers*, vol. 3, item 1539, msg, Eisenhower to Marshall, February 9, 1944, p. 1715.

164. Entry for February 17, 1944, Command

Diary, Spaatz Papers, Diary.

165. Zuckerman, *Apes to Warlords*, p. 228.

166. Entry for February 17, 1944, Command Diary, Spaatz Papers, Diary.

167. Entry for February 19, 1944, Command Diary, Spaatz Papers, Diary.

168. Msg K–3769, Spaatz to Arnold, Spaatz Paper, Diary.

169. Entry for February 19, 1944, Command Diary, Spaatz Papers, Diary.

170. Ibid.

171. Msg K–3769, Spaatz to Arnold, Spaatz Papers, Diary.

172. Msg F–347, Arnold to Spaatz, February 20, 1944, Command Diary, Spaatz Papers, Diary.

173. Butcher, *My Three Years with Eisenhower*, pp. 498–499; Hastings, *Bomber Command*, pp. 274–275; Craven and Cate, *Argument to V-E Day*, p. 80.

174. Tedder, *With Prejudice*, p. 508.

175. Ibid., pp. 508–509.

176. Chandler, *Eisenhower's Papers*, vol. 3, item 1575, memo, Eisenhower to Tedder, February 29, 1944, pp. 1755–1756.

177. Ibid.

178. Ibid.

179. Ibid.

180. Tedder, *With Prejudice*, pp. 510–511.

181. Ibid.

182. Butcher, *My Three Years with Eisenhower*, pp. 498–499.

183. Forrest C. Pogue, *United States Army in World War II*, subseries: *The European Theater of Operations, The Supreme Command* (Washington, D.C.: GPO, 1954), p. 124.

184. Murray, *Strategy for Defeat*, table LIII, p. 240.

185. Ibid., table LII, p. 239.

186. Ibid., table L, p. 235.

187. *AAF, Statistical Digest, World War II*, pp. 100–101, table 69, and pp. 254–255, table 158.

Chapter 10

The Luftwaffe Defeated

1. Ltr, Spaatz to Arnold, March 6, 1944, Spaatz Papers, Diary.

2. Butcher, *My Three Years with Eisenhower*, p. 499.

3. Chandler, *Eisenhower's Papers*, vol. 3, item 1585, msg B–252, Eisenhower to Marshall, March 20, 1944, pp. 1766–1767.

4. Ltr, Spaatz to Arnold, March 1, 1944, AFHRC file no. 168.491,AF/CHO microfilm reel A 1657A, frames 1079–1089.

5. Pogue, *The Supreme Command*, p. 124.

6. Msg C.O.S.(W)1210, Air Ministry to British Military Mission, Washington, D.C., March 13, 1944, Spaatz Papers, Diary; and CCS 520, Control of Strategic Bombing for OVERLORD, March 17, 1944, AF/CHO microfilm reel A 5535, frames 377–379.

7. Pogue, *The Supreme Command*, p. 125.

8. Ibid.

9. Ibid.

10. Interview, Hughes by Hopper, March 20, 1944.

11. Ibid.

12. Plan for the Completion of the Combined Bomber Offensive, March 5, 1944, Spaatz Papers, Subject File 1929–1945.

13. Ibid.

14. Rostow, *Pre-Invasion Bombing Strategy*, p. 31

15. Ibid., p. 32.

16. Plan for Completion of the CBO, March 5, 1944, Spaatz Papers, Subject File 1929–1945.

17. Tedder, *With Prejudice*, p. 519.

18. Pogue, *The Supreme Command*, p. 128.

19. Ltr, Spaatz to Arnold, March 6, 1944, Spaatz Papers, Diary.

20. Memo, Arnold to the Chief of Staff, subj: Combined Bomber Offensive, March 13, 1944, Arnold Papers, Correspondence.

21. Ltr, Giles to Spaatz, March 16, 1944, Spaatz Papers, Diary.

22. Tedder, *With Prejudice*, pp. 516–517.

23. Teletype conference, Spaatz to AAF HQ, Washington, D.C., March 16, 1944, Spaatz Papers, Diary.

24. Tedder, *With Prejudice*, pp. 518–519.

25. Chandler, *Eisenhower's Papers*, vol. 3, item 1601, memo, March 22, 1944, pp. 1782–1785.

26. Webster and Frankland, *The Strategic Air Offensive*, vol. 3, p. 28.

27. Ltr, Eaker to Arnold, April 8, 1944, AFHRC file no. 168.491, AF/CHO microfilm reel A 1658, frames 893–896.

28. CAS/Misc/61, Spaatz Papers, Diary.

29. Drew Middleton, "Boss of the Heavyweights," *Saturday Evening Post*, May 20, 1944. See also Hamilton, *Master of the*

Battlefield, p. 582.

30. CAS/Misc/61, Spaatz Papers, Diary.

31. Rostow, *Pre-Invasion Bombing Strategy*, p. 45.

32. CAS/Misc/61, Spaatz Papers, Diary.

33. Ibid.

34. Ibid.

35. Ltr, Eaker to Arnold, April 8, 1944, AFHRC file no. 168.491, AF/CHO microfilm reel A 1658, frames 893–896.

36. Craven and Cate, *Argument to V-E Day*, p. 81.

37. Webster and Frankland, *The Strategic Air Offensive*, vol. 3, p. 32. See also Rostow, *Pre-Invasion Bombing Strategy*, p. 52.

38. See Henry D. Lytton, "Bombing Policy in the Rome and Pre-Normandy Invasion Aerial Campaigns of World War II: Bridge-Bombing Strategy Vindicated and Railyard-Bombing Strategy Invalidated," *Military Affairs* (April 1983) pp. 53–58; Charles F. Kindleberger, "World War II Strategy," *Encounter* (November 1978) pp. 39–42; Walt W. Rostow, "The Controversy over World War II Bombing," *Encounter* (August–September 1980) pp. 100–101.

39. Hastings, *Bomber Command*, p. 277, cites conversation with Air Commodore Sidney O. Bufton of the Air Ministry Planning Staff.

40. Stephen E. Ambrose, *The Supreme Commander: The War Years of General Dwight D. Eisenhower* (Garden City, N.Y.: Doubleday, 1970), p. 372.

41. Ltr, Eaker to Arnold, April 8, 1944, AFHRC file no. 168.491, AF/CHO microfilm reel A 1658, frames 893–896.

42. Msg U–60193, Weekly Message no. 10, Spaatz to Arnold (Eyes Only), March 26, 1944, Spaatz Papers, Diary.

43. Zuckerman, *Apes to Warlords*, p. 236.

44. Memo, Spaatz to Portal, "Use of Strategic Bombers in Support of OVERLORD," March 31, 1944, Spaatz Papers, Diary.

45. Ibid.

46. Ibid.

47. Msg W–12257, Eisenhower to Marshall, March 1, 1944, Spaatz Papers, Diary.

48. Msg B–225, Eisenhower to Marshall, March 6, 1944, Spaatz Papers, Diary.

49. Ibid.

50. Entry for March 24, 1944, Hoyt S. Vandenberg Papers, Diary, box 1.

51. Ibid., Vandenberg Diary, March 27, 1944.

52. Ibid.

53. AEAF/MS. 22005, Policy Governing Bombing Attacks on Railway Centers by U.S.

IXth Air Force, March 10, 1944, Spaatz Papers, Diary.

54. Ltr, Spaatz to Leigh-Mallory, March 15, 1944, Spaatz Papers, Diary.

55. Ltr, Spaatz to Eisenhower, March 18, 1944, Spaatz Papers, Diary. See also ltr, Spaatz to Leigh-Mallory, March 18, 1944, Spaatz Papers, Diary.

56. Butcher, *My Three Years with Eisenhower*, p. 503.

57. Chandler, *Eisenhower's Papers*, vol.3, item 1549, memorandum [for the record], March 20, 1944, p. 1776.

58. Craven and Cate, *Argument to V-E Day*, p. 123.

59. Hastings, *Bomber Command*, p. 267.

60. COPC/S.501/10/INT, Combined Operational Planning Committee, "Fourth Periodic Report on Enemy Daylight Fighter Defenses and Interception Tactics. Period 3 March 1944–31 March 1944," April 6, 1944, Spaatz Papers, Subject File 1929–1945.

61. Eighth Air Force figures compiled from individual mission reports summarized in Freeman, *Mighty Eighth War Diary*. RAF losses compiled from two separate documents: COPC/S.501/10 INT, March 12, 1944, and COPC/S.501/10 INT, April 6, 1944.

62. *AAF, Statistical Digest, World War II*, table 102, p. 190.

63. Murray, *Strategy for Defeat*, table LII, p. 239, and table LIII, p. 240.

64. Msg K–4164, Weekly Message no. 8, Spaatz to Arnold (Eyes Only), March 11, 1944, Spaatz Papers, Diary.

65. Interview, Kepner by Hopper, July 15, 1944.

66. Minutes, Commanders' Meeting, January 21, 1943, AFHRC file no. 520.141-1, AF/CHO microfilm reel A 5871, frame 1217.

67. Interview, Gen. Earle E. Partridge by Thomas A. Sturm and Hugh N. Ahann, April 23–25, 1974, USAF Oral History Collection, AFHRC file no. K239.0512–729, p. 239. Partridge served as Doolittle's deputy commander from January to May 1944. In June 1944 he took over the Eighth's 3d Bombardment Division from Maj. Gen. Curtis E. LeMay. Before going to Britain, Partridge spent eight months as the operations officer and chief of staff of the Twelfth and Fifteenth Air Forces in the Mediterranean.

68. Minutes, Commanders' Meeting, January 21, 1943, AF/CHO microfilm 520.141–1 "Commanders' Meetings," reel A 5871, frame 1217. For examples of Doolittle's earlier thinking, see rpt, Doolittle to Arnold, subj: Escort

Fighters, May 22, 1943, and rpt, Doolittle to Arnold, subj: Long Range Fighters, May 23, 1943, both in Doolittle Papers, box 19. In these documents Doolittle speaks of sending fighters on low-level sweeps ahead of escorted bomber formations to catch enemy aircraft on their fields and to strafe and bomb the fields. He implied an aggressive stance on the part of the escorting fighters by noting their capabilities of either preventing attacking fighters from "getting set" or of driving away heavily armored twin-engine fighters.

69. Entry for February 3, 1944, Command Diary, Spaatz Papers, Diary.

70. Memo, General Hansell from Lt. Col. J. H. Goddard, subj: Notes on Staff Meeting Held in Room 3E1046, 2:30 p.m., February 7, 1944; Maj. Gen. B. M. Giles presiding, February 7, 1944, AFHRC "8th Air Force Policy" File.

71. AAF Evaluation Board, ETO, "Eighth Air Force Tactical Development, August 1943–May 1945,"July 1945, AFHRC file no. 520.04.11, p. 50. This source is also available within General Kepner's personal files, AFHRC file no. 168.6005–192, AF/CHO microfilm reel A 1722.

72. Air Corps Field Manual 1–5, "Employment of Aviation in the Army," April 15, 1940, chap. 4, sec. 3, para. 66, subpara. a, pp. 40–41; Army Air Forces Field Manual 1–5, "Employment of Aviation in the Army," January 18, 1943, chap. 4, sec. 3, para. 56, subpara. a, p. 35.

73. FM 1–5, January 18, 1943, chap. 4, sec. 3, para. 66, subpara. b, p. 36

74. Army Air Force Field Manual 1–15, "Tactics and Technique of Air Fighting," April 10, 1942, chap. 1, sec. 1, para. 3, subpara. c, p. 2.

75. FM 1–15, April 10, 1942, chap. 5, sec. 7, para. 62, p. 37.

76. Ibid.

77. Ibid.

78. AAF Evaluation Board, ETO, "Eighth Air Force Tactical Development, August 1943–May 1945," p. 127.

79. Ltr, Spaatz to Arnold, subj: Long Range Fighter Sweeps, April 10, 1944, AFHRC file no. 168.491, AF/CHO microfilm reel A 1658, frames 1065–1070.

80. Adolph Galland, The First and the Last: The German Fighter Force in World War II (Mesa, Ariz.: Champlin Museum Press, 1986), p. 276. This is a reprint of the 1955 British edition.

81. AAF Evaluation Board, ETO, "Eighth Air Force Tactical Development, August 1942–May 1945," p. 52.

82. Director of Operations (AD) Minute 20849, subj: "American Long-Range Fighter Tactics, 26 April 1944," PRO AIR 20/860.

83. Ltr, Spaatz to Arnold, subj: "Long-Range Fighter Sweeps, 10 April 1944," AFHRC File no. 168.491, AF/CHO microfilm reel A 1658, frames 1065–1070.

84. Ltr, Doolittle to Leigh-Mallory, March 22, 1944, Doolittle Papers, box 19.

85. Boylan, Long-Range Escort Fighter, pp. 181–182.

86. Memo, CG, VIII Fighter Command to CG, 8th Air Force, subj: "Tactics and Techniques of Long-Range Fighter Escort" (E–A–58), July 25, 1944, AF/CHO microfilm reel B 5200, frames 142–161.

87. FM 1–5, April 15, 1940, chap. 4, sec. 1, para. 59, subpara. b, pp. 37–38.

88. FM 1–5, January 18, 1943, chap. 4, sec. 1, para. 48, subpara. g, p. 32.

89. Murray, Strategy for Defeat, p. 244.

90. Ibid.

91. AAF Evaluation Board, ETO, "Eighth Air Force Tactical Development, August 1942–May 1945," p. 127.

92. Ibid., p. 50.

93. Hinsley, British Intelligence, vol. 3, part 1, pp. 320–323.

94. Roger A. Freeman, Mighty Eighth War Manual (London: Jane's, 1984), p. 72.

95. Ltr, The Air Surgeon, Maj. Gen. N. W. Grant, to Arnold, March 29, 1944, Arnold Papers, Official Decimal File, box 91.

96. British Air Ministry, Rise and Fall of the German Air Force, 1933–1945, p. 288. See also Boylan, Long-Range Fighter Escort, pp. 203–204.

97. British Air Ministry, Rise and Fall of the German Air Force, 1933–1945, p. 296.

98. Boylan, Long-Range Fighter Escort, pp. 208–210.

99. Josef Schmid and Walter Grabmann, "The German Air Force Versus the Allies in the West," vol. 2, "The Struggle for Air Supremacy over the Reich: 1 January 1944–31 March 1944," USAF Historical Study no. 158 (1954), p. 82. Lt. Gen. Schmid commanded the Luftwaffe's I Fighter Corps during 1944. His force had responsibility for the defense of central Germany. This unpublished work is part of the USAF's German air generals' monograph project, which produced forty-two studies dealing with various aspects of the war from the Luftwaffe's perspective.

100. Josef Schmid, "The Employment of the German Luftwaffe Against the Allies in the West, 1943 to 1945," vol. 3, "Air Battles over

the Reich's Territory in Defense of the Vital Resources of the German Luftwaffe from 1 April 1944 to D-Day (June 6, 1944)," p. 4.

101. British Air Ministry, *Rise and Fall of the German Air Force*, pp. 292–293. Murray, *Strategy for Defeat*, pp. 230–231.

102. Walter Grabmann, "German Air Force Air Defense Operations" USAF Historical Study no. 164, (1956), pp. 735–736.

103. Memo, "Tactics of Long-Range Fighter Escort," July 25, 1944, p. 2; AF/CHO microfilm reel B 5200.

104. Freeman, *Mighty Eighth War Diary*, p. 195.

105. Murray, *Strategy for Defeat*, pp. 242–243.

106. Msg K–4082, Spaatz to Arnold, March 7, 1944, Spaatz Papers, Cables. This message was prepared by Spaatz's staff.

107. Ibid.

108. COPC/S.501/10/INT, April 6, 1944, Spaatz Papers, Subject File 1929–1945.

109. Freeman, *Mighty Eighth War Diary*, p. 195.

110. Ibid., pp. 89–90.

111. Murray, *Strategy for Defeat*, p. 182.

112. Freeman, *Mighty Eighth War Diary*, p. 126.

113. Murray, *Strategy for Defeat*, p. 225.

114. Freeman, *Mighty Eighth War Diary*, pp. 90, 126, 213.

115. Schmid and Grabmann, "The GAF versus the Western Allies," vol. 2, pp. 186–187.

116. COPC/S.501/10/INT, April 6, 1944, Spaatz Papers, Subject File 1929–1945. My description of the raid relies heavily on information contained in this document.

117. Freeman, *Mighty Eighth War Diary*, p. 196.

118. Ibid., figures compiled from various mission summaries within the book.

119. Murray, *Strategy for Defeat*, table L, p. 235.

120. Ibid., appendix 4, p. 345.

121. Craven and Cate, *Argument to V-E Day*, p. 66.

122. Compiled from Freeman, *Mighty Eighth War Diary*.

123. COPC/S.501/10/INT, May 8, 1944, AF/CHO microfilm reel A 5219, frames 1422–1453.

124. Transcript, telephone conversation between Brig. Gen. Orvil A. Anderson and Maj. Gen. Frederick L. Anderson, April 28, 1944, Spaatz Papers, Subject File 1929–1945.

125. Msg U–60496, Weekly Message no. 11, April 2, 1944, Spaatz to Arnold, Spaatz Papers,

Diary.

126. Msg U–60771, Spaatz to Surles, April 9, 1944, Spaatz Papers, Diary.

127. Ltr, Spaatz to Giles, April 18, 1944, Spaatz Papers, Diary. See also ltr, Spaatz to Arnold, April 10, 1944, Spaatz Papers, Diary for a detailed history of the development of the USSTAF's ideas on fighter sweeps. As an overwhelming amount of anecdotal evidence demonstrated, U.S. fighter pilots took their briefings literally. They shot at cows in the fields, pedestrians, bicycle riders, farm carts, and any moving civilian or military vehicle. Not surprisingly the German population felt far more resentment toward fighter pilots, who appeared to make personalized attacks directed against individual Germans, than against bomber crews who killed, unseen, thousands of people from 20,000 or more feet up. Anecdotal evidence also suggests more retaliation by the German civil population against shot down fighter pilots than against bomber crews.

128. Memo, Statistical Control to CG, USSTAF, "Enemy Aircraft Destroyed on the Ground," April 18, 1944, Spaatz Papers, Diary.

129. *AAF Statistical Digest, World War II*, table 104, p. 198.

130. Barry D. Watts, *The Foundations of US Air Doctrine: The Problem of Friction in War* (Maxwell AFB, Ala.: Air University Press, 1984), pp. 80–81.

131. Compiled from Freeman, *Mighty Eighth War Diary*.

132. Murray, *Strategy for Defeat*, table L, p. 235.

133. *AAF Statistical Digest, World War II*, table 2, p. 8.

134. Murray, *Strategy for Defeat*, appendix 4, p. 345.

135. *AAF Statistical Digest, World War II*, table 102, p. 190.

136. Murray, *Strategy for Defeat*, tables LII and LIII, pp. 239–240.

137. Ibid., p. 278.

138. Compiled from Eighth Air Force mission reports in Freeman, *Mighty Eighth War Diary*.

139. Ibid.

140. Ltr, Arnold to Spaatz, April 3, 1944, Spaatz Papers, Diary.

141. Ltr, Arnold to Twining [and all other Air Force Commanders], February 11, 1944, Eaker Papers.

142. Ltr, Doolittle to VIII Fighter Command and All Bombardment Divisions, subj: Retention of Personnel Completing Combat Tour, February 17, 1944, Doolittle Papers, box

19.

143. 1st Endorsement, ltr, 8th AF to CG, AAF, "Policy on Relief of Combat Crews," March 4, 1944, Doolittle Papers, box 19.

144. Ibid.

145. Freeman, *Mighty Eighth War Diary*, p. 200.

146. Memo to Arnold from the Air Surgeon, March 29, 1944, Arnold Papers, Official Decimal File, box 91.

147. Msg U–60910, Spaatz to Arnold, April 13, 1944, Spaatz Papers, Diary. USSTAF Public Relations Office prepared this message and sent it over Spaatz's signature.

148. Transcript, telephone conversation between Lt. Gen. James H. Doolittle and Maj. Gen. Frederick L. Anderson, March 9, 1944, Spaatz Papers, Subject File 1929–1945.

149. Ibid.

150. COPC/S.501/10/INT, May 8, 1944 "Period 1 April 1944–30 April 1944. AF/CHO microfilm reel A 5219, frames 1404–1419.

151. Maj. Gen. Frederick Anderson's Official Journal, entry for April 12, 1944, Spaatz Papers, USSTAF file.

152. Entry for April 13, 1944, Anderson's Official Journal.

153. Entry for January 18, 1944, Command Diary, Spaatz Papers, Diary.

154. Ltr, Spaatz to Arnold, April 16, 1944. In this cover letter Spaatz explained the transmission of his letter to Portal, a copy of which he also sent to Arnold notated "not sent" and "copy given to Amb. Winant."

155. Ltr, Spaatz to Portal, April 13, 1944, Spaatz Papers, Diary.

156. Ltr, Portal to Spaatz, April 14, 1944, Spaatz Papers, Diary.

157. Ltr, Sinclair to Winant, [n.d.] enclosed in ltr, Winant to Spaatz, April 18, 1944, Spaatz Papers, Diary.

158. Ltr, Portal to Spaatz, April 14, 1944, Spaatz Papers, Diary.

159. Entry for April 17, 1944, Command Diary, Spaatz Papers, Diary.

160. Entry for April 19, 1944, Command Diary, Spaatz Papers, Diary.

161. Ibid.

162. Entry for April 20, 1944, Command Diary, Spaatz Papers, Diary.

163. Entry for May 14, 1944, Command Diary, Spaatz Papers, Diary.

164. Draft ltr, Spaatz to Arnold [ca. March 6, 1944], March 6, 1944], Spaatz Papers, Diary. This annotated draft does not indicate whether Spaatz based a finished letter on it.

165. Ibid., msg AX–621, Air Ministry to USSTAF, February 17, 1944.

166. Ltr, Frederick L. Anderson to AM Sir Douglas Evill, Air Ministry, March 5, 1944, Spaatz Papers, Subject File 1929–1945.

167. Teletype conference transcript, March 17, 1944, Spaatz Papers, Subject File 1929–1945.

168. Craven and Cate, *Argument to V-E day*, pp. 373–384.

169. Msg U–60045, Spaatz to Arnold, March 23, 1944, Spaatz Papers, Diary. This message contains the text of Wilson's directive, the MAAF reply, and Portal's reply to Wilson.

170. Ibid.

171. Ibid.

172. Msg WAR–13234, Arnold to Spaatz, March 23, 1944, Spaatz Papers, Diary.

173. Msg WAR–13235, Arnold to Portal, March 23, 1944, Spaatz Papers, Diary. Copy sent to Spaatz as well.

174. Ltr, Arnold to Dill, March 23, 1944, Arnold Papers "JCS" folder: box 43.

175. Msg AX–779, Portal to Arnold, March 25, 1944, Spaatz Papers, Diary.

176. Msg OZ–1638, Portal to Dill, March 25, 1944, Arnold Papers, Official File 1932–1946, box 49.

177. Msg U–60100, Spaatz to Arnold, March 24, 1944, Spaatz Papers, Diary.

178. Msg WAR–13745, Arnold to Spaatz, March 24, 1944, Spaatz Papers, Diary.

179. Msg 14086, Spaata Papers, Diary.

180. Msg AX–902, Portal to Arnold, March 26, 1944, Spaatz Papers, Diary.

181. Craven and Cate, *Argument to V-E Day*, p. 174.

182. Interview, Hughes by Hopper, June 13, 1944.

183. Webster and Frankland, *The Strategic Air Offensive*, vol. 4, appendix 49 (table xxxviii), p. 516.

184. Tedder, *With Prejudice*, p. 521.

185. H. L. Ismay, *The Memoirs of General Lord Ismay* (New York: Viking Press, 1960), p. 349.

186. Winston Churchill, *The Second World War*, vol. 5, *Closing the Ring* (London: Cassell, 1952), p. 466.

187. Chandler, *Eisenhower's Papers*, vol. 3, item 1630, ltr, Eisenhower to Churchill, April 5, 1944, pp. 1809–1810.

188. Tedder, *With Prejudice*, pp. 522–529.

189. Memo for the record, subj: Meeting of April 15, n.d. [April 15, 1944], Spaatz Papers, Diary.

190. D/SAC/TS.100, ltr, Tedder to Spaatz, April 19, 1944, Spaatz Papers, Diary.

191. Ibid., pp. 538–539; report of Col.

Seibert, G–2 for Gen. Bradley, n.d. [ca. April 19, 1944], Spaatz Papers, Diary.

192. Entry for April 19, 1944, Command Diary, Spaatz Papers, Diary.

193. Pogue, *The Supreme Command*, pp. 163–164, Ambrose, *The Supreme Commander*, p. 403.

194. Entry for April 19 , 1944, Command Diary, Spaatz Papers, Diary.

195. Transcript, telephone conversation between Spaatz and Anderson, April 20, 1944, Spaatz Papers, Diary.

196. F. L. Anderson's Official Journal, entry for April 19, 1944, Spaatz Papers, USSTAF file.

197. Ibid.

198. COPC/S.501/10/INT, May 8, 1944, AF/CHO microfilm reel A 5219, frame 1425.

199. F. L. Anderson's Official Journal, entry April 19, 1944, Spaatz Papers, USSTAF file.

200. Draft of teletype text to be sent to Arnold, April 8, 1944, Spaatz Papers, Diary, marked "never sent."

201. Craven and Cate, *Argument to V-E Day*, pp. 306–307.

202. Rostow, *Pre-Invasion Bombing*, p. 148, note 28. Rostow maintains that in a personal conversation with one of the authors of the British Official History of the Strategic Bomber Offensive, Noble Frankland, he was told that Spaatz had confirmed in an interview with Frankland his threat of resignation. In addition, see Hansell, *The Air Plan That Defeated Hitler*, pp. 235–236. Hansell, who cites no sources, also claims that Spaatz threatened to quit unless he got two days over the oil targets. Conversely, Frankland has stated in a letter to this author dated January 3, 1986 that he has no record in his interviews of Spaatz confirming the resignation threat. Frankland wrote, "Whether or not he [Spaatz] threatened to resign his command over the issue I do not know."

203. Entry for April 19, 1944, Command Diary, Spaatz Papers, Diary.

204. Ibid.

205. Craven and Cate, *Argument to V-E Day*, p. 175

206. Entry for April 20, 1944, Command Diary, Spaatz Papers, Diary.

207. COPC/S.501/10/INT, May 8, 1944, AF/CHO microfilm reel A 5219, frames 1412–1413.

208. Entry for April 21, 1944, Command Diary, Spaatz Papers, Diary.

209. Compiled from Freeman, *Mighty Eighth War Diary*.

210. *AAF Statistical Digest, World War II*, table 159, p. 255.

211. Murray, *Strategy for Defeat*, tables LII and LIII, pp. 239–240.

212. Interview, Spaatz by Shaughnessey, 1959–1960, p. 73.

213. Memo, Spaatz to Doolittle and Twining, March 2, 1944, Spaatz Papers, Diary.

214. Interview, Doolittle by Burch, Fogelman, and Tate, September 26, 1970.

Chapter 11
Final Preparations for the Invasion

1. Ltr, Spaatz to Arnold, May 10, 1944, Spaatz Papers, Diary.

2. *AAF Statistical Digest: World War II*, table 160, p. 256.

3. Notes of Meeting Held in the Air C.-in-C.'s Office, 6th May 1944, TLM/MS.136/15, May 11, 1944, Spaatz Papers, Diary.

4. Hinsley, *British Intelligence*, vol. 3, part 2, p. 104.

5. Ibid., p. 105.

6. Ibid., memo, Maxwell to Spaatz, May 16, 1944; COPC/S.501/10/INT., Combined Operational Planning Committee, "Sixth Periodic Report on Enemy Daylight Fighter Defenses and Interception Tactics, Period 1 May 1944–31 May 1944," June 29, 1944, Spaatz Papers, Subject File 1929–1945.

7. Freeman, *Mighty Eighth War Diary*, p. 243.

8. Murray, *Strategy for Defeat*, p. 273.

9. Galland, *The First and the Last*, p. 280.

10. Craven and Cate, *Argument to V-E Day*, pp. 176–177.

11. Albert Speer, *Inside the Third Reich* (New York: Macmillan, 1970), p. 346.

12. Ibid., pp. 346–347.

13. Freeman, *Mighty Eighth War Diary*, pp. 252–254.

14. AAF, *Ultra and the History of the United States Strategic Air Forces in Europe vs. The German Air Force* (Frederick, Md.: University Publications of America, 1985), pp. 98–99. This study was completed by USSTAF no later than September 24, 1945.

15. Ibid., p. 99.

16. Ibid.

17. Rostow, *Pre-Invasion Bombing Strategy*, p. 52.

18. Webster and Frankland, *The Strategic Air Offensive*, vol. 4, appendix 32, pp. 321–325.

19. AAF, *Ultra and USSTAF*, p. 104. For a full and personal appreciation of the value of ULTRA to USSTAF, see Diane F. Putney, ed., *ULTRA and the Army Air Forces in World War II* (Washington, D.C.: GPO, AF/CHO, 1987). For the issue of targeting the oil plants, see pp. 35–38. This is an interview with U.S. Supreme Court Justice Lewis F. Powell, Jr., who served as an ULTRA liaison officer attached to Spaatz's headquarters.

20. Hinsley, *British Intelligence*, vol. 3, part 2, pp. 502–503.

21. Msg AX–119, Portal to Bottomley, May 3, 1944, Spaatz Papers, Diary.

22. Interview, Hughes by Hopper, June 13, 1944. See also msg AX–119, CAS (Portal) to DCAS (Bottomley), May 3, 1944, Spaatz Papers, Subject File 1929–1945.

23. Craven and Cate, *Argument to V-E Day*, p. 179.

24. Webster and Frankland, *The Strategic Air Offensive*, vol. 4, appendix 49, p. 516.

25. Craven and Cate, *Argument to V-E Day*, p. 179.

26. Draft of proposed teletype to General Arnold, April 8, 1944, Spaatz Papers, Diary, marked "never sent."

27. Entry for April 22, 1944, Command Diary, Spaatz Papers, Diary.

28. Draft ltr, Spaatz to Eisenhower, April 22, 1944, marked "shown to General Eisenhower unsigned," Spaatz Papers, Diary.

29. Ibid.

30. Entry for April 23, 1944, Command Diary, Spaatz Papers, Diary.

31. Ibid.

32. Ibid.

33. Notes of meeting at General Wilson's HQ, April 30, 1944, Spaatz Papers, Diary.

34. Tedder, *With Prejudice*, p. 526.

35. Ibid., pp. 526–527.

36. Ibid., p. 528.

37. Ibid.

38. Chandler, *Eisenhower's Papers*, vol. 3, item 1658, msg, Eisenhower to Marshall, April 29, 1944, pp. 1838–1839.

39. Ibid., transcript, telephone conversation between Doolittle and Spaatz, April 22, 1944, Spaatz Papers, Subject File 1929–1945.

40. Tedder, *With Prejudice*, pp. 528–529.

41. Chandler, *Eisenhower's Papers*, vol. 3,

item 1662, ltr, Eisenhower to Churchill, May 2, 1944, pp. 1842–44.

42. Tedder, *With Prejudice*, p. 529.

43. Ibid., p. 530.

44. Ibid.

45. Ibid., pp. 530–531.

46. Churchill, *Closing the Ring*, pp. 466–467.

47. Ibid., p. 467.

48. AAF Evaluation Board, ETO "Effectiveness of Air Attack Against Rail Transportation in the Battle of France," June 1, 1945, p. 164, AFHRC 138.4-37. This study based its figures on statistics supplied by the *Defense Passive*, the French organization responsible for calculating casualties resulting from air attacks.

49. Draft ltr, Spaatz to Eisenhower, April 22, 1944, Spaatz Papers, Diary, marked "shown to General Eisenhower unsigned."

50. Rostow, *Pre-Invasion Bombing Strategy*, pp. 41–42.

51. Craven and Cate, *Argument to V-E Day*, pp. 374–375.

52. Ibid., p. 157.

53. Hinsley, *British Intelligence*, vol. 3, part 2, pp. 111–112.

54. Interview, Smith by Hasdorff and Parrish, June 7–8, 1976, pp. 84–85. Smith's fellow brigadier generals were David Schlatter, Richard Nugent, O. P. Weyland, and Ralph Stearley.

55. Rostow, *Pre-Invasion Bombing Strategy*, p. 62.

56. Msg U–61689, Spaatz to Arnold, May 4, 1944, Spaatz Papers, Subject File 1929–1945.

57. Rostow, *Pre-Invasion Bombing Strategy*, pp. 63–64.

58. TLM/MS.136/15, Minutes of Meeting of 6 and 11 May 1944, Spaatz Papers, Diary.

59. Rostow, *Pre-Invasion Bombing Strategy*, p. 64.

60. Lytton, "Bombing Policy," *Military Affairs* (April 1983), 56.

61. Rostow, *Pre-Invasion Bombing Strategy*, appendix D, pp. 116–118. This appendix contains a copy of a mission report prepared by the 365th's commanding officer.

62. Craven and Cate, *Argument to V-E Day*, p. 158.

63. AAF Evaluation Board, ETO, "Effectiveness of Air Attack Against Rail Transportation in the Battle of France," pp. 27 and 31, AFHRC 138.4-37.

64. Rostow, *Pre-Invasion Bombing Strategy*, p. 61.

65. Craven and Cate, *Argument to V-E Day*, p. 158.

66. Tedder, *With Prejudice*, p. 537.

67. AAF Evaluation Board, ETO, "Effectiveness of Air Attack Against Transportation in the Battle of France," p. 164, AFHRC file no. 138.4–37.

68. British Air Ministry, Air Historical Branch, RAF Narrative, "The Liberation of North West Europe," vol. 1, "AEAF Planning and Preparation," p. 173, citing minutes from Churchill to the British Chiefs of Staff and the Supreme Commander.

69. Msg S–51984, Smith to Marshall, May 17, 1944, Walter Bedell Smith Papers, Eisenhower Presidential Library, Abilene, Kans.; Walter Bedell Smith, *Eisenhower's Six Great Decisions: Europe 1944–1945* (New York: Longmans, Green, 1956), p. 38; Chandler, *Eisenhower's Papers*, vol. 3, note 3 to item 1630, p. 1810.

70. Blumenson, *The Patton Papers*, vol. 2, p. 456.

71. Draft of presentation, May 15, 1944, Spaatz Papers, Diary.

72. For an excellent discussion of Montgomery's briefing and the controversy generated by the phase-lines, see D'Este, *Decision in Normandy*, pp. 90–104.

73. Craven and Cate, *Argument to V-E Day*, p. 156.

74. British Air Ministry, Air Historical Branch, RAF Narrative, "The Liberation of North West Europe," vol. 1, "AEAF Planning and Preparation," p. 178.

75. Craven and Cate, *Argument to V-E Day*, pp. 158–159. I could find no record of aircraft losses attributed only to the bridge campaign. Given the low-altitude type of attack, the relative abundance of light antiaircraft artillery, and the Germans' desperate need to defend the bridges, losses were probably heavy.

76. USSBS, Transportation Division, *The Effects of Strategic Bombing on German Transportation* (Washington, D.C.: GPO, 1947), p. 53.

77. Craven and Cate, *Argument to V-E Day*, pp. 154–155.

78. Ibid., pp. 155, 160.

79. Tedder, *With Prejudice*, pp. 538–543; Zuckerman, *Apes to Warlords*, pp. 256–258.

80. Craven and Cate, *Argument to V-E Day*, pp. 162–166.

81. Ibid.

82. British Air Ministry, Air Historical Branch, RAF Narrative, "The RAF in the Bombing Offensive Against Germany," vol. 6, "The Final Phase, March 1944–May 1945," p. 25.

83. Entry for May 23, 1944, Vandenberg Papers, Diary, box 1.

84. Entry for June 1, 1944, Vandenberg Papers, Diary, box 1.

85. Ibid.

86. Entry for June 1, 1944, Command Diary, Spaatz Papers, Diary.

87. Entry for June 2, 1944, Vandenberg Papers, Diary, box 1.

88. Hinsley, *British Intelligence*, vol. 3, part 2, pp. 104–105.

89. Entry for June 3, 1944, Command Diary, Spaatz Papers, Diary.

90. Entry for June 3, 1944, Vandenberg Papers, Diary, box 1.

91. Entry for June 3, 1944, Command Diary, Spaatz Papers, Diary.

92. Entry for June 6, 1944, Command Diary, Spaatz Papers, Diary.

93. Ltr, Spaatz to Giles, June 27, 1944, Spaatz Papers, Diary; Craven and Cate, *Argument to V-E Day*, pp. 188–193.

94. British Air Ministry, *Rise and Fall of the German Air Force*, p. 329.

95. Ltr, Spaatz to Giles, June 27, 1944, Spaatz Papers, Diary.

96. Ltr, Arnold to Spaatz, n.d.[late February 1944], AFHRC File No. 168.491, AF/CHO microfilm reel A 1657A, frames 1082–1085.

97. Craven and Cate, *Argument to V-E Day*, p. 155.

98. Ibid.

99. Eighth Air Force Statistical Summary of Operations, August 17, 1942, May 8, 1945, June 10, 1945, p. 47.

100. Eighth Air Force Monthly Summary of Operations, December 1944, with year-end summary, n.d. [early January 1945], p. 17.

101. Freeman, *Mighty Eighth War Diary*, pp. 256–259.

Part Five
The Mortal Blow
Normandy to Berlin

Chapter 12
Summer 1944
CROSSBOW, THUNDERCLAP
and Strategic Bombing

1. Entry for June 17, 1944, Command Diary, Spaatz Papers, Diary.

2. Eighth Air Force Monthly Summary of Operations, June 1944, n.d. [July 1944], AF/CHO microfilm reel A 5874, frame 1398.

3. British Air Ministry, *Rise and Fall of the German Air Force*, pp. 329–330.

4. Hinsley, *British Intelligence*, vol. 3, part 2, p. 220.

5. Ibid. See also AF/CHO Research Collection, SRH-013, *Ultra: History of US Strategic Air Forces Europe vs. German Air Forces*, pp. 197–206.

6. SRH–013, *Ultra History of USSTAF*, p. 197.

7. Ibid., p. 196.

8. Ibid., pp. 201–202.

9. Hinsley, *British Intelligence*, vol. 3, part 2, pp. 220–221.

10. British Air Ministry, *Rise and Fall of the German Air Force*, pp. 332–333.

11. Pogue, *The Supreme Command*, p. 252.

12. Terraine, *A Time for Courage*, pp. 546–547.

13. Chandler, *Eisenhower's Papers*, vol. 3, note to item 1758, p. 1933.

14. Entry for June 18, 1944, Vandenberg Papers, Diary, box 1.

15. Entry for June 18, 1944, Command Diary, Spaatz Papers, Diary.

16. Ibid.

17. Craven and Cate, *Argument to V-E Day*, p. 528.

18. Ibid.

19. Ibid., p. 531.

20. Ibid.

21. Ibid.

22. Ltr, Spaatz to Eisenhower, June 28, 1944, Spaatz Papers, Diary. Craven and Cate, *Argument to V-E Day*, p. 880, note that the copy of the document available to them carried the notation, "Carried to General E. by Gen. S., June 29, 1944."

23. Chandler, *Eisenhower's Papers*, vol.3,

item 1763, msg, Eisenhower to Marshall, June 19, 1944, pp. 1936–1937.

24. Ibid., item 1771, memo, Eisenhower to C/S, SHAEF [Smith], June 23, 1944, pp. 1946–1947.

25. Ibid., item 1786, memo, Eisenhower to DSC, SHAEF [Tedder], June 29, 1944, pp. 1960–1961.

26. Ltr, Spaatz to Eisenhower, July 10, 1944, Spaatz Papers, Diary.

27. Ibid.

28. Ibid.

29. Entry for July 10, 1944, Command Diary, Spaatz Papers, Diary.

30. Ibid.

31. Ibid., ltr, Spaatz to Tedder, July 15, 1944.

32. Memo, subj: Joint Air Staff-USSTAF CROSSBOW Committee, F. L. Anderson to Spaatz, July 21, 1944, Spaatz Papers, Diary.

33. Craven and Cate, *Argument to V-E Day*, p. 533.

34. Ibid., p. 534.

35. Ibid., p. 540.

36. Minute, Portal to Churchill, June 20, 1944, PRO PREM 3/14/2.

37. Minute, ACAS(P)/8235, ACAS(I) to Under Secretary of State (C), June 22, 1944, PRO AIR 20/842.

38. Minute, Portal to Churchill, June 21, 1944, PRO PREM 3/14/2.

39. Entry for June 20, 1944, Command Diary, Spaatz Papers, Diary.

40. Eighth Air Force Target Summary, "Statistical Summary of All Bomber Attacks, Alphabetically by Location, Period 17 August 1942–8 May, 1945," n.d. [May 31, 1945], pp. 7–8, AF/CHO microfilm reel A 5875, starting at frame 610.

41. Memo to Brig. Gen. George C. Mc-Donald, Director of Intelligence, USSTAF, subj: Operation "SHATTER," June 27, 1944, AF/CHO microfilm reel A 5616, frame 523.

42. Minute VCAS 1803, VCAS to CAS, subj: CROSSBOW, July 2, 1944, PRO AIR

8/1229.

43. Extract from COS(44) 219th Meeting (O), July 3, 1944, PRO AIR 8/1229.

44. Ibid., extract from Minutes of COS(44) 220th meeting (O), July 4, 1944.

45. Ibid., minute, CAS (Portal) to DCAS (Bottomley), July 5, 1944.

46. Ibid., COS(44) 598 (O), subj: CROSSBOW: Question of Retaliation, July 5, 1944.

47. 222d Meeting of the British Chiefs of Staff, cited in memo, Kuter to Arnold, August 9, 1944, Spaatz Papers, Diary.

48. Memo by the Air Staff, subj: Attack on German Civilian Morale, July 22, 1944, PRO AIR 20/3227.

49. Memo to DCAS from D.B.Ops, S.6, July 28, 1944, PRO AIR 20/3227.

50. Entry for July 21, 1944, Command Diary, Spaatz Papers, Diary.

51. Memo, Anderson to Director of Operations, July 21, 1944, Spaatz Papers, Subject File 1929–1945.

52. See table [Eighth Air Force Tonnage Dropped by Type Target], n.d. [ca. late May 1945], AF/CHO microfilm reel A 5871, frame 1363. This is a work sheet or draft of statistical bombing information collected by USSTAF; the column "Towns & Cities" was dropped from the final publication of this compilation.

53. COS(44) 650(O), Attack on German Civilian Morale, August 2, 1944, PRO AIR 20/4831. See attached note "Operation THUNDERCLAP," August 1, 1944.

54. Ibid.

55. Joint Board Numbered Document 355 (Serial 707), subj: Joint Board Estimate of United States Over-All Production Requirements, September 11, 1941, AFHRC file no. 145.81–23, AF/CHO microfilm reel A1370, starting frame 1413.

56. Ltr, Kuter to Anderson, August 15, 1944, Spaatz Papers, Diary.

57. Memo for Maj. Gen. F. L. Anderson, subj: "Attack on German Civilian Morale," from Col. Charles G. Williamson, September 12, 1944, Spaatz Papers, Diary.

58. Extract from COS(44) 257th Meeting (O), August 3, 1944, PRO AIR 8/1229.

59. Draft D.B.Ops comments on Attack on the German Government Machine, Outline Plan by Joint Planning Staff, J.P.(44)203(O) Revised Preliminary Draft, August 15, 1944, PRO AIR 20/4831.

60. J.P.(44) 203 Final, Attack on the German Government Machine, August 17, 1944, PRO AIR 20/8152.

61. B.Ops.1.comments on Attack on the German Government Machine to Wing Commander Ford-Kelsey, August 6, 1944, PRO AIR 20/4831.

62. COS(44) 774(O), Minute (D(K) 4/4) by the Prime Minister, Attack on the German Government Machine, August 28, 1944 [Minute dated August 23, 1944], PRO AIR 20/8152.

63. Craven and Cate, *Argument to V-E Day,* pp. 638–639. This chapter demonstrated no understanding of the background of THUNDERCLAP and presented a somewhat confused account of the proposed operation.

64. "Notes of the 81st Allied Air Commanders' Conference Held on Thursday, 24th August 1944, at HQ AEAF—1100 Hours," Spaatz Papers, Subject File 1929–1945.

65. Ltr, Spaatz to Eisenhower, August 24, 1944, Spaatz Papers, Diary.

66. 1st endorsement, Eisenhower to Spaatz, August 28, 1944, Spaatz Paper, Diary.

67. Ltr, Spaatz to Arnold, August 27, 1944, Spaatz Papers, Diary.

68. Entry for September 9, 1944, Command Diary, Spaatz Papers, Diary.

69. Webster and Frankland, *The Strategic Air Offensive,* vol. 1, p. 89, citing a Joint Planning Committee Appreciation dated August 1, 1935.

70. *AAF Statistical Digest, World War II,* table 159, p. 255; Freeman, *Mighty Eighth War Diary,* pp. 256–282.

71. *AAF Statistical Digest, World War II,* table 159, p. 255.

72. Ibid.

73. Ibid., table 59, p. 255.

74. Ibid., table 60, p. 256.

75. Murray, *Strategy for Defeat,* p. 177.

76. British Air Ministry, *Rise and Fall of the German Air Force,* p. 285.

77. Freeman, *Mighty Eighth War Diary,* p. 362.

78. British Air Ministry, *Rise and Fall of the German Air Force,* p. 286.

79. Freeman, *Mighty Eighth War Diary,* pp. 361–362.

80. Chandler, *Eisenhower's Papers,* vol. 3, item 1786, memo, Eisenhower to Tedder, June 29, 1944, pp. 1960–1961.

81. Freeman, *Mighty Eighth War Diary,* pp. 283–307.

82. Ibid. See also *AAF Statistical Digest, World War II,* table 159, p. 255.

83. Roger Freeman, *The US Strategic Bomber* (London: Macdonald and Jane's, 1975), pp. 153–154. This work's section on operational statistics extracts most of the vital bomber statistics from the *AAF Statistical Digest, World War II,* and presents them in a

more compact, useful, and more widely available form.

84. SRH–013, *Ultra History of USSTAF*, p. 217.

85. Ibid., p. 225.

86. Daily Intelligence Summary, August 18, 1944, Spaatz Papers, Diary. Although unmarked, this appears to be an ULTRA summary.

87. Compiled from Freeman, *Mighty Eighth War Diary*, pp. 311–336.

88. COPC/S.501/10/INT. "Ninth Periodic Report of Enemy Daylight Fighter Defences and Interception Tactics, 1 August 1944–31 August 1944," September 15, 1944, AF/CHO microfilm reel A 5220, frames 1551–1570.

89. Craven and Cate, *Argument to V-E Day*, p. 298.

90. Hinsley, *British Intelligence*, vol. 3, part 2, p. 509.

91. *AAF Statistical Digest, World War II*, pp. 255–256, tables 159 and 160.

92. Speer, *Inside the Third Reich*, pp. 350–351.

93. Ibid.

94. Hinsley, *British Intelligence*, vol. 3, part 2, pp. 510–511.

95. Webster and Frankland, *The Strategic Air Offensive*, vol. 4, appendix 49 (table xxxviii), p. 516.

96. Speer, *Inside the Third Reich*, p. 406.

97. Craven and Cate, *Argument to V-E Day*, p. 306.

98. Ltr, Eaker to Arnold, June 1, 1944, AFHRC File no. 168.491, AF/CHO microfilm reel A 1658, frames 957–958.

99. Freeman, *Mighty Eighth War Diary*, p. 312.

100. Table, Inventory Aging Record, Heavy Bomber Combat Crew Experience Level, n.d. [late 1944], AF/CHO microfilm reel A 5614, frames 636–637.

101. Eighth Air Force Narrative Summary, July 1944, AF/CHO microfilm reel A 5814, frame 310.

102. Ltr, B. M. Giles to Spaatz, June 19, 1944, Spaatz Papers, Diary.

103. Ibid.

104. Ltr, Spaatz to Giles, July 21, 1944, Spaatz Papers, Diary.

105. Msg U–65737, Spaatz to Arnold, July 31, 1944, War Department Communications Center (WDCC) Message File, reel 828, Modern Military Field Branch, NARA.

106. Compiled from individual mission reports in Freeman, *Mighty Eighth War Diary*, pp. 234–306.

107. Freeman, *Mighty Eighth War Diary*, pp. 270–273.

108. Msg U–64841, Spaatz to Arnold, July 13, 1944 WDCC, reel 828.

109. Msg WARX–71515, Arnold to Spaatz and Eaker, July 27, 1944, Spaatz Papers, Diary.

110. Ibid.

111. Msg U–65658, Spaatz to Arnold, July 29, 1944, Spaatz Papers, Diary.

112. Ibid.

113. Ibid.

114. Ltr, Arnold to Spaatz, August 14, 1944, Spaatz Papers, Diary.

115. Ibid.

116. Ltr, Arnold to Col. James W. Wilson, subj: "Instructions," August 14, 1944, Spaatz Papers, Diary.

117. Memo, Lt. Col. James W. Wilson to CG, AAF, subj: Combat Crew Morale in the Eighth Air Force, September 15, 1944, AFHRC File no. 168.491, AF/CHO microfilm reel A 1658, frames 1429–1431.

118. Craven and Cate, *Argument to V-E Day*, pp. 306–307. See also the report of the USSTAF Surgeon General, Memorandum Report on Morale of Combat Crew Personnel of the Eighth Air Force, August 31, 1944, AFHRC File no. 519.701, AF/CHO microfilm reel A 5737, frames 188–189. This report undermined the credibility of the diplomatic reports by pointing out that the U.S. Consul interviewed only two crews.

Chapter 13

Summer 1944
Heavy Bombers in Close Air Support

1. Craven and Cate, *Argument to V-E Day*, p. 233.

2. Ibid., p. 237.

3. Gordon A. Harrison, *United States Army in World War II*, subseries: *The European Theater of Operations, Cross-Channel Attack* (Washing-ton, D.C.: OCMH, GPO, 1951), p. 284.

4. Tedder, *With Prejudice*, p. 552.

5. Zuckerman, *Apes to Warlords*, p. 268. Zuckerman also attended this meeting.

6. Craven and Cate, *Argument to V-E Day*, p. 620.

7. Entries for May and June 1944, Vandenberg Papers, Diary, box 1.

8. Entry for June 6, 1944, Vandenberg Papers, Diary, box.1.

9. Entry for June 7, 1944, Vandenberg Papers, Diary, box.1.

10. Interview, Spaatz by Hopper, June 27, 1945, p. 13.

11. D'Este, *Decision in Normandy*, p. 214. D'Este, who has based this section of his work on AEAF historical files has by far the most complete and reliable account of the air command situation in Normandy.

12. Ibid., p. 215.

13. Ibid.

14. Nigel Hamilton, *Master of the Battlefield*, p. 648.

15. Entry for June 15, 1944, Vandenberg Papers, Diary, box 1. In this reference Montgomery's old and famous desert army, the British 8th Army, was confused with the new 2nd British Army just established on the beachhead.

16. Zuckerman, *Apes to Warlords*, p. 268.

17. Entry for June 15, 1944, Vandenberg Papers, Diary, box 1.

18. D'Este, *Decision in Normandy*, p. 223.

19. Minutes of Daily Air Commanders' Meeting, June 15, 1944, Spaatz Papers, Subject File 1929–1945; Tedder, *With Prejudice*, p. 552.

20. Tedder, *With Prejudice*, p. 552.

21. Ibid.

22. D'Este, *Decision in Normandy*, p. 224.

23. Zuckerman, *Apes to Warlords*, p. 268. Zuckerman incorrectly identifies Schlatter as belonging to USSTAF rather than Ninth Air Force.

24. Ibid., p. 270.

25. Tedder, *With Prejudice*, p. 552.

26. Ibid.

27. Zuckerman, *Apes to Warlords*, p. 270.

28. Entry for June 15, 1944, Command Diary, Spaatz Papers, Diary.

29. Ibid.

30. Entry for June 17, 1944, Command Diary, Spaatz Papers, Diary.

31. Entry for June 27, 1944, daily reflections on the course of the battle by Air Chief Marshal Sir Trafford Leigh-Mallory, dictated to Flight Lieutenant Hilary St. George Saunders, June 5, 1944–August 15, 1944, PRO AIR 37/784.

32. Leigh-Mallory Diary, June 29, 1944, PRO AIR 37/784.

33. Leigh-Mallory Diary, July 1, 1944, PRO AIR 37/784.

34. Tedder, *With Prejudice*, pp. 557–559.

35. Ambrose, *The Supreme Commander*, p. 435.

36. Tedder, *With Prejudice*, p. 557.

37. Leigh-Mallory Diary, July 8, 9, 10, 1944, PRO AIR 37/784.

38. Tedder, *With Prejudice*, pp. 559–560.

39. D'Este, *Decision in Normandy*, p. 313.

40. British Air Ministry, Air Historical Branch, RAF Narrative, "The Liberation of North West Europe," vol. 4, "The Breakout and the Advance to the Lower Rhine, June 1944–September 1944," p. 23.

41. Zuckerman, *Apes to Warlords*, p. 276.

42. British Air Ministry, Air Historical Branch, RAF Narrative, "The Liberation of North West Europe," vol. 4, "Breakout and Advance," p. 24. This narrative contains a detailed description of Zuckerman's report.

43. Zuckerman, *Apes to Warlords*, p. 277.

44. Ambrose, *The Supreme Commander*, pp. 436–437.

45. Tedder, *With Prejudice*, p. 561.

46. Leigh-Mallory Diary, July 8, 9, 10, 1944, PRO AIR 37/784.

47. Ibid.

48. Leigh-Mallory Diary, July 11, 12, 1944, PRO AIR 37/784.

49. Tedder, *With Prejudice*, p. 565.

50. British Air Ministry, Air Historical Branch, RAF Narrative, "The Liberation of North West Europe," vol. 4, "Breakout and Advance," p. 52. This monograph has detailed examinations of several of the heavy-bomber ground support operations.

51. D'Este, *Decision in Normandy*, pp. 370–378. This book offers particularly good insights into British methods, performance, and personalities during the Normandy campaign.

52. See Webster and Frankland, *The Strategic Air Offensive*, vol. 3, pp. 166–173, for a discussion in the improvement in British accuracy for the last year of the war. Much of this improvement came from Bomber Command's use of electronic bombing aids, such as Oboe and Gee-H, whose accuracy surpassed that of the American-employed H2X. For similar coverage and a comparison of the average bomb weight carried by U.S. and British heavy bombers, see the Report of the British Bombing Survey Unit (BBSU), "The Strategic Air War Against Germany 1939–1945" (London: BBSU, 1947), pp. 42–50. A copy of this work can be found in the files of the AFHRC file no. 512.552–11(c). Effectiveness is a combination of accuracy and bomb damage. The evidence indicates that Bomber Command, on the whole, delivered more of its bombs closer to its aiming

points than USSTAF. In any case many British bombs were much larger than American ones and, when on target, inflicted a higher degree of damage. German reports of damage to oil targets after AAF and RAF raids speak of the greater damage caused by heavier British ordnance.

53. Tedder, *With Prejudice*, p. 571.

54. D'Este, *Decision in Normandy*, p. 385.

55. Leigh-Mallory Diary, July 18, 19, 1944, PRO AIR 37/784.

56. Ambrose, *The Supreme Commander*, p. 439.

57. Bradley, *A Soldier's Story* p. 330.

58. Weigley, *Eisenhower's Lieutenants*, p. 137.

59. Ralph Bennett, *Ultra in the West: The Normandy Campaign, 1944–1945* (New York: Charles Scribner's Sons, 1980), pp. 99–101.

60. Omar N. Bradley, Memorandum [for the Record], subj: "Combined Air and Ground Operations west of St. Lô on Tuesday, 25 July 1944," July 25, 1944, Chester B. Hanson Diaries, U.S. Army Military History Institute, Carlisle Barracks, Pa. This memo purports to have been written on the day of the second COBRA bombing. Although it was certainly written as a justification of Bradley's actions during the period, it seems entirely too polished and knowledgeable for a document written at the time and under stressful circumstances. I assume this memo was written some time after the event, perhaps soon after the war, and inserted in the files, probably by Hanson, Bradley's personal aide-de-camp. It was probably written closer in time to the actual events than Bradley's 1951 memoirs and is at least as authentic. See also Bradley, *A Soldier's Story,* p. 339.

61. Bradley, *A Soldier's Story*, p. 338.

62. Martin Blumenson, *United States in World War II*, subseries: *European Theater of Operations: Breakout and Pursuit* (Washington, D.C.: OCMH, GPO, 1961), p. 220. Blumenson's account of COBRA is by far the most detailed, accurate, and objective published to date.

63. Ibid.

64. Bradley, *A Soldier's Story*, p. 341.

65. Blumenson, *Breakout and Pursuit*, p. 220. See also the report by Col. Harold W. Ohkle to CG, USSTAF, August 14, 1944, subj: "Report on Investigation," Spaatz Papers, Subject File 1929–1945.

66. Blumenson, *Breakout and Pursuit*, p. 220.

67. Ibid.; Bradley, *A Soldier's Story*, p. 340.

68. Bradley, *A Soldier's Story*, p. 330.

69. Ibid., p. 339.

70. Ibid., p. 340. Bradley says Spaatz attended, but Vandenberg's diary implies that Spaatz did not attend. I could find no record in Spaatz's papers to confirm his presence. General Quesada in his USAF oral history interview of May 12–13, 1975, places Spaatz and Doolittle at the meeting.

71. Ibid., p. 341.

72. Ibid.

73. Blumenson, *Breakout and Pursuit*, p. 221.

74. Entry for July 19, 1944, Vandenberg Papers, Diary, box 1.

75. Interview, Lt. Gen. Elwood A. Quesada by Lt. Col. Steve Long and Lt. Col. Ralph Stephenson, May 12–13, 1975, USAF Oral History Collection, AFHRC file no. K239.0512–838.

76. Pogue, *The Supreme Command*, p. 271.

77. Chandler, *Eisenhower's Papers*, vol. 3, item 1833, msg S–55586, Eisenhower to Marshall, July 15, 1944, p. 2008. See also editor's notes to this source for Marshall's refusal.

78. Entries for July 19–22, 1944, Vandenberg Papers, Diaries.

79. Bradley Commentary on World War II, Chester B. Hansen Collection, U.S. Army Military History Institute, Carlisle Barracks, Pa.

80. Ibid.

81. Ibid.

82. D'Este, *Decision in Normandy*, p. 384. D'Este obtained the use of Tedder's diary from Tedder's son.

83. Tedder, *With Prejudice*, p. 564.

84. Ltr, Montgomery to Maj. Gen. Frank Simpson, Director of Military Operation, cited in R. Lamb, *Montgomery in Europe 1943–1944* (London: Buchan and Enright, 1983), pp. 126–127.

85. Tedder, *With Prejudice*, p. 564.

86. Entry for July 19, 1944, Vandenberg Papers, Diary; box 1.Interview, Smith by Hasdorff and Parrish, June 7–8, 1976, pp. 95–96.

87. Bradley, *A Soldier's Story*, p. 341.

88. Blumenson, *Breakout and Pursuit*, p. 221.

89. Special Report on Operations July 24 and 25, HQ, Eighth Air Force, n.d. [ca. August 9, 1944], AF/CHO microfilm reel B 5050, frame 1185; entry for July 23, 1944, Vandenberg Papers, Diary, box 1.

90. Minutes of the 53d Allied Air Commanders' Conference, July 24, 1944, Spaatz Papers, Subject File 1929–1945.

91. Craven and Cate, *Argument to V-E Day*, p. 230.

92. Blumenson, *Breakout and Pursuit*, p. 231.

93. Hinsley, *British Intelligence*, vol. 3, part 2, p. 229.

94. Bradley, *A Soldier's Story*, p. 347.

95. Entry for July 24, 1944, Vandenberg Papers, Diary, box 1.

96. Ibid.

97. Ibid.

98. Memo for Gen. Spaatz's Diary, subj: "Operation COBRA," from Maj. Gen. Frederick L. Anderson, July 24, 1944, Spaatz Papers, Diary.

99. Entry for July 24, 1944, Vandenberg Papers, Diary, box 1.

100. Bradley, *A Soldier's Story*, pp. 347–348; Bradley's memo for the record of July 25, 1944, Hanson Collection.

101. Hinsley, *British Intelligence*, vol. 3, part 2, p. 228.

102. Ibid.

103. Blumenson, *Breakout and Pursuit*, p. 240.

104. D'Este, *Decision in Normandy*, p. 393. See also Air P/W Interrogation Detachment Report, "A.P.W.I.U.(Ninth AF Adv.) 63/1945," May 29, 1945, Spaatz Papers, Subject File 1929–1945. Bayerlein was a favorite of postwar American interrogators because of his excellent English, which enabled him to present his case more sympathetically than some of his compatriots.

105. Hinsley, *British Intelligence*, vol. 3, part 2, p. 231.

106. Bennett, *ULTRA in the West*, p. 102.

107. Blumenson, *Breakout and Pursuit*, p. 246.

108. Ibid., p. 236. Blumenson bases his figures on a USSTAF report of August 14, 1944. A possible contributing factor to McNair's death was his complete deafness. He may not have been aware of dropping bombs until it was too late to take cover.

109. Ibid.

110. Entry for July 25, 1944, Diary of Chester B. Hanson, U.S. Army Military History Institute, Carlisle Barracks, Pa.

111. Craven and Cate, *Argument to V-E Day*, p. 234. Craven and Cate put the figure at thirty-five "heavies" and forty-two mediums. In his diary for July 26, Spaatz, in looking at the bomb plots presented to him by Doolittle, estimated that "approximately sixty heavy bombers dropped short." Entry for July 26, 1944, Command Diary, Spaatz Papers, Diary.

112. Craven and Cate, *Argument to V-E Day*, p. 234.

113. Ibid., p. 233.

114. Interview, Quesada by Long and Stephenson, May 12–13, 1975.

115. "Special Report on Operations July 24 and 25, 1944," Col. Walter K. Todd, Deputy Chief of Staff for Operations to Commanding General, Eighth Air Force, n.d. [ca. August 8, 1944], AF/CHO microfilm reel B 5050, frames 1181–1204.

116. Entry for July 26, 1944, Command Diary, Spaatz Papers, Diary.

117. Ibid.; see also "Minutes of Combat Wing and Group Commanders Meeting," HQ, First Bombardment Division, July 27, 1944, AF/CHO microfilm reel B 5050, frames 1283–1284, and memo to General Doolittle, subj: "Bombing of Tactical Targets in Support of the 1st Army Assault," n.d. [August 1, 1944?], AF/CHO microfilm reel B 5050, frame 1101.

118. Freeman, *Mighty Eighth War Manual* pp. 23, 47, 234. This recent work contains a most detailed and accurate account of day-to-day operations of the Eighth Air Force. Its description of the typical mission is unequaled.

119. Entry for July 26, 1944, Command Diary, Spaatz Papers, Diary.

120. Ibid.

121. Ltr, Brig. Gen. George C. McDonald, Director of Intelligence, USSTAF, to Brig. Gen. Thomas D. White, Assistant Chief of the Air Staff, Intelligence, July 25, 1944, Papers of George C. McDonald, Air Force Academy.

122. Ltr, White to McDonald, August 1, 1944, McDonald Papers, Air Force Academy. White's comment is in a handwritten postscript.

123. Eighth Air Force, Statistical Summary of Eighth Air Force Operations, 17 August 1942–May 1945, n.d. [May 31, 1945], p. 31, Table on Bombing Accuracy.

124. By mid-1944 the Eighth Air Force had approximately two B–17 groups for every B–24 group; Fifteenth Air Force had the opposite ratio. An absolutely fair comparison of bombing accuracy between the two forces would have to account for such factors as opposition over target, escort, weather over target, distance to the target, and availability and type of electronic aiming assistance. The following figures, which convey only a very rough measure of the Eighth's and Fifteenth's accuracy, are from the forces' final statistical reports (Statistical Summary of Eighth Air Force Operations, 17 August 1942–8 May 1945, prepared June 10, 1945. Fifteenth Air Force Summary of Its

Results and Operations, 1 November 1943–8 May 1945, prepared May 20, 1945).

	Eighth Air Force	Fifteenth Air Force
January 1944	35	31
February	39	18
March	31	19
April	29	18
May	37	23
June	40	33
July	37	33
August	45	44
September–October	38	45
November–December	25	34
January 1945	29	35
February	49	33
March	38	52
April	59	81

Eighth Air Force figures cite the percentage of bombs falling within 1,000 feet of the preassigned mean point of impact (MPI) on visual missions under conditions of good to fair visibility. Fifteenth Air Force figures merely give the total percentage of bombs within 1,000 feet of the briefed MPI, apparently without regard to visibility.

125. "Eighth Air Force to CG, USSTAF," all figures taken from Special Report of Operations, July 24, 25, 1944, AF/CHO microfilm reel B 5050 frames 1181–1197.

126. Eighth Air Force, Statistical Summary of Operations, 17 August 1942–8 May 1945, p. 31. Some of this increase in accuracy can be attributed to the equipping of some of the 2nd Air Division's B-24s with advanced radar aids not made available to the other divisions.

127. Ltr, Bradley to Eisenhower, July 28, 1944, Omar N. Bradley Papers, U.S. Army Military History Institute, Carlisle, Pa., Correspondence with Eisenhower.

128. Vandenberg officially became Commanding General of the Ninth Air Force on August 7, 1944.

129. Entry for August 5, 1944, Command Diary, Spaatz Papers, Diary; entry for August 5, 1944, Vandenberg Papers, Diary, box 1.

130. Entry for August 7, 1944, Command Diary, Spaatz Papers, Diary

131. Craven and Cate, *Argument to V-E Day*, pp. 250–251.

132. Weigley, *Eisenhower's Lieutenants*, p. 204.

133. Ltr, Doolittle to Spaatz, August 10, 1944, Doolittle Papers, box 18; Freeman, *Mighty Eighth War Diary*, p. 319.

134. C. P. Stacey, *Official History of the Canadian Army in the Second World War*, vol. 3, *The Victory Campaign: The Operations in North-West Europe, 1944–1945* (Ottawa: The Queen's Printer and Controller of Stationery, 1960), pp. 223–224.

135. Weigley, *Eisenhower's Lieutenants*, p. 204. Hamilton, *Master of the Battlefield*, p. 785, contains a misleading account of the Eighth's performance on August 8. In this hagiography of Montgomery the author claims that, after the brilliant initial Canadian breakout, bombers of Spaatz's Eighth Air Force ran amok, bombing their own troops and causing more casualties than on the first day of COBRA, when Collins had to close down the offensive and start again the following day.

136. "Report of Bombing Results by Units of 1st Bombardment Division, 8 August 1944," n.d. [ca. August 10, 1944], AF/CHO microfilm reel B 5050, frames 1647–1657.

137. Entry for August 9, 1944, Command Diary, Spaatz Papers, Diary.

138. Ibid.

139. Terraine, *A Time for Courage*, p. 661.

140. Stacey, *The Victory Campaign*, pp. 243–245.

Chapter 14

Stalemate on the German Frontier

1 Msg U–68483, Spaatz to Arnold, September 24, 1944, Spaatz Papers, Diary.

2. Ltr, Spaatz to Lovett, October 1, 1944, Spaatz Papers, Diary.

3. Haywood S. Hansell, Jr., *The Strategic Air War Against Germany and Japan: A Memoir* (Washington, D.C.: AF/CHO, GPO, 1986), p.

119.

4. Michael S. Sherry, *The Rise of American Air Power: The Creation of Armageddon* (New Haven, Conn.: Yale University Press, 1987), p. 259.

5. Ronald Schaffer, *Wings of Judgement*, p. 103.

722

6. Memo, Eaker to Spaatz, subj: "Items on Conference Agenda during General Spaatz's Visit to MAAF." August 29, 1944, Spaatz Papers, Diary.

7. Ltr, Spaatz to Arnold, August 27, 1944, Spaatz Papers, Diary.

8. Ibid.

9. Ltr, Spaatz to Lovett, September 1, 1944, Spaatz Papers, Diary.

10. Ltr, Spaatz to Arnold, September 1, 1944, Spaatz Papers, Diary.

11. Ibid.

12. Ltr, Spaatz to Arnold, August 27, 1944, Spaatz Papers, Diary.

13. Ltr, Spaatz to Arnold, September 1, 1944, Spaatz Papers, Diary.

14. Entry for September 1, 1944, Command Diary, Spaatz Papers, Diary.

15. Chandler, *Eisenhower's Papers*, vol. 4, item 1930, msg FWD-13605, Eisenhower to Marshall, September 2, 1944, p. 211.

16. Ibid., item 1931, msg FWD-13657, Eisenhower to Arnold, September 3, 1944, pp. 2112-2113.

17. Ltr, Arnold to Eisenhower, September 6, 1944, Spaatz Papers, Diary.

18. Ibid.

19. Ltr, Arnold to Spaatz, September 29, 1944, Spaatz Papers, Diary.

20. Matloff, *Strategic Planning 1943–1944*, p. 511.

21. Hastings, *Bomber Command*, p. 302.

22. Webster and Frankland, *The Strategic Air Offensive*, vol. 4, pp. 47, 50–51.

23. Terraine, *A Time for Courage*, p. 672.

24. Webster and Frankland, *The Strategic Air Offensive*, vol. 2, p. 80.

25. Hastings, *Bomber Command*, pp. 323–337. See also Webster and Frankland, *The Strategic Air Offensive*, vol. 3, pp. 80–93.

26. Webster and Frankland, *The Strategic Air Offensive*, vol. 3, p. 60, note 1.

27. Ibid., pp. 58–59.

28. Msg Octagon 29. Portal and Arnold to Bottomley and Spaatz, September 15, 1944, Spaatz Papers, Diary. See also Webster and Frankland, *The Strategic Air Offensive*, vol. 4, pp. 170–172, appendix 8, xxxix.

29. Webster and Frankland, *The Strategic Air Offensive*, vol. 3, p. 62.

30. Ltr, Arnold to Spaatz, n.d. [c.a. September 19, 1944], Spaatz Papers, Diary. This is misfiled in Spaatz's papers, having been erroneously annotated "23 October?" Spaatz's reply to this letter is dated September 30, 1944. This source appears to be Arnold's letter to Spaatz of September 19 cited in Craven and Cate, *Argument to V-E Day*, p. 622, note 80.

31. Ltr, Arnold to Spaatz, September 29, 1944, Spaatz Papers, Diary.

32. Chandler, *Eisenhower's Papers*, vol. 4, ltr, Eisenhower to Marshall, September 18, 1944, pp. 2157-2159 and ltr, Spaatz to Arnold, September 30, 1944, Spaatz Papers, Diary. Eisenhower described Spaatz as "disturbed." Spaatz spoke of Eisenhower as "disconcerted."

33. Butcher, *My Three Years with Eisenhower*, p. 673.

34. Ltr, Spaatz to Arnold, September 30, 1944, Spaatz Papers, Diary.

35. Chandler, *Eisenhower's Papers*, vol. 4, item 1954, msg FWD–14819, Eisenhower to Arnold, p. 2145.

36. Pogue, *The Supreme Command*, p. 274.

37. Ltr, Arnold to Eisenhower, September 6, 1944, Spaatz Papers, Diary.

38. Chandler, *Eisenhower's Papers*, vol. 4, item 1986, ltr, Eisenhower to A.H.M. Sinclair (Secretary of State for Air), September 2, 1944, p. 2180.

39. Pogue, *The Supreme Command*, p. 275.

40. Craven and Cate, *Argument to V-E Day*, p. 622.

41. Ltr, Spaatz to Lovett, September 20, 1944, Spaatz Papers, Diary.

42. Ltr, Spaatz to Lovett, October 1, 1944, Spaatz Papers, Diary.

43. Craven and Cate, *Argument to V-E Day*, pp. 666–668. The information cited by Craven and Cate, although dated after September 1944, pertains equally to this earlier period. Spaatz would surely have known of the relative inaccuracy of H2X by September 1, 1944.

44. Hinsley, *British Intelligence*, vol. 3, part 2, p. 512.

45. SHDCS/S.1020/44, Minute, Robb to CG, USSTAF subj: "Employment of Strategic Air Forces," September 17, 1944, Spaatz Papers, Diary.

46. Webster and Frankland, *The Strategic Air Offensive*, vol. 4, pp. 172–173, appendix 8, xl, has a complete text of this directive.

47. "Directive Agreed by D.C.A.S., R.A.F. and Lt. Gen. Carl Spaatz, 23 September 1944," Spaatz Papers, Diary.

48. Ibid. A list of "Relative Priorities" is attached to Spaatz's copy of the directive. For an example of how quickly these relative priorities would shift in the light of new perceptions, see TLM/F/S.34, "Notes of the 100th Air Commanders' Conference," September 26, 1944, Spaatz Papers, Diary.

49. TLM/F/S.34, "Notes of the 100th Air Commanders' Conference," September 26, 1944, Spaatz Papers, Diary.

50. TLM/F/S.34, "Notes of the 101st Air

Commanders' Conference," September 29, 1944, Spaatz Papers, Diary.

51. Ibid.

52. Ibid.

53. Craven and Cate, *Argument to V-E Day,* p. 639, implies that the HURRICANE plans were of solely British origin. However, Spaatz's Command Diary for early October, his correspondence, and the minutes of the 102d Air Commander's Meeting show that Spaatz and USSTAF not only participated heavily in the development of the schemes but initiated them.

54. Ltr, Spaatz to Lovett, October 1, 1944, Spaatz Papers, Diary.

55. Ltr, Spaatz to Arnold, October 4, 1944, Spaatz Papers, Diary.

56. Memo, Spaatz to CG's 8th and 15th Air Forces, subj: "Enemy Oil Production," October 3, 1944, Spaatz Papers, Diary.

57. Entry for October 3, 1944, Command Diary, Spaatz Papers, Diary.

58. Msg W–40454, Arnold to Spaatz, Spaatz Papers, Diary.

59. Pogue, *The Supreme Command,* pp. 302–308.

60. Chandler, *Eisenhower's Papers,* vol. 4, item 2063, msg S–63616, Eisenhower to Marshall, October 23, 1944, pp. 2247–2248.

61. Pogue, *The Supreme Command,* p. 308.

62. Craven and Cate, *Argument to V-E Day,* pp. 647–649.

63. Terraine, *A Time for Courage,* p. 675.

64. Webster and Frankland, *The Strategic Air Offensive,* vol. 3, p. 84, note 3.

65. Ibid., p. 68.

66. DCS/TS.100, "Notes on Air Policy to be Adopted with View to a Rapid Defeat of Germany," October 25, 1944, Spaatz Papers, Diary.

67. Ibid.

68. Ibid.

69. Ibid.

70. Hinsley, *British Intelligence,* vol. 3, part 2, p. 526.

71. Webster and Frankland, *The Strategic Air Offensive,* vol. 4, pp. 178–179 Appendix 8 xiii (b) is a copy of "Directive No. 2 for the Strategic Air Forces in Europe."

72. Ibid., vol. 4, pp. 177–178, appendix 8, xliii (a).

73. Ibid., vol. 3, p. 84, note 3.

74. Ibid., vol. 4, pp. 431–433, appendix 40.

75. The literature dealing with the Allies' pause at the German border, their logistics problems, and Eisenhower's decision to support Montgomery is voluminous, acrimonious, and tendentious. For some of the most rational

accounts, read Weigley, *Eisenhower's Lieutenants,* pp. 277–319; Charles B. MacDonald, *United States Army in World War II,* subseries: *The European Theater of Operations, The Siegfried Line Campaign* (Washington, D.C.: OCMH, GPO, 1963), pp. 119–175, and Ambrose, *The Supreme Commander,* pp. 504–552.

76. Memo for the CG, Eighth Air Force, subj: "Cargo Trucking Operations, 29 August–30 September," n.d. [October 1944], AF/CHO microfilm reel A 5875, frames, 1149–1154.

77. Ibid.

78. Ltr, Spaatz to Arnold, November 6, 1944, Spaatz Papers, Diary.

79. MacDonald, *The Siegfried Line Campaign,* p. 198.

80. Ibid.

81. Ltr, Kuter to Giles, November 3, 1944, AF/CHO, manuscript and collected material for proposed volume of the correspondence of Gen. H. H. Arnold, European Theater of Operations, item 220, pp. 540–542. This letter summarizes the reports of Col. Sidney F. Griffin and Lt. Col. Arthur C. Carlson.

82. Freeman, *Mighty Eighth War Diary,* pp. 348–349.

83. TLM/F/S.34, "Notes of the 98th Allied Air Commanders' Conference held at A.E.A.F., Versailles," September 20, 1944, Spaatz Papers, Subject File 1929–1945.

84. Freeman, *Mighty Eighth War Diary,* pp. 348-353.

85. Ltr, Spaatz to Lovett, December 13, 1944, Spaatz Papers Diary.

86. Ltr, Spaatz to Arnold, December 13, 1944, Spaatz Papers, Diary.

87. Craven and Cate, *Argument to V-E Day,* p. 667.

88. HQ, Eighth Air Force, Operational Analysis Section, "Report on Bombing Accuracy Eighth Air Force, 1 September–31 December 1944," pp. 5–7, April 20, 22, 1945, Spaatz Papers, Subject File 1929–1945.

89. USSBS, Military Analysis Division, *Bombing Accuracy: USAF Heavy & Medium Bombers in the ETO,* vol. 63 (Washington, D.C.: GPO, n.d. [ca. 1947]), p. 4.

90. Webster and Frankland, *The Strategic Air Offensive,* vol. 4, p. 335, appendix 32, iv: Report of 5th October, Speer to Hitler.

91. Ibid., vol. 4, p. 517, appendix 49, xxxix.

92. For German production, see ibid.; for the Eighth Air Force, see Eighth Air Force Monthly Summaries of Operations, September, October, November, and December 1944, AF/CHO microfilm reel A 5871, frames 927–1292; for the Fifteenth Air Force, see "Statistical Story of

the Fifteenth Air Force." n.d. [June 1945], p. 10, AF/CHO microfilm reel A 6432, frame 811; and for the RAF, see Webster and Frankland, *The Strategic Air Offensive,* vol. 3, pp. 84, 233–234.

93. Webster and Frankland, *The Strategic Air Offensive,* vol. 4, p. 516, appendix 49, xxxviii.

94. USSBS, Oil Division, *Oil Division Final Report,* vol. 109 (Washington, D.C.: GPO, 1947), p. 121.

95. Ibid., p. 4.

96. USSBS, Military Analysis Division, *Air Force Rate of Operations,* vol. 61 (Washington, D.C.: GPO, 1947), p. 33.

97. Ibid., pp. 66 and 85.

98. Memo 55–24, Headquarters Eighth Air Force, Office of the Commanding General, Standard Operating Procedures: Operations, subj.: Attack of Secondary and Last Resort Targets, October 29, 1944, AFHRC file no. 519.5991–1.

99. Freeman, *Mighty Eighth War Diary,* pp. 338–339.

100. Alfred C. Mierzejewski, "Wheels Must Roll for Victory: Allied Air Power and the German War Economy 1944–1945," Ph.D. dissertation, University of North Carolina at Chapel Hill, 1985, pp. 207–208.

101. Hinsley, *British Intelligence,* vol. 3, part 2, p. 526.

102. Mierzejewski, "Wheels Must Roll," pp. 282–283, 287.

103 Hinsley, *British Intelligence,* vol. 3, part 2, p. 527.

104. Mierzejewski, "Wheels Must Roll," pp. 298–299.

105. Ibid., p. 304.

106. COPC/S. 501/10/INT, "Tenth Periodic Report on Enemy Daylight Fighter Defenses and Interception Tactics. Period 1 September 1944–30 September 1944," October 15, 1944, AF/CHO microfilm reel A 5220, frames 158–1593.

107. Freeman, *Mighty Eighth War Diary,* pp. 354–355.

108. Ltr, Anderson to Arnold, September 3, 1944, Spaatz Papers, Diary.

109. Ltr, Arnold to Spaatz, September 21, 1944, Spaatz Papers, Diary.

110. Ltr, Doolittle to Spaatz, September 28, 1944, Spaatz Papers, Diary.

111. Ltr, Doolittle to Spaatz, October 18, 1944, Spaatz Papers, Diary.

112. Ibid.

113. Ltr, Spaatz to Lovett, October 1, 1944, Spaatz Papers, Diary.

114. Ltr, Spaatz to Arnold, October 4, 1944, Spaatz Papers, Diary.

115. Hinsley, *British Intelligence,* vol. 3, part 2, pp. 408–409.

116. Ltr, Spaatz to Arnold, October 4, 1944, Spaatz Papers, Diary.

117. "Notes on Conference at Bari," October 15, 1944, Spaatz Papers, Diary.

118. Ltr, Spaatz to Portal, October 20, 1944, Spaatz Papers, Diary.

119. Ltr, Spaatz to Robb, October 20, 1944, Spaatz Papers, Diary.

120. Hinsley, *British Intelligence,* vol. 3, part 2 , p. 525.

121. Ibid., vol. 3, part 2, p. 409.

122. Entry for October 21, 1944, Command Diary, Spaatz Papers, Diary.

123. MacDonald, *The Siegfried Line Campaign,* p. 390.

124. "Notes of the Allied Air Commanders' Meeting," November 7, 1944, Spaatz Papers, Diary.

125. MacDonald, *The Siegfried Line Campaign,* pp. 405–406.

126. Ibid., pp. 411–414; for the subsequent fighting see pp. 411–439.

127. Ltr, Spaatz to Arnold (Eyes Only) December 13, 1944, Spaatz Papers, Diary.

128. "Notes of Meeting Held at S.H.A.E.F. on Tuesday, 5 December, at 14:30 Hours to Discuss the Employment of Strategic Air Forces," Spaatz Papers, Diary.

129. Ibid.

130. Ibid.

131. Ibid.

132. Entries for December 6–8, 1944, Command Diary, Spaatz Papers, Diary.

133. Webster and Frankland, *The Strategic Air Offensive,* vol. 4, pp. 494–495, appendix 49, xxii.

134. Ibid., p. 500, appendix 49, xxvii.

135. Ibid., p. 325, appendix 32, iv.

136. A.D.I. (K) Rpt 373/1945, "The Birth, Life and Death of the German Day Fighter Arm as Related by Adolf Galland," August 15, 1945, p. 57, Spaatz Papers, Subject File 1929–1945.

137. Ibid.

138. *AAF Statistical Digest, World War II,* pp. 157–159, table 89.

139. British Air Ministry, *Rise and Fall of the German Air Force,* p. 373; see also A.D.I. (K) 373/1945, p. 59.

140. A.D.I. (K) Rpt 373/1945, p. 57.

141. Ibid., p. 59.

142. Ibid.

143. *AAF Statistical Digest, World War II,* p. 255, table 159.

144. Freeman, *Mighty Eighth War Diary,* pp.

375, 384, 386.

145. Ltr, Spaatz to Arnold, November 5, 1944, Spaatz Papers, Diary.

146. Ibid.

147. Ibid.

148. Ibid.

149. COPC/S.501/10/INT, "Twelfth Periodic Report on Enemy Daylight Fighter Defences and Interception Tactics, Period 3 November 1944–16 December 1944," December 26, 1944, AF/CHO microfilm reel A 5220, frames 1634–1658.

150. Ltr, Spaatz to Giles, December 15, 1944, Spaatz Papers, Diary.

151. Ltr, Arnold to Spaatz, November 30, 1944, AF/CHO microfilm reel A 1658, frame 1155.

152. Ltr, Giles to Spaatz, December 11, 1944, Spaatz Papers, Diary.

153. Ltr, Spaatz to Lovett, December 13, 1944, Spaatz Papers, Diary.

154. Ibid.

155. Ltr, Giles to Spaatz, June 8, 1944, Spaatz Papers, Diary.

156. Ltr, Arnold to Spaatz (Eyes Only) September 26, 1944, annotated "to Anderson for reply. CS," Spaatz Papers, Diary.

157. Ltr, Spaatz to Arnold (Eyes Only) October 10, 1944, Spaatz Papers, Diary.

158. Craven and Cate, *Men and Planes*, p. 46.

159. Ltr, Arnold to Spaatz, November 19, 1944, Spaatz Papers, Diary.

160. Ibid.

161. "Resume of General Arnold's Remarks on Saturday, 18 November, 12 Noon" [n.d.], Spaatz Papers, Diary.

162. Ltr, Arnold to Spaatz, November 26, 1944, Spaatz Papers, Diary.

163. Ibid.

164. Ltr, Spaatz to Arnold, December 9, 1944, Spaatz Papers, Diary.

165. Ltr, Spaatz to Vandenberg, December 12, 1944, Spaatz Papers, Diary.

166. Ltr, Brig. Gen. E. P. Curtis, Chief of Staff, USSTAF, to Lt. Gen. Ira C. Eaker, CG, MAAF, December 30, 1944, Spaatz Papers, Diary.

167. British Air Ministry, *Rise and Fall of the German Air Force*, p. 356.

168. Based on figures compiled from Freeman, *The U.S. Strategic Bomber*, pp. 153–157.

169. *AAF Statistical Digest, World War II*, table 90, p. 160 and table 89, p. 159.

170. Craven and Cate, *Argument to V-E Day*, p. 596.

171. Ibid., p. 595.

Chapter 15

Victory

1. Ltr, Spaatz to Lovett, May 2, 1945, Spaatz Papers, Diary.

2. CCS 166/1/D, January 21, 1943, title: The Bomber Offensive from the United Kingdom, cited in Matloff, *Strategic Planning 1943–1944*, p. 28.

3. USSTAF, Daily Staff Meeting, December 21, 1944, Spaatz Papers, Diary.

4. Ltr, Spaatz to Arnold, January 7, 1945, Spaatz Papers, Diary.

5. Freeman, *Mighty Eighth War Manual*, p. 241.

6. Minutes of a meeting held on December 20, 1944, Spaatz Papers, Diary.

7. Freeman, *Mighty Eighth War Diary*, pp. 398–400, 404.

8. Ibid., pp. 398–407.

9. Notes of meeting held in Chief of Staff's office, December 26, 1944, Robb Papers, RAF Museum.

10. Memo, Office of the Director of Operations, USSTAF, subj: Air Effort Against Tactical Targets for Period 16 December 1944–4 January 1945 Inclusive, January 5, 1945, Spaatz Papers, Diary.

11. Craven and Cate, *Argument to V-E Day*, p. 706.

12. Hinsley, *British Intelligence*, vol. 3, part 2, p. 449.

13. Craven and Cate, *Argument to V-E Day*, p. 711.

14. Hinsley, *British Intelligence*, vol. 3, part 2, pp. 443–450.

15. Ibid., pp. 444–449.

16. Entry for December 31, Command Diary, 1944, Spaatz Papers, Diary.

17. Entry for December 31, 1944, Hobart R. Gay Papers, Diary, U.S. Army Military History Institute, Carlisle Barracks, Pa. Gay was on Patton's staff.

18. Entry for January 1, 1945, Command Diary, Spaatz Papers, Diary.
19. Bradley and Blair, *A General's Life*, p. 363.
20. Entry for January 1, 1945, Command Diary, Spaatz Papers, Diary.
21. British Air Ministry, *Rise and Fall of the German Air Force*, p. 380.
22. Entry for January 2, 1945, Command Diary, Spaatz Papers, Diary.
23. Ambrose, *The Supreme Commander*, pp. 581–588; Pogue, *Organizer of Victory*, pp. 511–512.
24. Ltr, Kuter to Arnold, Roundup No. 1, January 28, 1945, Kuter's Notes on Trip to Malta & Yalta, AF/CHO.
25. Memo, USSTAF Directorate of Operations, to Col. F. Miller, January 5, 1945, Spaatz Papers, Diary.
26. British Air Ministry, *Rise and Fall of the German Air Force*, pp. 380–381.
27. COPC/S.510/10/INT., "Thirteenth Periodic Report of Enemy Daylight Fighter Defences and Interception Tactics," February 12, 1945, AF/CHO microfilm reel A 5520, frames 1670–1690.
28. Mierzejewski, "Wheels Must Roll," p. 329. The next few paragraphs are based almost exclusively on the exhaustive and authoritative research of Mierzejewski. I can offer only a quick gloss on the mass of detail and analysis contained in this outstanding work.
29. USSBS, Transportation Division, *The Effects of Strategic Bombing on German Transportation* (Washington, D.C.: GPO, 1947), vol. 200, p. 53.
30. Mierzejewski, "Wheels Must Roll," p. 332.
31. Ibid., p. 335.
32. Ibid., pp. 359–360, 368–369.
33. Ibid., pp. 376–377.
34. Ibid., p. 411.
35. Hinsley, *British Intelligence*, vol. 3, part 2, p. 607.
36. Mierzejewski, "Wheels Must Roll," p. 429.
37. Ltr, Arnold to Spaatz, December 30, 1944, Spaatz Papers, Diary.
38. Rpt, subj: "Allied Air Supremacy and German Jet Planes," Director of Intelligence, USSTAF, to Lt. Gen. Carl A. Spaatz, Janury 3, 1945, Spaatz Papers, Diary.
39. Webster and Frankland, *The Strategic Air Offensive*, vol. 4, appendix 49, xxxviii, p. 516.
40. Intelligence Report, subj: "Allied Air Supremacy and German Jet Planes," Director of Intelligence, USSTAF, to Lt. Gen. Carl A.

Spaatz, January 3, 1945, Spaatz Papers, Diary.
41. Ibid.
42. Ibid.
43. Entry for January 5, 1945, Command Diary, Spaatz Papers, Diary.
44. Hinsley, *British Intelligence*, vol. 3, part 2, p. 853.
45. Entry for January 5, 1945, Command Diary, Spaatz Papers, Diary.
46. Msg, Anderson to Spaatz, Janury 5, 1945, Spaatz Papers, Diary. See also entry for January 7, 1945, Vandenberg Papers, Diary, box 1; memo for the record, Lt. Gen. Giles, January 5, 1945, on conference with Anderson and Winant, AFHRC file no. 168.491. AF/CHO microfilm reel A 1658, frames 1463–1466.
47. SHAEF Meetings, January 6, 1945, Robb Papers, RAF Museum.
48. Entries for January 8, 9, 1945, Command Diary, Spaatz Papers, Diary.
49. Ltr, Spaatz to Arnold, January 7, 1945, Spaatz Papers, Diary. This letter is a reply to Arnold's of December 14, 1944.
50. Ltr, Arnold to Spaatz, December 30, 1944, AFHRC File no. 168.491, AF/CHO microfilm reel A 1658, frame 1178.
51. Ltr, Spaatz to Arnold, January 7, 1945, Spaatz Papers, Diary. This letter is a reply to Arnold's three letters of December 30, 1944.
52. SHAEF Meetings, January 9, 1945, Robb Papers, RAF Museum.
53. Ltr, Spaatz to Arnold, January 10, 1945, Arnold Papers, Correspondence with Field Commanders.
54. "Notes of the Allied Air Commanders' Conference held at S.H.A.E.F., 11 January, 1945, at 11:30 Hours," Spaatz Papers, Diary.
55. Minutes of USSTAF Staff Meeting, January 16, 1945, Spaatz Papers, Diary; msg, Air Staff SHAEF to Chairman Combined Strategic Targeting Committee, January 13, 1945, AF/CHO microfilm reel A 5543, frame 229.
56. Ltr, Spaatz to Arnold, January 16, 1945, Spaatz Papers, Diary.
57. Directive No. 3 for the Strategic Air Forces in Europe, Spaatz Papers, Diary.
58. Memo for General Kuter, subj: Comments on Strategic Directive No. 3 by AC/AS Plans, AFHRC File no. 168.491, AF/CHO microfilm reel A 1658A, frames 1471–1472.
59. Webster and Frankland, *The Strategic Air Offensive*, vol. 3, p. 97. In addition, see msg SX–588, Bottomley to Spaatz, January 15, 1945, AF/CHO microfilm reel A 5543, frame 155.
60. Msg U–68114, Curtis (signed Spaatz) to

Doolittle, January 16, 1945, AF/CHO microfilm reel B 5046, frame 1819.

61. Webster and Frankland, *The Strategic Air Offensive*, vol. 3, p. 99.

62. Minute, D.B.OPs (Bufton) to DCAS (Bottomley), January 22, 1945, PRO AIR 20/3227.

63. Minute, ACAS (Ops.) to DCAS, January 23, 1945, PRO AIR 20/3227.

64. Webster and Frankland, *The Strategic Air Offensive*, vol. 3, p. 100.

65. Ibid.

66. "Notes of the Allied Air Commanders' Conference held at S.H.A.E.F. on 25 January, 1945, at 11:30 Hours," Spaatz Papers, Diary, and msg UA–53417, Spaatz to Doolittle, January 28, 1945, Spaatz Papers, Cables.

67. SHAEF Meetings, January 24, 1945, Robb Papers, RAF Museum.

68. J.I.C.(45) 22 (O) (Final), subj: German Strategy and Capacity to Resist, January 21, 1945, PRO PREM 3/193/6A.

69. Webster and Frankland, *The Strategic Air Offensive*, vol. 3, p. 101.

70. Ibid.

71. Ibid., p. 103.

72. Ibid., vol. 4, p. 301, appendix 28, ltr, Bottomley to Harris, January 27, 1945.

73. Ibid., vol. 3, p. 104.

74. Msg S–77217, Bottomley to Portal, January 31, 1945, AF/CHO microfilm reel A 5543, frames 1405–1406.

75. Entry for January 28, 1945, Command Diary, Spaatz Papers, Diary. See also A–2 [Intelligence] Planning Notes for the Eighth Air Force, 28 January–3 February 1945, AF/CHO microfilm reel A 5884, frames 1639–1641. These notes centered on planning for oil missions if visibility allowed. Otherwise they concentrated on a Berlin strike. The note for February 3 spoke of a "verbal USSTAF directive that requires 400 aircraft on any of the four active synthetic oil plants" (frame 1641).

76. Msg SP–184, Spaatz to Doolittle, January 24, 1945, Spaatz Papers, Diary.

77. Msg UA–53417, Spaatz to Doolittle, January 28, 1945, Spaatz Papers, Cables; and [THUNDERCLAP Target List], January 28, 1945, Spaatz Papers, Subject File 1929–1945.

78. Tedder, *With Prejudice*, p. 659.

79. Combined Strategic Targets Committee, Minutes of the 16th Meeting held at the Air Ministry on Friday, 2nd February, 1945, AF/CHO microfilm reel A 5221, frame 1256; see also the THUNDERCLAP Target List, January 28, 1945, Spaatz Papers, Subject File 1929–1945. This list shows the "primary aiming points" as Friedrichstrasse (main line and underground station), the Air Ministry, Gestapo HQ, the Foreign Office and governmental agencies, the Alexanderplatz railway station, and two bridges over the River Spree.

80. Msg S–77217, Bottomley to Portal, January 31, 1945, AF/CHO microfilm reel A 5543, frames 1405–1406.

81. "Notes of the Allied Air Commanders' Conference held at S.H.A.E.F., on 1 February, 1945, at 11:30 Hours," Spaatz Papers, Diary.

82. Msg S–77217, Bottomley to Portal, January 31, 1945, AF/CHO microfilm reel A 5543, frames 1405–1406.

83. Ltr, Kuter to Arnold, Roundup No. 2, January 31, 1945, Arnold Papers, Correspondence.

84. Minutes of [USSTAF] Staff Meeting, January 26, 1945, Spaatz Papers, Diary.

85. Ltr, Kuter to Arnold, Roundup No. 2, January 31, 1945, Arnold Papers, Correspondence.

86. Msg War–29863 (Hearth 88), Giles to Kuter, signed Arnold, January 31, 1945, War Department Classified Message Center (WDCMC), NARA, microfilm reel 1347.

87. Msg Cricket–35, Kuter to Giles, February 1, 1945, AF/CHO microfilm reel A 5543, frame 1372.

88. Ltr, Anderson to Spaatz (Eyes Only), February 2, 1945, Spaatz Papers, Diary; *Foreign Relations of the United States Diplomatic Papers: The Conferences at Malta and Yalta 1945* (Washington, D.C.: U.S. Department of State, GPO, 1955), pp. 468–469, Minutes of 182d Meeting of the Combined Chiefs of Staff, January 30, 1945.

89. Ltr, Anderson to Spaatz (Eyes Only), February 2, 1945, Spaatz Papers, Diary.

90. Ibid.

91. Memo, R.A.L. [Lovett] to Arnold, January 9, 1945; enclosed in ltr, Arnold to Spaatz, January 14, 1945, Spaatz Papers, Diary.

92. Excerpts from memo, Kuter to Arnold, January 11, 1945; enclosed in ltr, Arnold to Spaatz, January 14, 1945, Spaatz Papers, Diary.

93. Ltr, Spaatz to Arnold, Febru007ary 5, 1945, Spaatz Papers, Diary.

94. Ltr, Anderson to Spaatz, (Eyes Only), February 2, 1945, Spaatz Papers, Diary.

95. Msg Cricket–40, Anderson to Spaatz, February 1, 1945, AF/CHO microfilm reel A 5543, frame 1354.

96. Msg UAX–53637, Spaatz to Twining, February 2, 1945, Spaatz Papers, Diary.

97. Minutes of [USSTAF] Staff Meeting, February 2, 1945, Spaatz Papers, Diary.

728

98. Msg UAX–53637, Spaatz to Twining, February 2, 1945, Spaatz Papers, Diary.

99. Msg CS–93–JD (REDLINE), Doolittle to Spaatz, January 30, 1945, AF/CHO microfilm reel B 5046, frame 1808. For Doolittle's opinions on the shortcomings of the B-24 as compared to the B-17 see ltr, Doolittle to Giles, January 25, 1945, AFHRC file no. 168.491, AF/CHO microfilm reel A 1657A, frames 827–831. Doolittle noted that the B-24 flew at 24,000 feet compared to the B-17's 28,000 feet, and therefore suffered higher flak losses.

100. Msg JD–104–CS (REDLINE), Spaatz to Doolittle, AF/CHO microfilm reel B 5046, frame 1818, January 30, 1945.

101. [Eighth Air Force] A–2 Planning Notes, January 30, 1945, AFHRC file no. 520.321, AF/CHO microfilm reel A 5884, frame 1639. Also see msg D–61064, Doolittle to Spaatz, February 2, 1945, and msg D–61068, Doolittle to Spaatz, February 2, 1945, AFHRC file no. 519.332 February 1–19, 1945.

102. Msg UA–53649, Spaatz to Doolittle, February 2, 1945, AF/CHO microfilm reel B 5046, frame 1809.

103. Memo (D–W–33), Major J. Rifkin, Assistant D/Ops, to DCS Ops, February 2, 1945, AF/CHO microfilm reel B 5046.

104. Msg CS–96–JD (REDLINE), Doolittle to Spaatz, February 2, 1945, Spaatz Papers, Cables.

105. Ibid. This notation is signed C. S. [Carl Spaatz].

106. Spaatz may have recalled portions of the prewar AWPD/1 plan in connection with bombing Berlin. AWPD/1 (tab. 3, p. 3) had stated, in August 1941, "Immediately after some very apparent results of air attacks on the material objective listed above [power plants, oil, and transportation] or immediately after some major set-back of the German ground forces, it may become highly profitable to deliver a large scale, all-out attack on the civil population of Berlin. In this event, any or all of the bombardment forces may be diverted for this mission." See also interview, Gen. Carl A. Spaatz by Murray Green, August 8, 1969, Green Collection on "Hap" Arnold, U.S. Air Force Academy Archives, Colorado Springs, Colo., p. 5. For an alternate view on THUNDERCLAP see Mark A. Clodfelter, "Culmination Dresden: 1945" *Aerospace Historian* XXVI, no. 3 (September 1979), 134–147 (in particular, pages 142–144).

107. Eighth Air Force Monthly Summary of Operations, February 1945, AF/CHO microfilm

reel A 5875, frame 333; Freeman, *Mighty Eighth War Diary*, pp. 432–433; "THUNDERCLAP Target List," Spaatz Papers, Subject File 1929–1945.

108. Memo D–M–8, HQ 1st Air Division, Office Director of Intelligence, subj: Immediate Interpretation Report No. 229, 4 February 1945, AFHRC file no. 525.332, AF/CHO microfilm reel B 5287.

109. Eighth Air Force Target Summary: Statistical Summary of All Bomber Attacks, 31 May 1945, pp. 7–8, AFHRC file no. 520.3084–1, AF/CHO microfilm reel A 5875, frames 618–619.

110. *New York Times*, February 6, 1945, citing Swedish news service stories based on reports from returning plane passengers.

111. Craven and Cate, *Argument to V-E Day*, p. 726.

112. Figures cited by Professor Doctor Olaf Groehler, Akademie der Wissenschaften der DDR, Zentralinstitute für Geschichte, Berlin, in letter to Mr. Herman Wolk, Office of Air Force History, March 6, 1990. Given the number of homeless, Professor Groehler assessed the raid as the heaviest to hit Berlin during the war.

113. 3rd Air Division Mission Report of February 3, 1945, n.d. [ca. early February 1945], Eighth Air Force Mission Reports, RG 18, NARA.

114. USSBS, Area Studies Division, *A Brief Study of the Effects of Area Bombing on Berlin, Augsburg, Bochum, Leipzig, Hagen, Dortmund, Oberhausen, Schweinfurt, and Bremen*, vol. 39 (Washington, D.C.: GPO, 1947), pp. 35–36.

115. Translation of Allied propaganda leaflet dropped on Holland, "The Flying Dutchman No. 101," February 5, 1945, AF/CHO microfilm reel A 5823, frame 150–151.

116. Sydney Gruson, "3000-Ton Blow Hits Berlin in Steady Bombing of Reich," *New York Times*, February 4, 1945, pp. 1 and 5.

117. Minutes of [USSTAF] Staff Meeting, February 5, 1945, Spaatz Papers, Diary.

118. Msg Argonaut–23, Anderson to Spaatz, February 5, 1945, AF/CHO microfilm reel A 5544, frame 703.

119. Msg USSTAF–MAIN–IN 15905, Spaatz to Anderson, AF/CHO microfilm reel B 5046, frame 699, February 5, 1945.

120. A–2 Planning Notes, AFGRC file no. 520.321, AF/CHO microfilm reel A 5884, frame 1640.

121. Ltr, Spaatz to Arnold, February 5, 1945, Spaatz Papers, Diary.

122. A–2 Planning Notes, February 13, 1945, AFHRC file no. 520.321, AF/CHO microfilm

reel A 5884, frame 1643.

123. Freeman, *Mighty Eighth War Diary*, p. 439; Eighth Air Force Monthly Summary of Operations, February 1945, AF/CHO microfilm reel A 5875, frames 313–382.

124. Alexander McKee, *Dresden 1945: The Devil's Tinder Box* (New York: E. P. Dutton, 1984), pp. 211–243, in particular, p. 225.

125. USSBS, Area Studies Division, *Area Studies Division Report*, vol. 31 (Washington, D.C.: GPO, 1947), p. 5, for an excellent discussion of Bomber Command's new techniques and accuracy.

126. USSBS, Physical Damage Division, *Fire Raids on German Cities*, vol. 193 (Washington, D.C.: GPO, 1947), pp. 1, 35–37, 47.

127. The bombing of Dresden has given birth to a large body of literature, both of accusation and justification. In addition to the previously cited works by David Irving and Alexander McKee, both highly critical of Allied policy, one should read the official AAF historical study on Dresden, "Historical Analysis of the 14–15 February 1945 Bombing of Dresden," prepared by Chief Historian Charles Angell in 1953, which can be found in the AF/CHO Dresden Subject File; and Melden E. Smith, "The Bombing of Dresden Reconsidered: A Study in Wartime Decision Making," unpublished Ph.D. dissertation, Boston University, 1971.

128. HQ, 1st Air Division, Office of the Director of Intelligence, "Immediate Interpretation Report No. 232, 0530 hours, 15 February 1945," AFHRC file No. 525.332, AF/CHO microfilm reel B 5288, frame 676.

129. Notes of the Allied Air Commanders' Conference held at S.H.A.E.F., Versailles, on Thursday, 15th February 1945, at 11:30, Spaatz Papers, Diary.

130. Eighth Air Force Monthly Summary of Operations, February 1945, p. 22; Freeman, *Mighty Eighth War Diary*, p. 440.

131. Craven and Cate, *Argument to V-E Day*, p. 731.

132. Excerpts of Broadcast of February 17, 1945, Spaatz Papers, Diary.

133. Msg UA–64471, Anderson to Arnold, February 19, 1945, Spaatz Papers, Diary.

134. Ibid.

135. Ibid.

136. Ltr, Kuter to Anderson, February 21, 1945, AF/CHO microfilm reel A 5534, frames 412–413.

137. Msg WAR–39722, Col. Rex Smith to Spaatz, signed Arnold, February 18, 1945, Spaatz Papers, Diary.

138. See the cover sheet for the January 31 Directive, which clearly indicates that Kuter's delegation received two copies, msg S–77217 (CM–IN–108), Bottomley to Portal, January 31, 1945, WDCMC, microfilm reel 1122. See also msg Cricket–35, Kuter to Giles, January 31, 1945, WDCMC, microfilm reel 1122; and Cricket–40, Anderson to Spaatz, signed Kuter, February 1, 1945, WDCMC, microfilm reel 1122.

139. Msg MX–46131 (WDCMC, CM–IN–13314), Kuter to Spaatz, February 13, 1945, WDCMC, microfilm reel 1152.

140. Msg WAR–37181, Giles to Kuter, February 14, 1945, WDCMC, microfilm reel 1352.

141. Msg UAX–64205 (WDCMC, CM–IN–14466), Spaatz to Kuter, February 14, 1945, WDCMC, microfilm reel 1152. Spaatz also sent a copy of this message to Giles.

142. Ibid.

143. Msg WAR–39222, Giles to Spaatz, February 17, 1945, Spaatz Papers, Diary.

144. Msg WAR–39730, Arnold to Spaatz, February 18, 1945, Spaatz Papers, Diary.

145. Memo, Anderson to Spaatz, February 19, 1945, Spaatz Papers, Diary.

146. Msg UA–64462, Spaatz to Arnold [for Giles], February 18, 1945. Spaatz Papers, Diary.

147. Msg UA–64470, Anderson to Arnold, signed Spaatz, February 18, 1945, Spaatz Papers, Diary.

148. Ibid.

149. Ibid., msg UA–64462.

150. Ibid., msg UA–64470.

151. Msg WAR-39954, Arnold to Spaatz, February 19, 1945, WDCMC, microfilm reel 1354.

152. Msg UA–64484, Anderson to Arnold, February 19, 1945, WDCMC, microfilm reel 1155.

153. Msg UA–64603, Anderson to Arnold, February 20, 1945, Spaatz Papers, Diary.

154. Ltr, Spaatz to Lovett, February 21, 1945. Spaatz Papers, Diary.

155. Msg Argonaut–43, Anderson to Spaatz, February 7, 1945, AF/CHO microfilm reel A 5544, frame 635. See also *FRUS: Malta-Yalta*, Minutes, Second Tripartite Military Meeting, February 6, 1945, pp. 641–644.

156. *FRUS: Malta-Yalta*, First Plenary Meeting, February 4, 1945, CCS minutes, p. 583.

157. Angell, *Analysis of the Bombing of Dresden*, pp. 14–16.

158. Ibid., p. 5.

159. Webster and Frankland, *The Strategic Air Offensive*, vol. 3, p. 44.

160. Notes of the Allied Air Commanders' Conference, March 1, 1945, Spaatz Papers, Diary.

161. Webster and Frankland, *The Strategic Air Offensive*, vol. 4, pp. 484–486, appendix 49, xiv.

162. HQ, Eighth Air Force, Operational Analysis Section, "Report on Bombing Accuracy, 1 September 1944–31 December 1944," April 20, 1945, Spaatz Papers, Subject File 1929–1945; interview, Spaatz by Green, August 8, 1969, p. 5.

163. Memo, Anderson to Director of Bomber Ops., subject: "Bombardment Policy in Regard to Enemy Occupied Territories," February 21, 1945, AF/CHO microfilm reel A 5534, frame 415; see also ibid., microfilm reel A 5534, frame 388, HQ, USSTAF, Office of the Deputy Commander, Operations, Circular, subj: "Bombardment Policy," March 1, 1945.

164. USSBS, Military Analysis Division, *Weather Factors in Combat Bombardment Operations in the European Theater*, vol. 62 (Washington, D.C.: GPO, 1947), p. 29.

165. Ltr, Spaatz to Marshall, March 13, 1945, Spaatz Papers, Diary.

166. Ltr, Spaatz to Arnold, March 14, 1945, Spaatz Papers, Diary.

167. Freeman, *Mighty Eighth War Manual*, p. 225.

168. Craven and Cate, *Argument to V-E Day*, p. 795, citing USSBS, *Oil Division Final Report*.

169. Eighth Air Force Monthly Summary of Operations, March 1945, AF/CHO microfilm reel A 5875, frame 455.

170. Eighth Air Force Monthly Summary of Operations, May 1944, AF/CHO microfilm reel A 5875, frame 1327.

171. Eighth Air Force Monthly Summary of Operations, June 1944, AF/CHO microfilm reel A 5875, frame 1398.

172. Eighth Air Force Target Summary, Statistical Summary of All Bomber Attacks, AF/CHO microfilm reel A 5875, frames 618–619.

173. Eighth Air Force Monthly Summary of Operations, February 1945, AF/CHO microfilm reel A 5875, frame 333.

174. See Eighth Air Force Target Summary, n.d., [ca. May 31, 1945], AF/CHO microfilm reel A 5875, starting frame 610; and Eighth Air Force Statistical Summary of Operations, European Theater, August 17–May 8, 1945, June 10, 1945, AF/CHO.

175. Eighth Air Force Monthly Summary of Operations, December 1944, with a summary of the year, AF/CHO microfilm reel A 5875, starting frame 129; table: Distribution of Bomb Tonnage by Type of Target.

176. Eighth Air Force Monthly Summary of Operations, May 1944, AF/CHO microfilm reel A 5874, frame 1317.

177. "A Review of Bombing Results January 1943–May 1945," n.d. AF/CHO microfilm reel A 5871, frame 1364. This list adds 1,425 tons for January 1945; otherwise, its monthly totals are exactly the same as those found in the Monthly Summary of Operations.

178. Msg UA–64603, Anderson to Arnold, signed Spaatz, February 20, 1945, Spaatz Papers, Diary.

179. USSBS, *Air Force Rate of Operations*, pp. 32, 56.

180. The Statistical Summary of Eighth Air Force Operations lists for Germany only 174,633 tons, not counting 6,520 tons dropped on "railroad shops and stations" and 5,409 tons on "communications centers." "A Review of Bombing Results" lists 199,524 tons on "Marshaling Yards."

181. USSBS, *Air Force Rate of Operations*, exhibit e.

182. Ibid., p. 85.

183. Eighth Air Force Statistical Summary of Operations, p. 41.

184. Eighth Air Force Monthly Summary of Operations, February 1945.

185. Derived from Eighth Air Force Target Summary, Statistical Summary of all Bomber Attacks, AF/CHO microfilm reel A 5875, starting frame 610.

186. Sherry, *The Rise of American Air Power*, pp. 252–254.

187. Mierzejewski, "Wheels Must Roll," p. 429.

188. Craven and Cate, *Argument to V-E Day*, p. 732.

189. "Summary of CLARION," Spaatz Papers, Diary.

190. Notes of the Allied Air Commanders' Conference, February 1, 1945, Spaatz Papers, Diary.

191. Ltr, Anderson to Spaatz, (Eyes Only), February 2, 1945, Spaatz Papers, Diary.

192. Msg XVAF E–0695, Twining to Spaatz, February 3, 1945, AF/CHO microfilm reel A 5544, frame 827.

193. Ltr, Spaatz to Anderson, February 5, 1945, Spaatz Papers, Diary.

194. USSBS, *The Effects of Strategic Bombing on German Transportation*, p. 16;

USSBS, Military Analysis Division, *The Impact of the Allied Air Efforts on German Logistics,* vol. 64a (Washington, D.C.: GPO, 1947), pp. 60–61.

195. Ltr, Anderson to Brig. Gen. Joe L. Loutzenheiser, Chief, Operational Plans Division, HQ, AAF, March 20, 1945, AF/CHO microfilm reel A 5534, frame 344–345.

196. Msg, Anderson to Spaatz, February 22, 1945, Spaatz Papers, Diary.

197. Freeman, *Mighty Eighth War Diary*, pp. 442–456.

198. Hinsley, *British Intelligence,* vol. 3, part 2, p. 613.

199. COPC/S. 501/10/INT, "Fourteenth Periodic Report on Enemy Daylight Fighter Defenses and Interception Tactics, Period 3 February–28 February 1945," March 5, 1945, AF/CHO microfilm reel A 5520, frames 1702–1719.

200. Craven and Cate, *Argument to V-E Day,* p. 722.

201. *AAF Statistical Digest, World War II,* p. 255, table 159.

202. Ibid., p. 256, table 160.

203. Webster and Frankland, *The Strategic Air Offensive,* vol. 4, p. 516, appendix 49, xxxviii.

204. Figures for USSTAF from "Review of Bombing Results," AF/CHO microfilm reel A 5871, frames 1363–1364.

205. Craven and Cate, *Argument to V-E Day,* p. 729.

206. Ibid.

207. COPC/S.501/10/INT, "Fifteenth Periodic Report on Enemy Daylight Fighter Defenses and Interception Tactics, Period 1 March–31 March 1945," April 11, 1945, AF/CHO microfilm reel A 5219, frames 1731–1760.

208. *AAF Statistical Digest, World War II,* p. 255, table 159.

209. Ibid., p. 256, table 160.

210. Ltr, Spaatz to Giles, March 11, 1945, Spaatz Papers, Diary.

211. Memo, Anderson to Spaatz, subject: Report on Jet Tactics Against Heavy Bombers on Mission of 18 March," March 19, 1945, AF/CHO microfilm reel A 5534, frame 355.

212. COPC/S.501/10/INT, "Fifteenth Periodic Report," April 11, 1945, AF/CHO microfilm reel A 5219, frames 1731–1760 [para. 39].

213. "Notes of the Allied Air Commanders' Conference, held at Forward S.H.A.E.F., Reims, on Wednesday, 21st March 1945, at 11:30 Hours," Spaatz Papers, Diary.

214. Ibid.

215. Notes of the Allied Air Commanders' Conference, Reims, March 29, 1945, Spaatz Papers, Diary.

216. Ibid.

217. Msg WX–43671, Marshall to Eisenhower, February 26, 1945, Spaatz Papers, Diary.

218. Msg WAR–47850, Marshall to Spaatz, Spaatz Papers, Diary.

219. Ltr, Spaatz to Chief of Staff, U.S. Army, "Report on Visit to Switzerland, 7–8 March 1945," March 10, 1945, Spaatz Papers, Diary.

220. Ibid.

221. Msg WAR–53409, Marshall to Spaatz, n.d. [ca. mid-March], Spaatz Papers, Diary.

222. Butcher, *My Three Years with Eisenhower,* pp. 769–770.

223. Ltr, Arnold to Eisenhower, September 4, 1944, Spaatz Papers, Diary.

224. Chandler, *Eisenhower's Papers,* vol. 4, pp. 2129–2131, item 1941, ltr, Eisenhower to Arnold, September 11, 1944.

225. Ibid., vol. 4, pp. 2367–2368, item 2191, msg S-71794, Eisenhower to Marshall, December 21, 1944.

226. Ibid., vol. 4, pp. 2424–2428, item 2237, ltr, Eisenhower to Marshall, January 12, 1945, and item 2238, msg S-74901/SG 962, Eisenhower to Marshall, January 14, 1944.

227. Ibid., vol. 4, pp. 2460–2461, item 2264, Conference Notes, January 28, 1945.

228. Ltr, Kuter to Arnold, January 28, 1945, Arnold Papers, Correspondence.

229. Eighth Air Force Monthly Summary of Operations, March 1945, AF/CHO microfilm reel A 5875, frame 403.

230. Vincent C. Jones, *United States Army in World War II,* subseries: *Special Studies, Manhattan: The Army and the Atomic Bomb* (Washington, D.C.: CMH, GPO, 1985), pp. 287–288; Freeman, *Mighty Eighth War Diary,* p. 464; Leslie R. Groves, *Now It Can Be Told: The Story of the Manhattan Project* (New York: Harper & Brothers, 1962), pp. 230–231; and msg SP-201, Spaatz to Marshall, March 15, 1945; and msg UAX–66143, Spaatz to Marshall, March 19, 1945, Spaatz Papers, Diary.

231. Notes of Allied Air Commanders' Conference, Reims, March 15, 1945, Spaatz Papers, Diary.

232. Ltr, Spaatz to Marshall, (Eyes Only), March 13, 1945, Spaatz Papers, Diary.

233. Notes of the Allied Air Commanders' Conference, Reims, March 8, 1945, Spaatz Papers, Diary.

234. Ltr, Spaatz to Giles, March 19, 1945, Spaatz Papers, Diary.

235. Msg MX–23614, US Military Mission in Moscow to Spaatz, April 3, 1945, Spaatz Papers, Diary.

236. [USSTAF] Weekly Staff Meeting No. 16, April 2, 1945, Spaatz Papers, Diary.

237. Webster and Frankland, *The Strategic Air Offensive*, vol. 3, p. 112.

238. Ibid., p. 117.

239. Ibid.

240. Dudley Saward, *Bomber Harris: The Story of Sir Arthur Harris, Marshal of the Royal Air Force* (Garden City, N.Y.: Doubleday, 1985), pp. 291–292, ltr, Bottomley to Harris, March 28, 1945.

241. Ibid., pp. 292–294, ltr, Harris to Bottomley, March 29, 1945.

242. Ibid., pp. 294–295, Minute, Churchill to Chief of the Air Staff, April 1, 1945.

243. Ibid., pp. 295–297, Note by the Air Staff, COS(45)238(0), Portal to Churchill, "Area Bombing."

244. Memo, F. L. Anderson, subj: "Comments Re Cablegram WAR 65558 (USSTAF IN-28993)," 10 April 1945, AF/CHO microfilm reel A 5616, frame 154.

245. Notes of the Allied Air Commanders' Conference, Reims, April 5, 1945, Spaatz Papers, Diary.

246. Eighth Air Force Monthly Summary of Operations, April 1945, AF/CHO microfilm reel A 5875, frames 509–580, p. 3.

247. Msg FWD–18890, Tedder to Spaatz, signed Eisenhower, April 10, 1945, Spaatz Papers, Diary.

248. Msg UA–67340, Spaatz to Doolittle, April 11, 1945, Spaatz Papers, Diary.

249. Directive No. 4 For the Strategic Air Forces in Europe, April 13, 1945, AFHRC File no. 168.491, AF/CHO microfilm reel A 1658, frame 857.

250. Msg JD–117–CS (REDLINE), Spaatz to Doolittle, April 16, 1945, Spaatz Papers, Diary.

251. Freeman, *Mighty Eighth War Diary*, pp. 496–497.

252. *AAF Statistical Digest, World War II*, p. 255, table 159.

253. Ibid., p. 256, table 160.

254. Craven and Cate, *Argument to V-E Day*, p. 752.

255. Butcher, *My Three Years with Eisenhower*, pp. 837–838. Butcher went with the press party and shared quarters with Spaatz and Tedder.

256. Tedder, *With Prejudice*, p. 685.

Chapter 16
Assessment

1. Webster and Frankland, *The Strategic Air Offensive*, vol. 3, p. 310.

2. Craven and Cate, *Argument to V-E Day*, p. 792.

3. Eighth Air Force Statistical Summary of Operations, June 10, 1945; Statistical Story of the Fifteenth Air Force, n.d. [ca. June 1945], AF/CHO microfilm reel A 6432, beginning frame 800.

4. Surprisingly, after almost fifty years, U.S. casualty figures are open to question. For AAF numbers I have used what is considered the definitive War Department/Department of the Army casualty report. See Department of the Army, Statistical and Accounting Branch, Office of the Adjutant General, "Army Battle Casualties and Nonbattle Deaths in World War II, Final Report, 7 December 1941–31 December 1946" (Washington, D.C.: Department of the Army, June 1, 1953), pp. 84–88. Unfortunately, this publication does not break down casualties by numbered air force or lower AAF unit. See p. 5 of the work for a summary chart which reveals that, overall, the AAF suffered 52,173 deaths among battle casualties. Nor does the AAF have comprehensive casualty reports for World War II-era numbered air forces and smaller units. For the Eighth Air Force, the Eighth Air Force Association offers a figure of approximately 26,000 deaths. Kenneth P. Werrell in "The Strategic Bombing of Germany in World War II: Costs and Accomplishments," *The Journal of American History* LXXIII (December 1986), p. 708, cites a figure of 29,000 deaths for USSTAF in Europe. This seems reasonable. Accurate casualty figures for the Fifteenth Air Force might well show that the organization made a more substantial contribution to European losses than is generally acknowledged. For Navy and Marine deaths, see Department of Defense, American Forces Information Service, *Defense 91: Almanac* (September/October 1991), p. 47, Chart Service Casualties in Major War and Conflicts (as of

September 30, 1990).

5. British Bombing Survey Unit. "The Strategic Air War Against Germany 1939–1945," pp. 242–243.

6. Webster and Frankland, *The Strategic Air Offensive*, vol. 4, appendices xl and xli, pp. 439–440.

7. Terraine, *A Time for Courage*, p. 682.

8. USSBS, Area Studies Division, *Area Studies Division*, vol. 31, (Washington, D.C.: GPO, 2nd ed., 1947), p. 3.

9. USSBS, *Summary Report (European War)* (Washington. D.C.: GPO, 1945), p. 15.

10. Ibid.

11. Hansell, *The Strategic Air War*, pp. 130–131.

12. R. J. Overy, *The Air War* (New York, N.Y.: Stein and Day, 1980), p. 157.

13. Sherry. *The Rise of American Air Power*, p. 254.

14. Schaffer, *Wings of Judgement*, p. 106.

15. John Keegan, "Berlin," *MHQ: The Quarterly Journal of Military History* II (Winter 1990). pp. 82–83.

16. Yitzak Arad, *Belzec, Sobibor, Treblinka: The Operation Rheinhard Death Camps* (Bloomington: Indiana University Press, 1987), p. 392.

17. Chandler, *Eisenhower's Papers*, vol. 4, item 2271, memo [for the Record], February 1, 1945, pp. 2466–2469.

18. Ltr, Bradley to Eisenhower, December 1, 1944, Bradley Papers, Correspondence with Eisenhower.

19. Interview, Doolittle by Burch, Fogelman, and Tate, September 26, 1970, p. 53.

Glossary

Glossary

A/Cmdr	Air Commodore
AAF	Army Air Forces, U.S. Army
AASC	Allied Air Support Command
ABC	American British Staff Conversations
ABC–1	Anglo-American agreement to make Germany the no. 1 enemy
ABC–2	Anglo-American agreement on allocation of U.S. aircraft production
ACM	Air Chief Marshal
ACS	Assistant Chief of Staff
ADGB	Air Defense of Great Britain
AEAF	Allied Expeditionary Air Force
AEF	American Expeditionary Force
AFB	Air Force Base
AFHQ	Allied Force Headquarters
AGF	Army Ground Forces, U.S. Army
AGWAR	Adjutant General, War Department
AHB	Air Historical Branch (RAF)
AI	Air Intelligence (RAF)
Air Corps	Army Air Branch 1926–1941
Air Service	Army Air Branch 1920–1926
AM	Air Marshal
AMC	Air Matériel Command
ANVIL/DRAGOON	Allied invasion of southern France, executed August 1944
AOC	Air Officer Commanding (RAF)
APHRODITE	Project to use radio controlled bombers to crash into German targets
AR	Army regulations
ARCADIA	Anglo-American conference in Washington, December 1941–January 1942
ARGUMENT	Joint operation against German aircraft industry by Eighth and Fifteenth Air Forces, February 1944
ASP	Air support party
AVALANCHE	Invasion of Italy at Salerno, executed September 1943
AVM	Air Vice-Marshal
AWPD	Air War Plans Division
AWPD/1	Air War Plans Division/ Plan Number 1 (1941)
AWPD/42	Air War Plan Division/ Plan (1942)
Bluie West 1	Narsarssuak, Greenland
BOLERO	Scheduled buildup of American forces in Britain, 1942

CCS	U.S.-British Combined Chiefs of Staff
CG	Commanding General
CINC	Commander in Chief
CLARION	Allied air operation against German rail system, February 1945
CNO	Chief of Naval Operations
CO	Commanding Officer
COBRA	Air support operation for breakout of American First Army at St. Lô, France, executed July 24–25, 1944
CORKSCREW	Invasion of Pantelleria, executed June 1943
COSSAC	Chief of Staff, Supreme Allied Commander, established 1943
CROSSBOW	Allied bombing effort to counter German V-1 and V-2 effort
CSTC	Combined Strategic Targeting Committee
DFC	Distinguished Flying Cross
DSC	Distinguished Service Cross
DSCAEF	Deputy Supreme Commander Allied Expeditionary Force
EAC	Eastern Air Command
EOU	Economic Objective Unit of OSS, stationed in U.S. Embassy, London. Provided targeting information to AAF
ETO	European Theater of Operations
ETO USA	European Theater of Operations, U.S. Army
FDM	Field Marshal (German)
Flak	German acronym for antiaircraft artillery (*Fliegerabwehrkanone*)
FLAX	Allied air operation to cut off German air transport into Tunisia, April 1943
FM	Field manual
GAF	German Air Force
GC and CS	Government Code and Cypher School
GOC	General Officer Commanding (British)
GOODWOOD	British attack on German positions in Normandy, executed July 18, 1944
GYMNAST	Plan to invade Casablanca
HB	Heavy bomber
HURRICANE I	Plan for Allied air operation against the Ruhr, not executed
HURRICANE II	Plan for Allied air operation against German communications, not executed
HUSKY	Invasion of Sicily, executed July 1943
IAF	Italian Air Force
IFF	Identification Friend or Foe
JCS	Joint Chiefs of Staff
JEB STUART	Plan for strategic fighter-bomber force in Europe, late 1944, not executed

738

JUNIOR	Code name for establishment of Twelfth Air Force
Luftwaffe	German Air Force, 1933–1945
MAAF	Mediterranean Allied Air Force
MAC	Mediterranean Air Command
MARKET-GARDEN	Allied airborne and land offensive across Holland, executed September 1944
MEW	Microwave Early Warning (Radar)
MTO	Mediterranean Theater of Operations
MTOUSA	Mediterranean Theater of Operations, U.S. Army
NAAF	Northwest African Air Forces
NAAFTCC	Northwest African Air Forces Troop Carrier Command
NACAF	Northwest African Coastal Air Force
NAPRW	Northwest African Photographic Reconnaissance Wing
NASAF	Northwest African Strategic Air Force
NATAF	Northwest African Tactical Air Force
NATO	North African Theater of Operations
NATOUSA	North African Theater of Operations, U.S. Army
OCAC	Office of the Chief of the Air Corps
OCAS	Office of the Chief of the Air Service
OCTAGON	Second Quebec Conference between the Americans and the British August–September 1944
OPD	Operations Plans Division, War Department General Staff
OSS	Office of Strategic Services
OVERLORD	The cross-channel invasion from Britain to Normandy, executed June 6, 1944
PFF	Pathfinder aircraft equipped with early versions of H2X radar
PINETREE	Code name for VIII Bomber Command and later Eighth Air Force Headquarters
POINTBLANK	American strategic bombing effort before the cross-Channel invasion, executed June 1943–May 1944
QUEEN	Heavy bomber mission in support of American First Army, executed November 1944
RAF	British Royal Air Force
RAFDEL	Royal Air Force Delegation to Washington D.C., 1939–1945
RAINBOW No. 5	Joint Army-Navy War Plan calling for the major effort against Germany and defense of the Pacific, partially executed immediately after Pearl Harbor
REDLINE	AAF communication circuit set up to provide private, high-level communication between senior AAF officers in Europe and in the Mediterranean

Reichsbahn	The German state railway system
ROUNDUP	Plan for Anglo-American invasion of France in Fall 1942, not executed
S/Ldr	Squadron Leader
SATIN	Plan for American offensive in Southern Tunisia, January 1943, not executed
SCAEF	Supreme Commander Allied Expeditionary Force
SHAEF	Supreme Headquarters Allied Expeditionary Force
SHATTER	Plan for bombing small towns in Germany, July 1944, not executed
SLEDGEHAMMER	Plan for Allied invasion of France in the spring of 1943, not executed
SOE	Special Operations Executive (clandestine British intelligence organization)
SOS	Service of Supply, U.S. Army
SUPER-GYMNAST	Invasion of North Africa, later became TORCH
THUNDERCLAP	Plan for terror bombing of Berlin, executed February 3, 1945
TORCH	Allied invasion of North Africa, executed November 8, 1942
ULTRA	British code name for intelligence gathered by decrypting German wireless communications enciphered on the Enigma machine in World War II
USAFBI	U.S. Army Forces in the British Isles
USMA	U.S. Military Academy, West Point, New York
USSBS	U.S. Strategic Bombing Survey
USSTAF	U.S. Strategic Air Forces in Europe
WAAC	Women's Auxiliary Army Corps, U.S. Army
WAC	Women's Army Corps, U.S. Army
WD	War Department
WDAF	Western Desert Air Force
WDFM	War Department Field Manual
WDGS	War Department General Staff
WEARY-WILLIE	Project to send radio-controlled war-weary heavy bombers against Germany, not executed
Wehrmacht	German Armed Forces, 1933–1945
WIDEWINGS	Code name Eighth Air Force and later USSTAF Headquarters
WPD	War Plans Division, War Department General Staff
"Y" Service	British radio-telephone intercept organization

740

Bibliography

Bibliography

Manuscript Collections

Library of Congress, Manuscript Division, Washington, D.C.

Papers of Carl Andrew Spaatz

These papers, which comprise 379 containers, form the foundation of this volume. They were given to the Library of Congress by General Spaatz and the U.S. Air Force in 1948. They are divided into eight series, two of which proved of particular importance to this book—Diary and Notebooks, 1910–1953, and Subject File, 1929–1945. The diary file does not consist of Spaatz's private recollections and reminiscences. Rather, it contains copies of correspondence, cables, reports, meetings, and office diaries arranged chronologically, and personally selected by Spaatz at the time he received them for inclusion in this file. I could find no evidence of a systematic exclusion of derogatory or sensitive material from this file. The Subject File, which makes up half the collection, is a mixture of nuggets of historical gold and trivia. This file grudgingly yields extremely valuable information about almost every imaginable aspect of the air war in Europe. Archivists at the Library of Congress note that, year in and year out, the Spaatz collection is heavily used by researchers.

Papers of Henry H. Arnold
Papers of Hoyt S. Vandenberg
Papers of Ira C. Eaker
Papers of James H. Doolittle
Papers of Nathan F. Twining
Papers of Frank M. Andrews

These collections, listed in order of their importance to this work, flesh out the full details of Spaatz's relationships with six of his most important contemporaries. The Arnold collection provides copies of Arnold-Spaatz and Arnold-Eisenhower correspondence unavailable elsewhere. Arnold's personal notebooks on the great Anglo-American political and military conferences supply unique insights into his and the AAF's thinking. Vandenberg's diary gives useful information on his relationship with Spaatz, the extent of Spaatz's control of the Ninth Air Force, and relationship with Leigh-Mallory. The Eaker,

Doolittle, and Twining collections contain occasional pieces of correspondence and insight into the thinking of both men.

Center for Air Force History (CAFH), Washington, D.C.

Microfilm Collection

This microfilm collection of at least 17,000 reels is one of three microfilm copies of the paper records of the Air Force Historical Research Center (AFHRC) at Maxwell AFB, Alabama. AFHRC and the Washington National Records Center, Suitland, Maryland, store the other two copies of this film. Among the varied items included on the microfilm are personal papers, USSTAF office files, historical files of numerous AAF organizations, series of Eighth Air Force and Fifteenth Air Force statistical reports, mission reports, and special reports on operations, tactics, and significant events. Unfortunately, the file does not have a detailed finding aid, thus researchers are reduced to time-consuming and often fruitless searches for pertinent material. AF/CHO refers to the center's former designation—The Office of Air Force History.

AF/CHO. Dresden Subject File.
AF/CHO. USAF Historical Research Studies Collection.
AF/CHO. Air Force Oral History Collection

> Interview of Maj. Gen. Frederick L. Anderson, K239.512-607
> Interview of Gen. Orvil Anderson, K239.512-898
> Interview of Gen. Samuel E. Anderson, K239.512-905
> Interviews of Lt. Gen. Arthur C. Agan, K239.512-857, 899
> Interviews of Gen. James H. Doolittle, K239.512-623, 625, 793, 799
> Interview of Maj. Gen. Edward P. Curtis, K239.512-875
> Interviews of Gen. Ira C. Eaker, K239.512-626, 627, 799, 868, 918
> Interviews of Lt. Gen. Barney M. Giles, K239.2512-779, 804
> Interviews of Maj. Gen. James P. Hodges, K239.512-565, 799
> Interview of Gen. Laurence S. Kuter, K239.512-810
> Interview of Gen. Lauris Norstad, K239.512-1116
> Interview of 1st Lt. Charles R. D'Olive, K239.512-612
> Interview of Gen. Earle E. Partridge, K239.2512-729
> Interview of Lt. Gen. Elwood R. Quesada, K239.512-838
> Interview of Gen. Frederic H. Smith, K239.512-903
> Interviews of Gen. Carl A. Spaatz, K239.512-583, 754, 755, 767
> Interview of Mrs. Carl A. Spaatz (Ruth), K239.512-1266
> Interview of Maj. Gen. Arthur Vanaman, K239.512-1030

The foregoing interviews and files contain unique information on controversial or obscure incidents or technical and doctrinal points. Like all oral histories, these must be used with circumspection.

Numbered AAF/USAF Historical Studies

39. Layman, Martha E. "Legislation Relating to the Air Corps Personnel and Training Programs, 1907–1939." (1945).
70. Hennessey, Juliette. "Tactical Operations of the Eighth Air Force, 6 June 1944–8 May 1945." (1952).
78. Goldman, Martin R. R. "Morale in the AAF in World War II." (1953).
88. Ackerman, Robert W. "The Employment of Strategic Bombers in a Tactical Role, 1941–1951." (1953).
158. Schmid, Josef, and Grabmann, Walter. "The German Air Force Versus the Allies in the West: The Air War in the West." (1954).
159. Schmid, Josef. "The German Air Force Versus the Allies in the West: The German Air Defense." (1954).
164. Grabmann, Walter. "German Air Force Air Defense Operations." (1956).

These works are of uneven quality but provide technical details not readily available elsewhere. The German generals monograph project (150–195) gives a valuable inside look at various aspects of the Luftwaffe.

U.S. Air Force Academy Library, Colorado Springs, Colorado

Papers of Lawrence S. Kuter
Papers of George C. McDonald

Kuter's papers supply useful information on his participation in the North African campaign, Eaker's removal from command of the Eighth Air Force, the Yalta Conference, and the Dresden controversy. McDonald served as Spaatz's intelligence chief throughout the war. His papers help to establish what Spaatz knew and when he knew it.

U.S. Army Military History Institute, Carlisle, Pennsylvania

Papers of Omar N. Bradley
Papers of Hobart Gay
Papers of Chester Hanson

This collection supplies useful information on the ground Army's attitude toward the AAF and Spaatz.

Royal Air Force (RAF) Museum, Hendon, England

Papers of Air Chief Marshal James Robb

These papers contain transcripts of high-level meetings at SHAEF during the Battle of the Bulge. They also supply handwritten notebooks of daily affairs in North Africa, North African photos, and notes by the marshal on William Welsh's Final TORCH Report.

Public Records and Documents, Unpublished

U.S. National Archives and Records Administration (NARA)

National Archives, Washington, D.C.

Record Group 18-Records of the Office of the Chief of the Air Corps

Record Group 107-Records of the Office of the Secretary of War
Assistant Secretary of War for Air Files

Record 165-Records of the War Department General Staff
Assistant Chief of Staff Files
Intelligence Files

Record Group 337-Records of the Army Ground Forces

Washington National Records Center, Suitland, Maryland

Record Group 18-Records of the Office of the Chief of the Air Corps
Air Adjutant General Central Cable Files

Reference Collection
War Department Classified Message Center File, 1942–1947

Eisenhower Presidential Library, Abilene, Kansas

Papers of Lloyd R. Fredendall
Unpublished portions of the Butcher Diary

The War Department Classified Message Center File is one of the most historically valuable and least-known collections of records dealing with U.S. military history. It contains microfilm copies of every message sent or received (including information copies of intratheater messages) by the War Department, the General Staff and all its branches, and by the GHQ, AAF, as well as transcripts of the wartime transatlantic teletype and telephone conversations between Marshall and Eisenhower, Roosevelt and Churchill, and all others who used the circuits. Although these records, unfortunately, cannot be searched by subject, a researcher who already has a reasonable citation, including date of origin, can obtain a copy of all of the key high-level messages and cables of the war. The Operations Division records contain information on training and high-level telegrams. G-3 and AGF records give background on air-ground relations and training manuals. The Fredendall Papers (one small folder) and Butcher's diary give insights into the North African campaign.

The Public Records Office (PRO), Kew, England

PRO AIR/2
PRO AIR/8
PRO AIR/9
PRO AIR/20
PRO AIR/23

The PRO contains records of the Air Ministry and miscellaneous correspondence from field commanders and is the most important source for Portal's and Bottomley's wartime thoughts and actions. The field correspondence gives crucial data from Coningham, Tedder, and Welsh.

PRO AIR/37

These records of Leigh-Mallory's Allied Expeditionary Air Force, including his daily post-D-day diary and many records concerning the background and formation of the AEAF, form a key source for the study of OVERLORD.

PRO AIR/41

These RAF historical monographs give the RAF's own view of its activities and include valuable documentation and insights not available elsewhere.

PRO CAB/101

These records contain copies of the British World War II official histories with additional information and backup documents not released at the time of publication.

PRO PREM/3

These records of the Prime Minister as Secretary of Defense and war leader provide Churchill's views unfiltered for postwar publication.

British Air Ministry, Air Historical Branch, London England

Unpublished, undated campaign narratives by the RAF:

Anglo-American Collaboration in the Air War over North West Europe

The Liberation of North West Europe
Vol. 1: The Planning and Preparation of the Allied Expeditionary Air Force for the Landings in Normandy
Vol. 4: The Breakout and the Advance to the Lower Rhine, June 1944–September 1944

The North African Campaign, November 1942–May 1943

The RAF in the Bombing Offensive Against Germany
Vol. 3: Area Bombing and the Makeshift Force, June 1941–February 1942
Vol. 4: A Period of Expansion and Experiment, March 1942–Janurary 1943
Vol. 5: The Full Offensive, February 1943–February 1944
Vol. 6: The Final Phase, March 1944–May 1945

The RAF narrative histories were security-classified monographs intended for internal RAF use; as such, they are unusually frank in their criticisms of both the RAF and its sister services. They are of uneven quality, but represent a valuable historical source well worth examination. Microfilm copies of all listed narratives but the first are available at the Center for Air Force History, Washington, D.C. The office also maintains an extensive annotated index of RAF records given to the PRO and backup documentation for its historical monographs.

Public Records and Documents, Published

U.S. Official Histories

Craven, Wesley Frank, and Cate, James Lea, eds. *The Army Air Forces in World War II*, 4 of 7 vols:

Vol. 1: *Plans & Early Operations, January 1939 to August 1942.* Chicago: University of Chicago Press, 1948.
Vol. 2: *Europe: Torch to Pointblank, August 1942 to December 1943.* Chicago: University of Chicago Press, 1949.
Vol. 3: *Europe: Argument to V-E Day, January 1944 to May 1945.* Chicago: University of Chicago Press, 1951.
Vol. 6: *Men and Planes.* Chicago: University of Chicago Press, 1955.

Craven and Cate, recently reprinted by the Center for Air Force History, is the starting point for any serious study of the AAF in World War II. One of its chief faults, however, is its lack of perspective concerning air problems. It tends to be subjective and is somewhat unreliable for enemy casualty and loss figures. On many doctrinal points it fails to present an objective viewpoint. Because the combat volumes are all well over thirty years old they lack the benefit of more recent scholarship. In addition, the source materials for several of the work's chapters seem to have been scattered or broken up, so it is difficult to identify and locate key documents used by the original authors. Despite quibbles about a few judgments and statistics, Craven and Cate nevertheless remains the authoritative history of the AAF during the war.

UNITED STATES ARMY IN WORLD WAR II

Subseries: The War Department

Cline, Ray S. *Washington Command Post: The Operations Division.*Washington, D.C.: OCMH, GPO, 1951.
Coakley, Robert W., and Leighton, Richard M. *Global Logistics and Strategy, 1943–1945.* Washington, D.C.: OCMH, GPO, 1968.
Leighton, Robert W., and Coakley, Richard M. *Global Logistics and Strategy, 1940–1943.* Washington, D.C.: OCMH, GPO, 1955.
Matloff, Maurice, and Snell, Edwin M. *Strategic Planning for Coalition Warfare, 1941–1942.* Washington, D.C.: OCMH, GPO, 1953.
Matloff, Maurice. *Strategic Planning for Coalition Warfare, 1943–1944.* Washington, D.C.: OCMH, GPO, 1959.
Watson, Mark S. *Chief of Staff: Pre-War Plans and Preparations.* Washington, D.C.: OCMH, GPO, 1950.

Subseries: The European Theater of Operations

Blumenson, Martin. *Breakout and Pursuit.* Washington, D.C.: OCMH, GPO, 1961.
Harrison, Gordon A. *Cross-Channel Attack.* Washington, D.C.: OCMH, GPO, 1951.
MacDonald, Charles B. *The Siegfried Line Campaign.* Washington, D.C.: OCMH, GPO, 1963.
Pogue, Forrest C. *The Supreme Command.* Washington, D.C.: OCMH, GPO, 1954.

Subseries: The Mediterranean Theater of Operations

Garland, Albert N., and Smyth, Howard McGaw. *Sicily and the Surrender of Italy.* Washington, D.C.: OCMH, GPO, 1965.
Howe, George F. *Northwest Africa: Seizing the Initiative in the West.* Washington, D.C.: OCMH, GPO, 1957.

Subseries: The Army Ground Forces and Miscellaneous

Beck, Alfred M.; Bortz, Abe; Lynch, Charles W.; Mayo, Lida; and Weld, Ralph. *The Corps of Engineers: The War Against Germany.* Washington, D.C.: CMH, GPO, 1985.
Holley, Irving Brinton, Jr. *Buying Aircraft: Matériel Procurement for the Army Air Forces.* Washington, D.C.: OCMH, GPO, 1964.
Jones, Vincent C. *Manhattan: The Army and the Atomic Bomb.*Washington, D.C.: CMH, GPO, 1985.
Palmer, Robert R.; Wiley, Bell I.; and Keart, William R. *The Procurement and Training of Ground Combat Troops.* Washington, D.C.: OCMH, GPO, 1948.
Treadwell, Mattie E. *The Women's Army Corps.* Washington, D.C.: OCMH, GPO, 1954.
United States Army. Office of the Chief of History. *The War Against Germany and Italy:*

Mediterranean and Adjacent Areas: The Pictorial Record. Washington, D.C.: OCMH, GPO, 1951.

The Army "green series," published by the Office of the Chief of Military History (OCMH), now the Center of Military History (CMH), and produced by the U.S. Government Printing Office (GPO), supplies information on air-ground support, technical aspects of procurement, and prewar planning. Pogue's volume on the Supreme Command, Matloff's two volumes on Strategic Planning, and Leighton's and Coakley's two volumes on logistics provide essential information on high-level planning and give adequate treatment to air issues.

United States Strategic Bombing Survey (USSBS)

Aircraft Division. *Industry Report*, Vol. 4, 2d ed. Washington, D.C.: GPO, 1947
Area Studies Division. *Area Studies Division Report*, Vol. 31. Washington, D.C.: GPO, 1947.
Area Studies Division. *A Brief Study of the Effects of Area Bombing on Berlin, Augsburg, Bochum, Leipzig, Hagen, Dortmund, Oberhausen, and Bremen*, Vol. 39. Washington, D.C.: GPO, 1947.
Military Analysis Division. *The Defeat of the German Air Force*, Vol. 59. Washington, D.C.: GPO, 1947.
Military Analysis Division. *Air Force Rate of Operations*, Vol. 61. Washington, D.C.: GPO, 1947
Military Analysis Division. *Weather Factors in Combat Bombardment Operations in the European Theater*, Vol. 62. Washington, D.C.: GPO, 1947.
Military Analysis Division. *Bombing Accuracy: USAAF Heavy & Medium Bombers in the ETO*, Vol. 63. Washington, D.C.: GPO, n.d. [ca. 1947].
Military Analysis Division. *The Impact of the Allied Air Effort on German Logistics*, Vol. 64a. Washington, D.C.: GPO, 1947.
Oil Division. *Oil Division Final Report*, Vol. 109. Washington, D.C.: GPO, 1947.
Physical Damage Division. *Fire Raids on German Cities*, Vol. 193. Washington, D.C.: GPO, 1947.
Summary Report (European War). Vol. 1. Washington, D.C.: GPO, September 30, 1945.
Transportation Division. *The Effects of Strategic Bombing on German Transportation*, Vol. 200. Washington, D.C.: GPO, 1947.

The Strategic Bombing Survey began its studies before the end of the war in Europe and collected an extraordinary amount of data about all phases of U.S. strategic bombing in Europe and Japan. The various published reports of this independent, but AAF-dominated, group deserve careful scrutiny by anyone interested in the technical aspects of the American strategic bombing offensive.

U.S. Government and Air Force Publications

Boylan, Bernard. *Development of the Long-Range Escort Fighter*. U.S. Air Force Historical Study No. 139. 1955.
Carter, Kit C., and Mueller, Robert, eds. *The Army Air Forces in World War II: Combat Chronology*. Washington, D.C.: AF/CHO, GPO, 1973.
Frisbee, John L. *Makers of the United States Air Force*. Washington, D.C.: AF/CHO, GPO, 1987.

Futrell, Robert Frank. *Ideas, Concepts, Doctrine: A History of Basic Thinking in the United States Air Force, 1907–1964.* Maxwell Air Force Base, Ala.: Air University Press, 1971.

Greenfield, Kent Roberts. *Army Ground Forces and the Air-Ground Battle Team: Including Organic Light Aviation.* Historical Study No. 35, Ft. Monroe, Va.: Air Ground Forces, 1948.

Greer, Thomas H. *The Development of Air Doctrine in the Army Air Arm, 1917–1941.* U.S. Air Force Historical Study No. 89. Maxwell Air Force Base, Ala.: Air University Press, 1955.

Hansell, Haywood S., Jr. *The Strategic Air War Against Germany and Japan: A Memoir.* Washington, D.C.: AF/CHO, GPO, 1986.

Kohn, Richard H., and Harahan, Joseph P., eds. *Air Superiority in World War II and Korea.* Washington, D.C.: AF/CHO, GPO, 1983.

Maurer, Maurer. *Aviation in the U.S. Army, 1919–1939.* Washington D.C.: AF/CHO, GPO, 1987.

_____, ed. *The U.S. Air Service in World War I*, Vols. 1 and 3. Washington D.C.: AF/CHO, GPO, 1978.

Momyer, William W. *Airpower in Three Wars.* Washington, D.C.: AF/CHO, GPO, 1978.

Mortensen, Daniel R. *A Pattern for Joint Operations: World War II Close Air Support, North Africa.* Washington, D.C.: AF/CHO and CMH, 1987.

Murray, Williamson. *Strategy for Defeat: The Luftwaffe, 1933–1945.* Maxwell Air Force Base, Ala.: Air University Press, 1983.

Osur, Alan M. *Blacks in the Army Air Forces During World War II: The Problem of Race Relations.* Washington, D.C.: AF/CHO, GPO, 1977.

Putney, Diane T., ed. *ULTRA and the Army Air Forces in World War II: An Interview with Associate Justice of the U.S. Supreme Court Lewis F. Powell, Jr.* Washington, D.C.: AF/CHO, GPO, 1987.

Thompson, Wayne, ed. *Air Leadership: Proceedings of a Conference at Bolling Air Force Base, April 13–14, 1984.* Washington, D.C.: AF/CHO, GPO, 1986.

U.S. Congress, House. *Select Committee Inquiry into the Operations of the United Air Services, Hearings.* 68th Cong., 2d Sess., 1924.

U.S. Department of State. *Foreign Relations of the United States: The Conferences at Cairo and Teheran.* Washington, D.C.: GPO, 1961.

U.S. Department of State. *Foreign Relations of the United States: The Conferences at Malta and Yalta, 1945.* Washington, D.C.: GPO, 1955.

U.S. Department of State. *Foreign Relations of the United States: The Conferences at Washington, 1941–1942, and Casablanca, 1943.* Washington, D.C.: GPO, 1968.

U.S. Military Academy. *The Howitzer 1914.* West Point: USMA, 1914.

U.S. National Security Agency. *ULTRA: History of US Strategic Air Force Europe vs. The German Air Forces.* NSA Special Research History No. 13, June 1945.

U.S. War Department. *Annual Reports of the Chief of the Air Service and Air Corps, 1921–1938.* Washington, D.C.: GPO, 1921–1938.

U.S. War Department. *Annual Reports of the Secretary of War, the Chief of Staff, and the Assistant Secretaries of War, 1919–1941.* Washington, D.C.: GPO, 1919–1941.

U.S. War Department. Office of Statistical Control. *Army Air Forces Statistical Digest, World War II.* Washington, D.C.: GPO, 1945.

Watts, Lt. Col. Barry D. *The Foundations of US Air Doctrine: The Problems of Friction in War.* Maxwell Air Force Base, Ala.: Air University Press, 1984.

The *AAF Statistical Digest* is a prime source for the quantitative analysis of AAF operations in this book. Murray's book provides data on both the AAF and the Luftwaffe, but, unfortunately, the author concluded his study in September 1944. One copy of the Annual Reports of the Secretary of War is available in the Army Library in the Pentagon, while a copy of the Reports of the Chief of the Air Corps is in the CAFH reference library. Greenfield's study gives the Army Ground Forces' view of close air support. Putney's work has an excellent introduction on World War II intelligence.

British Official Histories

Butler, J.R.M. *Grand Strategy.* Vol. 2: *September 1939–June 1941.* London: HMSO, 1957.

Ehrman, John. *Grand Strategy.* Vol. 5: *August 1943–September 1944.*London: HMSO, 1956.

Gibbs, Norman H. *Grand Strategy.* Vol. 1: *Rearmament Policy.* London: HMSO, 1976.

Great Britain, Air Ministry. *The Rise and Fall of the German Air Force, 1933–1945.* New York: St. Martin's Press, 1983.

Gwyer, J.M.A., and Butler, J.R.M. *Grand Strategy.* Vol. 3, parts 1 and 2: *June 1941–August 1942.* London: HMSO, 1964.

Hinsley, F. H. *British Intelligence in the Second World War: Its Influence on Strategy and Operations.* Vols. 1, 2, and 3 of 4 in 5 books. London: HMSO, 1979–1988.

Playfair, I.S.O., Flynn, F. C., Molony, C.J.C., and Toomer, S. E. *The Mediterranean and Middle East,* Vol. 2: *The Germans Come to the Help of Their Ally (1941).* London: HMSO, 1956.

Playfair, I.S.O., Molony, C.J.C., Flynn, F. C., and Gleave, F. L. *The Mediterranean and the Middle East.* Vol. 4: *The Destruction of the Axis Forces in Africa.* London: HMSO, 1966.

Richards, Denis. *The Royal Air Force, 1939–1945.* Vol. 1: *The Fight at Odds.* London: HMSO, 1953.

Richards, Denis, and Saunders, Hilary St. George. *The Royal Air Force.* Vol. 2: *The Fight Avails.* London: HMSO, 1954.

Roskill, S. W. *The War at Sea, 1939–1945.* Vol. 3, part 1: *The Offensive 1st June 1943–31st May 1944.* London: HMSO, 1960.

Webster, Charles, and Frankland, Noble. *The Strategic Air Offensive Against Germany, 1939–1945.* London: HMSO, 1961.
    Vol. 1: *Preparation* parts, 1, 2, and 3.
    Vol. 2: *Endeavor,* part 4.
    Vol. 3: *Victory.*
    Vol. 4: *Annexes and Appendices.*

Hinsley's works constitute the definitive British intelligence histories of the war. They have precise information on the all-important ULTRA organization as well as other sources of information. We are unlikely ever to get government information on the activities of Allied intelligence other than in this series. The Air Ministry history of the Luftwaffe, originally published in 1947 as a security-classified document, is based on Luftwaffe records captured by the British and postwar interrogations of Luftwaffe and other high Nazi officials. Because of the fragmentary nature of surviving Luftwaffe documentation—almost 90 percent of it was destroyed at the end of the war—the work still presents one of the best comprehensive views of the German air arm. Webster and Frankland's supply valuable operational, strategic, and statistical data. Playfair's volume, while glossing over some British shortcomings, is a good integrated history of the campaign. All British Official Histories are published through Her Majesty's Stationery Office (HMSO).

British Bombing Survey Unit (BBSU)

The Strategic Air War Against Germany, 1939–1940

This document, completed in 1947, is the final report of the BBSU. It served as a statistical basis for many of the assessments of bombing results contained in the British official history of the strategic bombing offensive and stands in its own right as a useful summary of the bombing campaign.

Dissertations

Davis, Richard Green. "The Bomber Baron: Carl Andrew Spaatz and the Army Air Forces in Europe, 1942–1945" (PhD., George Washington University, 1986).
Fanton, Jonathan Foster. "Robert A. Lovett: The War Years" (Ph.D., Yale University, 1978).
Flugel, Raymond Richard. "United States Air Power Doctrine: A Study of the Influence of William Mitchell and Giulio Douhet at the Air Corps Tactical School, 1921–1935" (Ph.D., University of Oklahoma, 1965).
Julian, Thomas Anthony. "Operation FRANTIC and the Search for American-Soviet Military Collaboration, 1941-1944" (Ph.D., Syracuse University, 1967).
Meilinger, Phillip Stanley. "Hoyt S. Vandenberg: The Life of a General" (Ph.D., University of Michigan, 1985).
Mierzejewski, Alfred C. "Wheels Must Roll for Victory: Allied Air Power and the German War Economy, 1944-1945" (Ph.D., University of North Carolina, Chapel Hill, 1985).
Reynolds, Jon A. "Education and Training for High Command: General Hoyt S. Vandenberg's Early Career" (Ph.D., Duke University, 1980).
Smith, Melden E., Jr. "The Bombing of Dresden Reconsidered" (Ph.D., Boston University, 1971).
Tate, James P. "The Army and Its Air Corps: A Study of the Evolution of Army Policy Towards Aviation, 1919–1941" (Ph.D., Indiana University, 1976).

Mierzejewski's work is a masterly exposition of the effects of Allied bombing on the German transportation system and the fatal damage done to the German war economy by the choking off of its coal distribution system. Tate shows that, contrary to myth, the Army made a sincere effort to support its air arm, despite limited resources. The works on Vandenberg and Lovett give useful details on the careers of those important men. Meilinger's work has recently been published by Indiana University Press.

Articles

Barnett, Lincoln. "General Spaatz: America's No. 1 Airman in Africa," *Life* (April 19, 1943): 72–84.
Beaumont, Roger. "The Bomber Offensive as a Second Front," *Journal of Contemporary History* XXII (January 1987): 3–19.
Bottomley, Norman H. "The Strategic Air Offensive Against Germany," *Royal United Services Institute Journal* XCIII (May 1948): 225–239.
Coningham, Arthur. "The Development of Tactical Air Forces," *Royal United Services Institute Journal* XCI (May 1946): 211–226.
Davis, Richard G. "Operation Thunderclap: the U.S. Army Air Forces and the Bombing of Berlin, "*The Journal of Strategic Studies* XIV (March 1991): 90–111.
_____. "Carl A. Spaatz and the Development of the Royal Air Force-U.S. Army Air Corps Relationship, 1939–1940," *The Journal of Military History* LIV (October 1990): 453–472.
_____. "RAF-AAF Higher Command Structures and Relationships, 1942–45," *Air Power History* XXXVIII (Summer 1991) : 20–28.

_____. "Bombing Strategy Shifts, 1944–45," *Air Power History* XXXVI (Winter 1989): 33–45.

Eaker, Ira C. "Part II: Memories of Six Air Chiefs," *Aerospace Historian* XX (December 1973): 188–197.

_____. "Gen. Carl A. Spaatz, USAF," *Air Force Magazine* LVII (September 1974): 43–53.

Holley, Irving B., Jr. "Of Sabre Charges, Escort Fighters, and Space Craft," *Air University Review* XXXIV (September–December, 1983): 2–11.

Jacobs, W. A. "Strategic Bombing and American National Strategy, 1941–1943," *Military Affairs* L (July 1986): 133–139.

Keegan, John. "Berlin," MHQ: *The Quarterly Journal of Military History* II (Winter 1990): 72–83.

Kindleberger, Charles F. "World War II Strategy," *Encounter* LIII (November 1978): 39–42.

Lloyd, Hugh. "Allied Air Power in the Mediterranean 1940–45," *Royal United Services Institute Journal* XCII (November 1947): 554–566.

Lytton, Henry D. "Bombing Policy in the Rome and Pre-Normandy Aerial Campaigns of World War II: Bridge-Bombing Strategy Vindicated and Railroad-Bombing Strategy Invalidated," *Military Affairs* XLVII (April 1983): 55–58.

McFarland, Stephen L. "The Evolution of the American Strategic Fighter in Europe, 1942–44." *The Journal of Strategic Studies* X (June 1987): 189–208.

Murray, Williamson. "Attrition and the Luftwaffe," *Air University Review* XXIV (March-April 1983): 66–77.

Rostow, Walt W. "The Controversy Over World War II Bombing," *Encounter* LV (August–September 1980): 100–102.

Simpson, Albert F. "Tactical Air Doctrine—Tunisia and Korea," *Air University Quarterly Review* IV (Summer 1951): 5–20.

Spaatz, Carl. "Strategic Air Power: Fulfillment of a Concept," *Foreign Affairs* XXV (April 1946): 385–396.

Sullivan, John J. "The Botched Air Support of Operation Cobra," *Parameters* XVIII (March 1988): 97–110.

Tedder, Arthur. "Air, Land and Sea Warfare," *Royal United Services Institute Journal* XCI (February 1946): 59–68.

"TRAINING: Experiment Proved?" *Time* (September 20, 1943): 66, 68.

Werrell, Kenneth P. "The Strategic Bombing of Germany in World War II," *The Journal of American History* LXXIII (December 1986): 702–713.

Wolk, Herman S. "Men Who Made the Air Force," *Air University Review*, XXV (September-October 1972): 9–23.

_____. "Prelude to D-Day: The Bomber Offensive," *Air Force Magazine* LVII (June 1974): 60–67.

Wyman, David S. "Why Auschwitz Was Never Bombed," *Commentary* LXV (May 1978): 137–146.

Tedder's and Coningham's RUSI lectures are important to understanding their views on air doctrine and its application during World War II.

Memoirs, Biographies, and Published Personal Papers

Ambrose, Stephen E. *The Supreme Commander: The War Years of General Dwight D. Eisenhower.* New York: Doubleday, 1970.

Arnold, Henry H. *Global Mission.* New York: Harper & Row, 1949.

Blumenson, Martin, ed. *The Patton Papers.* Vol. 2: *1940–1945.* Boston: Houghton Mifflin, 1974.

Bradley, Omar N. *A Soldier's Story.* New York: Henry Holt, 1951.

Bradley, Omar N., and Blair, Clay. *A General's Life.* New York: Simon & Schuster, 1983.

Brereton, Lewis H. *The Brereton Diaries: The War in the Pacific, Middle East and Europe, 3 October 1941–8 May 1945.* New York: William Morrow, 1946.

Butcher, Harry C. *My Three Years with Eisenhower, The Personal Diary of Harry C. Butcher, USNR*

Naval Aide to General Eisenhower, 1942–1945. New York: Simon & Schuster, 1946.

Carver, Michael, ed. *The War Lords: Military Commanders of the Twentieth Century.* Boston: Little, Brown, 1976.

Chandler, Alfred D., ed. *The Papers of Dwight David Eisenhower: The War Years.* 4 vols. Baltimore: John Hopkins Press, 1970.

Churchill, Winston S. *The Second World War.* Vol. 4: *The Hinge of Fate.* Boston: Houghton Mifflin, 1950.

Coffey, Thomas M. *HAP: The Story of the US Air Force and the Man Who Built It: General Henry H. "Hap" Arnold.* New York: Viking, 1982.

Eisenhower, David. *Eisenhower: At War, 1943–1945.* New York: Random House, 1986.

_____. *Crusade in Europe.* Garden City, N.Y.: Doubleday, 1948.

Ford, Corey. *Donovan of OSS.* Boston: Little, Brown, 1970.

Galland, Adolph. *The First and the Last: The Rise and Fall of the German Fighter Forces, 1938–1945.* New York: Henry Holt, 1954.

Groves, Leslie R. *Now It Can Be Told: The Story of the Manhattan Project.* New York: Harper & Brothers, 1962.

Hamilton, Nigel. *Master of the Battlefield: Monty's War Years, 1942–1944.* New York: McGraw-Hill, 1983.

Harmon, E. N., and MacKaye, Milton. *Combat Commander: Autobiography of a Soldier.* New York: Prentice-Hall, 1970.

Harris, Arthur. *Bomber Offensive.* New York: Macmillan, 1947.

Hurley, Alfred F. *Billy Mitchell: Crusader for Air Power.* New York: Franklin Watts, 1964.

James, D. Clayton. *A Time for Giants: The Politics of the American High Command in World War II.* New York: Franklin Watts, 1987.

Kelsey, Benjamin S. *The Dragon's Teeth.* Washington, D.C.: Smithsonian Institution Press, 1982.

Kingston-McClourghry, E. J. *The Direction of War: A Critique of the Political Direction and High Command in War.* New York: Praeger, 1956.

Larrabee, Eric. *Commander in Chief: Franklin Delano Roosevelt, His Lieutenants, and Their War.* New York: Harper & Row, 1987.

Lay, Beirne, Jr., and Bartlett, Sy. *Twelve O'Clock High!* New York: Ballantine Books, 1965.

Lowenheim, Francis L.; Langley, Harold D.; and Jonas, Manfred, eds. *Roosevelt and Churchill: Their Secret Wartime Correspondence.* New York: Saturday Review Press/E. P. Dutton, 1975.

Meilinger, Philli p. *Hoyt S. Vandenberg: The Life of a General.* Bloomington: Indiana University Press, 1989.

Mets, David R. *Master of Airpower: General Carl A. Spaatz.* Novato, Calif.: Presidio Press, 1988.

Montgomery, Bernard L. *The Memories of Field-Marshal the Viscount Montgomery of Alamein.* New York: World Publishing, 1958.

Parton, James. *"Air Force Spoken Here": General Ira Eaker & the Command of the Air.* Bethesda, Md.: Adler & Adler, 1986.

Pogue, Forrest C. *George C. Marshall: Ordeal and Hope, 1939–1942.* New York: Viking, 1966.

_____. *George C. Marshall: Organizer of Victory, 1943–1945.* New York: Viking, 1973.

Puryear, Edgar F. *Stars in Flight: A Study in Air Force Leadership.* Novato, Calif.: Presidio Press, 1981.

Roosevelt, Elliot. *As He Saw It.* New York: Duell, Sloan, and Pearce, 1946.

Saward, Dudley. *Bomber Harris: The Story of Sir Arthur Harris, Marshal of the Royal Air Force.* Garden City, N.Y.: Doubleday, 1985.

Sherwood, Robert E. *Roosevelt and Hopkins: An Intimate History.* New York: Harper & Brothers, 1950.

Slessor, John. *The Central Blue: Recollections and Reflections.* London: Cassell, 1956.

Smith, Walter Bedell. *Eisenhower's Six Great Decisions: Europe, 1944–1945.* New York: Longmans, Green, 1956.

Speer, Albert. *Inside the Third Reich.* New York: Macmillan, 1970.

Tedder, Arthur. *With Prejudice: The War Memoirs of Marshal of the Royal Air Force, Lord Tedder GCB.* Boston: Little, Brown, 1966.

Truscott, Lucian K. *Command Decisions: A Personal Story.* New York: E. P. Dutton, 1954.

Zuckerman, Solly. *From Apes to Warlords.* New York: Harper & Row, 1978.

Arnold's memoirs, although hastily ghost-written and poorly edited, are still superior to any biography written about him. Tedder and Zuckerman, both of whom knew Spaatz well, also yield important information, especially on the transportation plan. Eisenhower's papers are extremely valuable, especially if one is unable to make the haj to Abilene, Kansas, to check the originals. They must be used with care, however, because comments on personnel serving with or under him have been severely edited. Ambrose's biography of Eisenhower is probably the best military biography of the Supreme Commander. Anyone wishing to appreciate Spaatz's contributions as a pioneer aviator and as the second Commanding General of the AAF and the first Chief of Staff of the USAF should start with Mets's biography published in 1988, which covers Spaatz's entire career before, during, and after World War II, concentrating on Spaatz the man. Prior to the publication of Mets's book, Alfred Goldberg's fourteen-page article on Spaatz in *The War Lords* was the only published and reasonably widely available biography of Spaatz.

Monographs and Secondary Sources

Arad, Yitzak. *Belzec, Sobibor, Treblinka: The Operation Reinhard Death Camps.* Bloomington: Indiana University Press, 1987.

Beck, Earl R. *Under the Bombs: The German Home Front, 1942–1945.* Lexington: University Press of Kentucky, 1986.

Bennett, Ralph. *Ultra in the West: The Normandy Campaign of 1944–1945.* New York: Charles Scribner's Sons, 1980.

Bidwell, Shelford, and Graham, Dominick. *Fire Power: British Army Weapons and Theories of War, 1904–1945.* London: George Allen and Unwin, 1982.

Comparato, Frank E. *Age of Great Guns: Cannon Kings and Cannoneers Who Forged the Firepower of Artillery.* Harrisburg, Pa.: Stackpole, 1965.

Copp, Dewitt S. *A Few Great Captains: The Men and Events That Shaped the Development of U.S. Air Power.* Garden City, N.Y.: Doubleday, 1980.

_____. *Forged in Fire: The Strategy and Decisions in the Air War Over Europe, 1940–1945.* Garden City, N.Y.: Doubleday, 1982.

Davis, Burke. *The Billy Mitchell Affair.* New York: Random House, 1967.

D'Este, Carlo. *Decision in Normandy.* New York: E. P. Dutton, 1983.

Frankland, Noble. *Bomber Offensive: The Devastation of Europe.* New York: Ballantine, 1970.

Freeman, Roger A. *The US Strategic Bomber.* London: Macdonald and Jane's, 1975.

_____. *Mighty Eighth War Diary.* London: Jane's, 1981.

_____. *Mighty Eighth War Manual.* London: Jane's, 1984.

Freidel, Frank. *Over There: The Story of America's First Overseas Crusade.* New York: Bramhall House, 1964.

Gilbert, Martin S. *Auschwitz and the Allies.* New York: Holt, Rinehart and Winston, 1981.

Hansell, Haywood S. *The Air Plan That Defeated Hitler.* Atlanta: Higgins-McArthur/Longino and Porter, 1972.

Hastings, Max. *Bomber Command.* New York: Dial, 1980.

Irving, David. *The Destruction of Dresden.* New York: Holt, Rinehart and Winston, 1964.

Kahn, David. *The Codebreakers: The Story of Secret Writing.* New York: Macmillan, 1967.

Lewin, Ronald. *ULTRA Goes to War: The First Account of World War II's Greatest Secret Basd on*

Official Documents. New York: McGraw-Hill, 1978.

McKee, Alexander. *Dresden 1945: The Devil's Tinderbox*. New York: E. P. Dutton, 1984.

Mierzejewski, Alfred C. *The Collapse of the German War Economy, 1944--1945: Allied Air Power and the German National Railway*. Chapel Hill: University of North Carolina Press, 1988.

Morison, Samuel Eliot. *History of United States Naval Operations in World War II*. Vol. 9: *Sicily-Salerno-Anzio, January 1943–June 1944*. Boston: Little, Brown, 1954.

Orpen, Neil. *Airlift to Warsaw: The Rising of 1944*. Norman: University of Oklahoma Press, 1984.

Overy, R. J. *The Air War, 1939–1945*. New York: Stein and Day, 1981.

Rostow, W. W. *Pre-Invasion Bombing Strategy: General Eisenhower's Decision of March 25, 1944*. Austin: University of Texas Press, 1981.

Schaffer, Ronald. *Wings of Judgement: American Bombing in World War II*. New York: Oxford University Press, 1985.

Sherry, Michael S. *The Rise of American Air Power: The Creation of Armageddon*. New Haven: Yale University Press, 1987.

Stanley, Roy M. *World War II Photo Intelligence*. New York: Charles Scribner's Sons, 1981.

Terraine, John. *A Time for Courage: In the Royal Air Force in the European War, 1939–1945*. New York: Macmillan, 1985.

Verrier, Anthony. *The Bomber Offensive*. Rev. ed. London: Pan Books, 1974.

Weigley, Russell F. *Eisenhower's Lieutenants: The Campaign of France and Germany, 1944–1945*. Bloomington: Indiana University Press, 1981.

Winterbotham, F. W. *The Ultra Secret*. New York: Dell, 1979.

Wykeham, Peter. *Fighter Command: A Study of Air Defence, 1914–1960*. London: Putnam, 1960.

Wyman, David S. *The Abandonment of the Jews: America and the Holocaust, 1941–1945*. New York: Pantheon, 1984.

Roger Freeman's books on the Eighth Air Force, although written for trivia buffs, give an accurate and colorful picture of equipment, tactics, and operations of the American heavy-bomber forces in Europe. Weigley's book on northwestern Europe is the best single account of the campaign, while D'Este has written an excellent account of Normandy. John Terraine's work on the RAF also is worthwhile. Frankland's short work for the Ballantine War Series presents an interesting contrast to his official endeavors. In the Ballantine work Frankland draws conclusions apparently denied to him in an official role; for instance, he gives Spaatz the laurel for winning the bomber offensive. Schaffer's book is a well-researched, balanced account of the moral dilemma faced by the AAF when the pursuit of victory led it beyond precision bombing to city bombing. Sherry offers good research and stimulating writing in an ultimately unsuccessful attempt to apply anti-Vietnam War morality to American bombing in World War II. Both books make a stronger case for the immorality of bombing Japan than Germany, focusing on the AAF's massive fire raid on Tokyo and on the atomic bombing of Hiroshima and Nagasaki. The current social trends rejecting nuclear war and open racism, one unheard of and the other not questioned in the 1940s, make the war against Japan a hot topic of modern research. The atrocities and racism of the Japanese regime are dismissed as cultural differences. Such a case cannot be made for the Germans. They belonged to the mainstream of Western culture, were Caucasian to a fault, and committed atrocities on a numbing scale.

Unpublished Material

Cabell, C.P. Unpublished autobiography.
Hughes, Richard D'O. Unpublished autobiography.
Mets, David. Untitled manuscript biography of Spaatz, 1982.

The Hughes autobiography gives useful inside details on the Eighth Air Force and USSTAF. I thank Professor W. W. Rostow for giving me the wartime chapters of this work. The edited version of Mets's work, published under the title *Master of Air Power*, is included under Memoirs, Biographies, and Published Personal Papers above. This manuscript is particularly strong on Spaatz's pre-World War II career and benefits from Mets's numerous interviews with Spaatz's family and associates. General Cabell was one of the AAF's leading intelligence officers. He also served in combat, leading a wing of Eighth Air Force heavy bombers. He was present in Spaatz's headquarters at Park House on the day of the initial Big Week mission, and he gives an important account of the events of that evening. The CAFH archives contains a copy of this work.

Index

Index

1st Tactical: 319n
2d Tactical: 273n, 307, 309, 310, 318,
    338, 364, 409, 454, 456, 489, 521,
    526
Air Forces (numbered, U.S.)
    Fourth: 82, 88
    Eighth (*see individual entry under*
    Eighth Air Force)
    Ninth: 156, 196, 240, 249, 250,
        260–261, 262, 267, 273, 276, 277,
        278, 290, 299, 307, 309, 316, 317,
        318, 319, 323, 331, 332, 335, 336,
        338, 355, 357, 364, 371, 408, 414,
        417, 454, 456, 462, 466, 484, 485,
        489, 514, 515, 518, 533
    Twelfth: 103, 109–110, 114, 115, 116,
        124, 128, 130, 139, 141, 143, 144,
        145, 152, 156, 163, 171, 178, 185,
        196, 247, 249, 250, 261, 264, 265,
        273, 298, 319n, 354, 360, 417, 484,
        548, 564
    Thirteenth: 273
    Fifteenth: 223, 264–268, 273, 274,
        278, 283, 290, 315, 319, 321, 323,
        346, 351, 354, 358, 379, 383,
        384–390, 395, 400, 417, 434, 439,
        440, 443, 448, 479, 490, 500, 504,
        505, 506, 514, 526, 536, 549, 571,
        573, 574, 584, 587
Air Liaison Officer (ALO)
    function of: 149–150
    introduced in Sicily: 243
Airlift, supplies to the front: 501–503
Air Service Tactical School: 19
Air superiority
    AAF over Germany: 367, 367,
        373–379, 414–415, 570–571
    AAF on D-Day: 341, 414–418
    Allied: 531–532
    assessment of: 587
    defined: 75
    in North Africa: 121, 145, 299
    POINTBLANK and OVERLORD,
        requirements for: 303, 312, 333
    strategy, role in: 93, 109, 214–216,
        299
    U.S. loss of over Germany: 287
    USSTAF over Germany: 358
    WWII: 587, 588, 595
Air Support Control Headquarters (ASC)
    established in Middle East: 150
Air support doctrine. *See also* Close air
    support.

defined in North Africa: 210–220
Air supremacy. *See* Air superiority.
Air Transport Service: 189
Air War Plans Division (AWPD)
    formed: 60
    reports by: 60–62, 111–112
Alam Halfa, defense of: 150
Albany, New York: 4
Albert Canal, Belgium
    bridge targets at: 408
Alexander, Harold R.L.G.
    British Army Commander in Chief,
        Mediterranean: 181, 204
    Commander, 18 Army Group: 178,
        181
    Italian operations planned by: 250
    NAAF air support praised by: 256
    Pantelleria operations prepared by:
        231
    proposed as Commander of Allied
        ground forces, SHAEF: 536
Alexandria, Virginia: 67
Algeria
    Allied control of: 123
    Eisenhower hq in: 230
Algiers: 147, 177, 178, 186, 277
    AFHQ in: 173, 174
    Allied occupation of: 123, 128
    aviation engineers in: 145
    intelligence activity moved to: 190
    invasion forces' departure from: 137
    NAAF Hq moved from: 189
Algiers Task Force: 125
Allen, Terry
    Commander, 1st Inf Div: 203
Allied Air Commanders Conference:
    544, 546, 558, 564, 572
Allied Air Control Conference: 544,
    546, 558
Allied Air Forces
    replaced by NW African Air Forces:
        178
    structure of: 152–154
    weakness of: 171
Allied Expeditionary Air Force (AEAF)
    abolished: 484–489
    command and control in: 454
    command structure of: 307–318, 454,
        467
    heavy bombers for close air support
        used by: 482
    hq at Stanmore: 294
    operations, Mar–Apr 44: 364

353th Fighter: 288
355th Fighter: 384
360st Fighter: 512
3364th Fighter: 408
375th Bombardment: 260
388th Bombardment: 260
445th Bombardment: 512, 514
Groves, Leslie R.
  Chief, Manhattan Project: 579
Gruenther, Alfred M.
  C/S, U.S. Fifth Army: 230
Guam, Japanese attack on: 68
Guderian, Heinz: 205
  Chief, German General Staff: 580
  incapacitated in raid: 580

H2X: 543, 593. *See also* Radar
  accuracy of: 346, 492, 504–506, 508,
    521–522, 532, 543, 567, 570, 582
  B-17s equipped with: 296–298
  Berlin attacked with aid of: 543, 567
  bombing through overcast aided by:
    306, 328
  D-Day operations aided by: 414
  Dresden attacked with aid of: 556,
    559, 564
  forbidden over occupied countries:
    382
  Magdeburg attacked with aid of: 553
  permitted against targets in France:
    401
  Ploesti attacked with aid of: 388
  tracked by Germans: 440
  Zürich attacked with aid of: 575
Halberstadt, Germany, raid on: 303
Halifax, Lord
  Foreign Minister (British): 46
Halle, Germany
  communications center attacked at:
    572
Hallein, Germany, raid on: 584
Halverson, Harry A.
  record-setting *Question Mark* flight,
    participant in: 22–23
Hamburg, Germany: 89
  Battle of: 426
  RAF targets in: 48, 557
Hamilton, Nigel
  Pantelleria analyzed by: 238–239
Hamm, Germany
  raids on: 391, 410, 508
Hampton Court, England: 104

Hansell, Haywood S.: 60, 271, 322
  air planner, ETO: 101
  ACTS instructor: 30
  moved to Pacific for B-29 operations:
    311
  selection of targets, criticized for: 588
  strategic bombardment of Germany
    assessed by: 484, 527
  strategy refocused by: 111–112
Harmon, Millard F., Chief of Staff: 79
Harris, Arthur T.: 113, 147, 315, 409,
    545. *See also* RAF Bomber
    Command
  area bombing, views on: 506, 527,
    552, 564, 570, 581
  assessment of: 592
  background of: 95–96
  Berlin raid requested by: 432–433,
    544
  bomb damage photos used by: 102
  Chief, RAF Bomber Command: 82,
    240, 267, 309, 454, 470, 496, 500
  close air support with heavy
    bombardment agreed by: 517
  command arrangements assessed by:
    486
  objectives assigned to: 306
  OVERLORD command arrangements
    viewed by: 327, 334, 336–338, 353
  Portal, relationship with: 496–497
  preinvasion operations, views on: 411
  reprisal raids favored by: 437, 487
  strategic bombardment plans, views
    on: 348, 349, 351
  strategy of: 93–95, 329, 330, 570
  targeting directives issued to:
    492–493, 500
Harrison, Leland
  U.S. Minister to Switzerland: 575
Harrison, Ruth: 7
  Spaatz's wife: 5
Hart, Charles E.
  acting commander in France: 464
Hartle, Russell P.
  Commander, Oran Task Force: 127
Hawaii: 51
  air ferry route to Australia: 69
Heston Airfield, England: 481
Hickey, Lawrence
  Commander, XII Air Service
    Command: 242
  replaced: 242
High Wycombe, England: 83, 93,

jet threat of: 484, 500–501, 539–542,
573
losses to: 439, 519
losses, Jan–Feb 44: 339
losses, 14 Oct 43: 376
losses, 27 Sep 44: 511
losses, Aug 17, 43: 373–376
losses, Mar 44: 358
losses: 104
lured to fight: 332, 333, 392, 396,
562
neutralization of: 429–432, 490, 517
night fighters of: 358, 501
night raids on London: 51–52
pilot training in: 44
resurgence of: 500–501, 511–515,
518–523
signals of tapped: 533, 535
strategic bombardment, effects on: 596
strategic bombardment, defense
against: 358–379
strategic bombardment, target of: 266,
284, 298, 299–300, 350, 390, 395,
411
strength, North Africa: Nov–Dec 42:
140
strength, May 44: 396
strength, Jun 44: 425
strength, Oct 44: 514
strength, Sep 44: 526
strength, Dec 44: 517–519
strength, Mar 45
strength, Sicily: 240
tactics of: 368–369, 378, 512–513
transports at Bougie sunk by: 139
U.S. positions dive-bombed by: 172
Lutzkendorf, Germany, raid on: 398
Luxembourg: 513
Lyster, St. G.
Chief, British Naval Air Staff: 86

MacArthur, Douglas: 25
area of responsibility: 97
Chief of Staff, U.S. Army: 24–25
prestige of: 267
Mackay Trophy: 32
Magdeburg, Germany
AAF raids on: 398, 553, 556
RAF raid on: 45
Mainz, Germany
strained rail system in: 538
Maison Blanche

air facility in Algiers: 142, 145
Maknassy, Tunisia
Axis raid near: 176, 177
U.S. attack on: 172
Malaya, defense of: 146
Malta: 545, 579
agreements at: 560
RAF fields at: 190, 225, 231, 239
raid on: 146
Tripartite Conference at: 543, 545,
546, 547–548, 572
Manhattan Project: 579
Mannheim, Germany
Luftwaffe defense responsibility for
assigned: 369
Mantes-Gassicourt, France
raid on: 408
Marble Arch, Tripolitania
WDAF at: 147
March Field (later AFB), California: 23,
25
March of Time: 103
Mareth Line: 208
Axis attack at: 203
MARKET-GARDEN (Operation): 489
assessment of: 503–504
proposed by Montgomery: 501
scheduled: 438
Marquis of Lothian
Ambassador to U.S. (British): 41, 46
Marrakech, Africa: 173, 210
airfield at: 189, 230
ferry route terminus: 153
Senate committee visit to: 246
Marseilles, France
Tripartite Conference in: 543
Marshall, George C.: 38, 41, 57, 60, 68,
70, 79, 112, 113, 152, 136, 234,
249, 260, 272, 290, 299, 313, 335,
344, 354, 536, 548–549, 553, 564,
572, 578, 580
air support doctrine, views on:
212–214, 218
Andrews selected CG, ETO, by: 101
autonomous strategic bombardment
operation supported by: 267
AWPD/1 endorsed by: 435–436
bombing of Switzerland, reaction to:
575
bombing of Rome discussed by: 261
bombing cities, views on: 550, 561,
591
Casablanca Conference, views at: 162,

German ground force losses revealed
by: 464, 472
information on Battle of the Bulge
revealed by: 533
Luftwaffe activity, Sicily revealed by:
241
Luftwaffe movements, D-Day
revealed by: 425, 426
Luftwaffe shift to defend Germany
revealed by: 514
Luftwaffe strength, May 44 revealed
by: 396, 413
Luftwaffe transfer of fighters to
Eastern Front revealed by: 573
Luftwaffe weaknesses revealed by:
302–303
secret of in jeopardy: 199, 200
Union of Soviet Socialist Republics
(USSR): 69, 518. See also Dresden;
Eastern Front; Red Army.
Berlin and Leipzig raids requested by:
553, 561–562
Dresden bombing, role in: 563–564
Eastern Front assessed: 111, 157, 164,
549–552
German surrender to: 584–585
German military operations: 354
liaison with: 549
U.S. crews force-landed in: 450
winter offensive of: 543, 560
United Press: 562, 572
United States
aircraft production in: 38, 64–66,
112–113
creation of military aviation in: 594
defense, state of: 38
entry of into WWII: 45, 59
neutrality laws of: 40
press coverage of war in: 304
public opinion in: 160
war production efforts of: 590
United States Air Force. See also United
States Army Air Corps; United
States Army Air Service; United
States Army Air Forces.
autonomy advocated for: 245,
522–523, 594
doctrine of: 119
United States Armored Force
lack of air support voiced by: 135
United States Army: 51. See also Army
Groups; Armies; Corps; Divisions.
accidental death, causes in: 14

age and rank of officers in, 1931: 13
Axis in Tunisia defeated by: 200–210
blacks in: 259
bombed by U.S. aircraft: 470–471
Chief of Staff: 24–25, 57, 163
command post exercises in: 135
defense in Ardennes of: 533
doctrine in: 130–136
expansion of planned: 38–39
forces in Sicily: 244
forces in Tunisia: 164–184
heavy bomber, support for: 423–424,
517
historical account of operations in
Sicily by: 253
officer corps in: 12–13
preparation for WWII of: 60
promotion system in: 8
struggle over air support in: 210–220,
223
United States Army Air Corps: 32. See
also United States Air Force;
United States Army Air Forces;
United States Army Air Service.
budget allocation for: 14
designated: 24
doctrine of: 29, 31, 53, 132
expansion in: 37–39, 57, 61
field grade officers in: 10–12
observers in England from: 41–44
reorganized: 25
strength, 1939: viii
United States Army Air Forces
(USAAF). See also Allies;
Mediterranean Allied Air Forces;
Mediterranean Allied Strategic Air
Force; Mediterranean Allied
Tactical Air Force; United States
Air Force; United States Army Air
Corps; United States Army Air
Service; United States Strategic Air
Forces.
adverse publicity fought by: 584
aircraft capabilities of: 74
aircraft raids described: 371–372, 373,
408
Air Staff: 215, 383, 436–437,
548–549
air support doctrine for TORCH:
130–136
air support doctrine redefined by:
216–220
antishipping campaign of: 189–196